FUNDAMENTALS OF INTERNATIONAL FINANCE AND DEVELOPMENT: WHAT YOU NEED TO KNOW

■ ■ ■

by

Enrique Carrasco
University of Iowa College of Law

AMERICAN CASEBOOK SERIES®

Mat #41450045

American Casebook Series is a trademark registered in the U.S. Patent and Trademark Office.

© 2015 LEG, Inc. d/b/a West Academic
        444 Cedar Street, Suite 700
        St. Paul, MN 55101
        1-877-888-1330

West, West Academic Publishing, and West Academic are trademarks of West Publishing Corporation, used under license.

Printed in the United States of America

ISBN: 978-0-314-28795-3

PREFACE

It rocks to talk about international finance and development! But the subject matter freaks most people out because international finance seems really complex and they know nothing about it. And development? What the heck is that? "Why do I need to know any of this stuff?" Here's my answer: Because it has shaped your lives in one way or another. Yeah, it has, and as we go through my textbook you'll understand how and why. I'll get to another answer in just a sec.

First, though, let me tell you something about how I've approached writing the textbook. I'm the Director of the University of Iowa College of Law Center for International Finance & Development. I established the Center because I wanted to explain international finance and development in plain English to readers around the world. My textbook takes the same approach: I use plain English and otherwise explain jargon if I use it. It's written for those who know nothing about international finance (or finance) or development.

But the textbook is unlike any textbook you've seen, at least in law school. Lots of people would rather see paint dry than read about international finance. The stuff is so . . . not fun, they think. So I've brought my skills as a playwright to the textbook's topics. I use informal language and pepper the chapters with scenes I've written that'll help you understand the text. Lest you think I'm a playwright wannabe, I'm a member of The Dramatist Guild of America, thanks to a professionally produced play of mine in New York. I've written many other plays, a good number of them based on contracts cases. They've been self-produced at the University of Iowa College of Law.

Now to the other answer to the question, "Why do I need to know any of this stuff?" The bar has been telling law schools to train you better. I know that's not news to you. But do you know that your future employers want you to know something about global economic and financial events and developments? What if you're having lunch with a lawyer or client and she wants to discuss, say, the ongoing litigation involving Argentina's bonds? Are you going to excuse yourself and go throw up in the restroom? You can avoid those embarrassing moments by reading my textbook! You'll learn about lots of stuff, ranging from the work of the International Monetary Fund to issues facing emerging market economies such as Argentina. Or, I suppose, at lunch you can come up with ridiculous talking points that have no basis in reality and get fired or lose the client. Actually, if you do that with a straight face, you'll make partnership instantly!

But you might say, "Okay. So I need to know something about international finance, if only to sound hip at dinner parties with the Washington, D.C. elite in their really expensive but elegantly understated homes in Georgetown. But why do I need to know this 'development' stuff? It's not like I'm planning to go on any safaris in the near future. Does going to an all-inclusive resort in Cancun count? How about watching House Hunters International?"

Here's why you need to know something about development: The world in which the United States, Europe, and Japan rule economically will come to an end in your lifetimes. Yeah, these so-called "emerging market economies," such as China, India, and Brazil, are going to be pretty much in your face sooner or later. You gotta deal with it! So wake up and smell the curry!

The textbook is basically a story of international finance and development. Here's the format for most of the chapters: There's the "text" of the book where we explain the topic at hand. Notice that I just started using "we." I'm the sole author of this textbook, but I've had an army of students help me. Hence the "we" in the textbook. Getting back to the format, in most chapters you'll see what we hope you'll think are interesting quotes. Right after the text, we've provided profiles (many with photos) of some of the chapter's notable characters. As you read the text, there might be concepts or terms you need to understand better, such as the mechanics of the gold standard. So, we've provided a "What's Up with That?" section that gives you more information on the concepts or terms. Then there's a section called "Questions from Your Talking Dog" that will help you focus on the important points of the chapter for review purposes. The last part of the chapter will provide you with supplemental materials—excerpts of articles, legal provisions, etc. that give you the chance to explore the chapter's topics more deeply and provide a basis for class discussion. You'll notice that there are no footnotes in the text and in most of the supplements—we've stripped out most of the footnotes in the supps. We did this because we don't want you to get bogged down with citations and subliminal messages of happiness and wealth or the end of the world. But the text is supported in one way or another by the sources we've cited at the end of the textbook or by what the person living in my mouth told me.

Getting back to the story, it begins in Chapter 1 with the establishment of the International Monetary Fund (IMF) and the World Bank, the "Bretton Woods Institutions (BWIs)," in the 1940s. Those institutions established the framework for international finance and development that still informs how we look at things today. The BWIs' framers hoped a system of fixed exchange rates supervised by the IMF would bring order to the chaos that pretty much shut down the global economy in the inter-war period and led to the rise of Hitler. Yeah, for real. They hoped the World Bank would help reconstruct war-torn Europe. We give you the nuts and bolts of the BWIs and you'll get to meet a couple of soldiers, Brad and Mikey, and other characters. You'll also find out how a Cézanne ended up hanging over John Maynard Keynes' bed.

In Chapters 2 through 4, we tell you stories about the meaning of "development," the ground-shaking collapse of the "Bretton Woods System" (BWS)—the system of global fixed exchange rates—and the rise of the World Bank. As to the meaning of development, in Chapter 2 you'll be in on a conversation between Mitch, a cabbie, and Rachel, his fare. They talk about lots of things, ranging from feudalism to John Maynard Keynes' Theory of Unemployment. Before you say it, you'll find knowledgeable cabbies who are happy to talk your ears off—some of them are PhDs who can't find work at universities. Anyway, you'll also read about competing theories of development, from the "structuralists" to the Neo-Marxists. Did you know that in his student days, Karl Marx was known as "the Moor"?

In Chapter 3, you'll have a front row seat as we witness the economic turbulence in the 1960s that brought down the BWS. The story starts with the descent of Britain and the pound sterling, followed by distortions in the U.S. economy. You'll find out that the U.S. was thought of as "the banker to the world," and why that created problems, not just for the United States but for the whole system of fixed exchange rates. Then came the fateful evening in August 1971, when President Nixon came on T.V. Marge and Ben were watching the tube when he came on. Ben wasn't a happy camper. The story's epilogue tells you about the world after the collapse of the BWS. Did you know that President Johnson worked for a time as a custodian?

If President Nixon isn't your cup of tea (cup of tea? What's wrong with me?), check out the rock star at the Word Bank—Robert McNamara, one of President Kennedy's "best and brightest." In Chapter 4, we look at how in the 1960s the Bank turned away from European reconstruction to "project lending" for infrastructure—e.g., roads and power—in developing countries. Armed with a quantitative approach he learned at Harvard Business School, McNamara transformed the Bank, taking it into new areas of lending, such as health and nutrition, and measuring success on the numbers of loans the Bank churned out. Not the best approach, as you'll see. At the same time, in the 1970s the Global South collectively told the Global North they were royally pissed off. They demanded a "New International Economic Order (NIEO)" that would give them more voice and power in international finance and development. What does a thud sound like? By the way, did you know that one of the Bank presidents before McNamara called developing countries "retarded"? We kid you not.

In Chapter 5, we move to the 1980s and the Latin American debt crisis that led to the so-called "lost decade." The crisis began with Mexico's default on its foreign loans, loans with floating interest rates that it received from banks around the world who recycled "petrodollars." When the United States jacked up interest rates to kill U.S. inflation, the loans became too expensive to pay off. In this chapter you'll learn the nuts and bolts of Eurodollar loans. You'll also come to understand the "muddling through" approach that the IMF and other actors used to resolve the crisis, given that there isn't a global bankruptcy court. You'll have the pleasure of understanding what FASB 15 means. Then you'll be introduced to the infamous c-word: conditionality. Did you know that Federal Reserve Chair Paul Volcker—the guy who masterminded the interest-rate hike that some say caused a global recession—is a huge fly-fishing enthusiast?

In Chapter 6, we move to the 1990s and talk about the rise of "good governance and development," a framework driven by the IMF and the World Bank. We talk about the turn away from state-led development to "market-friendly" policies. You've probably heard about the "Washington Consensus" (WC) at some point in your life—whether you know it or not. Maybe on the back of a cereal box. The WC is all about shrinking government's role in development and deregulating markets. You'll get to see what it means and how people reacted to it. Then we talk about what corruption is, why it's bad, and a trip to Paris. We finish with something you definitely have heard and talked about: the rule of law. Did you know that the famous economist Joseph Stiglitz is a Hoosier?

In Chapter 7, we take a look at the blow-back the BWIs took on their 50th anniversary. Anniversaries aren't always happy times. You'll read about how non-governmental organizations (NGOs)—we talk about them first—pounced on the World Bank and IMF for all sorts of violations ranging from human rights abuses to environmental devastation. For example, you'll read about the disastrous Arun-III hydroelectric project in Nepal that resulted in the World Bank withdrawing from the project. As to the IMF, we have a look at the criticisms of the austerity measures it required in exchange for its loans—the dreaded "conditionality." The BWIs responded, of course. We concentrate on the creation of the Bank's Inspection Panel, which allows parties to bring a claim against the Bank for failure to follow its policies. We also take a look at the IMF's response to the conditionality criticism and the creation of its Independent Evaluation Office, which assesses the Fund's operations. Both Chapters 6 and 7 have a bottom line theme of transparency and accountability of government bodies and international financial institutions. Did you know that former World Bank president James Wolfensohn failed his high school final exam?

We swing to capital markets in Chapter 8. You need to know something about them to understand the chapters that follow. We talk about the internationalization of the capital markets—where stocks and bonds are issued and traded. You'll come to understand that global markets are really important to developing countries: because of low domestic savings rates, developing countries can more easily than ever borrow from savers. In the 1990s, private sources of capital, such as institutional investors buying stocks and bonds in a developing country, dwarfed official sources, such as loans and grants from one country to another. We also take a look at the rise of portfolio investment, otherwise called "hot money"— "hot" because it can move in and out of a country in a flash, leaving countries, especially developing countries, in ruins. Did you know that Singapore's financial center ranks number five in the world?

In Chapters 9 and 10, we peer into two major crises, the 1994–1995 Mexican financial crisis and the Asian financial crisis. Prior to the outbreak of Mexico's crisis, portfolio investment poured into the country. Good times all around. Tequila flowed everywhere. After all, after the 1980s debt crisis, Mexico made a bunch of market-based reforms—it was the thing to do given the global "market-friendly" development movement. Problem, though: all that incoming investment put enormous downward pressure on the peso, which was fixed at the time. At the same time, Mexico issued lots of short-term debt via "tesobonos." Then came a couple of political assassinations and an uprising in Chiapas, and all hell broke loose. The portfolio investors, those holding the "hot money," pulled out their investments in a blink of an eye. Mexico had to abandon its fixed exchange rate because its central bank was running out of foreign reserves. Mexico's tesobonos were about to mature—payment time. How do you say "disaster" in Spanish? But Mexico didn't default on its debt. The United States led a rescue of the country. Some said it was a bailout. Of Mexico or someone else? Hmmm. . . . Did you know that President Carlos Salinas (1988–1994) was at that point the youngest president in Mexico's history?

The major theme of Chapter 10 on the Asian financial crisis is "contagion." The crisis started in Thailand in February 1997 and spread like a contagion to the Philippines, Malaysia, Indonesia, and South Korea. Hot money is involved in the crisis as well. But here's the thing: these countries' economies weren't carbon copies of each other (have you actually seen carbon paper?). And yet the contagion spread, eventually hitting Russia and Brazil. Have you read the book or seen the movie "Perfect Storm"? Even you haven't, you know what the phrase means. In the Asian financial crisis, it was a perfect storm of fixed exchange rates, balance of payments problems, lack of financial transparency, speculators, hot money, short-term debt, weak financial sectors, corruption, and herd behavior— buffalos are part of this story. Who came to the rescue? The International Monetary Fund, of course. It went crazy with conditionality—tons of stuff the countries had to do in return for the Fund's loans. Many economists pounced on the Fund's handling of the crisis. Check it out and see what you think. Listen to the music as you read the movie script. Did you know that the speculator George Soros is known as "the man who broke the Bank of England"?

In Chapter 11 we tackle capital adequacy. It doesn't have a sexy name but it's really important that you understand the basics before we cover the global financial crisis and the European sovereign debt crisis. In this chapter you'll come to understand what capital adequacy means and why it's so important for banks. A bank's capital is, in short, its assets, such as loans it's made, minus its liabilities, such as savers' deposits with the bank. If a bank doesn't have enough capital to absorb its losses, such as bad loans, it might fail. Worse yet, if it's a big bank, its failure might pose a systemic risk to the whole financial system. Pretty much the end of the world. We introduce you to international standards of capital adequacy, Basel I and II, that most countries in the world have adopted—i.e., they've made the standards law in their countries. Here's the thing: These standards weren't good enough to prevent the global financial crisis. Because of relatively low capital levels, banks and other financial institutions stopped lending. The resulting credit freeze was at the heart of the crisis. Did you know that one guy said that part of Basel II was like "jumping off a cliff?"

Chapters 12 through 16 cover the global financial crisis, the worst crisis since the Great Depression, a crisis that has led to the Great Recession of stagnant economic growth globally. We've likened the crisis to a virus that isn't contained and becomes a pandemic. The virus is the subprime mortgage. But here's the question: How did a problem in one sector of mortgage lending morph into a global crisis? We're going to show you how. We begin in Chapter 12, starting with what many, but not all, people think started it all: the Federal Reserve's ultra-low interest rates. But then many other factors contributed to the subprime mortgage crisis, such as investors abroad pouring lots of money into mortgage securities, and a housing boom that led to reckless and fraudulent subprime lending. When interest rates rose, homeowners all over the place started defaulting on their mortgages, many of which had adjustable rates that reset to an unaffordable rate. Millions of homeowners were "underwater," meaning they owed more on their mortgages than their homes were worth. Brutal. The question many asked was whether the subprime crisis was caused by lending to low-income borrowers, especially minorities. You'll see the debate. We also ask you to think about whether financial deregulation played a part in the crisis. We hope you like the chapter's format, which in many instances uses the actual words of real people involved in the crisis. If you don't, deal with it.

In Chapter 13, we look at the virus's transmitting agent: securitization, which is a process of taking a non-liquid asset, such as car loans—they're non-liquid because you can't really set up a table outside of the lender's office and sell the loans to passersby—and turning it into tradable securities. Securitization is not a bad thing in and of itself. In fact, it's really important to the financial system, and we explain the basics. The problem was that it got way out of control. With the help of credit agencies, investment banks churned out so-called mortgage backed securities (MBSs) like brats at a football game. The MBSs were re-securitized into collateral debt obligations (CDOs), and then the CDOs were re-securitized into "CDOs squared" and the madness continued. It got so complex—brace yourself for the "synthetic" CDO—that only the math PhDs who created them could understand them. Throw in credit default swaps, where, say, Bank 1 pays premiums to Bank 2, which agrees to pay Bank 1 if some of Bank 1's loans go bad, and you'll end up in a padded cell foaming at the mouth.

In Chapter 14, we describe the pandemic, the crisis that became global because these assets spread globally, particularly in Europe. Via a series of "news alerts," you witness the carnage that developed as subprime mortgages tanked. The alerts begin with the bankruptcy of New Century Financial, a huge subprime lender. Then two hedge funds operated by Bear Stearns collapsed. As losses mounted, banks stopped lending. Central banks around the world coordinated massive injections of liquidity. The U.S. Federal Reserve, led by its Chair Ben Bernanke, created all sorts of facilities to stop the bleeding—something he was criticized for later. Not enough. Bear Stearns collapsed. Worried about systemic risk—that Bear was too big to fail, meaning that its collapse would threaten the viability of the entire financial system—the Fed engineered a rescue via JP Morgan. In the meantime, reports started percolating regarding the credit rating agencies' messed-up rating system. Then the U.S. government took over Freddie Mac and Fannie Mae, the two giant "government sponsored entities," because of bad MBSs they issued (and other problems). But the defining moment was when the Fed and Treasury Department refused to rescue Lehman Brothers, another big investment bank. After it filed for bankruptcy, the pandemic let loose its fury, leading to the government take-over of the insurance giant AIG. Faced with the end of the world as we know it, the U.S. government passed the Troubled Assets Relief Program (TARP), the funds of which eventually were used to inject capital into banks so they'd start lending again. There's much more in the chapter but that's enough for now.

Chapter 15 is devoted to the credit agencies' role in the crisis. Firms like Standard & Poor's are known as the "gatekeepers" because credit rating agencies (CRAs) are supposed to reliably rate debt securities for the markets. Without their ratings, investment banks could not have created MBSs or CDOs. But the CRAs messed up royally, resulting in massive downgrades of the securities, from AAA golden to junk. The gatekeepers failed to do their job. And the virus was let loose on the world. The chapter tells the story in a drama based on a true story. We follow the story with additional material on CRAs. Do you know where Wingecarribee Shire is?

We close our look at the global financial crisis in Chapter 16, the epilogue. There's tons of stuff that happened after the news alerts in

Chapter 14. It could fill a whole book. Each chapter of the crisis could fill a book for that matter. In Chapter 16, we cover the major developments. We tell you about the "toxic assets," all the MBSs and CDOs and other assets that no one would touch. Then we give you the highlights of the Dodd-Frank Act, the biggest reform of the financial markets since the Great Depression. We cover reforms in: the mortgage industry, securitization, CRAs, over-the-counter derivatives, and the Federal Reserve. You'll learn about the Financial Stability Oversight Council, created to address systemic risk. Then we hit Basel III, which reforms capital adequacy in light of the deficiencies in the regime that became clear during the crisis. We close the chapter with a look at the litigation against various actors in the crisis, including some of the big banks that cranked out what turned out to be crap. Do you know who Daniel Tarullo is? He's Quintin Tarantino's cousin. Not.

In Chapter 17 we deal with the European sovereign debt crisis, which was triggered by massive government spending to survive the global financial crisis. "Oh please, not another crisis!" you plead. Sorry, but this crisis will tell you about the European Union, the European Monetary Union (EMU), and the euro. The creation of the EMU and the euro was yet another step towards European integration, which has its roots in post-WWII aspirations that European countries would never wage war against each other again. You'll learn about monetary unions, and optimal currency areas. You know, stuff with which you can impress people at cocktail parties. There was quite a bit of debate whether a European monetary union was a good idea and whether the EMU would constitute an optimal currency area. Some worried about countries giving up control over monetary policy after the creation of the euro—the European Central Bank (ECB) would rule in that area. Others said the EMU wouldn't be an optimal currency area because, unlike the United States, there wouldn't be a common fiscal policy (tax and spending)—each member country would continue to set its own fiscal policy, subject to, as you'll see, some (unenforced) restrictions.

Despite all the potential downsides, they formed the EMU in three stages starting in 1990. The most important part of the process was the Maastricht Treaty on European Union, which entered into force in 1992. The treaty was important because it laid down the criteria for joining the EMU. One of the criteria was limited government borrowing and debt—remember, countries retain control over fiscal policy but not monetary policy. So governments' annual budget deficits can't exceed 3% of GDP and total outstanding debt can't be more than 60% of GDP. Knowing that countries would be tempted to exceed the limits, the treaty contains a "no bailout" clause forbidding countries from providing financial support to each other. And the Stability and Growth Pact (SGP) reinforces limits on fiscal deficits and debts, providing for fines if countries don't lower the percentages. The EMU was established in 1999 with eleven member countries adopting the euro. Greece joined the union in 2001. As of this writing, the Eurozone has 18 member countries.

Finally, a monetary union! The euro! But you'll see there were fundamental flaws with the EMU. Greece developed tons of debt and its fiscal deficits were out of control. It was teetering on the brink of defaulting on its sovereign bonds. Fearing that a Greek default could threaten other member countries' ability to pay on their sovereign bonds, Eurozone countries and the IMF put together a rescue package.

It didn't work. Ireland was the next domino to fall. Then Portugal. Then Spain. Then Italy. Oh, s___t! What to do? As you'll see, lots of things. The ECB engaged in extraordinary measures to pump liquidity into the Eurozone. Member countries established two temporary facilities, the European Financial Stability Facility and European Financial Stabilization Mechanism, and a permanent facility, the European Stability Mechanism, to make loans to countries in trouble. Understanding that the SGP did little to prevent excessive fiscal deficits and debt, the European Parliament passed a package of legislation that in part makes fines more likely for countries that breach the limits. Most EU members also agreed to a "fiscal compact," an intergovernmental agreement that requires the signatories to adopt balanced-budget rules via their constitutions or legislation. And realizing that banks were really vulnerable to the crisis, the EU is in the process of creating a banking union, which among other things gives the ECB new supervisory powers over all of the Eurozone's 6,000 banks.

In Chapter 18 we look at two really important development topics: the Millennium Development Goals (MDGs), and the debt relief movement. The MDGs developed from a United Nations resolution in the late 1990s that pledged to free people "from the abject and dehumanizing conditions of extreme poverty." What followed were eight goals ranging from eradicating extreme poverty and hunger, to promoting gender equality and empowering women, to ensuring environmental sustainability. You'll read about the criticisms of the MDGs, such as the claim that they're too narrow, and the rebuttals, such as the argument that the Goals are good benchmarks for progress. Speaking of which, we look at how the MDGs are measured, and the progress towards reaching them. The chapter then turns to the debt relief movement to forgive multilateral debt, such as debt to the World Bank and the IMF. We look at the arguments for and against debt relief, ranging from moral hazard to economic arguments. Then most of the rest of the chapter explains and evaluates the Heavily Indebted Poor Countries (HIPC) Initiative launched by the World Bank and the IMF in the mid-1990s. The Initiative has tried to reduce poor countries' debt to sustainable levels. Did you know that Kofi Annan, who served as the U.N.'s

Secretary General from 1997 to 2006, studied economics at Macalester College in Minnesota? The winters there are brutal.

In Chapter 19 we introduce you to what probably is the most dominant conception of "development" today: the Capabilities Approach (CA) pioneered by Nobel Laureate economist Amartya Sen along with the philosopher Martha Nussbaum. The CA is a reaction to measuring a person's well-being by per capita gross national product. It emphasizes the freedom of an individual to pursue the life she values. Mitch, the cabbie, and Rachel, the lawyer, are back with us. In a cab ride, Rachel explains the CA in fundamental terms. You'll learn about "functionings" (like eating), "functioning vectors" (a bunch of different functions a person might want), and the "capability set" (alternative functioning vectors from which the person can choose). Throw those terms down at a cocktail party, and people will both love and fear you. Not a bad combination with the right drink. Anyway, Sen asks, how much freedom does a person have to make those choices? And when you ask that question, you have to look at the ability of a person to convert income into functionings. For example, you and I may be able to buy the same bike with equal incomes. But if I'm disabled and you're not, I can't pursue the functioning of riding the bike but you can. What's up with that? Rachel covers other important aspects of the CA, including Nussbaum's contribution to the CA, focusing on the philosopher's top ten human capabilities. We finish by looking at the criticisms of the CA, ranging from claims that it's too complex to biting criticisms of a top ten list put together by a white woman in the United States. Did you know that Martha Nussbaum prefers a genetically-engineered baby elephant as a pet? That's for real. Would you want a genetically-engineered prof? Hmmm. . . .

Chapter 20 begins our look at emerging market economies (EMEs). What is an EME? Many of you have heard of the so-called BRICS: Brazil, Russia, India, China, and South Africa. Until recently, these countries have experienced pretty impressive economic growth. And they've also done lots of market-based reforms. They're also gaining more political influence on a regional and global scale. But why "emerging?" The idea is that, although they're becoming significant actors within the Global South, they're still marked by flawed policies, weak institutional structures, and pretty bad inequality. We use Brazil as an example of an EME. We look at how Brazil went through a phase of statist development policies followed by market reforms after the 1980s debt crisis. Brazil "emerged" under the presidency of Luis Ignacio da Silva, who was elected the president of Brazil in 2002. During his tenure, Brazil adopted orthodox economic policies, which led to pretty impressive economic growth. Brazil also pursued development programs that sought to improve the poor infrastructure that accounted for social exclusion. And yet Brazil has its problems, ranging from a cumbersome regulatory and legal framework to high inequality. Did you know that the current president Dilma Rousseff was a left-wing guerrilla in the 1960s?

Chapter 21 is broken up into ten sections, A through J. Unlike the rest of the textbook, each section begins with commentary followed by an excerpt we've chosen on the topic—no supplements. First we look at racism in Section A, using Brazil as an example. You'll read a really interesting piece on post-racialism in the context of the United States and Brazil. The author argues that Brazil's claim that it's a racial democracy is false, exposing the roots of post-racial "discourse" in Brazil in racial classifications intended to "whiten" the society.

In Section B, we look at inequality in EMEs, using a paper that examines rising inequality in Asia. The authors point out that Asia's rapid growth has led to increased inequality. The numbers are pretty stark. Some might say, "Why should we be concerned about inequality? That's just life." The authors argue that we should be concerned because high inequality stunts economic growth. They propose a number of policies that focus on equal opportunity, such as efficient fiscal policies and labor-friendly economic policies.

In Section C, we read about violence and the author's thesis that we shouldn't blindly push free markets and democracy without looking at a country's socioeconomic conditions. If you don't look at those conditions, free markets and democracy may flare up hatred between ethnic minorities, such as Chinese Indonesians, who dominate a country economically, and indigenous majorities that are far less well-off.

It seems like today the concept of transparency is all the rage. In Section D we look at the Right to Information Act in India. The author of our selection argues that while the Act appears to empower marginalized people, it may well disempower people by creating a narrow bureaucratic path to finding the information that people need.

In Section E, you'll learn about the movement for "financial inclusion" in developing countries. In many developing countries, many people don't have access to the formal financial system—e.g., services ranging from savings, to payments, to insurance. The problem is really bad in Africa. But technology and entrepreneurship, such as mobile phone messaging services, are changing the situation.

Another big issue is remittances—typically money that migrants send back to their families in their home countries. The flow of remittances has shot up recently. In Section F, the authors explore how the trend can be both helpful, such as lifting people out of poverty, as well as harmful, such as making corrupt officials less accountable because recipients of remittances won't feel as compelled to make government officials justify their actions.

In Section G, we explore the development of securities markets in EMEs, using China as an example. Securities markets are important to development as they attract foreign investors. But the money coming in is hot money that can cause problems. You've probably heard of the Federal Reserve's monetary policy—"quantitative easing"—that has flooded the market with U.S. dollars. This has prompted investors to move their money to EMEs, which caused the host countries' currencies to rise, which hurt their exports. As soon as the Fed started hinting that it would start raising interest rates to soak up some of the liquidity, investors in the EMEs pulled their investments out, even though the host countries' economic fundamentals weren't that bad. Policymakers have said that the best thing EMEs can do in a globalized financial market is to develop their financial markets so they can withstand external shocks. Looking at China, you'll see that its financial sector has developed pretty impressively, but it's still a bank-centered financial sector. Trading on the Shanghai and Shenzhen stock exchanges is still dominated by state-owned entities, and the trading is thin, volatile, and mispriced. And the legal framework looks good on paper but it doesn't really protect investors.

Islamic finance is the topic of Section H. It's something you should know about because sharia-compliant global assets are more than $1 trillion today. The first article we've chosen explains Islamic finance beyond what people mostly hear about—that it has to be "interest-free." There's an ethical component to Islamic finance that's absent in Western finance, at least the way most people view Western finance. You'll learn, for example, that because interest is prohibited, lenders actually become investors, and they share business risks with the entrepreneur in return for shares of the profits. The second article surveys Islamic banking in the United Kingdom, which has a very large Muslim community. Among other things, you'll read about the establishment of the Islamic Bank of Britain, which opened its doors in 2004.

In Section I, we look at a piece written by the greatest scholar in the history of the world. The piece looks at how the global financial crisis opened a window for emerging economies to gain more voice in the global financial order. The author reviews the G20 summits that were held during the financial crisis, starting with the summit in November 2008 in Washington, D.C. At that summit, the leaders understood that emerging economies could no longer remain voiceless in matters of international finance. Via the following summits, emerging economies gained greater voice in the new Financial Stability Board, an international body charged with, among other things, coordinating the implementation of global standards in international finance. The leaders made the G20, which includes emerging economies, the "premier forum" for international economic cooperation. Leaders also agreed that there would be quota reform at the IMF that would give emerging market and developing countries increased (but limited) voting power. You know about Dominique Strauss Khan and the "perp walk," right?

We end the textbook with Section J, which covers litigation by so-called "vulture funds" against Argentina. In 2001, Argentina defaulted on a massive amount of debt, including bonds it had issued. In 2005 and 2010, Argentina took a hard line with the bondholders and managed to get them to agree to a 70–75% reduction in the bonds' principal. But there were the so-called "holdouts," bondholders that refused to participate in the restructuring. Those bonds eventually made their way into the hands of hedge funds, otherwise known as vulture funds. The vulture funds sued Argentina in the federal district court for the southern district of New York. In November 2012, the judge ruled that when Argentina next paid interest on the restructured bonds it would have to pay the vulture funds in full— one hundred cents on the dollar. So check it out: a U.S. federal district court judge issued a ruling that threatened to upend global international finance with respect to bond restructuring and the so-called *pari passu clause* or "equal treatment" provision. OMG! A stay was put in place and Argentina appealed to the Court of Appeals for the Second Circuit.

The issue on appeal was whether the district court judge properly ruled that the vulture funds were entitled to full payment on their bonds even though the holders of the exchanged bonds were receiving only a fraction of their bonds' value. Virtually all of us in international finance viewed the oral arguments as the Super Bowl of international finance. We emptied the stores of chips, salsa, brats, and beer. Tailgating was crazier than any college football game. Jonathan Blackman of the prestigious firm Cleary Gottlieb represented appellant Argentina. Ted Olson, the former Solicitor General, represented appellees—the vulture funds. You'll read a portion of the oral arguments and you can judge who won. But when the appeals court issued its opinion, it was a slam dunk for plaintiffs, in part because of Argentina's defiant stance against the vulture funds. As of this writing, the parties are in negotiations but they're going nowhere.

Well, there you have it. Have a good ride.

* * * * * * *

I end with a good number of acknowledgments. This textbook has been a long-time in the making in the sense that my mission to demystify the world of international and development for global readers began with the posting of the "E-Book on International Finance & Development" back in the day. The idea for the E-Book arose from a seminar I held during the Asian financial crisis. Throughout the course of the year, my students and I worked to the point of exhaustion to produce the book. At the time we posted the E-Book, the World Wide Web was in its infancy. The E-Boook attracted lots of attention, both in the United States and abroad. Since then the staffers of my Center—law students—added tons of work product to the Center's website with the same mission: to explain international finance and development in plain English to our global readers. Many thanks to the following students who worked in one way or another to produce the Center's impressive work product: Ricardo Contreras, Sandra Blanco, Nicole Wendt, Maria Weidner, Saladin Al-Jurf, Roman Terrill, James Woepking, Eric Dorkin, Charles McClellan, Jane Ro, Wesley Carrington, HeeJin Lee, Alexandra Basak Russell, Jason Cox, Judith Faucette, Consuelo Valenzuela Lickstein, Amanda Bahena, Lindsay McAfee, Nichole Johnson, Taryn Dozark-Frideres, Erin Nothwehr, Sandra Quesada, Lia Menéndez, Karen Fasano Thomsen, Tim Christensen, Leah Badertscher, Alison Guernsey, Emily Marriott, Cody Edwards, Hristo Chaprazov, Keslie Brandlee, Carrie Harrington, David Winkler, Christina Humphreys, Emily Winfield, Michael Sarabia, Sofia Biller, Karen Helgeson, Yolanda Rivera, Sean Williams, Tarik Abdel-Monem, Kenneth Fukuda, Janel Vaughan, Anastasia Slivker, Josh Startup, Kyounghwa Kang, Nathan Jackson, Joe Larson, Megan Murray, Chuan Li, James Oliver, and Kylie Franklin.

The E-Book has had a good run. I've retired it along with the rest of the content on the Center's website. Now comes my textbook. A number of very able students helped me produce the book in the span of twelve months: Jordyn Lueker, Tom Butler, Kristymarie Shipley, Garrett Morales, Elizabeth Archer, Blerta Mileti, Scott Stottlemyre, Eric Schmitt, Sara Gardner, Andrew Magner, John McCarthy, Jared Knight, Danitza Loya, Lucas Carney, and Michael Sarabia. I'm particular indebted to Ms. Lueker, the textbook's Supervising Editor. She not only produced substantive research for much of the book, but she tirelessly coordinated all aspects of preparing it for submission to West. I wouldn't have finished the book within a year without her exceptional judgment and managerial skills.

My project of demystifying international finance via the E-Book wouldn't have been possible without the support and encouragement of Dean William Hines. His successors, Dean Carolyn Jones and Dean Gail Agrawal, have supported my mission as well. Senior Associate Dean Eric Andersen has always been a big fan of my Center. And Gordon Tribbey, Assistant Dean for Finance & Administration, has generously supported my Center's activities and the production of this textbook.

Before the creation of the E-Book, before the creation of my Center, before the creation of this textbook, four people dear to me thought I was just fine without the trapping of academia: Pamela, Skye, David, and Felipe. Right on.

ENRIQUE CARRASCO

October 2014

SUMMARY OF CONTENTS

TABLE OF CONTENTS

FUNDAMENTALS OF INTERNATIONAL FINANCE AND DEVELOPMENT: WHAT YOU NEED TO KNOW

CHAPTER 1

THE BRETTON WOODS INSTITUTIONS

■ ■ ■

We start the grand narrative of the textbook with a look at the International Monetary Fund (IMF) and the International Bank for Reconstruction and Development (IBRD), also known as the Bretton Woods Institutions (BWIs). They were formed at the conclusion of the United Nations Monetary and Financial Conference held in Bretton Woods, New Hampshire, July 1–22, 1944, on the eve of the end of World War II. They were precursors to the United Nations and other multilateral institutions formed after World War II and reflected the new spirit of "let's get along," more formally "cooperation among nations," especially in economic matters. As you'll see in this textbook, the operations of the BWIs have had a significant role in shaping the world as we know it today. This chapter will discuss what led to the formation of the BWIs and the functions they performed in the late 1940s and 1950s.

To understand this chapter and many that follow you need a basic grasp of balance of payments (BOP), a kind of snapshot of a country's financial position vis-à-vis the rest of the world. So take a look at supplement 1A and make sure you get the basics. Don't freeze up, okay? Relax and keep an open mind. If you can't, deal with it!

Much of this chapter deals with technical stuff that you need to know—check out supplement 1E, which will give you the big picture about the BWIs and international law. But we start here by putting the Bretton Woods Conference in context. Understand that violence, whether physical or economic, underlies the creation and perpetuation of international finance. And there are many characters involved in the drama of international finance, a good number of which are unseen. So we're going to start and end this chapter with a play, which is based on a true story.

Part One: "War and Finance"

(lights up)

Scene One

Setting: June 6, 1944, 6:30 a.m., Omaha Beach, Normandy, overcast sky, rough seas, a troop landing craft jerks its way toward the beach, which is obscured by smoke.

Characters:

    Brad: U.S. soldier, private

    Mikey: U.S. soldier, private

    Sam: U.S. soldier, sergeant

Brad: Hold it together, Mikey.

Mikey: We don't have a chance! Listen!

Brad: Shut up.

(Mikey throws up)

Sam: Ready for a little dip, boys? We're not going to make it to the beach. Smoke 'em if you got 'em.

Mikey: "Hail Mary, full of grace . . ."

Brad: What's your favorite ice cream, Mikey?

Mikey: What? Are you kidding me?

Brad: My favorite is strawberry.

(the landing craft ramp opens, bullets shower in)

Mikey (yelling): Chocolate!

Brad (yelling): We'll share a banana split, okay?

Mikey (yelling): Promise me we will, Brad!

(a bullet splits Brad's head open, spraying Mikey with blood)

Scene Two

Setting: June 30, 1944, 4:00 p.m., Mount Washington Hotel, Bretton Woods, New Hampshire. The hotel is surrounded by the scenic White Mount National Forest, which is dominated by Mount Washington rising majestically to 6,288 feet.

Characters:

    Jake: painter

    Sal: painter

Jake: Packed.

Sal: I heard over 700. From forty-four countries, I think. Places like Libraria—

Jake: Liberia, Sal.

Sal: That's what I said. Also, Equator.

Jake: Sal, it's Ecuador. Don't ya' rememba geography class?

Sal: Actually, I don't Jake. How about Iceland? Did I pronounce that right, teach?

Jake: Speaking of Iceland, they're complainin'.

Sal: For what? This place is gorgeous.

Jake: The weatha. They say it's cold. Heard Morgenthau—

Sal: Who?

Jake: Henry Morgenthau, Junia. Treasury Secretary of our United States of America, Sal. Did you know his grandfatha was an inventa of sorts? Came up with a tongue scrapa. Can you imagine that?

Sal: No, Jake, I can't imagine that. Don't want to.

Jake: Anyways, heard he wanted a pair of wool socks. Can you imagine that, Sal?

Sal: No, I can't imagine that, either, Jake. Wool socks in July.

Jake: Go figya . . . What they need is gasmasks. Just one month, Sal. One month to paint four hundred rooms. Paint still drippin' from the brushes. Am I right? Ridiculous.

Sal: Yeah, ridiculous. I would say that, Jake. Ridiculous.

Scene Three

Setting: July 1, 1944, 3:00 p.m., Mount Washington Hotel, Bretton Woods, New Hampshire, United Nations Monetary and Financial Conference.

Character:

    Henry Morgenthau, Jr.: U.S. Treasury Secretary

Secretary Morgenthau: "President Roosevelt has sent a message to the Conference . . . I request the Secretary General to read President Roosevelt's message.

Members of the Conference: I welcome you to this quiet meeting place with confidence and with hope. I am grateful to you for making the long journey here, grateful to your Governments for their ready acceptance of my invitation to this meeting. It is fitting that even while the war for liberation is at its peak, the representatives of free men should gather to take counsel with one another respecting the shape of the future which we are to win . . . This conference will test our capacity to cooperate in peace as we have in war. I know that you will all approach your task with a high sense of responsibility to those who have sacrificed so much in their hopes for a better world."

Scene Four

Setting: June 13, 1944, 11:00 a.m., 2011 Forsythe Drive, Des Moines, Iowa, home of Private Brad Jacobsen.

<u>Characters:</u>

Irma: Brad's mother

Henry Black: U.S. soldier, sergeant

(Irma is taking a strawberry pie out of the oven, knock on the front door)

Irma: Just a minute!

(she hurriedly puts the pie on the kitchen table and throws the oven mitts in the sink, walks through the living room, opens the front door and starts to tremble)

Black: Ms. Jacobsen?

(long pause)

Irma (in a whisper): Yes?

Black: I'm Sargent Henry Black.

(fade to black)

Part Two: Economic Violence

Those who attended the Bretton Woods Conference in New Hampshire wanted to establish a monetary system that would prevent the repetition of the chaos during the inter-war period (1918–1939):

- high inflation;
- restrictions on international trade (e.g., the infamous **Smoot-Hawley Act**) and payments;
- speculative capital flows (for example, when commodity prices plummeted after 1929, capital flows to commodity exporting countries dried up);
- **sharp movements in central banks' foreign reserves in countries with fixed exchange rate systems (the central banks used the foreign reserves to defend the fixed rate), and wildly fluctuating exchange rate movements in countries with floating exchange rates (determined by the markets);**
- gold shortages; and
- sharp drops in economic activity (deflation).

Pretty much the end of the world, right? To accomplish economic stability and growth, the IMF's founders agreed upon a "gold exchange standard." The reference to gold is important, so let's talk a bit about the **gold standard** before we explain the Bretton Woods System in more detail.

The system agreed upon at Bretton Woods was related to the gold standard period between 1870 and 1914. (You've heard some politicians wax eloquently about the gold standard, right?) Many hoped the BWIs would restore the perceived order of the gold-standard system, minus the standard's problems. That international monetary system required that each unit of a country's currency represent a certain weight of gold Central banks were required to keep an "official parity" between the country's currency and gold—eg. £5 per one ounce of gold. Maintaining the official parity required central banks to keep adequate stocks of gold as "reserves."

The gold-standard system hoped to encourage countries to maintain sound economic policies—technically called "balance of payments equilibrium" for all countries. The key to the system was the flow of gold from one country to another. An example might help. Suppose Country A is exporting more than it's importing, running a current account surplus ("surplus country"). Importing Country B ("deficit country") will not be able to finance all of its imports from Country A with loans from that country. So how will Country B pay for imports from Country A? Gold. So gold reserves would flow (think "river of gold") out of Country B and into Country A. This would cause price levels in Country A to rise, and price levels in Country B to decline. Can you figure out what happens next? No worries if you can't right now (but later . . .). Country A's exports would decline because they've become more expensive, and Country B's exports would increase because they've become cheaper. In an "automatic fashion," there would be a decline in Country A's current account surplus and a matching decline in Country B's current account deficit. And BOP equilibrium is restored! Not. In theory, the gold-standard system was supposed to operate automatically, requiring little government cooperation between countries or their central banks. In fact, countries often violated the "rules of the game" because they didn't want to risk unemployment (Country B) or inflation (Country A). And experience demonstrated that the burdens of adjustment under the standard fell disproportionately on deficit countries, which pursued policies that unnecessarily caused economic pain to preserve gold reserves.

After World War I, during the inter-war period, it was tough for the European countries to return to the pre-1914 economic world because of the war debts they owed to each other and to the United States. The Allies had depleted their reserves during the war due to imports of food and wartime supplies. After the war, reserves were further drained to service wartime debts. Because their reserves were low, their currencies were worth less. So, yeah, the European nations could not maintain the gold standard after the end of World War I. Although several countries returned to the gold standard in the mid-twenties, the system ultimately fell apart permanently in 1931. During the same period, commodity prices had soared due to speculation. But the market could not maintain the inflated prices of the oversupplied commodities indefinitely. Eventually commodity prices sank like the Titanic and the U.S. stock market crashed in 1929. The ensuing Great Depression intensified the demand for gold. Since commodity prices had sharply declined, export income had also tanked. To protect reserves, countries began to "hoard" gold and reserve currencies such as the U.S. dollar. This caused a shortage of gold and dollars.

To make matters worse, country after country began to devalue their currencies (i.e., reduce the currency's value vis-à-vis other currencies) to make exports cheaper to foreign buyers and make imports more expensive—so-called "beggar thy neighbor" policies (causing neighboring countries to become beggars—cheap). A country's goods become cheaper when it devalues its currency because another country buying these goods can buy more of the exporting nation's money with its own money. Since the goods are to be paid with the exporting country's currency and the price of the goods remains the same as before the devaluation, the goods are cheaper.

But here's the thing: Other countries also began to use this technique to avoid losing buyers for their goods. There was really no advantage to these "competitive devaluations." In fact, countries around the world, including the United States, implemented measures restricting trade and payments to reduce imports and protect their economies. All of this led to a severe drop in global economic activity. Like we said, pretty much the end of the world.

Part Three: From Chaos to Monetary Order: The Creation of the IMF

The U.S. Department of State invited forty-four governments (the Allied countries) to the Bretton Woods Conference. The invitations stated the purpose of the Conference was to "formulat[e] definite proposals for an International Monetary Fund, and possibly a Bank for Reconstruction and Development." The invitees came to Bretton Woods to figure out how they could establish a monetary order that would prevent the brutal problems during the inter-war period. (Actually, the major players had been exchanging ideas well before the Conference.) They also wanted to facilitate investment in economies where little private capital was expected to flow, namely the European economies. At bottom, they wanted to promote economic prosperity, which they hoped would promote peaceful relations. The war stuff got messy.

> *"The quiet and pleasant atmosphere of Bretton Woods provides a most fitting physical setting for the discussions of the Conference. ... I am sure we are all conscious of the fact that the outcome of the Conference will affect the shape of the peace and the welfare of generations to come."*
> —U.S. Treasury Secretary H. L. Morgenthau, Proceedings United Nations Monetary and Financial Conference, 73 (1944).

Given the inter-war experience, economic policymakers of the time viewed floating exchange rates—that is, rates determined by market forces—as destabilizing. They believed floating exchange rates were too susceptible to wild speculative swings, which had wreaked havoc on the global economy.

They also wanted to avoid competitive devaluations and the ensuing trade restrictions, which had brought trade to a virtual standstill.

The gold standard provided the stability policymakers wanted to pursue at the end of World War II, but the standard's negative aspects turned off the BWIs' founders. One of the principal founders, Lord John Maynard Keynes of Britain, was especially critical of the standard, calling it, get this, a "barbarous relic." A fixed exchange rate system *tied* to gold would do the trick: promote important domestic goals such as full employment and price stability (avoiding inflation). They also wanted a system that would allow countries to maintain sound external economic relations (healthy and balanced international trade and foreign investment— balance of payments equilibrium) without having to impose trade restrictions to, say, reduce imports.

> *"Those who advocate the return to a gold standard do not always appreciate along what different lines our actual practice has been drifting. If we restore the gold standard, are we to return also the pre-war conceptions . . . allowing the tides of gold to play what tricks they like with the internal price level and abandoning the attempt to moderate the disastrous influence of the credit cycle on the stability of prices and employment? [see The Mechanics of the Gold Standard below.] . . . In truth, the gold standard is already a barbarous relic. All of us, from the Governor of the Bank England downwards, are now primarily interested in preserving the stability of business, prices, and employment, and are not likely, when the choice is forced on us, deliberately to sacrifice these to the outworn dogma, which had its value once, of £3 : 17: 10½ per ounce."*
> —J. M. Keynes, "Alternative Aims in Monetary Policy" (1923), in Essays in Persuasion, 208 (1931).

Most of the discussions at Bretton Woods were related to figuring out how the IMF would operate, a subject that required much debate and analysis of technical issues relating to international monetary affairs. For example, although both the United States and the United Kingdom agreed that some sort of mechanism would have to be created to supply countries experiencing balance-of-payments deficits with temporary loans ("liquidity"), the two countries had serious disagreements over how resources would be made available. Keynes, representing a deficit country (the United Kingdom), wanted to create a system that would provide deficit countries with plenty of credit upon request. So he proposed an International Clearing Union (ICU) that would issue a new form of international money called "bancor." Bancor would have a fixed exchange rate with gold and all member currencies. The ICU would monitor lending from one country to another. Keynes wanted the ICU to issue about $26 billion in new money.

The United States responded, "uh . . . no." Represented by Harry Dexter White, the United States objected to Keynes' proposal because it would amount to a huge loan from the United States to the rest of the world. Unlike the Keynes plan, the White plan reflected the agenda of creditor nations, or more specifically the only expected creditor nation, the United States. The United States was golden. No, really, it had the highest level of gold reserves, its infrastructure was not damaged by the war, and neither was its economy. So it was probably going to be the main contributor to the liquidity mechanism. This prospect worried the U.S. negotiators. They wanted to avoid putting too many U.S. dollars into foreign hands, mainly because the U.S. Treasury and the U.S. Congress would probably not agree to such an outcome. Understandably, then, it was important for White to limit the extent to which the United States would be liable for financing the post-war adjustments of other countries. The United States also wanted the international institution to have the power to require deficit countries to adopt policies that would restore balance of payments equilibrium.

White addressed these concerns in a proposal for an International Stabilization Fund (ISF). To address the liability concern, the ISF plan, unlike the ICU proposal, required member countries to contribute their own currencies and gold to the ISF. Rather than borrowing directly from other countries (the ICU plan), deficit countries (refresh your memory by reviewing balance of payments) would have to obtain the currencies they needed from a fund established and operated by the ISF. Each member country's contribution would reflect their relative economic strength. The United States contribution would be limited to just under $3.5 billion, far less than its liability under Keynes' proposal.

The United States' other main concern—requiring countries to adopt sound economic policies—was reflected in a proposed rule that would require countries to comply with conditions set forth by the ISF in exchange for accessing the pool of currencies. This "conditionality" approach was intended to create longer-term stability by promoting economic and monetary policies that would help the borrowing country prevent future crises.

It was obvious to everyone the IMF would not be created without the approval of the United States and the United Kingdom. Both countries faced major challenges at home. The United States negotiators knew the U.S. Congress would not vote in favor of the ICU plan because elements of the plan were so unfamiliar to them, and because of their perception that the United States, as creditor, would be at a disadvantage. On the United Kingdom side, the British Parliament and public were not prepared to accept a plan based on a fixed exchange rate system. Why? Because a fixed exchange rate would completely deprive the nation of its sovereign right to control its monetary policy to protect its domestic economy (we'll get to this in a sec). They feared the sterling was going to be super weak and require the government's protection.

A series of compromises led to the creation of an international organization, the International Monetary Fund, which closely resembled the White plan. Member countries had to declare a par value and maintain it within one percent of parity. They could change the parity, in consultation with the IMF, if they were experiencing a "fundamental disequilibrium" (of the

BOP). After all, a major purpose of the Fund was to help member countries finance short- or medium-term BOP disequilibria. Given the United Kingdom's concerns, the IMF would raise no objection if the member requested less than a ten percent change. But Fund approval was required if the member country requested a further ten percent change or if the country's first request called for a change above ten percent. To reach compromise, the Conference's participants dropped White's proposal to tie lending to economic policy reform—"conditionality." But the IMF ultimately vindicated his approach when it adopted conditionality in the 1950s. "Yes!" says White as he makes a fist pump.

Part Four: The Bretton Woods System

The IMF Articles of Agreement ("Charter")—check out supplement 1B—are intended to be a Code of Good Conduct controlling member countries' monetary policies. Keep in mind that the Charter is a treaty and member countries who sign it are bound by the treaty's provisions. By signing the Charter, member countries agree "to carry out all of its obligations under this agreement" (Article XXXI, section 2(a)). The Code covers, among other things, obligations regarding exchange rates (Article IV), convertibility as well as the provision of information to the Fund (Article VIII), and obligations to consult and collaborate with the Fund (Articles IV and VIII).

> "Too often lawyers are men who turn poetry into prose and prose into jargon. Not so our lawyers here in Bretton Woods. On the contrary they have turned our jargon into prose and our prose into poetry. And only too often they have done our thinking for us."
>
> —J. M. Keynes, Proceedings United Nations Monetary and Financial Conference, 1241 (1944).

> "[The code of good conduct is] a remarkable development in international relations because it represents massive agreement on the introduction of the rule of law into an arena in which previously the discretion of states to act as they wish was almost wholly unlimited."
>
> —J. Gold, The International Monetary Fund and International Law: An Introduction, IMF Pamphlet Series, No. 4, 10–11 (1965).

Just as member countries have obligations under the Charter, the IMF has obligations to its member countries. Article I, which lists the purposes of the Fund, reflects the founders' view that the IMF's primary function should be to keep the international monetary system running smoothly. Monetary order, in turn, would promote economic growth and international trade, goals stated in Article I(ii). The IMF addresses these goals in various ways. Let's begin with a discussion of the Bretton Woods fixed exchange rate system (the "Bretton Woods System"), which is related to the gold exchange standard we mentioned earlier.

Par Value

According to the IMF's original Charter, all member countries declared a "par value" in terms of the U.S. dollar. How did this actually happen? The original member countries established par with the Fund's approval by fixing the domestic currency/dollar exchange rate based on market trades.

Remember, trade at that time was through the U.S. dollar—the strongest currency on the globe. How did the Fund determine whether the proposed par value was acceptable? As long as the par value did not impede exports, the fixed rate was fine. You can think of it this way: If a country proposed an exchange rate that overvalued its currency (to show the world that its currency rocked in terms of U.S. dollars), that rate would impede exports—not good if you want to promote trade and maintain a tolerable balance of payments. So market rates were a check on the par value a member country could declare. Once a member country fixed its currency to the dollar, say, French franc 5/1 U.S. dollar, it was automatically fixed to gold because the United States was responsible for holding gold at $35 an ounce. Member countries held reserves in U.S. dollars and gold and they had the right to sell dollars to the U.S. Federal Reserve (a central bank) for gold. Oh, yeah, once a member country fixed its rate, it had to think twice about ignoring the Fund's decision to deny a requested change of the declared par value. In 1948 the Fund denied France's request for a change in par value. France changed it anyway. What did someone in your life tell you about accepting the consequences of your actions? The Fund barred France from using its resources for six years (Article IV, section 6). A serious consequence, don't you think?

The founders believed this "gold exchange standard" would impose monetary discipline on member countries. As an example, let's say the central bank of Brazil decided to unduly expand the country's money supply. This would trigger loss of the central bank's reserves and make it harder to maintain its fixed exchange rate (the currency's par value). In theory, the United States would also be constrained because an expansion of its money supply would result in central banks holding more dollars, which they could present to the Federal Reserve for gold. As we'll discuss in Chapter 3, the problem with the par value system was that it was "asymmetric"—i.e., all countries except the United States had to worry about maintaining the fixed rate against the reserve currency—the U.S. dollar. This put the United States in a privileged position because it wasn't constrained in monetary policy. It could, and did, expand the money supply without having to defend an exchange rate. Disastrous. The Bretton Woods System worked reasonably well through the 1960s, even though member countries occasionally violated its rules. But the system was a big-time headache for countries as they tried to defend the par values. The late 1960s witnessed considerable financial and economic turbulence, which resulted in the collapse of the system in the early 1970s. Today the IMF Charter implicitly endorses a system of floating exchange rates primarily governed by market forces of supply and demand.

Pool of Funds and Quotas

Now, given the inter-war experience, the IMF's founders knew that countries wouldn't agree to maintain fixed exchange rates if this resulted in domestic unemployment—you know, the Great Depression thing (check out **trilemma** in What's Up). So the founders built flexibility into the system in various ways. As we've noted, one important aspect of flexibility involved establishing a pool of currencies member countries could use to help them with adjustments they would have to make to restore balance of payments equilibrium. So how was this pool created? The primary method was, and still is, through the member country's quota subscriptions.

The original Charter (Article III, section 3(b)) said that a member country was required to pay twenty-five percent of its subscription in gold or a combination of gold and U.S. dollars. After the creation in 1969 (first amendment of the Charter) of **special drawing rights** (SDRs), an international reserve asset created by the Fund, member countries could provide the twenty-five percent in reserve assets which includes SDRs, "hard currencies" of other member countries (e.g., the U.S. dollar, pound, yen), or gold. After the collapse of the BWS, the Fund amended the Charter to require that twenty-five percent of any increase in quotas be paid in SDRs or in currencies the Fund will accept. The member country can pay up to seventy-five percent of its quota subscription with its own currency.

Each member's quota subscription is determined by a revised **quota formula** that attempts to better reflect each member country's relative position in the global economy. While the formula is intended to recognize the growing importance of emerging economies in the global economy, it still favors the traditional advanced economies. For example, the United States gets 42,122.4 million SDRs (17.68 percent of the total quota), while Brazil gets 4,250.5 SDRS (only 1.79 percent of the total) and Palau gets 3.1 million SDRs (a barely noticeable 0.001 percent of the total). New member countries are given preliminary quotas in the same range as existing members with similar economic size and characteristics. These quotas are automatically reviewed every five years, but the Board can choose to review a particular country's quota at any time.

Quotas are serious in other ways. For example, quotas determine a member country's voting power. Instead of conducting its business based on a one-vote-per-country rule, the Fund uses a formula that gives a wealthy member country with a large quota (e.g., the United States) more voting power and influence than a small, poor country. Surprise! Officially, each IMF member country gets **basic votes**—the number of votes that result from the equal distribution among all the members of 5.502 percent of the aggregate sum of the total voting power—plus one additional vote for each SDR 100,000 of assigned quota. The United States, as the member country with the largest SDR quota, gets 421,961 votes at 16.75 percent of the total voting quota. Gabon, on the other hand, only gets 2,280 votes at 0.09 percent of the total votes. Actually, the Fund operates frequently by consensus, avoiding formal voting procedures. But voting power counts even in consensus decisions.

Quotas also determine the allocation of SDRs as well as access to its financial resources. A member can borrow up to 200 percent of its quota each year, and 600 percent of its quota cumulatively. But the Fund might give a member country extra resources in extraordinary situations. In Chapter 9 we'll tell you about how the Fund went way over the limit for Mexico.

IMF Lending

Although the IMF's assistance is usually referred to as "lending" or "loans," a member country actually "purchases" SDRs or other currencies from the Fund in exchange for its own currency and agrees to "repurchase" (buy back) its own currency at a later date. Because the member is charged for this transaction, the purchase or "drawing" looks like a loan, which is what we'll call the transaction for the sake of simplicity.

The loans from the Fund's General Resources Account can be used for any purpose relating to general balance-of-payments support, such as restoring reserves in the country's central bank or selling the acquired currency in the foreign exchange markets to stabilize exchange rates. Member countries have automatic access to a portion of the Fund's resources, called the "reserve tranche" (initially called the gold tranche). The idea behind the automatic access is that the member country needs some space to use Fund resources for any purpose consistent with the Fund's Charter to help it conduct its international monetary transactions—without falling on its knees and pleading with the Fund (so pathetic when you think about it). Oh, and what's a **tranche**? Its origin is French and it means a "slice." In a bit we'll tell you about tranches in stand-by arrangements. And, hey, if you can pronounce tranche as the French do, you would be the coolest person at a cocktail party.

Member countries seeking an IMF loan beyond the reserve tranche must convince the Fund they have a balance of payments need. As the amount of the loan increases beyond the reserve tranche (technically moving into the "first credit," followed by "upper credit," tranches), the IMF imposes conditions on the use of the funds, known famously (or infamously) around the world as "conditionality."

Conditionality refers to the explicit commitment by the member country to implement remedial measures in return for IMF assistance. The Fund didn't just make up the requirement. Take a look at Article I(v), which lists one of the purposes of the Fund, as well as Article V, section 3(a), and you'll see the message (actually command): "Member country, you can use the general resources of the Fund only *temporarily* and under *adequate* safeguards. We want our resources back! So get your friggin act together!"

Conditions can range from general commitments to cooperate with the Fund regarding domestic economic policy to presenting the Fund with specific measures the country intends to implement at specific points in time. Those measures typically have related to minor things, such as the domestic money supply, budget deficits, international reserves, external debt, exchange rates, and interest rates. Yeah, just minor things . . . As you'll see in other chapters, conditionality has evolved—in a controversial way.

Drawings in the upper credit tranches typically are associated with one to two year "stand-by arrangements" (similar to pre-approved lines of credit). The Extended Fund Facility (established in 1974) provides "extended arrangements" of three to four years, usually to address structural problems in the economy. Upper credit tranche drawings are released only after the member country has met economic performance targets—"performance criteria" in the biz.

The country's specific plans are outlined in a "Letter of Intent" presented to the IMF. In many cases it's actually a "Letter of What the IMF Has Told Us What We Will Do." Although formally the member country prepares and "presents" the Letter of Intent to the Fund, practically speaking the Fund wields a pretty big stick when it comes to the Letter's content. The lending process begins when a member country asks for assistance. The Fund staff then enters into negotiations with the borrowing member (usually the finance ministry) to chat about the amount, terms and conditions of the lending arrangement, or program. After the Fund staff and finance ministry agree on the terms, the Letter is submitted to the Fund. A Letter of Intent typically describes the BOP problems the member is experiencing and the policies the member will pursue to correct the problems with the assistance of the Fund financing. The Letter will usually include a memorandum with details of its economic and financial policies. The Fund's Executive Board Decision attaches the Letter to its decision to provide financing. To look at the real thing, do an internet search for "Thailand's August 14, 1997 Letter of Intent."

In addition to drawings from the General Resources Account, the Fund has established a number of other lending "facilities" designed for specific problems, such as the Extended Credit Facility, which succeeded the Poverty Reduction and Growth Facility and provides concessional loans with a zero interest rate through the end of 2014 (when the interest rate will again be reviewed) with a grace period of five and a half years for poor countries experiencing protracted balance of payments problems; the Standby Credit Facility, which provides financial assistance to low-income countries with short-term balance of payment needs; the Rapid Credit Facility, which provides rapid financial assistance with limited conditionality to low-income countries with an urgent need to balance payments; and the **Flexible Credit Line**, which provides conditionality-free financing for member countries facing an imminent crisis, provided they meet certain qualification criteria.

Convertibility

According to its Charter, one of the IMF's purposes is to facilitate the expansion and balanced growth of international trade. What's needed in part is a multilateral system of payments for the current account—e.g., trade—transactions. Convertibility is key. What's that? A member country's residents, companies, and governmental bodies must be able to use the country's currency or be able to acquire foreign currencies to settle international trade transactions.

But here's the thing: Although the doors of the BWS opened in 1946, it wasn't really functional until the late 1950s. Remember that European countries were really messed up after the war. Inconvertibility was a way to deal with persistent current account deficits that resulted from imports exceeding exports (remember, war-torn). Just to make sure you get it, suppose the Netherlands guilder was convertible in the 1947, and the Netherlands was running a current account deficit. It was obligated under the BWS to stay within the one-percent parity band. But the deficit would put downward pressure of the guilder. Holders of guilder deposits would dump them, putting more downward pressure on the currency. Speculators would "short" the currency, i.e, use borrowed funds to sell the guilder, putting even more downward pressure on the currency. Eventually the central bank would burn through all of its reserves to defend the fixed rate, using dollars in reserves to buy gilders in the market. There's the rub. The Netherlands, like other European countries, didn't have much by way of reserves. Not even IMF funds sufficed. Solution? Don't make the guilder convertible.

By the 1950s, the war-ravaged countries were back on their feet and producing. The United States' BOP was such (we'll talk about this in Chapter 3) that dollars were flowing to these countries, and their improved foreign reserves prepared them to engage in international trade. And to put icing on the cake, in 1959 the IMF increased quotas to be used for temporary BOP problems. By then the European currencies were convertible (Japan's yen was inconvertible until 1964). It was all good for the BWS to become fully functional.

You'll find the rules on convertibility in Article VIII of the Fund's Charter. With some exceptions (the major one being Article XIV, which allows a transitional convertibility period), member countries agree not to impose restrictions on payments and transfers relating to the current account. They also agree to avoid "discriminatory currency arrangements," that is, agreeing to a favorable arrangement with another member country without offering the same arrangement to all other member countries. That's just not a nice thing to do. "Multiple currency practices"—using different exchange rates for different transactions—are also a no-no (unless the Fund otherwise approves). Although historically member countries were slow to accept Article VIII obligations, 167 of the IMF's 184 member countries now say yes to the dress.

Funny, though, while Article VIII insists on avoiding restrictions on the current account, Article VI(3) allows capital account restrictions, called **capital controls.** Actually it's not funny. We talked about this a bit ago. Hot money—fast-moving capital—wreaked havoc with countries' economies during the inter-war period. So the negotiators at the Bretton Woods Conference were just fine with this text: "Members may exercise such controls as are necessary to regulate international capital movements . . ." In fact, the IMF may "request" a member country to impose capital controls to prevent the use of the Fund's general resources to meet "large or sustained" capital outflows. The Charter says "request" but it's pretty much a demand because if the country fails to use capital controls, the Fund can close the general resources spigot. But it's never done that. There's one catch to using capital controls: a member country can't use them to restrict current account transactions. In the 1990s, the Fund flirted with the idea of switching the Charter's default position from pro-capital controls to anti-capital controls (many economists say they don't work) but dropped the idea when the Asian financial crisis hit. Today the Fund has in so many words endorsed the "judicious" (nice word) use of capital controls.

Compliance with the Fund's Rules

Before we talk about member countries' compliance with Fund rules, let's talk about what's called the Fund's "corpus juris," or its body of law. There is, of course, the Fund's Articles of Agreement. And Article XII, section 2(g) says: "The Board of Governors, and the Executive Board to the extent authorized, may adopt such rules and regulations as may be necessary or appropriate to conduct the business of the Fund." The Board of Governors has adopted the By-Laws. The Executive Board has adopted the Rules and Regulations, subject to the review of the Board of Governors. The Boards' resolutions and decisions further define the Fund's law and policy.

Now let's get to member countries. Although people say that the IMF has no real authority to force members to comply with many Fund rules and policies, that's not really true in practice. Sure, letters of intent, stand-by arrangements and other IMF loans aren't contracts or any other type of legal obligation. So a failure to abide by a Letter of Intent or stand-by arrangement isn't a breach of contract that would enable the Fund or anybody else to sue the country.

Still, there are many other ways the IMF can apply pressure on countries to comply. First, conditionality allows the Fund to withhold funds if a member country doesn't comply with the loans's conditions. Second, members know that by violating the rules and policies of the IMF they may be shut out of the international capital markets—where the money is.

Third, the Fund can prohibit a member country from using the General Resources Account. Ninth, the IMF can kick the country out of the organization. In the only expulsion in the Fund's history, Czechoslovakia was thrown out in 1954 when it introduced a new par value without first conferring with the Fund. And fiftieth, through collaboration and consultation with member countries, the Fund tries to persuade and cajole countries into complying with rules and policies. But ask yourself this question: If the member country hasn't borrowed from the Fund and doesn't plan to, how much leverage does the Fund really have? This happened in the 2000s.

Technical Assistance

The IMF began to give countries technical assistance in 1964 when ex-colonies wanted help setting up their own central banks and ministries of finance. The Fund provides assistance in the areas of fiscal policy, monetary policy, banking, institution building, financial legislation, and statistics (which helps IMF surveillance). When the Fund is providing assistance in areas not directly related to economics, it still says it's all about economics. For example, the Fund provides technical assistance with financial legislation relating to laws that support a free market.

Standards and Codes

The IMF, along with the World Bank and other standard-setting bodies, such as the Basel Committee on Banking Supervision, has developed internationally recognized standards and **codes** in twelve areas, three of which the Fund has developed: data dissemination, fiscal transparency, and monetary and financial policy transparency. The standards and codes reflect "best practices." They aren't law in any sense. But member countries will request that a Report on the Observance of Standards and Codes be prepared and published to tell the world (including potential foreign investors) that they're abiding or attempting to abide by the best practices in question—like a stamp of approval. Remember the capital markets!

The IMF's Structure

There are two primary organs within the IMF: the Board of Governors and the Executive Board. The Board of Governors is the highest governance body. Each member country has one representative—typically its finance minister or the head of its central bank—on the Board of Governors, which meets once annually. Members of the Board of Governors also serve on two important committees. The International Monetary and Financial Committee (formerly the Interim Committee) considers amendments to the Fund's Charter, monitors developments in the global economy (such as global liquidity), watches out for events that might mess with the world financial system, and advises the IMF on the direction of its work. The Development Committee—a joint committee with the World Bank—advises the Board on policies and matters concerning developing countries.

Although the Board of Governors has delegated most of its powers to the Executive Board (we'll get to it in a sec), the Charter says the Board can't delegate certain decisions, such as deciding what'll be on the Fund's cafeteria menu, or deciding on admission of new member countries, making quota adjustments, issuing SDRs, and amending the Articles of Agreement (Articles III, XXVIII). After all, they have to have something to do. The Charter stipulates that the Fund can make most decisions by a simple majority. But some decisions regarding key aspects of the Fund, such as quota adjustment, require an 85 percent majority of the total voting power (Article III, section 2(c)). And guess who has veto power? You got it—the United States, with their relatively massive 16.75 percent of the vote.

The Executive Board chaired by the Fund's Managing Director, currently Christine Lagarde, manages the IMF's day-to-day operations. The Board consists of twenty-four Executive Directors, eight of whom represent individual countries (China, France, Germany, Japan, Russia, Saudi Arabia, the United Kingdom, and the United States). The remaining sixteen Executive Directors represent constituencies—groups of similarly situated (for example, geographically or linguistically) member nations. The Executive Board meets several times each week. Each Director has a weighted number of votes tied to the constituency's combined IMF quota. But in practice decisions by formal vote can be avoided in favor of general consensus. Kind of a cumbaya thing, but not.

The Fund's staff is subdivided into a number of regional and functional departments. Five regional departments cover operations for the entire world. Functional departments include Finance, Fiscal Affairs, the IMF Institute (which trains national finance officers), and various administrative departments (Legal, Policy Development, Research, External Relations, etc.). In 2001, the Executive Board also established the Independent Evaluation Office (IEO), which evaluates IMF operations and policies. Chapter 7 will address the IEO in more detail.

Part Five: The Functions and Structure of the World Bank Group

Although the Bretton Woods Conference's objectives formally mentioned "development," relatively little time was devoted to discussing the plight of "developing countries." Actually, creating the World Bank was an afterthought. You just have to look at what the main players spent most of their time on. Preparations for creating the IMF had been underway for close to five years. Although there were preliminary drafts of the World Bank Charter, they didn't receive nearly as much attention as the IMF Charter.

Here's what happened in a nutshell. In June 1944, just prior to the Bretton Woods Conference, a number of countries met in Atlantic City to prepare an agenda for the Conference. There, the United Kingdom submitted the "boat draft," the document was drafted on the Queen Mary, which became the basis for discussion at the Bretton Woods Conference. The main point of contention was whether "development" or reconstruction would be the World Bank's priority. The European nations were particularly interested in World Bank assistance for post-war reconstruction of infrastructure. But the delegations from developing countries were more interested in, well, development of their countries. Mexico proposed language for the World Bank's Charter that would make development a priority. That didn't go anywhere. But developing nations did succeed in introducing the language found in Article III, section 1(a) that says the Bank's facilities would be used with "equitable consideration to projects for development and projects for reconstruction alike." Throw the developing countries a bone, yo. Check out supplement 1C.

Other chapters will tell you about the evolution of the World Bank. We'll give you an overview here. The World Bank consists of the International Bank for Reconstruction and Development (IBRD) and the International Development Association (IDA), the latter created in 1960. Both institutions make loans to governments (or to public or private entities that have a government guarantee) for projects and programs related to "development," that is, loans designed to promote economic and social progress in member countries. But the IDA makes loans to very poor countries measured by per capita gross national income (GNI), currently less than $1,205—e.g., Benin. The loans are "concessional"—i.e., interest free, with a repayment period of 40 or 35 years (if blended with an IBRD loan) and a 10-year grace period. Wouldn't you like that kind of loan? The IBRD lends to middle-income countries with GNI per capita ranging currently from $1,206 to $12,475—e.g., Costa Rica. The loans aren't concessional. The interest is based on how much the Bank has to pay on its bonds (the "cost of funding" a Bank loan). Borrowers have a 3- to 5-year grace period, and 15 to 20 years to repay the loan.

Three other entities are associated with, but legally and financially independent of, the IBRD and the IDA: The International Finance Corporation (IFC), the International Center for Settlement of Investment Disputes (ICSID), and the Multilateral Investment Guarantee Agency (MIGA). Collectively, these five entities are known as the World Bank Group.

Now we'll describe the initial activities of the IBRD. We'll then briefly explain the work of the IFC, ICSID, and MIGA. Later chapters will address the World Bank's evolution.

The International Bank for Reconstruction and Development

The main purposes of the IBRD, outlined in Article I of its Charter—check out supplement 1D—are to promote economic development and reduce poverty. It tackles this stuff by providing loans, guarantees and technical assistance for projects and programs in member countries.

You might say, hey, wait a second—before we go further, what's the difference between the IBRD and the IMF? Fair question. The IBRD and the IMF are similar in several ways and they frequently coordinate their activities. Still, their operations differ in important ways. Like the IMF, the IBRD is a multilateral institution, meaning that the governments of member countries own it. Only countries that are members of the IMF can become members of the IBRD. In fact, virtually every country in the world is a member of both institutions.

The IBRD is also like the IMF to the extent that richer countries own a greater share of the IBRD and have more voting power than the poorer countries. When a country joins the IBRD, the number of shares it receives (representing ownership) will reflect its quota in the IMF, which in turn reflects the country's relative economic strength. Like the IMF, the IBRD's Charter calls for weighted voting—i.e., not a one-vote-per-country rule but a voting system giving the richer countries (e.g., the United States) more votes and influence than poorer countries (although decisions typically have been taken on a consensus basis).

Both institutions focus on economic matters. The IMF traditionally engaged in short-term balance-of-payments lending to help establish policies that would stabilize overheated economies (e.g., correct a distorted exchange rate). The Bank, by contrast, traditionally funded longer-term projects designed to promote economic growth (e.g., an irrigation project to increase commodity exports). Starting with the debt crisis of the 1980s and continuing through the financial crises of the 1990s, both institutions more closely coordinated their lending and their use of conditionality to promote fundamental and often-painful market reforms in developing countries and former socialist economies. The Bank now engages in "adjustment lending" aimed at helping countries modify their economic policies and structures— a focus that differs from project lending. The IMF's activities have also come to resemble the Bank's to the extent that the Fund (1) now concerns itself with structural issues as well as balance-of-payments problems and (2) no longer restricts itself to short-term lending.

Although the IMF manages a pool of currencies from which it makes loans to member countries, it likes to think of itself primarily as an institution that oversees an orderly international monetary system, as called for in its Charter. The IBRD has a different mandate: it describes itself as "something like a cooperative" whose primary function is to engage in multilateral development financing for the benefit of its member countries—middle-income and creditworthy lower-income (below $1000 per capita income) countries.

Members of the IBRD pay only a small portion of the value of their shares, which collectively constitutes "paid-in capital;" the remainder is called "callable capital" in the biz. Unlike the IMF, whose loans are funded primarily by its members' quota subscriptions, the IBRD primarily funds its lending by selling AAA rated bonds in the world's capital markets to pension funds, insurance companies, corporations and banks, as well as individuals. Because of the AAA rating (virtually no risk of default), the IBRD can borrow at relatively inexpensive rates and pass along the savings to borrowing members. (The IDA is funded by donations from the world's rich countries.)

So speaking of borrowing, what kinds of loans does the IBRD make? Initially, the IBRD stressed reconstruction over development, providing loans to war-torn European countries. With the advent of the **Marshall Plan**, which provided significant United States aid to reconstruct Europe, the IBRD switched from reconstruction lending to "project lending" in developing countries. Many of these countries had just achieved independence during the decolonization period (1955–1965) and governments were down for taking the same road industrialized countries had taken to achieve economic prosperity. So policymakers in both the developed and developing world promoted a development strategy encouraging massive investments in developing countries to help them "take off" economically through a modern industrialized sector. The resultant economic growth would "trickle down" to the poorest segments of society. Uh . . . okay, if you say so . . .

The IBRD's lending concentrated on developing a country's infrastructure, such as building electric power plants and implementing transportation projects. Electric power would encourage the creation of factories, which in turn would create non-agricultural jobs and increase the standard of living. Improved transportation would not only benefit industry, but agriculture as well by making it easier to take commodities to the markets. Sounds like a plan!

Interestingly (well, we think it's interesting), the IBRD was formed in part to promote private foreign investment via guarantees or participations in loans and other investments made by private investors. But most of the lending during this period was to government entities, which were better able to handle large projects than the relatively small, under-developed private sectors. This contributed to state-led development in many parts of the world. Just say "statism" and you're good.

The International Finance Corporation

The International Finance Corporation (IFC), formed in 1956, promotes private sector investment in poor countries that would otherwise not easily attract private investment. It does this by providing, among other things, long-term market-priced loans and equity financing for private sector projects, such as financial institutions. The IFC's participation in a project acts as a seal of approval, encouraging other private investors to become involved. So in equity finance, the IFC takes a stake ranging from five to twenty percent of a project's equity. When it's time for the IFC to exit the investment, it prefers to sell its shares through the domestic market, often selling its shares to the public ("public offering").

The Multilateral Investment Guarantee Agency

Established in 1988, the Multilateral Investment Guarantee Agency (MIGA) is the most recent addition to the World Bank Group. MIGA is an investment insurance agency that encourages foreign direct investment in developing nations by providing guarantees against political (noncommercial) risks. In this way, investors are more willing to invest in countries that may not be politically stable.

The International Centre for Settlement of Investment Disputes

The International Centre for Settlement of Investment Disputes (ICSID) was established by treaty in 1966 to provide a forum for arbitration or mediation of disputes between foreign investors and their host countries. Its purpose is to promote increased flows of international investment by providing a forum outside the host state for settlement of investment disputes. Parties can't be forced to use ICSID conciliation and arbitration services. But once they've consented to arbitration under the ICSID Convention, neither can withdraw unilaterally.

The World Bank's Structure

Similar to the IMF, a Board of Governors represents the Bank's member countries. All member countries have one representative on the Board of Governors, typically the minister of finance or minister of development. The Bank's ultimate policy-makers, the governors, meet once a year at the Annual Meetings of the Boards of Governors of the World Bank Group and the International Monetary Fund. The World Bank Group President, currently Jim Yong Kim, chairs the meetings of the Boards of Directors.

Like the IMF, the governors delegate specific duties to the Board of Directors, which consists of the World Bank Group President and twenty-five Executive Directors. Some duties are non-delegable, such as deciding on a cafeteria menu that's better than the IMF's, admitting new members, changing the amounts of capital stock, or suspending a member (Article V, sec. 2(b)). The Board usually meets at least twice a week. France, Germany, Japan, the United Kingdom, and the United States, the five largest shareholders, each appoint their own Executive Director, while the other member countries are put in groups represented by 20 elected Executive Directors.

Again similar to the IMF, the Bank uses a weighted system of voting: voting power is based on the member country's quota. Traditionally the United States selected the Bank's President because the U.S. was the largest shareholder and because of the importance of the U.S. capital markets for the Bank's bonds. As a quid pro quo, the Europeans selected the Fund's Managing Director. Emerging countries have raised holy hell over this and now, supposedly, the selection process is open, transparent, and merit-based. Say that again?

The other World Bank Group organizations have a parallel structure. Individuals who serve as Executive Directors for the IBRD typically serve as the Executive Directors in all other World Bank Group institutions, managing their day-to-day operations.

Part Six: "Morgenthau and Mikey"

Scene Five

Setting: July 1, 1944, shortly after 3:00 p.m., Mount Washington Hotel, Bretton Woods, New Hampshire, United Nations Monetary and Financial Conference.

Character:

    Henry Morgenthau, Jr.: U.S. Treasury Secretary

Secretary Morgenthau: "In many countries controls and restrictions were set up without regard to their effect on other countries. These devices became economic weapons with which the earliest phase of our present war was fought by the Fascist dictators. There was an ironic inevitability in this process. Economic aggression can have no other offspring than war . . . Our task, then, is to confer, and to reach understanding and agreement, upon certain basic measures . . . for the establishment of a sound and stable economic relationship among us . . . We are to concern ourselves here with essential steps in the creation of a world economy in which the people of every nation will be able to realize their potentialities in peace; will be able, through their industry, their inventiveness, their thrift, to raise their own standards of living and enjoy, increasingly, the fruits of material progress on an earth infinitely blessed with natural riches. This is the indispensable cornerstone of freedom and security. All else must be built upon this. For freedom of opportunity is the foundation for all other freedoms."

Scene Six

Setting: June 6, 1954, shortly after 3:00 p.m., 5419 W. Roosevelt Road, Nashua, New Hampshire.

Characters:

    Michael Swift: former private, U.S. Army

    Irma: Brad's mother

(Michael is fixing burgers for a barbecue that evening, knock on the front door)

Michael: Be there in a sec!

(he washes his hands quickly and jogs to the door and opens it)

Michael: Can I help you ma'am?

Irma: Michael Swift?

Michael: Yes, that's me.

Irma: Mikey?

(pause)

Michael: Nobody's called me that in a long time.

Irma: Can I take you to Wilson's Dairy? It's just a block away, near my hotel.

Michael: I'm sorry. Who . . . Do I know—

Irma: I kept this in a shoe box.

(she hands Mikey a letter, he stares at it)

Irma: How about a banana split with chocolate and strawberry ice cream?

(fade to black)

You Gotta Know Something About Them!

John Maynard Keynes

John Maynard Keynes, one of three children, was the son of a lecturer and Cambridge's first female mayor. He enrolled in the prestigious Eton College at age fourteen, and later earned a mathematics degree from Kings College in Cambridge. Although Keynes never earned a doctorate degree, he was appointed to a life fellowship at Kings College at the tender age of twenty-six. Here's a great story: He loved art—quite the collector. His art critic friend told him about some Impressionist paintings in France that they should grab for Britain's National Gallery. While the war raged on, Keynes and the director of the National Gallery, Sir Charles Holmes, went to Paris and successfully bid on a number of paintings. But Holmes didn't like Cézanne. He didn't want to buy "Pommes," a cool still life portrait. So Keynes bought it. When Keynes arrived at a farmhouse in Sussex, he found that the road to the house was too muddy. So he put the Cézanne in a hedge. In 1969, Duncan Grant, Keynes' lover, said "when he arrived here he said 'if you'd like to go down to the road, there's a Cézanne just behind the gate.'" Keynes hung the Cézanne over his bed. When he died in 1946 he bequeathed it to Kings College.

Harry "Dexter" White

Harry "Dexter" White, the youngest of seven children, was the son of an immigrant peddler. He served in the U.S. Army in the war against Imperial Germany before beginning his academic career with education from Columbia, Stanford, and Harvard. White was a high-ranking economist with the U.S. Treasury and one of the architects of the Fund. He was accused of passing federal documents to the Soviets—the stress of denying these charges before the House Un-American Activities Committee aggravated an existing heart condition and led to a fatal heart attack. Brutal.

Jim Yong Kim

Image of Jim Yong Kim by *www.dfat.gov.au* is licensed under CC BY 2.0

Jim Yong Kim is a Korean-American who grew up in Muscatine, Iowa. He was the quarterback of his high school's football team and point guard on the basketball team. Kim is currently serving as the twelfth President of the World Bank, after being nominated to the position by President Barack Obama. He's done some very cool stuff—he's worked with the World Health Organization and co-founded Partners in Health, which treats diseases in impoverished areas on four continents. He's been awarded a MacArthur "Genius" Fellowship, and was named one of America's 25 best leaders by U.S. News and World Report and one of the 100 most influential people in the world by TIME Magazine.

Christine Lagarde

Christine Lagarde is the mother of two sons, an attorney, and was once a member of the French national synchronized swimming team. As the first female chairman at the international law firm of Baker & McKenzie, Largarde specialized in anti-trust, labor, and mergers and acquisitions. She was the first woman to work as the Finance and Economy Minister of a G-7 country, the first woman to be elected the IMF's Managing Director, and was honored with a Forbes magazine rating of 2009's 17th most influential woman in the world. Right on. Lagarde regularly posts pictures on her Facebook page and tweets about her activities and thoughts—in April of 2013, she tweeted that "a 3-speed economy is not enough, we need a full-speed global economy & this requires action on all policy fronts."

Joseph Gold

Sir Joseph Gold was General Counsel of the IMF's legal department from 1960 until 1979. Born in London, England, he was knighted in 1980 by Queen Elizabeth II (no horse and armor, though). "Joe," as those close to him called him, always regretted not attending the Bretton Woods conference, especially since some of his work was key to the formation of the International Monetary Fund. No wonder, then, that he wrote a ton of stuff on international monetary law. Maybe his S.J.D. from Harvard helped? Sir Joseph donated a sizeable collection of his writings on monetary law to Southern Methodist University, where he was awarded an Honorary Doctor of Laws degree. And check it out: He had a passionate interest in literature. Just before he kicked the bucket, he donated over 3,000 items of the Irish author Samuel Beckett (who doesn't know *Waiting for Godot*?) to the University of Delaware, which is nationally known for its collection of Irish literature. How cool is that?

What's Up with That?

Fixed Versus Floating Exchange Rates

A country with a fixed foreign exchange rate declares to the world that it'll defend the fixed rate, say 5 balbos to 1 dolla. If speculative capital floods the country, the amount of balbos will increase in the economy (because the dollas are being converted to balbos). This will cause downward pressure on the balbo—i.e., the real value of the balbo should be, say, 7 balbos to 1 dolla. Because the country has to defend the fixed 5/1 rate, its central bank will be forced to use its foreign reserves (dollas) to buy balbos to reverse the downward trend. At a certain point, the central bank will run out of reserves. The markets will know at some point that the balbo will have to be devalued. In other words, the country will be forced to declare a new fixed rate or abandon the fixed rate regime altogether.

This doesn't necessarily happen to a country with a floating exchange rate system. In the scenario we've just described, the balbo's value would decline until the markets determine it's "at the right price." In theory, the central bank wouldn't intervene in this process. But in reality central banks in countries with a floating exchange rate intervene in the foreign exchange markets to prevent what otherwise would happen in the markets—either a depreciation (the currency's value declines) or appreciation (the currency's value increases). Like we said in the text, the changes can be significant and destabilizing.

The Mechanics of the Gold Standard

There're various ways to explain the mechanics of the gold standard. Here's one take on it and it's simplified so you can grasp how it works. Keep in mind the assumption that France, the deficit country, can't borrow enough from Germany to finance the deficit. Also understand that the system works only if countries allow unhindered flows of gold. And the central banks of each country are obligated to exchange domestic currency for gold at the fixed rate. If the gold flows freely, the so-called "price-specie-flow mechanism" (yeah, a mouthful) works wonders! The adjustment process is symmetrical, meaning both the surplus and deficit countries have to adjust—meaning taking the pain—equally. Equality of pain rocks! Well . . . not really, but let's start with the way it works *in theory*. We'll use bullet points to take you through it step by step.

- Trade between Germany and France; Germany is the surplus country (exporting more than importing), France is the deficit country (importing more the exporting)
- Germany exports shoes for DM10 each; France exports scarves for FF10 each
- DM is fixed at DM5/1 ounce of gold; FF is fixed at FF10/1 ounce of gold
- So the fixed cross-rate between Germany and France: DM1/FF2.
- Each country starts with 10 ounces of gold in reserves
- Hence Germany has DM50 money supply (10x5=50); France has FF100 (10x10=100)
- Every time France wants to buy a German shoe, the importer has to pay FF20
- If the French importer buys two shoes, it has to pay FF40
- The French importer goes to the French central bank and exchanges the FF40 for 4 ounces of gold
- The German exporter takes the 4 ounces of gold to its central bank and receives DM 20
- So France loses 4 ounces of gold to Germany, leaving it with 6 ounces in gold reserves
- Because France is obligated to hold its fixed rate at FF10/1 ounce, there are FF60 circulating (if FF10/1 ounce of gold, 6x10=60FF)
- The lower money supply in France is deflationary (price levels drop)
- Germany's reserves increases to 14 ounces of gold

- Because Germany is obligated to hold its fixed rate of DM5/1 ounce of gold, Germany's money supply increases to DM70 (14x5=70)
- The increase in the money supply sparks inflation in Germany—increased price levels
- Assume a deflation rate of 5% in France and a 5% inflation rate in Germany
- Germany's shoes are now DM10.50 (price level increases); France's scarves are now FF9.50 (price level drops)
- Because Germany's exported shoes will cost more, it will export fewer shoes and buy more French scarves
- Because France's scarves cost less, it will export more scarves and buy fewer German shoes
- This causes the level of reserves to decrease in Germany because it's buying more French scarves and the German importers will exchange DM for gold
- This also causes the level of reserves in France to increase because French exporters will exchange gold for FF
- So Germany's surplus will decrease, and France's deficit will decrease, until "equilibrium" is established, meaning the flows of gold subside because the price of the shoe and scarf return to DM10/FF10.

Check out this really important point: Under the gold standard each country has <u>no control over its monetary policy</u>. The money supply increases or decreases automatically. Put another way, if Germany were to increase its money supply, interest rates would decrease and holders of DM deposits would sell the DM to Germany's central bank for gold and invest a currency with a better return. Germany would start losing its gold reserves and ultimately be unable to defend the DM5/1 ounce gold exchange rate.

Some (but not many today) think this system is really cool because central banks can't increase the money supply willy-nilly, which brings more stability to international transactions. But there are drawbacks. We'll mention just two. First, under the gold standard (or any fixed exchange rate system) a country has no control over its monetary policy. It can't increase the money supply to promote employment—more money in circulation means (at least temporarily) more economic activity and more jobs. And b), if the system is based on gold, the gold-mining countries would hold lots of power over the system.

But, here's the reality: Countries violated the "rules of the game," the gold standard game. They cheated on their partners and the whole system! Surplus countries receiving gold (Germany in our example) thought, "Well, if we play by the rules of the game, we'll just speed up the process where our money supply will increase, we'll face this inflation thing, and lose our export surplus." So there was less of an incentive for Germany to let the automatic adjustment take place. But poor France, on the other hand, would eventually start to panic because of the loss of gold. So, because Germany wasn't doing its part to reduce the inflows of gold, France held much of the burden of the adjustment process. And sometimes this would cause deficit countries like France to adopt overly contractionary policies. They thought this would get them to the point where the process would reverse: France would start exporting more, which would add to its gold reserves. This whole symmetrical adjustment thing was a myth.

Because of the pain of adjustment, unemployment/inflation, countries also manipulated the mechanism in part by "sterilizing:" France's central bank would buy assets for FF, putting more FF in circulation. Germany would sell assets for DM, taking DM out of circulation.

Ahh . . . the games countries play.

The Trilemma

To better understand the Bretton Woods System as well as the difference between fixed and flexible exchange rates, you should know something about the so-called "impossible trinity," otherwise known as the "trilemma." So how does it work? A country can simultaneously choose two but not three of the following policy goals:

(1) independent monetary policy

(2) exchange rate stability

(3) free capital movements

The gold system embraced (2) and (3) at the expense of (1)—no independent monetary policy. The BWS went for (1) and (2)—capital movements were restricted. In other words, countries used capital controls so that they could pursue reasonable monetary policies to promote employment, and the par value system promoted exchange rate stability (par values could be adjusted within limits). As you'll see, after the collapse of the BWS, the United States elected (1) and (3), giving up (2). In practice, though, the trilemma is not as strict as it appears to be. Countries cheated in the gold standard—played tricks to get some of (1), and countries like the United States have intervened in the foreign currency markets to manage their exchange rates—tricks to get some of (2).

Capital Controls

A government or central bank sets capital controls to limit movement of capital in and out of a domestic economy. These controls can help protect a country's financial stability in the face of unpredictable capital inflows and outflows. Controls might include market-based controls on the volume and price of transactions, taxation of cross-border financial flows, or restrictions on the speed at which currency enters and exits a country. While the Fund allows for capital controls under Article VI, section 3, member countries have to follow the restrictions in Article VI, section 1. In its 2013 banking crisis, Cyprus, among other things, put controls on its banks with restrictions like €300 daily maximum cash withdrawals and required approval of transactions above €500,000.

Special Drawing Rights

The SDR plan first began to take shape in March of 1966 when the Managing Director at the time, Pierre-Paul Schweitzer, proposed a reserve-creating plan to apply to all members, to counter fears of a global liquidity shortage of reserve assets. Reserves of U.S. dollars in central banks continued to climb and countries began to restrict international transactions and borrow to meet balance of payments needs. SDRs were born on August 6, 1969 (First Amendment of the Articles of Agreement), valued at 0.888671 grams of fine gold (the amount of gold equal to one U.S. dollar). The SDR isn't a currency—it's an artificial reserve asset. It's a potential claim on the currencies of other IMF members, meaning that holders of SDRs can exchange them for "freely usable currencies" (currencies that are readily accepted in international trade—e.g., the U.S. dollar, the euro, and the yen). For example, Bolivia, whose currency is the boliviano (hardly anyone will touch it), can exchange its SDRs for U.S. dollars or euros or yen. The SDR is the unit of account of the IMF, which means that all computations (except one) relating to currencies are done in SDRs. And check it out: Other international organizations use the SDR as a unit of account, such as the Nordic Investment Bank. Even private parties can use it as a unit of account—e.g., commercial banks that accept deposits expressed in SDRs. Today's SDR is defined as a basket of currencies: the pound sterling, the euro, the Japanese yen, and the U.S. dollar. The Fund's Executive Board reviews the basket's composition every five years. In November 2010 (the latest review), the weights of the basket currencies were revised using the value of exports of goods and services, as well as the amount of reserves of respective currencies held by other IMF member countries.

Quota Formula

According to the IMF, "The current quota formula is a weighted average of GDP (weight of fifty percent), openness (thirty percent), economic variability (fifteen percent), and international reserves (five percent). For this purpose, GDP is measured through a blend of GDP—based on market exchange rates (weight of sixty percent)—and on PPP exchange rates (forty percent). The formula also includes a 'compression factor' that reduces the dispersion in calculated quota shares across members."

Most of the controversy is over GDP, openness, and economic variability. So let's break these down. Gross Domestic Product (GDP) is, put simply, the total monetary value of goods and services produced in a country during a specific time—usually in a year's time. Notice, though, that for purposes of the quota formula, GDP is a blend of market and purchasing power parity (PPP) exchange rates. PPP exchange rates, which emerging economies favor, reflect the U.S. dollar's higher purchasing power in developing and emerging economies—e.g., you can buy more haircuts for a dollar in China than you can in the United States. Not surprisingly, market exchange rates receive the higher weighting—sixty percent. What is at stake is quota shares: switching from a pure market exchange rate to a blended rate that includes a PPP exchange rate translates into reduced shares for the rich economies

What about openness, meaning financial openness? Basically, it's supposed to measure a country's integration into the world economy. Although there're different ways of measuring openness, its basic purpose is to gauge cross-border investment income flows. A number of economists (including IMF Directors) have criticized the inclusion of this metric because in part it overstates a country's integration into the global economy.

Variability is intended to capture the likelihood of a country having to use Fund resources. It's based on a country's vulnerability arising from external capital flows. Like openness, this metric is highly contested.

And the Fund wanted a "simple and transparent" quota formula. Yeah, right . . .

Basic Votes

Before the 2011 Sixth Amendment of the Charter, Article XII 5(a) stipulated that each member country would receive 250 basic votes. The Sixth Amendment changed the calculation of basic votes to make sure the ratio of total basic votes to total voting power is not eroded by quota increases. Notice that under the new formula, adjustment to basic votes will occur automatically. Changes won't require Fund action—and no Fund organ can interfere with the automatic adjustments. The new method of determining basic votes—which nearly tripled the number of basic votes—reflects the Fund's recognition of a dynamic global economy and the need to give low-income member countries increased participation and voice in the Fund.

Tranches

Here's a visual look at how tranches work. Notice how in column (b) a member country's use of the reserve tranche brings its purchases to 100% of its quota. Purchases above a member country's quota move it into the credit tranches.

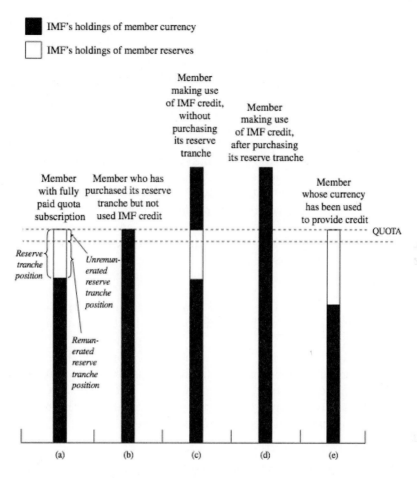

Situation (a): A member has paid its quota subscription in full and not drawn on its reserve tranche . . .

Situation (b): The member has drawn its reserve tranche in full. The reserve tranche purchase is not subject to charges (interest).

Situation (c): The member is using IMF resources but has not drawn its reserve tranche. The level of holdings in excess of the member's quota is subject to charges.

Situation (d): The member is using IMF resources, in addition to having drawn its reserve tranche. The level of holdings in excess of the member's quota is subject to charges.

Situation (e): The IMF has made use of the member's currency and pays the member remuneration on its enlarged reserve tranche position.

Source: *Financial Organization and Operations of the IMF*, Pamphlet Series No. 45, Sixth Edition, International Monetary Fund (2001)

Flexible Credit Line

The Flexible Credit Line (FCL) was established in March 2009 and does exactly what its name suggests: It gives qualified countries flexible lending both for crisis prevention and resolution. A "qualified" country is one with strong economic fundamentals and equally strong policy track records. It makes sense, then, that the usual conditionality isn't at play. The FCL is a renewable and non-concessional facility; the costs of drawings vary with the duration and amount of the loan. An approved member country can either draw on the credit line as soon as it's approved, or can wait and see if it's needed (this wait-and-see security isn't free—countries have to pay a commitment fee that's refunded only if they draw). If a member country draws from the FCL, the repayment period is between three and five years. Three countries, Mexico, Columbia, and Poland, have arrangements under the FCL. All three countries are taking the precautionary wait-and-see approach to the use of the FCL.

The Marshall Plan

Between 1948 and 1951 the United States provided about $13 billion in cash, goods and services to help Europe rebuild its war-torn economies. Under the plan, the United States provided aid to prevent people from starving in major war areas and to repair the economy. The goal was to rebuild the economies of Europe as quickly as possible. The plan was aimed at preventing the spread of communism in Western Europe and at stabilizing the international order in a way favorable to the development of political democracy and free market economies.

The Smoot-Hawley Tariff Act

Well, the name might sound "tariffying," but it really isn't that bad. Here's the scoop: the Smoot-Hawley Act is named after its sponsors, Senator Reed Smoot and Representative Willis C. Hawley, and it was signed into law on June 17, 1930. The Act, passed to protect the nation's farmers against competing foreign exports, jacked up tariffs big time. Although the Act didn't cause the Great Depression, it contributed to the global devastation and the destruction of trade among countries. Funny thing is that although the United States was seeking to help its own farmers, it really just ended up hurting trade. U.S. exports to Europe fell by two-thirds from 1929 to 1932. Stupid and brutal?

IMF Codes

Here's an example of one of the IMF's codes. We'll just give you a brief excerpt to give you an idea of what one of its codes looks like:

Code of Good Practices on Transparency in Monetary and Financial Policies: Declaration of Principles

III.   Public Availability of Information on Monetary Policy

3.1   Presentations and releases of central bank data should meet the standards related to coverage, periodicity, timeliness of data and access by the public that are consistent with the International Monetary Fund's data dissemination standards.

3.2   The central bank should publicly disclose its balance sheet on a preannounced schedule and, after a predetermined interval, publicly disclose selected information on its aggregate market transactions.

3.2.1   Summary central bank balance sheets should be publicly disclosed on a frequent and preannounced schedule. Detailed central bank balance sheets prepared according to appropriate and publicly documented accounting standards should be publicly disclosed at least annually by the central bank.

3.2.2   Information on the central bank's monetary operations, including aggregate amounts and terms of refinance or other facilities (subject to the maintenance of commercial confidentiality) should be publicly disclosed on a preannounced schedule.

3.2.3   Consistent with confidentiality and privacy of information on individual firms, aggregate information on emergency financial support by the central bank should be publicly disclosed through an appropriate central bank statement when such disclosure will not be disruptive to financial stability.

3.2.4   Information about the country's foreign exchange reserve assets, liabilities and commitments by the monetary authorities should be publicly disclosed on a preannounced schedule, consistent with the International Monetary Fund's Data Dissemination Standards.

QUESTIONS FROM YOUR TALKING DOG

1.   Thanks for adopting me. That cage was getting pretty old. Heck yeah, I love walks! It's almost a necessary thing, you know what I mean? Did you know I like international finance and development? Okay, yeah, it's kinda twisted. But I like to ask lots of questions when I take my walks—with you now, of course. Well, let's go then on our first walk. I'll try not to get too excited. So, here's the first question: Can you explain the "economic violence" that occurred between 1918 and 1939? Thank you. I was nervous about the first walk . . .

2.   Here's another: How did the gold standard work (or not)? And while you're at it, why did Keynes call it a "barbarous relic?"

3.   What was the fundamental purpose—Well, they sound rehearsed because I rehearsed them! So why, my friend, the Bretton Woods Conference (BWC) and the establishment of the BWIs?

4.   I can never keep the whole balance-of-payments thing straight. Can you tell me what's happening in a deficit country in a BOP crisis?

5.   Uhh . . . my tongue is hanging out because I'm thirsty. While you take me to the creek, can you tell me something about how the conference came about and how business was conducted? Did they start from scratch at the BWC? Who were the main negotiators?

6.   Okay, I got all that. But what was the primary purpose of the BWC? Did it deal with so-called development issues?

7.   I'm gonna go legal on you now (supplement 1E). What are the BWIs in terms of international law? What about its Charter? Juridical personality? Immunity? Customary international law?

8.   I'm on a roll, now. What's the Fund's purpose or purposes?

9.   Was the BWS a resuscitation of the gold standard? Yeah, that's a big word—resuscitation. I'm trying to expand my vocabulary.

10.   I've heard the founders were interested in both internal balance and external balance. What was that all about?

11.   What was the main bone of contention at the BWC? How was it resolved? . . . I get really pumped with this stuff. Sorry for the rapid fire.

12.   What a beautiful tree! Enough of that. So I've heard about a Code of Good Conduct. What was that about essentially?

13.   Let's get back to gold. How did the gold exchange standard of the BWS work? How did it impose monetary discipline? Was it a symmetrical system? Yeah, I'm pretty proud of the fancy words. I get to show off at cocktail parties. I mean doggie cocktail parties—better stuff than the swill humans drink.

14.   We've talked about how the gold standard was supposed to be symmetrical but wasn't. What about the BWS?

15.   How do quotas work?

16.   Can member countries borrow for any reason, say, to build a bridge—or a dog house?

17.   Here's a question that'll pop up in lots of our walks. Tell me something about conditionality. How does it work from a technical point of view and why can the Fund do that?

18. Take me through the process getting a loan from the Fund, say, that stand-by arrangement . . . arrangement. I've heard something about a purchase. What does that mean? And what the heck is a tranche?

19. What about this convertibility thing?

20. I thought the IMF was all about reducing barriers. What's up with capital controls?

21. By the way, how do you intend to discipline me? Speaking of which, how does the Fund make members comply with the rules?

22. What are these standards and codes the Fund's come up with?

23. Here's a basic one for you. What's the Fund's structure?

24. Was development a big issue at the BWC?

25. Tell me something about the difference between the Fund and the Bank.

26. Tell me what the IBRD does.

27. What's the World Bank Group?

28. What's your favorite ice cream?

29. What's the Bank structure? What? No! I still have a lot of energy to work out. I was caged up, man! Okay, okay. Tomorrow, then.

Chapter 1: Supplement

1A. *Balance of Payments (BOP)*

Understanding the basics of BOP will help you understand aspects of global economics and finance. As this excerpt illustrates, the BOP of a country is a snapshot of its macroeconomic relation with the rest of the world. Every financial crisis you'll study in this textbook will relate in some way to the BOP. To better understand the excerpt, we can start with a (very) simplified explanation of key concepts. So let's suppose Country A has a fixed exchange rate of 5 babos to 1 draga of Country B. (Yeah, babos and draga—corny, but we all do it.) Country A is buying more goods from abroad than it is selling abroad. So it has a "balance of payments deficit." In particular it has a "current account deficit"—not enough income (via exports) to pay for its imports. How does it finance this deficit? If it's in "balance of payments equilibrium," it's financing the deficit by inflows into the capital account, such as private international loans. But what happens when those loans dry up and the markets figure out that because of the current account deficit Country A will have to devalue its currency to increase its exports? Basically, a stampede. Both domestic and foreign holders of babos will rush to Country

A's central bank to exchange babos for draga. To defend its fixed exchange rate, the central bank will be forced to use its "official (foreign) reserves" of dragas to buy the babos the investors are selling to the bank. Country A is now in a "balance of payments crisis" because eventually the central bank will run out of reserves. So it devalues the babos to, say, 8 babos to 1 draga. But once it does that, the markets will lose faith (if such a thing exists) in the currency (better: the emperor has no clothes on!), resulting in further downward pressure on the babos. What might Country A do? As the excerpt explains, it has a number of options, including knocking on the IMF's door.

Todaro, Michael P; Smith, Stephen C., *Economic Development,*
11th Edition, © 2012, pp. 639–644.

The extension of our analysis beyond simple merchandise trade into areas related to the international flow of financial resources permits us to examine the balance of payments of developing nations. A balance of payments table is designed to summarize a nation's financial transactions with the outside world. It is divided into three components. Note that balance of payments tables are sometimes presented in a revised format that splits the current account into two parts (called the current account and the capital account) and labels what is here called the capital account the financial account. We retain the traditional approach to balance of payments accounting because most of the literature on developing-country debt and its ongoing treatment in the financial press is usually presented in that format. The current account focuses on the export and import of goods and services, investment income, debt service payments, and private and public net remittances and transfers. Specifically, it subtracts the value of imports from exports (the merchandise trade balance) and then adds flows of the net investment income received from abroad (e.g., the difference between interest and dividend payments on foreign stocks, bonds, and bank deposits owned by developing-country nationals and brought into the country, as opposed to being left overseas, and those securities, if any, of the developing country owned by foreigners plus repatriated profits of multinational corporations). Taking this total (A − B + C in Table 13.1), it subtracts item D, debt service payments, which represents a major component of heavily indebted poor countries current account deficits, and adds item E, net private and public remittances and transfers, such as money sent home by developing country nationals working abroad (e.g., Mexicans in the United States, Algerians in France, Pakistanis in Kuwait). The final result (A − B + C − D + E in Table 13.1) yields the current account balance—a positive balance is called a surplus, and a negative balance, a deficit. The current account therefore allows us to analyze the impact of various commercial policies, primarily on merchandise trade but also indirectly on investment income, debt service payments, and private transfers.

Table 13.1　A Schematic Balance of Payments Account

Exports of goods and services	A
Imports of goods and services	B
Investment income	C
Debt-service payments	D
Net remittances and transfers	E
TOTAL *current account* balance (A – B + C – D + E)	**F**
Direct private investment	G
Foreign loans (private and public), minus amortization	H
Increase in foreign assets of domestic banking system	I
Resident capital outflow	J
TOTAL *capital account* balance (G + H – I – J)	**K**
Increase (or decrease) in *cash reserve account*	L
Errors and omissions (L – F – K)	**M**

The capital account (financial account) records the value of private foreign direct investment (mostly by multinational corporations), foreign loans by private international banks, and loans and grants from foreign governments (as in the form of foreign aid) and multilateral agencies such as the IMF and the World Bank. It then subtracts an extremely important item, especially for the major debtor countries: what is called "resident capital outflow" in Table 13.1. To put its importance in perspective, during the 1980s debt crisis, wealthy nationals from many developing countries sent vast amounts of money into developed-nation bank accounts, real estate ventures, and stock and bond purchases; this capital flight is estimated to have had a value of up to half the total debt of some debtor nations at the peak of their debt problems. It dwarfed the receipt of private and public loans and investments and was a major contributor to the worsening balance of payments of many developing nations. Capital flight is also a chronic problem where autocratic governments have a shaky hold on power. The balance on capital account is therefore calculated as items G + H – I – J in Table 13.1. Again, a positive balance is a surplus and a negative one a deficit.

Finally, the cash account, or international reserve account (item L), is the balancing item (along with the "errors and omissions," item M, which reconciles statistical inequalities, but is sometimes used as a proxy for disguised or unrecorded capital flows) that is lowered (shows a net outflow of foreign reserves) whenever total disbursements on the current and capital accounts exceed total receipts. Table 13.2 presents a simple chart of what constitutes positive (credit) and negative (debit) items in a balance of payments table. Nations accumulate international cash reserves in any or all of the following three forms: (1) foreign hard currency (primarily U.S. dollars, but also Japanese yen, pounds sterling, or the European euro) whenever they sell more abroad than they purchase; (2) gold, mined domestically or purchased; and (3) deposits with the IMF, which acts as a reserve bank for individual nations' central banks (see Box 13.1).

Table 13.2   Positive and Negative Effects on Balance of Payments Accounts

Positive Effects (Credits)	Negative Effects (Debits)
1. Any sale of goods or services abroad (export)	1. Any purchase of goods and services abroad (import)
2. Any earning on an investment in a foreign country	2. Any investment in a foreign country
3. Any receipt of foreign money	3. Any payment to a foreign country
4. Any gift or aid from a foreign country	4. Any gift or aid given abroad
5. Any foreign sale of stocks or bonds	5. Any purchase from stocks or bonds from abroad

A numerical example might prove helpful at this point. In Table 13.3, a hypothetical balance of payments table for a developing country is portrayed. First, under the current account, there is a $10 million negative merchandise trade balance made up of $35 million of commodity export receipts (of which over 70%—$25 million—are derived from primary agricultural and raw material products), minus $45 million of mostly manufactured consumer, intermediate, and capital goods import payments. To this total we add $5 million in payments for the services of foreign shipping firms and $1 million of investment income receipts representing net interest transmitted on foreign bond holdings, subtract $15 million of debt service payments representing this year's interest costs on the accumulated foreign debt of the developing country, and add $2 million of remittance and transfer receipts derived from payments of domestic workers living overseas who send home part of their earnings. Together, all of these items add up to a deficit on current account of $27 million.

Table 13.3 A Hypothetical Balance of Payments Table for a Developing Nation

Item	Amounts (millions of dollars)			
A. *Current Account*				
Commodity exports			+35	
Primary products	+25			
Manufactured goods	+10			
Commodity imports			−45	
Primary products	−10			
Manufactured goods	−35			
Services (e.g. shipping costs)			−5	
Investment income			+1	
Debt-service payments			−15	
Net remittances and transfers			+2	
Balance on current account		−27		
B. *Capital Account*				
Private direct foreign investment			+3	
Private loans and portfolio investments			+4	
Government and multilateral flows (net)			+3	
Loans	+9			
Debt amortization	−6			
Resident capital outflow			−8	
Balance on capital account		+2		
Balance on current and capital accounts		−25		
C. *Cash Account*				
Net decrease in official monetary reserves			+25	
Balance on cash account		+25		

Turning to the capital account, we see that there is a net inflow of $7 million of foreign private investment, consisting of $3 million of direct investment from multinational corporations in the form of new local factories and $4 million in private loans (from international commercial banks) and private portfolio (stock and bond) investments by foreign individuals and mutual funds. There is also a net positive $3 million inflow of public loans in the foreign aid and multilateral agency assistance. Note that the gross inflow of $9 million in public loans and grants is partly offset by a $6 million capital outflow representing amortization (gradual reduction) of the principal on former loans. However, these figures were reversed in the 1980s—the outflow to repay accumulated debts exceeded the inflow of both public aid and new refinancing bank loans. As a result, a $35.9 billion net transfer from developed to developing countries in 1981 became a $22.5 billion transfer from poor to rich nations by 1990 (they turned positive again in the 1990s until substantial new problems emerged for some countries between 1997 and 2002).

Table 13.4 Before and After the 1980s Debt Crisis: Current Account Balances and Capital Account Net Financial Transfers of Developing Countries, 1978–1990 (billions of dollars)

Year	Current Account	Capital Account Net Financial Transfers
1978	−32.1	33.2
1979	+10.0	31.2
1980	+30.6	29.5
1981	−48.6	35.9
1982	−86.9	20.1
1983	−64.0	3.7
1984	−31.7	−10.2
1985	−24.9	−20.5
1986	−46.4	−23.6
1987	−4.4	−34.0
1988	−22.4	−35.2
1989	−18.4	−29.6
1990	−3.0	−22.5

Returning to Table 13.3, we see that a major reason for the perverse flow of financial capital from poor to rich nations was very high levels of resident capital outflow. This capital flight is estimated to have amounted to almost $100 billion during the first half of the 1980s from just five of the principal countries involved (Argentina, Brazil, Mexico, the Philippines, and

Venezuela) and almost $200 billion over the period 1976–1985. In Table 13.3, it is listed as an outflow of $8 million. The net result is a $2 million positive balance on capital account, bringing the total balance on current and capital accounts to a deficit of $25 million.

To finance this $25 million negative balance on combined current and capital accounts, our hypothetical country will have to draw down $25 million of its central bank holdings of official monetary reserves. Such reserves consist of gold, a few major foreign currencies, and special drawing rights at the IMF (these will be explained shortly). International reserves serve for countries the same purpose that bank accounts serve for individuals. They can be drawn on to pay bills and debts, they are increased with deposits representing net export sales and capital inflows, and they can be used as collateral to borrow additional reserves.

We see, therefore, that the balance on current account *plus* the balance on capital account must be offset by the balance on cash account. This is shown by the net *decrease* of $25 million in official monetary reserves. If the country is very poor, it is likely to have a very limited stock of these reserves. This overall balance of payments deficit of $25 million may therefore place severe strains on the economy and greatly inhibit the country's ability to continue importing needed capital and consumer goods. In the least developed nations of the world, which have to import food to feed a hungry population and possess limited monetary reserves, such payments deficits may spell disaster for millions of people.

Facing existing or projected balance of payments deficits on combined current and capital accounts, developing nations have a variety of policy options. For one thing, they can seek to improve the balance on current account by promoting export expansion or limiting imports (or both). In the former case, there is the further choice of concentrating on primary or secondary product export expansion. In the latter case, policies of import substitution (the protection and stimulus of domestic industries to replace previously imported manufactured goods in the local market) or selective tariffs and physical quotas or bans on the importation of specific consumer goods may be tried. Or countries can seek to achieve both objectives simultaneously by altering their official foreign-exchange rates through a currency devaluation that lowers export prices and increases import prices. Alternatively or concurrently, they can seek loans and assistance from the World Bank or the IMF. Traditionally, this has required that the countries follow very restrictive fiscal and monetary policies. These have been called *stabilization policies* by the IMF; and termed *structural adjustment* by the World Bank, which has made structural adjustment loans as part of this process. *Stabilization policies* and *structural adjustment*, both packages of preconditions for receiving loans, are popularly referred to as conditionality. These policies are designed to reduce domestic demand so as to lower imports and reduce the inflationary pressures that may have contributed to the "overvalued" exchange rate that slowed exports and promoted imports. In recent years, these institutions have shown somewhat less policy inflexibility, but it is not yet clear whether this trend will continue.

In addition, developing countries can try to improve the balance on their capital account by encouraging more private foreign direct or portfolio investment, borrowing from international commercial banks, or seeking more public foreign assistance (aid). But neither private foreign investment nor a majority of foreign aid comes in the form of gifts (outright grants). The receipt of loan assistance implies the necessity of future repayments of principal and interest. Directly productive foreign investments in, say, building local factories entail the potential repatriation of sizable proportions of the profits of the foreign-owned enterprise. [T]he encouragement of private foreign investment has broader development implications than the mere transfer of financial or physical capital resources.

Finally, developing nations can seek to modify the detrimental impact of chronic balance of payments deficits by expanding their stocks of official monetary reserves. One way of doing this is through the acquisition of a greater share of international "paper gold" known as special drawing rights.

1B. *Excerpts of IMF Articles*

You might think that reading the IMF's Charter is about as exciting as watching sidewalks crack. But it's not that bad. Actually, it's pretty cool when you think about how the Charter goes about constructing the IMF's mandate. Remember, the Fund's bound by the Charter. So if it goes beyond its mandate, it's acting ultra vires—beyond the scope of its powers. Let's start with the current Article 1. You know about the Fund's monetary function, which is embodied in 1(i). Is development part of its purpose? Is the Fund's purpose in part to promote trade by eliminating trade restrictions? You should be able to pick out the language relating to conditionality. Regarding original Article III, why not review quotas every year or every fifteen years? Let's look at original Article IV. You should see the tight link between par value and gold—after all, the Bretton Woods System was formally a gold exchange regime (and later became in effect a pure reserve currency regime). Check out section 7 of Article IV, which addresses uniform changes in par value. Yeah, it takes just a majority of the total voting power to make the uniform changes but look at the proviso. Go look at the voting power of each member country. How many countries have 10 percent or more of the total of the quotas? Article VIII is all about trade, right? And current Article XXVIII? The Golden Rule: Whoever owns the gold, rules. Look at the voting power again.

ARTICLE I (current)

Purposes

The purposes of the International Monetary Fund are:

(i) To promote international monetary cooperation through a permanent institution which provides the machinery for consultation and collaboration on international monetary problems.

(ii) To facilitate the expansion and balanced growth of international trade, and to contribute thereby to the promotion and maintenance of high levels of employment and real income and to the development of the productive resources of all members as primary objectives of economic policy.

(iii) To promote exchange stability, to maintain orderly exchange arrangements among members, and to avoid competitive exchange depreciation.

(iv) To assist in the establishment of a multilateral system of payments in respect of current transactions between members and in the elimination of foreign exchange restrictions which hamper the growth of world trade.

(v) To give confidence to members by making the general resources of the Fund temporarily available to them under adequate safeguards, thus providing them with opportunity to correct maladjustments in their balance of payments without resorting to measures destructive of national or international prosperity.

(vi) In accordance with the above, to shorten the duration and lessen the degree of disequilibrium in the international balances of payments of members.

The Fund shall be guided in all its policies and decisions by the purposes set forth in the Article.

Article III (original)

Quotas and Subscriptions

Section 3.   *Subscriptions: time, place, and form of payment*

* * *

(b) Each member shall pay in gold, as a minimum, the smaller of

(1) twenty-five percent of its quota; or

(2) ten percent of its net official holdings of gold and United States dollars as at the date when the Fund notifies

members under Article XX, Section 4(a) that it will shortly be in a position to begin exchange transactions.

Each member shall furnish to the Fund the data necessary to determine its net official holdings of gold and United States dollars.

(c)   Each member shall pay the balance of its quota in its own currency.

* * *

ARTICLE III (current)

Quotas and Subscriptions

Section 1.   *Quotas and payment of subscriptions*

Each member shall be assigned a quota expressed in special drawing rights. The quotas of the members represented at the United Nations Monetary and Financial Conference which accept membership before December 31, 1945 shall be those set forth in Schedule A. The quotas of other members shall be determined by the Board of Governors. The subscription of each member shall be equal to its quota and shall be paid in full to the Fund at the appropriate depository.

Section 2.   *Adjustment of quotas*

(a)   The Board of Governors shall at intervals of not more than five years conduct a general review, and if it deems it appropriate propose an adjustment, of the quotas of the members. It may also, if it thinks fit, consider at any other time the adjustment of any particular quota at the request of the member concerned.

(b)   The Fund may at any time propose an increase in the quotas of those members of the Fund that were members on August 31, 1975 in proportion to their quotas on that date in a cumulative amount not in excess of amounts transferred under Article V, Section 12(f)(i) and (j) from the Special Disbursement Account to the General Resources Account.

(c)   An eighty-five percent majority of the total voting power shall be required for any change in quotas.

(d)   The quota of a member shall not be changed until the member has consented and until payment has been made unless payment is deemed to have been made in accordance with Section 3(b) of this Article.

Section 3.   *Payments when quotas are changed*

(a)   Each member which consents to an increase in its quota under Section 2(a) of this Article shall, within a period determined by the Fund, pay to the Fund twenty-five percent of the increase in special drawing rights, but the Board of Governors may prescribe that this payment may be made, on the same basis for all members, in whole or in part in the currencies of other members specified, with their concurrence, by the Fund, or in the member's own currency. A non-participant shall pay in the currencies of other members specified by the Fund, with their concurrence, a proportion of the increase corresponding to the proportion to be paid in special drawing rights by participants. The balance of the increase shall be paid by the member in its own currency. The Fund's holdings of a member's currency shall not be increased above the level at which they would be subject to charges under Article V, Section 8(b)(ii), as a result of payments by other members under this provision.

(b) Each member which consents to an increase in its quota under Section 2(b) of this Article shall be deemed to have paid to the Fund an amount of subscription equal to such increase.

(c) If a member consents to a reduction in its quota, the Fund shall, within sixty days, pay to the member an amount equal to the reduction. The payment shall be made in the member's currency and in such amount of special drawing rights or the currencies of other members specified, with their concurrence, by the Fund as is necessary to prevent the reduction of the Fund's holdings of the currency below the new quota, provided that in exceptional circumstances the Fund may reduce its holdings of the currency below the new quota by payment to the member in its own currency.

(d) A seventy percent majority of the total voting power shall be required for any decision under (a) above, except for the determination of a period and the specification of currencies under that provision.

ARTICLE IV (original)

Par Values of Currencies

Section 1.   *Expression of par values*

(a) The par value of the currency of each member shall be expressed in terms of gold as a common denominator or in terms of the United States dollars of the weight and fineness in effect on July 1, 1944.

(b) All computations relating to currencies of members for the purpose of applying the provisions of this Agreement shall be on the basis of their par values.

Section 2.   *Gold purchases based on par values*

The Fund shall prescribe a margin above and below par value for transactions in gold by members, and no member shall buy gold at a price above par value plus the prescribed margin, or sell gold at a price below par value minus the prescribed margin.

Section 3.   *Foreign exchange dealings based on parity*

The maximum and the minimum rates for exchange transactions between the currencies of members taking place within their territories shall not differ from parity.

(a) in the case of spot exchange transactions, by more than one percent; and

(ii) (ii) in the case of other exchange transactions, by a margin which exceeds the margin for spot exchange transactions by more than the Fund considers reasonable.

Section 4.   *Obligations regarding exchange stability*

(a) Each member undertakes to collaborate with the Fund to promote exchange stability, to maintain orderly exchange arrangements with other members, and to avoid competitive exchange alterations.

(b) Each member undertakes, through appropriate measures consistent with this Agreement, to permit within its territories exchange transactions between its currency and the currencies of other members only within the limits prescribed under Section 3 of this Article. A member whose monetary authorities, for the settlement of international transactions, in fact freely buy and sell gold within the limits prescribed by the Fund under Section 2 of this Article shall be deemed to be fulfilling this undertaking.

Section 5.   *Changes in par values*

(a) A member shall not propose a change in the par value of its currency except to correct a fundamental disequilibrium.

(b) A change in the par value of a member's currency may be made only on the proposal of the member and only after consultation with the Fund.

(c) When a change is proposed, the Fund shall first take into account the changes, if any which have already taken place in the initial par value of the member's currency as determined under Article XX, Section 4. If the proposed change, together with all previous changes, whether increases or decreases,

(i) does not exceed ten percent of the initial par value, the Fund shall raise no objection;

(ii) does not exceed a further ten percent of the initial par value, the Fund may either concur or object, but shall declare its attitude within seventy-two hours if the member so requests;

(iii) is not within (i) or (ii) above, the Fund may either concur or object, but shall be entitled to a longer period in which to declare its attitude.

(a) Uniform changes in par values made under Section 7 of this Article shall not be taken into account in determining whether a proposed change falls with (i), (ii), or (iii) of (c) above.

(b) A member may change the par value of its currency without the concurrence of the Fund if the change does not affect the international transactions of members of the Fund.

(c) The Fund shall concur in a proposed change which is within the terms of (c)(ii) or (c)(iii) above if it is satisfied that the change is necessary to correct a fundamental disequilibrium. In particular, provided it is so satisfied, it shall not object to a proposed change because of the domestic, social, or political policies of the member proposing the change.

Section 6. *Effect of unauthorized changes*

If a member changes the par value of its currency despite the objection of the Fund, in cases where the Fund is entitled to object, the member shall be ineligible to use the resources of the Fund unless the Fund otherwise determines; and if, after the expiration of a reasonable period, the difference between the member and the Fund continues, the matter shall be subject to the provisions of Article XV, Section(b).

Section 7. *Uniform changes in par values*

Notwithstanding the provisions of Section 5(b) of this Article, the Fund by a majority of the total voting power may make uniform proportionate changes in the par values of the currencies of all members, provided all such change is approved by every member which has ten percent or more of the total of the quotas. The par value of a member's currency shall, however, not be changed under this provision if, within seventy-two hours of the Fund's action, the member informs the Fund that it does not wish the value of its currency to be changed by such action.

Section 8.   *Maintenance of gold value of the Fund's assets*

(a) The gold value of the Fund's assets shall be maintained notwithstanding changes in the par or foreign exchange value of the currency of any member.

(b) Whenever (i) the par value of a member's currency is reduced, or (ii) the foreign exchange value of a member's currency has, in the opinion of the Fund, depreciated to a significant extent within that member's territories, the member shall pay to the Fund within a reasonable time an amount of its own currency equal to the reduction in the gold value of its currency held by the Fund.

(c) Whenever the par value of a member's currency is increased, the Fund shall return to such member within a reasonable time an amount in its currency equal to the increase in the gold value of its currency held by the Fund.

The provisions of this Section shall apply to a uniform proportionate change in the par values of the currencies of all members, unless at the time when such a change is proposed the Fund decides otherwise.

* * *

ARTICLE V (current)

Operations and Transactions of the Fund

Section 1.   *Agencies dealing with the Fund*

Each member shall deal with the Fund only through its Treasury, central bank, stabilization fund, or other similar fiscal agency, and the Fund shall deal only with or through the same agencies.

Section 2.   *Limitation on the Fund's operations and transactions*

(a) Except as otherwise provided in this Agreement, transactions on the account of the Fund shall be limited to transactions for the purpose of supplying a member, on the initiative of such member, with special drawing rights or the currencies of other members from the general resources of the Fund, which shall be held in the General Resources Account, in exchange for the currency of the member desiring to make the purchase.

* * *

Section 3.   *Conditions governing use of the Fund's general resources*

(a) The Fund shall adopt policies on the use of its general resources, including policies on stand-by or similar arrangements, and may adopt special policies for special balance of payments problems, that will assist members to solve their balance of payments problems in a manner consistent with the provisions of this Agreement and that will establish adequate safeguards for the temporary use of the general resources of the Fund.

(b) A member shall be entitled to purchase the currencies of other members from the Fund in exchange for an equivalent amount of its own currency subject to the following conditions:

   (i)   the member's use of the general resources of the Fund would be in accordance with the provisions of this Agreement and the policies adopted under them;

   (ii) the member represents that it has a need to make the purchase because of its balance of payments or its reserve position or developments in its reserves;

   (iii) the proposed purchase would be a reserve tranche purchase, or would not cause the Fund's holdings of the purchasing member's currency to exceed two hundred percent of its quota;

   (iv) the Fund has not previously declared under Section 5 of this Article, Article VI, Section 1, or Article XXVI, Section 2(a) that the member desiring to purchase is ineligible to use the general resources of the Fund.

(c) The Fund shall examine a request for a purchase to determine whether the proposed purchase would be consistent with the provisions of this Agreement and the policies adopted under them, provided that requests for reserve tranche purchases shall not be subject to challenge.

* * *

   (ii) Each member whose currency is purchased from the Fund or is obtained in exchange for currency purchased from the Fund shall collaborate with the Fund and other members to enable such balances of its currency to be exchanged, at the time of purchase, for the freely usable currencies of other members.

* * *

Section 4.   *Waiver of conditions*

The Fund may in its discretion, and on terms which safeguard its interests, waive any of the conditions prescribed in Section 3(b)(iii) and (iv) of this Article, especially in the case of members with a record of avoiding large or continuous use of the Fund's general resources. In making a waiver it shall take into consideration periodic or exceptional requirements of the member requesting the waiver. The Fund shall also take into consideration a member's willingness to pledge as collateral security acceptable assets having a value sufficient in the opinion of the Fund to protect its interests and may require as a condition of waiver the pledge of such collateral security.

Section 5.   *Ineligibility to use the Fund's general resources*

Whenever the Fund is of the opinion that any member is using the general resources of the Fund in a manner contrary to the purposes of the Fund, it shall present to the member a report setting forth the views of the Fund and prescribing a suitable time for reply. After presenting such a report to a member, the Fund may limit the use of its general resources by the member. If no reply to the report is received from the member within the prescribed time, or if the reply received is unsatisfactory, the Fund may continue to limit the member's use of the general resources of the Fund or may, after giving reasonable notice to the member, declare it ineligible to use the general resources of the Fund.

* * *

Section 7.   *Repurchase by a member of its currency held by the Fund*

(a)   A member shall be entitled to repurchase at any time the Fund's holdings of its currency that are subject to charges under Section 8(b) of this Article.

(b)   A member that has made a purchase under Section 3 of this Article will be expected normally, as its balance of payments and reserve position improves, to repurchase the Fund's holdings of its currency that result from the purchase and are subject to charges under Section 8(b) of this Article. A member shall repurchase these holdings if, in accordance with policies on repurchase that the Fund shall adopt and after consultation with the member, the Fund represents to the member that it should repurchase because of an improvement in its balance of payments and reserve position.

(c)   A member that has made a purchase under Section 3 of this Article shall repurchase the Fund's holdings of its currency that result from the purchase and are subject to charges under Section 8(b) of this Article not later than five years after the date on which the purchase was made. The Fund may prescribe that repurchase shall be made by a member in installments during the period beginning three years and ending five years after the date of a purchase. The Fund, by an eighty-five percent majority of the total voting power, may change the periods for repurchase under this subsection, and any period so adopted shall apply to all members.

* * *

(i) All repurchases under this Section shall be made with special drawing rights or with the currencies of other members specified by the Fund. The Fund shall adopt policies and procedures with regard to the currencies to be used by members in making repurchases that take into account the principles in Section 3(d) of this Article. The Fund's holdings of a member's currency that is used in repurchase shall not be increased by the repurchase above the level at which they would be subject to charges under Section 8(b)(ii) of this Article.

* * *

(j)

(i) If a member's currency specified by the Fund under (i) above is not a freely usable currency, the member shall ensure that the repurchasing member can obtain it at the time of the repurchase in exchange for a freely usable currency selected by the member whose currency has been specified . . .

Section 8.   *Charges*

(a)

(i) The Fund shall levy a service charge on the purchase by a member of special drawing rights or the currency of another member held in the General Resources Account in exchange for its own currency, provided that the Fund may levy a lower service charge on reserve tranche purchases than on other purchases. The service charge on reserve tranche purchases shall not exceed one-half of one percent.

(ii) The Fund may levy a charge for stand-by or similar arrangements. The Fund may decide that the charge for an arrangement shall be offset against the service charge levied under (i) above on purchases under the arrangement.

(b) The Fund shall levy charges on its average daily balances of a member's currency held in the General Resources Account to the extent that they

(i) have been acquired under a policy that has been the subject of an exclusion under Article XXX(c), or

(ii) exceed the amount of the member's quota after excluding any balances referred to in (i) above.

The rates of charge normally shall rise at intervals during the period in which the balances are held.

(c) If a member fails to make a repurchase required under Section 7 of this Article, the Fund, after consultation with the member on the reduction of the Fund's holdings of its currency, may impose such charges as the Fund deems appropriate on its holdings of the member's currency that should have been repurchased.

* * *

Article VI (current)

Capital Transfers

Section 1.   *Use of the Fund's general resources for capital transfers*

(a) A member may not use the Fund's general resources to meet a large or sustained outflow of capital except as provided in Section 2 of this Article, and the Fund may request a member to exercise controls to prevent such use of the general resources of the Fund. If, after receiving such a request, a member fails to exercise appropriate controls, the Fund may declare the member ineligible to use the general resources of the Fund.

(b) Nothing in this Section shall be deemed:

(i) to prevent the use of the general resources of the Fund for capital transactions of reasonable amount required for the expansion of exports or in the ordinary course of trade, banking, or other business; or

(ii) to affect capital movements which are met out of a member's own resources, but members undertake that such capital movements will be in accordance with the purposes of the Fund.

Section 2.   *Special provisions for capital transfers*

A member shall be entitled to make reserve tranche purchases to meet capital transfers.

Section 3.   *Controls of capital transfers*

Members may exercise such controls as are necessary to regulate international capital movements, but no member may exercise these controls in a manner which will restrict payments for current transactions or which will unduly delay transfers of funds in settlement of commitments, except as provided in Article VII, Section 3(b) and in Article XIV, Section 2.

ARTICLE VIII (current)

General Obligations of Members

Section 1.　*Introduction*

In addition to the obligations assumed under other articles of this agreement, each member undertakes the obligations set out in this article.

Section 2.　*Avoidance of restrictions on current payments*

(a) Subject to the provisions of Article VII, Section 3(b) and Article XIV, Section 2, no member shall, without the approval of the Fund, impose restrictions on the making of payments and transfers for current international transactions.

(b) Exchange contracts which involve the currency of any member and which are contrary to the exchange control regulations of that member maintained or imposed consistently with this Agreement shall be unenforceable in the territories of any member. In addition, members may, by mutual accord, cooperate in measures for the purpose of making the exchange control regulations of either member more effective, provided that such measures and regulations are consistent with this Agreement.

Section 3.　*Avoidance of discriminatory currency practices*

No member shall engage in, or permit any of its fiscal agencies referred to in Article V, Section 1 to engage in, any discriminatory currency arrangements or multiple currency practices, whether within or outside margins under Article IV or prescribed by or under Schedule C, except as authorized under this Agreement or approved by the Fund. If such arrangements and practices are engaged in at the date when this Agreement enters into force, the member concerned shall consult with the Fund as to their progressive removal unless they are maintained or imposed under Article XIV, Section 2, in which case the provisions of Section 3 of that Article shall apply.

* * *

Section 5.　*Furnishing of information*

(a) The Fund may require members to furnish it with such information as it deems necessary for its activities, including, as the minimum necessary for the effective discharge of the Fund's duties, national data on the following matters:

(i)   official holdings at home and abroad of (1) gold, (2) foreign exchange;

(ii)   holdings at home and abroad by banking and financial agencies, other than official agencies, of (1) gold, (2) foreign exchange;

(iii)   production of gold;

(iv)   gold exports and imports according to countries of destination and origin;

(v)   total exports and imports of merchandise, in terms of local currency values, according to countries of destination and origin;

(vi)   international balance of payments, including (1) trade in goods and services, (2) gold transactions, (3) known capital transactions, and (4) other items;

(vii)   international investment position, i.e., investments within the territories of the member owned abroad and investments abroad owned by persons in its territories so far as it is possible to furnish this information;

(viii) national income;

(ix)   price indices, i.e., indices of commodity prices in wholesale and retail markets and of export and import prices;

(x)   buying and selling rates for foreign currencies;

(xi)   exchange controls, i.e., a comprehensive statement of exchange controls in effect at the time of assuming membership in the Fund and details of subsequent changes as they occur; and

(xii)   where official clearing arrangements exist, details of amounts awaiting clearance in respect of commercial and financial transactions, and of the length of time during which such arrears have been outstanding.

* * *

Section 6. *Consultation between members regarding existing international agreements*

Where under this Agreement a member is authorized in the special or temporary circumstances specified in the Agreement to maintain or establish restrictions on exchange transactions, and there are other engagements between members entered into prior to this Agreement which conflict with the application of such restrictions, the parties to such engagements shall consult with one another with a view to making such mutually acceptable adjustments as may be necessary. The provisions of this Article shall be without prejudice to the operation of Article VII, Section 5.

Section 7.   *Obligation to collaborate regarding policies on reserve assets*

Each member undertakes to collaborate with the Fund and with other members in order to ensure that the policies of the member with respect to reserve assets shall be consistent with the objectives of promoting better international surveillance of international liquidity and making the special drawing right the principal reserve asset in the international monetary system.

ARTICLE XII (current)

Organization and Management

Section 1.   *Structure of the Fund*

The Fund shall have a Board of Governors, an Executive Board, a Managing Director, and a staff, and a Council if the Board of Governors decides, by an eighty-five percent majority of the total voting power, that the provisions of Schedule D shall be applied.

Section 2.   *Board of Governors*

    (a) All powers under this Agreement not conferred directly on the Board of Governors, the Executive Board, or the Managing Director shall be vested in the Board of Governors. The Board of Governors shall consist of one Governor and one Alternate appointed by each member in such manner as it may determine. Each Governor and each Alternate shall serve until a new appointment is made. No Alternate may vote except in the absence of his principal. The Board of Governors shall select one of the Governors as Chairman.

    (b) The Board of Governors may delegate to the Executive Board authority to exercise any powers of the Board of Governors, except the powers conferred directly by this Agreement on the Board of Governors.

* * *

    (g) The Board of Governors, and the Executive Board to the extent authorized, may adopt such rules and regulations as may be necessary or appropriate to conduct the business of the Fund.

* * *

Section 3. *Executive Board*

(a) The Executive Board shall be responsible for conducting the business of the Fund, and for this purpose shall exercise all the powers delegated to it by the Board of Governors.

(b) The Executive Board shall consist of Executive Directors with the Managing Director as chairman. Of the Executive Directors:

　(i) five shall be appointed by the five members having the largest quotas; and

　(ii) fifteen shall be elected by the other members.

* * *

(g) The Executive Board shall function in continuous session at the principal office of the Fund and shall meet as often as the business of the Fund may require.

* * *

Section 4. *Managing Director and staff*

(a) The Executive Board shall select a Managing Director who shall not be a Governor or an Executive Director. The Managing Director shall be chairman of the Executive Board, but shall have no vote except a deciding vote in case of an equal division. He may participate in meetings of the Board of Governors, but shall not vote at such meetings. The Managing Director shall cease to hold office when the Executive Board so decides.

(b) The Managing Director shall be chief of the operating staff of the Fund and shall conduct, under the direction of the Executive Board, the ordinary business of the Fund. Subject to the general control of the Executive Board, he shall be responsible for the organization, appointment, and dismissal of the staff of the Fund.

(c) The Managing Director and the staff of the Fund, in the discharge of their functions, shall owe their duty entirely to the Fund and to no other authority. Each member of the Fund shall respect the international character of this duty and shall refrain from all attempts to influence any of the staff in the discharge of these functions.

(d) In appointing the staff the Managing Director shall, subject to the paramount importance of securing the highest standards of efficiency and of technical competence, pay due regard to the importance of recruiting personnel on as wide a geographical basis as possible.

Section 5.   *Voting*

(a) The total votes of each member shall be equal to the sum of its basic votes and its quota-based votes.

* * *

(c) Except as otherwise specifically provided, all decisions of the Fund shall be made by a majority of the votes cast.

* * *

Section 7.   *Publication of reports*

(a) The Fund shall publish an annual report containing an audited statement of its accounts, and shall issue, at intervals of three months or less, a summary statement of its operations and transactions and its holdings of special drawing rights, gold, and currencies of members.

(b) The Fund may publish such other reports as it deems desirable for carrying out its purposes.

Section 8.   *Communication of views to members*

The Fund shall at all times have the right to communicate its views informally to any member on any matter arising under this Agreement. The Fund may, by a seventy percent majority of the total voting power, decide to publish a report made to a member regarding its monetary or economic conditions and developments which directly tend to produce a serious disequilibrium in the international balance of payments of members. If the member is not entitled to appoint an Executive Director, it shall be entitled to representation in accordance with Section 3(j) of this Article. The Fund shall not publish a report involving changes in the fundamental structure of the economic organization of members.

ARTICLE XXVIII (current)

Amendments

(a) Any proposal to introduce modifications in this Agreement, whether emanating from a member, a Governor, or the Executive Board, shall be communicated to the chairman of the Board of Governors who shall bring the proposal before the Board of Governors. If the proposed amendment is approved by the Board of Governors, the Fund shall, by circular letter or telegram, ask all members whether they accept the proposed amendment. When three-fifths of the members, having eighty-five percent of the total voting power, have accepted the proposed amendment, the Fund shall certify the fact by a formal communication addressed to all members.

(b) Notwithstanding (a) above, acceptance by all members is required in the case of any amendment modifying:

  (i)   the right to withdraw from the Fund (Article XXVI, Section 1);

  (ii) the provision that no change in a member's quota shall be made without its consent (Article III, Section 2(d)); and

  (iii) the provision that no change may be made in the par value of a member's currency except on the proposal of that member (Schedule C, paragraph 6).

(c) Amendments shall enter into force for all members three months after the date of the formal communication unless a shorter period is specified in the circular letter or telegram.

ARTICLE XXXI (current)

Final Provisions

Section 2.   *Signature*

(a) Each government on whose behalf this Agreement is signed shall deposit with the Government of the United States of America an instrument setting forth that it has accepted this Agreement in accordance with its law and has taken all steps necessary to enable it to carry out all of its obligations under this Agreement.

1C. *Developing Countries' Voice at Bretton Woods*

This excerpt talks about the role of developing countries at the Bretton Woods Conference. Did they have much influence? Why might that have been a good thing, even at the expense of development issues? What do you think of the "universalism" thing?

E. Carrasco, "An Opening for Voice in the Global Economic Order: The Global Financial Crisis and Emerging Countries," *12 Oregon Rev. Int'l Law*, 182–186 (2010)

The primary purpose of the Bretton Woods Conference in July 1944 was not, of course, to improve the plight of developing countries. Instead, it was to fashion institutions that would supervise a "transition from a war-time economy to a peace-time economy in the United Nations." Invoking universalist themes embedded in the narrative of liberalism, U.S. Treasury Secretary Henry Morgenthau Jr. captured the essence of the task when he spoke at the inaugural plenary session of the conference:

"We are to concern ourselves here with essential steps in the creation of a dynamic world economy in which the people of every nation will be able to realize their potentialities in peace; will be able, through their industry, their inventiveness, their thrift, to raise their own standards of living and enjoy, increasingly, the fruits of material progress on an earth infinitely blessed with natural riches. This is the indispensable cornerstone of freedom and security. All else must be built upon this. For freedom of opportunity is the foundation for all other freedoms."

Accordingly, "an International Monetary Fund and possibly a Bank for Reconstruction and Development" would be created in order to advance liberalism's twin goals of postwar peace and prosperity. The IMF would promote international monetary cooperation and stability by enforcing a rule-based system of fixed but adjustable exchange rates (the "par value system"), promoting currency convertibility, and providing members with temporary (short-term) resources to cope with balance-of-payments adjustment. In addition to coordinating private investment, the World Bank would provide (long-term) loans, initially for use in postwar reconstruction of war-torn Europe.

The main players at the conference were the United States and the United Kingdom. The U.S. delegation faced isolationist sentiments in the U.S. Congress. In the United Kingdom, many feared the proposed system would jeopardize U.K. ties with the Commonwealth as well as import future U.S. deflation (1930s-style). Thus, both the U.K. and U.S. delegations concentrated on creating an international monetary system that would be acceptable in their respective domestic political arenas. The deliberations focused almost exclusively on complicated matters that were vital to such a system—e.g., rules relating to an international currency and multilateral clearing mechanism, drawing rights, par values, a transition period during which restrictions could be maintained on current account transactions, and the governance of the IMF.

Not surprisingly, then, the Conference treated development issues (e.g., structural impediments facing developing countries) "peripherally," at best. The slight treatment of development and developing countries was not due to inattentive participants from developing countries—a good number of them attended the Conference. The Indian delegation, for instance, led a campaign to include references to developing countries throughout the IMF's charter. Its efforts culminated in an unsuccessful attempt to add a phrase to the IMF's purposes that would have required the IMF "to assist in the fuller utili[z]ation of the resources of economically under-developed countries." The compromise limited development to an indirect purpose, making it a consequence of the IMF's direct purpose to "facilitate the expansion and balanced growth of international trade . . ."

The Mexican delegation experienced a similar result when it urged the drafters of the Bank's charter to consider "development" as well as "reconstruction." The Mexicans offered an amendment to the proposed language for Article III, Section 1 that would have required the Bank not only to "give equal consideration to projects for development and to projects for reconstruction" but also to "always" make "its resources and facilities . . . available to the same extent for either kind of project." The drafters ultimately adopted a softened version of the amendment, requiring the Bank to give "equitable consideration to projects for development and projects for reconstruction alike."

Brazil also attempted to stress developing country concerns at the conference. Because erratic commodity prices caused havoc with developing countries' balance-of-payments, the Brazilian delegation pressed for a conference "to promote stability of prices of raw materials and agricultural products and to formulate recommendations for attainment of a more balanced growth of international trade." The Brazilian's resolution, though adopted, took a back seat to the central issues identified above.

The treatment of development issues at the Bretton Woods Conference suggests that success was achieved in part by marginalizing the interests of developing countries. By doing so, the IMF and World Bank treaties clearly enshrined a "universal" proposition that motivated the conference in the first place—that an open international economy was the best prescription for global prosperity, which, in turn, would help maintain international peace.

Economic growth was at the heart of postwar liberalism. The Bretton Woods Institutions (BWIs), along with the General Agreement on Tariffs and Trade (GATT), were charged with promoting growth via international economic law governing trade and investment.

1D. *Excerpts of IBRD Articles*

Here's the World Bank's Charter. Is its sole mandate to lend to member country governments? Given the Bank's lending to member country governments, folks forget that part of its mandate is to act as a catalyst for private capital, if it's available. Articles III and IV set out the Bank's business of lending. Can the Bank make or guarantee loans for anything other than projects? What are the conditions for making a loan or providing a guarantee? If the Bank makes a direct loan, can the borrower repay in a currency other than the currency of the loan? Is there a provision that tells the Bank to butt out of domestic politics? Article V gives you a sense of how much the Board of Directors delegates to the Executive Board, except . . .

ARTICLE I

Purposes

The purposes of the Bank are:

(i)   To assist in the reconstruction and development of territories of members by facilitating the investment of capital for productive purposes, including the restoration of economies destroyed or disrupted by war, the reconversion of productive facilities and resources in less developed countries.

(ii) To promote private foreign investment by means of guarantees or participations in loans and other investments made by private investors; and when private capital is not available on reasonable terms, to supplement private investment by providing, on suitable conditions, finance for productive purposes out of its own capital, funds raised by it and its other resources.

(iii) To promote the long-range balanced growth of international trade and the maintenance of equilibrium in balances of payments by encouraging international investment for the development of the productive resources of members, thereby assisting in raising productivity, the standard of living and conditions of labor in their territories.

(iv) To arrange the loans made or guaranteed by it in relation to international loans through other channels so that the more useful and urgent projects, large and small alike, will be dealt with first.

(v)   To conduct its operations with due regard to the effect of international investment on business conditions in the territories of members and, in the immediate postwar years, to assist in bringing about a smooth transition from a wartime to a peacetime economy.

The Bank shall be guided in all its decisions by the purposes set forth above.

ARTICLE III

General Provisions Relating to Loans and Guarantees

SECTION 1.   Use of Resources

(a)   The resources and the facilities of the Bank shall be used exclusively for the benefit of members with equitable consideration to projects for development and projects for reconstruction alike.

(b) For the purpose of facilitating the restoration and reconstruction of the economy of members whose metropolitan territories have suffered great devastation from enemy occupation or hostilities, the Bank, in determining the conditions and terms of loans made to such members, shall pay special regard to lightening the financial burden and expediting the completion of such restoration and reconstruction.

SECTION 2.   Dealings between Members and the Bank

Each member shall deal with the Bank only through its Treasury, central bank, stabilization fund or other similar fiscal agency, and the Bank shall deal with members only by or through the same agencies.

SECTION 3.   Limitations on Guarantees and Borrowings of the Bank

The total amount outstanding of guarantees, participations in loans and direct loans made by the Bank shall not be increased at any time, if by such increase the total would exceed one hundred percent of the unimpaired subscribed capital, reserves and surplus of the Bank.

SECTION 4.   Conditions on which the Bank may Guarantee or Make Loans

The Bank may guarantee, participate in, or make loans to any member or any political sub-division thereof and any business, industrial, and agricultural enterprise in the territories of a member, subject to the following conditions:

(i) When the member in whose territories the project is located is not itself the borrower, the member or the central bank or some comparable agency of the member which is acceptable to the Bank, fully guarantees the repayment of the principal and the payment of interest and other charges on the loan.

(ii) The Bank is satisfied that in the prevailing market conditions the borrower would be unable otherwise to obtain the loan under conditions which in the opinion of the Bank are reasonable for the borrower. . . .

(iv) In the opinion of the Bank the rate of interest and other charges are reasonable and such rate, charges and the schedule for repayment of principal are appropriate to the project.

(v) In making or guaranteeing a loan, the Bank shall pay due regard to the prospects that the borrower, and, if the borrower is not a member, that the guarantor, will be in position to meet its obligations under the loan; and the Bank shall act prudently in the interests both of the particular member in whose territories the project is located and of the members as a whole.

(vi) In guaranteeing a loan made by other investors, the Bank receives suitable compensation for its risk.

(vii) Loans made or guaranteed by the Bank shall, except in special circumstances, be for the purpose of specific projects of reconstruction or development.

SECTION 5.   Use of Loans Guaranteed, Participated in or Made by the Bank

(a) The Bank shall impose no conditions that the proceeds of a loan shall be spent in the territories of any particular member or members.

(b) The Bank shall make arrangements to ensure that the proceeds of any loan are used only for the purposes for which the loan was granted, with due attention to considerations of economy and efficiency and without regard to political or other non-economic influences or considerations.

(c) In the case of loans made by the Bank, it shall open an account in the name of the borrower and the amount of the loan shall be credited to this account in the currency or currencies in which the loan is made. The borrower shall be permitted by the Bank to draw on this account only to meet expenses in connection with the project as they are actually incurred.

* * *

ARTICLE IV

Operations

SECTION 1.   Methods of Making or Facilitating Loans

(a) The Bank may make or facilitate loans which satisfy the general conditions of Article III in any of the following ways:

(i) By making or participating in direct loans out of its own funds corresponding to its unimpaired paid-up capital and surplus and, subject to Section 6 of this Article, to its reserves.

(ii) By making or participating in direct loans out of funds raised in the market of a member, or otherwise borrowed by the Bank.

(iii) By guaranteeing in whole or in part loans made by private investors through the usual investment channels.

(b) The Bank may borrow funds under (a) (ii) above or guarantee loans under (a) (iii) above only with the approval of the member in whose markets the funds are raised and the member in whose currency the loan is denominated, and only if those members agree that the proceeds may be exchanged for the currency of any other member without restriction.

* * *

SECTION 4.   Payment Provisions for Direct Loans

Loan contracts under Section 1 (a) (i) or (ii) of this Article shall be made in accordance with the following payment provisions:

(a) The terms and conditions of interest and amortization payments, maturity and dates of payment of each loan shall be determined by the Bank. The Bank shall also determine the rate and any other terms and conditions of commission to be charged in connection with such loan.

In the case of loans made under Section 1 (a) (ii) of this Article during the first ten years of the Bank's operations, this rate of commission shall be not less than one percent per annum and not greater than one and one-half percent per annum, and shall be charged on the outstanding portion of any such loan. At the end of this period of ten years, the rate of commission may be reduced by the Bank with respect both to the outstanding portions of loans already made and to future loans, if the reserves accumulated by the Bank under Section 6 of this Article and out of other earnings are considered by it sufficient to justify a reduction. In the case of future loans the Bank shall also have discretion to increase the rate of commission beyond the above limit, if experience indicates that an increase is advisable.

(b) All loan contracts shall stipulate the currency or currencies in which payments under the contract shall be made to the Bank. At the option of the borrowers however, such payments may be made in gold, or subject to the agreement of the Bank, in the currency of a member other than that prescribed in the contract.

(i) In the case of loans made under Section 1 (a) (i) of this Article, the loan contracts shall provide that payments to the Bank of interest, other charges and amortization shall be made in the currency loaned, unless the member whose currency is loaned agrees that such payments shall be made in some other specified currency or currencies. These payments, subject to the provisions of Article II, Section 9 (c), shall be equivalent to the value of such contractual payments at the time the loans were made, in terms of a currency specified for the purpose by the Bank by a three-fourths majority of the total voting power.

(ii) In the case of loans made under Section 1 (a) (ii) of this Article, the total amount outstanding and payable to the Bank in any one currency shall at no time exceed the total amount of the outstanding borrowings made by the Bank under Section 1 (a) (ii) and payable in the same currency.

(c) If a member suffers from an acute exchange stringency, so that the service of any loan contracted by that member or guaranteed by it or by one of its agencies cannot be provided in the stipulated manner, the member concerned may apply to the Bank for a relaxation of the conditions of payment. If the Bank is satisfied that some relaxation is in the interests of the particular member and of the operations of the Bank and of its members as a whole, it may take action under either, or both, of the following paragraphs with respect to the whole, or part, of the annual service:

(i) The Bank may, in its discretion, make arrangements with the member concerned to accept service payments on the loan in the member's currency for periods not to exceed three years upon appropriate terms regarding the use of such currency and the maintenance of its foreign exchange value; and for the repurchase of such currency on appropriate terms.

(ii) The Bank may modify the terms of amortization or extend the life of the loan, or both.

* * *

SECTION 10.   Political Activity Prohibited

The Bank and its officers shall not interfere in the political affairs of any member; nor shall they be influenced in their decisions by the political character of the member or members concerned. Only economic considerations shall be relevant to their decisions, and these considerations shall be weighed impartially in order to achieve the purposes stated in Article I.

ARTICLE V

Organization and Management

SECTION 1.   Structure of the Bank

The Bank shall have a Board of Governors, Executive Directors, a President and such other officers and staff to perform such duties as the Bank may determine.

SECTION 2.   Board of Governors

(a) All the powers of the Bank shall be vested in the Board of Governors consisting of one governor and one alternate appointed by each member in such manner as it may determine. Each governor and each alternate shall serve for five years, subject to the pleasure of the member appointing him, and may be reappointed. No alternate may vote except in the absence of his principal. The Board shall select one of the governors as chairman.

(b) The Board of Governors may delegate to the Executive Directors authority to exercise any powers of the Board, except the power to:

(i) Admit new members and determine the conditions of their admission;

(ii) Increase or decrease the capital stock;

(iii) Suspend a member;

(iv) Decide appeals from interpretations of this Agreement given by the Executive Directors;

(v) Make arrangements to cooperate with other international organizations (other than informal arrangements of a temporary and administrative character);

(vi) Decide to suspend permanently the operations of the Bank and to distribute its assets;

(vii) Determine the distribution of the net income of the Bank.

* * *

SECTION 3.   Voting

* * *

(b) Except as otherwise specifically provided, all matters before the Bank shall be decided by a majority of the votes cast.

SECTION 4.   Executive Directors

(a) The Executive Directors shall be responsible for the conduct of the general operations of the Bank, and for this purpose, shall exercise all the powers delegated to them by the Board of Governors.

(b) There shall be twelve Executive Directors, who need not be governors, and of whom:

  (i) five shall be appointed, one by each of the five members having the largest number of shares;

  (ii) seven shall be elected according to Schedule B by all the Governors other than those appointed by the five members referred to in (i) above . . . .

* * *

Executive Directors shall be appointed or elected every two years.

* * *

(e) The Executive Directors shall function in continuous session at the principal office of the Bank and shall meet as often as the business of the Bank may require.

* * *

SECTION 5.   President and Staff

(a) The Executive Directors shall select a President who shall not be a governor or an executive director or an alternate for either. The President shall be Chairman of the Executive Directors, but shall have no vote except a deciding vote in case of an equal division. He may participate in meetings of the Board of Governors, but shall not vote at such meetings. The President shall cease to hold office when the Executive Directors so decide.

(b) The President shall be chief of the operating staff of the Bank and shall conduct, under the direction of the Executive Directors, the ordinary business of the Bank. Subject to the general control of the Executive Directors, he shall be responsible for the organization, appointment and dismissal of the officers and staff.

(c) The President, officers and staff of the Bank, in the discharge of their offices, owe their duty entirely to the Bank and to no other authority. Each member of the Bank shall respect the international character of this duty and shall refrain from all attempts to influence any of them in the discharge of their duties.

(d) In appointing the officers and staff the President shall, subject to the paramount importance of securing the highest standards of efficiency and of technical competence, pay due regard to the importance of recruiting personnel on as wide a geographical basis as possible.

* * *

SECTION 8.   Relationship to Other International Organizations

(a) The Bank, within the terms of this Agreement, shall cooperate with any general international organization and with public international organizations having specialized responsibilities in related fields. Any arrangements for such cooperation which would involve a modification of any provision of this Agreement may be effected only after amendment to this Agreement under Article VIII.

* * *

SECTION 13.   Publication of Reports and Provision of Information

(a) The Bank shall publish an annual report containing an audited statement of its accounts and shall circulate to members at intervals of three months or less a summary statement of its financial position and a profit and loss statement showing the results of its operations.

* * *

(c) Copies of all reports, statements and publications made under this section shall be distributed to members.

* * *

1E. *The BWIs in International Law*

Here are the basics regarding the BWIs and international law. Hey! There IS such a thing as international law. Deal with it![*]

The Articles of Agreement

The Articles of Agreement ("Charters") of the BWIs are international treaties. The Charters delineate both what the Fund and Bank can and can't do, and what member countries have bound themselves to do and not do. The first Articles set forth each institution's purpose—see supplements 1B and 1D. In very broad terms, both are bound to promote economic growth and development of their member countries via facilitation of

---

[*]   This supplement is based in part on Professor Bradlow's chapter, *International Law and the Operations of the International Financial Institutions,* in <u>International Financial Institutions & International Law</u> (Daniel D. Bradlow & David B. Hunter eds., 2010).

international trade and monetary cooperation and stability. Each, however, has more specific mandates. For instance, the Bank's Charter binds the Bank to make project loans and only in "special circumstances" make policy-based, non-project loans (IBRD Articles of Agreement I(iv), III section (4)(vii)). The Fund's Charter binds it "to promote exchange stability, to maintain orderly exchange arrangements among members" and to provide its general resources on a temporary basis (and with adequate safeguards) to member countries experiencing balance of payments problems (IMF Articles of Agreement I(iii), (v)).

Juridical Personality

Now for just a bit of the law of international organizations. The IMF and the World Bank are international organizations with juridical personality. Since the BWIs were created by treaties, where states freely consented to create them, they have to have "juridical personality" in international law to pursue their objectives. They're subjects of international law and have international rights and duties, including the right to bring international claims. Theoretically, international organizations like the BWIs acquire this status because states that create them delegate some of their sovereign powers to them so they can pursue their purposes. So check out the Fund's Article IX(2): "The Fund shall possess full juridical personality, and, in particular, the capacity: (i) to contract; (ii) to acquire and dispose of immovable and movable property; and (iii) to institute legal proceedings." Article VII(2) of the Bank's Charter has the same language.

Adapting to Change

As you'll see in the narrative of the BWIs set out in this textbook, both institutions have evolved and adapted to changes in the world economic and financial order, if only to remain relevant. How can they do this if they're bound by a treaty? Creative lawyering! Here's how it works: When it comes to determining whether a particular operation complies with the Charter—which in many cases has language so general and ambiguous that you can drive a Mac truck through it—General Counsel of the Fund and Bank may issue an opinion. The Charters give the authority to interpret the Charters to their Executive Boards with a right to appeal to the Board of Directors (IMF Articles of Agreement XXIX; IBRD Articles of Agreement IX). They approve the legal opinions (most of them) and presto, they become authoritative decisions regarding interpretation of the Charter. If you want to check out a 2007 Fund decision that repeals and replaces a 1977 Decision on Surveillance Over Exchange Rate Policies, see: http://www.imf.org/external/np/sec/pn/2007/pn0769.htm#decision.

As you'll see in Chapter 6, when the World Bank decided to get into the good governance business, it appeared to be wading into member countries' political affairs, which its Charter prohibits. But the Bank's General Counsel came up with a test that would make just about any Bank involvement in domestic politics okay as long as the activity has a "direct, preponderant and clear" effect on the member country's *economic* development. The Fund doesn't have an explicit prohibition similar to the Bank, which has allowed it do the same thing. This "mission creep" is controversial. Some say the BWIs are on a slippery slope: What, if anything in a member country's affairs, is off limits? Others are cool with it because the BWIs need to adapt to change. If you're interested, have a look at these two articles: Daniel Bradlow, "Should the International Financial Institutions Play a Role in the Implementation and Enforcement of International Humanitarian Law?" 50 U. Kan L. Rev 695, 710 (2002), and Robert Hockett, "From Macro to Micro to 'Mission Creep': Defending the IMF's Emerging Concern with the Infrastructural Prerequisites to Global Financial Stability," 41 Columbia J. of Transnational Law 153, 177–78 (2002).

The BWIs as Signatories

The BWIs have signed various international agreements. For one, the IMF and the World Bank Group are specialized agencies of the United Nations and have signed agreements with it, which call for respectful consultation with the U.N., but otherwise say the BWIs can ignore the U.N.—except Article VII resolutions of the Security Council. The BWIs have also signed headquarters agreements with the United States and similar agreements with countries in which their offices are located. The most important provision in those agreements is immunity from suit in the courts of the host state.

Article VII, Section 3 of the Bank's Charter provides an exception to immunity. It states:

> Actions may be brought against the Bank only in a court of competent jurisdiction in the territories of a member in which the Bank has an office, has appointed an agent for the purpose of accepting service or notice of process, or has issued or guaranteed securities. No actions shall, however, be brought by members or persons acting for or deriving claims from members. The property and assets of the Bank shall, wheresoever located and by whomsoever held, be immune from all forms of seizure, attachment or execution before the delivery of a final judgment against the Bank.

Courts have interpreted this "facially broad waiver" narrowly: "[I]t is evident that the World Bank's members could only have intended to waive the Bank's immunity from suits by its debtors, creditors, bondholders, and those other potential plaintiffs to whom the Bank would have had to subject itself to suit in order to achieve its chartered objectives." Mendaro v. World Bank, 717 F.2d 610, 615 (D.C. Cir. 1983) (holding the Bank immune from employee's Title VII suit). Check out IMF Articles of Agreement, Article IX

(3): "The Fund, its property and its assets, wherever located and by whomsoever held, shall enjoy immunity from every form of judicial process except to the extent that it expressly waives its immunity for the purpose of any proceedings or by the terms of any contract."

We should mention one other international agreement: IBRD and IDA loan agreements to member countries. These and guarantee agreements are international agreements.

Customary International Law

We're going to cover just briefly the application of customary international law (CIL) to the IMF and the World Bank, primarily because, well, many wonder if it applies at all to the BWIs.

What is CIL? In contrast to treaties, CIL is considered the common law of international law. The idea that custom informs legal rules is ancient, going back at least to Roman law. Some of you have heard the simple CIL formulation: To determine if something has evolved into customary international law, you have to find consistent state practice regarding the matter (e.g., nations consistently exempt fishing vessels from being captured as a prize of war) as well as *opinio juris*, meaning that states follow the state practice out of a sense of legal obligation. There's many a pitched battle over both components of CIL.

As to the BWIs, one of the least controversial applications of CIL is that the Fund and Bank should respect their members' sovereignty. This can range from respecting the domestic procedures for implementation of a Bank loan—an international agreement—to refraining from interfering in a member state's domestic affairs. (The IMF avoids the first principle by contending that its stand-by arrangements are not contracts or international agreements.)

The pitched battle is over whether the BWIs are subject to CIL that *obligates* them to take into account human rights and the environment in their operations. For instance, some argue that the United Nations Declaration of Human Rights (UNDHR), which is not a treaty, is becoming CIL and therefore obligates the BWIs to promote human rights in its operations. The problem, though, is that the UNDHR is cast in such general language that it would be hard to come up with specific obligations that can be put into practice. And as to the environment, the Bank does formulate environmental impact assessments for its projects, but does it do so because it feels obligated to do so? The IMF's position is simple: "We're uncomfortable with any formal statement regarding our obligations to promote human rights and what we do has little impact on the environment." Really?

CHAPTER 2

DEVELOPMENT

■■■

Now that we've introduced you to international finance, we now turn to development, which was an afterthought at the Bretton Woods Conference. This chapter is divided into two parts. In Part I, Rachel and Mitch will tell you how the idea of "development" came into being. If you want the expanded version, it's in supplement 2A. Rachel's conversation with Mitch ends with Keynes because when the World Bank cranked into high gear, Keynesian economics was at its peak. In Part II we'll discuss different theories of development, beginning with the structuralist school of the 1940s and 50s and ending with the neoclassical revival of the 1980s. It's time for theatre now.

I. "RACHEL'S RIDE"

Setting: Chicago, winter evening, 2010

Characters:

   Rachel: third-year law student

   Mitch: cabbie

(lights up)

Rachel: O'Hare, please.

Mitch: You got it.

Rachel: How long do you think it will take?

Mitch: Are you in a rush or something?

Rachel: Kind of.

Mitch: We've hit the rush hour. It'll be slow going. Okay?

Rachel: I don't have much of a choice.

Mitch: No, you don't.

(pause)

Mitch: Law student?

Rachel: Excuse me?

Mitch: Law student. Are you a law student?

Rachel: Yes. I am. How did you—

Mitch: Where did I pick you up?

Rachel: Oh. Duh.

(pause)

Mitch: Let me guess. Third year?

Rachel: What?

Mitch: You look bored.

Rachel: Am I supposed to say thanks?

Mitch: I rarely hear that in my business . . . What's your business?

Rachel: What do you mean?

Mitch: What are going to do when you graduate?

Rachel: I'll be working at an NGO.

Mitch: A what?

Rachel: Non-governmental organization.

Mitch: Yeah, yeah. I got it. NGO. NGO. Like Greenpeace, right?

Rachel: Right.

Mitch: Doing what?

Rachel: Development stuff.

Mitch: Meaning?

Rachel: Helping countries.

Mitch: Wow. That's big time. Countries!

Rachel: I'm excited.

Mitch: You should be . . . So tell me, what's this development stuff all about?

Rachel: It's a long story.

Mitch: We have a long ride ahead of us. C'mon, don't you know cabbies like to talk?

Rachel: Okay, Mr. Cabbie. What do you want to know?

Mitch: What the heck does "development" mean?

Rachel: It depends on what point in time you ask that question.

Mitch: I'm not following.

Rachel: If development means having a government that one way or another tries to make your life better, that hasn't always existed.

Mitch: No kidding!

Rachel: I kid you not. Take feudal society. Serfs worked for vassals and the vassals sucked up to the Counts. Government's job was just to preserve the order. That meant people were born into their circumstances and they accepted that things wouldn't change.

Mitch: You stupid—

Rachel: What?

Mitch: No, not you. That idiot driver in the other lane.

Rachel: Oh.

Mitch: So tell me more.

Rachel: Then capitalism came into the picture—

Mitch: Wait, private equity firms existed back then?

Rachel: Ha. Since when do cabbies know anything about private equity?

Mitch: Hey, we can read.

Rachel: Sorry.

Mitch: You were saying? Capitalism?

Rachel: Right. A middle class arose. They upended the medieval thing and fought for the serfs but only because they needed labor for their factories.

Mitch: What's wrong with that? It's employment, right?

Rachel: Well, yeah, but it wasn't like the serfs found freedom.

Mitch: Not like Mel Gibson?

Rachel: He's bipolar.

Mitch: No, I mean, "Braveheart." You know, "Freeeeedommmm!"

Rachel: I haven't seen the movie.

Mitch: Get's kind of bloody. But that's Gibson.

Rachel: Your meter. This is going to be expensive.

Mitch: Take your mind off of that. Keep talking to me.

Rachel: Okay. Well, the middle class wanted stability by the end of the 15th century. So the "nation-state" was born with monarchs in control. They had private armies and they had to be paid. So they taxed for revenue to pay the armies.

Mitch: Now that's friggin' government.

Rachel: Right? So at that point the idea arose that government should promote economic growth—for more tax revenue.

Mitch: You know, I don't report tips to Uncle Sam.

Rachel: I didn't hear that.

(pause, Mitch puts something in his mouth)

Rachel: What are you doing?

Mitch: Chewing tobacco. Got a cup to spit.

Rachel: That's gross.

Mitch: It's my cab, Ms. Law Student. Just don't look. Check out the scenery.

Rachel: It's dark.

Mitch: Just imagine, then.

Rachel: I can't.

Mitch: Keep talking.

Rachel: Where was I?

Mitch: The nation-state.

Rachel: Right. Then came mercantilism, where the government was all about exporting as much as possible to get gold and silver.

Mitch: I like gold! See my chain?

Rachel: Uh . . . no.

Mitch: Let me show you.

Rachel: SO, anyway, then came the Industrial Revolution in Europe in the 18th and 19th centuries.

Mitch: Yeah, I remember that from high school. Industrial development, child labor, colonialism and all that jazz.

Rachel: Right. But do you remember that's when this whole idea of "developing countries" had its roots?

Mitch: How's that?

Rachel: They became suppliers of raw materials to the industrializing countries and they bought their manufactured goods.

Mitch: Raw materials . . . You mean like carrots?

Rachel: More like metals etc. needed to produce the manufactured goods.

Mitch: Gotcha.

Rachel: Then came—

Mitch: Adam Smith.

Rachel: How did—

Mitch: I've read his Wealth of Nations five times. When I'm waiting at O'Hare for a return fare to the city. Can be a long wait sometimes.

Rachel: Hmmm . . . So you know.

Mitch: Yeah, he trashed the mercantilists and argued for a more limited role for government. You know, stay out of the market, let it do its magic through self-interested individuals.

Rachel: Invisible hand.

Mitch: Yeah, but not totally. Government still had to do stuff the private markets wouldn't do, like national defense, laws, courts, etc . . .

Rachel: I'm impressed.

Mitch: Don't talk down to me. Cabbies are the intellectuals of this earth.

Rachel: Why's that?

Mitch: We see everything . . . Anyway, I like this. Let's keep going.

Rachel: Nothing better to do, I guess.

Mitch: Hey!

Rachel: Sorry.

Mitch: Just joshin' ya.

Rachel: Okay. Well, then came Karl Marx.

Mitch: Yeah, yeah, yeah . . . Exploitation of the workers. The proletariat masses take control of the system by overthrowing the bourgeoisie. Classless society.

Rachel: For Marx, economic development was tied to class struggle. He thought that trust in the government and cooperation with its goals were betrayals of the class struggle. The government's involvement in social reform was nothing more than the bourgeoisie's attempt to appease the workers and force them to abandon the struggle. Since the government reflects the will of the dominant class, it would never enact any law benefiting the subservient class.

Mitch: A Brecht play.

Rachel: What?

Mitch: I'm pulling over.

Rachel: Why?

Mitch: Nature's calling.

Rachel: Gross.

Mitch: Deal with it.

(Mitch leaves the cab, turning the engine off. Comes back minutes later.)

Rachel: Why did you turn off the car? I'm freezing.

Mitch: I'm trying to go green.

Rachel: Yeah, well, I'm white with cold.

Mitch: No, you're not.

Rachel: Yes I am.

Mitch: You might be cold, but you're not white.

Rachel: Look—

Mitch: Oh, yeah, we're post-racial.

Rachel: Race is a non-issue in this cab.

Mitch: Funny you should say that.

Rachel: What does that mean?

Mitch: Where did we leave off?

Rachel: No, tell me. What did you mean?

Mitch: Didn't black slaves help countries develop?

(pause)

Rachel: Are you going to charge me for your nature's call?

Mitch: Let's keep talking. What comes after Marx?

Rachel: Just don't get smart with me.

Mitch: I'm here to please. So after Marx?

Rachel: I think you know.

Mitch: Are we somewhere in the 19th or 20th century?

Rachel: In fact we are.

Mitch: Well?

Rachel: Then it was all about Alfred Marshall and Lenin.

Mitch: Alfred?

Rachel: Yes.

Mitch: I prefer Vladimir.

Rachel: What does that have to do with anything?

Mitch: We sound like a couple fighting.

Rachel: Look. First, I'm not your partner.

Mitch: We're on a ride together. An Aristotelian journey to a better place, a virtuous place.

Rachel: Stop with that cabbie, quasi-philosophy crap!

Mitch: Hmmm . . .

(car swerves violently)

Rachel: What are you doing? I'm about to throw up!

Mitch: I had to change a couple of lanes for the turnoff.

Rachel: Do all cabbies drive like you?

Mitch: Pretty much. So tell me about Alfred and Vladimir.

Rachel: Okay. Just don't make me sick.

Mitch: Deal.

Rachel: You know, we talk about globalization a lot today. But it was around at the beginning of the 20th century.

Mitch: Really!

Rachel: Absolutely! Capitalism ruled. If you were a European, you could travel just about anywhere and find the comforts of home.

Mitch: You mean like finding a Motel 9 anywhere you go?

Rachel: Well, kind of. But it was at that time that the idea of "developing countries/economies" really came into its own.

Mitch: Okay. Got that. Where do Alfred and Vladimir come in?

Rachel: Just hold on, Mr. Cabbie!

Mitch: Getting sassy with me?

Rachel: You want a good tip?

Mitch: SO, you were saying?

Rachel: Towards the end of the 1800s, neoclassical economists started looking at price not as a reflection of scarce resources but in terms of consumer preference and supply and demand.

Mitch: I'm with you.

Rachel: Alfred Marshall was a big neoclassical economist.

Mitch: I hate them.

Rachel: Neoclassical economists?

Mitch: No, just economists in general.

Rachel: They have their place.

Mitch: I suppose.

Rachel: They do. So Alfred—

Mitch: What about Fred?

Rachel: He said that economics was all about fully informed producers and consumers setting prices, leading to market efficiency.

Mitch: You mean, they're all on Facebook?

Rachel: Ha. No. But, anyway, Alfred's way of thinking is still with us.

Mitch: I know all about Vladimir, so we can skip him.

Rachel: Do you?

Mitch: Lenin didn't think like Marx. Marx thought the workers would revolt and a new socialist economy would be created. After the capitalist wealth was distributed, no more government. Lenin said, no dude. He said the proletariat class rocked and they would destroy the capitalist class. Government would be ruled by the proletariat. And they would go for government policies that would make our pocketbooks thicker.

Rachel: Can we stop?

Mitch: Why?

Rachel: Nature's calling.

Mitch: Gross.

Rachel: Deal with it!

Mitch: The next gas station is five miles away. Can you wait? You know, because it's gross otherwise.

Rachel: Stop this cab, now!

Mitch: Okay, okay. Calm down, will ya.

Rachel: You can keep the meter running!

Mitch: I want to hear the rest of your story.

Rachel: Fine!

(moments later Rachel gets back in the cab)

Rachel: What is that music?

Mitch: Alice in Chains.

Rachel: It's awful!

Mitch: What do you want to listen to?

Rachel: Let me think . . . Sinatra.

Mitch: I can do that.

(Strangers in the Night starts playing)

Rachel: Are we getting close?

Mitch: To what?

Rachel: The stupid airport, Mr. Cabbie!

Mitch: That's not what you're talking about.

Rachel: Hey, just do your job.

Mitch: I am.

Rachel: What does that mean?

Mitch: I'm just a cabbie. Taking you where you need to go.

Rachel: I'm going to San Diego.

Mitch: Really? You think?

Rachel: Look. Just stop and let me out.

Mitch: Sure. You have five miles to walk.

Rachel: So?

Mitch: You're wearing leg braces.

Rachel: Don't you dare!

Mitch: What happened after Fred and Vladimir?

Rachel: Why should I tell you?

Mitch: Because I'm a stupid cabbie who likes to talk.

Rachel: Go to hell!

Mitch: I'm already there. So, now that we're agreed where we are, tell me the end of the story.

Rachel: Why should I?

Mitch: I always finish a book. What's the last chapter?

Rachel: The Great Depression.

Mitch: Hard times.

Rachel: You could say that. Keynes knew that.

Mitch: John Maynard?

Rachel: He said the neoclassical economic thought doesn't explain the chronic unemployment.

Mitch: Theory of Unemployment.

Rachel: You've read it?

Mitch: O'Hare.

Rachel: So you know.

Mitch: I think so. He said that in a perfect economy money just keeps flowing around to keep everybody happy, from employers to employees.

Rachel: The circular flow of money.

Mitch: But why all the unemployment?

Rachel: Exactly!

Mitch: He said there were leakages in that perfect flow.

Rachel: Right!

Mitch: Yeah. Like people don't spend all their income.

Rachel: And that's not supposed to happen!

Mitch: So—

Rachel: Put more money into the economy to plug the leakages! So businesses would borrow money to make up for people not spending all of their income.

Mitch: The result—

Rachel: Ultimately, with all that money, businesses can't continue to invest, because their output won't increase!

Mitch: Unemployment.

Rachel: The solution. You know, right?

Mitch: No, you know.

Rachel: I do!

Mitch: Tell me.

Rachel: Have the government invest in areas that the private sector wouldn't be interested in—schools, roads, infrastructure . . . The government injects money but without getting into that cycle where businesses get to the point where they can't invest anymore!

Mitch: We're here.

Rachel: No!

Mitch: An NGO, huh?

Rachel: What?

Mitch: You're going to miss your flight.

Rachel: How much?

Mitch: No charge.

Rachel: What? No!

Mitch: It's cold out. Do you have a coat?

Rachel: Yes.

Mitch: Millions don't.

Rachel: What's your name?

Mitch: You know what a favela is, right?

Rachel: A slum in Brazil.

Mitch: Go there and ask that question.

(fade to black as Sinatra continues)

II. COMPETING THEORIES OF ECONOMIC DEVELOPMENT

Now that we've told you the grand story of the development of "development," we'll introduce you to four schools of economic thought that came into existence following World War II: (1) structuralism, (2) the linear-stages-growth model, (3) the neo-Marxist or dependency theory, and (4) the neoclassical revival of the 1980s. These schools fall under the general rubric of "development economics," a branch of economic analysis that responded to the perceived inability of classical, neo-classical, and Marxist economics to deal with the economic reality that plagued the poor countries of the world.

By the 1950s, it was possible to divide the world into two groups of countries—the poor and the wealthy. The wealthy group was composed of most of the Western European countries, Canada, and the United States. People living in these regions lived (and still live) with lots of material stuff and sucked up a large part of the world's resources. The other group—Latin America, Asia, and Africa—was poor, "underdeveloped," and contained almost seventy-five percent of the world's population. Economists and government policymakers, especially those in developing countries, began to look for reasons to explain this disparity and ways to eliminate it.

Part One: What Is Development Economics?

Let's begin by exploring the meaning of development economics.

We've said that the classical and neo-classical schools of economic thought are concerned primarily with the efficient and cost effective allocation of scarce resources and with the optimal growth of those resources over time. They hold that countries develop economically via the market. In a market economy, economic benefits flow to its participants from rational, self-interested, and voluntary acts. This behavior is efficient because it's based in part on the assumption of prices adjusting automatically to reflect fully informed people's transactions in the marketplace, and this produces the greatest overall economic growth. So if we were to ask an economist from either school why developing countries (or any country, for that matter) are experiencing economic growth problems, she'd try to find government-created barriers that restrict the free market. To stimulate growth, those inefficient barriers have to come down. This type of analysis and solution is universally applied—i.e., it doesn't radically change depending on the country being analyzed.

Political economy gives us a broader view of economic development. Like classical and neo-classical economists, political economists are concerned with the efficient and cost-effective allocation of scarce resources. But they bring a new coefficient—politics—into the development equation. When asking why some groups or countries are better off than others, political economists don't look solely at market forces for an explanation. They focus on the social and political mechanisms that economic/political groups, often elites, have created to control the allocation of scarce resources. Going back to Marx, Marxist political economy says that class struggle is a by-product of capitalism. Capitalism inevitably creates a conflict between the working class and the owners of capital. It doesn't matter what country you look at. The conflict may reach the same result: the social inequities will reach an intolerable point and the working class will trigger a socialist revolution that'll overthrow the capitalist regime. Who plays Brecht's Mother Courage on her wagon (not a horse this time)?

Development economics goes beyond the scope of either classical/neo-classical economics or political economy. It, too, is concerned with the efficient allocation of scarce resources. But its main concern is sustained economic growth over time that improves the standard of living for the masses who live in poverty in developing countries. So one of the main goals of development economics is the formulation of public policies designed to bring about rapid economic growth.

Like classical/neo-classical economists and Marxist economists, development economists see their role in society as model builders—they suggest models of economic growth for governments to follow. Development economists don't believe that a single model can be universally applied, given all the differences among developing countries. So development economics combines relevant concepts from traditional economic analysis with a broader multidisciplinary approach derived from looking at the historical and contemporary development experience of the specific region or country in question. Development economists typically first look at existing economic theories for inspiration or insight. They then modify or expand the theories to make them applicable to developing countries. Economists have used the resulting theories to explain the economic gap between developing and industrialized countries. The goal of

"*Even if the poverty trap is the right diagnosis [for poor developing countries], it still poses the question of why some impoverished countries are trapped and others are not. The answer often lies in the frequently overlooked problems of physical geography . . . Many of the world's poorest countries are severely hindered by high transport costs because they are landlocked; situated in high mountain ranges; or lack navigable rivers, long coastlines, or good natural harbors. Adam Smith was acutely aware of the role of high transport costs in hindering economic development. He stressed, in particular, the advantages of proximity to low-cost, sea-based trade as critical, noting that remote economies would be the last regions to achieve economic development . . .*"

—J. Sachs, The End of Poverty, 57–59 (2005)

development economics has been to pinpoint the geographic, cultural, political, economic, and institutional factors, both internal and external, that have clogged the pipeline of economic development.

Part Two: The Structuralist School

Although its influence has declined considerably, the structuralist school of development economics, most notably articulated by the theoretical writings of Raul Prebisch (see supplement 2C), has had a lasting impact on debates regarding development, especially regarding Latin America and other regions with similar problems.

> "As is well known, the proliferation of industries of every kind in a closed market has deprived the Latin American countries of the advantages of specialization and economies of scale, and owing to the protection afforded by excessive tariff duties and restrictions, a healthy form of internal competition has failed to develop, to the detriment of efficient production."
> —R. Prebisch, Towards a Dynamic Development Policy for Latin America, 71 (1963)

Industrialization

The structuralists focus on the mechanism by which "underdeveloped" economies transform their domestic economies from a traditional subsistence agricultural base into a rocking modern economy. A modern economy is defined as one in which most of the population is urban and the bulk of the country's output is in the form of manufactured products or services. Under this model, the ultimate question becomes how to expand the modern economy while contracting the indigenous traditional economy of the country or region. The objective of development is to trigger self-sustained economic growth through the structural transformation of underdeveloped economies. This can only happen by eliminating the underdeveloped country's reliance on foreign demand for its primary exports (raw materials) as the backbone fueling economic growth. Economic growth must be fueled through an expansion of the internal industrial sector.

Let's talk about how it all started. The structuralist school emerged in Latin America in the 1940s. In the latter part of the 19th century and the beginning of the 20th century, Latin American countries were exporters of raw materials. Classical economists, most notably David Ricardo, held that the region had a comparative advantage in raw materials, meaning they could produce raw materials more efficiently than other regions. If that's the case, they should concentrate on expanding exports of raw materials. But that's raw.

By the 1940s, Latin American economists began to attack this comparative advantage thing. They argued that export-led growth of raw materials was no longer a feasible path to economic development. "Hey (actually, 'Mira')," they said. "The prices of primary exports are tanking while the prices of manufactured products just keep going up!" It didn't help that the supply of manufactured goods was decreasing due to World War II. All of these factors messed up developing countries' economies big time. Given the low price developed countries paid for primary products, developing countries couldn't make enough money to pay for all of the imports they needed, including high-priced manufactured products. Kind of unfair, don't you think?

Many Latin American economists said the situation wouldn't improve following the War's conclusion. First of all, they noted that the advances in technology, which lowered the production costs of manufactured goods, weren't resulting in lower-priced imports. Structuralists pointed their finger at industrialized nations, "Mira, this is so injusto. You're not passing along the benefits of your advances to us. Instead, you're keeping the slice of the flan—okay, cake if you like that better—for yourselves. You know what we're talking about: increased profits for your manufacturers and higher worker's wages." Given these "structural" impediments in the world economy, the structuralists argued that developing countries had to pursue economic development through an expansion of the domestic industrial sector.

Second, they warned that, given the United States' role as the world's new industrial leader, the demand for raw materials would drop because the United States was rich in natural resources. Translation: The United States would be willing to buy raw materials abroad only if it was cheaper than extracting them at home. The post-War situation differed substantially from the glory days when Great Britain was the pre-eminent economic power but had few natural resources. Britain had to import raw materials to fuel its industries. This gave developing countries more bargaining power, power they would no longer have in the post-War world.

The Structure of Underdeveloped Economies

When thinking about the cause of underdevelopment, structuralist economists focused on the evolution of economic relationships between developed countries and the rest of the world. Developing countries were brought into the international economy to serve two purposes: (1) to supply cheap raw material, and (2) to purchase finished manufactured goods from industrialized economies. This gave rise to "enclave" economies in developing countries that expanded the primary product export sector at the expense of the industrial sector.

The structural relationships in the international economies led to a dual economic structure in developing countries, where a modern economy (the export sector) coexisted with a "backward" and undeveloped one. Governments maintained the modern sector not through internal innovations and advancement but by buying new technology from the developed countries. As long as dualism hung on, autonomous economic development would be impossible; that is, growth would depend on the industrial countries. Too much of anything is not a good thing, including dependence. (What about happiness? Hmmm . . .)

The Structural Transformation via Government Intervention

The structuralists argued that state intervention was key to bring about the structural changes that could lead to economic development. For example, government-imposed tariffs on imports were designed to kickstart the internal market by protecting new industries within the country—level the playing field between a manufacturer in an industrialized country and one in a developing nation. The rich countries tended to have better access to capital and technology as well as a more productive workforce. These factors enabled manufacturers in industrialized countries, say, steel producers, to produce a given product faster and cheaper than "infant industries"—steel producers in our example—in developing countries. In theory, the structuralists thought governments could lower or eliminate tariffs when the domestic industry had reached a level of development that enabled it to compete without the government-imposed protection. Get a lot of baby food.

Another important component of the structuralist approach was state-owned enterprises. The structuralists thought that, given the underdeveloped capital markets in developing countries, only the state could generate and manage the sizeable investments needed to industrialize. For example, in Brazil, by 1973 the government owned large chunks of key sectors—e.g., ninety-seven percent in telecommunications and sixty-three percent in mining. All of these policies, known collectively as "import-substitution," were geared at encouraging the country to industrialize. The state was charged with promoting a four-stage process of industrialization. The first stage was all about nondurable consumer goods such as textiles, food-stuffs, and pharmaceuticals. In the second stage, industries would use imported parts to produce consumer durable goods such as appliances, televisions, and automobiles. The third stage focused on the development of intermediate industries that would produce inputs for industries established during the first two stages. The final stage would see the rise of a capital goods industry that would provide heavy machinery and plant installations. What a plan!

Just to make sure you got it, the structuralists accepted that capitalism would lead to development. But they weren't convinced that the market alone could achieve the type of thriving capitalism that industrialized countries were enjoying. Governments of developing countries had to actively promote industrialization through government regulation of the economy.

Limited Success

While the structuralists made significant contributions to our knowledge of the process of development, their prescriptions weren't that successful.

Initially, the approach provided cool results in Latin America, especially for the large countries—Brazil, Mexico, and Argentina. After the onset of the debt crisis in the 1980s, the **Economic Commission for Latin America and the Caribbean (ECLAC)** reported that over the previous three decades the region's **gross domestic product (GDP)** grew at an annual average rate of 5.5%.

Yeah . . . well . . . countries that adopted the import-substitution model of development began to notice in the 1960s that government-led initiatives to industrialize couldn't effectively create the most important phase of industrialization relating to heavy machinery and plant installation. To make matters worse, heavy state involvement in the market created inefficiencies that eventually caused major internal and external economic problems. And the drive to industrialize led, ironically, to increased dualism in developing countries as the gap between the rich and the poor widened. Go figure . . .

Part Three: The Linear-Stages-of-Growth Model

The industrialized nations didn't pay much attention to the problems facing developing countries until the late 1940s and early 1950s. They approached the problems of the "Third World" only after they'd finished rebuilding much of Western Europe. Following World War II, most of the economies of Western Europe were royally messed up. The Marshall Plan for economic reconstruction came to the rescue. Europe's rapid re-industrialization would shape how policymakers in industrialized countries—we'll call them "the Global North guys" (and they were guys)—approached the economic problems of developing countries.

One thing should be clear at this point in our discussion: most folks thought that economic growth could only be achieved through industrialization. The Global North guys said that the constraints impeding economic growth in developing countries were mostly internal. Local institutions and social attitudes, especially those that negatively affected the rate of savings and investment, restricted growth. The Global North's view contrasted with the structuralists' view that developing countries' economic problems were due in large part to *external* factors.

The Global North guys thought the key to development was simple: implementation of a program providing for a massive injection of capital coupled with public sector intervention designed to accelerate the pace of economic development. This would compensate for the lack of internal savings and investment in developing countries. After all, this process was money in Western Europe via the Marshall Plan.

In this part, we look at Walt W. Rostow's stages-of-growth model of development. This isn't to say that Rostow's model was the only one or the best. But it was the model that came to rule in this strand of development economics.

Economic Development as a Linear Process

Rostow argued that advanced countries had all passed through a series of stages: (1) the traditional society, (2) the preconditions to take-off, (3) the take-off, (4) the drive to maturity, and (5) the age of high mass-consumption. Basically get old and fat.

In his view, the advanced countries had all passed the stage of take-off and had achieved self-sustaining growth. Developing economies were either in the "preconditions" or "traditional" stage. All they had to do to take-off (to reach self-sustaining growth) was to follow a certain set of development rules. Rostow defined take-off as a period when the degree of productive economic activity reaches a critical level and produces changes that lead to a massive and structural transformation of the economy and society. Think: Extreme Makeover.

A country could only reach the take-off stage (where's the tarmac?) if three criteria were satisfied. First, the country had to increase its investment rate, with investment amounting to no less than ten percent of the national income. The country could satisfy this requirement either through investment of the country's own savings or through foreign aid or foreign investment. The idea that increased investment leads to increased growth is based on the Harrod-Domar growth model, which, put simply, says that to grow economically countries must save and invest some percentage of **Gross National Product (GNP)**. Second, the country had to develop one or more substantial manufacturing sectors with a high rate of growth. Third, a political, social and institutional framework had to exist or be created to promote the expansion of the new modern sector.

Under this theory, economic growth was measured by a rising GNP. Given the low savings rates in developing countries, the government was responsible for creating a class of people who liked to save. The government also had to make sure that people who saved more would get a greater share of the national-income pie. Otherwise national income would be consumed rather than invested. Savings, good; consumption, bad!

You can see why this model was so widely accepted, right? It justified massive transfers of capital and technology from the North (industrialized countries) to the South (developing countries). At the same time, it provided a rationale for the massive concentrations of wealth that existed in developing countries.

Erroneous Assumptions

Despite its appeal, the Rostow model proved to be seriously messed up. The model blamed developing countries' stagnation on internal factors, namely a lack of internal savings and investment. The model assumed that if these components were injected into developing countries through foreign direct investment or aid—like injecting a turkey—economic growth would naturally (organic turkey) follow. This assumption was based, in part, on the success of the Marshall Plan in Europe. The model assumed that but for the low savings and investment rates, developing countries and Europe were the same for purposes of development.

They weren't. While post-World War II Europe lost its infrastructure and industrial base, social structures remained intact. It was a society rich in human resources—i.e., skilled labor and a competent managerial sector. It had a stable civil and criminal legal framework experienced in handling the many problems associated with capitalism. Developing countries' levels of human resources couldn't compare to those of Europe. So yeah, economic aid and foreign investment weren't enough to industrialize the region. If developing countries were to achieve sustained growth, the society itself had to be restructured. The linear-stages-of-growth model focused only on the symptoms of an ailing economic society. It never bothered to determine what factors led to a society that saved very little and invested even less.

Part Four: The Neo-Marxist Approach

One of the most controversial schools of development economics in the 1960s and 1970s focused on neo-Marxist theory. Neo-Marxist economists, particularly Paul Baran and Andre Gunter Frank (see supplement 2B), accepted Marxist philosophy in principle but argued that it had to be modified if it was to be applicable to developing countries. They argued that Marx didn't have sufficient information to develop a theory dealing with underdevelopment. Armed with

> *"It is in the underdeveloped world that the central, overriding fact of our epoch becomes manifest to the naked eye: the capitalist system, once a mighty engine of economic development, has turned into a no less formidable hurdle to human advancement."*
> —P. Baran, Political Economy of Growth, 249–50 (1957)

observations that Marx couldn't possibly have made, neo-Marxists made important theoretical departures from orthodox Marxist doctrine. We'll cover only two here.

First, neo-Marxists broadened the scope of orthodox Marxist doctrine by looking at exploitation among nations. As you saw in the cab ride, Marx's doctrine of surplus value said that the capitalist class was robbing the worker. The worker received only a fraction of the value of the product that his labor produced. The capitalists, the private owners of the factories and the machines, expropriated the difference. The neo-Marxists gave this theory an international dimension based on how nations behaved. They concluded that industrialized countries historically extracted surplus value from developing countries: Developed countries paid really low prices for the primary products, such as metals, imported from developing countries, transformed them into finished products, such as automobiles, and sold them back to developing countries at really high prices. This resulted in chronic poverty and misery in developing countries.

Second, neo-Marxists took issue with the orthodox Marxist theory that a social revolution is possible only after a country has undergone a capitalist transformation. The orthodox position would mean that a revolution couldn't occur in developing countries until industrialization ruled. Neo-Marxists argued that passing through the industrialization stage was impossible for many developing countries, given the theorists' observations that developing countries—"peripheral countries"—were stuck in a state of underdevelopment and unequal exchange with advanced capitalist nations—the "center".

The path to industrialization was difficult and even impossible to follow because, like we've said, developing countries were brought into the capitalist international economy as producers of cheap raw materials. So foreign capital flowed to and modernized only one sector of developing economies—the primary products sector. The by-product of this process was the destruction of indigenous industry, either directly or through neglect. Neo-Marxists claimed that foreign capitalists had no interest in developing local industries. And the local capitalists were happy as long as they could extract surplus labor from the peasantry and wage laborers. The surplus capital was either invested abroad or consumed via the purchase of luxury goods (from abroad, of course).

All of these factors contributed to static economies in developing countries, which meant they couldn't achieve capitalism. Solution? Neo-Marxists called upon the masses to engage in a socialist revolution without waiting for industrialization. The revolution would place the surplus value in the hands of the workers, who would invest in socialist development. Yeah . . . well . . .

The Flaws

Neo-Marxist theory was an important and provocative contribution to development economics, primarily because it questioned many assumptions supporting development theory based on capitalism. Still, the theory was subject to lots of criticism, especially the neo-Marxist-based "dependency theory," which said that developing countries' development was dependent on, and thwarted by, advanced capitalist countries.

Classically trained economists argued that heeding neo-Marxist calls for self-sufficient development would lead to economic stagnation in developing countries. Pointing to empirical evidence, Marxist economists claimed the neo-Marxists incorrectly concluded that developing countries couldn't achieve the capitalist mode that Marx thought necessary for a socialist revolution. Others noted that neo-Marxist theory failed to explain patterns of specialization in developing countries. Still others believed neo-Marxist theory was too formalistic to be useful.

Part Five: Basic Needs

Although the dependency school itself became the subject of critical analysis, the preoccupation in the 1970s with inequitable development eventually led other theorists to advance the "basic needs" model of development. In 1972, Dudley Seers first threw down this model when he questioned whether, given the increased inequality in developing countries, growth in per capita income alone could be used to measure development. Development economists began to offer alternative approaches that would consider the welfare of the poorest segments of society in developing countries. The World Bank, which also questioned the exclusive focus on GNP, recommended moderate income redistribution to the poorest forty percent of the population. Others called for significant land distribution.

But the basic needs model had its own problems. (What model doesn't?) Critics said the concept of meeting basic needs was incoherent and difficult to apply. The model would sacrifice economic growth for equity (a false dilemma, as policymakers would conclude later) and result in significant increases in public sector expenditures. The strategy emphasized labor-intensive, primary production at the expense of industrialization in developing countries. It didn't satisfy the South's call for a New International Economic Order (NIEO) (see Chapter 4). It also wasn't politically viable in nonsocialist developing countries due to the power of the landowning classes. Yeah, the basic needs model had issues.

Still, a radical, normative approach to meeting basic needs cropped up in the late 1970s. Its proponents assigned a high priority to meeting personal consumption requirements and access to employment. They also emphasized the importance of self-sustained growth and less dependent development through structural change and investment in human capital (e.g., education). The radical paradigm wanted to avoid the impediments of the import-substitution model of development, such as foreign exchange shortages, inadequate domestic demand, and price distortions. How? A more equal income distribution would create demand for domestically produced consumer goods and services provided by small- and medium-sized companies. The early phase of development would emphasize labor intensive means of production, including emphasis on primary goods for export. Large-scale industrial production of capital and intermediate goods would follow.

On the supply side, the model called for more equal asset distribution, primarily through land reform, to encourage local entrepreneurs and to promote the development of technical expertise. The state would promote redistributive development by pursuing pricing (subsidies and rationing) and market policies intended to affect the composition of demand. State controls over investment would also be used, where appropriate, to promote changes in composition of production. Eliminating price distortions and increasing public sector research into alternative technologies would promote appropriate production technologies. Popular participation would energize the entire process. Foreign aid and NGOs would also play visible roles. Yeah, let's do it!

Well . . . no . . . not all of it, at least. Given the perceived political resistance to the basic needs approach and the neoliberal counteroffensive (which began in the early 1970s and culminated in the IMF/World Bank adjustment programs of the 1990s), major voices of the approach argued for meeting basic human needs through improved public services and investment in human capital. This approach, which the World Bank adopted in the early- to mid-1980s, avoided radical and controversial redistributive policies by focusing on cost-effective, targeted expenditures on the poor.

Part Six: The Neoclassical Revival

Neoclassical theory experienced a resurgence in the 1980s. It's not coincidental that, during this same period, conservative political parties governed in most of the industrialized nations—e.g., United States, United Kingdom, Canada, and Germany.

Neoclassical economic theory dismissed neo-Marxist theory as flawed and unrealistic. It also rejected structuralists' claims that developing countries' problems were due to structural impediments in the international economy and that domestic structural flaws required significant state intervention in the economy.

To neoclassical economists, such as Jacob Viner and Bauer and Yamey, poorly designed economic policies and too much state interference led to economic stagnation in developing countries. They argued that to stimulate the domestic economy and promote the creation of an efficient market, developing country governments had to lose market restrictions and limit government intervention. This was to be accomplished through the privatization of state-owned enterprises, promotion of free trade, reduction or elimination of restrictions on foreign investment, and a reduction or elimination of government regulations affecting the market. These reform measures collectively were called "the Washington Consensus," which we'll get into in Chapter 6. Bottom line: market forces, not government intervention in the economy, would bring about development in stagnating economies.

This framework became the basis for the massive economic changes that occurred in Latin America after the onset of the debt crisis in the early 1980s and for the equally profound transformation of socialist economies after the Soviet Union, like, went away.

You Gotta Know Something About Them!

Paul Baran

Though he didn't formally attend school until he was eleven, Paul Baran became a noted economist and neo-Marxist. He moved from Europe to America as an adult where he lectured at Harvard and eventually become a member of the OSS (an early version of the CIA). In 1949, Baran joined the faculty at Stanford University. According to his contemporaries, Baran, though brilliant, wasn't always thrilled about writing and research. He, like many of us, probably would've rather spent his time talking about his ideas than turning them into formal papers.

Karl Marx

Karl, a good-looking but sarcastic guy, was known during his student days as Mohr (the Moor). Although his forefathers were Jewish, Karl's father Heinrich (a lawyer!) was baptized at age 35 in the evangelical faith. Karl was baptized in 1824. The Marx family abandoned the Jewish faith because in the 19th century, Jews were excluded from all public posts, including the practice of law. Before Prussian authorities ran him out of Germany, Marx had been living in Cologne where he edited a newspaper, The Rhenish Gazette, and met his wife. Eventually, he settled in London where he finally expired in his armchair in 1883.

Vladmir Lenin

Born Vladimir Ilich Ulyanov, Lenin was an exceptional student, but was expelled from university for his radical policies and his ties with his deceased (executed) "state criminal" of a brother. After finishing a law degree, he was arrested and exiled to Siberia for continuing to cause trouble. The cold of Siberia didn't stop him: When he returned home, he led the October Revolution. That was in October, we think. Anyway, assassins tried to blow him away. Six years later he kicked the bucket at age 54.

Alfred Marshall

Alfred defied his parents' hopes that he'd enter the clergy. He became instead a high priest in the academic world of mathematics. He eventually attended Cambridge and balanced concentrated mathematics study with "light" reading including Shakespeare, the Agamemnon, and Boswell's Life of Johnson. His claim to fame started with his publication Economics of Industry (1879), which he wrote with his wife, Mary Paley, and continued with his numerous contributions to microeconomic theory.

Raul Prebisch

Called "Latin America's Keynes," Prebisch studied and taught economics for twenty-five years. He also served as the general manager of the Central Bank of Argentina (which he in fact co-founded)—a position from which he was unceremoniously fired after eight years. He only found out about his displacement after his wife picked up the morning paper that announced it. Prebisch was ultimately known for his work within the United Nations system, starting with the Economic Commission for Latin America and then as founding secretary-general of the United Nations Conference on Trade and Development, which advocates for development policies that'll benefit developing countries.

Walt W. Rostow

Named after the poet, Walt Whitman, Rostow was born to an economic historian who had visions of greatness for his son. At age nineteen, he graduated from Yale and went on to win a Rhodes scholarship and serve as a major in the Army's covert Office of Strategic Services in World War II. He eventually pursued a career as a scholar and political advisor. He penned Kennedy's 1960 campaign slogan, "Let's get this country moving again."

Adam Smith

Born in Scotland, Adam Smith, the famed economist, was a member of the philosophy department at Oxford and a good friend of David Hume, a big name in philosophy. Interestingly, Smith saw himself first and foremost as a philosopher, and only secondarily as an economist. Though his famous concept of the invisible-hand promotes rational self-interest, Smith had a soft heart—he supported charity and benevolence. In fact, Smith was really concerned about poverty and inequality that existed in a market economy. Read his book, The Theory of Moral Sentiments. Pretty cool stuff. By the way, the photo is the best we could do.

What's Up with That?

GDP versus GNP

This is pretty dry stuff, but you gotta know this. Gross Domestic Product (GDP) and Gross National Product (GNP) both measure the size and strength of the economy but their definition, calculation and applications are different. GDP is a measure of national income, national output and national expenditure produced in a particular country. GNP equals GDP plus net property income from abroad, which includes the value of all goods and services produced by nationals, whether in the country or not.

Economic Commission for Latin America and the Caribbean

The Economic Commission for Latin America was established in 1948. The Commission added the Caribbean countries in 1984, becoming ECLAC. Stationed in Chile, it's one of five regional commissions of the United Nations. ECLAC rocks for most Latin Americans. It assists with the economic and social development of Latin America by strengthening economic ties and cooperation between countries, gathering and publishing economic and social data, advising governments, organizing conferences and workshops, and, among other things, bringing both regional and global perspectives to Latin American issues.

QUESTIONS FROM YOUR TALKING DOG

1.   Since I'm your vassal—I'm not? Then what's with the leash? Anyway, I want to know about the trajectory—yeah, it's a big word but I'm a smart dog—of development from feudalism to Keynesian economics?

2.   Development economics. Huh? Hey, I need a snack.

3.   I've seen you playing with Legos. That's like structuralism, right? What was that all about? Was it all good or did it have weaknesses like my right hip?

4.   You imported my doggie-sweater, right? Was that like import-substitution? Ok, so I'm way off. Then tell me about it. Good stuff?

5.   I'm feeling like a prof . . . hey, so what if I don't have tenure. Why was it almost inevitable that developing countries, especially those in Latin America, would adopt a statist model of development?

6.   I knew a dog called Rostow. What's up with his stages-of-growth model of development? Was it all good?

7.   I've seen you wear those Che Guevera t-shirts. So you can tell me about the neo-Marxist approach to development, right? Was it all cool? Don't call me pretentious! Want me to go on the carpet?

8.   I hate the dog food you give me. You say it's basic. I just have basic needs. What's the problem with that?

9.   I love the Mozart you play on your phone. That's classical, right? Ok, then, what are economists talking about when they talk about the neo-classical revival in the 1980s?

<u>Chapter 2: Supplement</u>

2A. *How the Idea of Development Got Started*

"Economic development" or "development" is a term that economists, politicians, and others have used frequently in the 20th century. But the concept has been in existence in the West for centuries. Modernization, Westernization, and especially Industrialization are other terms people have used when discussing economic development. Although no one is sure when the concept originated, most people agree that development is closely bound up with the evolution of capitalism and the demise of feudalism.

Development has lots of meanings. The meaning a particular person attaches to the term depends on her subjective view of the world. The meaning of development is not only a product of the individual's perspective but also of the particular period in time when the word is being uttered. So what do you do? Place the meaning in a historical context. We're going to keep our story simple. So if you're a PhD in history or philosophy, indulge us.

Part One: The Early Stages of Capitalism

Feudal Society

Following the collapse of the Roman Empire, the West experienced a time in which all effective public authority disappeared. Feudalism was a system whose ultimate goal was to create decentralized government. Check out this hierarchy: The system was based on a contractual relationship among members of the nobility in Europe, and it revolved around the most important warrior (no, not William Wallace of Braveheart) in the region—the Count. The Count maintained strict control over all the lesser warriors (lords) in his region. The lords accepted the Count as their Lord (or were forced to do so), thereby becoming vassals of the Count. The Count's duty was to protect the lords and settle any dispute that arose between them. Most importantly, the Count guaranteed that as long as the vassals remained loyal they'd be allowed to remain in possession of their land or fiefdoms. This pattern was replicated all over Europe.

So, a highly localized form of "government" evolved during the Middle Ages. It was all about control—control-freak-dom. Feudal government combined political and military service with landholding to prevent Medieval Europe from disintegrating into thousands of "seigneuries" (independent estates run by different lords). In other words, government was essentially a system of cooperation designed to protect and perpetuate the feudal system and to preserve order. Given society's vulnerability to unpredictable harvests, to whatever type of governance prevailed at the time, and to frequent wars, active and consciously designed government programs to improve the welfare of society simply didn't exist. If you're in that kind of world, the idea of a bureaucracy of government officials responsible for designing programs to provide people with a better standard of living is . . . well . . . give me another arrow.

It's a pretty evident thing that development policy as we think of it today did not exist in feudal society. For much of that period, a person did not witness or expect significant changes in society during his or her lifetime. His or her position in that society was pre-determined and fixed at birth. Serfs, who worked for the vassals, couldn't "move up" and become knights or barons; such mobility was generally unheard of. Individuals viewed themselves as victims of their destiny and environment. It never occurred to the average person that he could do something to achieve a life he valued (the fancy word is "agency") or that nature could be conquered.

But, hey, medieval society was not completely static. Change did occur. But it wasn't the product of a systematic approach that applied science and technology to produce material goods. That would have to wait for industrial revolution.

Transition to Capitalism

Exactly what fueled the transition from feudalism to capitalism in its early stages is a hotly debated issue. We'll probably never know. What is known is that government played a minor role in the process. The movement was a local one driven by dudes jacked up on ambition. Some were in search of fame, while others sought prestige. But most of all, they wanted personal financial gain. Development, or "progress," as the early bourgeoisie (the middle class) called it, was synonymous with the improvement of an individual's lot in society.

There was no general idea that anyone had to think about the welfare of society as a whole. People got rid of medieval institutions not because they felt that society as a whole would be better off, but because the early capitalists would be better off. They fought for the freedom of the serf with almost the same tenacity that they fought for free trade. A victory in both fields was crucial to their personal economic well-being. A free peasantry would provide the labor for the capitalist's factories and free trade would expand the market for the factories' manufactured goods. Right, we're not talking William Wallace's cry of freedom (you know, Mel Gibson playing Wallace in "Braveheart").

The Nation-State

Feudalism began to decline after its peak in the 13th century. By the end of the 15th century, the power of the feudal governments had eroded through wars and feudal rebellion. Banditry—yeah, bandits—was almost out of control. All of this messed up trade and commerce, which was being driven at the time by the emerging capitalist middle class. Then came the rise of the nation-state and the concentration of power in the hands of sovereigns, which laid the foundation for post-medieval progress and development.

In response to the strife of the period, various powerful rulers attempted to bring peace to Western Europe. These rulers became known as the New Monarchs. They consolidated the smaller feudal governments under the institution of monarchy, which became the legitimate form of public power. Dig it: loyalty and respect for the monarchy were obtained through force, marriage, or peaceful (and sometimes not-so-peaceful) negotiations. The monarchs especially sought out and received the support of the middle class townspeople, who were tired of the petty wars and abuses of the feudal lords that impeded economic activity. How petty!

The monarchs quickly realized that maintaining a strong central government was expensive. To maintain control of their nation-state they needed their own private army; they could no longer depend on the nobles for military purposes—wimps. Because they had to pay the private army, the monarchs realized that their survival was dependent on an important aspect of development—a growing and sound tax base. What's wild is that policymakers in the latter half of the 20th century encouraged developing countries to do the same thing!

Tax revenues could be increased in two ways: increasing the size of the tax base—the number of people that could be taxed—or stimulating an increase in production. Most rulers opted for a combination of the two. But wars to expand the tax base tended to cost a bunch, prompting rulers to stress increases in production. By this time, then, economic development became an objective of state policy. Gradually, the notion of promoting sustained increases in economic wealth became an independent and legitimate aspect of state policy, which came to be known as mercantilism.

Mercantilism

In its early phase, mercantilism was characterized by a nation-state's drive to accumulate gold and silver. This policy gradually gave way to one geared at building and maintaining a strong and self-sufficient economy. Government pursued self-sufficiency by putting the poor to work. The goal was to create full employment, and to discourage the bad stuff—you know, idleness, begging, vagabondage, that sort of thing. Government introduced new crafts and manufacturing processes into the country. It gave favorable treatment to merchants who created jobs at home and to those who sold their products abroad.

The government's goal was to increase the exports of manufactured products and reduce all imports except those necessary to produce manufactured goods. With its trading partners having to pay for their imports in either gold or silver, the result would be a favorable trade balance for the country—that is, more gold and silver would flow into the country than flow out. If a state were able to export more than it imported, at the end of the year it would be richer than its trading partners. Yeah, sitting on a pile of bling.

During this period capitalism was exported to the rest of the world. Creating new markets for manufactured goods fueled Europe's drive to explore and colonize. The Europeans viewed exploitation of colonies as a legitimate means of acquiring precious metals as well as the raw materials for export industries.

Part Two: Competitive Capitalism (1700–1860)

During the 18th and 19th centuries, thanks to the Industrial Revolution (remember reading about the catalytic steam engine in high school? . . . uhh . . . college?), capitalism ruled in Western Europe, which laid the groundwork for many of the elements of 20th century development policy. For example, mercantilism contributed to a shift in focus from agriculture to industrial development. The industrial sector was geared to the production of goods for consumption. It was composed of small firms that bought and sold their products freely in a very competitive open market. Production took place in factories, which churned out manufactured products using simple labor-intensive technologies.

The new factories for the most part required only unskilled labor. Skilled craftsmen found themselves replaced by machines with which they could not compete. So they were forced to join the army of unskilled workers populating the new factories. (That's called underemployment these days, right?) An unskilled factory worker earned more than his counterpart working in the fields. Still, that factory worker didn't earn enough to support a family. At times the wage was not even enough to provide for the worker's basic necessities. To survive, the entire family had to work. The work at the factories was so mechanical that a kid could perform it. Indeed, employers often preferred women and children because they didn't have to pay them much. Think Mugato in "Zoolander."

In the international arena, this era was characterized by a push to bring new regions into the capitalist sphere through colonialism, which since the 15th century had expanded Western European power and control to the East Indies and the Americas. So for example, the English East India Company became a quasi-governmental entity in the 18th century and, after the British defeated the French in the Seven Years War, went on to conquer India's mainland. After the Napoleonic Wars, the newly independent Latin American countries entered the world economy as suppliers of raw materials and consumers of manufactured goods. And the British Empire of the late 18th century ensured that Asia and Africa would perform the same function. The seeds of the "developed/developing country" dichotomy—loaded with exploitation.

Part Three: Classical Political Economy: Adam Smith and "Laissez Faire"

In 1776, Adam Smith published <u>Wealth of Nations</u>, where he criticized the concept of mercantilism. Smith's views regarding limited government intervention and free markets, better known as the "laissez faire" system, would become key components of one school of development policy that continues to this day.

Smith felt that the regulatory and monopolistic practices characteristic of mercantilism limited a country's economic growth. He thought the best way to increase the wealth of a nation was through the reduction of anti-growth barriers, such as government intervention. He criticized the cheerleaders of mercantilism and argued that the economic system was worldwide, and as such should not be burdened by political or national barriers. He called on governments to eliminate tariffs on traded goods. "Free trade," Smith would cry out from atop a horse (doing his best William Wallace impression)—he was Scottish after all.

Contrary to popular belief, Smith never proposed a complete ban on government involvement in the economy. He was okay with limited government intervention, arguing that a government's role should be limited to national defense, internal security, and the provision of reasonable laws and fair courts in which private disputes could be resolved without a fist fight.

Under Smith's model, government involvement in any area other than what we just mentioned would have a negative impact on economic growth.

This is because economic growth is determined by the needs of a free market and the entrepreneurial nature of private persons. If there's a shortage of a product, its price will rise, and will stimulate producers to produce more, while at the same time attracting new persons into that line of production. If there is an excess supply of a product (more of the product than people are willing to buy), prices will fall and producers will focus their energy and money in other areas where there is a shortage or where there is a need which no one has yet satisfied (thereby creating a new market). The theory of the market mechanism is pretty cool, right?

Smith argued that this system would be regulated by the self-interest of each individual capitalist. He believed that each individual knows his own interest better than anyone, especially the government. In Smith's model, the sum total of individual interests will maximize the general welfare and liberty of all. Where's the horse?

Part Four: Karl Marx and the Socialist Revolution

You probably know all this from TED Talks, but what the heck.

In 1867 Karl Marx published <u>Das Kapital</u>, a work that systematically and historically analyzed the capitalist system. His theories would provide much of the material for arguments that have opposed development models based on capitalism and the laissez faire system.

Marx lived at a time when capitalism was at its prime—it was spreading throughout the world. Members of the capitalist class had become masters of both the social and political spheres. Their power was the fruit of the industrial revolution and of the many political and military battles that the capitalist class had waged against the nobility. The capitalists had joined with the working class to wrestle power away from the nobility. The first great battle, the French Revolution, was fought in 1789. In 1848, once again beginning in Paris, the capitalists staged a new revolution with the help of the working class. The successful revolutions gave political control to the capitalists. According to Marx, this allowed the capitalist class to create a government that could exploit the working people. For Marx, the government was nothing more than a tool of the capitalist class.

Marx believed that just as the bourgeoisie (the capitalist middle class) had relied on revolutionary movements to wrestle power from the nobility, so, too, could the working class, called the "proletariat," eventually overthrow the bourgeoisie. The eventual fall of the bourgeoisie was not just desirable—it was inevitable. Marx reached this conclusion based on his economic theory of labor—you know, the surplus value thing. At the heart of it was the conclusion that the capitalist owner robbed the worker. The worker received only a fraction of the value of the product that his labor produced. The capitalist class kept the remainder. This theft eventually led to an economic crisis caused by overproduction—the vast majority of the population couldn't afford to consume the products the owners of capital produced. The capitalist's answer to this problem was the continual creation of new markets.

Marx saw capitalism as an historical necessity because it was the most productive and flexible economic system in human history—he thought it rocked. It could move capital and labor to meet demand faster than any of the previous systems that it'd replaced. But Marx refused to accept capitalism as the ultimate mode of production (economic system). He believed the system was plagued with internal contradictions that would inevitably lead to its destruction and replacement by a more advanced system.

According to Marx, the relations of production (the way people interact in a particular economic system) create different economic classes. For example, under the feudal economic system, two classes existed: the nobility and the peasantry. The dominant class, the nobility, created a system to maintain its position. Religion, government, laws, and morals reflected the needs of the dominant class and were used to perpetuate its position of power. As capitalism emerged, a new dominant class, the bourgeoisie, began to appear. The nobles and the bourgeoisie eventually clashed (and the nobles weren't so noble anymore).

Marx believed that the beginning of capitalism set its own final downfall into motion. He reasoned that the capitalist system cannot exist without workers. As more factories are built, more people will be forced to work in them. So under capitalism the army of workers will continually expand. With the expansion of capitalism around the world comes the global creation of a working class.

But Marx was convinced that the capital system is ruthless. Here's how he thought the dominoes would fall: in order to survive, capitalists must continually strive to out-produce one another. But not all capitalists will be able to compete. Capital will become concentrated in fewer hands. The bourgeoisie that are unable to compete will be forced to join the working class or perish. This process will continue until one day the proletariat masses will be able to take control of the system by overthrowing the bourgeoisie, resulting in a classless society. No new class will rise out of the ashes because class arises from economic differences, and capitalism will have eliminated these differences by making everyone a proletariat. Since the concepts of state, religion, morality, and laws are mechanisms to maintain class differences, they, too, will disappear. Yet, government will not be eliminated immediately. A limited form of government (a proletariat dictatorship) will be put in place to prevent a possible attack by any surviving (zombies?) bourgeoisie. This dictatorship will eventually become useless, and when it does, it'll "wither away."

For Marx, economic development was tied to class struggle. It could only be achieved as a class; individual achievement was not emphasized. Marx thought that trust in the government and cooperation with its goals were betrayals of the class struggle. The government's involvement in social reform was nothing more than the bourgeoisie's attempt to appease the workers and force them to abandon the struggle. Since the government reflects the will of the dominant class, it would never enact any law benefiting the subservient class.

Really, Marx viewed politics as a mechanism created by the bourgeoisie to confuse the workers and divide them. Political divisions fuel nationalism that, in turn, misleads workers from one country into believing that the workers of another country are enemies. Marx would argue, for example, that essentially there is no difference between the class relations in Mexico and those in the United States. Workers in both countries are being exploited.

This would be a good time to see a Brecht play.

Part Five: Imperialism and Economic Theory (1860–1945)

Capitalism ruled during the latter half of the 19th century and first half of the 20th. Alfred Marshall and Vladimir Lenin were two well-known thinkers whose theories about capitalism laid the groundwork for post-World War II development theory. Before describing their work, here's some background.

> "The hope that poverty and ignorance may gradually be extinguished derives indeed much support from the steady progress of the working classes during the nineteenth century. The steam engine has relieved them of much exhausting and degrading toil; wages have risen; education has been improved . . . A great part of the artisans have ceased to belong to the 'lower classes' in the sense in which the term was originally used."
>
> —A. Marshall, Principles of Economics, 3–4 (1890)

By the beginning of the 20th century it was safe to say that a truly global economy existed (today's globalization is not, after all, a new phenomenon). Most, if not all, of the characteristic traits of capitalism could be found almost anywhere in the world. A traveler could board a ship in England headed for the Americas, Africa, India or Asia with little or no concern of what he'd find there. If he were headed to a "modern" or civilized place, he'd be able to find anything that he could find at home. By this time, capitalism had helped spread Western European influences of science, weapons, industry, medicine, and lifestyle to almost every corner of the globe. Any corner void of capitalism's presence was considered savage or uncivilized, like if you didn't have a smartphone today.

Not all people, nor all regions, reaped the rewards of capitalism. Western European nations divided most of the world's economically underdeveloped areas among themselves in their spread of capitalism. As the capitalist modes of production spread around the world, capitalism replaced local industries and with them the livelihood of many local craftsmen in countries that came to be known as "developing countries/economies." The need for raw materials by the industrialized Western European countries—

that came to be known as "developed countries/economies"—led to a realignment of land use. Indigenous populations were driven out of their lands.

Western Europeans were no longer satisfied with purchasing what the "natives" could produce. They wanted goods of a type or in a quantity that local craftsmen could not provide. To get what they wanted, Europeans invested capital in, and transferred technology to, underdeveloped areas. The economies of these regions were assimilated into the capitalist market. Traditions and customs had to give way to progress. Indigenous people had to give up their lifestyles and join the working class. Their fortunes were now tied to the market. If the market thrived, they survived. In times of economic depressions, they starved.

Europe relied on its economic power and its modern military weapons—its force—to maintain control of the rest of the world. This colonial system was to remain in place until World War I. In fact, the imperialistic rivalries among the various European powers led to the Great War.

Towards the end of the 1800s, neoclassical economists started looking at price not as a reflection of scarce resources (that was the classical perspective) but in terms of consumer preference and supply and demand. Alfred Marshall, one of the big neoclassicals, explained demand based on marginal utility (the usefulness of an additional unit of a good as compared to the unit before it). Supply, then, was a result of marginal productivity (the cost of producing the last item of a given quantity). In the end, the result is that fully informed producers and consumers set prices, leading to market efficiency. Marshall's analysis remains influential today.

Marshall's thinking was also important in a larger sense—he tried to rationalize the imperialistic exploits of capitalism. He believed that capitalism would triumph over the challenge posed by the socialist movement. He argued that progress would abolish all classes; in the long run, every man would become a gentleman. This classless gentleman would be created through better education, a reduction in physical labor, shorter working hours, and a greater distribution of society's wealth. This process was not going to happen overnight, or through a revolution. This classless society was to be a by-product of capitalism. As capitalism advanced, the proletariat would be transformed from unskilled to skilled workers. "I'll have a crumpet with my tea after my polo game."

Marshall's ideas built upon the thinking of classical economists regarding the state. He thought the role of the state shouldn't be limited to providing external security and domestic law and order, as classical economists had argued. Marshall believed the state should also advance education, encourage trade unions, provide public health, restrict monopolies, and provide relief to the poor through employment. But he stopped there, as he agreed with the classical economists that the state should not otherwise intervene in the operation of the economy.

Just like Marshall, Vladimir Lenin liked the idea of capitalism and tried to rationalize it. But unlike Marshall, Lenin was not as optimistic about capitalism's long-term prospects. Given the conditions in Russia in the early 20th century, Lenin pushed for a socialist revolution sooner rather than later.

To understand Lenin's theories, first you have to understand the historical context in which he lived. Lenin was from Russia, which at the beginning of the 20th century was still a feudal society. Political power (and, to some extent, economic power) remained in the hands of the nobility. This is not to say that capitalistic modes of production or a capitalist class did not exist there. They both did. Using Marx's theory on the composition of a society, Russian society was composed of four classes: the peasantry, the nobility, the proletariat, and the bourgeoisie.

Given the state of global capitalism at the time, Lenin argued that capitalism had entered its highest and final stage—i.e., that the proletariat had firmly established and united itself as a class, and replaced the bourgeoisie as the revolutionary class. But he argued that the bourgeoisie, who viewed the proletariat as a threat, would hang with the nobility on many issues. This new alignment allowed many feudal practices to continue. The promised democratic freedoms would never materialize because the capitalist class was afraid that minor things, like freedom of speech, would allow the proletariat to organize and carry out its class struggle more effectively.

Lenin believed it was up to the proletariat to take over the struggle, with the peasantry as an ally. The end result would be that the proletariat and the peasantry would overthrow the capitalist state and establish a dictatorship. For real! But the dictatorship would be kind of a good one (?) because in part it would lose feudalism and establish conditions under which the proletariat could enjoy democratic freedoms.

Lenin's view of development differed from that of Marx. Marx believed that given the continual deterioration of the proletariat's plight and the continual concentration of economic forces in a smaller and smaller number of people, the capitalist system would be unable to perpetuate itself. The workers would revolt and a new socialist economy would be created. After the capitalist wealth was distributed, all forms of government would eventually wither away.

Lenin saw things a little differently. He expected the proletariat class to take an active role in bringing about that downfall of the capitalist class even before capitalism has eliminated all traces of feudalism. Because the state would not have generated the kind of wealth Marx had envisioned, Lenin's model required the state—in the form of a proletariat dictatorship—to pursue economic policies to generate wealth. You see where this is going in terms of the role of the state in the economy, right?

Part Six: John Maynard Keynes and the State

After the Great Depression, many policymakers stopped believing the neoclassical school's claim that the market would eventually bring prosperity and happiness for all. John Maynard Keynes was a student of Alfred Marshall and a supporter of the neoclassical school of thought. Keynes' later work provided policymakers with the justification needed for state-driven development.

The severity of the Great Depression of 1929, the resulting growth in unemployment, and the spectacular growth of the non-capitalist market in the USSR led many economists to think twice about the orthodox classical and neoclassical development theories. The traditional view saw unemployment in a capitalist economy as a short-term adjustment problem. The economy would eventually reach an equilibrium point where the supply of labor would equal the demand for labor. Given the high unemployment rate in the capitalist markets, economists began to doubt that employment was actually determined by supply and demand. Their skepticism had a point: the USSR's non-market economy of the 1930s didn't experience any unemployment.

So the neoclassical economists' view of the world, where supply and demand was in equilibrium in every market and every economic aspect, including employment, was determined by this equilibrium, no longer made sense. The capitalist world's rise in unemployment wasn't an isolated event limited to a particular geographical region or economic sector. Drastic countermeasures were needed to save the system, but these countermeasures couldn't be put in place until the cause of the problem was understood.

Keynesian economics was an attempt to explain why the capitalist economies were on the verge of collapsing. What factors led to the unemployment of millions of workers? Why did the output of goods and services drop so drastically when the supply of resources and the industrial base remained constant? Keynes felt that all of this could be explained if one understood the basics of unemployment. Through his Theory of Unemployment, Keynes attempted to explain the causes of the near-collapse of capitalism.

Keynes first examined the process of production. In any given period, a firm produces a certain quantity of goods. These goods are then sold, say for $100. It cost the firm $70 to produce the product. That $70 includes the cost of maintaining the plant and equipment, wages, administrative expenses, the cost of inputs (raw materials) and the cost of capital (the cost associated with having the capitalist's money tied up in the venture). The remaining $30 is the net profit for that time period. This represents the income of the firm's owner. But this isn't the total income produced by this firm. Keynes' theory holds that during the production period in question this firm actually produces an income of $100. The $70 cost-of-production figure represents income to other participants in the production process. So the worker receives part of that $70 in the form of wages, the managers in the form of salary, the landlord in the form of rent, and so on.

This simple model is applicable to the entire economy. The value of everything produced in the United States in a given period is equal to the total incomes received during the same period. So if all that is produced is to be sold, people must spend all of their income. Remember, under this theory, total income equals total production, and money moves from the businesses to the public in the form of wages, salaries, rents, and profits. It then flows back to the businesses when the public buys goods and services. Keynes termed this process "the circular flow of money." He argued that as long as people spent all of their income, businesses would be able to sell all of their production. As long as this equilibrium was maintained that process would continue.

Keynes argued that a perfect circular flow of money does not occur automatically. Not all money that leaves the business sector as a cost of production is returned to the business via public consumption of goods and services. Keynes identified three reasons—three leakages—for this phenomenon: (1) people don't spend all of their income, (2) people buy goods and services from foreign business sectors, and (3) people don't have control of all of their income (the state takes some of it in the form of taxes). If left uncorrected, the leakages would lead businesses to reduce production. The result would be unemployment.

Keynes said the effects of the leakages can be neutralized through a proportional infusion of money into the economy. The leakages caused by private savings will be offset if businesses expand their capital base by borrowing the funds that were saved. The import leakage can be offset if the country is able to export goods and services that equal the value of imports. The tax leakage can be plugged if the government spends on goods and services an amount equal to its tax revenue.

Inherent in this solution is its failure. The capitalist must expand his or her capital base to bring private savings back into the system. This expansion results in an expansion of the production capacity of the business sector. To recoup their investment, businesses must increase their output. This, by definition, leads to an increase in income, which, in turn, leads to higher savings.

This cycle repeats itself until it's no longer economically feasible for the business sector to continue to invest. The result is economic collapse (e.g., the Great Depression), unless someone finds a solution. Keynes saw government intervention as the solution.

He suggested that the vicious cycle could be avoided by injecting money back into the system without expanding the capital stock. In other words, increases in the money supply must not be allowed to expand the country's production capacity. Keynes proposed that when savings exceeded investment, the government should borrow the savings and spend that money on social projects. These projects, though, shouldn't be ones that would increase the productive capacity or reduce the investment opportunities of the business sector.

Following Keynes' thinking, the government should focus its investment in areas that the private sector wasn't interested in (because there was no profit): schools, roads, hospitals and other public services. This result in full employment would no longer be directly linked to the productive capacity of the business sector. The net result of this government action would be to restore economic equilibrium. The money that'd leaked out in the form of private savings would be pumped back into the economy without placing a strain on the business sector's need to invest.

In Keynesian economics, government involvement is crucial if the economy is to survive. Many of the participants at the Bretton Woods Conference embraced this ideology, which translated into state-led development policies.

2B. *Process of Underdevelopment*

Depending on the party you go to, saying you're a Neo-Marxist economist might be super cool. But before you do that, read this excerpt carefully. Do you really buy into his theory of underdevelopment as a product of being incorporated into the world capitalist system? Are his examples of Egypt and the Arabs of the Maghreb convincing? Was his stuff awesome back in the day but pretty stupid now?

A. G. Frank, <u>Dependent Accumulation and Underdevelopment</u>,
154–157 (1979)

The Islamic people of the Middle East and North Africa, who during the Middle Ages had not only achieved a high degree of civilisation and development and had—along with China—made essential technological and cultural contributions to Western Europe's ability to achieve subsequent development under capitalism, were not spared the development of underdevelopment as an essential result of this same historical process. As Sarç notes, first Ottoman industry and then her village handicrafts were destroyed by British manufactures after the latter country's victory over Napoleon in 1815. And as Luxemburg notes, this de-industrialisation was but the first step in harnessing the peasant economy and in subordinating the Turkish state to the needs of world capitalist development.

The most spectacular process of incorporating a Middle Eastern economy in the process of world capitalist development—and along with the Indian one of the classic case histories of the development of underdevelopment—occurred in Egypt. There Mohammed Ali had tried to incorporate his country in this historical process in the second quarter of the 19th century, while maintaining national control and stimulating national, including industrial, development. But all he succeeded in doing was effectively to pave the way for Egypt's incorporation in the process of world capitalist development under foreign control. His industrialisation policy failed in part because of Egypt's lack of sufficient political autonomy within the Turkish Empire, which made the necessary tariff that is cotton—development effort fruitless—and in fact turned it into an underdevelopment policy—because his major effort consisted in creating the productive and social structure necessary to produce cotton for export to Europe. Under his rule, Egyptian cotton exports rose from about £1.5 million in 1823 to £5 million in 1850. Then, as European control became effective in Egypt after Ali's rule, the export of cotton grew much more rapidly to £22 million by 1880 and to £60 million in 1913, though the real value grew much more still than these monopolistically priced official values. In the meantime, as the British Consul-General, Lord Cromer, who governed Egypt between 1883 and 1907, announced: 'The policy of the government may be summed up thus: (1) export of cotton to Europe subject to 1 per cent export duty; (2) imports of textile products manufactured abroad subject to 8 per cent import duty; nothing else enters into the government's intentions, nor will it protect the Egyptian cotton industry, because of the dangers and evils that arise from such measures . . . Since Egypt is by her nature an agricultural country, it follows logically that industrial training could only lead to neglect of agriculture while diverting the Egyptians from the land, and both these things would be disasters for the nation.' Twenty-five years later, Lord Cromer looked back and summarised what his policy has achieved: 'The difference is apparent to any man whose recollections go back some ten or fifteen years. Some quarters [of Cairo] that formerly used to be veritable centres of varied industries—spinning, weaving, ribbonmaking, dyeing, tent-making, embroidery, shoemaking, jewellry making, spice grinding, cooper work, the manufacture of bottles out of animal skins, saddlery, sieve making, locksmithing in wood and metal, etc.—have shrunk considerably or vanished. Now there are coffee houses and European novelty shops where once there were prosperous workshops.' . . . Abdel-Malek goes on to note:

> The wretchedness of city and country was countered by the enrichment of the large landed proprietors, who had finally found a regular customer in the occupying power. It was able to guarantee them incessantly growing wealth, since Egypt had become from end to end a gigantic cotton plantation for the factories of Lancashire. Thus was born the political alliance

between Great Britain and the large landowners, headed by the royal family, which was to dominate Egyptian political life for three-quarters of a century.

Thus, the same process of development of underdevelopment—colonial transformation of the economic and class structure and the consequent underdeveloped policy of the colonial ruling class, be it foreign or 'national'—was imposed by world capitalist development on Egypt as well.

Essentially the same process of capitalist underdevelopment befell the Arabs of the Maghreb, and especially of Algeria, which after 1830 was not only colonialised but even more colonialised by French capitalism. For the Maghreb as a whole, the process is reviewed by Amin; and the development of underdevelopment in Algeria is analysed by Lacoste et al. as indicated by their subtitles:

> The decline of the urban economy. It begins by the destruction of the towns and the definitive decadence of the traditional urban society . . . The decline of the rural economy . . . of the agricultural and pastoral activities . . . The demographic decline is no less important . . . Social regression and re-enforcement of feudalism . . . The inequality of the regimes is not only maintained but aggravated . . . The destruction of the economic structures broken up . . . The agricultural crisis and the famine (1866–1870) . . . Private speculation with the tribal lands . . . The new structures of agrarian colonization (1881–1900) and the conquest of the Sahara . . . The vineyard boom . . . The consequences of the crisis in wine-growing: land concentration and political predominance of big colonization . . . The other side of the colonial ledger: the pauperization of the Algerian peasantry. The peasantry excluded from the forest . . . The Moslem peasantry to sell its land . . . The extension of the speculative colonization . . . The degradation of the peasant condition and of Moslem agriculture. The proletarianization . . . The stagnation of [agricultural] techniques and the degradation of the soil . . . A policy favorable to the [European] colony and to the disadvantage of the [Algerian] fellah . . . The appearance of the underdevelopment of Algeria . . .

Thus, the same pattern and process of underdevelopment also repeat themselves in Algeria and the Maghreb in general.

2C. *Structuralist Analysis*

Prebisch was a rock star in his day. Why? The whole idea of structural impediments to development still resonates today. But what was the problem with structuralism? Think twice about going to a party and saying you're a structuralist economist.

R. Prebisch, "The Economic Development of Latin America and
its principal problems," *Economic Bulletin for
Latin America* (1950)

I.   Latin American and the high productivity of the United States

The United States is now the principal cyclical centre of the world, as was formerly Great Britain. Its economic influence over other countries is obvious, and in that influence, its enormous increase in productivity has played a vital part. It has profoundly affected foreign trade and, through its variations, the rate of economic development of the rest of the world and the international distribution of gold.

The Latin-American countries, with their high coefficient of foreign trade, are extremely sensitive to such economic repercussions. An examination of the implications of the phenomenon and the problems it presents is therefore opportune.

It is a well-known fact that, in the United States, prices have not fallen in proportion to the increase in productivity as the recent research of Mr. Fabricant has clearly shown. During the period covered by that research— the forty years preceding the Second World War—manufacturing production costs declined regularly and persistently. The movement of prices did not follow this pattern at all. The increase in productivity was not reflected in prices but in income. Wages and salaries rose as real costs fell. This did not account, however, for all the benefits of productivity, as an appreciable part of it was passed on in the form of a shorter working day.

The increase in income arising out of higher productivity sooner or later extends to all phases of economic life through the well-known process, which need not be recalled here. By virtue of that same process income has also increased in activities in which technical progress has been insignificant or non-existent, as in certain types of services. In some social groups the increase was very slow; meanwhile the rest of the community enjoyed advantages which, as the necessary adjustment took place, had to be yielded to the former. This transfer, however, was usually offset by new increases in wages resulting from still higher productivity.

This fact is pointed out as a good example of the type of adjustment to which the gradual industrialization of Latin America will necessarily give rise. As productivity increases with industrialization, wages will rise, thus causing a comparative increase in the prices of primary products. In this way, as its income rises, primary production will gradually obtain that share of the benefits of technical progress which it would have enjoyed had prices declined. As in the case of the lagging social groups mentioned above, it is evident that such adjustment will mean a loss of real income in the industrial sectors, which will, however, be limited by the import coefficient;

but in the long run, that loss can be well compensated by the benefit of subsequent technical developments

As mentioned before, since prices do not keep pace with productivity, industrialization is the only means by which the Latin-American countries may fully obtain the advantages of technical progress.

Another solution had, nevertheless, been found by the classical theory. If the advantages of technique were not passed on through prices, they would be extended to the same degree by the raising of income. We have just seen that this is precisely what happened in the United States, as well as in the other great industrial centres. It did not, however, occur in the rest of the world. It would have required, throughout the world, the same mobility of factors of production as that which characterized the broad field of the internal economy of the United States. That mobility is one of the essential assumptions of the theory. In fact, however, a series of obstacles hampered the easy movement of productive factors. Doubtless the high wages paid in the United States, as compared with those in the rest of the world, would have attracted large masses to that country, with a very adverse effect upon wages, tending to reduce the difference between them and those in the rest of the world.

Thus the observance of one of the essential rules of the classic game would have resulted in a considerable lowering of the standard of living of the United States, as compared with the levels actually achieved.

It is easily understandable that the protection of this standard of living, attained by great effort, should have prevailed over the uncertain advantages of an academic concept. But the classic rules of the game form an indivisible whole and, if one is eliminated, the others cannot logically serve as absolute standards governing relations between the centres and the periphery.

This point is the more worthy of consideration in that one of the consequences of the technical progress of the United States, so much greater than that of the rest of the world, has been another important departure from the rules.

As previously stated, the import coefficient of the United States has become extremely low, not more than 3 per cent. In 1929 it was 5 per cent. The decline is not new, but one of long standing. During the last hundred years, national income increased about two and a half times more than imports.

This phenomenon is largely explained by technical progress. Paradoxical as it may seem, increased productivity contributed to the strengthening of the United States' protective tariff policy, after that country had reached the stage of economic maturity. The explanation is simple. Over a given period of time, technical progress does not affect all industries equally. When higher wages resulting from the increased productivity of the more advanced industries are extended to the less advanced, the latter lose the advantage which had enabled them to compete with foreign industries paying lower wages. The significance of this factor will be appreciated from the fact that wages are twice or two and a half times as high in the United States as in Great Britain. Thus, tariff protection has been necessary for industries more efficient than their foreign competitors, but whose level of productivity is lower than the average for their own country. For instance, despite the great improvement of agricultural technique, some of the important branches of agriculture needed protection as a result of their relatively high incomes as compared with those of foreign competitors . . .

It is under these new conditions of international economy, that the process of industrialization has begun to develop in Latin America. The fundamental problem lies in adaptation to these conditions—in so far as they cannot be altered—while seeking new rules in keeping with the new circumstances.

Until that happens, and possibly with slight intervals, a persistent tendency toward disequilibrium will prevail. It is due, fundamentally, to the following fact: while, as we have seen, the import coefficient of the United States has been declining, the dollar imports of the Latin-American countries are tending to increase, thus compelling them to take defensive measures to lessen the effects. There are several reasons for this:

First: since technical progress has been greater in the United States than anywhere else, the demand for the capital goods necessary for industrialization is preferentially made upon that country.

Second: technical development continuously manifests itself in the form of new products which, by modifying existing ways of life, assume the character of new necessities, of new ways of spending the income of Latin America, generally substituting them for the previous forms of domestic expenditure.

Third: in addition to those products which have undeniable technical advantages, there are others toward which demand is diverted by the considerable persuasive power of advertising. New tastes are created which must be satisfied by imports, to the prejudice of those which could be satisfied locally.

That it is not possible to reduce the import coefficient at the centre on the one hand, and to allow it to increase freely in the periphery on the other, under the influence of the above factors, was fully proved by the serious events of the nineteen thirties. We now have sufficient perspective to understand their significance and to learn the lesson that they teach. One other fact must first be mentioned.

It has already been stated that the industrialization of Latin America, if wisely carried out, will open the way to a considerable increase in national income, by giving more productive employment to vast numbers of the population at present engaged in occupations of low productivity.

It can now be seen that the rise in income so far achieved has accentuated the influence of those factors on the demand for dollar imports. The greater the rise in income in these countries, therefore, the greater their need to import . . .

CHAPTER 3

THE FALL OF THE BRETTON WOODS SYSTEM

■■■

The fall of the Bretton Woods System (BWS) marked the end of a system of fixed exchange rates and a transition to floating rates for most of the world. Participants at the Bretton Woods Conference believed they had created a par value system that would impose global monetary discipline. Countries declared par values that they had to adhere to in most situations, and the United States committed itself to maintaining the price of gold at $35 an ounce. As we shall see, the system was fatally flawed and collapsed in 1971.

Let's think about this chapter like this: Imagine a town that's been flattened after a massive tornado. No houses remain erect, just huge piles of debris. People in shock. Hungry. Dark clouds obscure the sun, making everything seem hopeless. Eventually, a committee is formed to reconstruct the town. They decide to start by building a big, sturdy house at the center of the town as its anchor. Without realizing it, they build a critically flawed foundation. Still, the house goes up, christened "The Bretton Woods System." Confidence and hope is restored. The town comes back. It thrives. All will be good. Stable.

Not. Listen for the cracks in the foundation. They were exposed by the hot money that began flowing in the 1960s due, among other things, to the convertibility of Western European currencies (see Chapter 1) and to the expansion of the **Eurocurrency market**, where financial transactions in currencies other than the dollar (especially deutsche mark and Swiss franc) took off.

It's a gripping drama.

(lights up)

Act One: The Descent of Britain and the Pound Sterling

As you know from your high school history, the industrial revolution in Great Britain set it on a trajectory to rule the world in the 19th century. The sterling rocked. It was fully convertible into gold and used in about 60 percent of world trade. Just prior to WWI, it consistently ran current account surpluses. And because of this, Britain was the main exporter of capital (long-term) and the leading creditor country.

Then came WWI and a series of crises that ultimately led to the fall of the British Empire after WWII. In the meantime, the United States was rising as a global power, becoming a major exporter of capital and creditor country. By 1962 Great Britain's current account surplus had virtually disappeared. Thereafter, it lived the life of a deficit country. It just gets uglier, folks.

At the outset of the Bretton Woods System, the sterling was set at $4.03/£1. Britain, a debtor country by then, negotiated a loan with the United States, a condition of which was that Britain would allow holders of sterling receipts accumulated in trade transactions to convert them to dollars "as early as practicable" but no later than July 15, 1947 (the sterling became inconvertible in 1931). What's the sound of massive amounts of sterling being exchanged into dollars? It was so loud (bad) that five weeks later Britain suspended convertibility.

Things just got worse. Britain kept bleeding reserves to defend its parity. You know what has to happen eventually, right? In 1949, Britain devalued the sterling to $2.80/£1. But everybody saw the emperor had no clothes on. Britain struggled for a decade-and-a-half to defend that rate, aided in part by repeatedly going to the IMF trough.

Time for politics in this story. After being out of office for thirteen years, the Labour Party came back to power in 1964. But since it was in power when the government devalued the pound in 1949, it didn't want to begin its renewed reign by devaluing the currency—it's an ugly thing, especially for politicians.

Now, remember Britain was in deficit—too many imports and too few exports and desperate to find ways to bridge the gap. Labour's solution: raise tariffs to reduce imports and in essence subsidize exports. Domestically, it introduced a program that, among other things, restored free medical prescriptions and raised old age pensions. Lots of people in Britain might have liked what they saw in the program, but the international markets thought that Labour was crazy to worry about health and old age when the economy was going to hell in a handbasket. Holders of sterling quickly sold over £100 million. On November 23, 1964, the government raised the key interest rate to stop the selling. Not enough. The next day, Britain notified the IMF it wanted to draw $1 billion from a previously negotiated Standby Agreement. Not enough. Over the next twenty-four hours, the Federal Bank of New York feverishly called western central banks and put together $3 billion in short-term credit. "Come on! Back off dumping sterling!" It worked—temporarily.

Over the next three years Britain struggled to defend the sterling, sometimes winning, sometimes losing. But then came the war in the Middle East. Egypt closed the Suez Canal. (Go back to your history books—or Google, whatever.) Holders of sterling started dumping it—again. The

U.S. Federal Reserve and central banks in other countries tried desperately to support the sterling. On November 17, 1967, holders of sterling offered over $1 billion worth of the currency, but nobody was buying except the Bank of England. (It was obligated to do that under Article IV(3) of the Fund's Charter.)

It was over. On November 18, 1967, Chancellor of the Exchequer James Callaghan announced that the sterling would be devalued from $2.80/£1 to $2.40/£1 that night, a 14.3 percent drop. The Fund said in essence, "The U.K. has a fundamental disequilibrium [key phrase], so we're cool with the devaluation." President Johnson said the same thing. Soon thereafter the U.K. negotiated a $1.4 billion loan from the IMF.

CRACK

Act Two: The United States' Deteriorating Balance of Payments

Scene One: The Paradox of the United States Being Banker to the World

The United States began the 1960s with a major balance of payments problem that only worsened. Unlike the U.K.'s BOP problem, which involved *a current account* deficit, the U.S.'s problem was in the capital account—a *capital account* deficit. Specifically, lots of long-term capital was flowing out of the U.S. while at the same time it was accumulating short-term liabilities—claims on the U.S (we'll explain all of this in a sec). As you know, a current account deficit isn't necessarily bad if the deficit is being financed by flows into the capital account. A capital account deficit isn't necessarily bad, if that deficit is covered by a surplus in the current account. And the United States ran current account surpluses until 1971, when it went into deficit.

Between 1950 and 1957, the deficits averaged $1.3 billion annually. Lots of the outflow was long-term private and government capital. You might think this is worrisome but back in the day, lots of economists and policymakers thought it was all good because dollars were needed to help rebuild war-torn countries. Without those dollars that ultimately went into the foreign reserves of central banks, the recovery would've been slower. Think about it. If countries faced a BOP deficit, without dollars in reserves they faced the following options: (i) deflate the economy—unemployment; (ii) devalue—traumatic and restricted by BWS rules; (iii) erect trade barriers or; (iv) . . . uh . . . go to the IMF (which probably wouldn't have enough pot—oops, meant *in* the pot—to fix the problem). Now let's see, if you were president of one of the countries, which option would you pick? Hmmm . . .

You can see, then, that the United States was banker to the world. It was lending long-term (e.g., a thirty-year loan) and funding the loans by borrowing short-term (e.g., short-term deposits). Remember we just said that most of the U.S. capital outflows ended up in the foreign reserves of foreign central banks. Under the BWS, the central banks had short-term claims on the U.S: just like depositors can withdraw money from their accounts at the bank, the central banks had the right to exchange those dollars for gold. Can you see what's coming? Take a look at this:

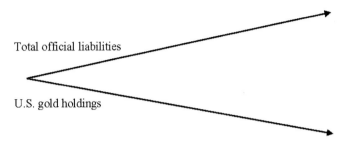

Total official liabilities

U.S. gold holdings

Yeah, that's right. By the 1960s, the short-term claims on the United States exceeded its gold stock. Uh-oh. Check it out, it's called the Triffin's paradox: Providing liquidity to the rest of the world via outflows of dollars threatened to undermine the very structure of the BWS.

CRACK

Scene Two: The Confidence Problem

Let's elaborate a bit on the Triffin's paradox, otherwise known as the "confidence problem." Supposedly, U.S. macroeconomic policy was constrained by the foreign central banks' right to convert dollars into gold. But except for a number of instances in the 1950s and 1960s, central banks didn't exercise that right because the dollar rocked and the gold supply wasn't keeping up with the expanding global economy.

In his 1960 book, <u>Gold and the Dollar Crisis</u>, the Yale economist Robert Triffin warned that eventually the foreign central bank holdings of dollars would exceed the United States gold stock. So if the BWS's "conversion right" had any teeth, the United States eventually would not be able to abide by its commitment to exchange dollars for gold at $35 an ounce. So if you were a foreign central bank, what would you do or think? Cash in your dollar chips to the U.S. Fed, right? And do it before other central banks beat you to it, lest you wind up at the end of

"Barring a drastic revaluation of gold prices, the maintenance of adequate reserve levels will thus continue to depend on the growth of foreign exchange reserves as a supplement to gold itself. This, however, cannot fail to increase further and further the vulnerability of the world monetary system to shifts of confidence—justified or unjustified—in the national currencies actually used as reserve media. A repetition of 1931 would, at some point, become well-nigh unavoidable."
    —R. Triffin, <u>Gold and the Dollar Crisis</u>, 87 (1960)

the line and there's no gold left. And, of course, all the central banks are thinking this way. Not good.

Let's put the looming crisis in sharper relief: In 1960, outflows of those short-term "deposits" we talked about spiked to almost $2.5 billion. As foreign central banks withdrew their deposits (exchanging dollars they collected for gold), the U.S. gold reserves took a nosedive. Between 1957 and 1967, gold reserves went from about $23 billion to about $12 billion.

> " 'I know everyone else think I worry about this too much,' he [Kennedy] said as we pored over what seemed like the millionth report on the subject [the balance-of payments problem]. 'But if there's ever a run on the bank, and I have to devalue the dollar or bring home our troops, as the British did, I'm the one who will take the heat. Besides it's a club that De Gaulle and all the others hang over my head. Any time there's a crisis or a quarrel, they can cash in all their dollars and where are we?' "
> —G. Bach, <u>Making Monetary and Fiscal Policy</u>, quoting Sorensen, Kennedy, 133 (1971).

On October 20, 1960, gold in the London market fetched $40 an ounce—above the $35 an ounce BWS anchor.

CRACK

Possible solutions: Increase the dollar price of gold. Instead of $35 an ounce, why not, say, $38 an ounce? This would seem like a reasonable solution, easing the pressure on gold. But it would also be inflationary. Besides it would just put more money into the pockets of the gold producers. But even worse, increasing the official price would create the expectation that further increases might not be far off. This would magnify the confidence problem.

Wait! How about this: Have the United States stop running BOP deficits and being banker to the world! Yes! Where's the after-party?

How do you spell "global disaster?" Back to Triffin's dilemma. Go ahead and do that and watch a global economic contraction of epic proportions as the international system loses the liquidity that the United States provided.

CRACK

> "Nobody could ever have conceived of a more absurd waste of human resources than to dig gold in distant corners of the earth for the sole purpose of transporting it and re-burying it immediately afterwards in other deep holes, especially excavated to receive it and heavily guarded to protect it."
> —R. Triffin, <u>Gold and the Dollar Crisis</u>, 89 (1960)

That's why Triffin thought it was stupid to base international reserves on a national currency or gold.

The Triffinesque solution that worked was the creation of an international reserve asset: **special drawing rights (SDRs)**. (In 1963, Edward Bernstein, formerly with the Fund, proposed a composite reserve unit (CRU), which ultimately morphed into SDR.) The IMF created the SDR as a reserve asset that could be used to settle international accounts. Here's how it worked: A deficit country could use its SDRs to obtain convertible currencies via another Fund member to fix its problems. After the Fund members agreed that creating SDRs would require a majority of 85% of the total voting power of the Board of Governors, the First Amendment took effect on July 28, 1969.

Scene Three: Stop the Bleeding

When the sterling took the dive in 1967, the market also lost confidence in the U.S. dollar. Market players began to dump the dollar. The 1967 fourth quarter payments

> "[I]n my judgment, the experience up to now with the operation of the special drawing rights facility has been highly successful, and it can be stated that the SDR has become established as a reserve asset."
> —P. Schweitzer, Managing Director, International Monetary Fund, in M. de Vries, <u>The IMF in a Changing World 1945–85, 79</u> (1986)

deficit on a liquidity basis stood at $7 billion. The trade surplus was almost gone. What to do? Well, to improve liquidity, one could raise taxes, tighten monetary policy, and reduce government spending. One could also increase the U.S. dollar price of gold, effectively devaluing the currency. Yeah . . . well . . . President Johnson was running for re-election. Forget about those options.

What's left? Stop the bleeding from the capital account! How? **Capital controls**! Remember, unlike the IMF Charter's commandment that "thou shalt not restrict current account transactions," it didn't similarly proscribe restriction on the capital account. Through an **Executive Order**, the President began a program that restricted overseas investments by U.S. multinational corporations (MNC). In essence the program clamped down on the amount of equity capital an MNC could use to make investments abroad. They could borrow if they wanted to expand abroad but they faced borrowing restrictions if they tried to borrow from U.S. banks. The program also required MNCs to repatriate more of their foreign subsidiaries' earnings. In addition to these measures, President Johnson also introduced measures to offset outflows of government capital, such as tying foreign aid to purchasing U.S. goods, and introducing a "Buy American" campaign for military expenditures abroad. (An Interest Equalization Tax was already in place to discourage outflows of portfolio investment—e.g. a 15% tax was imposed on purchases of foreign stock from a non-U.S. person.) It's all about liquidity.

Act Three: The Collapse of the London Gold Pool

As the value of the U.S. dollar continued its downward path, both private and government (central banks) holders of dollars sold the currency for gold, and under the BWS the United States was obligated to exchange dollars for gold on demand. After the United Kingdom devalued the pound sterling, market players rushed for gold: $580 million in about a week in November 1967.

CRACK

During the weekend immediately after the rush, the central banks of Belgium, Germany, Italy, the Netherlands, Switzerland, Great Britain, and the United States met and arranged credit swaps to defend the fixed price of $35 per ounce of gold.

This worked on and off during the rest of the year. But when news of the fourth quarter payments deficit of $7 billion hit the market, the speculators pounced. They figured they could make a tidy sum buying gold with dollars, knowing that the United States couldn't hold the dollar at $35 dollars an ounce. Check it out: Let's say a speculator borrows $350 and then sells the dollars for gold at $35 an ounce, receiving ten ounces of gold—called "shorting" the dollar in the biz. After devaluation, the value moves to, say, $75 an ounce. The speculator than buys back the dollars with her ten ounces of gold and gets $750. After she repays the loan with interest, say, $400, her profit is $350. Pretty sweet, yeah?

To defend the official price of the dollar against the speculators, the Federal Reserve Bank of New York, the Bank of England, and other European central banks formed the London Gold Pool. Its purpose was to intervene in the private gold market in London to defend the official price by either buying or selling gold—i.e., keeping the price of gold in the private market close to the official price. The Pool worked until the U.K. devaluation of the pound. Then, as we said, the speculators pounced: Between November, 1967 and March, 1968, the Pool bled about $2.5 billion to maintain the official parity of $35 an ounce.

CRACK

"I sent personal messages immediately to British Prime Minister Wilson, Prime Minister Aldo Moro of Italy, and West German Chancellor Kiesinger. It was imperative, I told them, that we cooperate in order to avoid financial disorders that could 'profoundly damage the political relations between Europe and America and set in motion forces like those which disintegrated the Western world in 1929 and 1933.' I also told them: 'The speculators are banking on an increase in the official price of gold. They are wrong.'"

—L.B. Johnson, The Vantage Point: Perspectives of the Presidency 1963–1969, 318 (1971).

"These decisions were reached early in the afternoon of March 14, a Thursday. The only point of disagreement among my advisers was whether we should close the London gold market on Friday or wait until after the weekend. We had lost $372 million to the speculators on March 14, and I decided we should move immediately. If the market remained open on Friday, we might well lose another billion dollars in gold, and I had had enough of the speculators."

—L.B. Johnson, The Vantage Point: Perspectives of the Presidency 1963–1969, 318 (1971).

The Bank of England closed the gold market on Friday, March 15, 1968. Over the weekend the central bankers met in Washington, D.C. On March 17, they issued this communiqué:

COMMUNIQUÉ ISSUED BY GOVERNORS
OF CENTRAL BANKS

March 17, 1968

The governors of the central banks of Belgium, Germany, Italy, the Netherlands, Switzerland, the United Kingdom, and the United States met in Washington on March 16 and 17, 1968 to examine operations of the gold pool, to which they are active contributors. The Managing Director of the International Monetary Fund and the General Manager of the Bank for International Settlements also attended the meeting.

The governors noted that it is the determined policy of the U.S. Government to defend the value of the dollar through appropriate fiscal and monetary measures and that substantial improvement of the U.S. balance of payments is a high-priority objective.

They also noted that legislation approved by Congress makes the whole of the gold stock of the nation available for defending the value of the dollar.

They noted that the U.S. Government will continue to buy and sell gold at the existing price of $35 an ounce in transactions with monetary authorities. The governors support this policy, and believe it contributes to the maintenance of exchange stability.

* * *

The governors agreed to cooperate fully to maintain the existing parities as well as orderly conditions in their exchange markets in accordance with their obligations under the Articles of Agreement of the International Monetary Fund. *The governors believe that henceforth officially held gold should be used only to effect transfers among monetary authorities, and, therefore, they decided no longer to supply gold to the London gold market or any other gold market. Moreover, as the existing stock of monetary gold is sufficient in view of the prospective establishment of the facility for special drawing rights, they no longer feel it necessary to buy gold from the market. Finally, they agreed that henceforth they will not sell gold to monetary authorities to replace gold sold in private markets.* (emphasis added)

* * *

Many experts in finance saw the newly established two-tier system as ringing the death knell for the U.S. dollar. It would no longer be "good as gold."

CRACK

Act Four: France and Germany Jolt the System

The late 1960s amounted to a last gasp for the BWS. It began with France under President de Gaulle. The spring of 1968 witnessed student demonstrations in Paris that morphed into huge protests that included workers. The unrest occurred at a time when wages in France and social welfare expenditures were sacrificed to strict fiscal and monetary policies. To quell the unrest, France increased the wages as well as prices for agricultural products, both of which stoked inflation. Facing internationally agreed trade liberalization, it put into place a series of measures that violated the agreed-upon trade measures.

The markets got spooked and started selling francs. President de Gaulle refused to consider a devaluation. In June, France drew its gold tranche from the IMF and imposed exchange controls (restrictions on the convertibility of the franc). In July, the Fed put together a $1.3 billion line of credit for France. But the selling of the franc continued. France desperately drew down on the line of credit and sold gold. It was burning its reserves. Those who sold francs bought the German mark because of rumors it was going to revalue the currency. Things were getting out of control. On November 20, the major foreign exchange markets of Europe shut down.

CRACK

Time for a meeting—this time in Bonn.

At the meeting of the industrialized countries' finance ministers and central bankers, the participants—but apparently not France—agreed, among other things, that France would devalue the franc by roughly 11%, but Germany wouldn't change its parity (Ja!). President de Gaulle would have none of it and in November announced to the world that France would not devalue! President de Gaulle declared, "What is happening in regard to our currency proves to us again that life is a struggle; that effort is a price of success, that salvation demands victory."

In June 1969, President de Gaulle lost the election and had to move out of the Élysée Palace. France announced an 11% devaluation of the franc. In September it negotiated a $985 million stand-by agreement with the Fund. A portion of the drawing came from the **General Arrangements to Borrow (GAB)**, which was created in 1962 to defend the monetary system.

So much for victory.

The flow of money from France to Germany put upwards pressure on the mark. Germany initially refused to revalue. Can you recall why that would be unpopular? A higher mark would hurt exports and light the flames of inflation.

Despite the commitment under the Fund Charter to keep its currency within one percent of par value, on October 24 Germany announced a 9.3% revaluation. Both the Fund and the United States in essence said it was understandable for Germany to depart from Fund rules, if only temporarily. And, of course, the revaluation would not affect the U.S. dollar one bit!

In November, the money that flooded into Germany reversed course on a dime. The world heard Germany's knock on the IMF's door for its gold tranche.

CRACK

The end was near.

Act Five: The System's Fatal Flaws

Let's review how the BWS was supposed to impose monetary discipline. If a foreign central bank decided to pursue an excessively expansionary monetary policy—pump more money into the economy to give it a kick-start—the bank would witness downward pressure on the domestic currency. Since it had to maintain the fixed exchange rate, it would have to use dollars in reserve to buy its domestic currency to relieve the downward pressure on the currency. But it couldn't do that forever because it would eventually run out of reserves and become unable to maintain the fixed rate, which it promised to do under the system.

Theoretically, the BWS also constrained U.S. monetary policy. If the Federal Reserve excessively expanded money supply, foreign banks would accumulate dollars. Under the BWS, the United States was obligated to exchange those dollars for gold, which would lead to a depletion of U.S. gold. Also, if the Fed unduly expanded money supply, the United States would be unable to maintain the official price of gold at $35 an ounce—there would be upward pressure on the price of gold (e.g., $36 an ounce). But here's the thing: Because the dollar was the global reserve currency and because the United States had no obligation to fix the dollar to other currencies—all that it had to do was maintain the price of gold at $35 an ounce—the monetary policy of the United States was, in fact, not constrained. That was a key problem with the BWS.

CRACK

Act Six: The Death of the Bretton Woods System

Most people agree that the beginning of the end of the BWS occurred in the mid-60s, which witnessed increased U.S. spending because of the Vietnam conflict and President Johnson's "**Great Society.**" This was accompanied by an expansionary monetary policy in the United States—printing money to finance growing government budget deficits. This fueled inflation—it rose from 2% in 1965 to about 6% in late 1970, falling to just above 4% in August 1971. We've talked about the deterioration of the U.S. balance of payments and the losses of gold. All of this led private investors to sell U.S. dollars and convert them to pounds, deutsche marks or francs. This led to further downward pressure on the dollar. The markets became convinced that the dollar had to be devalued against all the major European currencies.

The hot money flowed into the German mark, the Swiss franc, the Dutch guilder and other European currencies. To try to keep the system from crumbling, in May 1971 the European central banks absorbed huge U.S. dollar inflows.

CRACK

But it was too much. On May 5, 1971, five European central banks announced they would no longer support the dollar. They closed their foreign exchange markets for the week.

CRACK

In the same month, Germany allowed the mark to float; so, too, did the Netherlands with the guilder. Other European countries changed their par values. Although Fund rules didn't permit Germany and the Netherlands to allow their currencies to float, the Fund saw the writing on the wall.

CRACK

The BWS's death was near.

President Nixon's position during the turmoil in May was in so many words, "we'll study the situation and the proposals to fix the system (such as widening the bands or allowing small incremental changes—a 'crawling peg') but really the markets should figure this out."

In the meantime, faith in the value of the dollar continued to plummet. The United States was hemorrhaging gold. By August, gold stocks stood at $10 billion, as compared to $25 billion in 1949. Central banks around the world held over $30 billion in U.S. dollars.

CRACK

Then came the evening of August 15, 1971, when President Nixon went on the radio and television and shocked the world.

> "[Treasury Secretary] Connally began his contribution by saying: 'It is generally assumed we are going to have to move. We have to close the gold window.' Together with a price and wage freeze, and an import tax of 10–15 percent, this action, he told the President, would make 'the international finance people . . . realize you moved across the board strongly. This would be acting in consonance with the way people view you—great statesmanship and great courage. That's the right posture for you—a man ready to make far-reaching moves.' To [Chairman of the Federal Reserve Board] Burns's arguments, Connally replied: 'So the other countries don't like it. So what?'; and when Burns added that they might retaliate, 'Let 'em. What can they do?'"
> —H. James, International Monetary Cooperation Since Bretton Woods, 219 (1996)

"Global Finance and the Brady Bunch"

<u>Setting</u>: A living room in Portland.

"Marge, isn't it time for the Brady Bunch?"

"Yes, I think so, dear."

"Is Nixon doing a guest appearance on the show?"

"That would be something, wouldn't it? He's so handsome!"

"I don't think this is the Brady Bunch, Marge."

"Why don't we listen to him, Ben? He seems to be saying something important."

"I'm going to make myself a bologna sandwich—extra mayo 'cause I can't watch my favorite show."

The Challenge of Peace

Good evening:

I have addressed the Nation a number of times over the past 2 years on the problems of ending a war. Because of the progress we have made toward achieving that goal, this Sunday evening is an appropriate time for us to turn our attention to the challenges of peace . . .

We are going to take . . . action—not timidly, not half-heartedly, and not in a piecemeal fashion . . . the time has come for a new economic policy for the United States. Its targets are unemployment, inflation, and international speculation.

In recent weeks, the speculators have been waging an all-out war on the American dollar . . . I have directed the Secretary of the Treasury to take the action necessary to defend the dollar against the speculators . . .

I have directed Secretary Connally to suspend temporarily the convertibility of the dollar into gold or other reserve assets, except in amounts and conditions determined to be in the interest of monetary stability and in the best interest of the United States. (emphasis added)

Now, what is this action—which is very technical—what does it mean for you?

Let me lay to rest the bugaboo of what is called devaluation.

If you want to buy a foreign car or take a trip abroad, market conditions may cause your dollar to buy slightly less. But if you are among the overwhelming majority of Americans who buy

American-made products in America, your dollar will be worth just as much tomorrow as it is today.

The effect of this action, in other words, will be to stabilize the dollar.

Now, this action will not win us any friends among the international money traders. But our primary concern is with the American workers, and with fair competition around the world.

To our friends abroad, including the many responsible members of the international banking community who are dedicated to stability and the flow of trade, I give this assurance: The United States has always been, and will continue to be, a forward-looking and trustworthy trading partner. In full cooperation with the International Monetary Fund and those who trade with us, we will press for the necessary reforms to set up an urgently needed new international monetary system. Stability and equal treatment is in everybody's best interest. I am determined that the American dollar must never again be a hostage in the hands of international speculators . . .

As we move into a generation of peace, as we blaze the trail toward the new prosperity, I say to every American: Let us raise our spirits. Let us raise our sights. Let all of us contribute all we can to this great and good country that has contributed so much to the progress of mankind.

Let us invest in our Nation's future; and let us revitalize that faith in ourselves that built a great nation in the past and that will shape the world of the future.

Thank you, and good evening.

And on that day, a Sunday, the Bretton Woods System died.

CRASH

The next Sunday Ben sat in heavenly bliss as he watched Florence Henderson. He thought she was beautiful . . .

(fade to black)

Epilogue

After President Nixon's speech that closed the gold window, the major European foreign exchange markets closed for over a week. In December, the Group of Ten convened in the Commons Room of the Smithsonian Institution's Old Red Castle in Washington, D.C. to try to revive some semblance of the BWS—see supplement 3A. The negotiation led to the Smithsonian Agreement. Essentially, the U.S. dollar was devalued to $38 an ounce, non-reserve countries agreed to revalue their

> *"I know that may seem to be an overstatement, but when we compare this agreement with Bretton Woods, which, of course, was the last very significant agreement of this kind, we can see how enormous this achievement has been . . . indeed, the most significant event that has occurred in world financial history."*
> —Weekly Comp. Pres. Docs. 1670 (1971)

currencies against the dollar, and the Fund's Executive Board adopted a temporary arrangement with wider exchange rate margins. It's all good! Not.

The Smithsonian Agreement was short-lived. After another speculative attack against the pound sterling in June 1972, the U.K. allowed the currency to float, which caused sixteen other countries to float their sterling-pegged currencies. By February 1973, most of the fixed exchange rates fell, including Japan's yen. The United States devalued the dollar again to $44.22 an ounce, which triggered a massive flow out of the U.S. dollar on Thursday, March 1, 1973. The next day foreign exchange markets around the world closed down. Upon reopening, the major currencies floated against each other. Most developing countries maintained a fixed rate to defend their currencies. A group of European countries—Belgium, Denmark, France, Germany, Luxembourg, the Netherlands, Norway, and Sweden—agreed to coordinate their currencies against each other in what became known as "the snake." The two major cornerstones of the System—the gold convertibility of the dollar and the par value system—were gone. The Smithsonian Agreement was dead.

The turbulence that followed the collapse of the BWS prompted the IMF to establish a Committee on Reform of the International Monetary System and related issues. Negotiations focused on amending Article IV of the Fund's Charter, which governed the par values of currencies. It wasn't long before the two main positions crystalized. France along with lots of other countries wanted a Charter provision that would ultimately lead to an adjustable par value system—back to the BWS. The United States wouldn't have any part of it. It insisted on an Article IV that would give member countries the right to float their currencies without asking the Fund for permission. There was no way that it would go back to a system where the United States was obligated to maintain a fixed exchange rate system. The compromise was that the Charter would allow member countries to choose their own exchange rate systems. But an adjustable par value system—

back to the BWS—could be adopted by an 85% majority of the Fund's total voting power.

In January 1976, the IMF's Interim Committee (a Fund committee focused on monetary policy) met in Kingston, Jamaica, where they announced the Second Amendment of the Fund's Charter, which, among other things, implicitly endorsed a new world of floating exchange rates via a new Article IV.

In the new world, collaboration would be the name of the game. Section 1 of the amended Article IV reads:

> Recognizing that the essential purpose of the international monetary system is to provide a framework that facilitates the exchange of goods, services, and capital among countries, and that sustains sound economic growth, and that a principal objective is the continuing development of the orderly underlying conditions that are necessary for financial and economic stability, each member undertakes to collaborate with the Fund and other members to assure orderly exchange arrangements and to promote a stable system of exchange rates. In particular, each member shall:
>
> > (i)   endeavor to direct its economic and financial policies toward the objective of fostering orderly economic growth with reasonable price stability, with due regard to its circumstances;
> >
> > (ii)   seek to promote stability by fostering orderly underlying economic and financial conditions and a monetary system that does not tend to produce erratic disruptions;
> >
> > (iii)   avoid manipulating exchange rates of the international monetary system in order to prevent effective balance of payments adjustment or to gain an unfair competitive advantage over other members; and
> >
> > (iv)   follow exchange policies compatible with the undertakings under this Section.

The principle underlying the new Article IV is that in a system of floating exchange rates each member country has a duty to collaborate with the Fund to ensure "orderly economic and financial conditions." (See more in supplement 3B.) Without stable economies in member countries, a floating exchange rate system would be disastrous. Remember the chaos before the adoption of the BWS?

Collaboration as a principle is not enough. The revised Article IV calls upon the IMF to engage in surveillance of the international monetary system and member countries must provide information to help it do its job. Here's the text of Section 3:

(a)   The Fund shall oversee the international monetary system in order to ensure its effective operation, and shall oversee the compliance of each member with its obligations under Section 1 of this Article.

(b)   In order to fulfill its functions under (a) above, the Fund shall exercise firm surveillance over the exchange rate policies of members, and shall adopt specific principles for the guidance of all members with respect to those policies. Each member shall provide the Fund with the information necessary for such for surveillance, and, when requested by the Fund shall consult with it on the member's exchange-rate policies. The principles adopted by the Fund shall be consistent with cooperative arrangements by which members maintain the value of their currencies in relation to the value of the currency or currencies of other members, as well as with other exchange arrangements of a member's choice consistent with the purposes of the Fund and Section 1 of this Article. These principles shall respect the domestic social and political policies of members, and in applying these principles the Fund shall pay due regard to the circumstances of members.

If the information provided to the Fund indicates that the member country's economy is becoming unstable—e.g., it's putting restrictions on current transactions or payments for balance of payments purposes—the Managing Director can informally begin discussions with the member country to figure out what the heck is going on. Otherwise, it usually engages in annual Article IV consultations with each member country to determine whether its economic policies, including its exchange rate regime, are consistent with section 1 of Article IV.

Procedurally, a group of Fund economists go to the member country to discuss its economy with government and central bank officials. The mission's staff also may consult with politicians and members of civil society. Then they go back to the Fund and blab about the country and the Executive Board sends its reactions to the country. As you'll see later in the textbook, the content of the discussions with member countries has expanded beyond looking strictly at the economy. Today, there's also regional and global surveillance.

You Gotta Know Something About Them!

Lyndon B. Johnson

Lyndon B. Johnson was born in a small farmhouse in rural Texas. He worked a variety of odd jobs before attending college, including custodial work, road construction, and elevator operation. Even though—or perhaps because—he struggled in school, he earned his teaching degree and served as both the principal and a teacher at a Mexican-American school and as a public speaking teacher (he led his debate team to the district championships!). You don't think of school principals as being forgetful, but on his wedding day, Johnson forgot to buy Lady Bird a wedding ring—oops—so a friend had to run out and buy one for him. After his time as Commander in Chief, Johnson retired to his ranch in Texas, where he was delivered briefing papers from Henry Kissinger every Friday by a White House jet.

Richard Nixon

Richard Nixon was born in California to a service-station owner and a lemon farmer. He was both an athlete and an actor in his early years. He played basketball in college (and got his teeth smashed in), and played character parts such as the Innkeeper in John Drinkwater's *Bird in Hand*. His early political life wasn't successful—he lost his high-school election for student body president. He shook off the loss, though, and attended Duke University Law School and served as a Navy lieutenant commander in the Pacific (but never saw any actual combat). Nixon was accused of improperly using donor funds when campaigning as Eisenhower's vice president in 1952, but the only thing he would admit was accepting one political gift—a cocker spaniel named Checkers. When the first U.S. astronauts landed on the moon during his first few months as President, he called them from the Oval Office to say it was, for every American, "the proudest day of our lives."

Charles de Gaulle

Charles de Gaulle was born in Lille, France and was the 6'5' son of a Jesuit headmaster. He joined the French military where he was wounded multiple times and held in several German prisoner of war camps until the end of WWI. De Gaulle rose through the ranks of the military, but had to flee France for England after he refused to accept France's surrender to Germany in WWII. He returned after Paris's liberation from Germany and was elected the President of France's Fifth Republic. He retired to his estate in Colombey-les-Deux-Eglises where he finished his memoirs.

James Callaghan

James Callaghan, known by some as "Big Jim" or "Sunny Jim," was born in Portsmouth England. He grew up in great poverty, but that didn't prevent him from achieving great things: he's the only person in history to have held all four top positions in the U.K. government (Chancellor of the Exchequer from 1964–1967, Home Secretary from 1967–1970, Foreign Secretary from 1974–1976, and Prime Minister from 1976–1979). A member of the Labour Party, he was known as especially "un-presidential" with his approachable and open style with his cabinet. But this photo of Callaghan doesn't make him look so sunny.

What's Up with That?

Eurocurrency Markets

Eurocurrency is currency deposited in banks outside the currency's home country. So, for example, a dollar deposited in a London bank is a Eurodollar, yen is a Euroyen. You can even have a Euroeuro. Although London was, and still is for the most part, the home of the Eurocurrency markets, today there Eurocurrency markets in other places such as Singapore—e.g. you can have a Eurodollar deposit in Singapore. All are considered "offshore" markets.

Eurocurrency was born in the 1950s during the Cold War, when the Soviets moved their dollars from the United States to Europe out of fear that the United States would expropriate their dollar deposits. This created the

"Eurodollar," the most important Eurocurrency today. By 1966, the Eurodollar market expanded into a Eurocurrency market with a gross size over $20 billion. By 1970, its size was about $57 billion.

Why did the Eurocurrency market develop? Because banks wanted to avoid domestic regulations that increased their costs. In the United States, these regulations included: reserve requirements on time deposits; a regulation that prohibited interest on demand deposits and placed a ceiling on time deposits; FDIC premia; fed, state, local tax; and lending limits.

By establishing branches or subsidiaries in the lightly-regulated London market, U.S. banks could become more profitable by offering higher deposits and making loans with competitive rates. As of 2003, the Eurodollar market stood at $15,926 billion.

Capital Controls

A government or central bank sets capital controls to limit movement of capital in and out of a domestic economy. These controls can help protect a country's financial stability in the face of unpredictable capital inflows and outflows. Controls might include market-based controls on the volume and price of transactions, taxation of cross-border financial flows, or restrictions on the speed at which currency enters and exits a country. While the Fund allows for capital controls under Article VI, section 3, member countries have to follow the restrictions in Article VI, Section 1. In its recent banking crisis, Cyprus, among other things, put controls on its banks with restrictions like €300 daily maximum cash withdrawals and required approval of transactions above €500,000.

Here's all of Article VI, Capital Transfers:

Section 1.   *Use of the Fund's general resources for capital transfers*

(a)   A member may not use the Fund's general resources to meet a large or sustained outflow of capital except as provided in Section 2 of this Article, and the Fund may request a member to exercise controls to prevent such use of the general resources of the Fund. If, after receiving such a request, a member fails to exercise appropriate controls, the Fund may declare the member ineligible to use the general resources of the Fund.

(b)   Nothing in this Section shall be deemed:

(i)   to prevent the use of the general resources of the Fund for capital transactions of reasonable amount required for the expansion of exports or in the ordinary course of trade, banking, or other business; or

(ii)   to affect capital movements which are met out of a member's own resources, but members undertake that such capital movements will be in accordance with the purposes of the Fund.

Section 2.   *Special provisions for capital transfers*

A member shall be entitled to make reserve tranche purchases to meet capital transfers.

Section 3.   *Controls of capital transfers*

Members may exercise such controls as are necessary to regulate international capital movements, but no member may exercise these controls in a manner which will restrict payments for current transactions or which will unduly delay transfers of funds in settlement of commitments, except as provided in Article VII, Section 3(b) and in Article XIV, Section 2.

Executive Order

The President of the United States issues executive orders to manage the activities of the Executive Branch. These orders are typically directed at agencies rather than individuals. Once signed, the White House sends an order to the Office of the Federal Register, which then numbers and publishes them. U.S. Presidents historically used executive orders to supplement acts of Congress, but times of emergency, such as WWI and the Great Depression, greatly expanded their use. For example, President Franklin D. Roosevelt issued 654 orders in his first year of Presidency alone to implement his New Deal program. It's important to realize, though, that these orders don't always automatically have the full force of the law—you may remember the "Steel Seizure Case" in which President Truman issued an executive order to seize most of the country's steel mills, but the Supreme Court said he didn't have the authority to do that.

Special Drawing Rights

The SDR plan first began to take shape in March of 1966 when the Managing Director at the time, Pierre-Paul Schweitzer, proposed a reserve-creating plan to apply to all members, to counter fears of a global liquidity shortage of reserve assets. Reserves in U.S. dollars in central banks continued to climb and countries began to restrict international transactions and borrow to meet balance of payments needs. SDRs came into existence on August 6, 1969 (First Amendment of the Articles of Agreement), valued at 0.888671 grams of fine gold (the amount of gold equal to one U.S. dollar). The SDR is not a currency, but rather an artificial reserve asset. It's a potential claim on the currencies of other IMF members, meaning that holders of SDRs can exchange them for "freely usable currencies" (currencies that are readily accepted in international trade—e.g., the U.S. dollar, the euro, and the yen). For example, Bolivia, whose currency is the boliviano (hardly anyone will touch it), can exchange its SDRs for U.S. dollars or euros or yen. The SDR is the unit of account of the IMF, which means that all computations (except one) relating to currencies are done in SDRs. And check it out: Other international organizations use the SDR as a unit of account, such as the Nordic Investment Bank. Even private parties can use it as a unit of account— e.g., commercial banks that accept deposits expressed in SDRs. Today's SDR is defined as a basket of currencies: the pound sterling, the euro, the Japanese yen, and the U.S. dollar. This basket composition is reviewed every five years by the Fund's Executive Board. In November 2010 (the latest review), the weights of the basket currencies were revised using the value of exports of goods and services, as well as the amount of reserves of respective currencies held by other IMF member countries.

General Arrangements to Borrow

Before the General Arrangements to Borrow was established in 1962, the IMF didn't have the resources for large-scale borrowing if, for example, both the United States and the U.K. experienced a reserve shortage. The Fund didn't have enough non-dollar and non-sterling reserves to fulfill the U.S. and U.K.'s potential borrowing requests (remember, when a member country borrows from the Fund, it is borrowing other currencies). After much negotiation led by Per Jacobsson (the Fund managing director), ten countries and central banks—later to be known as the Group of Ten (G-10)—agreed to provide a collective $6 billion to the IMF in case of a such a crisis. Jacobsson saw this kind of global participation as essential to the stability of the world economy. The GAB is available for the participants of the G-10, but others can use it in certain circumstances. In 1998, the New Arrangements to Borrow (a similar credit arrangement between the IMF and 38 member countries and institutions) was established to supplement the GAB.

Great Society

President Lyndon B. Johnson's Great Society was a series of domestic programs to put an "end to poverty and racial injustice." It was the United States' largest social reform agenda since President Roosevelt's New Deal. In a speech at the University of Michigan in May 1964, President Johnson challenged the United States to join together to form a Great Society: "Your imagination, your initiative, and your indignation will determine whether we build a society where progress is the servant of our needs, or a society where old values and new visions are buried under unbridled growth. For in your time we have the opportunity to move not only toward the rich society and the powerful society, but upward to the Great Society." Programs were implemented for education, civil rights, the environment, the arts and humanities, and especially to eliminate poverty. Many Great Society programs still exist today: we've all heard of Head Start, Job Corps, Medicare, and Medicaid.

QUESTIONS FROM YOUR TALKING DOG

1.   You might have rescued me from an animal shelter, but that doesn't mean I'm dumb. When I was in . . . my prison run, I read a lot. Yes, I did. I didn't join the weight-lifting dudes. So, what factors contributed to the U.K.'s crisis in the 1960s?

2.   Here's a clever question for you, my owner: How did the United States' BOP deficit differ from the U.K.'s? Why was it necessary?

3.   What was significant about Triffin's paradox? I'm on a roll here.

4.   What was the "confidence problem" all about? Hey, don't you like to snuggle with me?

5.   Why was October 20, 1960 a crack in the BWS's foundation?

6.   What introduced liquidity into the global monetary system and how did it work? No, I'm not going to stop the questions until you turn off "Housewives on Steroids" on cable.

7.   Can you explain how President Johnson's executive order related to the trilemma? Yeah, I know what that is. I read widely.

8.   How did swaps keep the BWS afloat? Stop harassing me. Just answer my questions.

9.   Can you explain how speculators make money by betting on a currency— e.g., shorting it? Don't you dare call me short!

10.   I know you love that (cheap) golden chain around your neck. That reminds me: What was the purpose of the London Gold Pool and what was significant about establishing a two-tier system? Okay, so I sound formal. So what?

11.   Here's another formal one: What do the crises during the 1960s demonstrate about "internal" and "external" concerns?

12.   Do you value me? Really! Then why are you talking about a devaluation being humiliating?

13.   GAB? Is that like gossip? No? Then what was it about?

14.   Why was the BWS asymmetrical? No, you're not going to sleep! Drink some coffee and answer my question: Why was it congenitally flawed?

15.   What was the United States' position regarding the correction of its deficit?

16.   How did the Fund's Charter complicate what would in effect be a devaluation of the dollar?

17. You're tired of my questions? Here's one that's different: Would *you* eat a bologna (miscellaneous debris) sandwich on white bread with extra mayo?

18. Okay, that grossed you out. Let's get back to business. Were speculators the culprits behind the fall of the BWS?

19. What's with the Smithsonian Agreement? I think I lifted my leg on that building not too long ago.

20. I love French dogs like the Briard. So can you explain France's adoption of dual exchange markets? How was this possible under Article VIII of the Fund's Charter? Okay, yeah, this isn't about French dogs.

21. This was a tweet—I use Twitter all the time—from some economist: Why would some countries be concerned about having the United States improve its BOP situation (which had moved into a current account deficit)?

22. What was the essence of the Second Amendment of the Fund's Charter? Key elements?

23. What was the major function of the IMF after the collapse of the BWS?

24. What are arguably the merits of flexible exchange rates?

25. Okay, fine! I was just trying to have a conversation with you. Oh, no heavy stuff? Okay, then, one last question: Why did Ben have a crush on Florence Henderson?

Chapter 3: Supplement

3A. *Exchange Rate Realignment*

Garritsen de Vries is the Fund's Historian. This excerpt gives you an inside look at the Fund as the BWS collapsed. According to the author's account, what were the fundamental flaws of the BWS? What do you think of the U.S. arguments regarding how realignment should proceed? The major fight was between the United States and Europe. But, hello, what about developing countries? Can you imagine being the Managing Director of the Fund at this time? Would you like to have the fate of the global economy in your hands? Keep in mind as you read that for every deficit country there's a surplus country. We end the excerpt with U.S. Treasury Secretary Connally's analysis of the problem. Three months later, the key players maneuvered through the politics of realignment to reach the Smithsonian Agreement, which, as you know, was short-lived.

M. Garritsen de Vries, *Road to the Smithsonian Agreement* in
The International Monetary Fund 1966–1971:
Volume 1: Narrative (1976)

EXCHANGE RATE REALIGNMENT—A SENSITIVE ISSUE

The second issue to which the Managing Director referred in the Executive
Board meeting of August 16—that of realignment of the exchange rates of
the major industrial nations—was an extremely sensitive one. There were
many officials and economists who regarded the U.S. dollar as overvalued,
at least in relation to some of the currencies of the EEC countries—such as
the deutsche mark, the Netherlands guilder, and the Belgian franc—and
in relation to the Japanese yen. At a minimum it was now generally
recognized that a realignment of the par values of the industrial countries
had somehow to be achieved. Just how the readjustment of exchange rates
was to be effected, however, was not so clear. Although there had been
informal hints at least as far back as 1968 that countries with surpluses
should revalue their currencies vis-a-vis the dollar, the authorities of the
countries experiencing the most protracted surpluses—the Federal
Republic of Germany and Japan—fearing that reduced levels of exports
might endanger their rates of economic growth, continued to be very
reluctant to do so. Moreover, monetary officials of most of the EEC
countries, centering at attention on the prolonged balance of payments
deficit of the United States, had for some time considered a change in
exchange rates through an increase in the dollar price of gold to be
essential. Because of the severe aggravation of inflationary pressures in
the United States and the substantial enlargement of the U.S. balance of
payments deficit following a sizable expansion of U.S. military
expenditures in Viet-Nam, European officials believed more strongly than
ever that corrective action was up to the United States.

U.S. Position on Dollar Devaluation

The management of the Fund had been in touch informally with the U.S.
authorities throughout the first seven months of 1971, especially after the
first week of May, and knew the position of the U.S. authorities to be
sharply different from that being expressed by European officials.
Moreover, as the speeches reported in the preceding chapter indicate, the
U.S. authorities had begun openly to state their views. They took the
position that the responsibility for correcting the chronic imbalances in
international payments—the U.S. deficit on the one side and the surpluses
of several other industrial countries on the other side—ought to be shared.
More explicitly, they believed that the U.S. payments deficit resulted at
least partly because the United States for many years had been
shouldering a very heavy share of the defense costs of Western Europe,
Japan, and other militarily allied countries, and because the trading
arrangements of the EEC and of Japan did not permit the liberal entry of

U.S. goods. Therefore, countries with surpluses ought to revalue their currencies and some concessions ought to be made in respect of military burden—sharing and trading arrangements. Especially was it imperative that changes be made in the common agricultural policy of the EEC, which was hampering U.S. exports of agricultural goods to European countries, and in restrictions on imports by Japan, which were preventing a correction of the large U.S. trade deficit with that country.

In addition to wanting action on these broad fronts, the U.S. monetary authorities had another problem—how to attain a realignment of the exchange rates for the major currencies without changing the dollar price of gold. They had stated on a number of occasions, and again on August 15, 1971, that they would not devalue the dollar. (*De facto* depreciation of the dollar vis-a-vis other major currencies that might take place in exchange markets following the suspension of official convertibility was not, of course, devaluation in terms of gold. Indeed, market depreciation of the dollar against other currencies could be construed as tantamount, economically, to appreciation of other currencies in terms of the dollar.)

The way in which the par value system had been implemented since its establishment made it difficult for the United States to take action on the exchange rate for the dollar. Market intervention was the main technique by which members of the Fund ensured that spot rates between their currencies and the currencies of other members stayed within prescribed margins around par values. Thus an intervention currency was necessary, and margins came to be defined in terms of the intervention currency. As the strongest convertible currency after World War II, the dollar rapidly became the principal intervention currency and the currency in terms of which most margins were stated. The United States, for its part, fulfilled its exchange rate obligations by opting to buy and sell gold freely—that is, without limit-for the settlement of international payments. In these circumstances, the United States assumed a basically passive role in the exchange market: exchange rates of other currencies vis-a-vis the dollar were determined not by U.S. actions but by actions of the central banks of other countries.

Because of this operation of the par value system, there was a belief on the part of some officials that there was no method by which the United States could actually devalue the dollar. In fact, some knowledgeable monetary officials believed that the par value system had to function in this way under the Fund's Articles of Agreement and that in effect the Articles of Agreement, which contained a definition of the dollar in terms of gold, even precluded a change in the dollar price of gold.

But, more importantly, there were a number of basic economic reasons why devaluation of the dollar by raising the price of gold was being avoided. For one thing, it was considered possible that other countries would also raise the price of gold in terms of their currencies, thereby undoing the desired effect of realigning the dollar vis-a-vis these other currencies. Moreover, the dollar was the major reserve currency of the world. For a number of reasons, many countries had accumulated large holdings of dollars since World War II. To avoid jeopardizing the stability of the dollar, several countries, especially after 1965, had refrained from exercising their right to convert these holdings in to gold. Devaluation of the dollar would have an adverse effect on the value of countries' reserves of dollars.

There was another consideration governing the attitudes of the U.S. monetary authorities toward devaluation of the dollar—that an appropriate realignment of the dollar vis-a-vis the currencies of other industrial nations might well have to be considerably larger than those countries were prepared to accept. In their view, it was imperative that the U.S. deficit be converted into a surplus, at least for a few years. Should the dollar be devalued in 1971 and the size of the devaluation prove to be too small, perhaps because other countries would not initially be prepared to agree to a large enough change, it would be extremely awkward, and would shake confidence in the dollar, to devalue it in terms of gold again later.

The adverse reactions in the United States to the possibility of a formal devaluation of the dollar were strengthened by still another factor. There were many U.S. officials and economists who firmly opposed any action that might enhance the role of gold in the international monetary system; hence there was concern, and even anxiety, that an increase in the official dollar price of gold incidental to a devaluation of the dollar in terms of other currencies might have such an effect. The risk of enhancing the status of gold in the monetary system was believed to be especially great if there should have to be a second devaluation of the dollar.

Over time, the conviction had grown in U.S. Government circles that the only way in which the United States could take action on the rates of exchange between the dollar and other currencies was to break the link between the dollar and gold. For instance, the report of the President's Commission on International Trade and Investment Policy, submitted to the President in July 1971, pointed out that the problems of the deteriorating trade balance were compounded by the dollar's pivotal role in the monetary system as an intervention currency and a reserve currency; therefore, the United States did not have ready recourse to the remedy of a change in its exchange rate. The report of the Subcommittee on International Exchange and Payments of the Joint Economic Committee of Congress likewise emphasized that the legal link between the dollar and the price of gold and the role of the dollar as the chief intervention currency effectively limited any U.S. initiative to alter dollar exchange rates, and, in effect, suggested the need to break that link.

* * *

MR. SCHWEITZER'S CONCERNS AND RESPONSES

At a meeting in Brussels on August 19, 1971, the finance Ministers of the EEC decided that a reform of the international monetary system, including a restructuring of par values, was necessary, and that to this end they would take "a common initiative" within the appropriate international institutions, naming the Fund in particular. Meanwhile, to enable exchange markets to reopen on Monday, August 23, they agreed that the rates between the U.S. dollar and five of the six currencies of the EEC countries—the Belgian franc, the deutsche mark, the Italian lira, the Luxembourg franc, and the Netherlands guilder—would be freely determined in exchange markets; there was to be a dual market for the French franc (see the following section). They further agreed that the EEC countries would work out among themselves techniques for market intervention in order to minimize the degree of rate fluctuation among their own currencies. They emphasized that it was important for the operation of EEC agricultural policy that fluctuation among the rates for their own currencies be limited. The common agricultural policy, in turn, was indispensable for the achievement of greater economic and monetary union among the six countries of the EEC.

The Managing Director was apprehensive lest, in the existing circumstances, the international monetary situation deteriorate beyond repair. If exchange markets reopened on August 23 on their own terms, there was not the slightest chance, he thought, that the rates quoted would bear any resemblance to an appropriate pattern of exchange rates. Moreover, if the U.S. import surcharge was retained for long, it would distort trade and make the achievement of a satisfactory pattern of rates difficult, if not impossible. There was, he believed, a real danger that countries might resort to restrictions on trade, exchange controls, and multiple exchange rates, such as had prevailed in the late 1940s and early 1950s, and which would be very hard to remove. Yet, as he remarked to the Executive Directors on Thursday, August 19, the U.S. authorities did not appear to be in a hurry to bring the existing difficulties to an end, nor did the EEC countries seem to have agreed on a solution.

The situation presented serious problems not only for the industrial countries but also for the developing and other primary producing members, which were worried about the adverse effects of exchange rate fluctuations, the accompanying uncertainties, and the U.S. import surcharge. Many of them were unsure what exchange rate policies to pursue and were asking for advice from the management and staff of the Fund. Mr. Schweitzer was also concerned that the vast majority of countries would not have a chance to participate in any solution.

Keeping in close communication with the Executive Directors and with the top officials of the EEC, the BIS, and the Group of Ten, the Managing

Director in consultation with the senior staff formulated his positions. The staff of the Research Department had already been working not only on a possible new pattern of exchange rates but also on ways in which the operation of the international monetary system might be improved. The staff of the Legal Department had been working on draft amendments to the Articles of Agreement governing changes in exchange rates and margin requirements . . . and on other possible changes in the Articles. The General Counsel proposed a program of work that would encompass the study by the Executive Directors of all alternatives for a reformed international monetary system, including proposals that would involve the broadest kinds of amendments to the Articles of Agreement. The Economic Counsellor presented the calculations discussed above and put forward for consideration by the Executive Directors a paper outlining a new framework for the monetary system. The Area Departments examined the implications for all members of a realignment of the currencies of the major industrial members. The Treasurer's Department and the Legal Department suggested ways to adjust the Fund's holdings of currencies and to continue operations in the General Account and the Special Drawing Account.

Several Initiatives

Thus, when Mr. Schweitzer addressed the Executive Board on August 19, he stressed that the whole of the international monetary system was at stake and that he thought the Fund could, and should, take the initiative. The Fund was in a unique position, he said, to propose a comprehensive and impartial solution to both the procedural and the substantive problems that had been raised . . .

With the Executive Board's concurrence, the Managing Director sent a message to all Governors of the Fund on August 19. Recent developments, he cabled, gave great cause for concern but at the same time created the opportunity for strengthening the system. Unless prompt action was taken, the prospect was for disorder and discrimination in currency and trade relationships, which would seriously disrupt trade and undermine the system that had served the world well and had been the basis for effective collaboration for a quarter of a century. Piecemeal approaches to change were not likely to yield beneficial results even for a single country, much less for the whole community of countries represented in the Fund, and he considered it vitally important that action be "prompt, collective, and collaborative." This action was the assigned task of the Fund, and the Fund was in a position to make a contribution of great importance to the establishment of a better monetary system. He intended to press for rapid progress toward agreement on appropriate exchange rates and other measures that would restore the monetary system to effective and lasting operation.

In the next few days, many of the Governors, especially those for the developing members, cabled their support of the Managing Director's efforts. It became evident almost at once, however, that the Group of Ten was not yet ready to proceed. On Friday, August 20, Mr. Benson advised Mr. Schweitzer that there was insufficient support among the Group of Ten for an immediate ministerial meeting; he had therefore requested Mr. Ossola, then chairman of the Deputies of the Group of Ten, to convene a meeting of the Deputies "at the earliest possible date."

Mr. Schweitzer's grave concern about the monetary situation was revealed to the world when, in the following week, he appeared twice on television. In an interview on Monday morning, August 23—as exchange markets were reopened and a variety of exchange rates prevailed, many involving fluctuations in the rates for the U.S. dollar—Mr. Schweitzer was asked for his view about a change in the dollar price of gold as a way to improve the situation. He replied that a whole new pattern of exchange rates was necessary, and that "in my opinion it would be normal for the U.S. to make a contribution." The next day, August 24, he was asked whether a change in the price of gold in terms of the U.S. dollar would be a major contribution to solving the international imbalance problem. He again replied in such a way as to suggest that, in a new pattern of exchange rates, the dollar might have to be redefined in terms of gold.

Mr. Schweitzer's statements on this subject reflected his interest in currency realignment as the first essential step to improving the world monetary situation. In this regard he was especially mindful of the problems that would confront the United States if it decided to devalue. In his opinion, the view that dollar devaluation was not possible deprived the United States, alone among nations, of the use of a vital instrument of balance of payments adjustment, namely, a change in the exchange rate for its currency. Given these circumstances, Mr. Schweitzer acted on his belief that public statements by the Managing Director of the Fund could help to prepare the way for dollar devaluation and for a quick realignment of exchange rates. But there were press reports that the U.S. monetary authorities, believing that the time was not ripe for action, did not welcome public expression of views about dollar devaluation.

VARIETY OF EXCHANGE RATES INTRODUCED

In the week after the U.S. suspension of official convertibility, the Managing Director also asked the Executive Directors to communicate to all member countries a statement in which the Fund called attention to the undertaking of each member under Article IV, Section 4 (a), "to collaborate with the Fund to promote exchange stability, to maintain orderly exchange arrangements with other members, and to avoid competitive exchange alterations," and in which each member was requested to advise the Fund

promptly and in detail of the exchange measures and practices applied in
its territories.

It was evident from the replies that members were resorting to a number
of exchange rate expedients. Several members advised the Fund that,
notwithstanding their desire to maintain orderly exchange rates, they no
longer found it possible to observe margins around their par values. Most
of the industrial members in Europe (Austria, Belgium, Denmark, the
Federal Republic of Germany, Italy, Luxembourg, the Netherlands,
Norway, Sweden, and the United Kingdom) and Japan were letting the
exchange rates for their currencies float. The rate for the Canadian dollar
also continued to float.

The exchange rates of some European currencies and of the Japanese yen
were under strong upward pressure, but the monetary authorities of these
countries were intervening in the markets so as to limit upward
movements.

The currencies of Australia, Burma, Iraq, Ireland, Malaysia, New Zealand,
Singapore, and a number of other sterling area members were pegged to
sterling, and so they too were, in effect, floating against the dollar. Several
developing countries—including the Khmer Republic, the Libyan Arab
Republic, Portugal, Somalia, and Viet-Nam—likewise introduced floating
rates for their currencies. The rates for the currencies of Afghanistan,
Brazil, Colombia, Korea, Lebanon, the Philippines, and the Yemen Arab
Republic continued to fluctuate, as they had prior to August 15.

A few members introduced dual exchange markets. For example, France
did so with effect from August 23, 1971. The official market was reserved
for transactions for trade and trade-related items and for government
exchange dealings; these transactions were to take place at rates based on
the par value. A separate market—the financial market—was established
for all other authorized transactions, primarily capital transactions; these
were to take place at freely fluctuating rates . . .

Many members of the Fund, however, continued to apply the same fixed
U.S. dollar rates for their currencies, although some of them widened the
margins around their par values within which the dollar rates could
fluctuate. Members that kept the same fixed dollar rates included most of
those in Latin America, African members other than those in the French
franc area, and several members in Asia, Europe, and the Middle East.
Several members, including Ceylon, Ghana, India, Kenya, Nigeria,
Pakistan, South Africa, the Sudan, Tanzania, and Uganda, changed the
peg for their currencies from sterling to the dollar.

The French dual market was a multiple currency practice and thus, unlike
a single fluctuating exchange rate, produced exchange rates in a form that
the Fund could approve under the Articles. The Executive Board approved
this practice until the end of 1971. Toward the end of the year, they

extended that approval until the next Article VIII consultation with France . . .

GROUP OF TEN MEETINGS

Mr. Schweitzer was informed by Mr. Benson on August 25 that a meeting of the Finance Ministers and Central Bank Governors of the Group of Ten was being called for September 15 and 16 in London, and he was invited to attend. The ministerial meeting was preceded by a meeting of the Deputies of the Group of Ten in the Fund's Paris Office on September 3 and 4. The Economic Counsellor attended the Deputies' meeting and reported to the Executive Directors that the Deputies had considered the views of the Under Secretary for Monetary Affairs in the U.S. Treasury, Mr. Volcker, on the outlook for the U.S. balance of payments and the aims of the U.S. authorities. These aims included the restoration of a basic position of long-term equilibrium, together with a modest surplus at least for a few years in order to restore confidence in the U.S. dollar. Much at attention was directed to the magnitude of the improvement needed in the U.S. balance of payments. Any lessening of the U.S. deficit necessarily had counterparts in reduced surpluses by other countries, and the implication of surpluses by the United States was deficits by other countries. Some countries now in surplus saw in any reduction of these surpluses the specter of recession. Obviously, the greater the improvement expected in the U.S. position and the more rapidly it was to be achieved, the stronger the actions that were required. Hence, important negotiations hinged on estimates of the magnitude of the turnaround to be attained in the U.S. payments position and when it was to be achieved.

Mr. Dale spelled out the details to the Executive Directors. The U.S. authorities believed that the U.S. overall balance had to be improved by at least $13 billion. The projections of the U.S. Government for 1972, in the absence of corrective measures, was for a trade deficit of about $5 billion and a deficit on basic balance, that is, a current account and long-term capital deficit, of about $10 billion. The authorities considered a $13 billion turnaround to be a minimum. It did not allow for the momentum which the pace of deterioration had gained nor for the lag which would occur before the effects of new measures, including exchange rate changes, took place. Furthermore, such a figure provided for only modest capital outflow to developing countries and for virtually no net long-term capital flow to the rest of the developed world. In particular, it assumed that Canada would not resort to the New York bond market for any great amounts and that European and other developed countries would not make much use of the New York securities market on a net basis.

On September 13, 1971, just before the ministerial meeting of the Group of Ten, the Finance Ministers of the EEC countries reached agreement on the common position that they would take at the meeting. That position included, inter alia, the need for realignment against gold of the currencies of all industrial countries, including the dollar, and the removal of the U.S. import surcharge. The differences between the positions of the industrial countries meant that when the Finance Ministers and Central Bank Governors of the Group of Ten met on September 15 and 16 very little could be agreed except generalities. The Ministers and Governors agreed only that a very substantial adjustment was required to redress the position of the United States, with corresponding adjustments in the positions of other countries; that a large part of this adjustment would have to come about by selective currency realignment; and that "fair world trading arrangements and [military] burden-sharing" would have to be considered. Differences in view continued on the key issues: exchange rates, the approximate magnitude of the necessary improvement to be achieved in the U.S. position, and the timing of the removal of the U.S. import surcharge. It was evident that multilateral negotiations of a major and complex nature lay ahead.

In the course of the London meeting, Mr. Schweitzer put forward a list of the substantive problems requiring discussion, including fundamental monetary reform, and expressed his concern about the continuation of the disarray in exchange rates. He stressed to the Ministers and Governors, as he had to the Executive Directors, his view that the pattern of exchange rates which was emerging did not provide a satisfactory basis for a more permanent pattern. He pointed out that many countries had already made contributions toward the needed currency realignment, noting that the currencies of Canada, the Federal Republic of Germany, and the Netherlands had floated upward vis-a-vis the dollar even before August 15 and that the currencies of Belgium, Italy, Japan, Sweden, and the United Kingdom had been floating upward since that date. So far, there had been no contribution from the United States, and he considered it unlikely that a solution could be found to the realignment problem if one major country refused to accept its share of adjustment. After an adequate move by the United States, the remainder of the realignment would have to be brought about by changes in the rates of the other currencies.

The Finance Ministers and Central Bank Governors of the Group of Ten met again, less than two weeks later, in Washington, on September 26, 1971, the day before the opening of the Annual Meeting, but again no agreement was reached. What talks about trade might take place, whether the United States would remove the surcharge before new parities were negotiated, and what new parities would be agreed were issues that were still being hotly debated. European officials were pressing hard for new parities. The monetary authorities of France, in particular, were insisting on a change in the dollar price of gold. That the United States had a different view was evident in the remarks of Mr. Connally (United States) at a press conference after the Group of Ten meeting on September 26. In accordance with the established procedures of that Group for rotating the chairmanship, Mr. Connally had just succeeded Mr. Benson as chairman for the coming year. He characterized "the gold question" as primarily "a political problem, not an economic one," and rather than a "premature decision regarding parities," he proposed a "general clean float" of major exchange rates (*clean* referring to the absence of official intervention in exchange markets).

3B. *Amended Article IV of the Fund's Charter*

Here's the rebirth of Article IV of the Fund's Charter after the collapse of the BWS. What's the Fund's role now? What is the fundamental objective of Article IV and why? Why is surveillance so important? What exactly is going on in Article IV, Section 2? Why is it highly unlikely that a par value system will come back? What language at least pays lip service to member countries' sovereignty?

Article IV

Obligations Regarding Exchange Arrangements

Section 1.   *General obligations of members*

Recognizing that the essential purpose of the international monetary system is to provide a framework that facilitates the exchange of goods, services, and capital among countries, and that sustains sound economic growth, and that a principal objective is the continuing development of the orderly underlying conditions that are necessary for financial and economic stability, each member undertakes to collaborate with the Fund and other members to assure orderly exchange arrangements and to promote a stable system of exchange rates. In particular, each member shall:

(i)   endeavor to direct its economic and financial policies toward the objective of fostering orderly economic growth with reasonable price stability, with due regard to its circumstances;

(ii) seek to promote stability by fostering orderly underlying economic and financial conditions and a monetary system that does not tend to produce erratic disruptions;

(iii) avoid manipulating exchange rates or the international monetary system in order to prevent effective balance of payments adjustment or to gain an unfair competitive advantage over other members; and

(iv) Follow exchange policies compatible with the undertakings under this Section.

Section 2.   *General exchange arrangements*

(a) Each member shall notify the Fund, within thirty days after the date of the second amendment of this Agreement, of the exchange arrangements it intends to apply in fulfillment of its obligations under Section 1of this Article, and shall notify the Fund promptly of any changes in its exchange arrangements.

(b) Under an international monetary system of the kind prevailing on January 1, 1976, exchange arrangements may include (i) the maintenance by a member of a value for its currency in terms of the special drawing right or another denominator, other than gold, selected by the member, or (ii) cooperative arrangements by which members maintain the value of their currencies in relation to the value of the currency or currencies of other members, or (iii) other exchange arrangements of a member's choice.

(c) To accord with the development of the international monetary system, the Fund, by an eighty-five percent majority of the total voting power, may make provision for general exchange arrangements without limiting the right of members to have exchange arrangements of their choice consistent with the purposes of the Fund and the obligations under Section 1 of this Article.

Section 3.   *Surveillance over exchange arrangements*

(a) The Fund shall oversee the international monetary system in order to ensure its effective operation, and shall oversee the compliance of each member with its obligations under Section 1of this Article.

(b) In order to fulfill its functions under (a) above, the Fund shall exercise firm surveillance over the exchange rate policies of members, and shall adopt specific principles for the guidance of all members with respect to those policies. Each member shall provide the Fund with the information necessary for such surveillance, and, when requested by the Fund, shall consult with it on the member's exchange rate policies. The principles adopted by the Fund shall be consistent with cooperative arrangements by which members maintain the value of their currencies in relation to the value of the currency or currencies of other members, as well as with other exchange arrangements of a member's choice consistent with the purposes of the Fund and Section 1 of this Article. These principles shall respect the domestic social and political policies of members, and in applying these principles the Fund shall pay due regard to the circumstances of members.

Section 4.   *Par values*

The Fund may determine, by an eighty-five percent majority of the total voting power, that international economic conditions permit the introduction of a widespread system of exchange arrangements based on stable but adjustable par values. The Fund shall make the determination on the basis of the underlying stability of the world economy, and for this purpose shall take into account price movements and rates of expansion in the economies of members. The determination shall be made in light of the evolution of the international monetary system, with particular reference to sources of liquidity, and, in order to ensure the effective operation of a system of par values, to arrangements under which both members in surplus and members in deficit in their balances of payments take prompt, effective, and symmetrical action to achieve adjustment, as well as to arrangements for intervention and the treatment of imbalances. Upon making such determination, the Fund shall notify members that the provisions of Schedule C apply.

Section 5.   *Separate currencies within a member's territories*

    (a)   Action by a member with respect to its currency under this Article shall be deemed to apply to the separate currencies of all territories in respect of which the member has accepted this Agreement under Article XXXI, Section 2(g) unless the member declares that its action relates either to the metropolitan currency alone, or only to one or more specified separate currencies, or to the metropolitan currency and one or more specified separate currencies.

    (b)   Action by the Fund under this Article shall be deemed to relate to all currencies of a member referred to in (a) above unless the Fund declares otherwise.

CHAPTER 4

THE RISE OF THE WORLD BANK AND THE NIEO

∎∎∎

In Chapter 3 we addressed the dramatic fall of the Bretton Woods System (BWS). We turn away from monetary affairs to focus on the rise of the World Bank and the Global South's call for a New International Economic Order (NIEO) in the turbulent decade of the1970s. As the IMF redefined its role in the dust of the collapsed BWS, the World Bank arose as *the* stage for development, and Robert McNamara was the rock star who jumped into the mosh pit of developing countries. At the same time, the NIEO roared to life, only to whimper to its death by the end of the decade. Let's begin the drama with the World Bank.

(lights up)

Act One: The Awakening of the World Bank

Scene One: The Bank Opens Its Doors

The International Bank for Reconstruction and Development ("Bank") opened for business on June 25, 1946 on H Street in Washington, D.C. But when the doors swung open, the Bank said, "Uh . . . are we going to be a permanent gig or are we in business just long enough to reconstruct Europe?" If reconstructing Europe were its only purpose, the Bank would have closed its doors by the late 1950s (initially it made a small number of reconstruction loans). By that time, thanks to the Marshall Plan, good times had returned to Western Europe. And when the European currencies became convertible in the mid-1950s (see Chapter 1), capital started flowing again to the countries that would form the "developed" part of the world. The Bank was supposed to provide longer-term, low-interest-rate reconstruction loans to countries that were starved for capital. "Uh . . . now what do we do?"

> "The Bank, said a Swiss newspaper in March 1947, 'was born under an unlucky star.' Its activity to date could be summed up in a single word: 'zero.' This harsh assessment of an institution widely hailed at the close of the Bretton Woods conference three years earlier was not confined to the notoriously tough-minded Swiss. Under the most charitable of judgments, the early years of the World Bank would have to be characterized as inauspicious."
> —E. Mason & R. Asher, <u>The World Bank Since Bretton Woods</u>, 36 (1973)

Enter stage left: developing countries or, what many folks called them then, "underdeveloped" countries—now called the "Global South" a lot. Remember from Chapter 2 that development economists, from the structuralists to the neo-Marxists, said the Global North—developed countries—rigged the global system against the Global South. And we're not even talking about the colonized countries. With the wave of decolonization, particularly in Africa, the Bank had new clients who said to the Global North, "Hey, we're sovereigns just like you. We need money to do what you guys have done."

And the Bank smiled.

Scene Two: Project Lending

The Bank met its clients' needs by making loans for projects—"project lending" in the biz. This wasn't just a whim. Article I of the Bank's Charter (see supplement 1D), which lists its purposes, says one purpose is "[t]o arrange the loans made or guaranteed by it in relation to international loans through other channels so that the more useful and urgent projects, large and small alike, will be dealt with first." Article III(1)(a), which addresses the use of the Bank's resources, mandates that the Bank consider projects for development and reconstruction alike. And (4)(vii) allows non-project lending only in "special circumstances"—we'll talk about this in another chapter.

The funny thing is that at the Bretton Woods Conference the United States wanted a more relaxed approach that would allow the Bank to make other types of loans. But focusing on Bank projects was useful for a number of reasons. They had a clear beginning and end. Because of that, borrowing countries didn't view Bank lending as cramping what they did domestically. And project lending gave everyone the impression that the Bank, a multilateral institution, was comprised of technocrats who couldn't possibly be actors in the Cold War drama. Hmmm . . .

Most of the Bank's project lending to governments (the Bank can't lend to private entities without a government guarantee) went to the power and transportation sectors—infrastructure lending. Why is that, you ask? Power outages were common, especially in Latin America and Asia. Power . . . that's kind of important to any country but really important to countries trying to "develop," don't you think? And the railroads and highways were a mess. Check this out: Because it was such a pain to transport potatoes to Rio de Janeiro from other parts of the country, Brazil imported potatoes from the Netherlands. You heard right, the Netherlands! There's something wrong with that development picture.

Let's look at Mexico for another example. In October of 1960, the Mexican government received a U.S. $25 million loan to build thirteen road projects. An IBRD report found that because the number of vehicles using Mexico's roads had more than doubled since 1950, the project was necessary to improve existing roads to manage the increased traffic. The upgraded roads would also connect isolated but populated and developed areas with other parts of Mexico, and connect commercial centers with important ocean ports.

The creation of the International Development Association (IDA) in 1960 marked an expansion of lending beyond typical infrastructure—e.g., agriculture and education. You know from Chapter 1 that the IDA makes concessional loans to poor countries, so when it was created a whole bunch of new clients came in. Keeping the poor countries in the IDA (trapped in there, really) protected the **Bank's AAA credit rating**, which benefitted the Bank's borrowers. The rating allowed the Bank to borrow more cheaply, which translated into cheaper loans to its member country borrowers.

Scene Three: The Bank's First Four Presidents

So who was presiding over all of this Bank activity? Men! American men! Remember the golden rule? Whoever owns the gold, rules. Since the United States threw down one-third of the capital to establish the Bank, it controlled the Bank. From the outset it was understood that the United States would have the prerogative of picking an American as Bank President. The Europeans picked the IMF's Managing Director. Having people—men—from other parts of the world head the Bank and the Fund? Forget about it!

Let's look at the first four Presidents. First came Eugene Meyer, a former Wall Street investment banker who almost immediately got into a fight with the U.S.'s executive director over how to run the bank. Meyer lasted just six months on the job. Then came John McCloy, a lawyer! He went to Harvard Law School and became a partner at Cravath five years after joining the firm. (Yeah, that partnership track exists only in your dreams.) After World War II, he became a name-partner of Milbank, Tweed, Hope, Hadley and McCloy, which led to the chairmanship of Chase Manhattan Bank. McCloy led the World Bank for a little over two years. During that short time he started turning the Bank from reconstruction to development in large part because that was an important way to contain the Soviet threat in the Cold War.

> *"I could stay and fight these bastards, and probably win in the end, but I'm too old for that."*
>
> —Eugene Meyer, quoted in J. Kraske et al., <u>Bankers with a Mission: The Presidents of the World Bank, 1946–91</u>, 31 (1996)

Then came another Eugene, Eugene Black, a banker (Chase National Bank). His presidency lasted thirteen years—from 1949 to 1962! During that time he raised lots of capital for the Bank (he secured the Bank's AAA rating) and expanded and

> " 'Yet the essence of successful economic development, and therefore the essential task of the Bank, is precisely to bring new enterprises into being and new techniques into effective use in economically retarded areas—and the more retarded the country the more urgent and challenging is our task.' "
> —Eugene Black quoted in J. Kraske et al., <u>Bankers with a Mission: The Presidents of the World Bank, 1946–91</u>, 99 (1996)

internationalized the Bank's staff. He also presided reluctantly over the creation of the IDA (he understandably wanted to protect the Bank's AAA rating). He was much more enthusiastic over the opening of the International Finance Corporation (IFC) in 1956. The IFC is essentially an investment bank that takes a minority share in foreign direct investment (FDI) in developing countries.

In 1963 George Woods, another Wall Street investment banker, took over the Bank's helm. Woods had a bad temper but when he was in a good mood he pushed the Bank in the direction of development. He increased the Bank's agricultural loans and cooperated with United Nations agencies, such as the United Nations Educational, Scientific, and Cultural Organization (UNESCO), to fund education. In 1967, he proposed forming a group of experts to study how resources could be used more effectively to promote development.

Why were virtually all of these Presidents Wall Street bankers? A bit ago we said that at the outset the Bank was supposed to provide longer-term, low-interest-rate reconstruction loans to European countries. But when it was conceived the idea was that it would act as a guarantor of FDI in host countries. Very quickly, though, the Bank realized that the FDI flows weren't large enough for reconstruction projects. So it had to become a lender. Slight problem: The Bank didn't have the resources to make loans—member countries contributed very little to the Bank's pot when it opened its doors.

> "[T]here wasn't a Wall Street man who would touch the [Bank's] bonds with a ten-foot pole."
> —R. Oliver, <u>George Woods and the World Bank</u>, 41 (1995)

The solution: Issue bonds in the capital markets, especially to Wall Street investors. But to get investors to buy the bonds, the Bank had to convince them that it was trustworthy. That's where the Bank Presidents' Wall Street connections paid off. They were able to convince investors that the Bank would lend only to creditworthy borrowers. And the best vehicle for lending was for "productive" projects. You can see, then, that in the early years the Bank saw itself *as a bank,* not as a development institution. When President Black secured the AAA rating, the sweetest rating possible, the Bank's bonds were golden.

Before the next Bank President enters the stage, we need to talk about development and how that concept was changing in the 1960s and 1970s.

Scene Four: The Concept of Development

The post-colonial push to develop economically resulted in pretty cool growth rates. Gross national product (GNP) per capita for developing countries as a group averaged 3.4% a year during 1950–1975, faster than any group of countries in any comparable period before 1950. But the averages masked big differences in wealth between countries. For example, Brazil, Somalia, Trinidad and Tobago, and Turkey grew at an annual average of 3.7% per capita between 1950 and 1975. The growth picture wasn't nearly as good for South Asia and much of Africa: less than 2% per capita during the same period.

Income inequality within developing countries was also a fact of life despite economic growth. Most of the increases in income were concentrated in sectors directly involved in what became a state-led process of development. Typically, the government sector, those employed in industries, and those who otherwise had special ties to the government or to foreign investors benefited the most. The push to develop led to great migrations of people from rural areas to big cities, where many couldn't find jobs. And the push to industrialize (the import substitution model we discussed in Chapter 2) favored industry over agriculture, which led to increased poverty in rural areas.

Some theorists and policymakers said chill: The gap between the rich and the poor would eventually shrink with increased economic growth (the **Kuznets inverted-U curve**). They believed that if government policy favored the sectors that appeared to be thriving, the whole country would be better off. And the wealth would "trickle down" to the poorer sectors of society. But in the 1960s, many realized that the trickle-down approach to development wasn't working. In fact, some believed that benefits were defying physics and "trickling up."

The preoccupation in the 1970s with inequitable development led some economists to reject the idea that growth in per capita income alone could be used to measure development. But this raised the nagging question whether growth would have to be sacrificed for equity. You can't have your cake and eat it, too.

Well, maybe you can. The publication of *Redistribution and Wealth* in 1974 by economist Hollis Chenery and his associates at the World Bank marked a "semiofficial" rejection of what was a false dilemma. They trashed the idea there was an inevitable and permanent trade-off between distribution of assets/income and growth. Since the "objectives of growth and equity may not be in conflict," economic policies in developing countries could combine growth objectives with distributive concerns—check out supplement 4C. The growth-with-equity economic analysis created the opening for McNamara.

(lights down; fireworks go off on stage; Bruce Springsteen's "Born in the U.S.A" blares out [yeah, the song was released in 1984 but it's perfect for this staging]; lights up; enter McNamara in 1968 stage left)

Scene Five: Robert McNamara, the Rock Star

McNamara led the Bank in a head-first dive into development, with an emphasis on poverty alleviation—check out his speech in supplement 4A. He was one of the "best and the brightest" of President Kennedy's administration. A man on a mission, McNamara viewed the Bank as a tool to accomplish the goal of attacking and resolving developing countries' problems.

> "No one would ever mistake McNamara for a European; he was American through and through, with the American drive, the American certitude and conviction . . ."
> —A. Halberstam, The Best and the Brightest, 215 (1973)

And he believed he had the training to wield the tool. He went to Harvard Business School, where he was inculcated with the mindset of setting goals and using quantitative

> "Why, then, did I leave? It was not because I was ill, although newspapers reported such stories, and the president told his aides he was worried I might commit suicide, as had Truman's first defense secretary, James V. Forrestal. It has since become a common assumption that I was near emotional and physical collapse. I was at loggerheads with the president of the United States; I was not getting answers to my questions; and I was tense as hell. But I was not under medical care, not taking drugs except for an occasional sleeping pill, and never contemplated suicide."
> —R. McNamara, NcNamara in Retrospect: the Tragedy and Lessons of Vietnam, 313 (1995)

> "Thus if one had asked the international development community what credentials a World Bank president should have, Robert McNamara would have been one of the least qualified."
> —D. Kapur et al., The World Bank: It's First Half Century, Vol. 1, 5 (1997)

methods to achieve them. He applied the same approach during his time in the military and to his consulting work that led to his appointment as president of the Ford Motor Corporation. As Secretary of Defense, McNamara's style put the military under civilian control, but ultimately knocked heads with President Johnson over the conduct of the Vietnam War. He left the administration for the World Bank, his managerial zest to solve problems unfazed.

When McNamara became Bank President, he followed through with George Woods' proposal and asked former Canadian Prime Minister Lester B. Pearson to form a commission to study the past twenty years of development experience and make recommendations for the future. Published in 1969, the Pearson Commission lauded the Bank for its "formidable experience of development finance." It situated the Bank at the center of multilateral lending for development, coordinating its work with the **regional development banks** and the International Monetary Fund.

McNamara wasted no time. In 1968, the can-do Bank President told the Board of Governors, "I believe that globally the Bank Group should during the next five years lend twice as much as during the past five years. This means that between now and 1973 the Bank Group would lend in total nearly as much as it has lent since it began operations twenty-two years ago." Check it out: The volume of new loans grew from $847 million in 1967–1968 to $1.4 billion in 1968–1969! And that was just the beginning. His quantitative training at Harvard Business School . . .

> *"We are in the business of dealing in numbers—numbers of people, numbers of dollars, numbers of tons of food produced. How on earth can you run this place without thinking in those terms?"*
> —Robert MacNamara quoted in J. Kraske et al., Bankers with a Mission: The Presidents of the World Bank, 1946–91, 118–119 (1996)

McNamara's Moral Mission

But McNamara wasn't just about numbers—he had morals, which informed his mission of equitable growth. We have to share with you an extended portion of his famous 1973 address to the Bank's Board of Governors in Nairobi, Kenya. It rocks. You might want to listen to a digitized recording of the speech on the World Bank's website.

> "Relative poverty means simply that some countries are less affluent than other countries, or that some citizens of a given country have less personal abundance than their neighbors. That has always been the case, and granted the realities of differences between regions and between individuals, will continue to be the case for decades to come.
>
> But absolute poverty is a condition of life so degraded by disease, illiteracy, malnutrition, and squalor as to deny its victims basic human necessities.
>
> It is a condition of life suffered by relatively few in the developed nations but by hundreds of millions of the citizens of the developing countries represented in this room. Many of you have cause to know far better than I that:
>
> - One-third to one-half of the two billion human beings in those countries suffer from hunger or malnutrition.
> - 20% to 25% of their children die before their fifth birthdays. And millions of those who do not die lead impeded lives because their brains have been damaged, their bodies stunted, and their vitality sapped by nutritional deficiencies.
> - The life expectancy of the average person is 20 years less than in the affluent world. They are denied 30% of the lives those of us from the developed nations enjoy. In effect, they are condemned at birth to an early death.

- 800 million of them are illiterate and, despite the continuing expansion of education in the years ahead, even more of their children are likely to do so.

This is absolute poverty: a condition of life so limited as to prevent realization of the potential of the genes with which one is born; a condition of life so degrading as to insult human dignity—and yet a condition of life so common as to be the lot of some 40% of the peoples of the developing countries. And are not we who tolerate such poverty, when it is within our power to reduce the number of afflicted by it, failing to fulfill the fundamental obligations accepted by civilized men since the beginning of time?

I do not wish you to interpret my remarks as those of a zealot. But you have hired me to examine the problems of the developing world and to report to you the facts. These are the facts . . .

[I]n my view the fundamental case for development assistance is the moral one. The whole of human history has recognized the principle—at least in the abstract—that the rich and the powerful have a moral obligation to assist the poor and the weak . . .

The basic problem of poverty and growth in the developing world can be stated very simply. The growth is not equitably reaching the poor. And the poor are not significantly contributing to growth.

Despite a decade of unprecedented increase in the gross national product of the developing countries, the poorest segments of their population have received relatively little benefit. Nearly 800 million individuals—40% out of a total of two billion—survive on incomes estimated (in U.S. purchasing power) at 30 cents per day . . .

The need to reorient development policies in order to provide a more equitable distribution of the benefits of economic growth is beginning to be widely discussed. But very few countries have actually made serious moves in this direction . . .

. . . While most countries have broadened the statements of their development goals to include references to reducing unemployment and increasing the income of the poor—as well as emphasizing traditional growth in output—they still measure progress toward these complex objectives with a single measuring rod: the growth of GNP."

New Areas of Lending

McNamara's "growth with equity" approach was stamped on the programs the Bank initiated. Although the typical lending continued, McNamara's mission to wipe out absolute poverty expanded the Bank's lending—lots of it—to new areas: health and nutrition, urban development (including urban poverty), water supply and sewerage, education (especially for primary schooling and adult education and literacy), rural development focusing on the small landholders, and population control. Just looking at Sub-Saharan Africa, this type of lending mushroomed, from 123 projects in the 1960s to 583 in the 1970s.

Let's look at a population control project. In what would be the Bank's second stab at family planning (and the first project to be financed by the IDA), in March 1971, McNamara approved a $4.8 million concessional loan to the Republic of Tunisia for a "population project." McNamara's report cited problems with Tunisia's existing family planning program, which reached only 2.5% of women of childbearing age, lacked organization, and had issues with overcrowding in maternity hospitals. The Bank project tried to improve these existing services with technical assistance—things like management consultations and assessments on the best use of resources. The loan would also fund the construction of four maternity hospitals, two rural maternity centers, and twenty-nine maternal and child health centers.

Now let's look at two contrasting education projects. One project involved a non-concessional $9.5 million loan in 1973 to expand and relocate the University of Singapore (one of two higher education universities in the country at the time) with aim of preparing for future demand for skilled high-level people in engineering, architecture, and business. The other was a $3.5 concessional loan in 1971 to the Republic of Congo to improve curricula, provide teacher training, and build facilities in the primary and secondary levels.

Good stuff, right? Let's keep reading.

McNamara's Report Card

During the McNamara years, the steroid-injected Bank grew much bigger and complex. It had to because of the pressure to lend. Ever the quant, McNamara's Bank measured success by output instead of on the outcome of particular projects. Total Bank lending went from $734.8 million in 1968 to $5.173 billion in 1980. But so many of the loans were duds.

They failed because they were inappropriate for the locality, and otherwise failed to reach the people the project intended to help. Let's take a look at a few examples. Take for instance the rural development program focusing on the small landholder. At the annual meeting of the Bank in Nairobi in 1973, McNamara announced that over a five-year period Bank lending would increase by 40% over the previous five-year period, with much of the lending going to the rural sector, where poverty was widespread. Although millions benefitted from the program, the success of improving the productivity of the small landholder was questionable and the poorest of the poor—those without land—benefitted indirectly at most. The ambitious program hardly fulfilled McNamara's goal of putting countries on a path of poverty eradication.

Let's take a look at Tanzania. McNamara's Bank made a slew of project loans for livestock, cashew nut, tobacco, and cotton. It also made loans to improve education, which focused on secondary schools, teacher training centers, vocational training centers, community centers, a rural health center, and a medical school to boot. They all were pretty much screwed up. Why? A major problem was that the Bank's growth-with-equity approach failed to take into account the institutional weaknesses of the governments responsible for implementing the programs. Bottom line: His top-down, quantitative approach didn't work.

Yet another problem dealt with human rights, which would come back to haunt the Bank in the 1990s. Critics charged that it turned a blind eye to extremely controversial ways the borrowing government implemented projects. Take the $10 million loan to the Tanzanian government to improve the productivity and living standards of farm families in a region of the country. McNamara's Bank was convinced the loan was a good bet to demonstrate the growth-with-equity approach in a country whose president, Julius Nyerere, flew the banner of African socialism. Slight problem, though: The government's program involved large-scale forced resettlement of the rural folk into villages. In a 1975 review of the program, the Bank said in essence, "we just don't know if this villagization [is that even a word?] thing will work." It didn't. A subsequent Bank review of the project said the Bank had lost its perspective as an "honest broker."

> *"In the early 1970s, development experts and public interest development groups began to criticize the prevailing trickle-down theory of development. Despite McNamara's efforts to broaden the lending policy of the Bank, the institution came under attack for supporting regimes that were persistent violators of human rights and for not doing enough to aid the poor . . . The problem was worsened by the rapid growth of lending under the dynamic leadership of McNamara, which stimulated a considerable increase in public and congressional attention to Bank policies and practices."*
>
> —C. Gwin, "U.S. Relations with the World Bank, 1945–1992," in D. Kapur et al., The World Bank: Its First Half Century, 211 (1997)

And the United States didn't have his back. McNamara caught flak from the Nixon administration—which wasn't crazy about him. The Treasury Department and others felt the Bank, a multilateral institution, was taking something at the gym to make it beastly and putting the Bank beyond the U.S.'s control. This was not cool since U.S. bilateral aid, where the U.S. could exert political leverage, was shrinking. Then there was the Bank's U.S. Executive Director who charged that the Bank was way over-lending, threatening the Bank's ability to borrow. And "Hey, we're not down with the Bank's support for state-led development," said the Treasury. What's really strange was that as hard as McNamara tried to focus on poverty alleviation, Congress grew frustrated in the late 1970s at the lack of progress.

> *"According to the press, McNamara was not the first choice of Republican President Nixon . . . McNamara 'had irritated many important leaders in the Nixon administration. They had thought that, as an American, McNamara should be responsive to policy nudges, but over and over again he proved to be unnudgeable.'"*
> —C. Gwin, "U.S. Relations with the World Bank, 1945–1992," in D. Kapur et al., <u>The World Bank: Its First Half Century</u>, 211 (1997) (quoting W. Clark, "Robert McNamara and the World Bank," *Foreign Affairs, vol. 6*, 176 (fall 1981)

When Ronald Reagan was elected, the administration indicated it would emphasize bilateral over multilateral aid for foreign policy reasons. U.S. funding of the Bank would require greater emphasis on private markets.

McNamara left the Bank in 1981. He was one of a kind—check out supplement 4B. His drive and passion transformed the Bank like no other President. He pushed the envelope—which made it a lightning rod for criticism from the U.S. left and right political spectrum. Ironically, his push for growth with equity raised tensions between the Global North and South. Let's get to that now.

Act Two: The New International Economic Order

(Aretha Franklin singing "R-E-S-P-E-C-T, Find out what it means to me")

As McNamara was attempting to tackle poverty at the World Bank, the Global South looked at the global state of affairs and said, "enough." They used the United Nations to call for a "New International Economic Order" (NIEO).

Scene One: The Roots

It's pretty clear in the story we've sketched out about McNamara's Bank, that the world in the 1970s was not an equitable world. When decolonization came about, the Global South said to the Global North, "You've exploited us and that's why you're rich. It's our turn and you owe us big time." They had a good reason to be pissed. They saw their share of the world's wealth diminish despite 5.5% percent annual average economic growth during the 1960s. Grant-based aid from the developed world steadily decreased. But aid-tied loans from the Global North—loans conditioned upon the debtor country buying goods from developed countries at artificially high prices—increased.

> *"[T]he prosperity of the West is derived, to a large extent from the draining the wealth and exploitation of the labour of the peoples of the Third World, and that their economic apparatus, imposing though it be, rests on fragile and vulnerable foundations."*
> —U. N. Speech by Algerian Foreign Minister Abdelaziz Bouteflika, 1975 in J. Singh, <u>A New International Economic Order</u>, 20 (1997)

To make matters worse, debt was piling up. From 1965 to 1972, the debt of the G-77 developing countries rose at an average rate of 15% per year, reaching $100 billion by the end of that period. By 1979, G-77 debt had climbed to $400 billion. The Global South argued that the global economic system made debt repayment a pain, as the meager income developing countries received from raw material exports was used to pay for the much more expensive imports of manufactured products from the developed countries.

Given the golden rule, would the NIEO spring out of the World Bank or IMF? Uh . . . no. Remember the system of weighted voting in both institutions: it put rich countries in the driver's seat. The Global South opted for a strategy through the United Nations, where the one-nation-one-vote rule carried the day.

Scene Two: The Push

On behalf of the **Non-Aligned Movement**, Algerian President Houari Boumediene made a request to the Secretary General for a Special Session at the U.N. to pursue the NIEO program then being finalized at the 1973 Nonaligned Summit-Conference in Algiers. At the Sixth Special Session of the U.N. Assembly held in April 1974, the NIEO came to life with the adoption of two U.N. General Assembly resolutions: the "Declaration on the Establishment of a New International Economic Order" and the "Programme of Action on the Establishment of a New International Economic Order."

> *"[The Declaration] was "a significant political document, but it does not represent unanimity of opinion in the Assembly. To label some of these highly controversial conclusions as agreed is not only idle, it is self-deceiving."*
> —U.S. Ambassador John Scali, in J. Singh, <u>A New International Economic Order</u>, 9 (1997)

In December 1974, the General Assembly adopted a re-articulation of the "Declaration" and "Programme" (the two resolutions adopted in May) in a resolution titled, "Charter of Economic Rights and Duties of States," which is generally referred to as the NIEO Charter—see supplement 4D. This resolution passed by a vote of 120 for, 10 abstentions, and 6 against— Belgium, Denmark, the German Federal Republic, Luxembourg, the United Kingdom, and the United States.

The NIEO's ideology was based on the concepts of sovereignty and sovereign equality. It called for negotiations with industrialized countries to modify the philosophical, juridical, and institutional principles and structures of the existing international economic order. Basically a new global order—piece of cake.

Given the NIEO's ambitions, its agenda was . . . like . . . HUGE! The Charter emphasized the right of each nation to manage its own economic resources free from any outside interference. It also suggested changes to the terms of international trade, based on the fundamental principle that all states have the right to engage in trade regardless of their political, economic, or social system. Commodities were to be traded at "stable, remunerative and equitable prices," which would increase the income of poor producers and stabilize the trade flows of developing countries. The rich countries would lose their subsidies (especially in agriculture), so that small developing-country producers wouldn't have to compete as much with them. And then there was the demand for non-reciprocal treatment, i.e., the Global North would give preferential treatment to the Global South's imports without asking for anything in return.

Monetary and financial issues, focusing on the IMF, were also on the agenda. The NIEO Charter stressed the need "[t]o take fully into account the requirements of developing countries for, and their ability to contribute to, balance-of-payments finance [and] to increase the over-all participation of developing countries in the decision-making process of the Fund." The 1976 Manila Declaration declared that "the system of voting in the IMF and the World Bank should be reformed to accord developing countries greater representation and weight in decision-making in these institutions." The G-77 also argued that "the conditionality attached to drawings from the IMF by developing countries should take fully into account the structural problems of economies of the developing countries." The NIEO Programme of Action called for increased liquidity in the international monetary system through an additional allocation of special drawing rights **(SDRs)**, and it also stipulated that a link between SDRs and development aid should exist for those countries in need.

In the Seventh Special Session in September 1975, the Global North responded with a U.N. resolution titled "Development and International Economic Co-operation," which responded to a number, but not all, of the NIEO's demands, such as confirming the developed countries' commitment to set aside 0.7 percent of their GDP as **official development assistance (ODA)** to developing nations. It also mentioned establishing a link between SDRs and development assistance, which the IMF *should* consider but only *when* it considers creating more SDRs to increase international liquidity. Although the Global North viewed the resolution as reflecting a new consensus on a new global order, it was intended to maintain the existing economic order (sounds pretty incompatible with the *New* International Economic Order), but give development assistance via more liberal trade, by the transfer of aid and technology (through international organizations other than the U.N.), and by the creation of programs for the stabilization of commodity prices.

> *"[T]here must be consensus, first and foremost, on the principle that our common development goals can be achieved only by cooperation, not by the politics of confrontation. There must be consensus that acknowledges our respective concerns and our mutual responsibilities. The consensus must embrace the broadest possible participation in international decisions. The developing countries must have a role and a voice in the international system, especially in decisions that affect them. But those nations who are asked to provide resources and effort to carry out the decisions must be accorded a commensurate voice."*
>
> —U.N. Ambassador Daniel Moynihan, U.N. Speech, 1975 in J. Singh, <u>A New International Economic Order</u>, 23 (1997)

Scene Three: The Failure

Nobody doubts that the Global South acquired a sense of voice through the NIEO agenda. After all, the U.N. resolution on Development and International Economic Co-operation was hailed as a key marker in the inevitable change in the global order that would benefit the Global South. But the NIEO never amounted to much more than talk. The NIEO's staggering lack of success was due largely to its very purpose for existing in the first place—the lack of power developing nations held in international relations. The G-77 and Nonaligned Movement in particular tried to remedy the lack of individual strength with strength in numbers, even though such a large group of countries inevitably had differing goals based on national best interests.

The rich countries didn't exactly support the idea of putting their place at the top of the economic food chain in jeopardy. Even the more modest reforms got shot down by the Global North, and here we mention just a few. The Global North interpreted the NIEO demands as a call for reparations for past harm, which made economic relations appear to be a zero-sum game where the developing nations' gain would mean an equivalent loss for the developed nations. Developed countries also felt that they had nothing to gain from increasing aid to the developing world as they would still be blamed for the economic failure of any developing country, regardless of how poorly governments managed their economies.

The developed world's loudest complaint against NIEO ideology was that it was hypocritical considering the domestic politics of many developing countries. Governments that had done little to solve internal inequality were more than willing to ask for a solution in international organizations. A major part of the problem was that even though the growth-with-equity approach to development had taken hold in the 1970s, developing countries for the most part still clinged to the trickle down approach. They ostensibly cared about the marginalized and vulnerable and they believed they could help them by pushing for economic growth.

> *The U.N. Committee on Development Planning in 1975 "touched upon another aspect of the development debate – the need for a new internal economic order, to go along with a New International Economic Order. As the committee indicated, most of the dominant issues of development have to be thrashed out domestically. The debate on a new international economic order has centered so far on international arrangements and institutional structures. Any radical changes at the international level would not, however, be fully effective without radical economic and social transformation within national boundaries."*
>
> —J. Singh, A New International Economic Order, 17 (1997)

The NIEO saw its mission as just, imperative, and humane. But while seeking the mission on the international plane, many NIEO countries were violating human rights and oppressing their citizens. Not cool. Many of these countries were not democracies (a legacy of colonialism?), yet they insisted international finance institutions become more democratic, specifically the IMF and World Bank.

And, of course, there was great dispute over the legal significance of the NIEO. In response to the Global South's claims that the NIEO resolutions reflected **customary international law**, critics argued the nonbinding resolutions were merely moral or political statements, at best constituting "soft law" (not really legally binding but not completely void of legal significance). On top of this, the deep divisions between the North and South left much of the NIEO's business unfinished. In the end, it met a quiet death (or lapsed into a coma) after the late 1970s.

(fade to black as Simon & Garfunkel's "Bridge Over Troubled Water" plays)

You Gotta Know Something About Them!

Robert McNamara

Robert Strange McNamara was born in Oakland, California. Robert's parents weren't formally educated. His father was the sales manager of a wholesale shoe firm. They were good parents: they were determined to give their children every opportunity via education. "Their resolve shaped my life," said McNamara. His sister said, "We had a very happy home life. The only thing nontypical about it was Bob. Even as a little boy my brother was terrific. He was something special." McNamara majored in economics at Berkeley. He liked sports but he wasn't very good at it. But he was a tenacious guy.

Eugene Black

Eugene was a southern boy, born in Atlanta, Georgia. Mint juleps, anyone? His grandfather, Henry Grady, was a big-time figure in the Reconstruction Era, arguing that the South had to get its act together by looking at the North. Eugene's dad was a high-flying banker who first became head of the Federal Reserve Bank in Atlanta and then Chair of the Fed. After graduating from the University of Georgia with a Latin major, Eugene enlisted in the U.S. Navy—the Army wouldn't take him because of a heart murmur. When he came back to civilian life, he spent some time with a New York investment firm selling bonds and meeting with bankers and investors. Eugene wasn't all work and no play—he was really into Balzac. He was also heavy into Shakespeare.

What's Up with That?

AAA Credit Rating

In the context of sovereign bonds, a credit rating from a credit rating agency (CRA) such as Standard & Poor's assesses the creditworthiness of governments that issue bonds. Investors use the ratings when deciding whether to buy sovereign bonds. A "AAA" rating, the highest rating possible, is the CRA's judgment that the sovereign issuer in question is highly likely to service its debt on time and in full—i.e., it's highly unlikely to default on the bond. Risk-averse investors like to hear that and some institutional investors can't hold bonds with a lower rating. AAA bonds are very safe and for that reason, the return on the bonds is not very high. And as we noted in the text, that allows the Bank to lend at lower interest rates.

Kuznets Inverted-U Hypothesis

In a paper published in 1955, the economist Simon Kuznets suggested that income distribution would worsen in the early stages of economic growth. But over time, the gap in income would shrink. Ergo, the inverted Kuznets curve. Why? Because economies typically go through structural changes. For example, you're likely to see an increase in inequality with the transition from traditional low-income rural sectors to higher-income industrial sectors. The inequality gap lessens as the economy grows. Although the hypothesis is a main-stay in development economics, not all economists agree with it.

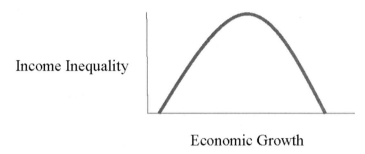

Income Inequality

Economic Growth

Regional Development Banks

Regional Development Banks (RDBs) are Multilateral Development Banks (MDBs) that were founded to promote development in their regions. They give low-interest loans and grants to low- and middle-income countries for things like agriculture, health, and education. There are four RDBs that typically are associated with the other MDBs—the World Bank Group: the Inter-American Development Bank (IDB), founded in 1959; the African Development Bank (AFDB), founded in 1964; the Asian Development Bank (ADB), founded in 1966; and the European Bank for Reconstruction and Development (EBRD), founded in 1991. Each RDB has its own legal and operational status and is owned by both regional and non-regional member governments (the U.S. government is a member of all four RDBs).

G-77 and Non-Aligned Movement

The Group of 77 (G-77) was established in June 1964 by seventy-seven U.N. developing countries to voice their collective economic interests. The G-77 used their strength in numbers to enhance their negotiating power within the U.N. and to encourage South-South economic cooperation. The G-77 produces action programs, declarations, agreements on development issues, and conclusions and recommendations on current events. Today the G-77 has swelled to more than 130 members but retains its historic name.

The Non-Aligned Movement (NAM) is a movement of more than 100 member countries representing the interests of developing countries. The NAM evolved from a 1955 meeting between twenty-nine countries—most of which were former colonies—to discuss shared concerns and interests. The Movement was largely shaped by the Cold War—it wanted to keep its members neutral in world politics and prevent them from getting caught up in power struggles. Today the Movement continues to work on issues relating the international economic order. In his 2004 opening remarks at a NAM conference, the President of South Africa Thabo Mbeki listed "the eradication of poverty and underdevelopment, securing peace and stability for ourselves, [and] ensuring a democratic inclusive situation" as their objectives. He added, "We have no other global political instrument except the Non-Aligned Movement to help us to address these goals."

Special Drawing Rights

The SDR plan first began to take shape in March of 1966 when the IMF Managing Director at the time, Pierre-Paul Schweitzer, proposed a reserve-creating plan to apply to all members, to counter fears of a global liquidity shortage of reserve assets. Reserves in U.S. dollars in central banks continued to climb and countries began to restrict international transactions and borrow to meet balance of payments needs. SDRs came into existence on August 6, 1969 (First Amendment of the Articles of Agreement), valued at 0.888671 grams of fine gold (the amount of gold equal to one U.S. dollar). The SDR is not a currency, but rather an artificial reserve asset. It's a potential claim on the currencies of other IMF members, meaning that holders of SDRs can exchange them for "freely usable currencies" (currencies that are readily accepted in international trade—e.g., the U.S. dollar, the euro, and the yen). For example, Bolivia, whose currency is the boliviano (hardly anyone will touch it), can exchange its SDRs for U.S. dollars or euros or yen. The SDR is the IMF's unit of account, which means that all computations (except one) relating to currencies are done in SDRs. And check it out: Other international organizations use the SDR as a unit of account, such as the Nordic Investment Bank. Even private parties can use it as a unit of account— e.g., commercial banks that accept deposits expressed in SDRs. Today's SDR is defined as a basket of currencies: the pound sterling, the euro, the Japanese yen, and the U.S. dollar. This basket composition is reviewed every five years by the Fund's Executive Board. In November 2010 (the latest review), the weights of the basket currencies were revised using the value of exports of goods and services, as well as the amount of reserves of respective currencies held, by other IMF member countries.

Official Development Assistance (ODA)

ODA is comprised of medium- and long-term concessional loans (including a grant element of at least twenty-five percent—effectively a ten percent discount rate) and grants from multilateral (e.g., the World Bank) and bilateral (U.S. government) sources. ODA is intended to promote economic development in the countries and territories in the Development

Assistance Committee's (DAC) list of ODA recipients. The DAC is part of the Organisation for Economic Co-operation and Development (OECD), and its list includes a range of countries, from "least developed countries," such as Benin, to "upper middle income countries and territories," such as Jordan.

Customary International Law

It's dangerous to try to define customary international law (CIL) when we're asking what's up with that. An ancient concept, CIL boils down two questions: First, is there reasonably consistent state practice? For example, do most, if not all, states leave fisherman alone in a war? Second, do states feel they are under a legal obligation to conform to the state practice—what we call *opinio juris* in the biz. So do states leave the fisherman alone because they feel legally obligated to do so? It's rare to have a state say, "Yup, we feel a legal obligation to leave those fisherman alone." That's where legal scholars and judges can come into play and say, "In my learned opinion, I believe the consistent state practice and all of the surrounding circumstances, including historical evidence, demonstrate sufficient *opinio juris* to constitute customary international law." United Nations resolutions of the General Assembly are really problematic in terms of CIL. The U.N.'s Charter doesn't give the General Assembly the power to make law. But resolutions could be viewed as evidence of CIL. The International Court of Justice at the Hague has used resolutions in this way. Bottom line: General Assembly resolutions are at best what's called "soft law"—not really legally binding but not completely void of legal significance. What's up with that?

QUESTIONS FROM YOUR TALKING DOG

1.   So what if it's raining? I gotta stretch my legs and find a tree. So put on a jacket and answer this question: Why did the IBRD switch from reconstruction to development?

2.   Why can't the World Bank give you a loan so that you can buy decent dog food for me? You know, the canned food that could feed an entire village of starving children somewhere in the world?

3.   Yeah, it's coming down pretty hard. I like it. So let me ask. From a political point of view, why did project lending make sense? What is project lending, anyway?

4.   Can you remind me again what the difference is between IBRD and IDA lending?

5.   Do you envy John McCloy for making partner at Cravath in just five years? Don't worry, I'll still lick your face!

6.   I've seen some pretty dumb dogs, but how can countries be "retarded" in Black's words? And a follow-up: Did these World Bank Presidents, including McNamara, know anything about development?

7.   There's a tree! While I do my business, tell me what that "growth with equity" thing was all about?

8.   You've told me that McNamara was all about numbers, but he had a moral code, didn't he? I don't know why I ask because I have no idea what morals are other than you won't throw me in the microwave.

9.   So this guy was a rock star, huh? How did McNamara change the World Bank? Why did he change things?

10.   It sounds like they never had fights in the McNamara house. C'mon! Really? By the way, if you don't throw me that bone I'll rip your throat out. So what if I'm a Chihuahua!

11.   Before we turn around, tell me about McNamara's legacy.

12.   Was he like a really smart pit-bull? The one next door is really stupid.

<u>Chapter 4: Supplement</u>

4A. *McNamara's Pivotal 1966 Speech*

This speech turned heads before McNamara became World Bank President. McNamara's rhetoric. Hmmm . . . The frightening thing about it is that lots of folk at that time thought of developing countries in the same way. What does he mean when he says, "Without development, there can be no security"? Does he bring you to tears? Or at least prompt you to give him a standing ovation?

D. Hughes & R. McNamara, "Security in the Contemporary World," *Congressional Record* 112 (1966)

SECURITY IN THE CONTEMPORARY WORLD

Robert S. McNamara, Secretary of Defense
before the American Society of Newspaper Editors
Montreal, Canada, May 18th, 1966

Any American would be fortunate to visit this lovely island city, in this hospitable land. But there is a special satisfaction for a Secretary of Defense to cross the longest border in the world and realize that it is also the least armed border in the world. It prompts one to reflect how negative and narrow a notion of defense still clouds our century.

There is still among us an almost eradicable tendency to think of our security problem as being exclusively a military problem—and to think of the military problem as being exclusively a weapons-system or hardware problem.

* * *

From the point of view of combat readiness, the United States has never been militarily stronger. We intend to maintain that readiness. But if we think profoundly about the matter, it is clear that this purely military posture is not the central element in our security. A nation can reach the point at which it does not buy more security for itself simply by buying more military hardware. We are at that point. The decisive factor for a powerful nation already adequately armed is the character of its relationships with the world.

In this respect, there are three broad groups of nations: first, those that are struggling to develop; secondly, those free nations that have reached a level of strength and prosperity that enables them to contribute to the peace of the world; and finally, those nations who might tempted to make themselves our adversaries. For each of these groups, the United States, to preserve its intrinsic security, has to have distinctive sets of relationships. First, we have to help protect those developing countries which genuinely need and request our help and which, as an essential precondition, are willing and able to help themselves.

* * *

The Developing Nations

First, the developing nations. Roughly 100 countries today are caught up in the difficult transition from traditional to modern societies. There is no uniform rate of progress among them, and they range from primitive mosaic societies fractured by tribalism and held feebly together by the slenderest of political sinews to relatively sophisticated countries well on the road to agricultural sufficiency and industrial competence.

This sweeping surge of development, particularly across the whole southern half of the globe, has no parallel in history. It has turned traditionally listless areas of the world into seething cauldrons of change.

On the whole, it has not been a very peaceful process.

In the last 8 years alone there have been no less than 164 internationally significant outbreaks of violence, each of them specifically designed as a serious challenge to the authority, or the very existence, of the government in question. Eighty two different governments have been directly involved.

What is striking is that only 15 of these 164 significant resorts to violence have been military conflicts between two states. And not a single one of the 164 conflicts has been a formally declared war. Indeed, there has not been a formal declaration of war anywhere in the world since World War II.

The planet is becoming a more dangerous place to live on, not merely because of a potential nuclear holocaust but also because of the large number of de facto conflicts and because the trend of such conflicts is growing rather than diminishing. At the beginning of 1958, there were 23 prolonged insurgencies going on about the world. As of February 1, 1966, there were 40. Further, the total number of outbreaks of violence has increased each year: In 1958, there were 34; in 1965, there were 58.

The Relationship of Violence and Economic Status

But what is most significant of all is that there is a direct and constant relationship between the incidence of violence and the economic status of the countries afflicted. The World Bank divides nations on the basis of per capita income into four categories: rich, middle income, poor, and very poor.

The rich nations are those with a per capita income of $750 per year or more.

The current U.S. level is more than $2,700. There are 27 of these rich nations. They possess 75 percent of the world's wealth, though roughly only 25 percent of the world's population.

Since 1958, only one of these 27 nations has suffered a major internal upheaval on its own territory. But observe what happens at the other end of the economic scale.

Among the 38 very poor nations those with a per capita income of under $100 a year not less than 32 have suffered significant conflicts. Indeed, they have suffered an average of two major outbreaks of violence per country in the 8 year period. That is a great deal of conflict.

What is worse, it has been predominantly conflict of a prolonged nature. The trend holds predictably constant in the case of the two other categories: the poor and the middle income nations. Since 1958, 87 percent of the very poor nations, 69 percent of the poor nations, and 48 percent of the middle income nations have suffered serious violence.

There can, then, be no question but that there is an irrefutable relationship between violence and economic backwardness. And the trend of such violence is up, not down.

Now, it would perhaps be somewhat reassuring if the gap between the rich nations and the poor nations were closing and economic backwardness were significantly receding. But it is not. The economic gap is widening.

By the year 1970 over one half of the world's total population will live in the independent nations sweeping across the southern half of the planet. But this hungering half of the human race will by then command only one sixth of the world's total of goods and services. By the year 1975 the dependent children of these nations alone children under 15 years of age will equal the total population of the developed nations to the north.

Even in our own abundant societies, we have reason enough to worry over the tensions that coil and tighten among under-privileged young people and finally flail out in delinquency and crime. What are we to expect from a whole hemisphere of youth where mounting frustrations are likely to fester into eruptions of violence and extremism?

Annual per capita income in roughly half of the 80 underdeveloped nations that are members of the World Bank is rising by a paltry 1 percent a year or less. By the end of the century these nations, at their present rates of growth, will reach a per capita income of barely $170 a year. The United States, by the same criterion, will attain a per capita income of $4,500.

The conclusion to all of this is blunt and inescapable: Given the certain connection between economic stagnation and the incidence of violence, the years that lie ahead for the nations in the southern half of the globe are pregnant with violence.

U.S. Security and the Newly Developing World

This would be true even if no threat of Communist subversion existed as it clearly does. Both Moscow and Peking, however harsh their internal differences, regard the whole modernization process as an ideal environment for the growth of communism. Their experience with subversive internal war is extensive, and they have developed a considerable array of both doctrine and practical measures in the art of political violence.

What is often misunderstood is that Communists are capable of subverting, manipulating, and finally directing for their own ends the wholly legitimate grievances of a developing society.

But it would be a gross oversimplification to regard communism as the central factor in every conflict throughout the underdeveloped world. Of the 149 serious internal insurgencies in the past 8 years, Communists have been involved in only 58 of them—8 percent of the total—and this includes seven instances in which a Communist regime itself was the target of the uprising.

Whether Communists are involved or not, violence anywhere in a taut world transmits sharp signals through the complex gangli of international relations; and the security of the United States is related to the security and stability of nations half a globe away.

But neither conscience nor sanity itself suggests that the United States is, should or could be the global gendarme. Quite the contrary. Experience confirms what human nature suggests: that in most instances of internal violence the local people themselves are best able to deal directly with the situation within the framework of their own traditions.

The United States has no mandate from on high to police the world and no inclination to do so. There have been classic cases in which our deliberate non-action was the wisest action of all. Where our help is not sought, it is seldom prudent to volunteer. Certainly we have no charter to rescue floundering regimes who have brought violence on themselves by deliberately refusing to meet the legitimate expectations of their citizenry.

Further, throughout the next decade advancing technology will reduce the requirements for bases and staging rights at particular locations abroad, and the whole pattern of forward deployment will gradually change.

But, though all these caveats are clear enough, the irreducible fact remains that our security is related directly to the security of the newly developing world. And our role must be precisely this: to help provide security to those developing nations which genuinely need and request our help and which demonstrably are willing and able to help themselves.

Security and Development

The rub comes in this: We do not always grasp the meaning of the word "security" in this context. In a modernizing society, security means development.

Security is not military hardware, though it may include it. Security is not military force, though it may involve it. Security is not traditional military activity, though it may encompass it. Security is development. Without development, there can be no security. A developing nation that does not in fact develop simply cannot remain "secure." It cannot remain secure for the intractable reason that its own citizenry cannot shed its human nature.

If security implies anything, it implies a minimal measure of order and stability. Without internal development of at least a minimal degree, order and stability are simply not possible. They are not possible because human nature cannot be frustrated beyond intrinsic limits. It reacts because it must.

Now, that is what we do not always understand, and that is also what governments of modernizing nations do not always understand. But by emphasizing that security arises from development, I do not say that an underdeveloped nation cannot be subverted from within, or be aggressed upon from without, or be the victim of a combination of the two. It can. And to prevent any or all of these conditions, a nation does require appropriate military capabilities to deal with the specific problem. But the specific military problem is only a narrow facet of the broader security problem.

Military force can help provide law and order but only to the degree that a basis for law and order already exists in the developing society: a basic willingness on the part of the people to cooperate. The law and order is a shield, behind which the central fact of security—development—can be achieved.

Now we are not playing a semantic game with these words. The trouble is that we have been lost in a semantic jungle for too long. We have come to identify "security" with exclusively military phenomena, and most particularly with military hardware. But it just isn't so. And we need to accommodate to the facts of the matter if we want to see security survive and grow in the southern half of the globe.

Development means economic, social, and political progress. It means a reasonable standard of living, and the word "reasonable" in this context requires continual redefinition. What is "reasonable" in an earlier stage of development will become "unreasonable" in a later stage.

As development progresses, security progresses. And when the people of a nation have organized their own human and natural resources to provide themselves with what they need and expect out of life and have learned to compromise peacefully among competing demands in the larger national interest then their resistance to disorder and violence will be enormously increased.

Conversely, the tragic need of desperate men to resort to force to achieve the inner imperatives of human decency will diminish.

Military and Economic Spheres of U.S. Aid

Now, I have said that the role of the United States is to help provide security to these modernizing nations, providing they need and request our help and are clearly willing and able to help themselves. But what should our help be? Clearly, it should be help toward development. In the military sphere, that involves two broad categories of assistance.

We should help the developing nation with such training and equipment as is necessary to maintain the protective shield behind which development can go forward.

The dimensions of that shield vary from country to country, but what is essential is that it should be a shield and not a capacity for external aggression.

The second, and perhaps less understood category of military assistance in a modernizing nation, is training in civic action. Civic action is another one of those semantic puzzles. Too few Americans and too few officials in developing nations really comprehend what military civic action means. Essentially, it means using indigenous military forces for nontraditional military projects, projects that are useful to the local population in fields such as education, public works, health, sanitation, agriculture—indeed, anything connected with economic or social progress.

It has had some impressive results. In the past 4 years the U.S. assisted civic action program, worldwide, has constructed or repaired more than 10,000 miles of roads, built over 1,000 schools, hundreds of hospitals and clinics, and has provided medical and dental care to approximately 4 million people.

What is important is that all this was done by indigenous men in uniform. Quite apart from the developmental projects themselves, the program powerfully alters the negative image of the military man as the oppressive preserver of the stagnant status quo.

But assistance in the purely military sphere is not enough. Economic assistance is also essential. The President is determined that our aid should be hardheaded and rigorously realistic, that it should deal directly with the roots of underdevelopment and not merely attempt to alleviate the symptoms. His bedrock principle is that U.S. economic aid—no matter what its magnitude—is futile unless the country in question is resolute in making the primary effort itself. That will be the criterion, and that will be the crucial condition for all our future assistance.

Only the developing nations themselves can take the fundamental measures that make outside assistance meaningful. These measures are often unpalatable and frequently call for political courage and decisiveness. But to fail to undertake painful, but essential, reform inevitably leads to far more painful revolutionary violence. Our economic assistance is designed to offer a reasonable alternative to that violence. It is designed to help substitute peaceful progress for tragic internal conflict.

The United States intends to be compassionate and generous in this effort, but it is not an effort it can carry exclusively by itself. And thus it looks to those nations who have reached the point of self-sustaining prosperity to increase their contribution to the development and, thus, to the security of the modernizing world.

* * *

. . . Who is man? Is he a rational animal? If he is, then the goals can ultimately be achieved. If he is not, then there is little point in making the effort.

All the evidence of history suggests that man is indeed a rational animal but with a near infinite capacity for folly. His history seems largely a halting, but persistent, effort to raise his reason above his animality. He draws blueprints for utopia. But never quite gets it built. In the end he plugs away obstinately with the only building material really ever at hand [*sic*] his own part-comic, part-tragic, part-cussed, but part-glorious nature.

I, for one, would not count a global free society out. Coercion, after all, merely captures man. Freedom captivates him.

4B. *McNamara's Bank*

What a driven, smart, and manipulative dude as well as a control freak! And he wasn't even a lawyer! Check it out: He consulted with Norman

Borlaug. Any idea how important Borlaug was? Where was he born? Yeah, that's right, IOWA. There's an elementary school in Iowa City named after him. As you'll see, McNamara said "I don't want this to be known as McNamara's Bank."... C'mon!!

J. Kraske et al., *Robert S. McNamara: Champion of the Developing World* in <u>Bankers with a Mission</u>, 204–211 (1996), © **World Bank**

From the moment McNamara walked into the Bank, there had been no question who was in charge. He dominated the Bank, its staff, its board of executive directors, and almost any other audience that needed to be controlled in the pursuit of his mission. He relied on his ability to work hard and to absorb large amounts of written material on every relevant subject. He was always better prepared than anybody else and quicker on his feet than those with whom he dealt.

Toward the end of his tenure in the World Bank, McNamara reflected on his managerial orientation: "My background was a background of establishing objectives for institutions and then pursuing those objectives in effective ways . . . I always felt that business leadership had two primary responsibilities: one was to the stockholders of the firm and one was to the society they were part of. And the objectives we formulated were in those terms." Earlier, he had said of his style as a manager: "The role of a public manager is very similar to the role of a private manager; in each case he has the option of following one of two major alternative courses of action. He can either act as a judge or a leader . . . . I have always believed in and endeavored to follow the active leadership role as opposed to the passive judicial role.

McNamara recognized that he needed the support of the executive directors and the governors whom they represented. He was consequently determined to ensure that he obtained the backing of the executive directors with a minimum of fuss. William Clark, vice president for external relations, described the first board meeting McNamara chaired on April 9, 1968. "The meeting went extremely badly. One by one, the executive directors attacked a staff paper on the effects of devaluation on the Bank's assets." McNamara called a meeting of the president's council and expressed his dismay: "In three hours nothing had been achieved, and there had been no single mention of development. He had come to the Bank to deal with development issues, . . . not to participate in a debating society. In future, no proposal should be taken to the board unless it was already firmly established that it had the support of the majority of the voting power."

McNamara took pains to avoid any outward manifestation of his dominating role. He encouraged the executive directors to speak out on issues and gave them the opportunity to discuss policy and operational matters at length. Without exception, he treated them with respect and conveyed the sense that their importance grew along with that of the Bank. His sense of accountability to the Bank's shareholders compelled him to ensure that the board was fully informed. He presented the board with a growing flow of issue papers and action programs. Although this practice conveyed his view of the importance of the board as an institution, the preparation of elaborate papers on every conceivable issue was also a way of overwhelming the executive directors. He kept them busy while he was running the Bank. Of course, he read every paper that went to the board himself. In board discussions he knew the weaknesses of every project and could always answer the questions raised better than his staff. He made it a point to rephrase questions asked by the executive directors to make sure that staff in their answers addressed the real issues. If the staff gave the wrong answer, he would provide the right answer. All the while, he would be patient. He never criticized staff members who had made a mess of things, leaving that job to his vice president. You knew you had botched it if he turned to the vice president and asked him to comment further.

McNamara would usually summarize the discussion at the conclusion of a meeting. He would do that brilliantly, often condensing many hours of discussion succinctly and masterfully. But in the process, some of the directors would find that their objections had somehow been glided over and that the conclusion reflected what McNamara had wanted all along. So there was a growing sense among the executive directors that they were being manipulated.

This feeling became more pronounced as the McNamara presidency advanced. The board members' resentment grew as McNamara succeeded in raising their sense of their own importance but not their sense of effective participation. They spent more time consulting with each other outside the board meetings, coordinating their positions. On critical issues they might come to a board meeting with, in effect, a board position already arrived at, even with designated speakers in some instances. To defuse the situation, McNamara began to meet informally with the board outside the board room, in his own office, to thrash out sensitive issues before they came before the board. This transferred the deliberations and the decisionmaking process from the board room to his own office.

McNamara's behavior was determined in part by his view of large meetings. To him the purpose of large meetings was to ratify decisions; consequently they had to be controlled. He did not believe in the value of debates in facilitating the exchange of views. He felt uncomfortable with large numbers of people in the room. Dissent in large meetings became a challenge to his authority, and challenges had to be put down. This earned him the reputation of being intolerant of others' views. In contrast, those who dealt closely with him, one on one, regarded him as considerate, interested, and approachable—as someone who liked to be informed and challenged in private discussions.

The number of people in the Bank who dealt directly with McNamara remained limited. He relied on Burke Knapp, the senior vice president, operations, to run the Bank and execute his programs. He valued Knapp's experience and judgment. Until he retired, Knapp represented the traditions of the Bank established during the Black period, especially the strong belief in the value of the Bank's project work. He was able to reconcile those traditions with the boldness of McNamara's approach. Ernest Stern, who eventually succeeded Knapp as senior vice president, operations, was the only one who kept up with McNamara. He was able to match McNamara in the breadth and detail of the treatment of issues, and the president consulted him on a broad range of issues. Otherwise, McNamara relied on people to perform particular functions. He would turn to Chenery on economic matters, to Baum and Yudelman on rural development issues, to Cargill and Rotberg on IDA and financial matters, and to William Clark to get in touch with people, especially outside the United States.

When he needed to stimulate his thinking, McNamara seemed to give much more of his time and attention to people outside the Bank. He kept up an intensive flow of communications with people such as Barbara Ward, Maurice Strong, David Rockefeller, and a number of other public figures who gave him new ideas. He also liked to talk directly to experts on technical subjects that interested him—with Norman Borlaug on high-yielding wheat or with Daniel Benor on agricultural extension—and so add to his already formidable arsenal of information.

McNamara remained invisible to the majority of the Bank's staff. He did not walk the corridors of the Bank, never dropped into other people's offices, never ate in the Bank's executive dining room, let alone the cafeteria. As a result, the attitude of the staff toward him remained ambivalent. Everyone admired and respected his leadership. They were pleased with his thrust into rural development and urban development, the poverty focus of the institution, and the desire to be more effective as a development institution. But while they felt proud to be part of the Bank's mission, they also worried that they might not count, that they were just "data gatherers."

McNamara relied on his personal assistants and his managers, resisting strenuously any suggestions to be more outgoing. Davidson Sommers, who had been the Bank's general counsel in the 1950s and worked as a consultant for the president for about ten years, recalls that he wrote a memorandum to McNamara advising him of the poor state of internal communications. McNamara called him into his office and said, "Dave, you're absolutely right. Those guys don't know how to manage." Sommers pointed out that middle-level managers needed a model and that McNamara could improve the morale of the institution if he would take some time to walk around the Bank and stick his head in a few offices. McNamara replied, "Oh, Dave, I don't want to do that. I don't want this to be known as McNamara's Bank." In fact, even the practice of monthly senior staff meetings attended by departmental managers progressively fell into disuse. He rejected the suggestion that he address larger staff gatherings with the argument that he could not possibly contribute to such a meeting the equivalent in value of the time wasted by a large audience of staff members. Understandably, McNamara had "a reputation for being remote and for not getting to know people in the Bank very well."

McNamara preferred written communications to oral reports. This was a matter of efficiency—he felt that he could read much faster than anyone could talk—but it was also a question of being in control. The way to gain McNamara's attention was to give him a memorandum on which he could focus. For his trips he required elaborate briefing books, which he perused thoroughly, as his marginal notations showed. Every meeting required a detailed written brief. Although there were specific instructions about the length and format of briefing papers, he never complained about the volume of briefing materials prepared for him. Of course, he preferred whenever possible to have numbers and tables.

McNamara had arrived at the Bank with a well-established reputation as a modern manager who had successfully run large organizations through the use of systems analysis. Peter Cargill was mocking his colleagues when he reported to his staff about one of the first encounters between McNamara and the senior managers of the Bank, "Everybody was trying to be cute by asking McNamara about the merits of systems analysis." Although the term was apparently never used in the Bank, the spirit of systems and of control certainly pervaded the Bank in those years. Evaluations of his role as a manager—the field on which his professional reputation was based—were mixed. Some thought that he was a superb manager who achieved institutional objectives with maximum efficiency. Others felt that his tendency to centralize decisionmaking and his attention to detail prevented a more effective use of the staff's potential and the necessary strengthening of institutional safeguards.

Given McNamara's success as a leader, it is fair to ask whether his transformation of the institution would be lasting. He had surely come to personify the Bank as nobody before or after him. He had so shaped the Bank to represent his views, his style, and his methods that the Bank had become "McNamara's Bank." This fateful dependence had created a management problem: it would be very difficult for a newcomer to take over and run the institution, especially a newcomer with less energy than McNamara had brought to the job.

McNamara's Legacy

Although McNamara claimed that he was anxious to leave the Bank at the end of his second term, he had been in fact very eager to accept a third term. It was a sign of his dedication to the mission of the Bank, however, that he announced abruptly in June 1980 that he would leave before completing his third five-year contract. He may have had personal reasons for wanting to quit. The principal consideration, however, seems to have been his recognition that the shift to conservatism, already plainly evident in the United Kingdom, would shape the outcome of the 1980 presidential elections in the United States. The task of the Bank, the fight against poverty, had hardly begun. The challenges of the approaching decade of the 1980s would be daunting, and he thought they called for a continuity of leadership he would no longer be able to provide.

The Bank McNamara left in 1981 was completely transformed from the institution he had entered thirteen years earlier. It was a much larger organization. It was also much more complex. Its membership had continued to expand, and with the People's Republic of China's assuming full participation, it was well on its way to becoming a universal organization. Its popular name, World Bank, had become appropriately descriptive of the institution and of the global role it now played.

4C. *Growth and Inequality in Asia*

In the text we discuss the false choice between economic growth and equity. This excerpt from an IMF publication makes the point that income inequality is an impediment to economic growth. The authors use Asia as an example. What's your reaction to their analysis? Note the difference between poverty reduction and inequality. By the way, financial inclusion is an important topic today. We'll get to that in Chapter 21.

R. Balakrishnan et al., "An Achilles' Heel,"
Finance and Development (2013)

An Achilles' Heel

Inequality threatens Asia's growth miracle

Over the past 25 years, Asia has grown faster than any other region of the world, leading many to label the coming years the "Asian Century." With the region's successful integration into the global marketplace and its large middle class increasingly coming to the fore, there are good reasons to think that the world economy will increasingly shift toward Asia in the coming decades.

However, Asia's fortunes are threatened by a surge in inequality that has accompanied that quarter century of growth. Paradoxically, the same growth that reduced absolute poverty has created a widening wedge between haves and have-nots. This polarization has not only tarnished the region's economic achievements but, left unaddressed, could leave Asia's promise unfulfilled. As a consequence, policymakers throughout the region are looking for ways to arrest rising inequality and make growth more inclusive.

We look at what lies behind this worsening income distribution, why it matters, and what can be done to make Asian economic growth more inclusive.

Inclusive growth matters

Society should be interested in confronting inequality of income and wealth not just for ethical reasons but because it also has more tangible implications.

For a given growth rate, rising inequality typically means less poverty reduction. A growing body of research also shows that income disparities are associated with worse economic outcomes, including lower growth and greater volatility. At a fundamental level, income inequality is now widely thought to retard growth and development, for such reasons as limiting the accumulation of human capital in a society (see "More or Less," in the September 2011 F & D). Recent work by Berg and Ostry (2011) also argues that unequal societies are less likely to sustain growth over a long period.

The most commonly used summary measure of income distribution is the Gini index. It varies from zero, which signifies complete equality because everyone has the same income, to 100, where there is total inequality because just one person has all of it. The lower the Gini index, then, the more equitably income is distributed among the various members of society. Relatively egalitarian societies like Sweden and Canada have Gini indices between 25 and 35, whereas most developed economies are clustered around 40. Many developing economies have Gini indices that are even higher.

Changes over time in a country's Gini index can help demonstrate whether economic growth has been "inclusive"—that is, whether its benefits are increasingly shared by people at all income levels. A falling Gini index would suggest that the distribution of income is becoming more even.

More narrowly, we could home in on the most vulnerable—say, for example, the bottom 20 percent of the population—and see how much of the fruits of growth accrue to them. For example, we could ask how a 1 percent increase in national income affects them. If their incomes rise by at least 1 percent, growth can be said to be inclusive. But if the incomes of the poor rise by less, growth is not inclusive, because it leaves them relatively worse off.

Asia's blemished record

Over the past two and a half decades, growth in most Asian economies has been higher, on average, than in other emerging markets. This growth has enabled significant reductions in absolute poverty—the number of people living in extreme poverty (on less than $1.25 a day) was almost halved, from more than 1.5 billion in 1990 to a little over 850 million in 2008. Despite this impressive overall record in poverty reduction, Asia is still home to two-thirds of the world's poor, with China and India together accounting for almost half . . .

Poverty and inequality in India and China

Poverty in China and India has been considerably reduced since the two largest countries began their economic takeoffs—three decades ago in China, two in India.

China's poverty fell fastest during the early 1980s and mid-1990s, spurred by rural economic reforms, low initial inequality, and access to health care and education opportunities. In 1981, China was one of the world's poorest nations with 84 percent of the population living on less than $1.25 a day— then the fifth-largest poverty incidence in the world. By 2008, 13 percent were in poverty, well below the developing economy average. India has also reduced poverty, although at a slower rate than China. In 1981, 60 percent of Indians lived on less than $1.25 a day, fewer than in China. By 2010, the share fell to 33 percent, but was two and a half times higher than in China.

However, inequality has increased in both countries. According to official estimates, China's Gini (where zero represents the most equal income distribution and 100 the most unequal) increased from 37 in the mid-1990s to 49 in 2008. India's Gini ticked up from 33 in 1993 to 37 in 2010, according to the Asian Development Bank (2012). There is also significant inequality based on gender, caste, and access to social services.

Between one-third and two-thirds of overall inequality in China and India reflects a widening of disparities between rural and urban areas, as well as between regions.

Moreover, inequality has increased across Asia. This is a new phenomenon for the region and contrasts starkly with its dramatic period of economic takeoff in the three decades before 1990. "Growth with equity" was the mantra during this period, as Japan and the Asian tigers were able to combine fast growth with relatively low—and in many cases falling— inequality. Asia's recent dismal record on inequality is therefore a stunning turnaround.

From an international perspective, inequality has risen faster in Asia over the past 25 years than in any other region (see Chart 1). The rise has been especially pronounced in China and east Asia, leaving Gini indices in many parts of the region between 35 and 45. That is still lower than in most sub-

Saharan African and Latin American countries, which typically have Ginis in the range of 50. But countries in Latin America and sub-Saharan Africa (as well as in the Middle East and North Africa) have on average bucked the global trend and reduced inequality in the past quarter century, shrinking the gap between them and Asia.

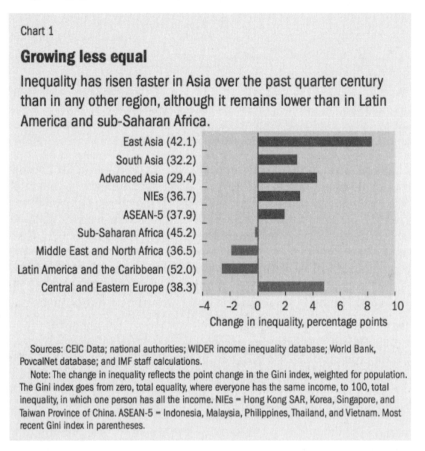

Chart 1

Growing less equal

Inequality has risen faster in Asia over the past quarter century than in any other region, although it remains lower than in Latin America and sub-Saharan Africa.

Change in inequality, percentage points

Sources: CEIC Data; national authorities; WIDER income inequality database; World Bank, PovcalNet database; and IMF staff calculations.

Note: The change in inequality reflects the point change in the Gini index, weighted for population. The Gini index goes from zero, total equality, where everyone has the same income, to 100, total inequality, in which one person has all the income. NIEs = Hong Kong SAR, Korea, Singapore, and Taiwan Province of China. ASEAN-5 = Indonesia, Malaysia, Philippines, Thailand, and Vietnam. Most recent Gini index in parentheses.

In particular, even as the purchasing power of Asia's citizens has grown, the incomes of the bottom 20 percent have not risen as much as those of the rest of the population (see Chart 2). This is true both in relatively less developed economies, including China and much of south Asia, and in more advanced economies like Hong Kong SAR, Korea, Singapore, and Taiwan Province of China. Asia's experiences are a marked contrast to those of emerging market economies in other parts of the world, in particular in Latin America, where the incomes of the bottom 20 percent have risen by more than those of other sections of the population since 1990. So while Asia has undoubtedly led the globe in terms of rates of growth over the past 25 years, the nature of that growth has arguably been the least inclusive among all emerging regions.

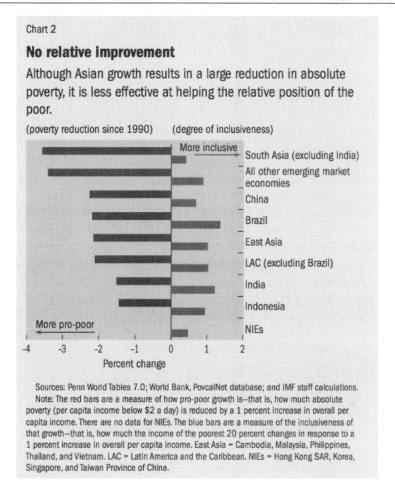

Chart 2

No relative improvement

Although Asian growth results in a large reduction in absolute poverty, it is less effective at helping the relative position of the poor.

(poverty reduction since 1990)   (degree of inclusiveness)

More inclusive →   South Asia (excluding India)

All other emerging market economies

China

Brazil

East Asia

LAC (excluding Brazil)

India

Indonesia

More pro-poor ←   NIEs

-4   -3   -2   -1   0   1   2

Percent change

Sources: Penn World Tables 7.0; World Bank, PovcalNet database; and IMF staff calculations.
Note: The red bars are a measure of how pro-poor growth is—that is, how much absolute poverty (per capita income below $2 a day) is reduced by a 1 percent increase in overall per capita income. There are no data for NIEs. The blue bars are a measure of the inclusiveness of that growth—that is, how much the income of the poorest 20 percent changes in response to a 1 percent increase in overall per capita income. East Asia = Cambodia, Malaysia, Philippines, Thailand, and Vietnam. LAC = Latin America and the Caribbean. NIEs = Hong Kong SAR, Korea, Singapore, and Taiwan Province of China.

Less inclusive

Rising inequality has been an almost global phenomenon over the past two and a half decades, with Gini indices generally ticking up across advanced and developing economies. Many analysts have attributed the rise at least in part to international forces beyond the control of any one country, such as globalization and technological change that favors skilled workers over unskilled ones.

The difference between the Asian experience and that of the rest of the world suggests that, in addition to global factors, there may be some specific features of Asia's growth that have exacerbated the rise of inequality in the region. Addressing these factors—which our analysis suggests include fiscal policies, the structure of labor markets, and access to banking and other financial services—may hold the key to broadening the benefits of Asia's growth, and hence sustaining it. In particular, increases in spending on education, years of schooling, and the labor share of income, as well as policies that expand access to financial services, significantly increase the inclusiveness of growth—that is, how much the income of the poorest rises when average incomes increase. Asia has fallen behind in many of these areas.

Public spending on the social sector is low, as a result of policy choices: The relatively low amount of public spending on health and education in Asia points to an important potential role for fiscal (tax and spending) policy in strengthening inclusiveness (see Chart 3). In advanced economies, taxes and transfer policies (such as those dealing with welfare and unemployment) have been estimated to reduce inequality on average by about one-quarter, based on Gini indices. In contrast, the redistributive impact of fiscal policy in Asia is severely restricted by lower tax-to-GDP ratios, which average half of those in advanced economies and are among the lowest in developing regions (Bastagli, Coady, and Gupta, 2012). The result is substantially lower levels of social spending. Greater reliance on less progressive tax and spending instruments also adds to inequality. In Asia, indirect taxes, such as those on consumption of goods and services, account for half of tax revenue, compared with less than one-third in advanced economies. Such taxes are paid disproportionately by the poor.

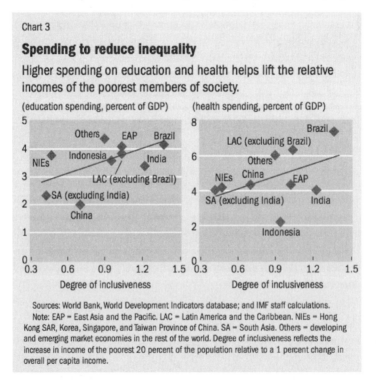

Chart 3

Spending to reduce inequality

Higher spending on education and health helps lift the relative incomes of the poorest members of society.

Sources: World Bank, World Development Indicators database; and IMF staff calculations.
Note: EAP = East Asia and the Pacific. LAC = Latin America and the Caribbean. NIEs = Hong Kong SAR, Korea, Singapore, and Taiwan Province of China. SA = South Asia. Others = developing and emerging market economies in the rest of the world. Degree of inclusiveness reflects the increase in income of the poorest 20 percent of the population relative to a 1 percent change in overall per capita income.

The labor share of income has shrunk considerably: In the past two decades across Asia there has been a significant decline in labor's share of total income and an increase in the share that goes to capital, averaging about

15 percentage points, according to the Asian Development Bank (2012). This contributes to inequality because capital income tends to go to wealthier people, while poor people who work in the formal sector earn most of their income from wages. Technological change is part of the reason the capital share of national income has risen—and also part of the reason economic growth does not trigger as big an increase in demand for labor as it used to. But part of the changes in the capital-labor share of income may also be attributable to a deliberate bias toward industries that have a high capital-to-labor ratio in some parts of Asia. That tilt is reflected in their manufacturing and export-led policies, relatively low employment gains compared with their rapid growth rates, and the concentration of wealth in the hands of corporations rather than households. In addition, rising inequality is linked to the relatively weaker bargaining power of workers. Many workers in Asia toil in the mainly unregulated informal sector, which depresses wages. Moreover, even in the formal sector, lower-skilled workers have little to no bargaining power to raise relative wages.

Financial access is thin: Lack of access to finance is a major impediment in many parts of Asia, where more than half the population and a significant proportion of small and medium-sized enterprises have no connection to the formal financial system of banking, insurance, or securities. Research has demonstrated that financial development not only promotes economic growth but also helps apportion it more evenly. This is because lack of access to financial services and costs associated with transactions and contract enforcement take the biggest toll on poor people and small-scale entrepreneurs, who typically lack collateral, credit histories, and business connections. These deficiencies make it almost impossible for poor people to obtain financing, even if they have projects with high prospective returns. By fostering the development of financial markets and financial instruments—such as insurance products that make it easier for businesses and individuals to cope with shocks such as accidents or death—governments can both spur growth and help ensure that it is distributed more equitably.

Improving performance

So, on this basis, what types of policies might help Asian economies redress the recent period of less inclusive growth?

Fiscal policies: Asian governments must increase spending on education, health, and social protection, while maintaining fiscal prudence. Part of this could be achieved by raising tax-to-GDP ratios, particularly through a more progressive tax system or by broadening the base of direct taxes to boost the redistributive impact of fiscal policy. At the same time, targeted social expenditures aimed at vulnerable households could be increased. Conditional cash transfer programs—which require a specific socially desirable action from a household, such as increased school attendance or vaccinations—are on the rise in low-income emerging market economies. Brazil's Bolsa Familia and Mexico's Opportunidades are two of the largest such programs and are considered successful in raising the incomes of the poor.

Labor market policies: Labor policies that enhance rural employment programs, increase the number of workers in the formal sector and reduce the size of the informal sector, remove impediments to labor mobility, and enhance worker training and skills could disproportionately help lower-skilled members of the labor force. In addition, the introduction of, or increases in, minimum wages has also been advocated in some countries to support the income of low-earning workers. For example, China's announcement in February 2013 of a 35-point plan to tackle income inequality included a provision to raise minimum wages to at least 40 percent of average salaries across most regions by 2015. In general, we found that inclusiveness is positively associated with the degree of employment protection and minimum wage levels (see Chart 4).

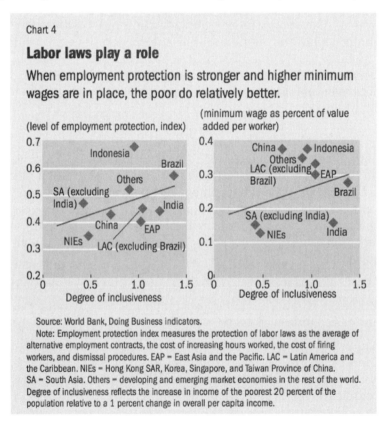

Chart 4

Labor laws play a role

When employment protection is stronger and higher minimum wages are in place, the poor do relatively better.

Source: World Bank, Doing Business indicators.
Note: Employment protection index measures the protection of labor laws as the average of alternative employment contracts, the cost of increasing hours worked, the cost of firing workers, and dismissal procedures. EAP = East Asia and the Pacific. LAC = Latin America and the Caribbean. NIEs = Hong Kong SAR, Korea, Singapore, and Taiwan Province of China. SA = South Asia. Others = developing and emerging market economies in the rest of the world. Degree of inclusiveness reflects the increase in income of the poorest 20 percent of the population relative to a 1 percent change in overall per capita income.

Financial access: Recommendations based on international experience include expanding credit availability by promoting rural finance, extending microcredit (modest loans to small entrepreneurial operations), subsidizing lending to the poor, promoting credit information sharing, and developing venture capital markets for start-up businesses.

Follow through

If Asian countries pursue policy measures to broaden the benefits of growth, notably enhanced spending on health and primary and secondary education, stronger social safety nets, labor market interventions for lower-income workers, and financial inclusion, they could stem the tide of rising inequality.

Many of these policies have the added potential to reduce the bias toward capital and large corporate entities, broadening the benefits of growth for household incomes and consumption. In this way, they could also facilitate the needed change in Asia's economic model from external to domestic demand that would prolong the region's growth miracle and support global rebalancing. The stakes are high. Without action to redress inequality, Asia may find it difficult to sustain its rapid rates of growth and take a position at the center of the world economy in the years to come.

4D. *Charter of Economic Rights and Duties of States*

CERDS reflects a framework of development that prevailed in the 1970s. Can you describe it looking only at the Charter? To what extent are its elements legitimate? To what extent are its elements hypocritical? What is justice according to the Charter?

Charter of Economic Rights and Duties of States
GA Res. 3281(xxix), UN GAOR, 29th Sess.,
Supp. No. 31 (1974) 50

The General Assembly,

Recalling that the United Nations Conference on Trade and Development, in its resolution 45 (III) of 18 May 1972, stressed the urgency to establish generally accepted norms to govern international economic relations systematically and recognized that it is not feasible to establish a just order and a stable world as long as a charter to protect the rights of all countries, and in particular the developing States, is not formulated.

Recalling further that in the same resolution it was decided to establish a Working Group of governmental representatives to draw up a draft Charter of Economic Rights and Duties of States, which the General Assembly, in its resolution 3037 (XXVII) of 19 December 1972, decided should be composed of forty Member States.

Noting that, in its resolution 3082 (XXVIII) of 6 December 1973, it reaffirmed its conviction of the urgent need to establish or improve norms of universal application for the development of international economic relations on a just and equitable basis and urged the Working Group on the Charter of Economic Rights and Duties of States to complete, as the first step in the codification and development of the matter, the elaboration of a final draft Charter of Economic Rights and Duties of States, to be considered and approved by the General Assembly at its twenty-ninth session.

Bearing in mind the spirit and terms of its resolutions *3201 (S-VI)* and *3202 (S-VI)* of 1 May 1974, containing, respectively, the *Declaration* and the *Programme of Action* on the Establishment of a New International Economic Order, which underlined the vital importance of the Charter to be adopted by the General Assembly at its twenty-ninth session and stressed the fact that the Charter shall constitute an effective instrument towards the establishment of a new system of international economic relations based on equity, sovereign equality and interdependence of the interests of developed and developing countries.

Having examined the report of the Working Group on the Charter of Economic Rights and Duties of States on its fourth session, transmitted to the Generally Assembly by the Trade and Development Board at its fourteenth session.

Expressing its appreciation to the Working Group on the Charter of Economic Rights and Duties of States which, as a result of the task performed in its four sessions held between February 1973 and June 1974, assembled the elements required for the completion and adoption of the Charter of Economic Rights and Duties at the twenty-ninth session of the General Assembly, as previously recommended.

Adopts and solemnly proclaims the following Charter:

Charter of economic rights and duties of states

Preamble

The General Assembly,

Reaffirming the fundamental purposes of the United Nations, in particular the maintenance of international peace and security, the development of friendly relations among nations and the achievement of international co-operation in solving international problems in the economic and social fields,

Affirming the need for strengthening international co-operation for development,

Declaring that it is a fundamental purpose of the present Charter to promote the establishment of the new international economic order, based on equality, sovereign equality, interdependence, common interest and co-operation among all States, irrespective of their economic and social systems,

Desirous of contributing to the criterion of conditions for:

a. The attainment of wider prosperity among all countries and of higher standards of living for all peoples,

b. The promotion by the entire international community of the economic and social progress of all countries, especially developing countries,

c. The encouragement of co-operation, on the basis of mutual advantage and equitable benefits for all peace-loving States which are willing to carry out the provisions of the present Charter, in the economic, trade, scientific and technical fields, regardless of political, economic or social systems,

d. The overcoming of main obstacles in the way of economic development of the developing countries,

e. The acceleration of the economic growth of developing countries with a view to bridging the economic gap between developing and developed countries,

f. The protection, preservation and enhancement of the environment,

Mindful of the need to establish and maintain a just and equitable economic and social order through:

a. The achievement of more rational and equitable international economic relations and the encouragement of structural changes in the world economy,

b. The creation of conditions which permit the further expansion of trade and intensification of economic co-operation among all nations,

c. The strengthening of the economic independence of developing countries,

d. The establishment and promotion of international economic relations, taking into account the agreed differences in development of the developing countries and their specific needs,

Determined to promote collective economic security for development, in particular of the developing countries, with strict respect for the sovereign equality of each State and through the co-operation of the entire international community,

* * *

Reiterating that the responsibility for the development of every country rests primarily upon itself but that concomitant and effective international cooperation is an essential factor for the full achievement of its own development goals.

Firmly convinced of the urgent need to evolve a substantially improved system of international economic relations,

Solemnly adopts the present Charter of Economic Rights and Duties of States.

Chapter I

Fundamentals of international economic relations

Economic as well as political and other relations among States shall be governed, inter alia, by the following principles:

- a.   Sovereignty, territorial integrity and political independence of States;

- b.   Sovereign equality of all States;

* * *

- g.   Equal rights and self-determination of peoples;

* * *

Chapter II

Economic rights and duties of states

Article 1

Every State has the sovereign and inalienable right to choose its economic system as well as it political, social and cultural systems in accordance with the will of its people, without outside interference, coercion or threat in any form whatsoever.

Article 2

1.   Every State has and shall freely exercise full permanent sovereignty, including possession, use and disposal, over all its wealth, natural resources and economic activities.

2.   Each State has the right:

- a.   To regulate and exercise authority over foreign investment within its national jurisdiction in accordance with its laws and regulations and in conformity with its national objectives and priorities. No State shall be compelled to grant preferential treatment to foreign investment;

- b.   To regulate and supervise the activities of transnational corporations within its national jurisdiction and take measures to ensure that such activities comply with its laws, rules and regulations and conform with its economic and social policies. Transnational corporations shall not intervene in the internal affairs of a host State. Every State should, with full regard for its sovereign rights, cooperate with other States in the exercise of the right set forth in this subparagraph;

c.   To nationalize, expropriate or transfer ownership of foreign property, in which case appropriate compensation should be paid by the State adopting such measures, taking into account its relevant laws and regulations and all circumstances that the State considers pertinent. In any case where the question of compensation gives rise to a controversy, it shall be settled under the domestic law of the nationalizing State and by its tribunals, unless it is freely and mutually agreed by all States concerned that other peaceful means be sought on the basis of the sovereign equality of States and in accordance with the principle of free choice of means.

* * *

Article 4

Every State has the right to engage in international trade and other forms of economic co-operation irrespective of any differences in political, economic and social systems. No State shall be subjected to discrimination of any kind based solely on such differences. In the pursuit of international trade and other forms of economic co-operation, every State is free to choose the forms of organization of its foreign economic relations and to enter into bilateral and multilateral arrangements consistent with its international obligations and with the needs of international economic co-operation.

* * *

Article 7

Every State has the primary responsibility to promote the economic, social and cultural development of its people. To this end, each State has the right and the responsibility to choose its means and goals of development, fully to mobilize and use its resources, to implement progressive economic and social reforms and to ensure the full participation of its people in the process and benefits of development. All States have the duty, individually and collectively, to co-operate in eliminating obstacles that hinder such mobilization and use.

Article 8

States should co-operate in facilitating more rational and equitable international economic relations and in encouraging structural changes in the context of a balanced world economy in harmony with the needs and interests of all countries, especially developing countries, and should take appropriate measures to this end.

Article 9

All States have the responsibility to co-operate in the economic, social, cultural, scientific and technological fields for the promotion of economic and social progress throughout the world, especially that of the developing countries.

Article 10

All States are juridically equal and, as equal members of the international community, have the right to participate fully and effectively in the international decision-making process in the solution of world economic, financial and monetary problems, inter alia, through the appropriate international organizations in accordance with their existing and evolving rules, and to share in the benefits resulting therefrom.

Article 11

All States should co-operate to strengthen and continuously improve the efficiency of international organizations in implementing measures to stimulate the general economic progress of all countries, particularly of developing countries, and therefore should co-operate to adapt them, when appropriate, to the changing needs of international economic co-operation.

* * *

Article 13

1.   Every State has the right to benefit from the advances and development in science and technology for the acceleration of its economic and social development.

2.   All States should promote international scientific and technological co-operation and the transfer of technology, with proper regard for all legitimate interests including, inter alia, the rights and duties of holders, suppliers and recipients of technology. In particular, all States should facilitate the access of developing countries to the achievements of modern science and technology, the transfer of technology and the creation of indigenous technology for the benefit of the developing countries in forms and in accordance with procedures which are suited to their economies and their needs.

3.   Accordingly, developed countries should co-operate with the developing countries in the establishment, strengthening and development of their scientific and technological infrastructures and their scientific research and technological activities so as to help to expand and transform the economies of developing countries.

4.   All States should co-operate in research with a view to evolving further internationally accepted guidelines or regulations for the transfer of technology, taking fully into account the interest of developing countries.

Article 14

Every State has the duty to co-operate in promoting a steady and increasing expansion and liberalization of world trade and an improvement in the welfare and living standards of all peoples, in particular those of developing countries. Accordingly, all States should co-operate, inter alia, towards the progressive dismantling of obstacles to trade and the improvement of the international framework for the conduct of world trade and, to these ends, co-ordinated efforts shall be made to solve in an equitable way the trade problems of all countries, taking into account the specific trade problems of the developing countries.

* * *

Article 16

1.   It is the right and duty of all States, individually and collectively, to eliminate colonialism, apartheid, racial discrimination, neo-colonialism and all forms of foreign aggression, occupation and domination, and the economic and social consequences thereof, as a prerequisite for development. States which practise such coercive policies are economically responsible to the countries, territories and peoples affected for the restitution and full compensation for the exploitation and depletion of, and damages to, the natural and all other resources of those countries, territories and peoples. It is the duty of all States to extend assistance to them.

* * *

Article 17

International co-operation for development in the shared goal and common duty of all States. Every State should co-operate with the efforts of developing countries to accelerate their economic and social development by providing favourable external conditions and by extending active assistance to them, consistent with their development needs and objectives, with strict respect for the sovereign equality of States and free of any conditions derogating from their sovereignty.

Article 18

Developed countries should extend, improve and enlarge the system of generalized non-reciprocal and non-discriminatory tariff preferences to the developing countries consistent with the relevant agreed conclusions and relevant decisions as adopted on this subject, in the framework of the competent international organizations. Developed countries should also give serious consideration to the adoption of other differential measures, in areas where this is feasible and appropriate and in ways which will provide special and more favourable treatment, in order to meet the trade and development needs of the developing countries. In the conduct of international economic relations the developed countries should endeavour to avoid measures having a negative effect on the development of the national economies of the developing countries, as promoted by generalized tariff preferences and other generally agreed differential measures in their favour.

Article 19

With a view to accelerating the economic growth of developing countries and bridging the economic gap between developed and developing countries, developed countries should grant generalized preferential, non-reciprocal and non-discriminatory treatment to developing countries in those fields of international economic co-operation where it may be feasible.

* * *

Article 22

1.   All States should respond to the generally recognized or mutually agreed development needs and objectives of developing countries by promoting increased net flows of real resources to the developing countries from all sources, taking into account any obligations and commitments undertaken by the States concerned, in order to reinforce the efforts of developing countries to accelerate their economic and social development.

2.   In this context, consistent with the aims and objectives mentioned above and taking into account any obligations and commitments undertaken in this regard, it should be their endeavour to increase the net amount of financial flows from official sources to developing countries and to improve the terms and conditions thereof.

3.   The flow of development assistance resources should include economic and technical assistance.

* * *

Article 28

All States have the duty to co-operate in achieving adjustments in the prices of exports of developing countries in relation to prices of their imports so as to promote just and equitable terms of trade for them, in a manner which is remunerative for producers and equitable for producers and consumers.

* * *

CHAPTER 5

THE 1980s DEBT CRISIS AND THE LOST DECADE

■ ■ ■

In this chapter we'll tell you about the first major financial crisis after the fall of the Bretton Woods System, the 1980s debt crisis. It was a big deal in a lot of ways—we're going to concentrate on Latin America (there's a supplement on Africa's experience—5C). First, it gave the International Monetary Fund (IMF) a highly visible role in crisis management. Although many observers criticized the Fund (and the World Bank) for its handling of the crisis, it helped bring about a system (however muddled) that eventually resolved it. The Fund was able to do this by bringing together commercial banks, debtor countries, and other entities involved in the crisis. Oh, are you wondering whether there's a global bankruptcy court— yeah, many of the debtor countries in the crisis were bankrupt—that could've taken care of this? In your dreams.

The debt crisis also illustrated the IMF's deep involvement in development issues. With the collapse of the Bretton Woods System of fixed exchange rates, the Fund, some say, became an institution without a purpose. The debt crisis gave the IMF a reason for existing. Along with the World Bank, the IMF required debtor countries to implement market-based reforms via adjustment programs in exchange for financial assistance—conditionality. The programs were controversial, especially relating to their social costs. The crisis brought Latin America's economic growth to a halt. That's why you hear people say it was the "lost decade of development." It took years for the region's poverty rates to fall back to pre-crisis levels (which were high to begin with).

Once we give you the basics, we'll show you how this stuff worked "on the ground," using Chile as an example. You might want to go back to the first supplement in Chapter 1 to refresh your memory about balance of payments before you read this chapter. We also highly recommend that you read the explanation of **bank capital and loan loss reserves** at the end of the chapter.

So here we go with the saga. The exchange in Part One is based on a true story.

Lights, camera, action.

Part One: The Earthquake

"The Call"

Setting: Thursday, August 12, 1982, 10:00 a.m., office of IMF Managing Director, Jacques de Larosiere

Characters:

> Jacques de Larosiere, IMF Managing Director
>
> Jesus Silva Herzog, Mexico's Secretary of Finance
>
> José Angel Gurría Treviño, Mexico's principal debt negotiator
>
> Sterie T. Beza, IMF Deputy Director, Western Hemisphere Department
>
> Paul Volker, Federal Reserve Chairman
>
> Donald Regan, U.S. Treasury Secretary

(the phone rings in Larosiere's office)

Larosiere: Jesus.

Silva Herzog: It won't work.

Larosiere: What?

Silva Herzog: It's over, Jacques.

Larosiere: But Beza. He's been there a week. We need the data. We can't approve the facility without it. You know this. The end of August is the best we can do.

Silva Herzog: He did the best he could.

Larosiere: What do you mean he did the best he could? You drew $700 million on the swap line with the Federal Reserve. And the dual exchange market to isolate the speculators—

Silva Herzog: We can't hold them off forever. This comes as a surprise to you?

Larosiere: Of course not. But I thought you would give us more time.

Silva Herzog: How can we give anyone more time? The banks are the problem and you know it. Jose informed me yesterday. They're refusing to roll over the principal due Monday. We don't have the reserves, Jacques.

(long pause)

Silva Herzog: We're defaulting.

Larosiere: What are you saying? Do you know what an earthquake this will cause?

Silva Herzog: I've closed down the exchange markets.

Larosiere: My god.

Silva Herzog: Made it more expensive for banks to buy foreign exchange from the central bank. Dollar-denominated deposits will be payable only in pesos. I've sent letters to our creditors. They now know. We can't pay the principal come Monday.

Larosiere: The capital markets won't touch you for a decade if you do this.

Silva Herzog: I've called Volcker and Regan.

(very long pause)

Silva Herzog: Jacques?

Larosiere: Yes.

Silva Herzog: I'm flying up to see you. I'll be there at three.

Part Two: How It All Began: Recycling and Scissors

Petrodollar Recycling

Why did Mexico's Secretary of the Treasury decide that Mexico would default on its external debt? The answer begins with the "petrodollar recycling" of the 1970s. During that period, the price of oil jacked up seriously—oil prices quadrupled in 1973–74. Oil-exporting countries in the Middle East were swimming dollars. What to do with all that money? Do the environmentally-friendly thing: recycle!

Policymakers in developed countries and even the IMF encouraged a recycling of the petrodollars to developing countries, especially to oil importers. So the oil countries took their petrodollars and deposited them in banks in the **Eurodollar market** in London and big U.S. and Japanese banks. Having identified a lucrative market, U.S. European, and banks around the world opened the petrodollar lending spigot to governments and state-owned entities (as well as to private companies) in developing countries. Developing countries, particularly in Latin America, were also eager to borrow relatively cheap money from the banks, especially the large "money-center" U.S. banks, to fuel their growth.

> *"Administration, including me, told the large banks that the process of recycling petrodollars to the less developed countries was beneficial, and perhaps a patriotic duty."*
>
> —L. Seidman, Full Faith and Credit: The Great S&L Debacle and Other Washington Sagas, 38 (1993)

"Money to Be Made"

<u>Setting</u>: Big, money-center, bank office, 1970s

<u>Characters</u>:

    Chairman of the big bank: Chair

    Banker in the big bank: Banker

Chair: Shall we make some money?

Banker: Is the Pope Catholic?

Chair: Let's do $600 million.

Banker: Nice round number. Venezuela wants it.

Chair: Start making the calls for the slices.

Bankers: I'm on it.

Chair: The Japanese will jump on this. So will our regionals.

Banker: Nice piece of the pie for them.

Chair: Who can resist the spread?

Banker: The sweetest slice of pie imaginable.

The bankers are talking about the typical loans they made with Eurodollars: syndicated, medium-term (five or six years) jumbo Eurodollar loans. Typically, a single large bank would not itself make the whole loan. As the "lead managing bank," it would find "participating banks" around the world that would take a slice of the loan. Those banks just want to make a profit but don't want to do any of the work. So they let the lead managing bank, other managing banks (say, a big Japanese bank that would coordinate participations in Asia) and the "agent bank" (coordinating payments, etc.) take care of everything. The loans, typically comprised of one-, three- or six-month "advances," are funded by one-, three-, or six-month Eurodollar deposits. They're floating rate loans because every time those advances are rolled over they are re-priced based on the prevailing London Interbank Offered Rate (LIBOR).

Here's a (really) simplified example based on the scene: A syndicate of banks makes a five-year, $600 million floating rate Eurodollar loan to Venezuela. The loan stipulates a three-month "interest period," meaning three-month advances. A U.S. participating bank takes a $10,000 slice of the loan. At the beginning of the loan, the participating bank will go to the London interbank market and take a three-month deposit at the prevailing LIBOR (Libo Rate), let's say it's 3%. At the end of that three-month deposit it has to pay 3%. This is its "cost of funding" its slice of the loan. So the interest rate on the advance to the borrower will be based on the 3% the participating bank has to pay on the deposit. That advance will be rolled-over throughout the term of the loan, which means that at the end of the first three-month deposit the bank will go back to the London interbank market and take another three-month deposit at the prevailing rate, say, LIBOR is now 4%. Now the interest rate on the advance to the borrower will be based on 4% for the next three months. This is the "floating" rate aspect of the loan because the interest rate changes based on LIBOR for the life of the loan.

Now notice that we're saying that the advance's interest rate is "based" on LIBOR. There's another "fixed" part of the interest rate charged to the borrower. It's called the "margin" or "spread" in the biz. The spread will be calculated based on the perceived risk of the borrower and represents the bank's profit for the most part. Let's assume a margin of 1–1/8% is agreed upon. This means that every three months the interest the borrower has to pay is LIBOR plus the spread. Taking our numbers, the interest rate on the first advance would be 4–1/8% and 5–1/8% on the second. Have a look at supplement 5D for some provisions from an actual Eurocurrency loan. But remember the big picture. Banks in this syndicated loan are doing the typical work of a bank: they take short-term liabilities—the Eurodollar deposits—and turn them into long-term assets—the five-year loan.

Getting back to the borrowers in the crisis, Latin American countries were growing pretty well in the 1970s. Real domestic product averaged about 6% annually for a decade or more before the quadrupling of oil prices in 1973–1974, and between 4% and 5% during the rest of the decade. Not bad. They borrowed syndicated loans from the banks to pursue their development via various projects (many of which failed). They also borrowed from the banks to cover BOP deficits that developed after the oil hike. Inflation increased the price of imports (oil, of course), and as you'll in a sec, exports dropped. Between 1973 and 1975, the current account deficits of non-oil-exporting countries rose from about $8 billion to $31 billion. That's a serious jump.

The Scissors Thing Leading to Default

The lending and borrowing was a frenzied party. Check it out: In Latin America foreign debt mushroomed from $29 billion in 1970 to $159 billion in 1978, a worrisome development that was not lost on economists and government officials. But, hey, why take the punch bowl away when everybody is partying?

> *"The most immediate worry is that the stability of the U.S. banking system and by extension the international financial system may be jeopardized by the massive balance of payments lending that has been done by commercial banks since the oil price hike."*
>
> —U.S. Senate Committee on Foreign Relations, Subcommittee on Foreign Relations, *International Debt, the Banks, and U.S. Foreign Policy*, 95th Cong., 1st sess., 5 (1977)

Well, the party did come to a halt with the global recession in the early 1980s, triggered by Federal Reserve Chair Paul Volcker's hike in interest rates to stem U.S. inflation. A significant drop in debtor countries' exports combined with high global interest rates triggered a "scissors" phenomenon: Debtor countries' income from exports dropped while their foreign debt became more expensive because the loans carried floating interest rates that increased along with global rates. During the 1980–1982 period, the debt/export ratio for Latin American countries rose from 226% to 354%, while the interest/export ratio climbed from 18% to 44%. These ratios are critical indicators of a debtor country's ability to meet its foreign debt payments, since they compare the country's stock of debt and the outflow of foreign exchange in debt service (interest payments) to the inflow of foreign exchange from exports. The burdensome foreign debt payments were compounded by

> "Well, by the standards of a lot of countries, by Latin American standards, it wasn't so bad [in 1979]. But the inflation rate had gotten into double digits, more than 10 percent. Double-digit inflation is a terrible thing—and it got up to 14 or 15 percent on a monthly basis for a while, shortly after I became chairman of the Fed. It was the biggest inflation and the most sustained inflation that the United States had ever had."
>
> —P. Volcker, PBS Interview

massive capital flight—outward transfers of money by private individuals and entities in developing countries. After Mexico, Brazil defaulted.

Then Venezuela.

Then Argentina.

Then Chile.

Welcome to the Latin American Debt Crisis.

"Panic"

Setting: Office in U.S. Treasury

Characters:

    Two Treasury officials: TO1, TO2

    Chairman of a big U.S. bank: Chair

TO1: What's your exposure?

Chair: Big.

TO2: My house is big. Give us the number.

Chair: $10 billion.

TO1: Holy—

TO2: Capital?

Chair: 5.

TO1: Jesus . . . 10 in dead loans and only 5 to absorb it.

TO2: You idiots—

Chair: Lose the tone. You don't scare me.

TO1: If this gets out, all hell will break loose.

Chair: You know what you have to do.

TO2: Let you sonofabitches go under.

Chair: Really? What would hell on earth look like?

TO1: We back off. No write-offs.

Chair: Right.

TO2: Wrong. We'll be all over you. You're going to raise the cushion. And when we think it's time, you're going to write this crap off.

Chair: Can you pass me another danish?

(TO1 begins to pass the tray to Chair and TO2 slaps it away violently)

TO2: Get the hell out of here.

The prospect of massive defaults posed grave problems for creditor countries, such as the United States. Government regulators discovered that commercial bank creditors, particularly the big U.S. ("money center") banks, such as Citicorp, had dangerously low levels of **capital** that could be used to absorb losses resulting from massive loan defaults, which exposed them to collapse (check out supplement 5A).

"Unlike some European regulatory authorities, immediately after the Mexican crisis U.S. banking officials did not require that large reserves be set aside on the restructured LDC [less developed country] loans or on the succeeding arrearages by other LDC nations Such a policy was not feasible at the time and might have caused a financial panic because the total LDC portfolio held by the average money-center bank was more than double its aggregate capital and reserves at the end of 1982 .... Thus, regulatory forbearance was also granted to the large banks with respect to the establishment of reserves against past-due LDC loans ... [T]his forbearance was necessary because seven or eight of the ten largest banks in the U.S. might have been deemed insolvent, a finding that would have precipitated an economic and political crisis."

—FDIC's Public Information Center, An Examination of the Banking Crises of the 1980s and Early 1990s, 207 (1997)

What to do? Hey, don't look for an orderly resolution of the crisis, such as a global bankruptcy court.

Part Three: The "Muddling Through" Approach

Maybe no global bankruptcy court, but check it out: The principal players in the crisis—governments, banks, the IMF, and the World Bank—averted a collapse of the international financial system by resorting to case-by-case debt

"There are no general rules, and the solution to yesterday's problem is not the answer to today's question. The solution for the Kingdom of Oz simply will not work for the Republic of Zo."

—A. Mudge, 'Sovereign Debt Restructure: A Perspective of Council to Agent Banks, Bank Advisory Groups and Servicing Banks," Journal of Transnational Law, 60 (1984)

restructuring negotiations, popularly known as the "muddling through" approach. It was all about doing a series of work-outs with hundreds of commercial bank creditors throughout the world via Bank Advisory Committees (BACs) or Steering Committees, which were comprised of banks with the greatest exposures (loans) to debtor countries. For example, Chile's BAC was comprised of twelve banks chaired by Manufacturers

Hanover Trust. Similar work-outs for bilateral loans, i.e., government-to-government loans such as a loan from the U.S. Export-Import Bank to Nigeria (much of the lending to Africa was bilateral), took place under the auspices of the **Paris Club**.

> *"[Critics argue that the] IMF's role as honest broker in debt crises is . . . overblown. In the absence of the IMF . . . why couldn't private lenders and borrowers strike a deal as they did in 1914."*
> —M. Bordo & H. James, "The International Monetary Fund: Its Present Role in Historical Perspective," 19 (1999)

The IMF played a critical role in the muddling through process. Referred to as the "honest broker," the Fund informed the creditor banks that it would not approve standby or extended arrangements until the banks had committed themselves to new money contributions.

Under the "muddling-through" approach, commercial banks agreed to (1) provide balance of payments financing in the form of "new money" (new loans) to debtor countries, and (2) stretch out external debt payments—"extending maturities." Hmm . . . more loans to a strapped debtor country. What exactly was going on?

"Insanity"

Setting: two lawyers at the firm's water cooler

Lawyer 1: I don't get it. Banks are lending more money to deadbeat borrowing countries?

Lawyer 2: Yeah.

Lawyer 1: That's idiotic!

Lawyer 2: Not really. It's the game.

Lawyer 1: What game would that be?

Lawyer 2: FASB 15.

Lawyer 1: Frisbee?

Lawyer 2: Financial Accounting Standards Board Statement No. 15.

Lawyer 1: You're an accountant?

Lawyer 2: No, but we're lawyers.

Lawyer 1: So we can be anybody at any given point in time.

Lawyer 2: Need I say more? Anyway, FASB 15 essentially says the banks don't have to recognize a loss on a restructured loan as long as the borrower regularly pays enough to equal the balance on the loan. *(See supplement 5B.)*

Lawyer 1: So the loans go in and come right back out to the banks.

Lawyer 2: The games we play, my friend.

Part Four: Conditionality

In return for the restructuring, debtor countries agreed to abide by IMF and World Bank stabilization and structural adjustment programs intended to correct domestic economic problems that gave rise to the crisis. The distinction between IMF and Bank programs was often blurred in practice because of the close collaboration between the two institutions and the complementary nature of their programs. Both programs carried "conditionality," releasing funds in installments and requiring recipients to meet **performance criteria** for each installment.

The IMF's stabilization programs applied short-term "emergency" measures intended to reduce domestic demand for goods and services— think of it like dousing water on a fire, an economy on fire in this case. The idea behind stabilization is that a drop in demand will result in a reduction of the current account deficit (more imports than exports), which the IMF believed was one of the major causes of the financial crises in debtor countries. In most cases, governments reduced demand by cutting public expenditures, devaluing the country's currency (debtor countries typically had fixed exchange rate regimes), and reducing the money supply. The expenditure-cutting included drastic cuts in infrastructure (e.g., roads, bridges, and dams), freezing state employees' wages or laying off state employees, reducing consumer subsidies, and cutting health and education expenditures. (Pretty brutal, huh?) Central banks devalued the currency in part to reduce imports and increase exports. Authorities reduced the money supply to check inflation.

In Chapter 4, we talked about how the Charter requires the World Bank to make "project" loans. But there's the "special circumstances" exception in Article III, section 4(vii) ("Loans made or guaranteed by the Bank shall, except in special circumstances, be for the purpose of specific projects . . ."). The World Bank did policy-based lending through structural adjustment loans (SALs) and sector adjustment loans (SECALs), medium- to long-term loans that supported structural changes to improve supply and prevent the recurrence of a crisis. The World Bank structural adjustment programs complemented stabilization efforts by shooting for economic efficiency, which, in turn, would increase the domestic supply of goods and services. Although the programs differed among countries, they shared two themes: liberalization of domestic and foreign trade, and privatization of often large and inefficient public enterprises. Domestic liberalizations included abolishing price controls, freeing interest rates, ending credit rationing, and establishing a capital market. Liberalization of external trade typically included reduction of high tariffs, elimination of quotas on imports and import licenses, abolition of export duties and licenses, devaluation of the currency (hence reducing the price of exports), and product diversification. Public enterprises were also subject to market discipline via privatizations, reduction or abolition of subsidies, and other streamlining measures. Pretty much remaking the whole economy.

Part Five: From Debt Fatigue to Debt Reduction

Debt Fatigue

After a few years of repeated restructuring deals, "debt fatigue" began to appear. Bank executives dragged their butts to emergency rooms begging for vitamin B shots. Not really, but it's a good visual! New loans to debtor countries plummeted as commercial bank creditors contemplated the (unthinkable) possibility that debtor countries were facing insolvency—bankruptcy—rather than a temporary drop in their ability to pay back the foreign debt—a liquidity crisis.

> *"There is simply no mechanism for a national government to be thrown into bankruptcy proceedings. This is inherent in the nature of national governments, which are not liquidated even under the most adverse financial situations. [T]hey do not cease to exist."*
> —W. Wriston, Risk and Other Four Letter Words, 151 (1986)

In October 1985, U.S. Treasury Secretary James Baker proposed a strategy, dubbed the Baker Plan, which tried to alleviate the debt fatigue. The plan was designed to kick-start growth in fifteen highly indebted countries (including five non-Latin American countries: Yugoslavia, the Philippines, Nigeria, the Ivory Coast, and Morocco) through $29 billion in new lending by commercial banks and multilateral institutions in return for structural economic reforms such as privatization of state-owned entities and deregulation of the economy. But the strategy failed because the projected financing didn't materialize and, to the extent it did, the new lending just added to debtor countries' already crushing debt burden. Can you imagine that! The region's total external debt (public and private) rose from $333 billion in 1982 to $446 billion in 1987. But that's not all, folks! To make matters worse, during this period Latin American debtor countries were making massive net outward transfers of resources. In other words, annual transfers abroad, such as interest payments on external debt, exceeded inward transfers—from just 1981 to 1982 the resource transfer went from an inflow of $31.7 billion to an outflow of $7.8 billion. Brutal.

In light of what appeared to be a problem that wouldn't go away, government officials, academics, and private entities began to propose plans that would provide debtor countries with debt relief rather than debt restructuring. The proposals were driven by prices for **debt trading on the secondary market**, which slid from an average of 65% of its nominal value in 1986 to 28% in 1989. One proposal involved debt relief through an "international debt management authority." Such an entity would have used funds from the IMF, the World Bank, and other sources to buy developing country debt from commercial banks at a discount—using the secondary market as a guide. The discount would've been passed along to debtor countries that agreed to make economic reforms.

In the meantime, various debtor countries suspended debt payments and fell out of compliance with, or otherwise refused to adopt, IMF adjustment programs. The nerve! This led Secretary Baker in April 1987 to suggest a "menu of options" approach (picture a cafeteria) intended to bring flexibility to the case-by-case approach. Baker's suggestion envisioned commercial banks choosing from a menu financial options that would be more attractive to them. For example, creditor banks could slide along their trays and choose loans for trade and projects, or traditional balance-of-payments financing, or new money bonds, which could be attractive to banks because of enhanced transferability and because debtor countries would be less likely to default on bonds—harder to restructure. But this virtual smorgasbord wasn't enough to entice banks that had grown (sick and) tired of their continued involvement in the crisis.

"Bye, Bye Miss American Pie"

Setting: Big bank office, late 1980s

Characters:

>   Chairman of the big bank: Chair

>   Banker in the big bank: Banker

Banker: Menu of options . . .

Chair: I'm not hungry. Let's just do it.

Banker: What?

Chair: Call these dead loans just that. Up the **loan-loss reserves**. We're leaving this dance.

Banker (singing): Bye, bye, Miss American Pie.

Chair: You're a lounge lizard now? Shall I pull out the karaoke machine?

Banker: Just remembering the good ole' days.

One month after Baker's announcement, Citicorp made its move: it announced a $3 billion increase to its loan loss reserves against its troubled loans to debtor countries, a move that other U.S. banks followed. The writing was on the wall: major U.S. banks didn't expect to be repaid and wanted to wash their hands of the crisis.

The Brady Initiative

The Brady Initiative, announced in March 1989 by U.S. Treasury Secretary Nicholas F. Brady, marked a change in U.S. policy towards the debt crisis. Given the persistently high levels of foreign debt, the Initiative shifted the focus of the strategy (finally) from increased lending to voluntary, market-based debt reduction (reduction of outstanding principal) and debt service reduction (reduction of interest payments) in exchange for continued economic reform by debtor countries.

Debtor countries obtained significant (but not massive) debt relief under the Brady Initiative through: (1) direct cash buybacks; (2) exchange of existing debt for "discount bonds" (bonds issued by the debtor country with a reduced [discounted] face value but carrying a market rate of interest); (3) exchange of existing debt for "par bonds" (bonds that carry the same face value as the old loans but carry a below-market interest rate); and (4) interest rate reduction bonds (bonds that initially carry a below-market interest rate that rises eventually to the market rate). Commercial bank creditors that didn't want to participate in a debt or debt service reduction option could choose to give debtor countries new loans or receive bonds created from interest payments owed by debtor countries. Debtor countries sweetened the deals by providing "enhancements" on the cafeteria menu, such as principal collateral via **U.S. Treasury zero coupon bonds** and interest collateral. We'll give you a simple description of the Brady Bond process:

- A number of banks have X amount of non-performing loans they made to, say, Mexico, meaning they produce no revenue. So they want these loans off their books.
- The banks take those loans and exchange them for par bonds from Mexico. When those bonds mature, Mexico has to pay.
- The banks then sell those bonds to investors on the secondary market, where they trade.
- Mexico purchases zero-coupon Treasury bonds (with funds it received from the IMF, World Bank and other sources) with maturities that match the maturities of the par bonds. The Treasury bonds, which collateralize the par bond's principal, are put in escrow at the Federal Reserve.
- At the Brady Bond's maturity date, the investor receives payment on the bond that Mexico issued. The investor knows that if Mexico defaults on the bond, it'll receive the principal collateral: Rather than paying Mexico on the zero-coupon bond, the Treasury's payment goes to the investor.
- To cover the possibility that Mexico will miss an interest payment, cash may be used to collateralize on a rolling basis a certain number of interest payments on the Brady Bond, say, interest payments over a six-month period.

Commercial bank creditors agreed to Brady deals with a good handful of countries, including Argentina, Costa Rica, Mexico, Nigeria, the Philippines, Venezuela, Uruguay and Brazil. Brazil's $44 billion Brady deal provides a good example, with its six options. It's a bit complex, but you need to see it:

1) A collateralized discount bond which reduces eligible debt by 35% of its face value. The primary collateral will be 30-year U.S. Treasury zero-coupon bonds. The interest rate on the bonds is LIBOR plus 13/16ths.

2) A collateralized par bond that will pay 4% in years 1 to 5, 5.75% in year 6 and 6% in years 7 to 30. U.S. Treasury zero-coupon bonds also will provide the collateral.

3) Front-loaded interest reduction bonds paying 4% in the first year and rising to LIBOR plus 13/16ths in years 7 to 15.

4) New money: Creditors can provide new money up to 18.18% of eligible debt.

5) Temporary interest relief under a restructuring mechanism.

6) Front-loaded interest capitalization bonds, with an interest rate that rises from 4% for the first year to 8% for years 7 to 20.

In the meantime, Latin American countries made substantial economic reforms. In 1991, the region registered capital inflows that exceeded outflows for the first time since the onset of the debt crisis. This led some observers to proclaim that the debt crisis was over for major Latin American debtor countries.

Brady Bonds postscript: By May 1994, eighteen countries agreed to Brady Bond deals that shaved off $60 billion in debt. Forgiveness . . . nothing like it. In 1994, Brady Bonds accounted for 61% of total trading in emerging market debt ($1.68 trillion). Their share dwindled to about 2% of total trading by 2005. By mid-2006, most Brady Bonds were gone. They were either exchanged or bought back by debtor countries in public or private deals on the secondary market.

Part Six: How It Worked with Chile

Here we're going to take a look at how it happened "on the ground" by looking at Chile's experience in the crisis. The author was actually on the ground in Santiago. You should go there sometime. The empanadas and wine are to die for. And take a weekend to go to Viña del Mar. So cool. And then you should go—wait a second, this is a textbook, not a travel guide. So here's an excerpt from yours truly. You'll see references to "cooperation." That's because the author analyzed debt restructuring via game theory. You know, Simon says negotiate.

E. CARRASCO, "CHILE, ITS FOREIGN COMMERCIAL BANK CREDITORS AND ITS VULNERABLE GROUPS: AN ASSESSMENT OF THE COOPERATIVE CASE-BY-CASE APPROACH TO THE DEBT CRISIS"

Law and Policy in International Business, 319–322, 329–352 (1993)

Looking at absolute figures, one might be tempted to conclude that Chile's predicament in 1982 was mild compared to other Latin American debtor countries. In 1982, Brazil, Mexico, and Argentina, the three major debtor countries in terms of their absolute external debt, carried total external debt of approximately $92.2 billion, $86 billion, and $43.6 billion, respectively. Chile, on the other hand, carried only $17.3 billion of external debt in that year. In relative terms, however, Chile suffered one of the most severe debt burdens in all of Latin America. In 1982, for example, Chile had the highest external debt relative to its GDP: 130 percent, compared to 50 percent in Brazil and 75 percent in Argentina. Moreover, Chile owed eighty-five percent of its debt to foreign commercial banks, compared to a range of forty percent to sixty percent for other Latin American countries . . .

The ultimate objective for Chile since 1982, as for other debtor countries, has been to resume economic growth and development by obtaining access to the voluntary international lending market. The intermediate objectives have been to seek relief from onerous debt servicing obligations and to cover the "financing gap," i.e., the projected deficit in the debtor country's balance of payments. In other words, Chile sought what Lee Buchheit has called "a period of respite."

But as Ralph Reisner has aptly stated: "[T]he underlying financial issues dividing the parties were of gargantuan proportions. What was frequently at stake was nothing less than the economic viability of entire countries and some of the largest financial institutions in the world." On one side of the table, debtor countries argued that the crisis was due in large part to "external" factors, such as the worldwide recession of the early 1980s and the accompanying economic stagnation of the developed countries, the drop in international commodity prices, and high international interest rates. Debtor nations argued further that they were devoting virtually all of their scarce foreign exchange to external debt payments, which they could not possibly continue to make in accordance with the loan agreements. Making such payments was counterproductive, because by doing so debtor countries were forsaking economic development. On the other side of the table, commercial bank creditors argued that the debtor countries' plight was due in large part to waste and economic inefficiency. They pointed out that debt forgiveness would raise significant regulatory and accounting problems and pose a moral hazard the possibility that debtor countries would deliberately aggravate their economic problems in order to qualify for debt relief . . .

At the outset of the crisis, the cooperative approach called for a procedural and substantive negotiating structure whereby debtor countries, on a case-by-case basis, would receive infusions of "new money" from commercial bank creditors in addition to multilateral funding and have their external debt restructured. Commercial bank creditors, on the other hand, would maintain the integrity of their loan portfolios by receiving timely interest payments. Moreover, IMF conditionality would enhance the likelihood of repayment of their loans to these countries.

Most of the players at least publicly adhered to the belief, eventually enshrined in the Baker Plan, that cooperative efforts to accomplish the intermediate objectives would lead to fulfillment of the ultimate objective. Jesus Silva-Herzog, who served as Secretary of the Treasury of Mexico from 1982 to 1986, captured the debtor country's view when he wrote:

> The strategy that was followed after those initial moments [after the announcement in August 1982 of the Mexican moratorium] was to give borrowers time and additional resources to help them handle their problems. The restructuring of payments into longer maturities, the addition of new money, and the imposition of severe domestic economic adjustments, together with the recovery of economic activity in the rich countries, were expected to make it possible for the debtor countries to resume economic growth, comply with their financial obligations, and gradually return to the international capital markets.

A U.S. banker voiced similar sentiments reflective of a value creating approach:

> The central issues under negotiation are who will bear the costs of economic adjustment and how these costs will be distributed among the major groups of players. It is a game with high stakes. Governments can fall. Banks can collapse. Credit agencies may be crippled. In spite of these stark realities, debt restructurings can be a positive sum game. All players benefit when a sovereign debt restructuring works. This fact motivates all of the players to stay at the bargaining table. However, despite their common interest in a successful restructuring, the players will not necessarily benefit equally.

The numerous debt restructuring negotiations, such as between Mexico, Brazil, Venezuela, Argentina, and Chile and their respective commercial bank creditors, that have taken place since the outbreak of the crisis indicate that most of the players have continued to adhere to this value-creating belief even though value-claiming quite clearly has taken place. The banks have claimed value: Debtor countries have made net outward transfers of approximately $25 billion annually while receiving few new money loans. And debtor countries have engaged in value claiming: debtor countries have fallen out of compliance with IMF structural adjustment programs and otherwise have periodically halted external debt payments . . .

The success of negotiations to achieve the intermediate objective, given the value-creating aspect of the case-by-case approach, depended heavily on the flow of accurate information between the parties. The gathering and processing of information was a daunting task, however. Debtor countries, for example, had to ascertain precisely how much public and private sector debt they carried and who carried it. They also had to review any legal, economic, and political factors that would bear on restructuring external debt. Commercial bank creditors—Chile had approximately 500—carried different exposures to debtor countries, were subject to different regulatory regimes, and approached the crisis with many different and often conflicting points of view.

1.   The Bank Advisory Committee

In view of this problem, the IMF, the World Bank, and the central banks and finance ministries of the industrialized countries backed the idea of creating committees of the debtor countries' major creditor banks. Usually known as Bank Advisory Committees (BACs) or Steering Committees, these committees acted as the primary forum for engaging in the complex process that would create value for the players in the debt crisis. Chile's BAC was comprised of twelve commercial bank creditors chaired by Manufacturers Hanover Trust.

Constituting a committee of a debtor country's commercial bank creditors to facilitate debt rescheduling was not a new idea. For example, after encountering balance-of-payments difficulties in the mid-1970s, Peru sought, among other things, to reschedule medium- and long-term debt owed to its 285 commercial bank creditors. Initially, Peru attempted to negotiate separately with each national group of creditor banks, but that approach failed because of creditor banks' (particularly the U.S. banks') demands that all commercial bank creditors be treated equally. A steering committee was subsequently formed, comprised of banks with the highest exposure to the country.

BACs have not acted as paid advisors to debtor countries, and therefore do not represent them in debt restructuring negotiations. Nor, as a matter of law, have they acted as agent for the universe of Chile's commercial bank creditors, although in practice they have "represented" the creditors at the negotiating table. Given the importance of accurate information to the value-creating process of negotiation, BACs have played a central role in gathering, processing, and disseminating information. They have also played a key role in "marketing" the product—the deal—generated through negotiations based on the information.

2. Procedure

Chile's debt negotiations followed a pattern that is generally applicable to other negotiations between Latin American debtor countries and their commercial bank creditors.

a. *Gathering Information*

The task of gathering information may begin with a presentation (in New York City) to the BAC by high-level government official, usually the debtor country's Minister of Finance. The Minister uses this occasion to transmit information regarding the country's economic situation, its macroeconomic program, and its external financing needs.

Prior to the commencement of the actual negotiations, the BAC's economic subcommittee visits the country along with personnel from the IMF and the World Bank to gather data on the country's economy for transmission to the BAC. The data is used, among other things, to calculate the financing gap for which new money loans would be needed. The financing gap, which is covered by bilateral and multilateral funding as well as loans from commercial bank creditors, may be estimated through the use of an economic macro model, comparing a debtor country's projected current account deficits and reserve changes, net scheduled amortizations, and other capital outflows with the country's projected financial inflows from direct foreign investment, international agencies, and bilateral sources. Based on such estimations, Chile's commercial bank creditors were asked to contribute new money equal to 10.95 percent of their exposure to the country as of June 31, 1983—the so-called "base date." In 1984, the percentage was lowered to 6.75 percent of exposure as of the base date.

Other subcommittees or special units have been formed to gather specific information. For example, because a high level of external debt emanated from Chile's private sector, the BAC in 1984 formed a subcommittee comprised of five of its members to analyze the situation. The subcommittee studied various issues relating to the private sector, such as Chile's bankruptcy laws and exchange rates, as well as efforts to restructure the external debt of the country's largest private sector debtors.

The proposition that cooperation can evolve and thrive in negotiations by breaking up large and complex issues appears to be borne out by the continued if not expanded role of BAC subcommittees in negotiations for debt relief under the Brady Initiative. In Venezuela's negotiations, for example, subgroups were created for debt reduction, debt service reduction, and new money. These subgroups conducted the initial negotiations directly with Venezuela before returning to the BAC with the results.

b.   *Processing of Information*

The processing of information takes place during the actual negotiations between the debtor country and its commercial bank creditors. During this phase, the negotiators use the information that has been gathered to answer complex financial and legal questions. The BACs have formed Asset Enhancement Units to help answer these questions. These entities study the viability of debt restructuring proposals and coordinate the strategies being followed by the debtor countries. Cross-membership among the various BACs to Latin American debtor countries enhances the processing function. Citibank, for example, has chaired practically all of such BACs.

c.   *Marketing the Deal*

Once the information is processed, the BACs are responsible for disseminating the information through the "term sheet" to the international financial community, including all of the debtor country's commercial bank creditors. The term sheet embodies the agreement in principle between the BAC and the debtor country as to the major financial issues, such as "who pays; lends or defers payment of how much, when and at what price." Significant legal issues that envelop the deal are also addressed. The term sheet is accompanied by a communication from the debtor country regarding its economic policies as well as a statement of support for the deal by the BAC, the IMF, the World Bank and, lately, the IDB.

After transmission of the term sheet, a delegation from the debtor country along with members of the BAC and representatives of the World Bank and the IMF commence the "road show," a series of visits to the world's financial centers intended to "sell" the deal to the rest of the country's commercial bank creditors. At this juncture, the BAC's membership becomes very important to the value-creating process. The debtor country selects banks that can most effectively influence the entire pool of the country's commercial bank creditors. Because Chile owed approximately fifty percent of its external debt to U.S. banks, seven major U.S. banks sat on the committee, including Manufacturers Hanover as Chair of the BAC. Citibank was chosen to coordinate the relations with the financial institutions in the Northeast corridor, while Bank of America was asked to perform the same task with the banks on the Pacific Coast. The Bank of Nova Scotia represented the Canadian banks. The Bank of Tokyo represented the Japanese banks, which held at least ten percent of Chile's external debt. The remaining three spots were held by Credit Suisse, representing the Swiss, French, Italian, and Spanish banks; Dresdner Bank, representing the German, Scandinavian, Belgian, Dutch, and Austrian banks; and Midland Bank, representing the British, Portuguese, and Arab banks.

d.   *Executing the Agreements*

The term sheet usually asks the commercial bank creditors to commit to the deal promptly, and "early participation fees" have been used to get a "critical mass" of banks (ninety percent or more) to sign up. North American lawyers for the BAC then draft the agreements that embody the deal. The drafts are delivered to the debtor country for review and comment. Many Latin American debtor countries have retained North American counsel to assist them in this process. After the required number of commitments have been received, the debtor country delegation meets with the BAC to negotiate the contours of the final draft. One of the central purposes of these negotiations is to ensure that final agreements accurately reflect the agreement in principle embodied in the term sheet.

Once the final drafts have been prepared, they are delivered to the BAC for a final review and thereafter to all of the country's remaining commercial bank creditors. Commentary from these banks is transmitted to the chair of the BAC, who in turn passes along pertinent commentary to the debtor country and its counsel.

This process, which can take several months or more, culminates with a signing ceremony in New York, usually in the offices of counsel to the BAC. As in the commencement of the negotiations, the Minister of Finance delivers a speech that emphasizes the importance of the deal to the debtor country. The Minister also reviews the economic problems of the country as well as the steps being taken to address such problems.

3.   The Role of Precedent

Precedent is a key, yet malleable concept under the case-by-case approach. The use of precedent in the debt crisis has created the expectation that a rule or decision that arises out of a particular set of circumstances will be applied in the future to a sufficiently similar set of circumstances. The key question, of course, is whether a set of circumstances is sufficiently similar to warrant application of an existing rule or decision. Both debtor countries and commercial bank creditors have devoted considerable time and energy debating this question. Over the course of the past decade, precedent nevertheless has contributed to the durability of the system and, in turn, to the evolution of cooperation.

Mexico provided important precedents at the outset of the crisis. Several months after announcing its "standstill" on payments of external debt, Mexico proposed what in essence was a "three-pronged" debt restructuring plan comprised of involuntary lending by the commercial bank creditors, debt rescheduling and economic reform. First, Mexico, with the assistance of the IMF, "invited" each of its commercial bank creditors to contribute "new money" equal to seven percent of its exposure to Mexico as of August 22, 1982. Second, Mexico proposed to reschedule over an eight-year period public sector debt to commercial banks maturing between August 22, 1982 and December 31, 1984. Third, and of great importance to commercial creditor banks, Mexico agreed to an Extended Fund Arrangement with the IMF whereby Mexico would receive $3.9 billion over a three-year period, provided it could implement various economic reforms set forth by the IMF.

In 1984, Mexico proposed that debt restructuring be stretched over a greater period of time, thus creating the "multi-year restructuring agreement," or MYRA. Brazil, Argentina, Venezuela, Chile, and other Latin American debtor countries adopted Mexico's model, albeit with various modifications and variations. In each debt restructuring exercise after the Mexican "threshold agreements," both the debtor country and its commercial bank creditors scrutinized restructuring agreements signed by other countries for approaches or provisions that could present favorable or unfavorable precedents. A U.S. banker aptly captured the significance that precedent had gained in sovereign debt restructuring:

> Crafting a solution to the international debt crisis involves a case by case approach in that each restructuring is negotiated individually with separate bank advisory committees. The process takes on generic elements, however, because each settlement sets a precedent for ongoing and future negotiations. Individual agreements are tailored to the specific economic and political needs of countries but the "style" of the settlement sets the "fashion trend" for future negotiations. There is no better example of this phenomenon than the Mexican restructuring agreement of 1984, the style of which has set the benchmark for acceptable agreements involving other debtor countries. Now, regardless of their respective economic needs and abilities to pay, all of the major debtors negotiate for the 1984 Mexican terms.

Chile used the Mexican precedent in 1985 to obtain a MYRA for approximately $4.5 billion in principal maturing in the years 1985 through 1987. In a popular use of precedent, Chile argued for lower interest rates in 1988, pointing to the lower rates Argentina and Mexico obtained in earlier negotiations with their commercial bank creditors.

Although commercial bank creditors were more likely to distinguish than to follow previous agreements, they occasionally used precedent affirmatively. In 1986, for example, John Reed, President of Citibank, suggested that Chile pursue a credit facility modeled after an Ecuadorian facility that was tied to Ecuador's oil production, a suggestion that Chile ultimately rejected. In 1988, Chile's BAC used Mexican and Brazilian precedent to suggest that Chile offer early participation fees to those banks that made expeditious commitments to new money proposals.

Chile also set precedents for other Latin American debtor countries. In 1985, for example, Chile entered into a co-financing agreement with the World Bank whereby: the Bank guaranteed fifty percent of a $300 million loan from Chile's commercial bank creditors, a precedent that Mexico and other Latin American debtor countries eventually followed. Chile's retiming of interest payments from a quarterly to a semi-annual basis in 1985 was followed by Argentina and Venezuela. Mexico and the Philippines used the debt reduction mechanisms Chile employed in 1988, such as cash buy-backs of external debt and debt-for-debt exchanges, in their negotiations under the Brady Initiative.

4. Legal Aspects

The agreements that were hammered out between commercial bank creditors and debtor countries at the outset of the crisis were based on standard provisions of Eurodollar loan agreements. Two types of provisions, as modified for sovereign debt restructure, have encouraged cooperation: (i) those that require the debtor country to make periodic reports regarding their economic and financial state of affairs; and (ii) those that seek to ensure equal treatment among similarly situated creditors.

a. *Disclosure*

. . . Prior to the debt crisis, debtor countries did not transmit much information regarding their financial and economic affairs to their private lenders. Debtor countries considered such reporting to be unduly cumbersome and inappropriate. Creditors perhaps thought such information was unnecessary. Covenants in post-1982 agreements, however, have required debtor countries to provide commercial bank creditors with detailed reports of their economic performance and financial condition. Debtor countries have also been required to disclose reports generated for and by the IMF under an IMF standby or Extended Fund Arrangement. And because such facilities may expire prior to the expiration of the multiyear restructuring or new money agreements, some debtor countries have agreed to "enhanced Article IV consultation" procedures that require the IMF staff and the debtor country to make a mid-year report on the country's economy.

Transparency must be a two-way street, of course. Commercial bank creditors, especially in the United States, have been subject to extensive reporting and disclosure requirements. For example, banks are required to publicly disclose loans that have been placed on "non-accrual" status. Under Financial Accounting Standard 15 they must disclose in their financial statements the effects on their incomes of interest relief in "troubled debt restructurings."

b. *Equal Treatment*

As noted above, in the mid-1970s Peru abandoned its efforts to negotiate separately with each national group of creditor banks after the banks complained that they were not being treated equally. The principle of equal treatment among similarly situated creditors has been critical to the evolution of cooperation in the, debt restructuring process. As Buchheit and Reisner have stated:

> [T]he creditors exist in a kind of balance of terror; each has its full panoply of legal rights in the face of a massive default,

but any attempt to enforce those rights will jeopardize the position of all creditors. The clear message is that a move toward the courthouse by a few lenders would risk a stampede by many lenders; thus damaging perhaps irretrievably the interests of all lenders. Whether one chooses to view these statements as an appeal to the moral responsibilities of creditors, inter se or as a blunt assertion of what in another context is called "mutually assured destruction," the result is an effort to replicate in a sovereign debt context the functional equivalent of the "automatic stay" protection accorded to corporate debtors who seek the protection of a domestic bankruptcy filing.

The equal treatment principle is enshrined primarily in *pari-passu*, negative pledge, mandatory prepayment, sharing, and cross-default clauses. The *pari-passu* clause, which is usually set forth as a representation and warranty and a covenant, seeks to ensure that the loan in question will not be subordinated in right of payment to other indebtedness of the borrower. The negative pledge clause is related to the *pari-passu* clause in that it seeks to prevent the borrower from pledging its assets in favor of other creditors.

Mandatory prepayment clauses also seek to ensure equal treatment by requiring the debtor country to make ratable payments of restructured debt should it decide to make repayments prior to their due date. And sharing clauses have discouraged commercial bank creditors from abandoning the pack to try to collect from the debtor country more than other commercial bank creditors could receive. Under a sharing clause, recipients of unequal payments are required to share proportionately with the rest of the commercial bank creditors. Finally, complicated cross-default clauses in restructuring agreements have entitled commercial bank creditors of a particular public sector obligor to declare a default if any other public sector obligor defaults under any other credit agreement . . .

At the outset of the debt crisis, commercial bank creditors assumed that debtor countries could put their economic houses in order relatively quickly and thereby return to the voluntary lending markets and normal debt service. The assumption proved to be wrong, however. Commercial bank creditors came to realize sometime in 1984 that debtor countries perhaps faced a state of insolvency (unable to amortize their external debt) rather than illiquidity (temporarily unable to gather enough foreign exchange to service their external debt). Consequently, the banks became increasingly reluctant to engage in debt restructuring exercises, especially the new money component. Their reluctance grew as major U.S. banks increased their capital throughout the decade and added significantly to their loan loss reserves. Intransigence reached a peak during the negotiations with Mexico for debt and debt service reduction under the Brady Initiative. The deterioration in cooperation was due in part to the breakdown of the equal treatment principle—debt relief deals have required waivers of the sharing, negative pledge, and mandatory prepayment clauses—and to the perception on the part of debtor countries that cooperation had paid off solely for commercial bank creditors . . .

Cooperation has also managed to survive in the debt crisis because of actual or threatened modifications of the payoffs third party efforts to increase the costs of defection or the reward for cooperation. The IMF's withholding of approval of standby arrangements pending commitments by commercial bank creditors to a deal with the debtor country is an example of this technique. The U.S. Federal Reserve has also acted to change the payoffs. During the Mexican negotiations under the Brady Initiative, the Fed threatened banks with the possibility of imposing new reserve requirements. The Fed has also increased the reward by liberalizing regulations that govern debt/equity conversions in debtor countries. As noted in Part I, funding from the U.S. Treasury, the IMF, the World Bank, and the IDB has allowed debtor countries to sweeten their deals with the banks by providing "enhancements" in the form of principal and interest collateral. Recently, of course, debtor countries have also been induced to cooperate by the Enterprise for the Americas Initiative, which has offered forgiveness of official debt as well as free trade in exchange for cooperative behavior.

In Chile's case, the stalemate was broken frequently by the familiar actors outside the BAC, namely, the IMF, the World Bank, the Federal Reserve, and the U.S. Treasury Department. The Federal Reserve Bank of New York, a representative of which regularly attended Chile's BAC meetings, was a particularly useful ally for Chile. At times, the Chilean negotiating team could successfully persuade these other actors to place pressure on the BAC to agree to a proposal Chile had put on the negotiating table, such as Chile's proposal to re-time interest payments. The BAC, on the other hand, was equally capable of persuasion. For example, it managed to convince the IMF and the World Bank that Chile should provide a guarantee for restructured debt of the private financial sector originally due during the 1985–87 period. The BAC also persuaded the IMF and the World Bank to nod in the banks' favor when they insisted that Chile restructure its official external debt through the Paris Club in order to meet its financing needs.

C.   *The Deals*

Chile's initial exchanges with its commercial bank creditors illustrate the emergence of cooperative behavior. Given the heavy emphasis on the role of the private sector in Chilean development, the government took the position at the outset of the debt crisis that a large portion of Chile's external debt—private sector debt— was not its problem: These debtors and their foreign commercial bank creditors had to work things out themselves. The banks, which viewed their debtor to be the country as a whole, did not agree. Consequently, all credit, including critical short-term trade lines, was swiftly shut down. After this initial non-cooperative behavior (mutual defections), which resulted in both parties being worse off, Chile was "nice" and began its approach to the debt crisis by starting with the cooperative choice. The banks reciprocated. Thus, Somerville and his negotiating team very skillfully manipulated the system described above to secure deals with Chile's commercial bank creditors that provided malice of payments financing, postponed payments of principal, and lowered interest payment elements which other Latin American debtor countries pursued after 1982. Agreements with the IMF and the World Bank played an integral role in these deals. The bulk of the deals, which included agreements with official creditors, occurred in six phases spanning from 1983 to 1989.

As to Chile's financing gap, commercial bank creditors agreed to lend $3.165 billion in new money pursuant to agreements signed in 1983, 1984, and 1985. The banks did not contribute new money to help cover the financing gap for 1987 and 1988. Instead they agreed to re-time interest rate payments on new money and restructured debt falling due between 1988 and 1992 from a semi-annual to an annual basis. Critical short-term trade credit facilities amounting to approximately $6.7 billion were signed in 1983, 1985, 1987, and 1989.

The IMF and the World Bank also contributed to Chile's financing needs. The IMF approved a Standby Arrangement and Compensatory Facility totaling 795 million SDRs in 1983, an Extended Fund Arrangement and Compensatory Facility totaling 820.6 million SDRs in 1985, an extension of the 1985 Compensatory Facility in the amount of 75 million SDRs in 1988, and a Standby Arrangement for 64 million SDRs in 1989. In 1985, the World Bank co-financed $300 million in new money by providing a guarantee for 50 percent of the amount. In the same year, the Bank provided a $750 million structural adjustment loan that was disbursed in three tranches between 1985 and 1988.

The rescheduling of public sector and publicly guaranteed private financial sector external debt to commercial bank creditors, covering approximately $8.95 billion in payments originally scheduled to mature during the years 1983–1991, occurred in 1983, 1985, and 1987. In 1985, 1987, and 1988 the restructuring and new money agreements were amended, in part, to reduce the spread on interest payments and re-time them. By the end of Somerville's tenure, the spread was reduced from 2.125 percent over the London Interbank Offered Rate (LIBOR) or 2 percent over the U.S. prime to LIBOR plus 13/16ths for restructured debt and LIBOR plus 7/8ths for new money (the U.S. prime rate was eliminated).

In 1988, given the emerging idea of using a "menu of options" to allow commercial bank creditors to pick from a variety of debt or debt service reduction options, Chile and its commercial bank creditors agreed to various measures intended to introduce more flexibility in the management of Chile's external debt. First, Chile could use reserves from its Copper Stabilization Fund to buy back up to $500 million of external debt at a discount. Second, Chile could prepay external debt in pesos to those creditors that agreed to lend new money for investments in the country. Third, Chile could guarantee up to $500 million in new money loans from the banks, with the new loans receiving priority in repayments. Finally, a portion of the "old debt" could be swapped at a discount for new debt.

As to official creditors, Chile restructured debt through the Paris Club twice during Somerville's tenure. In 1985, Chile's BAC, as well as the World Bank and the IMF, insisted that Chile could meet its financing needs in part by restructuring official external debt, seventy percent of which was owed to the United States and Japan. Accordingly, Chile rescheduled $223.8 million in payments falling due in 1985 and 1986, resulting in $150 million in debt service relief for those years. Chile returned to the Paris Club for the same reason in 1987, restructuring $166.4 million in 1987 and 1988 maturities.

Of course, Chile's reduction in external debt is also attributable to the debt swap program Chile established in 1985. The program has functioned primarily through Chapters XVIII (used primarily by Chilean residents) and XIX (available to foreign investors and non-resident Chileans) of Chile's Compendium of Rules on

International Exchange. Under Chapter XVIII, Chilean residents can use repatriated capital or foreign exchange from the internal parallel foreign exchange market to acquire, through auctions, discounted Chilean external debt (with maturities exceeding one year). These investors then arrange prepayment with the debtor and can use the proceeds for any purpose. Under Chapter XIX's debt-to-equity conversion program, a foreign investor or non-resident Chilean may exchange Chilean external debt (with maturities exceeding one year) for an equity investment in the country, for cash, or for peso denominated notes (in the case of Central Bank debt) that can be sold in the domestic secondary market. The proceeds of such sales are used for equity investments in the country. If the foreign investor is also a creditor of the firm in which he plans to invest the proceeds of the swap, the transaction is accomplished through another investment law, D.L. 600. Chile's debt-to-equity program generated $9.7 billion in swaps between 1985 and 1990. During the first three-and-a-half years of the program such swaps accounted for twenty-nine percent of Chile's medium- and long-term debt to commercial banks as of 1985 . . .

Part Seven: The Lost Decade of Development

A great number of observers dumped on the IMF and the World Bank for their handling of the debt crisis. They argued that the poor, women, children and other groups (indigenous peoples) suffered disproportionately as a result of stabilization and structural adjustment programs (SSAPs) during the 1980s. As Latin America's economies stagnated (experiencing zero or negative economic growth), per capita income plummeted, poverty increased, and the already wide gap between the rich and the poor widened further. The debt crisis seriously eroded whatever gains had been made in reducing poverty through improved social welfare measures over the preceding three decades. These developments led policymakers to label the 1980s "the lost decade of development."

Post-crisis studies of the impact of SSAPs helped policymakers figure out if the programs had a negative impact on poverty and income distribution. The studies showed that SSAPs had mixed effects. Some studies indicated that SSAPs had adversely affected the poor and increased the gap between the rich and the poor in developing countries. This is because SSAPs resulted in lower wages for laborers and increased unemployment. Funds earmarked by governments or the World Bank for "social safety nets" fell short of the amount required to prevent overall increases in poverty.

As you might expect, other studies showed that SSAPs were not as bad as critics claimed. Some pointed out that the impact of SSAPs varied from country to country—they weren't uniformly bad across developing countries. Others showed that the plight of the poor could be improved after the implementation of SSAPs. For example, an overvalued exchange rate can reduce agricultural exports by making them more expensive for foreign consumers, thereby impoverishing people in the agricultural sector. A devaluation may improve those exports by making them less expensive and may indirectly increase the income of the rural poor. Still other studies indicated that avoiding adjustment or implementing adjustment policies that departed from IMF/World Bank criteria resulted in skyrocketing inflation, which disproportionately hurt the poor who use most of their income for consumption.

Here's another portion of the author's article that describes what happened in Chile in the wake of adjustment (pp. 355–359):

B.   *The Regressive Impact of Structural Adjustment*

Although Chile's experience may be a success in many ways on the international plane, the domestic adjustment process was painfully regressive. The costs of such adjustment were not addressed or internalized effectively by the cooperative approach described in Part III.

1.   Overview of Adjustment Policies

Patricio Meller, who has written extensively on the Chilean adjustment process, has pointed out that the post-1982 adjustment process in Chile witnessed various important policy changes. In his view, Chile experienced three phases in its adjustment. The government adopted: (i) the now well-known contractionary policies in 1982–1983 to close the expenditure-output gap; (ii) expansionary policies in 1984 to address the internal disequilibrium; and (iii) policies in 1985 aimed at changing relative prices through real devaluation, given the recognition that Chile's external disequilibrium was a long-term problem.

As discussed above, the Chilean government's initial response to the crisis was to rely on the automatic adjustment mechanism. After the devaluation in June of 1982, the government experimented with several exchange-rate policies within a three month period. Monetary policy reflected similar confusion. The recession and devaluations reduced the economy's liquidity. The authorities attempted but ultimately failed to pursue an active monetary policy through increases in the M1 money supply.

As to Chile's agreements with the IMF, the 1983–1984 IMF Standby Arrangement prescribed orthodox contractionary adjustment measures, including depreciation of the peso, reduction of wages, a cautious monetary policy, fiscal restraints, and maintenance of a market-based open economy. The arrangement was revised in 1984 in light of Chile's failure to meet certain performance criteria. Given the high unemployment rate in Chile (above twenty percent at that time), the government and the IMF agreed to an expansionary policy that would allow a higher public deficit. The increase in public investment was financed by a hike in rates and tariffs of public utilities and postponement of tax reform.

The 1985–1987 IMF Extended Fund Facility envisioned significant reductions in the current account deficit, a reduction in inflation, attainment of a small balance-of-payments surplus in each phase of the program, and moderate economic growth fueled by Chile's exports. The goals would be accomplished by: (i) maintaining a high real exchange rate via crawlingpeg minidevaluations; (ii) continued adherence to the wage restraint policy; (iii) fiscal restraint; (iv) a monetary policy aimed, inter alia, at eliminating Central Bank subsidies and recapitalizing the banking system; and (v) orderly external debt service that would eventually shift Chile's source of external credit from commercial banks to multilateral and official sources. The Chilean economic authorities followed the performance criteria faithfully and at the end of the period exceeded the IMF's targets for the current account, the economic growth rate, the balance of payments, and the public sector deficit.

As noted above, the World Bank and the IMF worked with Chile to support the government's positions with its commercial bank creditors during the 1985–86 negotiations. The Structural Adjustment Loan from the World Bank, which complemented the IMF adjustment program, addressed three structural issues: (i) diversification of exports; (ii) increased public savings through reduction of inefficient public social programs and tax reform to increase public revenues; and (iii) financial reform aimed at recapitalizing the financial system, providing saving incentives to private firms, and eliminating subsidies to borrowers.

In sum, the World Bank and the IMF programs envisioned medium and long-term adjustment measures. The adjustment measures were complemented by a work-out with Chile's commercial bank creditors-debt restructuring and new money. Increases in domestic savings, which required great sacrifices by certain segments of the Chilean population, would be transferred out of Chile in the form of interest payments to the commercial bank creditors. As Meller has noted,

[T]he renegotiation of foreign debts imposed a heavy future burden on the Chilean economy. In bargaining with commercial banks, the Chilean government had to provide public guarantees for unguaranteed, private debts, thus eliminating the possibility of major write-offs in case-by-case negotiations among private agents. In this way, the government "socialized" among Chilean society (present and future) large private losses that could not be serviced or repaid . . .

Between 1982 and 1988, the net outward transfer of real resources in external debt service averaged approximately $800 million per year.

2.   Regressive Aspects

Chile's resolve to be the good debtor required certain segments of the population to make greater sacrifices than others.

a.   *The Favored*

The Central Bank of Chile played a key role in preventing the collapse of the domestic financial system: "Whereas previously the Central Bank had pursued a policy of minimum intervention in the liberalised domestic financial market and in capital movements, from 1983 on it became the primary domestic financial intermediary, the conduit for the bulk of foreign credit disbursement." The Central Bank, for example, provided: (i) public guarantees of private financial sector external debt; (ii) a preferential exchange rate for foreign currency debtors; (iii) a conversion scheme ("dedollarization") whereby dollar debt could be swapped for peso debt at a preferential exchange rate; and (iv) subsidized interest rate swaps with Chilean commercial banks. In 1985, the Central Bank also purchased approximately $2.4 billion in risky loans made by domestic banks." At the end of the day, the government, in effect, bailed out the two largest *grupos* in Chile.

The government also implemented regressive tax measures by focusing on taxation of expenditures and encouraging savings through tax credits while reducing corporate taxes and marginal income tax rates. Intervened banks and companies were reprivatized through a "popular capitalism" program that some say amounted to "a free gift to high-income groups (those affected by marginal tax rates of at least 30 percent)." In 1986, the government began selling off traditional state-owned enterprises, such as various public utilities and the national airline. Foreign investors, using steeply discounted Chilean external debt purchased on the secondary market and redeemed by the Central Bank at par value, participated in these privatizations, prompting

Meller to observe that the government played "Santa Claus" to foreigners, as well as to Chilean high income groups.

b.   *The Vulnerable*

Meanwhile, the post-1982 economic adjustment measures resulted in a twenty percent per capita reduction of public social expenditures, mainly in health, education, and housing. Yet approximately fifty percent of health and education expenditures and seventy-seven percent of housing expenditures benefitted the lowest forty percent of the income group in Chile. Real wages plummeted by more than twenty percent at the outset of the adjustment phase and remained close to that level for several years thereafter. Construction and industrial workers as well as underpaid public sector employees suffered disproportionate losses in this regard." The unemployment rate exceeded 31 percent in 1983 and remained above the 1980 level (17 percent) until 1987, when it dropped to 13.9 percent. More than half of the unemployed were in the lowest fifth of the income group." Consumption per capita dropped by fifteen percent as a result of the stabilization. By 1988, the share of total consumption by households in the highest 20 percent of the income group stood at 54.6 percent, compared to a 12.6 percent share for the lowest 40 percent of the income group. "Given the real devaluations that took place throughout this period and the different composition of consumption baskets among the socio-economic groups, the highest twenty percent income group lost approximately eleven percent less in purchasing power than those in the lowest forty percent income group."

Although the poor (working and unemployed) and working class suffered disproportionately throughout the adjustment process in Chile, the government targeted social expenditures on the very poor and most vulnerable, including pregnant mothers and children under six. Moreover, the government implemented emergency job programs to combat unemployment. At the height of the crisis (1983), these programs employed approximately 500,000 people. Although these programs were useful in some, respects, some observers have noted that they provided grossly inadequate subsidies and were otherwise laden with stigma . . .

"The Spread"

Setting: Present day, a law school office filled with stacks of admissions files

Characters:

Professor Thomas Swanson, son of Chairman of the big bank

Professor Joy Anderson

Anderson: This is an interesting file.

Swanson: Stands out?

Anderson: It does.

Swanson: Tell me.

Anderson: Her name is Liliana Dominguez.

Swanson: California? Texas? New York?

Anderson: Chile. Santiago. She moved to the states when she was a kid.

Swanson: Anything else?

Anderson: Her essay. You should read it.

Swanson: Let me see it. (reads part of the essay to himself)

"I'm a survivor of the 'Lost Decade' in Latin America. In 1986, my father lost his job. He was a statistician in the Banco Central, the country's central bank. He told me many fathers lost their jobs. 'It's for the good of our country,' he told me. We left Chile in 1987 for the United States to find a better life. We ended up in a small town in the northeast, where my father found a job cleaning offices. That's the best he could do. But I knew he was humiliated.

I remember the day. It was a Friday in 1989 when I returned early from school because the heat let us out early. I found my mother crying at our small kitchen table. She had a letter in her hand. It was in my father's handwriting. The letter said he quit his job and left us. He left us to find a man who was the Chairman of a big bank. He was going to ask the man whether it was worth the spread. I didn't know what that meant then. I learned about it in a finance course in undergraduate school.

I never saw my father again . . . With my law degree, along with my MBA, I hope to work in investment banking. Maybe I might find my father. When he vacuums my office."

Swanson: Her LSAT score is in the gutter. We can't risk it.

Anderson: Your call.

Swanson: We have to live with the calls we make, don't we?

(pause)

Anderson: That's pretty cryptic, Thomas.

Swanson: Do you know what a spread is?

(fade to black)

You Gotta Know Something About Them!

James Baker

James A. Baker, III has been around the White House for some time. Although we've focused on his role in the Treasury, he also assumed the role of Secretary of State, White House Chief of Staff and advisor to the President, Personal Envoy of the UN Secretary General, and a host of other high-ranking positions. James has been a senior partner at his grandfather's (James Addison Baker, founder of Baker & Botts LLP) firm since 1993.

Nicholas F. Brady

Nicholas Brady's father, James Brady, worked in investments and rubbed shoulders with the likes of the Rockefellers, the du Ponts, and the Mellons. His great-grandfather, Anthony Brady, worked closely with Thomas Edison. After studying at Yale and Harvard, Nicholas became a U.S. senator (New Jersey), and served as the Treasury Secretary from 1988 to1993. Nicholas recently offered to donate $50,000 (and an extra $100,000 on certain conditions) to the Warrior-Scholar project—an organization focused on helping veterans transition from military to college life.

Jacques De Larosiere

Jacques De Larosiere served as the Managing Director of the IMF from 1978 to 1987. Today he serves as the President of the Observatoire de l'Epargne Européenne, a position he took on after he retired as the advisor to the chairman of BNP Paribas (a huge global banking group). Between (and before) these positions, he worked in international finance in other capacities. You would think these high-finance guys are all about caviar and champagne. Not Jacques. In an interview in 1997, he said, "I cannot understand excess. When I was growing up in Paris, my family never took a taxi; that was frowned upon . . . I always look at the marginal taxpayer . . . and ask myself if I were that person, could I afford five-star hotels and lavish receptions?"

Paul Volcker

While Mr. Larosiere was serving at the IMF, Paul Volcker was serving as chairman of the U.S. Federal Reserve. Appointed by President Carter in 1979, Volcker held this position until 1987 when President Reagan appointed Alan Greenspan in his stead. Recently, Volcker has been memorialized in part of the Dodd-Frank Reform Act of 2010 in a section of that law entitled the "Volcker Rule." Today, however, Paul has retired from the spotlight (he served as chairman of the Obama Administration's Economic Advisory Board until 2011) and has taken up private life. He's a huge fly-fishing enthusiast and told Forbes Magazine shortly after his retirement that he had a number of fishing trips planned already; a fitting close to the career of someone who was quite the "big fish" in his own field.

What's Up with That?

Eurocurrency Markets

As we said in the text, foreign commercial banks, including U.S. banks, made Eurocurrency loans to developing countries. Eurocurrency is currency deposited in banks outside the currency's home country. So, for example, a dollar deposited in a London bank is a Eurodollar, yen is a Euroyen. You can even have a Euroeuro. Although London was, and still is for the most part, the home of the Eurocurrency markets, today there are Eurocurrency markets in other places such as Singapore—e.g. you can have a Eurodollar deposit in Singapore. All are considered "offshore" markets.

Eurocurrency was born in the 1950s during the Cold War, when the Soviets moved their dollars from the U.S. to Europe out of fear that the U.S. would expropriate their dollar deposits. This created the "Eurodollar," the most important Eurocurrency today. By 1966, the Eurodollar market expanded into a Eurocurrency market with a gross size over $20 billion. By 1970, its size was about $57 billion.

Why did the Eurocurrency market develop? Because banks wanted to avoid domestic regulations that increased their costs. In the United States, these regulations included: reserve requirements on time deposits; a regulation that prohibited interest on demand deposits and placed a ceiling on time deposits; FDIC premia; fed, state, local tax; and lending limits.

By establishing branches or subsidiaries in the lightly-regulated London market, U.S. banks could become more profitable by making loans with competitive rates. As of 2003, the Eurodollar market stood at $15,926 billion.

Paris Club

It's not about wine and baguettes. The Paris Club is a forum in which sovereign borrowers on an ad hoc basis can restructure loans made by governments or by private lenders with a creditor-government guarantee. Government agencies, such as the Agency for International Development, the Export-Import Bank, and the Commodity Credit Corporation in the United States, typically provide such public sector credit. Private debt to official creditors (e.g., Ex-Im Bank loan to a private borrower through a supplier credit program) can also be restructured under the auspices of the Paris Club if the government in which the private borrower is located cannot provide the borrower with foreign exchange to service the debt.

Bank Capital and Loan Loss Reserves

This stuff is important, so don't let your eyes glaze over. A bank's balance sheet is comprised in part of assets and liabilities. Assets typically consist of loans to its customers. Liabilities represent that bank's debt and traditionally consist of deposits—yeah, like when you deposit money in your bank. If the total value of a bank's assets exceeds that bank's liabilities, the amount of that difference is the bank's capital. So why do regulators require banks to hold a certain amount of capital—say, capital equal to 10% of assets? We'll just mention two reasons. First, capital acts like a cushion to absorb losses so that the bank doesn't fail. The concern is not so much that that particular bank will fail as it is that the failure will cause other banks to fail—what we call "systemic risk" in the biz. Second, it may prevent "moral hazard." You see, a bank may engage in risky business, such as making a bunch of risky but maybe really profitable loans. If the bank loans go sour and the government rescues the bank, it's likely to keep engaging in the risky, possibly even riskier, stuff because it knows the government will come to the rescue. But bank capital includes shareholders' equity. If the bank loses its shirt, so too will the shareholders. So the thinking is that the shareholders will police the bank. That's good in theory . . . in theory.

Now let's talk about loan loss reserves. A bank adds to its loan loss reserves because it recognizes that some borrowers won't repay their loans. If that's the case, the bank must write off the bad debt. It does so by setting aside a portion of its earnings and putting it into the loan loss reserves account. When the bank does this, it's retaining earnings and by doing that adding to the difference between the bank's assets and its liabilities. This increases the bank's capital. Keep in mind that when a bank does add to its loan loss reserves, it isn't necessarily at that time writing off the bad debt. It may wait to formally write it off. When it does formally write it off, the bank's assets are reduced by the amount of the write off. The write off also reduces the bank's capital. But keep in mind that at the time of the write off, the bank's reported earnings won't be affected because they were reduced earlier to make the contribution to the loan loss reserve account.

Performance Criteria

Performance criteria are specific and measurable conditions that borrowing member countries have to meet before they can receive loans beyond the first tranche. The conditions are related to macroeconomic variables like monetary and credit aggregates, a minimum level of international reserves, fiscal balances, or a maximum level of government borrowing. While "officially" the member country has the responsibility of selecting and following through with these conditions, in reality the IMF chooses what must be done (because really, these measures are meant to safeguard IMF resources). And that's the problem. Because borrowing countries had no "ownership" of the criteria, they often couldn't meet them. In reality we could call them "non-performance" criteria.

Debt Trading on the Secondary Market

Banks make loans to borrowers, right? We can call that the "primary market"—i.e., lenders to borrowers. The banks can then sell the loans on the "secondary market" to other investors. In the big time, a bunch of banks get together to make a big "syndicated loan." Once the loan is made to the borrower, the banks can sell their slice of the loan on the secondary market. The trading desks of big investment banks handle the trades among investors. Brady Bonds also traded on the secondary market.

Treasury Zero Coupon Bonds

Generically, zero coupon bonds are pretty easy to understand. Most people understand that bonds pay regular interest on the principal—coupon payments. Zero coupon bonds are just that—no coupons, no interest payments to the bondholder. Instead, investors buy these at a pretty big discount from the face value—what it's worth when it matures (time for the bond issuer to pay up). When the bond matures, the investor gets a lump sum comprised of the initial payment it made at the discount plus what amounts to the interest on the bond—what's called "imputed interest" in the biz. U.S. Treasury bonds are supposed to be a golden investment because it's the U.S. Treasury—not exactly a slouch.

QUESTIONS FROM YOUR TALKING DOG

1.   You love to recycle your gin bottles, don't you? An environmentally-conscious alcoholic. Just kidding! Put my leash on and let's go. It's a sunny day. Sorry about that lame joke. But I saw you were reading something on the 1980s. I got lots of questions for ya' on this walk. Let's start with petro-dollar recycling. What was that all about?

2.   Why's a bank part of indirect finance? I mean, how does it make money?

3.   Those Eurodollar jumbo loans you mentioned at the house. Why are they floating rate loans?

4.   Why did developing countries borrow so much?

5.   I thought scissors are what you use to trim my cute tail. Yeah, it is. What's with the scissors thing in the crisis?

6.   I don't get it. Why didn't the U.S. regulators force the banks to write off the bad loans immediately?

7.   I've seen you muddling mojitos. Is that what happened in the crisis? If it was, they must have had lots of fun! Or does that "muddling through" thing mean something else?

8.   Is the Paris Club in Iowa or France? What do they do in this club? Good dancing?

9.   Here's a ten million dollar question: What the heck is FASB 15? Before you explain, can you give me a horse tranquilizer?

10.   You're always mentioning conditionality. You even bark it out when you sleep. What was that all about in the crisis?

11.   What was the difference between the Baker Plan and Brady Initiative? Just the names?

12.   What was the difference between "discount bonds" and "par bonds?" And "enhancements," what was that all about? Can I get an enhancement? Maybe a better bed?

13.   Tell me how debt restructuring worked on the ground in Chile. By the way, where can we get some empanadas? I'm hungry.

14.   What's a "financing gap" and how was it filled?

15.   Are we lost? I don't recognize this alley. While we're figuring out our bearings, why do they call the crisis "the lost decade of development?" Who was hurt the most?

16.   Loan loss reserves? Tell me how they work.

17.   Let's take a break under this tree. Good. Now. Can you tell me something about Africa's foreign debt?

18.   I like debates. Tell me about the debate regarding the impact of SSAPs on income distribution? What? That's not above my head! I read your casebooks, don't I?

19. I'm getting sleepy under this shade. Can you read Eurocurrency loan provisions to me? That'll put me out really fast.

Chapter 5: Supplement

5A. *U.S. Commercial Banks and the Developing Country Debt Crisis*

In the 1980s, Jeffrey Sachs went from country to country advising governments how to cope with the crisis. This excerpt nails the games U.S. commercial banks played, with the help of regulators. Query: Were the games necessary to prevent an implosion of the U.S. financial markets?

J. Sachs & H. Huizinga, "U.S. Commercial Banks and the Developing Country Debt Crisis," NBER Working Paper No. 2455, Brainard, William C., and Gerry L. Perry, eds., Brookings Papers on Economic Activity 1987: 1. pp. 555–557.
© 1987 The Brookings Institution

THE DEBT CRISIS of the less developed countries broke out in August 1982, with the announcement by Mexico that it would be unable to meet debt obligations then falling due. Since then, more than forty developing countries have been forced to reschedule debts with commercial bank creditors and to seek additional lending and other forms of relief from the international financial community. From the inception of the debt crisis, the primary U.S. concern has been the risks to the major U.S. commercial banks, whose exposure in the developing countries has significantly exceeded their total bank capital.

Table 1 shows the exposure of the U.S. banks in the major debtor countries at the end of 1986. The exposure is divided by size of bank (the nine largest banks, as against the rest of the U.S. banks) and by type of claim (on the public sector, as against the private sector). The concentration of the claims is high: the exposure of the top nine banks in just the top four countries, Argentina, Brazil, Mexico, and Venezuela, accounts for $41 billion, or 45 percent of total U.S. bank exposure shown in the table. The top nine banks account for a remarkable 65 percent of total exposure of U.S. banks in Latin America. Sovereign loans, those to foreign public sector borrowers, account for about two-thirds of U.S. bank lending to the less developed countries (LDCs).

Table 1. Claims of U.S. Banks in the LDC Debtor Countries, End-1986
Millions of dollars except as noted

| Country | Claims of top nine banks | | Claims of all other banks | | Secondary market | |
	Public	Other	Public	Other	Bid price[a] (dollars)	Value of all public debt
Argentina	3,961	1,967	1,677	919	47.0	2,650
Bolivia	41	2	34	19	10.0	8
Brazil	10,176	5,183	3,822	3,229	55.0	7,699
Chile	2,850	1,296	1,097	1,219	67.0	2,644
Colombia	968	560	236	384	81.0	975
Costa Rica	204	10	169	33	33.0	123
Dominican Republic	286	35	78	28	42.0	153
Ecuador	1,161	197	712	101	45.0	843
Gabon	34	10	3	0	82.0	30
Guatemala	28	7	14	30	72.0	30
Honduras	84	19	33	38	38.0	44
Ivory Coast	217	57	74	17	60.0	175
Jamaica	158	13	24	9	37.0	67
Liberia	24	493	5	126	5.0	1
Malawi	25	12	1	4	74.0	19
Mexico	8,960	4,393	5,571	4,732	53.0	7,701
Morocco	405	282	65	140	65.5	308
Nicaragua	17	8	41	0	5.0	3
Nigeria	404	263	144	92	28.0	153
Panama	261	1,117	114	701	64.0	240
Peru	511	307	383	145	11.0	98
Philippines	2,611	1,092	942	462	67.0	2,381
Poland	290	73	89	17	43.0	163
Romania	93	22	14	11	87.0	93
Senegal	20	2	6	0	61.0	16
Sudan	31	6	1	1	2.0	1
Uruguay	653	45	162	69	68.0	554
Venezuela	4,206	2,301	1,355	1,251	67.0	3,726
Yugoslavia	965	350	413	337	70.0	965
Zaire	8	4	1	0	24.5	2
Zambia	69	4	2	2	18.0	13
Total	39,721	20,131	17,282	14,116	. . .	31,878
Percent of capital	85	43	25	20	. . .	27

Sources: Federal Financial Institutions Examination Council, "Country Exposure Lending Survey: December 1986," Statistical release E-16 (126) (April 24, 1987); Salomon Brothers, Inc., *Indicative Prices for Less Developed Country Bank Loans* (July 27, 1987).

a. Bid price for a $100 claim on the secondary market as of July 1987.

The debt management strategy pursued by the United States and the official financial community since 1982 has been geared toward the protection of the large commercial banks, at least on a short-run accounting basis. U.S. policy has been to maintain current interest servicing by the debtor countries to the U.S. banks and to avoid any explicit debt forgiveness or even capitalization of interest payments. U.S. regulators have applied lax prudential standards to banks with large LDC exposures, allowing them to carry almost all such exposure on the books at face value, though its value on the secondary market is heavily discounted. Banks have also been allowed to count as current income all the interest payments they receive on the loans, even those payments made possible only by new "involuntary" loans to the debtor country.

By acting as if all is normal, the regulators have hoped to accomplish three things: to keep the debtor countries from halting interest payments or promoting alternative proposals for debt forgiveness; to keep the banks from withdrawing precipitously from the debtor countries; and to keep depositors and other creditors of the banks from withdrawing precipitously from the banks. In a limited sense that strategy has worked. Worst-case scenarios of financial panic have been avoided, and the banks have been given time to increase their capital ratios. U.S. bank exposure in the problem debtor countries as a percentage of the book value of primary capital has declined significantly since 1982, as shown in table 2. The regulatory laxness may, however, have hindered the adjustment of the U.S. banks to the crisis by allowing them to move slowly in rebuilding their capital base. Some banks have paid unduly large dividends at the expense of their capital in recent years, because they have been allowed to overstate their economic incomes.

Table 2. Exposure in the Debtor Countries as a Percentage of Bank Capital, Various Periods, 1982–86[a]

Region	End-1982	Mid-1984	End-1986
All U.S. banks			
All LDCs	186.5	156.6	94.8
Latin America	118.8	102.5	68.0
Africa	10.2	7.7	3.2
Nine major banks			
All LDCs	287.7	246.3	153.9
Latin America	176.5	157.8	110.2
Africa	19.3	14.3	6.0
All other banks			
All LDCs	116.0	96.1	55.0
Latin America	78.6	65.2	39.7
Africa	3.8	3.3	1.3
Addendum			
Total bank capital (billions of dollars)			
All U.S. banks	70.6	84.7	116.1
Nine major banks	29.0	34.1	46.7
All other banks	41.6	50.6	69.4

Source: Federal Financial Institutions Examination Council, "Country Exposure Lending Survey," April 25, 1983, October 15, 1984, and April 24, 1987, issues.

a. Exposures are total amounts owed to U.S. banks after adjustments for guarantees and external borrowing. Total exposures are calculated for all LDCs (OPEC, nonoil Latin America, nonoil Asia, nonoil Africa); Latin America (nonoil Latin America plus Ecuador and Venezuela); and Africa (nonoil Africa plus Algeria, Gabon, Libya, and Nigeria).

However well the regulatory treatment has papered over the crisis, it has not solved it. Nor has it hidden that fact from the debtors, the banks, or the marketplace. Despite the official optimism of the United States and the creditor community regarding the debt crisis and despite the seemingly relaxed attitudes of the U.S. regulators, most market participants have conceded that much of the LDC debt will not be repaid. A good indicator of long-term expectations regarding LDC claims is the price of those claims on the secondary market. Column 5 of table 1 records the secondary bid price for a $100 claim, as of July 1987. The price for claims on Argentina, Brazil, and Mexico is in the range of $45–$55. The average price for the entire U.S. bank portfolio, weighted by exposure in the various countries, is $55.90 per $100 claim. The $57 billion of U.S. bank exposure to foreign governments in table 1 has a secondary market value of $31.9 billion.

Although many bankers and U.S. administration spokesmen try to argue that the secondary market price of U.S. debt is a poor guide to more general market sentiments concerning the LDC debt, stock market prices of the commercial banks closely reflect the secondary market valuation of the LDC exposure. As pessimism has grown over the value of the LDC claims in banks' portfolios, equity prices of banks have dropped.

The fact that stock market prices have been discounted helps to explain the current eagerness of banks to sell their LDC exposures at a discount, since they can accept a capital loss in the books without further depressing their market value. Citicorp's decision this past spring to increase its loan loss reserves against Latin American exposure (an action that was followed by the other major banks in the United States and abroad) appears to be a prelude to a policy of selling off the LDC exposure at a significant discount. As we discuss later, this new policy of selling off debt may have important implications for public policy in this area.

We organize our discussion of these developments in the following manner. First, we briefly consider the underlying causes of the growing market discount on the LDC debt. Then we turn to an analysis of how the banks and regulators have responded to the crisis since 1982. Next, we examine the evidence that the stock market is now valuing the LDC debt at the substantial discounts reflected in the secondary market. Finally, we explore the implications of the market discount for the future of debt negotiations and for debt relief.

Why the LDC Debt Sells at a Discount

The shortcomings of the current U.S. debt management strategy have not gone unnoticed. In a 1986 study Sachs pointed out that most of the optimistic assessments of the debt crisis ignored the internal economic dislocations caused by the large debt overhang. Most optimistic observers have viewed the debtor countries' problem purely in terms of external parameters such as OECD growth, world interest rates, and global commodities prices. They have failed to take account of the economic and political disarray within the debtor countries that has resulted from, or has at least been greatly aggravated by, the debt crisis: low rates of national saving and investment, large budget deficits, and recourse to inflationary finance.

Most of the LDC debtors have little real prospect of servicing the interest due on their external debt in the next few years. In the past five years, they have made significant net resource transfers to the creditors. Latin America, for example, has transferred about 5 percent of GNP per year. But despite these transfers, the debt-export ratios of the major debtor countries have risen, not fallen. (See table 3.)

Recent increases in certain primary commodity prices, apparently in a lagged response to the depreciation of the dollar, gave rise to hope that the export prospects of the LDCs would improve. Ironically, however, most of the price increases have been for nonfood primary commodities produced mainly in the developed countries or in the Asian developing countries, most of which are not in crisis. The prices for sugar, wheat, beef, coffee, and cacao, the main Latin American commodity exports, continue to be deeply depressed. Moreover, international interest rates have risen significantly during 1987.

Table 3. Ratio of External Debt to Exports, 1982, 1984, 1986, and 1987[a]

Percent

Country	1982	1984	1986	1987[b]
Argentina	405	461	536	554
Brazil	339	322	425	471
Chile	333	402	402	370
Colombia	191	254	198	235
Ecuador	239	259	333	464
Mexico	299	292	413	366
Nigeria	84	158	300	310
Peru	269	356	497	551
Philippines	269	309	308	309
Venezuela	84	158	322	278
Total	264	290	385	385

Source: Morgan Guaranty Trust Company of New York, *World Financial Markets* (June–July 1987), p. 4, table 6.

a. The debt-export ratio is the average gross external debt as a percentage of exports of goods, services, and private transfers.

b. Projections.

Many of the major debtor countries are in fiscal turmoil, even after sharp cuts in government spending in recent years. The interest due on the foreign debt constitutes such a large proportion of government expenditures (around 30 percent in many of the debtor countries) that it stands in the way of budgetary reform. The voters in the new democracies in Latin America are not content to absorb further fiscal austerity for the sake of foreign creditors. The recent rise in interest rates will intensify the fiscal pressures. The large fiscal deficits are now being financed in large part through an expansion of credit by the central banks, a process that will result in high inflation. For several years, inflation has been at triple-digit annual rates in Argentina, Brazil, and Peru. It topped a 150 percent annual rate in the spring and summer of 1987 in Mexico. The 20,000 percent hyperinflation in Bolivia was brought under control only after Bolivia stopped all interest payments on the external bank debt.

One result of the internal economic disarray has been a burgeoning of unilateral actions on the debt, particularly in the democratic countries in Latin America. Bolivia, Brazil, Costa Rica, the Dominican Republic, Ecuador, Honduras, and Peru have all unilaterally suspended part or all of the interest servicing on their foreign debt in the past two years. In Argentina and Mexico, the two major debtor countries that have not suspended, the banks found it necessary in 1987 to relend much of the interest due in order to forestall a unilateral suspension of payments.

Mexico received approximately $6 billion in bank credits, and Argentina recently signed an agreement for $2 billion in new bank credits.

Three other large debtors, Chile, the Philippines, and Venezuela, have been servicing their debts recently without substantial refinancing of interest. Chile, of course, is not so much a model debtor country as a model authoritarian country whose government can impose the requisite domestic austerity to make it possible to service the debt. In the Philippines, internal instability at first prevented the Aquino government from taking a tough stand with creditors. The government therefore signed a rescheduling agreement in 1987 with no concerted lending from the banks. But there is now a good chance that a unilateral partial suspension of debt servicing will be declared by the Philippine Congress. In Venezuela, as well, the government is under fierce political pressure to abandon its recent debt rescheduling agreement. Even the government's own political party has called for reopening negotiations to achieve debt relief.

In debt agreements negotiated in the past year, the banks have lost ground. In the first round of reschedulings, in 1983, debt was recontracted with an interest rate spread of about 2 percentage points over LIBOR (the London Interbank Offered Rate). In the second round of reschedulings, in 1984–85, the spread fell to about 1.2 percentage points. In the recent round, the spread has fallen further, to less than 1 percentage point. Similarly, commissions have declined, and the maturities and grace periods on the rescheduled debts have also increased.

It is thus not difficult to understand the growing discount on LDC paper in the secondary market. The economies in most cases are not getting better, and the countries are increasingly demanding more concessions in reflection of that reality. Moreover, the international macroeconomic environment, particularly regarding interest rates and commodity prices, remains unsatisfactory. Detailed price quotations on the secondary market have been available only for the past year, with several investment banks now circulating price sheets, but all indications are that the discount has been growing and the prices falling over the past few years . . .

Patterns of Debt Management by the Banks and Bank Regulators

In response to the debt crisis, U.S. banks have virtually stopped making new loans to the problem debtor countries, with the little new lending that remains being confined to specific bailout packages. Bank earnings, for the most part, did not suffer until 1987, when banks set aside reserves to cover possible losses on LDC claims. Under pressure from regulators, the banks increased their primary capital base and thereby reduced the ratio of LDC exposure to capital.

BANK EXPOSURE IN THE LDCs

The change in bank lending is illustrated in table 5. Although the widely publicized negotiated loan agreements are termed "new money" packages, U.S. bank exposure to the problem debtor countries fell in absolute dollar amount during 1982–86, after rising rapidly during 1979–82. The absolute decline in lending belies the myth that the banks have continued throughout the crisis to provide net "new money" to the debtor countries, though at a reduced rate of increase. The widely publicized concerted lending agreements in recent years have been loans to governments. As table 5 shows, claims on the public sector rose 53 percent during 1982–86. But claims on the private sector declined 48 percent. At the same time that the banks have been providing "new money" to governments, they have been withdrawing loans from the private sector. Three other factors can also account for the differential growth in claims on the public and private sectors. To some extent, private sector debts have become public sector debts as governments have taken over some of the foreign obligations of the private sector since the beginning of the debt crisis. Secondly, the decline in exposures to the private sector represents, in part, a write-off of claims on the private sector, rather than an amortization of loans. Third, declines in exposure also reflect sales by the banks of their LDC claims, or declines due to debt-equity swaps. Given the published data it is impossible to distinguish changes in exposure due to new loans, amortizations, write offs, sales, swaps, or public sector assumptions of private sector debt.

The notion of "new money" is also misleading because most "new money" packages after 1982 have involved considerably less in new loans than is due to the same creditors in interest. Thus, even when Mexico or Argentina gets a so-called new loan after months of hair raising negotiations, the check is still written by the debtor government to the commercial bank. Technically, the net resource transfer (equal to new lending net of amortizations and interest payments) to the debtors is negative. These negative net resource transfers point up one of the fallacies in a popular argument against LDC default—that if a country defaults, it will be not be able to attract new bank money. Losing new money will be of little concern to a debtor country if the reduction in interest payments achieved by default exceeds the new money that the country is able to borrow by not defaulting.

Table 5. Changes in Bank Loan Exposure, 1979–86

Country	Percentage change in exposure, 1979–82			Percentage change in exposure, 1982–86		
	Total	Public	Private	Total	Public	Private
Argentina	71	165	41	4	84	−44
Bolivia	−31	−8	−54	−75	−70	−84
Brazil	50	78	38	10	92	−36
Chile	147	17	226	6	267	−50
Colombia	47	83	35	−33	19	−57
Costa Rica	−12	27	−35	−16	42	−81
Dominican Republic	33	10	65	−15	49	−75
Ecuador	29	22	33	7	147	−77
Gabon	−33	−35	2	−72	−76	−30
Guatemala	−47	57	−54	−60	27	−75
Honduras	−34	30	−57	−9	17	−38
Ivory Coast	46	42	63	−43	−41	−50
Jamaica	11	8	19	−22	−05	−68
Liberia	−16	−43	−15	−67	−55	−67
Malawi	−20	−41	46	−54	−49	−61
Mexico	113	131	102	−3	50	−38
Morocco	15	−23	121	18	27	9
Nicaragua	−2	70	−76	−84	−84	−84
Nigeria	149	54	501	−51	−39	−63
Panama	31	485	24	−61	−3	−65
Peru	82	27	139	−47	−2	−72
Philippines	43	99	18	−11	45	−53
Poland	−18	13	−33	−69	−44	−89
Romania	−31	−28	−34	−50	−15	−79
Senegal	−1	−35	251	−62	−38	−94
Sudan	8	28	−56	−82	−83	−67
Uruguay	230	492	65	1	28	−59
Venezuela	34	28	38	−21	15	−47
Yugoslavia	−71	−85	−64	−11	250	−64
Zaire	−39	−37	−73	−91	−94	21
Zambia	25	−11	231	−60	−39	−92
Overall exposure	42	52	36	−12	53	−48

Sources: Federal Financial Institutions Examination Council, "Country Exposure Lending Survey," various issues.

The pattern of concerted lending packages among the debtor governments also illustrates the venerable economic adage, "If you owe your bank £100, you're in trouble; if you owe your bank £1,000,000, then he's in trouble." Very systematically, it is the countries with large debts that have been able to bargain for new lending from the banks . . .

BANK EARNINGS

Ironically, during 1982–86 the debt crisis did not have a serious adverse effect on the reported current *earnings* of the banks, even though it called into question their very solvency. While doubts grew about the long-term willingness of the debtor countries to service their debts and while principal repayments were postponed for many years in the course of reschedulings, most LDCs continued to service the interest due, though sometimes only after the banks loaned them some of the money to do so. Even when interest payments were clearly tied to new loans, the bank regulators allowed the banks to report the interest received in full as current income, rather than, for example, requiring that part of the interest be allocated to loan loss reserves, and therefore not be counted as current income.

As shown in table 7, reported net income rose between 1980 and 1986 for all of the nine major banks, with the conspicuous exception of BankAmerica, which suffered major losses on its domestic loan portfolio. In some cases the measured income was even enhanced by the crisis, because in 1983 and 1984 many of the rescheduling agreements involved significant front-end fees and an increase in the interest rate spreads built into the loan agreements. As table 8 shows, the share of LDC assets on a nonaccrual basis at the end of 1986 is only slightly higher than the ratio of domestic loans on a nonaccrual basis.

Table 6. Medium-Term Concerted Lending as a Percentage of Debt Outstanding from Private Financial Institutions, 1983–86

Percent

Country	1983	1984	1985	1986	Average, 1983–86
Argentina[a]	12	18	0	0	8
Bolivia	0	0	0	0	0
Brazil	11	14	0	0	6
Chile	35	16	9	0	15
Colombia	0	0	29	0	7
Congo	0	0	0	9	2
Costa Rica	0	0	0	0	0
Dominican Republic	0	0	0	0	0
Ecuador	20	0	0	0	5
Gabon	0	0	0	0	0
Guatemala	0	0	0	0	0
Honduras	0	0	0	0	0
Ivory Coast	0	0	4	0	1
Jamaica	0	0	0	0	0
Liberia	0	0	0	0	0
Madagascar	0	0	0	0	0
Malawi	0	0	0	0	0
Mexico	11	6	0	8	6
Morocco	0	0	0	0	0
Nicaragua	0	0	0	0	0
Nigeria	0	0	0	4	1
Panama	0	0	3	0	1
Peru	16	0	0	0	4
Philippines	0	18	0	0	5
Senegal	0	0	0	0	0
Sudan	0	0	0	0	0
Togo	0	0	0	0	0
Uruguay	18	0	0	0	5
Venezuela	0	0	0	0	0
Yugoslavia	41	0	0	0	10
Zaire	0	0	0	0	0
Zambia	0	0	0	0	0

Sources: Authors' calculations with data from World Bank, *World Debt Tables: External Debt of Developing Countries, 1986–1987* (World Bank, 1987); World Bank, *World Debt Tables, Second Supplement* (World Bank, 1987); and Maxwell Watson and others *International Capital Markets: Developments and Prospects, 1986*, Occasional Paper 43 (IMF, December 1986). For each year, we calculate the ratio of the concerted loan CL_t to the disbursed debt at time $t-1$, D_{t-1}.

a. In 1987 Argentina received a concerted loan amounting to 5 percent of its 1986 outstanding loans.

Table 7. Bank Reported Net Income, 1980–87

Millions of dollars

Bank	1980	1981	1982	1983	1984	1985	1986	1987[a]
Citicorp	449	531	723	860	890	998	1058	−999
BankAmerica	643	445	390	391	346	337	−518	−929
Chase Manhattan	354	412	308	430	406	565	585	−832
Manufacturer's Hanover	229	252	295	337	353	408	411	−1103
J. P. Morgan	342	348	394	460	538	705	873	952
Chemical	174	205	241	301	341	390	402	−703
Security Pacific	181	206	234	264	291	323	386	112
First Interstate	225	236	221	247	276	313	338	−165
Bankers Trust	214	188	223	260	307	371	428	−151
First Chicago	63	119	137	184	86	169	276	−438

Sources: Compustat data base and Keefe, Bruyette, and Woods, Inc., *Keefe Nationwide Bankscan* (July 17, 1987).
a. Projected.

Table 8. Percentage of Bank Exposure to Latin America on Nonaccrual and Percentage of Other Bank Assets on Nonaccrual, End-1986[a]

Bank	Latin debt	Other assets
Citicorp	3.8	1.6
BankAmerica	6.1	3.6
Chase Manhattan	3.0	2.0
Manufacturer's Hanover	0.8	3.0
J. P. Morgan	1.8	0.8
Chemical	1.3	2.3
Security Pacific	1.6	1.9
First Interstate	4.4	1.7
Bankers Trust	3.5	1.5
First Chicago	2.4	2.1
Average	2.9	2.0

Source: Based on data from Salomon Brothers, *Review of Bankperformance, 1986* (Salomon Brothers, 1987).
a. Nonaccrual loans are loans in which interest is credited by the bank on a cash basis rather than as it accrues. Latin exposure includes loans to Argentina, Chile, Mexico, and Venezuela.

In assessing the effects of the debt crisis on measured earnings, one must draw a distinction between the bank claims on the public sector and those on the private sector. For the sovereign, or public sector, loans, the vast bulk of interest due has been paid on a timely basis. Among the major debtors before 1987, only Argentina fell behind on interest payments on sovereign debt, in 1984 and early 1985. Brazilian sovereign debt has been in suspension since February 20, 1987. By contrast, private debtors in Argentina, Mexico, and Venezuela have had periods of fairly significant arrearages on their debt, though by the end of 1986 most of those arrearages had been eliminated. Also, an unknown proportion of the private debt has been lost forever in the form of firmlevel bankruptcies or in debt workouts with the creditors at slightly concessionary rates.

Only in 1987 have the income statements of the banks begun to suffer, as some of the larger debtors, especially Brazil, have suspended interest payments and, more important, as banks have made significant additions to loan loss reserves. Because of loan loss provisions, the large U.S. banks posted losses of about $10 billion in the second quarter of 1987.

It is useful here to make clear the meaning of the recent additions to loan loss reserves by Citicorp and the other leading banks. Table 9 shows the size of the additions and the share of Latin American exposure that is now covered by the reserves. That share is calculated by subtracting all domestic nonperforming assets from the banks' total loan loss reserves. The net reserves are then compared with the exposure in Latin America. Citicorp's stated goal was to cover 25 percent of its Latin American exposure.

Since the loan loss reserves are "unallocated," that is, not tied to particular loans, or even to particular countries, they do not involve a write-down in value of particular assets. More obviously, they do not involve any forgiveness by the banks of any part of the debts owed by the developing countries. The increase in unallocated reserves reduces reported income of the banks, but it does not reduce taxable income. On the balance sheet, the increase is a transfer from shareholders' equity to loan loss reserves. It does not affect measured primary capital of the bank because U.S. bank regulators count loan loss reserves as part of primary capital.

The addition to reserves does not affect the cash flow of the banks. In that sense it is a cosmetic move only. In the future, if the banks write off some portion of their LDC exposure, either by selling the assets at a discount or by settling with the countries at below-market terms, they will be able to charge the losses to the loan reserves without any effect on reported income. At that point, however, the capital base of the bank would shrink, and the taxable earnings of the bank would fall in line with the write-off. Thus, by accepting large reported losses now, the banks will be better placed to report positive earnings in the future, even if the LDC loans go sour.

Table 9. Bank Loan Loss Reserves, Net and as a Percentage of Latin Exposure[a]
Millions of dollars except where noted

Bank	Loan loss reserve, end-1986	+ Loan loss reserve addition, 1987	− Domestic nonper-forming assets	= Net loan loss reserve	Net reserve as percent-age of ex-posure to Latin four
Citicorp	1,698	3,000	2,022	2,676	27
BankAmerica	2,172	1,100	3,148	124	2
Chase Manhattan	1,065	1,600	980	1,685	26
Manufacturer's Hanover	1,008	1,700	1,761	947	14
J. P. Morgan	910	0	316	594	14
Chemical	669	1,100	1,015	754	18
Security Pacific	729	500	1,132	97	7
First Interstate	536	750	1,238	48	4
Bankers Trust	591	700	526	765	28
Average	1,042	1,161	1,349	854	16

Sources: Authors' calculations with data from *New York Times*, July 2, 1987; Salomon Brothers, *Review of Bankperformance, 1986.*
a. Data on loan loss reserves are updated through July 2, 1987; all other data are for end-1986. Latin exposure includes loans to Argentina, Brazil, Mexico, and Venezuela.

CAPITAL ADEQUACY

Even before the debt crisis hit, U.S. bank regulators had judged that the capital-asset ratios of U.S. banks were insufficient. New regulations promulgated in the early 1980s called for a rise in the ratio of primary capital to total assets, from the prevailing low levels of about 4 percent to levels of 5.5 percent. Total capital (primary capital plus certain types of qualifying subordinated debt) was required to rise to 6 percent of total bank assets.

A vast literature on banking regulation has stressed the need for such prudential limits. Banks are highly leveraged institutions, subject to the possibility of large fluctuations in net worth and also to various incentive problems. A small decrease in the average value of a bank's assets can dramatically reduce the bank's net worth and even drive the bank into bankruptcy. Moreover, because banks are operating with borrowed funds and because most of those funds are insured by federal deposit insurance, bank managers may have the incentive to take excessive gambles if bank capital is too low a share of total assets. If the gamble goes well, the shareholders enjoy an enormous proportional return to their claims. If the gamble goes poorly, the shareholders lose only the small amount of the net worth, and the deposit insurance institution must make up the difference to the depositors.

Table 10. Bank Primary Capital as a Percentage of Total Assets, 1980–86

Bank	1980	1981	1982	1983	1984	1985	1986
Citicorp	3.8	4.1	4.2	4.9	5.9	6.2	6.8
BankAmerica	4.0	3.9	4.3	5.1	5.8	6.1	6.9
Chase Manhattan	3.8	4.2	4.7	5.4	6.4	6.9	7.0
Manufacturer's Hanover	3.6	3.8	4.6	5.0	5.7	6.3	7.2
J. P. Morgan	4.7	5.1	5.6	6.9	7.0	8.0	8.3
Chemical	3.7	3.9	5.0	5.5	6.3	7.0	7.2
Security Pacific	4.9	4.7	4.9	5.3	5.8	6.4	6.4
First Interstate	5.1	5.0	5.0	5.8	6.1	6.2	6.1
Bankers Trust	3.5	4.0	4.5	5.6	6.2	6.4	6.5
First Chicago	4.7	4.3	5.0	5.6	6.1	7.2	8.3
Average	4.2	4.3	4.8	5.5	6.1	6.7	7.1

Source: Salomon Brothers, *Review of Bankperformance*, various editions.

Another aspect of prudential supervision, one that was obviously overlooked in the 1970s and early 1980s, is the requirement that the bank not commit more than 15 percent of its capital in loans to any borrower. In fact, the loans to the Brazilian government and to the Mexican government greatly exceeded 15 percent of capital for many of the large U.S. banks, but the rule was not invoked because the regulators allowed the banks to treat the various official borrowers, such as parastatals, central government, and development banks, in Mexico and Brazil as distinct borrowers even though they were all backed by the same government guarantee. In the event, all of the loans to all of the borrowers went bad at the same time. The multiple borrowers indeed reflected a single risk, as might have been expected.

On paper, the capital adequacy rules have been enforced, and the capital base of the U.S. banks has been strengthened. But at least some of the improvement reflects accounting conventions rather than an actual strengthening of bank balance sheets. For bank capital to protect the bank from bankruptcy and to forestall adverse incentive problems, it should consist mostly of shareholders' equity, and it should be properly valued. But the measure of primary capital used for capital adequacy requirements includes both equity and loan loss reserves. Thus, even when the banks make loan loss provisions because they anticipate future losses on assets, *measured* primary capital is unaffected, because the loan loss provision involves a transfer between shareholders' equity and loan loss reserves, both of which are fully counted in primary capital. Moreover, because the LDC claims are carried in the books at full face value, and until recently were not covered by loan loss provisions, the book values of shareholders' equity clearly overstated the market value of shareholders' equity.

Table 11. Bank Shareholders' Equity as a Percentage of Total Assets, 1981–June 1987

Bank	1981	1982	1983	1984	1985	1986	June 1987
Citicorp	3.6	3.7	4.3	4.2	4.4	4.6	2.7
BankAmerica	3.4	3.7	4.2	4.3	3.8	3.8	3.0
Chase Manhattan	3.9	3.9	4.3	4.5	5.0	5.1	3.2
Manufacturer's Hanover	3.2	3.9	4.2	4.3	4.6	5.0	2.7
J. P. Morgan	4.5	4.6	5.7	5.7	6.3	6.6	6.2
Chemical	3.5	4.1	4.5	4.9	4.9	5.1	3.0
Security Pacific	4.0	3.9	4.4	4.2	4.5	4.5	3.3
First Interstate	4.3	4.4	4.7	4.9	5.1	4.9	3.3
Bankers Trust	3.9	3.7	4.4	4.6	4.9	4.7	3.4
First Chicago	3.7	3.9	4.8	4.8	5.3	5.9	n.a.
Average	3.8	4.0	4.6	4.6	4.9	5.0	3.4

Source: *New York Times*, July 2, 1987; and Salomon Brothers, *Review of Bankperformance*, various editions.
n.a. Not available.

Thus, U.S. banks enjoyed rising capital-asset ratios during 1982–86, as shown in table 10, but suffered a significant decline in the ratio of shareholders' equity to assets as of mid-1987 (table 11), when the banks made a substantial increase in loan loss reserves. The conclusion seems to be that the regulators have raised the ratio of shareholders' equity to total assets but little in the 1980s. Because the loan loss reserves on the Latin American claims still cover no more than 25 percent of the Latin exposure and because the markets are signaling a discount on the debt of perhaps 45 to 50 percent, it seems clear that shareholders' equity is still overstated on account of the LDC debt, even after the additions to loan loss reserves.

Regulatory laxness, a "business as usual" attitude, certainly contributed to the failure of the banks to make a greater advance in rebuilding their equity base. It was clear from the beginning of the debt crisis that at least some of the interest earnings on the LDC debt should have been regarded as fictitious, particularly when leading debtors required new involuntary loans to meet interest payments on existing debts. Prudent regulators might have required that the banks build up capital in part by reducing dividend payouts. But the major banks have maintained dividend payout ratios since 1982 as if the debt crisis had not occurred, as is evident in table 12. BankAmerica was particularly flagrant. Even when its earnings were falling because of bad domestic loans, not to mention bad foreign loans, it continued to pay significant dividends, leading to a sharp rise in the ratio of dividends to income. Now the bank is fighting for survival.

Our conclusion that banks have rebuilt capital slowly must be tempered to the extent that other assets of the banks are undervalued on the books relative to true market values. One reason to think that other assets are indeed undervalued is that, as we show in the next section, the market values of many of the large banks were at or above their book values as of the summer of 1987, despite the clear evidence that the market values of their LDC claims were far below their book values.

We attempted to create an equity-asset ratio based solely on market values rather than book values, by calculating the market value of overall bank assets as the sum of the market value of bank equity and the book value of bank liabilities. We assumed that the banks' liabilities, which are mostly short-term fixed-income liabilities, have a market value equal to book value. We then took the ratio of the market value of equity to the constructed market value of assets. We found that on average for the ten large banks, the ratio of equity at market value to assets rose from 3.2 percent in 1983 and 3.6 percent in 1984 to 5.5 percent in June 1987, suggesting some real increase in capital adequacy. The sharp decline in the stock market in October 1987 has probably pushed the market-based ratio of equity to assets back down sharply, close to the levels of 1984.

There would be one practical implication for LDC debt management if the banks' non-LDC claims are carried on the books at below-market value. As the losses on the LDC assets are realized, for example, by sales of debt in the secondary market, the banks would be able to cushion the effect on their overall capital by selling off other assets that are undervalued on the books and taking the capital gains. Citicorp began to adopt this strategy in the fall of 1987 by selling a part of its real estate equity at a significant capital gain to offset the reported losses on its LDC portfolio . . .

Table 12. Dividend Payout Ratios for Ten Banks with Large LDC Exposure, 1980–86

Bank	1980	1981	1982	1983	1984	1985	1986
Citicorp	35	37	31	29	32	32	35
BankAmerica	33	50	59	70	86	−43[a]	0
Chase Manhattan	28	27	44	32	41	30	31
Manufacturer's Hanover	37	37	38	37	45	38	37
J. P. Morgan	35	37	37	36	34	29	27
Chemical	31	29	34	34	36	34	34
Bankers Trust	20	28	27	27	27	26	26
Wells Fargo	36	36	33	33	32	30	28
Marine Midland	23	26	28	29	38	29	28
Irving Bank	28	28	37	36	36	32	31
Average	31	33	37	36	41	31[b]	28

Source: Salomon Brothers, *Review of Bankperformance*, various editions.
a. BankAmerica paid a dividend of $1.16 per common share despite losses of $2.68 per share.
b. Excluding BankAmerica.

Latin American Exposure and the Market Valuation of Commercial Banks

The regulators and banks have so far operated as though claims on the LDCs are worth their full face value, despite overwhelming evidence to the contrary. The stock markets, however, have seen through the accounting veil and written down the value of banks with heavy exposures in the problem debtor countries . . .

* * *

5B. *Statement of Financial Accounting Standards No. 15 (as issued in 1977)*

Read it and weep. Really. No, for real: those in the biz know this by heart. Remember, if you're a lawyer, you can be anybody at any given point in time. Can you identify the key passages that lawyers focused on in the crisis?

> Portions of FASB Statement No. 15, Accounting by Debtors and Creditors for Troubled Debt Restructurings, copyrighted by the Financial Accounting Foundation (FAF), 401 Merritt 7, PO Box 5116, Norwalk, CT 06856–5116, are reprinted with permission. Complete copies of Statement 15 are available from the FAF

FASB 15: Accounting by Debtors and Creditors for Troubled Debt Restructurings

1.   This Statement establishes standards of financial accounting and reporting by the debtor and by the creditor for a troubled debt restructuring. The Statement does not cover accounting for allowances for estimated uncollectible amounts and does not prescribe or proscribe particular methods for estimating amounts of uncollectible receivables.

2.   A restructuring of a debt constitutes a troubled debt restructuring for purposes of this Statement if the creditor for economic or legal reasons related to the debtor's financial difficulties grants a concession to the debtor that it would not otherwise consider. That concession either stems from an agreement between the creditor and the debtor or is imposed by law or a court. For example, a creditor may restructure the terms of a debt to alleviate the burden of the debtor's near-term cash requirements, and many troubled debt restructurings involve modifying terms to reduce or defer cash payments required of the debtor in the near future to help the debtor attempt to improve its financial condition and eventually be able to pay the creditor. Or, for example, the creditor may accept cash, other assets, or an equity interest in the debtor in satisfaction of the debt though the value received is less than the amount of the debt because the creditor concludes that step will maximize recovery of its investment.

3.   Whatever the form of concession granted by the creditor to the debtor in a troubled debt restructuring, the creditor's objective is to make the best

of a difficult situation. That is, the creditor expects to obtain more cash or other value from the debtor, or to increase the probability of receipt, by granting the concession than by not granting it.

4.   In this Statement, a receivable or payable (collectively referred to as debt) represents a contractual right to receive money or a contractual obligation to pay money on demand or on fixed or determinable dates that is already included as an asset or liability in the creditor's or debtor's balance sheet at the time of the restructuring. Receivables or payables that may be involved in troubled debt restructurings commonly result from lending or borrowing of cash, investing in debt securities that were previously issued, or selling or purchasing goods or services on credit. Examples are accounts receivable or payable, notes, debentures and bonds (whether those receivables or payables are secured or unsecured and whether they are convertible or nonconvertible), and related accrued interest, if any. Typically, each receivable or payable is negotiated separately, but sometimes two or more receivables or payables are negotiated together. For example, a debtor may negotiate with a group of creditors but sign separate debt instruments with each creditor. For purposes of this Statement, restructuring of each receivable or payable, including those negotiated and restructured jointly, shall be accounted for individually. The substance rather than the form of the receivable or payable shall govern. For example, to a debtor, a bond constitutes one payable even though there are many bondholders.

5.   A troubled debt restructuring may include, but is not necessarily limited to, one or a combination of the following:

a.   Transfer from the debtor to the creditor of receivables from third parties, real estate, or other assets to satisfy fully or partially a debt (including a transfer resulting from foreclosure or repossession).

b.   Issuance or other granting of an equity interest to the creditor by the debtor to satisfy fully or partially a debt unless the equity interest is granted pursuant to existing terms for converting the debt into an equity interest.

c.   Modification of terms of a debt, such as one or a combination of:

1.   Reduction (absolute or contingent) of the stated interest rate for the remaining original life of the debt.

2.   Extension of the maturity date or dates at a stated interest rate lower than the current market rate for new debt with similar risk.

3.   Reduction (absolute or contingent) of the face amount or maturity amount of the debt as stated in the instrument or other agreement.

4.   Reduction (absolute or contingent) of accrued interest.

6.   Troubled debt restructurings may occur before, at, or after the stated maturity of debt, and time may elapse between the agreement, court order,

etc. and the transfer of assets or equity interest, the effective date of new terms, or the occurrence of another event that constitutes consummation of the restructuring. The date of consummation is the time of the restructuring in this Statement.

7.   A debt restructuring is not necessarily a troubled debt restructuring for purposes of this Statement even if the debtor is experiencing some financial difficulties. For example, a troubled debt restructuring is not involved if (a) the fair value of cash, other assets, or an equity interest accepted by a creditor from a debtor in full satisfaction of its receivable at least equals the creditor's recorded investment in the receivable; (b) the fair value of cash, other assets, or an equity interest transferred by a debtor to a creditor in full settlement of its payable at least equals the debtor's carrying amount of the payable; (c) the creditor reduces the effective interest rate on the debt primarily to reflect a decrease in market interest rates in general or a decrease in the risk so as to maintain a relationship with a debtor that can readily obtain funds from other sources at the current market interest rate; or (d) the debtor issues in exchange for its debt new marketable debt having an effective interest rate based on its market price that is at or near the current market interest rates of debt with similar maturity dates and stated interest rates issued by nontroubled debtors. In general, a debtor that can obtain funds from sources other than the existing creditor at market interest rates at or near those for nontroubled debt is not involved in a troubled debt restructuring. A debtor in a troubled debt restructuring can obtain funds from sources other than the existing creditor in the troubled debt restructuring, if at all, only at effective interest rates (based on market prices) so high that it cannot afford to pay them. Thus, in an attempt to protect as much of its investment as possible, the creditor in a troubled debt restructuring grants a concession to the debtor that it would not otherwise consider.

* * *

STANDARDS OF FINANCIAL ACCOUNTING AND REPORTING

* * *

Accounting by Creditors

* * *

Modification of Terms

* * *

31. If, however, the total future cash receipts specified by the new terms of the receivable, including both receipts designated as interest and those designated as face amount, are less than the recorded investment in the receivable before restructuring, the creditor shall reduce the recorded investment in the receivable to an amount equal to the total future cash

receipts specified by the new terms. The amount of the reduction is a loss to be recognized according to paragraph 35. Thereafter, all cash receipts by the creditor under the terms of the restructured receivable, whether designated as interest or as face amount, shall be accounted for as recovery of the recorded investment in the receivable, and no interest income shall be recognized on the receivable for any period between the restructuring and maturity of the receivable.

* * *

Related Matters

* * *

35. Losses determined by applying the provisions of paragraphs 28–34 of this Statement shall, to the extent that they are not offset against allowances for uncollectible amounts or other valuation accounts, be included in measuring net income for the period of restructuring and reported . . .

* * *

38. Legal fees and other direct costs incurred by a creditor to effect a troubled debt restructuring shall be included in expense when incurred.

* * *

5C. *African Debt*

This excerpt gives you a sense of the debt crisis in Africa. Some questions for you: In general, what kind of debt did African countries carry? How did Africa's debt profile differ from Latin America's? Any trends? What does this author think of the "muddling through" approach we described in the text? Yeah . . . he wouldn't agree with some of what Carrasco says in 5A.

P. S. Mistry, FONDAD, *African Debt: Dimensions and Characteristics*, in <u>African Debt Revisited: Procrastination or Progress?</u> 17–23 (1992)

The disbursed and outstanding debt of Africa stood at just over $270 billion at the end of 1990 . . .

. . . African debt, in both of its two sub-regions [(Northern and Sub-Saharan Africa)], has ballooned since 1982 although there has been very little new borrowing for development investment since then. Debt has kept growing more rapidly in sub-Saharan Africa between 1986–90 than in North Africa . . . Whereas all categories of debt have increased relatively slowly for North African debtors between 1986–90, the sub-Saharan region has experienced particularly rapid growth in debt obligations to *official* creditors. That region's outstanding indebtedness to bilateral creditors grew by over $23 billion between 1986–90 despite cancellations of concessional debt while its indebtedness to multilateral creditors grew by a further $14 billion. In the latter case, obligations to the World Bank (and its soft-loan affiliate, IDA) grew by over $8 billion, while those to other multilateral creditors (mainly the African Development Bank and EEC) grew by a further $6 billion. Debt owed to the IMF actually fell by about $600 million. The IMF, as we shall see later, extracted a significant quantum of net resources from sub-Saharan Africa between 1986–90 resulting in other creditors effectively financing debt service payments to that agency.

. . . It is now acknowledged as a commonplace that the debt problems of middle-income debtors (in North Africa and elsewhere) are largely with commercial creditors (mainly banks) while those of sub-Saharan Africa are mainly with official creditors (chiefly OECD governments). Taking the sub-Saharan region as a whole (including Nigeria and Cote d'Ivoire), the proportion of debt owed to private creditors (including short-term debt) is nearly 34% while in the case of North Africa it is 42%; not that great a difference. In absolute terms the amount of debt owed to private creditors by sub-Saharan countries at the end of 1990 was considerably larger than for North Africa; $55 billion vs $45 billion respectively. North Africa's largest debtor, Egypt (1989 per capita income of $640) owed more of its debt to official creditors (69%) than sub-Saharan Africa's largest debtor, Nigeria (1989 per capita income of $250) which owed private creditors 54% of its total debt. Nigeria and Cote d'Ivoire between them owed private creditors over $28 billion at the end of 1990, or over 50% of the total amount owed by the sub-Saharan region to private creditors. Excluding these two countries, the rest of sub-Saharan Africa owed private creditors nearly $27 billion or 24% of a total debt of $115 billion; a proportion that is larger than generally recognized.

Other noteworthy features are the relative shifts in proportions of debt due to different categories of creditor between 1982 and 1990 for both sub-regions in Africa. The exposure of private creditors in North Africa's total debt structure declined moderately from over 50% in 1982 to just under 42% in 1990, while in the case of sub-Saharan Africa the shift was much more pronounced; it fell from nearly 51% to below 34%. The same was true for offsetting increases in exposure on the part of bilateral and multilateral creditors. In North Africa, bilateral exposure grew from 40% in 1982 to nearly 45% in 1990 while multilateral exposure grew from 9% to 13%. In sub-Saharan Africa bilateral exposure grew more rapidly, from 28% in 1982 to nearly 40% of total debt in 1990, while multilateral exposure over the same period grew more modestly than is commonly thought i.e. from 21% to 26%.

In examining the reasons for these shifts, three essential features need to be borne in mind: (a) only multilateral banks provided Africa with substantial amounts of new money on the long-term debt account between 1982–90; (b) bilateral governments, particularly from OECD countries, of course substantially stepped up their grant flows to sub-Saharan Africa, and even more to Egypt, between 1982–9—but, on their debt accounts, most of the increase reflects the impact of repeated reschedulings with interest being capitalized and compounded rather than flows of new money; and (c) though private creditor exposure increased by $10 billion over the 1982–90 period for North Africa and by $18 billion for sub-Saharan Africa (the increase being concentrated almost entirely in Nigeria and Cote d'Ivoire) this again did not represent flows of net new money but the impact of reschedulings. In fact, a considerable amount of the new money provided by the multilaterals to Africa between 1982–90 has gone into financing debt service payments to private creditors, and between 1986–90, to the IMF.

In relative terms Africa's debt burden worsened considerably between 1982 and 1990 as the continent's output stagnated and exports fell with the relative performance of the two sub-regions being markedly different . . . North Africa's debt ratios deteriorated (vulnerable as they are to movements in world energy prices which collapsed in the late 1980s) throughout the previous decade but did not fare quite as badly as those for sub-Saharan Africa. For the latter region the debt/GNP ratio deteriorated from under 39% in 1982 to over 110% in 1990 whilst the debt/exports ratio nearly doubled from 188% to over 345%. These 1990 ratios are much worse than those for the other two heavily indebted regions of the developing world: Latin America (48% and 261% respectively) and Eastern Europe (50% and 140% respectively). Comparatively they indicate the urgency of reducing debt burdens of low-income countries in Africa by significant amounts in acknowledgement of the region's reduced economic circumstances and capacity.

Seen from an African debtor's point of view, debt crisis "management" in Africa between 1982–90 can only be judged to have failed dismally. Creditors, however, often express a more positive opinion about the achievements of the period. The international financial system did not collapse. Creditors did not have to take as hard a hit in financial and economic terms as they had originally feared. Only a handful of weak creditor banks went under. Creditor economies pulled out of the recession of 1980–82 within 16 months to enjoy nearly eight subsequent years of sustained growth. Debtor economies, on the other hand, were sucked into a deeper and longer recession than anyone could have imagined. Sub-Saharan GNP (in current dollars) kept falling from over $200 billion in 1980 to a nadir of under $133 billion in 1987 before staging a weak recovery to an estimated $143 billion in 1990. Between 1982–90, Africa's external debt doubled. In North Africa it grew by less than 60%. South of the Sahara it increased by over 225% when donors were attempting to ensure that the opposite happened. As will become evident in the next section of this paper, debt service payments also ballooned; as did interest arrears. With regional

GDP and exports falling, this resulted in a much more onerous debt burden in 1990 than in 1982, relative to Africa's (and particularly sub-Saharan Africa's) capacity to repay.

Unlike debtor countries in the Western Hemisphere, Africa did receive positive net transfers throughout the 1980s largely because of expanded grant aid flows, especially food aid and emergency relief. Whereas, net transfers from all sources of external finance (including net private foreign investment and net official loans and grants) to countries in the Western Hemisphere, for example, were negative throughout the 1980s net transfers for sub-Saharan Africa were significantly positive throughout— thanks largely to expanded official bilateral grant flows. Net transfers *from all external sources* to Africa amounted to $23.4 billion in 1981 but averaged less than $8 billion between 1982–90 even though official grants increased from $7 billion in 1981 to nearly $14 billion in 1990. For sub-Saharan Africa, *annual average net transfers* from all sources of $11 billion in 1981–82 fell to less than $6 billion in 1983–85 before recovering to $12.6 billion between 1986–90. During the decade, official grants to sub-Saharan Africa increased steadily from $6 billion in 1981 to nearly $12 billion in 1990.

It is difficult to see these levels of grant assistance being sustained, leave alone increased in real terms, in the face of new competing claims in other parts of the Second and Third worlds. The impressively large positive net transfer figures for sub-Saharan Africa (which arise partly because a steadily increasing amount of scheduled debt service has simply not been paid and arrears have been permitted to build-up), raise serious questions about why sub-Saharan economies have not yet responded to the debt relief and adjustment ministrations of creditors. They strengthen arguments which suggest that further debt relief through reduction will therefore not solve the structural problems of Africa's low-income economies which are inhibiting a supply response commensurate with the external assistance effort. Part of the reason may well be that too large a part of expanded grant assistance has been provided for food aid, emergency relief and to support debt service payments to multilateral agencies rather than to finance development investment for growth.

5D. *Loan Agreement Provisions*

The restructured loans to borrowers in the debt crisis were jumbo syndicated Eurocurrency loans. The loan's casts of characters are the borrowers (companies or governments), the lead manager (the bank that makes the loan happen), other managing banks (managing lending banks in a region of the world, typically the United States, Europe, and Japan in the loans of the debt crisis), participating banks (banks in each region that want to make a slice of the loan), and the agent bank, which acts as an administrator of the loan—e.g., coordinating payments.

Below are typical provisions you'll find in Eurocurrency loans. The loans are typically medium term, e.g. five years, with one, three, or six month advances that are rolled over and re-priced with each rollover. Why is, say, a six-month advance re-priced when it's rolled over? Why six months? Why are these loans called "floating rate loans?" In such a loan, what is the base rate and what is the margin or spread? Why those two components? The base rate reflects "the cost of funding." What does that mean? What does the margin or spread represent? What's the purpose of the "change in circumstances" provision and whom does it favor? What provision indicates that banks are the greatest socialist when it comes to loan repayments? What's the purpose of the "no liens" (negative pledge) provision? Some call the cross-default provision the "nuclear button." Why might that be? In reality, would that button ever be pressed in a debt crisis? Check out the waiver of sovereign immunity. Why the waiver? What do you think of the limitation of liability? Finally, wouldn't the loan state the governing law is the law of the Borrower?

"<u>Advance</u>" means . . . an advance by a Bank to the borrower . . .

<u>Making the Advances</u>. On the day of each Borrowing, each Bank through its Lending Office shall deposit in freely transferable and same day funds . . . in the appropriate Agent's Account in amount in the Loan Currency of such Bank equal to the amount of the Advance to be made by such Bank in such Loan Currency as part of such Borrowing.

"<u>Interest Rate</u>" means Domestic Rate, LIBO Rate, Fixed Rate or Existing Fixed Rate.

"<u>LIBO Rate</u>" means, for each Interest Period for a LIBO Deposit Account:

    (a) with respect to each Deposit Currency in which a LIBO Deposit Account may be opened (except Pounds Sterling), the average (rounded upward, if necessary, to the nearest whole multiple of one-sixteenth of one percent (1/16%) per annum) of the rates per annum at which deposits in such Deposit Currency for such Interest Period are offered by each of the LIBO Reference Banks for such Deposit Currency to prime banks in the London interbank market at 11:00 A.M. (London time) (or as soon thereafter as practicable) two Quotation Days before the first day of such Interest Period for a period equal to such Interest Period and in an amount approximately equal to the Quotation Amount . . .

"<u>LIBO Rate Margin</u>" means, for each LIBO Rate Deposit Account, 13/16% per annum.

SECTION 3.05.   <u>Interest on LIBO Deposit Accounts</u>. The Central Bank shall pay interest on each unpaid principal amount on deposit in each LIBO

Deposit Account at a rate equal to all times during each Interest Period for such amount to the sum of

(i) the LIBO Rate for such Interest Period for the Deposit Currency in which such Deposit Account is denominated and

(ii) The LIBO Rate Margin for such Deposit Currency . . .

SECTION 5.07. <u>Changes in Circumstances</u>. (a) If at any time after the date of this Agreement either

(i) the introduction of or any change in applicable law, rule or regulation or in the interpretation or administration thereof by any central bank or other governmental authority, or

(ii) the compliance, in accordance with normal banking practice, by any Bank (or its Lending Office) with any guideline, request or directive by (x) any such central bank or other governmental authority (whether or not having the force of law) . . .

<u>shall</u>

(1) subject any Bank (or its Lending Office), to any tax, duty or other charge with respect to this Agreement, the Guaranty or its Deposit Accounts, or

(2) change the basis of taxation of payments to any Bank (or its Lending Office) of the principal of or interest on its Deposit Accounts or in respect of any other amounts due under this Agreement or the Guaranty (except for (A) changes in the rate of tax on the overall net income of a Bank (or its Lending Office) or (B) Other Taxes, in each case imposed by the jurisdiction in which such Bank's principal executive offices or Lending Office is located, or by any central bank or other governmental authority in any such jurisdiction), or

(3) impose, modify or deem applicable any reserve, special deposit or similar requirements against assets or, deposits with or for the account of, or credit extended by, any Bank (or its Lending Office) which is obligated to maintain any Deposit Account (other than any increase that is specially taken into account in the computation of an Interest Rate for such Deposit Account) . . .

and the result of any of the foregoing is

(A) to increase the cost to any Bank (or its Lending Office) of maintaining or funding any of its Deposit Accounts, or

(B) to reduce the amount of any sum receivable by a Bank (or its Lending Office) hereunder or under the guaranty, then the Central Bank shall, from time to time, within ten Business Days of a demand by such Bank (with a copy of such demand to the Agent), pay for the account of such Bank such additional amount or amounts as will compensate such Bank for such increased cost or reduction.

SECTION 8.01.   Covenants of the Central Bank . . .

(a) Obligations Pari Passu. Ensure that at all times its obligations under this Agreement constitute direct unconditional general obligations of the Central Bank ranking at least pari passu in right of payment with all other unsecured External Indebtedness of the Central Bank now or hereafter outstanding.

(b) No Liens [Negative Pledge]. Not create or suffer to exist any Lien upon or with respect to any of its present or future properties (including, without limitation, International Monetary Assets) or revenues, in each case to secure or otherwise provide for payment of External Indebtedness of any Person . . .

SECTION 10.01. Events of Termination . . .

(e) Cross Defaults. (i) An "event of Default" under [this loan agreement] shall occur [when] . . .

(B) any Other Obligor shall fail to pay on any due date for payment thereof (whether at maturity, upon acceleration or otherwise) any amount with respect to any of its External Indebtedness (other than External Indebtedness owed to IBRD) and such failure shall continue for at least two Business Days after notice given by a Bank to the Central Bank and the Guarantor (with a copy to the Agent) or by the Agent to the Central Bank and the Guarantor that such obligation is overdue . . .

SECTION 11.03. Limitations on Liability of the Agent and the Bank Advisory Committee for Venchala.

(a) The Agent. Neither the Agent nor any of its Affiliates, directors, officers, agents or employees shall be liable for any action taken or omitted to be taken by it or them in connection with this Agreement . . . except for its or their own gross negligence or willful misconduct . . .

(b) The Bank Advisory Committee for Venchala. No member of the Bank Advisory Committee for Venchala, as such, shall have any duties or obligations whatsoever with respect to this Agreement or any other document or any matter related hereto.

SECTION 12.07. <u>Jurisdiction: Immunities.</u>

(a) Consent to Jurisdiction.

    (i) The Central Bank hereby irrevocably submits to the non-exclusive jurisdiction of any New York State or Federal court sitting in New York City, the High Court of Justice in London and of any competent Federal court in Venchala in any action or proceeding arising out of or relating to this Agreement . . . The Central Bank hereby irrevocably waives to the fullest extent it may effectively do so, that defense of any inconvenient forum to the maintenance of such action or proceeding . . .

(c) <u>Immunities</u>. To the extent that the Central Bank has or hereafter may acquire may acquire any immunity from jurisdiction of any court or from any legal process (whether . . . attachment prior to judgment, attachment in aid of execution . . .) with respect to itself or its property, the Central Bank hereby irrevocably waives such immunity in respect of its obligations under this Agreement . . .

SECTION 12.08. <u>Disputes Between the Guarantor and the Banks: Jurisdiction Over the Guarantor.</u>

(a) Arbitration.

    (i) If any dispute, difference or question relating to the performance, interpretation or construction of this Agreement . . . shall arise with respect to a claim or demand for payment . . . [the dispute, difference or question may be referred] to arbitration . . .

(b) <u>Waiver of Immunities</u>. To the extent that the Guarantor is or becomes entitled to any immunity from any judicial proceedings or from execution of judgment in Venchala . . . or from the enforcement therein of any arbitration decision on the grounds of sovereignty or otherwise in respect of any matter arising out of or relating to its obligations under this Agreement, the Guarantor does hereby and will irrevocably and unconditionally agree not to plead or claim any such immunity with respect to its obligations or any other matter under or arising out of or in connection with this Agreement . . .

SECTION 12.11. <u>Governing Law</u>. This Agreement shall be governed by, and construed in accordance with, the laws of the State of New York, United States.

CHAPTER 6

DEVELOPMENT IN THE 1990S

■■■

In this chapter we're going to talk about two major themes that arose in the 1990s, the "market-friendly" approach to development and good governance. Market-based reforms were rooted in the structural adjustment programs (SAPs) of the International Monetary Fund (IMF) and the World Bank in the 1980s. But the market-friendly approach married with good governance made its official debut in 1992 with the Bank's publication of "Governance and Development." It was a virtual playbook for developing countries to get the development thing right. The Bank addressed, among other things, the role of government, public sector management, accountability, decentralization, the rule of law, conflict resolution, information transparency, and corruption.

We're not going to slog through all of that. We'll limit ourselves largely to two key themes of the 1990s: the market-friendly approach and the corruption strand of good governance, with a focus on the rule of law. The stuff on corruption will deal with the concept itself (with examples). For U.S law on anti-corruption and the international scene, have a look at supplement 6C.

I. MARKET-FRIENDLY DEVELOPMENT

The market-based reforms of the 1990s were a continuation of the structural reforms in countries after the 1980s debt crisis. The disintegration of the Soviet Union and the socialist bloc in Eastern Europe provided additional opportunity to introduce a market-driven framework of development. Both the World Bank and the IMF played big-time roles in promoting the market-friendly approach and promoting their use around the world.

Market-friendly policies typically emphasized non-inflationary growth, fiscal discipline (i.e., wise government spending), high savings and investment rates, trade and foreign investment liberalization, privatization, and domestic market deregulation. Unlike the state-centric development models adopted in many regions of the world after World War II, the 1990s model shrunk the State's role considerably. Policymakers argued that while the state must perform functions that the private sector can't or won't perform (it's called "**market failure**" in the biz), such as maintaining a functional legal system, it shouldn't involve itself heavily in the market. Let private actors in the market do their thing and, unlike inefficient state-owned entities (SOEs), they'll generate greater economic growth and wealth in the long run. (How that wealth is distributed is another matter.)

The market-friendly framework of development eventually became associated with the "Washington Consensus," (WC) a term coined by the economist John Williamson in 1989. He identified a set of reforms he believed policymakers in Washington could agree were needed in Latin America:

- Fiscal discipline to combat deficits that led to balance of payments crises and high inflation.
- Reordering public expenditure priorities to target the poor.
- Tax reform to broaden the tax base with moderate marginal tax rates.
- Liberalizing interest rates in the context of a broader financial liberalization.
- A competitive exchange rate.
- Trade liberalization.
- Liberalization of inward foreign direct investment.
- Privatization of state-owned entities.
- Deregulation of the economy to ease barriers to entry and exit.
- Property rights for the informal sector.

The WC, which spread well beyond Latin America, was based on three broadly accepted concepts: (1) macroeconomic discipline, (2) a market economy, and (3) openness to the world in the context of trade and foreign direct investment. The policies that constituted the WC were intended to combat the "global apartheid" perspective, which claimed that developing countries weren't part of the orthodox economic world because they pursued a flawed development model that included inflation, state-led industrialization, and import substitution. (See supplement 6A.) Let's take a look at how two of the WC reforms, privatization and trade liberalization, played out in Mexico, Zimbabwe, and Kenya, respectively.

Mexico

Mexico's story starts with its 1917 Constitution. It provided the juridical basis for expanding the State's control over the economy. During the import-substitution period in the 1950s (see Chapter 2) the State came to own steel mills, coal mines, paper mills, and oil refineries. By 1982 the state-driven model of development resulted in State ownership of more than 1,155 heavily subsidized entities in all sectors of the economy, especially energy and infrastructure. Check it out: SOEs employed 4.4% of the labor force and 30% of fixed capital formation. This development model produced the "Mexican Miracle": Between World War II and 1981, Mexico's gross domestic product (GDP) grew at an average annual rate of 6.1%. By today's standards, that rocks.

But then came the Latin American debt crisis (see Chapter 5), which obliterated economic growth. SAPs fundamentally restructured the economy. Between 1982 and 2003, Mexico reduced its SOEs from 1,155 to 210. Constitutional reforms led to widespread liquidation of SOEs and additional privatizations, which accelerated in the late 1980s and early 1990s. By 2003 the government privatized strategic areas of the economy, such as public utilities, ports, airports, toll roads, and railroads. Privatization on steroids! (As to the trade-liberalization component of the WC, in 1994 Mexico joined the United States and Canada to form the North American Free Trade Agreement (NAFTA), the world's largest free trade area when measured by total GDP.)

Critics of Mexico's privatization argued that the program resulted in higher prices, reduced wages, and reduced government revenues. Others responded with analysis that diminishes price hikes and lower wages and shows higher profitability resulting from increased efficiency. And higher profitability translates into increased government revenue via taxation. Still others noted that privatization allowed entrepreneurs to form alliances and otherwise restructure their business.

But privatization wasn't a panacea for economic growth: it didn't work. Between 1982 and 1997, annual GDP averaged only 1.8%. The Mexican Miracle had vanished. In all fairness, though, many economies (except East Asian countries and Chile) experienced a downturn during this period. In the United States, GDP per capita fell from 2.4% in 1940–80 to 1.5% in 1980–1994. Brazil's rates for the same period dropped from 3.5% to –0.5. And let's not forget Mexico's recession after the 1994 financial crisis, which we'll cover in Chapter 9.

Zimbabwe & Kenya

Most African governments started liberalizing the agricultural sector in the 1980s as part of the SAPs. The measures included promoting private sector involvement and privatizing, deregulating consumer/producer prices, and eliminating subsidies. As with virtually all SAPs, economists are divided over whether liberalization has been a good idea, with some saying it has improved food security and others arguing the opposite.

But the biggest problem in assessing WC-based reforms is that implementation has been slow and marked by reversals. Let's look first at Zimbabwe and trade reforms in the context of food security in remote rural areas. There, the government imposed price controls on maize meal in 1998, five years after the IMF/WB SAPs required the government to abandon them. The grain SOE price discriminated, selling lower to big milling firms than others. It also controlled the export and import of maize. While renewed State controls of the market helped some players in the economy (e.g., local milling and retailing), and even though the controls appeared to reduce poverty in the rural hinterlands, some economists argued that allowing more private sector involvement would've been a better tool to reach the poor.

Kenya's experience illustrates not a reversal of reforms in the maize market but the impediments to it. In the 1980s, conditional lending sought to liberalize the maize market. But cronyism and rent-

> *"African states have made strong progress with many of the reforms, which helps explain, in part, the continent's improved economic performance in recent years. Economic growth in Africa is expected to average 3.1 percent this year and 4.2 percent next year—more than twice the average in 1984–93 and marginally higher than the average for all developing countries."*
>   —T. Manuel, "Africa and the Washington Consensus: Finding the Right Path," *Finance & Development,* 18 (2003)

> *"[T]he Washington Consensus model implemented across Latin America dictated a form of capitalism that concentrated income, reduced employment opportunities, and restricted social rights."*
>   — C. Wylde, International Political Economy Series: Latin America After Neoliberalism: Development Regimes in Post-Crisis States

seeking—the well-connected and politicians seeking to monopolize government subsidies (more about rent-seeking in a minute)—mucked up important marketing decisions. Tariffs on maize imports, price support (the subsidies) and high transportation costs caused maize prices to rise well above prices globally.

Bottom line: The WC was a lightning rod for heated debate regarding development policy. The IMF has been a strong proponent of the WC. But there've been strong opponents of the WC that made arguments that reflect some of the problems with the WC that we just looked at.

The economist Joseph Stiglitz is a prominent critic of the WC. He argues that the WC rested on a flawed belief in market fundamentalism, the idea that markets rule and always get things right. But markets in and of themselves don't produce efficient outcomes. In other words, it's almost impossible to have markets that work perfectly without the need for government. To have such a market you need fully informed actors— perfect information, when in fact it's common to find information "asymmetries." And you can't have "externalities" like pollution produced by economic activity, or any need for public goods such as national defense (have a look at "market failure" in What's Up with That?). For this stuff you need, OMG, government! Sure, governments in developing countries were messed up when the WC arose, but the WC caused a radical and unnecessary shift to market fundamentalism. Stiglitz has outlined a "post-Washington Consensus consensus" (PWC) that recognizes a more robust role for government—other than merely enforcing contract and property rights. You have to have an efficient government that addresses externalities and provides public goods. The PWC is more inclusive in that it involves the participation of developing countries. It doesn't take a cookie-cutter approach to reforms that ignores differing economic conditions among countries. Countries should be allowed to experiment and find what works for them. There's a role for an efficient state that works together with the market. And a successful development process shouldn't focus solely on GDP growth but also take into account sustainable and equitable development that doesn't ignore issues such as income distribution and female education.

II. GOOD GOVERNANCE AND THE WORLD BANK

The market-friendly approach to development won't work if the governments don't behave themselves. It makes sense, right? A market economy can't rock unless the government follows transparent, predictable, and stable rules—rules that are corruption-free. Can any of us say we're in favor of non-transparent government with unpredictable rules that reek of corruption? That's like saying, "I want to grow up to be despot!" Actually . . . that might not . . . Let's not go there. Let's be good boys and girls, straight or gay, and talk about the C word.

Part One: How the Bank Justified Its Anti-Corruption Agenda

As we said, we're going to concentrate on the corruption strand of good governance. But first let's have a look at how the World Bank defined governance when it got into this business in the 1990s and how it justified doing so. The impetus for the Bank's governance agenda began with an important study of Sub-Saharan Africa. It laid out what the region had to do by way of governance to promote development. The Bank defined governance as "the manner in which power is exercised in the management of a country's economic and social resources for development." It focused on three aspects of governance: (1) the form of political regime; (2) the process by which authority is exercised in the management of a country's resources; and (3) the capacity of governments to design, formulate and implement policies and discharge functions. The Bank couldn't touch the first aspect—its Charter says no way. But the last two aspects became central to the Bank's good governance agenda.

> *"Africa requires not just less government but better government . . . [M]any governments are wracked by corruption and are increasingly unable to command the confidence of the population at large . . ."*
> —Quoting Senegal's President Abdou Diouf, World Bank, Sub-Saharan Africa: From Crisis to Sustainable Growth, A Long-Term Prospective Study, 3 (1989)

> " '[B]oth voices in and outside the Bank interpreted the "concern with governance,' to be a significant break from previous parameters. The legal department urged great caution in not overstepping the Bank's requirement to remain non-political. Some member countries, such as China, accused the Bank of attempting to infringe on their sovereignty, and while some NGOs welcomed what they interpreted as a loosening of the Bank's distinctions between political and economic conditionalities, others protested at the 'brazenly patronizing interference' of the Bank."
> —T. Polzer, "Corruption: Deconstructing the World Bank Discourse," *Development Studies Institute*, 14 (2001)

But here's the thing: once you start down the governance path, where do you stop? That's where Ibrahim Shihata, the Bank's General Counsel, comes in. He asked this question: To what extent can the Bank engage in governance matters with its member countries given Article IV of the Bank's Charter: "The Bank and its officers shall not interfere in the political affairs of any member; nor shall they be influenced in their decisions by the political character of the member or members concerned. Only economic considerations shall be relevant to their decisions, and these considerations shall be weighed impartially in order to achieve the purposes stated in Article I."

Shihata noted that economic considerations, which the Bank could safely address, often relate to how a member country handles its resources, which smells a bit political. But he argued that political events in the member country can't be ignored if, say, they jeopardize the country's ability to keep its commitments under a Bank loan. And the Bank's work in civil service and legal reform, while related to politics, has a direct effect on how the member country runs its economy—which is within the Bank's mandate in Article I of the Charter (review the supplement in Chapter 1 on the Bank's Charter if you have to). So, check it out, he came up with this test: "The staff have to establish the case for the direct economic effect in a clear and unequivocal manner. For it to be taken into account, such economic effect has to be preponderant . . . when these considerations are associated with political actions or flow from political events, they have to be of such impact and relevance as to make them a Bank concern . . ." Isn't that lovely lawyer's language? Maybe you can do that too when you grow up! Hey, there's enough wiggle room in that test to drive a Mac truck through it. In fact, it has allowed the Bank to become involved in domestic issues that relate to basic human rights. See for yourself: In 1994, the Bank (and the IMF) got Burkina Faso to make a commitment to crack down on female genital mutilation in exchange for loans.

Now that we've had a glimpse of a lawyer's wizardry, let's look at a fact of life that will always create jobs for lawyers: corruption.

Part Two: What Is Corruption and Why Is It Bad?

What Is It?

> *"In a state where corruption abounds, laws must be very numerous."*
> —Publius Cornelius Tacitus, Roman historian, circa AD 56–177.

Most of us feel about corruption what Justice Stewart said about porn: "I know it when I see it." But around the world people see things differently—no, we're not talking about porn.

> *"The common 'Western' conception of corruption, including that used by the Bank, depends on the existence of a public domain which is recognisably separate from a private sphere, with different codes of acceptable conduct in each . . . this distinction between public and private is far from universal and is predicated on a particular European cultural and historical experience."*
> —T. Polzer, "Corruption: Deconstructing the World Bank Discourse," Development Studies Institute, 18–19 (2001)

Corruption, the C word. There are so many different shades of it. The United Nations Development Programme has collected thirteen terms that in one way or another reflect corruption, including insider trading (where people try to make tons of money by trading stock based on non-public information). But let's just work with the World Bank's generic definition of corruption: "The abuse of public office for private gain." That's a good start but let's put meat on those corrupt bones.

Corruption comes in many flavors. **Transparency International**, an NGO whose mission is to expose the stinking rot of corruption (so multinational corporations can compete on a level playing field to exploit—sorry, to secure a mutually beneficial relationship with developing countries), has identified three types of corruption. You got your "grand corruption," where high level officials divert public funds to their Swiss bank accounts and in doing so mess up the government's central functions and policymaking. On the other end you have your "petty corruption," where low level officials hold their hands out for "grease payments" from regular folks who just want access to basic services so they can get on with life. Then you have your "political corruption" when the corrupt government players don't want money—they want power! What does Nietzche say about the "will to power?" Never mind, that's too deep for power-mongering.

Why Is It Bad News?

There's a bunch of stuff that's not cool about it. Let's start with what's called "rent seeking" in the biz. The use of bribery has given civil servants tremendous power and allow people who pay bribes a privileged form of access—rent seeking. Here are some examples: People might bribe officials to gain access to scarce benefits, such as import and export permits, government contracts, or one of a limited number of licenses to open a business enterprise. Check out this scene:

"A Trip to Paris"

<u>Setting</u>: Department of Trade

<u>Characters</u>:

James: Director of the Office of Import Quotas

Nelson: President of the Association of Domestic Auto Industry

Nelson: Word is you're thinking of scraping the quota.

James: You heard right. Tea?

Nelson (tersely): No.

James: You should be more polite, Nelson. Rude people don't get what they want.

Nelson: Don't you support your country's auto industry?

James: I'm no less the patriot than you. (James sips on his tea) Come now, Nelson, shall we avoid being lame?

Nelson: Don't patronize me.

James: Then don't try to tell me the junk you produce is better than what we can get from Vlamaria. You should be thankful for the protection we've given you all these years.

Nelson: We need more time.

James: For what? To learn how to assemble a dashboard correctly?

(long pause and then Nelson throws a thick envelope on James' desk; James takes a long look at it and then locks eyes with Nelson)

James: Do you think I'm a peasant? Do you?

Nelson: How much more?

James: So you can charge our good citizens outrageous prices for a product that breaks down a block off the lot?

Nelson: Who's being lame now?

James: My assistant will tell you how much and where to wire it.

Nelson: And us?

James: Two more years.

Nelson: Five.

James: It will cost you, Nelson.

Nelson: We'll pay.

James: Wait for his call. He'll give you all the information you need.

Nelson: I'm sure he will. He must be quite the expert by now.

James: Oh, Nelson, the mistress wants me to take her to Paris for a week. We travel first class.

Nelson: Rot in hell, James.

James: I'll think about it but only after I've taken her to the Musée d'Orsay. Who's your favorite, Nelson, Degas or Monet?

You can see that the government's import quota provides an opportunity for the domestic auto industry to engage in rent-seeking via a bribe. The result? The domestic auto industry can charge consumers prices that are higher than they would be if the better imported cars were allowed unrestricted access to the economy. And the lack of competition via the quota doesn't give the domestic auto industry much of an incentive to improve domestic cars.

Rent seeking may be had via payments for services connected with obtaining inside information (such as inside information on contract specifications), or the expediting of an official procedure (such as a reduction in paperwork). Bribes can also operate to prohibit others from sharing in a benefit, such as owners of an illegal business paying police investigators to raid their competition, or an owner of a legal business entity paying officials to place excessive constraints on the competition or requesting that the official deny the license application of a potential competitor. In short, rent seekers will pay whatever price to officials to hog it all. Economists and policymakers universally agree that this type of rent seeking is economically wasteful and further distorts an economy infected by corruption.

Rent-seeking is not the only bad news. Corruption also creates a barrier to firms that want to enter the market. Corrupt players in the market will do whatever is necessary to keep their transactions secret. The secrecy causes lots of problems. Market participants need information to engage in transactions—without the information markets can't function optimally. Because corrupt players have created a private club of sorts, they don't trust outsiders. And because many of the contracts in the club are unenforceable, the players will only deal with each other lest they lose a lot of money.

Here are a couple of other problems with corruption. It may lead to inflexible prices. Once corrupt market players have settled on the amount of a bribe, the price mechanism may not function properly, that is, prices won't accurately reflect market changes. Corruption can also be a pain for foreign investors, which means they'll walk away. If investors become convinced that a corrupt government is likely to become unstable, they won't risk their money. This may lead to less innovation, the consequences of which will ripple through the economy. Ultimately, it's bad for consumers: they pay higher prices for possibly inferior products.

Enough recitation. Let's take a look at corruption in infrastructure projects, a fairly recent focus of the World Bank. You know from Chapter 4 that project lending is the meat and potatoes of Bank lending, and that infrastructure is pretty important for development. To make sure the projects comply with Bank policies and ultimately succeed, you gotta root out that stinking corruption! And we're not talking about something insignificant. Low-income countries need big time financing to do infrastructure projects, like up to 9% of GDP. In 2007, the Bank's Development Committee said one way of ensuring the success of infrastructure projects is to strengthen communication. Before we get to that, let's talk about how corruption messes up these types of projects.

So look down and check out all the possibilities of corruption—and rent seeking—that can find its way into a project cycle. Corruption can start with project planning. For example, corrupt politicians can take bribes from corrupt businesses to influence what project will be selected and approved. It's almost like the project is selected because it'll be a corruption cow. This bleeds into project design. But it's in the contracting process and bid evaluation where bribes and kick-backs fly fast and furious to secure lucrative contracts involved in the project. This is the "grand corruption" we talked about. Then you can see how corruption screws up the contract implementation phase. Let's take project delays. In the contract between the contractor and the (in all likelihood) the government, if either party is found at fault for delaying the completion of the project the other party may be entitled to damages. Let's see now, who decides whether there's been a breach of the contract in this regard? Let's find that person and give him or her an all-expenses paid trip to Paris. Yeah, let's do that!

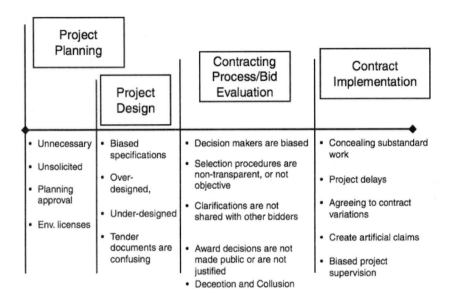

Source: L. Hass et al., World Bank, "Setting Standards for Communication and Governance: The Example of Infrastructure Projects" (2007)

Studies show the costs corruption in infrastructure projects is staggering, gobbling huge chunks of GDP. And this type of corruption can hurt the poor the hardest if corruption boosts prices and the poor need the services the most, like a project to build a toll road that may be really important for poor farmers.

So to fix this problem the Bank says you have to promote inclusive, transparent communication that allows all phases of the project to be monitored. Check this out:

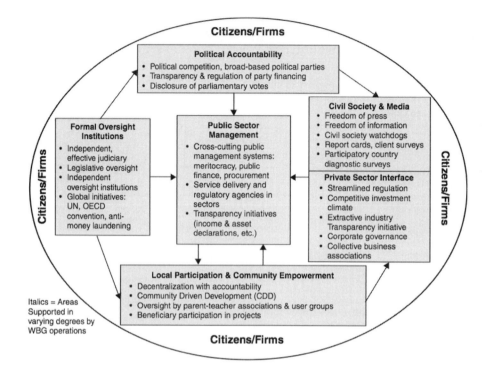

Source: L. Hass et al., World Bank, "Setting Standards for Communication and Governance: The Example of Infrastructure Projects" (2007)

Pretty, isn't it? There's some important stuff there, like an independent judiciary, freedom of the press and of information, corporate governance, and oversight by parents. Don't get mom started!

Let's look briefly at an infrastructure project in Sierra Leone in 2003, just as it was coming out an 11-year war with rebels. The country was in shambles. The project involved completion of a hydroelectric project that was abandoned in 1997 because of the conflict. Just as the project preparations got into swing, the government passed legislation that promoted transparent, inclusive, accountable and sustainable governance with responsibilities reaching down to local councils. The World Bank and the government appointed professionals in communications. The communication process helped deal with everything from tribal conflicts to mistrust of government. And the project was completed.

And life is good. Hmmm . . . You think?

Part Three: Combating Corruption: Promoting the Rule of Law

At the outset of the chapter we mentioned the Bank's 1992 publication, "Governance and Development," which launched the Bank's crusade to combat corruption through good governance. The Bank's argument was that good governance was essential to effective, equitable development in the context of the market-friendly approach to development in the 1990s. In the Bank's view, corruption thrives on poor governance, characterized by, among other things, weak institutions, an inadequate legal framework, government—rather than market—allocation of scarce resources, underpaid civil servants (they resort to bribes because they don't make enough to make ends meet), excessive government regulations, an uncertain policy framework, and "closed" decisionmaking . . . Sorry, ran out of breath on that list. Anyway, corruption ultimately hits the country's vulnerable groups the hardest. That really sucks, don't you think? Now we could address each of these problems, but since you're lawyers-in-the making, we'll limit ourselves to the Bank's views on improving the legal framework for development.

The Bank views the rule of law as the most important aspect of economic development, as it provides economic actors with reliable and stable rules that allow them to plan and pursue their activities in the market-friendly framework of development. The 1992 report identified five "critical elements" of the rule of law for purposes of development which to us may seem like no-brainers.

> *"The Rule of Law is not a Western idea, nor is it linked up with any economic or social system . . . As soon as you accept that man is governed by law, and not by whims of men, it is the Rule of Law."*
> —Adetokunbo A. Ademola, Chief Justice of Nigeria (1961), quoted in World Bank, "Governance and Development," 22 (1992)

Here they are with some examples of what the Bank became involved in. Lights down, time for PowerPoint.

- There is a set of rules known in advance.
  - It assisted countries in publishing official gazettes that set forth new laws.
  - It insisted that countries not issue decrees that were inconsistent with new laws or with amendments required as a condition for project lending.
  - It assisted countries in trying to make their laws consistent with market reforms—e.g., ensuring that the country's constitution recognizes private property rights.
- The rules are actually in force.
  - As a preliminary matter, the Bank noted that merely transplanting laws from one country to another may not work because they don't take into account local conditions—a swipe at the **"law and development"** movement.
  - It assisted with improving laws relating to tax collection.
  - It helped countries change security laws to allow financial institutions to pursue foreclosure—e.g., changing a law to drop the requirement of going to court to get a judgment

and allow direct execution of foreclosure on collateral pledged under a loan.

Hey, stop snoring!

- There are mechanisms to ensure application of the rules, given that the rule of law constrains governments as well as private citizens.
  o Noting the practical importance of the delegation of discretionary authority by the legislative to the executive branch, it advised countries on how to improve administrative bodies.
  o It assisted countries in removing obsolete and contradictory regulations to promote administrative decisions based on clear and relevant rules—e.g., assisting a country in establishing effective banking regulation.

Slap yourself—or a fellow student—to stay awake!

- Conflicts are resolved through binding decisions of an independent judicial body.
  o Given the importance of contract enforcement to the market-friendly development framework, the Bank worked with countries to strengthen the judicial branch, which in many developing countries (1) was not truly independent, (2) was overworked, (3) lacked adequate facilities, and (4) lacked adequately trained personnel.
  o It assisted countries in establishing judicial efficiency— e.g., helping a country establish commercial courts that allowed financial institutions to resolve suits against defaulting borrowers within a reasonable period of time rather than ten to fifteen years.
  o It began to assist countries in training judges in economics and business law.

Find toothpicks for your eyelids if you have to!

- There are procedures for amending rules when they no longer serve their purpose.
  o Noting the importance amending laws in a predictable manner, Bank projects provided training and technical assistance to a country's legal offices—e.g., Ministry of Justice.

Lights up. Wipe the glaze off your eyes! This might help: An example of what the Bank tried to do in Ecuador. In 1995, the Bank approved a $10.7 million loan to assess the state of the legal and judicial system and to provide recommendations that formed the basis for the Judicial Reform Project. The project tried to involve stakeholders—players with skin in the game such as development agencies and NGOs—to formulate a judicial reform strategy. The project had four components: (1) a pilot program dealing with case administration and information support in lower courts; (2) a pilot Alternative Dispute Resolution (ADR) mechanism tied to the courts; (3) a Program for Law and Justice to address, among other things, modernization of property registration, a professional development program, a study on the state of legal education, and legal service pilots for poor women; and; (4) development of court infrastructure standards.

The Bank assessed the project in 2003, concentrating on the legal service pilots for women. It reported that overall the results were positive. The data showed that women who went to the legal clinics were better off than women who didn't use them. For instance, clients were more likely to receive child support payments, and less likely to be victims of domestic violence after separation. The clients also felt more empowered to assert their rights. (For more, see supplement 6B.) But keep in mind two things: First, the main purpose of the assessment was to set a baseline for assessing other similar Bank projects, not to change Ecuador's laws to better empower poor women. (Wouldn't the Bank's Charter prohibit it from doing that? Hmmm . . .) Second, it's the World Bank assessing itself. Enough said.

In 1997, the World Bank issued a report titled, "The State In A Changing World." Abiding by its market-friendly approach to development, the Bank said (triumphantly), "much of the developing world has had to face up to the failure of state-dominated development strategies." Still, it didn't dismiss the state entirely. An "effective state" is necessary to complement the private marketplace. And guess what's critical to that role? Yes, the rule of law! In discussing how to improve the "capabilities" of the state in developing countries, the report stressed the importance of an independent judiciary to ensure the accountability of the executive and legislative branches. It also made an astonishing statement: "Writing laws is the easy part; they need to be enforced if a country is to enjoy the benefits of a credible rule of law." Did a lawyer write this? Sorry, but that statement doesn't pass the laugh test.

The Bank's rule of law agenda continues in the 21st century. While its definition of the rule of law now includes the recognition and protection of human dignity and stresses accessibility of justice to all, its market-friendly approach remains embedded in its work: "[A] well-functioning legal and judicial system allow the state to regulate and empower private individuals to contribute to economic development by confidently engaging in business, investments, and other transactions." Now, let's see, where does human dignity come into play? Oh, yeah, that's right, empowering private individual to become more confident in the market place. And life is good . . .

Hey, no joking. Amartya Sen—you know, the Nobel Laureate who's written about "development as freedom" (we'll talk about him in Chapter 20)—thinks that the ability of the individual to trade in the marketplace is part of freedom and human dignity.

Human dignity. Pretty cool. And if a market-friendly framework promotes it, that's way cool. But that's a big "if," isn't it? See you tomorrow boys and girls . . . with human dignity.

You Gotta Know Something About Them!

Ibrahim Shihata

Ibrahim Shihata rocked. He graduated from Cairo University Law School at age 20, and received his Doctor of Juridical Science degree from Harvard seven years later. Unlike other bios we've provided, here we'll give you an excerpt of Shihata's obit, written by James Wolfensohn, then President of the World Bank: "It is with profound sadness that I received the news that Dr. Ibrahim F. I. Shihata, general counsel of the World Bank from 1983 to 1998, passed away on 28 May. 'Mr. Shihata'—as everyone here came to know Ibrahim—was an exceptional man. A lawyer—one of the greatest international jurists of the twentieth century; an expert on international development with an unequivocal commitment to the cause of poverty reduction . . . During his 15 years with the Bank, as general counsel, Ibrahim was involved in every major policy discussion and senior managers continually looked to him for advice. With his brilliant mind, broad knowledge of history and powers of persuasion, he issued a series of legal opinions that enabled the Bank to respond to the rapidly changing needs of its membership during that time. He was at his best, perhaps, when he was at the Board, usually being asked to give the final opinion on a contentious issue, which he always did with objectivity, integrity and good humour . . . One of his proudest achievements, and a lasting legacy, was his role in the establishment of the Multilateral Investment Guarantee Agency (MIGA)—of which it can truly be said that he was the principal architect. He . . . played a key role in the establishment of the Inspection Panel . . . On behalf of everyone at the Bank Group, I am extending our deepest condolences to Ibrahim's wife, Samia S Farid, and their three children Sharif, Yasmine and Nadia. Our hearts are with them."

John Williamson

John Williamson is a Brit who attended the London School of Economics and Princeton University. Check it out: he speaks Portuguese—he taught economics at Pontifica Universidade Católica do Rio de Janeiro. Not a bad place to teach. He calls the Washington Consensus his "child"—his daughter even calls it her illegitimate brother.

Joseph Stiglitz

Image of Joseph E. Stiglitz by the Government of Thailand is licensed under CC BY 3.0

Joseph Stiglitz is a Hoosier born in Indiana. Yup! His parents weren't economists. His father was an insurance agent and his mother taught remedial English at Purdue. But his uncle, a highly successful lawyer, could've played an economist on TV (remember, lawyers [think they] can do anything). Joseph got his undergrad degree in economics from Amherst University. While he was there he railed on the fraternities because they were a pain—socially divisive. The school banned them years later. Joseph received his Ph.D. from MIT in 1967 and became a professor at Yale just three years later. He's taught all over the place, including some places you might have heard of— Princeton, Stanford, MIT, Oxford. He's currently at Columbia University. For sure you know he was Chairman of the Council of Economic Advisors in the Clinton Administration. No biggie. From there he spent some time as Chief Economist and Senior Vice President of the World Bank. No biggie. He's also advised President Obama. In 2002, he wrote an earthquake of a book titled, Globalization and Its Discontents, where, among other things, he railed on the IMF. (But the IMF still exists. Darn!) He was named one of *Time's* "100 most influential people in the world" in 2011. And oh, yeah—he won the Nobel Prize for Economics in 2001. No biggie.

What's Up with That?

Market Failure

Markets can be very efficient in the sense that private actors in the markets do the best job of allocating scarce resources and providing what we all need or want. But sometimes they fail. There are many examples of market failure. We're going to give you just two, one dealing with public goods and the other with property and contract rights.

Let's use national defense as a "public good." Everybody benefits from a national defense that prevents attacks on the country. And there's no way to exclude people from enjoying the safety of national defense. Private businesses see no way to benefit from providing national defense because, since a business can't charge "users" of national defense, the cost to each business will exceed the benefits it receives from providing it. This is an example of a market failure because private actors won't provide what is needed. That's where governments come in. They have to provide national defense because the private sector won't do it or won't provide it adequately.

Now let's look at property and contract rights. Suppose you live in an area where houses aren't abundant. You want to sell your house for the best price possible. So as you live in it, you pay for upkeep and maybe just before you sell the house you make improvements to the house that you know will increase the selling price. Because of the improvements, you can sell the house for, say, $50,000 more than if you had not done the upkeep or improvements. So you're better off by that amount, the buyer has a nice house, the value of your neighbor's house may improve, the government will receive more revenue via property taxes, etc . . . This is what's called a Pareto efficient outcome: no one is worse off, you and others are better off, and the scarce resource—the house—finds its highest valued use. The market works and that's cool. But what if you lived in a world where property rights and contract enforcement didn't exist? In that world, you couldn't be sure you owned the house or you couldn't be sure that the sales contract would be enforced. If that were the case, would you have any incentive to maintain your house and make improvements?

Transparency International

Transparency International (TI) is an NGO founded by former World Bank regional program director Peter Eigen in 1993 with the apparent purpose of fighting corruption. TI is famous for its Corruption Perceptions Index (CPI), which measures levels of perceived corruption in the public sector around the world. TI gets this information from a combination of surveys and assessments of corruptions from various institutions. It published the first CPI in 1995, ranking 45 countries. As of the 2012 Index, TI ranked 176 countries: the U.S. is 19, Peru is 83, Greece is 94, and Egypt is 118 (the higher the number ranking, the higher the perceived corruption—so 1 is the least corrupt and 176 is the most). Some hail the CPI for giving governments an incentive to fight corruption in their own public institutions. But critics say that the CPI is based on perceptions rather than actual incidents of corruption and that TI's rankings aren't necessarily a reflection of actual corruption in a country. They also point out that the surveys used to gather data aren't consistent, and that the perceptions gathered by the surveys aren't measuring the public's opinion, but rather the opinion of external organizations.

Law and Development

During the Cold War, funding from the U.S. government, private foundations such as the Ford and Rockefeller Foundations, and international organizations enabled scholars to write about and advise on non-communist strategies to modernize "Third World" nations through legal reform. Inspired by the work of Max Weber, scholars believed that an autonomous, consciously designed, and universal legal system could help replicate the development path of Western industrialized societies. Yes! But by the early 1970s, scholars had some serious reservations about the "liberal legalist model." No! In a soul searching article titled "Scholars in Self-Estrangement: Some Reflections on the Crisis in Law and Development Studies in the United States," David Trubek and Marc Galanter confessed:

> "Law and development studies are in crisis because some scholars have come seriously to doubt the liberal legal assumptions that 'legal development' can be equated with exporting United States institutions or that any improvement of legal institutions in the Third World will be potent and good. They have come to see that legal change may have little or no effect on social economic conditions in Third World societies and, conversely, that many legal 'reforms' can deepen inequality, curb participation, restrict individual freedom, and hamper efforts to increase material well-being."

The law and development "movement" basically died then, but was raised from the dead in the 1980s when legal reform was tied to U.S. funding to improve criminal justice systems in developing countries. Lock up those outlaws!

QUESTIONS FROM YOUR TALKING DOG

1.　Hey, what's with this "market-friendly" development thing you keep mumbling about? I just ate so we can chill before our walk.

2.　I was just reading a book on my nightstand about the "Washington Consensus." Let's talk about that. Can you get me a cup of coffee?

3.　You hate it when I whine. But wasn't Williamson a big whiner about the WC? He's against that bipolar thing. Does he take medication for that?

4.　You think he was pretty much right? Or was he a neoliberal devil? I *do* know what neoliberalism is! Hayek! No, I didn't sneeze!

5.　You can pet my tummy if you tell me all about good governance and corruption. But first, how the heck could Chihuahua, I mean, Shihata get around the Bank's Charter that prohibits it from messing around with domestic politics?

6.　Might there be a donut in the cabinet? You know, for my coffee. While you're looking, tell me what the heck is a "grease payment?" That sounds gross.

7.   I know about all the evils of corruption. But I really dig—yeah, sometimes I do—the stuff about corruption in infrastructure projects. Can I have a biscuit after you tell me about it? I'm hungry, okay?

8.   Rule of law? You should know this stuff cold. Get it right or I'll flunk you.

9.   I was just watching a documentary about Ecuador. Take me to the Galapagos, will ya? Pero primero explicame el proyecto— . . . I've been taking classes. Ok, in English: But first, tell me about that cool World Bank project there.

<u>Chapter 6: Supplement</u>

6A. *The Washington Consensus*

Here you get to hear it from the man who started it all. As you read it, think about these questions: Who did he use as his knocking board on the merits of the Washington Consensus? Not exactly Marxist economists. He does admit that some of his initial formulations could've been more carefully crafted given what we now know. Cool. But what's his bottom line about his list? Does he over-estimate its importance? Or does he get it just about right to the extent that various constituencies used the list to serve their own purposes? Is it all about him? Ask Martha Nussbaum about the perils of making a list of universals (see Chapter 20). What's more presumptuous, "Washington Consensus" or "Universal Convergence?"

J. Williamson, "A Short History of the Washington Consensus"
in <u>The Washington Consensus Reconsidered: Towards a
New Global Governance</u> (2004)

Content of the Original List

The ten reforms that constituted my list were as follows.

1.   **Fiscal Discipline**. This was in the context of a region where almost all countries had run large deficits that led to balance of payments crises and high inflation that hit mainly the poor because the rich could park their money abroad.

2.   **Reordering Public Expenditure Priorities**. This suggested switching expenditure in a progrowth and propoor way, from things like nonmerit subsidies to basic health and education and infrastructure. It did *not* call for all the burden of achieving fiscal discipline to be placed on expenditure cuts; on the contrary, the intention was to be strictly neutral about the desirable size of the public sector, an issue on which even a hopeless consensus-seeker like me did not imagine that the battle had been resolved with the end of history that was being promulgated at the time.

3. **Tax Reform**. The aim was a tax system that would combine a broad tax base with moderate marginal tax rates.

4. **Liberalizing Interest Rates**. In retrospect I wish I had formulated this in a broader way as financial liberalization, stressed that views differed on how fast it should be achieved, and—especially—recognized the importance of accompanying financial liberalization with prudential supervision.

5. **A Competitive Exchange Rate**. I fear I indulged in wishful thinking in asserting that there was a consensus in favor of ensuring that the exchange rate would be competitive, which pretty much implies an intermediate regime; in fact Washington was already beginning to edge toward the two-corner doctrine which holds that a country must either fix firmly or else it must float "cleanly".

6. **Trade Liberalization**. I acknowledged that there was a difference of view about how fast trade should be liberalized, but everyone agreed that was the appropriate direction in which to move.

7. **Liberalization of Inward Foreign Direct Investment**. I specifically did not include comprehensive capital account liberalization, because I did not believe that did or should command a consensus in Washington.

8. **Privatization**. As noted already, this was the one area in which what originated as a neoliberal idea had won broad acceptance. We have since been made very conscious that it matters a lot how privatization is done: it can be a highly corrupt process that transfers assets to a privileged elite for a fraction of their true value, but the evidence is that it brings benefits (especially in terms of improved service coverage) when done properly, and the privatized enterprise either sells into a competitive market or is properly regulated.

9. **Deregulation**. This focused specifically on easing barriers to entry and exit, not on abolishing regulations designed for safety or environmental reasons, or to govern prices in a non-competitive industry.

10. **Property Rights**. This was primarily about providing the informal sector with the ability to gain property rights at acceptable cost (inspired by Hernando de Soto's analysis).

First Reactions

The three American discussants whom I had invited to react to my paper were Richard Feinberg (then at the Overseas Development Council), Stanley Fischer (then Chief Economist at the World Bank), and Allan Meltzer (then as now a professor at Carnegie-Mellon University). Feinberg and Meltzer were intended to make sure that I had not represented as consensual anything that one or other side of the political spectrum would regard as rubbish, while Fischer would play the same safeguard role as regards the IFIs.

Fischer was most supportive of the basic thrust of the paper, saying that "there are no longer two competing economic development paradigms" and that "Williamson has captured the growing Washington consensus on what the developing countries should do." But he pointed to some areas that I had not commented on and where sharp disagreements remained, such as the environment, military spending, a need for more comprehensive financial reform than freeing interest rates, bringing back flight capital, and freeing flows of financial capital. It was not my intent to argue that controversy had ended, so I would not take issue with his contention that there remained sharp disagreements on a number of issues (including the desirability of capital account liberalization). And my initial paper did indeed formulate the financial liberalization question too narrowly.

Meltzer expressed his pleasure at finding how much the mainstream had learned (according to my account) about the futility of things like policy activism, exploiting the unemployment/inflation tradeoff, and development planning. The two elements of my list on which he concentrated his criticism were once again the interest rate question (though here he focused more on my interim objective of a positive but moderate real interest rate than on the long run objective of interest rate liberalization) and a competitive exchange rate. The criticism of the interest rate objective I regard as merited. His alternative to a competitive exchange rate, namely a currency board, would certainly not be consensual, but the fact that he raised this issue was my first warning that on the exchange rate question I had misrepresented the degree of agreement in Washington.

Feinberg started off by suggesting that there really was not much of a consensus at all, but his comment mellowed as it progressed, and he concluded by saying that there was convergence on key concepts though still plenty to argue about. His most memorable line does not appear in his written comment but consisted of the suggestion that I should have labeled my list the Universal Convergence rather than the Washington Consensus, since the extent of agreement is far short of consensus but runs far wider than Washington. He was of course correct on both points, but it was too late to change the terminology.

The point about how much more apt it would have been to refer to a universal convergence rather than a Washington consensus was rubbed home in a fourth comment, by Patricio Meller of CIEPLAN in Santiago de Chile. In the months that followed I participated in several meetings where I not only argued that the policies included in my ten points were in fact being adopted fairly widely in Latin America, as our conference had confirmed, but also that this was a good thing and that lagging countries should catch up. I know that I never regarded those ten points as constituting the whole of what should be on the policy agenda, but perhaps I was not always as careful in spelling that out as I should have been.

The two points in my original list that seem to me in retrospect least adequate as a summary of conventional thinking are the two identified by Allan Meltzer, namely financial liberalization and exchange-rate policy. The agenda for financial liberalization went broader than interest rates, to include most importantly the liberalization of credit flows, and (as Joe Stiglitz has often pointed out) it needed to be supplemented by prudential supervision if it were not to lead almost inexorably to financial crisis. We already had the experience of the Southern Cone liberalization of the late 1970s to emphasize that point, so I clearly should not have overlooked it. On exchange rate policy

I fear I was guilty of wishful thinking in suggesting that opinion had coalesced on something close to my own view, whereas in fact I suspect that even then a majority of Washington opinion would have plumped for either the bipolar view or else (like Meltzer) one of the poles. In arguing that lagging countries should catch up with the policy reforms on my list, I argued on occasion that the East Asian NICs had broadly followed those policies. A Korean discussant (whose name I regret to say escapes me) at a conference in Madison challenged this contention; he argued that their macro policies had indeed been prudent, but also asserted (like Alice Amsden and Robert Wade) that their microeconomic policies had involved an active role for the state quite at variance with the thrust of points 4 and 6–9 of my list. I think one has to concede that some of the East Asian countries, notably Korea and Taiwan, were far from pursuing laissez-faire during their years of catch-up growth, but this does not prove that their rapid growth was attributable to their departure from liberal policies, as critics of the Washington Consensus seem to assume axiomatically. There were after all two other East Asian countries that grew comparably rapidly, in which the state played a much smaller role. Indeed, one of those— namely Hong Kong—was the closest to a model of laissez-faire that the world has ever seen. It would seem to me more natural to attribute the fast growth of the East Asian NICs to what they had in common, such as fiscal prudence, high savings rates, work ethic, competitive exchange rates, and a focus on education, rather than to what they did differently, such as industrial policy, directed credit, and import protection.

Incidentally, one should compare the policy stance of Korea and Taiwan with that of other developing countries, not with a textbook model of perfect competition. Most of the countries that failed to grow comparably fast were even less liberal. So even if it was wrong to treat the East Asian NICs as pin-up examples of the Washington Consensus in action, it is even more misleading to treat them as evidence for rejecting microeconomic liberalization. That controversy cannot be resolved by any simple appeal to what happened in East Asia. But arguments about the content of the Washington Consensus have always been secondary to the wave of indignation unleashed by the name that I pinned on this list of policy reforms. Some of the reformers obviously believed that I had undercut their local standing by calling it a "Washington" agenda, and thus suggesting that these were reforms that were being imposed on them rather than being adopted at their own volition because they recognized that those were the reforms their country needed. When I invented the term I was not thinking of making propaganda for economic reform (insofar as I was contemplating making propaganda, it was propaganda for debt relief in Washington, not propaganda for policy reform in Latin America). From the standpoint of making propaganda for policy reform in Latin America, Moisés Naím (2000) has argued that in fact it was a good term in 1989, the year the coalition led by the United States emerged victorious in the Cold War, when people were searching for a new ideology and the ideology of the victors looked rather appealing. But it was a questionable choice in more normal times, and a terrible one in the world that George W. Bush has created, where mention of Washington is hardly the way to curry support from non-Americans. It was, I fear, a propaganda gift to the old left.

Varying Interpretations

To judge by the sales of *Latin American Adjustment: How Much Has Happened?*, the vast majority of those who have launched venomous attacks on the Washington Consensus have not read my account of what I meant by the term. When I read what others mean by it, I discover that it has been interpreted to mean bashing the state, a new imperialism, the creation of a laissez-faire global economy, that the only thing that matters is the growth of GDP, and doubtless much else besides. I submit that it is difficult to find any of these implied by the list of ten policy reforms that I presented earlier.

One event that I found extraordinary was to learn that many people in Latin America blamed the adoption of Washington Consensus policies for the collapse of the Argentine economy in 2001. I found this extraordinary because I had for some years been hoping against hope that Argentina would not suffer a collapse like the one that occurred, but was nonetheless driven to the conclusion that it was highly likely because of the fundamental ways in which the country had strayed from two of the most basic precepts of what I had laid out. Specifically, it had adopted a fixed exchange rate that became chronically overvalued (for reasons that were not its fault at all, let me add), and—while its fiscal deficits were smaller than in the 1980s—it had not used its boom years to work down the debt/GDP ratio. Its fiscal policy as the crisis approached was not nearly restrictive enough to sustain the currency board system. None of the good reforms along Washington Consensus lines that Argentina had indeed made during the 1990s—trade liberalization, financial liberalization, privatization, and so on—seemed to me to have the slightest bearing on the crisis. Yet Latin American populists and journalists, and even a few reputable economists, were asserting that the Washington Consensus was somehow to blame for the Argentinean implosion. I am still hoping to learn the causal channel they have in mind.

One has to conclude that the term has been used to mean very different things by different people. In fact, it seems to me that there are at least two interpretations of the term beside mine that are in widespread circulation. One uses it to refer to the policies the Bretton Woods institutions applied toward their client countries, or perhaps the attitude of the US government plus the Bretton Woods institutions. This seems to me a reasonable, well-defined usage. In the early days after 1989 there was not much difference between my concept and this one, but over time some substantive differences emerged. The Bretton Woods institutions increasingly came to espouse the so-called bipolar doctrine (at least until the implosion of the Argentine economy in 2001, as a direct result of applying one of the supposedly crisis-free regimes), according to which countries should either float their exchange rate "cleanly" or else fix it firmly by adopting some institutional device like a currency board. As pointed out above, that is directly counter to my version of the Washington Consensus, which called for a competitive exchange rate, which necessarily implies an intermediate regime since either fixed or floating rates can easily become overvalued. Again, the Bretton Woods institutions, or at least the IMF, came in the mid-1990s to urge countries to liberalize their capital accounts, whereas my version had deliberately limited the call for liberalization of capital flows to FDI. Both of those deviations from the original version were in my opinion terrible, with the second one bearing the major responsibility for causing the Asian crisis of 1997. But there were also some highly positive differences, as the Bank and Fund came to take up some of the issues that I had not judged sufficiently major in Latin America in 1989 to justify inclusion. I think in particular of institutional issues, especially regarding governance and corruption, in the case of the Bank, and financial sector reform as reflected in standards and codes in the case of the Fund. And by the late 1990s both institutions had replaced their earlier indifference to issues of income distribution by a recognition that it matters profoundly *who* gains or loses income.

The third interpretation of the term "Washington Consensus" uses it as a synonym for neoliberalism or market fundamentalism. This I regard as a thoroughly objectionable perversion of the original meaning. Whatever else the term "Washington Consensus" may mean, it should surely refer to a set of policies that command or commanded a consensus in some significant part of Washington, either the US government or the IFIs or both, or perhaps both plus some other group. Even in the early years of the Reagan administration, or during Bush, it would be difficult to contend that any of the distinctively neoliberal policies, such as supply-side economics, monetarism, or minimal government, commanded much of a consensus, certainly not in the IFIs. And it would be preposterous to associate any of those policies with the Clinton administration. Yet most of the political diatribes against the Washington Consensus have been directed against this third concept, with those using the term this way apparently unconcerned with the need to establish that there actually was a consensus in favor of the policies they love to hate.

Why should the term have come to be used in such different ways? I find it easy enough to see why the second usage emerged. The term initially provided a reasonable description of the policies of the Bretton Woods institutions, and as these evolved the term continued to refer to what these currently were.

What puzzles me is how the third usage became so popular. The only hypothesis that has ever seemed to me remotely plausible is that this was an attempt to discredit economic reform by bundling a raft of ideas that deserve to be consigned to oblivion along with the list of commonsense proreform proposals that constituted my original list. This was doubtless facilitated by the name that I had bestowed on my list, which gave an incentive to anyone who disliked the policies or attitudes of the US government or the IFIs to join in a misrepresentation of the policies they were promoting.

In any event, surely intellectual integrity demands a conscientious attempt in the future to distinguish alternative concepts of the Washington Consensus. Semantic issues may not be the most exciting ones, but being clear about the way in which terms are being used is a necessary condition for serious professional discussion. The practice of dismissing requests for clarification as tedious pedantry should be unacceptable. Perhaps then more critics would follow the example of the Korean discussant to whom I referred earlier who laid out precisely which elements of my original agenda he objected to. Or if a critic chooses to use the third concept, then surely he should say that he is talking about a concept of the Washington Consensus that has never commanded a consensus in Washington.

6B. *Judicial Reform in Ecuador*

This is an excerpt of the World Bank's 2003 assessment of the Bank-funded Judicial Reform Project in Ecuador, which we mentioned in the chapter. The assessment was carried out under the auspices of the Bank's Legal Vice Presidency. It attempts to determine the extent to which legal aid programs improve the plight of one of the most vulnerable segments of Ecuadorian society: poor women with children (the most vulnerable of the vulnerable are black and indigenous women). It does so by narrowing the assessment to child support payments, and narrowing it further to mothers that had separated from their spouse or partner who fathered their child(ren). Although we haven't included the discussion of relevant Ecuadorian law, the assessment notes that, among other things, the amount of child support is determined by the judge, taking into account the needs of the child and the provider's economic means and needs. What risk(s) does this raise in Ecuador? Take a look at the first sentence under "Methodology" and the following bracket (from a footnote). Why pose the purpose of the assessment in those terms? Does the assessment limit itself to its purported purpose? Another purpose of the assessment, which we didn't include, was to assess the best mix of quantitative and qualitative data for future evaluations of similar projects.

International Bank for Reconstruction, "Impact of Legal Aid:
Ecuador" (2003)

Introduction

Legal Aid Initiative and the Need for Evaluation

The World Bank's (1994) assessment of Ecuador's judicial sector found, among other things, that there were virtually no legal resources for poor women suffering domestic violence or trying to obtain legal entitlements such as child support. The Bank's Judicial Reform Project, approved in 1996, took this into account in its design.

The Program for Law and Justice component included a Special Fund created to counter-balance top-down reforms by financing demand-driven solutions to the problem of access to justice, among other issues. Specifically, the subcomponent *Legal Services Pilots for Indigent Women* gave partial grants to local non-governmental organizations (NGOs) that provided legal and complementary services to qualified women and their children. The goal of these grants was to enable poor women to obtain and secure their legal entitlements and begin to take action that would improve their socio-economic positions. The program supported the work of three local NGOs: *Centro Ecuatoriano para la Promoción y Acción de la Mujer (CEPAM), Corporación Mujer a Mujer, and Fundación María Guare.* These organizations provide not only legal information and representation, but also complementary services such as psychological counseling and referrals to shelters for battered women. The geographical area served corresponds to three major cities (Quito, Guayaquil, and Cuenca) and two urban outskirts (Duale and Santa Elena). Financing for the NGOs was initially granted for the period April 1998 through March 2000, and was later extended until 2002. The total budget of the Program for Law and Justice exceeded US$1.6 million dollars; the Legal Services Pilot addressed in this evaluation represents less than US$400,000.

The intervention has several important characteristics that warrant an impact evaluation. First, the program tests an innovative approach to poverty reduction. Ecuador's Legal Aid for Indigent Women was the first Bank-financed project to include a legal aid component aimed squarely at poor women and their children. Similar initiatives are currently being implemented under grants in Sri Lanka and Jordan.

Second, the program improves our understanding of the link between improved access to justice and poverty reduction, a topic that has been the focus of some research in the past few years . . .

Third, the program was designed to have the highest poverty impact on a group in society that is particularly vulnerable. Single women with children are among the poorest people in Ecuador and their living standards are consistently inferior to those of men. In addition, they are the victims of violence and abuse that affect not only their emotional well being, but their ability to escape poverty as well. In a study of the economic costs of domestic violence toward women, Morrison and Orlando (1999) found that domestic violence has a large, negative impact on women's earnings.

In order to simplify the analysis, we focus our attention on the effectiveness of the program in changing the economic status of women by means of improving their access to child support awards. Data were derived mainly from survey instruments designed for this purpose and administered in coordination with personnel from local NGOs.

Beyond the specific findings about the legal aid program in Ecuador, this report places emphasis on drawing methodological lessons that might be used to evaluate similar activities in other countries. Thus, we discuss at length the methodologies used, their strengths, and short-comings. Perhaps the most important lesson drawn is that, because legal and judicial reform projects may entail outcomes difficult to quantify, it is important to combine both quantitative and qualitative evaluation techniques.

Methodology

The ultimate question in evaluating the economic effect of the activities in Ecuador is, "Were women who had access to legal aid and related services better off than women who did not have such access, holding other factors equal?" [This is the ultimate question as to the *direct* economic effects of the project.] To simplify the analysis and facilitate comparisons with other activities, we focus on a single category of cases: situations in which mothers had separated from the spouse or partner who fathered their child(ren). We consider whether access to legal aid:

1. Translates into better legal results (obtaining a favorable judgment entitling them to child support, or a favorable settlement or decision in paternity or custody disputes);

2. Translates into better economic conditions for poor mothers and their children;

3. Decreases a woman's chances of being battered;

4. Improves women's access to justice by improving their knowledge of their legal rights;

5. Improves women's access to justice by lowering the "transaction costs" of asserting a claim;

6. Improves women's access to justice by affecting how they made the decision whether or not to assert their legal claims;

7. Translates into any objective improvement in the situation of children; and

8. "Empowers" women, either subjectively or objectively.

Our economic task is to analyze the welfare consequences of a particular legal aid clinic's program aimed at helping poor women in Ecuador . . . .

* * *

Data Used in this Evaluation

To measure the impact of the activities in Ecuador, we primarily draw on two sources, a survey of 180 women who had used the legal aid program and a control group of 182 similarly situated women who did not have access to legal aid, and three focus groups of a total of 24 mothers eligible for legal aid, of whom 14 were legal aid clients and 10 were non-clients . . .

We also rely on the Bank's previous reports and assessments of gender issues in Ecuador, including those related specifically to this activity. Finally, we use secondary sources describing Ecuador's laws and socio-economic situation, such as Ecuador's latest LSMS survey (*Encuesta de Condiciones de Vida*, 1988–1989) conducted by its census bureau (INEC).

In seeking to develop a model for evaluating other legal aid clinics, we also draw heavily on research the World Bank has previously undertaken or commissioned in the areas of justice reform, gender and development.

Results

By almost any conceivable measure, the legal aid clinics were a success. The answer to every item in our earlier list of questions addressed is "yes."

1. Legal aid clients attain better legal results than non-clients. The intervention increases the probability of obtaining a child support award by 20 percentage points. This is in comparison with non-clients after controlling for relevant factors.

2. Legal aid clients attain better economic results than non-clients. The intervention increases the probability of actually receiving a child support payment by 10.4 percentage points. This is in comparison with non-clients after controlling for relevant factors.

3. Legal aid clients report drastically lowered rates of severe physical violence. While nearly half of all women in both the study group and the comparison group report suffering severe physical violence from their former spouse or partner during the relationship, those women with legal aid report lower levels of violence after separation. Virtually identical rates of severe physical violence prior to the separation are reported by legal aid clients and non-clients (47.6 percent and 49.4 percent, respectively). After the separation, the rate of such violence for legal aid clients is more than halved, to 22.9 percent, while for non-clients the decline was less significant (to 33.5 percent). As noted below, even after controlling for other possibly relevant factors, this translates into a significant reduction (by 17 percentage points) of the probability of such violence for clients in comparison to non-clients.

4. Legal aid helped narrow the information gap that prevents some mothers from seeking the child support to which they are entitled. Legal aid clients are more likely to assert their legal rights to child support than non-clients. Moreover, among those women who did not assert claims, clients were less likely than non-clients to cite "lack of knowledge" as a reason for not asserting a claim.

5. Legal aid lowered the transaction costs of asserting a claim. The main deterrent to using the judicial system is the perception that courts are corrupt, nontransparent, and biased against women. Legal aid helps by cutting through the red tape and otherwise reducing transaction costs.

6. Legal aid clients show a high level of customer satisfaction and have a more positive outlook toward the judicial system. They are more likely than non-clients to recommend seeking child support "to a friend who is thinking about it."

7. Legal aid had positive intergenerational impact. Specifically, receiving child support payments increases the probability of

the child attending school by 4.8 percentage points. In addition, the legal aid clinics have an indirect impact on the child's attendance rate by decreasing the incidence of domestic violence after separation (physical violence after separation decreases the child's probability of attending school by 4 percentage points).

8. Legal aid empowers women. In the focus groups, women describe important non-monetary gains from CEPAM's intervention, such as improved self-esteem and help in coping with the aftermath of domestic violence. When asked what they had learned from legal aid, women speak of ending a situation in which they had felt alone and helpless.

* * *

Focus Group Results

. . . Below is a summary of the major findings from the focus groups, which to some extent corroborate the survey results.

* * *

Obstacles to obtaining legal aid

The main deterrent to using the judicial system is the perception that courts are corrupt, nontransparent, and biased against women. CEPAM helps by cutting through the red tape and otherwise reducing transaction costs. CEPAM clients reported that they were able to negotiate the judicial system notwithstanding its problems.

Fear of physical violence and other forms of retaliation is another major concern for mothers when deciding whether to seek child support, which is consistent with the results of the survey.

"I went [to the authorities] only once because he found out about it and threatened to beat me up. I already had problems with him because he wanted to take my daughter away from me . . . He said he could take her because I did not have a job to support her, because I was too young."

* * *

Gender Issues

This evaluation has shown that the specific legal aid clinic accomplished what legal aid clinics are supposed to do: help clients. For all the reasons discussed above, CEPAM clients were better off legally, economically, and subjectively than non-clients in the study group.

The activity we are evaluating brings together two aspects of the World Bank's mission and goals. It is part of a legal and judicial reform project which aims to promote the rule of law and includes integrated gender aspects to increase women's ability to enforce equality in rights and resources.

Some of the most important links between gender and growth through human capital have to do with women's "empowerment." The empowerment of women is, like the diminution of poverty, one of the Millennium Development Goals of the Bank. As World Bank publications (2002b) and (2001) point out, the interrelation of gender inequality and poverty is both intricate and pervasive.

The primary pathways through which gender systems affect growth are the productivity of labor and/or and the allocative efficiency of the economy, specifically through:

- Investments in human capital, especially girls' and women's education and health;
- Investments in physical capital, especially women's access to capital or to the formal sector employment it creates; and
- The functioning of markets and institutions.

The concept of "empowerment" resists quantification. We may not be able to measure empowerment directly, but we do know that empowerment of women is linked not only to higher incomes for women and their families, but also to intergenerational effects on child schooling, nutrition and survival.

Legal aid is by definition designed to "empower" women by increasing their access to justice. Yet the linkage between legal aid and some of the benefits associated with women's empowerment may not be provable in an individual activity, because the scale of the activity is too small to support this kind of analysis.

In this case we actually were able to show a link between women's empowerment and certain development indicators: The children of legal aid clients were more likely to still be in school than the children of non-clients.

* * *

6C. *U.S. v. Kay: The Foreign Corrupt Practices Act*

We include United States v. Kay to introduce you to the U.S.' anti-corruption statute, the Foreign Corrupt Practices Act. The opinion will give you a good overview of a very complex statute. You know how to read opinions well by now. So we'll leave it up to you to discuss the issue in the case and how the Fifth Circuit resolves it. Question: Is anything beyond a "grease payment" permissible? Are grease payments even exempt?

United States v. Kay, 359 F.3d 738 (5th Cir. Tex. 2004)

United States v. Kay

Plaintiff-appellant, the United States of America ("government") appeals the district court's grant of the motion of defendants-appellees David Kay and Douglas Murphy ("defendants") to dismiss the Superseding Indictment ("indictment") that charged them with bribery of foreign officials in violation of the Foreign Corrupt Practices Act ("FCPA"). In their dismissal motion, defendants contended that the indictment failed to state an offense against them. The principal dispute in this case is whether, if proved beyond a reasonable doubt, the conduct that the indictment ascribed to defendants in connection with the alleged bribery of Haitian officials to understate customs duties and sales taxes on rice shipped to Haiti to assist American Rice, Inc. in obtaining or retaining business was sufficient to constitute an offense under the FCPA. Underlying this question of sufficiency of the contents of the indictment is the preliminary task of ascertaining the scope of the FCPA, which in turn requires us to construe the statute.

The district court concluded that, as a matter of law, an indictment alleging illicit payments to foreign officials for the purpose of avoiding substantial portions of customs duties and sales taxes to obtain or retain business are not the kind of bribes that the FCPA criminalizes. We disagree with this assessment of the scope of the FCPA and hold that such bribes could (but do not necessarily) come within the ambit of the statute. Concluding in the end that the indictment in this case is sufficient to state an offense under the FCPA, we remand the instant case for further proceedings consistent with this opinion. Nevertheless, on remand the defendants may choose to submit a motion asking the district court to compel the government to allege more specific facts regarding the intent element of an FCPA crime that requires the defendant to intend for the foreign official's anticipated conduct in consideration of a bribe (hereafter, the "quid pro quo") to produce an anticipated result—here, diminution of duties and taxes—that would assist (or is meant to assist) in obtaining or retaining business (hereafter, the "business nexus element"). If so, the trial court will need to decide whether (1) merely quoting or paraphrasing the statute as to that element (as was done here) is sufficient, or (2) the government must allege additional facts as to just what business was sought to be obtained or retained in Haiti and just how the intended quid pro quo was meant to assist in obtaining or retaining such business. We therefore reverse the district court's dismissal of the indictment and remand for further consistent proceedings.

I.   FACTS AND PROCEEDINGS

American Rice, Inc. ("ARI") is a Houston-based company that exports rice to foreign countries, including Haiti. Rice Corporation of Haiti ("RCH"), a wholly owned subsidiary of ARI, was incorporated in Haiti to represent ARI's interests and deal with third parties there. As an aspect of Haiti's standard importation procedure, its customs officials assess duties based on the quantity and value of rice imported into the country. Haiti also requires businesses that deliver rice there to remit an advance deposit against Haitian sales taxes, based on the value of that rice, for which deposit a credit is eventually allowed on Haitian sales tax returns when filed.

In 2001, a grand jury charged Kay with violating the FCPA and subsequently returned the indictment, which charges both Kay and Murphy with 12 counts of FCPA violations. As is readily apparent on its face, the indictment contains detailed factual allegations about (1) the timing and purposes of Congress's enactment of the FCPA, (2) ARI and its status as an "issuer" under the FCPA, (3) RCH and its status as a wholly owned subsidiary and "service corporation" of ARI, representing ARI's interest in Haiti, and (4) defendants' citizenship, their positions as officers of ARI, and their status as "issuers" and "domestic concerns" under the FCPA. The indictment also spells out in detail how Kay and Murphy allegedly orchestrated the bribing of Haitian customs officials to accept false bills of lading and other documentation that intentionally understated by one-third the quantity of rice shipped to Haiti, thereby significantly reducing ARI's customs duties and sales taxes. In this regard, the indictment alleges the details of the bribery scheme's machinations, including the preparation of duplicate documentation, the calculation of bribes as a percentage of the value of the rice not reported, the surreptitious payment of monthly retainers to Haitian officials, and the defendants' purported authorization of withdrawals of funds from ARI's bank accounts with which to pay the Haitian officials, either directly or through intermediaries—all to produce substantially reduced Haitian customs and tax costs to ARI. Further, the indictment alleges discrete facts regarding ARI's domestic incorporation and place of business, as well as the particular instrumentalities of interstate and foreign commerce that defendants used or caused to be used in carrying out the purported bribery.

In contrast, without any factual allegations, the indictment merely paraphrases the one element of the statute that is central to this appeal, only conclusionally accusing defendants of causing payments to be made to Haitian customs officials:

for purposes of influencing acts and decisions of such foreign officials in their official capacities, inducing such foreign officials to do and omit to do acts in violation of their lawful duty, and to obtain an improper advantage, in order to assist American Rice, Inc. in obtaining and retaining business for, and directing business to American Rice, Inc. and Rice Corporation of Haiti. (Emphasis added)

Although it recites in great detail the discrete facts that the government intends to prove to satisfy each other element of an FCPA violation, the indictment recites no particularized facts that, if proved, would satisfy the "assist" aspect of the business nexus element of the statute, i.e., the nexus between the illicit tax savings produced by the bribery and the assistance such savings provided or were intended to provide in obtaining or retaining business for ARI and RCH. Neither does the indictment contain any factual allegations whatsoever to identify just what business in Haiti (presumably some rice-related commercial activity) the illicit customs and tax savings assisted (or were intended to assist) in obtaining or retaining, or just how these savings were supposed to assist in such efforts. In other words, the indictment recites no facts that could demonstrate an actual or intended cause-and-effect nexus between reduced taxes and obtaining identified business or retaining identified business opportunities.

In granting defendants' motion to dismiss the indictment for failure to state an offense, the district court held that, as a matter of law, bribes paid to obtain favorable tax treatment are not payments made to "obtain or retain business" within the intendment of the FCPA, and thus are not within the scope of that statute's proscription of foreign bribery. The government timely filed a notice of appeal.

II. ANALYSIS

A. Standard of Review

We review de novo questions of statutory interpretation, as well as "whether an indictment sufficiently alleges the elements of an offense." As a motion to dismiss an indictment for failure to state an offense is a challenge to the sufficiency of the indictment, we are required to "take the allegations of the indictment as true and to determine whether an offense has been stated."

"[I]t is well settled that an indictment must set forth the offense with sufficient clarity and certainty to apprise the accused of the crime with which he is charged." The test for sufficiency is "not whether the indictment could have been framed in a more satisfactory manner, but whether it conforms to minimum constitutional standards"; namely, that it "[(1)] contain [ ] the elements of the offense charged and fairly inform[ ] a defendant of the charge against which he must defend, and [(2)], enable[ ] him to plead an acquittal or conviction in bar of future prosecutions for the same offense."

Because an offense under the FCPA requires that the alleged bribery be committed for the purpose of inducing foreign officials to commit unlawful acts, the results of which will assist in obtaining or retaining business in their country, the questions before us in this appeal are (1) whether bribes to obtain illegal but favorable tax and customs treatment can ever come within the scope of the statute, and (2) if so, whether, in combination, there are minimally sufficient facts alleged in the indictment to inform the defendants regarding the nexus between, on the one hand, Haitian taxes avoided through bribery, and, on the other hand, assistance in getting or keeping some business or business opportunity in Haiti.

B.   Words of the FCPA

"[T]he starting point for interpreting a statute is the language of the statute itself." When construing a criminal statute, we "must follow the plain and unambiguous meaning of the statutory language." Terms not defined in the statute are interpreted according to their "ordinary and natural meaning . . . as well as the overall policies and objectives of the statute." Furthermore, "a statute must, if possible, be construed in such fashion that every word has some operative effect." Finally, we have found it "appropriate to consider the title of a statute in resolving putative ambiguities." If, after application of these principles of statutory construction, we conclude that the statute is ambiguous, we may turn to legislative history. For the language to be considered ambiguous, however, it must be "susceptible to more than one reasonable interpretation" or "more than one accepted meaning."

The FCPA prohibits payments to foreign officials for purposes of:

> (i)   influencing any act or decision of such foreign official in his official capacity, (ii) inducing such foreign official to do or omit to do any act in violation of the lawful duty of such official, or (iii) securing any improper advantage . . . in order to assist [the company making the payment] in obtaining or retaining business for or with, or directing business to, any person.

None contend that the FCPA criminalizes every payment to a foreign official: It criminalizes only those payments that are intended to (1) influence a foreign official to act or make a decision in his official capacity, or (2) induce such an official to perform or refrain from performing some act in violation of his duty, or (3) secure some wrongful advantage to the payor. And even then, the FCPA criminalizes these kinds of payments only if the result they are intended to produce—their quid pro quo—will assist (or is intended to assist) the payor in efforts to get or keep some business for or with "any person." Thus, the first question of statutory interpretation presented in this appeal is whether payments made to foreign officials to obtain unlawfully reduced customs duties or sales tax liabilities can ever fall within the scope of the FCPA, i.e., whether the illicit payments made to obtain a reduction of revenue liabilities can ever constitute the kind of bribery that is proscribed by the FCPA. The district court answered this question in the negative; only if we answer it in the affirmative will we need to analyze the sufficiency of the factual allegations of the indictment as to the one element of the crime contested here.

The principal thrust of the defendants' argument is that the business nexus element, i.e., the "assist . . . in obtaining or retaining business" element, narrowly limits the statute's applicability to those payments that are intended to obtain a foreign official's approval of a bid for a new government contract or the renewal of an existing government contract. In contrast, the government insists that, in addition to payments to officials that lead directly to getting or renewing business contracts, the statute covers payments that indirectly advance ("assist") the payor's goal of obtaining or retaining foreign business with or for some person. The government reasons that paying reduced customs duties and sales taxes on imports, as is purported to have occurred in this case, is the type of "improper advantage" that always will assist in obtaining or retaining business in a foreign country, and thus is always covered by the FCPA.

In approaching this issue, the district court concluded that the FCPA's language is ambiguous, and proceeded to review the statute's legislative history. We agree with the court's finding of ambiguity for several reasons. Perhaps our most significant statutory construction problem results from the failure of the language of the FCPA to give a clear indication of the exact scope of the business nexus element; that is, the proximity of the required nexus between, on the one hand, the anticipated results of the foreign official's bargained-for action or inaction, and, on the other hand, the assistance provided by or expected from those results in helping the briber to obtain or retain business. Stated differently, how attenuated can the linkage be between the effects of that which is sought from the foreign official in consideration of a bribe (here, tax minimization) and the briber's goal of finding assistance or obtaining or retaining foreign business with or for some person, and still satisfy the business nexus element of the FCPA?

Second, the parties' diametrically opposed but reasonable contentions demonstrate that the ordinary and natural meaning of the statutory language is genuinely debatable and thus ambiguous. For instance, the word "business" can be defined at any point along a continuum from "a volume of trade," to "the purchase and sale of goods in an attempt to make a profit," to "an assignment" or a "project." Thus, dictionary definitions can support both (1) the government's broader interpretation of the business nexus language as encompassing any type of commercial activity, and (2) defendants' argument that "obtain or retain business" connotes a more pedestrian understanding of establishing or renewing a particular commercial arrangement. Similarly, although the word "assist" suggests a somewhat broader statutory scope, it does not connote specificity or define either how proximate or how remote the foreign official's anticipated actions that constitute assistance must or may be to the business obtained or retained.

Third, absent a firm understanding of just what "obtaining or retaining business" or "assist" actually include, the parties' remaining arguments prove little. For instance, the separation of the statutory prohibition into two aspects—(1) seeking to induce a foreign official to act in consideration of a bribe (quid pro quo) (2) for purposes of assisting in obtaining or retaining business (business nexus)—provides little insight into the precise scope of the statute. The government may be correct in its contention that the quid pro quo requirement expands the scope of the statute, because Congress otherwise could have dispensed with the quid pro quo requirement entirely and simply prohibited only those payments resulting directly in obtaining or retaining business contracts. It is at least plausible, however, as defendants argue, that the quid pro quo requirement was not necessarily meant to expand the statutory scope, but instead was meant to distinguish acts of a foreign official in his official capacity from acts in his private capacity. Similarly, defendants might be right in urging that the business nexus element restricts the scope of the statute to a smaller universe of payments than those made to obtain any advantage; yet it is conceivable that this restriction was included to exempt more marginal facilitating payments, but not the types of payments that defendants are accused of making.

Neither does the remainder of the statutory language clearly express an exclusively broad or exclusively narrow understanding of the business nexus element. The extent to which the exception for routine governmental action ("facilitating payments" or "grease") is narrowly drawn reasonably suggests that Congress was carving out very limited categories of permissible payments from an otherwise broad statutory prohibition. As defendants suggest, however, another plausible implication for including an express statutory explanation that routine governmental action does not include decisions "to award new business to or to continue business with a particular party," is that Congress was focusing entirely on identifiable decisions made by foreign officials in granting or renewing specific business arrangements in foreign countries, and not on a more general panoply of competitive business advantages.

The fourth and final interpretive factor, the statute's title—"Foreign Corrupt Practices Act"—is more suggestive of a relatively broad application of its provisions, but only slightly so. By itself, such a generic title fails to make one interpretation of the statutory language more persuasive than another, much less establish one as the only reasonable construction of the statute. In sum, neither the ordinary meaning nor the provisions surrounding the disputed text are sufficiently clear to make the statutory language susceptible of but one reasonable interpretation. Inasmuch as Congress chose to phrase the business nexus requirement obliquely, and to say nothing to suggest how remote or how proximate the business nexus must be, we cannot conclude on the basis of the provision itself that the statute is either as narrow or as expansive as the parties respectively claim.

C.   FCPA Legislative History

As the statutory language itself is amenable to more than one reasonable interpretation, it is ambiguous as a matter of law. We turn therefore to legislative history in our effort to ascertain Congress's true intentions.

1.   1977 Legislative History

Congress enacted the FCPA in 1977, in response to recently discovered but widespread bribery of foreign officials by United States business interests. Congress resolved to interdict such bribery, not just because it is morally and economically suspect, but also because it was causing foreign policy problems for the United States. In particular, these concerns arose from revelations that United States defense contractors and oil companies had made large payments to high government officials in Japan, the Netherlands, and Italy. Congress also discovered that more than 400 corporations had made questionable or illegal payments in excess of $300 million to foreign officials for a wide range of favorable actions on behalf of the companies.

In deciding to criminalize this type of commercial bribery, the House and Senate each proposed similarly far-reaching, but non-identical, legislation. In its bill, the House intended "broadly [to] prohibit[ ] transactions that are corruptly intended to induce the recipient to use his or her influence to affect any act or decision of a foreign official . . ." Thus, the House bill contained no limiting "business nexus" element. Reflecting a somewhat narrower purpose, the Senate expressed its desire to ban payments made for the purpose of inducing foreign officials to act "so as to direct business to any person, maintain an established business opportunity with any person, divert any business opportunity from any person or influence the enactment or promulgation of legislation or regulations of that government or instrumentality."

At conference, compromise language "clarified the scope of the prohibition by requiring that the purpose of the payment must be to influence any act or decision of a foreign official . . . so as to assist an issuer in obtaining, retaining or directing business to any person." In the end, then, Congress adopted the Senate's proposal to prohibit only those payments designed to induce a foreign official to act in a way that is intended to facilitate ("assist") in obtaining or retaining of business.

Congress expressly emphasized that it did not intend to prohibit "so-called grease or facilitating payments," such as "payments for expediting shipments through customs or placing a transatlantic telephone call, securing required permits, or obtaining adequate police protection, transactions which may involve even the proper performance of duties." Instead of making an express textual exception for these types of non-covered payments, the respective committees of the two chambers sought to distinguish permissible grease payments from prohibited bribery by only prohibiting payments that induce an official to act "corruptly," i.e., actions requiring him "to misuse his official position" and his discretionary authority, not those "essentially ministerial" actions that "merely move a particular matter toward an eventual act or decision or which do not involve any discretionary action."

In short, Congress sought to prohibit the type of bribery that (1) prompts officials to misuse their discretionary authority and (2) disrupts market efficiency and United States foreign relations, at the same time recognizing that smaller payments intended to expedite ministerial actions should remain outside of the scope of the statute. The Conference Report explanation, on which the district court relied to find a narrow statutory scope, truly offers little insight into the FCPA's precise scope, however; it merely parrots the statutory language itself by stating that the purpose of a payment must be to induce official action "so as to assist an issuer in obtaining, retaining or directing business to any person."

To divine the categories of bribery Congress did and did not intend to prohibit, we must look to the Senate's proposal, because the final statutory language was drawn from it, and from the SEC Report on which the Senate's legislative proposal was based. In distinguishing among the types of illegal payments that United States entities were making at the time, the SEC Report identified four principal categories: (1) payments "made in an effort to procure special and unjustified favors or advantages in the enactment or administration of the tax or other laws" of a foreign country; (2) payments "made with the intent to assist the company in obtaining or retaining government contracts"; (3) payments "to persuade low-level government officials to perform functions or services which they are obliged to perform as part of their governmental responsibilities, but which they may refuse or delay unless compensated" ("grease"), and (4) political contributions. The SEC thus exhibited concern about a wide range of questionable payments (explicitly including the kind at issue here) that were resulting in millions of dollars being recorded falsely in corporate books and records.

As noted, the Senate Report explained that the statute should apply to payments intended "to direct business to any person, maintain an established business opportunity with any person, divert any business opportunity from any person or influence the enactment or promulgation of legislation or regulations of that government or instrumentality." We observe initially that the Senate only loosely addressed the categories of conduct highlighted by the SEC Report. Although the Senate's proposal picked up the SEC's concern with a business nexus, it did not expressly cover bribery influencing the administration of tax laws or seeking favorable tax treatment. It is clear, however, that even though the Senate was particularly concerned with bribery intended to secure new business, it was also mindful of bribes that influence legislative or regulatory actions, and those that maintain established business opportunities, a category of economic activity separate from, and much more capacious than, simply "directing business" to someone.

The statute's ultimate language of "obtaining or retaining" mirrors identical language in the SEC Report. But, whereas the SEC Report highlights payments that go toward "obtaining or retaining government contracts," the FCPA, incorporating the Senate Report's language, prohibits payments that assist in obtaining or retaining business, not just government contracts. Had the Senate and ultimately Congress wanted to carry over the exact, narrower scope of the SEC Report, they would have adopted the same language. We surmise that, in using the word "business" when it easily could have used the phraseology of SEC Report, Congress intended for the statute to apply to bribes beyond the narrow band of payments sufficient only to "obtain or retain government contracts." The Senate's express intention that the statute apply to corrupt payments that maintain business opportunities also supports this conclusion.

For purposes of deciding the instant appeal, the question nevertheless remains whether the Senate, and concomitantly Congress, intended this broader statutory scope to encompass the administration of tax, customs, and other laws and regulations affecting the revenue of foreign states. To reach this conclusion, we must ask whether Congress's remaining expressed desire to prohibit bribery aimed at getting assistance in retaining business or maintaining business opportunities was sufficiently broad to include bribes meant to affect the administration of revenue laws. When we do so, we conclude that the legislative intent was so broad.

Congress was obviously distraught not only about high profile bribes to high-ranking foreign officials, but also by the pervasiveness of foreign bribery by United States businesses and businessmen. Congress thus made the decision to clamp down on bribes intended to prompt foreign officials to misuse their discretionary authority for the benefit of a domestic entity's business in that country. This observation is not diminished by Congress's understanding and accepting that relatively small facilitating payments were, at the time, among the accepted costs of doing business in many foreign countries.

In addition, the concern of Congress with the immorality, inefficiency, and unethical character of bribery presumably does not vanish simply because the tainted payments are intended to secure a favorable decision less significant than winning a contract bid. Obviously, a commercial concern that bribes a foreign government official to award a construction, supply, or services contract violates the statute. Yet, there is little difference between this example and that of a corporation's lawfully obtaining a contract from an honest official or agency by submitting the lowest bid, and—either before or after doing so—bribing a different government official to reduce taxes and thereby ensure that the under-bid venture is nevertheless profitable. Avoiding or lowering taxes reduces operating costs and thus increases profit margins, thereby freeing up funds that the business is otherwise legally obligated to expend. And this, in turn, enables it to take any number of actions to the disadvantage of competitors. Bribing foreign officials to lower taxes and customs duties certainly can provide an unfair advantage over competitors and thereby be of assistance to the payor in obtaining or retaining business. This demonstrates that the question whether the defendants' alleged payments constitute a violation of the FCPA truly turns on whether these bribes were intended to lower ARI's cost of doing business in Haiti enough to have a sufficient nexus to garnering business there or to maintaining or increasing business operations that ARI already had there, so as to come within the scope of the business nexus element as Congress used it in the FCPA. Answering this fact question, then, implicates a matter of proof and thus evidence.

In short, the 1977 legislative history, particularly the Senate's proposal and the SEC Report on which it relied, convinces us that Congress meant to prohibit a range of payments wider than only those that directly influence the acquisition or retention of government contracts or similar commercial or industrial arrangements. On the other end of the spectrum, this history also demonstrates that Congress explicitly excluded facilitating payments (the grease exception). In thus limiting the exceptions to the type of bribery covered by the FCPA to this narrow category, Congress's intention to cast an otherwise wide net over foreign bribery suggests that Congress intended for the FCPA to prohibit all other illicit payments that are intended to influence non-trivial official foreign action in an effort to aid in obtaining or retaining business for some person. The congressional target was bribery paid to engender assistance in improving the business opportunities of the payor or his beneficiary, irrespective of whether that assistance be direct or indirect, and irrespective of whether it be related to administering the law, awarding, extending, or renewing a contract, or executing or preserving an agreement. In light of our reading of the 1977 legislative history, the subsequent 1988 and 1998 legislative history is only important to our analysis to the extent it confirms or conflicts with our initial conclusions about the scope of the statute.

2.   1988 Legislative History

After the FCPA's enactment, United States business entities and executives experienced difficulty in discerning a clear line between prohibited bribes and permissible facilitating payments. As a result, Congress amended the FCPA in 1988, expressly to clarify its original intent in enacting the statute. Both houses insisted that their proposed amendments only clarified ambiguities "without changing the basic intent or effectiveness of the law."

In this effort to crystallize the scope of the FCPA's prohibitions on bribery, Congress chose to identify carefully two types of payments that are not proscribed by the statute. It expressly excepted payments made to procure "routine governmental action" (again, the grease exception), and it incorporated an affirmative defense for payments that are legal in the country in which they are offered or that constitute bona fide expenditures directly relating to promotion of products or services, or to the execution or performance of a contract with a foreign government or agency.

We agree with the position of the government that these 1988 amendments illustrate an intention by Congress to identify very limited exceptions to the kinds of bribes to which the FCPA does not apply. A brief review of the types of routine governmental actions enumerated by Congress shows how limited Congress wanted to make the grease exceptions. Routine governmental action, for instance, includes "obtaining permits, licenses, or other official documents to qualify a person to do business in a foreign country," and "scheduling inspections associated with contract performance or inspections related to transit of goods across country." Therefore, routine governmental action does not include the issuance of every official document or every inspection, but only (1) documentation that qualifies a party to do business and (2) scheduling an inspection—very narrow categories of largely non-discretionary, ministerial activities performed by mid—or low-level foreign functionaries. In contrast, the FCPA uses broad, general language in prohibiting payments to procure assistance for the payor in obtaining or retaining business, instead of employing similarly detailed language, such as applying the statute only to payments that attempt to secure or renew particular government contracts. Indeed, Congress had the opportunity to adopt narrower language in 1977 from the SEC Report, but chose not to do so.

Defendants argue, nevertheless, that Congress's decision to reject House-proposed amendments to the business nexus element constituted its implicit rejection of such a broad reading of the statute. The House bill proposed new language to explain that payments for "obtaining or retaining business" also includes payments made for the "procurement of legislative, judicial, regulatory, or other action in seeking more favorable treatment by a foreign government." Indeed, defendants assert, the proposed amendment itself shows that Congress understood the business nexus provision to have narrow application; otherwise, there would have been no need to propose amending it.

Contrary to defendants' contention, the decision of Congress to reject this language has no bearing on whether "obtaining or retaining business" includes the conduct at issue here. In explaining Congress's decision not to include this proposed amendment in the business nexus requirement, the Conference Report stated that the "retaining business" language was not limited to the renewal of contracts or other business, but also includes a prohibition against corrupt payments related to the execution or performance of contracts or the carrying out of existing business, such as a payment to a foreign official for the purpose of obtaining more favorable tax treatment . . . The term should not, however, be construed so broadly as to include lobbying or other normal representations to government officials.

At first blush, this statement would seem to resolve the instant dispute in favor of the government; however, the district court interpreted Congress's decision to leave the business nexus requirement unchanged as a determination not to extend the scope of the statute. The court thus declined to defer to the report because, in the court's estimation, the legislative history "consist[ed] of an after-the-fact interpretation of the term 'retaining business' by a subsequent Congress more than ten years after the enactment of the original language."

We agree that, as a general matter, subsequent legislative history about unchanged statutory language would deserve little or no weight in our analysis. The Supreme Court has instructed that "the interpretation given by one Congress (or a committee or Member thereof) to an earlier statute is of little assistance in discerning the meaning of that statute." In this case, moreover, Congress's enactment of subsequent legislation did not include changes to the business nexus requirement itself.

Nevertheless, the Supreme Court has also stated that "[s]ubsequent legislation declaring the intent of an earlier statute is entitled to great weight in statutory construction." And, we have concluded that Congress is "at its most authoritative [when] adding complex and sophisticated amendments to an already complex and sophisticated act." Although in 1988 Congress refused to alter the business nexus requirement itself, it did enact exceptions and defenses to the statute's applicability, both of which the pertinent Conference Report language helps to explain vis-à-vis the statute's overall scope. And it must be remembered that clarifying the scope of the 1977 law was the overarching purpose of Congress in enacting the 1988 amendments. Thus, the legislative history that the district court rejected as irrelevant in fact explains how the 1988 amendments relate to the original scope of the statute and concomitantly to the business nexus element.

First, the Conference Report expresses what is implied by the new affirmative defense for bona fide expenditures for the execution or performance of a contract. The creation of a defense for bona fide payments strongly implies that corrupt, non-bona-fide payments related to contract execution and performance have always been and remain prohibited. Instead of leaving this prohibition implicit, though, the Conference Report's description of "retaining business" explained that this phrase, and thus the statutory ambit, includes "a prohibition against corrupt payments related to the execution or performance of contracts . . ."

Similarly, in its 1988 statutory description of routine governmental action, Congress stated that this exception does not include decisions about "whether, or on what terms . . . to continue business with a particular party," which must mean, conversely, that decisions that do relate to "continu[ing] business with a particular party" are covered by, i.e., are not excepted from, the scope of the statute. The Conference Report, in turn, states that "retaining business" means "the carrying out of existing business," thereby simply repeating statutory intent without explaining it. We discern no meaningful distinction between the phrase "continuing business" in the statutory text, and "carrying out of existing business" in the Conference Report.

Third, the Conference Report states that "retaining business" should not be construed so broadly as to include lobbying or "other normal representations to government officials." This statement directly reflects the Conference Committee's decision not to include language from the House bill focusing on legislature and regulatory activity so as to avoid any interpretation that might curb legitimate lobbying or representations intended to influence legislative, judicial, regulatory, or other such action. Thus, like other language of the report, far from being irrelevant to Congress's intentions in 1988, this provides a direct explanation of why Congress elected not to include the newly proposed language.

The remaining contested language in the 1988 Conference Report states that "retaining business" includes—covers—payments such as those made "to a foreign official for the purpose of obtaining more favorable tax treatment." We know that the SEC was concerned specifically with these types of untoward payments in 1977, and that Congress ultimately adopted the more generally-worded prohibition against payments designed to assist in obtaining or retaining business. This specific reference in the Conference Report therefore appears to reflect the concerns that initially motivated Congress to enact the FCPA. But even if this language is not dispositive of the question, the rest of the passage does reflect Congress's purpose in passing the 1988 amendments, and therefore deserves weight in our analysis.

Finally, it is inaccurate to suggest, as defendants do, that this report language constituted an attempt to insert by subterfuge a meaning for "retaining business" that Congress had expressly rejected in conference. The only language that Congress chose not to adopt regarding the business nexus requirement concerned payments for primarily legislative, judicial, and regulatory advantages. Corrupt payments "related to the execution or performance of contracts or the carrying out of existing business" have no direct connection with the proposed language on legislative, judicial, and regulatory action, and thus were not part of the proposed amendment.

3.   1998 Legislative History

In 1998, Congress made its most recent adjustments to the FCPA when the Senate ratified and Congress implemented the Organization of Economic Cooperation and Development's Convention on Combating Bribery of Foreign Public Officials in International Business Transactions (the "Convention"). Article 1.1 of the Convention prohibits payments to a foreign public official to induce him to "act or refrain from acting in relation to the performance of official duties, in order to obtain or retain business or other improper advantage in the conduct of international business." When Congress amended the language of the FCPA, however, rather than inserting "any improper advantage" immediately following "obtaining or retaining business" within the business nexus requirement (as does the Convention), it chose to add the "improper advantage" provision to the original list of abuses of discretion in consideration for bribes that the statute proscribes. Thus, as amended, the statute now prohibits payments to foreign officials not just to buy any act or decision, and not just to induce the doing or omitting of an official function "to assist . . . in obtaining or retaining business for or with, or directing business to, any person," but also the making of a payment to such a foreign official to secure an "improper advantage" that will assist in obtaining or retaining business.

The district court concluded, and defendants argue on appeal, that merely by adding the "improper advantage" language to the two existing kinds of prohibited acts acquired in consideration for bribes paid, Congress "again declined to amend the 'obtain or retain' business language in the FCPA." In contrast, the government responds that Congress's choice to place the Convention language elsewhere merely shows that Congress already intended for the business nexus requirement to apply broadly, and thus declined to be redundant.

The Convention's broad prohibition of bribery of foreign officials likely includes the types of payments that comprise defendants' alleged conduct. The commentaries to the Convention explain that " '[o]ther improper advantage' refers to something to which the company concerned was not clearly entitled, for example, an operating permit for a factory which fails to meet the statutory requirements." Unlawfully reducing the taxes and customs duties at issue here to a level substantially below that which ARI was legally obligated to pay surely constitutes "something [ARI] was not clearly entitled to," and was thus potentially an "improper advantage" under the Convention.

As we have demonstrated, the 1977 and 1988 legislative history already make clear that the business nexus requirement is not to be interpreted unduly narrowly. We therefore agree with the government that there really was no need for Congress to add "or other improper advantage" to the requirement. In fact, such an amendment might have inadvertently swept grease payments into the statutory ambit—or at least created new confusion as to whether these types of payments were prohibited—even though this category of payments was excluded by Congress in 1977 and remained excluded in 1988; and even though Congress showed no intention of adding this category when adopting its 1998 amendments. That the Convention, which the Senate ratified without reservation and Congress implemented, would also appear to prohibit the types of payments at issue in this case only bolsters our conclusion that the kind of conduct allegedly engaged in by defendants can be violative of the statute.

4.　Summary

Given the foregoing analysis of the statute's legislative history, we cannot hold as a matter of law that Congress meant to limit the FCPA's applicability to cover only bribes that lead directly to the award or renewal of contracts. Instead, we hold that Congress intended for the FCPA to apply broadly to payments intended to assist the payor, either directly or indirectly, in obtaining or retaining business for some person, and that bribes paid to foreign tax officials to secure illegally reduced customs and tax liability constitute a type of payment that can fall within this broad coverage. In 1977, Congress was motivated to prohibit rampant foreign bribery by domestic business entities, but nevertheless understood the pragmatic need to exclude innocuous grease payments from the scope of its proposals. The FCPA's legislative history instructs that Congress was concerned about both the kind of bribery that leads to discrete contractual arrangements and the kind that more generally helps a domestic payor obtain or retain business for some person in a foreign country; and that Congress was aware that this type includes illicit payments made to officials to obtain favorable but unlawful tax treatment.

Furthermore, by narrowly defining exceptions and affirmative defenses against a backdrop of broad applicability, Congress reaffirmed its intention for the statute to apply to payments that even indirectly assist in obtaining business or maintaining existing business operations in a foreign country. Finally, Congress's intention to implement the Convention, a treaty that indisputably prohibits any bribes that give an advantage to which a business entity is not fully entitled, further supports our determination of the extent of the FCPA's scope.

Thus, in diametric opposition to the district court, we conclude that bribes paid to foreign officials in consideration for unlawful evasion of customs duties and sales taxes could fall within the purview of the FCPA's proscription. We hasten to add, however, that this conduct does not automatically constitute a violation of the FCPA: It still must be shown that the bribery was intended to produce an effect—here, through tax savings—that would "assist in obtaining or retaining business."

* * *

III. CONCLUSION

We cannot credit the district court's per se ruling that the fiscal benefits of the mal-administration of foreign revenue laws by foreign officials in consideration for illicit payments by United States businessmen or business entities can never come within the scope of the FCPA. Just as bribes to obtain such illicit tax benefits do not ipso facto fall outside the scope of the FCPA, however, neither are they per se included within its scope. We are satisfied that—for purposes of the statutory provisions criminalizing payments designed to induce foreign officials unlawfully to perform their official duties in administering the laws and regulations of their country to produce a result intended to assist in obtaining or retaining business in that country—an unjustified reduction in duties and taxes can, under appropriate circumstances, come within the scope of the statute.

As the district court held the indictment insufficient based on its determination that the kind of bribery charged in the indictment does not come within the scope of the FCPA, that court never reached the question whether the indictment was sufficient as to the business nexus element of the crime, for which the charging instrument merely tracked the statute without alleging any discrete facts whatsoever. As we conclude that the business nexus element of the FCPA does not go to the core of criminality of that statute, we hold that the indictment in this case is sufficient as a matter of law. For the foregoing reasons, therefore, the judgment of the district court dismissing the indictment charging defendants with violations of the FCPA is reversed and the case is remanded for further proceedings consistent herewith.

REVERSED and REMANDED.

CHAPTER 7

THE BWI'S 50TH ANNIVERSARY

■■■

In 1994, the World Bank and the IMF, remember, collectively called the Bretton Woods Institutions or BWIs, turned fifty years old. While most birthdays are occasions to party, not everyone was in a mood to celebrate.

The partiers observed that the BWIs (as well as the international trading rules called the General Agreement on Tariffs and Trade), despite their flaws, had accomplished much of what their founders intended: a more peaceful world and increased global prosperity through liberalized economies. All three institutions operated in an era of increased globalization, which created tremendous opportunities for developing countries.

But the somber ones, largely non-governmental organizations (NGOs), thought differently. Among the most visible and vocal of BWI critics, a campaign called "Fifty Years Is Enough," was established to trash the BWI's on their anniversary. In 1994, the campaign included more than two-hundred religious, labor, human rights, and environmental organizations from more than fifty countries across the globe. They launched their criticisms in light of increased poverty, unemployment, and social disintegration that accompanied globalization. More than one billion people lived in poverty and the gap between the rich and the poor widened, both within countries and between them. Approximately 730 million people around the world were unemployed, underemployed, or working poor. In Chapter 4, we talked about the push for "growth with equity" in the 1970s, as manifested in McNamara's World Bank. In the 1990s, the BWI's critics stressed what we could call "growth with marginalization."

With this in mind, we're going to look at some of the main criticisms of the BWIs, and their responses. But before we do that, we're going to explore the world of NGOs, since their role in the world of international finance and development increased considerably in the 1990s.

I. NGOs: WHAT THEY ARE AND WHAT THEY DO

So what are NGOs, what do they do, and do they all get along?

What They Are

Numbering in the tens of thousands, NGOs are groups of individuals organized for virtually any purpose or issue, ranging from sexual discrimination to the rights of disabled people. Neighborhoods, professionals, and religious groups are but a few of the wide variety of constituencies that NGOs represent. NGOs may carry out programs on a grassroots level, such as providing disaster relief. They can be organized on a national level and deal with specific concerns of an individual country. They can also be international in scope, tackling global problems.

As you might have guessed, NGOs can range greatly in size, from the tiny local NGO to mammoth groups such as the environmental-activist and policy organization Greenpeace. They receive their funding from many sources, including donations, fees, foundations, governments, and international organizations. They're called NGOs because they're private entities that aren't established by a government or by an agreement among governments.

Unlike states, NGOs don't enjoy formal recognition ("legal personality") under international law, although they've achieved recognition as private legal organizations under the domestic laws of various countries. For example, an NGO can register itself as a legal entity in the United States. They've also obtained "consultative status" with international (and regional) organizations. If you look at Article 71 of the United Nations (U.N.) Charter, it permits NGOs to establish consultative relations with the Economic and Social Council, allowing them to provide the U.N. with technical advice and to express the views of the public. Treaties may grant NGOs "observer status," such as the 1987 Montreal Protocol on Substances that Deplete the Ozone Layer. So both environmental and industrial NGOs can attend the convention's meetings and intervene in plenary sessions. But they can't propose amendments to the treaty.

What They Do

NGOs do lots of things. We'll talk about just four but important functions. First, they do lots of monitoring. They monitor governments to make sure they're on the up and up. For example, the Supreme Court of Indonesia allowed an Indonesian NGO, Friends of the Earth Indonesia (WALHI), to file a complaint against President Suharto for his alleged diversion of nearly $200 million designated for reforestation projects to a budding aircraft industry. They also monitor international organizations especially regarding development policy. NGO advocacy led to the World Bank's establishment of the environmental assessment (EA) procedure in 1989. The EA calculates possible environmental consequences in the early stages of a proposed project.

Second, NGOs provide technical expertise to governments and international organizations. For example, large NGOs from the Global

North, such as Greenpeace, as well as many from developing countries used their observer status to become integrally involved in the negotiations leading to the 2001 Stockholm Convention, which calls for the global elimination of toxic chemicals, including PCBs and DDT.

Third, NGOs play an important role in disseminating information to the public, which they can do instantly today via the Internet. For example, in August 1995, a dam broke at the Omai Gold Mine in Guyana and released more than 325 million gallons of cyanide into the Essequibo River. The mining company said there was absolutely no threat to animal or sea life. But international NGOs, working through sources of information close to the scene of the spill, claimed that the site of the accident was an "environmental disaster area." The press in the United States relied on these NGOs' accounts for most of its information about the dam break.

> *"POPs weaken the immune systems of whales and polar bears, contaminate the food supply of Inuit communities in the Arctic, and are wreaking havoc in wildlife and people throughout the world," said Clifton Curtis, director of WWF's global Toxics Programme. "The Stockholm POPs Convention will ban or severely restrict these dangerous chemicals. WWF looks forward to working with convention parties to effectively implement this carefully crafted treaty . . . The Stockholm Convention is unique in attacking the problem at its source, banning outright or severely restricting some of the world's most dangerous chemicals."*
> —"Landmark Toxics Treaty to Become Law," at http://wwf.panda.org/wwf_news/index.cfm?11364/Landmark-toxics-treaty-to-become-law (2004)

Fourth, NGO advocacy has led to fundamental rethinking of the development framework. During the 1990s, there was much talk about NGOs (and other non-state actors, such as multinational corporations) contributing to the erosion of traditional notions of sovereignty, threatening to push the nation state off center-stage in the drama of development. Dramas, of course, are about change. The script of the 1990s had the state losing control over its domestic affairs. This led to a blurring of the line between "domestic" and "international" law. Sovereignty's perceived erosion intensified throughout the 1990s, largely influenced by the fall of the Soviet Union, advances in communications technology, and a globalized economy. NGOs took advantage of the confusion on stage to push for "participatory development" and "people-centered development," which refer to grassroots, decentralized development from the ground up, rather than from the top down (the traditional government-driven approach).

Their Limitations

Although NGOs made important and positive contributions to development policy in the 1990s, they also created problems. We'll briefly cover some of the criticisms that you should consider when thinking about the stormy decade.

"Governments . . . increasingly challenge the numbers and motives of civil society organizations in the United Nations— questioning their representation, legitimacy, integrity or accountability. Developing country Governments sometimes regard civil society organizations as pushing a 'Northern agenda' through the back door." "We the Peoples: Civil Society, the United Nations and Global Governance. Report of the Panel of Eminent Persons on United Nations–Civil Society Relations."

—United Nations General Assembly, 58th session, Strengthening of the United Nations System, 7 (2004)

As NGO's presence increased in the 1990s, governments in developing countries started to fear that NGOs would cramp their sovereign power. Result? Close monitoring and regulation. For example, Arab and Asian countries often limited NGOs' ability to take a public stance on human rights and other issues that they held to be vital national interests.

Another problem was that sometimes NGOs failed to see the big picture. Most NGOs are created with very specific mandates tied to their funding. The narrow focus on one particular issue frequently excludes the wider context, which limits their effectiveness in emerging economies and may lead to fragmentation of civil society. At the very least, the activity of thousands of NGOs can create distracting noise and information bottlenecks.

While international NGOs, dominated by the Global North, have played important roles in international finance and development, NGOs in the Global South have gained their own strength and voice. This has resulted in friction between and among NGOs, with developing-country NGOs often resenting being pushed around by the big time groups.

"Activists tend to depict campaigns as resulting from the international equivalent of a 911 call: Southern NGOs in distress reach out to Northern organizations, which feel morally compelled to respond. Academic writing on the subject has largely accepted this explanation. However, accumulating evidence indicates that Northern NGOs' involvement in international advocacy may be prompted by organizational goals that have little to do with local requests for aid."

—C. Pallas & J. Urpelainan, "Mission and Interests: The Strategic Formation and Function of North-South NGO Campaigns," 401 Global Governance 19 (2013)

"[I]nternational NGOs collectively are not conduits from 'the people'. . . from the bottom up. Rather, they are a vehicle for international elites to talk to other international elites about the things . . . that international elites care about." K. Anderson, "The Ottawa Convention Banning Landmines, the Role of International Non-governmental Organizations and the Idea of International Civil Society,"

—European Journal of International Law 11, no. 1, 118 (2000)

II. CRITICISMS OF THE BWIs

Now that we have a good sense of NGOs and what they do, let's move to the battle between NGOs and the BWIs. In the 1980s and 1990s, NGOs trashed the World Bank and IMF for contributing to environmental devastation, and for using conditionality to wreck economies. Let's start with the Bank.

Part One: The World Bank

NGOs spent a great deal of time attacking the environmental consequences of the World Bank's project lending. The Bank's dam project in Nepal was one of a wave of dam projects in developing countries. It's one of the most infamous examples of a project gone haywire.

The Arun-III hydroelectric project in Nepal was huge project intended to generate 201 MW of electricity from the River Arun. It also called for a construction of a seventy-three mile access road through the Arun valley to the dam. The project's price tag was about US $800 million, $136.1 of which would be a loan from the International Development Bank (IDA), the Bank's concessional arm (see Chapter 1). To prepare for the road, the government expropriated land and forced people on the route to resettlement, only to abandon the road project.

The project sparked a widespread firestorm of controversy. While supporters argued that the country desperately needed electricity, opponents claimed that the electricity would be unaffordable. They also stressed that the huge project, which would result in increased government debt, would crowd out other important development projects. Green Scissors, a coalition of Friends of the Earth and the National Taxpayers Union Foundation, said the project was a risky investment, and noted the Asian Development Bank's conclusion that the project would "risk severe erosion, stream disruptions, floods and landslides." If these criticisms weren't enough, NGOs claimed that public involvement by the Nepalese— at both local and national levels—had been nonexistent because the Bank withheld crucial technical information on the project from the parties.

The project led to the first ever official complaint filed with the World Bank's Inspection Panel, which we'll describe in just a second. After the Panel's investigation, Bank President Wolfensohn directed the Bank in 1995 to withdraw from the project.

The Arun-III dam is not the only Bank-financed project that NGOs jumped on. Here are a few more:

> *"Large complex projects require institutions like the World Bank to weigh the benefits against the risks and then decide on their feasibility. The judgment made over a year ago in the case of Arun came out in favor of the project after substantial internal debate. Irrespective of whether that was the right or wrong decision at the time, I concluded that under today's circumstances . . . the risks to Nepal were too great to justify proceeding on the project."*
> —President James Wolfensohn quoted in R. Bissell, "The Arun III Hydroelectric Project, Nepal," Demanding Accountability: Civil-Society Claims and the World Bank Inspection Panel, 38 (2003)

- The Sardar Sarovar Dam in India, which displaced over 240,000 people. This population was relocated to sites with poor land, no clean water, and no electricity. The World Bank withdrew from this project in 1993.
- The Polonoroeste Frontier Development Scheme in Brazil, which also led to mass human resettlement, this time in formerly pristine rain forests; the project also resulted in significant deforestation of an area of rainforest equal in size to Great Britain.
- The Pak Mun Dam in Thailand destroyed critical fisheries on the Mun River, impoverishing the people who relied on the fish as a source of income.
- The Singrauli in India, where twelve open-pit coal mines resulted in pollution that tainted the region's water, food crops, and fish stocks. Over 300,000 people were relocated to complete the project, many to slums that lacked basic sanitation facilities and no possibility for securing land rights.

NGOs cited these examples to show the world that the greatest burdens of environmentally harmful projects fell disproportionately on the poorest segments of the population. The rich folks could pretty much avoid the harmful stuff. Now let's talk about resettlement.

Resettlement

Today, we can't fathom being forced by the government to move from one part of the country to another. (But let's not forget President Roosevelt's executive order to relocate Japanese Americans during WWII, which was upheld by the Supreme Court in the infamous Korematsu decision.) But that's what happened in the 1990s with World Bank money involved. Forced resettlement programs often compel native populations to leave traditional tribal lands or relocate from densely populated to less-densely populated areas. The use of forced resettlement as a component of Bank-funded projects appeared at that time to be prevalent: one study completed by the World Bank said that one in seven dollars spent by Bank-funded projects included forced resettlement. (Check out supplement 7A for a human rights take on resettlement.)

Let's take a look at resettlement in Indonesia. In 1994, Indonesia boasted the world's largest resettlement program under its transmigration policy. The Bank supported the Transmigration Program through seven projects totaling $560 million.

It began in the 1950s, and in roughly forty years the government moved hundreds of thousands of poor farming families from the highly populated islands of Java, Bali, and Madura to less-populated islands in the Indonesian archipelago. Indonesian officials claimed that the program helped the country develop and gave poor families a chance to lead a better life via land ownership.

But NGOs pointed to a survey finding that transmigrants were unable to improve their living standards on eighty percent of the resettlement sites. Many of the farming families had been relocated to rainforest areas that didn't support agriculture. Another challenge for Indonesian transmigrants arose in cases where relocation sites were already inhabited by indigenous tribes who responded violently to the arrival of transmigrant settlers.

Officials touted the program as voluntary and said that transmigrants received relocation assistance in the form of housing and agricultural support. But NGOs claimed that based on the government's own data, neither of these promises was fulfilled. Transmigrant populations were composed of the poor, the powerless, and the unpopular; specifically, farmers, beggars and vagrants, and political prisoners. The government relocated these groups to make way for industrial and tourism projects. NGOs also said that the government used transmigrants to provide cheap labor for new economic sectors that the government wanted to develop.

Now to the Fund.

Part Two: The International Monetary Fund

NGOs also used the 50th anniversary to blast the IMF. Before we talk about specific criticisms of the Fund, we'll mention a few criticisms that were common to the Fund and Bank. First, critics accused the Fund and Bank of being dominated by U.S. banks. This criticism was rooted in the 1980s debt crisis, which we discussed in Chapter 5. The essence of the argument was that U.S. banks drove the restructuring of the debt in a way that favored their balance sheets at the expense of debtor countries that had to undergo painful structural adjustment programs required under the loans from the Fund and the Bank. Second, both the Bank and the Fund operated behind a veil of opacity, which would get stripped away relatively quickly by global civil society—the big NGO players in the transparency drive: International NGO Network, Bank Information Center, the Center of International Environmental Law, Friends of the Earth, Environmental Defense, Urgewald, IFI-Watch, Corner House, Halifax Initiative, and FoE-Japan. Heard of them?

Conditionality

For the IMF, the principal criticism was the conditionality attached to its loans. As you may recall from Chapters 1 and 5 (review them to make sure you understand this stuff), the Fund's Charter calls on it to protect its resources. So when it gives a loan to a member country, it wants to make sure it gets its money back and that the member country will fix its economy so it won't have to come back to the Fund hat in hand.

That may make sense, but many critics said the elements of conditionality—many of them—were all wrong. NGOs claimed that the Fund was misguided by imposing harsh austerity programs as conditions for the loans. It set unreasonable targets to try to achieve balance of payments equilibrium. In its attempt to do this, the Fund tried to dampen demand by requiring borrowers, among other things, to devalue their currency and cut the money supply—resulting in higher interest rates, and cut government spending, including cuts in social spending. As described in Chapter 5, this led to increased unemployment and poverty, in many cases (but not all, as you saw in the case of Chile) hitting the most vulnerable the hardest.

Part Three: Lending to Countries with a History of Human Rights Violations

We'll close with the condemnation of the BWI's for lending to repressive or authoritarian governments. For example, in the late 1970s, Chile (under Augusto Pinochet), Uruguay (under Juan Maria Bordaberry), Argentina (under Leopoldo Galtieri), and the Philippines (under Ferdinand Marcos) received hundreds of billions of dollars in loans from the BWIs, even though these countries used repressive tactics, including torture, against their own citizens. Yet, with Brazil, the World Bank refused to make loans to Brazil's democratically-elected Goulart administration (1961–1964), but approved lending to Branco's military dictatorship in 1964. Here's another well-known example dealing with South Africa and Portugal (keep in mind this is before Shihata):

M. DARROW, BETWEEN LIGHT AND SHADOW: THE WORLD BANK, THE INTERNATIONAL MONETARY FUND AND INTERNATIONAL HUMAN RIGHTS LAW

The Bank's early views concerning the breadth of its mandate were aired in the 1960s during the course of the Portuguese and South African loan controversies. In December 1965 the UN General Assembly adopted two resolutions calling upon "the specialised agencies of the UN to take necessary steps to deny technical and economic assistance" to the governments of South Africa and Portugal because of their respective apartheid and colonial policies were in violation of the UN Charter. The General Assembly's requests were renewed in 1967, at which time the World Bank was in the process of evaluating loan proposals for both countries. While the loans were still pending, the then IBRD President circulated the UN Resolutions to the Bank's Executive Directors, with a statement in the following terms:

> [T]he Bank's Articles provide that the Bank and its officers shall not interfere in the political affairs of any member and that they shall not be influenced in their decisions by the political character of the member or members concerned. Only economic considerations are to be relevant to their considerations. Therefore, I propose to continue to treat requests for loans from these countries in the same manner as applications from other countries . . . I am aware that the situation in Africa could affect the economic development, foreign trade and finances of Portugal and South Africa. It will therefore be necessary in reviewing the economic condition and prospects of these countries to take account of the situation as it develops.

When invited by the General Assembly to explain why the Bank could not comply with the Resolutions, the IBRD General Counsel argued that the "political" prohibition in the Bank's Article's had two purposes. Firstly, to prevent the possibility of using Bank financing as leverage against any Bank member in order to advance the political aims of any other member or group of members. Secondly, to assure the private capital market that economic, rather than political, considerations would guide the Bank's financial decisions. The UN legal counsel rejected the IBRD's contentions, expressing doubt that Article IV of the IBRD articles "was intended to preclude considerations dealt with in the

[South African and Portuguese] resolutions which involved international obligations under the Charter."

Hmmm . . . Let's see, on the one hand member countries are concerned about any particular country calling the shots about their domestic order (which member country would that be?), and on the other hand the World Bank must assure holders of the Bank's bonds that their investments are golden even if Bank funding is going to torturers.

International finance is violence.

III. THE BWIs RESPOND

The BWI's responses to its critics were carefully crafted, holding steady to core institutional principles while agreeing to fashion policies that acknowledge participatory development and "country ownership" of programs. We start, as we should, with the BWI's Charters.

Part One: Charter Limitations

As an initial matter, both the Fund and the Bank responded to the critics by saying, "Before you tear us apart, keep in mind that we're bound by our Charters . . . well . . . kind of."

In the early 1990s, the Bank recognized that its responsiveness to criticism required it to walk a fine line because its Charter prohibits it from interfering with the domestic politics of member countries. According to Article IV, Section 10 of the Charter, neither the institution nor its officers may "interfere in the political affairs of any member, nor shall they be influenced in their decisions by the political character of the member . . . [O]nly economic considerations shall be relevant to their decisions, and these considerations shall be weighed impartially."

As we discussed in Chapter 6, to stick with this mandate, the Bank formulated a test to distinguish between "economic" factors, which it can take into account, and "political" factors, which it can't. Not surprisingly, this test, which focuses on whether a factor has a "direct and obvious economic effect" relating to the Bank's work, is, like, crazy hard to apply. Check it out: By the mid-1990s, Bank lending supported civil service reform, judicial reform, family planning, reform of universities, access to health care, and the list goes on. Uh . . . none of this messes with a member country's political affairs? C'mon!

As to the IMF, by the mid-1990s the Fund's Article IV consultations (see Chapter 3) would touch upon health care, housing, labor markets, military spending, etc. even though Article IV(3)(b) of its Charter says as to surveillance over exchange arrangements: "These principles shall respect the domestic social and political policies of members, and in applying these principles the Fund shall pay due regard to the circumstances of members." Respect? Due regard? C'mon!

Here's geopolitics line-drawing at work: Remember the collapse of the Soviet Union and the subsequent BWI-aided transition of emerging nations from communist governments with planned economies to democratic governments with market-based economies? Developing countries didn't like this. They felt that the BWIs were diverting funds for the political ends of "democratizing and liberalizing" former Communist nations. Using the BWIs for geopolitics? Neva!

Part Two: The Bank

The Bank's major response to its critics regarding the "collateral damage" of its projects was the creation of the Inspection Panel. Before we get to that, let's briefly cover some specific responses to the environment and resettlement criticisms.

The Environment and Resettlement

In response to the environmental criticisms, one of the Bank's major steps was to incorporate Environmental Action Plans (EAPs) in its Country Assistance Strategies (CAS). CAS are created for borrowers from the International Development Association and International Bank for Reconstruction and Development (IBRD—the original Bank). A CAS provides a framework of development prepared by the member country in consultations with the country's civil society and other stakeholders to help the Bank coordinate its activities with the country, especially regarding poverty alleviation. EAPs are prepared by the member country to identify its environmental issues and assist the Bank in designing its project lending accordingly.

> "[Country ownership is] undermined by the extent to which the consultants hired at the instigation of the Bretton Woods institutions ensure that the letters and documents . . . are 'acceptable' and meet the standards of the two institutions for project proposals. Hence the official presentation of ownership should be interpreted for what it is: a legitimizing strategy for a particular political ideology."
> —G. Anders, "Good Governance as Technology: Towards an Ethnography of the Bretton Woods Institutions," in The Aid Effect: Giving and Governing in International Development, 53 (2005)

This is big picture stuff. Notice that the member country is supposed to formulate both the CAS and the EAP. This reflects the "country ownership" approach as a response to the criticism that the Bank (and the Fund) dictated what needed to be done in a member country—which usually resulted in failure.

Now to indigenous peoples. The World Bank's policy on Indigenous Peoples requires that the borrower country develop an Indigenous Peoples Plan (IPP) in consultation with the indigenous community when undertaking a project that could affect the interests of indigenous people. This policy makes sure not only that the communities support the project, but also that they enjoy the project's benefits. The policy also sets out general requirements for the relocation of indigenous populations (also known as involuntary resettlement). The borrower country must first seek alternatives to relocation. But if relocation is unavoidable, the country has to mitigate and compensate the affected population.

The Inspection Panel

The creation of the Bank's Inspection Panel was a big deal. Finally, the Bank would be accountable for all of its sins! The Inspection Panel would see to it! Repent, sinner Bank, repent! International financial institutions can't quite do that. Still, the Bank's Inspection Panel spawned similar bodies at the regional development banks. This excerpt lays out how it works and its strengths and weaknesses.

E. CARRASCO & A. GUERNSEY, "THE WORLD BANK'S
INSPECTION PANEL: PROMOTING TRUE ACCOUNTABILITY
THROUGH ARBITRATION"

Cornell International Law Journal, 578–579, 583–602 (2008)

Introduction

In September 1993, the World Bank (the Bank) created the Inspection Panel (the Panel). The creation of the Panel was, at the time, an unprecedented effort to increase the Bank's accountability. Prior to the establishment of the Panel, the Bank had engaged in a number of projects that devastated local populations and caused significant environmental damage . . .

Lewis Preston, then President of the World Bank, commissioned an independent review of the project, known as the Morse Commission (the Commission). The Commission's report revealed that the Bank had pervasively failed to follow its own social and environmental policies in project lending. Another internal review of the Bank, known as the Wapenhans Report, described a "culture of approval" at the Bank—an attitude that emphasized increasing the Bank's loan portfolio without adequately taking into account the social and environmental consequences of the project lending. After unrelenting pressure from environmental and human rights non-governmental organizations (NGOs), the World Bank established the Inspection Panel with the hope of bringing transparency to the Bank's project lending.

* * *

II. Inspection Panel Procedure and Evolution

Since its inception, the Inspection Panel's role has been to address the concerns of those who are "affected by Bank projects and to ensure that the Bank adheres to its operational policies and procedures in the design, preparation, and implementation of such projects." In theory, the Panel fulfills its role by providing an independent forum where those harmed by a World Bank-financed project can complain. Panel-member Werner Kiene has stated that the Inspection Panel differs from many accountability and recourse mechanisms. In his view, the Panel represents a shift in development paradigms—it is a mechanism of "development-by-below," whereby beneficiaries of Bank policies are able to demand responses to problems themselves. Although the Inspection Panel has increased the World Bank's accountability, critics have pointed to various flaws that limit the Panel's effectiveness.

A.   The 1993 Resolution Establishing the Inspection Panel

Pursuant to the 1993 Resolution that established the Inspection Panel, the Panel is composed of a group of "three members of different nationalities from Bank member countries." The President of the World Bank nominates these members, and the Bank's Executive Directors ultimately appoint them. In an effort to help maintain the Panel's independence from the larger Bank, anyone who has worked as Bank staff in the two years prior is prohibited from serving on the Panel. Moreover, once having served on the Panel, Panel members cannot work for the Bank again . . .

B.   Standing to Bring Request Review Before the Panel

The Panel's operating procedures explicitly limit access to the Panel via standing requirements. First, the procedures authorize complaints only from a "group" of people, not an individual. The 1996 Clarification defines a group as "any two or more persons who share some common interests or concerns." Second, the group must claim that "an action or omission of the Bank . . . to follow its own operational policies and procedures during the design, appraisal and/or implementation of a Bank-financed project"— which includes both project lending and developmentpolicy lending—will have an "actual or threatened material adverse effect on the group's rights or interests." In other words, there must be a clear connection between the harm that the affected people are suffering, or are about to suffer, and the Bank's policy.

For example, in the Lesotho Highlands Water Project in South Africa the Inspection Panel refused to recommend remedial measures because of a lack of causation. In that case, the claimants complaint to the Inspection Panel stated that African townships were going to suffer a "dramatic increase in water prices for what was Africa's largest-ever dam project," and that the "[B]ank's technical advice to the South African government[ ] resulted in a distortion of water management policies and placed a disproportionate cost on poor townships." The Inspection Panel did not recommend an investigation, however, because "there [did] not appear to be a connection between these conditions and any observance or not by the Bank of its own policies and procedures. Rather, they appear to be a part of the enormous legacy and odious burden of apartheid."

Third, even if the Requester can satisfy this requirement, before filing such a claim the Requester is required to take steps "to bring the matter to the attention of [Bank] Management with a result unsatisfactory to the Requester." The Panel has indicated that "[i]t is useful, if possible, for Requesters to attach copies of any correspondence between affected people and the Bank to demonstrate that steps had been previously taken to try to get complaints resolved."

Parties other than the affected parties are authorized to file claims with the Inspection Panel as well. For example, any one of the Bank's Executive Directors may request an investigation. The procedures also authorize local or foreign representatives, such as NGOs, acting on the explicit instructions of affected people to bring requests to the Panel. In the case of foreign representation, however, "the Panel will require clear evidence that there is no adequate or appropriate representation in the country where the project is located." According to Panel procedures, the circumstances warranting non-local representation must be "exceptional." This requirement emerged as a compromise between NGOs in developed countries that wanted to represent affected peoples in foreign nations and borrowing-country governments that "feared intervention of foreign parties" in their relationships with their citizens and "the increased politicization and internationalization of their domestic issues." . . .

In the history of the Inspection Panel, there has only been one instance in which the Board has permitted wholly non-local representation: the China Western Poverty Reduction Project. When this project was first implemented, people in the affected area feared they would be harmed if they spoke against it and instead sent letters to an NGO in Washington, D.C., the International Campaign for Tibet (ICT), with the aim of "seeking international assistance in raising concerns about the devastating impacts of th[e] project on local peoples." The Tibetan Government in Exile also sought ICT's help in filing a claim with the Panel.

In its request for inspection on behalf of the affected persons, the ICT included an annex detailing the basis for its representational authority. ICT claimed that the "exceptional" threshold had been met because "local people affected by the . . . [p]roject [were] unlikely to access . . . information about the existence of the Inspection Panel, or to have access to NGOs in their country who would be able to provide documentation about the existence of the Panel or the Bank's policies and procedures." Even assuming the presence of NGOs, however, the ICT argued that no one in Tibet could "safely bring a claim" because of the Chinese's treatment of dissidents. Ultimately, the Board never commented upon ICT's eligibility and the Panel's request for a determination of the issue, but it did authorize an inspection.

The operating procedures outline the precise requirements for what a Requester must include in the request to the Panel. Generally, the Requester must include a description of the project at issue, "an explanation of how Bank policies, procedures or contractual documents were seriously violated," the harm that the party suffered, and what steps the Requester has already taken to resolve the issue with the Bank. If the party is not sure what policies apply, the Panel will identify what policies, if any, are implicated "[o]n the basis of the factual situation and elements of harm presented." The Panel provides a model form for those who wish to request inspection, although a simple letter with all of the relevant information is also sufficient.

C.   Subject Matter Jurisdiction

There are limitations on the subject matter jurisdiction of the Inspection Panel. Its procedures only empower the Panel to review Bank compliance with its 1) operational policies, which "establish the parameters for the conduct of operations [and] also describe the circumstances under which exceptions to policies are permissible and . . . who authorizes exceptions;" 2) bank procedures, which "explain how Bank staff carry out the policies set out in the [operating procedures] by spelling out the procedures and documentation required to ensure Bank wide consistency and quality;" and 3) operational directives, which "contain a mixture of policies, procedures, and guidance."

The Panel is not authorized to investigate Bank compliance regarding actions of "other parties (such as the borrowing government, the implementing agency, a corporation, the [International Finance Corporation,] IFC, or the [Multilateral Investment Guarantee Agency,] MIGA)." Also precluded [are] "[c]omplaints filed after the closing date of the loan," or when less than 5% of the loan is outstanding. The claim is also precluded if the Panel has already inquired into a matter on a previous request, unless the Requester is able to show that there is new evidence or new circumstances surrounding the issue . . .

D.   The Panel's Action on a Request

Once the Panel receives a request, the "process can be . . . divided into three stages: registration, eligibility, and investigation." During the registration component, the Panel makes the Bank and the public aware that a Requester has filed a complaint and completes a quick review to ensure that the group has standing and that the Panel has jurisdiction over the claim. The Panel's operating procedures do not provide a specific time-line within which this registration review must take place, but they do require that the Panel "promptly register the Request, or ask for additional information, or find the Request outside the Panel's mandate." For the most recent requests that the Panel receives, the complaints are registered within a week. The Panel views this first step as an "administrative" one, the primary purpose of which is to prevent "complaints that are obviously outside its mandate, that are anonymous, or that are manifestly frivolous."

Generally, whether or not the Panel can register the request is fairly clear. For example, in 1995, the Inspection Panel refused to register a request filed by a number of Chilean citizens and a Chilean NG0. The Requesters claimed that the International Finance Corporation (IFC), a part of the bank that provides loans to private companies, "had violated [the Bank's] relevant policies regarding indigenous peoples and environmental assessment and failed to supervise properly the implementation of the project." The Inspection Panel concluded, however, that its mandate clearly limited its investigatory powers to projects under the IBRD and the IDA. Because the Panel did not have power over IFC projects, it refused to investigate.

Once a claim is registered, the eligibility phase begins, and the Panel forwards the complaint to the Bank's President. The Bank's Management, through the Bank's President, must respond to the Panel's inquiry within twenty-one business days, providing evidence that the Bank "has complied, or intends to comply with the Bank's relevant policies and procedures." When the Panel receives Management's response, it has another twenty-one business days to evaluate whether Management has truly remedied, or intends to remedy, the problem.

One factor that the Panel may consider when deciding whether to recommend an investigation is whether Management "dealt appropriately with the subject matter of the request . . . [and] demonstrated clearly that it has followed the required policies and procedures." If so, then this may weigh in favor of recommending no further action. Yet, in instances where Management and the Requester cannot easily reconcile their views regarding the Bank's compliance with its policies and/or the source of the alleged harm, the Panel may choose to recommend an investigation. Additionally, it is expected that if Management admits that it failed to follow the Bank's policies, in its response to the claim it should propose "remedial actions and a timetable for implementing them.

However, the decision whether to recommend an investigation is not just based on the request and Management's response. The Panel also has the power to conduct a preliminary study, which may entail a visit to the project site. Although this preliminary evaluation is not required, the idea behind such a visit is to ensure that the Panel makes "an informed recommendation about an investigation to the Board . . ." In addition to a substantive inquiry into the merits of the compliant, during this phase the Panel conducts a more thorough review of the eligibility of the Requesters themselves.

Thus, after reviewing the claimant's request, Management's response, information from third parties, and any preliminary findings, the Panel will make a recommendation to the Board indicating "whether the matter should be investigated" more thoroughly. This recommendation is referred to as the Eligibility Report.

Under the Resolution establishing the Panel, only the Board had the power to officially authorize the Panel to proceed with an investigation. After the 1999 Clarifications, which were developed in response to the criticisms of the Working Group on the Second Review of the Inspection Panel, the Board agreed (except for in limited circumstances) to authorize investigations on a no-objection basis.

The Panel ostensibly begins investigating soon after the Board's approval of the Panel's investigation request; however, no specific timeline is included in the operating procedures. Panel investigations typically consist of visits to the project site, interviews with the affected people or their representatives, and conversations with government officials and the authorities in charge of the project. The Panel also interviews Bank staff and Management. All of these conversations are supposed to remain confidential, and "the 1999 Clarifications stress the need for the

Panel to keep the profile of its in-country activities low and to make it clear that the Panel is investigating the Bank (not the borrower)." The Panel may also hire outside consultants who are recognized specialists in the subject areas related to the Requesters' claim.

After ruling on whether the Bank is in compliance with its policies and procedures, the Inspection Panel submits its findings to the Bank's Management and the Board. The Panel does not propose remedial measure and "does not have the power to issue an injunction, stop a project, or award financial compensation for harm suffered." The Bank's Management reviews the Panel's findings and must submit a response to the Board within six weeks. If it chooses to do so, Management is able to make remedial recommendations in this report. The Bank officially refers to these reports as "compliance plans"—although they have also been referred to as "action plans." The plans describe "the measures [that Management] intends to adopt to address the problems of non-compliance of the project expressed in the Panel's report."

The Board reviews the Panel's findings in conjunction with Management's recommendations. Although the Board is empowered to "ask the Panel to check whether Management has made appropriate consultations about [any proposed] remedial measures with affected people, . . . the Board has not done so as of 2003." The Board is then required to contact the initial Requester within two weeks of considering the Panel's report and Management's response, informing him or her of the investigation's results and "the action decided by the Executive Directors, if any."

The length of a Panel investigation varies greatly—from a number of months to over a year—and there is no timeline set forth in the Panel Resolution or its operating procedures . . .

III. Criticisms of the Inspection Panel

Each year the demand for the Panel's attention increases, with July 1, 2006 to June 30, 2007 as the Panel's busiest year to date . . .

Despite the increasing use of the Panel's procedures, there are numerous criticisms of the Panel's work, and critics often question whether the Panel truly increases the World Bank's accountability. According to these critics, the Panel is not an adequate accountability mechanism because it has a limited mandate, a limited ability to grant relief, and generally lacks the independence from the Bank necessary to make it a wholly effective institution.

A.   Panel's Inability to Grant Relief

The inability of the Panel to grant relief is one of the most-cited problems with the Inspection Panel. First, the Panel has very limited authority to recommend any type of remedial measure to the Bank—the Panel is not a problem-solving entity, and under its operating procedures it is expected to opine solely on whether the Bank complied with its own policies. It also follows, then, that the Panel has no authority to provide compensation to affected communities. Furthermore, just as the Panel is generally precluded from proposing and providing remedies, so are the affected parties who initiated the investigatory process in the first place.

Because the Panel is unable to provide relief, both the Panel and affected communities often look to Management for aid. The Bank does have a limited ability to provide injunctive relief, but its power to halt a project depends on the stage of the project. Board authorization for an inspection of a project that has not yet begun does not automatically mean that the Bank also intends the preparatory work on the project to cease. If the Bank does so intend, however, Management has the power "to suspend the Bank's preparatory work, or the Board may request it to do so pending the outcome of inspection in cases where the prevailing circumstances require such a measure." Furthermore, "[t]he Panel . . . may also indicate whether . . . suspension of preparatory work . . . would be needed for the purpose of its inspection (if, for example, the continuation of such work would have the potential of making the alleged harm irreversible)." This tactic appears to be little used, although Dana Clark has indicated that it could have been invoked in the National Thermal Power Corporation's (NTPC) Power Generation Project in Singrauli, India, to halt the "forced eviction" of villagers from the project area before the inspection could take place.

The Bank also has the power to grant injunctive-type relief by halting or cancelling loan disbursement. As a general matter, because the financial demands to complete a project without the Bank's support are prohibitively high, an order to stop disbursement functions as the equivalent of an order to halt the entire project . . .

It is not the Bank's practice, however, to provide compensation for harms that the Inspection Panel identifies. Consequently, an increased ability for the Panel and the Bank to grant relief—both injunctive and compensatory—to parties affected by the Bank's failure to follow its own policies and procedures would dramatically increase the effectiveness of the Panel and its responsiveness to claimant communities.

B.   The Bank's Failure to Follow Through with Remedial Plans

Not only is the Panel unable to propose relief based on its investigatory findings, but the Board has "explicitly prohibited the panel from having an oversight role in [the] management-generated action plans" that the Bank designs as remedial responses to the problems that the Inspection Panel uncovers. Unfortunately, at the same time the Bank prevents Panel oversight of these remedial plans, the Board itself, has failed to entirely fulfill its responsibility to follow up on the proposed plans.

For example, in the case of the Yacyreta Hydroelectric Project in Argentina/Paraguay, claimants filed a request for inspection asserting that the Bank had violated its policies relating to the "environment, resettlement, wildlands, information disclosure, indigenous peoples, and project supervision, among others." After an extremely contentious investigation, the Inspection Panel found that the Bank had violated numerous policies and procedures. In developing its action plan in response, however, Management did not consult with local communities and failed to publish its action plan in Spanish so that the affected communities could understand the outcome of the investigation. Six years after the Board first considered the Panel report, "bank management had done little to follow up to ensure that the action plans were being implemented," and the Board did not intervene . . .

C.   Limited Panel Independence

An additional criticism of the existing system is, that the Panel is not entirely independent from the Bank as a whole. First, in relation to the Panel's autonomy, critics have claimed that "as an interior body of the Bank itself, its ideas cannot be completely independent of the ideology of that institution." Because the Panel is an arm of the Bank, it is by definition an institution with a de facto World Bank bias and consequently acts with the interests of the institution in mind and not necessarily with the interests of the affected communities.

In addition, some critics have argued that the Bank's ability to interfere with the Panel's work (either at the investigation or the remedy stage), and the lack of the Panel's ability to prevent such interference, also compromises its status as an independent body . . .

D.   Obstacles to the Access of Panel's Procedures

Critics of the Panel also regularly raise concerns over the equity of the access to Panel procedures and the resulting pro-Management bias. Specifically, once the affected parties (or their agents) have requested an inspection, the parties are not given the opportunity to address the Panel's findings, Management's response, or review any of the information about their claim prior to the Board decision on how to proceed. Thus, while the Board considers Management's recommendations, the original Requesters are pushed aside, and the Board "ignore[es] the experience, knowledge, and preferences of the people who triggered the process in the first place."

Coupled with the Management bias inherent in the Bank's relief process, there are a number of structural obstacles to filing complaints, and parties may find that the Panel has excluded their claim on procedural grounds. For example, the Panel does not have the power to investigate projects in cases where "the loan financing the project has been substantially disbursed." As critics point out, however, "many problems with projects [that the Bank finances] don't show up until years after the funds are disbursed;" thus, for these people, "there simply is no official recourse." For example, in the second request associated with India's NTPC Power Generation Project, the Inspection Panel refused to register the complaint because the "Request was filed after the loan financing the project closed." Any and all harms emerging thereafter were simply not redressable.

* * *

Well, the Inspection Panel had its problems, but it was still a pretty major step towards accountability. Check out supplement 7B.

Part Three: The IMF

We're going to concentrate on the IMF's response to the core criticism that the Fund's conditionality imposed "harsh austerity measures." We'll finish this chapter with a look at the Fund's Independent Evaluation Office.

Deal With It

The Fund's response to those harsh things as part of its conditionality was: "Your economy was really messed up when we got involved. Had you not swallowed the 'harsh' medicine, your country would be worse off, including your poor." Proving the counterfactual is always tough (it seems easier for economists than for lawyers). But countries that borrow from the Fund really do have serious economic problems that need fixing. If they're not fixed, the capital markets won't touch them when they need the money the most. If there aren't flows into the capital account of the country's balance of payments (BOP) (see the supplement in Chapter 1), bad things will happen, like debt default. If that happens, you can kiss the capital markets goodbye for a good chunk of time.

Oh, and then there's another thing, says the Fund:

"The Politician's Cover"

Setting: A dark underground garage; a sweaty politician, Fund guy in a trench coat

Politician: Your conditionality is intolerable! An insult to our sovereignty! You're causing so much misery! Damn you!

(Fund guy takes a drag on a cig)

Fund: C'mon, you know how this works. You have to be quoted in the papers saying that, right?

Politician (eyes popping out): Not just any papers. The National News, they favor me.

(Fund guy takes another long drag on his cig, looks at it if as it has all the answers)

Fund: Isn't it your enemies that you have to convince? That we're the boogie-man? That you had to do this because the IMF's an evil monster that can stuff this down your throat?

(Politician grabs the Fund guy by his trench coat lapels)

Politician: And I have no choice.

Fund: Exactly.

(Politician takes a step back)

Politician: And that's how I fix the problems while not getting thrown out.

(Fund guy takes a long drag on his cig, throws it down, blows the smoke out his nose, and puts the cig out with his foot)

Fund: We're here to please.

Politician: Your conditionality is intolerable! An insult to our sovereignty! You're causing so much misery! Damn you!

(Fund guy looks straight into the eyes of the Politician)

Fund: Say it again with more conviction.

And real quick. The criticism that U.S. banks dominated the Fund? Hey, we forced them to be part of the restructuring process in the 1980s. So there!

The Softening of Conditionality? (Say that again?)

Conditionality can be brutal. And the IMF has a heart (after all, corporations are people). While defending structural adjustment as an integral tool to promoting economic health, the Fund's approach to conditionality changed a bit. The Fund would get less anal (just a bit) about BOP adjustment, contractionary monetary policy to kill inflation, and exchange rate devaluation, and pay more attention to keeping prices and exchange rates stable. Conditionality began to encompass poverty alleviation, environmental protection, military expenditures, and good governance. These topics were also covered in Article IV consultations (see Chapter 3).

The Fund's heart didn't stop there. Recognizing that there is a human component of structural adjustment, it began speaking of social "safety nets," programs designed to cushion the effects of adjustment programs on vulnerable segments of society. Because economists noted that a good portion of government spending intended for the poor was absorbed by the relatively well-off segments of society, the safety net programs would be "targeted" at the vulnerable. So, for example, a food subsidy program was re-worked to make sure funds actually helped the poor obtain basic foods.

For the Fund, it was all about "high quality" economic growth (aka growth with equity). This approach married the "human" component of the Fund's policies with stable macroeconomic policies,

"We have to help member countries achieve conditions for "high-quality growth," by which I mean growth that is sustainable, that respects the environment, that brings lasting full employment and poverty reduction, and that fosters greater equity through increased equality of opportunity."
—Camdessus, Managing Director, IMF, "Income Distribution and Sustainable Growth: The Perspective from the IMF at Fifty," June 1, 1995.

market-based trade and investment policies, and principles of good governance including transparency, participatory development, and accountability.

Yes, the Fund has a heart! But it's not bleeding . . .

Independent Evaluation Office

"[A] separate evaluation office that is carefully structured to be, to the fullest extent possible, independent from management and the Executive Board can establish a reputation with the outside world that its reports are indeed, objective, and can thus contribute more to the confidence of the public at large in the institution than can be achieved by any internal units, however capable and independent-minded its staff."
—*Review of Experience with Evaluation in the Fund* (2000)

The drumbeat for transparency and accountability in the 1990s was so unrelenting that the IMF caved and established an Independent Evaluation Office (IEO) in 2000—but not without kicking and screaming. Here's an excerpt that explains the road to the IEO's establishment.

D. PERETZ, "A BRIEF HISTORY OF THE IEO" IN INDEPENDENT EVALUATION AT THE IMF: THE FIRST DECADE

(2012)

This brief history of the IEO is written to help mark the office's tenth anniversary. It covers some of the events that led up to the creation of the IEO, the initial vision for the office, and the key events in the IEO's 10-year history . . . The focus is on the institutional history rather than on the substance of the IEO's work, which is covered elsewhere. The Part ends with an assessment of IEO's successes and of some recurrent institutional issues that continue to be the subject of debate.

Pre-History

In a sense, the genesis of the IEO can be traced back at least 20 years, to the late 1980s/early 1990s when discussions began on its creation. Evaluation offices with greater or lesser degrees of independence have a longer history at the multilateral development banks than at the IMF . . . Before the late 1980s, the IMF Executive Board and Management saw independent evaluation as an activity that might be appropriate for development agencies but not for an institution like the Fund. Not until the late 1980s/early 1990s did a few Board members begin to suggest that the IMF too could benefit from having an independent evaluation office. This was the start of a long and difficult process leading to the IEO's eventual birth in September 2000.

In January 1993, the Board discussed a statement by Managing Director Michel Camdessus and a report by a staff task force that recommended the creation of an evaluation office at the Fund. The report referred to this office as independent, although the task force was recommending that the Director be appointed by and accountable to the IMF Managing Director . . . There was wide support in the Board from both developed and developing country chairs to create the office, led by Executive Directors representing Brazil (then the Dean of the Board) and the United Kingdom, albeit with different opinions on many details. A few Directors noted their opposition or reservations, but in most cases also noted their willingness to join a consensus in favor of setting up the office. [Creating an] "Independent Evaluation Office was shelved, with Management citing continued lack of Board consensus combined with staffing and resource pressures in the Fund as reasons for lack of further action.

Those who continued to press for the creation of an evaluation office over the next few years saw a hardening of Management's opposition, possibly reflecting a concern that an independent unit could end up "second-guessing" Management, despite mounting external and internal pressures to act. The pressures included an explicit call by G-7 finance ministers . . . for the creation of an independent evaluation office at the Fund . . .

Instead, Camdessus suggested a different approach to evaluating Fund activities . . . [The] Managing Director . . . said he had come to the view that such use of outside experts would be a less costly, less bureaucratic, and more refreshing approach than setting up a separate evaluation office. In January the following year, Camdessus formally proposed this approach to the Board: Management and the Board would experiment with commissioning a series of independent external evaluations and would review the experience after some two to three years . . .

An Evaluation Group of Executive Directors (EG) was convened in July 1996, with terms of reference that were adopted by the Board in September that year, and commissioned three external evaluations in the period 1996–99.

- "External Evaluation of the ESAF," carried out by a group led by Kwesi Botchwey (former Finance Minister of Ghana);
- "External Evaluation of Fund Surveillance," carried out by a group led by John Crow (former Governor of the Bank of Canada); and
- "External Evaluation of the Fund's Research Activities," carried out by a group chaired by Professor Frederic S. Mishkin (former Director of Research at the Federal Reserve Bank of New York).

These evaluations produced important findings, conclusions, and recommendations. For example, "External Evaluation of Fund Surveillance" (the Crow Group report) urged the Fund to concentrate its resources on the most systemically important countries, and to focus its work on the international aspects of the systemically important countries' policies—and in particular on the interface of financial sector and macroeconomic policies of the systemically important countries. These conclusions came to be echoed in several subsequent IEO reports and remained valid 10 years later.

However, Executive Directors and many external stakeholders saw shortcomings with the Fund's reliance on external evaluations. As anticipated, the experience was reviewed by the EG at the end of the three-year trial period; and a report was considered by the Board in early 2000 . . .

The EG review also took account of external opinions on independent evaluation at the Fund. At the time there were mounting calls from external stakeholders for the establishment of a permanent independent evaluation office at the Fund. These were fueled in part by widespread criticisms of the Fund's handling of the late 1990s capital market crises in East Asia and elsewhere. The EG review noted reports by groups of NGOs calling for the establishment of a separate independent evaluation office . . .

Establishment of the IEO

The Initial Vision

In making its recommendations in early 2000, the EG emphasized several features that its members considered essential for an independent evaluation office. In a sense these constituted the initial vision of the founders of the IEO:

- " . . . an [Independent Evaluation Bank] EVO . . . reporting directly to, but operating at 'arms length' from, the Board, and with effective independence from management."
- " . . . [the EVO] must complement existing [self-] evaluation efforts by augmenting the potential scope of evaluation where Fund expertise may be limited . . . ."
- " . . . it must enhance the credibility of evaluations to observers outside the Fund . . . . Even if it were internally accepted that current self-evaluation was wholly objective, the perception outside the institution that such bias exists, in and of itself, undermines the ability of the Fund to undertake its work."
- The evaluation office would "need to include a transparent and efficient mechanism for systematic follow-up [of its recommendations]."

* * *

. . . The general approach to establishing the EVO was endorsed by the Board in April 2000, and a few days later by the International Monetary and Financial Committee (IMFC). Discussions continued over the summer of 2000, with the main features of the office being agreed at Board meetings in August and September 2000.

Terms of reference (TOR) for the evaluation office were agreed at the September 2000 meeting and subsequently reported to the IMFC . . . Their key features are:

- a mission of promoting learning in the Fund as well as improving the Board's oversight (thus giving the evaluation office the two standard functions of independent evaluation—learning and accountability—although the latter had been and remained the Board's main concern);

- a work program to be decided by the Director after a broad process of consultation;
- a variety of measures to buttress the independence of the Director and staff;
- a strong presumption that reports would be published; and
- a budget set by the Board separately from the general IMF budget (the main concrete sense in which the evaluation office is accountable to the Board).

* * *

The last set of decisions in making the IEO operational was taken in August 2002 when the Director in consultation with the Board adopted standard rules and processes for the review and publication of evaluation reports and other documents produced by the IEO. These rules and processes, which constitute the basis for those in place a decade later, stipulated that:

- The IEO will give units in the Fund whose activity is being evaluated an opportunity to comment on preliminary assessments. The evaluators will incorporate all factual corrections that may surface but are free to take account of or ignore any comments on substantive aspects of the assessment.
- When an evaluation report has been completed it will be transmitted to Management and the EG and circulated to the Executive Board. At this point, no changes to the document can be made other than purely factual corrections.
- IMF Management will be provided an opportunity to prepare written comments.
- Reports will be discussed by the Board, and a Summing Up of the discussion prepared.
- Reports, if published, will include written comments received from Management and staff, and any IEO responses thereto, along with the Summing Up of the Board's discussions.

The First Five Years (2002–06)

Establishing the Office and Setting the Work Program

The office was fully staffed by early 2002 . . . The Director began a process of consultation on the IEO's work program shortly after his appointment in July 2001. An initial list of 34 possible evaluation topics was prepared and published for consultation with members of the Executive Board and other interested internal and external groups, including representatives of civil society and academics in Washington, Europe, and Africa. Following these discussions, 15 topics were chosen for the IEO's initial medium-term program. The choice gave priority to topics that had been the subject of controversy or criticism, were of the greatest interest to the Fund's wide range of member countries, and offered the greatest learning potential.

Initial Evaluations: Setting the Pattern

Three topics were chosen from the list to be evaluated during FY2003: Prolonged Use of IMF Resources; Capital Account Crises; and Fiscal Adjustment in IMF-Supported Programs. Work on all three started in parallel. The mix was deliberate, including one topic—capital market crises—that was bound to raise controversial issues, and two that focused more on internal IMF processes but were thought likely to offer good learning opportunities. There were extensive processes of consultation and checking: the office felt it should be especially thorough in its work on these initial evaluations, knowing they would help establish its reputation and at the same time set precedents for its future work. The first IEO evaluation report—Evaluation of Prolonged Use of IMF Resources—was issued in September 2002 and the next two were completed by August 2003 . . .

Processes that were developed in the course of the first few evaluations set a pattern that continues today.

- The chosen project leader and team produce a concept note, setting out the main questions to be addressed and methods to be used, and this is used as a basis for a brainstorming session with a group of knowledgeable external advisors.
- Based on this the IEO prepares a draft issues paper which is posted on the IEO website and used as a basis for discussion with the Board, Management, staff, and external stakeholders. A final issues paper is then posted setting out the scope of the evaluation, main questions, methods, and work plan.
- Methods used include (internal and external) document reviews, surveys, interviews, statistical analyses, and/or preparation of background papers.
- Towards the end of the evaluation a further workshop with external advisors and experts is held to discuss emerging conclusions and recommendations. Often these workshops give rise to further questions and suggestions requiring further work.

- A draft evaluation report is prepared and reviewed within the IEO and by selected external advisors.

- The revised draft report is then sent to IMF staff for written comment, typically within three to four weeks. These comments are meant to focus on factual errors and inaccuracies. Where appropriate, relevant country authorities are also given an opportunity to correct factual errors.

- After careful review, taking account of all comments, the IEO Director approves the final version of the evaluation report, for circulation initially to the Evaluation Committee and IMF Management.

* * *

The Lissakers Report: Evaluating the Evaluators

As noted above, the IEO's initial terms of reference provided for an external evaluation of the office after a period, to assess its effectiveness and to consider possible improvements to its structure, mandate, operations, or terms of reference. To do the job the Board chose an independent panel in September 2005, chaired by Karin Lissakers (former U.S. Executive Director at the Fund). The panel reported in March 2006.

The panel concluded that the IEO had served the IMF well, but also identified "certain weaknesses and . . . trends that are cause for concern about its future," noting the "biggest challenge facing the IEO [as being] to avert the tendencies, pressures, and practices that may push it in the direction of becoming bureaucratized, routinized, and marginalized." . . .

These recommendations reflect the panel's findings, which include the following:

- While IEO reports had led to some improvements, both Board and Management had paid too little attention to systematic follow-up.

- Management and staff should take an open and constructive approach to the IEO's findings . . .

- Too many evaluations had focused on process issues and not enough on issues of systemic and strategic institutional importance . . .

- There had been insufficient engagement with governments and other stakeholders—an important way of getting the IEO's messages across.

The panel also expressed a concern that in one case the IEO "had accommodated management and staff sensibilities to the

342

detriment of the information value of its evaluation and its contribution to Board oversight."

The Executive Board considered the Lissakers Report on April 26, 2006 and endorsed some but not all of these findings . . . A few Directors suggested that the practices for submitting the IEO's draft reports to Management and staff for comment should be reviewed. There was much discussion of the panel's concern that the IEO's independence could have been compromised . . . by pressures from Management to alter draft reports . . .

With one exception—that no changes were made to the policy on the IEO's access to information—the recommendations from the Lissakers Report were broadly implemented by the IEO Director and the Board over the following two years . . .

New follow-up mechanisms were introduced. In January 2007 the Board agreed on a new framework for follow-up to IEO reports. This requires:

- Management to provide, soon after the Board's discussion of each IEO report, a forward-looking Management Implementation Plan (MIP) for the recommendations endorsed by the Board; and
- Management to present to the Board an annual Periodic Monitoring Report (PMR) on the state of implementation of Board-endorsed recommendations and MIPs.

* * *

IEO's outreach and communications strategy was strengthened. Outreach was revamped following the Lissakers Report, and strengthened to the extent possible . . . Most importantly, the IEO launched a new website in early 2007, giving easy access to all IEO material and reports . . .

* * *

IEO practices regarding Management and staff review of draft evaluation reports were clarified. In December 2007, the Director of IEO confirmed his intention to maintain the practice of allowing Management and staff the opportunity to comment on draft reports, while acknowledging that interaction with IMF staff at this stage of an evaluation could be perceived as potentially compromising the independence of views of the evaluation team. His decision was based on an earlier review initiated by the IEO, and took account of the concerns about IEO's independence that had been raised during the Board discussion of the Lissakers Report. He proposed that any subsequent material changes reflected in the final version of the evaluation report would be explained to the Board and recorded in an internal memorandum, along with a redlined version to facilitate subsequent internal reviews or external panels reviewing the IEO's work. He also confirmed that the IEO has no obligation to take on board any such comments received.

* * *

As of November 2013, the IEO had completed twenty-one evaluations. We won't talk about all of them—you can go to the IEO website and check them out. We'll look briefly at a February 2013 evaluation regarding the role of the IMF as a "trusted advisor." The global financial crisis in 2007–2008 prompted the question whether member countries have confidence in the Fund's advice. To what extent is it a trusted advisor? The report noted that views of the Fund as a trusted advisor differed by region. Uh . . . yeah! Latin America, Asia, and large markets were "the most skeptical" while the advanced countries were "the most indifferent." LOL. But after the crisis, the Fund's image improved, and the evaluation's purpose was to figure out how the Fund could maintain the positive image.

The evaluation made three conclusions. First, Article IV mission teams "should consult early with country authorities on their key areas of interest." Second, the Fund staff should consult with country authorities to develop a strategic plan and "promote an ongoing dialogue and close working relationship with Executive Directors." Third, to address "concerns about lack of evenhandedness," the Fund should "incorporate early and openly the views of all countries during the preparation of its major policy papers . . ." Dude, this is cutting edge evaluation!

You see, that's part of the problem with the IEO and its evaluations. Given its structure, can it really be brutally critical of the Fund? The Fund's Executive Board appoints the IEO's Director, whom they can fire at any time. The Board establishes the IEO's budget. Although the 2007 procedural tweaking calling for forward-looking Management Implementation Plans and annual Periodic Monitoring Reports was a good step forward, keep in mind that the IEO can't make a binding decision that the Fund has acted *ultra vires*—in violation of its Charter. So is the IEO's main function to legitimize the Fund? Are its evaluations just (inadequate) window dressing intended to persuade global civil society that the Fund believes in transparency and accountability? Hmmm . . .

Part Four: NGOs Become Buddies with the BWIs

The BWIs at 50 realized that NGOs weren't going to go away. What's that saying . . . keep your friends close but your enemies closer. Well . . . maybe that's overstating it a bit. But it's pretty safe to say that the Bank and Fund initially saw NGOs as a major pain in the butt. But why live with stress?

After all, the 1990s was all about "participatory development." We'll get back to this in a sec.

Let's look at the Bank. Little by little NGOs became involved in discussions with the Bank about its operational policies, something that never would have happened before the 1990s. NGOs became particularly involved in policy dialogue regarding poverty and the environment. In the 1990s, NGOs were invited to a series of conferences on those topics. And given NGOs' pressures on the Bank to become more transparent, in 1994 it established the Public Information Center that made available many documents that previously had not seen the light of day.

Now the Fund. Get lost! Okay, we're exaggerating a bit. Although the Fund, unlike the Bank, is a monetary institution and doesn't do project lending, it couldn't ignore the participatory development thing. And the IMF was part of the poverty

> *"The new participatory approach adopted by the IMF in its poverty eradication efforts incorporates an important role for civil society and the IMF recognizes the contribution that NGOs are making to poverty reduction. What the IMF is trying to achieve now is not to reinvent the NGO's role in the poverty reduction process, but simply to make it clear that we are ready to join forces so as to move decisively towards our shared objectives."*
> —S. Pereira Leite, Assistant Director, Office in Europe, IMF, Speech, Sept. 2001

> *"[S]uccessful poverty reduction programs require "ownership," which in turn requires democratic consultation and full participation by stakeholders in developing the strategy. A question that is often asked is what should we do if the national government, which should be in the driver's seat, pays only lip service to the participatory process. My answer is that we should push the government gently in the right direction; but, in the end, it is civil society that will have to demand more participation in the development process."*
> —S. Pereira Leite, Assistant Director, Office in Europe, IMF, Speech, Sept. 2001

eradication thing, too. So, little by little, it began cooperating with NGOs because of their strengths in, among other things, (1) advocacy, (2) helping design realistic structural adjustment programs, and (3) monitoring and evaluating poverty reduction efforts.

IV. SOCIAL DEVELOPMENT

We close the chapter with a look at an U.N. summit that captured what became a widely accepted framework for development, a framework that the BWIs ultimately accepted.

The process of "growth with marginalization" prompted the United Nations to sponsor the World Summit for Social Development in Copenhagen, Denmark. Held in 1995, the Summit's purpose was to develop a "new organizing concept" to address a post-Cold War world that failed to fulfill liberalism's universal promise of peace and prosperity. The deliberations focused on three core issues relating to Article 55 of the U.N. Charter: (1) the alleviation and reduction of poverty; (2) the expansion of productive employment; and (3) the enhancement of social integration, particularly of the more disadvantaged and marginalized groups.

The Summit embraced a definition of development thickened by forty years of experience. Under a people-centered framework of social development, the governments urged a political, economic, ethical and spiritual vision for social development that is based on human dignity, human rights, equality, respect, peace, democracy, mutual responsibility and cooperation, and full respect for the various religious and ethical values and cultural backgrounds of people. Is that pretty much the kitchen sink?

This vision of development was participatory, calling for the full participation of people in formulating, implementing and evaluating decisions relating to the functions of their societies. Put another way, the Summit envisioned an "enabling environment for social development," i.e., "an economic, political, social, cultural and legal environment that will enable people to achieve social development." Enabling. That's an agency thing. No, not like insurance.

By the mid-1990s, the BWIs were down with that. Like we said, Bank-funded operations took into account health, education, and other matters relating to social welfare. Even the IMF covered things like health care, environment, and military expenditures in its Article IV consultations with member states.

OMG!

You Gotta Know Something About Them!

James Wolfensohn

President of the World Bank from 1995 to 2005, James Wolfensohn, known as the "Renaissance banker," is a native Australian who was born to struggling immigrant parents during the Great Depression. He failed his high school final exam, but was still admitted to the University of Sydney—at age sixteen! James represented his country in the 1956 Olympics. Not a big deal . . . He worked briefly as a lawyer in Australia before earning his MBA from Harvard in 1959. In the 1960s, he worked as an investment banker in London. Eventually he made his way back to the United States in 1970 and did investment banking in New York. James became a naturalized U.S. citizen in 1980 with the hopes of succeeding Robert McNamara as World Bank President. Check it out: He started studying cello when he was 41 and played at Carnegie Hall on his 50th, 60th, and 70th birthdays. The 60th was with Yo-Yo Ma and the 70th was with Bono!

QUESTIONS FROM YOUR TALKING DOG

1.   What's with these "NGOs?" Non-Great-Dane Owners? No? Well, stop shoveling those chips into your mouth and tell me about non-governmental organizations. What kind of status do they have in international law? Why are they important when it comes to international finance and development? But everybody thinks they're all that, right? Tell me.

2.   I was just checking out Facebook—yeah, I'm on it. That's how I get my news. Shut up and eat your chips. Anyway, like I was trying to say, the World Bank and the IMF were getting trashed in the mid-1990s. Tell me about it, but first give me a swig of your beer, I mean your horse urine. Okay, let's start with the World Bank. What were people complaining about?

3.   I'm not into conspiracy theories, but do you think the IMF and World Bank worked for the U.S. banks?

4.   It seems like the first and last thing some people complain about is IMF conditionality. What was their beef in the 1990s? Speaking of beef, I need some food up in me. How about a cheeseburger, extra pickles and no onions.

5.   Human rights. That leaves me out, doesn't it? Okay, let's not go there—for now. But tell me about human rights and the BWIs.

6.   I think I made out what you were saying between chomps and swigs. But now that you can talk to me, tell me about how the World Bank responded to getting trashed. First, tell me about this Charter stuff.

7.   The establishment of the Inspection Panel was a big deal, right? Why did people think it needed to be established? Can anybody bring a claim? Can it be any kind complaint, say a claim alleging the Bank violated human rights? What's the procedure? Can the IP decide on its own to investigate? The IP looks cool to me. But not everyone has a dog's intellect. What did people complain about?

8.   Sure, let's talk about the IMF. What's this about the Fund providing political cover? Softening conditionality? Are you kidding me? Is the Independent Evaluation Office just like the IP?

9.   Back to NGOs. Did the BWIs finally figure out they can be useful?

10.   Social development. You mean how to hold a conversation? Okay, what does it mean? Did the concept have any impact?

11.   Dude, are you serious that Wolfensohn played cello with Bono? I've spent the past year trying to find Bono's glasses online. Hey! I'm a cool dog. And yeah,

I sing while you're in the shower. Deal with it! And throw me one of those treats . . . Fine! I'll act all cute for you. Fine!

Chapter 7: Supplement

7A. *Resettlement*

This policy piece on the World Bank's involuntary resettlement policy doesn't pull any punches. It documents in a very compelling way the terrible hardships endured by those who are forced to resettle with the support of World Bank funding. The critique of the Bank's Safeguard Policy on Involuntary Resettlement is couched in human rights language. Does the Bank's Charter require it to take into account human rights when funding a project? Does this critique argue that it does? What exactly is its human rights argument? If you were the Bank, how would you react to the recommendation that the Bank should undertake human rights impact assessments for its projects—with the listed metrics in paragraph 48? Regarding the project in Box 4, did the Inspection Panel conclude that the Bank violated human rights? Section 6 is all about participatory development. Makes sense, right? Any downsides? What do you make of the reparations/effective remedy argument?

N. Bugalski and D. Pred, "Reforming the World Bank Policy on Involuntary Settlement: Submissions to the World Bank Safeguards Review," Inclusive Development International, International Accountability Project, Bank Information Center and Housing and Land Rights Network— Habitat International Coalition (2013)

1.   Introduction

1.   The rights to adequate housing and security of the person and home are basic tenets of human rights law, and serve to protect individuals and communities from being forcibly displaced from their homes, lands and livelihoods. Despite these guarantees in international law, every year approximately 15 million people are forcibly displaced to make way for development projects such as mines, oil and gas pipelines, urban renewal schemes, mega-dams, ports and transportation infrastructure. Direct impacts from these projects, including land and real estate speculation, changes in land use and access to natural resources and environmental pollution, further escalate the number of displaced people.

2.   While land acquisition and eviction may be necessary in exceptional circumstances, displacement caused by development largely occurs in a manner that violates human rights and leads to the increased impoverishment of the displaced. Evictions are often accompanied by egregious corruption, the use or threat of violence to force people from their homes, lands and livelihoods, and the undemocratic imposition of so-called "development" projects. Those impacted by forced evictions and

displacement face a number of well-documented specific risks and human rights violations, including: homelessness; loss of livelihoods; food insecurity; psychological trauma; negative health impacts; loss of health status; increased morbidity and vulnerability, especially among women and children; economic and cultural marginalization; and, social disintegration. Forced evictions are also inherently discriminatory, as it is the poor and marginalized sections of the population, with few exceptions, who are required to move out of the way for development projects.

3.   The objectives of the World Bank Policy on Involuntary Resettlement, now set out in Operational Policy 4.12, are to avoid or minimize involuntary resettlement; to make any resettlement activities a sustainable development program, including through project benefit-sharing and meaningful consultation of affected persons; and to assist displaced persons in their efforts to improve, or at least restore, livelihoods and living standards. The Policy requires a resettlement plan or a resettlement policy framework for projects that have displacement impacts. It extends assistance to people who do not own property but are nonetheless affected by development projects, including groups with communal and/or traditional tenure arrangements, renters, wage-earners and those without legally recognized rights to land and property that they occupy or use.

4.   With more than one million people affected by forced displacement and involuntary resettlement from active Bank projects at any given point in time, the policy remains an important human rights safeguard for affected people living in countries with incomplete or inadequate legal and regulatory frameworks. However, evidence suggests that the policy often fails to achieve its core objective of avoiding or mitigating adverse impacts of displacement and that Bank projects have frequently caused violations of human rights. Problems related to involuntary resettlement have been the third most cited complaint in cases submitted to the Inspection Panel. The number of such cases is likely to rise in view of the expansion of the Bank's core business of infrastructure development, unless a concerted effort is made to strengthen mechanisms and processes for the implementation and supervision of the Policy.

5.   It is imperative that with the World Bank's review of its safeguard policies, the protections that exist in OP 4.12 are not lost through the weakening of its scope and content. Rather, the review must be used as a process to identify areas in which the Policy falls short of human rights standards, and how the policy—and compliance with the policy—needs to be strengthened to ensure that it conforms to international human rights law and that marginalized people are not made to suffer the impacts of development, but rather become its primary beneficiaries.

6.   As organizations dedicated to defending and promoting people's rights to adequate housing, land and natural resources, we submit these comments to the World Bank with a view to supporting the Bank in

undertaking a rigorous review of its safeguard policies and ensuring that its future operations respect and help realize human rights, especially of the most vulnerable. We look forward to engaging with the World Bank throughout the Safeguards Review process to support the adoption of stronger policies, and we will do so in close collaboration with other groups with firsthand experience monitoring involuntary resettlement.

7. These comments highlight areas of the World Bank's policy and practice on involuntary resettlement that are in particular need of updating and aligning with international law and contemporary best practices. While some aspects of the current safeguards meet these standards and should be retained, other elements of the Policy are in urgent need of upgrading if the Bank is to ensure that it does not contribute to the global crisis of forced displacement. We recognize that it is not in the Bank's power to put an end to the epidemic of human rights abuses conducted in the name of development; however, when global public funds are used to finance development, the strongest possible international standards to protect human rights must apply. This will have direct impacts for people affected by Bank-financed projects and has the potential for catalytic effects on international resettlement policy and practice.

* * *

2. Policy Scope

11. OP/BP 4.12 covers economic and physical displacement that result from Bank-financed projects and are caused by the involuntary taking of land. This reflects the impetus for the original version of the policy: the violent forced eviction of some 60,000 people to make way for the Bank-financed Sobradhinho Dam in Brazil. In recognition that other activities connected to Bank projects in diverse sectors can cause displacement, the current policy also covers such activities when, in the judgment of the Bank, they are: directly and significantly related to the Bank-assisted project; necessary to achieve the project's objectives; and carried out contemporaneously with the project. The policy makes clear that it covers direct economic and social impacts of physical or economic displacement resulting from land acquisition or "other activities" described above. It also covers the involuntary restriction of access to legally designated parks and protected areas resulting in adverse impacts on livelihoods. All components of the project that result in involuntary resettlement, regardless of the source of financing fall under the scope of the policy.

12. Despite the important expansion of the scope of the policy beyond displacement caused by land acquisition, the scope remains problematic and overly narrow because:

- It does not explicitly cover displacement that occurs in the project area prior to, or in anticipation of, Bank involvement in a project;

- It does not explicitly cover temporary displacement or lost access to assets or resources;
- It does not cover the involuntary restriction of access to resources that people depend upon other than those in legally designated parks and protected areas;
- It does not cover displacement that occurs because of a project's adverse impacts on the environment or natural resources that people depend upon;
- It does not cover indirect social and economic impacts, or indeed impacts on all human rights, despite the fact that addressing these can be critical to mitigating the risk of impoverishment, and failing to address them will place the burden of these impacts on those displaced; and
- It does not cover resettlement that is voluntary in nature, but, nonetheless, requires measures to safeguard against impoverishment and other adverse impacts and to maximize development benefits.

* * *

A sustainable development and human rights-based approach to resettlement, by its nature, does not only address the direct impacts of resettlement. [T]he anticipated human rights impacts of resettlement should be assessed and then addressed through appropriate safeguard measures. This requires much more than an assessment of "immediate consequences" such as impacts on current assets, living standards, and incomes of affected persons. It also requires an assessment of, inter alia, the potential for lost access to resources and opportunities for self-development to which they would have otherwise had access. Without addressing these impacts, the short and long-term risks of impoverishment will not be mitigated.

* * *

5.   Human Rights Impact Assessment and Due Diligence

46. The state-of-the-art in impact assessments has advanced considerably since the World Bank last reviewed its Involuntary Resettlement Policy. In particular, the importance of conducting human rights impact assessments of development investments has been broadly acknowledged. Given the unusually high risk of human rights violations during involuntary resettlement, and conversely, the opportunities for advancing the enjoyment of a range of human rights through a well planned and executed resettlement project, the revised policy should require human rights impact assessments be conducted during project preparation. Undertaking human rights impact assessments is a precondition for ensuring that the Bank is not complicit in human rights violations as a result of displacement

caused by its projects. It is also an essential foundation for designing Resettlement Plans and Process Frameworks that effectively achieve policy objectives, including conceiving and executing resettlement as a sustainable development program and improving the livelihoods and standards of living of those resettled.

47. An assessment of potential impacts on human rights looks not only at current assets, living standards, and incomes of affected households and communities, as currently required by the policy, but it also covers the potential for lost resources and opportunities for self-development to which they would have otherwise had access. These resources and opportunities relate to economic development, social and cultural fulfillment, and civil and political activity and protections. In other words, they relate to the full range of civil, political, economic, social and cultural rights. The way in which the enjoyment of these rights is likely be affected by displacement, for individuals, households and disaggregated groups—*both positively and negatively*—is thus the subject matter of a comprehensive human rights impact assessment. Anything short of this is failing to capture the real and full implications of involuntary resettlement on people's lives. Without the kinds of questions and scoping human rights impact assessments elucidate, many critical risks—and opportunities—can remain invisible.

48. A comprehensive human rights impact assessment of a resettlement process involves the following:

- The collection of disaggregated baseline data on household organization, assets, living standards, productive activities and skills, incomes and access to basic services.

- The collection of disaggregated baseline data on household access to resources and opportunities, including sustenance and livelihood opportunities; educational and recreational facilities, especially for youth; health services and resources; community, social and cultural resources and facilities; and opportunities to participate in public and community affairs and to engage in mechanisms for State-citizen interface. Information on the barriers to accessing these resources and opportunities for all affected persons or particular groups is also collected.

- The collection of data on community organization and communal assets, productive activities, skills and resources.

- The collection of data and studies on patterns of exclusion, marginalization and discrimination faced by affected persons, including for example affected women, children, disabled persons, the elderly, and ethnic and other minorities.

- Studies on social and cultural characteristics, including systems and institutions that may be affected by displacement.

- An assessment of the likely negative impacts on the current situation (assets, living standards, income, livelihoods, etc.) and opportunities for self-development (due to the level, range and quality of access to resources and opportunities) of affected persons as a result of physical and/or economic displacement or restrictions on access to natural resources, unless those impacts are mitigated. A variety of options for mitigation measures are identified and explored. Particular attention should be paid to the potential disproportionate impacts of displacement on vulnerable and marginalized groups such as people with disabilities, children, women, the elderly and minorities and the design on corresponding special mitigation measures.

- An exploration of the possibilities for improving the current situation (assets, living standards, income, livelihoods, etc.), expanding opportunities for self-development (due to the level, range and quality of access to resources and opportunities) and reversing exclusion, marginalization and discrimination through a variety of tailored resettlement, rehabilitation and development options.

49. The human rights impact assessment should be conducted through participatory processes to the fullest extent possible, with all data verified at the household and community level. The options for mitigating losses, improving access to resources and opportunities and reversing marginalization should be presented in an accessible form to affected persons. The human rights impact assessment will thus inform the decision making of affected persons during the resettlement planning process or the development of a process framework to address impacts of restrictions on access to resources . . . The Bank should ensure that the findings of the impact assessment are ultimately reflected in Resettlement Plans or Process Frameworks. The absence of a comprehensive *ex ante* human rights impact assessment to inform Resettlement Plans and Process Frameworks will almost certainly preclude genuinely successful and sustainable outcomes.

50. A series of *ex post* human impact assessments at regular intervals are also necessary to ensure that policy objectives are being met and the human rights of affected persons, and disaggregated groups, especially those identified as (formerly) vulnerable and marginalized, are fully respected. *Ex post* impact assessments should measure the extent to which resources are being appropriately utilized to progressively realize human rights for project-affected persons. Corrective action plan, if required, should be based on *ex post* impact assessments.

51. In addition to the above, as part of its due diligence, the Bank should undertake an independent human rights risk assessment of the

Resettlement Plan, Policy Framework or Process Framework once a draft is developed. Displacement carries significant risks of human rights violations, including forced evictions and regressions in the enjoyment of a range of human rights. These risks are heightened by poor resettlement planning and implementation due to capacity constraints and/or a lack of political will to respect people's rights. The level of such risks in the given governance environment needs to be thoroughly assessed by the Bank, including by examining the borrower and responsible agency's record and experience with resettlement, and mitigated accordingly.

* * *

Box 4: Ghana/Nigeria Western African Pipeline Project

The West African Gas Pipeline Project involves the construction of a new pipeline system that will transport natural gas from Nigeria to Ghana, Togo and Benin. In Nigeria, the development of the pipeline involves the displacement of people associated with the acquisition of 144 hectares of land for the right of way (ROW) and ancillary facilities. The 25-meter-wide ROW traverses 23 communities made up of approximately 90,000 people.

In 2006 the Inspection Panel received a request for investigation by affected communities asserting that the Project would cause irreparable damage to their land and destroy their livelihoods.

In its investigation report the Panel observed that "[m]any of the problems . . . can be linked to the lack of adequate socio-economic data gathered as a foundation for actions relating to resettlement." Inadequate information had been collected on, inter alia, the number of displaced persons, and relatedly, the local land tenure systems that determined who had user rights to the acquired land; the proportion of each family's holdings that had been acquired and thus the impact on land-based livelihoods; and the socioeconomic risks to vulnerable persons. Averages and aggregates were used to inform the socio-economic analysis and safeguard measures, rather than specific individual and household data. A small subset of households was used to estimate the Project's impact on all displaced households. The failure to collect sufficient and appropriate data, and to undertake comprehensive socio-economic analyses of the data, resulted in extremely insufficient compensation payments, well below replacement value, as well as an absence of other measures to ensure the restoration of living standards. In short, the lack of data meant that the actual impoverishment risks were not measured or mitigated by the resettlement action plan. As articulated by the Panel, "the absence of adequate baseline information makes it impossible to ensure that the impacts and potential impoverishment risks facing local people are properly addressed." Moreover, despite the fact that the operation of an existing pipeline was essential for gas to flow through the new pipeline, the environmental and socioeconomic secondary impacts "upstream" and "downstream" of the

Project were not assessed. The Panel found that associated facilities and supply areas should be viewed as an inter-connected system in defining the project's area of influence for the purposes of socio-economic assessment.

The Panel also highlighted the lack of due diligence on the part of Bank Management in determining whether the agency responsible for resettlement had the capacity to carry out the resettlement action plan. The Panel was unable to find a formal assessment of the agency's past experience and capacity, despite indications of a poor record that included direct warnings by civil society groups in an open letter to the Bank President about human rights violations and conflicts related to the project prior to the Bank's involvement.

The Panel found that these failures amounted to violations of current Bank policy and procedures. The case also underscores the need for both greater clarity on policy requirements with respect to the collection of data and socio-economic analysis, and greater scope and depth of impact assessments in order to inform mitigation measures that will effectively safeguard against risks of impoverishment and human rights violations.

Source: World Bank Inspection Panel, Investigation Report, Ghana: West African Gas Pipeline Project (2008).

* * *

6. Access to Information, Consultation and Active Participation in Decision Making

54. The importance of access to information and opportunities for participation and consultation for affected people during the resettlement process is firmly established. The magnitude of implications of involuntary resettlement on the lives of people displaced is of such high order that it would be manifestly unjust and unconscionable to exclude affected people from enjoying a significant degree of control over decision making. Moreover, the policy objective of conceiving and executing resettlement activities as sustainable development programs can only be met in practice if fundamental aspects of the process reflect the needs, priorities and choices of affected people. These notions are reflected to some degree in the current policy, which requires borrower-governments to include in their resettlement planning instruments "measures to ensure displaced persons are (i) informed about their options and rights pertaining to resettlement; and (ii) consulted on, offered choices among, and provided with [. . .] resettlement alternatives." The policy also requires that displaced persons and their communities, and any host communities, be "offered opportunities to participate in planning, implementing, and monitoring resettlement."

55. Case research shows, however, that these policy requirements have not routinely translated into meaningful consultation of and active

participation in decision-making processes by affected people. In 12 of 15 requests submitted to the Inspection Panel since 2001 that raised non-compliance with OP 4.12, inadequate access to information and consultation formed part of the complaint. In these instances, the failure to ensure the active participation of affected people in resettlement planning, implementation and monitoring resulted in poor resettlement results that did not meet policy objectives . . .

56. Currently, there is also no requirement that affected people are informed of their right to access the Inspection Panel and the method for doing so. This omission must be corrected: Creating awareness about these rights and channels for claiming them is an essential measure to address prevailing power asymmetries and improve accountability.

57. Second, there is no definition or explanation of "meaningful consultation" in the current policy. Consultation in practice often amounts to little more than top-down information sessions, carried out by parties with a financial stake in the outcome, during which affected people are told what they will be offered and where they will be resettled. In the worst cases the requirement for consultation devolves into manufacturing "consent" through duress. A clear articulation of the components and characteristics of meaningful consultation in Bank policy would constitute an obvious and simple step in facilitating improved practice . . . .

58. Third, both the weaknesses in current practice and the policy objective of treating resettlement as a sustainable development program, point to the need for a new approach to engaging affected people in the process of resettlement. For certain elements of the process, there should be a shift beyond the notion of merely consulting affected people, to the provision of independent advice and technical assistance to give people greater control over decision making related to resettlement. This shift should support greater inclusion of marginalized groups in decision making processes. It should also incorporate proactive efforts to elevate the degree of control in decision making exercised by women, in recognition of the disproportionate impacts of evictions and displacement that they face.

59. Done properly, this could change the paradigm of resettlement processes by providing affected people with the knowledge, resources and tools necessary to enable them to develop and implement, with all necessary support, appropriate parts of the resettlement plan. Resettlement activities, as envisaged, would evolve into a genuine community-driven development initiative based on the priorities set by beneficiaries. This would require corresponding planning methodologies, the injection of appropriate resources and ongoing investment in the communities over a sufficient time period.

* * *

11. Reparations and Access to an Effective Remedy

97. The World Bank's Safeguard Policies are designed to prevent Bank-financed operations from causing adverse impacts. Nonetheless, history has demonstrated that some Bank-assisted activities inflict substantial harm upon people, constituting a gross violation of human rights. Project-affected persons and communities are entitled under international law to remedy and reparations for violations of human rights. These entitlements involve a range of measures that States have a duty to ensure. Even in well planned and resourced resettlement processes, backed by good intentions—mistakes are made and unanticipated harms are caused. In these cases, affected people have a right to a timely and effective remedy.

98. There is currently no guaranteed right to remedy within the World Bank safeguards and accountability framework. Even when the Inspection Panel concludes that harm has been caused to affected people as a result of non-compliance with operational policies, there is no mechanism in place to ensure that the harm is redressed. Without such a mechanism, those whose rights have been violated must rely on Bank Management and the Board's goodwill to take appropriate remedial action, as well as the cooperation of borrower governments, which is not always forthcoming, as illustrated by the Albania Coastal Zone Management Project and the Cambodia Land Management and Administration Project (see Box 11). This fundamental accountability gap threatens to render the safeguard policies and Inspection Panel meaningless for people who are harmed as a result of Bank-supported operations.

* * *

Recommendations on Ensuring Access to an Effective Remedy

1.   The revised policy should guarantee the right to an effective remedy, including the right to reparations, for people who have suffered human rights violations and other harms resulting from displacement and resettlement. Special provisions should be made to enable women to access their right to remedy, including through legal aid.

2.   The policy should require that independent, accessible and transparent grievance mechanisms are established at the local level for every project that induces involuntary resettlement.

3.   The policy and Bank procedures should provide recourse for affected people to seek remedies, including where appropriate compensatory damages, if they are found by the Inspection Panel to have suffered harm as a result of a Bank operation. These provisions should be stipulated in the legal agreement with the borrower.

7B. *The Inspection Panel: Transparency Plus Accountability*

Transparency is all the rage, right? These authors don't think so. Real accountability is needed to push institutions to change. But how do you do that on the international plane? Enforceable hard-law rules? What do the authors think? Does their discussion of the Panel persuasively support their thesis?

T. Hale and A. Slaughter, "Transparency: Possibilities and Limitations," *30 Fletcher F. World Aff. 153* (2006)

Riding a train between Princeton and New York, the ethicist Peter Singer found himself seated next to a talkative man. After answering many questions about his profession, Singer finally managed to inquire as to his fellow traveler's occupation. "I'm a transparency maintenance worker," the man replied. Thinking he had discovered an advocate of truth and responsibility, Singer excitedly asked his seatmate what institution or organization he monitored. Confused, the man replied, "I wash windows."

Singer's mistake was an honest one. The concept of transparency has spread imperialistically out of the good governance canon and into popular parlance. The window-washer's usage notwithstanding, in this paper transparency will be used to denote any kind of measure that publicizes information about an institution's behavior, such as monitoring, reporting, or simply responding to inquiries.

Commonly recognized as a desirable institutional value for everything from corporations to governments, transparency in recent years has developed from a buzzword into a substantive policy tool, particularly in efforts to make transnational actors more socially and environmentally responsible. Openness and disclosure have been demanded of such diverse organizations as international financial institutions, transnational corporations, and nation-states. In each of these cases, transparency is touted as a tool of accountability—a way to make global institutions more responsive and thus begin to fill globalization's "democracy deficit."

But can merely exposing the behavior of an actor—be it a corporation, an intergovernmental organization, or even a country—actually affect how it behaves? Transparency is often used as a synonym for accountability, but real accountability requires more than monitoring. In order to hold a person or organization accountable, it is necessary not only to know what they are doing, but also to have some way to make him do something else.

Knowledge is the first step toward enforcement, which domestically is generally carried out by government regulators and courts. If a corporation pollutes the environment or exploits its employees, it can be fined and its managers can be held criminally liable.

At the international level, these formal legal solutions are rarely available. Does this mean that international transparency mechanisms are toothless, as some critics claim? Not necessarily. In this article we identify several levers that activists and international lawyers can use to bring real, coercive pressures to bear at the international level. When these tools— which include market pressure, personal and institutional values, and even dialogue with society—are available, transparency mechanisms can go beyond mere monitoring to provide actual enforcement.

Some critics dismiss such pressures as too soft or overly informal to regulate behavior, but experience suggests they can be surprisingly coercive. The key issue, however, is not the larger debate between hard and soft regulation, but rather how and under what conditions transparency can promote accountability. As transparency-based policies expand in both rhetoric and practice, careful study of the exact ways they can and cannot make global actors more accountable is needed in order to distinguish effective governance policies from public relations stunts.

Furthermore, well-constructed transparency mechanisms may be a useful tool for policymakers who increasingly find traditional regulation unsuitable to complicated transnational problems. Consider the proposal by some activists [to] regulate all transnational corporations through a body of international law enforced by the United Nations: the technical challenges of such a regulatory effort would overwhelm any intergovernmental agency, and it is highly unlikely that a single body of global law and a single global regulator would be seen as legitimate by businesses. Transparency mechanisms—if properly understood and well implemented—may be sufficiently flexible to help overcome these challenges.

To understand how these issues work in practice, consider the following three transparency mechanisms: one that seeks to regulate corporations, another that targets an international organization, and a third aimed at nation-states.

REMEMBER THE SULLIVAN PRINCIPLES?

Beginning in the late 1970s, U.S. corporations operating in South Africa faced a slew of criticism from civil rights activists, students, church groups, and others who believed that U.S. investment in South Africa bolstered the white minority regime. While some activists called for complete withdrawal and divestment, others argued that U.S. corporations could serve as a progressive force for change.

This reformist line was championed by the Reverend Leon H. Sullivan, a civil rights activist from Philadelphia who also served on the board of General Motors. Working with corporations invested in South Africa, Sullivan developed a set of principles for firms to follow, such as desegregating workspaces, promoting non-whites to positions of authority, and donating to local educational and health charities.

Because the principles were voluntary and many in the activist community doubted that anything short of full withdrawal would have any effect on the apartheid regime, Sullivan and his partners needed some way to make their commitments credible. In 1978 they contracted Arthur D. Little, a respected consulting firm, to collect data on corporate compliance and publish that information in an annual report. Corporations were evaluated according to each of the Sullivan Principles and given an overall ranking: "making good progress," "making acceptable progress," or "needs to be more active." Through this system, the behavior of U.S. firms operating in South Africa was made somewhat transparent.

However, the information about corporate behavior that was actually generated and publicized by these reports was sketchy, at best. Arthur D. Little evaluated corporations against largely imprecise and subjective criteria, forcing the reports' authors to wax Orwellian at times. For example, for the principle concerning the promotion of non-whites, a high score was defined as "quite considerable" progress, a middle score as "somewhat considerable," and a low score as "slight or no advancement." In the third report, nearly 70 percent of companies were placed in the middle category, leaving observers to wonder what exactly "somewhat considerable" progress meant. As one activist wrote, "to trust the efficacy of the Sullivan Principles requires a great deal of faith."

Despite these limitations, many institutions looking to promote change among U.S. corporations in South Africa used the Sullivan Principles as a way to target the economic pressure they applied. In 1993, the Investor Responsibility and Research Center (IRRC) counted 255 state and municipal laws limiting government procurement from, or public investment in, companies doing business in South Africa. Many of these laws invoked the Sullivan Principles, allowing the governments to do business with firms that participated or received high rankings, while prohibiting economic interaction with firms that were not signatories or performed poorly in the rankings.

Other types of investors also relied on the Sullivan reports to direct their economic pressure. A sizeable number of private universities interviewed by the IRRC stated that they routinely supported shareholder resolutions demanding compliance with the Sullivan Principles and would not hold stock in companies that had not signed them. Many church groups, private foundations, and even private banks followed suit.

That so many socially-conscious investors were willing to use the Sullivan Principles in spite of their many defects suggests that even a small amount of transparency can create economic pressure. It also suggests that a stronger, more revealing transparency mechanism might have had even more coercive effects on U.S. corporations in South Africa. Indeed, the fact that corporations fought efforts to strengthen the reporting system and make their actions more visible reinforces this conclusion.

But even if transparency were an effective way to channel economic pressure against noncompliant corporations, the question remains whether or not such pressure actually improved the lot of non-white South Africans. A 1985 IRRC study compared the performance of Sullivan signatories to that of non-signatories in order to determine, as the report's title bluntly asks, "Does Signing the Sullivan Principles Matter?" The IRRC indeed found that signatories outperformed nonsignatories in several areas, such as equitable pay rates, promotion of nonwhite managers, and donations to local communities. In itself, this finding might be unsurprising, given that the corporations most likely to sign the Sullivan Principles were also likely to be the most socially responsible. Interestingly, however, the report also found that the areas in which signatories were more responsible than nonsignatories were precisely those areas measured in the annual report. The report found no statistical difference between signatories and nonsignatories in areas in which corporate behavior was not publicized. In other words, U.S. corporations only improved their social performance when firm behavior was exposed.

A WATCHDOG AT THE WORLD BANK

Throughout the 1980s and early 1990s, the World Bank came under heavy criticism from environmentalists, human rights activists, and indigenous peoples' associations. These groups contended that many of the bank's lending projects were violating environmental and social safeguard policies and harming the very people and places they were supposed to help.

In 1993, following the controversial Narmada Dam project that was heavily criticized for displacing indigenous people, the bank created an independent Inspection Panel to serve as an internal watchdog. Any person negatively affected by a bank project—or, in some cases, an organization acting on that person's behalf—can file a complaint with the panel. If the panel deems the complaint within its mandate, a full investigation commences. To gather evidence, the panel holds interviews, conducts field visits, and takes submissions from outside experts, bank staff, affected stakeholders, and NGOs. Its goal is to determine whether the bank has violated any of its environmental or social policies. The end result is a factual assessment of the bank's compliance with its own policies, which is presented to the bank board and then released to the public.

The Inspection Panel is effectively an "information court." It has a plaintiff, a defendant, and a panel of judges. Evidence is collected and weighed to determine whether the defendant has violated a certain set of established rules. But unlike most courts, the Inspection Panel's judgments have no formal legal consequences. They simply paint an ostensibly accurate and objective picture of bank behavior; they make it transparent.

How effectively has this information court provided remedies to people hurt by bank lending projects? In one case involving a poverty alleviation project in western China, the panel review ultimately led to the end of bank involvement in the project. Of the 25 cases for which data was available, six others prompted large changes in bank projects, such as allocation of further funding for displaced people or the revision of environmental assessments. Seven other cases resulted in smaller changes or further study of the issues in question. The remaining eleven resulted in no changes.

Those asking the question "does the Inspection Panel work?" will be unsatisfied by those numbers because it is unclear how many of the 25 cases should have resulted in large changes, how many in small changes, and how many were in fact spurious. We have no baseline against which to measure the panel's record.

For our purposes, however, the results are quite interesting. They show that in over half of the cases brought before the panel, the mere release of information changed bank behavior—and that in a quarter of the cases, this change was substantial. Given that the panel's findings had no hard consequences, why should the bank have changed its policies in any of the cases?

Two factors may help answer that question. First, the cases that resulted in the most extensive project changes were the ones on which NGOs like the Center for International Environmental Law lobbied hardest. Cases with high levels of public activism achieved significant change in 60 percent of cases, compared with only 15 percent of less attention-grabbing cases.

Second, change at the bank seems driven by the extent to which a case is connected to the bank's institutional values—its underlying sense of identity. The panel process contains a preliminary fact-finding stage that allows the bank to review stakeholder grievances and potentially reform a project before a factual record is published. At this stage of the game, bank officials are not yet exposed to public shame, so their motivations for changing policy likely stem from their own values—internal transparency. Of the six cases resolved in the preliminary stage, two achieved large policy changes and the remainder achieved mid-level results. These results are substantially better than the success rate for cases that went to the full investigation stage, suggesting that transparency can alter an institution's behavior simply by showing where its actions conflict with its own values.

TRADE AND TRANSPARENCY IN NORTH AMERICA

In 1992, the United States, Mexico, and Canada signed the North American Free Trade Agreement (NAFTA), an unprecedented and controversial step toward continental economic integration. Before the measure passed in the U.S. Congress, environmentalists insisted that a separate treaty be linked to NAFTA to ensure that economic integration would not come at the cost of the North American environment. The North American Agreement on Environmental Cooperation (NAAEC), as the treaty was named, created an intergovernmental body called the Commission on Environmental Cooperation (CEC), with headquarters in Montreal.

One of the CEC's principal tasks is to investigate citizens' complaints that the NAFTA parties have failed to enforce their environmental laws, as the NAAEC requires. The citizen submission process functions as another information court, investigating the parties' compliance with environmental laws and publishing its findings as factual records. While the CEC process goes one step beyond the World Bank panel by allowing the United States, Canada, and Mexico to use a CEC report as the basis for formal legal sanctions against each other under the NAAEC, they have never invoked that provision. Instead, citizens have depended on the informal sanction of activist pressure to compel compliance with the NAAEC.

How have they fared? On balance it seems that the CEC has been less effective than the World Bank panel. For example, in the high-profile Cozumel case, the CEC's findings led to improvements in Mexican environmental law but failed to stop the specific violation at issue—the building of a cruise ship pier in environmentally sensitive waters in the Gulf of Mexico. Of 26 completed CEC cases, four resulted in high levels of policy change, seven in medium changes, and the remainder in negligible changes. Again, these results are less interesting to us than the question of what made some cases more successful than others.

As in the World Bank example, we find that activist pressure was an important predictor of successful cases. While only 15 percent of all cases yielded high results, cases with high levels of advocacy achieved substantial policy changes 30 percent of the time. Only 20 percent of the cases with substantial activism yielded no result.

HOW AND WHEN TRANSPARENCY POLICIES WORK: THREE UNDERAPPRECIATED FORCES

The above examples suggest three forces that, when empowered by transparency, can sometimes alter the behavior of global actors—markets, dialogue with civil society, and institutional values. These forces can change how institutions act even in the absence of formal legal structures, but their scope and power depend on a number of conditions.

Market Pressure

Economic pressure can bring about social change only when significant numbers of consumers and investors are willing to apply it. If buyers do not care enough about an issue to differentiate "good" products from "bad" ones and potentially pay a premium for the "good" product, markets will not direct suppliers toward socially conscious behavior.

Additionally, some actors are more vulnerable to market pressure than others. For example, companies that make products for mass consumption rely heavily on brand image to sell their goods. Many of the most prominent transnational corporations—Nike, McDonalds, Toyota—fall into this category. Conversely, companies that make generic goods or sell primarily to other businesses do not depend on public goodwill for sales and are therefore less susceptible to consumer pressure. Mining companies like Anglo-American or Rio Tinto are a good example. However, these corporations may still be vulnerable to pressures from capital markets, as was seen in the South African example.

Dialogue with Civil Society

The above examples suggest that transparency mechanisms work better when activists incorporate the information into their dialogue with the institutions they are trying to hold accountable. Why might this occur?

First, information courts like the World Bank Inspection Panel and the CEC provide a concrete forum for grievances. Brushing off stakeholders' criticisms is not an option because the Inspection Panel and the NAFTA commission create a process in which the Bank and the NAFTA parties are compelled to engage with their critics.

Second, beyond simply providing a forum in which dialogue can occur, these transparency mechanisms moderate the exchange by highlighting where each side's claims diverge from reality. Information courts are not just talking shops; they are places where actors have to face the facts if they wish to remain credible. Transparency mechanisms compel actors to tell the truth, enhancing the standing of those with valid claims against targeted institutions, which—unless they cooperate—find their credibility significantly diminished.

Third, by dividing credible information from specious claims, transparency mechanisms serve an important "editing" function. Robert Keohane and Joseph Nye argue that in informational politics there exists a "paradox of plenty: a plentitude of information leads to a poverty of attention." Transparency mechanisms cut through the flood of information and countervailing claims to focus stakeholders' attention on the facts.

Institutional Values

The experience of the World Bank suggests that transparency mechanisms can make use of institutional values to change behavior by demonstrating to organizations how their actions are contrary to their core principles. It should come as no surprise that the World Bank, an organization whose mission is infused with a powerful ethos of poverty alleviation, is susceptible to such pressures. The fact that we found little evidence for values-driven behavioral change among the Sullivan Principles companies or the NAFTA countries likely reflects the different values held by many corporations and the difficulty states have in hewing to a defined institutional ethos.

THE FUTURE OF TRANSPARENCY

Understanding transparency mechanisms is important not only because they and their accompanying rhetoric have become so pervasive but because transparency represents a promising direction in which to develop innovative governance tools.

We argued before that transnational regulation is often seen—at times correctly—as both technically impracticable and politically illegitimate. However, transparency-based systems may be able to avoid the technical limitations of traditional regulation by distributing functions across the full spectrum of relevant players. No single regulatory entity would be required to collect compliance information and punish violations. Instead, actors would monitor and enforce standards against themselves, their peers, and their opponents using the three levers discussed above. In the World Bank and CEC cases, it was mostly NGOs that served this function. NGOs were also instrumental to the use of the Sullivan Principles, but universities, state and local governments, and private banks—with their substantial financial assets—were the main regulators.

Regarding legitimacy, it is politically easier to get an organization to agree to discuss something than to do something. Many corporations, international organizations, and states are unwilling to agree to be bound by a common standard or law. However, they are likely willing—or can be made willing—at least to discuss problems with relevant stakeholders. What that organization may not realize, however, is that mere discussion may greatly increase the likelihood of action.

CONCLUSION

So who could be opposed to transparency? Who could be in favor of opacity or, worse still, obscuration? Small wonder that transparency has become the rallying cry of good global governance. However, in order for transparency to handle the tasks that policymakers and activists envision for it, it must be seen as a conduit to regulation, not as regulation itself. Consider the cases presented in this paper: if it were not for socially conscious investors, the Sullivan Principles would have done little to improve the lives of black South Africans working for U.S. corporations under apartheid. But for activists and the personal values of World Bank staff, the Inspection Panel's findings would fall on deaf ears. And but for environmentalist pressure and media attention, the CEC would have little effect on environmental enforcement in North America.

Seeing transparency in this way alerts us to its limits. Policymakers seeking to use transparency mechanisms as a means of regulation must understand that they are unlikely to succeed in environments where market pressures do not exist, activist groups are poorly organized, and the targeted institutions' internal values run contrary to the program's goals.

Still, this conception of transparency also highlights some important possibilities. The fact that mere information can create accountability at the global level by marshalling concrete pressures against international actors suggests an intriguing path to global regulations that are at once effective, technically feasible, and politically viable. This finding should give hope to anyone committed to making global institutions more responsive to the people whose lives they affect. Transparency may be an egregiously overused and poorly understood buzzword, but beneath the rhetoric lies a valuable—if circumscribed—tool for transnational accountability.

CHAPTER 8

CAPITAL MARKETS

■■■

This chapter will give you a basic understanding of the international capital markets as they existed during their evolution throughout the 1990s. Know this stuff and you'll be good with other chapters to come, especially those relating to the Mexican and Asian financial crises.

Part One: What Are Capital Markets?

Capital markets are markets where savers—people, companies, and governments with more money than they need (because they save some of their income)—transfer those funds to people, companies, or governments that have a shortage of funds (because they spend more than their income). Stock and bond markets are two major capital markets. Capital markets channel money from those who do not have an immediate productive use for it to those who do—it's all about economic efficiency, folks.

When savers make investments, they convert cash or savings (risk-free assets) into risky assets. And since all investments are risky in some way, the only reason a saver would put cash at risk is if the returns on the investment are greater than returns on holding risk-free assets. Buying stocks and bonds and investing in real estate are common examples. The savers hope that the stock, bond, or real estate will "appreciate," or grow in value.

For example, suppose Rafael and Kamali make $50,000 in one year, but they only spend $40,000 that year. They can invest the $10,000—their savings—in a mutual fund (pools of money managed by an investment company) investing in stocks and bonds all over the world. Kamali and Rafael know that making such an investment is riskier than keeping the $10,000 at home or in a savings account. But they hope that over the long-term the investment will yield greater returns than cash holdings (money under the bed) or interest on a savings account. The borrowers in this example are the companies that issued the stocks or bonds that are part of the mutual fund portfolio. Because the companies have spending needs that exceed their income, they finance their spending needs by issuing securities in the capital markets.

Rafael and Kamali's investment is an example of "direct" finance, where the companies borrowed directly by issuing securities to Kamali and Rafael in the capital markets. But not all borrowing is done directly. "Indirect" finance involves a financial intermediary between the borrower and the saver. For example, if Rafael and Kamali put their money in a savings account at a bank, and then the bank lends the money to a company (or another person), the bank is an intermediary. Financial intermediaries are the matchmakers of the capital markets—they connect savers and borrowers who otherwise might never find each other.

Remember, capital markets are all about efficiency. In our example, Rafael and Kamali want to productively invest their savings of $10,000. And companies are out there that have great business ideas but no funds to carry them out. The capital markets are a cool way to shift that $10,000 from Rafael and Kamali to the companies that hope to put it to good use. If there were no capital markets, Rafael and Kamali might have kept their $10,000 under the bed or in a low-yielding savings account. The companies might have put off or canceled their business plans. And that's just not a happy ending, is it?

Part Two: The Structure of Capital Markets

So to get a handle on structure, let's first take a look at primary and secondary markets. The primary market is where new securities (stocks and bonds are the most common) are issued. The corporation or government agency that needs funds (the borrower) issues securities to buyers in the primary market with the help of big investment banks that underwrite the securities. In other words, the bank says, "hey borrowers, for a fee, we'll sell your securities to the public and we guarantee that they'll sell for at least 'x' dollars each." But this business of issuing new securities is only half of the story. The other half is in the secondary market. So what is it?

The secondary market is just that—secondary. First, a borrower issues securities to buyers in the primary market. Second, those buyers trade their securities with other investors. That arena is what we call the secondary market, and it's where the vast majority of capital transactions take place. The secondary markets you've heard about a lot are the New York Stock Exchange for stocks, and the **bond markets** for debt.

The next thing we've got to look at is what kinds of securities we're dealing with. One type is what we call a debt instrument. Savers who purchase debt instruments are creditors. Creditors, or debt holders, receive future income or assets in return for their investment. The most common example of a debt instrument is a bond (essentially a loan that an individual gives to a borrower—a government, company, city, etc.). In return, the investor gets interest payments (usually at a fixed rate) for the life of the bond and receives the principal when the bond matures.

Another kind of security is stock—the one most people are familiar with. When investors (savers) buy stock, they become owners of a "share" of a company's assets and earnings. If a company is successful, the price that investors are willing to pay for its stock usually rises and shareholders who bought stock at a lower price stand to make a profit—buy low, sell high. But if a company doesn't do so well, just the opposite might happen. Stock prices go down and shareholders lose money. So let's go back to Rafael and Kamali. If they put their money in stocks, they are buying equity in the company that issued the stock.

Part Three: Internationalization of Capital Markets in the Late 1990s

One of the most important developments since the 1970s has been the internationalization, and now globalization, of capital markets. Let's look at some of the basic elements of these international capital markets.

> *"Every nation on planet earth was poor at some point. What made the difference was tapping into global trade and capital markets. That is the way to go."*
> —African Development Bank President Donald Kaberuka, Speech at the Eastern and Southern African Trade and Development Bank, December 19, 2012

Integrated International Markets

Basically, the international capital markets deal with any transaction having an international dimension via closely integrated domestic markets. So how do people doing business in the international capital markets connect? Since the late 1990s, sophisticated communications systems have allowed people all over the world to conduct business from wherever they are. The major world financial centers where people do business include, among other places, Hong Kong, Singapore, Tokyo, London, New York, and Paris.

The foreign exchange (FX) market is key to the smooth functioning of the international capital markets. In the late 1990s, it was enormous, with market turn-over (the amount of currency that is traded, bought and/or sold) well above $1 trillion daily. (The average daily turnover in traditional foreign exchange markets is currently around $4.9 trillion.) Let's check out some examples of just how important the FX market is. Commercial banks use it to help facilitate corporate transactions—e.g., allowing a Canadian company to import from Japan and pay in yen, even though the income for the Canadian company is Canadian dollars. Corporations use the market to help counterbalance currency risk—i.e., the risk that a company loses money due to fluctuations in the exchange rate. Speculators use the market to make money by gambling on which way the exchange rate will go.

Let's get back to securities. It's not hard to find examples of securities that trade in the international capital markets. Foreign bonds are a typical example of an international security (e.g., a bond sold by a Korean company in Mexico denominated in Mexican pesos). Another kind of bond is a Eurobond, which is denominated in a currency other than that of the country in which it is sold (e.g., a bond denominated in Japanese yen that is sold in France). In the late 1990s, the Eurobond became the primary bond of choice in the international marketplace. Over 80% of new issues in the international bond market were Eurobonds. The primary reason for their popularity is that because they can be repaid in any of several predetermined currencies, the issuing company can choose the currency it prefers, be it yen, euros, pounds, or another currency. When the holding period is over, the holder chooses the most preferable currency at that time. This partially protects buyers from exchange rate fluctuations.

One last thing before we move on to portfolio diversification. Maybe you've heard of American Depositary Receipts (ADRs) or Global Depositary Receipts (GDRs). In the late 1990s, these were used extensively in the privatization of public enterprises in developing and transitioning (i.e. socialism to capitalism) countries (check out supplement 8A). ADRs and GDRs are certificates issued by a depositary bank, representing shares of stock of a foreign corporation held by the bank. Countries that began to privatize public enterprises included The People's Republic of China, India, and many Latin American countries such as Chile, Mexico, Bolivia, and Brazil. Chile was the first Latin American country to truly embrace privatization and used ADRs to open the path for Latin American countries to access Western capital markets. Brazil privatized several large state owned enterprises (SOEs) including Telebras (the formally state-owned monopolistic telephone system) in 1998.

Portfolio Diversification

A major benefit of the internationalization of capital markets is the diversification of risk. Individual investors, major corporations, and individual countries all usually try to diversify the risks of their financial portfolios. Why? Because people are generally risk-averse. In other words, they would rather get relatively small, but consistently positive returns on investments than go for potentially huge returns on investments that fluctuate wildly where the risk for loss is equally huge. This relationship between risk and returns is something that all portfolio investors look at.

During the 1990s, as emerging market economies (EMEs) became more stable, investment in EME companies increased as investors started to view international investment as a way to diversify their portfolios and reduce risk. (Check out supplement 8B for an overview of capital flows and EMEs.) Some of the benefits for investors in diversifying their portfolios internationally included higher returns (than in their domestic market); participation in the growth of a foreign market; and, of course, lowering their portfolio risk. Since more and more investors started recognizing these benefits in the 1990s, portfolio investment in EME financial markets started to increase greatly.

The Principal Actors

<u>Commercial Banks and Governments</u>: Remember from chapter 5 that the major form of sovereign debt in the 1970s and 1980s was loans from foreign commercial banks. Although commercial bank lending continued to be important in some regions of the world, the 1990s witnessed the rise of bonds as the major form of sovereign debt in the Global South, in part because investors in the Global North chased after higher yields (see supplement 8B). Still, banks competed fiercely to retain and grow market share. Guess where lots of the lending occurred? Check out chapter 10 on the Asian financial crisis.

<u>Non-bank Financial Institutions and Corporations</u>: During the late 1990s, insurance companies, pension and trust funds, and mutual funds from many countries began to diversify into international markets. And corporations tapped into foreign funds via issuance of stocks and bonds, and foreign bank loans.

Changes Critical to Development

Let's take a look at why many observers say we entered an era of global capital markets in the 1990s. This whole process was attributable to the existence of offshore markets (foreign banks, corporations, deposits that are located outside of national borders), which came into existence decades prior because corporations and investors wanted to escape domestic regulation. The existence of offshore markets in turn forced countries to liberalize their domestic markets, like removing capital controls (transaction tax or limitations on buying/selling national currency at market rate). This dynamic created greater internationalization of the capital markets. Until the 1990s, capital markets in the United States were larger and more developed than markets in the rest of the world. But during the 1980s and 1990s, the relative strength of the U.S. market decreased considerably as the world markets began to grow at phenomenal rates. Three primary reasons account for this phenomenon. Let's check them out.

First, citizens around the world (and especially the Japanese) were increasing their personal savings. Second, many governments had further deregulated their capital markets since 1980, allowing domestic companies more opportunities abroad, and giving foreign companies the opportunity to invest. Finally, technological advances made it easier to access global markets. Information could be retrieved more quickly, easily, and cheaply than ever before. Investors in one country could get their hands on more detailed information about investments in other countries, and they could obtain it easily. So in the late 1990s we witnessed the globalization of markets—i.e., the increased integration of domestic markets into a global economy. Don't mistake this for the process of internationalization, though, which connected less integrated domestic markets of the past with offshore markets.

The global capital markets became critical to development. Developing countries, like all countries, have to encourage productive investments to promote economic growth. If the countries have domestic savings, the savings can be used to make productive investments. But, historically, developing countries have suffered from low domestic savings rates. Thanks to global capital, developing countries added to domestic savings by borrowing savings from abroad. In 1993, Latin America countries borrowed $44.7 billion in foreign funds.

Part Four: Sources of Capital

There are two sources of capital: private and public, and they're both very important to the economies of the world. When capital from these sources moves across borders, you get what we call capital flows. Those flows then are recorded in the balance of payments account. But there are some important differences between private and public sources, so let's get things straight.

Private

Foreign direct investment (FDI) and portfolio investment (both debt and equity flows) are important sources of private capital. Check them out.

First there's FDI. FDI is capital that corporations invest in countries other than their own—hence the foreign bit. For instance, imagine a Japanese company that starts a joint venture (50–50) with a Mexican company based in Mexico. This kind of capital isn't nearly as liquid as portfolio investment (and it's a lot less volatile). Since an investment is generally considered FDI only if the foreign corporation owns at least ten percent of voting stock in the company it's investing in, FDI funds are usually medium- to long-term investments. You just don't pull that much capital out on a whim.

Now, we just said that portfolio investment is "liquid." It's actually more than liquid—it's HOT, what we call "hot money" in the biz. Portfolio investments are from individuals or institutional investors that sink their money into the stock and bond markets. But, as you will see, portfolio investors can (and will) head for the exit door, removing their money from a country almost instantaneously. Very liquid, yeah?

Public

Now let's talk about the other side—public sources of capital. They include official non-concessional loans of both multilateral and bilateral aid and official development assistance (ODA), which is made up of grants and concessional multilateral and bilateral loans. Brace yourselves.

Let's start with multilateral and bilateral official non-concessional loans. Yeah, it's a mouth full, so let's break it down. First, the "official" title just means they come from either multilateral or bilateral creditors or donors. The "non-concessional" part means that the loan is based on market rates, must be repaid, and isn't partly grants. And then there's the multilateral/bilateral distinction. Official non-concessional multilateral aid consists of loans that come from the IMF, the World Bank, regional development banks, and other intergovernmental agencies. For instance, in 2008, the International Bank for Reconstruction and Development, part of the World Bank group, gave Colombia a customized loan aimed at providing students with financial aid on terms that would make it easier for them to pay off their debt. By contrast, official non-concessional bilateral aid means loans that come from sovereign governments and their central banks or other agencies (i.e., bilateral donors/creditors), including export credit agency loans.

Then you've got your ODA and concessional loans. ODA refers in part to official public grants that are legally binding commitments and provide a specific amount of capital available to disburse for which no repayment is required. The total amount of ODA in 1995 was $78 billion and decreased to about $65 billion a few years later in 1999. Asia and sub-Saharan Africa were the largest and most stable of the ODA beneficiaries, hovering around $20 billion per year, while Central and South America received a fraction of that aid, about $5 billion.

Concessional bilateral aid refers to aid from governments, central banks, and export credit agencies that contains a partial grant element (25% or more), or that partially forgives the loan. Similarly, concessional multilateral aid contains a partial grant, or forgiveness of the loan, and comes from many of the same sources as non-concessional multilateral aid.

Private Capital in the Late 1990s

During the 1990s, the sources of capital for developing countries changed in a major way. In 1990, net long-term resource flows to developing countries (private and public sources of capital) was $101.9 billion. Of that, approximately 57% was from official loans or grants, and the remaining 43% came from private sources. Just five years later, in 1995, only 28% of the resources were from official sources, with the remaining 72% from private sources. And yet the amount of official funding in dollar terms remained relatively constant. So what does that mean was happening to private funding? It was off the charts. From the 1990 figure of $44 billion, private sources increased to an average of $124 billion.

And it wasn't just one particular type of private funding that increased during those five years—all of them were skyrocketing. Portfolio equity flows went from $4 billion to over $22 billion. Foreign direct investment went from $25 billion to $90 billion. Private debt flows went from $15 billion to almost $25 billion. Some big changes in the sources of funds for developing countries, right?

So why was this happening? For one thing, international portfolio diversification became more prevalent every day: insurance companies, mutual funds, pension funds, and securities houses were looking to diversify. They also had more funds than ever to invest. Worldwide, portfolios were absorbing an increasing share of aggregate savings. These portfolios were coming more and more under the control of professional fund managers. The "pros" are generally more apt to diversify in the international marketplace. Around 1991, there were around 100 professional global managed funds, with a value of just under $200 billion. By the end of the decade, there were about 430 global funds worth nearly $700 billion.

As overall international portfolio diversification grew, so did the share of international portfolio diversification that went to developing countries. For example, according to the IMF, the five largest industrial countries in the late 1990s (U.K., U.S., Japan, Germany and France) increased their international investments from $100 billion in 1980 (about 5% of assets) to $900 billion in 1993 (more than 7% of assets). In 1987, $0.50 of every $100 of foreign portfolio investment went to emerging markets. By 1993, that figure increased to $16 of every $100. Net capital inflows to developing countries as a percentage of world savings more than doubled (from 0.8% to 2%) between 1990 and 1993.

Capital flows to developing countries were quickly bringing the world closer to a seamless global marketplace in the late 1990s, but the growth of global institutional investors also changed the nature of the funds that were being pumped into emerging markets. Suddenly, they were based more on short-term liquidity and performance than long-term business ventures. And sure, developing countries can take some precautionary measures to protect themselves from the risks of these volatile cash flows. The central bank can intervene in foreign exchange markets and the government can impose capital controls. During the early part of the 1990s, the central banks of Thailand and Mexico pegged their currency to the dollar to help stabilize the exchange rate. But massive—massive—and instantaneous withdrawals of funds from a country can wreck its economy despite the theoretical precautionary measures. As the Mexican and Asian financial crises illustrate, the dangers of these sorts of capital flows are very real and very powerful.

> "The [International Monetary Fund] has shifted its thinking on . . . what is a sensible toolkit for emerging countries when faced with volatile capital flows. So, there was recognition that in instances where you face severe volatility of capital flows, some form of management of those capital flows could be sensible. In other words, where it is not due to your own domestic policy being out of sync with your economic fundamentals but simply because of the vicissitudes of the global capital markets, some sort of capital flow management was sensible."
> —Tharman Shanmugaratnam, Chairman, International Monetary and Financial Committee, Transcript of the IMFC Press Briefing, April 21, 2012

Net private capital flows to major emerging market economies fell to about $200 billion in 1997, from a peak of $295 billion in 1996. And just prior to this dramatic decline was the Mexican financial crisis. Capital flows to Mexico reached $104 billion between 1990 and 1994—20 percent of the capital flows to all EMEs during that time. In the fourth quarter of 1993, Mexico had a private capital inflow of just $7.7 billion. By the time 1995's fourth quarter rolled around, the inflow became a private capital *outflow* of $4.3 billion. A few years later came the Asian crisis. The five economies most affected by the crisis (South Korea, Indonesia, Thailand, Malaysia and the Philippines) had an inflow of $93 billion in 1996. In 1997, they had a combined outflow of $12 billion. That's a net change of $105 billion in a single year! Danger, Will Robinson.

You Gotta Know Something About Them!

Singapore

Singapore is an economic powerhouse not only in Southeast Asia, but also in the world, ranking as a top 5 (number 4) financial center. It's also one of the busiest ports in the world (top 5), in addition to having one of the largest per capita incomes in terms of purchasing power parity. It's a founding member of Association of South East Asian Nations (ASEAN), a regional organization designed to promote political and economic cooperation. Singapore rocks because it's one of the original Four Asian Tigers (the others being Taiwan, South Korea, and Hong Kong) that has become the second freest economy according to the Index of Economic Freedom in 2011. What's the Index? It's a partnership between the Wall Street Journal and the Heritage Foundation (think tank) and together they track global economic freedom. Check it out: Singapore consistently ranks at the top of the least corrupt countries according to Transparency International, an NGO that measures corruption. While the economy is free, there are stringent laws regarding drug use—possession of drugs is a capital offense—which has led to one of the lowest drug usage rates in the world.

London

Now that we've looked at an Eastern economic powerhouse, let's look at a Western powerhouse. London, according to finance professionals surveyed by Financial Times, is the most competitive financial center in the world. It's the world's biggest center for foreign exchange trades according to TheCityUK, a lobbyist group. The Atlantic, a magazine targeted at "thought leaders," thinks London is pretty awesome too, ranking it the second most economically powerful city in the world, after NYC. The MasterCard Worldwide Centers of Commerce Index, which checks out global financial centers, thinks highly of London, ranking it the top commercial center. It's an important part of the U.K., too, as the finance sector in the city makes up 10% of the United Kingdom's GDP.

What's Up with That?

Bond Market

Let's look at the bond market, which is huge. It consists mainly of government issued securities and corporate debt securities. The bond market is a whole lot bigger than the stock market and is really important to the public and private sectors. In 2011, the global capital stock was $212 trillion, with bonds making up $157 trillion, nearly 75%. The U.S. capital market is about 64% bonds and 36% stocks for a combined total of nearly $60 trillion. Why is there such a large difference between the sizes of stock markets compared to bond markets? Because governments have a ton of debt, especially the United States. And while only corporations issue stock, both governments and corporations issue bonds.

QUESTIONS FROM YOUR TALKING DOG

1. Are you ready to go? C'mon, I wanna play in the leaves, yo. While you're throwing your jacket on, tell me: who the heck are Rafael and Kamali? I'm just wondering.

2. Capital markets. Direct, indirect, primary, secondary, stocks, bonds. What? No, I'm not having a stroke. They sound like important words. Explain.

4. Here's a good pile. Take the leash off. Fine. Tell me about ADRs (See also supplements 8A.)

5. Yeah, I'm *so* interested in the link between internationalization of the capital markets and portfolio investment. (cough, just get me to the next pile)

6. Offshore markets? Let me guess. Markets that aren't on a beach. You did see that coming, right?

7. What's so hot about portfolio investment? Am I hot? And while you're at it, what's the big deal with private capital flows in the 1990s?

Chapter 8: Supplement

8A. *American Depositary Receipts: A Basic Explanation*

American Depositary Receipts (ADRs) became a critical conduit in the capital markets of the 1990s. This supplement will give you a really good understanding of how ADRs work. Joseph Velli's article explains the basics of ADRs—good stuff.

Joseph Velli, "American Depositary Receipts: An Overview,"
17 Fordham Int'l L.J., 38 (1994)

INTRODUCTION

I would like to thank everybody involved for providing me with this opportunity to speak to you about the wonderful world of American Depositary Receipts ("ADRs"). Today I will attempt to provide you with an overview of the ADR market. I will talk about the different types of ADR programs available, and I will talk about the growth that has occurred over the last several years.

Before I start, though, I thought it would be useful to set the stage a little bit. I just want to mention a few points. As Bill Decker mentioned earlier, for the first time, last year Glaxo, a non-U.S. company out of the United Kingdom, was the most actively traded stock on the New York Stock Exchange ("NYSE"). That, in and of itself, is very impressive. About 275 billion Glaxo ADRs were traded on the NYSE traded last year. But what I think is more impressive is that over 350,000 U.S. investors own Glaxo ADRs, and Glaxo's market capitalization here in the United States is approximately U.S.$20 billion. So the trading volume is impressive, but so is the number of shareholders and their market capitalization.

It is also important to realize that, excluding Canadian companies, the vast majority of non-U.S. companies use ADRs when they decide to list in the United States. In fact, some of these companies are more actively traded in the United States than in their home country. For example, for Hong Kong Telecom out of Hong Kong, Repsol out of Spain, Telemex out of Mexico, there is more trading volume both in share terms and in dollar terms in the United States than in their respective home countries.

I. ADRs: GENERAL BACKGROUND

A. Operation of ADR Programs

What are ADRs? How do they work? Very simply, an ADR is a receipt that is issued by a U.S. depositary bank, such as The Bank of New York, that actually represents the shares that are held overseas. So the ADR is merely a receipt that is issued in certificate form in the United States that represents the actual shares of a non-U.S. company.

Once the ADR program is established, the ADRs trade freely in the United States, like any other U.S. security. They can trade on the over-the-counter market or they can trade on one of the exchanges, such as NASDAQ, the American Stock Exchange ("ASE"), or the NYSE. ADRs can also be used to raise equity capital.

I think one recent trend is that people have gotten away from calling depositary receipts "American depositary receipts." Now, they basically either call them "global depositary receipts" ("GDRs"), or simply, as I prefer, "depositary receipts." In order not to confuse anybody, though, I will use the most common term, "ADRs."

The best way to understand how an ADR works is to look at an example of a trade. Again, let's go back to Glaxo, which trades on the NYSE. Glaxo did not raise capital here; the company simply listed on the NYSE without conducting a public offering.

DEPOSITARY RECEIPT SETTLEMENT

Let's assume that the very first trade takes place here in Glaxo's ADRs. A U.S. investor, whether it's an institutional investor or a retail investor, would simply call up his U.S. broker and say, "Buy me 1,000 or 10,000 Glaxo ADRs." In many cases the investor is not even aware that he is buying an ADR; all he really knows is that he's investing in Glaxo. So he calls up his broker (for argument's sake Merrill Lynch or Goldman Sachs) and says, "Buy me 1,000 Glaxo ADRs."

The broker, because there are no ADRs outstanding here, goes to the foreign market, in this case the London market, buys 1,000 Glaxo shares off the London exchange, deposits those actual shares with the depositary bank (for example The Bank of New York) and then the depositary bank issues 1,000 ADRs in the U.S. marketplace. So the shares are deposited by the broker and The Bank of New York would issue 1,000 ADRs. That's how an ADR is created.

Once the ADR is issued and outstanding, it freely trades like any other security. In the very next trade, if another investor calls up his broker and says, "I want to buy 500 Glaxo ADRs," the broker has a choice: he can either buy the ADR that is already existing in the U.S. marketplace, or he can repeat the process just described by going to the London Stock Exchange.

The last point on the trading aspect is what we call ADR cancellation. If I own 1,000 Glaxo ADRs and want to sell those ADRs, but cannot find a buyer, I simply would cancel those ADRs and sell the actual shares back into the home market, in Glaxo's case, in London. Thus, ADRs can be created or issued, they can be transferred here like any other U.S. security, or they can be canceled.

B. *Rationale Behind Establishing ADR Programs*

There are several different reasons why non-U.S. companies establish ADR programs. Some of them were covered today and I will not harp on them. Basically, companies establish ADR programs as a way of entering the U.S. markets to, hopefully, tap some demand for their securities. Many companies have found that by establishing ADR programs and enabling U.S. investors to buy their ADRs, they are able to get a better valuation for their share price. There are a couple of reasons for this.

First, in many industries or many sectors here, such as the telecommunications sector, the U.S. investment community may put a higher valuation or price/earnings ratio ("P/E") on that sector. As a result, if you are a company in France and you're in the telecommunications business and your P/E in France is 14 and the P/E in the United States for telecom stocks is somewhere around 18, by establishing an ADR program you should receive a higher valuation for your shares.

Second, the simple fact of a non-U.S. company establishing an ADR program here, enabling U.S. investors to buy the shares simply here, usually translates into a higher stock price for the company.

Third, companies establish ADR programs as a means of raising capital in the United States. In many cases, when a company is making an offering, their home market cannot absorb it—for example, YPF, an Argentine oil company, earlier this year did a U.S.$3 billion global offering that was part of a privatization. There was no way YPF was going to be able to raise U.S.$3 billion in the Argentine market. As a result, they raised roughly U.S.$500 million locally, they raised U.S.$2 billion in the United States, and U.S.$500 million in Europe.

Companies also establish ADR programs for other reasons. A great example is Roche, the Swiss pharmaceutical company. Roche established an ADR program for one reason: they have about 40,000 U.S. employees who wanted to invest in the parent company. By establishing an ADR program, the company was able to give their executives in the United States stock options, it was able to offer a 401-K savings plan for their U.S. employees, and the program enabled the U.S. employees to buy Roche ADRs.

C. *Investor Perspective*

From the investor's standpoint, U.S. investors buy ADRs for three main reasons: convenience, cost, and liquidity. From the convenience side, ADRs trade and settle just like any other U.S. security. There is no difference between buying Glaxo ADRs and buying IBM, AT&T, or General Motors stock. It works exactly the same way, you pay the same commission rates. ADR dividends are paid in U.S. dollars and they settle just like any other

U.S. security. So there is virtually no difference between buying and selling an ADR and buying and selling any other U.S. security.

On the cost side, ADRs also offer a lot of advantages as compared to what we call "direct" investing, meaning buying Glaxo shares directly in the U.K. market. There are three major cost advantages from a U.S. investor's standpoint.

First, custody fees are avoided. If I buy Glaxo shares in London, or an institution buys them in London, you have to appoint a global custodian to hold the shares in London. That global custodian could charge you anywhere from ten to forty basis points annually. By buying an ADR, which settles and clears in the United States, U.S. investors avoid that charge.

Second, foreign exchange rates on dividends are better on ADR dividends. Typically, when the depositary bank pays dividends and converts, in Glaxo's case Pound Sterling, into U.S. dollars, because we are converting such a large sum of money, we are able to get a better rate than if you as an investor went to your bank and tried to cash a £10 cheque. So the foreign exchange rates are better in dividends.

Third is what I call "failed trade financing." Because ADRs settle according to U.S. principles and they settle in the United States, very rarely does a trade fail. What I mean by "fail" is if an investor buys the ADRs and they are not delivered on the settlement date, resulting in the failure of the trade. The failed trade rate in the United States for ADRs is less than 0.5%. If an investor buys shares directly in places like Brazil, Chile—not so much in Latin American anymore; they've straightened it out—but still in places like Italy, Spain, China, the failed trade rate could be substantially higher. As a result, the investor would have to finance his position, and that cost could add up over time.

II.   ADR PROGRAMS

Type	Act	Registration	Disclosure	Cost	Listing	Raise Capital
Unsponsored	1933	F-6	None	0	OTC	No
	1934	12G3-2(b)	None			
Sponsored Level I	1933	F-6	None	$ 5,000	OTC	Not Now
	1934	12G3-2(b)	None	$ 20,000		
Sponsored Level II	1933	F-6	None	$200,000	Exchange	Not Now
	1934	20-F	Detailed	$500,000		
Sponsored Level III	1933	F-1	Rigorous	$400,000	Exchange	Yes - U.S., Global
	1934	20-F	Detailed	$900,000		
Private DR	1933	None	Euro-Style	$100,000	Portal	Yes - U.S., Global
	1934	12g3-2(b)		$400,000		

A. *Unsponsored ADR Programs*

There are essentially two types of ADR programs: unsponsored and sponsored. I am not going to spend a lot of time on unsponsored ADRs. The key thing to remember about unsponsored ADRs is they are absolutely obsolete, and there are a lot of hidden costs and problems associated with unsponsored ADRs. In fact, since 1983, there have only been three new unsponsored ADR programs established.

B. *Sponsored ADR Program*

What has taken their place is what we call sponsored ADRs. Simply, the word "sponsored" means that the company is appointing a U.S. depositary bank and the company is sponsoring their entry into the U.S. capital markets. As a result, there is a service contract in place and the investor can be relatively assured of the type of service and information they are going to receive on an ongoing basis.

1. Level I, II, and III ADR Programs

There are essentially three types of sponsored ADRs: Sponsored Level I, Level II, and Level III.

A Sponsored Level I ADR trades over-the-counter in the United States on the pink sheets. You establish a Level I program by establishing what is known as an information exemption under the Securities Exchange Act of 1934 (the "Exchange Act"). Basically, all a company has to do is supply the Securities and Exchange Commission ("SEC") with any material information they produce and distribute locally in their home country and they can obtain an exemption from registration.

A Level I program, because the company is not registered fully with the SEC, cannot be listed on an exchange and a Level I program cannot be used to raise capital. However, many companies have found that by establishing a Level I program, because it's very easy to do and is a low-cost way of entering the U.S. market, they use it as their first step into the U.S. public markets. They establish a Level I program, they start an investor relations exercise, and they start building up a core group of U.S. investors.

Level II is when a company decides to list on one of the exchanges. In order to list on one of the exchanges you have to file a Form 20-F under the Exchange Act, which again means essentially complying or reconciling to U.S. accounting and disclosure requirements. For some companies this could be costly and difficult; for other companies it shouldn't be a problem.

Level III ADRs is when a company decides to make a public offering in the U.S. marketplace. Typically, as was discussed today, this requires filing a Form F-1 with the SEC, which again requires complying with U.S. accounting and disclosure procedures.

We have found, over time, that the vast majority of companies that come into the U.S. market start off with a Level I ADR program and then upgrade over time. The upgrading could take anywhere from six months to ten years, but eventually companies with Level I programs upgrade to either a listing on the NYSE, the ASE, or NASDAQ.

In fact, Glaxo is a prime example. The company started out with a Level I program that lasted for approximately one year. It was able to build up a core group of U.S. investors. Eventually Glaxo upgraded to the NYSE.

If I could just mention one other point on listing, our position, and what we usually recommend to companies, is that they should not get too excited about a Level I program. Their management must fully realize that it's only a starting step and their visibility, unless they have an unbelievably good story to tell U.S. investors, is going to be very limited. Typically, a Level I company can expect to obtain anywhere between three to six percent of its shareholder base in the United States through such a program. What we have found is that when they do a listing and they upgrade it, whether they do a Level II or Level III, their U.S. investor base will materially increase. If a company has four percent U.S. shareholder base with a Level I, they could expect somewhere between ten to fifteen percent with a Level III.

2.   Common Misconceptions

As Bill Decker mentioned this morning, we typically run into a lot of misconceptions or misinformation in the marketplace. Many companies do not realize that there are different types of ADR programs. Some are very easy to establish, some are more difficult because of accounting and legal issues; some are very cheap to establish; and some cost significant amounts of money.

The biggest misconception right now in the marketplace is that there is a difference between ADRs and GDRs. There is absolutely no difference between an American Depositary Receipt and a Global Depositary Receipt. They work exactly the same way. What will happen is with a Level III ADR or with a private placement under Rule 144A of the Securities Act of 1933 ("Rule 144A" or "144A"), the underwriter will determine what to call the depositary receipt. If a big portion of the offering is taking place in Europe, the underwriter will call the depositary receipt a GDR, trying to get away from tainting the security by calling it an "American Security." If the majority of the offering takes place in the United States, then the underwriter will call it an ADR.

3.   Growth of the ADR Market

Regarding the growth of the market, at the end of 1993, we are projecting that there will be approximately 990 ADR programs. Over the course of 1993, we are projecting that about 110 new ADR programs will be established. The reason why the numbers for 1992 and 1993 don't match up is that a lot of companies are obviously converting from unsponsored to sponsored and some companies go through mergers, bankruptcies, and other reorganizations. But from 1992 to 1993 we are projecting that over 110 new companies will establish ADR programs, which will be a record.

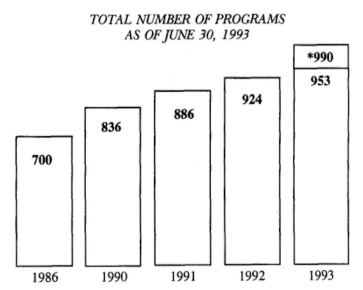

TOTAL NUMBER OF PROGRAMS
AS OF JUNE 30, 1993

*Year-end projection
∎Includes all Depositary Receipt programs except 144A Depositary Receipt programs

The largest ADR markets are the United Kingdom, Australia, and Japan. These three markets represent approximately half of the ADR marketplace. What is of interest is that over the last three years, the fastest growing part of the world for ADR programs in terms of percentage has been Latin America. It started off in Mexico three years ago, and now it has spread to Argentina, Brazil, Chile, Peru, and Colombia. Latin America, for the last three years, has clearly been the fastest-growing segment of the ADR market.

PERCENTAGE OF TOTAL DEPOSITARY RECEIPT PROGRAMS BY COUNTRY AS OF JUNE 30, 1993

As of June 30, 1993 there were 953 Depositary Receipt programs

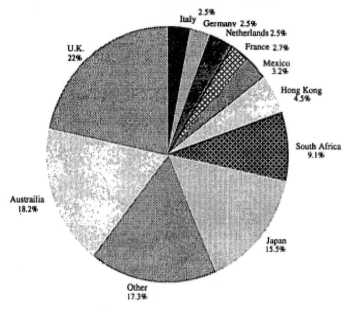

■ Excludes 144A Depositary Receipt programs

Going forward, we expect that, for the next few years, Latin America will remain one of the fastest-growing, but we expect Southeast Asia to eventually overtake Latin America. In fact, earlier this year, Shanghai Petrochemical was the first company out of China to do an ADR offering and listing on the NYSE. We expect that, within the next eighteen months, somewhere between twelve to twenty companies from China will have ADR programs here. In fact, we are currently working on four ADR programs for Chinese companies. Hong Kong is also another fast growth market for ADRs. Out of the top fifty companies in Hong Kong, forty-three have ADR programs, all of which have been established over the last year.

We are projecting that, by the end of 1993, there will be about 251 companies with ADR programs listed here on one of the exchanges. The majority of these companies are listed on the NYSE. Again, the type of ADR program that is used to list on an exchange is either a Level II or a Level III ADR. In order to list, as was discussed by Bill Decker and Frode Jensen, essentially you have to comply with U.S. accounting and disclosure standards, just like any other U.S. company would.

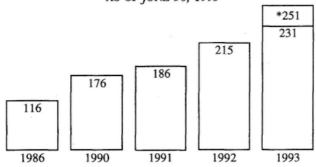

TOTAL NUMBER OF LISTED DEPOSITARY RECEIPT
PROGRAMS ON NYSE, AMEX AND NASDAQ
AS OF JUNE 30, 1993

*Year-end projection

There are a couple of reasons for the rapid pick-up in listings. One is, many companies that established Level I programs two or three years ago had a very favorable experience in the U.S. marketplace and are now upgrading to a listing on an exchange. The second reason is that many companies are simply coming into the market, skipping Level I and Level II ADRs, and doing public offerings straight-away to take advantage of the favorable market conditions that exist today.

For 1993, we are projecting about U.S.$182 billion worth of ADRs will trade here on one of the exchanges. That is up significantly compared to 1992, when U.S.$125 billion worth of ADRs traded.

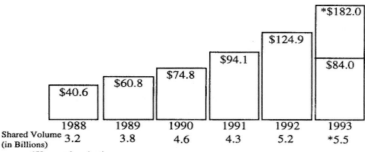

ANNUAL DOLLAR VOLUME OF DEPOSITARY RECEIPTS
LISTED ON NYSE, AMEX AND NASDAQ (TRADING VOLUME
IN BILLIONS OF DOLLARS)

*Year-end projection
■ Trading volume data is for Depositary Receipts listed on exchanges only.
During the first six months of 1993, this accounted for 231 of tthe total 953 programs.

There are a couple of reasons for this. First, which is pretty obvious, there are more listings. The more listings, the more trading volume. But what I think is more important is that we have seen a clear trend over the last few years where domestic portfolio managers—of pension money, mutual funds, etc.—are starting to invest internationally by using ADRs. They are not buying shares directly overseas, but their first steps into this market for traditional domestic portfolio managers will always be through the ADR mechanism. We also see a lot of retail interest in ADRs. Approximately 30% of the ADR trading volume is by retail investors.

This chart below shows some of the most actively traded ADRs in the United States. About U.S.$16 billion of Royal Dutch ADRs were traded in the United States last year. One of the things I always hear is that large institutional investors don't buy ADRs, that only retail investors buy ADRs. Well, I don't know about you, but my family clearly does not buy U.S.$15 billion worth of securities. So the message is that large institutional investors do buy ADRs and they actively trade ADRs.

TOP 20 SPONSORED DEPOSITARY RECEIPTS*
AS OF JUNE 30, 1993

Company	Country	Share Volume	Dollar Volume	Exchange
Glaxo Holdings	U.K.	274,799,000	$5,253,110,494	NYSE
Telefonos de Mexico Ser L	Mexico	254,317,200	12,930,880,394	NYSE
Royal Dutch Petroleum	Netherlands	174,911,200	15,591,366,306	NYSE
Hanson PLC	U.K.	160,747,800	2,879,921,644	NYSE
British Petroleum	U.K.	116,782,000	6,089,377,100	NYSE
Ericsson Telephone "B" Shares LM	Sweden	88,625,500	3,256,187,231	NASDAQ
SmithKline Beecham	U.K.	58,637,400	1,768,871,875	NYSE
Wellcome PLC	U.K.	52,861,600	646,370,044	NYSE
Memorex Telex	Netherlands	49,692,800	22,747,031	NASDAQ
Unilever	Netherlands	45,730,700	5,028,425,044	NYSE
Senetek PLC	U.K.	45,146,100	117,389,408	NASDAQ
News Corporation	Australia	45,115,700	1,854,475,500	NYSE
YPF S.A.	Argentina	43,407,400	957,675,763	NYSE
Reuters Holdings	U.K.	42,473,300	2,583,684,525	NASDAQ
Phillips	Netherlands	38,353,100	532,210,944	NYSE
Imperial Chemical Industries	U.K.	36,586,300	2,235,510,356	NYSE
TOTAL "B" Shares	France	36,251,800	848,214,713	NYSE
Repsol	Spain	28,898,900	706,565,350	NYSE
Telefonica de Espana	Spain	27,472,200	903,727,956	NYSE
Automated Security (Holdings)	U.K.	27,202,800	128,727,131	NYSE

* by Share Volume

For 1993, we are projecting that there will be about thirty-five public offerings, Level III-type ADRs, which is up significantly since 1992. There are a couple of reasons. One is privatizations; many countries around the world are going through a privatization exercise, selling off their state enterprises and listing their securities around the world. They do that typically through a public offering in the United States. The other reason is that non-U.S. companies are simply taking advantage of the favorable markets here in the United States, so they're raising capital here. And, in many cases, the capital they are raising here is at a much better cost than it would be in their home country.

For 1993, we are projecting approximately U.S.$8 billion in new capital will be raised by non-U.S. companies. Again, that is up significantly compared to last year. We have also tended to see the size of the offerings increase over the last year or two. As I said, YPF raised U.S.$2.3 billion; Wellcome PLC raised U.S.$1.5 billion last year, so some of these offerings are quite big through ADRs.

III. *RAISING CAPITAL IN U.S. MARKETS*

There are essentially two ways a non-U.S. company can raise capital in the United States: they can make a public offering or make a private placement under Rule 144A.

A. *Public Offerings*

The advantages of doing a public offering are simple. By doing a public offering, the company is going to be treated like any other U.S. company that is traded in the public markets. These issues are going to have access to the fullest possible investor base. Finally, there are virtually no restrictions on the resale of the securities in the United States. So they are taking optimal advantage of the U.S. public markets by making a public offering.

However, public offerings are not without their disadvantages. The lead-in time may be prohibitive. As Bill Decker mentioned, it can be done in six months; but compare that to a Rule 144A [private] offering, which can be done in two months or less.

Secondly, costs are higher. Because a public offering requires SEC registration, the cost can be substantial for some companies, depending on their internal accounting records, acquisitions they have made in the past, etc. You can easily expect if you are doing a public offering for the bill to run anywhere between U.S.$500,000 to U.S.$1 million.

* * *

B. *Private Placement Offerings under Rule 144A*

Let me describe Rule 144A in laymen's terms. Basically, a company can make a private placement to Qualified Institutional Buyers ("QIBs") here in the United States. Because it is a private placement the company does not have to register with the SEC. They do usually issue an offering memorandum that describes the company and other factors that are relevant to the offering, and some financial information as well, but they do not have to register or conform to U.S. accounting or U.S. disclosure requirements.

Once the offering is done and the private placement offering is completed to these QIBs, the so-called large investors can trade these 144A depositary receipts among themselves. They don't have to wait two or three years to get out of it; they're not restricted in that sense; they can sell their ADRs to another QIB—or, probably more importantly, under Regulation S, they can cancel the ADR and sell the actual shares back into the home country.

Typically, a 144A offering will be for a company that is not in a position to register with the SEC in the United States, or is making a worldwide global offering and simply wants to raise a small amount of money in the United States. A "small amount of money" could be anywhere from U.S.$30 to U.S.$50 million. Once they get past the U.S.$50 million mark, it becomes difficult to place the shares under 144A, and more than likely the company will do a public offering if they want to enter the U.S. market.

A lot of companies also use Rule 144A as a stepping stone into the U.S. market. What I mean by that is once a company does a 144A offering, they can either at a later stage upgrade through listing a different ADR program on the NYSE, or they can do what is known as an exchange offer, where essentially they take their privately placed securities, register them with the SEC, and the securities become freely traded on one of the exchanges.

Private placements under 144A offer an issuer many advantages. First, a placement under 144A involves a relatively short lead-in time of only a couple of months. Second, 144A private placements do not require SEC registration, so the cost is substantially lower than doing a public offering. I should not say "substantially lower" any longer. There have been some 144A deals that have been done where it would have been more cost advantageous to do a public deal rather than a 144A deal.

There are, however, certain disadvantages to Rule 144A. It is a private placement; you only can sell your securities to QIBs. Even though 144A was intended to create a resale market among these large institutional investors, the fact of the matter is the market has not developed to the extent that people thought it would. Companies can use Rule 144A to raise a small amount of capital, but they are not going to be able to build a trading market here under 144A.

One of the innovations that has occurred on this side to help overcome the shortcomings of a 144A offering, especially as it relates to restrictions on resales and liquidity, is that now, typically, companies also establish what is known as a Level I ADR for the U.S. public markets that trades side-by-side with a 144A program. You have to be careful when you take this approach that you have the proper safeguards built into both the Level I and the 144A facility so that there's no leakage between the two programs.

In 1993 the 144A market basically died. In 1991 and 1992 it was pretty substantial. In 1992, about U.S.$3.8 billion was raised in equity under 144A ADR offerings. This year it is probably going to be somewhere around U.S.$500 million. The reason is that companies are learning that if they really want to take advantage of the U.S. markets, they have to do a public offering.

144A DEPOSITARY RECEIPT MARKET

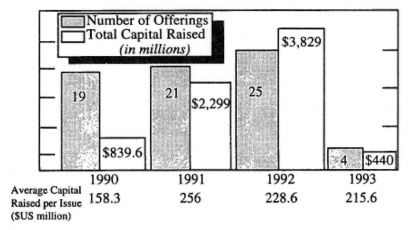

	1990	1991	1992	1993
Average Capital Raised per Issue ($US million)	158.3	256	228.6	215.6

■ In the first six months of 1993, there were 5 Depositary Receipt private offerings; 4 of which were Rule 144A.

There are some companies for whom it still makes good sense to do a 144A offering, but more and more companies are realizing that, "Yes, we could raise some money in the United States, but we're not going to be able to build a liquid market for our shares here under 144A." So they are doing public offerings instead.

Here are some sample 144A deals that have happened over the last couple of years.

SAMPLE 144A TRANSACTIONS

Date	Company	Amt. ($mm)	Industry	Type of DR Offering
12/90	U.K. Generating Cos.	575	Utility	U.S. Only
3/91	U.K. Regional Electric Cos.	175	Utility	U.S. Only
4/91	Vitro	37	Glass	U.S. Only
5/91	Samsung Electronics	35	Electronics	Global
6/91	STET	25	Telecommunications	U.S. Only
12/91	Grupo Situr	51	Hotel/Leisure	Global
3/92	Telecom Argentina	270	Telecommunications	Global
4/92	Australian Consolidated Press	23	Publishing	U.S. Only
4/92	Cemex	461	Cement	Global
5/92	Reliance Industries	150	Conglomerate	Global
6/92	Asia Cement	61	Cement	Global
10/92	Roche Holdings	275	Chemical	U.S. Only
10/92	Philippine Telephone	316	Telecommunications	Global
7/93	Woolworths Limited	27	Specialty Retailing	Global

IV. *ROLE OF THE DEPOSITARY*

The last thing I want to talk to you about is the role of the depositary. A depositary bank, such as The Bank of New York, has basically three roles.

First, we act as the depositary bank. That means that we are responsible for assisting the brokers who trade ADRs—such as Merrill Lynch, Goldman Sachs, First Boston—in issuing and canceling ADRs. As I described earlier, when somebody buys Glaxo shares in London and they decide to issue ADRs, they deposit them with The Bank of New York, and we issue the ADRs. That function is called a depositary function. Those types of transactions account for about ten to fifteen percent of the trading volume in ADRs.

Second, the depositary bank basically acts as the non-U.S. company's transfer agent in the United States. As transfer agent, the depositary bank is responsible for maintaining shareholder records, disbursing dividend payments, sending out proxy notices, etc. So the same type of functions we would perform for a U.S. company as a transfer agent, we perform for a company with an ADR program.

The last function of the depositary bank is that of an administrator. Basically, we help the company understand how to reach U.S. investors and how to promote their securities in the U.S. market; we help them put on "road shows" in the United States, i.e. investor presentations; 19 and, more importantly, we are constantly supplying the company with information regarding their ADR program—which brokers are trading their ADRs, what price they're trading at, how many ADRs are outstanding, and who their shareholders are.

* * *

8B. *1997 IMF Report on Emerging Economy Capital Markets*

Although this IMF report was issued after the Mexican financial crisis we talk about in the next chapter, the excerpt gives you a good snapshot of what the capital markets were all about for emerging economies in the mid-1990s. Although the excerpt contains lots of IMF-speak, don't let that scare you away from understanding important themes. How many of them can you find? As you go on your hunt, think about the components of the international capital markets discussed in the excerpt: foreign direct investment, portfolio investment, the bond and equity markets, and international bank lending.

IMF, "International Capital Markets: Developments,
Prospects, and Key Policy Issues" (1997)

Annex I

Recent Developments in Emerging Capital Markets

As the effects of the Mexican peso crisis on investor sentiment continued to wane, a number of factors helped propel private capital flows to the emerging markets from $192.8 billion in 1995 to a new peak of $235.2 billion during 1996. These factors included, first, the low level of interest rates in Japan and Germany and the compression of corporate bond spreads in the United States, which prompted fixed-income investors in the mature markets to move down the credit spectrum and search for higher yields on emerging market debt. Second, improved economic performance in many emerging markets reduced perceived credit risks. Third, institutional investors in the mature markets continued to seek the benefits of portfolio diversification in the emerging markets. Fourth, innovations in financial markets improved the ability of investors to manage exposures and risks to emerging markets, increasing the attractiveness of such investments. Fifth, continued financial and capital account liberalization in many emerging markets encouraged inflows. Finally, improvements in the availability and quality of information on emerging markets facilitated improved asset selection and assessment.

Underlying the surge of total private flows in 1996 were both strong foreign direct investment (FDI) and portfolio flows. FDI continued to grow rapidly, representing the largest component of flows, while portfolio flows almost doubled. As portfolio flows rebounded vigorously, bank lending flows fell off, though they continued to grow strongly to particular regions, such as Asia. Across the emerging markets, during 1996 and into 1997, investor sentiment shifted away from Asia in view of the regional slowdown, concerns about the current account deficits of some countries, and uneasiness about the state of the property and financial sectors, in favor of Latin America, where growth picked up, inflation slowed, and there was visible progress in strengthening and restructuring banking systems. The growth of total flows to Asia moderated, while flows to Latin America more than doubled, rising above the previous highs of 1993. While flows to the Middle East and Europe grew strongly, flows to Africa and the transition economies declined. As through the first half of the decade, the aggregate reserves of the emerging market countries continued to grow during 1996, and almost half of the net inflows were accumulated as reserves. Compared with the turbulence during late 1994 and 1995, emerging foreign exchange markets were relatively calmer in 1996 and early 1997. Though certain systemically important emerging markets remained susceptible to speculative attack, these pressures remained localized. In mid-May 1997, however, as the Thai baht came under severe speculative attack, pressures spilled over to a number of other countries, both within and outside the region, where international investors saw parallels in economic circumstance and structure.

The surge in portfolio flows during 1996 was associated with a spectacular boom in emerging debt markets, while emerging equity markets continued to recover from the trough following the Mexican crisis. There were dramatic improvements in the liquidity of emerging debt markets and steep reductions in the volatility of returns on both debt and equity markets. The bond market rally sparked a sharp shift in the structure of emerging market primary external financing toward increased bond issuance and a reduced reliance on syndicated bank lending. Spreads on new bond issues fell across the board, while maturities lengthened. The favorable environment encouraged a number of new entrants into the market and led several borrowers to restructure existing liabilities at improved terms. By early 1997 spreads on emerging market debt had declined to their previous historic lows—of late 1993 and early 1994—leading to concerns that yields may have reached their lower limits in adequately compensating for risk. Although trading activity continued to increase, returns fell off sharply during the first quarter of 1997. Expected returns on emerging market equity—earnings-price ratios adjusted for growth—rose steadily during 1996 and into 1997, buoyed by upward revisions to forecasts of growth, while volatility declined. Adjusted for volatility, returns, particularly in Latin America, looked increasingly favorable relative to those in the mature markets. The increase in emerging market equity prices during 1996 accelerated in the first quarter of 1997, again particularly in Latin America. In the international syndicated loan market, a reduced demand for bank financing by emerging market borrowers coincided with rising supply, and strong competition among banks created considerable pressures on pricing and weakened loan structures, also raising concerns as to whether risks were being sufficiently priced. Refinancings accounted for almost a fifth of new syndications of medium-and long-term loans in 1996, and over a third in Latin America.

This annex discusses emerging market financing, with a focus on recent developments during 1996–97. The first section discusses net capital flows in the balance of payments, the behavior of international reserves, and developments in foreign exchange markets. The following sections discuss developments in emerging debt markets, equity markets, mutual funds dedicated to emerging markets, and international bank lending.

Capital Flows, Reserves, and Foreign Exchange Markets

Capital Flows in the Balance of Payments

In spite of several unfavorable developments, total private capital flows to emerging markets during the 1990s have proven remarkably resilient . . . Increases in interest rates in the mature markets during the course of

1994, the Mexican peso crisis and "Tequila" (contagion) effects that followed, and occasional high volatility in the mature assets markets all had only temporary and localized effects on these flows. Similarly, during 1996 the strong performance of many of the mature equity markets, uncertainties relating to the course of interest rates in the mature markets, and perceived vulnerabilities in some of the systemically important emerging market countries failed to deter the overall volume of private flows to emerging markets, which grew by 22 percent to a new record of $235.2 billion. For the first time in the 1990s, private capital flows to the emerging markets exceeded total (private plus official) capital flows in 1996, and $13.2 billion in net repayments of official flows meant that total capital flows actually declined from $232.0 billion in 1995 to $222.0 billion in 1996. Net official flows were negative not only to Latin America, reflecting the substantial repayments by Mexico of the official assistance extended in the aftermath of the crisis, but also to the Middle Eastern, European, and transition economies.

A key characteristic of the surge in private capital inflows to the emerging markets during the 1990s, and one that has been critical in underpinning the resilience of total private flows during the period, has been the steady growth of FDI flows. Encouraged by continued capital account liberalization and the easing risks of a reversal of sentiment against the emerging markets have concomitantly diminished and that, were such a reversal to occur, the consequences would not be severe. Underlying this belief are several notions. First, that FDI flows, by their nature, tend to be "long-term," in that they are driven by positive longer-term sentiment in favor of emerging markets and, therefore, less likely to be reversed than relatively "short-term" portfolio flows. Second, since FDI entails physical investment in plant and equipment, it would, in fact, be difficult to reverse.

* * *

The events surrounding the Mexican crisis certainly help support this view. Even as portfolio flows to Latin America switched from a net inflow of $60.8 billion during 1994 to a net outflow of $7.5 billion in 1995, substantial net inflows of FDI continued, declining only modestly, from $21.5 billion to $19.9 billion. However, there are a number of features of both the data on FDI flows, and the historical behavior of FDI flows, that suggest caution in interpreting the growth in importance of such flows as imparting an enduring resilience to capital flows to emerging markets.

Several factors suggest that the proportion of FDI in total flows as measured by balance of payments data may overstate the importance of these flows. First, the balance of payments differentiation between FDI flows and portfolio flows is arbitrary. Foreign investment in the equity of a company above a critical proportion of outstanding equity is classified as FDI, whereas that below the critical threshold is classified as portfolio equity investment. In reality, small differences above the critical level are unlikely to represent any substantially longer-term intentions of the investor, as compared with those below. Second, if the foreign company undertaking the FDI borrows locally to finance the investment, say from a local bank, depending on the form of incorporation of the company locally, the setup of the plant may count as FDI while the bank lending could show up as a capital outflow, reducing the proportion of net bank lending in overall flows and raising the proportion of FDI flows. Finally, there are sometimes tax or regulatory advantages to rerouting domestic investment through offshore vehicles and these factors have likely overstated the growth of FDI in recent years. The most commonly cited example of such rerouting of domestic investment is that by Chinese enterprises through Hong Kong, because of the tax advantages of doing so. With regard to the reversibility of FDI flows, while it may, in principle, be more difficult and expensive to sell physical rather than portfolio assets, physical assets, nevertheless, can still be sold, albeit typically at a discount, and in the end the sentiment for reversal will be weighed against the discount. There is little reason to expect the discount to always be prohibitive . . . [R]esearch indicates that, historically, for both industrial and developing countries, FDI and other flows labeled "long-term" according to the traditional balance of payments definition have generally been as volatile as, and no more predictable than, flows labeled "short-term."

* * *

Foreign Exchange Markets

A cornerstone of macroeconomic management in most emerging markets in response to the surge in capital inflows during the 1990s has been sustained central bank intervention to prevent nominal exchange rate appreciation, and emerging market currencies have, with few exceptions, either been pegged or depreciated in nominal terms over the period . . . In response to episodes of reversals in flows, authorities have relied on their reserve holdings to resist downward pressures on nominal exchange rates. Since the adjustment of real exchange rates can take place through the adjustment of either nominal exchange rates or domestic prices, preventing nominal exchange rate adjustment shifts the pressure to domestic prices. Forcing adjustment through goods prices can—if goods prices are slow to adjust—reduce the volatility of real exchange rates in the event that the sources of pressure for change—capital flows—themselves tend to be reversed frequently. An important consideration, therefore, is the nature of the capital flows—whether they are temporary and likely to be reversed or they are of a more permanent nature. The substantial buildup of reserves during the 1990s, and the limiting of nominal exchange rate movements, suggests that capital inflows into the emerging markets have tended to be treated as short term. The strategy of intervention and of limiting nominal exchange rate movements has increasingly given rise to uncertainty on the part of market participants as to the sustainability and future course of exchange rate management.

* * *

Bond Markets

Several factors acted in concert to create a spectacular rally in emerging debt markets during 1996. These included, first and perhaps foremost, the low-yield environment in the mature markets. While interest rates remained at low levels in Japan and Germany, there was a compression of spreads on the U.S. corporate bond market as improved business prospects lowered perceived corporate credit risk. This spurred fixed-income investors from the mature markets to search for higher yields on emerging debt markets during 1996 and into 1997. Second, improvements in underlying fundamentals in many emerging markets resulted in both formal upgrades of sovereign credit ratings and in perceptions of reduced credit risks. Third, the continued diversification of the portfolios of institutional investors from the mature markets into the emerging markets boosted the ongoing process of securitization in international capital markets. Fourth, Japanese and European retail interest in emerging market debt continued to be sustained at high levels.

The coincidence of these factors interacted to reinforce interest in emerging debt markets. First, as lower perceived credit risks narrowed spreads, one of the ways investors sought to pick up yield was to seek out longer-maturity issues. This favorable environment prompted several sovereign borrowers to launch new issues to restructure existing liabilities at improved terms and reduce refinancing risk by extending the maturity profile of their external debt. This further lowered perceived credit risks, reinforcing demand and narrowing spreads. By creating more comprehensive yield curves for emerging market debt, the new, longer-term sovereign issues improved the ability of international investors to manage, diversify, and hedge their exposures, enhancing the desirability of these instruments. These issues also set benchmarks for domestic corporate bonds, thereby increasing the access of these entities to international bond markets. Second, the decline in spreads also led investors to move down the credit spectrum in search of higher yields, facilitating the entrance of several new—that is, first-time—borrowers, both sovereign and corporate, hence increasing the size and breadth of the market. Finally, increased investor interest was associated with dramatic improvements in the liquidity of emerging debt markets, enhancing the attractiveness of these instruments.

* * *

Equity Markets

As several of the mature equity markets reached new highs in 1996, emerging equity markets continued to recover from the trough in early 1995, though cumulative returns since the peak in 1994 remained negative. The effects of the Mexican crisis continued to fade, and the volatility of equity prices—in both Latin America and Asia—subsided during 1996 and into 1997 to levels prior to the crisis, while the recovery of economic prospects in Latin America boosted forecasts of earnings growth. These factors combined to make emerging market equity look increasingly attractive relative to the mature markets, and price increases in Latin America accelerated in early 1997. The recovery in emerging equity markets in 1996 was accompanied by increased liquidity for most markets as turnover rose but new issuance remained subdued. While overall flotations of new equity by the emerging markets continued to decline, there were marked differences across regions, as placements by Latin American entities rebounded while those by Asian entities fell. There was an increased reliance on international issuance across regions, however, and the volume of international issuance increased.

* * *

. . . Equity funds continue to represent the majority of funds, around 90 percent in 1996, though this share has declined steadily from an estimated 98 percent in 1990, while the share of bond funds, which account for almost all of the remainder, has steadily increased from 2 to 10 percent, and multi-asset funds have remained negligible. Bond funds have been more significant among the dedicated "emerging market" and Latin American funds, where their shares had risen to 19 and 17 percent, respectively. Among Asian funds, on the other hand, bond funds continue to represent a modest share, around 3 percent at end—1996.

Figure 31. Emerging Market Mutual Funds (in billions of U.S. dollars)

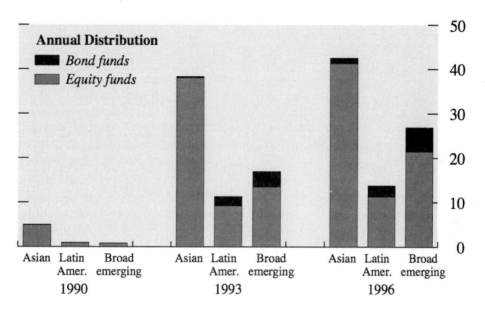

International Bank Lending

Syndicated Loans

The international syndicated loan market for emerging market borrowers during 1996 and the first quarter of 1997 was, albeit to differing extents across regional segments, characterized by moderating demand for bank lending that coincided with a rising supply of loanable funds. This mismatch created considerable downward pressure on pricing and caused loan structures to weaken. The favorable pricing of emerging market bonds caused borrowers increasingly to turn away from bank lending in favor of the longer maturities and less burdensome restrictions offered by fixed-income instruments, while favorable conditions in the loan market itself encouraged refinancing, which accounted for almost a fifth of new medium- and long-term syndications. On the other hand, the low level of interest rates in the mature markets and the tightening of interest margins on loans in these markets caused banks to look increasingly to the emerging markets for higher yields. The resulting intense competition among banks for lending to emerging market entities pushed down spreads, cut fees, increased tenor, and resulted in a weakening of loan covenants.

Following the sharp increase in syndicated bank lending to emerging markets during 1995 of over 36 percent due to the increased costs of borrowing on bond and equity markets in the aftermath of the Mexican crisis, the total volume of syndicated lending rose more modestly during 1996 by 6.4 percent to $79.7 billion . . . Lending to Asian countries continued to grow robustly, however, increasing by 22 percent and accounting for the largest share of bank lending, 62 percent in 1996, up from 54 percent in 1995. Lending to the European emerging markets also rose strongly, increasing by 9.0 percent, while the volume of loans extended to Latin America grew more modestly, by 5.4 percent, and declined to Africa and the Middle East. In the first quarter of 1997, the total volume of syndicated lending to the emerging markets dropped off by 2.4 percent relative to the average quarterly pace during 1996. Lending to the European emerging markets fell sharply, to half its pace during 1996, while lending to Asia (–2.4 percent) and the Middle East (–1.6 percent) declined moderately. By contrast, loan volumes to Latin America picked up, growing by a strong 38 percent, and lending to Africa recovered. The proportion of refinancings in new syndications for emerging market entities grew from the unusually high level of 17 percent in 1995 to 19 percent in 1996 (Table 20), with particularly strong increases to Latin America, Europe, and the Middle East. Average interest margins on new loans to the emerging markets as a whole, after having risen modestly in 1995, declined from 105 basis points to 88 basis points in 1996 (Table 20). The rise in spreads during 1995 had been localized to loans to Latin American entities, while average spreads on loans to the other emerging market regions had narrowed. The compression of spreads during 1996 was most evident in the Latin American and European emerging markets, where margins sometimes fell to levels close to those of the most highly rated international borrowers, again raising concerns as to whether risks were being mispriced.

During 1996, refinancings accounted for around 36 percent of new medium- and long-term syndications to Latin America, while average margins on loans declined steeply, from 181 basis points in 1995 to 109 basis points. An example of the levels to which competition pushed spreads was provided in September by the five-year $500 million refinancing loan by Codelco, a Chilean copper conglomerate, which priced at LIBOR plus 22.5 basis points. The proportion of refinancings in new syndications to Latin America moderated in the first quarter of 1997 to 27 percent, margins appeared to bottom out, and average margins remained unchanged. The deterioration in loan covenants, such as restrictions on the gearing ratio of the borrower and the double pledging of assets as collateral, was most evident in mid-1996 when three unsecured loans by Argentine companies were put up for syndication without financial covenants. In another unprecedented deal, in December 1996 the Central Bank of Argentina arranged a collateralized $6.1 billion contingent repo facility with international private sector banks to provide liquidity to the domestic banking system.

Average margins on loans to the European emerging markets fell from 131 basis points in 1995 to 88 basis points in 1996, and further to 73 basis points in the first quarter of 1997. The National Bank of Hungary pushed pricing to an all-time low for the region by refinancing a $350 million loan, priced at LIBOR plus 50 basis points signed in August 1996, at LIBOR plus 20 basis points in December. This rapid decline, also enjoyed by other Hungarian borrowers, coincided with the country's membership in the OECD, which reduced capital requirements for lenders against loans to various Hungarian entities. The keen competition among banks for high-yielding loans was evidenced in April 1997 by the $2.5 billion syndication for Gazprom, the Russian gas and oil company, which priced at LIBOR plus 200 basis points and was three times oversubscribed.

Table 20. Emerging Market Medium-and Long-Term Syndicated Loan Commitments: Interest Margins and Refinancings

	1990	1991	1992	1993	1994	1995	1996	1997:Q1
				(In basis points)				
Interest margins[1]								
Emerging markets	56	80	103	90	100	105	88	92
Africa	84	119	106	53	126	91	46	37
Asia	56	88	99	84	94	85	85	104
Europe	47	106	112	105	162	131	88	73
Middle East	98	51	86	109	91	60	83	72
Western Hemisphere	74	88	113	127	58	181	109	98
				(In percent)				
Refinancings								
Emerging markets	3.1	10.5	4.1	4.9	7.5	16.6	18.5	18.4
Africa	—	37.3	—	—	5.6	48.5	19.8	51.9
Asia	2.3	4.3	6.6	5.6	7.7	16.0	16.5	17.4
Europe	4.4	3.6	3.4	2.2	2.4	3.7	13.0	3.9
Middle East	—	0.8	—	13.4	4.3	0.9	14.7	—
Western Hemisphere	5.8	28.4	2.9	2.7	24.0	22.5	36.3	26.5

The robust growth of syndicated lending to the Asian emerging markets was underpinned by the continued expansion of lending to the financial and property sectors and for infrastructure financing. Infrastructure financing increasingly took the form of project finance which, by allowing for a separation of risks specific to the project from the overall balance sheet of the parent company, can provide higher yields. Project finance accounted for 32 percent of medium-and long-term syndications to the region during 1996. In terms of the number of project financing arrangements worldwide, the emerging markets of Indonesia, Thailand, China, India, and Hong Kong, China, have been among the top 10 most active countries in the world. These have included projects in power, telecommunications, water, and transport. Project financing has been particularly popular in Hong Kong, China, with the largest number of deals outside the United States, driven by the surge in building ahead of the territory's handover to China this year. Compared with the sharp pickups in the share of refinancings in total syndications to Latin America and the European emerging markets during 1996, the share in Asia remained steady at around 16 percent and was essentially unchanged in the first quarter of 1997. Average interest margins on syndicated lending to Asia remained unchanged in 1996 at 85 basis points, then rose to 103 basis points in the first quarter of 1997.

* * *

CHAPTER 9

THE MEXICAN CRISIS

∎∎∎

Now that we have a basic understanding of capital markets, especially in the 1990s, in the next two chapters we'll look at two major financial crises: the 1994–1995 Mexican financial crisis, and the 1998 Asian financial crisis. To better understand these chapters, we recommend that you review the essentials of balance of payments in supplement 1A.

In the 1990s, capital flows became increasingly volatile as a result of the growing importance and influence of private institutional investors. They manage massive flows of quickly moving short-term capital called portfolio investment or "hot money." The 1994–1995 Mexican financial crisis will show you how portfolio investment can leave a country in economic ruin.

The crisis raised lots of questions. How did Mexico contribute to the crisis? What was the IMF's role in the crisis and did it make mistakes? (Check out supplement 9A.) How about the United States? Why didn't the U.S. let Mexico resolve the crisis on its own with the help of the IMF? Was the bailout really about bailing out Mexico or about bailing out (U.S.) foreign investors?

To understand what happened in the 1994–1995 Mexican crisis, we need to get some basics under our belt. We'll start with institutional investors.

Part One: Institutional Investors

The major development in the private international capital markets in the 1990s was the significant rise in portfolio investment—hot money—in developing countries. After Mexico's debt crisis of the 1980s (see Chapter 5), it, like other debtor countries, turned to bonds—in Mexico's case "tesobonos" (which we'll explain in a minute). Who bought Mexico's bonds? Institutional investors making portfolio investments. It was the thing to do back in the day: Portfolio investment went through the roof, increasing more than eleven-fold from the late 1980s to 1993.

Portfolio Investment

Portfolio investment differs from foreign direct investment (FDI). With FDI, the investors take an equity stake in the company. This means the investor's and the company's other ownership interests are linked together for the long term. In return for this stability of ownership, the foreign direct investor gets a degree of influence over the management of the business enterprise. Portfolio investments are assets in the form of marketable securities (debt and equity) generally held for a short term and are more liquid than FDI. Investors can sell the securities almost instantly. The share of institutional investment in emerging markets increased big time in the 1990s. Until the Mexican financial crisis in 1995, institutional investors accounted for sixty-six percent of gross capital inflows into Latin America, while FDI accounted for only thirty percent. Many of the institutional investors in Latin America were from the United States, and most of their money found its way to Mexico, which was in the midst of market-based reforms—remember, the 1990s was the decade of the "market-friendly" approach to development.

Portfolio investment in emerging markets was much more volatile than FDI. For example, while portfolio flows into Mexico went from a net inflow of $60.8 billion in 1994 to a net capital outflow of $7.5 billion in 1995, FDI only fell from $21.5 billion to $19.9 billion over the same time span. Despite the 1994–1995 crisis, foreign direct investors still saw the real growth possibilities in Mexico. Given that Mexico rebounded relatively quickly from the crisis, the foreign direct investors' long-term strategy appeared to pay off.

Of the various institutional investors in the 1990s, pension funds, mutual funds, and insurance companies became the most prominent players in the capital markets of the developed countries. Hedge funds (risky investment vehicles used by really rich people and institutions to make—or lose—lots of money) also became an important player in the world of institutional investing. Large institutional investors made up an even larger part of the investor base in the world's financial markets, which translated into increased market power. United States institutional investors easily controlled the largest pool of funds among the OECD countries (comprised of advanced and emerging economies), with pension funds and insurance companies being the major players.

The Role of Institutional Investors

Why are institutional investors so prevalent in the financial marketplace? You never put all your eggs in one basket, right? The same rule applies to investments—you don't put all of your money into, say, Facebook. You diversify—find other companies to invest in as well. The large institutional investor allows a small investor—let's call her Juanita—to spread her money across a wider range of financial instruments than she could do individually. Juanita would have to pay too much in—get ready for economist speak—transaction costs (i.e., the costs in time and money incurred in researching, making, managing, withdrawing, or transferring investments) when spreading only a modest amount of money over a number of different investments. The institutional investor pools together an enormous number of small investors like Juanita. Measured against the size of this pool of money, the transaction costs of diversification drop greatly. So check it out, if ten private investors individually invested their money in diversified portfolios, each of them would incur transaction costs in making those investments. If those ten investors pool their money together and have their investment managed by a single financial firm, then—assuming their money is invested identically—the totality of transaction costs will be one tenth of what they would've been had they invested individually. Isn't that neat?

The Risks to Host Countries

The small investor poses little danger to the market, or even to a particular stock, because the investor's percentage of ownership is so small. Even the sale of a small investor's entire holdings in a modestly sized publicly traded company won't trigger a large-scale sale of the stock. But then, take your large institutional investors, they can cause large price swings in a particular stock with a large purchase or sale. A large investor's sale of a big holding in a publicly traded stock can potentially trigger sales by other large investors as the other large investors might think that the investor selling off the holdings has some information indicating the under-performance of the stock. Even if the company doesn't suffer from some mysterious malady (e.g., low earnings), large sales can lead to self-fulfilling prophecies as sale after sale creates the impression that the stock is in trouble. We call that "herd behavior" in the biz—you know, all those buffalo just aren't thinking that rationally (see Chapter 10 for more info on buffalos).

> *"The former finance minister of Mexico Jesús Silva Herzog characterized this phenomenon as a "twenty-one year old pushing a button," leading to the exit of billions of dollars from Mexico in a matter of seconds in the aftermath of its peso devaluation . . . their behavior was united not by institutional linkages but by the herd mentality."*
>
> —S. N. Katada, Banking on Stability: Japan and the Cross-Pacific Dynamics of International Financial Crisis Management, 158 (2001)

Here's another major risk: Foreign institutional investors can create problems because of the size of their capital inflows into an emerging economy. Why? Because a large influx of foreign capital—e.g., U.S. dollars that'll be converted into the domestic currency—can affect the value of the domestic currency. If the value of the domestic currency "floats," that is, the currency's value is determined by the market (supply and demand), then currency traders will pay less for the currency as the incoming capital increases the supply of the currency. If the value of the domestic currency is "pegged" or fixed to the value of a foreign currency, that is, if the country of Venala tells the world that it will exchange six sucras (its currency) for one dola, the strongest currency in the world ("hard currency"), then an increase in the money supply will not be met with a change in, i.e., lowering of, the traded price of the sucra. The greater the difference between the fixed value of the sucra and its perceived "true" value—meaning it's "overvalued," the greater the potential for attacks on the sucra by currency speculators. They'll bet that Venala eventually will be forced to "devalue," or lower, the value of the sucra. Suppose Venala devalues its currency to, say, eight sucras to the dola. If the speculator borrows (big time) to acquire the sucras and sells the sucras at the 6:1 exchange rate and buys the currency at 8:1, it will profit from the difference in the sell and buy rates (it's the old adage, "sell high, buy low"). The overvaluation also means that the overvalued domestic currency can purchase more imports than it otherwise could. At the same time, the country's exports will suffer because the overvalued currency will make them expensive for consumers abroad. Increased imports combined with decreased exports may lead to troublesome deficits in the country's current account.

What if those capital inflows suddenly reverse themselves resulting in massive outflows? It may be bad news for that developing country. Here are the basic mechanics: The institutional investor sells its investments and receives domestic currency. It then converts the domestic currency into another foreign currency, say the U.S. dollar, and quits the country. Other investors, both foreign and domestic, see this happening and they do the same thing. This is what's called capital flight, and it drains the central bank's reserves, which might make it difficult for the country to service its debt (long- and short-term) denominated in U.S. dollars. To attract more foreign currency reserves, the host country might raise interest rates to make foreign investment more attractive. But this can cause problems for the economy. For example, investment in the economy might head south if borrowing becomes more expensive. We're talking economic slowdown. When the country can least afford it. Now let's get to Mexico's crisis.

Part Two: The 1994–1995 Crisis

The Mexico of the 1990s owes much to the policies of the 1980s. The decade was plagued by inflation, which averaged nearly 70 percent annually, including three years when it exceeded 100 percent (1983, 1987 and 1988). The government pursued statist policies typical of many other Latin American economies. Import tariffs were set at very high rates. Many of Mexico's major industrial sectors were government-dominated monopolies. Like we said in Chapter 5, Mexico borrowed a ton from foreign commercial banks and suffered a significant debt crisis, which led the country to declare a default on its foreign debt in August 1982. After that, Mexico struggled to find new sources of foreign capital—foreign banks said bye-bye, even as capital escaped its borders.

In the late 1980s, Carlos Salinas became President of Mexico. A firm believer in free markets, President Salinas privatized nearly all of Mexico's state-owned industries. These "new" private companies turned to the growing Mexican equities market. Dig it: Portfolio investment increased from an annual average of $5.4 billion for the period 1986–90 to $67.9 billion in 1993 alone. Bottom line, Mexico reduced its dependence on credit debt by turning to equity financing. This level of equity financing in an emerging economy can be both a blessing and a curse.

As foreign investors saw Mexico as a more stable and "user friendly" environment, they increased their holdings of Mexican stocks, all the while bringing more and more capital into Mexico. To further entice foreign investors, the Mexican government put in place a **fixed exchange rate** in the form of a trading band on the peso vis-à-vis the U.S. dollar. In 1987, the band's lower limit was set at MXN 3.0562/USD 1, with an upper limit that was to increase by MXN 0.0004 each day—we call it a "crawling peg" in the biz. By 1993, that upper limit hovered around MXN 3.19.

Destabilization: The Deadly Mix of a Fixed Exchange Rate, Portfolio Investment, and Tesobonos

Because of the increase in the domestic money supply—as, e.g., U.S. dollars were exchanged for pesos—and the peg to the dollar, Mexico's money supply increased without a corresponding decrease in the value of the peso. An overvalued peso increased imports (they became artificially cheaper) and decreased exports (they became artificially more expensive). Going back to balance of payments, when a country spends more on imports than it receives in export proceeds, it has a "current account deficit."

Mexico financed the current account deficit with a surplus in its "capital account." So long as Mexico had a capital account surplus, the current account deficit could be sustained without too much fear of a balance of payments crisis. But here's the thing: the increase in the Mexican money supply fed inflation. The overvalued peso began to strain its peg to the U.S. dollar. Peso-holders began to speculate that the peg didn't reflect economic reality. They figured the government would be forced to devalue the peg. You know what's coming, right? Peso-holders exchanged their pesos for the far more stable U.S. dollar. The speculative exchanges depleted the central bank's foreign currency reserves, and the cycle fed upon itself. The more pesos that were exchanged for U.S. dollars, the less stable the peg became, as holders of pesos feared that the government would run out of U.S. dollars and they would be left holding worthless paper. As a result, still more people exchanged pesos for U.S. dollars, which, in turn, weakened the peg further and nearly erased the central bank's foreign exchange reserves.

The Mexican government accumulated an enormous amount of short-term, dollar denominated debt—U.S. $29.2 billion—by issuing "tesobonos." They were essentially bonds that guaranteed institutional investors that they wouldn't lose money if the Mexican government decided to devalue the peso. Simply stated, the Mexican government owed a lot of people a lot of U.S. dollars, and it was obligated to fully repay its creditors in a short amount of time. You know where this is going, right?

Politics further complicated the situation. Mexico faced an uncertain political future with the assassination of the ruling party's presidential candidate, Luis Donaldo Colosio, in March of 1994, and the assassination of the ruling party's number two man, Jose Francisco Ruiz Massieu, in August of 1994. The ruling party, particularly in the figure of Finance Minister Pedro Aspe, had committed itself to maintaining the peg at all costs. The fear of a ruling party loss in the upcoming elections further undermined the viability of the peg. Although the ruling party survived the August elections, the beginning of Ernesto Zedillo's presidency witnessed violence in **Chiapas** in December of 1994. Uncertainty as to how the President would react prompted the early stages of "capital flight" from Mexico's private capital markets.

Mexico Devalues

The Mexican government finally devalued the peso on December 20, 1994. When a government with a fixed exchange rate regime devalues the currency, it tells the world that it'll no longer purchase its own currency in exchange for a foreign currency at the previously announced exchange rate. The government could then announce a new peg or it could simply let the currency float in the world currency market. The Mexican government chose a new peg. The rate changed from MXN $3.4172 to MXN $4.0016 pesos per dollar, a 15 percent devaluation of the peso.

It's all good, right? Not. Many holders of pesos didn't believe the new peg could survive. More capital fled the country as institutional investors dumped their peso-denominated equities before another anticipated devaluation of the peso. On December 22, 1994, the Mexican government gave up and let the peso float. By March of 1995, the peso was trading at MXN $7.45 pesos to the dollar.

All of this wreaked havoc on Mexico's weakely structured banking sector. The capital flight drained the banks of their U.S. dollar deposits, which caused a liquidity crisis. After the devaluation, the peso value of dollar-denominated loans shot way up. After the devaluation, borrowers of dollar loans would need, say, seven pesos to pay off one dollar rather than three pesos at the pre-devaluation exchange rate. We'll cover capital adequacy in Chapter 11, but for now just understand that banks didn't have enough money to cover possible losses stemming from those suddenly expensive loans. And many of the banks' borrowers began to default—lots of bad loans piling up.

But the immediate problem was Mexico's short-term debt. In 1994, foreigners bought 40% of Mexican treasury notes and held stocks accounting for 30% of market capitalization (where market capitalization is equal to the total current trading value of each outstanding share of stock multiplied by the current trading price of the stock.) When this significant sum of money left the country in anticipation of a devaluation (capital flight,) Mexico's foreign exchange reserves dropped as low as U.S. $6 billion, peanuts for a central bank. But here's the clincher: Just as Mexico's foreign exchange reserves were plummeting its tesobonos were maturing. Big problem!

The Rescue

What was the world to do? Would they show Mexico some tough-love, letting it figure the situation out for itself, or was someone going to jump in and help? Many voices in the United States objected to the idea of a bailout—in their eyes, Mexico *wasn't* too big to fail. Because of the role that institutional investors played in bringing about the crisis, many people felt that a bailout would essentially go straight into the pockets of those investors. And concerns about moral hazard—i.e., bailing out Mexico would just encourage it to follow reckless policies—followed right on the tail of those criticisms. The United States wasn't alone in its reluctance, either. Japanese and European governments were less than thrilled with the idea of a bailout. But Mexico is a major U.S. trading partner, and a prolonged crisis there could have had serious economic and political implications for the United States.

On January 2, 1995, the United States organized a line of credit—U.S. $18 billion—to stabilize the exchange rate. Half of the funds came from the United States, $1 billion from Canada, $5 billion from the Bank for International Settlements (BIS), and $3 billion from foreign commercial banks. The financial package did little to reassure jittery investors because it barely covered the global tesobono debt. As of January 1995, Mexico had sold billions of dollars of tesobonos, the majority of which were owned by foreigners. Part of the Mexican government's initial plan was to issue new bonds with longer maturities and higher interest rates, hoping that the bonds would encourage holders of approximately $10.3 billion in tesobonos to roll them over.

But the bond sell-off continued. On January 12th, the United States proposed a U.S. $40 billion loan-guarantee plan for Mexico, which required Congressional approval. The plan quickly ran into difficulties as various members of the U.S. Congress insisted that Mexico raise its minimum wage, curb illegal immigration, and clamp down on drug trafficking in return for the aid. And some members viewed the loan package as bailing out wealthy investors who gambled in Mexico and lost. Congressional hedging on the recovery plan prompted more investors to sell. The peso collapsed another fifteen percent.

After officially receiving word of the initial plan's political death on January 30th, the Clinton administration, led by U.S. Treasury Secretary Robert Rubin, quickly put together an alternative U.S. $50 billion loan package that by-passed Congress and calmed the markets. Contributions came from the IMF ($18 billion), the BIS ($10 billion), and foreign commercial banks ($3 billion). The package also included $20 billion in U.S. loans and loan guarantees funded by the **Exchange Stabilization Fund**. In the event of default, Mexico agreed to divert proceeds from oil exports to the Federal Reserve Bank of New York.

> *"... there had been a poll in the paper that morning which said that by 79 to 18, the American people were against—strongly against my giving financial assistance to Mexico .... I said, okay, let's don't do it .... Let's tell him, sorry. Then a year from now when Mexico is still reeling, when people have been hurt south of Mexico, when we have another million illegal immigrants, when there are more narcotics coming across the border, when every Mexican hates our guts because they think we're greedy and selfish and uncaring about our neighbors and people ask me what in the daylights are you doing letting this mess develop, my answer is going to be, well, on the day I could have stopped it, there was a poll saying 79 percent of you were against it. And it quieted all the opposition ..."*
> —President Clinton, Council Awards Dinner (2010)

In June 1994, the World Bank approved a U.S. $1.51 billion loan package for Mexico, $1 billion of which was used to help Mexico restructure its banking sector. Remember that Mexico's banks got socked in the crisis. To help them out, the government did three things: (i) to address the withdrawal of deposits, it gave the banks short-term loans to help them with liquidity; (ii) to address low capital levels—raise more money, the government bought debt securities issued by the banks; and (iii) to address the mounting bad loans, the government bought a fraction of those loans from the banks. By way of reforms, the government improved bank regulation, ranging from strengthening bank supervision to establishing new capital adequacy rules.

Meanwhile, the IMF and the Mexican government entered into a stand-by arrangement which in part provided Mexico with an immediate cash injection (**special drawing rights**). Of the nearly $18 billion in total IMF commitments (688.4 percent of Mexico's quota—the highest proportion that'd ever been given), almost $8 billion was available immediately after the agreement was concluded. The Fund made the other $10 billion conditional on Mexico's meeting certain economic performance criteria—good ole conditionality. The criteria were part of an extensive economic reform package which the Mexican government agreed to implement as a condition of receiving the IMF's assistance. The reforms included reduced government expenditures, increased interest rates, and further privatization of state-owned industries.

Ultimately, Mexico was able to survive its liquidity crisis without having to default on its debt obligations. But the IMF's conditions, coupled with the economic problems caused by the peso devaluation, created severe economic hardship throughout the first half of 1995. Still, many in the international financial community thought all of this had to happen to prevent contagion—what became known as the "tequila effect" (a strange label as tequila—especially bad tequila—causes memory loss, not contagion). Mexico's crisis caused stock exchanges in Latin America to plummet, especially in Brazil and Argentina. Investors started pulling their money out of the countries, causing havoc with exchange rates. Even countries outside of Latin America—Hungary, Turkey, Indonesia, Malaysia, and Thailand—starting having problems. There was another reason Mexico had to be saved: The United States and the IMF wanted to reassure developing countries, and the world for that matter, that the "free market" model Mexico had adopted still rocked.

Part Three: The IMF's Post Crisis Adjustments

The speed at which foreign institutional investors fled the Mexican stock market, and the severity of the crisis resulting from the peso devaluation, convinced the IMF that it needed to adjust to the new realities of the global economy. Throughout 1994, the Fund had failed to adequately monitor the financial situation that ultimately devastated the Mexican economy. A United States Government Accounting Office Report revealed the Mexican government had provided outdated and inaccurate financial data to the IMF throughout 1994. Busted! To help prevent future crises, the Fund needed access to more and better information from member governments. The Fund was also worried that if another crisis were to erupt elsewhere, it wouldn't have the financial resources to come to the rescue. With these concerns in mind, the IMF began to consider certain adjustments and improvements to its own operations.

In June of 1995, the leaders of the G-7 (Canada, France, Germany, Italy, Japan, the United Kingdom, and the United States) held their annual meeting in Halifax, Nova Scotia (they discussed the global economy, among other things). The Summit's participants had to confront the fact that the world's financial markets differed radically from the markets of the glory days of the Bretton Woods Conference. Change was the order of the day. The summit leaders called for a number of reforms, including enhanced surveillance to provide early warnings of crises, additional financial mechanisms to help the IMF respond, and a new borrowing arrangement to backstop the Fund.

Data Dissemination

The Mexican crisis prompted the IMF to devise a method to have member countries disclose key economic data to the markets in a timely way. So the Fund encouraged member countries to report monthly on certain core economic indicators, such as exchange rates, international reserves, central bank balance sheet, the external current account balance, external debt/debt service, and **gross domestic product/gross national product**. And the data dissemination standards were born!

The data dissemination standards have three components. The Fund issued the special data dissemination standards (SDDS) in 1996 to guide members in disclosing their macroeconomic data to the public. In 1997, it established the general data dissemination standards (GDDS) to provide guidance to member countries with less developed statistical systems on how to best publish economic data. After the 2008 global financial crisis, it issued the SDDS Plus to address economies with systemically important financial sectors, meaning financial sectors that can negatively affect other financial sectors regionally or globally if they rock or tank. Some of the data include sectoral balance sheets, general government operations and general government gross debt, financial soundness indicators, and debt securities.

The Fund also created the Dissemination Standards Bulletin Board (DSBB), which discloses the SDDS information to the public. The Fund still maintains the DSBB on its website. For countries seeking access to the private international capital markets, the SDDS allows private investors to more accurately assess the risks associated with particular countries. Seventy-one member countries have subscribed and currently meet SDDS specifications for data gathering and publication.

The "Emergency Financing Mechanism" and the New Arrangements to Borrow

The IMF also began to make its surveillance more "continuous." Annually, or occasionally biannually, the Fund visits every member country to engage in what are called "Article IV consultations" during which Fund staff pour over the country's books and, maybe over coffee (or something stronger), have a chat with folks from the central bank and/or ministry of finance about the country's economic policies (see Chapter 3).

The IMF also created the Emergency Financing Mechanism (EFM) in 1995 to provide rapid responses to future financial crises. Limited only to "exceptional circumstances," the emergency financing mechanism enables the Fund to secure rapid Board approval (within 48–72 hours) for loans with streamlined—not gobs of—conditionality. The most recent EFM loans were in 2010 for Greece (SDR 26.4 billion, 3,212 percent of quota) and for Ireland (SDR 19.5 billion, 2,322 percent of quota).

As to the Fund's firepower in future financial crises, it had then been operating under the General Arrangements to Borrow (GAB), which gave the Fund access under exceptional circumstances to SDR 17 billion from central banks of eleven countries, with the approval of the GAB's participant countries. But it needed more if all hell broke loose! Solution? Come up with something new: the New Arrangements to Borrow (NAB). The NAB doubled the amount of SDRs available in a crisis to SDR 34 billion (currently SDR 370.0 billion).

You Gotta Know Something About Them!

Pedro Aspe

During the Mexican Financial Crisis, Pedro Aspe worked as the Minister of Finance for the Mexican government. Today he is the Co-Chairman of Evercore Partners, Inc., an investment bank in the United States, and is the founder and CEO of Protego, another boutique investment bank. If this weren't enough, outside of the finance world Pedro is also an academic. He has served as a professor at the Instituto Tecnológico Autónomo de México in Mexico City since 1995, and is also a member of the Visiting Committee for the Department of Economics at the Massachusetts Institute of Technology.

Carlos Salinas

Image of Carlos Salinas de Gortari is licensed under CC BY 2.0.

Carlos Salinas, Mexico's president from 1988 until 1994, won the 1988 election as a representative for the Institutional Revolutionary Party. He became the youngest president in Mexico's history. During his presidency, Pedro helped Mexico achieve a great deal of economic growth (though this would end in the 1994 financial crisis) and also made Mexico a part of NAFTA. Towards the end of his presidency, both financial and family crises hit hard. In 1994, Salinas' brother, Raul, was accused of ordering the murder of his ex-brother-in-law and political rival Jose Francisco Ruiz Massieu. He was convicted and sentenced to 50 years in jail, though this conviction was overturned a few months later. Just a year later, Raul's wife was arrested for trying to access his bank accounts in Switzerland, which authorities suspected were linked to drug trafficking. Raul himself, then, was formally accused of having acquired hundreds of millions of dollars by illegal means in 1996. To add to this, 2004 saw the murder of Carlos' other brother, Enrique. Although it was clear from the crime scene that Enrique's death had been at the hands of another individual, the case has yet to be solved. Today, Carlos has exiled himself and moved to Ireland, leaving Mexico and the public's resentment for him far in the distance.

Robert Rubin

The son of a lawyer, Robert Rubin was born in New York City and raised in lovely Miami Beach. After he graduated from Harvard College with a degree in economics (highest honors), he started at Harvard Law School but quit after three days! Three days! He preferred blue to crimson, graduating instead from Yale Law School and then spending two years at Cleary, Gottlieb, Steen & Hamilton in New York. But practicing at a blue chip law firm wasn't enough for Robert. He joined Goldman Sachs, and during his 26 years there, he rose to the position of co-chairman. Robert then became President Clinton's connection to Wall Street. Throughout his career as the Secretary of the Treasury in the Clinton administration, Rubin played a part in deregulation of the derivatives market and in repealing the Glass-Steagall Act (separating commercial banking from investment banking). Though at the time he and some other big names (such as Larry Summers and Alan Greenspan) thought that deregulation would rock, many now believe deregulation played a major role in bringing about the financial crisis of 2008. Despite being an incredibly busy man, Robert manages to find the time for a few extracurriculars, including fly-fishing.

What's Up with That?

The Allure of Fixed Exchange Rate Systems in Developing Countries

The central banks of developing countries have often adopted a fixed exchange rate monetary policy. In fact, during the 1990s nearly seventy developing countries were using some variety of fixed exchange rate system. Why? Two key reasons: credibility and reduced rates of inflation. When the central bank of an emerging economy assures the public that its currency may be exchanged for USD or some other hard currency at a fixed rate, foreign and domestic investors are more likely to believe that incurring foreign denominated debt carries little risk. Since the exchange rate is fixed, the weaker currency can (in theory) be exchanged for the stronger currency at a perfectly predictable rate at any time. This stimulates investment and allows the economy to grow. Since the nominal value of the emerging economy's currency is pegged to a hard currency, inflation in the emerging market should, in theory, slow to the rate of inflation of the peg currency, which is often lower and less volatile than the rate of inflation one might expect to see in the emerging market's currency. But we know that when an emerging economy attempts to maintain a fixed exchange rate despite slowing growth and diminishing reserves of hard currency, the results can be disastrous.

Uprising in Chiapas

On January 1, 1994, when the North American Free Trade Agreement (NAFTA) went into effect, the Zapatista National Liberation Army (EZLN) seized cities and towns in Chiapas. Within hours, the army responded, killing over 100 people. The two-year uprising was led by "Subcomandante Marcos," who famously wore a black ski mask. Marcos, who actually was a well-educated a son of a prosperous furniture retailer, aired grievances against NAFTA and neoliberalism in Mexico. He focused on the plight of poor indigenous groups—e.g., over 1 million people, mainly indigenous people, didn't have access to health care. In February 1966, the EZLN signed the San Andres Accords with the Mexican government, which recognized the autonomy of indigenous groups in Mexico.

Exchange Stabilization Fund

The ESF is a reserve fund of the United States Treasury Department used to maintain currency stability. It evolved from the Gold Reserve Act of 1934, which required the Treasury to have a stabilization fund to deal in gold, foreign exchange, and other kinds of credit and securities. It's made up of U.S. dollars, foreign currencies, and SDRs. The Secretary of the Treasury is in charge of all operations of the ESF. Use of the Fund is purely a function of the Execute Branch so Congress has to butt out.

Special Drawing Rights

The SDR plan first began to take shape in March of 1966 when the Managing Director at the time, Pierre-Paul Schweitzer, proposed a reserve-creating plan to apply to all members, to counter fears of a global liquidity shortage of reserve assets. Reserves in U.S. dollars in central banks continued to climb and countries began to restrict international transactions and borrow to meet balance of payments needs. SDRs came into existence on August 6, 1969 (First Amendment of the Articles of Agreement), valued at 0.888671 grams of fine gold (the amount of gold equal to one U.S. dollar). The SDR is not a currency, but rather an artificial reserve asset. It's a potential claim on the currencies of other IMF members. The SDR is the unit of account of the IMF. Today's SDR is defined as a basket of currencies: the pound sterling, the euro, Japanese yen, and the U.S. dollar. This basket composition is reviewed every five years by the Fund's Executive Boards. In November 2010 (the latest review), the weights of the basket currencies were reviewed using the value of exports of goods and services, as well as the amount of reserves of respective currencies held, by other IMF member countries.

GDP Versus GNP

Gross Domestic Product (GDP) and Gross National Product (GNP) both measure the size and strength of the economy but their definition, calculation and applications are different. GDP is a measure of national income, national output and national expenditure produced in a particular country. GNP equals GDP plus net property income from abroad, which includes the value of all goods and services produced by nationals, whether in the country or not.

QUESTIONS FROM YOUR TALKING DOG

1. What are we going to talk about today? Another crisis in Mexico, huh? Okay, where do we start? Portfolio investment. Tell me about it, but put my window down first.

2. And you're saying institutional investors made most of these types of investments? Who were these investors? I know they were institutional. Boy, I walked into that one. What type of institutions?

3. I always thought foreign investment was a good thing. You're telling me it can cause problems, especially portfolio investment? Like how? Does it matter if the host country has a floating or a fixed exchange rate system? Slow down. I wanna take in the changing foliage.

4. So the crisis starts with the reforms after the 1980s debt crisis? That seems ironic.

5. What kind of exchange rate was in place before the crisis?

6. Okay, give me the blow-by-blow. It seems to be all tied to the peg and the . . . the tesobonos—short-term debt. Got it.

7. Devaluation is humiliating, isn't it? I mean, the word itself is grim.

8. And the word "bailout" is pretty interesting. Who was being bailed out?

9. That's amazing. President Clinton just went around Congress after the first rescue package. How did he do that? Clever guy. And he never inhaled . . .

10. I thought you would never get to the IMF. What did it do?

11. I agree. After every crisis there seems to be a lot of hand wringing. "We gotta do something about this!" So go ahead, tell me about stuff that was done after the crisis. When you're finished, let's go to the pumpkin patch. The doggie one. I can't handle little kids right now.

Chapter 9: Supplement

9A. *Lessons from the Mexican Crisis*

Camdesuss's analysis is spot on in many ways. How so? But what's the bottom line in his address? Convincing the world that the IMF is still relevant? Note what he says: "So here again we have a full agenda." Happy times for the Fund?

M. Camdessus, Address: "Drawing Lessons from the Mexican
Crisis: Preventing and Resolving Financial Crises—
the Role of the IMF" (1995)

It is a great pleasure for me to be with you this morning, to share some thoughts on how, as you are considering how to forge a free trade area in the Americas, we in the IMF can create an environment amicable to it, by helping to prevent and resolve the financial crises of the next century. This is certainly the role of the IMF as the central institution of the international monetary system. The recent crisis in Mexico provides a focus for such thoughts. What did it signify, and what are its lessons, for economic policy, for the Americas, for the international community, and for the IMF? But before addressing these questions, we must be clear about how the crisis arose, and how it was managed.

As I shall argue later, the increased challenges we face today in preventing and resolving international financial crises are, paradoxically, to a large extent a consequence of economic progress. Mexico's crisis illustrates this: it can be understood only in the context of the country's economic progress of the past decade. From 1988 to 1993, with the active support of the IMF, Mexico strengthened the process of macroeconomic stabilization and structural transformation that began in the wake of the 1982 debt crisis. Its strategy aimed at attaining external viability and laying the foundations for private-sector-led growth. It was based on tight financial policies; the use of the exchange rate as a nominal anchor; comprehensive structural reforms, including privatization and trade and exchange liberalization; and a major restructuring of external debt.

The result was remarkable success on many fronts. A reduction in the fiscal deficit was achieved that should be an inspiration for many countries. Inflation was reduced from 160 percent in 1987 to 8 percent in 1993. Economic growth recovered from an average not much higher than zero in 1985–88 to 3 percent in 1989–93. The restructuring of external debt paved the way for a resumption of access to international financial markets, and private capital inflows surged, contributing to a large increase in international reserves. Mexico therefore entered 1994 with a strengthened economy, and an economy more deeply integrated into global markets, with its membership in NAFTA and impending accession to membership of the

OECD as well as its commitments to an open exchange and trade regime promising to lock in many of the important reforms it had implemented.

So what went wrong? I would point to a number of factors. First, there were still weaknesses in Mexico's economic position at the start of 1994 that contained the seeds of the crisis that eventually occurred. In particular, the external current account deficit, running at 6 1/2 percent of GDP in 1993, was very large by most standards, and was being financed largely by short-term capital inflows. A steep real appreciation of the peso and a major deterioration in the private sector's saving performance had contributed to the emergence of this deficit. Its sustainability was questionable, and indeed in February last year, at the conclusion of its regular consultation with Mexico, the IMF "stressed the need to lower the external current account deficit . . . to reduce the economy's vulnerability to a sudden reversal in capital flows."

But in the event, Mexico's weak external position was exacerbated in 1994 both by a series of unfavorable developments at home and abroad and by shortcomings in Mexico's policy response, partly owing to the political hiatus following the elections in August. The uprising in Chiapas at the start of the year was the first in a series of dramatic adverse domestic developments that are well known; and also from early 1994 Mexico was confronted with a substantial rise in world interest rates, which prompted international investors to reassess the share of their portfolios invested in emerging markets. All these developments tended to weaken the peso. And the policy response was not adequate, the outgoing administration leaving to the new administration the responsibility of defining the adjustment strategy that was called for. And indeed the country suffered a lot from the frequent Latin American problem of too long a time span between election and inauguration. The peso was allowed to depreciate within its band, but the vulnerability of the economy was increased by the replacement of peso-denominated government debt by Tesobonos, instruments indexed to the U.S. dollar. The current account deficit widened further, to 8 percent of GDP for 1994 as a whole. All these factors contributed to the eruption of the crisis last December.

Before considering the lessons of this experience, we must also be clear about how the crisis was resolved—I am confident enough to use these words today—and turned into a manageable problem. It was not resolved by the devaluation of December 20. Nor was it resolved two days later when, after a further massive loss of international reserves, the peso was allowed to float. This merely delivered another blow to confidence, and the peso continued to depreciate sharply, as financial markets questioned Mexico's ability to service its short-term debt. The fact is that confidence was not restored and the crisis was not resolved until two components were securely in place—a stringent adjustment program designed in close collaboration with the IMF, and a large-scale international financial rescue package in support of that program. This package has three elements. The IMF approved on February 1 an 18-month stand-by credit of $17.8 billion in support of Mexico's program for 1995–96, of which $7.8 billion was made available immediately. The other two elements, both dependent on Mexico's arrangement and policy understandings with the IMF are, of course, $20 billion in swaps and guarantees from the U.S. Exchange Stabilization Fund, and $10 billion of short-term support from the G-10 central banks through the BIS (Bank for International Settlements).

The IMF arrangement with Mexico is the largest ever approved for a member country, both in absolute amount and in relation to the country's quota in the Fund. Why such exceptional support? For a very simple reason, which is the very basic mandate of the IMF. Take Article I of our Articles of Agreement—it states that it is the IMF's mission: "To give confidence to members by making the general resources of the Fund temporarily available to them under adequate safeguards, thus providing them with opportunity to correct maladjustments in their balance of payments without resorting to measures destructive of national or international prosperity." On January 31 of this year, this was the problem: either large-scale financial assistance was put in place together with the support of the U.S.—and the IMF was the only institution in a position to extend it without delay—or Mexico had no solution other than to resort to "measures destructive of national or international prosperity", such as a moratorium on foreign debt or a re-imposition of trade and exchange restrictions, with a major risk of the spread of such measures to a number of countries.

As a matter of fact, there was a distinct risk of systemic repercussions. In the weeks following the eruption of the crisis, equity and currency markets came under pressure, most noticeably in Latin America but also in a number of more distant emerging market economies, including in Asia. These immediate spillover effects indicated that Mexico's crisis could raise doubts, unwarranted by fundamentals, about the viability of policies in other countries as well. A major interruption in the flow of capital to developing countries could have ensued, and thus one of the driving forces of global growth in recent years could have vanished.

But the exceptional assistance provided to Mexico was warranted equally by the strength of the program adopted and Mexico's track record of macroeconomic and structural adjustment. It is ambitious, aiming in particular to cut the external current account deficit to less than 1 percent of GDP in 1995 and to contain the inflationary effect of the peso's depreciation. Economic growth is projected to resume next year. To achieve these goals, the program is centered on a further tightening of the fiscal position and a strong monetary policy. The program also pursues further the strategy of privatization and liberalization of activities previously reserved for the public sector, and includes a number of measures to protect the poorest from the short-term adverse effects of the adjustment process.

There are by now encouraging indications that the program has taken hold. Mexico's trade balance was in surplus in the first quarter, in contrast with a $4.3 billion deficit in the same quarter of 1994. The peso has recovered from a low of 8.1 per dollar in early March to less than 6, and an easing of domestic interest rates also indicates that the financial situation is stabilizing. Problems certainly remain, but if the authorities continue to implement the program steadfastly and consistently, Mexico's economy is headed toward recovery, and given the acceleration of reforms in this program it should emerge from the crisis—and let me emphasize this— stronger than before.

This has been a testing experience for Mexico and the international financial community. What does it signify, and what are its lessons?

Mexico's crisis has been described as the first financial crisis of the 21st century, meaning the first major financial crisis to hit an emerging market economy in the new world of globalized financial markets. And this says a lot about its significance. The increasing international integration of financial markets in the past 10–15 years has brought great benefits, by fostering a more efficient allocation of global savings and boosting investment and growth in many countries. But there is a downside: vastly increased financial flows across national borders have also made countries that participate in international financial markets more vulnerable to adverse shifts in market sentiment: such shifts, though generally related to concerns about economic fundamentals and policy shortcomings, can often be delayed, sudden, massive, and destabilizing. Furthermore, financial globalization has increased the speed with which disturbances in one country can be transmitted to others. So financial globalization, though both a product of and a contributor to the economic progress of our time, has heightened the challenges of preventing and resolving financial crises.

And it is no accident that this crisis hit one of the most successful developing economies. An essential ingredient in the success of Mexico in the past decade—as with all other successful developing economies—has been its increased openness to the world economy and integration into international financial markets.

Thus, as I said at the beginning, the challenges that now have to be addressed are to a large extent a consequence of economic progress. And it would be an egregious mistake to seek to prevent financial crises by reverting to a closed economic system with exchange controls and less open markets: to do this would be to try to turn the clock back and forego the benefits of globalization. This is well understood by the Mexican authorities, who quite appropriately have been addressing Mexico's problems without resorting to that approach again.

So how should the challenges of financial crises be addressed? What are the lessons from Mexico about the conduct of economic policy, the role of the IMF, and international cooperation more generally?

As regards economic policy, I would emphasize four lessons. First, openness to international financial markets today imposes an obligation of unfailing discipline on economic policy. Vigilance and discipline provide the most effective deterrent and defense against financial market setbacks. Mexico's crisis demonstrated impressively the costs that can arise when a country lowers its guard and allows markets to exercise their discipline instead. A similar lesson was shown, for instance, by Argentina's very quick reaction to the crisis. By transforming the crisis into an opportunity to address in depth the worrying signs of weakness in its provincial banks, Argentina, with strong support from the IDB, World Bank, and IMF, has paid a great service not only to itself but to the Americas and the world at large. With the situation under control in Mexico and Argentina, the systemic risk was well-contained.

Second, large external current account deficits are dangerous, especially when they are being used to support domestic consumption and are being financed by short-term capital inflows. They are dangerous because they are not likely to be sustainable. This applies even when, as in Mexico's case, the fiscal position is strong and the external deficit largely reflects weak private sector saving. With the benefit of hindsight, Mexico's fiscal position should have been even stronger, to contain the country's dependence on easily reversible capital inflows. (Let me add in parentheses here that it is striking that large external deficits and weak national saving performance have been the Achilles' heel of all three NAFTA economies in recent years. In fact, during 1989–93 the United States, Canada, and Mexico were three of the four largest users of foreign capital in the world. Mexico is certainly not the only member of NAFTA that must face the imperative of addressing its economic imbalances.)

Third, Mexico's devaluation in December illustrates not only that it is inherently difficult to adjust a pegged exchange rate even when such a change is called for, but also that sound and credible accompanying macroeconomic measures are essential to provide a firm basis for market expectations and to make the new exchange rate sustainable.

Fourth, Mexico's crisis illustrates the costs of failure to publish regularly and in good time information about key economic indicators. The crisis arose in the way it did partly because the scale of the problem only became apparent at the time of the devaluation, and took the financial markets by surprise. If information about international reserves and other key variables had been published more frequently and with a shorter time lag, the efficiency of market discipline and the chances of a smoother adjustment would clearly have been enhanced.

These are a few of the main lessons that have emerged from Mexico's crisis for individual countries. But what are the lessons for the IMF? The crisis and its resolution have confirmed the urgency of action to enable the Fund to provide more help for countries in both preventing and resolving such crises. It has therefore confirmed the appropriateness of the attention we had already been giving, especially in the context of the IMF's 50th anniversary, to the need to ensure that the Fund is fully equipped to serve its purposes in the new environment of globalization.

The IMF's work in helping to prevent crises is carried out mainly through the exercise of its responsibility for surveillance over the international monetary system and members' exchange rate policies. IMF surveillance is an international cooperative effort aimed at improvements in policies, the prevention of policy mistakes, and the promotion of exchange market stability and sustainable growth. It is conducted mainly through the annual consultations held with all individual member countries and through regular discussions in our Executive Board on the world economic outlook and global financial market developments. In recent years the Fund has taken action to make surveillance more continuous and effective, and significant progress has been made. But Mexico's crisis showed that further adaptations are needed to make surveillance strong enough to minimize the risk of the eruption and spread of crises in the new global environment:

- First, data: stricter requirements need to be applied concerning the regular and timely communication by countries to the IMF of data on key economic indicators; and the Fund also needs to make more use of financial market data in monitoring developments. We shall also be working toward the establishment of standards for the timely publication of economic data by members to enable markets to work more efficiently;

- Second, more continuous policy dialogue: not only must countries be willing to keep the IMF informed of developments and seek its opinion on issues they are facing, but the Fund's internal procedures must be adapted to foster dialogue more effectively in the intervals between our regular consultations, particularly when countries have just ended an adjustment program with the Fund;

- Third, better focused surveillance: especially given its limited resources, the Fund must focus more effectively on countries at risk, and countries where financial tensions are most likely to have spillover effects. And surveillance must also focus more carefully on financial flows and their sustainability;

- Fourth, more pointed and candid surveillance: in its policy dialogue with member countries the Fund must be prepared to be more critical and demanding—yes, even more critical and demanding than in the past.

These are some of the items on our agenda of action to strengthen surveillance. I fear that implementing it will not be a straightforward matter: experience shows that while countries tend to be very eager for surveillance over others, they are less keen on surveillance over themselves. It will be a critical challenge for international policy cooperation and for the IMF.

But even with the most effective IMF surveillance, crises are likely to occur from time to time; and the IMF must also ensure that it has the means to provide countries with financial assistance adequate to contribute effectively to their resolution. It was able to do so in the case of Mexico, by resorting to its exceptional circumstances clauses. There have been a number of other large Fund financial arrangements in recent months, most notably in support of programs of stabilization and reform in Argentina, Russia, and Ukraine. Because of these and other expected commitments, the Fund's liquidity position, adequate at present, is projected to weaken considerably over the next two years. The Fund's resources are probably sufficient for our normal business during this period, and if emergencies call for it, the General Arrangements to Borrow (GAB) from some of our largest member countries can be activated. But we must look beyond the next couple of years, and see what action needs to be taken to ensure that the Fund's resources are strong enough to meet the demands the Fund may face in the closing years of this century and beyond. This was agreed by our Interim Committee, and following their preliminary discussion we shall in the next few months be considering a number of courses of action:

- The first priority is the Eleventh General Review of Quotas, which are our member countries' capital subscriptions to the IMF. This review must be initiated expeditiously, and while it should be concluded by March 1998 at the latest we should complete our work earlier if possible, before the end of 1996. This quota review should in my assessment lead roughly to a doubling in quotas, in order to ensure that the size of the Fund keeps pace with the growth in the world economy since the last review in 1990 and takes some account of the increased scale of international financial flows that now characterize the system;

- Second, we shall be reviewing the role of the General Arrangements to Borrow and exploring ways to increase the potential resources available to the Fund through borrowing from our members;

- Third, when considering ways in which temporary financing could help the IMF discharge its responsibilities at times of emergency, we must consider how the SDR—the international reserve asset that the IMF can create in special circumstances—could be instrumental in the introduction of safety-net arrangements, whereby SDRs could be issued on a temporary basis or lent to countries in support of strong policy programs in the context of a liquidity crisis. I am suggesting that this idea be considered with particular attention together with, but hopefully before, a wide-ranging review of the role and function of the SDR;

- Fourth, we shall be examining ways to ensure the continued availability of concessional balance of payments assistance to low-income countries following the expiration within the next few years of the existing enhanced structural adjustment facility (ESAF). One possibility to be considered is the sale of a modest part of the Fund's gold holdings and the use of earnings from the invested profits of such sales, combined with bilateral contributions from member countries, to provide the subsidy element that is needed;

- Finally, we shall be exploring the possibility of developing arrangements for more orderly international debt adjustment, taking into account the experience with debt reorganization under national laws. Consideration of this approach raises a number of complex economic, political, and legal issues, and I should emphasize that our work on this is still very exploratory.

So here again we have a full agenda.

I have indicated a number of ways in which the IMF will be seeking in the period ahead to increase its effectiveness in helping countries both to prevent and to resolve financial crises. Some, on the surveillance side, are already being implemented, while others are in stages of preliminary exploration. These efforts are as essential as they are challenging, because the increasing globalization of the world economy makes effective international monetary cooperation at the global level—an effective IMF— more important than ever before. Regional cooperation of course also has an essential role to play, and has contributed vitally to economic progress in Mexico and throughout this hemisphere. But Mexico's crisis had global, not only regional, repercussions; its resolution required financial assistance at the global level; and the adjustment that Mexico is now undergoing, though affecting mainly the United States and other countries in this hemisphere, has been having effects much further afield, including by contributing to some extent to the weakness of the U.S. dollar. Mexico's crisis was of global significance, and its resolution required global cooperation.

In trade relations as in international monetary relations, global cooperation is essential: regional cooperation is important, but it is not enough. NAFTA represents an important achievement in outward-looking regional cooperation that is already contributing to the advancement of prosperity in Mexico and its partner countries. The initiative for a free-trade area in the Americas—the subject of this conference—reflects the strong sense of community in this hemisphere and a conviction that the mutual advantage of nations requires cooperation in economic relations. It was this same conviction that led at the global level to the Uruguay Round agreement. That agreement, with the establishment of the WTO (World Trade Organization), has strengthened the institutional framework for pursuing global trade liberalization through multilateral cooperation. And that is essential. A critical element will be the resolution of trade disputes under strengthened multilateral rules. With the conclusion of the Uruguay Round, one had good reason to expect that unilateralism would recede and that the rule of law would prevail over the law of the jungle. I trust that that expectation can indeed be realized, and that global cooperation will prevail in international trade as in monetary relations.

The next crisis of the 21st century, like Mexico's crisis, will also be of global significance, affecting this hemisphere even if it originates outside it. We must be ready to face it, and for that we must now meet the challenge of making the IMF as strong and effective as the world economy of the 21st century needs it to be. It is gratifying that the Interim Committee is guiding us in this direction, and I am sure that the G-7 Summit in Halifax next month will give added impetus to our work. And we shall of course be counting on the support of the United States, which has contributed so much to rising global prosperity as a pillar of multilateral economic cooperation in the past 50 years.

CHAPTER 10

THE ASIAN FINANCIAL CRISIS

■■■

In this chapter we hop from Latin America to Southeast Asia and the Asian financial crisis ("AFC"), popularly known as the "Asian Contagion." It began with Thailand in February 1997 and, like a contagion, spread to the Philippines, Malaysia, Indonesia, and South Korea ("Asian financial crisis countries"—AFCCs). Prior to the onset of the crisis, the AFCCs rocked. People referred to their growth as "the Asian Miracle." But their economies had soft spots, some spots really soft. Here's the thing, though: They had different economic profiles. The Philippines, Malaysia, Indonesia, and South Korea were not replicas of Thailand. So what? Foreign banks and investors didn't care. Like a herd of buffalo, they bolted from all of the AFCCs. And when capital inflows quickly dried up, the AFCCs had to abandon their fixed exchange rates. What followed was brutal.

Have you read the book *Perfect Storm* by Sebastian Junger and/or seen the movie (the book is better) with George Clooney? Both are based on the true story of a 1991 nor'easter that eventually formed into a frightening cyclone and sank the *Andrea Gail* and its six-man crew of fishermen from Gloucester, Massachusetts. The idea behind the perfect storm is that atmospheric conditions come together uniquely to form the "perfect" storm.

Since the movie (book), people have used the term frequently to describe any number of elements that come together to form, in some if not many cases, an unexpected disaster. It's this sense of the term that we're going to use in this chapter because no one foresaw that an economic crisis in one country, Thailand, would morph quickly into a major regional crisis, and even hit Russia and Brazil. We're going to use a (heavily allegorical) remake of the movie (because most of you may have heard of the movie but not the book—hey, we're not saying you don't read books) as a vehicle to tell the crisis's story. Keep in mind that, like all movies (and plays), the writer doesn't try to cover every possible aspect of the story—that's bad writing. The AFC is complex and there are competing views of what caused it. This script will cover what most observers agree upon.

The movie begins with *The Thailand* sailing into the Gulf of Thailand (yeah, it's not quite the North Atlantic Ocean—use your imagination!). The perfect storm forms and endangers not just *The Thailand* but also *The Philippines, The Malaysia, The Indonesia,* and *The South Korea.* Since we don't speak Thai or any of the other languages of the AFCCs (we know, shame on us), the dialogue is in English. We recommend you listen to the indicated music as you read the chapter.

Time for the movie.

"Concession stand is still open! Popcorn, candy, and soda at outrageous prices! Be an idiot and buy some! You can crunch and slurp as loudly as you want but turn off your cellphones! Hey, you! Yeah, you with the brain-dead smile. Stop texting, or sexting, or whatever you're doing with that . . . that thing that has ruined real human interaction! (Announcer's cell phone goes off.) Oops. I thought I had it on vibrate."

The theatre darkens and you watch thirty minutes of previews of mostly worthless movies and questionable body spray.

Setting for I and II: *The Thailand* at sea prior to and during 1997

Characters:

     Ricardo: Crewmember

     Krista: Skipper of *The Thailand*

Setting for III: 2000, a pub in South Carolina

Characters:

     Henry: Old fisherman

     Seth: Law student

Setting for IV: *The IMF Conditionality* comes to the rescue

Characters:

     Crew of *The IMF Conditionality* and other boats in distress

Setting for V: present day, cable show: Global Perspectives

Characters:

     Janet Singh

     Seth Haber

I. BEFORE THE PERFECT STORM

Part One: A Sunny Day for "The Thailand" When It Sets to Sea

("Appalachian Spring: Allegro," Aaron Copland)

Thailand's economy, like those of the other AFCCs, was money before the crisis. From 1985 to 1995, Thailand's average annual GDP growth was 9.8%. Not too shabby. But why? Let's talk exports first. Between 1988 and 1995, exports grew at 28% per year. The growth was fueled by a saturated domestic market, an appreciation of other Asian currencies, and low labor costs and favorable tax and tariff treatment to attract large multinational corporations, such as Data General and Seagate, both U.S. based, and Minibea, from Japan.

> Richard Bruce, a portfolio manager with Rowe Price-Fleming, referring to investing in Asia: *"We think its long-term record of superior growth will continue through 1996 and 1997 and 1998."*
> —Quoted in "Mutual Funds Quarterly Report; The Forecast Looks Brighter for Adventure Travel," *The New York Times* (1996)

Thailand also enjoyed sweet capital flows. Both foreign and domestic capital helped shoot up the domestic investment ratio, which rose from 28.2% in 1985 to 41% in 1995. Between 1990 and 1996, foreign capital inflows averaged 10.3% of GDP. Offshore borrowing by Thai banks and companies accounted for most of the inflows (7.6% of GDP), with portfolio investment (we'll get to this in a sec) and foreign direct investment (FDI) making up for the rest. Most of the AFFCs had similar inflows, except Malaysia, which, for the most part, relied on FDI.

Thailand's pegged exchange rate kept it on a smooth sail. Just before the crisis, it pegged the baht to a basket of foreign currencies (such as the yen, deutschmark, and pound sterling) dominated by the U.S. dollar. In June 1997, the U.S. dollar/baht exchange rate was $1/24.5 baht. Foreign investors liked it and poured capital into the economy. This translated into skyward investment and trade.

And it didn't hurt that Thailand's government appeared to be fiscally prudent. Government consumption between 1985 and 1995 remained tame at an average annual rate of 4.9%. Fiscal deficits moved from 3.7% of GDP to a 3% surplus in the same time period.

(*The Thailand* is gently cutting through calm, shining water, seagulls flying above)

Ricardo: What a great day to take'r out, huh, skip?

Krista: Can't ask for anything better.

Ricardo: Calm seas . . .

Krista: The sun . . . Cool breeze. Just right.

Ricardo: Feels good, huh, skip!

Krista: Hmmm . . .

Part Two: Meanwhile the Perfect Storm Begins to Form

("Sail," AWOLNATION)

What *The Thailand* didn't know was that it was sailing into an epic disaster. Here's how the perfect storm came together.

A Sudden Ominous Wave Rolls Across the Sea: Exchange Rates

Like Thailand, the other AFFC countries maintained fixed or pegged exchange rate regimes—their domestic currencies were tied either to one foreign currency or a basket of currencies (usually the dollar, yen, or deutschmark). You know by now the advantages and disadvantages of a fixed exchange rate, right? . . . Right? Okay, well, developing countries with "soft" currencies tie them to "hard" currencies, like the dollar, to tell the world it's safe to invest in the country—no foreign exchange rate risk. But the downside is that you have to maintain the declared rate. So if there's upward or downward pressure on the domestic currency, usually the country's central bank will intervene in the foreign exchange markets to either sell or buy their currency, respectively.

But here's the thing we've talked about: The fixed exchange rate is like a bull's eye for speculators/investors. In most cases, the domestic currency is over-valued, or at least perceived to be. So the speculators/investors borrow lots—and we mean lots—of money, and bet the fixed rate will break—it's called "shorting the currency" (more on this in just a sec).

Wind Suddenly Picks Up: Balance of Payments Problems

Like Thailand, the other AFCC economies were rocking before the crisis, and this included impressive growth in exports, ranging from semiconductors to textiles. Foreign investors believed that exports would continue to grow and that the market would continue to absorb the exports.

Well, guess what? The party ended. Eventually there was an oversupply of exported goods on the market. And the AFCCs couldn't look to **Japan** or the United States to save the day because their economies weren't all that hot. Result: current account deficits.

As you know, current account deficits are not a disaster so long as they are financed by inflows to the capital account. The AFCCs had lots coming in. For example, Indonesia, Thailand, Malaysia, and the Philippines had capital inflows twice as large as their respective current account deficits in 1990–1994. But there were problems with these inflows. For one, the AFCC's financial systems were liberalized too quickly and weren't equipped to handle the capital inflows. And the inflows were converted into lots of short-term debt in local currency—e.g., dollars to baht. South Korea's short-term debt was 67% of total debt in 1997. And much of the lending disregarded the borrower's riskiness. Banks lent to borrowers they were too chummy with.

Dark Clouds Move In: Lack of Financial Transparency

We're back to transparency. Observers have said that due maybe in part to cultural factors (communitarian society emphasizing order, group harmony, and respect for authority—we discount this explanation pretty much to zero), the AFCCs lacked financial transparency. They didn't follow

international accounting standards, which would have allowed foreign investors to assess the financial health of the corporate sector. Few had an accurate picture of the high levels of short-term debt. Nor were people able to see the concentration of capital, especially in real estate (Thailand). And no one really had a good handle on the amount of bad debt banks were sitting on. For example, as South Korea pursued the restructuring of its financial sector after its crisis, the government reported that as of June 1998, total non-performing loans (NPLs) stood at 118 trillion won. But subsequent estimates put the NPLs at 136 trillion won. An eighteen trillion won discrepancy. You read that right: eighteen *trillion*!

But, despite the lack of transparency, investors still poured money into the AFFCs. When you're having a great party, why close the bar?

Sharks Start To Circle

Speculators, like George Soros' Quantum Fund and Julian Roberson's Tiger Management, smelled there was money to be made. Lots of it. Let's review how speculators make money by shorting the currency. We're going to use hypothetical exchange rates and use one form of speculation to keep the explanation understandable. Let's say a speculator borrows 100 baht and then sells the baht at an exchange rate of 10baht/$1. It now has $10. After devaluation the exchange rate is 20baht/$1. The speculator then buys back the baht with the $10 and receives 200 baht. After it repays the loan with interest, say, 110 baht, it's left with 90 baht in profit. Pretty sweet, yeah?

> *"I know I am taking a big risk to suggest it, but I am saying that currency trading is unnecessary, unproductive and immoral,"* Mr. Mahathir said . . . *"It should be stopped. It should be made illegal. We don't need currency trading. We need to buy money only when we want to finance real trade."*
> —"Soros Calls Mahathir A 'Menace' to Malaysia," *The New York Times* (1997)

Notice what shorting does: When speculators/traders sell the baht in massive quantities, they're putting tremendous downward pressure on the targeted fixed currency, forcing the central bank to burn through its reserves to buy their domestic currency. The central bank might decide to jack up interest rates to deter the speculators—if borrowing baht becomes more expensive, it squeezes their profit margins. But raising interest rates may have negative effects on the entire economy. Eventually reserves will be so low that the government will be forced to abandon the peg. The currency then plummets in value and the speculators/investors laugh all the way to the bank. The speculators will win almost every fight with a central bank—the central bank brings a knife to the fight, but the speculators bring a gun.

Hot Air Rising

Another problem with the capital inflows: Portfolio investment—"hot money"—poured into the AFCCs, except for Malaysia. What is portfolio investment and why is it hot? Foreign investors (largely institutional—

mutual funds, pension funds, and insurance companies) invest in highly liquid debt and equity securities, ranging from government debt securities to stock in non-financial corporations. Unlike FDI, portfolio investors have no managerial responsibilities in the entities they invest in. You can see why it's hot, right? It comes in quickly and, because the investment is highly liquid, it leaves in a flash, which can create huge problems for the host country, especially a developing country.

As the Hot Air Rises There's Surrounding Air Just Waiting . . .

Foreign banks saw an opportunity to make money by generously lending to the AFCCs. Japanese banks accounted for most of the lending. For example, in June 1997 Japanese banks held about 35% of the claims on Asian counterparties, European banks held 36%, and North American banks only 10%.

(cut to a uniformed woman, sweat glistening on her furrowed brows, looking intensely at the radar)

Coast Guard: *Thailand,* please acknowledge . . . *Thailand* . . . We don't like what the radar's showing. *Thailand* . . . Pick up . . . It could be very bad . . . *Thailand* . . . *Thailand* . . . Acknowledge, dammit! This could be disastrous. *Thailand*!

Part Three: The Thailand Starts Creaking

("Scary Monsters and Nice Sprites," Skrillex)

Current Account Deficits Knock into the Ship

Between 1991 and 1994, Thailand's current account deficits hovered around 5.5% of GDP. It got worse in the next two years, jumping to 8%. What pushed the percentages up was primarily a steep rise is real wages between 1982 and 1994: 70%. Not good for Thailand as its exports, such as semiconductors and textiles, were labor intensive. In 1996 (all but the last month), exports of labor-intensive products dropped 14.6%.

Like we said, a current account deficit itself is not an immediate worry as long as there's plenty of capital flowing into the economy. In Thailand's case, as well as the other AFCCs, the capital flows kept coming because interest rates were low in the industrialized world and investors were seeking higher returns—the so-called "yield hunt." But a long-term deficit means long-term capital inflows. The country gets addicted to the capital and may not do what it has to do to reduce the deficit. It's high after all. And when the country's economic fundamentals don't look right? The sharks start circling *The Thailand.*

Problems with the Financial Sector Make the Ship Pitch Violently

Before the 1990s Thailand's financial system was pretty much closed to outsiders, providing it with insulation from external problems. But starting in 1989, the government began to liberalize the sector in hopes of increasing economic growth. The reforms included (1) removal of the interest rate ceiling that banks and other financial firms could charge; (2) relaxation of capital controls, which included allowing foreign currency denominated accounts; (3) removal of the requirement that banks hold a specified amount of government bonds, which allowed them to structure their assets (e.g., loans) to best suit their needs; and (4) the establishment of a securities and exchange commission. Sounds good, right? Especially in the "market-friendly" decade of the 1990s, which we talked about in Chapter 6.

But the Achilles' heel of the reforms was the creation of the Bangkok International Banking Facilities (BIBF) in 1993. The BIBF consisted of forty-nine domestic and foreign banks that held licenses that allowed them to borrow offshore and then relend the borrowed funds to Thai borrowers. The government set up the BIBF for a number of reasons which could be boiled down to one goal: it wanted to expand investment in the country with cheap capital as well as promote international trade and in the process turn Bangkok into a world class financial capital.

But observers have said the BIBF was established too early. The government didn't have effective prudential controls (controls on lending) and its financial sector supervision kind of sucked. And here's the clincher: Thailand's central bank kept interest rates high to limit aggregate demand and control inflation. The BIBF license holders saw this as a money-making opportunity: borrow dollars (or yen) at a low interest rate and then relend the dollars (or yen) domestically at a higher interest rate, making a profit on the "spread."

And a wide river of borrowed money flowed into Thailand, money that was transformed into short-term debt.

The relending of the dollars would prove to be disastrous. The new borrowers exchanged the dollars for baht—for their domestic transactions. The increased demand for baht put upward pressure on the pegged exchange rate. Because the government was committed to defending the exchange rate—after all, that's what it promises to do—the central bank had to put more baht into circulation (by selling baht and buying foreign currencies).

Then came the classic "money multiplier effect." When the new borrowers spent the baht, the recipients of those baht would then likely deposit the baht in a bank, which would then make more loans. This triggered an economic "bubble," fed by increased real estate values that would eventually burst. Why real estate? Lenders required real estate as collateral. The skyward ascent of property values encouraged more lending.

And some say that "crony capitalism" contributed to Thailand's crisis because of the moral hazard it created. The theory goes that Thailand's financial institutions had close ties to powerful government officials. Example: The Bangkok Bank of Commerce (BBC) was sitting on a huge pile of bad debt—in 1991, 27% of its assets were nonperforming and it got worse. When the problem hit the streets, there was . . . yes, ladies and gentlemen, a run on the bank! But the government was there to save the day to the tune of $7 billion to save the bank. And guess what: Many of the bad loans were made to the very politicians who used public money to rescue the bank. Foreign lenders saw this as an implicit government guarantee of a bailout—very sweet for the foreign lenders.

But, this was very bad for *The Thailand*. There was no way many of those loans would be repaid, but because of the lack of transparency no one really knew the extent of the problem. And even when it got around that there was a problem, the loans kept coming, to the point where the ratio of short-term external liabilities to foreign reserves exceeded 100% (true for Korea and Indonesia as well). Foreign banks not only relied on the government's implicit guarantee but also on an international bailout a la Mexico's crisis a few years earlier. Moral hazard. It's a killer, man.

In the meantime, the overinvestment in real estate came home to roost. The bubble burst. Real estate developers defaulted left and right, causing most of Thailand's finance companies to go under. A bloodbath.

(cut to rough, angry seas)

Ricardo: Skip, somethin's not right.

Krista: Everything's fine. I'm controlling it. Everything. It's good.

Ricardo: The boys don't think so.

Krista: That's because you're all boys. I need men.

Ricardo: That's not fair, skip.

Krista: Take a look out there. What do you see?

Ricardo: I don't like what I see. It's scary, skip.

Krista: Then put blinders on. That's what boys do.

Ricardo: We should do something . . .

(The Thailand shudders)

Ricardo: Did you feel that, skip?

Krista: What I feel is your fear. Get the hell outta here. You're just a boy. A baby. Go put your diapers on.

Ricardo: Babies become men when the chop threatens to break us apart. The sea's turning against us, skip. We're men now. We have to be.

Krista: Then get the men up here. *The Thailand*'s never betrayed me. Ever!

II. *THE THAILAND* IS SUCKED INTO THE PERFECT STORM

("Redefine," Incubus, which spikes our adrenaline and makes us write in the present tense)

February 5, 1997: All Hell Breaks Loose

A Thai property developer named Somprasong Land fails to make a $3.1 million scheduled interest payment on its Eurobond loan, defaulting on the loan. The Thai stock market had already fallen 45% from its high in 1996 and it falls another 2.7% after the default.

Finance One, one of the largest financial institutions in Thailand, was a BIBF licensee that played the borrow-cheap-relend-dear game. When property values drop, many of its loans become "non-performing," meaning "you can kiss repayment of the loan goodbye."

In an attempt to assure foreign investors that their money is safe, the finance minister tries to arrange a merger of Finance One but fails and resigns. The new finance minister makes an unannounced visit to the central bank and finds out that nearly all of the central bank's $30 billion in foreign reserves is committed to forward contracts (committed to being sold at some point in the future). In light of this shocking revelation, the government allows Finance One, with over $30 billion in non-performing loans in late February, to fail—no publicly-funded bailout. This spooks foreign banks and institutional investors.

A Massively Strong Current Causes The Thailand to List Violently

Foreign commercial banks shut off the loan spigots, and inflows turn into outflows. Loans from Japanese banks, with the largest exposure to Thailand, turn into a negative-$12 billion outflow between mid-1997 and mid-1998. Other foreign banks follow suit. All told, Thailand loses $23 billion in foreign bank loans over the same period.

Portfolio investment turns outward on a dime—huge outflows of hot money. (The AFCCs witnessed a swing of almost $105 billion in 1997—11% of pre-crisis GDP.) As the crisis hits Thailand, holders of baht desperately exchange the currency for dollars (or yen and some other hard currency). Result? Fewer dollars coming in, and LOTS of dollars going out. The baht keeps getting dumped into the marketplace but the central bank doesn't have the foreign reserves to soak it all up.

May 1997: Krista Tries to Right the Ship

The Thai central bank attempts to defend the currency peg. It uses $5 billion in reserves to buy baht on the open market. Reserves fall to a low of

$33 billion. The government raises interest rates from 10% to 12.5%, but this just encourages the BIBF licensees to lend more.

The central bank is caught between a rock and a hard place. It can either drastically raise interest rates (and it does raise interest rates somewhat) or it can let the baht float. Jacking up interest rates will help protect the peg but it'll be a body blow to a weakened economy. But abandoning the baht's peg will be humiliating. Worse yet, debtors who have to repay short-term debt will face insolvency because after abandoning the peg the currency will plummet, meaning debtors will need far more baht to pay off, say, $1 of debt. The central bank decides to try and defend the baht. It uses unannounced currency swaps (borrowing a currency it needs for its reserves and repaying later) to buy some time. It's a futile effort.

July 2, 1997: The Thailand's Windows Blow Out and the Sea Pours In

Thailand's government allows the baht to float against the dollar. The baht immediately depreciates by 15–20%. By July 1998, the exchange rate would drop to 41 baht to the dollar from its June 1997 peg of 24.5/$1.

The Sharks Feed

Speculators, like George Soros and Julian Robertson, make millions. Champagne corks pop and wild, testosterone-driven parties break out at Quantum Fund and Tiger Management. Yachts for everybody!

> *"Mahathir, 71, who has overseen Malaysia's growth during his 16-year rule, charged that Soros aimed to stop the fast-growing region in its tracks. 'All these countries have spent 40 years trying to build up their economies,' Mahathir said before the conference, 'and a moron like Soros comes along with a lot of money' and undermines them."*
>
> —"Malaysian Leader, Soros Trade Barbs," *Los Angeles Times* (1997)

We know it's not good for the screenplay but actually most analysts now agree that speculators didn't bring down the AFFCs. What brought them down was the

> *"On Sunday, Mr. Soros said: 'Dr. Mahathir suggested banning currency trading. This is such an inappropriate idea that it doesn't deserve serious consideration. Interfering with the convertibility of capital at a moment like this is a recipe for disaster. Dr. Mahathir is a menace to his own country.'"*
>
> —"Soros Calls Mahathir A 'Menace' To Malaysia," *The New York Times* (1997)

burst of the economic bubble, the drop in exports, the large amounts of short-term debt that became very expensive to repay after the devaluation (can you figure out why?), insufficient foreign reserves, a huge drop in foreign loans, and killer outflows of portfolio investment.

But, hey, we can say this movie is *based* on a true story. That way we can write whatever we want!

The Thailand Comes Closer to the Whirlpool's Vortex

Getting back to Thailand, its economy was in a freefall. The government had to close fifty-six finance companies by December of 1997. It took over four commercial banks to prevent the banking sector from imploding. It also axed infrastructure projects. Even the Thai military cut back its spending. Public sector employees' paychecks took a 20% hit. Thousands of Thais lost their jobs.

The sudden reversal of hot money was a killer for all East Asian countries. Thailand saw a swing of over $26 million between 1997 and late 1998. In 1996, the AFCCs enjoyed net private capital inflows of about $102 billion, which turned negative in 1998 to the tune of about –$27 billion. Thailand went from over $18 billion to over –$8 billion in the same period.

> Vorachan Vinyarath, a Thai wallpaper salesman: *"When Thailand was in a good economic situation, I think people were overspending . . . . We need an economist with a talented tongue to persuade those foreign investors to come back."*
> —"A Thai Business Wonders, Will It All Crumble?" *Los Angeles Times* (2007)

Brutal.

Starting in July, 1997, Thailand suffered through six consecutive quarters of negative GDP growth.

Brutal.

(*The Thailand* is being tossed about violently in a brutal, unforgiving sea)

Ricardo: Tell us, skip. We need to know. Prepare. You know?

Krista: Do you pray, young man?

Ricardo: No, skip.

Krista: That makes two of us.

(*The Thailand* lurches upward into an angry wave)

Krista: You're married, aren't you?

Ricardo: Yes, I am, skip.

Krista: What's her name?

Ricardo: His name is Matthew.

(Krista looks at Ricardo and smiles)

Krista: Blow him a kiss. That might be as good as a prayer.

Ricardo: Sure, skip. I will. A kiss for all of us.

(A wave pounds into the boat, knocking Krista out)

III. THE STORM SUCKS IN *THE PHILIPPINES, THE MALAYSIA, THE INDONESIA,* AND *THE SOUTH KOREA*

Okay, so thanks to stubborn Krista, *The Thailand* got sucked into the perfect storm. But *The Philippines, The Malaysia, The Indonesia,* and *The*

South Korea had no such Krista and were minding their own business. So why did they get sucked in?

Roll the film.

Part One: The Philippines, The Malaysia, and The Indonesia

(The camera focuses squarely on Henry, an old fisherman with a craggy face. He's nursing a mug of beer. A cigarette looks like it's permanently attached to his lips. Pan out to show an old run down pub, the floor strewn with peanut shells and other unknown [don't want to know] debris. Seth, a law student researching the perfect storm of the Asian financial crisis, sits across from Henry.)

Seth: So I understand that you were in South Korea in 1997. Is that right?

Henry: Yes, sir.

Seth: Sailing?

Henry: Fishin.'

Seth: Right, right. How did you find yourself way over there?

Henry: Went on an adventure of sorts.

Seth: Sounds like fun! Haha . . . ha . . . ha . . .

(silence as camera focuses on Henry's deadpan face)

Seth: Well . . . okay . . . so you witnessed the storm, the perfect storm, unfold?

Henry: I did. Wasn't pretty. Fact, it was god-awful.

Seth: I know all the trouble started with *The Thailand*, but why did the other boats get hit? Can you tell me what happened in your own words?

Henry: That's all I got, my own words . . .

Seth: Right! Of course!

Henry: Need a beer?

Seth: No, thanks. Do you think I might be able to get a caramel mocha latte with a touch of peppermint?

(silence as camera focuses on Henry's deadpan face)

Seth: Okay, then, may I start asking you questions?

Henry: Keep fillin' my mug and I'll talk.

Seth: Sure. No problem, it's the law school's money anyway . . .

(silence as camera focuses on Henry's deadpan face)

Seth: I'm not getting off to a good start, am I?

Henry: You're fine. Shoot me a question.

Seth: How did the other boats get caught in the perfect storm?

Part Two: The Dangerous Whirlpool

("Dies Irae," theme from "The Shining")

(shot of a massive whirlpool in an angry sea darkened by menacing thunder clouds)

Henry: I've been fishin' 'bout thirty-five years and never seen it, a whirlpool, I mean. But I'm guessin' that most folks at some point in their lives—me included—imagine gettin' caught in one. Form in different ways, you know. Somofim' when opposing currents collide. When that happens, you could say there's "perfect chaos." Water starts chasin' water. For no reason, really. Maybe panic, I suppose. Like people chasin' each other to get to their bank on Main Street, a perfectly fine bank, based on a mere rumor that a bank on Fifth Street 'sbout to go under. I saw that once. (pause) Yes sir, when most of us think of the pool, we don't think of the swirlin' water goin' down a drain. We think of a massive and deadly hole in the sea, a hole created by panic. That kinda whirlpool'll devour anything drawn into it. Destruction is a certainty, if not death. Davy Jones' Locker. We fear it.

(pause the film)

What Henry is describing is "herd behavior," which fed the contagion. The concept didn't originate with the Asian financial crisis; it's much older than that. Essentially there's a chaotic event—like when Thailand goes under—and investors panic, pulling their money out of the other AFCCs even though their economic profiles differed from Thailand's. Due in part to a lack of transparency, once some investors headed for the door, the others saw this and rushed for the doors too, even though they might not have known why the initial investors were fleeing. Think: a stampede of buffalo. Herd behavior. They're not going to stop and say, "Well, now wait a minute. Let's look carefully at each country to determine whether the conditions warrant pulling our money out." Of course not! They're stupid buffalo! And they don't even talk in the first place!

Thailand's devaluation of the baht after having burned through its reserves triggered the contagion. Foreign investors in the other AFCCs, from banks to portfolio investors who were in the countries purely for yield, bolted for fear of being last in line and losing everything. So what if South Korea's economy was putting the country on the cusp of becoming "developed" in 1997, whereas Indonesia's economy was still typical of a "developing" country?

Remember the buffalo. They leave a devastated landscape in their wake.

(roll the film)

Part Three: The Whirlpool Drags in the Other Ships

("Phantom Limb," Alice in Chains)

Henry: As *The Thailand* was fightin' for her life, the whirlpool's whip hit **The Philippines**. Like *The Thailand*, when she set out she looked fit. Fact she was a newer ship than *The Thailand*. Some sort of improvements, actually. Lookin' at her you'd a thought she'd cut through the water just fine. Turns out she had somof same problems. Buyin' more fish than she sold. Started borrowin' too much from them greedy banks. Made the same mistake of agreein' to pay back the damn loans real quick.

(Henry takes a long pull on his beer)

Still, she hit the pool's devil of a current. One second she's goin' for'd, next she's goin' the opposite direction. Started to list, just like *The Thailand*. Skipper tried best he could to fight back. But she ran so low on fuel, she finally gave up. It was July 11, just a few days after *The Thailand* gave up.

(Henry lights another cigarette)

Seth: Are those Camels? You guys like those, huh.

(silence as camera focuses on Henry's deadpan face)

Seth: Another beer?

Henry: I'm gettin' dry with all this talk.

Seth: Waiter!

Henry: There ain't no waiter. This place look fancy to you?

Seth: No, no not at all. It's a cool place. Smelly, but cool.

Henry: The beer.

Seth: Sure. Sure. Be right back. Can I go to the bathroom first?

(silence as camera focuses on Henry's deadpan face)

Seth: Be right back.

(Seth comes back with a beer)

Seth: Nice and cold. Freezing, really.

Henry: The only way to drink horse urine. My favorite.

Seth: What a pleasant thought . . . Anyway, what happened after *The Philippines* got caught?

Henry: **The Malaysia** was just southwest of *The Philippines*. Smooth seas for her, too, when she took off. N'fact, some envied her 'cause she looked so good. Sure, she was doin' same thing the other two did. Buyin' more fish than sellin'. Them quicky loans risin'. Still, her debt wasn't that bad, and most of 'em loans still gave her a bit of time to pay 'em back—not like the quickies.

(Henry takes a pull on his cigarette and follows it up with a long pull on the beer)

Henry: One thing was dif'rent from the other two.

Seth: What was that?

Henry: When she got in trouble, she was in a stable current. She shouldn't have listed, but she did. She fought back. No use, though. She gave up in late July. Couple weeks later **The Indonesia** went down, even though the fella who owned her patched her up good and she was sellin' lots of fish.

Seth: How tragic!

Henry: A warm beer is tragic. A fisherman at sea knows the risk.

Seth: Could be a fisherwoman.

(silence as camera focuses on Henry's deadpan face)

Seth: I mean a woman who fishes . . . But not, no . . . with a pole . . . not, you know, like a kid fishing for . . . sunfish or anything . . . maybe trout . . . no, bass. Yeah, bass. They're big, aren't they?

(silence as camera focuses on Henry's deadpan face)

Seth: Do they serve wine here? Merlot is my favorite!

(silence as camera focuses on Henry's deadpan face)

Henry: Son, man or woman, we call 'em skipper.

Seth: Right on!

(silence as camera focuses on Henry's deadpan face)

Seth: Why don't we just get back—

Henry: Let's do that—

Seth: The perfect storm. *The South Korea* was next. Right?

Henry: She was big. Still . . .

Seth: Tell me about it.

Henry: It's complicated.

Seth: I can look it up on Wikipedia, if you want.

(silence as camera focuses on Henry's deadpan face)

Henry: I gotta book that explains it.

Seth: Where did you get it?

Henry: Washed ashore.

Seth: Where's it from?

Henry: Iowa.

Seth: Iowa? But all they have there are corn, pigs, and cows.

(silence as camera focuses on Henry's deadpan face)

Seth: Maybe not . . .

(Henry throws the book on the table)

Henry: Have a look.

Seth: Pretty neat. "*South Korea and the Asian Financial Crisis: A Perfect Storm*," by . . . Henry . . .

Henry: Yeah.

Seth: You? But—

Henry: I'm abd in South East Asian Studies.

Seth: Ph.D.? But you don't . . . I mean you talk like . . .

Henry: I've been working on it a long time. I prefer it over scholar-speak.

(Seth looks at Henry for the longest time)

Seth (blurts out): Will you read to me, Henry? Please?

Henry: I need a cold one.

Seth: I think I'll have one, too!

(Seth comes back with two freezing mugs and chugs his, wiping his mouth with the back of his hand and grinning like an idiot)

(Henry begins to read from his book)

Henry: To understand what happened to South Korea in the Asian financial crisis, we have to start with the "chaebols." Explaining in detail what they were and how they functioned would take several pages, so we're going to cut to the chase. A chaebol was a network of firms controlled by a founding family. The control could be direct, where the family would hold a controlling interest in the firms. Or it could be indirect, such as established a base firm that controlled subsidiaries, which held shares in each other—cross shareholding. All in the family, right?

Chaebols were created through a fire sale of Japanese assets after the Second World War. The South Korean government gave them import and production monopolies in exchange for political contributions. Hmmm . . . Aside from money exchanging hands, giving the chaebols monopolies was part of the state-led model of development South Korea and the other "Asian Tigers" (Hong Kong, Singapore, and Taiwan) pursued at the time. The government targeted sectors of the economy that they thought would propel the country forward economically. And it worked. It was called the "Asian Miracle" because of the stunning growth rates, collectively about 10% annually for decades. When the crisis hit Korea was the tenth largest economy.

So how did chaebols come to rule? The heavy and chemical industries drive (HCI drive) initiated in 1973. The HCI drive targeted six strategic industries: steel, nonferrous metal, shipbuilding, electronics, machinery, and chemical industries. The government directed banks to make lots of cheap loans to the chaebols and it worked: HCI export products rose from 4.8% of total exports in 1970 to 30% in 1995. And the debt kept piling up. Check this out: The top thirty chaebols borrowed so heavily that the average debt to equity ratio was 333%. Two of the chaebols that went bankrupt after the collapse, Sammi and Jinro, had respective debt to equity ratios of 3,245% and 8,598%! How do you spell: INSANE LEVERAGE!

But you couldn't see the debt mountain growing because of the chaebol structure—no large shareholder base to answer to. To make things worse, the chaebols began to borrow foreign currency overseas and converted the currency into won. Short-term debt—not good.

Like the AFCCs, South Korea's current account deficit began to increase: It was only 2% of GDP in 1995, but had increased to 4.9% of GDP in 1996. But during the first half of 1997, the current account deficit shrank and in fact moved into surplus in June.

The deficits were financed by the capital account. Problem, though: 54.9% of the capital inflows were in the form of . . . You guessed it—short-term debt. But nobody really saw what was coming. People saw that overall debt was only 25% of GDP and they thought Korea had its debt under control. But once the capital inflows turned into outflows, the debt wasn't rolled over. Yeah, a pretty serious liquidity problem.

South Korea, like the AFCCs had a fixed exchange rate in the form of a tight "band" within which the won moved up or down. The won was tied to the U.S. dollar. Not a bad thing in and of itself. But as the dollar appreciated, so did the won, making exports—especially semiconductors— less competitive. We just showed you the numbers. There was another problem: its short-term debt dwarfed its foreign exchange reserves. When the crisis hit, the ratio of short-term debt to reserves was 210.6% ($34.1 billion in reserves June 1997). Bad. Thailand's ratio was 141.1%, the Philippines' was 72.6%, Indonesia's was 162.9%, and Malaysia's was 60.9%.

In the meantime chaebols were starting to tank into bankruptcy. In April, 1997, the government put together an anti-bankruptcy pact. Here's how it worked: A state entity, the Korean Asset Management Corporation, bought non-performing assets from the chaebols, which injected them with liquidity they desperately needed. Then a group of commercial and state banks agreed to extend credit and defer payments for ninety days.

Then the chaebol Kia happened. In June, 1997, Kia started going down. The government put Kia into the bankruptcy pact. In September, creditors refused to extend any more credit to Kia. In October, the government intervened and kicked the management out, effectively nationalizing Kia.

The end was near. Korea's central bank was intervening in the market to defend the won. Because foreign capital inflows dried up, the central bank started burning reserves. It claimed it had $30 billion in reserves when in reality reserves were half that amount.

The sharks fed, leaving the won's bloody carcass floating in the sea of the foreign exchange market. The won/U.S. dollar exchange rate dropped from 850/$1 in June 1997 to 1,290/$1 in July 1998.

On November 21, the Korean government, having given up defending the won, announced it would seek support from the IMF.

(cut to Seth, he has tears in his eyes as he looks at Henry)

Henry: Whatcha cryin' for, kid.

Seth: My dad used to read to me like that . . . You remind me of him.

Henry: You mean he reeks of horse urine and rotten fish?

(Seth rubs his eyes with his shirt sleeve and then looks at Henry)

Seth: He did, Henry. He did . . . And I loved it.

(Henry smiles)

Henry: How about two cold ones, son.

Seth: I'd like that. Very much.

Henry: Waiter?

(fade to black)

IV. THE RESCUE

(*The Thailand* is sinking from the weight of the water that's poured into the ship)

Ricardo: I thought you were dead, skip.

Krista: Maybe I am, which means you're dead, too.

Ricardo: I don't think so, skip. I just peed in my pants.

(Krista gives Ricardo a weary smile)

(long pause)

Ricardo: Skip! Look!

Krista: I'm seeing double. What?

Ricardo: Nine o'clock. See it? I can't believe it, skip! It's *The IMF Conditionality*! We're going to make it, skip!

("Ride of the Valkyries" Wagner)

Krista: I hope I *am* dead.

> "Nobody likes the International Monetary Fund; if anyone did, it would be a bad sign."
> —P. Krugman, The Return of Depression Economics and the Crisis of 2008, 115 (2009)

Why does Krista hope she's dead? Because the IMF sought to fundamentally restructure the AFCCs' economies via "structural" conditionality on steroids. At the height of the crisis, IMF arrangements with Korea, Thailand (do an internet search for Thailand's August 14, 1997 Letter of Intent), and Indonesia included a staggering 94, 73, and 140 structural conditions, respectively—many of which failed. How crazy is that? (The U.S., World Bank, Asian Development Bank, and Japan contributed to most of the packages.)

As we'll see in a bit, much of what the IMF required was all wrong. First, though, let's look at the "rescue" efforts. And, no, we're not going to talk about all of the conditions—that would be, like, crazy on steroids.

Part One: The IMF Conditionality Rescues The Thailand

(A massive ship, *The IMF Conditionality* comes abreast *The Thailand*)

IMF Captain: You're in bad shape.

Krista: What a news flash!

IMF Captain: You want us to help you?

Krista: I prefer torture, but I'm willing to talk.

IMF Captain: About what?

Krista: How we're going to fix the situation.

(IMF Captain throws a brief case aboard *The Thailand*)

IMF Captain: Open it.

(Krista opens it and finds a Letter of Intent)

Krista: Like I said, I prefer torture.

After Thailand devalued the baht, it entered into negotiations with the IMF, with the talks focusing on austerity measures. Sorry, did we say "negotiations?" You all have heard of contracts of adhesion, right? Take it or leave it. On August 20, 1997, the IMF announced a $17.2 billion support package with $3.9 billion from the Fund. The aid was intended to increase investor confidence and rebuild the central bank's foreign reserves. The conditionality was staggering. Check it out:

- High interest rates were imposed to combat inflation and restore the baht's value. They were relaxed in 1998 as the economy had begun to contract.

- Thailand, which had a budget deficit of 2.5% of GDP—not that bad—just prior to the IMF loan, had to raise excise taxes to reach a budget surplus of 1% of GDP.

- Bad loans, which totaled 2.7 trillion baht, had to be declared non-performing (NPLs)—i.e., forget about being repaid—after 6 months instead of 12.

- For at least the next ten years Thailand had to allow foreign majority ownership in financial institutions. At the time, Thailand, like many other developing countries, limited foreign ownership to 49% of the firm.

- Thailand had to create by royal decree (like an executive order) a new Financial Sector Restructuring (FRA) agency. It was formed to oversee the liquidation of fifty-eight financial institutions.

- Banks and financial firms had to increase their minimum capital from 8.5% of assets to 12%. This was above international standards, and proved too demanding. So the government allowed them to return to the minimum.

- Auditors of financial institutions had to comply with Thailand's auditing regulations.

- The central bank had to create the Thai Asset Management Corporation to assist in debt restructuring negotiations between debtors and creditors. (In 2001, the government created the Thai Asset Management Corporation to buy NPLs.)

- The central bank had to suspend liquidity lines to ailing financial institutions. (Bank consolidation followed. Eight commercial banks were merged with other banks between December 1997 and November 1999.)

- The central bank had to disclose the level of foreign reserves every two weeks. (As exports increased because of the depreciated baht, the central bank rebuilt its reserves.)

- No easy monetary policy.

- Thailand had to amend its bankruptcy laws. In April 1998, it amended the Bankruptcy Act to improve reorganization of viable companies, but the change proved ineffective because of the tons of distressed debt. (The Act was further amended in March 1999 to improve creditor rights.)

- Thai food for all IMF staff upon demand until the world comes to an end or the IMF ceases to exist, whichever comes later. What's another stipulation?

Part Two: The IMF Conditionality Rescues The Philippines and The Malaysia Tells the IMF to Take a Hike

(The IMF Conditionality comes abreast The Philippines and The Malaysia)

The Philippines

IMF Captain: It's *The Philippines*—again.

First Mate: She's a pain.

IMF Captain (to the boat): This is the second time.

Skipper: Don't remind me. Just get us out.

IMF Captain: We get to check out your boat and make sure it's really seaworthy. Deal?

Skipper: Do I have a choice?

The Philippines was already hooked up with an IMF loan. It used part of the loan to cover the $2 billion in foreign reserves it burned during the crisis. When the original loan expired, the Philippines entered into a $1.1 billion standby facility with the Fund. The quid pro quo (conditionality)? High interest rates, stricter loan loss provisions and higher capital requirements for banks, fiscal surpluses (so the government is taking in more revenue that it's spending), and total liberalization of the capital account.

The Malaysia

IMF Captain: What?

Skipper: We don't need or want your assistance.

IMF Captain: You're out of your mind, *Malaysia*. You won't survive.

Skipper: Watch us.

IMF Captain: Suit yourself. Helmsman, turn her about.

Unlike the other AFCCs, Malaysia didn't look for or want IMF assistance. First, it tried the typical adjustments to end speculation on the ringgit, such as raising interest rates and cutting government spending. It also pegged its exchange rate at 3.8 ringgit per dollar (a 10% hike in from the pre-crisis FX rate), and cut interest rates to boost the economy.

They didn't work. So it imposed extensive capital controls: it required all ringgit asset transactions to go through an authorized domestic intermediary, and it banned repatriation of investments held by foreigners for one year to stop capital outflows. Because FDI was so important to Malaysia, the government exempted it from the capital controls and allowed

> "The IMF believes that any restrictions imposed on the movement of capital [are] not conducive to building investor confidence."
> —IMF spokesman, quoted in "IMF Suggests Malaysian Move is a Disincentive," *Asian Wall Street Journal* (1998)

unlimited repatriation of FDI profits and dividends. The government gradually lifted the capital controls after February, 1999.

Malaysia improved its BOP by raising tariffs to curb luxury imports. Tariffs were raised to over 800% for cars! To promote exports, Malaysia lowered tariffs for items that would promote tourism, such as clothing and footwear. Make Malaysia a "shopping paradise." Who could resist buying new shoes!

It's impossible to say whether Malaysia would have been better off had it accepted IMF assistance—you know, the counterfactual thing. But check it out: Malaysia's recovery took only two years while Thailand and Indonesia needed five years.

What's interesting is that, unlike Thailand, Indonesia, and South Korea, Malaysia's government survived the crisis. Malaysia's Prime Minister Mahathir ruled with an iron fist. He imprisoned political rivals, banned rallies, and prohibited students from doing what they like to do: protest. The Prime Minister was a pretty controversial guy during the AFC. He blamed the crisis on foreigners, especially Jews, zeroing in on George Soros. And he was into conspiracy theory, claiming the United States conspired against Malaysia. Yet the capital flight that led to Malaysia's crisis was domestic in origin—Malaysians. Those with means have a way of protecting what they have. Happens all the time.

Part Three: The IMF Conditionality Rescues The Indonesia

(The IMF Conditionality comes abreast *The Indonesia)*

IMF Captain: This one's a real gem.

First Mate: Rotten.

IMF Captain (to the boat): This is going to cost you.

Skipper: A certainty. How much?

The announcement of an IMF package at the end of October—$18 billion from the IMF, the World Bank, and the Asian Development Bank supplemented by additional funding—temporarily stemmed the slide of the rupiah's value. In return, Indonesia agreed to various reforms including a budget surplus of 1% of GDP. It also agreed to overhaul the banking system—it closed sixteen banks. The first IMF package was not enough to stabilize the currency. In January 1998, the IMF and World Bank made it clear that Indonesia was not fully committed to the IMF's conditionality, in particular meeting the budget surplus. The markets clobbered the rupiah: within two days it fell from Rp 7000 to Rp 10,000 to the dollar. Then came the second rescue package with a raft of conditions ranging from trade and foreign investment liberalizations to privatization. Still, the crisis continued, with riots against the ethnic Chinese.

Part Four: The IMF Conditionality Rescues The South Korea

(The IMF Conditionality comes abreast *The Thailand)*

IMF Captain: You're a big one with big problems.

Skipper: Only in your eyes.

IMF Captain: You want to get smart with me?

Skipper: Why no your lordship. May I kiss your ring?

IMF Captain: That's more like it.

Skipper (mumbles): I wish I could gut you like a fish.

IMF Captain: What was that?

Skipper: I said I wish I could get you fresh fish.

On December 3rd of 1997, Korea had to turn to the IMF for assistance, and received a $57 billion support package—with conditionality that would choke a horse. Here we go with bullet points again, and we won't include all of the Fund's stipulations:

- Review the remaining restrictions on corporate foreign borrowing, including short-term borrowing.
- Lose restrictions on foreign ownership of land and real estate.
- Lose the limits on foreign investment in Korean equities.
- Reach a current account deficit of 1% of GDP or less for 1998 and 1999.
- Keep inflation at 5% or less.
- Slow GDP growth rate to 3% for 1998 (to allow a steady recovery by 1999.
- Balance the budget by raising taxes and reducing spending.
- Remake the financial sector.
  - o The General Banking Law and Financial Industry Act was amended to make 100% foreign ownership possible. This further liberalized Korea's economy by allowing easier acquisitions of Korean companies.
  - o Businesses had to become more transparent with consolidated financial statements.

   o The central bank had to become more independent and its sole mandate would be to control inflation.

   o The central bank governor would be selected by presidential appointment (after legislative approval) instead of being appointed by the Ministry of Finance and Economy (MOFE).

   o The central bank governor, rather than the MOFE, would become the chairman of the bank's monetary board.

   o The Financial Supervisory Commission (FSC) similar to the Securities Exchange Commission was created to supervise the financial sector.

   o The FSC would control a new Financial Supervisory Board (FSB), which would create license business activities and create new supervisory rules relating to the operations of Korea's financial institutions.

- Privatize the steel industry.
- Reform the cheabols (more about this in a sec).
- The government had to allow banks to fail. By April 2000, the total number of banks in Korea fell from thirty-three to twenty-three. (Non-bank financial institutions faced even more closures, totaling 430 institutions by April 2000, a 79% decrease in the number of non-bank financial institutions from 1997.)

Despite the loan announcement Korea's descent into the whirlpool's vortex continued. Capital flight continued, as much as $1 billion per day. The stock market was nose-diving. So was the won, falling at one point to 2000 won/$1 per dollar. Brutal.

To stop the descent, South Korea had to deal with the drop in liquidity. The IMF loan helped. The government and thirteen international banks agreed to convert $21.8 billion in short-term debt into longer-term government-guaranteed loans. The current account reached a surplus thanks in large part to a drop in imports.

In the meantime, the government had to deal with a ton of bad assets held by financial institutions. Korea initially thought that bad assets totaled about 100 trillion won. But under international accounting standards the actual amount was 112 trillion won as of March 1998. Via the Korean Asset Management Cooperation, the share of non-performing loans fell to 8.7% by December 1999, down from 14.5% in March 1998. In total, the government used 101.7 trillion won dealing with this problem. (Non-bank financial institutions' non-performing loans actually increased to 23.2% in December 1999, up from 9.6% in March 1998.).

Back to the chaebols. With pressure from the World Bank, the top Chaebols finally agreed with the Korean government to make reforms, signing an agreement in December of 1998. First on the list was increased transparency. Chaebols had to start releasing consolidated financial statements. No more illegal internal transactions between them. Affiliate payment guarantees had to disappear. Paid-in capital had to increase. Asset-liability ratios had to be lowered to 200%.

And that's not all! Chaebols had to change their business structures. Reforms would be focused on the leading companies in each group. Non-leading companies would be separated from the individual groups. Bad companies had to be closed or sold, which reduced the companies from 264 to 130 companies by the end of 1999). Chaebols began borrowing less. The debt ratios for the top four chaebols decreased from 473% (five Chaebols) to 173.9% in 1999.

Finally, chaebols had to fund the creation of 1000 McDonalds in South Korea for good measure.

V. IMF CRITICISM

Setting: Cable show: Global Perspectives, hosted by Janet Singh, present day

Janet: Welcome to Global Perspectives. Today we are pleased to have with us Professor Seth Haber, a noted expert in law and the economics of the Global South. Dr. Haber is a *summa cum loud* graduate of University of Werock Law School. After clerking for the U.S. Supreme Court, he acquired a Ph.d in economics from the University of Fearme. Once again, welcome to the show.

Seth: Thank you. A pleasure to be here.

Janet: As you know, this is the last in our series of looking back at the Asian financial crisis, and in particular the role of the International Monetary Fund or IMF. Before we get into some of the details, can you tell us what the overall legacy of the IMF's involvement in the crisis is?

Seth: An overwhelming negative legacy. No question about it.

> *"IMF is the "Typhoid Mary of emerging markets, spreading recessions in country after country."*
> —J. Sachs, quoted in "IMF Shouldn't Get Money Without Reform" *New York Times* and *International Herald Tribune* (2009)

Janet: Generally speaking, what were the criticisms?

Seth: It's hard to know where to start, really. But to put it in its most fundamental terms, the Fund misdiagnosed the problems in each of the countries involved in the crisis—we can call them the AFCCs. It then imposed excessive conditions on the loans it made to them.

Janet: So-called "conditionality."

Seth: Precisely.

Janet: Professor Joseph Stiglitz was quite a visible critic, was he not?

Seth: Indeed he was. Given that he's a Nobel laureate in economics and the former senior vice-president and chief economist of the World Bank, his criticisms carried a great deal of weight. Professor Paul Krugman, also a Nobel laureate, was a notable critic.

Janet: In a nutshell could you tell us what Professor Stiglitz found troublesome about the IMF's involvement?

Seth: He said the IMF made two fundamental errors. The first was to insist in the late 1980s and early 1990s on financial sector liberalization, in more technical terms, liberalization of the capital account.

Janet: Meaning the inflows and outflows of capital, such as loans, foreign direct investment, portfolio investment, and the like.

Seth: Exactly.

Janet: And the second error?

Seth: To demand fiscal austerity and high interest rates, which might have been appropriate for Latin American countries. They suffered from very high inflation rates and overheated economies. But the AFCCs didn't have high inflation rates and their economies needed "re-heating."

Janet: Can you give us examples of these misdiagnoses?

Seth: Sure. Let's take the conditionality imposed on the Philippines.

> *"I would ask people from the IMF why they had put a particular provision in to the loan agreement, for instance that the central bank had to focus exclusively on inflation —inflation had not been a problem in Korea—and they would say 'oh we always do that'. Or you would ask, 'why privatize the Korean steel industry?' It was one of the most efficient in the world, which was making profits not losses and contributing to government revenue, and they would say 'because we always do it'."*
>
> —J. Stiglitz, quoted in "The Contented Malcontent," *The Guardian* (2002)

Janet: Why do you say imposed? Doesn't the country propose the changes it must make?

Seth (smiles): Fiction is beautiful, isn't it?

Janet (smiling back): It has its place. So the Philippines?

Seth: Well, here's a laundry list of sorts. First, the IMF demanded high interest rates to stop inflation and speculation. But this wrecked highly indebted firms and increased the number of non-performing loans on the banks' books. It also demanded that banks immediately adopt stricter loan loss provisions and higher capitalization requirements, which further destabilized the financial sector.

Janet: For our viewers, by loan loss provisions you mean the capital banks have to set aside to cover bad loans.

Seth: Yes.

Janet: And higher capital requirements means banks had to hold more capital relative to their assets, such as loans.

Seth: Correct. To give an example, instead of holding $5 in capital for every dollar in assets—loans, a bank would have to hold $10 in capital for every dollar. In a crisis, it's very hard for banks to raise capital, such as issuing stock.

Janet: So the other way to comply with the higher capital requirements was to lend less, contracting the economy. But the AFCCs desperately needed economic growth.

Seth: Exactly. And the IMF didn't realize at the time that the AFCC's financial sectors were fragile in the first place. Take Indonesia. The IMF made the country close sixteen banks in September of 1997. But the closures combined with tightened monetary policies pushed the Indonesian banking system to the brink. People lost confidence in the banking system. There were actually runs on the banks. In May 1998, the line stretched a kilometer outside of the doors of Bank of Central Asia during the economic meltdown that followed the fall of President Suharto.

Janet: He was quite corrupt, wasn't he?

Seth: A grand thief, I would say.

Janet: Other errors?

Seth: I'll mention two others. First, the IMF insisted on fiscal surpluses, meaning, among other things, steep cuts in government spending and hikes in taxes. But this was the wrong medicine for the patient. The Philippines needed to run fiscal deficits—meaning government spending— for a period of time to promote economic growth.

Janet: But not all economists agree with that Keynesian approach—deficit spending.

Seth: That's right. Deficit spending is always a contentious issue. (*See Supplement 10E*)

Janet: Getting back to the tax hikes.

Seth: Sure. Much of the tax revenue was to come from tariffs on imports, but imports plummeted when the peso dropped in value after the government gave up trying to defend the fixed exchange rate. Second, the IMF was adamant about complete liberalization of the capital account. But an open capital account allowed some of the capital inflows, especially portfolio investment—so called "hot money"—to turn on a dime and become destructive outflows during the crisis. Stiglitz pointed out that India and China, that did not have wide open capital accounts, escaped the harshest aspect of the crisis.

Janet: Is it accurate to say that the IMF attempted to essentially remake the economies of the AFCCs?

Seth: It is.

Janet: But weren't many of the reforms necessary?

Seth: No doubt but the IMF's remedies only made things worse. And some of the structural reforms were irrelevant. For example, the IMF's insisted that Indonesia end the monopoly on cloves. Although monopoly had its problems, breaking it up was irrelevant to stabilizing the rupiah.

Janet: Might—

Seth: If I might—

Janet: Sure.

Seth: A major problem with structural conditionality was that it prevented borrowing countries, and key stakeholders in the countries, from developing a sense of ownership of the adjustment programs—which ultimately resulted in significant program failure rates. And what's interesting is that borrowing countries gamed conditionality by complying with the conditions during the program and thereafter dropping or reversing the reform policies. Bottom line: critics claimed that structural conditionality reflected ideology without addressing the actual conditions in the borrowing countries.

Janet: Might all of these problems be related to the IMF's very structure?

Seth: Stiglitz spared no words. He voiced what virtually everyone has known about the IMF: the United States, which favors creditors, dominates the institution. The IMF in effect bailed out the banks that willingly, perhaps recklessly, lent to the AFFCs.

Janet: The bottom line?

Seth: The IMF lost it credibility, and it had little to start with.

Janet: All of these changes must have been painful for the AFCC's citizens.

Seth: Conditionality hit the poorest, of course, especially women and children. (*See supplement 10C*) The price of basic foodstuffs went through the roof. There were riots in the streets of Jakarta. People died. Hungry people in Indonesia destroyed shops—many owned by ethnic Chinese who dominated commerce—in search of food. Unemployment skyrocketed. In South Korea, labor unions took to the streets and clashed with riot police.

Janet: It just occurred to me that there's a link between violence and international finance.

Seth: International finance is violence.

Janet: Something to ponder, I suppose. So did the IMF ignore the criticisms?

Seth: It didn't apologize. It never would. It insisted the AFCCs' economies had to be reformed, and without IMF assistance the countries would have been worse off. It did make two concessions of sorts. First, it said, "well, maybe our surveillance could've been better so that we could've seen the crisis forming." (S*ee Supplement 10A)* Second, some of the Executive Board's Directors questioned whether fiscal contraction was the right medicine for the AFFCs.

> *"As World Bank President, Mr James Wolfensohn, visits Indonesia, [a correspondent] finds out how the people are coping with the fall-out of the bank's over-optimistic economic forecasts for the region amid soaring prices for basic foodstuffs. Two slim young mothers in bare feet, each holding a baby boy, stood on the edge of the small crowd gathered in a north Jakarta truck yard on Wednesday to welcome World Bank President, Mr James Wolfensohn. Not that Tina and Maemunah had any idea who he was or why he had come to their poor Kalibaru suburb. Smiling gracefully as Indonesians do even when life treats them cruelly, they explained that they just were hanging around in the hope that someone might be giving out rice. These are the people who feel the full force of Indonesia's economic collapse. The two women each earn about 7,000 rupiahs (less than $1) a day selling cooked rice and this sum is fast depreciating as prices shoot up. 'An egg used to cost 250 rupiahs, now it is 400,' said Maemunah. 'Rice was 1,000, it went up to 1,500.' Tina, whose husband died in a motor-cycle accident, continued the list: vegetable oil was up from 1,500 to 4,000 a litre; milk from 2,300 to 3,000, she said."*
>
> —"Tension rises in Indonesia as people left hungry," *Irish Times* (1998)

Janet: But you must agree that the countries are better off today.

Seth: They are doing much better today than in 1997–98. (*See Supplement 10B*) But that's like saying you climbed out of a deep hole, in part created by the IMF. There's no way you couldn't be better off.

Janet: What about the IMF conditionality. Did it change in any way?

Seth: In 2000, the IMF began looking at its structural performance criteria and decided to streamline conditionality. The revised conditionality guidelines were adopted in 2002. The guidelines tried to rein in structural conditionality by requiring "parsimony" when setting conditions and by requiring that the conditions be "critical" to the achievement of the program goals. But the revisions had little effect on the IMF's use of structural conditionality.

Janet: Was there any attempt to fix things on a more global level?

Seth: There was a lot of talk about a "New International Financial Architecture." But that's what it was—a lot of talk. The only concrete result of all the talk was the creation of the Financial Stability Forum, whose mandate was to oversee actions to identify vulnerabilities in the international financial system. It was a pretty obscure forum until the 2008 global financial crisis.

Janet: Thank you, Professor Haber, for a very informative discussion. We always like to end the show with a question that reveals the human side of our guests.

Seth: Haha.

Janet: You've accomplished so much in so little time. What or who inspired you to pursue your impressive trajectory?

Seth: A fisherman.

Janet: Captain Ahab?

Seth: Henry.

Janet: Where and when did you meet him?

Seth: In 2000, in a smelly bar in South Carolina.

Janet: How did he inspire you?

Seth: He taught me how to drink horse urine.

(immediate cut to a commercial)

* * *

(*The Thailand* is still in choppy water but not in danger of sinking; the whole crew is on deck looking exhausted)

Ricardo: Skip! We made it through! You were right. It was torture working with *The IMF Conditionality*.

Krista: ym eman si atsirk.

Ricardo: What skip?

Krista: i evah neeb demrofer.

Ricardo: Skip. Are you okay?

Krista: i ma a retteb atsirk won.

Ricardo: Skip! What's wrong?

Krista: i ma a retteb atsirk won. i ma a retteb atsirk won. i ma a retteb atsirk won.

Ricardo: What have they done!

Krista: i ma a retteb atsirk won. i ma a retteb atsirk won. i ma a retteb atsirk won. i ma a retteb atsirk won. i ma a retteb atsirk won. i ma a retteb atsirk won.

(Ricardo and the crew look sadly and mystified at their skipper)

(Four Walls "Act I, scene VII" John Cage)

(fade to black)

Part Five: Epilogue

Not long after the Asian Contagion hit the AFFC's, Russia hit rough waters. Few foresaw the hit. After several years of economic decline, Russia was on an upward trajectory. Inflation dropped from 800% in 1993 (can you wrap your mind around that?) to 6% in July of 1998 and GDP was showing signs of growth.

But Russia had a big soft spot. It's a big producer and exporter of commodities, ranging from minerals to oil. In August 1998, commodity prices sunk to their lowest levels. This was a body blow to the current account: commodities accounted for 70% of Russia's merchandise trade.

Then what? Yeah, capital flight. Between May and August of 1998 $4 billion went for the exit door. On July 20, 1998, the IMF issued Russia an emergency loan of $11.2 billion with $4.8 billion to be disbursed immediately. Not enough to stem the liquidity problem. On top of that the Russian legislature balked at the Fund's conditionality, which included cutting government expenditures, with most cuts in public programs like health care and education. Investors got rattled, even though Russia agreed to most of the Fund's demands.

To protect the ruble, Russia's central bank hiked interest rates from 47% in May to 200% in August. No use. Foreign reserves plummeted. Finally, on August 17, 1998 Russia allowed the ruble to depreciate by more than 70%. The ruble went from about 6 rubles/$1 to 28 rubles/$1 by December of 1999. Russia's GDP decreased by 5% by the end of the year. Brutal.

And Soros? After the ruble devaluation, Soros' announced that his fund had lost $2 billion in Russia. Financial karma, dude.

In the fall of 1997, Brazil carried a budget deficit and its economy was on the brink of deflation—decreasing price levels and a negative inflation rate. Exports were dropping and imports mushroomed. In October 1997, the speculators pounced. The assault resulted in . . . right, a reduction in foreign exchange reserves and capital flight. On September 11, 1998, investors withdrew more than $2 billion despite the central bank raising interest rates to 50%. Brutal.

Brazil kept bleeding capital: net outflows of $33.7 billion from second half of 1998 to the first quarter of 1999. Not even a $41 IMF loan—with conditionality requiring interest rate hikes, spending cuts, and higher taxes—could stop the capital flight. The central bank burned $37 billion in foreign reserves to protect the real. Finally, on January 16, 1999, Brazil abandoned its currency band (a form of a fixed exchange rate) and floated the real. It ended up losing 30% of its value. The central bank brings a knife to the fight . . .

Not much substantive reform followed the AFC other than the Financial Stability Forum (FSF). It initially convened 1999 to respond to failures in the financial regulatory system. In the wake of the financial crises of the 1990s, there was a push to create a New International Financial Architecture that would better address problems as they arose and better coordinate financial supervision and regulation on an international scale—supplement 10D. The FSF was part of this push, with the particular goal of promoting the harmonization of standards among international financial organizations and institutions.

The FSF's initial members consisted of the finance minister, central bank governor, and a supervisory authority from each of the G-7 countries, as well as representatives from the IMF, World Bank, Bank for International Settlements ("BIS"), Organization for Economic Cooperation and Development ("OECD"), and standard-setting bodies such as the Basel Committee on Banking Supervision ("BCBS").

The FSF's initial work was underwhelming. The most ambitious project was the adoption of a Compendium of Standards, intended to harmonize and make the many sets of standards published by standard-setting bodies more workable. The FSF flagged "Twelve Key Standards" for priority in implementation, such as the IMF's Code of Good Practices on Fiscal Transparency, the IASB's International Accounting Standards, and IOSCO's Objectives and Principles of Securities Regulation. It also published reports that gathered dust.

You Gotta Know Something About Them!

Gordon Gekko

Oops. Wrong guy.

George Soros

Image of George Soros by World Economic Forum is licensed by CC BY 2.0.

George Soros fled Nazi occupied Europe during World War II and has now become one of the world's premier hedge fund managers. He's famously (infamously) known as "the man who broke the bank of England" in 1992. It was a great drama and here's the essence of it. Britain and Germany were two of eight European countries that fixed their rates against each other in 1978 in the European Monetary System (EMS). For a number of reasons, the EMS became very unstable in 1992 and the speculators moved in. Britain was in a recession and needed to follow an expansionary monetary policy. Because of the way the system worked, Germany had to do the same but refused to do so because of the dangers of inflation. That's when the speculators, including Soros, pounced on the pound, selling (shorting) the pound furiously. Britain ultimately gave up and withdrew from the IMF on September 16, 1992. George walked away with a cool . . . one billion dollars. Take that Dr. Evil!

Prime Minister Mahathir Mohamad

Born in northern Malaysia, Mahathir Mohamad became an army doc who later hung his own shingle. But he had political ambitions! So he turned his open/closed sign to "closed." He was elected to parliament in 1964, and that's where it all started. After dissing then-Prime Minister Abdul Rahman in the wake of the 1969 race riots, Mahathir was thrown out of Malaysia's dominant political party, the United Malays National Organization (UMNO). A passionate writer, he wrote a book during his political exile called The Malay Dilemma, which analyzed why the Malay people weren't economically better off than the ethnic Chinese and argued, among other things, that that Malays had the right to control immigration, define citizenship, and control the content of their kids' education. The book also explained that affirmative action would help Malays move up the business chain. The Minister of Home Affairs thought the book was out of control and banned it in Malaysia (but it was published in Singapore, so Malays were able to get their hands on it). Mahathir was reinstated in the UMNO in 1972 after Rahman resigned. Mahathir himself became Prime Minister in 1981. He did great things for the Malaysian economy, but if you're in to civil liberties, he wasn't exactly a rock star: He altered the constitution to restrict the interpretive power of the Supreme Court and temporarily banned *The Asian Wall Street Journal* for writing negative articles about him and his administration.

What's Up with That?

Japan's Lost Decade

You should know something about Japan's "lost decade." It's widely used as an example of government doing too little, too late to tackle a crisis. The crisis was triggered when the bubble in land and stock prices burst in 1992. And guess what: Japanese banks made tons of real estate loans. Hence a huge, we mean huge, nonperforming loan (NPL) crisis that tanked the Japanese economy for over a decade. Check it out: Between 1992 and 2007, Japan's banks posted credit losses of about ¥99 trillion (about $950 billion). When it was all said and done, between 1992 and 2000 the government spent ¥86 trillion (17% of GDP) to solve the NPL problem.

Why the lost decade? Lots of reasons, but the big one most people talk about is delay. The government didn't really get the seriousness of the problem quick enough. And the actions it did take were nickel and dime stuff. It wasn't until 1998 that the government injected public funds to capitalize the banks: ¥1.7 trillion. That might look like a big number but it wasn't nearly enough given the size of the bad debt problem. And it also was too slow to buy NPLs from healthy banks. There's also some history here. Prior to the crisis, Japan's banks were heavily regulated under a "convoy" system, meaning that the regulators made sure that every bank would survive regardless of its problems. But there was a quid pro quo: banks had to channel household savings to the industrial sector as Japan rebuilt after World War II. It worked, right?

And then you have your public outrage. For example, in the mid-90s seven housing loan corporations—non-bank financial institutions—called "jusen" imploded with losses of approximately ¥6,410 billion. About ¥680 billion in taxpayer money was used. The public resented it so much that it was almost impossible to think about using public funds to fix the banking problem. Let's not forget policy problems. Take deposit insurance. As bank failures mounted, the government enacted a deposit guarantee program that fully covered deposits and interbank transactions. While this had its up sides—for example, calming depositors, it also had a major downside: it helped the weak banks survive when they should've been shut down, and it made it harder for the healthier banks to recover.

Throw in some macroeconomic problems like a huge fiscal deficit, a good handful of political wrangling, and a pinch of culture—the consensus thing, and you got yourself a lost decade.

International Accounting Standards

As the text points out, it's really important for investors, governments, and multilateral financial institutions such as the IMF to have an accurate picture of a financial institution's health. So financial reporting is key. But the problem is that different countries have used different accounting standards (each country's standards are referred to as their "generally accepted accounting principles"—GAAP), and in many developing countries the standards have been . . . well, let's just say pretty lax. That's where standard-setting bodies come in—bodies that issue standards they hope countries will adopt (i.e., the soft law we've talked about).

Starting in 1973 with the establishment of the International Accounting Standards Committee (IASC), accounting experts from around the world have tried to come up with one set of standards, "international accounting standards" (IAS). In 2001, the International Accounting Standards Board (IASB) succeeded the IASC, and thus far has adopted thirteen "international financial reporting standards" (IFRS) which amend or otherwise adopt some of the IAS. For example, some of the inter-related standards relevant to the ASF's problems with reporting bad debt are IFRS 7 on disclosing the exposure of financial instruments to risk, the IAS 32 on principles relating to presentation in financial instruments, and IFRS 9, which specifies how an entity should classify and measure financial assets and liabilities (which eventually will replace IAS 39).

All of this sounds nice and sweet, but as soon as you say "international" accounting standards, the world starts quarreling. Only until recently the United States has argued that U.S. GAAP rocks and that the IFRS just doesn't do the job. But that position really riled the European Union, which agreed to adopt the IFRS from 2005. In 2006 the IASB and the Financial Accounting Standards Board, the U.S. (private) body that issues accounting standards, agreed to accelerate the convergence between U.S. GAAP and the IFRS. In 2007, the U.S. Securities and Exchange Commission allowed non-U.S. companies to report using IFRS, and it's in the process of figuring out how and when U.S. companies should use IFRS.

Emerging market economies (EMEs) are in the process of adopting the IFRS. South Africa started in 2005 and others have established timelines to adopt them. Argentina, Mexico, and Russia have been the most recent EMEs to them. As to the AFCCs, let's look at Thailand's progress . . . . Uh . . . it hasn't adopted them and instead issued its own standards which it says are compatible with the 2009 IFRS. (silence as camera focuses on Henry's deadpan face) Here's what the country says about adopting the IFRS: "Within Thailand the process of adoption requires a good understanding of IFRS in the context of the Thai people and business. Many do not see the need for adoption as the size of their company is small. Confidence in adopting IFRS has been undermined by the financial crises in the US and EU. Constant changes to the standards have a destabilising effect and therefore many are reluctant to move forward." In all fairness to Thailand and other EMEs/developing countries, the process of converting from domestic GAAP to the IFRS is complex and expensive. And many developing countries just don't have the financial infrastructure and expertise to convert. Hey, have you read some of these standards? Only twisted accountants get off on this stuff—just like twisted lawyers get off on the rule against perpetuities.

The Philippines

The Philippines' exchange rate regime was similar to Thailand's although it differed from the peg insofar as the peso could move up or down within a "band." Before the AFC, the Philippines seemed to be cruising. A rising GDP helped it grow out of a recession in the early 1990s. It tamed inflation, and trade was up. Its short-term debt was small compared to other AFCCs; FDI dominated until 1996. It had also made regulatory reforms in the banking sector, such as single borrower limits, required provisions for loan losses, and tighter auditing requirements.

But, like Thailand, the Philippines was running high current account deficits, caused by an appreciating peso and tariff reductions. Also like Thailand, Filipinos borrowed more and more dollars overseas at lower interest rates. In 1997, foreign bank lending increased 22.4%—short term loans. Bad news.

The contagion hit the Philippines shortly after Thailand went down. Portfolio investors rushed for the exit door. The downward pressure on the peso was something fierce. The central bank increased overnight lending rates from 10% to 15% in an attempt to stop the peso's dive. As the peso's band became increasingly unsustainable, the central bank desperately raised overnight lending rate from 15% to 24% on July 3. It also burned $2 billion of its $11 billion in foreign reserves to defend the band. It gave up on July 11, letting the peso float. It fell 9.8% against the dollar. In June 1997, the peso/U.S. dollar exchange rate was 2.5/$1. By July 1998 it had fallen to 4.1/$1. Brutal.

Malaysia

Malaysia's economy rocked up to the onset of the crisis. Low inflation and budget surpluses. Foreign debt appeared to be under control. And unlike the other AFFCs, most of its capital inflows took the form of foreign direct invest, which is far less "hot" than portfolio investment, which can turn on a dime. And its stock market rocked. It was all good.

Maybe not *all* good. Foreign debt tripled from 1994 to 1997, with short-term debt growing in leaps and bounds. Private sector debt surged. Portfolio investment started coming in. Banks began making risky loans.

The first attack on the pegged ringgit (like Thailand) came on July 28, 1997. The central bank tried briefly to defend it but gave up. The ringgit then began its steady descent into the whirlpool's vortex, from 2.5 ringgit/$1 in June 1997 to 4.1/$1 in July 1998.

Indonesia

In the first half of 1997, Indonesia's economy was cruising. Economic growth was averaging about 8% per annum over a decade, inflation had fallen to under 6%, and the budget was under control, as was the exchange rate and balance of payments. The speculators attacked the rupiah shortly after Thailand allowed its currency to float on July 2. The government widened the exchange rate band but the speculators forced the rupiah to float, starting on August 14. With the rupiah going to hell in a handbasket, the government hiked up interest rates, but that put a vice on the economy, hitting the construction and property development sectors, and eventually the banking system that was heavily exposed to the property sector.

QUESTIONS FROM YOUR TALKING DOG

1.   Yeah, I remember watching it. Who eats swordfish? I know you don't. Anyway, I'm thinking of doing a documentary about the Asian financial crisis. You know a lot about it. Can I ask you some questions? Thanks. Well first, how were the economies of the AFCCs doing before the crisis hit? You know, like GDP growth, balance of payments, capital flows, etc.

2.   Did all of them have the same exchange-rate regime? Pros and cons?

3.   I've read that the AFCCs' financial systems were liberalize too quickly. Why was that a problem? Yeah, I know, I'm asking good questions. It would be a nightmare to have a stupid talking dog.

4.   We've talked about transparency on other walks. Was that a problem in this crisis?

5.   I know I'm short! That's a sensitive subject. Oh, shorting the currency. Sorry. So what does that mean?

6.   Hot money? What's that?

7.   Just like transparency, foreign bank lending is something we talk about all the time. What happened in this crisis?

8.   So Thailand gets in trouble first, right? Give me the blow-by-blow, especially with the Bangkok International Banking Facilities, and short-term debt.

9.   Why was Finance One such a big deal?

10.   And then came the capital outflows?

11.   The pegged exchange rate was a killer, huh. Tell me again.

12.   I'm not sure how I feel about speculators. Didn't the Prime Minister of Malaysia have an issue with them?

13.   I know that after Thailand, the Philippines, Malaysia, Indonesia, and South Korea fell like dominoes. You can tell me about the Philippines, Malaysia, and Indonesia after dinner. Can we have Thai food, by the way? I'm sick of that miscellaneous debris you feed me. What I want to know for the documentary is why the other Asian countries were affected by Thailand's fall, even though their economies weren't carbon copies of each other.

14.   Now let's talk South Korea. Those chaebols are fascinating. Tell me about them.

15.   Was South Korea's crisis basically the same as the others?

16.   I want to make the IMF a big part of my script. I want to know about conditionality, with specific examples. Go. No, I'm not telling you to fetch. Well . . . maybe I am.

17.   Some big time economists pounced on the IMF pounced, right? Tell me about their critique. Okay, there's a laundry list. Just give it to me, and I'll decide what stays in.

<u>Chapter 10: Supplement</u>

10A. *Fischer Speech*

This supplement provides a speech by Stanley Fischer, First Deputy Managing Director of the IMF, given in the midst of the AFC. How would you characterize its overall tone? He correctly notes that the crisis was not solely due to the AFCC's economic policies. What do you think of his counterfactual argument—i.e., had the IMF not become involved the crisis would've been worse? After the collapse of the BWS, the Fund has constantly sought to justify its existence. Do you see any of this in Fischer's speech?

Address by Stanley Fischer, First Deputy Managing Director of
the International Monetary Fund: "The Asian Crisis: A View
from the IMF" Midwinter Conference of the Bankers'
Association for Foreign Trade (1998)

As the crisis has unfolded in Asia, the IMF has become, at least for this brief moment in history, almost a household name. But even if the institution has become more well known, its role in Asia and more broadly in the world economy is not widely understood. Thus, I am very pleased to have this opportunity to discuss the Asian crisis, what the IMF is doing to help contain it, and the institution's wider role in the international monetary system.

Asia's economic success

The crisis in Asia has occurred after several decades of outstanding economic performance. Annual GDP growth in the ASEAN-5 (Indonesia, Malaysia, the Philippines, Singapore, and Thailand) averaged close to 8 percent over the last decade. Indeed, during the 30 years preceding the crisis per capita income levels had increased tenfold in Korea, fivefold in Thailand, and fourfold in Malaysia. Moreover, per capita income levels in Hong Kong and Singapore now exceed those in some industrial countries. Until the current crisis, Asia attracted almost half of total capital inflows to developing countries—nearly $100 billion in 1996. In the last decade, the share of developing and emerging market economies of Asia in world exports has nearly doubled to almost one fifth of the total.

This record growth and strong trade performance is unprecedented, a remarkable historical achievement. Moreover, Asia's success has also been good for the rest of the world. The developing and emerging market economies of Asia have not just been major exporters; they have been an increasingly important market for other countries' exports. For example, these countries bought about 19 percent of U.S. exports in 1996, up from about 15 percent in 1990. Likewise, the dynamism of these economies helped cushion the impact of successive downturns in industrial economies on the world economy during 1991–93. In recent years, they have also been a source of attractive investment returns. For all these reasons, the developing and emerging market economies of Asia have been a major engine of growth in the world economy.

So what went wrong? Let me start with the common underlying factors.

The origins of the crisis

The key domestic factors that led to the present difficulties appear to have been: first, the failure to dampen overheating pressures that had become increasingly evident in Thailand and many other countries in the region and were manifested in large external deficits and property and stock market bubbles; second, the maintenance of pegged exchange rate regimes for too long, which encouraged external borrowing and led to excessive exposure to foreign exchange risk in both the financial and corporate sectors; and third, lax prudential rules and financial oversight, which led to a sharp deterioration in the quality of banks' loan portfolios. As the crises unfolded, political uncertainties and doubts about the authorities' commitment and ability to implement the necessary adjustment and reforms exacerbated pressures on currencies and stock markets. Reluctance to tighten monetary conditions and to close insolvent financial institutions has clearly added to the turbulence in financial markets.

Although the problems in these countries were mostly homegrown, developments in the advanced economies and global financial markets contributed significantly to the buildup of the imbalances that eventually led to the crises. Specifically, with Japan and Europe experiencing weak growth since the beginning of the 1990s, attractive domestic investment opportunities have fallen short of available saving; meanwhile, monetary policy has remained appropriately accomodative, and interest rates have been low. Large private capital flows to emerging markets, including the so-called "carry trade," were driven, to an important degree, by these phenomena and by an imprudent search for high yields by international investors without due regard to potential risks. Also contributing to the buildup to the crisis were the wide swings of the yen/dollar exchange rate over the past three years.

The crisis erupted in Thailand in the summer. Starting in 1996, a confluence of domestic and external shocks revealed weaknesses in the Thai economy that until then had been masked by the rapid pace of economic growth and the weakness of the U.S. dollar to which the Thai currency, the baht, was pegged. To an extent, Thailand's difficulties resulted from its earlier economic success. Strong growth, averaging almost 10 percent per year from 1987–95, and generally prudent macroeconomic management, as seen in continuous public sector fiscal surpluses over the same period, had attracted large capital inflows, much of them short-term—and many of them attracted by the establishment of the Bangkok International Banking Facility in 1993. And while these inflows had permitted faster growth, they had also allowed domestic banks to expand lending rapidly, fueling imprudent investments and unrealistic increases in asset prices. Past success also may also have contributed to a sense of denial among the Thai authorities about the severity of Thailand's problems and the need for policy action, which neither the IMF in its continuous dialogue with the Thais during the 18 months prior to the floating of the baht last July, nor increasing exchange market pressure, could overcome. Finally, in the absence of convincing policy action, and after a desperate defense of the currency by the central bank, the crisis broke.

Contagion to other economies in the region appeared relentless. Some of the contagion reflected rational market behavior. The depreciation of the baht could be expected to erode the competitiveness of Thailand's trade competitors, and this put some downward pressure on their currencies. Moreover, after their experience in Thailand, markets began to take a closer look at the problems in Indonesia, Korea, and other neighboring countries. And what they saw to different degrees in different countries were some of the same problems as in Thailand, particularly in the financial sector. Added to this was the fact that as currencies continued to slide, the debt service costs of the domestic private sector increased.

Fearful about how far this process might go, domestic residents rushed to hedge their external liabilities, thereby intensifying exchange rate pressures. But the amount of exchange rate adjustment that has taken place far exceeds any reasonable estimate of what might have been required to correct the initial overvaluation of the Thai baht, the Indonesian rupiah, and the Korean won, among other currencies. In this respect, markets have overreacted.

So, in many respects, Thailand, Indonesia and Korea do face similar problems. They all have suffered a loss of confidence, and their currencies are deeply depreciated. Moreover, in each country, weak financial systems, excessive unhedged foreign borrowing by the domestic private sector, and a lack of transparency about the ties between government, business, and banks have both contributed to the crisis and complicated efforts to defuse it.

But the situations in these countries also differ in important ways. One notable difference is that Thailand was running an exceptionally large (8 percent of GDP) current account deficit, while Korea's was on a downward path, and Indonesia's was already at a more manageable level (3 1/4 percent of GDP). These countries also called in the IMF at different stages of their crises. Thailand called on the IMF when the central bank had nearly run out of usable reserves. Korea came still closer to catastrophe, a situation which has improved following the election of Kim Dae-Jung, the forceful implementation of the IMF-supported program even before he takes office, and the start of discussions with commercial banks on the rollover of Korea's short-term debt.

Indonesia, on the other hand, requested IMF assistance at an earlier stage, and at the start—in early November—the reform program seemed to be working well. But questions about the implementation of the program and the President's health, as well as contagion from Korea, all took their toll. Last week, after intense consultations and negotiations with the IMF, President Suharto decided to accelerate the reform program. Important measures to deal with banking sector difficulties and to increase confidence in the banks should be announced in the next few days. Corporate sector debt difficulties will have to be dealt with in a way that preserves the principle that the solution is primarily up to individual debtors and their creditors. The Philippines, for its part, has not escaped the turmoil, but its decision to extend the IMF-supported program that it had already been implementing successfully for several years has helped mitigate the effects of the crisis.

IMF-supported Programs in Asia

The design of the IMF-supported programs in these countries reflects these similarities and differences. All three programs have called for a substantial rise in interest rates to attempt to halt the downward spiral of currency depreciation. And all three programs have called for forceful, up-front action to put the financial system on a sounder footing as soon as possible.

To this end, non-viable institutions are being closed down, and other institutions are required to come up with restructuring plans and comply—within a reasonable period that varies according to country circumstances—with internationally accepted best practices, including the Basle capital adequacy standards and internationally accepted accounting practices and disclosure rules. Institutional changes are under way to strengthen financial sector regulation and supervision, increase transparency in the corporate and government sectors, create a more level playing field for private sector activity, and open Asian markets to foreign participants. Needless to say, all of these reforms will require a vast change in domestic business practices, corporate culture, and government behavior, which will take time. But the process is in motion, and already some dramatic steps have been taken.

The fiscal programs vary from country to country. In each case, the IMF asked for a fiscal adjustment that would cover the carrying costs of financial sector restructuring—the full cost of which is being spread over many years—and to help restore a sustainable balance of payments. In Thailand, this translated into an initial fiscal adjustment of 3 percent of GDP; in Korea, 1 1/2 percent of GDP; and in Indonesia, 1 percent of GDP, much of which will be achieved by reducing public investment in projects with low economic returns.

Some have argued that these programs are too tough, either in calling for higher interest rates, tightening government budget deficits, or closing down financial institutions. Let's take the question of interest rates first. By the time these countries approached the IMF, the value of their currencies was plummeting, and in the case of Thailand and Korea, reserves were perilously low. Thus, the first order of business was, and still is, to restore confidence in the currency. Here, I would like to dispel the notion that the deep currency depreciations seen in Asia in recent months have occurred by IMF design. On the contrary, as I noted a moment ago, we believe that currencies have depreciated far more than is warranted or desirable. Moreover, without IMF support as part of an international effort to stabilize these economies, it is likely that these currencies would have lost still more of their value. To reverse this process, countries have to make it more attractive to hold domestic currency, and that means temporarily raising interest rates, even if this complicates the situation of weak banks and corporations. This is a key lesson of the "tequila crisis" in Latin America 1994–95, as well as from the more recent experience of Brazil, Hong Kong, and the Czech Republic, all of which have fended off attacks on their currencies over the past few months with a timely and forceful tightening of interest rates along with other supporting policy measures. Once confidence is restored, interest rates should return to more normal levels.

Let me add that companies with substantial foreign currency debts are likely to suffer far more from a long, steep slide in the value of their domestic currency than from a temporary rise in domestic interest rates. Moreover, when interest rate action is delayed, confidence continues to erode. Thus, the increase in interest rates needed to stabilize the situation is likely to be far larger than if decisive action had been taken at the outset. Indeed, the reluctance to tighten interest rates in a determined way at the beginning has been one of the factors perpetuating the crisis. Higher interest rates should also encourage the corporate sector to restructure its financing away from debt and toward equity, which will be most welcome in some cases, such as Korea.

Other observers have advocated more expansionary fiscal programs to offset the inevitable slowdown in economic growth. The balance here is a fine one. As already noted, at the outset of the crisis, countries need to firm their fiscal positions, to deal both with the future costs of financial restructuring and—depending on the balance of payments situation—the need to reduce the current account deficit. Beyond that, if the economic situation worsens, the IMF generally agrees with the country to let automatic stabilizers work and the deficit to widen somewhat. However, we cannot remain indifferent to the level of the fiscal deficit, particularly since a country in crisis typically has only limited access to borrowing and since the alternative of printing money would be potentially disastrous in these circumstances.

Likewise, we have been urged not to recommend rapid action on banks. However, it would be a mistake to allow clearly bankrupt banks to remain open, as this would be a recipe for perpetuating the region's financial crisis, not resolving it. The best course is to recapitalize or close insolvent banks, protect small depositors, and require shareholders to take their losses. At the same time, banking regulation and supervision must be improved. Of course, we take individual country circumstances into account in deciding how quickly all of this can be accomplished.

In short, the best approach is to effect a sharp, but temporary, increase in interest rates to stem the outflow of capital, while making a decisive start on the longer-term tasks of restructuring the financial sector, bringing financial sector regulation and supervision up to international standards, and increasing domestic competition and transparency. None of this will be easy, and unfortunately, the pace of economic activity in these economies will inevitably slow. But the slowdown would be much more dramatic, the costs to the general population much higher, and the risks to the international economy much greater without the assistance of the international community, provided through the IMF, the World Bank, and bilateral sources, including the United States.

Most major industrial countries appear well positioned to absorb the adverse effects of the Asian crisis. In the United States, consumer spending and investment remain strong and incoming data for the fourth quarter point to further robust growth in output and household spending. Consumer confidence remains at or near all-time highs, and the unemployment rate stood at 4.7 percent in December, only slightly above the November rate of 4.6 percent, which was the lowest rate in 24 years. Direct measures of prices indicate that inflationary pressures are receding, and the strong dollar and weak import and commodity prices suggest that this trend will continue for a while longer. Nevertheless, it does not take a great deal of imagination to see how the problems in Asia could take on larger proportions, with more profound effects on global growth and financial market stability. That is why the international community has decided to work together through the IMF to try to overcome the crisis in a way that does the least damage to the global economy.

Moral Hazard

Of course, not everyone agrees with the international community's approach of trying to cushion the effects of such crises. Some say that it would be better simply to let the chips fall where they may, arguing that to come to the assistance of countries in crisis will only encourage more reckless behavior on the part of borrowers and lenders. I do not share the view that we should step aside in these cases. To begin with, the notion that the availability of IMF programs encourages reckless behavior by countries is far-fetched: no country would deliberately court such a crisis even if it thought international assistance would be forthcoming. The economic, financial, social, and political pain is simply too great; nor do countries show any great desire to enter IMF programs unless they absolutely have to.

On the side of the lenders, despite the constant talk of bailouts, most investors have made substantial losses in the crisis. With stock markets and exchange rates plunging, foreign equity investors have lost nearly three-quarters of the value of their equity holdings in some Asian markets. Many firms and financial institutions in these countries will go bankrupt, and their foreign and domestic lenders will share in the losses. International banks are also sharing in the cost of the crisis. Some lenders may be forced to write down their claims, especially against corporate borrowers. In addition, foreign commercial banks are having to roll over their loans at a time when they would not normally choose to do so. And although some banks may benefit from higher interest rates on their rollovers than they would otherwise receive, the fourth quarter earnings reports now becoming available indicate that, overall, the Asian crisis has indeed been costly for foreign commercial banks.

In effect, we face a trade-off. Faced with a crisis, we could allow it to deepen and possibly teach international lenders a lesson in the process; alternatively, we can step in to do what we can to mitigate the effects of the crisis on the region and the world economy in a way that places some of the burden on borrowers and lenders, although possibly with some undesired side effects. The latter approach—doing what we can to mitigate the crisis—makes more sense. The global interest, and indeed the U.S. interest, lies in an economically strong Asia that imports as well as exports and thereby supports global growth.

Simply letting the chips fall where they may would surely cause more bankruptcies, larger layoffs, deeper recessions, and even deeper depreciations than would otherwise be necessary to put these economies back on a sound footing. The result would not be more prosperity, more open markets and faster adjustment, but rather greater trade and payments restrictions, a more significant downturn in world trade, and slower world growth. That is not in the interest of the United States, nor of any other IMF member.

Role of the IMF

If I am emphatic on that point, it is because the IMF was founded in the hope that establishing a permanent forum for cooperation on international monetary problems would help avoid the competitive devaluations, exchange restrictions, and other destructive economic policies that had contributed to the Great Depression and the outbreak of war. The international economy has changed considerably since then, and so has the IMF. But its primary purposes remain the same; they are (and here I quote from the IMF's Articles of Agreement):

"to facilitate . . . the balanced growth of international trade, and to contribute thereby to . . . high levels of growth and real income"—and we have consistently promoted trade liberalization;

"to promote exchange rate stability, to maintain orderly exchange arrangements among members, and to avoid competitive exchange depreciation"; and

to provide members "with opportunities to correct maladjustments in their balance of payments, without resorting to measures destructive of national or international prosperity."

Our approach to these tasks is straightforward: it is to encourage all members to pursue sound economic policies and to open their economies to trade and investment. It is also to seek to avert crises by keeping close watch on member countries' economies and to warn them when trouble threatens. Sometimes we succeed, in that we warn countries and they take action. Sometimes we warn, but our advice is not followed, even when it is timely and on the mark. And sometimes despite our continuous efforts to strengthen our surveillance over member policies and performance, we might see some of the key elements of an emerging crisis, but fail to draw their full implications. We will continue to seek to strengthen surveillance—but it would be unrealistic to expect that every crisis can be anticipated.

When crisis does strike, the IMF has been willing to act in accordance with its purposes to deal with major problems confronting the international economy. On numerous occasions, the IMF has helped provide the expertise and vision needed to come up with pragmatic solutions to important international monetary problems, and it has helped mobilize the international resources to make them work. This was true during the energy crisis in 1973–74, when the IMF established a mechanism for recycling the surpluses of oil exporters and helping to finance the oil-related deficits of other countries. It was true in the mid-1980s, when the IMF played a central role in the debt strategy. It was true in 1989 and after, when the IMF helped design and finance the massive effort to help the 26 transition countries cast off the shackles of central planning. And it was true in 1994–95, when the IMF came forward to help avert Mexico's financial collapse—and to prevent the crisis from spilling over into the markets, forcing other countries to resort to exchange controls and debt moratoria, and possibly causing a dramatic disruption in private capital flows to developing countries. Because of the authorities' efforts and IMF support, Mexico's markets remained open and capital continued to flow.

There is no denying that each of these crises has been difficult—especially for the IMF members most adversely affected. In each case we, the IMF and the international community as a whole, learned from our experiences. And in each case, it is clear that without Fund assistance, things would have been much worse. The IMF's effectiveness derives from the fact that as an international institution with a nearly global membership, it can carry on a policy dialogue with member countries and make policy recommendations in situations where a bilateral approach would not be accepted. At the same time, the IMF provides a mechanism for sharing the responsibility of supporting the international monetary system among the entire international community.

IMF Resources

Part of that shared responsibility is to provide resources to the IMF. Let me emphasize that the IMF is not a charitable institution, nor does it carry out its operations at taxpayers' expense. On the contrary, it operates much like a credit union. On joining the IMF, each member country subscribes a sum of money called its quota. Members normally pay 25 percent of their quota subscriptions out of their foreign reserves, the rest in their national currencies. The quota is like a deposit in the credit union, and the country continues to own it. The size of the quota determines the country's voting rights, and the United States, with over 18 percent of the shares, is the largest shareholder. Many key issues require an 85 percent majority, so that the United States effectively has a veto over major Fund decisions.

When a member borrows from the Fund, it exchanges a certain amount of its own national currency for the use of an equivalent amount of currency of a country in a strong external position. The borrowing country pays interest at a floating market rate on the amount it has borrowed, while the country whose currency is being used receives interest. Since the interest received from the IMF is broadly in line with market rates, the provision of financial resources to the Fund has involved little cost, if any, to creditor countries, including the United States.

As you are no doubt aware, the Fund's membership has recently agreed to increase IMF quotas by 45 percent, about $88 billion, which will raise the capital base of the institution to some $284 billion. The United States' share of this increase would be nearly $16 billion. In addition, the Fund has taken steps to augment its financial resources through the agreement on the New Arrangements to Borrow (NAB). Under the NAB, participants would be prepared to lend up to about $45 billion when additional resources are needed to forestall or cope with an impairment of the international monetary system, or to deal with an exceptional situation that poses a threat to the stability of the system.

These are large sums. They are often described as an expense to the taxpayer. We are deeply aware in the IMF that our support derives ultimately from the legislatures that vote to establish their countries' quotas—their deposits—in the IMF. We must justify that support. But it must also be recognized that contributions to the IMF are not fundamentally an expense to the taxpayer; rather, they are investments. They are an investment in the narrow sense that member countries earn interest on their deposits in the IMF. Far more important, they are also an investment in a broader sense, an investment in the stability and the prosperity of the world economy.

Thank you.

10B. *The AFCCs a Decade Later*

Here we have a speech by Mr. David Burton, Director of the Asia & Pacific Department, IMF, nearly a decade after Fischer's speech. How do they differ in tone and substance? In 2007 (one year before the global financial crisis), Asia was much better off than in 1997. Do you see any subtext in Burton's statement that Asia "is once again the most dynamic region in the world economy"? Chapter 3 explains the Trilemma. Did the crisis induce the AFCCs to change the binary? Is it a "clean" binary? Because so many countries fall out of compliance with Fund conditionality, the Fund finally got the idea of "country ownership." The last paragraph before the conclusion describes the Fund's efforts to address the Fund's "democratic deficit."

Speech by David Burton, Director of the Asia & Pacific Department, IMF, "Asia and the IMF: 10 Years After the Asian Crisis," conference organized by the Woodrow Wilson Center for International Scholars (2007)

Good morning. It is a great pleasure to be here today at this interesting conference on the tenth anniversary of the Asian financial crisis.

Both Asia and the IMF have changed in many important ways in response to the Asia crisis and its aftermath. A decade later, Asia has made considerable progress in strengthening its economic foundations, and is once again the most dynamic region in the world economy. For its part, the IMF has retooled itself to better help its membership cope with increasing economic and financial globalization. Today, I will talk about these changes, focusing on those aimed at adapting to financial globalization. But let me first go back briefly to the crisis itself.

The crisis

The Asia crisis was unprecedented in its nature and virility. With the exception of Thailand, traditional macroeconomic imbalances were not evident beforehand, and did not play a major role. Instead, financial and corporate sector weaknesses, not fully apparent at the time, were at the root of the crisis. Other ingredients included pegged exchange rates that encouraged excessive unhedged foreign borrowing; inadequate reserve levels; and a lack of transparency, not least about the true levels of usable reserves. Indeed, lack of information really was a major impediment to understanding what was happening and making appropriate policy recommendations.

This mixture set the stage for the sudden reversal of investor sentiment and international capital that took place and exacerbated its effects. Doubts about the soundness of financial institutions and corporates spread quickly across national borders. This set off a vicious circle of capital outflows, plummeting exchange rates, and crippling balance sheet effects. Private demand collapsed and output in the most affected countries declined sharply. And the underdevelopment of social safety nets exacerbated the social and economic impact of the slumps.

As private creditors were stampeding for the exits, the international community, working through the Fund, provided substantial financing. At the same time, governments in the region adjusted policies, increasingly taking strong and appropriate actions. Also, steps were taken to involve the private sector in providing financing. After some initial adjustments, the approach eventually turned the tide; confidence began to recover and capital to return, though not before substantial damage had been done by the crisis. As you can see from the slide [shown below], output recovered quickly, with the most determined reformers—notably Korea and Malaysia—performing the strongest.

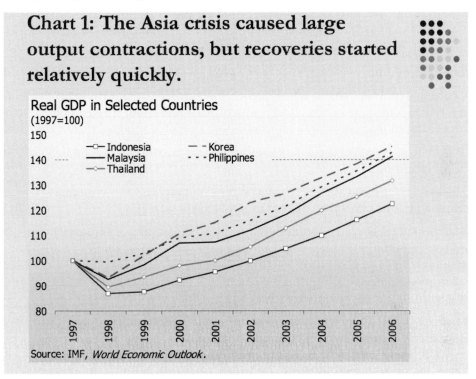

Chart 1: The Asia crisis caused large output contractions, but recoveries started relatively quickly.

Real GDP in Selected Countries
(1997=100)

Source: IMF, *World Economic Outlook*.

What were the lessons learned from the crisis, and what progress has been made in applying them? Here I will focus on questions related to financial liberalization and openness:

First let me mention one wrong lesson that fortunately was not drawn—namely that it was safest for Asian countries to withdraw from globalization. Despite the crisis, Asia has continued to embrace globalization, and today the region plays an even bigger role in the world economy than in the mid-1990s. Instead, the reforms undertaken in the region over the past decade have been geared to equip it to benefit more from globalization and to cope with its attendant risks, especially those associated with mobile international capital.

In this connection, an important lesson we have learned, supported by work done at the Fund and elsewhere, is that to reap the potential gains that financial globalization offers and to avoid the attendant risk of higher volatility, macroeconomic frameworks and financial sectors must be robust. This means meeting certain standards of institutional quality, governance and transparency—preconditions that were not adequately met in Asia prior to the crisis.

We have also learned much more about the interlinkages between the balance sheets of the financial, corporate, government, and household sectors, and about how disturbances in one sector can quickly spread to the others. This has helped to improve the ability of country authorities and the Fund to identify weaknesses and vulnerabilities that previously might have gone undetected.

Changes in Asia

Countries in Asia over the past decade have made considerable progress in applying these lessons. They have strengthened their policy and institutional frameworks to an impressive extent, reducing vulnerabilities.

Let me first mention three key areas where improvements have been made at the national level.

First, many countries have strengthened macroeconomic policy frameworks in several respects. In particular:

Substantial reserve cushions have been built up, as an important line of defense against possible future market volatility. Up to a point this is good, although too large a buffer of this type can be costly to maintain. Also, continued reserve buildups can come at the expense of an unbalanced and unsustainable pattern of growth.

Many countries have adopted more flexible exchange rate systems. This has allowed for more effective absorption of shocks, including shifts in investor sentiment. Flexible exchange rates also allow interest rates to be set more in response to domestic conditions, and help to avoid an under assessment of exchange risks by banks and corporations. The move toward exchange rate flexibility, however, has not been uniform in Asia, with some countries moving faster than others—as is evident from chart 2 [seen below]. In particular, the limited flexibility so far in China makes it more difficult for other countries to allow their exchange rates to strengthen. And this has been reflected in continued reserve buildups in some cases.

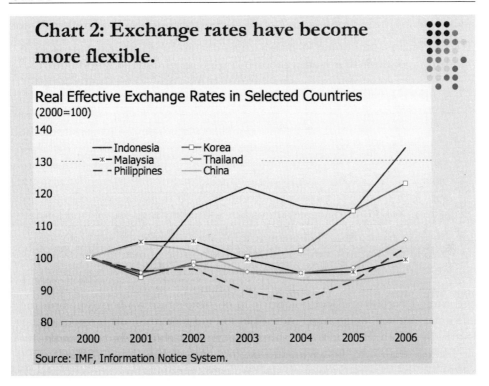

Chart 2: Exchange rates have become more flexible.

Real Effective Exchange Rates in Selected Countries
(2000=100)

Source: IMF, Information Notice System.

A second area is transparency, where transparency of policies and availability of information have improved markedly. Asian authorities, with the help of the IMF under its transparency initiatives, now routinely publish more high frequency information, including about their external debt and reserves. With many of the region's central banks having moved to inflation targeting frameworks, statements about monetary conditions and policy developments are also now regularly published.

Third, Asian countries have undertaken important efforts to reform financial sectors and improve corporate governance. These reforms include overhauling regulatory and supervisory systems, raising accounting standards, and strengthening shareholder rights. In the banking system, this has been reflected in a marked reduction in non-performing loans—this is true for all the countries most affected by the crisis. At the same time, overgeared corporations have substantially reduced their debt levels, with debt equity ratios sharply reduced across the board (see chart 3 [below]). The lessons of the crisis have also spawned a number of regional initiatives aimed at increasing the financial integration and resilience of the region through increased policy dialogue, reserve sharing arrangements and capital market development.

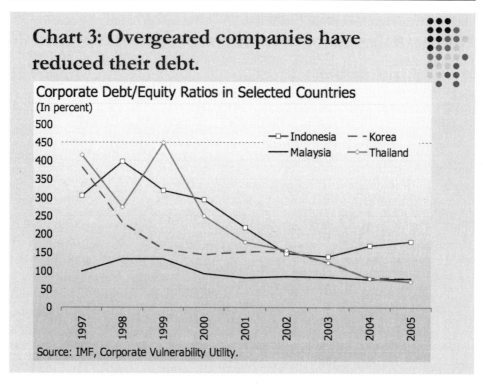

Chart 3: Overgeared companies have reduced their debt.

Corporate Debt/Equity Ratios in Selected Countries
(In percent)

Source: IMF, Corporate Vulnerability Utility.

Information exchange and policy dialogue have been stepped up since the crisis through various fora including ASEAN and ASEAN+3, with the crisis perhaps creating a stronger sense of regional identity.

Under the ASEAN+3 framework, a system of bilateral swap arrangements (the Chiang Mai Initiative) was set up after the crisis. Earlier this month, a plan was announced to strengthen this mechanism by turning it into a reserve pooling arrangement. The IMF supports this initiative, seeing it as a useful complement to its own financing.

In order to broaden and deepen regional capital markets, efforts are underway to promote local bond markets, with a view to developing and diversifying sources of funding in Asia. Government initiatives in this area, including under the Asian Bond Market Initiative and the two Asian Bond Funds, are facilitating a bottom up process of integration.

As a result of these changes at both the national and regional level, the strength and resilience of Asia's financial sectors have been enhanced, making the region better placed to benefit from the globalization of finance. Indeed, over the past year emerging Asia has been able to handle well two moderate bouts of global financial market turbulence, recovering quickly from each episode. However, the regional economy remains to be tested by a major disturbance to global financial markets.

Continuing challenges from capital flows

Nevertheless, Asia continues to face challenges from its increasing financial integration at the global and regional levels. One issue that officials in many countries are currently grappling with is how to deal with surges in capital inflows. While net inflows have been relatively constant in recent years, gross inflows and outflows have both risen sharply (see chart 4 [below]). The increase in outflows is particularly noteworthy. It reflects a growing desire of Asians to invest outside their home countries. This is a natural and healthy result of Asia's growing financial integration with the global economy.

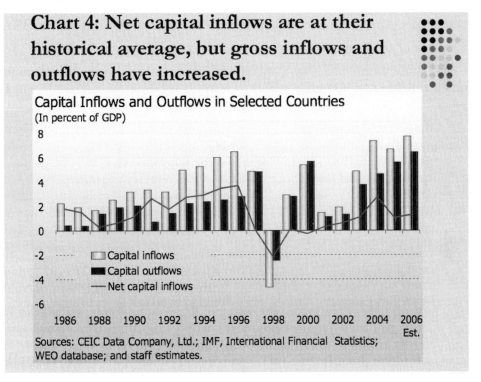

Chart 4: Net capital inflows are at their historical average, but gross inflows and outflows have increased.

Capital Inflows and Outflows in Selected Countries
(In percent of GDP)

Legend:
- Capital inflows
- Capital outflows
- Net capital inflows

Sources: CEIC Data Company, Ltd.; IMF, International Financial Statistics; WEO database; and staff estimates.

As well as increasing in scale, gross capital flows in the region have also become more volatile. A particular concern here is that surges in inflows can put strong upward pressure on currencies; can provide additional— sometimes unwanted—loanable funds in the financial sector, potentially contributing to asset price bubbles; and, perhaps most importantly, can create a risk that funds might flow out more quickly than they came in.

A temptation may be to address these concerns by imposing some form of capital controls to discourage speculative inflows. While the use of capital controls cannot be entirely ruled out, it can be very difficult to do in practice in these circumstances, and is often counterproductive. There is evidence to suggest that capital controls tend to be particularly easily circumvented when they are imposed on previously liberalized systems. Also, in those circumstances controls can create doubts about the future direction of policy, potentially discouraging foreign direct investment.

Surges in capital inflows seem for the time being to be a feature of financial globalization. And there is no "magic bullet" for dealing with them. The best short-run policy response appears to be a combination of exchange rate flexibility, and limited intervention to smooth exchange rate movements. Over the longer term, further steps to develop and deepen financial markets, including in the context of regional financial integration, can also help. Further liberalization of restrictions on outflows, as warranted by the pace of financial market reform, can also support deeper integration and potentially offset swings in capital inflows.

Changes at the Fund

I would now to turn to how the IMF has changed in response to the Asia crisis, touching on just a few areas.

First, we have substantially raised the importance of financial sector surveillance, and of integrating this work more closely with our traditional macroeconomic analysis. The focus is on identifying potential vulnerabilities in the financial sector, and appropriate policy responses. This is now a central part of our dialogue with member countries. We have done a lot of work over the last decade to better understand how vulnerabilities in the financial sector can be transmitted to other sectors of the economy, and vice versa. We also follow developments in capital markets more closely than before, and analyze their potential implications for economic and financial stability.

Second, we now do more analysis at multilateral and regional levels, to complement our country-level work. The goal is to better capture common trends and actual and potential spillovers, especially from financial market developments.

Third, we are also assessing whether our financing tools for crisis prevention can be improved, and whether we can agree on a new liquidity instrument that would be both useful to, and used by, emerging market countries.

Fourth, we have learned better the importance of country ownership. We give prominence to the government's own priorities in program design. And we have streamlined the conditions attached to our lending so that they cover only issues critical to macroeconomic stability and growth.

Finally, we are moving ahead with governance reform. The objective is to ensure that voice and representation in the Fund better reflect the realities of today's global economy. We took an important step at our Annual Meetings in Singapore where the Fund's Governors agreed to a two-year program of change, starting with increases in quotas for China, Mexico,

Korea, and Turkey. The Governors also agreed that the next stage should involve further increases in quotas for the Fund's most dynamic members, while making sure that the voice of low income countries is protected. The second stage is to be completed no later than September 2008. Dynamic emerging market countries, including those in Asia, must feel that they have an adequate voice in the Fund—that the Fund is their institution, and not one run by others and in which they have inadequate voice.

Concluding thoughts

I would like to conclude by touching on the role now of the IMF in Asia. This has changed a lot since the Asia crisis. We no longer have programs with emerging market countries, as you know. But this is in fact a normal and desirable state of affairs—it was the Asia crisis and the aftermath that were the aberrations. We continue to be closely engaged with our members in Asia, both at a national level and in regional fora. This engagement is based very much on two-way dialogue, in which the Fund can bring global economic perspectives and the experience of the membership at large to bear on national and regional economic issues; and in which the Asian perspective can be brought to global economic questions. We also provide considerable technical assistance and training to members in the region. The primary objective in all of this is to ensure financial stability both in the region, but also at the global level where Asia in an increasingly important player.

Thank you.

10C. *The Children*

In the chapter, Seth says in the interview that international finance is violence. This supplement provides the Executive Summary of a UNICEF report on the impact of the AFC on vulnerable groups, with a focus on children, in Thailand, Malaysia, South Korea, and Indonesia. In what ways is Seth right? In what ways is he completely wrong? If international finance is violence, how well did these countries protect their vulnerable from its brutality?

N. Jones & H. Marsden, "Assessing the Impacts of and Responses to the 1997–98 Asian Financial Crisis through a Child Right's Lens: Including Children in Policy Responses to Previous Economic Crises," United Nations Children's Fund (2010)

Executive Summary

The 'miracle' of East Asian economic growth was brought to a standstill when the Asian financial crisis hit in 1997, unleashing a range of economic, political and social consequences across the region and exposing this transformation as fragile and unstable. This paper examines the macro-micro impacts of the 1990s crisis in order to assess the impact pathways through which macroeconomic shocks affected children, youth and caregivers, and the extent to which different packages of economic and social policy responses mitigated the negative impacts on child wellbeing. It focuses on four countries most affected by the crisis: Indonesia, South Korea, Malaysia and Thailand.

The motivation for this study is as follows. The recent food, fuel and financial crises have sparked considerable debate as to how the effects of the resulting shocks on vulnerable populations in developing countries can best be mitigated. In light of the greater prevalence and distinctive nature of childhood poverty, it is important to ensure these discussions integrate age- and gender-specific considerations, and a more nuanced understanding of how previous economic shocks have affected children could help inform these debates. This study therefore seeks to add to this knowledge gap by drawing out important lessons from the experience of the Asian 1997/98 financial crisis, arguing that a review a decade after the 1990s crisis is particularly valuable because it allows for an assessment not only of the short-term effects of a major macroeconomic shock on child wellbeing but also of its more medium-term effects. More generally, given that 2009 is the 20th anniversary of the UN Convention on the Rights of the Child, it is obviously timely to consider the extent to which children's rights have been affected by major economic and social policy choices and to tease out relevant learning for future crisis contexts . . .

Impacts of the Asian economic crisis: Assessing transmission belts from the macro through micro levels on children and caregivers

Macro-level shocks

The Asian economic crisis was triggered after the Thai government allowed the baht to float in July 2007, which led to a crisis of confidence not only in the Thai economy but also among the Asian Tigers more generally. As the contagion effect from Thailand spread, the region experienced sudden capital flight and the drying up of liquidity. Reversing sometimes decades of positive economic growth, gross domestic product (GDP) growth contracted sharply and inflation spiked for food and consumer goods and services. This in turn led to sudden and widespread unemployment and a reduction in the value of real wages. Overall, Indonesia was most negatively affected, followed by Thailand, and both countries endured the highest social costs, including sharply decreased remittance flows, and took the longest to recover from the crisis aftermath. In Malaysia and Korea, the stronger pre-crisis macroeconomic health of both countries afforded the government greater fiscal space within which to intervene, and as a result the recovery time was shorter, but not without considerable pain.

Meso-level impacts on human development, poverty and inequality

At the meso level, these macro-level shocks resulted in a sharp increase in poverty in the four countries, and had the greatest impact on Indonesia. Urban areas were most negatively affected, partly because of their proximity to markets and rising food and commodity prices, but rural areas—where most of the poor resided—were also significantly impacted. Poor agricultural producers, faced with the rising price of inputs and, in the case of Indonesia, the effects of the El Niño drought, struggled to take advantage of rising food prices.

In terms of age-specific impacts, young people and new entrants to the labour market were especially affected by the financial shock and subsequent unemployment, underemployment and lack of opportunities. The employment impacts also fell heavily on older people, especially women, who generally lacked the skills and education to find new employment sources following retrenchment.

With important implications for the paper's focus on children and caregivers, there is considerable evidence to suggest that the Asian financial crisis impacted men and women differently, with the gender development index ranking worsening for all the case study countries except Korea. Overall male unemployment rates increased more in all countries, but women's overall labour force participation was significantly lower pre-crisis and women appear to have been more vulnerable to deteriorating conditions of work. Those concentrated in low or semi-skilled jobs in the hard-hit service and industrial export-oriented sectors were especially vulnerable. There are also reports that women found it more difficult in comparison with men to find new work post-retrenchment, and increasingly sought new forms of income in the informal sector, often of a precarious and risky nature, including sex work. Evidence of men entering into new and insecure work is a gap in the findings.

Micro-level impacts on households

The micro-level impacts of the crisis were multiple, although they varied significantly between male- and female-headed households.

Diminishing household expenditure and consumption: Households were forced to make expenditure and consumption cutbacks in the quantity and quality of food and services in the face of declining purchasing power and reduced incomes. Overall, household expenditure decreased and the share allocated to food increased, but this often involved a switch to less and lower quality food. Spending on health also declined. The utilisation of health facilities decreased in Indonesia, Korea and Malaysia, but increased in Thailand, although there was a significant shift away from private services to lower-quality public services. By contrast, the evidence suggests that although households struggled with the costs of education, these were largely maintained at the expense of luxury goods. Children may have also borne the brunt of cutbacks in terms of recreation activities and clothes, as evidence from Indonesia suggests.

Intra-household dynamics: The limited evidence that exists on the gendered intra-household impacts of the crisis suggests mixed effects. In some cases, changing economic circumstances arguably opened up new opportunities to shift unequal gender relations as women were accorded greater decision-making power in households owing to higher contributions to household income. In other cases, however, unequal gender relations are also reported to have been magnified, with women having less access to household resources and more demanding time burdens.

Reproduction, nurture and care: The financial crisis impacted on the care economy and generally resulted in larger care burdens for women and also girls. In addition, there was an increase in gender-based violence, breakdown of familial relationships and divorce rates. Fertility patterns also changed, with more couples reportedly choosing to wait for the economy to recover before having children.

Psychological impacts: The crisis is found to have had detrimental impacts on the psychological health and suicide rates of adults, with notable gender differences. While the spill-over impacts on children and youth are poorly documented, evidence from other contexts suggests that the effects are likely to have been negative and considerable (e.g., Kahn et al., 2004).

Impacts on children's rights

. . . Survival: Importantly, basic health indicators such as life expectancy and infant and child mortality rates were protected throughout the crisis years across the four countries. Downward trends in malnutrition also continued, but there was an increase in short-term malnutrition in Indonesia. Here, mothers buffered the impacts of the crisis from their children, but increased anaemia among pregnant women impacted infants' micronutrient deficiency. In terms of health-seeking behaviour, children's (less than three years old) contact with immunisation services decreased in Indonesia, and there is some evidence of increased morbidity during the crisis years from Indonesia and Thailand. Overall, there was a decline in the use of child health services, with the exception of Thailand, where private service usage shifted significantly towards public services.

Development: Household spending (although constrained) and government safety nets appear to have protected children's right to education relatively well and fewer working opportunities encouraged greater enrolments . . . .

Protection: The evidence on the effects of the crisis on children's right to protection is more limited and fragmented, but existing evidence suggests that there were important implications for the quality and quantity of care children received from caregivers, heightened risk of child abuse and mixed impacts on children's engagement in child labour. First, in terms of care, the number of children living on the streets increased in Indonesia and Thailand and they were at increased risk of sex work, drug use and crime. There was also an increase in child abandonment and children taken into care in all four countries. Increased poverty among women in general and rising rates of female migration in Indonesia in particular suggests that there may have been additional impacts on care time and quality. This is an area which requires further research.

Another area of significant concern, but about which there was no evidence of the direct impacts on children, is the implications of the rising incidence of mental ill-health as a result of the crisis on especially men but also women. Evidence from other contexts (e.g., Kahn et al., 2004) suggests that parental mental ill-health can have serious negative implications for child wellbeing and this is therefore an area that should also be monitored in the context of the current crisis.

Second, in terms of violence against children, there is some limited evidence of rising rates of child abuse from Thailand and Malaysia, associated with sudden parental unemployment and reduced working hours in the latter. However, there is more ample evidence about rising rates of gender-based conflict and violence, and it can therefore be hypothesised that these dynamics are likely to have had negative physical and psychological spill-over effects on children also.

Third, there is mixed evidence on child labour, most likely owing to data constraints. In Indonesia, older children appeared to have shouldered the burden by working longer hours, especially girls in terms of unpaid domestic work. The number of children in work or looking for work declined overall . . .

Policy responses

. . . **Social sector reform and investment in basic services:** Overall, the paper's analysis highlights an important tension between cutting social expenditure on basic services and increasing that on social protection. Indonesia and Thailand had a more limited resource base and greater debts when the financial crisis struck, hampering their ability to protect these spheres, and so significant cutbacks in basic services were made (some in crucial areas, such as reproductive health and preventative health care measures in Thailand). Social protection packages were later scaled up (Thailand) and designed largely from scratch (Indonesia), with the help of external funds in order to mitigate the worst effects on the poor. Malaysia and Korea had greater resource bases and fiscal space, allowing them greater freedom to protect spending on health and education. Malaysia actually increased its social sector spending, allowing the government to build on its already comparatively strong social service structures and programmes. Korea too was able largely to maintain social spending, with some slight dips in crisis years, combined with a push towards privatisation of the health system.

Social protection: Informal social protection mechanisms through family and community links are reported to have proved critical in shielding negative crisis impacts on the poor and children, especially in the immediate aftermath of the crisis before formal social protection programmes were brought in or scaled up, and for those without access to these. However, these also came under threat in some contexts as social capital and social cohesion eroded, reflected in rising rates of crime and violence, homelessness and drug abuse and falling community participation.

* * *

10D. *G22 Reports*

Seth says that talk about a New International Financial Architecture was just that, talk. In 1998, the G-22 issued a report that explained the agendas of two working groups: strengthening domestic financial systems and managing international financial crises. This excerpt includes executive summaries of the agendas of the latter two working groups. When you look at it, there's not much that's "new." What in view of the G22 is the best way of strengthening domestic financial systems, given increased global financial integration? As to the working group on international financial crises, what do you see that might be "new?" Avoiding government-induced moral hazard? Contractual arrangements that can introduce payment flexibility and risk sharing? Choice of exchange rate regime? Effective national insolvency regimes? The importance of the IMF? The one thing that the report did foresee is the increased incorporation of "collective action causes" (CACs) in bonds.

Working Groups of the G22, Reports on the International
Financial Architecture: "Strengthening Financial Systems" &
"International Financial Crises" (1998)

Report of the Working Group on Strengthening Financial Systems

EXECUTIVE SUMMARY

Like many crises before it, the international financial crisis that began in Asia clearly demonstrates the importance of robust and efficient domestic financial systems. Weak banking systems and poorly developed capital markets contributed to the misallocation of resources that led to the crisis. Key to the strengthening of domestic financial systems is the implementation of sound practices for supervision, settlement, accounting and disclosure. This requires close international cooperation and collaboration among those in the official sector who are involved in the supervision of financial systems.

Implementation of sound practices requires that, first, there be a consensus on what constitutes sound practices. In many areas of banking supervision and securities regulation, international consensus has been reached and principles or standards have been established. In other areas, there still is a need to define best practices and develop standards. Standards should be developed in a collaborative manner to ensure that both the developed and emerging world have a voice in the standard-setting processes. The inclusion of a wider range of countries helps to ensure that the standards developed are more widely adopted in a timely fashion.

> **The Working Group endorses this broad international consultative process for the development and refinement of sets of standards and sound practices.**

The implementation of sound practices depends on incentives to do so. These can be in the form of market-based incentives, either alone or in combination with official or regulatory incentives. The global nature of financial markets highlights the importance of international cooperation among those in the official sector involved in the supervision of financial systems. The Working Group looked at ways to best foster cooperation and coordination to ensure consistent application and to make best use of the limited resources available to help strengthen financial systems.

STANDARDS

The Basle Committee on Banking Supervision (BCBS) has produced the *Core Principles for Effective Banking Supervision* and the International Organisation of Securities Commissions (IOSCO) has produced the *Statement of Objectives and Principles of Securities Regulation* and *International Disclosure Standards for Cross-Border Offerings and Initial Listings by Foreign Issuers*. These, along with the IMF's *Special Data Dissemination Standard,* represent a significant contribution to efforts to strengthen financial systems and should be implemented rapidly.

> **The Working Group endorses these existing sets of principles and underscores the importance of their rapid implementation.**

The Working Party considers it essential to develop sets of sound practice in the area of corporate governance. Economies become vulnerable to systemic stress when a large number of individual firms fails to formulate and pursue prudent business strategies, to establish and apply effective systems of internal control, and to monitor and manage the full range of financial and commercial risks to which they are exposed. The Working Group attaches particular importance to elements of corporate governance and structure relating to risk management and control—most notably the management of liquidity and foreign exchange risk. The mismatch between the maturity of foreign currency assets and liabilities in national banking systems must not get too far out of line with the capacity of the domestic authorities to supply foreign currency liquidity from the official reserves and any contingent financing that may be available.

> **The Working Group considers it essential that sets of sound practices in the area of corporate governance continue to be developed, and supports the related efforts of the OECD and the BCBS. The Working Group encourages the prompt implementation of the BCBS recommendations regarding internal controls. The Basle-based committees, working together with the IFIs, should also consider the management of both domestic and foreign currency liquidity in different sectors. The IMF should give priority to work on the macroeconomic dimensions of liquidity and related risks.**

The lack of well-developed money and capital markets is another important root cause of banking crises. The Working Party emphasised the importance of fostering the emergence and growth of these markets where they are not found currently and will seek concrete ways to give momentum to their development.

SAFETY NETS

In the crisis in Asia the authorities faced difficult choices in considering whether, and on what terms, they would offer support so that financially troubled banks and non-bank entities could meet their obligations. Explicit safety net arrangements help to reduce the risk of indiscriminate extension of public guarantees. Yet care must be taken in designing them, as poorly designed or overly generous arrangements dull incentives to monitor risks, thereby increasing the likelihood of the crises they aspire to deal with. A well-designed set of explicit, ex ante procedures with pre-ordained hierarchies of claims and/or loss sharing arrangements reduces the need for ad hoc, ex post actions. The Group stresses the importance of identifying criteria to determine the appropriate limits on the extension of public guarantees.

Having in place a well-designed framework for the resolution process in the case of a future systemic crisis will alter expectations by the public and by institutional investors and may thus help to enhance financial stability. The Group's report introduces some basic guidelines and urges that they be developed further in a collaborative effort, drawing on the experience of various international fora.

> **The Working Group recommends adopting, implementing and enforcing a method of structured early intervention in the banking sector which includes a well-considered set of**

mechanisms to ensure a consistent, timely and graduated response by supervisors.

Depositor protection schemes are also part of the financial safety net. Among their most important goals are: increasing the stability of the financial system by reducing the risk of bank runs and contagion, and assisting small depositors who typically do not have the capacity to monitor the soundness of banks.

The Group encourages the BCBS, with substantive input from the IMF and the World Bank, to develop guidelines for deposit insurance with emphasis on measures to reduce moral hazard and adverse selection.

Insolvency regimes are also an important part of an economy-wide safety net because they serve to make the risks and consequences of a failure of a corporate entity easier to quantify for all parties involved and lower the prospect of ad hoc, ex post assistance or guarantees which distort incentives. The Working Group on International Financial Crises developed key principles and features of effective insolvency regimes for commercial entities.

The Working Group supports the key principles and features of insolvency regimes in view of their importance for enhancing financial stability.

When ex post actions are necessary, however, it is important to distinguish between restructuring banks and other financial institutions in "normal times" (defined by the absence of systemic risk within the financial system and through the economy at large) and in crisis situations. The Working Group will continue in its efforts to develop guidelines for restructuring of financial institutions in normal and crisis situations.

IMPLEMENTATION OF STANDARDS AND SOUND PRACTICES

Market discipline should be employed to promote the implementation of sound practices. However, such discipline does not work without adequate transparency and appropriate incentives to price risk. The lack of international consensus on sound practices for loan valuation, loan-loss provisioning and credit risk disclosure seriously impairs the ability of market analysts as well as regulators to understand and assess the risks inherent in a financial institution's activities.

The Working Group supports the ongoing work of the BCBS in the improvement of asset valuation and loan loss provisioning and underscores the importance of IASC completing its set of core accounting standards.

It may make sense for financial market participants to establish a mechanism for developing collective, publicly available assessments of key aspects of national financial infrastructure—such as the supervisory systems for financial institutions; accounting and disclosure practices; corporate governance; legal regimes relevant to investment, including arrangements for dealing with insolvency; and payment and settlement systems.

> **The Working Group recommends that the official sector initiate a dialogue with relevant private organisations, professional groups and institutions on how the private sector can more effectively utilise the information that is now, or will become, available on the key institutional aspects of national financial systems.**

Among regulatory tools, the Basle Capital Accord is an excellent example of a relatively straightforward regulatory device that has proved useful in focusing attention on the importance of bank capital. The Accord is under review, motivated in part by a desire to foster improved risk evaluation and management in conditions where the nature of banks' activities and financial techniques are undergoing rapid change.

> **The Working Group advocates timely progress on this review of the Basle Capital Accord.**

Access to major financial markets for emerging market institutions is an important element in the effort to strengthen financial systems. An international consensus on concrete criteria to be used by national authorities when determining conditions for market access could help to ensure equitable conditions for market entry and to prevent competition in laxity.

> **The Working Group is of one view on the benefits of open access, but recognises that it should not occur in such a way as to undermine the quality of supervision. Principles guiding national practices with respect to market access for banks should be developed jointly by industrial and emerging market countries. The IFIs could provide a forum for such efforts.**

Conditionality for IFI programmes is a powerful means of fostering implementation of standards and sound practices and the Working Group supports the application of conditionality to measures pertaining to financial stability, recognising that the proper sequencing must be carefully considered as well as the impact on social stability, particularly in crisis situations.

Official oversight is another way in which implementation can be encouraged. The particular type and combination of oversight mechanisms (conditionality, surveillance, peer review, comprehensive technical assistance programmes) that are most suitable for enhancing financial stability will vary from country to country.

> **The Working Group is of the view that all countries should go through some process of independent assessment, subject to the condition that the process meets certain minimum standards and contains a core set of elements.**

With respect to surveillance, the IMF has the advantage of having a well established surveillance mechanism that covers all member countries. However, it lacks the resources and expertise to conduct financial sector surveillance alone. The World Bank, on the other hand, has greater resources and expertise in this field, but its country coverage is limited. The Working Group recommends that financial sector surveillance be anchored in the IMF's surveillance process but benefit from expertise at the World Bank and elsewhere. Serious consideration of using peer reviews as a component of, or complement to, financial sector surveillance is warranted.

INTERNATIONAL COOPERATION

At present, supervision of the global financial system is fragmented both functionally and geographically, while global financial markets are becoming increasingly integrated. Geographical fragmentation is addressed through cooperation among different international groupings of functional supervisors, and the functional separation by cooperation among international groupings of banking, securities and insurance supervisors in the Joint Forum. The Working Party exchanged views on the adequacy of these arrangements and how they can be improved or reformed.

> **The Group also endorses the G-7 *Principles for Information Exchange,* and urges their implementation in industrial and emerging market countries.**

The Group also considered global oversight of—and accreditation mechanisms for—supervisors to promote coordination across functions and to help support the independence of supervisors. To this end some members suggested seeking the involvement of the private sector. Other possible approaches include an international group of eminent experts to consult with supervisory authorities, and consideration of standards for internal managerial audits of supervisors.

Cooperation among IFIs and international groupings—to ensure effective surveillance and develop sets of sound practices—is important for strengthening financial systems. The Group discussed the need for enhanced cooperation among the IFIs (including regional MDBs) and international regulatory groupings, but has not yet developed thorough and concrete proposals.

The Group agreed that it would not be feasible to overhaul the IFIs, or set up a new large international financial institution. The division of responsibilities should reflect operational efficiency, avoid extending into each others' core activities, and enhanced accountability. In areas where responsibilities are shared, the IFIs need to ensure collaboration. The Group sees considerable promise in the following innovations:

- a Financial Sector Policy Forum in which finance ministry, central bank, regulatory and IFI representatives could meet to discuss international financial sector issues, across functional levels, and with full inclusion of systemically important emerging markets;
- a system for the exchange of information on financial sector regulatory and supervisory methods and findings; and
- a process of coordination or a clearing house to match demands from individual countries for technical assistance in financial regulation matters with the supply of experts.

The Group welcomes the setting up of the Basle Core Principles Liaison Group and plans for cooperation between the World Bank and IMF, including the creation of the Financial Sector Liaison Committee to adapt the division of work to country-specific situations, foster dissemination of standards and sound practices and help optimise the use of resources and facilitate joint work. The subject of enhanced cooperation will be explored further by the Working Group.

Report of the Working Group on International Financial Crises

EXECUTIVE SUMMARY

The larger scale and greater diversity apparent in recent capital flows to emerging markets have been of immense benefit both to emerging market countries and the world as a whole. However, they also allow crises to erupt and spread more quickly and with greater force than in the past. These new risks make it more essential than ever that countries pursue sound domestic policies to minimise their vulnerability to contagion.

Over the past year, many investors have suffered significant losses on certain emerging market debt instruments. As a result, there has been a general withdrawal of funds from emerging markets without respect for the diversity of prospects facing those countries. This report does not aim to address the critical current issues arising from this contagion. Rather, it focuses on the architecture required for the future. The international community has an interest in encouraging credit and investment decisions based on careful analysis that is focused on the long-term strengths and fundamentals of the economies involved. *Moreover, it is critical that the international financial system strengthen its ability to limit and better manage international financial crises, including appropriate roles for the official community and private sector.*

This report identifies a range of policies and institutional innovations that could help prevent international financial crises and facilitate the orderly resolution of the crises that may occur in the future. It highlights questions that would have to be addressed in the context of a particular crisis, given the circumstances at the time and the types of instruments that are contributing to the crisis. It seeks to identify for further consideration principles that could help guide debtors, their private creditors and the official community in answering these often difficult questions. In particular, this report identifies for consideration policies that could help reduce the frequency and limit the scope of future crises, improve creditor coordination, and promote the orderly, cooperative and equitable resolution of the international financial crises that occur in the future. Some of the recommendations will require further examination and will take time to implement. The report should not be considered an agenda for addressing the problems currently being experienced in many emerging markets.

POLICIES THAT COULD HELP REDUCE THE FREQUENCY AND LIMIT THE SEVERITY OF INTERNATIONAL FINANCIAL CRISES

The number and depth of recent payments crises have highlighted the critical importance of adopting policies to reduce their frequency and limit their severity. A range of policies can contribute to crisis prevention and help limit the scope of the crises which do occur. A number of these are examined in the reports of the other two Working Groups. This report highlights four issues in particular: limiting the scope of government guarantees; expanding the use of innovative financing arrangements that provide emerging markets with greater insurance against periods of market volatility; maintaining appropriate exchange rate regimes; and implementing effective insolvency and debtor-creditor regimes.

Implicit or explicit access to government resources on subsidised terms distorts market incentives and may encourage private debtors and creditors to take excessive risks.

Limiting, to the extent possible, the range of economic and financial activity that is covered, implicitly or explicitly, by government guarantees and ensuring that those guarantees which are offered are as explicit as possible and are "priced" appropriately, so as to reflect the risks being insured by the government, would contribute critically to crisis prevention.

The Working Group recognises the role of the government in protecting smaller depositors in the banking system and the overall integrity of the payments and financial system. However, preserving the stability of the financial and payments system does not require protecting individual banks, their managers or their equity owners from the risk of failure. (See the report of the Working Group on Strengthening Financial Systems for more detailed recommendations on the management of the financial safety net.)

Recent events have highlighted the continued vulnerability of many emerging markets to external shocks and the consequent need for the prudent management of their external liabilities.

> **The Working Group encourages the development and greater use of innovative financing techniques that could provide, depending on the nature of the arrangements, either greater payments flexibility or the assurance of new financing in the event of adverse market developments.**

Arrangements that could provide more flexibility in payments and greater risk sharing among debtors and creditors include: pre-negotiated options that would allow the debtor to extend automatically the maturity of certain obligations, debt instruments under which repayments would be reduced in certain precise, contractually defined circumstances, or other insurance-type products. Contractual arrangements that would provide assured new financing or guaranteed liquidity in the event of market volatility include the contingent credit and liquidity facilities that several countries have recently negotiated. Such contingent credit and liquidity lines may provide additional liquidity at a lower cost than holding a comparable quantity of reserves and may also exert useful ex ante policy discipline. Governments should use such lines prudently, just as they should use their reserves prudently, and, in particular, should not use them as a means of postponing adjustment.

The choice of an exchange rate regime is one of the most critical policy choices any country can make. This report does not seek to resolve the complex issues associated with the choice of an exchange rate regime; it seeks only to identify certain issues so as to help policy-makers avoid policy mistakes which can contribute to an international financial crisis. It should be emphasised that the policy mistakes which can contribute to an international financial crisis can occur in the context of any exchange rate regime.

Recent events in Asia have highlighted the critical importance of strong insolvency and debtor-creditor regimes to crisis prevention, crisis mitigation and crisis resolution. Effective national insolvency regimes contribute to crisis prevention by providing the predictable legal framework needed to address the financial difficulties of troubled firms before the accumulated financial difficulties of the corporate sector spill over into an economy-wide payments crisis. Such a predictable framework is also essential to the orderly resolution of corporate financial difficulties, and thus is an essential element of any regime for orderly and cooperative crisis management. Among the most important basic objectives of an insolvency regime are: to maximise the ex post value of the firm, whether it is liquidated or reorganised; to provide a fair and predictable regime for the distribution of assets recovered from debtors; and to facilitate the provision of credit for commercial transactions by providing an orderly regime for the distribution of the proceeds of debtors' assets . . .

POLICIES TO ENCOURAGE CREDITOR COORDINATION

Difficulties associated with creditor coordination can preclude the orderly and cooperative resolution of international financial crises, as actions taken by an individual creditor in pursuit of its own self-interest, narrowly defined, can reduce the potential resources available for all creditors, in part, by failing to create a framework that provides the debtor with the time and incentives needed to adopt and implement the policy adjustments required for orderly crisis resolution. Certain contractual clauses—the collective representation clause, the majority action clause and the sharing clause—could be incorporated into the legal documentation of sovereign bonds issued in foreign offerings in order to encourage more effective creditor coordination should difficulties occur.

> **To encourage the adoption of such "collective action clauses", the Working Group recommends that their governments give consideration to: (i) engaging in educational efforts with identified constituencies in major financial centres to promote the use of collective action clauses in sovereign and quasi-sovereign bonds issued in foreign offerings; (ii) identifying sovereign and quasi-sovereign issuers likely to come to their markets soon and encouraging such issuers to use the collective action clauses; and (iii) examining the use of such clauses in their own sovereign and quasi-sovereign bonds issued in foreign offerings.**

The Working Group discussed the possible merits and potential difficulties associated with the creation of new channels to enhance communication between the IMF, other international financial institutions and private market participants and emphasised the need for any arrangement to be fair and transparent.

PROMOTING THE ORDERLY, COOPERATIVE AND EQUITABLE RESOLUTION OF INTERNATIONAL FINANCIAL CRISES

Recent events have highlighted how the larger scale and greater diversity of recent capital flows to emerging markets generate the risk that payments crises can erupt more quickly and can be larger in scope than in the past. The assistance and support of the IMF and other international financial institutions for their members in the event of a crisis, in the context of a strong programme of policy adjustments, remain critically important.

> **The IMF must have sufficient resources to remain capable of catalysing policy reform and the restoration of market confidence. Therefore, it is essential to implement rapidly the agreed IMF quota increase and to put into place the New Arrangements to Borrow (NAB).**
>
> **Countries that anticipate possible difficulties should seek early assistance from the IMF, in order to reduce the risk that they will be placed in a position where they lack sufficient resources to meet their debt obligations in full. The combination of adjustment and financing typically associated with IMF assistance should be sufficient to resolve most payments difficulties and should continue to constitute the normal framework for managing and resolving international financial crises.**

The size, sophistication and heterogeneity characteristic of recent international capital flows have reduced the relevance of the procedures used in the past to ensure an appropriate private sector role in resolving severe international financial crises. In particular, many such procedures were developed and proved effective during the 1980s, in an era when a small number of large international banks provided most capital flows to emerging markets.

> **The same capacity for innovation that enabled the private sector to help create markets for a range of new emerging market debt instruments should be applied to modernise existing procedures and institutions or to develop new practices that will contribute to the orderly and cooperative resolution of future crises.**

Such innovation is required because the scale of private capital flows significantly exceeds the resources that can reasonably be provided by the official community, even with the needed quota increase to bolster IMF resources and other measures to supplement the ability of international financial institutions to provide emergency liquidity during severe financial crises. Moreover, the perception that sufficient official financial assistance may be made available to allow a country to meet all contractual obligations without some form of appropriate private sector involvement may distort the incentives of both creditors and debtors, encouraging some creditors to take unwarranted financial risk and some debtor countries to follow inappropriate policies.

A country that anticipates possible difficulties meeting the terms of debt contracts, public or private, should immediately undertake appropriate policy adjustments to enhance its capacity to meet those obligations. The international community has a clear interest in assuring that no country suspends debt payments as an alternative to policy reform and adjustment, given the costs associated with even a temporary suspension of payments.

Countries should make the strongest possible efforts to meet the terms and conditions of all debt contracts in full and on time.

Nonetheless, it is unlikely that temporary interruptions in payments on some debt obligations would never occur, particularly if there were to be unanticipated adverse market developments. In cases where an interruption in debt payments is unavoidable, a voluntary, cooperative and orderly debt restructuring, combined with the adoption of a strong programme of policy reform to enhance the debtor's payments capacity, constitutes the most efficient means of crisis resolution.

When the government of a crisis country faces the possibility that either it or a significant portion of the country's private sector may be unable to meet their obligations on time and in full, the government should initiate discussions with private creditors aimed at achieving a voluntary agreement on a strategy for addressing the country's debt problems.

In some circumstances, a purely voluntary approach may be impractical. In particular, it might consume so much time that it would lead to an erosion of confidence that would be contrary to the collective interest of creditors and debtors in a cooperative and equitable workout.

Recent experience has underscored the fact that unilateral actions, especially if they substitute for reform and adjustment, are highly disruptive.

In those extreme cases where a temporary suspension of payments cannot be avoided, experience indicates that a disorderly workout is against the interests of debtors, creditors and the international community.

A disorderly workout fails to promote the common interests of all parties in prompt and equitable crisis resolution in two ways: first, it fails to maintain incentives for the debtor to pursue a programme of strong and sustained policy adjustments that will allow the rapid restoration of market access and help maintain the value of outstanding creditor claims, and second, the absence of a rapid and cooperative restructuring of payments can itself contribute to poor economic performance, leading to a reduction in the total resources available for debt service. In extreme cases, it is particularly important for the government of the crisis country to maintain an open and transparent approach to the country's private creditors and work with them to achieve a cooperative, orderly restructuring of contractual obligations.

> **In such extreme cases, the interests of all parties in orderly and cooperative restructuring of contractual obligations can be furthered by devising an enhanced framework for future crisis management that would allow the international community to signal its willingness to provide conditional financial support, where appropriate, in the context of a temporary payments suspension, in certain limited circumstances.**

Such an informal signal should be provided only if, in the judgment of the international community, a government's decision to suspend debt payments reflects the absence of reasonable alternatives, if the government is undertaking strong policy adjustments and if the government is engaged in good faith efforts with creditors to find a cooperative solution to the country's financial difficulties. Such a signal has been provided in certain exceptional cases during previous crises, so as to support a comprehensive and credible programme of policy reform and to encourage the negotiation of a cooperative agreement with creditors that places the country on a sustainable payments path, thus promoting the collective interests of both debtors and creditors.

> **The Working Group supports an IMF policy decision to indicate its willingness to consider providing financial support for policy adjustment, despite the presence of actual and/or impending arrears on the country's obligations to private creditors, including arrears on marketable debt instruments. Such a signal should be provided only if: the governmen though its maze of compliments were t of the crisis country is not interrupting debt payments as an alternative to reform and adjustment; it is implementing a strong programme of policy reform; it is making a good faith effort to work with creditors in finding a cooperative solution to the country's financial difficulties; and international support is critical to the success of a strong adjustment programme.**

In some cases governments facing the need for a comprehensive restructuring of debt payments arising from an extreme international financial crisis have imposed temporary capital and exchange controls in order to buttress a temporary suspension of payments. The use of such controls should be considered only in exceptional circumstances and in conjunction with IMF-supported programmes of policy adjustments to create the conditions required for the restoration of financial and macroeconomic stability and the ultimate restoration of currency convertibility. Even in such circumstances, it may be determined that the large costs associated with the suspension of convertibility, given the extensive ties created by modern financial markets, exceeds the possible contribution such measures could make to limiting balance of payments pressures.

Several factors are likely to determine the speed with which a country regains market access, including: the policy measures adopted by the government; the stance of the IMF and the official community more broadly towards the government's policy decisions; and the approach the government adopts towards its private creditors. Recent events have demonstrated that a financial crisis in one country can augment greatly market pressure on other countries. In such circumstances, the official sector may want to provide additional financing to countries which are pursuing appropriate policies but who nevertheless face increased pressure.

10E. *Kenneth Rogoff's Response to Stiglitz*

Seth's references to Stiglitz are based on the economist's widely-read book, Globalization and its Discontents. The book is well worth your read. Stiglitz is a pretty confident guy. Maybe too confident. Check out what another prominent economist, Kenneth Rogoff, has to say about him and his criticisms of the IMF.

K. Rogoff, "An Open Letter to Joseph Stiglitz, Author of
Globalization and Its Discontents" (2002)

An Open Letter
By Kenneth Rogoff,
Economic Counsellor and Director of Research,
International Monetary Fund

To Joseph Stiglitz,
Author of *Globalization and Its Discontents*
(New York: W.W. Norton & Company, June 2002)

Washington D.C., July 2, 2002

At the outset, I would like to stress that it has been a pleasure working closely with my World Bank colleagues—particularly my counterpart, Chief Economist Nick Stern—during my first year at the IMF. We regularly cross 19th Street to exchange ideas on research, policy, and life. The relations between our two institutions are excellent—this is not at issue. Of course, to that effect, I think it is also important, before I begin, for me to quash rumors about the demolition of the former PEPCO building that stood right next to the IMF until a few days ago. No, it's absolutely not true that this was caused by a loose cannon planted within the World Bank.

Dear Joe:

Like you, I came to my position in Washington from the cloisters of a tenured position at a top-ranking American University. Like you, I came because I care. Unlike you, I am humbled by the World Bank and IMF staff I meet each day. I meet people who are deeply committed to bringing growth to the developing world and to alleviating poverty. I meet superb professionals who regularly work 80-hour weeks, who endure long separations from their families. Fund staff have been shot at in Bosnia, slaved for weeks without heat in the brutal Tajikistan winter, and have contracted deadly tropical diseases in Africa. These people are bright, energetic, and imaginative. Their dedication humbles me, but in your speeches, in your book, you feel free to carelessly slander them.

Joe, you may not remember this, but in the late 1980s, I once enjoyed the privilege of being in the office next to yours for a semester. We young economists all looked up to you in awe. One of my favorite stories from that era is a lunch with you and our former colleague, Carl Shapiro, at which the two of you started discussing whether Paul Volcker merited your vote for a tenured appointment at Princeton. At one point, you turned to me and said, "Ken, you used to work for Volcker at the Fed. Tell me, is he really smart?" I responded something to the effect of "Well, he *was* arguably the greatest Federal Reserve Chairman of the twentieth century" To which you replied, "But is he smart like *us*?" I wasn't sure how to take it, since you were looking across at Carl, not me, when you said it.

My reason for telling this story is two-fold. First, perhaps the Fund staff who you once blanket-labeled as "third rate"—and I guess you meant to include World Bank staff in this judgment also—will feel better if they know they are in the same company as the great Paul Volcker. Second, it is emblematic of the supreme self-confidence you brought with you to Washington, where you were confronted with policy problems just a little bit more difficult than anything in our mathematical models. This confidence brims over in your new 282 page book. Indeed, I failed to detect a single instance where you, Joe Stiglitz, admit to having been even slightly wrong about a major real world problem. When the U.S. economy booms in the 1990s, you take some credit. But when anything goes wrong, it is because lesser mortals like Federal Reserve Chairman Greenspan or then-Treasury Secretary Rubin did not listen to your advice.

Let me make three substantive points. First, there are many ideas and lessons in your book with which we at the Fund would generally agree, though most of it is old hat. For example, we completely agree that there is a need for a dramatic change in how we handle situations where countries go bankrupt. IMF First Deputy Managing Director Anne Krueger—who you paint as a villainess for her 1980s efforts to promote trade liberalization in World Bank policy—has forcefully advocated a far reaching IMF proposal. At our Davos [World Economic Forum] panel in February you sharply criticized the whole idea. Here, however, you now want to take credit as having been the one to strongly advance it first. Your book is long on innuendo and short on footnotes. Can you document this particular claim?

Second, you put forth a blueprint for how you believe the IMF can radically improve its advice on macroeconomic policy. Your ideas are at best highly controversial, at worst, snake oil. This leads to my third and most important point. In your role as chief economist at the World Bank, you decided to become what you see as a heroic whistleblower, speaking out against macroeconomic policies adopted during the 1990s Asian crisis that you believed to be misguided. You were 100% sure of yourself, 100% sure that your policies were absolutely the right ones. In the middle of a global wave of speculative attacks, that you yourself labeled a crisis of confidence, you fueled the panic by undermining confidence in the very institutions you were working for. Did it ever occur to you for a moment that your actions might have hurt the poor and indigent people in Asia that you care about so deeply? Do you ever lose a night's sleep thinking that just maybe, Alan Greenspan, Larry Summers, Bob Rubin, and Stan Fischer had it right— and that your impulsive actions might have deepened the downturn or delayed—even for a day—the recovery we now see in Asia?

Let's look at Stiglitzian prescriptions for helping a distressed emerging market debtor, the ideas you put forth as superior to existing practice. Governments typically come to the IMF for financial assistance when they are having trouble finding buyers for their debt and when the value of their money is falling. The Stiglitzian prescription is to raise the profile of fiscal deficits, that is, to issue *more* debt and to print *more* money. You seem to believe that if a distressed government issues more currency, its citizens will suddenly think it more valuable. You seem to believe that when investors are no longer willing to hold a government's debt, all that needs to be done is to increase the supply and it will sell like hot cakes. We at the IMF—no, make that we on the Planet Earth—have considerable experience suggesting otherwise. We earthlings have found that when a country in fiscal distress tries to escape by printing more money, inflation rises, often uncontrollably. Uncontrolled inflation strangles growth, hurting the entire populace but, especially the indigent. The laws of economics may be different in your part of the gamma quadrant, but around here we find that when an almost bankrupt government fails to credibly constrain the time profile of its fiscal deficits, things generally get worse instead of better.

Joe, throughout your book, you condemn the IMF because everywhere it seems to be, countries are in trouble. Isn't this a little like observing that where there are epidemics, one tends to find more doctors?

You cloak yourself in the mantle of John Maynard Keynes, saying that the aim of your policies is to maintain full employment. We at the IMF care a lot about employment. But if a government has come to us, it is often precisely because it is in an unsustainable position, and we have to look not just at the next two weeks, but at the next two years and beyond. We certainly believe in the lessons of Keynes, but in a modern, nuanced way. For example, the post-1975 macroeconomics literature—which you say we are tone deaf to—emphasizes the importance of budget constraints across time. It does no good to pile on IMF debt as a very short-run fix if it makes the not-so-distant future drastically worse. By the way, in blatant contradiction to your assertion, IMF programs frequently allow for deficits, indeed they did so in the Asia crisis. If its initial battlefield medicine was wrong, the IMF reacted, learning from its mistakes, quickly reversing course.

No, instead of Keynes, I would cloak your theories in the mantle of Arthur Laffer and other extreme expositors of 1980s Reagan-style supply-side economics. Laffer believed that if the government would only cut tax rates, people would work harder, and total government revenues would rise. The Stiglitz-Laffer theory of crisis management holds that countries need not worry about expanding deficits, as in so doing, they will increase their debt service capacity more than proportionately. George Bush, Sr. once labeled these ideas "voodoo economics." He was right. I will concede, Joe, that real-world policy economics is complicated, and just maybe further research will prove you have a point. But what really puzzles me is how you could be *so* sure that you are 100 percent right, so sure that you were willing to "blow the whistle" in the middle of the crisis, sniping at the paramedics as they tended the wounded. Joe, the academic papers now coming out in top journals are increasingly supporting the interest defense policies of former First Deputy Managing Director Stan Fischer and the IMF that you, from your position at the World Bank, ignominiously sabotaged. Do you ever think that just maybe, Joe Stiglitz might have screwed up? That, just maybe, you were part of the problem and not part of the solution?

You say that the IMF is tone deaf and never listens to its critics. I know that is not true, because in my academic years, I was one of dozens of critics that the IMF bent over backwards to listen to. For example, during the 1980s, I was writing then-heretical papers on the moral hazard problem in IMF/World Bank lending, an issue that was echoed a decade later in the Meltzer report. Did the IMF shut out my views as potentially subversive to its interests? No, the IMF insisted on publishing my work in its flagship research publication *Staff Papers*. Later, in the 1990s, Stan Fischer twice invited me to discuss my views on fixed exchange rates and open capital markets (I warned of severe risks). In the end, Stan and I didn't agree on everything, but I will say that having entered his office 99 percent sure that I was right, I left somewhat humbled by the complexities of price stabilization in high-inflation countries. If only you had crossed over 19th Street from the Bank to the Fund a little more often, Joe, maybe things would have turned out differently.

I don't have time here to do justice to some of your other offbeat policy prescriptions, but let me say this about the transition countries. You accuse the IMF of having "lost Russia." Your analysis of the transition in Russia reads like a paper in which a theorist abstracts from all the major problems, and focuses only on the couple he can handle. You neglect entirely the fact that when the IMF entered Russia, the country was not only in the middle of an economic crisis, it was in the middle of a social and political crisis as well.

Throughout your book, you betray an unrelenting belief in the pervasiveness of market failures, and a staunch conviction that governments can and will make things better. You call us "market fundamentalists." We do not believe that markets are always perfect, as you accuse. But we do believe there are many instances of government failure as well and that, on the whole, government failure is a far bigger problem than market failure in the developing world. Both World Bank President Jim Wolfensohn and IMF Managing Director Horst Köhler have frequently pointed to the fundamental importance of governance and institutions in development. Again, your alternative medicines, involving ever-more government intervention, are highly dubious in many real-world settings.

I haven't had time, Joe, to check all the facts in your book, but I do have some doubts. On page 112, you have Larry Summers (then Deputy U.S. Treasury Secretary) giving a "verbal" tongue lashing to former World Bank Vice-President Jean-Michel Severino. But, Joe, these two have never met. How many conversations do you report that never happened? You give an example where an IMF Staff report was issued prior to the country visit. Joe, this isn't done; I'd like to see your documentation. On page 208, you slander former IMF number two, Stan Fischer, implying that Citibank may have dangled a job offer in front of him in return for his cooperation in debt renegotiations. Joe, Stan Fischer is well known to be a person of unimpeachable integrity. Of all the false inferences and innuendos in this book, this is the most outrageous. I'd suggest you should pull this book off the shelves until this slander is corrected.

Joe, as an academic, you are a towering genius. Like your fellow Nobel Prize winner, John Nash, you have a "beautiful mind." As a policymaker, however, you were just a bit less impressive.

Other than that, I thought it was a pretty good book.

Sincerely yours,

Ken

CHAPTER 11

CAPITAL ADEQUACY

■■■

> *"As a scholar of the Great Depression, I honestly believe that September and October of 2008 was the worst financial crisis in global history, including the Great Depression."*
>
> —Quoting Fed Chairman Ben Bernanke, in B. Born, "Deregulation: A Major Cause of the Financial Crisis," Harvard Law & Policy Review, 233 (2011)

We're about to cover the 2008 global financial crisis, the worst crisis since the Great Depression. As we'll see, banks, and their "capital adequacy" as we say in the biz, were at the heart of the crisis. So we have to talk about what bank capital is, why it's important, and how it's regulated. We're going to concentrate on the Basel Accords, the first two here. "Yuck," you might say, "I'd rather watch paint dry." Well, you have to know this stuff, so deal with it. We'll try to inflict as little pain as possible. We'll keep it simple as best we can—this stuff can get pretty complex. You'll notice that there are no profiles or supplements for this chapter. You'll see them in Chapter 18, where we'll talk about post-crisis Basel III.

> *"Modern finance is complex, perhaps too complex. Regulation of modern finance is complex, almost certainly too complex. That configuration spells trouble. As you do not fight fire with fire, you do not fight complexity with complexity. Because complexity generates uncertainty, not risk, it requires a regulatory response grounded in simplicity, not complexity."*
>
> —"The Dog and the Frisbee," Speech given by Andrew Haldane, Executive Director Financial Stability, Bank of England, at the Federal Reserve Bank of Kansas City's 366th Economic Policy Symposium, Jackson Hole, Wyoming, August 31, 2012

Let's get started, shall we?

Part One: What Is Bank Capital and Why Is It Important?

Balance Sheet

Like any business, a bank has a balance sheet that shows its assets, liabilities, and equity. A bank's assets are mainly loans that they make. Now bankers don't call mom (actually it's whoever answers the phone) for money to make loans. They "fund" their loans via deposits people and businesses place with the bank. The deposits are their liabilities. They convert their liabilities into assets and make money on the "spread," the difference between the interest they pay on the deposits and interest they charge on the loans. And the difference between a bank's assets and its liabilities is its equity—its capital. So:

$100 in loans – $50 in deposits = $50 in capital

Protecting Against Insolvency

Why is it that capital so important? Let's start with protecting against bank insolvency. What happens when the bank has $25 in loans and $50 in deposits?

$$\text{\$25 in loans} - \text{\$50 in deposits} = \text{\$} - 25 \text{ in capital}$$

Negative $25 in capital. Yeah, that bank's going down—it's insolvent. Why might it have gone from $100 to $25 in assets? Its borrowers defaulted on their loans to the tune of $75. The bank has to write off that bad debt against its capital. If, though, the bank has $1000 in assets and $50 in liabilities, its capital would be $950.

$$\text{\$1000 in assets} - \text{\$50 liabilities} = \text{\$950 in capital}$$

Even if it has to take a $75 hit, its capital would still be in the black.

$$\text{\$950 in assets} - \text{\$75} = \text{\$875 in capital}$$

But bad loans are not the only threat to a bank's solvency. What if the bank has $100 in assets and $50 in liabilities—deposits—and it takes a hit of $5 in bad loans, leaving it with $45 in capital? Putting aside deposit insurance, what if the bank's depositors see that hit, panic, and form a line outside of the bank demanding their deposits back, which generally speaking they can do? Who cares if it's irrational behavior—it's a run on the bank. If they demand the $50, the bank might not be able to liquidate the $95 in loans— say, sell the loans to another bank—quickly enough to pay the depositors. Or if it does, it might have to sell its assets at "fire-sale" prices (way below their market value). How will it pay the depositors? With its remaining $45 in capital. Here's the math:

$$\text{\$100 in assets} - \text{\$50} = \text{\$50 in capital}$$

$$\text{\$50} - \text{\$5 in bad loans} = \text{\$45 in capital}$$

$$\text{\$45 in capital} - \text{\$50 run on the bank} = -\text{\$5 in capital}$$

Yeah, that bank's going down, unless other banks help it out or the Fed (our central bank) comes to the rescue.

Systemic Risk

But who cares about one bank—well if you're not a depositor or shareholder of the bank (we'll get to them in a second)? Banks go under all the time. In 2012 fifty-one U.S. banks sank into insolvency. No biggie. Here's the fear, though: a run on one bank becomes a run on many banks. Now we're talking "systemic risk." That's what happened between 1929 and 1933, when deposit insurance didn't exist (the Federal Deposit Insurance Corporation (FDIC) wasn't created until 1934). The first wave of bank panic was from October 1930 to January 1931. It started when crop failures led to bank failures in Missouri, Indiana, Iowa and a few other states, which in turn created a widespread panic among depositors to try to convert their deposits into currency. The runs continued. By 1933, the number of commercial banks shrank from 25,000 to 14,000, a forty percent decline. Brutal.

The 2008–2009 financial also dealt with systemic risk but of a different sort. Take Bear Stearns, one of the largest investment banks globally before it crashed in 2008. It had thousands of counterparties, ranging from banks such as J.P. Morgan to hedge funds. It was so systemically important (not everybody agreed) that in March 2008 the Federal Reserve arranged a deal to have J.P. Morgan buy Bear, initially for $2 a share! More on Bear in Chapter 16.

Protecting Against Moral Hazard

The other major function of bank capital is to guard against "moral hazard." Here's the problem: Banks take risks—e.g., make risky loans—to pursue profits. What if the bank takes a major hit to its capital because of its risky behavior? That's where "market discipline" comes into play—supposedly. The idea behind capital is that the bank's shareholders will feel the pain when capital—the bank's equity—takes a big hit. So it's in their best interest to police the bank. But market discipline is weakened with deposit insurance and the expectation of a government bailout. Without effective market discipline, the bank is likely to continue to engage in even riskier behavior. That's moral hazard. So the thinking is that increased capital requirements will help guard against that (but even this is disputed). But here's the thing: What if the banking crisis crosses borders and countries differ in their regulation of bank capital? Enter stage left: the Basel Accords (I, II, and III).

Part Two: What Led to International Regulation of Bank Capital?

Prior to 1988, international standards governing bank capital didn't exist, even though major banks had international operations. The wake-up call came on June 26, 1974. On that day German regulatory authorities yanked the banking license of Bankhaus Herstatt, a medium-sized bank in Cologne, Germany. But the impact of its failure wasn't limited to Germany. There were unsettled transactions between Herstatt Bank and U.S. banks, where the U.S. banks ("counterparties") had already paid Herstatt deutschmarks and were expecting U.S. dollars the next day. Didn't happen. The German government shut down Herstatt after the close of Germany's inter-bank payment system. Yeah, heavy counterparty losses ensued.

> *"[Bankhaus Herstatt] had been started in 1727 by Johann David Herstatt . . . as a silk mill and trading firm."*
> —Jerry Markham, <u>A Financial History of the United States, Vol. III,</u> 20 (2002)

The Herstatt fiasco led the **Bank for International Settlements (BIS)** to set up a standing committee in 1974 comprised of the Group of Ten central bank governors. It was originally called the Committee on Banking Regulations and Supervisory Practices and eventually morphed into the Basel Committee on Banking Supervision (BCBS). The BCBS's membership has increased significantly since then, now counting forty-four central bankers and regulators.

The BCBS is a forum for its members to discuss issues and problems relating to bank regulation. Initially, the BCBS coordinated non-substantive procedural issues: the Basel Concordat, issued in 1976, allocated home/host supervisory duties of international banks. The BCBS's issuance of rules on capital adequacy in 1988, Basel I, marked its move to substantive rules— standards. That's why it's called a "standard-setting body." The standards it issues are not "hard law" like U.S. banking and corporate law. They are not binding on national governments—we don't have a

> *"[A]doption of [U.S. capital adequacy] rules meets international expectations for U.S. implementation of the Basel III capital framework. This gives us a firm position from which to press our expectations that other countries implement Basel III fully and faithfully."*
> —Daniel Tarullo, "Dodd-Frank Implmentation," Before the Committee on Banking, Housing, and Urban Affairs, U.S. Senate, Washington, D.C. July 11, 2013

global government that can enforce global law. But a lot of countries adopt the standards for one reason or another. That's why Basel I (and II and III) are considered "soft law," meaning the standards are not law but countries think they're pretty persuasive and more or less comply with the standards even though there aren't any formal sanctions for failing to comply. International financial law as a whole is considered soft law. Is that a good or bad thing?

Part Three: Basel I

Why Basel I?

Now let's talk about why, apart from Herstatt's failure, the BCBS felt the need to issue standards on capital adequacy. Since the Committee's establishment, international banking and business grew at an increasing rate. Some of the largest and most internationally active banks had low capital levels. Not safe.

But there was another problem with countries having different capital adequacy rules: unfair competition. Suppose you have two banks governed by two different capital standards, where Bank A is required to hold an amount of capital equal to 2% of its assets, and Bank B is required to hold an amount of capital equal to 8% of its assets. If Bank A has $100 in capital, Bank A can lend up to $5,000. But for Bank B that same $100 in capital only allows it to lend up to $1,250. "Not fair," cried the countries with regs requiring higher capital levels. "We want a level playing field!"

Then came in 1988 came the "International Convergence of Capital Measurement and Capital Standards," which has since become known as the Basel I Capital Accord, or simply Basel I. Remember, Basel I (and II and III) is not a treaty. It's a set of rules that a country can decide to adopt—in most cases without domestic legislation (central banks have regulatory authority to adopt the rules). And although Basel I was intended only for internationally active banks, countries around the world adopted the Accord for their banks—soft law. By the mid-2000s, about 120 countries had adopted it, some for the "prestige" factor (e.g., developing countries telling the world that they rock), some prodded to do so by the International Monetary Fund. The United States and the European Union applied the Accord to all of their banks.

The Rules

<u>Risk-Weighting</u>

Prior to Basel I, most countries used a straight leverage ratio, meaning capital had to be a certain percentage of assets regardless of the riskiness of the assets. So if the leverage ratio is 10% and a bank has $1 million in assets, it would have to have $100,000 in capital. The Accord changed this. To determine capital adequacy, the bank's assets would be adjusted for risk, otherwise known as the bank's risk-weighted assets (RWA). To be considered adequately capitalized under Basel I, a bank had to maintain a capital ratio of 8%, meaning the bank's capital had to equal at least 8% of the bank's risk-weighted assets. Looking at the asset's risk makes sense, right? The required level of capital should be proportionate to not only the quantity of a bank's assets, but also to the asset's quality—the risk of loss in the assets. The riskier assets (i.e., those that have a higher chance of default, or loss) should be offset by a higher amount capital.

To take into account asset risk, Basel I established four risk categories or "buckets" (0%, 20%, 50%, and 100%) into which each of the bank's assets would be placed. Riskier assets were placed in higher-percentage brackets, which meant that more of that asset's value was included in a bank's RWA total, which, in turn, meant that a bank's capital requirement would increase. Here's a simplified table:

Risk-Weight Category	Types of Assets Included in the Risk Category
0%	Cash; assets involving the governments of OECD countries
20%	Assets involving banks located in OECD countries; cash items in the process of collection
50%	Loans secured by mortgages on residential property

Risk-Weight Category	Types of Assets Included in the Risk Category
100%	Assets involving businesses; personal consumer loans; assets involving non-OECD governments (unless the transaction is denominated and funded in the same currency)

So, looking at risk, holding cash poses no risk of loss to the bank. That's why cash was in the 0% risk category, which meant that the bank would not have to include the value of its cash in its total RWA. Likewise a loan made to a government that's a member of the **Organisation for Economic Co-operation and Development (OECD)**, such as the United States, was perceived as low-risk. Into the 0% risk bucket we go! But then we move to assets such as commercial loans (i.e., loans made to businesses), which are perceived to be high-risk, and we're at 100%. The next step: The bank had to have capital equal to at least 8% of RWA. Let's do the numbers:

- Bank 1 makes four $1000 loans to IBM.
  - Risk Weight: 100%
  - Hence $4000
  - Capital equals 8% of risk-weighted assets
  - Result: the bank must set aside $320 in capital
- Bank 2 holds two Treasury bonds at $1000 each and two long-term loans to OECD banks at $1000 each.
  - Risk Weight for TBs: 0%
  - Risk Weight for LT OECD loans: 20%
  - 20% of $2000 = $400
  - Capital equals 8% of risk-weighted assets
  - Result: bank need only set aside $32 in capital.

What counted as capital, you ask? It can get pretty complicated (and defining what counts was controversial) so we'll keep it simple. Basel I (as well as II and III) broke down capital into two components: Tier 1 and Tier 2 capital. Tier 1 capital consisted of higher-quality forms of capital—"core capital"—because the items, such as common stock, have lower priority of repayment in the event a bank becomes insolvent, meaning they have the greatest ability to absorb asset losses. Put another way, holders of the bank's common stock get wiped out. Sorry shareholders of common stock . . . but not really because you took the risk.

Tier 2 contained capital that was considered less reliable—e.g., subordinated debt, which the bank doesn't need to pay back until it has paid all its senior debt holders. So the bank can use the proceeds from issuing subordinated debt to pay other liabilities. Basel I rules said a bank's Tier 1 capital had to equal 4% of RWA. Its total capital, comprised of Tier 1 and 2 capital, had to equal at least 8% of RWA. Basel I also had a formula for converting off-balance sheet items (contingent assets, like an unused portion of a home equity loan) to come up with the total RWA.

Criticisms of Basel I

The critics were all over Basel I. We'll focus on risk weighting and the arbitrage it encouraged. Let's start with risk-weighting. Critics saw Basel I's bucket approach to risk-weighting assets as arbitrary, overly broad, and not nearly sensitive enough to the risks of a bank's assets. Each bucket contained assets with very different levels of risk. Here's an example of the problem. Take commercial loans to private borrowers. The Accord assigned all types of commercial loans a 100% risk-weighting, requiring the bank to include the entire value of the loan in the total of its RWA. But, come on, not all commercial loan borrowers pose the same amount of risk. A loan to a well-established company is far less risky than a loan to a start-up company. Even a secured loan to a private borrower—where the borrower puts up assets as collateral—was thrown in the bucket. Is a mortgage loan, which gets tossed in the 50% bucket, really less risky than the secured loan to a business? The United States insisted on the risk weight for mortgage loans—called "credit allocation" in the biz. Finally, take the 0% allocation for OECD assets. The United States and Greece pose similar credit risks? Come on!

> *"Perhaps the most fundamental problem with the Basel I standards stems from the fact that they attempt to define and measure bank portfolio risk categorically by placing different types of bank exposures into separate 'buckets'. Banks are then required to maintain minimum capital proportional to a weighted sum of the amounts of assets in the various risk buckets. That approach incorrectly assumes, however, that risks are identical within each bucket and that the overall risk of a bank's portfolio is equal to the sum of the risks across the various buckets."*
>
> —Anupam Prakash, "Evolution of the Basel Framework on Bank Capital Regulation," Reserve Bank of India Occasional Papers, Vol. 29, No. 2, Monsoon 92 (2008)

Now let's all say "regulatory arbitrage." Basel I's risk-weighting approach encouraged banks to engage in it. Think about it. If a bank wanted to avoid having to hold more capital or otherwise comply with the capital/asset ratio, it would hold government bonds with a zero risk weighting. Ergo, no capital costs. And it would avoid making consumer or business loans, which carried 100% risk weighting. How do you spell "credit crunch?" But not everyone agreed that Basel I caused a reduction in bank lending.

As the criticisms of Basel I mounted, the members of the BCBS decided that reform was in order. After several years of negotiations and consultations, in 2004 the BCBS released a set of revisions to Basel I, titled "International Convergence of Capital Measurement and Capital Standards: A Revised Framework," also known as Basel II.

Part Four: Basel II

Basel II takes a "Three Pillar" approach to bank regulation. We're just going to look at Pillar I, which focuses on calculating capital adequacy (Pillars II and III deal with supervisory review standards and market discipline issues).

Features of Basel II and How They Address Basel I's Faults

A few things before we look at Basel II. The new Accord doesn't completely throw out Basel I. Basel II still requires that a bank's total capital equal at least 8% of the bank's risk-weighted assets. It continues to assess a banks' capital adequacy using the same capital adequacy ratio. And it doesn't alter Basel I's definition of capital.

Pillar I is designed to correct the deficiencies of Basel I: changing the method of measuring credit risk, i.e., the risk in the bank's assets. The idea is to calculate risk more accurately, which the drafters thought would reduce regulatory arbitrage. Pillar I's approach to measuring credit risk actually consists of two approaches: the standardized approach (SA) and the "internal ratings-based (IRB) approach," which has two variations: the foundation IRB (F-IRB) and the advanced IRB (A-IRB).

The SA is the least complex so that's what we're going to focus on. It keeps the risk bucket approach to figure out risk weighting. But it differs from Basel I in a couple of ways. First, the SA expands the number of risk buckets from four to six. In addition to the 0%, 20%, 50%, and 100% risk categories used under Basel I, the SA also includes a 150% risk category.

The SA also changes how an asset is tossed into a risk bucket by looking at asset risk more carefully—supposedly. It does this by using credit-rating agencies, such as Standard & Poor's and Moody's, to assign risk. So if a commercial borrower receives a AAA rating from Standard & Poor's (its opinion of the obligor's creditworthiness), that loan is placed in the 20% risk bucket. Under Basel I, all commercial loans, regardless of the creditworthiness of the borrower, were placed in the 100% risk bucket. If a borrower isn't rated by a credit agency, the SA automatically places that loan in the 100% risk bucket.

Under the SA, the risk-weighting depends not only that asset's credit rating, but also on whether that asset represents a claim on a government. After all, government assets pose less risk, right? Hmmm . . . Anyway, here are two tables that show the approach.

Credit Rating (S&P)	Government Risk-Weighting
AAA to AA-	0%
A+ to A-	20%
BBB+ to BBB-	50%
BB+ to B-	100%
Below B-	150%
Unrated	100%

Credit Rating (S&P)	Private Counterparty Risk-Weighting
AAA to AA-	20%
A+ to A-	50%
BBB+ to BB-	100%
Below BB-	150%
Unrated	100%

The SA is the simplest method to calculate credit risk in Pillar I, so it's easy to apply to small banks. But for the larger banks, Basel II has two IRB approaches, the F-IRB and the A-IRB. Unlike the SA, the F-IRB and A-IRB allow banks to use their own internal methodologies to determine the risk level of their assets (the primary difference between the two being that under A-IRB banks can set more of the metrics to determine credit risk). Remember, under the SA, banks use external ratings to risk-weight their assets. Because the IRB approaches are so complicated, banks can use them only if they convince their regulators they have wizards who know how to use them.

Criticisms of Basel II

Just like Basel I, Basel II has its problems. We're going to concentrate on the criticisms of the standardized approach. One real problem is that the approach uses rating agencies to determine asset risk. But one of the major causes of the global financial crisis was that credit rating agencies got it all wrong—their ratings of securities were way off. Since the rating agencies were paid by those they were supposed to rate, critics questioned the ratings' reliability and objectivity.

There's another big problem with the SA. It doesn't specify which rating agency a bank has to use. So banks can use different rating agencies (e.g. S & P, Moody's, etc.), each of which have their own way of assigning ratings. Critics also point out that the SA doesn't do a good job of differentiating among unrated borrowers, where it simply assigns them a 100% risk rating. So the SA is just like Basel I: it lumps borrowers of varying degrees of risk in the same risk category. Go figure . . .

Regarding the IRB approaches, they seem good in theory—attempting to calibrate risk more accurately, but in practice they sucked. They were so complex that the regulators had no clue how to assess the banks' methodologies. They amount to nothing more than the banks regulating themselves. They also encourage banks to hold lower amounts of capital during good economic times (why not, life is good!), which means that when

> "[Because] the IRB approaches are essentially untested, the regulators adopting them are taking at least a leap of faith and, critics fear, possibly a leap off a cliff."
> —Daniel Tarullo, Banking on Basel, 6 (2008)

bad times hit, they won't have enough capital—i.e., they would be up a creek without a paddle. What are they going to do? They can increase retained earnings by reducing dividends to shareholders. Boy, that would be really good news to the banks' owners! They can also issue equity or debt. In the middle of a financial crisis? Good luck. Or they can reduce their lending. Yeah, that's the ticket! Put another way, the IRB approaches increase the likelihood of aggravating a financial crisis. It's called "procyclical" in the biz—"pro" meaning making things worse.

Given the problems, it's not surprising that Basel II's implementation was choppy. The two big players, Europe and the United States, took different paths toward implementing the Accord. The European Union applied the Accord to all of its banks starting 2007. The U.S. took a much slower approach in part because of concerns that Basel II would result in substantially lower capital levels. It was in the process of starting a test run for the big banks when the crisis struck in 2008 and stopped the Accord's implementation in its tracks.

But even before the crisis, talks on how to improve Basel II were underway. The crisis put a spotlight on the problems. In the fall of 2010 the BCBS released Basel III (formally titled, "A Global Regulatory Framework for More Resilient Banks and Banking Systems"). We'll check it out in Chapter 18.

What's Up with That?

Bank for International Settlements

The Bank for International Settlements (BIS) is the world's oldest international financial institution. It was established to deal with reparations following World War One. When the reparations issue faded, the BIS became known as the "central bank for central banks." Its mission is to promote monetary stability and communication between central banks and the financial community. The BIS holds regular meetings of central bank governors and other senior officials to discuss the global economy. It also conducts research and compiles statistics in areas like monetary stability and policy, exchange rates, financial markets, and central bank governance. Through seminars and workshops, the BIS works with the BCBS to provide financial sector supervisors with the latest information on market practices to help them improve and strengthen their financial systems. The BIS also provides banking services to, among other things, help central banks manage their foreign reserves (an average of 4% of global foreign exchange reserves have been invested by central banks with the BIS over the past few years).

The Organisation for Economic Co-operation and Development

Officially created in 1961, the OECD is like a fraternity. It's comprised of 34 advanced and emerging economies. They basically keep each other informed as to what's going on with each other's economies and help each other out if one of the countries has a problem they don't know how to tackle. To do this, the OECD collects and analyzes a bunch of data on a variety of topics affecting people's lives, like taxes, pension systems, leisure time, and school systems. It then uses this information to make recommendations to its members to fight poverty and increase the social well-being of their citizens. OECD member countries can participate in peer reviews to monitor their economic development—these reviews are really what keep the OECD running effectively. Everyone wants to look good in front of peers, right?

QUESTIONS FROM YOUR TALKING DOG

1.   Did you know I was a banker in my previous life? I was a pig. Get it? Piggy bank. Don't groan so loud out here. Okay, let's talk bank capital. Why is it important? Go ahead and throw some numbers at me.

2.   I've heard of runs on banks. How does that work?

3.   Systemic risk, huh? Why should we be more worried about that?

4.   It seems like you've talked about moral hazard on most of our walks. So tell me how bank capital protects against moral hazard.

5.   Shouldn't regulation of bank capital be a domestic thing? Why international?

6.   Is Basel I some sort of law? If not, why would any country adopt it?

7.   Leverage ratio. Risk weighting. What's the difference? Risk buckets? When I think of a bucket, I think of the beach. Not quite the same, huh.

8.   Give me some numbers so that I can understand this stuff.

9.   Wait a second. What the heck counts as capital?

10. Basel I wasn't all that. I can see why, but tell me more. Regulatory arbitrage. That sounds cool. I'll remember it for a cocktail party. Tell me about it so that I have it straight.

11. So the sequel is Basel II. What's different about the sequel?

12. Now we got pillars, huh? Tell me about pillar I. Can I lift my leg on it?

13. No kidding! The Standardized Approach uses credit rating agencies? What a good one! How does it work?

14. Say what? Internal ratings-based approach? Tell me about it in one sentence. I'm not sure how much more of this I can take.

15. I can see one huge criticism of Basel II. Using credit rating agencies, right?

16. The IRB approaches were procyclical? Who makes up these words?

17. Was Basel II adopted? Do I really care? Can I go after that squirrel now?

CHAPTER 12

THE VIRUS: SUBPRIME MORTGAGES

■ ■ ■

Here we'll tell you about the virus that was at the root of the financial pandemic: subprime mortgages. Of course, those mortgages alone weren't lethal. As you'll see, other conditions existed to turn subprime mortgages into a lethal virus.

This chapter's format differs from previous chapters. It consists of a series of scenes that move back and forth in time. A good portion of the dialogue is an adaption of published pieces. We've used a talk show host format to deliver portions of the published pieces. All the published stuff will be in quotes. We've relied heavily on The Financial Crisis Inquiry Report solely for factual information that virtually all observers agree upon. The Born piece is much more opinionated. We've included it because the question whether deregulation allowed the virus to spread with relative ease is a hot topic that will run throughout the story of the crisis. We also use "News Alerts," which aren't quotations of any publications but are based on various sources. Otherwise, the dialogue is fictional but, except for "The Airport Connections," "The Renter," and "Surviving the Bad Things," it reflects what really happened based on our research. Don't ignore it!

We don't delve into mortgage regulation in our coverage of the crisis. It's important, but explaining the complex network of regulations, especially those of federal regulatory agencies—a product of a crazy regulatory framework that puzzles most people in other parts of the world—would stop the chapter's momentum in its tracks. As some of the "interviews" suggest, federal regulators were out to lunch and state regulators were understaffed and overwhelmed. We've included a supplement at the end of the global financial crisis chapters that will give you an overview of this stuff.

We won't say much more here except this: As we hope you've realized thus far, there are real people and real lives in the narrative of international finance. The global financial crisis is no different. We've used this chapter to remind you of this.

(Lights up)

June 25, 2003

News Alert: In economic news, Federal Reserve Chairman Alan Greenspan has lowered the Fed Funds rate to 1%, a 45-year low. The Fed Chair lowered the key rate in 2001 from 6.5 percent to 1.75 percent after the bursting of the bursting of the Internet and technology bubble as well as the September 11 terrorist attacks.

"The Airport Connections"

<u>Setting</u>: An airport, February 2004

<u>Characters:</u>

>Phil Angelides
>
>Pepe Johnson
>
>Brooksley Born
>
>Cheryl Black
>
>John Henderson
>
>Juan
>
>Leticia

(Angelides approaches a pretzel kiosk)

Angelides: May I have one and a bottle of water, please.

Cheryl: Small or large bottle?

Angelides: Small is fine.

(Cheryl places the pretzel in the bag and grabs a bottle of water)

Cheryl: $4.75 please.

Angelides: Here's six. Keep it.

Cheryl: Thank you.

Angelides: You're welcome.

(Angelides turns away from the kiosk and runs into Johnson, causing Angelides to drop the pretzel)

Johnson: So sorry, buddy.

Angelides: No worries.

(Angelides turns back to Cheryl)

Angelides: Uh, ma'am. May I have another—

Johnson: Hey, this was completely my fault. I'll pay. Here.

(Johnson hands Cheryl a ten dollar bill, Cheryl glances at a red tattoo on Johnson's forearm)

Cheryl: That's a fancy tattoo, if you don't mind my saying.

Johnson: Goes with my hair. Haha!

(Cheryl hands Angelides a pretzel)

Angelides: Thanks, to both of you.

(Angelides walks off at a brisk pace)

Cheryl: Would you like a pretzel?

Johnson: No thanks. Have to watch my figure!

Cheryl: I guess we all do.

Johnson: Have a nice day.

Cheryl: You as well.

(outside of airport, Angelides gets into what appears to be a family car)

Juan: Familia. Bad for business.

Leticia: We're cab drivers—

Juan: Cabbies. I like that better.

Leticia: Be patient.

Juan: I've tried to tell that to my landlord but it hasn't helped.

(Born approaches Leticia)

Born: Are you available?

Leticia: No. Sorry. Rules say you have to take the first cab.

Born: Okay. Thank you.

Juan: That rule bites.

Leticia: Have you ever stopped to think that we need rules?

Juan: I'm not answering that question.

Leticia: Juan, it was rhetorical.

Juan: Your big words . . . rhetorical . . .

(a limo pulls up, Johnson gets in)

John: Good afternoon, sir!

Johnson: Hello.

John: Trump Tower, right?

Johnson: Absolutely.

John: I'll have you there in no time!

Johnson: That's the attitude!

John: Always do your best. That's how I see it.

Johnson: You see it right . . . How's the business? What's your name, by the way?

John: John. John Henderson. Business is awesome! I actually own part of the company—Henderson's Limousine Services.

Johnson: Good for you, John!

John: It's just temporary, though.

Johnson: How so?

John: I'm going on to bigger and better things! You know, the American Dream!

Johnson: Dream big, my man.

John: May I ask what you do, sir?

Johnson: Own a mortgage company.

"Liquid Fuel and Houses"

> Financial Crisis Inquiry Commission, "The Financial Crisis
> Inquiry Report: Final Report of the National Commission on the
> Causes of the Financial and Economic Crisis in the United
> States" (2011)

Setting: Cable Show: "Today's Big Issues" 2011

Characters:

> Masika, the Host
>
> Guest: Phil Angelides, Chairman, the Financial Crisis Inquiry Commission

Masika: Good evening. In our continuing series on the crisis, tonight we explore the Federal Reserve's interest rate policy in the early 2000s and how it might have contributed to the crisis, in particular the link between low interest rates and the housing boom. It's my pleasure to welcome Mr. Phil Angelides, Chairman of the Financial Crisis Inquiry Commission. Thank you for being with us this evening.

Angelides: My pleasure.

Masika: To begin, Mr. Angelides, can you remind us what the Federal Reserve did with interest rates prior to the outbreak of the crisis?

Angelides: Surely. "From June 2003 through June 2004, the Federal Reserve kept the federal funds rate—"

Masika: That's the Fed's key rate that is the basis for all other interest rates.

Angelides: Correct. "The Federal Reserve kept the federal funds rate low at 1% to stimulate the economy following the 2001 recession. Over the next two years, as deflation fears waned, the Fed gradually raised rates to 5.25% in 17 quarter-point increases."

Masika: What was problematic about keeping the interest rate low?

Angelides: "In the view of some, the Fed simply kept rates too low too long. John Taylor, a Stanford economist and former under secretary of treasury for international affairs, blamed the crisis primarily on this action. If the Fed had followed its usual pattern, he told the FCIC, short-term interest rates would have been much higher, discouraging excessive investment in mortgages. [Taylor said the] 'boom in housing construction starts would have been much more mild, might not even call it a boom, and the bust as well would have been mild.' "

Masika: Is he right?

Angelides: "Ben Bernanke and Alan Greenspan disagree. Both the current and former Fed chairman argue that deciding to purchase a home depends on long-term interest rates on mortgages, not the short-term rates controlled by the Fed, and that short-term and long-term rates had become de-linked . . . When the Fed started to raise rates in 2004, officials expected mortgage rates to rise, too, slowing growth. Instead, mortgage rates continued to fall for another year. The construction industry continued to build houses, peaking at an annualized rate of 2.27 million starts in January 2006—more than a 30-year high."

Masika: That doesn't seem to make sense.

Angelides: "As Greenspan told Congress in 2005, this was a 'conundrum.' One theory pointed to foreign money. Developing countries were booming and—vulnerable to financial problems in the past—encouraged strong saving. Investors in these countries placed their savings in apparently safe and high-yield securities in the United States. Fed Chairman Bernanke called it a 'global savings glut.' "

Masika: So we have to think globally when we talk about our country's crisis.

Angelides: Indeed. "As the United States ran a large current account deficit, flows into the country were unprecedented. Over six years from 2000 to 2006 U.S. Treasury debt held by foreign official public entities rose from $0.6 trillion to $1.43 trillion; as a percentage of U.S. debt held by the public, these holdings increased from 18.2% to 28.8%. Foreigners also bought securities backed by Fannie and Freddie, which, with their implicit government guarantee, seemed nearly as safe as Treasuries. As the Asian financial crisis ended in 1998, foreign holdings of GSE securities held steady at the level of almost 10 years earlier, about $186 billion. By 2000— just two years later—foreigners owned $348 billion in GSE securities; by 2004, $875 billion . . . [F]ormer Fed governor Frederic Mishkin told [us], 'You had a huge inflow of liquidity. A very unique kind of situation where poor countries like China were shipping money to advanced countries because their financial systems were so weak that they [were] better off shipping [money] to countries like the United States rather than keeping it in their own countries. The system was awash with liquidity, which helped lower long-term interest rates.' "

Masika: I see. I've heard of the so-called yield hunt. Was this part of the influx of money?

Angelides: Yes. "Foreign investors sought other high-grade debt almost as safe as Treasuries and GSE securities but with a slightly higher return. They found the triple-A assets pouring from the Wall Street mortgage securitization machine."

Masika: We'll cover securitization in our next program. But for now what you're talking about is taking a bunch of mortgages, pooling them, and creating a security, a so-called mortgage-backed security. And a portion of that security is rated AAA, apparently just about as safe as Treasury bonds.

Angelides: Correct. "Paul Krugman, an economist at Princeton University, told the FCIC, 'It's hard to envisage us having had this crisis without considering international monetary capital movements. The U.S. housing bubble was financed by large capital inflows. So were Spanish and Irish and Baltic bubbles. It's a combination of, in the narrow sense, of a less regulated financial system and a world that was increasingly wide open for big international capital movements.' It was an ocean of money."

Masika: If we move to the housing bubble, can you tell us how low interest rates fueled the housing industry?

Angelides: "With the recession over and mortgage rates at 40-year lows, housing kicked into high gear—again. The nation would lose more than 340,000 nonfarm jobs in 2002 but make small gains in construction. In states where bubbles soon appeared, construction picked up quickly. California ended 2002 with a total of only 2,300 more jobs, but with 21,100 new construction jobs. In Florida, 14% of net job growth was in construction. In 2003, builders started more than 1.8 million single-family dwellings, a rate unseen since the late 1970s. From 2002 to 2005, residential construction contributed three times more to the economy than it had contributed on average since 1990."

Masika: So there was a boom in housing construction, but there had to be demand.

Angelides: Of course. "Low rates cut the cost of homeownership: interest rates for the typical 30-year fixed-rate mortgage traditionally moved with the overnight fed funds rate, and from 2000 to 2003, this relationship held . . . By 2003, creditworthy home buyers could get fixed-rate mortgages for 5.2%, 3 percentage points lower than three years earlier. The savings were immediate and large. For a home bought at the median price of $180,000 with a 20% down payment, the monthly mortgage payment would be $286 less than in 2000. Or to turn the perspective around—as many people did—for the same monthly payment of $1,077, a homeowner could move up from a $180,000 home to a $245,000 one.”

Masika: Big move!

Angelides: Let me give you some more numbers.

Masika: I'm just about overloaded!

Angelides: The numbers are important. “As people jumped into the housing market, prices rose, and in hot markets they really took off . . . In Florida, average home prices gained 4.1% annually from 1995 to 2000 and then 11.1% annually from 2000 to 2003. In California, those numbers were even higher: 6.1% and 13.6%. In California, a house bought for $200,000 in 1995 was worth $454,428 nine years later . . . Nationwide, home prices rose 9.8% annually from 2000 to 2003—historically high, but well under the fastest-growing markets.”

Masika: Thank you, Mr. Angelides, for a very informative and numbers-laden discussion.

Angelides: You're welcome.

“Housing prices were rising so rapidly—at a rate that I'd never seen in my 55 years in the business—that people, regular people, average people got caught up in the mania of buying a house, and flipping it, making money. It was happening. They buy a house, make $50,000 . . . and talk at a cocktail party about it . . . . Housing suddenly went from being part of the American dream to house my family to settle down—it became a commodity. That was a change in the culture . . . . It was sudden, unexpected.”
—Quoting Angelo Mozilo, CEO of Countrywide Financial, in “The Financial Crisis Inquiry Report: Final Report of the National Commission on the Causes of the Financial and Economic Crisis in the United States,” 5 (2011)

“Cabbies Talk Subprime”

Setting: An airport taxi stand, December 3, 2005

Characters:

> Juan, cabbie
>
> Leticia, cabbie, maybe smarter than Juan

Leticia: How's it looking?

Juan: You tell me. We're on the back end . . . Too many of them have family picking them up.

Leticia: Familial love. Bad for business. Brutal.

Juan: Very. Speaking of business, my last fare was a reporter from the Times. What was her name . . . It'll come to me . . . Mara, yeah, Mara Wales. Was on her way to do a TV show or something. She was talking to me about subprime mortgage loans. Didn't quite get it. You know anything about them?

Leticia: Of course.

Juan: Do you have to say that? Of course. You always say that. Of course.

Leticia: Done?

Juan: For now.

Leticia: Subprime mortgages. Made to borrowers who don't qualify for "prime," otherwise known as "conventional," loans. The "sub" means the borrower's credit history is messed up, assuming he has a credit history. You heard of the FICO score?

Juan: Is that how you get into law school?

Leticia: Are you seriously—

Juan: Hey, we're moving up!

Leticia: You're so miserably transparent, you know that?

Juan: Of course.

Leticia: Anyway, FICO is an acronym for the private consulting group Fair Isaac Housing Corporation. A higher FICO score means you're golden, with the best score being 850 and 350 the worst. A FICO score of about 720 or higher and you're looking at a conventional mortgage. 620 or lower means you're in the subprime gutter.

Juan: I was in the gutter last night. So I qualify?

Leticia: You're so loveably lame, Juan.

Juan: Make up your mind. Am I miserably transparent or loveably lame?

Leticia: How about miserably lame or transparently loveable.

(pause, Juan stares at Leticia)

Leticia: Anyway, back to subprime. Stuff like low income, lots of credit cards, being late on loan payments, defaulting, filing for bankruptcy, and being unemployed would put you in line for a subprime.

Juan: That sounds like me.

Leticia: You buying a house, Juan?

Juan: No, but I'm messed up like that. You got a smoke?

Leticia: I quit.

Juan: What! First familial love. Now this?

Leticia: Grow up, Juan.

Juan: I've tried but this is as tall as I'm going to get.

Leticia: Let me keep explaining.

Juan: I shouldn't have asked.

Leticia: Subprime mortgages don't just go to gutter borrowers.

Juan: You've always had a way with words.

Leticia: Of course. They can go to borrowers with good credit. It's how the mortgage is put together. The lender might specialize in high-cost loans that aren't conventional. They won't be your staple thirty-year fixed loan, which goes back to the Depression.

Juan: Are you a historian now?

Leticia: I'm a History Channel fanatic. Anyway subprimes can be quirky, you know, like the 2/28 hybrids.

Juan: Better gas mileage.

(pause, Leticia stares at Juan)

Leticia: A 2/28 hybrid is a mortgage that's fixed for two years, after which it becomes adjustable. They call them adjustable rate mortgages, ARMs, very common in subprimes—about 75% of them. After the fixed period, the ARMs adjust every so often based on where the interest rate might be. Most of them have a 2% adjustment cap.

Juan: That sounds reasonable, even to an unreasonable guy like me.

Leticia: Maybe. Make mortgages affordable when you first get them. Some lenders use teaser rates to get the borrowers in the door.

Juan: Why am I thinking—

Leticia: Say one more word and I'll find a good gutter for you, Juan. Anyway a teaser rate might be 1% or 2%.

Juan: I still don't see the problem.

Leticia: But what if interest rates climb into the heavens?

Juan: Eternal life?

Leticia: More like your monthly mortgage payments suddenly climb into the heavens. Suddenly you're struggling to make the payments.

Juan: Sounds more like hell.

Leticia: Here's another factoid for you; subprimes don't all go to low-income folks who want to buy their first house.

Juan: The American Dream, right?

Leticia: Since World War II. Home ownership means you've made it.

Juan: One day, one day, Leticia, I'll have my own place. Maybe in Seattle.

Leticia: It's over-rated. But, Juan, over half of the subprimes are issued to homeowners who want to refinance a mortgage to take cash out of the home equity. Not first-time homeowners. The refi homeowners end up with an even bigger mortgage. Called a cash-out.

Juan: Yeah, well I need a cash-in. I hate familial love.

"Subprime Rising"

> Financial Crisis Inquiry Commission, "The Financial Crisis
> Inquiry Report: Final Report of the National Commission
> on the Causes of the Financial and Economic Crisis
> in the United States" (2011)

Setting: Cable Show: "Today's Big Issues" 2011

Characters:

Masika, the Host

Guest: Phil Angelides, Chairman, The Financial Crisis Inquiry Commission

Masika: Welcome back to our program, Mr. Angelides.

Angelides: My pleasure.

Masika: This evening we want to explore the rise of subprime mortgages. Does this story start with the rising housing values we've discussed?

Angelides: Yes, it does. "Homeownership increased steadily, peaking at 69.2% of households in 2004. Because so many families were benefiting from higher home values, household wealth rose to nearly six times income, up from five times a few years earlier . . . Higher home prices and low mortgage rates brought a wave of refinancing to the prime mortgage market. In 2003 alone, lenders refinanced over 15 million mortgages, more than one in four—an unprecedented level. Many homeowners took out cash while cutting their interest rates. From 2001 through 2003, cash-out refinancings netted these households an estimate $427 billion . . ."

Masika: What did they do with the cash?

Angelides: "According to the Fed's 2004 Survey of Consumer Finances, 45.0% of homeowners who tapped their equity used that money for expenses such as medical bills, taxes, electronics, and vacations, or to consolidate debt; another 31.0% used it for home improvements; and the rest purchased more real estate, cars, investments, clothing, or jewelry."

Masika: What happened when the refinancing boom was over?

Angelides: "The refinancing boom was over, but originators still needed mortgages to sell to the Street. They needed new products that, as prices kept rising, could make expensive homes more affordable to still-eager borrowers. The solution was riskier, more aggressive, mortgage products that brought higher yields for investors but correspondingly greater risks for borrowers . . . Subprime mortgages rose from 8% of mortgage originations in 2003 to 20% in 2005. About 70% of subprime borrowers used hybrid adjustable-rate mortgages (ARMs) such as 2/28s and 3/27s—mortgages whose low 'teaser' rate lasts for the first two or three years, and then adjusts periodically thereafter."

Masika: So many terms!

Angelides: "The securitization machine began to guzzle these once-rare mortgage products with their strange-sounding names[, for example] I-O—"

Masika: I-O?

Angelides: Interest-only.

Masika: Is that where the borrower pays only the interest on the loan? Puts off paying principle?

Angelides: Exactly. Then you've got your ninja loans, that's no income, no job, no assets.

Masika: Are you kidding me?

Angelides: I kid you not. "In this new market, [lenders], most of them non-depositary companies—not your typical commercial bank—competed fiercely; Countrywide Financial Corporation took the crown."

Masika: Thank you, Mr. Angelides.

Angelides: You're welcome.

"I Want A Beautiful House"

Setting: Office of Predators R Us Mortgage Brokers, Inc. December 1, 2005

Characters:

    Ryan: Mortgage officer

    Cheryl Black: Borrower

    Bob: Mortgage officer

Ryan: Hi, Ms. Black. You were smart to pick up on our Interest Rate Reduction Notification from our Department of Loan Reprocessing.

Cheryl: I thought it was a government mailing because that official-looking eagle emblem.

Ryan: Those eagles! But, hey, good news, Cheryl, you'll be in the house of your dreams soon!

Cheryl: Oh my goodness!

Ryan: Now we won't be able to swing what we call a prime mortgage.

Cheryl: What's that?

Ryan: Don't worry yourself about that.

Cheryl: No, tell me. Prime. That means the best type of loan, doesn't it?

Ryan: Not necessarily. For you, the best type of loan—

Cheryl: Is a prime. But you're not going to give me one, are you?

Ryan: I'm sorry, no. Your income is pretty low and you were unemployed for a time, right?

Cheryl: Yes. But now I have a steady job.

Ryan: Selling pretzels at the airport.

Cheryl: That's right.

Ryan: Look, Cheryl, we've looked at your credit report and you have a lot of credit cards open. You have quite a few delinquent payments.

Cheryl: Can we stop talking about this? You said I could buy my house.

Ryan: I did! And we have a great product for you, Cheryl. It's an ARM that fits you perfectly!

Cheryl: That a joke?

Ryan: Keep my day job, right. Sorry. Adjustable Rate Mortgage. Your interest rate for the first two years is just 1%. Isn't that sweet, Cheryl?

Cheryl: And after that?

Ryan: Then the interest rate adjusts every now and then.

Cheryl: Now and then?

Ryan: Six months. Every six months.

Cheryl: How's it adjusted?

Ryan: Lots a questions, huh. The rate depends on the market rate. But, hey, don't worry about the details. You want that house, right? Am I right?

Cheryl: Yes, but—

Ryan: We can make it happen for you, Cheryl. Our ARM is like the key to your house. Take the key. Open the front door. Walk into your home. *Your* home, Cheryl. Don't walk away from this. You'll regret it. Let us help you.

Cheryl: Okay. Yes. I really want that house.

Ryan: I know, Cheryl. And the great thing about this is that the value of that house is only going to go one way and that's up. It'll be a great investment.

(Cheryl signs the papers and leaves, Bob walks by Ryan's desk)

Bob: Another one?

Ryan: Yup. Business is sweet. Very sweet, Bobby boy!

Bob: Did she pick up on it?

Ryan: The prepayment penalty? It's all good. Didn't have a clue.

"I Want A Beautiful Deck"

Setting: Office of "We Can Give You Cash-Out Instantly—For a Price" Mortgage Broker, December 1, 2005

Characters:

     Sarah: Mortgage Officer

     John Henderson: Borrower

Sarah: Well, Mr. John "I've got a great ARM" Henderson, good news!

John: Tell me, Sarah!

Sarah: You'll be able to build that deck you've been dreaming about!

John: Yes!

Sarah: Smart thing to refinance now when interest rates are almost non-existent.

John: Absolutely! So what kind of loan are we talking about? I qualify for a conventional, right? My FICO is 750!

Sarah: Sure, John. But why do that when we can give you a deal sweeter than a prime. And we don't need to deal with all those docs. Your word is good enough!

John: Really?

Sarah: We've got a great ARM with an interest rate so low you'll laugh—1% fixed for the first two years and it adjusts every six months based on market interest rates.

John: One percent for two years is awesome, Sarah. But after two years I'm gambling on interest rates. A thirty-year fixed—

Sarah: That's old school, John. ARMs are where it's at. If interest rates move against you, we'll just refi.

John: Okay. Alright, then. Let's go for it!

Sarah: No down side, John. Now, let's look at some numbers. You have roughly $50,000 in equity and your balance on the mortgage is $150,000. We can refi with the ARM so that you can pull out the 50, pay off some or all of your debt and still have money left over for that deck of yours. I bet you can't wait to have a big party on it!

John: You know it!

Sarah: You had better invite me!

John: Well, yeah, of course, Sarah!

Sarah: The new mortgage will be for $200,000. But don't worry about it, John, because the value of your place is only going to go one way and that's up. It's smart for you to do this. We can offer you the best deal!

John: Let's party!

Sarah: You better get started on those invitations!

John: I'm working on the list now!

(John and Sarah signs papers and John leaves; Sarah picks up the phone)

Sarah: Snagged another one. Wanted prime but took the chump to the ARM trough and he ate it up. (pause) No, now it's two percent every time we take them to the trough—$4,000 on this one. Not a bad spread. (pause, laughs) Yeah, well, I'm gonna buy my own island. Beat that!

"The Penalty"

Setting: An airport taxi stand, December 15, 2005

Characters:

    Juan, cabbie

    Leticia, cabbie

Leticia: I was just reading an interesting report by the Center for Responsible Lending.

Juan: That's all you do. Read reports. Don't forget. You drive a cab. Read a trashy novel.

Leticia: I do. When I take a bubble bath. Happy?

Juan: Delirious.

Leticia: Can I tell you about this report?

Juan: Familial love kills business.

Leticia: So this report is about prepayment penalties on subprime mortgages.

Juan: What is that?

Leticia: Let's say you have a $150,000 mortgage and you want to pay it all off early. If there's a prepayment penalty, you usually have to throw down a wad equal to six months' interest. So let's say a subprime has a ten percent interest rate. The penalty would be $6,000.

Juan: Mucho dinero.

Leticia: That's right. Did you know that the median net worth for Latinos in 2002 was just $7,932? Even worse for African Americans, $5,998.

Juan: I see where you're going with this.

Leticia: Only a sliver of prime loans have prepayment penalties. Subprimes? Eighty percent.

Juan: Holy—

Leticia: And listen to this.

Juan: Yeah.

Leticia: The report found that borrowers of color are more likely to have loans with the penalties. What they did was look at zip code areas where more than half of the people were minorities. They found that people in those zip codes were 35% more likely to have prepayment penalties than borrowers in zip codes where people of color were less than 10% of the communities.

Juan: This is depressing me, Leticia.

Leticia: Let me make you suicidal.

Juan: Do you have to? It's such a nice day. Sunny. Cute clouds.

Leticia: So most of us hold our net wealth in the equity of our homes. So what if a Latina subprime borrower works hard to improve her credit and wants to refinance out of the subprime and into a cheaper mortgage. Prepay.

Juan: She loses a chunk of her equity in the house.

Leticia: Correcto, Juan.

Juan: Wait a second. Your example. A $6,000 penalty. If she can't pay that?

Leticia: Subprime twilight zone. You never get out. The mortgage industry makes a pretty good argument, though. Prepayment penalty in exchange for a lower interest rate.

Juan: Makes sense.

Leticia: But it's not true, says another report by that Center.

Juan: You wouldn't have any Prozac on you.

Leticia: I gave it up last month. I'm fine with hallucinations.

(Cheryl, smiling widely, walks past the Juan and Leticia)

Juan: What's up Cheryl? Another day, another dollar?

Cheryl: What would an airport be without hot pretzels!

Juan: How many in one day?

Cheryl: Thousands!

Leticia: You're a happy one today!

Cheryl: I just bought a house!

December 2006

News Alert: Nonprime loans account for an increasing share of the overall mortgage market, rising from 12% in 2000 to 34% in this year. Over the same period, the dollar volume of nonprime mortgages originated annually has climbed from $100 billion to $600 billion in the subprime market and from $25 billion to $400 billion in the Alt-A market. The Alt-A market involves nonprime mortgages that are made to borrowers who are close to qualifying for a prime mortgage but are riskier borrowers because there's limited documentation of income or assets.

"A Predator Falls"

> Based on E. Rhodes, "The party's over at Kirkland mortgage company," *The Seattle Times* (2006)

Setting: Cable Show: "Today's Big Issues" December 3, 2006

Characters:

Mara Wales, Times Reporter

Masika, the Host

Masika: Tonight I have the pleasure of speaking with Ms. Mara Wales, a reporter for the Times. Welcome, Ms. Wales.

Mara: Happy to be here.

Masika: You've written a very compelling account of the demise of the mortgage company Atua Financial, which filed for bankruptcy in June. Tell us the story, starting with Pepe Johnson.

Mara: Mr. Johnson is an interesting fellow. He was a high school soccer superstar and played in Europe in the early 90s instead of going to college right away.

Masika: What club did he play for?

Mara: A team sponsored by an obscure pub in England.

Masika: Not exactly the Premier League.

Mara: No, but I understand the beer was good.

Masika: Haha. Now he returned to the states in the mid-90s, graduated from college with a business degree, and opened Atua in the late 1990s, correct?

Mara: Yes, at a time when interest rates were at 30-year lows. He didn't waste time building his empire. By the early 2000s, Atua was so big that Johnson built a massive headquarters complete with an olympic-size swimming pool, a skateboard park, and a hundred-foot rock climbing wall.

Masika: Wow! Impressive.

Mara: He wasn't your average mortgage broker. He wore his hair in dreadlocks, dressed only in shorts and soccer jerseys, and had a bright red tattoo of a soccer ball on his forearm with the inscription "strikers are greedy."

Masika: So how did this striker become so successful?

Mara: He did refinancings and his target clients were people with poor credit histories. Those borrowers were limited to subprime loans, much more expensive than prime loans but very profitable for Atua.

Masika: But it would seem to make sense that a lender has to take into account a borrower's riskiness. Subprime loans fill a need, correct?

Mara: Of course. But it was Mr. Johnson's business practices that were a problem.

Masika: How so?

Mara: Atua enticed borrowers by sending them mailings that looked like a government mailing. You had to look really hard to find "Atua" in the fine print. He also hired telemarketers to swamp homeowners with calls, regardless of whether they were on the national Do Not Call List.

Masika: Weren't those tactics deceptive and misleading? Did the state government go after him?

Mara: It did. But nothing came of it except a small fine. In the meantime, his business grew exponentially. In 2005, he received the Entrepreneur of the Year Award from the chamber of commerce.

Masika: Was it all about profitability?

Mara: Fast money and little training.

Masika: A lethal combination I would think.

Mara: Mr. Johnson admitted that his loan officers really had no experience in the mortgage business. Most of them were high school graduates who worked at fast food chains and gyms. They heard about Atua by word of mouth. They went from making the minimum wage to earning $100,000 by working the phones.

Masika: That is nothing short of frightening.

Mara: Sara Gaulding, an experience loan officer there, told me that those kids had no clue what a credit report was. They had no idea what they were selling. Just get the borrower hooked somehow and make money hand over fist.

Masika: My goodness. Doesn't the state require mortgage loan officers to have training or be licensed?

Mara: Not currently.

Masika: Can you tell us something about what it was like to work at Atua?

Mara: It was like an out-of-control college party. Beer, gin, and tequila and who knows what else everywhere. Some of the areas of the building reeked of urine and vomit. When the phone calls when into high gear, many of the staff would egg each other on by shouting "Snagged twenty idiots in ten minutes. Beat that, bitches!"

Masika: So what brought an end to the party?

Mara: According to Mr. Johnson, his business depended on mortgage refinancings. When interest rates rose, that business plummeted. Atua tried to adjust by trying to close more complex loans but in the end it wasn't sustainable. And things kept going downhill for Atua.

Masika: How so?

Mara: The state regulatory agency received dozens of complaints claiming that Atua failed to get the borrower's signature on key documents, that it forged documents or failed to provide federally required documents, and that it charged excessive fees. It turned out that Atua violated many federal and state laws.

Masika: This is staggering. Were there any ethical employees at Atua?

Mara: Sure there were. A loan officer told me she refused to go forward with a loan for a seventy-year-old woman who clearly didn't understand what was going on. There were others who refused to succumb to the "always be closing the subprimes" attitude that prevailed at Atua.

Masika: To finish up, can you tell us how Atua Financial met its end?

Mara: The state imposed a hefty lien on Atua for unpaid taxes. Hundreds of workers lost their jobs. Atua's creditors sued. A group of the ethical employees hired a lawyer to file a class action suit against Atua, but the lawyer advised them that it would be futile because Atua was asset-less. They were outraged that nothing could be done to make Mr. Johnson feel the pain they were enduring.

Masika: And Mr. Johnson?

Mara: He's on the brink of personal bankruptcy.

March 12, 2007

News Alert: New Century Financial Corporation, one of the largest subprime mortgage lenders, filed for Chapter 11 bankruptcy reorganization today. It's expected that it will cut 3,200 employees, or 54% of its work force. Between 2005 and 2007, New Century made at least $75.9 billion in subprime loans. In its filing, it said it would not be able to pay $8.4 billion in repayments to its lenders, which include Bank of America, Morgan Stanley, Citigroup, Barclays Bank, and UBS. New Century's descent began when it announced on March 2 that two criminal probes were commenced against it. Its auditor, KPMG, express doubt about the company's ability to survive, especially since its creditors announced they would no longer finance the company. A week later New Century's stock lost 78% of its value, which prompted the New York Stock Exchange to suspend trading in the company's shares. Established in 1996, New Century went from 50 employees to 7,200 people in 2006. The rise in its stock price was equally impressive, going from $9.67 in June 1997 to $66.95 in December 2004. However, in the second half of 2006 New Century hit strong headwinds as mortgage rates rose. Much of its business was in California, Florida, New York, and Arizona, states that witnessed the steepest decline in home values after the housing bubble burst, leading to a glut of new homes. Rising delinquencies and defaults by its subprime borrowers led to its collapse.

> *"Lax or practically non-existent government oversight created what criminologists have labeled 'crime-facilitative environments,' where crime could thrive,"*
>
> —Quoting Henry N. Pontell, Professor of Criminology at the University of California, Irvine, in testimony to the Commission in "The Financial Crisis Inquiry Report: Final Report of the National Commission on the Causes of the Financial and Economic Crisis in the United States," 161 (2011)

> *"I don't think anyone can credibly argue that [mortgage fraud] is more important than the war on terror. Mortgage fraud doesn't involve taking loss of life so it doesn't rank above the priority of protecting neighborhoods from dangerous gangs or predators attacking our children."*
>
> —Quoting Alberto Gonzales in "The Financial Crisis Inquiry Report: Final Report of the National Commission on the Causes of the Financial and Economic Crisis in the United States," 163 (2011)

"Fraud Free For All"

> Financial Crisis Inquiry Commission, "The Financial Crisis Inquiry Report: Final Report of the National Commission on the Causes of the Financial and Economic Crisis in the United States" (2011)

Setting: Cable Show: "Today's Big Issues" 2011

Characters:

   Masika, the Host

   Guest: Phil Angelides, Chairman, The Financial Crisis Inquiry Commission

Masika: Good evening. This evening's program is devoted to the fraud that arose in the mortgage industry during the years prior to the crisis. It's my pleasure to welcome Mr. Phil Angelides, Chairman of the Financial Crisis Inquiry Commission. Thank you for being with us this evening.

Angelides: My pleasure.

Masika: What was the extent of the fraud?

Angelides: "Ann Fulmer, vice president of business relations at Interthinx, a fraud detection service, told the FCIC that her firm analyzed a large sample of all loans from 2005 to 2007 and found 13% contained lies or omissions significant enough to rescind the loan or demand a buyback if it had been securitized. The firm's analysis indicated that about $1 trillion of the loans made during the period were fraudulent. Fulmer further estimated $160 billion worth of fraudulent loans from 2002 to 2007 resulted in foreclosures, leading to losses of $112 billion for the holders."

Masika: Those are staggering numbers. Could you tell us what government bodies are responsible for monitoring mortgage fraud?

Angelides: "The responsibility to investigate and prosecute mortgage fraud violations falls to local, state and federal law enforcement officials. On the federal level, the Federal Bureau of Investigation investigates and refers cases for prosecution to U.S. Attorneys, who are part of the Department of Justice. Cases may also involve other agencies, including the U.S. Postal Inspection Service, the Department of Housing and Urban Development, and the Internal Revenue Service. The FBI, which has the broadest jurisdiction of any federal law enforcement agency, was aware of the extent of the fraudulent mortgage problem. FBI Assistant Director Chris Swecker began noticing a rise in mortgage fraud while he was the special agent in charge of the Charlotte, North Carolina, office from 1999 to 2004."

Masika: So getting back to the numbers, how could that much fraud go undetected?

Angelides: A number of reasons. First of all, fraud usually isn't investigated unless the property goes into foreclosure. Second, "[a]according to Fulmer, experts in the field—lenders' quality assurance officers, attorneys who specialize in loan loss mitigation, and white-collar criminologists—say the percentage of transactions involving less significant forms of fraud, such as relatively minor misrepresentations of fact, could reach 60% of originations. Such loans could stay comfortably under the radar, because many borrowers made payments on time." Third, the system for catching data of fraud were inadequate. Keep in mind that mortgage fraud investigation had to compete with other important matters facing the country, such as terrorism.

Masika: Clearly, but just to be clear, even with all the federal agencies you've mentioned, fraud essentially slipped through the cracks?

Angelides: It's really a matter of regulatory coverage—jurisdiction at the federal level. "For example, suspicious activity reports, also known as SARs, are reports filed by FDIC-insured banks and their affiliates to the Financial Crimes Enforcement Network (FinCEN), a bureau within the Treasury Department that administers money-laundering laws and works closely with law enforcement to combat financial crimes. SARs are filed by financial institutions when they suspect criminal activity in a financial transaction. But many mortgage originators, such as Ameriquest, New Century, and Option One, were outside FinCEN's jurisdiction—and thus the loans they generated, which were then placed into securitized pools by larger lenders or investment banks, were not subject to FinCEN review."

Masika: Our viewers are surely wondering how that jurisdictional gap existed in the first place. But what about at the state level?

Angelides: "As mortgage fraud grew, state agencies took action."

Masika: Can you give us an example?

Angelides: "In Florida, Ellen Wilcox, a special agent with the state Department of Law Enforcement, teamed with the Tampa police department and Hillsborough County Consumer Protection Agency to bring down a criminal ring scamming homeowners in the Tampa area."

Masika: How was this criminal ring organized?

Angelides: "Its key member was Orson Benn, a New York-based vice president of Argent Mortgage Company, a unit of Ameriquest. Beginning in 2004, 10 investigators and two prosecutors worked for years to unravel a network of alliances between real estate brokers, appraisers, home repair contractors, title companies, notaries, and a convicted felon in a case that involved some 130 loans."

Masika: A convicted felon. Incredible. So how did this network operate?

Angelides: "According to charging documents in the case, the perpetrators would walk through neighborhoods, looking for elderly homeowners they thought were likely to have substantial equity in their homes. They would suggest repairs or improvements to the homes. The homeowners would fill out paperwork, and insiders would use the information to apply for loans in their names."

Masika: It seems like this was identity theft, really.

Angelides: No doubt about it. "Members of the ring would prepare fraudulent loan documents, including false W-2 forms, filled with information about invented employment and falsified salaries, and take out home equity loans in the homeowners' names. Each person involved in the transaction would receive a fee for his or her role; Benn, at Argent, received a $3,000 kickback for each loan he helped secure."

Masika: Everybody gets a piece of the fraud.

Angelides: That's how it worked. "When the loan was funded, the checks were frequently made out to the bogus home construction company that had proposed the work, which would then disappear with the proceeds."

Masika: What about the victims of the horrible scam?

Angelides: "Some of the homeowners never received a penny from the refinancing on their homes. Hillsborough County officials learned of the scam when homeowners approached them to say that scheduled repairs had never been made to their homes, and then sometimes learned that they had lost years' worth of equity as well. Sixteen of 18 defendants, including Benn, have been convicted or have pled guilty."

Masika: To close our program, can you sum up for us what can only be characterized as a regulatory debacle.

Angelides: Let me put it in the words of "Ed Parker, the head of mortgage fraud investigation at Ameriquest, the largest subprime lender in 2003, 2004, and 2005. [He] told the FCIC that fraudulent loans were very common at the company. 'No one was watching.' "

May 2008

News Alert: An estimated 8.5 million homeowners owe more on their home loans than their home's value, known technically as "negative equity," and popularly known as being "underwater." Over the past year, first mortgage defaults rose from 1.5 million to 2.2 million. Many of the defaulting borrowers have lost employment, victims of the softening job market. This development can be traced to 2006. Based on first mortgage data, defaults on subprime mortgages soared in 2006 to nearly 1 million on an annualized basis from 775,000 in 2005. Experts attributed the surge in defaults to rising interest rates and falling home prices. Most defaulting borrowers were "flippers," speculators who bought and sold property quickly for profit. A second wave of defaults in the subprime mortgages hit the housing sector in 2007. Experts attributed the surge to adjustable rate mortgages that originated in 2005. Most of these ARMs had low fixed interest rates for the first two years, followed by periodic adjustments based on market rates. With interest rates climbing, the first reset spiked monthly mortgage payments to unmanageable levels in many cases. Defaults rose from 1 million in 2006 to 1.5 million to 2007.

"The Reset"

Setting: An airport taxi stand, December 3, 2007

Characters:

    Juan, cabbie

    Leticia, cabbie

Juan: How's the hustle?

Leticia: $175. You?

Juan: $175.50

Leticia: Actually, it's $180. You?

Juan: $180.50

Leticia: What's up with this fifty cent thing?

Juan: It's my way of being taller than you.

Leticia: You've got some—

Juan: Yeah, yeah . . . serious issues. Thanks for reminding me—for the millionth time.

(pause)

Leticia: The news these days. Terrible, don't you think?

Juan: Absolutely, absolutely, no doubt. Just horrible. Horrendous. The darkest days . . .

(Leticia stares at Juan)

Leticia: You don't know what I'm talking about, do you?

Juan: I'm transparent, right?

Leticia: Loveably so, Juan.

Juan: Okay. Tell me about the terrible news. Is the sky falling?

Leticia: Some would say that.

Juan: Better get my cab in the garage.

Leticia: So many people losing their homes, especially the subprime borrowers.

Juan: Those 3/45s.

(Leticia looks at Juan, who's smiling at her)

Leticia: I'm not going to take the bait.

Juan: Hey, you're breaking the rules of the game, Leticia.

Leticia: That's what this whole subprime thing has been, a game.

Juan: In any game, someone wins and the other loses.

Leticia: Hmmm . . . maybe . . . But in this game, everybody thought they were winning. There wouldn't be losers. Buying your first house. The American Dream. The Ownership Society. Everybody should own a home. The government subsidizes it by making interest on mortgages tax deductible. Government policy pushes lenders to lend to minority communities that have been shut out of financing.

Juan: What's wrong with that?

Leticia: Some say we're in this mess because of that policy, at least it's one of the causes. Besides, many other countries don't have this own-your-own-home fetish.

Juan: Yeah, but if you work hard and save your pennies, why shouldn't you feel proud to buy your first house?

Leticia: You're right.

Juan: Finally.

Leticia: Even those who had homes and did a cash-out refi thought they were winners. Pay off some debt, build a new deck, maybe buy some jewelry. Or maybe just sell and buy a bigger, better house.

Juan: Like those that popped up in Uppity Estates.

Leticia: Yeah, like those.

Juan: The builders make money. They can't stop building.

Leticia: It's a party. Your most important asset is your house. And there's only one way the value of your house is going to go and that's up. A great party, Juan.

Juan: Everybody likes a great party.

Leticia: Especially the New Centuries of this world.

Juan: Even I heard about that. Those lenders made serious money.

Leticia: By preying on borrowers.

Juan: But is it really fair to jump on them, as if this whole thing is their fault?

Leticia: Juan, are you engaging me in a serious conversation?

Juan: I have my weaknesses.

Leticia: We all do . . . And we can be stupid. Like borrowers not taking responsibility. Not asking questions. Not reading what they're signing.

Juan: Is a victim of fraud stupid?

Leticia: Absolutely not. The regulators, the ones who could've stopped all this crap, many of them were out to lunch. You can call that stupid.

Juan: And what about the flippers. Weren't they complicit in this whole thing?

Leticia: Complicit? You know what that means?

Juan: I'm listening to a self-improvement tape. You know, self-esteem. It's important for people like me.

Leticia: You crack me up, Juan.

(long pause, Leticia looks at the grey sky while Juan uses his jacket sleeve to remove a spot on the cab; Juan suddenly stops and looks at Leticia)

Juan: Hey, I haven't seen Cheryl, lately. You?

Leticia: The pretzel company she worked for shut down. Lost her job.

Juan: That bites.

Leticia: Went by her house—

Juan: You know where she lives?

Leticia: We became buddies. She had me over now and then for coffee. She was so happy in that house. You could see it.

Juan: Why past tense?

Leticia: She lost it. Remember those ARMs I told you about?

Juan: I do.

Leticia: Her monthly payments shot up when the interest rate reset. Tried to refinance but the prepayment penalty trapped her.

Juan: Where's she now?

Leticia: Don't know. I asked her neighbors. They had no clue.

Juan: Life sucks sometimes.

Leticia: You have to be prepared.

Juan: For what?

Leticia: For the bad things that come to you. You have to fight as hard as you can. As hard as you can, Juan.

(pause)

Juan: You're up. Good luck with the hustle.

Leticia: Take care.

(John gets into the cab)

Leticia: Where to?

John: 2719 Heart Lane.

Leticia: It'll take about an hour.

John: Not in a hurry.

(they drive through a middle class neighborhood)

Leticia: All these foreclosure signs.

John: Lots.

Leticia: I was telling my friend about how bad it is.

John: It's pretty ugly.

Leticia: If I'm not mistaken, your house is in this type of neighborhood.

John: Pretty similar.

Leticia: I guess you still own yours.

John: You guessed right.

Leticia: Told my friend about all the homeowners who're losing their houses because their ARMs reset to a much higher interest rate. Do you have one, if you don't mind my asking?

John: I do.

Leticia: Did your loan reset?

John: Yup. But I think I'll survive. Sold part of my business to make ends meet. This can't last forever.

Leticia: I hope not.

(they arrive at John's house)

Leticia: That'll be an even $80.

John: Here you go.

(John hands Leticia $100)

Leticia: You wouldn't have an envelope, would you?

John: Sorry, I'm not in the habit of carrying envelopes with me. Why do you need one, if you don't mind *my* asking?

Leticia: I want to send this to someone.

John: Think it's a good idea to send someone cash?

Leticia: Stupid, isn't it.

John: Your heart's in the right place, I suppose.

Leticia: You think?

John: Is she sick?

Leticia: I don't know.

John: Send her a check.

Leticia: Good idea.

(pause)

John: Are you okay?

Leticia: Bad things come to us, don't they?

John: Sorry?

Leticia: Have a nice evening. Thanks for the tip.

John: Take care of yourself.

"Of Government, Communities and Finance"

<u>Setting</u>: Cable Show: "Today's Big Issues" 2011

Characters:

Masika, the Host

Anila Gupta, Professor of International Finance

Masika: Good evening. Tonight we explore another aspect, a controversial one, of the subprime mortgage crisis, that is, to what extent did low-income borrowers of subprime mortgages contribute to the crisis. Our guest is Professor Anila Gupta, Professor of International Finance, who has written extensively on this topic. Welcome, Professor Gupta.

Gupta: I'm happy to be here.

Masika: To begin with, what was the basic debate all about?

Gupta: Putting it simply, the debate centered on whether government policies helped trigger the crisis by promoting, sometimes pushing for, increased lending to low-income households in the form of subprime mortgage loans. The arguments focus on the Community Reinvestment Act of 1977, and Fannie Mae and Freddie Mac, both known as the government-sponsored entities or GSEs.

Masika: Let's start with the CRA. Can you tell us briefly about that law?

Gupta: Surely, the CRA was passed because of the discrimination low- and moderate-income communities faced in the credit markets, including the practice of redlining.

Masika: And that was about banks refusing to lend in particular communities, am I right about that?

Gupta: You are.

Masika: Do I get an "A" for that?

Gupta: Haha! Of course!

Masika: So, Professor, can you tell us the essence of the CRA? What it tries to do.

Gupta: Certainly. Under the CRA the four federal banking agencies are—

Masika: What are those four?

Gupta: My apologies.

Masika: No apologies necessary.

Gupta: The four are the Federal Reserve, the Federal Deposit Insurance Corporation, the Office of the Comptroller of the Currency, and the Office of Thrift Supervision. They encourage the banking institutions they supervise to help meet the credit needs of their communities. And this includes low- and moderate-income areas.

Masika: Are the banks incentivized in some way to do this type of lending?

Gupta: The banks' regulators will look at the extent to which the banks have served their local communities, including their lower-income households, when they consider banks' applications for mergers, acquisitions, and branches.

Masika: A powerful incentive.

Gupta: Especially for the bigger banks.

Masika: How exactly do the regulators measure the banks' efforts?

Gupta: Although the CRA doesn't stipulate targets or goals, the reality is that the regulators do look at the numbers regarding lending to lower-income groups. It's important to keep in mind, though, that the statute emphasizes that banks' should lend safely and soundly.

Masika: Does the CRA say anything about borrowers borrowing safely and soundly?

Gupta: No, but in a sort of paternalistic way borrowers supposedly will borrow safely and soundly because that's supposedly the only type of lending the bank should be engaged in.

Masika: I think we get the subtext of your comment pretty easily.

Gupta: We live with "shoulds." Banks should lend safely and soundly, and borrowers should borrow prudently. That normative notion is honored in the breach quite often. Hence, we have financial crises.

Masika: Indeed. Now, can we move to the GSEs, and can you tell us briefly what they are and how they work. Why are they called government-sponsored-entities or GSEs?

Gupta: Let me preface my explanation, if I might. I'm sure your viewers know that the GSEs were taken over by the government during the crisis, in part because of some of the things we're going to talk about. As we speak, the government is deliberating over the restructuring of the GSEs.

Masika: Thank you, Professor. That's important to keep in mind tonight. So, once again, why are Fannie Mae and Freddie Mac called government-sponsored-entities or GSEs?

Gupta: It's because they are in a sense hybrid institutions. They look like private entities because they have private shareholders who are entitled to the GSEs' profits. But, although they aren't government owned, they have government appointees on their boards and can borrow from the Treasury Department. Because of that, everyone has understood that Fannie and Freddie were backed by the full faith and credit of the United States.

Masika: And that was important to fulfill their mandate of providing affordable financing for housing, correct.

Gupta: You get another "A"!

Masika: Thank you, Professor! So, briefly, how did they work?

Gupta: They did two things to pursue their mandate. First, they bought mortgages from banks that conformed to the GSE standards. This allowed the banks to make more mortgage loans. The GSEs then would package the loans into securities, mortgage-backed securities that they guaranteed against default. That process of turning the mortgages into securities is called securitization.

Masika: Thank you, Professor. What was the second thing they did?

Gupta: They also borrowed from the market at cheap rates and bought mortgage-backed securities produced by other banks.

Masika: And this, too, promoted mortgage lending but a step removed, right?

Gupta: Right. There were banks on the other end that were selling their mortgages so they could make more loans.

Masika: Got it. Now we can address the debate you framed for us.

Gupta: I think it's best to talk about the debate by discussing the views of Professor Raghuram Rajan, who is championed by the political right, and Professor Paul Krugman, who is championed by the political left.

Masika: Very good. Let's start with Professor Rajan. He's a Professor of Finance at University of Chicago's Booth School of Business, correct?

> *"But I believe owning something is a part of the American Dream, as well. I believe when somebody owns their home, they're realizing the American Dream . . . and we saw that yesterday in Atlanta, when we went to the new homes of the new homeowners. And I saw with pride first hand, the man say, welcome to my home. He didn't say, welcome to government's home: he didn't say, welcome to my neighbor's home: he said, welcome to my home . . . he was a proud man . . . and I want that pride to extend all throughout our country."*
> —Quoting George W. Bush, in R. Rajan, Fault Lines, 37 (2010)

Gupta: Yes. Here's Professor Rajan's argument. In the 1990s, the Clinton and Bush administrations pushed to increase lending to low-income borrowers. Under the Clinton administration, the Department of Housing and Urban Development or HUD increased pressure on the GSEs to allocate more funding for low-income housing.

> *"This past year, I directed HUD Secretary Henry G. Cisneros . . . to develop a plan to boost homeownership in America to an all-time high by the end of this century . . . expanding home ownership with strengthen our nation's families and communities, strengthen our economy, and expand this country's great middle class. Rekindling the dream of homeownership for America's working families can prepare our nation to embrace the rich possibilities of the twenty-first century."*
> —Quoting Bill Clinton, in R. Rajan, Fault Lines, 36 (2010)

Masika: What about the Clinton administration and the CRA?

Gupta: President Clinton also turned up the screws on CRA enforcement, which Rajan argues led to increased mortgage lending to low-income borrowers.

Masika: Does Professor Rajan place all the blame on the Clinton administration?

Gupta: Not at all. Rajan doesn't spare President George W. Bush. In his view, President Bush also pushed the GSEs to focus on low-income borrowers. The consequence of this pressure was that the GSEs increased their portfolio of subprime loans.

Masika: So his argument is that government policies essentially forced banks and the GSEs to lower their standards for lending?

Gupta: Yes, and he adds that the all of this encouraged frenzied subprime lending by mortgage lenders in the private sector. His bottom line is that politicians, in many cases looking for votes, pushed for more lending to low-income households. This caused the price of houses to increase to the point that low-income borrowers couldn't afford to make the mortgage payments. He cites to statistics, of course. He's noted that after 2006, default rates of subprime loans to low-income borrowers tripled the rates of defaults of prime loans.

Masika: Everything thus far has focused on the lenders. What about the borrowers?

Gupta: Excellent question. Professor Rajan argues that borrowing by low-income households wasn't demand driven. After all, he argues, why would poor people go out and buy a house when they're barely making ends meet? In his view, government policy triggered supply-driven credit to low-income borrowers.

Masika: In other words, poor people didn't exercise choice when they borrowed. The credit flowed in and they loaded up on it, like silly people.

(awkward pause)

Masika: So what is the argument on the other side, the argument by Professor Paul Krugman, the Economics Nobel Laureate at Princeton?

Gupta: Professor Krugman absolutely disagrees with Professor Rajan. As to Professor Rajan's position on the CRAs, Professor Krugman has said, in his words, it "has been refuted over and over again." He argues that the boom in subprime lending was the work of mortgage companies not subject to the CRA. He also argues that in the run-up to the crisis, securitization by the GSEs—the issuance of mortgage-backed securities—dropped while securitization rose in the private sector.

Masika: Has Professor Rajan provided a rebuttal?

Gupta: Yes, a very lively one. He pointed out that Krugman's data for the GSEs is based on *total* residential mortgage originations. Instead, you have to look at the GSEs' *subprime* residential mortgage originations. By his estimations, between 2004 and 2006 the GSEs bought $434 billion in subprime mortgage-backed securities. In 2004, the GSE purchases of subprimes accounted for 44% of the market in these securities.

Masika: What about the role of the CRA?

Gupta: Professor Rajan cites a study by the University of Chicago that concludes that banks about to undergo a CRA examination increased their lending to low-income borrowers, and that those loans were 15% more likely to be delinquent a year after the loan was made.

Masika: So does Professor Krugman lose the debate, at least as to the CRA?

Gupta: Not necessarily. In November 2008, the staff of the Board of Governors of the Federal Reserve produced a study to determine whether the CRA in fact was a root cause of the crisis. According to the study, if you look at the data, in 2006 two-thirds of mortgage loans were non-CRA loans. They were made to middle- and upper-income borrowers. Only 10% of all loans were CRA loans to low-income borrowers.

Masika: That's in line with what I know.

Gupta: And, according to the study, if you look at the data for 2005 and 2006, the peak years of subprime lending, independent mortgage companies, not CRA-covered banks, made about half of all the higher-priced, subprime loans. You could also look at the 90-day or more delinquency rates. The numbers between January 2006 and April 2008 are high regardless of income, although they're slightly higher in lower-income areas.

Masika: What explains that?

Gupta: It's not surprising because lower-income borrowers have few or no assets to withstand economic shocks.

Masika: Final question, Professor. Who wins the debate?

Gupta: I would say that Professor Krugman has a formidable opponent.

Masika: Nothing like a good fight.

Gupta: Life would be boring otherwise.

Masika: No doubt, Professor Gupta. Thank you very much for shedding light on this controversial issue.

Gupta: You're most welcome.

"The Renter"

Setting: Offices of an apartment landlord, 2010

Characters:

    Heidi & Francis, employees of landlord's company

Heidi: 306 is three months behind in his rent.

Francis: Who's in that place?

Heidi: Some guy. Heard he was a high flyer. Made money hands over fists.

Francis: What. An investment banker gone bust?

Heidi: Nah. I hear he made his money selling mortgages.

Francis: You're kidding. And he rents an apartment now?

Heidi: Go figure . . . Anyway, what are we going to do with this slouch?

Francis: You talk to the landlord, not me. I just work here.

Heidi: It's always gotta be me. Why is that?

Francis: You have the people skills to deal with the boss.

Heidi: Stuff it, Francis.

(Heidi walks to the boss's office and knocks on the door, hears "come in", she opens the door and steps in)

Heidi: Mr. Henderson, we have a slouch in 306.

"Liquid Fuel Mixes with Deregulation"

> B. Born, "Deregulation: A Major Cause of the Financial Crisis,"
> *Harvard Law & Policy Review* (2011)

Setting: Cable Show: "Today's Big Issues" 2011

Characters:

Brooksley Born, Partner, Arnold & Porter

Masika, the Host

Masika: Good evening. We have a very special program for you tonight. Our guest is Brooksley Born, who was a Commissioner on the Financial Inquiry Commission from mid-2009 until February 2011. She was a distinguished partner of the law firm Arnold & Porter, and served as Chair of the Commodities Futures Trading Commission from 1996 to 1999. Welcome to the program Ms. Born.

Brooksley: My pleasure to be here.

Masika: Tonight we look back at the global financial crisis. I'm very interested in your views of financial regulation having served as Commissioner.

Brooksley: "My recent service as a member of the Financial Crisis Inquiry Commission ('FCIC') brought home to me how important it is for us to reexamine the role of business regulation. We are now experiencing the tragic results of thirty years of deregulatory pressures in the financial sector. The FCIC quite rightly concluded that failures in financial regulation and supervision along with failures of corporate governance and risk management at major financial firms were prime causes of the financial crisis engulfing this country in 2007 and 2008. As the report recently issued by the FCIC documents, decades of deregulation and failure to regulate newly emerging

> "[P]rospective subprime losses were clearly not large enough on their own to account for the magnitude of the crisis . . . Rather, the system's vulnerabilities, together with gaps in the government's crisis-response toolkit, were the principal explanations of why the crisis was so severe and had such devastating effects on the broader economy."
> —Quoting Fed Chairman Ben Bernanke, in B. Born, "Deregulation: A Major Cause of the Financial Crisis," *Harvard Law & Policy Review*, 232 (2011)

financial markets, firms, and products led to a financial system that was extremely fragile and vulnerable to a full-blown crisis when the U.S. housing bubble collapsed."

Masika: How did this state of fragility come about in your view?

Brooksley: "The FCIC found that these vulnerabilities in our financial system were the direct result of a growing belief in the self-regulating nature of financial markets and the ability of financial firms to police themselves. Former Fed Chairman Alan Greenspan—a laissez-faire economist—championed these beliefs during his nineteen years in office. With support from large financial services firms, their trade associations, and like-minded economists, he was able to persuade a number of policy makers in several successive presidential administrations, members of Congress, and federal financial regulators to support deregulatory efforts on the false assumption that self-regulation would be sufficient to protect the financial system and our economy against excesses in the market."

> "[I]t is critically important to recognize that no market is ever truly unregulated. The self-interest of market participants generates private market regulation. Thus, the real question is not whether a market should be regulated. Rather, the real question is whether government intervention strengthens or weakens private regulation."
> —Quoting Fed Chairman Alan Greenspan, in B. Born, "Deregulation: A Major Cause of the Financial Crisis," *Harvard Law & Policy Review*, 232 (2011)

Masika: You say trade associations. Can you give a sense of the lobbying involved in this whole thing?

Brooksley: "The FCIC found that the financial sector devoted enormous resources to its effort to convince federal policy makers of the need for deregulation. In the decade leading up to the financial crisis, the sector spent $2.7 billion on federal lobbying efforts, and individuals and political action committees ('PACs') related to the sector made more than $1 billion in federal election campaign contributions."

Masika: That's staggering.

Brooksley: "As a result of these pressures, significant regulatory gaps developed in the financial system including the lightly regulated shadow banking system that grew to rival the traditional banking system in size and importance and the enormous market in deregulated over-the-counter derivatives. A number of investment banks grew to be of systemic importance without adequate oversight.

> *"As a scholar of the Great Depression, I honestly believe that September and October of 2008 was the worst financial crisis in global history, including the Great Depression."*
> —Quoting Fed Chairman Ben Bernanke, in B. Born, "Deregulation: A Major Cause of the Financial Crisis," *Harvard Law & Policy Review,* 233 (2011)

Institutional supervision of large bank holding companies, commercial banks, and thrifts was gradually weakened, allowing them to engage in riskier activities. Mortgage lending standards deteriorated, and securitization of mortgage-related assets burgeoned with little regulatory scrutiny. These developments created the conditions that caused the collapse of the housing bubble to turn into a major financial crisis."

Masika: Did you voice your concerns when you were Chair of the U.S. Commodity Futures Trading Commission, the "CFTC"?

Brooksley: "During the late 1990s, as chair of the . . . CFTC, I participated in the debate . . . about whether the over-the-counter derivatives market should be regulated. The CFTC was concerned that the rapidly growing and opaque market posed dangers to market participants and the financial system as a whole and asked whether a regulatory scheme similar to that imposed on futures and options markets would significantly reduce those dangers. Deregulatory forces prevailed in the debate . . ."

Masika: So regulation of derivatives was the key issue?

Brooksley: Not quite. "[T]he FCIC investigation revealed that financial deregulation was not limited to the derivatives market, but has been pervasive, extending to mortgage lending, securities regulation, and institutional supervision, among other areas . . . The FCIC found that there was an explosion in risky mortgage lending accompanied by a significant deterioration in mortgage lending standards in the years leading up to the financial crisis, with many mortgage lenders ignoring borrowers' ability to repay their loans. Because lenders no longer held loans for the duration of the mortgages, but instead sold them to mortgage securitizers, they passed on the risks of the loans and had little incentive to maintain high lending standards. In addition, lenders made many predatory loans designed to impose high interest payments or other terms increasing the yield on the loans."

Masika: Respectfully, Ms. Born, you speak as if regulation on mortgages didn't exist. Is that truly the case?

Brooksley: "The FCIC found that the Fed had the statutory authority to regulate the terms of mortgages issued by all lenders nationwide and to address predatory lending practices under the Home Ownership and Equity Protection Act of 1994. The Fed was well aware of the widespread abuses in mortgage lending practices, having received reports from lenders, consumer advocates, and its own staff about the increase in risky mortgage lending and the falling underwriting standards. But the Fed refused to take action effectively to regulate this irresponsible lending . . . Despite [the] efforts [of the current chairman of the Federal Deposit Insurance Corporation, Sheila Blair,] and those of Fed governor Edward Gramlich, the Fed refused to strengthen its regulations to stop the predatory lending . . . because of its deregulatory attitude . . . "

> *"I think nipping this in the bud in 2000 and 2001 with some strong consumer rules applying across the board that just simply said you've got to document a customer's income to make sure they can repay the loan, you've got to make sure the income is sufficient to pay the loans when the interest rate resets, just simple rules like that . . . could have done a lot to stop this."*
> —Quoting Sheila Blair, FDIC Chair, in B. Born, "Deregulation: A Major Cause of the Financial Crisis," *Harvard Law & Policy Review*, 234 (2011)

> *"The mind-set was there should be no regulation; the market should take care of policing, unless there already is an identified problem. We were in the reactive mode because that's what the mind-set was of the '90s and the early 2000s."*
> —Quoting Scott Alvarez, General Counsel, Federal Reserve Bank, in B. Born, "Deregulation: A Major Cause of the Financial Crisis," *Harvard Law & Policy Review*, 234 (2011)

"Surviving the Bad Things"

Setting: Office of Staff, January 7, 2010

Characters:

> Susan, Commission Staffer
>
> Phil Angelides
>
> Brooksley Born
>
> Cheryl Black, Legal Intern
>
> Steve: Receptionist

Susan: How are the questions for Blankfein coming, Cheryl?

Cheryl: Almost done. I want to get them right.

Susan: Is that what they tell you at Georgetown?

Cheryl: Yes. They didn't tell you that at Yale?

Susan: We questioned whether the concept of right really exists.

Cheryl: It does. There's what's right and what's wrong.

Susan: You sound pretty sure of yourself.

Cheryl: I've lived it.

(Born enters)

Born: Are you harassing my interns again, Susan?

Susan: Isn't that my job?

Born: Absolutely, especially when they're at the top of their class. And how is my star intern?

Cheryl: I'm great, Ms. Born.

Born: Are you writing killer questions for me?

Cheryl: I hope so.

Born: Are you free for lunch tomorrow?

Cheryl: Sure.

Born: Let's meet here at noon. You pick the spot.

Cheryl: Thanks, Ms. Born.

(Angelides enters)

Angelides: Oh Susan, oh Susan! Where are my questions for Dimon?

Susan: They're on your desk, Mr. Angelides.

Angelides: Now why would you put them there? You know I can't find anything on my desk!

Born: Phil, have you met Cheryl Black, my intern?

Angelides: I haven't had the pleasure.

(Angelides shakes hands with Cheryl)

Cheryl: Good to meet you, Mr. Angelides.

Angelides: The same. I hear you're a star at Georgetown.

Cheryl: I try my best.

Angelides: Well, whatever you're doing is working. Keep it up. Susan, let's attack my desk.

(Susan and Angelides walk into the hallway)

Angelides: She's an older student. What's her background?

Susan: Not sure. She doesn't talk about it much. I heard at some point she worked at an airport, doing what, I don't know.

Angelides: Hmmm . . . C'mon, let's find the buried treasure.

(Steve enters the Commission office)

Steve: Cheryl?

Cheryl: Yeah.

Steve: Someone's here to see you.

Cheryl: Who?

Steve: I didn't catch her name.

Cheryl: I'll be out in a sec.

Steve: Sure thing.

(Cheryl saves her file on the computer, makes a note on a yellow pad, and walks to the reception room)

(she enters the reception room, long pause)

Leticia: Hi.

Cheryl: Oh my god, Leticia.

Leticia: You could've said goodbye.

(pause)

Cheryl: I was humiliated. I couldn't bear seeing you.

Leticia: It wasn't your fault. You know that, right?

Cheryl: It won't happen again.

Leticia: Not to a kick-ass lawyer.

(pause)

Leticia: Here's a question for you, Ms. Cheryl Black, Esquire. What do you do when bad things come to you?

Cheryl: Fight.

Leticia: As hard as you can.

Cheryl: As hard as you can.

(fade to black)

You Gotta Know Something About Them!

Alan Greenspan

Alan Greenspan was Fed Chair from 1987 to 2006. In his high school days he rubbed elbows with famed musician Stan Katz. Check it out: Alan played the clarinet—even went to Juilliard to play but then transferred to NYU. He doesn't play the clarinet these days—piano instead. Back in the day, Alan was Chairman of the Council of Economic Advisers for the Ford administration. After stepping down as Fed Chair, he did what lots of former government officials do: He founded an economic consulting firm, Greenspan Associates LLC, which advises investment banks, hedge funds, and government agencies. Alan has received some cool honors from governments all over the world: Honorary Knighthood by Queen Elisabeth II; the Legion of Honor in 2000 by the French government; and the Presidential Medal of Freedom from George W. Bush in 2005. But the most dubious honor is that Time magazine named him one of "25 people to blame for the financial crisis."

Raghuram Rajan

Raghuram Govinda Rajan is a rising star. He's the 23rd Governor of the Reserve Bank of India, having taken over the position in 2013. He was the IMF's Chief Economist and Director of Research from 2003–2006. He's currently on leave of absence from the University of Chicago's graduate business school—he's a little busy with monetary policy in India. He's received a bunch of awards, including the Financial Times-Goldman Sachs prize for best business book in 2010, and the Fischer Black Prize for the best finance researcher under the age of 40. He's also got a pretty cool blog! When he's not blogging, he plays tennis and squash.

Paul Krugman

Paul Krugman. Let's see, where do we start with this rock star? He's a prof at Princeton University, a Centenary Professor at the London School of Economics, the 2008 Nobel Laureate in Economics, and—most important—an op-ed columnist for the New York Times. The Econ Journal Watch polled him as one of the favorite economists of America. The Asia Times has even called him the "Mick Jagger of political/economic punditry." He's also a member of the G30 (Group of Thirty), an international body of academics and leading financiers who examine financial and economic issues. In his spare time, he's written or edited 20 books and 200 professional journal articles and acted as a consultant to the Federal Reserve Bank of New York, the World Bank, the IMF, the UN, and Portugal and the Philippines. Paul and his wife, Robin Wells, also an economist, currently live in a Japanese style home with their two cats, Doris Lessing, and Albert Einstein. When they have time, they chill in their condo in St. Croix.

Brooksley Born

Brooksley Born is cool. She's a graduate of Stanford Law, where she served as the first woman president of the Stanford Law Review. Rock on! In the 1970s she joined the law firm of Arnold & Porter, working part-time because she was raising her children. And, yeah, she was promoted to partner. In 1996, she became the head of the Commodity Futures Trading Commission (CFTC), after President Clinton nominated her. During her time at the CFTC, she clashed with Alan Greenspan over deregulating the markets. In 2009, she was awarded the John F. Kennedy Library Foundation's Profile in Courage Award, which is given to public servants that make courageous decision. The award was in recognition for her efforts as the head of the CFTC. She fought the good fight. In 2009, Nancy Pelosi appointed her a commissioner for the Financial Crisis Inquiry Commission. These days, when she's not in D.C., Brooksley spends time in Squirrel Island, Maine. She and her husband really like the water, like really: they own a 32-foot sailboat and a 28-foot powerboat.

Phil Angelides

Phil Angelides was appointed the Chairman of the Financial Crisis Inquiry Commission in 2009, which was tasked with investigating the events surrounding the global financial crisis. Phil has politics in his blood. While in college, he tried to run for Sacramento City Council. He tried again—unsuccessfully. When he was the Chairman of the California Democratic Party from 1991 to 1993, he helped Bill Clinton win California in the presidential election. After his time with the California Democratic Party, he ran for State Treasurer, losing in 1994 but winning in 1998, and again in 2002. In 2006, he was the democratic nominee for California governor. But he lost to The Terminator, Arnold Schwarzenegger. And guess what, he's not a lawyer. OMG!

QUESTIONS FROM YOUR TALKING DOG

1.   Things are different now, aren't they? I don't get as many treats from you. You're feeding me garbage food. It started in 2007, didn't it? The biggest crisis since the Great Depression. We're going to have a lot of walks on this one. Sure, let's start with the Federal Reserve's interest-rate policies before the crisis. Tell me about them?

2.   What is this "conundrum" that Greenspan talked about in 2005? And what's up with the so-called "global savings glut?" Why is that relevant to anything?

3.   I'm tired of our apartment. When are we going to move into a house? Speaking of which, tell me about the housing boom that led up to the crisis.

4.   Subprime mortgage? It's a mortgage that's not prime, right? Beyond that, I don't know. Want to tell me? Were they just for poor people? Can you give me some examples? Do you have a treat in your pocket?

5.   An adjustable rate mortgage sounds like a neat thing. Why was it a problem then?

6.   I'm going to tell you the same thing about prepayment penalties. They make sense. What was the problem?

7.   Are you kidding me? Mortgage brokers got a percentage for steering borrowers to more expensive subprime loans?

8.   Yeah, I know what predators are. Great Danes who will eat me for breakfast. Predatory lending? Sounds sleazy, so for sure I want to know more.

9.   So you got all these subprime mortgage lenders making lots of money. When did the party stop?

10.   The stuff you're telling me! Rampant fraud. Talking above you? Okay, lots of fraud. Tell me more. And don't skip the regulators.

11.   Underwater? Flippers? Massive defaults? When was all this happening? Sounds like the end of the world.

12.   Who hasn't heard of the Community Reinvestment Act? I'm a dog and I've even heard about it. Pretty political. Let's talk politics.

13.   Fannie Mae and Freddie Mac? What musical was that . . . I'm not playing dumb. Sometimes I do, but not now. So tell me about them and why they're even relevant to the crisis.

14.   Brooksley Born? Don't tell me, a lawyer. Why am I not surprised. Probably big-time, right? She had a bone to pick with deregulation? What you mean by that? And since we're on the subject, watch the chicken bones in the garbage. They're tempting.

CHAPTER 13

THE VIRUS SPREADS: SECURITIZATION

■ ■ ■

The subprime mortgage crisis was a pretty bad thing. But here's the question: why did problems with one type of mortgage in the United States morph into a global financial crisis? In other words, how did the subprime virus spread beyond the mortgage market? The transmitting agent was securitization.

Put simply, securitization is a process of turning non-liquid assets, such as car loans, into tradable debt securities—bonds. The bond's principal and interest flow from cash flows generated by the pool of assets. It's a big business. We're talking trillions of dollars, even before the crisis hit. Why would that be the case? Because lots of bad, greedy, unscrupulous, dirty, rotten people do securitizations? Not really, at least, not last time we checked. Well . . . some . . . maybe.

Anyway, securitization has been around for a long time and it's a critical part of our financial system. As you'll see, a properly structured securitization is a win-win outcome. So, conceptually, securitization isn't in and of itself a bad thing. But it got out of control. The securitization machine sucked in the virus—subprime mortgages—and, given problems with the machine, transmitted it all too readily to the world.

The lecture below will give you all of the essentials. Warning: This stuff might make your head spin, especially the synthetic CDO stuff. In this scenario you will meet one Hector Loco. Ask yourselves whether you would encounter a Mr. Loco on Main Street, USA if you tried to explain this stuff to him.

Enough said. Put your gloves and masks on and let's get to work. Oh, lest you think we forgot to include a profile, Hector Loco is our guy for this chapter.

<u>Setting</u>: Lecture Hall, Werock College of Law, present day

<u>Characters</u>:

> Professor Henry Levine
>
> Professor Janet Patterson
>
> Hector Loco, student
>
> Student 1

Student 2

(lights up)

Patterson: Welcome, once again, faculty, students, and staff, to the second program in our series that looks back at the global financial crisis. We are exceptionally pleased that Professor Henry Levine will be speaking to us today regarding securitization and how it played a role in the crisis. Professor Levine graduated from our College of Law well before many of you were born. I know this embarrasses him, but that's why we're here!

(audience laughs)

Patterson: Professor Levine has authored dozens of books and hundreds of articles, all of which he donated to Recycling R Us, which will process his publications into toilet paper. According to his website, he is an expert in nothing. Still, he has something intelligent to say now and then. Please join me in welcoming Professor Levine.

(applause, Patterson and Levine shake hands)

Levine: Thanks, Janet.

Janet: You're most welcome. (whispering) Henry . . .

Levine: Yeah?

Janet: There's a firecracker in the audience. Watch out for him.

Levine: What's his name?

Janet: Hector Loco.

Levine: Loco. That's crazy, right?

Janet: You'll find out.

Levine: Thanks. I know how to handle locos.

What the Heck Is Securitization?

Levine: Thank you, Professor Patterson, for your kind and nonsensical introduction. I'm super pleased to be here to tell you, as Professor Patterson said, something about the securitization process and the role it played in the global financial crisis of 2008. The term might sound intimidating but it's really not, at least most of it. So let's begin. Securitization is the process of pooling assets and turning them into securities that are sold to investors. The biz usually distinguishes between mortgage-backed securities (MBS) and asset-backed securities (ABS). Let's deal with ABS first to get the basics—we're keeping it simple because otherwise we'll be here for a month.

Loco: That's wild, man!

Student 1: Shut up, Loco!

(silence)

Levine: Most of the terms we're about to look at will also apply to MBS.

Part One: ABS

The Receivables

Levine: Many of you have taken out loans to buy a car or get an education—

Loco: Hey! Do you know how much—

Levine: Let's not go there, okay?

Loco: I'm the consumer! I pay your salary!

Levine: I think about that every day Mr. . . .

Loco: Loco.

Levine: Yes, Mr. Loco, I'm your bitch.

(audience guffaws)

Loco: You got that right!

Levine: May I continue?

Loco: It's all you, man!

Levine: All sorts of assets can be securitized, from car loans, to student loans, to equipment leases, to payments that customers make to a company. Let's say a wholesale soccer equipment company, "Soccer R Us," has ongoing accounts with retail soccer stores around the country. The retail stores make regular payments to Soccer R US. Those payments, what are called the *receivables*, are the first step in securitization. When you securitize, you pool together those receivables and turn them into securities.

The Originator

Loco: Wait a second! Who's doing what? And while we're at it, why?

Levine: Let's take it step by step, Mr. Loco.

Loco: I'm down for that!

Levine: Okay. Soccer R Us is called the *originator*. It'll sell the receivables. As to the "why" question, the company might want to sell the receivables—which might not be marketable—and, among other things, use the money to pay off debt it's incurred.

The Special Purpose Vehicle, Arranger, and the Servicer

The originator will sell the receivables to a securitization company called a *"special purpose vehicle"* or SPV—you'll also see the term "special purpose entity" or SPE, which is set up by a bank or banks—we call them the *arranger or arrangers*. In ABSs generally, the SPV may be a corporation, a limited partnership, a limited liability company, or a trust formed just for the purpose of buying the receivables.

Loco: Wait a second! Dude, where does the SPV get the money to buy the receivables?

Levine: Respectfully, Mr. Loco, as soon as you drop the Red Bull, I'll tell you.

(auditorium breaks out laughing)

Levine: Let's resume, shall we? The SPV will issue securities via an underwriter to investors, say 90-day commercial paper (CP)—unsecured short-term debt. They buy the securities and presto, the SPV now has the money to buy the receivables! The SPV will then use those receivables to pay up on the CP when it matures. This process repeats itself through the life of the receivables. Although Soccer R Us has sold the receivables, it will collect the payments from the retail stores, take care of arrears, etc. So the originator in this case is also the *servicer*, and receives a fee for its administrative services.

Rating Agencies

Loco: Wait a second! Who's going to buy unsecured debt—the CP—backed by what might turn out to be crappy receivables???

Levine: Dude, one more sip . . .

(auditorium erupts in laughter)

Levine: Okay, so, to make the securities attractive to investors, the banks arranging the securitization will get a rating agency, say, Standard & Poor's, to slap a AAA rating on the CP. Golden. The banks might also throw in enhancements to cover the possibility that some of Soccer R Us's customers might default (credit enhancement) or be late on their payments (liquidity enhancement). Super golden. Check out this screen:

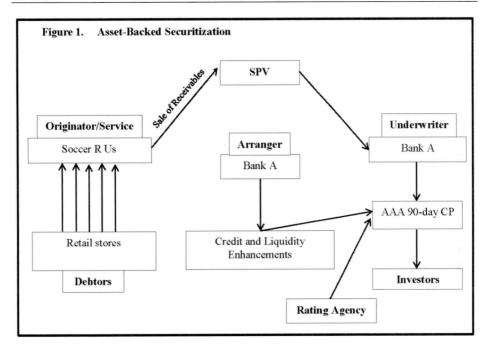

Figure 1.   Asset-Backed Securitization

Loco: What do all those boxes mean, man??

Levine: It means everybody wins.

Loco: Hey, man, the retail stores don't get their debt forgiven. That majorly sucks! Debt sucks!!

Student 1: You suck, Loco!

(laughter)

Levine: Deal with it, Mr. Loco. Actually, the retail stores do benefit to the extent that Soccer R Us's balance sheet adjustments, paying off debt, result in low prices for the retailers. Besides, forgiving the retailers' debt would gut the securitization. Let's look at all the other players. Soccer R Us, the originator, gets to pay off debt, which will improve its balance sheet. Soccer R Us, as the servicer, receives fees for being the administrator. The bank or banks get lots of fees for everything they do, from being arranger, underwriter, and enhancement provider. The credit rating agency gets paid. And the investors get primo securities.

Loco: Where's the after party, man???!!

Levine: The detox center is a block away.

(the auditorium breaks out in hoots and laughter)

True Sale and Bankruptcy Remote

Levine: Before we go to MBS, I'm going to go legal on you.

Loco: Earth to Mr. Levine, we're in a law school.

Levine: Really? I thought for sure we were in a psych ward.

(laughter, a yellow pad goes flying in the direction of Loco)

Levine: Now remember the SPV will have assets parked with it during the securitization. Do you think the investors will touch the CP if there's a chance that somebody might grab those receivables? Not with a ten-foot pole. So the lawyers have to make sure two basic requirements are met. First, you have to have a "true sale." That means no bull. The originator really has to sell the receivables and have no residual interest in them. Some courts use a "resemblance" test. We can call it the smell test: does the transfer look/smell like a sale or is it more like a pledge of assets? If you end up working in the field, you'll draft opinion letters for your clients giving them comfort that the receivables in the securitization will not be included in the transferor's bankruptcy estate.

Loco: Yeah, man, I can do that!

Levine: Cool. It's an important skill.

Loco: Yeah, man, I'm all about skills!

Levine: No doubt.

Loco: Gwen Stefani rocks!

(silence, bewildered looks in auditorium)

Levine: Okay. Second, the deal has to be "bankruptcy remote."

Loco: Huh?

Levine: Suppose Soccer R Us goes bankrupt. The trustee's job is to find and grab all of Soccer R Us' assets. Suppose the trustee could grab the assets in the SPV? You can kiss the investors goodbye. The SPV has to be bankruptcy remote—the trustee can't touch it. What if the SPV goes bankrupt? Kiss the investors goodbye again. The SPV itself has to be bankruptcy remote, meaning it can have only a hint of debt. Lawyers will take care of this through contractual provisions and the SPV's Charter.

Part Two: MBS

Levine: Now that we've got the lingo down, let's get to MBS. MBS involve the same basic process, although now you're pooling mostly single-family mortgages as well as retail and office mortgages. Time for a little history. MBS go back to the 1970s. The Government National Mortgage Association—GNMA, popularly called Ginnie Mae, guaranteed the first mortgage-backed security in 1970. Back then they were so-called "pass-through" securities because loans were combined into pools and the mortgage payments "passed through" to the holders of the securities on a pro-rate basis. The MBS that Ginnie produces have explicit backing of the full faith and credit of the U.S. government. Then came Fannie Mae and Freddie Mac, the government-sponsored-entities—GSEs.

Loco: Ginnie, Fannie, Freddie . . . Uh-huh . . . Ginnie, Fannie, Freddie . . . Uh-huh.

Student 1: Shut up, fool!

Levine: Almost finished. Fannie and Freddie are called government-sponsored entities because although they were created by federal legislation, they've been privatized into publicly traded shareholder corporations with some government control, for example, the choice of board members. The GSE's began issuing collateralized mortgage obligations, which, unlike pass-throughs, reconfigure the flows into different classes called "tranches," which means "slice" in French. Fannie and Freddie MBS are not explicitly guaranteed by the U.S. government, but the market always believed that the government wouldn't allow Fannie and Freddie Mac to fail. Keep that in mind as you study the crisis. Anyway, commercial and investment banks entered the securitization market when they realized that there was a market for mortgages that didn't conform to the standards required by the GSEs. The MBS the banks issue are typically called "private label MBS."

So much for the history. Let's start with the originators in a MBS. Some originators are banks—

Loco: Since when do banks sell the mortgages they make?

Levine: Great question.

Loco: Yeah, I rock!

Student 1: You sink like one, too, Loco!

Levine: To answer your question, back in the day when banks approved mortgages to their customers, they looked carefully at the customer's credit rating, etc. It was called originate-to-hold, meaning the bank would hold onto the mortgage loan. That changed to the originate-to-distribute approach—banks and other financial institutions originated the mortgages knowing that as soon as they signed the papers, they would sell the mortgages.

Loco: Like, cranking them out, yeah?

Levine: Cranking. But there might be good reasons for banks to sell their loans. As you know from a previous talk, banks have to hold a certain amount of capital based on the loans they make. A bank might want to manage its capital levels by selling the loans. And it's kind of hard for a bank to sell loans directly to investors. So why not convert them into a marketable security? Banks also face interest rate risk, meaning the risk that they might have to pay a higher interest rate on deposits—their liabilities—than the yield on their loans—their assets. So if the bank has a bunch of fixed-rate, low yielding loans, it could sell those loans to manage its interest-rate risk.

Loco: I love risk! I would be a kick-ass banker, with a caddie.

Student 1: Zip it, Loco!

Levine: Non-depository specialized lenders—called monolines—were also originators. In 2006, the top five originators were HSBC, New Century Financial, Countrywide, Citigroup, and WMC Mortgage. In addition to earning fees from the borrowers, originators make a profit when they sell a pool of mortgages to an SPV. For example, an originator will sell a portfolio of mortgages with the principal of $100 million for $102 million, for a $2 million profit. Not bad.

Loco: I could buy a yacht with that!

Levine: I prefer sailboats.

Loco: Oh, you're one of those!

Levine: And I'm at peace with that. Now let's talk about the arranger. The arranger coordinates the sale of pools of mortgages from the originator to the SPV. The arranger can also be the originator, and it does a number of things: performs due diligence of the originator, creates the SPV, which will issue the debt securities to the investors, consults with the credit agencies, completes any filings with the SEC, and is underwriter of the securities. The arranger makes money by charging fees to the investors and by premia investors pay on securities. The top five arrangers/issuers in 2006 were Countrywide, New Century, Option One, Fremont, and Washington Mutual.

When securitizing mortgages, the arranger has to have a warehouse lender.

Loco: You mean people who would lend warehouses or lenders that live in warehouses? Be clear, my man!

(a highlighter goes flying through the air towards Loco)

Levine: Somehow the arranger has to fund the mortgages until the securitization is finalized. This isn't a problem when the arranger is a depository institution/commercial bank, which funds its mortgages from its deposits. But monoline arrangers—that is, non-depository institutions—need loans from a third-party lender to fund loans that are "warehoused" until they are sold. Warehouse lenders, who aren't certain about the value of the mortgages, protect themselves by, say, requiring what we call in the biz "over-collateralization." For example, a warehouse lender will make a $9 million loan against collateral of $10 million of underlying mortgages.

Okay, so the mortgages are sold to the SPV and it starts issuing securities. The asset manager acts as agent for the investor.

Loco: Hey, what if the manager is an idiot and buys a bunch of junk?

Levine: Well, you have the reputation of the arranger. And why not have the asset manager do due diligence on the arranger and originator? And let's not forget the sweeteners, such as credit enhancements that the arranger can provide.

Next in the assembly line is the credit rating agency. Like our ABS example, credit rating agencies assign ratings to the mortgage-backed securities issued by the SPV. They calculate the amount of credit enhancement that's required based on an estimated loss distribution and on that basis slap a credit rating on the securities. The CRA will do only limited due diligence of the arranger and originator.

Then comes the servicer, which collects the loan payments, makes advances of unpaid interest by borrowers to the SPV, accounts for principal and interest, does customer service for the mortgagors, holds the escrow relating to property taxes and insurance, contacts delinquent borrowers, and supervises foreclosures. Of course, the servicer collects a fee for its services.

Loco: Fees, fees, fees!!! Are you getting a fee for this show you're putting on?

Levine: Academia isn't as crass as the financial industry. We receive honoraria.

Loco: Same difference!

Levine: We're intellectuals, Mr. Loco.

Loco: You're nothing more than self-promoting entrepreneurs.

Levine: But in the service of humanity.

Loco: Let's get a big, fat amen from the audience!

(silence)

Levine: Because of the importance of the servicer's responsibilities, credit rating agencies will take into account the quality of the servicer and their ratings are intended to gauge the servicer's ability to prevent or mitigate losses due to changing market conditions. The top five servicers in 2006 were Countrywide, J.P. Morgan Chase, Citigroup, Option One, and America West.

Finally we come to the investors. As you know, the investors provide the funding for the SPV's purchase of mortgage pools that underlie the MBS.

Here's a visual on the securitization of mortgage backed securities:

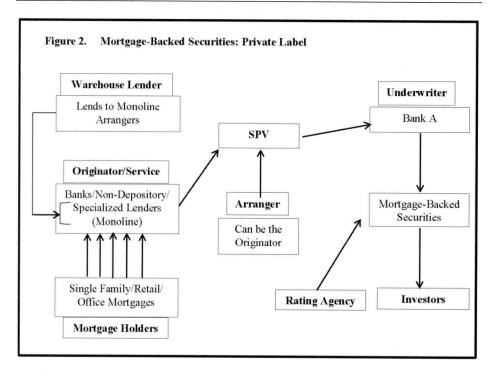

Loco: But wait a second! How can you take piece of crap subprime mortgages and turn them into AAA securities???

Levine: What are you holding behind your back, Mr. Loco?

Loco: I'm scratching my back. I think there's a pimple there.

Levine: Uhhh . . .

Loco: Come scratch it for me!

Levine: I'll take a rain check on that.

(a pack of post-its goes flying in Loco's direction)

Levine: Anyway, check this out:

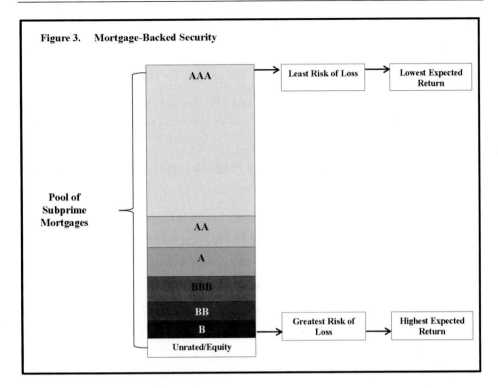

Figure 3.   Mortgage-Backed Security

To answer your question, Mr. Loco, there are at least three ways to turn doo-doo into gold. First, as you can see, the MBS is sliced up into the tranches we talked about. All the tranches below are "subordinated" to the AAA tranche, meaning investors holding this "senior" tranche will be paid first. So if the subprime mortgage holders start defaulting, the lower tranches will lose out first, starting with the unrated tranche—a buffer, as you'll see in a sec—and moving up, with AAA being the last in line to lose. Another way to look at it is a waterfall. When the payments come in from the holders of the subprime mortgages they go first to the AAA tranche. If there's a shortfall in the waterfall, the lowest tranches will feel it first. Notice, though, that in exchange for enjoying the lowest risk of loss, the AAA tranche will get the lowest return. The gamblers, like hedge funds, go for the lower tranches, like the B tranche, for a higher return.

The second way of turning doo-doo into gold is "over-collateralization," meaning the amount of the principal of the mortgage pool exceeds the principal balance of the MBS issued by the SPV. For example, the mortgage pool might be, say, $100,000, to pick a number, and the total principal of the MBS is $90,000. This creates the unrated equity tranche that you can see.

The third way is to create an "excess spread."

Loco: Like raspberry jam?

Mr. Levine: Your favorite?

Loco: On beef jerky, man!

Levine: Hmmm . . . well . . . getting back to the excess spread, put simply, the spread is the difference between the interest payments the SPV receives from the mortgage holders and the costs associated with issuing the MBS. So, for example, the SPV receives mortgage interest payments of 8% and the costs of the deal amount to 6%. Do the numbers and you have an excess spread of 2%. Check it out: the excess spread has to be wiped out before the tranches start getting wiped out, starting with equity tranche. Sweet for the investors, don't you think?

Loco: Yeah!

Levine: Can we get an amen?

(auditorium says "amen" in unison)

Part Three: Re-Securitization: CDOs

Levine: MBSs can be "resecuritized" through collateralized debt obligations (CDOs), which arose in the 1990s. This was a form of "structured finance." The original CDOs were "asset-backed," meaning the SPV could be stuffed with any kind of debt, bonds, loans or other instruments. Like asset-backed securitization, these CDOs were initially created for balance sheet purposes. For example, banks managed the amount of capital they needed to hold by putting together CDOs to get rid of loans—assets—on their books. CDOs gradually morphed from balance-sheet types to CDOs created by asset managers and institutional investors to get sweet returns via arbitrage—i.e., they made more money on the assets' return than the interest they had to pay on the debt instruments distributed to investors.

Loco: Arbitrage, man. I could drop that at a party and be really cool!

Student 1: You'd get thrown out the window, Loco!

Loco: That would be cool, too. Like, with glass in my teeth, man!

(a half-eaten apple goes flying through the air towards Loco)

Levine: Folks, check this out: By 2007, residential MBS constituted 56% of the assets in CDOs. The multi-trillion-dollar CDO market was highly standardized and global, attracting all sorts of investors. To standardize the market, CDOs were sliced up into tranches like the MBS. So the top tranche would have a AAA rating—the senior tranche—and be the first to receive the flow from the assets. The waterfall would then flow to the tranches below the senior tranche—the mezzanine and junior tranches. The same inverse relationship between risk and return applies. Each tranche appeals to a different kind of investor—the senior tranche is for low-risk investors such as banks or insurance companies, the mezzanine level appeals to the investor who is looking for a medium-risk security, and the junior class is for the highly leveraged investor such as a hedge fund. Credit ratings agencies such as Moody's, Standard and Poor's, and Fitch provide the risk profile of the underlying assets. Have a look at this visual:

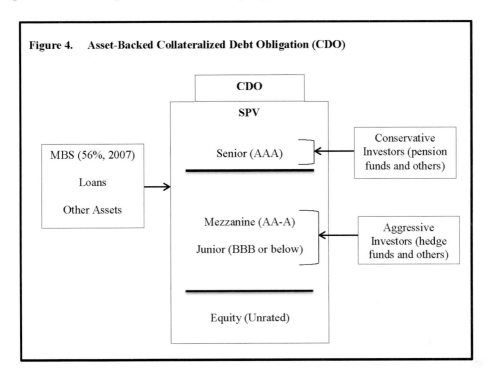

Figure 4.   Asset-Backed Collateralized Debt Obligation (CDO)

A CDO was so much fun to put together, why stop with a plain CDO? CDOs could be comprised of other CDOs. SPVs, managed by commercial and investment banks, would buy short-term CDOs and then issue long-term CDOs (often called a CDO-squared) with a higher interest rate. Why even stop there! The prevalence of CDOs-squared in the market led to the CDO-cubed credit derivatives and beyond. The CDOs got so complicated that only the mathematicians who wrote them understood what was going on. But, hey, as long as everybody's making money . . .

Loco: (shoots up, starts bobbing up and down and snapping his fingers and yells at the top of his voice) Show me the money! Show me the money!

Student 1: You suck, Loco! Sit your lousy-Cuba-Gooding-Junior-impersonation-butt down!

(a sub sandwich goes whistling through the air towards Loco)

Levine: Is that tuna? My favorite.

(laughter)

Levine: Believe it or not, things get crazier. In the late 1990s, "synthetic" CDOs came on stage.

Loco: You mean like polyester?

Levine: A leisure suit.

Loco: A what?

Levine: Google it.

Levine: To understand a synthetic CDO, we have to look at figure 4 again. Notice that the investors assume the credit risk of the portfolio of the assets owned by the SPV. In a synthetic CDO, the SPV doesn't own anything. The assets are merely "referenced"—you'll see this in a minute. Banks might do this because they want to retain the legal ownership of the assets but transfer the risk. They do that via credit derivatives, particularly credit default swaps (CDS).

Loco: Credit what?

Levine: Credit default swap. It's basically insurance. Let's suppose the bank has made a bunch of loans and there's always credit risk associated with those loans, right? Well, to protect itself against this risk the bank could enter into a credit default swap with a counterparty, another financial institution. The bank is called the "protection buyer," and the counterparty is called the "protection seller." The deal is that the protection buyer will make periodic payments to the protection seller, like insurance premiums. If the borrowers default on loans and the credit default swap contract stipulates that that is a "credit event," the protection seller must either buy the assets at the contract price or pay the bank the difference between the contract price and the market value of the loans. And check this out: Since the CDS is considered a swap, not insurance, it was virtually unregulated! And no one knew exactly how large the CDS market was before the crisis hit. Some said it had a notional value—

Loco: Man, stop using that jargon crap with us.

Levine: My bad, Mr. Loco. Notional amounts are used in derivatives. Let's take a credit default swap. Suppose a bank has loans totaling $1 million. The $1 million—the notional amount—is used to figure out what the premiums will be and what the payout will be if there's a credit event.

Loco: That's better.

Levine: Getting back to my point, just before the crisis people were throwing around $50–$60 trillion in notional value.

Loco: That's insane, man!

Student 1: Friggin' A!

Loco (to Student 1): Are you my friend now?

Student 1: Hell no!

Levine: Now that we understand credit default swaps, let's look at a synthetic CDO. Brace yourselves.

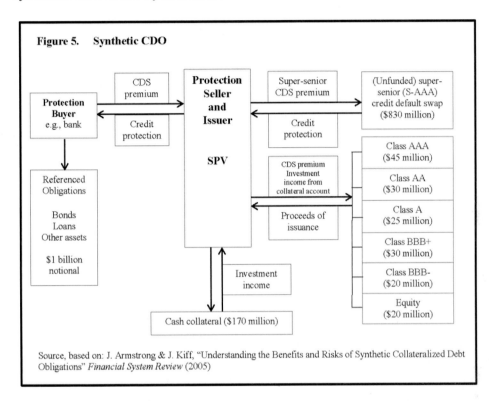

Figure 5.   Synthetic CDO

Source, based on: J. Armstrong & J. Kiff, "Understanding the Benefits and Risks of Synthetic Collateralized Debt Obligations" *Financial System Review* (2005)

Starting on the left, you have your referenced obligations—a portfolio of assets with a $1 billion notional amount. Notice that the SPV doesn't own that portfolio—it's just put together for purposes of the synthetic CDO. Also notice that the protection buyer on the left could be a bank—buying protection to the tune of $1 billion—the referenced obligations. So it enters into a credit default swap with the SPV, the protection seller. The protection buyer will make premium payments to the SPV. Let's look at the SPV. Notice that it's also the issuer of the securities to the investors on the right, with the highest funded tranche being Class AAA. By funded I mean that those investors actually pay for the securities issued by the SPV. The four tranches above the equity tranche are funded as well. Since, unlike the asset-backed CDO in figure 4, the funds from the investors aren't used to buy assets, they're instead used to buy very safe AAA securities treasury bonds and placed in the cash collateral account.

Looking from left to right, the return on the investments in the collateral account as well as the premiums from the protection buyer will run to the investors in the waterfall fashion. If the assets in the references obligations start defaulting, the CDO will first start using the assets in the collateral account to compensate the protection buyer for the losses. Once those run out, the investors will start getting hit, starting with the initial Class BBB securities.

But notice where most of the money is—the unfunded super-duper-senior tranche. It's the safest tranche and so it gets to drink from the waterfall first in return for the smallest return. This helps the synthetic CDO work funding-wise because most of the liability is there and that tranche will receive a comparatively small return. Another way of looking at the super senior tranche is that it's a separate credit default swap with the protection buyer. The bank/protection buyer is on the asset side and the super senior tranche is on the liability side—for every asset in these deals there has to be a liability. So if you look at the whole figure, you'll see that this synthetic CDO is a huge credit default swap between the protection buyer—the bank way on the left—and the investors way on the right, who are essentially the protection sellers, with the super senior tranche having a separate CDS with the protection buyer.

Why this craziness? When they were first putting this stuff together they thought everybody was going to win. The bank/protection buyer covers its risk, the asset managers—could be the bank—get fees, and investors can choose the risk/return profile that they want. Take, for example, institutional investors who are hunting for a better yield but can't invest in high-yielding, non-investment grade bonds. The CDO is the answer!

The Virus Goes Global

Investors from around the world doing the yield hunt, typically insurance companies, pensions funds, and hedge funds, gobbled up the CDOs. European banks loaded up on MBS and CDOs. In China, a booming economy based on the country's ability to produce low-cost goods for the world led to a lot of wealth. Chinese investors, like those in Europe and the United States, wanted somewhere safe to put their investments. They started with Treasury bonds, which were safer than other instruments, and then loaded up on the same securities.

And no one suspected that a toxic pandemic was just around the corner . . .

(commotion in the audience)

Student 1: Loco!

Student 2: What's going on?

Student 1: He's trying to eat his textbook!

Student 2: Which one?

Student 1: What the #$%@ does it matter?

Student 2: Some taste better than others.

Student 1: Loco, spit that crap out. Hold him down!

(they pull the pages out of Loco's mouth)

Student 1: Are you okay, Loco?

(Loco gasps)

Loco: It's a @#$% casino, man!

(Loco bolts out of the hall)

Loco: IT'S A CASINO. NOTHING MORE!!!

(the hall eventually empties, a bit later Levine walks to his car and Loco approaches)

Levine: That was quite a show.

Loco: I do my best.

Levine: To hide.

(pause)

Levine: You're good at it.

Loco: Yeah, I suppose.

Levine: My shadow is really pretty small, son.

Loco: Not small enough.

Levine: Hector Loco . . . What a name.

Loco: It works, don't you think?

(Levine opens his car door)

Loco: What time is your flight?

Levine: Couple of hours.

(Levine looks at Loco lovingly and hugs him)

Loco: They won't understand any of this.

Levine: Teach them in your study group. You'll do a better job than me.

Loco: Maybe.

Levine: I love you, son.

Loco: I love you, too, mom.

QUESTIONS FROM YOUR TALKING DOG

1.   Do we really have to go out? It's too cold. Oh, *you* need the exercise! Well, what's the topic of conversation today? Securitization. Yeah, I'm ready. First, though, what the HECK does that mean?

2.   We can start with asset-backed securities. Break it down for me. Like, what kind of stuff can be securitized?

3.   I get what receivables means. Originator? Tell me.

4.   Special purpose vehicle? Is that like a dog car? Why is that kind of thing necessary?

5.   This jargon is making this walk very unpleasant. Arranger? Servicer?

6.   Yes, I've heard of rating agencies. What's their role in this stuff?

7.   Why is this example you're giving me such a neat thing?

8.   Why do you set me up like this? No, I don't know what true sale and bankruptcy remote mean. Just tell me, and don't embarrass me again.

9.   Time for a history lesson? Wait, wait. What's the difference between Ginnie Mae, and Fannie Mae and Freddie Mac?

10. Private label, is that like scotch?

11. Originate-to-hold? Originate-to-distribute? What do those mean?

12. I don't get it. Why would banks want to be originators?

13. Monolines? Slow down and explain that to me. What's the point of the warehouse lender?

14. Tell me who else is on this assembly line. Can you draw a picture for me?

15. Yeah, I see that piece of crap. No, I don't know how to turn it into gold. Tell me how it worked with mortgage-backed securities and these subprime loans you've been talking about. Subordination, overcollateralization, excess spread. You can't just throw those words at me. Explain!

16. Re-securitization? When will this end? Never? OMG! CDOs? You'll owe me big time! Tell me about them.

17. Asset-backed CDOs? Draw me a picture.

18. CDOs squared? Are you kidding me? What are those?

19. Synthetic CDOs? Why synthetic? It's all about credit default swaps? What the heck are those?

20. Uhh . . . you need to explain that whole thing to me. And draw me a picture. When we're through, I'm going to throw myself in front of a car. Just kidding! Give me a hug.

CHAPTER 14

OUTBREAK

■■■

I. THE VIRUS ATTACKS THE GLOBE

March 12, 2007

1. <u>News Alert:</u> New Century Financial Corporation, one of the largest subprime mortgage lenders, filed for Chapter 11 bankruptcy reorganization today. It's expected that it will cut 3,200 employees, or 54% of its work force. Between 2005 and 2007, New Century made at least $75.9 billion in subprime loans. In its filing, it said it would not be able to pay $8.4 billion in repayments to its lenders, which include Bank of America, Morgan Stanley, Citigroup, Barclays Bank, and UBS. New Century's descent began when it announced on March 2 that two criminal probes were commenced against it. Its auditor, KPMG, expressed doubt about the company's ability to survive, especially since its creditors announced they would no longer finance the company. A week later New Century's stock lost 78% of its value, which prompted the New York Stock Exchange to suspend trading in the company's shares. Established in 1996, New Century went from 50 employees to 7,200 people in 2006. The rise in its stock price was equally impressive, going from $9.67 in June 1997 to $66.95 in December 2004. However, in the second half of 2006 New Century hit strong headwinds as mortgage rates rose. Much of its business was in California, Florida, New York, and Arizona, states that witnessed the steepest decline in home values after the housing bubble burst, leading to a glut of new homes. Rising delinquencies and defaults by its subprime borrowers led to its collapse.

June 7, 2007

2. <u>News Alert:</u> Bear Stearns, the Wall Street investment bank, has suspended redemption in one of its two hedge funds, its High-Grade Structured Credit Strategies Enhanced Leverage Fund. As of April 30th, the fund, which invested heavily in CDOs backed by subprime mortgages, was down 23% for the year. Investors reportedly sought to redeem approximately $250 million before Bear shut down redemptions. Although the fund posted healthy returns over its first four months, it sustained mounting losses early in the year as the subprime mortgage market imploded. As the fund's name suggests, it is highly leveraged, with some sources reporting a ratio of 3 to 1, meaning that it borrows three dollars for

every dollar invested in the CDOs. High leverage can be very profitable if the assets rise in value, but it can destroy a hedge fund in short order if the market drops.

June 22, 2007

3.   News Alert: Bear Stearns has pledged up to $3.2 billion in loans to rescue one of its hedge funds, the Bear Stearns High-Grade Structured Credit Fund, that is collapsing because of bad bets on subprime mortgages. Bear is also negotiating with banks to rescue the second, larger fund, High-Grade Structured Credit Strategies Enhanced Leverage Fund. Market watchers see Bear's pledge as a pre-emptive move to prevent lenders, such as Merrill Lynch and Deutsche Bank, from seizing the securities and dumping them on the market, which could expose the investment bank and the market to catastrophic losses.

July 17, 2007

4.   News Alert: Bear Stearns' two hedge funds, which invested in AAA tranches of CDOs, have collapsed. In a letter sent to investors, Bear Stearns revealed that its Bear Stearns High-Grade Structured Credit Fund had lost more than 90% of its value, while the Enhanced Leverage Fund's capital had virtually disappeared. The hedge funds' demise was precipitated by Bear Stearns lenders' who demanded more collateral, which forced the cash-poor investment bank to sell its CDOs. This only worsened Bear's position as the securities plummeted in value when they were dumped on the market. The hedge funds ultimately sold nearly $4 billion in CDOs.

July 31, 2007

5.   News Alert: Bear Stearns two hedge funds, the Bear Stearns High-Grade Structured Credit Fund and the Bear Stearns High-Grade Structured Credit Enhanced Leveraged Fund, have filed for Chapter 15 bankruptcy.

August 9, 2007

6.   News Alert: BNP Paribas SA, France's biggest bank, has blocked withdrawals from three investment funds because of its inability to value their holdings following losses in the U.S. subprime mortgage market. The funds' assets, about €1.6 billion ($2.2 billion), dropped 20 percent in less than two weeks. About a third of the funds' assets are in subprime securities rated AA or higher. NIBC Holding NV, a Dutch investment bank, reported today that it has lost at least €137 million on U.S. subprime securities this year. BNP's spokesman said it was impossible to calculate the value of the funds given the lack of prices for some securities. In related news, the European Central Bank has injected €95 billion into the euro zone banking system. This is the largest such intervention in overnight rates by the ECB since September 11, 2001.

August 10, 2007

7.   <u>News Alert:</u> Over the past 48 hours, central banks in Europe, Asia and North America have injected over $300 billion into their banking systems in an attempt to stave off what is becoming a global crisis as credit markets seize up. In the United States, the Federal Reserve pumped $38 billion into the banking system, the largest single-day liquidity operation since September 19, 2001.

September 14, 2007

8.   <u>News Alert:</u> The Bank of England has extended emergency funding to Northern Rock, a large British mortgage lender. The move comes after investors withdrew support of Northern Rock amid worries that it could face short-term difficulties raising capital in the wholesale market.

October 25, 2007

9.   <u>News Alert:</u> Merrill Lynch has announced a $2.24 billion loss in the third quarter due mainly to the $7.9 billion write-downs on CDOs and subprime mortgages.

October 26, 2007

10.   <u>News Alert:</u> Countrywide Financial has reported its first loss in 25 years, a third-quarter loss of $1.2 billion on about $1 billion in write-downs.

November 5, 2007

11.   <u>News Alert:</u> Citigroup CEO, Chuck Prince, has resigned after an announcement that Citigroup may have to write down up to $11 billion in bad debt from losses in the subprime mortgage crisis.

November 13, 2007

12.   <u>News Alert:</u> Bank of America has announced it will have to write off $3 billion of bad debt.

November 15, 2007

13.   <u>News Alert:</u> Barclays has confirmed a $1.6 billion write-down in the month of October due to its holdings of subprime securities. The bank also stated that more than €5 billion in its holdings of subprime securities could lead to more write-downs in the future.

November 21, 2007

14.   <u>News Alert:</u> Freddie Mac, a government-sponsored entity that buys mortgages and packages them into securities, has reported a record-breaking $2 billion loss for the third quarter stemming from the mortgages it holds. This compares to a $715 million loss the previous third quarter.

578 OUTBREAK CH. 14

December 3, 2007

15. <u>News Alert:</u> Moody's has announced that it has or might cut the ratings of $116 billion of debt held by Structured Investment Vehicles (SIVs), entities sponsored predominantly by banks worldwide that have invested in mortgage-backed securities and CDOs. The assets have plummeted in value due to the subprime mortgage crisis. Market analysts suspect that credit rating agencies gave SIVs with subprime debt overly favorable ratings.

December 10, 2007

16. <u>News Alert:</u> UBS has announced $10 billion more in write-downs associated with its holdings of subprime securities. This brings the total write-downs for UBS to $13.7 billion thus far. However, analysts from Deutsche Bank believe UBS still has approximately $9 billion in exposure.

December 12, 2007

17. <u>News Alert:</u> In an effort to unfreeze interbank lending, the United States Federal Reserve has announced the creation of the Term Auction Facility to provide the banking sector with additional liquidity. The TAF provides funding for up to thirty-five days. Banks can use a wide range of securities as collateral. The Fed also approved reciprocal currency arrangements, known as swap agreements, which will provide $20 billion to the European Central Bank and $4 billion to the Swiss National Bank.

December 20, 2007

18. <u>News Alert:</u> Bear Stearns has reported its first quarterly loss in its 84-year history of $854 million. Bear also wrote down $1.9 billion on Bear's mortgage holdings.

January 15, 2008

19. <u>News Alert:</u> Citigroup, the largest bank in the US, has reported a $9.83 billion loss in the fourth quarter, with an $18.1 billion write down on its subprime mortgage-related exposure. The bank also announced it would raise $12.5 billion in new capital to shore up its balance sheet. $6.88 billion will come from the Government of Singapore Investment Corporation.

January 21, 2008

20. <u>News Alert:</u> Global stock markets in London and Europe suffered the biggest one day loss since September 11, 2001. The FTSE 100 index fell 5.5%, wiping out £76 billion in market value as investors sell off equity for the safety of government bonds

January 22, 2008

21. <u>News Alert:</u> A new panic in the global credit market has led the Fed to cut its key interest rate by 75 basis point, the largest inter-meeting cut in Fed history.

February 28, 2008

22. <u>News Alert</u>: AIG has announced a $5.2 billion loss for the fourth quarter of 2007, the second consecutive quarter of losses. Most of the losses are related to write downs of $11.12 billion relating to revaluation of a large credit default swap portfolio. AIG has written $78 billion in credit default swaps, which may be problematic for the insurer if the housing market continues its downturn.

March 3, 2008

23. <u>News Alert</u>: UK's largest bank, HSBC, has reported a $17.2 billion loss on write downs of its U.S. mortgage portfolio.

March 10, 2008

24. <u>News Alert</u>: Rumors are circulating on Wall Street that Bear Stearns could be experiencing liquidity problems. Investors have responded to the rumors by selling Bear's stock. In related news, Lehman Brothers cut 5% of its workforce across all lines of business. The 1,425 people who were let go join the ranks of 4,000 Lehman employees who received pink slips in the last year.

March 11, 2008

25. <u>News Alert</u>: In an effort to boost liquidity in the troubled MBS market, the Fed has created the Term Securities Lending Facility (TSLF). The facility will offer primary dealers—financial firms that conduct transactions with the fed in the open market operations—up to $200 billion in treasury securities for 28 days, accepting AAA-rated private mortgage backed securities as collateral. The creation of the TSLF exposes the Fed to possible default on the MBS securities, with the losses falling upon taxpayers.

March 12, 2008

26. <u>News Alert</u>:

CNBC's David Faber: "It's been a hard week for the shares of Bear Stearns as the firm has been buffeted by constant rumors of a looming liquidity problem. Bear maintains that its balance sheet, capital positions, all strong . . . Joining me now first is Alan Schwartz. He is Bear Stearns' president and CEO . . . Why is all this out there to begin with? What do you think is causing these rumors?"

Alan Schwartz: "Well you know it's very hard to say. Why do rumors start? If I had to speculate, I would say that you know last week was a difficult time in the mortgage business . . . Some people could speculate that Bear Stearns might have some problems in there since we're a significant player in the mortgage business. None of those speculations are true . . . Part of the problem is that when speculation starts in a market that has a lot of emotion in it and people are concerned about the volatility, then people will sell first and ask questions later. And that creates its own momentum. We put out a statement, I did, that our liquidity and balance sheet are strong . . . We don't see any pressure on our liquidity, let alone a liquidity crisis."

March 13, 2008

27. News Alert: Bear Stearns has reported that its liquid assets have dropped to $2 billion caused largely by loss of investor confidence in light of the rumors of illiquidity. This reflects a loss of $15 billion in cash and cash equivalents in two days as reported by the SEC on March 11.

March 14, 2008

28. News Alert: Bear Stearns has set up an emergency funding agreement with JP Morgan Chase (JPMC) to access liquidity if needed.

March 16, 2008

29. News Alert: JPMC has announced it will acquire Bear Stearns for $2 per share. The Federal Reserve Bank has agreed to lend JPMC $30 billion to cover Bear's long-term assets to alleviate the need for a fire sale. Sources say that on March 14 Treasury Secretary Paulson and New York Fed President Geithner told Bear's CEO, Alan Schwartz, that he had to make a deal to be taken over by this evening.

March 24, 2008

30. News Alert: JPMC has raised its price on Bear Stearns to $10 per share after the original merger at $2 per share fell through because of legal errors and opposition by Bear shareholders.

April 8, 2008

31. News Alert: The International Monetary Fund has released a new estimate on credit crunch losses. The Fund now projects the losses to be upwards of $945 billion. It cautioned, however, that the estimate could go much higher if new developments like the Bear Stearns bailout materialize.

May 2008

32. News Alert: An estimated 8.5 million homeowners owe more on their home loans than their home's value, known technically as "negative equity," and popularly known as being "underwater." Over the past year, first mortgage defaults rose from 1.5 million to 2.2 million. Many of the defaulting borrowers have lost employment, victims of the softening job market. This development can be traced to 2006. Based on first mortgage data, defaults on subprime mortgages soared in 2006 to nearly 1 million on an annualized basis from 775,000 in 2005. Experts attributed the surge in defaults to rising interest rates and falling home prices. Most defaulting borrowers were "flippers," speculators who bought and sold property quickly for profit. A second wave of defaults in the subprime mortgages hit

the housing sector in 2007. Experts attributed the surge to adjustable rate mortgages that originated in 2005. Most of these ARMs had low fixed interest rates for the first two years, followed by periodic adjustments based on market rates. With interest rates climbing, the first reset spiked monthly mortgage payments to unmanageable levels in many cases. Defaults rose from 1 million in 2006 to 1.5 million to 2007.

May 22, 2008

33. News Alert: Moody's has announced an internal investigation into its rating process, declaring that up to $4 billion of complex debt products were incorrectly rated AAA because of faulty computer models. New York Senator, Charles Schumer, has called upon the SEC to investigate the matter.

June 16, 2008

34. News Alert: Lehman Brothers has reported a $2.8 billion second quarter loss marking the first loss in the company's fourteen year history under public ownership.

June 26, 2008

35. News Alert: The SEC has announced it will attempt to reduce its own reliance on credit ratings. The SEC is recommending that explicit references to credit ratings—forty-four—be dropped from its market rules. SEC chairman, Christopher Cox, stated that some of the SEC regulations implicitly assume that securities with high credit ratings are liquid and have lower price volatility, which has been proved wrong by the credit crisis.

July 8, 2008

36. News Alert: The SEC has disclosed that credit rating agencies failed to manage conflicts of interest in assigning ratings to the complex financial instruments backed by subprime mortgages. The findings of the SEC probe follow months of investigations to determine whether the rating agencies failed to follow their usual procedures to publish higher ratings for complex financial products. SEC chairman Christopher Cox said that the volume of rating requests caused employees to cut corners in rating the complex securities.

July 13, 2008

37. News Alert: The fate of Freddie Mac and Fannie Mae has become grimmer as investors short the GSEs stock, causing the shares to plummet in value.

The U.S. Treasury and Federal Reserve have released a roadmap indicating how they will protect Freddie Mac and Fannie Mae from insolvency. Because of their need for short-term financing, the mortgage companies are vulnerable to a sudden loss of market confidence in carrying out their day-to-day business. Although government officials did not announce a detailed bailout package, they made it clear that they will provide a liquidity backstop if needed. The Treasury conceded that this may include a large injection of public funds.

July 14, 2008

38. News Alert: More details have surfaced about the plan to rescue Freddie Mac and Fannie Mae. The government said it will approach Congress for the authority to give unlimited funds to make sure that Fannie Mae and Freddie Mac do not fail. The Federal Reserve announced it will provide Freddie and Fannie emergency funds on the same terms as banks should it become necessary.

August 19, 2008

39. News Alert: Former IMF chief economist, Kenneth Rogoff, has warned that the credit crunch may lead to the failure of a large U.S. bank within months. "The worst is yet to come," says Rogoff. In his view, the credit crisis will likely lead to consolidation in the U.S. financial sector and Fannie Mae and Freddie Mac will cease to exist in their present form.

August 20, 2008

40. News Alert: Lehman Brothers has held secret talks to sell up to 50% of its shares to South Korean or Chinese investors. The talks reportedly broke down because Lehman was asking too high of a price. Shares in Lehman Brothers have fallen almost 85% since early 2007.

September 7, 2008

41. News Alert: The U.S. government has taken control of Freddie Mae and Fannie Mac in what could become the world's largest financial bailouts. The plan includes a government injection of $100 billion to each troubled mortgage lender to ensure that they can meet their debts. The government will also buy mortgage bonds backed by the companies starting with $5 billion and provide unlimited liquidity until the end of next year.

September 11, 2008

42. News Alert: Lehman Brothers has announced plans to shrink its size to survive the crisis. The news came after Lehman reported its worse loss ever of $3.9 billion for the third quarter spurred by $7.8 billion in credit-related write-downs. CEO Dick Fuld has told analysts that Lehman was in one of its toughest periods in its 158-year history but would pull through.

September 13, 2008

43. News Alert: Major banks have devised a rescue package to buy Lehman Brothers. Bank of America appears to be the leading contender and it is considering a joint takeover bid with JC Flowers and China

Investment Co., the Chinese sovereign wealth fund. Both Moody's and Standard & Poor's have said they will cut Lehman's credit ratings if the bank fails to find a buyer, further crippling Lehman's ability to raise funds. The U.S. Treasury and Federal Reserve have refused to use public funds to close a rescue the investment bank.

September 14, 2008

44. <u>News Alert:</u> Merrill Lynch has entered into talks to be acquired by Bank of America. This comes after Bank of America removed itself from the bidding for Lehman Brothers because the government refused to supply financial assistance with the acquisition.

In related news, American International Group (AIG) is seeking to raise $10 to 20 billion in equity from private investors to shore up its balance sheet. AIG has also petitioned the Fed to borrow from the discount window to help stabilize its business operations. Because of its exposure to the real estate and credit default swaps market, the ratings agencies have threatened to downgrade AIG if it does not raise the much needed capital.

September 15, 2008

45. <u>News Alert:</u> Lehman Brothers has announced it will file for Chapter 11 bankruptcy as acquisition talks with Bank of America have broken down.

The European Central Bank (ECB) has allotted €30 billion in a one-day liquidity operation to counter the effects of Lehman's bankruptcy. The Bank of England has announced that it will offer £5 billion of extra reserves to help stabilize the markets. Both banks said that European banks will now be short of cash because their loans to Lehman Brothers will now be tied up in bankruptcy proceedings.

In other news, a deal between AIG and New York insurance regulators will allow the insurance company to access $20 billion of assets from its subsidiaries in an attempt to add liquidity and prevent a credit downgrade. Despite the deal, all of the major rating agencies have downgraded AIG's long-term debt, which could trigger billions of dollars in collateral payments on its derivative trades.

September 16, 2008

46. <u>News Alert:</u> The Federal Reserve announces it will lend AIG $85 billion in emergency funds, giving the government a 79.9% stake in the company. The government stake was implemented to prevent existing shareholders from benefiting from the bailout.

In other news, trading has been suspended on the Russian stock exchanges Micex and RTS. This comes after a 20% drop in response to the crisis in the US. In an effort to stabilize, the Russian central bank has injected $14.16 billion in emergency one-day funds into the money market.

September 17, 2008

<u>47.</u> <u>News Alert:</u> A money market fund managed by Reserve Management Corporation (RMC) has "broken the buck" as its net asset value (NAV) has dropped below $1 per share. This is the first time since 1994 that this has happened to a money market fund. It was caused by RMC's decision to write $785 million held in Lehman Brothers debt down to zero, and a large increase in redemptions. The run on RMC prompted other money market mutual fund companies to hold on to their cash rather than investing in commercial paper or certificates of deposit. Their decision not to invest in the term funding markets has cut off important sources of short-term funding for banks and corporations that sell the securities.

In development abroad, central banks around the world have announced $180 billion emergency injection to provide liquidity and halt the escalating crisis. This was in response to the lack of lending between banks that had occurred in the U.S. and UK following the AIG bailout.

September 18, 2008

<u>48.</u> <u>News Alert:</u> The credit markets are virtually frozen. Given the uncertainties surrounding the solvency of financial firms, interbank lending has come to a halt. Banks have become reluctant to lend to each other, which is essential to funding their positions and managing their liquidity. The inability of banks to borrow funds from other banks has led to a drop in lending to businesses and consumers.

September 19, 2008

<u>49.</u> <u>News Alert:</u> In an effort to save the $3,400 trillion mutual funds market, the U.S. Treasury has announced it will insure money market funds in an attempt to prevent a run on the funds. And President Bush has approved use of up to $50 billion from the Exchange Stabilization Fund to insure the holdings of any publicly offered money market mutual fund. Fed has created the Asset-Backed Commercial Paper Money Market Mutual Fund Liquidity Facility to extend loans to U.S. depository institutions and bank holding companies to finance their purchases of asset-backed commercial paper from money market mutual funds.

At the SEC, the agency has issued a ban on the short-selling of 799 financial stocks. The ban is expected to last for 10 days but could last up to 30.

At the Treasury Department, Secretary Paulson has urged Congress to pass legislation that will allow the government to buy toxic mortgage securities from the banks. The proposal will give the Treasury authority to purchase up to $700 billion of the troubled assets by issuing Treasury securities.

September 22, 2008

50. <u>News Alert:</u> The Federal Reserve has announced that Goldman Sachs and Morgan Stanley have been approved to become deposit-taking bank holding companies, which subjects them to regulation by the Fed, including capital requirements. They were last of the big five Wall Street investment firms after the disappearance of Bears Stearns, Merrill Lynch, and Lehman Brothers.

CHAIRMAN CHRISTOPHER COX, SPEECH: "TESTIMONY CONCERNING TURMOIL IN U.S. CREDIT MARKETS: RECENT ACTIONS REGARDING GOVERNMENT SPONSORED ENTITIES, INVESTMENT BANKS AND OTHER FINANCIAL INSTITUTIONS," BEFORE THE COMMITTEE ON BANKING, HOUSING, AND URBAN AFFAIRS, UNITED STATES SENATE, BY U.S. SECURITIES AND EXCHANGE COMMISSION

Chairman Dodd, Ranking Member Shelby, and Members of the Committee, thank you for inviting me here today to discuss the turmoil in the U.S. credit markets and the efforts of the Securities and Exchange Commission, in concert with the Department of the Treasury, the Federal Reserve, and other regulators to protect investors and our markets. I should say at the outset that my testimony is on my own behalf as Chairman of the SEC, and does not necessarily represent the views of the Commission or individual Commissioners.

Last week, by unanimous decision of the Commission and with the support of the Secretary of the Treasury and the Federal Reserve, the SEC took temporary emergency action to ban short selling in financial securities. We took this action in close coordination with regulators around the world . . .

First and foremost, the SEC is a law enforcement agency, and we have devoted an extraordinary level of enforcement resources to hold accountable those whose violations of the law have contributed to the subprime crisis and the loss of confidence in our markets . . . The reason for this aggressive enforcement investigation is the significant opportunities that exist for manipulation in the $58 trillion CDS market, which is completely lacking in transparency and completely unregulated . . .

The SEC's own program of voluntary supervision for investment bank holding companies, the Consolidated Supervised Entity program, was put in place by the Commission in 2004. It borrowed capital and liquidity measurement approaches from the commercial banking world—with unfortunate results similar to those experienced in the commercial bank sector. Within this framework, prior to the spring of 2008, neither commercial bank nor investment bank risk models contemplated the scenario of total mortgage market meltdown . . .

The creators of the Consolidated Supervised Entity program in 2004 had designed it to operate on the well-established bank holding company model used by regulators not only in the United States but around the globe. They decided that the CSE rules would permit the parent holding company to calculate its capital adequacy using an approach consistent with either of the Basel standards, adopted by the Basel Committee on Banking Supervision. But the market-wide failure to appreciate and measure the risk of mortgage-related assets, including structured credit products, has shown that neither the Basel I nor Basel II standards as then in force were adequate. Each had serious need of improvement.

As a result, since March 2008, the SEC and other groups in which we participate have focused on improving standards for capital, liquidity, and risk management in both commercial and investment banking. Following the sale of Bear Stearns, groups such as the Senior Supervisors Group, the Financial Stability Forum, the International Organization of Securities Commissions, and the Basel Committee all pointed to the need to strengthen and improve these standards . . .

As a matter of prudence, investment banks are urged to maintain capital and liquidity at levels far above what would be required. But beyond highlighting the inadequacy of the pre-Bear Stearns CSE program capital and liquidity requirements, the last six months—during which the SEC and the Federal Reserve have worked collaboratively with each of the CSE firms pursuant to our Memorandum of Understanding—have made abundantly clear that voluntary regulation doesn't work. There is simply no provision in the law that authorizes the CSE program, or requires investment bank holding companies to compute capital measures or to maintain liquidity on a consolidated basis, or to submit to SEC requirements regarding leverage. This is a fundamental flaw in the statutory scheme that must be addressed, as I have reported to the Congress on prior occasions.

Because the SEC's direct statutory authority did not extend beyond the registered broker dealer to the rest of the enterprise, the CSE program was purely voluntary—something an investment banking conglomerate could choose to do, or not, as it saw fit.

The failure of the Gramm-Leach-Bliley Act to give regulatory authority over investment bank holding companies to any agency of government was, based on the experience of the last several months, a costly mistake. There is another similar regulatory hole that must be immediately addressed to avoid similar consequences. The $58 trillion notional market in credit default swaps—double the amount outstanding in 2006—is regulated by no one. Neither the SEC nor any regulator has authority over the CDS market, even to require minimal disclosure to the market . . .

Mr. Chairman, I appreciate this opportunity to discuss the current market turmoil, the policy choices that Congress now faces, and the SEC's actions to maintain orderly markets and protect investors in this crisis.

September 24, 2008

51. <u>News Alert:</u> We interrupt this program for an address from President Bush to the nation:

Good evening. This is an extraordinary period for America's economy.

Over the past few weeks, many Americans have felt anxiety about their finances and their future. I understand their worry and their frustration.

We've seen triple-digit swings in the stock market. Major financial institutions have teetered on the edge of collapse, and some have failed. As uncertainty has grown, many banks have restricted lending, credit markets have frozen, and families and businesses have found it harder to borrow money.

We're in the midst of a serious financial crisis, and the federal government is responding with decisive action.

We boosted confidence in money market mutual funds and acted to prevent major investors from intentionally driving down stocks for their own personal gain.

Most importantly, my administration is working with Congress to address the root cause behind much of the instability in our markets.

Financial assets related to home mortgages have lost value during the housing decline, and the banks holding these assets have restricted credit. As a result, our entire economy is in danger.

So I propose that the federal government reduce the risk posed by these troubled assets and supply urgently needed money so banks and other financial institutions can avoid collapse and resume lending.

This rescue effort is not aimed at preserving any individual company or industry. It is aimed at preserving America's overall economy.

It will help American consumers and businesses get credit to meet their daily needs and create jobs. And it will help send a signal to markets around the world that America's financial system is back on track.

I know many Americans have questions tonight: How did we reach this point in our economy? How will the solution I propose work? And what does this mean for your financial future?

These are good questions, and they deserve clear answers.

First, how did our economy reach this point? Well, most economists agree that the problems we're witnessing today developed over a long period of time. For more than a decade, a massive amount of money flowed into the United States from investors abroad because our country is an attractive and secure place to do business.

This large influx of money to U.S. banks and financial institutions, along with low interest rates, made it easier for Americans to get credit. These developments allowed more families to borrow money for cars, and homes, and college tuition, some for the first time. They allowed more entrepreneurs to get loans to start new businesses and create jobs.

Unfortunately, there were also some serious negative consequences, particularly in the housing market. Easy credit, combined with the faulty assumption that home values would continue to rise, led to excesses and bad decisions.

Many mortgage lenders approved loans for borrowers without carefully examining their ability to pay. Many borrowers took out loans larger than they could afford, assuming that they could sell or refinance their homes at a higher price later on.

Optimism about housing values also led to a boom in home construction. Eventually, the number of new houses exceeded the number of people willing to buy them. And with supply exceeding demand, housing prices fell, and this created a problem.

Borrowers with adjustable-rate mortgages, who had been planning to sell or refinance their homes at a higher price, were stuck with homes worth less than expected, along with mortgage payments they could not afford.

As a result, many mortgage-holders began to default. These widespread defaults had effects far beyond the housing market.

See, in today's mortgage industry, home loans are often packaged together and converted into financial products called mortgage-backed securities. These securities were sold to investors around the world.

Many investors assumed these securities were trustworthy and asked few questions about their actual value. Two of the leading purchasers of mortgage-backed securities were Fannie Mae and Freddie Mac.

Because these companies were chartered by Congress, many believed they were guaranteed by the federal government. This allowed them to borrow enormous sums of money, fuel the market for questionable investments, and put our financial system at risk.

The decline in the housing market set off a domino effect across our economy. When home values declined, borrowers defaulted on their mortgages, and investors holding mortgage-backed securities began to incur serious losses.

Before long, these securities became so unreliable that they were not being bought or sold. Investment banks, such as Bear Stearns and Lehman Brothers, found themselves saddled with large amounts of assets they could not sell. They ran out of money needed to meet their immediate obligations, and they faced imminent collapse.

Other banks found themselves in severe financial trouble. These banks began holding on to their money, and lending dried up, and the gears of the American financial system began grinding to a halt.

With the situation becoming more precarious by the day, I faced a choice, to step in with dramatic government action or to stand back and allow the irresponsible actions of some to undermine the financial security of all.

I'm a strong believer in free enterprise, so my natural instinct is to oppose government intervention. I believe companies that make bad decisions should be allowed to go out of business. Under normal circumstances, I would have followed this course. But these are not normal circumstances. The market is not functioning properly. There has been a widespread loss of confidence, and major sectors of America's financial system are at risk of shutting down.

The government's top economic experts warn that, without immediate action by Congress, America could slip into a financial panic and a distressing scenario would unfold . . . [O]ur country could experience a long and painful recession.

Fellow citizens, we must not let this happen. I appreciate the work of leaders from both parties in both houses of Congress to address this problem and to make improvements to the proposal my administration sent to them.

There is a spirit of cooperation between Democrats and Republicans and between Congress and this administration. In that spirit, I've invited Senators McCain and Obama to join congressional leaders of both parties at the White House tomorrow to help speed our discussions toward a bipartisan bill.

I know that an economic rescue package will present a tough vote for many members of Congress. It is difficult to pass a bill that commits so much of the taxpayers' hard-earned money.

I also understand the frustration of responsible Americans who pay their mortgages on time, file their tax returns every April 15th, and are reluctant to pay the cost of excesses on Wall Street.

But given the situation we are facing, not passing a bill now would cost these Americans much more later.

Many Americans are asking, how would a rescue plan work? After much discussion, there's now widespread agreement on the principles such a plan would include.

It would remove the risk posed by the troubled assets, including mortgage-backed securities, now clogging the financial system. This would free banks to resume the flow of credit to American families and businesses . . .

In close consultation with Treasury Secretary Hank Paulson, Federal Reserve Chairman Ben Bernanke, and SEC Chairman Chris Cox, I announced a plan on Friday.

First, the plan is big enough to solve a serious problem. Under our proposal, the federal government would put up to $700 billion taxpayer dollars on the line to purchase troubled assets that are clogging the financial system.

In the short term, this will free up banks to resume the flow of credit to American families and businesses, and this will help our economy grow.

Second, as markets have lost confidence in mortgage-backed securities, their prices have dropped sharply, yet the value of many of these assets will likely be higher than their current price, because the vast majority of Americans will ultimately pay off their mortgages.

The government is the one institution with the patience and resources to buy these assets at their current low prices and hold them until markets return to normal.

And when that happens, money will flow back to the Treasury as these assets are sold, and we expect that much, if not all, of the tax dollars we invest will be paid back . . .

The Treasury Department recently offered government insurance for money market mutual funds. And through the FDIC, every savings account, checking account, and certificate of deposit is insured by the federal government for up to $100,000 . . .

Once this crisis is resolved, there will be time to update our financial regulatory structures. Our 21st-century global economy remains regulated largely by outdated 20th-century laws . . .

In the long run, Americans have good reason to be confident in our economic strength. Despite corrections in the marketplace and instances of abuse, democratic capitalism is the best system ever devised.

It has unleashed the talents and the productivity and entrepreneurial spirit of our citizens. It has made this country the best place in the world to invest and do business. And it gives our economy the flexibility and resilience to absorb shocks, adjust, and bounce back.

Our economy is facing a moment of great challenge, but we've overcome tough challenges before, and we will overcome this one.

I know that Americans sometimes get discouraged by the tone in Washington and the seemingly endless partisan struggles, yet history has shown that, in times of real trial, elected officials rise to the occasion.

And together we will show the world once again what kind of country America is: a nation that tackles problems head on, where leaders come together to meet great tests, and where people of every background can work hard, develop their talents, and realize their dreams.

Thank you for listening. May God bless you.

September 29, 2008

52. <u>News Alert:</u> The U.S. House of Representatives has voted against the $700 billion bailout bill proposed by the Treasury. The markets reacted negatively. The S & P 500 fell 8.8%—its worst drop since 1987—and the Dow Jones Industrial Average fell 777.68 points—its worse points decline ever.

Globally, central banks have pumped more cash into the beleaguered credit markets. The Fed has more than doubled its swap lines with the European Central Bank and other central banks from $290 billion to $620 billion.

The European Central Bank along with the governments of the Netherlands, Belgium, and Luxemburg have agreed to partially nationalize Fortis, the European banking and insurance giant.

One of Germany's biggest lenders, Hypo Real Estate (HRE), has been rescued by the German government after a €50 billion liquidity crisis. HRE has been given a €35 billion lifeline by German private sector banks, the Bundesbank, and the European Central Bank.

In Iceland the government has taken control of Glitnir, the country's third largest bank. The government put €600 million of equity into the bank. Regulators have blamed the credit squeeze and Glitnir's inability to obtain short-term financing. David Oddsson, central bank governor, said that, without intervention, Glitnir would have ceased to exist within weeks.

September 30, 2008

<u>53.</u> <u>News Alert:</u> The Securities and Exchange Commission has issued a clarification on fair value accounting. The mark-to-market rule has been blamed by many to have exacerbated the credit crisis by forcing banks to write down their assets. The clarification stipulates that fair value assumes an orderly transaction between market participants and distressed or forced liquidation sales are not orderly.

October 1, 2008

<u>54.</u> <u>News Alert:</u> The collapse of Sigma Finance marks the end of the era of structured investment vehicles. Sigma was the last surviving SIV, a debt fund that borrowed short-term commercial paper in order to lend long at a higher interest rate. Sigma managed $27 billion and was the oldest member of the SIV industry that once controlled over $400 billion. The decision to liquidate was made after JP Morgan cut Sigma's last funding line.

October 3, 2008

<u>55.</u> <u>News Alert:</u> The revised Senate-approved bailout plan has passed through the U.S. House of Representatives and has been signed into law by President Bush. The Emergency Economic Stabilization Act establishes the Troubled Assets Relief Program or TARP, which gives the Treasury Department the power to purchase $700 billion in toxic assets on banks' balance sheets.

October 6, 2008

<u>56.</u> <u>News Alert:</u> French President, Nicolas Sarkozy, currently holding the rotating presidency of the European Union, is hosting an emergency summit on the global financial crisis in Paris. Leaders of France, Germany,

UK, and Italy met and agreed that Europe will not allow any bank to fail and file for bankruptcy. Sarkozy said that the European Union will stand behind their banking and financial institutions. Measures to protect banks could include liquidity from the central banks, targeted measures for individual banks or a reinforcement of bank deposit guarantees.

October 22, 2008

57. News Alert: The White House has announced it will hold a G-20 meeting on November 15, 2008. The global financial summit is expected to focus on the credit crisis and steps that can be taken to improve the world economy.

November 12, 2008:

58. News Alert: Treasury Secretary Paulson has announced that the government will no longer pursue the plan to buy toxic assets under the $700 billion troubled asset relief program or TARP. Mr. Paulson said that, given the worsening market conditions, the Treasury must to act quickly. Purchasing troubled assets would take time to implement. The better approach would be to inject capital into the banks. "Although the financial system has stabilized, both banks and non-banks may well need more capital given their troubled asset holdings, projections for continued high rates of foreclosures and the stagnant U.S. and world economic conditions," Paulson said. The Capital Purchase Program was established on October 14 to infuse banks with capital. On October 28, $125 billion was injected into nine banks considered systemically important: Bank of America, Bank of New York Mellon, Citigroup, Goldman Sachs, JP Morgan Chase, Morgan Stanley, State Street, Wells Fargo, and Merrill Lynch.

November 13, 2008

59. News Alert: President Bush Discusses Financial Markets and World Economy Federal Hall National Memorial.

New York, New York

> . . . We live in a world in which our economies are interconnected. Prosperity and progress have reached farther than any time in our history. Unfortunately, as we have seen in recent months, financial turmoil anywhere in the world affects economies everywhere in the world. And so this weekend I'm going to host a Summit on Financial Markets and the World Economy with leaders from developed and developing nations that account for nearly 90 percent of the world economy. Leaders of the World Bank, the International Monetary Fund, the United Nations, and the Financial Stability Forum are going to be there, as well . . .

> The leaders attending this weekend's meeting agree on a clear purpose—to address the current crisis, and to lay the foundation

for reforms that will help prevent a similar crisis in the future . . . So this summit will be the first of a series of meetings.

It will focus on five key objectives: understanding the causes of the global crisis, reviewing the effectiveness of our responses thus far, developing principles for reforming our financial and regulatory systems, launching a specific action plan to implement those principles, and reaffirming our conviction that free market principles offer the surest path to lasting prosperity.

First, we're working toward a common understanding of the causes behind the global crisis. Different countries will naturally bring different perspectives, but there are some points on which we can all agree:

Over the past decade, the world experienced a period of strong economic growth. Nations accumulated huge amounts of savings, and looked for safe places to invest them. Because of our attractive political, legal, and entrepreneurial climates, the United States and other developed nations received a large share of that money.

The massive inflow of foreign capital, combined with low interest rates, produced a period of easy credit. And that easy credit especially affected the housing market. Flush with cash, many lenders issued mortgages and many borrowers could not afford them. Financial institutions then purchased these loans, packaged them together, and converted them into complex securities designed to yield large returns. These securities were then purchased by investors and financial institutions in the United States and Europe and elsewhere—often with little analysis of their true underlying value.

The financial crisis was ignited when booming housing markets began to decline. As home values dropped, many borrowers defaulted on their mortgages, and institutions holding securities backed by those mortgages suffered serious losses. Because of outdated regulatory structures and poor risk management practices, many financial institutions in America and Europe were too highly leveraged. When capital ran short, many faced severe financial jeopardy. This led to high-profile failures of financial institutions in America and Europe, led to contractions and widespread anxiety—all of which contributed to sharp declines in the equity markets.

These developments have placed a heavy burden on hardworking people around the world. Stock market drops have eroded the value of retirement accounts and pension funds. The tightening of credit has made it harder for families to borrow money for cars or home improvements or education of the children. Businesses have found it harder to get loans to expand their operations and create jobs. Many nations have suffered job losses, and have serious concerns about the worsening economy. Developing nations have been hit hard as nervous investors have withdrawn their capital.

We are faced with the prospect of a global meltdown. And so we've responded with bold measures. I'm a market-oriented guy, but not when I'm faced with the prospect of a global meltdown. At Saturday's summit, we're going to review the effectiveness of our actions.

Here in the United States, we have taken unprecedented steps to boost liquidity, recapitalize financial institutions, guarantee most new debt issued by insured banks, and prevent the disorderly collapse of large, interconnected enterprises. These were historic actions taken necessary to make—necessary so that the economy would not melt down and affect millions of our fellow citizens.

In Europe, governments are also purchasing equity in banks and providing government guarantees for loans. In Asia, nations like China and Japan and South Korea have lowered interest rates and have launched significant economic stimulus plans. In the Middle East, nations like Kuwait and the UAE have guaranteed deposits and opened up new government lending to banks.

In addition, nations around the world have taken unprecedented joint measures. Last month, a number of central banks carried out a coordinated interest rate cut. The Federal Reserve is extending needed liquidity to central banks around the world. The IMF and World Bank are working to ensure that developing nations can weather this crisis.

This crisis did not develop overnight, and it's not going to be solved overnight. But our actions are having an impact. Credit markets are beginning to thaw. Businesses are gaining access to essential short-term financing. A measure of stability is returning to financial systems here at home and around the world. It's going to require more time for these improvements to fully take hold, and there's going to be difficult days ahead. But the United States and our partner[s] are taking the right steps to get through this crisis.

In addition to addressing the current crisis, we will also need to make broader reforms to strengthen the global economy over the long term. This weekend, leaders will establish principles for adapting our financial systems to the realities of the 21st century marketplace. We will discuss specific actions we can take to implement these principles. We will direct our finance ministers to work with other experts and report back to us with detailed recommendations on further reasonable actions.

One vital principle of reform is that our nations must make our financial markets more transparent. For example, we should consider improving accounting rules for securities, so that investors around the world can understand the true value of the assets they purchase.

Secondly, we must ensure that markets, firms, and financial products are properly regulated. For example, credit default swaps—financial products that insure against potential losses—should be processed through centralized clearinghouses instead of through unregulated, "over the counter" markets. By bringing greater stability to this large and important financial sector, we reduce the risk to our overall financial systems.

Third, we must enhance the integrity of our financial markets. For example, authorities in every nation should take a fresh look at the rules governing market manipulation and fraud—and ensure that investors are properly protected.

Fourth, we must strengthen cooperation among the world's financial authorities. For example, leading nations should better coordinate national laws and regulations. We should also reform international financial institutions such as the IMF and the World Bank, which are based largely on the economic order of 1944. To better reflect the realities of today's global economy, both the IMF and World Bank should modernize their governance structures. They should consider extending greater voter—voting power to dynamic developing nations, especially as they increase their contributions to these institutions. They should consider ways to streamline their executive boards, and make them more representative.

In addition to these important—to these management changes, we should move forward with other reforms to make the IMF and World Bank more transparent, accountable, and effective. For example, the IMF should agree to work more closely with member countries to ensure that their exchange rate policies are market-oriented and fair. And the World Bank should ensure its development programs reflect the priorities of the people they are designed to serve—and focus on measurable results.

All these steps require decisive actions from governments around the world. At the same time, we must recognize that government intervention is not a cure-all. For example, some blame the crisis on insufficient regulation of the American mortgage market. But many European countries had much more extensive regulations, and still experienced problems almost identical to our own.

History has shown that the greater threat to economic prosperity is not too little government involvement in the market, it is too much government involvement in the market. We saw this in the case of Fannie Mae and Freddie Mac. Because these firms were chartered by the United States Congress, many believed they were backed by the full faith and credit of the United States government. Investors put huge amounts of money into Fannie and Freddie, which they used to build up irresponsibly large portfolios of mortgage-backed securities. And when the housing market declined, these securities, of course, plummeted in value. It took a taxpayer-funded rescue to keep Fannie and Freddie from collapsing in a way that would have devastated the global financial system. And there is a clear lesson: Our aim should not be more government—it should be smarter government.

All this leads to the most important principle that should guide our work: While reforms in the financial sector are essential, the long-term solution to today's problems is sustained economic growth. And the surest path to that growth is free markets and free people.

This is a decisive moment for the global economy. In the wake of the financial crisis, voices from the left and right are equating the free enterprise system with greed and exploitation and failure. It's true this crisis included failures—by lenders and borrowers and by financial firms and by governments and independent regulators. But the crisis was not a failure of the free market system. And the answer is not to try to reinvent that system. It is to fix the problems we face, make the reforms we need, and move forward with the free market principles that have delivered prosperity and hope to people all across the globe.

Like any other system designed by man, capitalism is not perfect. It can be subject to excesses and abuse. But it is by far the most efficient and just way of structuring an economy. At its most basic level, capitalism offers people the freedom to choose where they work and what they do, the opportunity to buy or sell products they want, and the dignity that comes with profiting from their talent and hard work. The free market system provides the incentives that lead to prosperity—the incentive to work, to innovate, to save, to invest wisely, and to create jobs for others. And as millions of people pursue these incentives together, whole societies benefit.

Free market capitalism is far more than economic theory. It is the engine of social mobility—the highway to the American Dream. It's what makes it possible for a husband and wife to start their own business, or a new immigrant to open a restaurant, or a single mom to go back to college and to build a better career. It is what allowed entrepreneurs in Silicon Valley to change the way the world sells products and searches for information. It's what transformed America from a rugged frontier to the greatest economic power in history—a nation that gave the world the steamboat and the airplane, the computer and the CAT scan, the Internet and the iPod.

Ultimately, the best evidence for free market capitalism is its performance compared to other economic systems. Free markets allowed Japan, an island with few natural resources, to recover from war and grow into the world's second-largest economy. Free markets allowed South Korea to make itself into one of the most technologically advanced societies in the world. Free markets turned small areas like Singapore and Hong Kong and Taiwan into global economic players. Today, the success of the world's largest economies comes from their embrace of free markets.

Meanwhile, nations that have pursued other models have experienced devastating results. Soviet communism starved millions, bankrupted an empire, and collapsed as decisively as the Berlin Wall. Cuba, once known for its vast fields of cane, is now forced to ration sugar. And while Iran sits atop giant oil reserves, its people cannot put enough gasoline in its—in their cars.

The record is unmistakable: If you seek economic growth, if you seek opportunity, if you seek social justice and human dignity, the free market system is the way to go. And it would be a terrible mistake to allow a few months of crisis to undermine 60 years of success . . .

We're facing this challenge together and we're going to get through it together. The United States is determined to show the way back to economic growth and prosperity. I know some may question whether America's leadership in the global economy will continue. The world can be confident that it will, because our markets are flexible and we can rebound from setbacks. We saw that resilience in the 1940s, when America pulled itself out of Depression, marshaled a powerful army, and helped save the world from tyranny. We saw that resilience in the 1980s, when Americans overcame gas lines, turned stagflation into strong economic growth, and won the Cold War. We saw that resilience after September the 11th, 2001, when our nation recovered from a brutal attack, revitalized our shaken economy, and rallied the forces of freedom in the great ideological struggle of the 21st century.

The world will see the resilience of America once again. We will work with our partners to correct the problems in the global financial system. We will rebuild our economic strength. And we will continue to lead the world toward prosperity and peace.

Thanks for coming and God bless.

II. THE NEWS ALERTS PUT IN CONTEXT

We deliberately didn't include an introduction in this chapter. The point of the news alerts is to have you witness how the crisis deepened to the point where it spread to Europe and caused people to say that it was the greatest crisis since the Great Depression. What we're going to do here is comment on some of the news alerts to give you greater context and understanding of the crisis and how it unfolded. Given the structure of this chapter, we've decided that our friendly talking dog will take a nap.

Part One: March–December 2007

Mortgage Brokers Start Tanking

We began the chapter with a news alert that we included in Chapter 12—when mortgage brokers started tanking because of toxic subprime mortgages.

Bear Stearns' Hedge Funds

In news alerts 2–5 you witness the collapse of Bear Stearns' two hedge funds, a collapse that signaled the beginning of a downward spiral that would lead to the collapse of Lehman Brothers. The alerts pretty much speak for themselves. The hedge funds loaded up on AAA tranches of CEOs, using lots of leverage, which, as the alerts indicate, could make investments very profitable or result in catastrophic losses depending on where the market goes. As CDOs began tanking, lenders began demanding more collateral. What did the hedge funds do? They sold $3.8 billion in CDOs, which, of course, caused CDOs prices to plunge, the last thing these hedge funds needed. As of March 2008, banks and securities firms globally had written down—because of mark-to-market accounting—over $181 billion.

Global Write-Downs

News alerts 6–14 show you that the virus spread to Europe. Everywhere you turned, banks were writing off toxic mortgage-backed assets. Central banks globally saw Armageddon approaching and flooded the banking systems with liquidity to stave off a credit freeze. Two other alerts dealing with Northern Rock, a British mortgage lender, and Freddie Mac, spelled more trouble on the way. Let's talk briefly about each.

Northern Rock primarily raised money by participating in the wholesale market and by securitizing mortgages. Money in the wholesale market comes from financial institutions, governments, and other entities, instead of from the customer deposits that serve as the main source of funding for most commercial banks. These entities loaned money to Northern Rock and other financial institutions for short periods of time and they had the option of either letting Northern Rock keep the money longer (roll over the loan) or withdrawing their money if they were not happy with Northern Rock's financial position. To securitize mortgages, Northern Rock packaged a bunch of mortgage loans into bonds that were sold to investors. Although the bank grew for more than a decade, it ultimately ran into trouble.

When the mortgage crisis hit in 2007, the lenders in the wholesale market stopped rolling over their loans to Northern Rock and pulled their money out of the bank. They also stopped making new loans to Northern Rock. This caused a liquidity crisis in August 2008 that prevented the bank from issuing new loans and deprived it of the funding it needed to continue operating. Northern Rock was forced to ask the BoE for help on August 13, 2008.

The FSA, the BoE and the Treasury worked together to deal with Northern Rock's financial problems, and the BoE recognized that it would possibly have to act as a lender of last resort to the bank. First, though, the regulatory bodies attempted to find a stronger bank to buy Northern Rock in lieu of nationalizing it. Lloyds TSB, another British bank, offered to buy Northern Rock if the BoE would lend it £30 billion to complete the deal. But the BoE refused because the three regulatory authorities agreed that it would be inappropriate to subsidize one bank's takeover of another bank. Without the loan, the deal fell through and British regulators were unable to broker a Northern Rock sale. On September 13, 2007, the BoE finally decided to provide emergency funding to Northern Rock.

As to Freddie Mac, the jump in losses, due to subprime loans going sour, was a tremor before the earthquake that was about to hit Fannie and Freddie.

Structured Investment Vehicles

In news alert 15 you see the grim plight of Structured Investment Vehicles (SIVs). During the crisis, SIVs purchased mostly highly rated medium- and long-term fixed income assets, such as mortgages, tranches of pools of mortgages, and/or CDOs. An SIV funded itself with cheaper, mostly short-term highly rated commercial paper (CP). The SIV sponsor, often a bank, made money in a couple of ways: (i) management and custody fees, and (ii) the spread, i.e. the difference between the SIV's funding costs—the rate on CP, and the cash flow—the return on the mortgage assets. The SIV faced various risks such as credit risk, the potential default in the value of assets, and liquidity risk, the inability to fund the assets. Since liabilities are shorter-term than the assets, there had to be continuing funding of assets over time—repeated issuance of CP. In September 2007, there was at least $100 billion in SIV assets.

SIVs got into trouble when subprime assets began to default. When the market began to seize up in August 2007, it became harder to issue CP. CP investors became reluctant to hold CP as the default rate of subprime mortgage backing the SIVs' assets began to climb. In the fall of 2007, the U.S. Treasury urged Bank of America, Citigroup, and JP Morgan to develop a "Super SIV" that would hold the mortgage assets during the liquidity crunch. The Super SIV never came to be. Instead, many banks, facing reputational risk, put "off-balance sheet" SIV assets on their balance sheets, even though they had no legal obligation to do so. This required banks to hold more capital.

The Federal Reserve

In news alert 17, you learn of the Federal Reserve's creation of the Term Auction Facility (TAF). It was the first of several facilities created to pump liquidity into the financial sector. It was an extraordinary effort to rescue the financial sector and otherwise to save the economy—but not everybody was crazy about what the Fed did and how it ran up its balance sheet to the moon. Let's have a look at some of the facilities.

The TAF was an extension of the discount window. The Fed can increase liquidity by lowering its key rate, the federal funds rate (see news alert 21). That rate decreased from 5.25% in August 2007 to 0 to .25% in July 2009. In a liquidity crunch the Fed can also use a lending tool called the discount window, which allows banks to borrow from the Fed at the discount rate. To discourage unnecessary use of the discount window, the discount rate is usually higher than the fed funds rate. During the crisis, banks were reluctant to borrow from the discount window. So the Fed created the Term Auction Facility (TAF), which auctioned reserves to banks in exchange for collateral. It was just like the discount window but it didn't carry the stigma. Lending under the facility peaked at $493 billion in March 2009.

News alert 25 tells you about the creation of the Term Securities Lending Facility (TSLF). Instead of borrowing just overnight, the TSLF allowed primary dealers to borrow up to $200 billion of treasury securities for 28 days. This was important because treasury securities are used in repurchase agreements or "repos," a short-term form of financing. For example, if a financial firm wants to borrow money on a short-term basis, it can sell the treasury securities to a counterparty and after a certain period of time repurchase them. The loans under the TSLF could be collateralized with private-label MBS with an AAA rating, agency commercial mortgage-backed securities, and other agency obligations.

Although it's not in a news alert, the Fed created the Primary Dealer Credit Facility in March 2008, which extended credit to primary dealers against a wide range of investment-grade securities.

News alert 49 mentions the creation of Asset-Backed Commercial Paper Money Market Mutual Fund Liquidity Facility (AMLF) immediately after the money market fund managed by Reserve Management Corporation (RMC) "broke the buck" (news alert 47). That facility extended loans to U.S. depository institutions and bank holding companies to help them buy asset-backed commercial paper from money market mutual funds. The banks acted as intermediaries to assist the commercial paper market. In October 2008, the Fed created the Commercial Paper Funding Facility (CPFF) to buy three-month highly rated U.S. commercial paper, whether secured or unsecured, from issuers. Unlike the AMLF, under the CPFF the Fed helped CP issuers directly.

Bear Stearns

News alert 18 is the beginning of the end for the investment bank Bear Stearns.

Part Two: January–March 2008

The New Year witnessed continued global bank losses and panic as things got worse. News alert 22 reveals AIG's mounting losses tied to credit default swaps. But the major episode in this period is the downfall of Bear Stearns as revealed in news alerts 24 and 26–30. This is a story about the evaporation of liquidity within days of a very interconnected financial firm. Must you rescue it to prevent a meltdown in the financial sector?

Bear Stearns

Bear Stearns was an 85-year-old investment bank with about 14,000 employees. Not only did it produce its own MBS but it also owned residential mortgage originators—churning out what would become toxic assets. The securities were sold to institutional investors, like hedge funds and pension funds, but Bear kept some on its balance sheet. The rumors indicated in alert 24 (March 10, 2008) related to reports that European financial institutions refused to do fixed income (like bonds) trades with Bear. As word got around in Wall Street, U.S. fixed-income firms and stock traders decided to stop doing business with Bear. Other firms then became very hesitant to do business with Bear. As the rumors of Bear's demise intensified, the investment bank's hedge fund clients pulled their cash out and money market funds reduced their holdings of Bear's short-term debt. And if this wasn't enough, a bunch of institutional investors that had taken out credit default swaps with Bear as protection seller tried to undo those trades. Yet, as news alert 26 tells you, Bear's CEO Alan Schwartz went on CNBC and said there wasn't a problem with Bear's liquidity. Hmmm . . .

As news alert 27 indicates, Bear's liquidity cushion of reserves plummeted. News alert 28 tells you that Bear reached out to J.P. Morgan for a loan. The Fed came into the picture and they decided that something had to be done to prevent widespread panic. Bear Stearns' liquidity position turn out to be so bad that on March 14 the Fed decided it would make a loan short-term loan via the discount window.

But there was a problem: Bear wasn't a commercial bank, so the Fed didn't regulate it—the SEC did. Solution? The Fed invoked Section 13(3) of the Federal Reserve Act, which stipulates:

> "In unusual and exigent circumstances, the Board of Governors of the Federal Reserve System, by the affirmative vote of not less than five members, may authorize any Federal reserve bank, . . . to discount for any individual, partnership, or corporation, notes, drafts, and bills of exchange when such notes, drafts, and bills of exchange are indorsed or otherwise secured to the satisfaction of the Federal Reserve bank: *Provided*, That before discounting any such note, draft, or bill of exchange for an individual, partnership, or corporation the Federal reserve bank shall obtain evidence that such individual, partnership, or corporation is unable to secure adequate credit from other banking institutions . . ."

The Fed used this provision, which hasn't been used since the Great Depression, to provide a loan to J.P. Morgan for up to $30 billion of Bear's assets. Word was that the Fed had to do this because J.P. Morgan was reluctant to take on Bear's crappy portfolio. J.P Morgan acquired Bear in a stock-for-stock buyout valued at $2 a share for Bear's stock. (Later raised to $10 per share—see news alert 20).

The Fed's intervention was controversial. On the one hand, people, including Treasury Secretary Paulson, argued that saving Bear would prevent severe financial instability. But there was another problem: Bear held $46 billion in mortgages, MBS, and ABS. If it failed, it would have to dump the toxic securities on the market, which would force other firms to write down similar assets. We're talking meltdown. On the other hand, there were those who argued that intervening would contribute to moral hazard, meaning that if a badly performing firm is saved, it's likely to continue performing badly knowing that it will be rescued again.

Part Three: April–September 7, 2008

In this period, losses related to the virus kept rising. News alert 32 might look familiar—we used it in Chapter 14. It indicates how bad things got for homeowners as the virus took hold. News alerts 33 and 36 reveal the credit rating agencies' faulty ratings process and conflicts of interest, which led to massive rating downgrades. News alert 35 shows you how CRA ratings were hardwired into SEC regulations. Starting with news alerts 34 and 37, we begin to see the downward trajectory of Lehman Brothers and the GSEs, Fannie Mae and Freddie Mac. We'll see what happens to Lehman in a minute. The big story in this period is what happened to the GSEs.

So why did the government take over Fannie and Freddie and inject the GSEs with billions of dollars? In Chapter 15, we explained what the GSEs do, so we won't repeat that here. Let's start with their regulation. In 1991, Congress began developing a regulatory scheme to oversee the GSEs, and it created the Office of Federal Housing Enterprise Oversight (OFHEO) (replaced in July 2008 by the Federal Housing Finance Agency (FHFA)). When Congress created the OFHEO, it also amended the GSEs' charters to include an affordable housing mission. In 1999, for example, the GSEs reached an agreement with HUD that by 2001, half of the mortgages they guaranteed would be made to low-income borrowers.

To achieve government-set housing goals, the GSEs used increasingly lax underwriting standards that contributed to their increased exposure to risky debt. Between 2005 and 2007, 57% of the mortgages acquired by Fannie Mae were characterized as subprime. For Freddie Mac it was 61%. As of August 2008, the GSEs held or guaranteed a combined total of over $1 trillion in unpaid principal balance exposures on subprime loans.

OFHEO was aware of the GSEs' risky practices. It routinely noted the increased exposure of the GSEs to subprime default risk, but it didn't do anything about it. Its examinations of the GSEs regularly concluded that they both had sufficient capital and prudent credit-risk management. Meanwhile, the GSEs pursued profit for their shareholders. In 2000, Fannie reported earnings of $4.448 billion, up from $3.912 billion in 1992.

But here was the killer: The GSEs were skating on very thin ice capital wise. It turns out they were highly leveraged—severely undercapitalized: They owned or guaranteed $5.3 trillion of mortgages with capital less that 2%! By the end of December 2007, Fannie was in deep trouble: It revealed that it had only $44 billion in capital to absorb nearly $3 trillion in assets and guarantees. And there was no way capital could be raised given the market conditions. Just before the government take-over, FHFA investigations revealed gross mismanagement at the GSEs and accounting practices that hid their serious problems. Then came conservatorship.

Part Four: September 11–28, 2008

Lehman Falls

News alerts 42–25 report the fall of Lehman Brothers, the 157-year-old investment bank. At the time of news alert 42, regulators question whether the $28 billion in capital that Lehman reported was really worth that much, given that the market value of its assets, especially commercial real estate loans, was probably pretty low. Many officials, including the market, believed that Lehman was on its way to the grave. It would be yet another

Bear Stearns—withdrawal of funds and lending, wiping out capital and liquidity in a matter of days.

And that in fact started happening. Financial firms and pension funds reduced their exposure to Lehman. Asian central banks did the same. Repo financing also started drying up. In a repo—a repurchase agreement—Lehman would buy overnight commercial paper collateralized with what became illiquid securities—mortgage related securities—and buy the securities back. It got so bad that commercial paper counterparties refused to do repos with Lehman. To raise capital, the firm considered getting an investment from Korea Development Bank, among other things. The markets plunged when news circulated that the Korean bank would not provide any funds to Lehman.

When Lehman announced its $3.9 billion third-quarter loss, a number of large money funds reduced their exposure to Lehman. The Fed then began deliberating what to do with Lehman after Bank of America decided not to do the deal to buy Lehman. Rescuing the investment bank would raise a moral hazard problem, that is, the Fed would send a signal that it would rescue any firm that is too big to fail, which would encourage firms to engage in the very behavior that led to the crisis, knowing that they would be bailed out. Yet Lehman's bankruptcy would be catastrophic according to some officials. In the end, officials decided that Lehman wouldn't be rescued. On the day that Lehman filed for bankruptcy, the Dow lost more than 500 points. People lost their entire investments. The banks bankruptcy reverberated through Lehman's empire—subsidiaries, affiliates, creditors, and employees. Insolvency proceedings of the subsidiaries commenced in eighteen foreign countries.

Lehman's bankruptcy sparked heated debate about the wisdom of that decision. Many believed the government's decision was mistaken and revealed inconsistent policy. See for yourself: As you can see in news alert 45, on the day that Lehman filed, the ECB allotted €30 billion in a one-day liquidity operation. The Bank of England announced its own liquidity operation.

In news alert 47, you learn that the money market fund managed by Reserve Management Corporation "broke the buck", meaning that its net asset value dropped below one dollar per share. It had to write down millions of dollars in Lehman's debt. This caused a run on money market mutual fund companies as investors panicked that they would lose their money. Because of the run, money market mutual fund companies stocked up on cash and stopped investing in commercial paper and certificates of deposit, which are critical for financial firms' short-term funding. In news alert 49, you learn that both the Treasury and the Fed the acted to calm money market investors.

At the SEC, the agency issues a ban on short-selling of financial stocks—investors are betting against them. In news alert 15, you learn that Goldman Sachs and Morgan Stanley became deposit-taking banking holding companies, which subject them to regulation by the Fed, including capital requirements. In the same news alert, you see the testimony of SEC Chairman Christopher Cox, in which he places the blame for the problems with the investment banks on weak regulation.

In news alert 48, you learn that the credit markets have become virtually frozen, a death knell not just for the financial markets, but also for the greater economy.

In news alert 51, you read President Bush's address to the nation as the crisis continued to deepen. You witness someone who is deeply committed to "free enterprise" having to explain to the nation why government intervention is desperately required. He announces a $700 billion government program that will remove the "toxic assets" off the banks' balance sheets so they can begin to lend again.

Was it a mistake to let Lehman fail?

AIG

News alerts 44–46 report on the bailout of American International Group (AIG), a huge insurer with a global operation. Because AIG was mostly an insurance company, the federal Office of Thrift Supervision, not the Fed or the FDIC, regulated it at the holding company. The U.S. subsidiaries were regulated by the states.

AIG's problems began with a small company unit based in London called AIG Financial Products (AIGFP). AIG allowed the unit's executives to operate the unit with nearly complete autonomy from the parent company. It was a small unit, with just 377 employees, and when it first opened it sold only low-risk, run-of-the-mill financial products. But in the late 1990s, the unit began selling insurance packages on collateralized debt obligations (CDOs). CDOs were popular with investors, as those holding the lower tranches could receive sizeable returns as long as people continued to make payments on their mortgages. Because of the risk involved in these investments, AIG sold the investor credit default swaps (CDS). As protection seller, AIG promised to pay up if defaults occurred in the underlying mortgage pool.

AIGFP reportedly described the CDSs as "almost a sure thing" and built up a nearly $500-billion portfolio of swaps. By the end of September 2007 the credit crisis had hit AIGFP hard. Because AIG set up AIGFP as a bank instead of as an insurer, and because of the particular way in which it arranged its contracts, the London-based unit had to provide its trading partners with collateral when the value of the mortgage loans packaged in the insured CDOs declined. When Lehman started tanking, and the credit rating agencies downgraded AIG, the counterparties on the credit default swaps demanded between $14 and $15 billion in collateral payments. Since AIGFP didn't have enough money to fulfill the CDS contracts as the value of the insured CDOs decreased, its corporate parent, AIG, had to cover the losses. Basically, the small AIGFP unit destabilized the entire company as subprime mortgage defaults mounted and the company faced crippling CDS liability.

AIG's losses from the CDSs were huge and the company didn't have the capital to pay off all of the customers who had entered into CDS agreements. By the second week of September 2008, AIG had no choice but to disclose its financial problems to the Fed and ask for a $40 billion bridge loan to prevent investment losses from causing a downgrade in its credit ratings.

Initially, the Fed and the U.S. Treasury refused to bail out AIG and instead attempted to broker a deal with JPMorgan Chase and Goldman Sachs to get AIG private financing, but this didn't work out. This left the Fed with only two options: bail AIG out or let it collapse. Because AIG was so large and deeply interconnected with the global economy, letting AIG collapse could have potentially caused major economic damage around the world. Additionally, everyone insured by AIG or who invested in its financial products would have suffered financial losses. AIG, in the Fed's view, was too big to be allowed to fail. So the Fed, relying on Section 13(3) of the Federal Reserve Act, chose to save AIG. On September 16, 2008 it agreed to provide the insurance company with $85 billion in federal funds. The bailout gave the Fed an eighty percent controlling stake in AIG, which effectively nationalized the insurer.

The government's initial bailout wasn't enough to solve AIG's problems, so the Fed and the Treasuries Troubled Asset Relief Program (TARP) provided additional funds. Ultimately, AIG received $184.6 billion in assistance from the government. In return, the government received a 92% ownership share in the company.

The Consequences of Deregulation

News alert 50 signals the end of the big five investment firms. Chairman Cox's testimony before the Senate committee raises a couple of spectacular failures of deregulation. First, he notes that manipulation was possible in the huge credit default market, which was completely unregulated.

Then he talks about the failure of the Consolidated Supervised Entities (CSE) program. Here's the story in a nutshell. The Graham-Leach-Bliley Act created a regulatory hole regarding investment bank holding companies: there was no statutory scheme that addressed how and by whom investment bank holding companies with specialized bank affiliates should be supervised. It is within this context that the SEC adopted the voluntary CSE program in 2004. The CSE program was created for and limited to the five independent investment banks in the US: Merrill Lynch, Goldman Sachs, Morgan Stanley, Lehman Brothers, and Bear Stearns.

A key aspect of the CSE was that it allowed the investment banks' broker-dealers to compute net capital using an alternative method based on Basel II. In other words, the broker-dealers were exempt from the SEC's standard net capital rule, which placed a ceiling on broker-dealers. Among other things, that rule limited aggregate indebtedness to 15 times the broker-dealer's net capital—most broker dealers followed the rule. The CSE's alternative net capital rule, which relied on Basel capital rules, had no similar limitation. The result was predictable: all five of the investment banks' debt-to-equity leverage ratios went through the roof—Bear Stearns' leverage ratio was 33 to 1 before it collapsed.

Let's get back to why the CSE was limited to the big five investment banks. Let's go the European Union (EU). The EU's Financial Conglomerates Directive required regulatory supervision at the parent company level of financial conglomerates that included a regulated financial institution, such as a broker dealer. The directive had an exemption for foreign financial conglomerates that were regulated by their home countries in a way that was deemed equivalent to the directive. U.S. commercial banks fell under this exemption because they are subject to supervision at the bank holding company level by the Fed. But U.S. investment banks had no similar SEC oversight over their parent companies. The independent U.S. investment banks, fearing they would be regulated by European regulators, persuaded the SEC to come up with the CSE as a form of equivalent regulation that would satisfy the terms of the directive and give the investment bank's immunity from European regulation.

After Bear Stearns collapsed, a government report ripped apart the CSE. It noted that Bear was compliant with the CSE's capital and liquidity requirements just before the collapse. It also noted that the SEC knew about Bear's problems but did nothing about it.

But that begs the question: Why didn't the regulators do something? Well, may they just didn't understand Basel II. This happens more often than you think—the regulators can't regulate because they don't get it. But it probably comes down to what Chairman Cox said: The program was voluntary. The investment banks could leave the program if they felt like it. The SEC had no authority to order a CSE firm to, say, reduce its debt to equity ratios. The best it could say was, "Would you mind?"

In September 2008, the SEC announced it was ending the CSE program.

Part Five: September 29–November 13, 2008

The Creation of the Trouble Assets Relief Program (TARP)

News alert 52 reports on a bombshell: On October 3, 2008, the U.S. House of Representatives voted against the Treasury's $700 billion bailout plan. Politicians clashed over the wisdom of the bailout, in many instances on ideological grounds. As you can see, the decision rocked the markets. In the meantime, global financial sectors were going to hell in hand-basket. After the politicians were warned of a global meltdown if they refused to support the administration's plan, President Bush signed the Emergency Economic Stabilization Act into law. The EESA created TARP, giving the Treasury Department the authority and money to purchase the so-called toxic assets on banks' balance sheets. But it proved impossible to value the toxic assets. Too high a price and taxpayers would have to shoulder the burden. Too low a price and the financial firms would take a hit to their capital positions because of the write off. News alert 58 tells you that the government decided instead to use TARP to inject funds directly into banks to help their capital positions, which they hoped would thaw the credit freeze and enable banks to lend again.

The Mark-to Market Controversy

News alert 53 reports on an SEC clarification of the mark-to-market accounting rule, FAS 157, pending additional interpretive guidance by the Financial Accounting Standards Board (FASB), the U.S. accounting body, and its international counterpart, the International Accounting Standards Board (IASB). Essentially, the rule says that if you acquire securities that you intend to trade in the near future—the "trading book," you have to "mark" the security to the current market price periodically. As the crisis worsened, financial firms increased their write-downs apparently due marking-to-market accounting rules—"fair value" accounting. Some recommended suspending fair value accounting, arguing that it was procyclical, meaning the rule just made things worse. But FASB and the IASB rejected the recommendation. They pointed to the need to provide investors with transparent information.

FAS 157 (2006) defines fair value in terms of "the price in an orderly transaction between market participants to sell an asset or transfer a liability in the principal (or the most advantageous) market for the asset or liability." From the outset of the crisis, financial institutions complained that FAS 157 didn't provide enough guidance to measure assets in illiquid markets. FASB then released FAS 157–3 on October 10, 2008. FAS 157–3 clarified that fair value is not the price an asset would receive in a distressed sale or "fire sale." FASB also clarified measuring fair value in inactive markets in FAS 157–4, issued on April 9, 2009. FAS 157–4 states that the fair value of an asset is not the price that the asset would generate in a distressed or fire sale. The FAS 157–4 release acknowledged that, "some constituents observed an emphasis on the use of the so-called last transaction price (or quoted price) as the sole or primary basis for fair value even when a significant adjustment to the transaction price (or quoted price) may be required or when other valuation should be considered." This led to a misapplication of FAS 157. FAS 157–4 states, "In the Board's view, a significant decrease in the volume and level of activity for the asset or liability is an indication that transactions or quoted prices may not be determinative of fair value because in such market conditions there may be increased instances of transactions that are not orderly. In those circumstances, further analysis of transactions or quoted prices is needed, and a significant adjustment to the transactions or quoted prices may be necessary to estimate fair value in accordance with Statement 157." Anecdotal evidence and market evidence suggested that the new guidance in FAS 157–4 alleviated the problem of people relying too heavily on the use of the so-called last transaction price (or quoted price) as the sole or primary basis for fair value even when a significant adjustment to the transaction price (or quoted price) may be required or when other valuation should be considered. After several major studies on the issue, it appeared that fair value accounting didn't significantly contribute to the crisis.

A Global Problem

News alerts 56–59 show you that by late 2008 everyone knew that the crisis was now a global one, and it had to be resolved globally. The G-20 meeting in November was the first of several summits held to figure out how to resolve the crisis. News alert 58 gives you a sense of how difficult it must have been for a Republican President, who fiercely believed in "free market capitalism," to support government measures in the United States that, in some cases, amounted to nationalization of firms.

You Gotta Know Something About Them!

Ben Bernanke

Ben Bernanke received his B.A. in economics from Harvard (summa cum laude) and his Ph.D. from MIT. He was appointed a Federal Reserve Governor in 2002, and four years later he stepped up to be Fed Chair. In 2010, he was appointed to a second term. Ben is a smart guy. He skipped the first grade, won the South Carolina state spelling bee at age 12, and got the highest SAT score in South Carolina in the year he took it. The son of a pharmacist (dad) and substitute teacher (mom), he played the saxophone in his high school marching band. How good was his march? Hmmm . . . In college Ben worked as a waiter at South of the Border during summer breaks. Did he get good tips?

Hmmm . . . He even did a little stint in construction where he helped to build a hospital. Ben in a hardhat. Hmmm . . . Ben, you *are* human, even though you held the fate of the world in your hands as Fed Chair!

Henry Paulson

Henry Paulson had a long career in the private sector before going public. After graduating from Dartmouth College in 1968, he went to Harvard in 1970 and earned his M.B.A. After a stint as staff assistant in the Nixon White House, Hank joined Goldman Sachs in Chicago, where he climbed his way to Chairman and CEO of the company. In 2006, George W. Bush appointed him Treasury Secretary (after asking him three times to take the position). During the financial crisis, he was at the center of the action, urging weak banks such as Lehman Brothers and Merrill Lynch to find buyers and helping put together the purchase of Bear Stearns by JP Morgan. Hank was also an important architect of the TARP bailouts; he worked with people such as Timothy Geithner to convince Congress to pass a measure giving the Treasury broad authority to buy mortgage-backed securities. Check it out: His initial proposal for such authority was only about three pages long! How many pages would a lawyer have written? In college, Hank played football and garnered an honorable mention all-American offensive lineman. Probably helped him lay down the law in the crisis. He's not all about finance: An avid conservationist, Hank was Chairman of The Nature Conservancy for two years starting in 2004. A traitor to conservatives? He doesn't think so.

Christopher Cox

Christopher Cox has spent time in both the public and private sectors, and had a long career as a member of Congress. He received his B.A. from the University of Southern California in 1973, distinguishing himself by graduating magna cum laude in only three years. But that's not all. Christopher received an M.B.A. from Harvard Business School and a J.D. from Harvard Law School in 1977, earning both degrees simultaneously. He was even an editor of the Harvard Law Review. After a year as a law clerk to U.S. Court of Appeals Judge Herbert Choy, Christopher joined the law firm of Latham & Watkins and specialized in venture capital and corporate finance from 1978 to 1986. He then served in the White House as Senior Associate Counsel to President Reagan. Following his stint at the White House he ran for a seat in the House of Representatives to represent California, and won in 1989, beginning a 17-year career in Congress where he would gain a reputation as a conservative Republican who argued for less financial regulation. In 2005, Christopher was appointed SEC Chairman by President George W. Bush. Then came the global financial crisis, a pretty rocky time for him—critics blamed the SEC for lax oversight. Christopher is an avid reader of Ayn Rand. At Harvard, he was a member of a small extra-curricular group called "Harvard Law Students for Reagan." Christopher is fluent in Russian, and in the early 1980s he founded Context Corporation, which published the English translation of the Soviet Union's daily newspaper Pravda.

CHAPTER 15

CREDIT RATING AGENCIES AS GATEKEEPERS

■■■

As with most pandemics, we can see a footprint of fault in the path to the global financial crisis. In Chapter 12 we looked at subprime mortgage lending, the virus itself. The fault footprint was marked by (1) Fed monetary policy, (2) borrowers who didn't bother to understand the loans they signed or engaged in fraud, and (3) lenders—originators—who preyed on financially unsophisticated borrowers by foisting really complex products on them.

In Chapter 13 we looked at the transmission of the virus via securitization, explaining how the various players helped transform subprime mortgages into MBSs and CDOs. We had our hands full explaining the basics of these securities. So here we very briefly give you more of the footprint. First, the arrangers—purchasers of the pool of mortgages—failed to do their due diligence on the originators. Had they looked more closely at what the originators were up to, they would have seen the virus. Second, the asset managers, such as JPMorgan Investment Advisors, Inc., who managed the assets of investors such as pension funds, moved portfolios from corporate bonds to MBSs and CDOs for higher yields (which meant more cha-ching for the managers) without doing due diligence on the arrangers (and originators). Then the pandemic hit, as we witnessed in Chapter 14.

Of course, the credit rating agencies (CRAs) played an important part in this drama, in the massive creation of MBSs and CDOs. They're known as the gatekeepers (like auditing companies) because they're supposed to expertly rate debt securities based on the risk of default, with an AAA rating signifying the lowest probability of default—golden. In theory, it's an efficient way to monitor the quality of debt securities issued by private firms and governments. Sure, every investor could do its own risk analysis (some of the big institutional investors might do that), but that could be very costly, maybe so costly that they wouldn't bother. Without an entity or entities to monitor, and in most cases publicly publish their expert views on the quality of debt securities, investors would run great risks and issuers would struggle with accurate pricing of their securities.

But what if the gatekeepers, the last line of defense against the virus, fail to do their job? In this chapter, we'll witness the human consequences of that failure. We're not suggesting that they're most to blame. As you read this encounter, ask yourselves whether the investors should shoulder some of the blame for the crisis by over-relying on the CRAs' ratings.

The encounter is based on a true story about Wingecarribee Shire, an idyllic space in Australia and its encounter with the virus. Like most of the stuff in this textbook, you can write a whole book about the CRAs and the crisis. To preserve the flow of the encounter, we've put some background and detail into the "What's Up with That?" section and into the quotes. Oh, and the talking dog isn't around for this chapter. (Relieved?) It doesn't seem necessary. No bios either, but you can do what playwrights do: imagine the life story of William and David—picture them in your mind.

Now, get off of Facebook and check this out.

"The Gatekeeper's Reckoning"

Setting: 1:00 a.m., law office, New York, present day

Characters

    David: lawyer

    William: janitor

(lights up)

William: May I empty your trash, sir?

David: Sure. Thanks. Let me get out of the way.

(David stands up and William empties the trash can, noticing many empty cans of energy drinks; David catches William looking at the cans)

David: I know. Ridiculous. They fill the whole trash can.

William: To each his own, sir.

David: I live here. Catch a cat nap now and then.

William: A twenty-four hour operation, isn't it, sir.

David: We're global. Time zones keep us busy.

William: It would seem we're all connected, sir.

David: You bet. And you can drop the "sir." Call me David.

(William returns the trash can to its spot and faces David; David sits, William doesn't move)

William: Okay. David.

David: There we go.

(William turns to leave)

David: Wait. How about you?

William: Me?

David: Your name, sir!

William: Smith.

David: No, I mean your first name.

William: William.

David: Can I call you Bill?

William: I prefer William, if you don't mind.

David: Not at all. William it is.

(pause)

David: You're new here, aren't you?

William: My first week, sir.

David: David.

William: Yes, David.

(David pulls a bottle of 18-year-old scotch and two tumblers from his desk drawer)

William: Quite nice.

David: Have some with me, to celebrate your first week.

William: Thank you, but no.

David: C'mon, William. You're almost done, right? I can use a break before I call Singapore. Sit down and have a bit, just a bit. We can talk. It's important for me to know the staff.

William: Why is that?

David: It's in my best interest, William. I have the cleanest carpet of all the offices on the floor.

(pause)

David: That was a joke, William.

William: You're quite the comedian.

David: David.

William: David.

(David pours some scotch)

David: Let's press restart. William, how nice of you to stop by. Please have a seat. You have a moment, don't you?

William: But your work—

David: Will always be there. Sit, please. You look thirsty. How about a bottle of primo spring water? Got some in the little fridge here.

(Williams sits upright in an office chair facing David, David unscrews the bottle cap and hands William the water)

William: Thank you . . . David.

David: No problem.

(William holds the bottle on his lap, doesn't drink; David puts his stocking feet on his desk, takes a drink of scotch)

David: Are you Australian, William?

William: Yes, I am. My accent—

David: I know it well.

William: How so?

David: Scuba diving. Heron Bommie.

William: The Great Barrier Reef.

David: Spectacular. Spent a week there just last June.

William: First time?

David: Been there about a dozen times. How about you?

William: A bit beyond my budget. Quite a ways from my town in any event.

David: Where's that?

William: Burrawang. In Wingecarribee Shire.

(David takes a long pull, all the while looking at William, long pause)

David: Wingecarribee Shire. I've heard of it. About two hours from Sydney, yeah?

William: Indeed.

David: Beautiful place . . . I've been told.

William: Quite. Eucalyptus trees, roos, koalas, wallabies . . .

David: Why did you leave such an idyllic place for the craziness of New York?

William: I lost my church.

David: Your church?

William: Yes, my church. Not very big, but good congregants. I was the pastor. I lost it in 2008. My church.

(David takes another long pull and pours more scotch)

David: Sorry.

William: For what?

David: Your loss. Your church.

(William stares at David)

David: Drink, William. It's good water, don't you think?

(William doesn't drink)

William: What do you do, if you don't mind my asking?

David: Not at all, William. I'm a corporate lawyer.

William: What do corporate lawyers do?

David: Lots of stuff. I do finance. Everything from project finance to Eurobonds.

William: Bonds?

David: Yes. Sort of international bonds.

William: Sounds complex. You must have considerable expertise.

David: I would like to think so, William.

William: How have you come about it?

David: Degrees in business and law. Then lots of hard work.

William: Here? I mean, you've become an expert in finance here?

(David takes a pull)

David: I was at a credit agency before I came here.

William: Credit agency. What is that?

David: They're private companies that rate the creditworthiness of companies or countries that issue debt securities, like bonds.

William: Creditworthiness?

David: Their ability or willingness to pay a debt.

William: This is quite interesting. May I ask you about these agencies? Could you spare a few moments?

David: Of course. I told you I needed a break.

(David takes a drink)

David: You haven't touched your water, William.

(William takes a sip of water)

David: What you want to know?

William: How many of these agencies are there?

David: There're two U.S. **firms that dominate the market**, Standard & Poor's and Moody's. Fitch Ratings, a British firm, has a slice of the market but not as big. Then you got a bunch of little fish.

William: So if I understand correctly, these firms issue ratings so people know how profitable these . . . securities, debt securities will be.

David: Not quite. Credit agencies aren't like investment analysts that make recommendations on whether to buy, sell or hold a security. Their ratings are useful because they're a standard way to figure out whether it's worth lending to a company or government and at what price—you know, the interest rate on a bond.

William: I see. They're sort of gatekeepers, aren't they?

David: Precisely, William.

William: They tell the world if a security is gold or trash?

(David takes his feet off the desk)

David: That's a colorful way of putting it.

William: What's the gold rating? The best gold?

David: Triple A.

William: And the trash?

David: If you use **Moody's ratings**, anything below BBB loses its "investment grade" status and become speculative. Sometimes it's called junk.

William: Trash.

David: Sure. Trash.

William: Such a range. **How do they do it**?

David: They look at a bunch of data ranging from the issuer's financial position to the quality of management.

William: Data. It seems that it's at the heart of the ratings. How do they collect it?

(David starts putting his shoes on)

David (looking at his shoes): Good questions, William. Typically there's a team of raters with a lead analyst.

William: Were you a lead analyst, David?

(David stops tying his shoes and looks at William)

David: Yes.

William: Hmmm . . . What did you do?

David: I coordinated the gathering and analysis of the data. Then presented it to the rating committee. It decides what rating the debtor or the financial instrument will receive.

William: Who pays for all of this?

(David finishes tying his shoes and stands up)

David: The issuer, William.

William: Are you saying that the very firm that has asked you to rate its securities is paying you?

David: Yes. **The issuer pays the credit rating agency**.

(William, still sitting upright, takes a sip of water)

William: You said you were a lead analyst. When? Perhaps 2008?

David: William, this has been a great conversation, but I have to start preparing for my call to Singapore.

William: May I finish my water, David?

David: Sure.

(William takes a sip of water)

David: Why don't you chug it.

William: You didn't answer my question.

David: What question was that?

William: Were you an analyst in 2008?

David: Yes, I was.

William: So you were turning trash into gold, weren't you? Taking subprime mortgages and turning them into mortgage-backed securities with triple A slices. The same with collateralized debt obligations.

David: You seem to know a lot about finance for a janitor.

William: I've had a number of years to read books. After all, David. I lost my church.

David: I said I was sorry, pastor. Build a new one. I'll make a sizeable donation.

(William takes a sip)

William: Have a seat, David.

David: Thank you, but no.

William: "Let's hope we are all wealthy and retired by the time this house of cards falters." Does that sound familiar? Was it in an email you sent to an analyst on your team?

(David walks to the office door and tries to open it and can't)

William: Please, have a seat, David.

David: Open this door!

William: You and the others rated thousands of these securities worth trillions of dollars on paper **without really knowing what you were doing**. You conspired with your clients to maximize profits by making sure you could create securities with big slices of gold. Gold that was actually trash. But why would you care, David? You and your clients were making money hand over fist. You sold your soul to the devil. All for revenue.

(David reaches in his pocket for his cell phone)

William: Are you looking for this?

(William stands up and raises his hand holding David's cell phone)

William: Don't even bother with your office phone.

David: Look, Mr. Pastor-turned-wacked-out janitor, everybody had a hand in it—borrowers, mortgage brokers, investment banks, just to name of few. And let's not forget about the investors, they blindly bought the stuff. They looked at the ratings as if we were making investment recommendations. We weren't. And they should've known that. Everybody was having a party, including the investors, including Wingecarribee Shire. And what about the ultimate gatekeepers, the **regulators**? Why don't you creep them out?

William: There wouldn't have been a party without the gold, and you helped create it, David. The party came to an end in 2007, didn't it? The housing market collapsed. Then all of you downgraded billions of dollars of these securities. The gold was downgraded to junk. Within a year, nearly $2 trillion securities were downgraded.

David: What do you want from me?

William: You haven't asked me, David. Aren't you curious?

David: Asked you what?

(William approaches David, standing close to him)

William: Why I lost my church. My lovely church in Burrawang.

(David rushes to the wall and starts pounding)

William: There's no one here, David. Unusual, isn't it.

David: Let me out of here, please!

William: My church along with others in the township of Wingecarribee Shire invested in the securities. The gold slices. I was hoping to build a children's wing for my church. Many families in my church. Then the gold turned into trash. Into trash, David! We lost everything! Everything, David!

(pause)

William: My families left. I preached to a nearly empty church.

(pause)

William: I lost my church, David. It was torn down . . . God abandoned me. Abandoned Wingecarribee Shire.

(long pause)

David: If I could take it all back—

William: You all were the gatekeepers . . .

(William goes to his cart and pulls out a hammer and slowly approaches David)

David: What are you doing?

William: Those securities weren't trash, really. No, that's not the right word, David.

David: Please put that down.

William: They were a deadly virus.

David: I left the agency. I couldn't stay there.

William: You could've contained the virus. But you did the opposite. And the virus went global, all the way to Wingecarribee Shire.

(long pause)

David: I'm truly sorry, William. Please don't hurt me.

William: Do you pray, David?

(David starts trembling)

David: I used to.

William: I as well. I want to pray again.

(pause)

David: You can build another church . . . in Burrawang.

William: Why do you think I'm here?

David: I'm sorry? What?

(William raises the hammer)

William: Are you good with a hammer, David?

(fade to black)

What's Up with That?

The History of Credit Rating Agencies

Here's the history of credit rating agencies (CRAs) in a nutshell. Moody's, established by John Moody, issued its first public bond ratings in 1909. Then Poor's Publishing Company followed by Standard Statistics Company in 1922—in 1941 Standard and Poor's merged. Fitch Publishing Company began its business in 1924. The firms made money by putting together manuals to help investors figure out whether a bond's principal and interest would be repaid.

How did these three firms come to dominate the market? Good question. Well, we start with U.S. bank regulators. In 1936, they prohibited banks from investing in speculative securities—only investment grade. And of course that was determined by the CRAs' rating manuals. Then came the state insurance regulators who said the same thing to insurance companies: to figure out how much capital insurance companies had to hold, the regulators looked at the ratings the CRAs gave to the bonds the insurance companies bought. The same thing happened in the 1970s with federal pension regulators.

A major thing happened in the 1970s. In 1975, the Securities Exchange Commission (SEC) set minimum capital requirements for broker-dealers based on the riskiness of their portfolios. But instead of references to rating manuals, the SEC essentially froze the market by ruling that only the ratings of a "nationally recognized statistical rating organization" (NRSRO) would be acceptable—and named the three existing firms as NRSROs! Well, heck, soon all the financial regulators jumped in and did the same thing. CRAs essentially became "hardwired" into regulations. For example, a federal regulation issued under the Investment Company Act of 1940 requires that money market funds invest in debt that's been rated by an NRSRO. Even private contracts use them—e.g., if a party's credit rating falls, it might trigger the posting of more collateral. And you know about Basel II's Standardized Approach.

In the early 1970s, the CRAs' business model changed from "the investor pays" to "the issuer pays" model. Nobody can really put a finger on exactly why this happened, but one explanation is that fast photocopying machines would allow investors to just copy ratings manuals, depriving the CRAs of serious money. "Issuer pays" raises a conflict of interest you say? Well, yeah, kinda:

Rating agency: We'll give you a higher rating if you give us a higher fee.

Issuer: We're shopping around for the best credit rating agency. What can you offer us?

Rating agency: We'll bump up your ratings if you'll keep your business with us.

Although the Credit Rating Agency Reform Act of 2006 opened up the barrier somewhat and resulted in seven more credit agencies to be designated as NRSROs, the big three still dominate.

Moody's Ratings

Moody's assigns ratings based on a scale, with "Aaa" designating the highest quality securities (minimal credit risk)—gold, and "C" designating the lowest rated securities, which typically have little prospect for recovery and are often in default—trash. In between the two ratings, from most creditworthy to least, are the following ratings: Aa, A, Baa, Ba, B, Caa, and Ca. The classifications "Aa" through "Caa" can have numerical modifiers, with "1" representing the higher end of the generic rating, "2" representing a mid-range ranking, and "3" indicating the lower end of the ranking. For example, an asset rated "Aa1" would be of slightly higher quality than an asset rated "Aa2," even though both fall into the "Aa" rating. Hmmm . . .

The Ratings Process

While each CRA has its own unique rating procedures, the general process is similar across most CRAs. A credit rating is based on both quantitative and qualitative values. Quantitative data may include (1) data from the issuer about its financial position, especially data on cash flow relative to debt obligations, (2) data the agency gathers on the industry, competitors, and the overall economy, and (3) legal advice relating to an issuance. Qualitative data may include (1) data from the issuer about management, policy, business outlook, and accounting practices, and (2) data gathered by the agency relating to competitive position, quality of management, long-term industry prospects, and economic environment.

A rating is typically reached by a team of raters under the direction of a lead analyst. A debtor or financial instrument to be rated is assigned to the analyst team that specializes in that debtor or instrument's industry. Analysts begin by collecting information on the entity they are rating. Once the data is collected, the analysts evaluate the data and decide how much weight to give to each factor in the analysis. The analysts present their weighting proposals to the overall rating committee, which then decides what rating the debtor or the financial instrument will receive. Before publishing the rating, the CRA informs the debtor of the rating and the reasons behind the rating. If the debtor disagrees with the proposed rating, it may attempt to provide further information to adjust the rating. If a rating is a "point in time rating," the CRA's involvement in the rated entity terminates once it publishes the rating. But for most ratings, the CRA continues to monitor the issuer and/or its securities on an ongoing basis.

The process differs when rating structured products such as MBSs and CDOs. In fact, the rating process is kind of the reverse of CRAs' process for rating corporate bonds. Why? Because the issuer of a structured product decides beforehand what rating it wants for each tranche. So here's the process in a nutshell: An issuer of say, an MBS, sends the CRA data on a pool of loans, such as principal amount, geographic location, and borrowers' credit history. The lead analyst will analyze the loan pool and propose a tranche structure with accompanying ratings. The analyst uses models to predict what percentage of loans would default and how much could be recovered under a severe stress test. Based on the results, the MBS would have to be structured in such a way that would protect the highest tranche. So if the issuer tells the CRA that it wants a certain structure for the security, the analyst is supposed to check the proposed structure to see if it meets the model's requirements. If the analyst says the issuer's proposed structure is a no-go, the issuer can just stick with the analyst's ratings, which might give the highest tranche a AA rating. Or if the issuer wants that senior tranche to be AAA, it will have to make adjustments in the structure. (Or the issuer can say go to hell and go to another CRA.) Once the issuer and the CRA settle on a structure, the analyst will do a final review, including a review of legal documentation, and submit the proposal to the ratings committee, which will either approve the structure or adjust it. Check it out: the CRA usually is paid only if the credit rating is issued. Hmmm . . .

Flawed Ratings and Downgrades

It's clear as day now that CRAs held an overly optimistic view of the housing market and the default rates for subprime mortgages. S&P executives admitted that many of the assumptions underlying mortgage-related ratings from 2005 to 2007 were erroneous. Even as the subprime market began to unravel in the United States during 2007, many of the MBSs continued to receive or maintain AAA ratings. As the housing market worsened and many mortgages went into default, investors questioned the validity of the AAA ratings. In April 2007, S&P announced that it was adjusting the method of rating subprime mortgages and the instruments incorporating them. They admitted that the previous model, which was introduced in 2002, didn't fit the current housing market. All three CRAs adopted some internal reforms ranging from improving the effectiveness of the analytical methodologies to providing a clearer picture of the credit characteristics of structured finance ratings. Could this have been done to forestall regulation? Hmmm . . .

As the housing market worsened and foreclosures increased during the summer and fall of 2007, the CRAs downgraded billions of dollars of MBSs and CDOs. Many formerly AAA-rated securities were downgraded five levels to a speculative grade, otherwise known as "junk." In the third quarter of 2007, CRAs downgraded $85 billion in mortgage securities. In the fourth quarter alone, $237 billion in MBSs were downgraded. In the first quarter of 2008, an additional $739 billion in MBSs were downgraded, and $841 billion were downgraded in the second quarter of 2008. That amounts to nearly $2 trillion in downgrades in those four quarters alone. Insurers of MBSs and CDOs found themselves with insufficient capital to meet all the claims from the failing instruments. Many MBS and CDO holders found their once valuable assets to be worthless. Brutal.

Pre-Crisis Regulation of CRAs

The CRAs are private entities. They haven't been subject to much regulatory oversight. Like we said, in the United States, the SEC recognizes CRAs through its "nationally recognized statistical rating organization" (NRSRO) designation. Now a CRA can operate without NRSRO or any other formal recognition status. But, hey, for issuers, NRSRO status is golden because many federal and state laws require the designation.

Until the passage of the Credit Rating Agency Reform Act of 2006 ("the 2006 Act"), the NRSRO requirements were pretty hard to figure out. The NRSRO designation was a major barrier to new CRAs. The 2006 Act made it easier for competing agencies to gain NRSRO status, but the Act didn't change the underlying CRA model. Those supporting the 2006 Act believed that a greater number of CRAs might improve accountability, affordability, innovation and the overall quality of ratings.

The 2006 Act follows the general thrust of federal securities laws: provide full and accurate disclosure of material information so that the investing public can make informed decisions. So the Act requires a CRA that registers as an NRSRO to disclose information such as ratings performance, conflicts of interest, and the procedures used in determining ratings. The 2006 Act mandates that the SEC grant NRSRO registration to any CRA that applies and has been in the rating business at least three consecutive years before submitting its NRSRO application, unless the SEC finds that "the applicant does not have adequate financial and managerial resources to consistently produce credit ratings with integrity and to materially comply with the [SEC prescribed] procedures and methodologies."

But this wasn't enough, or the right type of, regulation to monitor the CRAs' role in creating the monster machine that churned out complex structured products—e.g., MBSs and CDOs.

CHAPTER 16

EPILOGUE

■■■

The crisis continued after the series of news alerts in Chapter 14. Bailouts continued. For instance, in November 2008, the U.S. government bailed out Citigroup to the tune of $45 billion. Starting in December of the same year, the government began bailing out General Motors and Chrysler to the ultimate tune of $79.7 billion. In January 2009, the government bailed out Bank of America to the tune of $138 billion. Downgrades continued, banks were shut down, and the Fed and central banks around the world continued to pump liquidity into the system. The U.S. economy then entered into "the Great Recession." As of this writing, we're still slowing climbing out of it. In this chapter, we're going to give you a little dénouement, of sorts. We'll start with resolution of the "toxic assets"—you know, the crappy MBS, etc., and a quick look at repayment of TARP bailouts.

I. TOXIC ASSETS AND TARP

Remember that originally the idea was to use government funds to buy the toxic assets from the banks. But they decided instead to inject capital into the banks, hoping they would start lending again. From the outset a number of economists argued that the better approach was to inject capital into banks so they could start lending again. Besides, how exactly was the government going to price the toxic assets? If they over-valued the junk, the taxpayers would take the hit. If the low-balled the junk, banks would take a hit to their capital, the last thing they need.

But, wait a second, what happened to the toxic assets? In March 2009, the Treasury announced the Public-Private Investment Program (PPIP). The idea was to leverage private funds with government funds to take the toxic loans or securities off the banks' balance sheets. Private investors chose the assets they wanted to purchase with partial guarantees or matching money from the government. The loan part of PPIP didn't go past a single pilot sale in September 2009. A total of $18.6 billion was disbursed under the PPIP. All of the government money has been repaid with over $3 billion in income—no losses.

By 2010, a lot of the TARP programs were gone or winding down. Although initial estimates of taxpayer exposure ran as high as $23.7 trillion, today the figure shows that most of the money provided under these programs was paid back in full with interest (with some write-offs). Even the programs that still have balances have generated net income that exceeds the principal outstanding. The Federal Reserve, for example, has already received more money than it paid out in the various facilities.

II. DODD-FRANK

The U.S. response to the crisis was the enactment of the Dodd-Frank Street Reform and Consumer Protection Act in July 2010. Spanning 2,300 pages and requiring more than 400 rules, many of which are not promulgated yet, the Dodd-Frank Act is the most sweeping financial reform since the Great Depression. There is no way we can explain all of Dodd-Frank here—we would be crazy to do that. We're just going to concentrate on aspects of Dodd-Frank that relate to the major themes in our chapters. And even then, we're going to keep it short and sweet. We're going to cover mortgage reform, securitization and credit rating agencies, the Fed, systemic risk, and credit default swaps, an "over-the-counter" derivative. (Yeah, there's important stuff in Dodd-Frank regarding executive compensation—many of the execs were out of control, looking only at short-term profit-making. We'll save this topic for another day.)

Part One: Mortgage Reform

The Dodd-Frank Act enacted a two-pronged response to subprime mortgage crisis, the Mortgage Reform and Anti-Predatory Lending Act (Mortgage Reform Act), and the Bureau of Consumer Financial Protection.

The Mortgage Reform Act, which requires a lot of rulemaking, provides support for homeowners in a number of ways. We're going to concentrate on home buying. It changes mortgage loan origination to "assure that consumers are offered and receive residential mortgage loans on terms that reasonably reflect their ability to repay the loans and that are understandable and not unfair, deceptive or abusive." So all mortgage originators have to be qualified and they're prohibited from mischaracterizing residential mortgage loans that are available to consumers. And they can't receive extra compensation for steering consumers to loans that consumers have no reasonable way of repaying, that don't provide the consumer with a net tangible benefit, or that are predatory—e.g. excessive fees.

No more ninja loans, either. The creditor has to make a reasonable and good faith determination of the consumer's ability to pay based on verified and documented information. What a concept! As to prepayment penalties, the Mortgage Reform Act requires the lender to offer the consumer a residential mortgage that doesn't include prepayment penalties, but the consumer can choose a mortgage with terms that include a prepayment penalty.

An originator who is held liable of breaching the Morgtage Reform Act is required to pay the plaintiff actual damages or three times the total compensation to the originator plus costs and reasonable attorney fees.

Now let's look at the Bureau of Consumer Financial Protection, an executive agency that regulates consumer financial products or services under federal law. Its objective is to implement and enforce federal consumer financial law so that consumers have access to financial products or services, such as real estate loans, and that those products and services are fair, transparent, and competitive. Sounds like a good principle in light of what you've just read. Beneath the principle is the Bureau's mandate to ensure that consumers are given understandable information to make responsible decisions, and that they're protected from discrimination and unfair, deceptive or abusive acts and practices.

You're lawyers in the making, so of course you want to know how the Act defines unfair, deceptive and abusive acts. You probably know what deceptive means. An act or practice is unfair if the Bureau has a reasonable basis to conclude that the act or practice causes or is likely to cause substantial injury to consumers which they can't reasonably avoid, and that the injury is not outweighed by countervailing benefits to consumers or to competition.

As to abusive acts or practices, the Bureau will conclude that they're abusive if they materially interfere with the consumer's ability to understand a term or condition of a consumer financial product or services, or if they take unreasonable advantage of (i) a consumer's inability to understand the material risks, costs or conditions of the product or service, or (ii) the consumer's inability to protect his/her interests in choosing or using a consumer financial product or service, or (iii) a consumer's reasonable reliance on, say, a mortgage broker to act in the consumer's interests.

The Act establishes a Consumer Financial Civil Penalty Fund that will hold any civil penalties from judicial and administrative actions under federal consumer financial laws. That money will be used to pay victims of violations of federal consumer financial laws and otherwise be used for consumer education and financial literacy programs.

Part Two: Securitization and Credit Rating Agencies

Securitization

In Chapter 13, we said that securitization as a concept is pretty neat and really important to finance, but that it got out of control and helped spread the virus. One reason for that was that issuers of private-label MBSs didn't stand to lose anything—they assumed no risk of loss if the securities tanked. Put another way, issuers had no "skin in the game."

The Act changes this by requiring issuers to retain at least 5% of the credit risk, unless the securities underlying loans meet risk-reducing standards. The Act also requires issuers to make greater disclosures regarding the underlying assets.

Credit Rating Agencies

The Act tightens the belt on CRAs—NRSROs—and undoes the regulatory hardwiring. To start off, it creates an Office of Credit Ratings at the SEC to keep an eye on CRAs and fine them if warranted. The SEC is also required to examine NRSROs at least once a year and release it findings to the public. Considering the screw up with CRA's methodologies, the Act requires NRSROs to disclose their methodologies, and their ratings track record. As to conflicts of interest, the Act prohibits compliance officers from working on ratings, methodologies, or sales and requires NRSROs to put into place procedure to monitor movement of employees from NRSROs to clients they've rated. And as to the hardwiring, the Act calls upon the elimination of NRSROs ratings from statutes and regulations. One other major change: Prior to Dodd-Frank, CRAs were exempt from liability for material misstatements or omissions in registration statements of publicly issued securities—i.e., liability under section 11 of the Securities Act. Now, they are subject to the same liability as other experts whose opinions are used in the registration statement—e.g. accountants. When sued, the CRAs claimed protection under the First Amendment, the argument being that they issue opinions just like newspapers whose views are subject to public disagreement and debate. That argument is not playing well in the courts today.

Part Three: The Federal Reserve

The Fed was heavily criticized for its use of Section 13(3) of the Federal Reserve Act in the bailouts of Bear Stearns and AIG. And the critics didn't like how the Fed did so much stuff behind closed doors. The Dodd-Frank Act responded to the critics in two ways. First, the Act prohibits the Fed from using Section 13(3) from making emergency loans to an individual entity. The Treasury Secretary has to give the Fed the okay, and no loans to insolvent firms. And the borrowers have to put up enough collateral to protect taxpayers from assuming any losses. Second, to promote more transparency, the Fed has to disclose information about its emergency lending, its use of the discount window, and its open market operations.

Part Four: Systemic Risk

The crisis highlighted the problem with systemic risk, that is, the too-big-to-fail problem. Dodd-Frank responded to the problem big time. First it created the Financial Stability Oversight Council, which is made up of ten federal financial regulators, an independent member, and five non-voting members. The Council is charged with looking for emerging risks in the financial system and putting together a response. It'll make recommendations to the Fed on matters relating to capital, leverage, liquidity, and risk management. Based on a two-thirds vote and a vote of the chair of the Council, the Council can require that a non-bank financial company be regulated by the Fed if that company poses a systemic risk. With a two-thirds vote and a vote of the chair, it can approve a Fed decision to require a large firm to divest some of its holdings if it poses a systemic risk. As to capital standards, the Council can impose a 15–1 leverage requirement upon a company if that company poses a systemic risk.

Second, Dodd-Frank attempts to end bailouts by, among other things, requiring the big, complex financial firms to submit so-called "funeral plans." The plans are supposed to show how the firm can be shut down in a rapid and orderly way. If they don't submit acceptable plans, regulators can require high capital levels and put restrictions on the firm's growth—maybe even requiring a divestment.

Part Five: Over-the-Counter Derivatives: Credit Default Swaps

In the Outbreak, folks realized that credit default swaps were completely unregulated. It was a huge market and nobody really knew the extent of counter-party risk. It was a really scary thing. Dodd-Frank addresses this problem by giving the SEC and the Commodities Futures Trading Commission (CFTC) authority to regulate over-the-counter derivatives such as credit default swaps. The Act requires mandatory clearing for some credit default swaps, which means that the counter-parties have to do the deal in most cases through a clearing broker.

III. CAPITAL ADEQUACY

A major theme of the crisis was the freezing of the credit markets, which dried up lending. The banks stopped lending because they were afraid of sitting on bad assets, which would require them to take a write-off. Write-off = hit to capital. It was pretty evident that something had to be done to improve capital positions to prevent another killer credit freeze. This brings us back to capital adequacy and the Basel Accords. Here we're going to tell you about Basel III, most of which has been implemented in the United States—have a look at supplement 16B.

Even before the crisis, talks on how to improve Basel II were underway. The crisis put a spotlight on the problems. In the fall of 2010 the BCBS released Basel III (formally titled, "A Global Regulatory Framework for More Resilient Banks and Banking Systems"). Basel III doesn't replace Basel II. Basel III's primary goal is to improve banks' ability to absorb asset losses without affecting the rest of the economy—the systemic risk we've talked about. It does this by attempting to improve the quantity and quality of bank capital.

Regulatory Capital

Basel III's definition of regulatory capital is more restrictive and emphasizes greater quality. It retains the Tier 1 and 2 distinction, but limits their composition to capital that's better able to absorb losses. Under Basel III, Tier 1 capital must be mostly "core capital,' which consists of equity stock and retained earnings. And many items that were included in a bank's capital calculation under Basel II, including some forms of subordinated debt, are excluded under Basel III. Under the Accord, banks are required to maintain an amount of Tier 1 capital equal to at least 6% of risk-weighted assets (RWA), a 2% increase over the current 4%. And banks will have to hold an amount of core capital equal to at least 4.5% of RWA. Under Basel I and II, core capital had to represent only 2% of RWA. The total amount of core capital that banks are required to hold increases to 7% if you include the capital conservation buffer, which we'll talk about in a second. Because the capital transformation will take time, items that will no longer qualify as "capital" under Basel III will be phased out of a bank's capital calculation over a ten-year period starting in 2013.

Now let's talk about quantity. By the time participating countries fully implement Basel III in 2019, banks are expected to maintain a total capital ratio of 10.5%, an increase from the 8% requirement under Basel II. As with Basel I and Basel II, banks under Basel III must maintain a minimum total capital ratio of at least 8% of RWA. But under Basel III, after a bank has calculated its 8% capital requirement, it has to hold an additional capital "conservation buffer" equal to at least 2.5% of its RWA, which brings the total capital requirement to 10.5% of RWA. The conservation buffer's purpose is to make sure banks have enough capital levels to absorb asset losses, especially during periods of financial and economic stress.

To combat procyclical behavior, Basel III requires banks to maintain a "counter-cyclical buffer." The buffer will range from 0%–2.5% of RWA. You can look at it as an extension of the capital conservation buffer because it requires banks to have higher levels of capital during good economic times. So when bad times hit, banks can avoid drastic measures that will only worsen the crisis (stop lending to comply with the capital asset ratios). If you assume a counter-cyclical buffer of 2.5%, Basel III could require banks to maintain a capital level at least equal to 13% of its total RWA. Buffers, buffers everywhere!

Leverage Ratio

We're back to the future. Basel III brings back the straight leverage ratio, which requires banks to maintain an amount of capital that's at least equal to 3% of the bank's total assets. Remember, before Basel I, regulators used only a leverage ratio. Keeping it simple has its advantages, doesn't it? Banks had to begin reporting their leverage ratios to their domestic regulators beginning on January 1, 2013. And starting on January 1, 2015, banks will be required to disclose their leverage ratios to the public.

Global Systemically Important Banks

Given the theme of this chapter, systemic risk, we should also tell you about Basel III's rules regarding global systemically important banks (G-SIBs). Banks that operate globally will be designated G-SIBs based on, among other things, their size, interconnectedness, global activity, and complexity—using twelve indicators ranging from cross-jurisdictional liabilities and claims to the amount of **over-the-counter derivatives**. Once a bank is designated a G-SIB, it has to meet a progressive initial Common Equity Tier 1 capital requirement ranging from 1% to 2.5% depending on the bank's global interconnectedness. To prevent a G-SIB from becoming even more systemically important on a global scale, Basel III assesses an additional 1% surcharge. These additional capital requirements will be phased in between January 2016 and the end of 2018, becoming effective on January 1, 2019. The BCBS urges national authorities to require banks with a leverage ratio exceeding EUR 200 billion to publicly disclose the twelve indicators used in the assessment methodology.

Liquidity Coverage Ratio

Basel III has also introduced a "liquidity coverage ratio" (LCR). Recall that we said in a bank run, it might not be able to liquidate its assets quickly enough or it might have to sell assets at "fire-sale" prices, requiring it to burn its capital. One of the lessons of the financial crisis was that banks and other financial institutions had a really tough time liquidating assets, which they desperately needed to do. The LCR addresses the problem by requiring that banks have enough "high-quality liquid assets" (HQLA) they can convert at market value into cash immediately via the private markets during periods of financial stress. An example of a HQLA is a Treasury bond, which is assigned a 0% risk-weight under Basel II's Standardized Approach. That asset is as liquid as water! The LCR will be phased in over a five-year period, starting in 2015.

Critique of Basel III

Critics never want to shut up. There are those who say that Basel III's increased capital levels will only reduce lending. For example, if a bank has $100 worth of capital, under Basel II it could lend up to $1250 of risk-weighted loans ($100 would be the 8% minimum capital level required by Basel II). But when Basel III is fully implemented, that same $100 of capital could now represent up to 13% of the bank's total risk-weighted assets, which means the bank can lend only up to $770. If banks substantially reduce their lending, what happens to economic growth? The studies come up with differing predictions.

Other critics say that higher capital levels will hurt bank profits. Banks will compensate for the lost income from their reduced lending ability by increasing interest rates on their loans. And guess who will be willing to pay the higher rates? Less creditworthy borrowers. Hmmm . . .

But there are those who think Basel III's capital levels are too low. They point out that in the global financial crisis, many of the banks, especially those in the United States, already had capital levels at or above the Basel III levels. Some studies suggest that minimum capital ratios should be closer to 15%–20%!

Maybe the biggest criticism of Basel III is what it fails to do. Many of the criticisms of Basel II go unaddressed in Basel III. For example, Basel III doesn't address the problems with Basel II's methods of assigning risk to a bank's assets—it does nothing to change the calculation of the bank's risk-weighted assets and leaves in place the use of external rating agencies to determine risk. And Basel III doesn't do anything to harmonize the IRB approaches to prevent banks from coming up with radically different capital ratios. There's always tomorrow!

IV. MAKING THEM PAY

What about suing the bastards? The encounter you read in Chapter 15 is based on a real story. Here's its resolution: In September 2012, the Federal Court of Australia held that the Australian branch of Lehman Brothers, formerly Grange Securities, was liable for breach of contract, negligence, breach of fiduciary duty, and misleading and deceptive conduct in its financial and investment advice to the plaintiffs, the three local Councils, including Wingcarribee Shire. The plaintiffs claimed that they suffered losses relating to their holdings of synthetic collateralized debt obligations (SCDOs) and other complex securities. Prior to hiring Grange as asset manager, the Councils followed a conservative investment strategy, investing in low risk assets. Under contracts with Grange, it began trading in SCDOs. But, the court noted, among other things, that the Councils were not financially sophisticated and that the SCDOs could only be understood by experts.

How about the United States? Issuing banks have faced lawsuits from a number of actors ranging from investors and shareholders (class actions or derivative actions) to the U.S. government, with settlements totaling in the billions of dollars. We'll just tell you a bit about government actions. It's gone after a bunch of big banks and reached over $100 billion in settlements, including $13 billion and $7 billion settlements with JPMorgan and Citigroup, respectively. The big kahuna came in August 2014, when the Department of Justice reached a record-breaking $16.65 billion civil settlement with Bank of America relating to federal and state claims that BOA and its subsidiaries, Countrywide Financial and Merrill

Lynch, packaged and sold rotten residential mortgage-backed securities (RMBS) and CDOs without telling investors of key facts regarding the quality of the securitized loans. For example, Merrill cranked out the securities saying they were all good when in fact many of the underlying loans sucked. BOA did an $850 million securitization telling investors that the securitization was backed by prime mortgages when in fact many of the mortgages were messed up. Countrywide basically did the same thing, telling investors that the originating loans were good to go when in fact they too were messed up. And check it out: Both Countrywide and BOA fraudulently sold crap mortgages to Fannie and Freddie.

The settlement included a $5 billion penalty under the Financial Institutions Reform, Recovery and Enforcement Act (FIRREA—signed into law in 1989 in the wake of the 1980s savings and loan crisis). Most of the rest of the money went to settle federal and state claims of fraud and to make BOA help people who were shafted by its conduct—e.g., loan modifications to help homeowners come out from underwater (so that their home would be worth more that the mortgage) and new loans to creditworthy borrowers who really need new loans. The settlement doesn't release individuals from civil liability and both BOA and its subs as well as individuals can still be prosecuted for criminal wrongdoing. But here's the thing: Very few individuals have been held accountable for the pain they caused. The case most people have heard about is the 2010 $67.5 million civil fraud settlement between the Securities and Exchange Commission and Angelo Mozilo, the Bronx street fighter who reigned over Countrywide while it swindled investors. As of this writing, word is that Los Angeles prosecutors may go after Mozilo and other Countrywide execs on civil charges.

As to CRAs, in February 2013, the DOJ (private actors, such as pension funds have sued the CRAs as well) brought a FIRREA-based civil lawsuit against Standard & Poor's alleging that the CRA inflated its ratings of RMBS and CDOs to bring in more cha-ching while at the same time telling investors, including federally-insured financial institutions, that their ratings were objective. How do you spell "fraud?" The latest on the street is that S & P has decided to settle for $1 billion, far short of the $5 billion the DOJ wants.

You Gotta Know Something About Them!

Daniel Tarullo

Born in Boston, Massachusetts, Daniel Tarullo eventually landed at the University of Michigan Law School, where he became the Article and Book Editor of the Michigan Law Review. He practiced law in Washington, D.C. before joining the Clinton administration, where he held several senior positions, including Assistant to the President for International Economic Policy and President Clinton's personal representative to the G7/G8 group of industrialized nations. Daniel is currently serving on the Board of Governors of the Federal Reserve System, where he emphasizes capital planning to prevent another financial catastrophe. He's also a law professor (formerly at Harvard and Princeton Universities and currently at Georgetown University), and teaches courses in international financial regulations and banking law. Daniel is not all about economics: he also has a passion for reading, especially Faulkner and Eliot.

What's Up with That?

Over-the-Counter Derivatives

A derivative is a financial instrument that derives its cash flows, and therefore its value, by reference to an underlying instrument, index or reference rate. There are four basic types of derivatives. A forward contract obligates one party to buy, and the other party to sell, a specific asset for a fixed price at a future date. A futures contract is a forward contract that is standardized and traded on an exchange. A swap contract is an agreement between two parties to exchange a series of cash flows—e.g., fixed-interest rate payments for floating-rate interest payments. An option contract is a contract between two parties, which gives one party the right but not the obligation to buy or sell an underlying instrument for a specified price on or before a specified date. In the over-the-counter market the counterparties execute a derivatives transaction directly with each other. The advantage of the OTC market is that a derivatives contract can be tailored to the needs of the counterparties. Forward contracts are OTC instruments. Most swaps are traded OTC. In an OTC trade the counterparties have no assurance that either will perform. A buyer might decide not to buy or a seller might decide not to sell. In an exchange trade, the exchange itself (actually a clearing house associated with the exchange) guarantees that the counterparties will perform their obligations. The

Dodd-Frank law passed after the global financial crisis changes some of this.

QUESTIONS FROM YOUR TALKING DOG

1. No, I don't need a tarp. The grass is just fine. You mean something else? The Troubled Asset Relief Program? Yeah, you talked about it. Did the government put a lot of money into the banks with that stuff? What did they ever do with those toxic assets?

2. If I were a taxpayer, I would probably be pretty teed off about all of my money that was used to bail out these reckless firms and companies. Did we get all of our money back?

3. Do I really need to know all about Dodd-Frank? I don't think so. I don't care that we're taking a long walk today, just stick to the basics. And don't forget to throw me a bone.

4. So what about mortgage reform? Is it all about providing more information to people? Or is it more than that?

5. What about securitization? Why any changes in the first place? Does Dodd-Frank do anything about credit rating agencies?

6. Yeah, a lot of people like to complain about the Federal Reserve these days. What exactly did it do wrong? Does Dodd-Frank do anything about it?

7. You know, I've always thought that systemic risk is like porn—you know it when you see it. I guess not. So what does Dodd-Frank do about that kind of thing?

8. Of course I want to know what Dodd-Frank does about credit default swaps. Shoot.

9. Back to capital adequacy, huh? Basel III. That sounds like a movie sequel. I don't think it's as much fun, though. So tell me how Basel III improves upon Basel II, please. Yuck. Start with regulatory capital. Does Basel III require more? I'm an idiot for asking this, but in what way does it require more?

10. Back to the future with this leverage ratio thing? Tell me.

11. How does Basel III deal with the big girls and boys, you know, the big banks?

12. It's not just about capital but liquidity too, am I right? I know, I'm a smart dog. All small dogs are smart.

13. So people have problems with Basel III? How so? And when you finish, get this bug out of my eye.

14. Ahhh, that's better, thanks. One other question, did anybody sue the bastards who caused all this crap?

<u>Chapter 16: Supplement</u>

16A. *Congressional Testimony*

Here we go back to how the crisis started. We give you the Congressional testimony of two homeowners who experienced the pain of the crisis. The first Congressional witness is Audrey Sweet. Should she and her husband have realized that what they were told was too good to be true? Did she fail to perform her own due diligence? If so, should one overlook that given what appears to be Countrywide's fraudulent conduct? The second witness is Nettie McGee, who was 65 years old when she bought her home. How do you picture Ms. McGee in your mind? A physically and mentally weak old woman made to sign a forty-page document in a small room? What narrative do you draw from the testimony of these two individuals? The Dodd-Frank Act addresses both financial literacy and unfair lending practices.

> S. Hrg. 110–237, "A Local Look At The National Foreclosure Crisis: Cleveland Families, Neighborhoods, Economy Under Siege From The Subprime Mortgage Fallout", 17–19 (2007)

On false confidence lenders/brokers gave unqualified borrowers, setting them up to fail.

My name is Audrey Sweet. When my husband and I did our home loan search, we believed that these responsible lenders were probably doing us a favor. We were then introduced to a real estate agent who said she could take care of everything. We were so excited that finally, someone was going to give us a chance. She took us to the Countrywide Home Loans office and we began our home search. When we finally found one we liked, the agent said that the seller and lender would do all sorts of things to give us a home. It was as though everyone was doing us a favor. When you match that with our lack of funds, our lack of knowledge about mortgages, credit, finances and less then [sic] stellar credit, we were a dream come true, at least to the broker. When we were finally told the amount of the monthly mortgage payment, we were shocked. When we expressed our concern, we were told not to worry about it. We would be able to refinance to a better rate in a year.

We just had to prove ourselves. We requested that the property taxes be escrowed, but were told that if we did, the loan would no longer be affordable and we would not be approved. In the excitement of the moment, I did not focus in on the fact that I was just told that my income would not support the expense of both the mortgage and property taxes.

He knew that I would eventually lose my home, yet went forward with the loan. I lived up to my end of the deal by paying my mortgage, but neither he nor Countrywide lived up to their commitment.

Of course, the refinancing never happened and we've been since falling behind on our mortgage from time to time, but we've managed to bring it current each time. I did end up seriously neglecting the property taxes.

In March of this year, Countrywide took action and paid back the taxes, a total of $3,493.51. I fully expect that they would do this to protect their interest in the property. However, I did not expect what came next. In April, I received a letter from Countrywide, informing me that my monthly payment was to increase by $658 effective in June for the next 12 months, because our back taxes had been paid by Countrywide.

In addition, our rate was set to adjust up in February 2008. It was written in our loan document that it can only adjust up, never down. $387.72 of this increase was attributed to the shortage amount. However, when you multiply that by the 12 months it was to be effective, that comes to $4,652.64.

I have yet to receive a clear explanation of what that amount was to cover. This new payment, in my experience with Countrywide's lack of willingness to help, prompted me to call ESOP, Empowering and Strengthening Ohio's People, also known as the Eastside Organizing Project. In preparing for my visit to ESOP, I began to look over my home loan documents and discovered several things I had apparently overlooked until then. First, was that my gross monthly income was recorded as $726 more than it actually was. Second, I have two sets of loan documents, one that was created 10 days before we closed and another from the day of closing.

The closing date document lists my assets as $9,400 in my Charter One megaccount. I've never had $9,400 in the bank. The final item I noticed was that the tax amount listed on the appraisal report was $1,981.34, which comes to about $165 a month.

Countrywide listed my taxes as $100 a month. Again, looking back to my mortgage application experience, I was embarrassed. I remember how I felt so undeserving of a loan, because I'd been turned down so many times before and I realized that I finally made a 30-year mistake.

Once I realized that Countrywide was counting on my feeling this way, I became angry. I began to see how I had been taken advantage of, and was hoping that my initial feeling of embarrassment would keep me from sharing my experience with anyone.

However, that would mean I would lose my home, and I have decided not to let that happen. When I first came to ESOP in April 2007, various resources have been presented that I would not know of otherwise. One service ESOP is offering me is a weekly conference call with Countrywide. These phone calls were essential to my result with Countrywide, as there were witnesses to every promise and excuse given.

While the calls were helpful to keep my case in their face, they also showed how little Countrywide cared. The same modification was offered twice. I had declined both times, as this did not fit what I could afford.

Although I have asked repeatedly for the following information, I have yet to receive it. The name of the compliance officer working on my case, the amount of the tax payment, and the $9,400 asset and the documentation to support this. After these talks, I would usually end up feeling defeated. However, ESOP continued to encourage me. Without their support, I would have given up long before the issues were resolved.

Once Countrywide finally received a report from their compliance person, I received a call from them. They said that while what happened with my loan was not exactly illegal, there were definitely things that should have been done better. Since then, the contact with Countrywide repeatedly refer to what happened with my loan as a special circumstance. In June, Countrywide executives met with ESOP to talk to their borrowers.

At that meeting, I was struck by their less than willing attitude to help people keep their homes. They refused to answer any questions and refused to sign a letter of commitment with ESOP to work with their borrowers. I'm going to wrap up because I've gone over my time. But basically since then, they referred me to a program with Third Federal Savings and Loan, where they educate home buyers on home buying process, credit and finances, and I was able to refinance with them with a fixed rate of 7.2 percent. That's where I'm at now with my taxes escrowed.

S. Hrg. 110–511, "The Looming Foreclosure Crisis: How To
Help Families Save Their Homes," 6–7 (2007)

On inadequate loan counseling

In 1997, I began renting my current home on South Aberdeen Street. I rented it for 2 years with an option to buy. When I finally bought my first home in 1999, for $80,000, I was 65 years old. I made the payment for 6 years. I had a fixed rate mortgage and I knew what to expect each month: it was $735 every month. I was able to make my payments and pay my taxes. I could afford all of my bills.

Then in October of 2005, the sheriff came to my door to tell me that my backyard was going to be sold for auction for $5,000 because of an unpaid tax bill. I paid the taxes on my house every year. I just didn't know that I had two tax bills, one for my house and one for my backyard. The tax bill for my backyard had been sent to an address across town for years, since and before I moved in. I was desperate to keep my backyard and my beautiful trees, but I had to pay the city $5,000 and I had to do something fast because I would lose my yard.

I didn't have $5,000 in the bank. I live on Social Security and I get some rent from my daughter. Then I saw a commercial on TV about refinancing your home. I thought if I refinanced, I could get money to pay the tax bill and keep my yard. I called the number and a broker came to visit me the next day. He wrote down my personal information, and a week and a half later he called me and asked me to come down to sign the papers.

After I arrived at the crowded office, I was taken into a small room, handed about 40 pages, and told where to sign. The woman in charge of the closing stood over me and turned the pages as I signed them. The whole process took about 10 minutes. I thought I was signing a fixed-rate loan. Then, with no explanation of the loan, I was sent out the door. The mortgage company paid the taxes to the county.

Then, to my surprise, they called me a few days later to come back and get a check for $9,000. I didn't know they had me borrowing the extra $9,000. When I asked about it, the mortgage company said that I could use it for bills. I thought it was a good idea, so I used the money to pay some bills and fix my plumbing problem. I started paying the loan back. The payments were about the same as my original loan. It's been difficult at times, but I have never missed a payment.

A month and a half ago, in October of this year, I got a letter from my mortgage company that said that on December 1, my payment was going up from $706 to $912. I called the mortgage broker, but he doesn't work there anymore. I thought I signed a fixed-rate mortgage. I had no idea my payment would jump almost 25 percent. My interest rate went from 7.8 to 10.87, and eventually it will go higher.

I don't know how to make my payments now. They are higher than my Social Security check. The only reason I can get by now is because my daughter pays me a little rent. Right now, my lawyers from the Legal Assistance Foundation in Chicago are trying to help me negotiate with my lender, but we don't know if the bank will agree to lower my interest rate back where it was before.

I know I will lose my home that I waited my entire life to own if I can't get my original rate back. Many people who could originally afford their mortgage payments are losing their homes because they have an adjustable rate mortgage. Please help people like me, please, who waited their entire lives to own their homes. Please help me.

16B. *Statement by Tarullo on Capital Adequacy*

The Dodd-Frank Act established the Financial Stability Oversight Council comprised of federal financial regulators. The Council monitors systemic risk including capital levels. This Statement by Daniel Tarullo, a member of the Fed's Board of Governors, is pretty interesting for a number of reasons. That the Fed, the OCC, the FDIC have made major rulemakings on capital regulation is really impressive, given the complexity of the subject matter. Why do you think that might be the case? Why does Tarullo go out of his way to cast the U.S. regulatory efforts as a reflection of Basel III? Other than preventing bank insolvency, what other very important purpose does a strong capital level serve? Note the reference to the Collins Amendment. Why the Amendment? Do the exceptions for community banks make sense? To test your understanding of the bank capital, why does Tarullo stress the increase in common equity capital? How is systemic risk addressed? How does the statement reflect the idea that Basel's capital levels are floors?

D. Tarullo, Statement: "Dodd-Frank Implementation" (2013)

For release on delivery 11:00 a.m. EDT

July 11, 2013

Statement by Daniel K. Tarullo
Member
Board of Governors of the Federal Reserve System
before the Committee on Banking, Housing, and Urban Affairs
U.S. Senate Washington, D.C.
July 11, 2013

Chairman Johnson, Ranking Member Crapo, and other members of the Committee, thank you for the opportunity to testify on the Federal Reserve's activities in mitigating systemic risk and implementing the Dodd-Frank Wall Street Reform and Consumer Protection Act of 2010 (Dodd-Frank Act).

With the third anniversary of the Dodd-Frank Act upon us, it is a good time to reflect on what has been accomplished, what still needs to be done, and how the work on the Dodd-Frank Act fits with other regulatory reform projects. Indeed, the deliberate pace and multi-pronged nature of the implementation of the act—occasioned as it is by complicated issues and decisionmaking processes—may be obscuring what will be far-reaching changes in the regulation of financial firms and markets. Indeed, the Federal Reserve and other banking supervisors have already created a very different supervisory environment than what was prevalent just a few years ago.

Today, I will review recent progress in key areas of financial regulatory reform, with special—though not exclusive—attention to implementation of the Dodd-Frank Act, including how that law affects the regulation of community banks. I will also highlight areas in which proposals are still outstanding and, in a few cases, in which we intend to make new proposals in the relatively near future.

Implementation of Basel III Capital Rules

Let me begin by noting the completion of our major rulemakings on capital regulation.

Although most of the provisions in these rules do not directly implement provisions of the Dodd-Frank Act, implementation of that law is occurring against the backdrop of implementation of the Basel III framework.

This month, the Federal Reserve, the Office of the Comptroller of the Currency, and the Federal Deposit Insurance Corporation (FDIC) approved final rules implementing the Basel III capital framework, as well as certain related changes required by the Dodd-Frank Act. The rules establish an integrated regulatory capital framework designed to ensure that U.S. banking organizations maintain strong capital positions, enabling them to absorb substantial losses on a going-concern basis and to continue lending to creditworthy households and businesses even during economic downturns.

The rules increase the quantity and improve the quality of regulatory capital of the U.S. banking system by setting strict eligibility criteria for regulatory capital instruments, by raising the minimum tier 1 capital ratio from 4 percent to 6 percent of risk-weighted assets, and by establishing a new minimum common equity tier 1 capital ratio of 4.5 percent of risk-weighted assets. The rules also require a capital conservation buffer of 2.5 percent of risk-weighted assets to ensure that banking organizations build capital during benign economic periods so that they can withstand serious economic downturns and still remain above the minimum capital levels. In addition, the rules improve the methodology for calculating risk-weighted assets to enhance risk sensitivity and incorporate certain provisions of the Dodd-Frank Act, such as sections 171 and 939A. The rules also contain certain provisions, including a supplementary leverage ratio and a countercyclical capital buffer, that apply only to large and internationally active banking organizations, consistent with their systemic importance and their complexity. The rules will have several important consequences.

First, they consolidate the progress made by banks and regulators over the past four years in improving the quality and quantity of capital held by banking organizations. Second, they remedy shortcomings in our existing generally applicable risk-weighted asset calculations that became apparent during the financial crisis. In so doing, they also enhance the effectiveness of the Collins Amendment, the scope of which we have extended through these rules by applying standardized floors to capital buffer, as well as minimum requirements. Third, adoption of these rules meets international expectations for U.S. implementation of the Basel III capital framework. This gives us a firm position from which to press our expectations that other countries implement Basel III fully and faithfully.

In crafting these rules, the banking agencies made a number of changes to the 2012 proposals, mostly to address concerns by community banks. For example, the new rules maintain current practice on risk weighting residential mortgages and provide community banking organizations the option of maintaining existing standards on the regulatory capital treatment of "accumulated other comprehensive income" (AOCI) and pre-existing trust preferred securities. These changes from the proposed rule are meant to reduce the burden and complexity of the rules for community banks while preserving the benefits of more rigorous capital standards. Most banking organizations already meet the higher capital standards, and the rules will help preserve the benefits of the stronger capital positions banks have built under the oversight of regulators since the financial crisis.

* * *

All financial institutions subject to the new rules will have a significant transition period to meet the requirements. The phase-in period for smaller, less complex banking organizations will not begin until January 2015, while the phase-in period for larger institutions begins in January 2014.

Stress Testing and Capital Planning Requirements for Large Banking Firms

Important as higher capital requirements and a better quality of capital are to the safety and soundness of financial institutions, conventional capital requirements are by their nature somewhat backward-looking. First, they reflect loss expectations based on past experience.

Second, losses that actually reduce reported capital levels are often formally taken by institutions well after the likelihood of losses has become clear. Rigorous stress testing helps compensate for these shortcomings through a forward-looking assessment of the losses that would be suffered under stipulated adverse economic scenarios, so that capital can be built and maintained at levels high enough for the firms to withstand such losses and still remain viable financial intermediaries. In the middle of the financial crisis, the Federal Reserve created and applied a stress test to the nation's largest financial firms. The next year, Congress mandated stress tests for a larger group of firms in the Dodd-Frank Act. This fall, we will extend the full set of stress testing requirements to the dozen or so banking organizations with greater than $50 billion in assets covered in the Dodd-Frank Act but not fully covered in our previous stress tests.

Regular, comprehensive stress testing, with published results, has already become a key part of both capital regulation and overall prudential supervision. In the annual Comprehensive Capital Analysis and Review (CCAR), the Federal Reserve requires each large bank holding company to demonstrate that it has rigorous, forward-looking capital planning processes that effectively account for the unique risks of the firm and maintains sufficient capital to continue to operate through times of extreme economic and financial stress. CCAR and Dodd-Frank Act stress tests have shown the significant supervisory value of conducting coordinated cross-firm analysis of the major risks facing large banks.

The Federal Reserve has used stress testing and its broader supervisory authority to prompt a doubling over the past four years of the common equity capital of the nation's 18 largest bank holding companies, which collectively hold more than 70 percent of the total assets of all U.S. bank holding companies. Specifically, the aggregate tier 1 common equity ratio— which is based on the strongest form of loss-absorbing capital—at the 18 firms covered by the stress test has more than doubled, from 5.6 percent at the end of 2008 to 11.3 percent at the end of 2012. That reflects an increase in tier 1 common equity from $393 billion to $792 billion during the same period.

Enhanced Prudential Requirements for Large Banking Firms

Sections 165 and 166 of the Dodd-Frank Act require the Federal Reserve to establish a broad set of enhanced prudential standards, both for bank holding companies with total consolidated assets of $50 billion or more and for nonbank financial companies designated by the Financial Stability Oversight Council (Council) as systemically important. The required standards include capital requirements, liquidity requirements, stress testing, single-counterparty credit limits, an early remediation regime, and risk-management and resolution-planning requirements. The sections also require that these prudential standards become more stringent as the systemic footprint of a firm increases.

The Federal Reserve has issued proposed rules to implement sections 165 and 166 for both large U.S. banking firms and foreign banks operating in the United States. In addition, earlier this week the federal banking agencies jointly issued a proposal to implement higher leverage ratio standards for the largest, most systemically important U.S. banking organizations. We have already finalized the rules on resolution planning and stress testing, and we are working diligently this year toward finalization of the remaining standards.

On liquidity, we will also be implementing the Basel III quantitative liquidity requirements for large U.S. banking firms. We expect that the federal banking agencies will issue a proposal later this year to implement the Basel Committee's Liquidity Coverage Ratio for large U.S. banking firms. These quantitative liquidity requirements would complement the stricter set of qualitative liquidity standards that the Federal Reserve has already proposed pursuant to section 165 of the Dodd-Frank Act.

On capital, we will be proposing risk-based capital surcharges on the most systemically important U.S. banking firms. The proposal will be based on the risk-based capital surcharge framework developed by the Basel Committee for global systemically important banks, under which the size of the surcharge will increase with a banking firm's systemic importance. These surcharges are a critical element of the Federal Reserve's efforts to force the most systemic financial firms to internalize the externalities caused by their potential failure and to reduce any residual subsidies such firms may enjoy as a result of market perceptions that they may be too big to fail. We anticipate issuing a proposed regulation on these capital surcharges around the end of this year.

* * *

16C. *Implementation of Basel III*

This Basel Committee report on Basel III implementation is an example of what the Committee does in addition to promulgating standards. How does the report reflect potential problems with the "soft law" of financial regulations? Notice the reference to "fostering public confidence in regulatory ratios." Why bother saying that? Basel 2.5 addresses a bank's "trading book," which records trading of securities. The assets in the trading book are not held for very long, whereas the assets in the banking book are. The BCBS issued 2.5 because banks were engaging in arbitrage: they moved assets to the trading book, which had lower capital requirements. Why might developing countries choose not to adopt Basel III but Basel II instead?

Basel Committee on Banking Supervision, "Report to G20
Leaders on monitoring implementation of Basel III
regulatory reforms" (2013)

* * *

Summary

This is the fourth report from the Basel Committee on Banking Supervision to update G20 Leaders on progress in implementing the Basel III regulatory reforms. The last update was issued in April 2013. The report provides an overview of the Committee's Regulatory Consistency Assessment Programme (RCAP), which includes (i) monitoring the progress of Basel Committee members in adopting the globally agreed Basel III standards; and (ii) assessing the consistency of national or regional banking regulations with the global Basel III standards and analysing the outcomes that are produced by those regulations. The report also includes an overview of the progress made in finalising outstanding components of the Basel III regulatory reforms.

Of the 27 jurisdictions that comprise the Basel Committee, 25 have now issued the final set of Basel III based capital regulations. Indonesia and Turkey have draft rules in place and efforts are under way to finalise them. Most recently, the European Union and the United States issued final regulations in June and July 2013, respectively. In addition, a number of members have begun to move towards introducing regulations for the liquidity and leverage ratios, as well as the requirements that apply to firms designated as global systemically important banks (G-SIBs) and domestic systemically important banks (D-SIBs).

The Basel Committee's periodic monitoring of Basel III's quantitative impact indicates that internationally active banks continue to build capital, and appear well placed to meet the full set of fully phased-in minimum Basel III capital requirements ahead of the 2019 deadline. In the six months to December 2012, the average Common Equity Tier 1 (CET1) capital ratio of large internationally active banks rose from 8.5% to approximately 9% of risk-weighted assets. In addition, the aggregated capital shortfall of those banks that still have capital ratios below the fully phased-in 2019 CET1 requirements continues to decrease: the shortfall is now well below half the aggregate annual profits of the industry (which in 2012 totalled over €400 billion). Despite this progress and in the light of the current challenging global economic environment, banks and national authorities must remain particularly vigilant to actual and potential deterioration in banks' asset quality in order to ensure further improvement in capital adequacy. Adjustments may also be required as the process of implementation of finalised capital regulations deepens further.

The Committee's assessment programme of Basel III implementation remains on track. The Committee recently concluded an assessment of the consistency of Switzerland's capital regulations with the Basel III standards, and is currently assessing China, Brazil and Australia. It is encouraging to note that those jurisdictions that have undergone an assessment of their final rules have so far promptly rectified identified issues and are continuing with regulatory reforms. The RCAP process has thus far helped improve member jurisdictions' consistency with the Basel III standards. As a result, regulations to adopt and implement Basel III standards are stronger than would otherwise have been the case absent the Committee's efforts at monitoring and assessing implementation. However, the Committee has also published studies of banks' calculations of risk-weighted assets in both the banking and trading books. The results revealed material variations in the measurement of risk-weighted assets across banks, even for identical hypothetical test portfolios. The Committee is actively considering possible policy reforms to improve the comparability of outcomes. In doing so, it needs to ensure an optimal balance between the risk sensitivity of the framework and its complexity.

The Committee, in accordance with agreed timelines, continues to work to finalise a few remaining policy-related elements of the Basel III framework. Timely adoption of Basel III standards, ensuring good quality implementation of national regulations that are consistent with the globally-agreed Basel III standards, and improving the reliability of risk-weighted asset calculations remain key priorities of the Committee over the medium term.

Progress report on Basel III implementation

Full, timely and consistent implementation of Basel III remains fundamental to building a resilient financial system, fostering public confidence in regulatory ratios and providing a level playing field for internationally active banks. To aid in the adoption of Basel III regulatory standards and their implementation, the Basel Committee has put in place the Regulatory Consistency Assessment Programme (RCAP) to monitor, review and report on Basel III implementation. The programme broadly consists of two parts: (i) monitoring, which includes the monitoring of standards adoption by member jurisdictions and of banks' progress in raising capital and liquidity buffers to meet the new minimum standards; and (ii) assessments and review studies, which include the assessments of local regulations and their consistency with the Basel standards, and reviews of banks' calculations of capital ratios, risk-weighted assets and other regulatory outcomes.

This report provides an update on the work done by the Basel Committee since the previous update issued in April 2013. In particular, the report outlines the progress made on: (i) the adoption of rules by member and non-member jurisdictions; (ii) the assessments of regulatory consistency and outcomes; and (iii) the policy reform of outstanding elements of the Basel framework.

(i) Adoption of Basel III standards

Member jurisdictions have made considerable progress since the last report was published in April 2013. More details regarding the implementation status of each member jurisdiction can be found in the tables in Annex 1, which includes summary information about the next steps and the implementation plans being considered.

Capital

Basel II

Of the 27 Basel Committee member jurisdictions, 24 have implemented Basel II fully. The United States, which is one of the three jurisdictions yet to fully implement Basel II, has issued final regulations on Basel II;

however, its largest banks are still on parallel run for implementing the advanced approaches. The remaining two jurisdictions (Argentina and Russia) have also initiated the process to complete the implementation of Basel II.

Basel 2.5

The number of member jurisdictions who have fully implemented Basel 2.5 is 22. Of the other five members, the United States has issued the remaining part of the rules, which will come into force in 2014. Argentina, Indonesia, Mexico and Russia have either partially adopted Basel 2.5 or have initiated steps to do so.

Basel III

Of the 27 member jurisdictions, 11 have now issued final Basel III capital rules that are legally in force. The number of members that have issued final rules but not yet brought them into force has increased to 14 (this includes Argentina, Brazil, Korea, Russia, the United States and the nine EU member states that are members of the Basel Committee). The two remaining member jurisdictions (Indonesia and Turkey) have issued draft rules.

Leverage

The Basel Committee is currently in the process of finalising the details of the Basel III leverage ratio standard. The agreed start date for banks to begin disclosing their leverage ratios is 1 January 2015 (see also Section (iii) below). Some member jurisdictions have already initiated steps in preparation for the introduction of this new requirement. This should assist in prompt implementation once a final international standard is agreed.

Liquidity

Regarding the adoption of regulations relating to the Liquidity Coverage Ratio, 11 member jurisdictions have issued final rules (South Africa, Switzerland and EU member states), while four member jurisdictions have started the implementation process by issuing draft rules (Australia, Hong Kong SAR, India and Turkey). The agreed start date for the phase-in of liquidity requirements is 1 January 2015.

Systemically important banks

With regard to the global systemically important banks (G-SIBs) and domestic systemically important banks (D-SIBs) requirements, only two member jurisdictions (Switzerland and Canada) have so far issued final regulatory rules and begun to enforce them. Ten member jurisdictions have issued the final set of regulations, which are not yet in force (South Africa and EU member states). The remaining member jurisdictions have not yet issued draft rules. The agreed start date to phase in the requirements is 1

January 2016. However, to enable timely implementation of the requirements, the Committee has agreed that national jurisdictions will adopt official regulations/legislation consistent with the Basel III standards that establish the reporting and disclosure requirements by 1 January 2014.

Non-Basel Committee/non-EU jurisdictions

Several non-Basel Committee member jurisdictions are reporting the adoption and implementation of Basel II, 2.5 and III standards. In July 2013, the Financial Stability Institute (FSI) issued its annual progress report on Basel adoption in jurisdictions that are neither members of the Basel Committee nor members of the EU. The report updates the FSI's previous progress report and provides results as of end-May 2013.

The FSI survey questionnaire was sent to over 100 non-Basel Committee/non-EU jurisdictions, and 74 jurisdictions responded. Compared to 2012, there has been significant progress in the efforts to adopt Basel capital standards . . . Among the surveyed jurisdictions, 54 have either implemented Basel II or are in the process of implementation, 16 have implemented Basel 2.5 or are in the process of implementation, and 26 have implemented Basel III or are in the process of implementation.

* * *

(ii) Assessing consistency and outcomes

As part of the RCAP, the Committee has started to assess in detail the consistency of local regulations implementing the Basel III risk-based capital standards. The assessments cover the substance of the local regulations, but also their form, ie whether the rules are laid down in regulatory instruments that are binding from a regulatory and supervisory perspective.

In 2012, the Basel Committee assessed the final capital regulations in Japan, and the draft capital regulations in the European Union and the United States. The Committee continued with assessments of Singapore and Switzerland, published in March and June 2013, respectively. The Committee is currently in the process of assessing China, Brazil and Australia. New assessments of the European Union, United States and Canada will commence in the second half of 2013, and be published in 2014 . . . The Basel Committee urges jurisdictions to address material inconsistencies between domestic regulations and the globally agreed Basel standards identified by the final assessments under the RCAP. The Committee will monitor implementation progress in future assessments as well as analyse prudential outcomes.

The assessments are demonstrably contributing to greater consistency in the national adoption of Basel III standards. For example, in the case of Japan, Singapore and Switzerland, the regulatory authorities promptly resolved a number of initial assessment findings by amending the domestic regulations that implement Basel III capital standards (see table below). These amendments have contributed to a more consistent domestic implementation of the Basel framework, and thus set a positive precedent for future RCAP assessments and for the implementation process as a whole.

Overview of assessment outcomes			Table 1
Assessed member jurisdiction	Publication date of assessment	Number of regulatory changes, amendments, and clarifications made by a member jurisdiction during the assessment	Overall assessment grade
Japan	October 2012	5	Compliant
Singapore	March 2013	15	Compliant
Switzerland	June 2013	22	Compliant

Studies on regulatory outcomes

As part of RCAP, the Basel Committee has initiated studies to examine the consistency of risk-weighted assets (RWAs) measurement by banks that use internal model approaches. Following its first report on the measurement of market risk RWAs, issued in January 2013, the Committee published a second report in July 2013 on the regulatory consistency of RWAs for credit risk in the banking book. The banking book study draws on supervisory data from more than 100 major banks, as well as additional data on sovereign, bank and corporate exposures collected from 32 major international banks as part of a portfolio benchmarking exercise.

The banking book study reveals that there is considerable variation across banks in average RWAs for credit risk across banks. While most of the variation can be explained by broad differences in the composition of banks' assets, reflecting differences in business models and risk preferences, there is also material variation driven by diversity in bank and supervisory practices with regard to measuring credit risk.

* * *

Annex 1: Monitoring adoption status of Basel III

The Basel III framework builds upon and enhances the regulatory framework set out under Basel II and Basel 2.5. The tables herein therefore review members' regulatory adoption of Basel II, Basel 2.5 and Basel III.

- Basel II, which improved the measurement of credit risk and included capture of operational risk, was released in 2004 and was due to be implemented from year-end 2006. The Framework consists of three pillars: Pillar 1 contains the

- minimum capital requirements; Pillar 2 sets out the supervisory review process; and Pillar 3 corresponds to market discipline.
- Basel 2.5, agreed in July 2009, enhanced the measurements of risks related to securitisation and trading book exposures. Basel 2.5 was due to be implemented no later than 31 December 2011.
- In December 2010, the Committee released Basel III, which set higher levels for capital requirements and introduced a new global liquidity framework. Committee members agreed to implement Basel III from 1 January 2013, subject to transitional and phase-in arrangements.

In November 2011, G20 Leaders at the Cannes Summit called on jurisdictions to meet their commitment to implement fully and consistently Basel II and Basel 2.5 by end-2011, and Basel III starting in 2013 and completing by 1 January 2019. In June 2012, G20 Leaders at the Los Cabos Summit reaffirmed their call for jurisdictions to meet their commitments. This message was reiterated in Moscow in February 2013 by the G20 Finance Ministers and Central Bank Governors.

Methodology

The data contained in this annex are based on responses from Basel Committee member jurisdictions. The following classification is used for the status of adoption of Basel regulatory rules:

1. Draft regulation not published: no draft law, regulation or other official document has been made public to detail the planned content of the domestic regulatory rules. This status includes cases where a jurisdiction has communicated high-level information about its implementation plans but not detailed rules.

2. Draft regulation published: a draft law, regulation or other official document is already publicly available, for example for public consultation or legislative deliberations. The content of the document has to be specific enough to be implemented when adopted.

3. Final rule published: the domestic legal or regulatory framework has been finalised and approved

4. Final rule in force: the domestic legal and regulatory framework is already applied to banks.

In order to support and supplement the status reported, summary information about the next steps and the implementation plans being considered by members are also provided for each jurisdiction. In addition to the status classification, a colour code is used to indicate the implementation status of each jurisdiction.

The table is also available on the Basel Committee's website (www.bis.org/bcbs). The web version includes links to relevant domestic regulations.

Green = implementation completed; Yellow = implementation in process; Red = no implementation.

Country	Basel II	Basel 2.5	Basel III			
			Risk-based capital	G-SIB / D-SIB requirements	Liquidity (LCR)	Leverage ratio[26]
Argentina	3, 4	1, 4	3, 4	1	1	
	(3) Final Pillar 3 rules published on 8 February 2013 will come into force on 31 December 2013. (4) Final rules for Pillar 1 credit risk and Pillar 2 came into force on 1 January 2013.	(1) Revisions to the Basel II market risk framework (July 2009): market risk amendments to reflect Basel 2.5 are considered a lower priority given the limited activity in Argentina. (4) Enhancements to the Basel II framework (July 2009): rules relating to enhancements to securitisation came into force on 1 January 2013.	(3) Final Pillar 3 rules published on 8 February 2013 will come into force on 31 December 2013. (4) Final rules for Pillars 1 and 2 came into force on 1 January 2013.			
Australia	4	4	4	1	2	
					Revised draft standards issued in May 2013 based on the January 2013 BCBS revisions.	
Belgium	4	4	(3)	(3)	(3)	
			(Follow EU process)	(Follow EU process)	(Follow EU process)	(Follow EU process)
Brazil	4	4	3	1	1	
			Final rules published on			

[26]   The Basel Committee is currently in the process of finalising the details of the Basel III leverage ratio standard. Classification scores for the implementation status will be assigned once the leverage ratio standard is finalised. The agreed start date for banks to begin disclosing their leverage ratios is 1 January 2015.

Country	Basel II	Basel 2.5	Basel III			
			Risk-based capital	G-SIB / D-SIB requirements	Liquidity (LCR)	Leverage ratio[26]
			1 March 2013 will come into force on 1 October 2013.			
Canada	4	4	4	3, 4	1	
			Requiring banks to meet an "all-in" basis – thereby meeting 2019 capital levels but phasing out non-qualifying capital instruments.[27]	(3) Capital rules take effect in January 2016 (4) Final rules issued and additional supervisory expectations and disclosure obligations in effect.	Domestic process has begun and public consultation will commence in October 2013.	Domestic process begun to consider alignment of current Assets-to-Capital Multiple to Basel III leverage requirements.
China	4	4	4	1	1	
				The CBRC is reviewing the specific D-SIB supervisory framework. D-SIB surcharge of 1% has been applied to the five largest Chinese banks since 2010.		A domestic leverage ratio requirement of 4% has been in effect since 2012.
France	4	4	(3)	(3)	(3)	
			(Follow EU process)	(Follow EU process)	(Follow EU process)	(Follow EU process)
Germany	4	4	(3)	(3)	(3)	

[27]   Final rules for the credit valuation adjustment (CVA) issued on 10 December 2012 will come into force on 1 January 2014.

Country	Basel II	Basel 2.5	Basel III			
			Risk-based capital	G-SIB / D-SIB requirements	Liquidity (LCR)	Leverage ratio[26]
			(Follow EU process)	(Follow EU process)	(Follow EU process)	(Follow EU process)
Hong Kong SAR	4	4	4	1	2	
			Final rules on minimum capital standards and associated disclosure requirements took effect on 1 January 2013 and 30 June 2013, respectively. Rules on capital buffers expected to be issued in 2014.	Rules on G-SIB / D-SIB requirements expected to be issued in 2014 (likely in conjunction with rules on capital buffers).	Undertaking industry consultation on implementation of LCR. Rules on LCR expected to be issued in 2014.	Rules on disclosure of leverage ratio expected to be issued in 2014.
India	4	4	4	1	2	
			Footnote[26]		Draft guidelines issued in February 2012. Final rules on LCR are being formulated.	Guidelines issued in May 2012. Leverage Ratio monitoring started from quarter ending June 2013.
Indonesia	4		2	1	1	
		Securitisation exposures are insignificant and prospects remain highly subdued for any material issuance. Furthermore, no bank opts to adopt	Regulation on Basel III capital is to be issued in 2013.	BI is currently conducting a study to determine the appropriate D-SIB framework that fits with the nature of the	BI has started dialogues with supervisors and the banking industry to reach a common interpretation of elements required in	Leverage ratio discussed in Basel III consultative paper released in June 2012.

[26] Final rules for the credit valuation adjustment (CVA) issued for implementation from 1 January 2014. Composition of capital disclosure rules implemented from 1 July 2014. Rules on capital requirements for banks' exposures to central counterparties (CCPs) issued for implementation from 1 January 2014.

Country	Basel II	Basel 2.5	Basel III			
			Risk-based capital	G-SIB / D-SIB requirements	Liquidity (LCR)	Leverage ratio[26]
		the internal model approach (IMA) for market risk. Nevertheless, a consultative paper on Basel 2.5 is to be issued in 2013 to seek the industry's comments on the possible changes to BI's relevant regulations eg BI's 2005 regulation concerning asset securitisation for banks and BI's 2007 regulation concerning market risk internal model.		Indonesian financial system.	the 2013 LCR.	
Italy	4	4	(3)	(3)	(3)	
			(Follow EU process)	(Follow EU process)	(Follow EU process)	(Follow EU process)
Japan	4	4	4	1	1	
			Rules covering capital conservation buffer and the countercyclical buffer not yet issued. Draft regulations expected in 2014/15.			
Korea	4	4	3	1	1	
			Final regulation was published on 3 July 2013 and it will come into force on 1 December 2013.			
Luxembourg	4	4	(3)	(3)	(3)	
			(Follow EU process)	(Follow EU process)	(Follow EU process)	(Follow EU process)

Country	Basel II	Basel 2.5	Basel III			
			Risk-based capital	G-SIB / D-SIB requirements	Liquidity (LCR)	Leverage ratio[26]
Mexico	4	1, 4	4	1	1	
		(1) Other than the Pillar 2 provisions, which have been partially implemented, the remaining aspects will be implemented in 2013. (4) Pillar 2 provisions have been partially implemented.	Rules on banks' exposure to central counterparties (CCPs) not yet issued.			
The Netherlands	4	4	(3)	(3)	(3)	
			(Follow EU process)	(Follow EU process)	(Follow EU process)	(Follow EU process)
Russia	1, 4	1, 4	3	1	1	
	(1) Draft regulations for Pillars 2 and 3 are being developed. They are planned to be published during 2013. (4) Simplified standardised approach for credit risk, simplified approach for market risk and the Basic Indicator Approach for operational risk implemented.	(1) Draft regulations for Pillars 2 and 3 are planned to be published during 2013. (4) Final regulation on the revised standardised approach for market risk in force since 1 February 2013.	Regulation for capital definition and capital adequacy ratios published in February 2013 with draft amendments published in July 2013. Reporting under the new capital rules started at 1 April 2013 with 1 January 2014 being the effective date of their implementation as a regulatory requirement.	Methodology of D-SIB determining is planned to be published for public consultation in 2013.	Draft regulation for LCR developed and planned to be published in 2013.	Draft regulation for leverage ratio planned to be published in 2013 with the parallel run period starting from third quarter of 2013.

Country	Basel II	Basel 2.5	Basel III			
			Risk-based capital	G-SIB / D-SIB requirements	Liquidity (LCR)	Leverage ratio[26]
Saudi Arabia	4	4	4	1	1	
Singapore	4	4	4	1	1	
						See footnote[29]
South Africa	4	4	4	3	3	
	See footnote[30]		A directive has been recently issued which has the effect that the capital charge for credit valuation adjustment (CVA) risk on banks' exposures to ZAR-denominated OTC derivatives and non-ZAR OTC derivatives transacted purely between domestic entities will be zero-rated for the course of	The requirements related to G-SIB/ D-SIB has already been incorporated into the Regulations (Basel III) that were implemented with effect from 1 January 2013. Subsequently the BSD issued a directive to banks regarding the application of the amended capital framework, which	The requirements related to the calculation of and reporting to the BSD of LCR have already been incorporated into the Regulations (Basel III) that were implemented with effect from 1 January 2013, which is currently primarily being used for monitoring purposes. Subsequently the BSD	The requirements related to the calculation of and reporting to the Bank Supervision Department (BSD) of a leverage ratio have already been incorporated into the Regulations (Basel III) that were implemented with effect from 1 January 2013, which is currently primarily

[29]   MAS has published and implemented requirements on the calculation of the leverage ratio and reporting to MAS in MAS Notice 637, based on the rules published in the Basel III text dated 16 December 2010 (revised 1 June 2011). The Basel rules on the Leverage Ratio are expected to be updated by the end of 2013 for the implementation of the disclosure requirement by 1 January 2015, and the final Basel rules on the Leverage Ratio are expected to be published in 2017. MAS will reference these revisions in the Basel rules and implement them in their regulations accordingly.

[30]   The Regulations that contain the Basel II, Basel 2.5 and Basel III requirements are available at www.resbank.co.za/publications/detail-item-view/pages/publications.aspx?sarbweb=3b6aa07d-92ab-441f-b7bf-bb7d1b1bedb4&sarblist=21b5222e-7125-4e55-bb55-58fd3333371e&sarbitem=5442.

Country	Basel II	Basel 2.5	Basel III			
			Risk-based capital	G-SIB / D-SIB requirements	Liquidity (LCR)	Leverage ratio[26]
			2013, ie until 31 December 2013.[31]	includes the requirements related to G-SIBs / D-SIBs.[32]	issued a directive to banks to incorporate the updated LCR framework issued by the Basel Committee during January 2013.[33]	being used for monitoring purposes.
Spain	4	4	(3)	(3)	(3)	
			(Follow EU process)	(Follow EU process)	(Follow EU process)	(Follow EU process)
Sweden	4	4	(3)	(3)	(3)	
			(Follow EU process)	(Follow EU process)	(Follow EU process) The Basel Committee's December 2010 LCR is implemented and in force.[34]	(Follow EU process)
Switzerland	4	4	4	4	4, 1	
				Final rule in force for G-SIBs and D-SIBs.	(4) Published requirements for monitoring period for LCR until end 2014.	Test reporting planned for the fourth quarter of 2013. Requirements for LR monitoring

[31] This came about as a result of the limited time between the finalisation by the Basel Committee of the proposed rules and the intended date of implementation, and the absence of a domestic central counterparty for domestic OTC derivatives transactions.

[32] The directive is available at www.resbank.co.za/publications/detail-item-view/pages/publications.aspx?sarbweb=3b5aa07d-92ab-441f-b7bf-bb7dfb1bedb4&sarblist=21b5222e-7125-4e55-bb65-58fd3333371e&sarbitem=5686.

[33] The directive is available at www.resbank.co.za/publications/detail-item-view/pages/publications.aspx?sarbweb=3b5aa07d-92ab-441f-b7bf-bb7dfb1bedb4&sarblist=21b5222e-7125-4e55-bb65-58fd3333371e&sarbitem=5626.

[34] The rule is available at http://fi.se/Folder-EN/Startpage/Regulations/Regulatory-Code/FFFS-201206/.

Country	Basel II	Basel 2.5	Basel III			
			Risk-based capital	G-SIB / D-SIB requirements	Liquidity (LCR)	Leverage ratio[26]
					Published qualitative requirements for liquidity risk management. (1) Started discussion with industry on draft LCR rules. Consultation of draft ordinance planned for Oct 2013. Enactment planned for first quarter of 2014.	period planned for mid-2014.
Turkey	4	4	2	1	2	
			Draft regulations issued in February 2013.		Draft regulation issued in July 2013.	Draft regulation issued in March 2013.
United Kingdom	4	4	(3)	(3)	(3)	
			(Follow EU process)	(Follow EU process)	(Follow EU process)	(Follow EU process)
United States	4	3, 4	3	1	1	
	Parallel run ongoing: all Basel II mandatory institutions are required to implement the advanced approaches to credit risk and operational risk. Banks have made significant progress in implementation efforts and those institutions in parallel run are reporting both Basel I and Basel II regulatory capital ratios to supervisors on a	(4) Final market risk capital requirements, which incorporate Basel 2.5, became effective on 1 January 2013. (3) Other Basel 2.5 revisions included as part of the final Basel III rule approved in July 2013, effective 1 January 2014.	Final Basel III rule approved in July 2013, effective 1 January 2014.	US agencies currently anticipate issuance of a notice of proposed rulemaking to implement the G-SIB framework by year-end 2013, pending finalisation of this framework by the Basel Committee.	US agencies currently anticipate issuance of a notice of proposed rulemaking with regard to the LCR by year-end 2013.	Leverage ratio included in final Basel III rule approved in July 2013 and effective 1 January 2014. Existing US leverage ratio remains in effect. Basel III leverage ratio reporting begins 1 January 2015, and compliance with minimum requirements begins 1 January 2018.

Country	Basel II	Basel 2.5	Basel III			
			Risk-based capital	G-SIB / D-SIB requirements	Liquidity (LCR)	Leverage ratio[26]
	quarterly basis. US institutions in parallel run remain subject to Basel I capital requirements.					
European Union	4	4	3	3	3	
			The agreement between the European Parliament and the EU Council on the legislative texts implementing Basel III and further measures regarding sound corporate governance and remuneration structures published in the Official Journal[25] on 27 June 2013 with a date of application of 1 January 2014. The legislative texts are Directive (No 2013/36) and Regulation (No 575/2013). Where necessary, detailed technical standards will be prepared by EBA and adopted by the Commission on a timely	Mandatory G-SIB and optional D-SIB buffers implemented by Article 131 of Directive No 2013/36 with date of application of 1 January 2016.	LCR to be implemented by a delegated act to be adopted by the Commission before 30 June 2014 for application in 2015 (cf Article 460 Regulation No 575/2013).	Mandatory disclosure of leverage ratio from 1 January 2015 (cf Articles 451 and 521 of Regulation 575/2013).

[25]   Available at http://eur-lex.europa.eu/JOHtml.do?uri=OJ:L:2013:176:SOM:EN:HTML.

21   Progress report on Basel III implementation

Country	Basel II	Basel 2.5	Basel III			
			Risk-based capital	G-SIB / D-SIB requirements	Liquidity (LCR)	Leverage ratio[26]
			basis.			

Annex 2: Adoption of Basel standards by non-Basel Committee/non-EU jurisdictions: 2013 FSI survey

The FSI survey covers the same scope as the BCBS survey—jurisdictions' regulatory adoption of Basel II, Basel 2.5 and Basel III.

Methodology

For the status of adoption of Basel regulatory rules, the FSI uses the same classification adopted by the Basel Committee: (1) Draft regulation not published; (2) Draft regulation published; (3) Final rule published; (4) Final rule in force. If a jurisdiction gets classification of 2, 3 or 4 for at least one subsection of Basel II, Basel 2.5 or Basel III, the jurisdiction will be deemed to be in the process of implementing the rules.

Tables

Basel II: Implemented / in the process of implementation (54 as of end-May 2013)

Jurisdiction	Jurisdiction	Jurisdiction	Jurisdiction
Armenia Bahrain	Georgia	Madagascar	Philippines
Bangladesh	Gibraltar	Malaw Malaysia	Qatar
Barbados	Guatemala	Mauritius	Republic of Macedonia
Bermuda	Guernsey	Montenegro	Serbia
Bolivia	Honduras	Morocco	Seychelles
Bosnia and Herzegovina	Iceland	Mozambique	Sri Lanka
Cayman Islands	Isle of Man	Namibia Nepal	Thailand
Chinese Taipei	Jersey	New Zealand	The Republic of
Colombia	Jordan	Norway Oman	Belarus
Congo	Kosovo	Paraguay	Uganda
Costa Rica	Kuwait	Peru	United Arab Emirates
Dominican Republic	Lebanon	Uruguay	Zimbabwe
Egypt	Liechtenstein		
	Macao		

Basel 2.5: Implemented / in the process of implementation (16 as of end-May 2013)

Jurisdiction	Jurisdiction	Jurisdiction	Jurisdiction
Bahrain	Egypt	Lebanon	Nepal
Barbados	Gibraltar	Liechtenstein	Norway
Cayman Islands	Iceland	Malawi	Uganda
Chinese Taipei	Jersey	Morocco	United Arab Emirates

Basel III: Implemented / in the process of implementation (26 as of end-May 2013)

Jurisdiction	Jurisdiction	Jurisdiction	Jurisdiction
Bolivia	Kosovo	Norway	The Republic of Belarus
Chinese Taipei	Lebanon	Peru	Uganda
Colombia	Malaysia	Philippines	United Arab Emirates
Costa Rica	Morocco	Qatar	Uruguay
Egypt	Namibia	Republic of	Zimbabwe
Georgia	Nepal	Macedonia	
Gibraltar	New Zealand	Serbia	
		Thailand	

16D. *Bailouts and Political Accountability*

This excerpt addresses an important aspect of the crisis's resolution: the political legitimacy of bailouts. Systemic risk is a big theme of the crisis, but what does it mean? When we say that a firm is too big to fail or that it's too interconnected to fail, we are typically talking about systemic risk because the firm's failure is likely to affect the entire financial system, if not the economy. But this author suggests that systemic risk is actually a political issue. What do you think of his idea of using the median voter to determine the social tolerance of economic harm? Is it a practical metric? Is he right that a leave-it-to-the-regulators approach is mistaken? What about his argument that regulators should take into account the response of a median voter to her decisions in a crisis? The article has a good discussion of Dodd-Frank's ex-ante and ex-post provisions regarding systemic risk. Regarding OLA, how does one determine "socially unacceptable loss allocations"? As you know, the Fed's use of section 13 (3) of the Federal Reserve Act during the crisis provoked much controversy. As the author indicates, the Fed used this provision to bail out Bear Stearns and to create the various lending facilities used to combat the crisis. Do you agree with his assessment of its use? It seems like transparency is important to just about everything in life. Here, the author argues that transparency is a way to keep regulators politically accountable. In his discussion of the AIG bailout, he argues that transparency would have prevented the US government from using taxpayer dollars to bail out foreign banks. Doesn't that feed into xenophobia? The author says that political accountability "is not necessarily a good thing." What do you think? What do you think of his argument that the Fed should not have resolution authority? What about a council of regulators? And the use of haircuts in terms of political accountability?

A. J. Levitin, "In Defense of Bailouts," *99 Geo L.J. 435* (2011)

INTRODUCTION

The financial crisis of 2007–2009 witnessed a spectacular parade of bankruptcies, distressed sales, and bailouts of major financial and industrial firms. The government response to the crisis was haphazard. Some failed firms were resolved through the bankruptcy process without government assistance. Others were resolved in bankruptcy but with government financing. Yet others were resolved through FDIC resolution processes. Some were sold in government-blessed distressed transactions, while others were sold with guarantees from the Federal Reserve or bailed out with direct loans from the Federal Reserve. Government-sponsored housing finance enterprises Fannie Mae and Freddie Mac were bailed out first with limited, and then with open-ended, commitments of preferred stock investment from the U.S. Treasury. And under the Trouble Asset Relief Program (TARP), 842 companies—including auto manufacturers, banks, finance companies, investment companies, insurance companies, and mortgage servicers—received direct capital investment from the U.S. Treasury.

The government's handling of the crisis provoked widespread dissatisfaction because of its haphazardness, because of its lack of transparency, and because of the use of taxpayer dollars to support private companies, many of which had engaged in activities that contributed to the crisis. Although Congress approved some bailout activities, much of the government intervention in the market was through the Federal Reserve, an agency designed to be insulated from political influence.

The bailouts' processes and results—in which some firms' creditors took losses while others' did not—fueled popular outrage and undercut the bailouts' political legitimacy. The bailout of AIG, in particular, stirred great public backlash because of its lack of transparency, the lack of loss sharing between the government and AIG's creditors, and the sizeable bonuses AIG paid out after the bailout. Bailouts are often multistage affairs, and the severity of the popular backlash means that it will be difficult for the government to intervene to stem further economic collapse, either domestically or globally. Indeed, the ability to respond adequately to future crises will be limited by dissatisfaction with the legitimacy of the response in 2007–2009. Recognition of the problems with the federal response to the financial crisis made addressing the systemic risks posed by systemically important—or "too-big-to-fail" (TBTF)—firms a centerpiece of the financial regulatory reform agenda.

This Article explores the political and economic tensions in systemic risk regulation and TBTF resolution. It sets forth a new definition of systemic risk that is sensitive to bailouts' political accountability and legitimacy problems. It also challenges several widely held conceptions about systemic risk and sets forth a framework for analyzing bailout structures with an eye towards enhancing their political legitimacy . . .

* * *

I.   TOO BIG TO FAIL AND SYSTEMIC RISK

A.   DEFINING SYSTEMIC RISK

1.   Existing Definitions

The starting point for considering responses to the systemic risk is to define it. The term systemic risk is not a term of art with a precise, generally accepted definition. There have been numerous attempts to define the term "systemic risk." None has yielded a simple, precise, meaningful, and easy-to-use definition. Existing definitions are at once too narrow and too vague and fail to account for the political nature of systemic risk responses.

The existing literature has generally identified systemic risk as the risk of a single firm's failure having substantial negative effects on the broader economy. As far as it goes, this definition is fine. It is not an especially useful definition for thinking about whether a particular firm's failure truly poses systemic risk or how responses to systemic risk should be structured.

The existing literature has not attempted to deal with the question of how much of an impact on the broader economy is sufficient to make a risk "systemic." Instead, definitions simply posit that the impact must be "substantial," or "a good deal bigger and worse" than the failure of any one firm, or have "significant adverse effects on the real economy," or present the risk of "clear and significant damage to the real economy."

Some definitions have attempted slightly more specificity, such as "substantial volatility in asset prices, significant reductions in corporate liquidity, potential bankruptcies and efficiency losses" or "resulting in increases in the cost of capital or decreases in its availability, often evidenced by substantial financial-market price volatility." These definitions, however, are still keyed to a "substantial" metric, without being able to define "substantial" in reference to anything in particular. Thus, E. Gerald Corrigan, the President of the Federal Reserve Bank of New York, argued that it is necessary to distinguish between disruptions versus crises, with only the latter being systemic. Corrigan, however, did not provide a method for distinguishing between disruptions and crises, leading economist Lawrence H. Summers to posit that "The issue of what constitutes a financial crisis is semantic."

What sort of risk is systemic is only semantic in the sense that there is not an objective metric against which it can evaluated. Exactly what level of impact is unacceptable is a variable matter; one observer might judge a risk to be systemic, another not. This type of loose definition is not a firm basis on which to build policy. Accordingly, it is worth approaching the definitional question *da capo*.

Taken literally, systemic risk is the risk posed to a "system." But the risk posed by what? And to which system?

The risk is posed by the inability of a firm or number of firms to honor their obligations as they come due. The definition of the system will vary by context; systemic risk has been a concern in payment systems for decades, but when discussed in that context, it is the risk that the particular financial technology system—say the wire transfer system—will go down because of a participant firm's failure. The ultimate impact of such a system failure could be far-reaching, but the concern is really about the particular system itself, not the downstream effects.

Other times, the system in reference is variously the "depository system," the "banking system," or even the "financial system"—the latter seemingly covering all of financial intermediation. Again, the term is being used to refer to a discrete system. In these contexts, however, and even in the payment system context, the implied (but often unvoiced) concern is that the failure of a financial intermediation system would affect the real economy.

2.   A Political Definition of Systemic Risk

Thus, as used in this Article, systemic risk is not a concern about a discrete technology system or even about the system of financial intermediation, but a concern about the broader economy. The failure of a technology system for payments clearance might have far-reaching consequences, or might not. Only if the risk's realization would have such far-reaching consequences would we call it systemic in the sense used in this Article.

Thus, we might define systemic risk as the risk that the failure of a particular quantum of institutions will result in a socially unacceptable macroeconomic contraction. Put differently, systemic risk is the risk of socially unbearable macroeconomic consequences of microeconomic failures.

There are three critical points about this definition. First, it is not about an absolute measure of macroeconomic impact from an individual firm's failure, but about whether society is willing to tolerate that level of macroeconomic impact. This is a political, rather than an economic, question. So conceived, systemic risk is ultimately a political issue, not an economic issue. Therefore, we need to look to a political, rather than an economic, measure of systemic risk.

The best measure we have of social tolerance of economic harm is electoral expression. Accordingly, this Article uses the median voter as the metric for social tolerance of macroeconomic impact.

Although the median voter is a good electoral guide in a democracy, the median voter might well make poor choices that he or she will later regret. The median voter has less than perfect information, suffers from cognitive biases, and is far from knowledgeable about financial markets. Put differently, the median voter is not an expert and may not know what is good for him or her. Why should such an individual's anxieties be the metric of systemic risk?

The reason we should defer to as frail and imperfect a metric as the median voter is that absent the median voter's support, government's ability to take the technical steps necessary to respond to financial crises is constrained. Political legitimacy is critical for ensuring that government responses to financial crisis are effective. Serious crises often require repeated government actions, and the perceived legitimacy of one governmental action affects the government's range of actions in the future. If the government response is seen as an overreaction, the political blowback can dissuade regulators from taking future actions, even if prudent. The ability of government to respond effectively to financial crises is determined in large part by whether the median voter perceives a crisis that merits governmental response.

It is also worthwhile to consider the alternative approach to using a median voter metric—relying on regulatory expertise to identify systemic risk. Although there are problems with the ability of the median voter's evaluative process, the case for placing the systemic risk determination in the hands of expert regulators is far from convincing.

Experts—including financial regulators—frequently disagree as to the causes of and solutions for financial crises. Experts themselves suffer from cognitive biases and have less than perfect information, particularly during financial crises. They also frequently fail to agree on the proper course of action. And to the extent that a financial crisis can be attributed, in part, to regulatory failures, the very existence of a crisis casts doubt on the expert regulators' ability to handle one. For example, the same regulators who oversaw the build-up of the housing bubble and the expansion of shadow banking were the same people responsible for managing the crisis response in 2008.

There is also good reason to question the value of regulators' expertise producing optimal outcomes. U.S. regulators failed to use the six months after Bear Stearns's failure in March 2008 to prepare for the difficulties that came to a head in September 2008. The decision to permit Lehman Brothers to file for bankruptcy arguably exacerbated the financial crisis of 2008, and had consequences beyond those anticipated by regulators. Lehman Brothers is hardly an isolated incident. The Federal Home Loan Bank Board's 1982 decision to change regulatory capital accounting procedures to permit a longer amortization period for "supervisory goodwill" for savings and loans (S & Ls) exacerbated the S&L crisis. This move was intended to facilitate the purchase of failed S&Ls by solvent S&Ls, but instead enabled insolvent S & Ls to continue operating. The insolvent S&Ls responded by making double-or-nothing bets on the commercial real estate market, which, when they flopped, only deepened their insolvency.

The point here is not that expertise (and experience) is useless, but that experts are fallible, just like median voters, and we should be hesitant to overrate the value of expertise when gauging systemic risk. Moreover, few expert regulators are truly shielded from political pressure.

The solution, this Article proposes, is to meld political legitimacy and expertise by developing procedures that regularize governmental response to systemic risk. If procedures that are put in place *ex ante* are followed during a crisis, compliance with those procedures alone increases the legitimacy of the response. Procedure can thus substitute for legitimacy. Proceduralizing the implementation of bailouts (but not their contents other than in broad terms) is the best way for balancing expertise and political legitimacy.

There are limits to this median voter metric. Voting is an expression of many things, which suggests that instead of a simple median voter approach, it might be better to use a probabilistic voting model that accounts for the numerosity and density of voters that find the macroeconomic consequences unacceptable. This model should also measure how this electoral issue ranks among the median voter's other concerns. Economic security, however, is often a critical and overriding electoral issue when it arises, so the median voter metric might suffice.

For purposes of this Article, the distinction between a median voter and a probabilistic voter is not crucial. Instead, what is important is that social risk tolerance is gauged electorally, thereby tying responses to systemic risk to political legitimacy. Because of this electorally-linked definition of systemic risk, it is important that the governmental body that determines whether a risk is systemic, and therefore how to respond, be politically responsive to the median voter. If the government is sensitive to the political consequences of its decision-making, it will attempt to act in accordance with its perception of the median voter's macroeconomic risk tolerance in order to maximize its electoral appeal. Aligning systemic risk response with political accountability is an important step in guaranteeing the perceived political legitimacy of the response. This Article's definition, then, sees systemic risk as ultimately a political expression of social risk tolerance, rather than a measurable economic construct, equivalent to default risk, currency-conversion risk, or interest-rate risk.

There are inherent difficulties in gauging median voter preferences. Median voter preferences cannot be gauged accurately or in real time.

Preferences may in fact be dynamic as they change in response to informational or situational changes. Our primary tool for gauging voter preferences is elections, but elections do not necessarily express voters' revealed preferences on any particular issue, and typically do so with some delay from the time when a risk's character is being gauged. Voting is generally on a limited menu of candidates, each of whom represents a bundle of positions on various issues, rather than positions on a particular issue. Moreover, voting is generally local, rather than national. The only national election—for President and Vice President—occurs only once every four years and through the Electoral College, rather than by direct popular vote.

Thus, what is ultimately being gauged is what median voter preferences are likely to be at the next moment of electoral discipline. The median voter measure is not an actual measure of median voter preferences, but instead a measure of the *perception* of future median voter preferences at a particular electoral moment. This measure introduces the problem of misperception of future median voter preferences and over- or under-compensation of perceived risk due to electoral risk averseness. On the other hand, it has the benefit of gauging voter preferences in the future, after some delay. The median voter is likely to be incompletely informed about a financial crisis while the crisis is happening; delay likely improves the information available to the median voter.

Because of the impossibility of perfectly measuring median voter preferences (not to mention the potentially dynamic nature of these preferences), the best that can be done is to try to maximize the political accountability of systemic risk policy. This means placing policy decisions in the hands of more, rather than less, politically accountable entities. The more politically accountable a decision-making entity, the more it will attempt to gauge median voter preferences. Tying systemic risk policy to political accountability in this manner is far from perfect, but greater political accountability via electoral discipline, however imperfect, enhances the legitimacy, and therefore the effectiveness, of systemic risk response . . .

Third, this definition of systemic risk is in no way restricted to financial firms. Treatments of systemic risk generally focus exclusively on financial institutions with the implicit assumption that nonfinancial firms do not generate systemic risk. They also measure macroeconomic impacts in terms of the cost or availability of capital.

A view of systemic risk that fails to look beyond financial institutions is too narrow. While financial firms may be a particular locus of systemic risk, such systemic risk can derive from nonfinancial firms and from entities like state and local governments as well. This Article views macroeconomic impacts more broadly. Not only are costs and availability of capital measures of macroeconomic impact, but so too are factors such as unemployment and reduced economic output (in other words, productivity).

Moreover, when we expand our view of systemic risk to nonfinancial firms, the geographic scope of systemic risk changes. Financial institutions in the United States, and indeed the world, are well integrated; the market for capital is both national (as with retail deposits) and global (hence the carry trade). Thus, when systemic risk is viewed solely as a matter of financial institutions, it makes sense to measure macroeconomic impacts in national or global terms. But when we also include nonfinancial firms in the universe of systemic risk, it is necessary to look at regional macroeconomic effects, such as regional unemployment.

At some point, to be sure, there is a limit to how small of an economic region can be reasonably used to analyze systemic risk. Because this Article views systemic risk in terms of social norms—how much of an economic downturn will a society tolerate—there is inherent fluidity in the geographic scope involved, and it will often relate to the political clout of a particular region. For example, a sharp economic downturn in unrepresented, peripheral territories like Guam or Puerto Rico might not be viewed as socially unacceptable by the national electorate, whereas an equivalent downturn in a metropolitan center, such as New York City, in a populous and politically powerful state such as California, or in an electorally critical region, such as Ohio, might be.

Under this Article's definition, systemic risk is not quantifiable in economic terms. In some circumstances, a 1% increase in the cost of capital or unemployment might be a sufficient macroeconomic impact to make an individual firm's failure pose a systemic risk; in other situations, the threshold might be a 10% increase. While systemic risk is about individual firms' failure having broader economic consequences, what makes such consequences systemic or not is ultimately a valuation driven by social norms and political culture. Systemic risk is ultimately a political, rather than an economic, matter . . .

* * *

II. THE LIMITS OF SYSTEMIC RISK REGULATION

One approach to systemic risk is to try to mitigate or eliminate it through *ex ante* regulation. This can be done by eliminating firms or practices that create systemic risk, monitoring systemic risk, and responding as needed before crisis occurs, ensuring that firms are more resilient to financial mishaps, and ensuring that firms can be resolved more easily . . .

* * *

I. THE DODD-FRANK ACT

The approach taken by Congress in the Dodd-Frank Wall Street Reform and Consumer Protection Act (Dodd-Frank) incorporates many of the previously discussed approaches to systemic risk regulation. Titles I and II of Dodd-Frank deal with systemic risk regulation and resolution authority. Dodd-Frank's general approach to systemic risk is to emphasize improved macroprudential monitoring and regulation for financial firms and to provide a liquidation procedure for bank holding companies (BHCs) and systemically important nonbank financial companies (NFCs). Dodd-Frank thus puts great weight on reducing systemic risk through *ex ante* regulation but consigns ex post risk mitigation to a receivership process . . . That adds little flexibility that does not already exist in bankruptcy resolutions of BHCs and bankruptcy-eligible NFCs.

Title I of Dodd-Frank is focused on *ex ante* systemic risk regulation. It creates a regulatory entity charged with monitoring systemic risk and extends prudential regulatory powers. Dodd-Frank establishes the Financial Stability Oversight Council (FSOC) comprising ten voting members—the Treasury Secretary, the Federal Reserve Board Chairman, the Comptroller of the Currency, the Director of the newly created Bureau of Consumer Financial Protection, the Securities and Exchange Commission Chairman, the Federal Deposit Insurance Corporation Chairperson, the Commodities Futures Trading Commission Chairperson, the Federal Housing Finance Agency Director, the Chairman of the National Credit Union Administration Board, and an independent insurance expert appointed by the President—and five nonvoting members.

The FSOC is charged with identifying risks to the financial stability of the United States, promoting "market discipline, by eliminating expectations on the part of shareholders, creditors, and counterparties of such companies that the Government will shield them from losses in the event of failure," and responding to "emerging threats to the stability of the United States financial system." The FSOC is to be supported in its work by an Office of Financial Research, and funded by assessments on large BHCs—those with consolidated assets of over $50 billion—and systemically important NFCs.

The FSOC's duties are primarily limited to monitoring the U.S. economy and making recommendations for action to the primary regulators of various financial institutions. The FSOC cannot undertake prudential regulation on its own. The only prudential authority it has requires a prior determination by the Federal Reserve Board (the Fed) that a firm poses a systemic risk. In such a case, and only for large BHCs (holding more than $50 billion in consolidated assets) and systemically important NFCs, the

FSOC may, by a two-thirds majority vote, limit mergers and acquisitions, restrict the offering of financial products, require the termination of activities, impose conditions on the firm's activities, or require asset sales.

Although the FSOC's prudential authority is limited, Dodd-Frank establishes expanded prudential regulation for BHCs—already subject to Federal Reserve regulation—and certain NFCs determined by the FSOC to be systemically important and thus subject to Fed regulation. As part of its prudential regulation, the Fed is directed to set risk-based capital and leverage requirements, liquidity requirements, overall risk management requirements, nonbinding resolution plan and credit exposure report requirements, and concentration limits. The Fed is also authorized to impose contingent capital requirements, enhanced public disclosure requirements, short-term debt limits, and other prudential standards it deems appropriate. Dodd-Frank further requires BHCs with assets over $10 billion and publicly traded nonbank financial companies to establish a risk committee on their boards, and requires periodic stress testing by both regulators and the firms themselves. The Fed is also empowered to require early remediation actions by BHCs and NFCs.

Dodd-Frank incorporates all of these potential approaches to *ex ante* regulations. For BHCs, it imposes regulatory costs on bigness by imposing assessments and some regulatory requirements based on asset size. For NFCs, it imposes costs on bigness and interconnectedness by subjecting these firms to the Fed's prudential regulation and assessments. Dodd-Frank creates a type of firewall through its adoption of the Volcker Rule, limiting the proprietary trading and investing activities of depositaries. It requires living wills and more robust microprudential regulation to improve capital structures. Executive compensation is not itself directly regulated by Dodd-Frank, but the Act does have provisions for all publicly traded companies—including TBTF firms—enhancing compensation committee independence, providing increased disclosure and improved reporting of executive compensation, and subjecting executive compensation to a nonbinding shareholder vote. The assessments on large BHCs and NFCs to fund oversight and the costs of receiverships function somewhat like an insurance fund. The creation of the FSOC provides a systemic risk regulator with the ability to intervene *ex ante* on an ad hoc basis . . .

No matter how well *ex ante* regulation is done, it can only mitigate, but not eliminate, systemic risk. Some quantum of systemic risk will always exist. The remaining risk must be addressed ex post, once a crisis has emerged, through resolution. The following section considers the importance of resolution systems and the inherent inability of bankruptcy-type resolution regimes to deal with TBTF firms . . .

III. TOO BIG TO FAIL RESOLUTION

* * *

C. BANKRUPTCY VERSUS BAILOUTS: AN ILLUSORY CHOICE

* * *

2.   The Dodd-Frank Act's Orderly Liquidation Authority

Unfortunately, in the Dodd-Frank Act, Congress chose to subscribe to the fiction that bailouts can be banned. Dodd-Frank is formally titled as "An Act . . . to end 'too big to fail', to protect the American taxpayer by ending bailouts . . . ," and one of its provisions specifically prohibits "Federal Government Bailouts of Swaps Entities," while another prohibits taxpayer funding of resolutions. Thus, Dodd-Frank provides for an "Orderly Liquidation Authority" (OLA) for systemically important firms that is essentially an FDIC bank receivership model applied to bank holding companies and systemically important nonbank financial companies. In terms of maximizing value of the failed firm's assets, OLA is quite flexible. Even though OLA formally permits only liquidation, not reorganization, a functional reorganization could be achieved through the sale of all or substantially all assets to a new company. But in terms of loss allocation, OLA has only slightly greater flexibility than Chapter 7 bankruptcy, because it is bound to a priority scheme from whence deviation is not permitted for policy concerns.

The OLA process has a complex procedural trigger. First, there must be a determination of systemic risk: a process colloquially called "three keys turning." This determination requires a two-thirds vote of the Federal Reserve Board (key one) plus a two-thirds vote from the FDIC (key two), unless the firm is a broker-dealer or insurance company, in which case a two-thirds vote from the SEC or the approval of the Director of the Federal Insurance Office is substituted for the FDIC vote. After the systemic risk determination is made, it must be ratified by the Treasury Secretary, in consultation with the President (key three). The Treasury Secretary must document the decision and make reports to Congress and the public, subject to a subsequent GAO review. If the determination is ratified, notice is provided to the firm and FDIC. If the firm acquiesces, the FDIC is appointed as receiver. Otherwise, the Treasury Secretary must petition the United States District Court for the District of Columbia to appoint the FDIC as receiver. The court has twenty-four hours to make a ruling or the FDIC is automatically appointed as receiver. The receivership can last up to five years.

Once the FDIC is appointed as receiver for an OLA process, an automatic stay goes into place, and the FDIC proceeds to liquidate the firm. The liquidation itself is similar to an FDIC bank receivership, meaning that the FDIC acts as receiver for the failed firm and is in charge of adjudicating claims and maximizing the value of the firms' assets, including using a bridge financial institution arrangement, avoidance powers, and providing post-receivership funding (equivalent to DIP financing).

The receivership process is subject to its own priority scheme that requires absolute priority as well as equal treatment for similar creditors in most cases. Deviation from the priority system is only allowed for cases in which it would maximize the value of the firm's assets or reduce losses from the resolution; there is no authority to deviate priority to reduce systemic risk, nor is there authority to guarantee the obligations owed to third parties. The FDIC is also empowered to recoup the prior two years' compensation paid to a current or former senior executive or director who is substantially responsible for the failed condition of the firm.

The FDIC's expenses in the receivership process are to be funded by an "Orderly Liquidation Fund," which is to be funded through assessments on bank holding companies with more than $50 billion in consolidated assets and systemically important nonbank financial companies. Dodd-Frank also includes a cryptic provision that "[t]axpayers shall bear no losses from the exercise of any authority under this title." Although this provision likely means that taxpayers shall not bear any of the costs of the U.S. government as receiver, it could be read to provide that the U.S. government as pre-receivership creditor shall not incur any losses in a liquidation, so that any government losses would be recovered from assessments on financial institutions.

The major distinctions between the OLA process and a Chapter 11 process are whether there is a formal versus de facto ability to reorganize; the use of government as receiver, rather than a debtor in possession or trustee; slightly different priority schemes; and the process being run through an administrative agency, rather than though a court. These differences give the FDIC much more control over the process, but they do little to actually ensure that the process is better able to contain the systemic consequences of the firms' failure. Whether OLA will be followed in future crises will depend on whether it will produce socially acceptable distributional outcomes. If an OLA proceeding would result in socially unacceptable loss allocations, it is likely to be abandoned either for improvised resolution or for the statutory framework to be stretched, as with the Bankruptcy Code in GM and Chrysler, to permit outcomes not intended to be allowed.

* * *

IV. BAILOUT STRUCTURES

* * *

Bailout structures need to ensure political legitimacy in order to ensure efficacy. The ability to respond adequately to later stages of a crisis or future crises depends on the perceived political legitimacy of the initial crisis response. If a crisis response provokes a political backlash because it is perceived as illegitimate, it can hobble the ability of government to respond to future crises even when such responses would be in accord with social risk tolerance thresholds. Crisis responses are often built upon the model of previous responses, and backlash against a particular response can distort future responses and result in government permitting socially unacceptable macroeconomic harms to occur.

1.   Historical Bailout Mechanisms

* * *

The Fed's statutory authority as LOLR has evolved over time. When the Fed was established in 1913, it was authorized to lend solely to member banks via rediscounting (at the "discount window"). Rediscounting involved the Fed advancing funds to its member banks on the security of loans that the member banks had made. Thus, if a member bank failed to repay its loan to the Fed, the Fed would keep the underlying loan as collateral. Originally, the only eligible collateral was commercial and agricultural loans; government securities were not acceptable collateral. The Fed's rediscounting powers were gradually expanded to allow for greater flexibility in collateral.

The July 1932 legislation that expanded the [Reconstruction Finance Corporation]'s powers to permit it to lend to entities other than financial institutions also expanded the Fed's authority by adding section 13(3) to the Federal Reserve Act. Section 13(3) allowed the Fed, "[i]n unusual and exigent circumstances," with supermajority consent of five of the seven Fed governors, "to discount for any individual, partnership, or corporation, notes, drafts, and bills of exchange . . . that are indorsed or otherwise secured to the satisfaction of the Federal Reserve bank" if there was "evidence that such individual, partnership, or corporation is unable to secure adequate credit accommodations from other banking institutions."

Two years later, the Fed's authority was further expanded with the addition of section 13(b) to the Federal Reserve Act, which allowed regional Federal Reserve banks to make advances of working capital to established businesses, if these businesses were unable to find capital elsewhere. The Fed's Section 13(b) authority for making such loans was revoked in 1958 and transferred to the nascent Small Business Administration. Authority to discount notes, drafts, and bills of exchange for nonbanks under section 13(3) remained, however, and in 1991, as part of a major overhaul of the bank regulatory system, the requirement that the assets discounted for nonbanks be "of the kinds and maturities made eligible for discount for member banks under other provisions of this Act" was removed, as well as language that prohibited the discounting under section 13(3) of "notes, drafts, and bills covering merely investments or drawn for the purpose of carrying or trading in stocks, bonds, or other investment securities" other than U.S. government securities.

Section 13(3) was probably never intended as a source of bailout authority. Neither its language nor the circumstances of its adoption lend themselves to such an interpretation. Thus, section 13(3) does not require any sort of finding of systemic risk. The terminology did not exist when section 13(3) was first drafted, but even the "unusual and exigent circumstances" requirement does not necessarily indicate systemic risk, just market disruption.

Nor does section 13(3) indicate that it is meant to authorize any sort of rescue financing. The language refers to firms being unable to find financing elsewhere, but assumes that the firms can post sufficient collateral for rediscounting. That is, section 13(3) was designed to address liquidity problems, not solvency problems. A bailout often involves the latter, as well as the former (to the extent they are distinguishable). Finally, it is worth noting what is missing in section 13(3): the ability to either guarantee debts or lend on an unsecured basis. True LOLR bailout authority would include both.

When viewed in historical context, it is even harder to see section 13(3) as a bailout statute. When the statute was enacted in 1932, systemic risk was already a reality; the problem at hand during the Great Depression was that financial institutions were unwilling to lend, even to creditworthy borrowers. The Fed's section 13(3) authority, like the RFC lending authority it backstopped, was intended as a response to market failures, rather than firm failures. Neither the RFC nor the Fed was authorized to act as a bailout agency. Each was instead authorized to be a literal LOLR for when the market was frozen. Indeed, this was Congress's interpretation when it last revisited section 13(3) in 1991, as evidenced by Congress's decision to place the 1991 amendment under the section heading of "Emergency Liquidity," a heading which does not imply a power to recapitalize insolvent firms or address systemic risk.

The Fed has used its section 13(3) powers "sparingly"; between 1932 and 1936, the Fed made 123 direct loans under section 13(3), totaling about $1.5 million. It is not clear whether any of these loans were bailouts per se. The Fed again invoked section 13(3) in 1966 and 1969 to offer loans to S&Ls and savings banks that were having trouble raising capital because of interest rate ceilings from Regulation Q, but no loans were actually granted. Thereafter, section 13(3) was not used again until March 11, 2008. Not surprisingly, the Fed's LOLR authority for nonbanks was noted by only four contemporary legal articles prior to the financial crisis, only one of which gave it more than passing reference.

Beginning in March 2008, however, the Fed routinely invoked its section 13(3) authority for all of its market interventions. First, on March 11, 2008, the Fed established the Term Securities Lending Facility (TSLF), which allowed primary dealers in U.S. government securities—investment banks—to borrow U.S. government securities on a full-recourse basis, provided that such privileged dealers posted government-backed or investment-grade securities (including MBS) as collateral. Subsequently, Section 13(3) provided the authority for an extension of nonrecourse credit to JPMorgan Chase Bank to provide assistance to Bear Stearns (which ultimately led to the creation of Maiden Lane LLC), as well as the creation of various lending facilities. These newly established lending facilities included the Primary Dealer Credit Facility (PDCF), the Asset-Backed Commercial Paper Money Market Mutual Fund Liquidity Facility (AMLF), the Commercial Paper Funding Facility (CPFF), the Money Market Investor Funding Facility (MMIFF), and the Term Asset-Backed Securities Loan Facility (TALF). The Fed also relied upon section 13(3) to provide assorted support for AIG. As David Wessel has noted, through these programs, the Fed was substituting itself for the shadow banking system "one market at a time."

The United States has never had a formal bailout mechanism. Section 13(3) of the Federal Reserve Act was dragooned into this role, but that is not its intended purpose; it was meant to be a credit backstop for creditworthy firms facing frozen financial markets, rather than a tool to rescue individual failing firms. Section 13(3) was intended as a response to market failures, rather than firm failures. Similarly, the RFC was not a bailout agency. As with section 13(3), the RFC was intended to deal with market failure, not firm failure. Section 13(3) was always intended to provide liquidity support, not solvency support.

Indeed, the difficulty that the Fed encountered when dealing with AIG was that liquidity and solvency support bled into each other, and the Fed ultimately found itself acting in a solvency support role. The liquidity—solvency divide is treacherous, and its successful navigation is an inherent LOLR problem. But even though LOLRs do not always successfully navigate the divide and avoid solvency support, the alternative is the unrealistic option of not having LOLRs at all. The truth is that there is no commitment device that can actually prevent governments from undertaking LOLR activity; when scared, governments bail, as shown by the United States in 1992 (bailing out Mexico absent authority), the United States in 2008 (stretching section 13(3) authority), and the European Union in 2010 (bailing out Greece despite a no-bailouts clause in the E.U. Treaty). This sort of disregard for the law in times of crisis can be fairly criticized, but binding ourselves to eschew LOLR behavior would amount to an economic suicide pact.

The history of LOLR activity in the United States reflects the tensions that exist in designing bailout mechanisms. Three interrelated tradeoffs exist:

risk of over-or-under authorization, political accountability, and speed of response . . .

* * *

3.   Political Accountability

This Article defines systemic risk as the risk of socially unacceptable macroeconomic consequences from the failure of individual firms. This definition hinges on what level of macroeconomic consequences is socially unacceptable. Determination of social standards is a political judgment by the entity with authority to authorize a bailout. The question is which entity is most likely to gauge social risk tolerance correctly, which is in turn a question of political accountability.

More accountable entities are more likely to correctly gauge social risk tolerance. This means these entities' actions are more likely to be perceived as legitimate. Legitimacy is important not just for its own sake, but for instrumental purposes. Technocratic autonomy needs political legitimacy to function. If one bailout is perceived as illegitimate, later ones might be harder to sell politically even if they correctly respond to social risk tolerance. In order to ensure that bailouts track actual social risk tolerance, it is critical that they be perceived as politically legitimate when they are used.

Whether Congress or administrative agencies are more politically accountable is a central debate in administrative law scholarship. Some scholars argue that agencies are accountable politically through presidential control of agencies, and that accountability legitimates agency action. This accountability, they argue, makes agencies more responsive than Congress to prevailing political preferences. This model of legitimating accountability breaks down, however, when it is applied to independent agencies, where accountability through the removal power is limited. Consider, for example, the Fed, where governors are appointed for fourteen-year terms . . .

Transparency is a key element of accountability, and Congress and agencies also differ in terms of transparency. Generally, there is greater transparency in congressional action. For major legislation, roll call votes are common, and there is the stylized theater of floor debates and sometimes even committee hearings. All of these actions take place in full view of the public, even if the deal-making does not. Moreover, the terms of legislation are public.

For agencies, transparency varies. When undertaking a bailout, agencies do not proceed using notice- and comment-rulemaking; instead, they proceed simply by doing deals. The process by which these deals are authorized and the terms of the deals are often not public, or not public until well after the fact. For example, the Board of Governors of the Fed did not release the minutes of its meetings from March 14 and 16, 2008, when it authorized under section 13(3) the Primary Dealer Credit Facility and the bailout of Bear Stearns, until June 27, 2008. I have been unable to locate any public record of the Board's minutes from its March 11, 2008, meeting when Section 13(3) was invoked for the first time to authorize the Term Securities Lending Facility.

Indeed, regulators often want to keep the facts of intervention private because of concerns about the impact of full information on the market. Thus, citing concerns about potential market impacts, the Fed refused initially, even in the face of congressional request, to release the identities of the counterparties of AIG that received direct bailout payments from Maiden Lane III, LLC, a special purpose subsidiary of the Federal Reserve Bank of New York, as agent for the Board of Governors of the Fed. The Fed is particularly opaque in its actions, especially when it acts through regional Reserve Banks that are not part of the federal government proper. Nor is Treasury, which bridles at oversight, a model of transparency.

Part of transparency and accountability is also a willingness to explain actions to the public. Whereas Congress (or at least individual congressmen) typically explains its actions to anyone who is willing to listen, agencies are much more tight-lipped, except when called before Congress.

Lack of communication can also undercut the legitimacy of a bailout. For example, Fed Chairman Ben Bernanke clearly articulated the potential harms of AIG's failure, but only to a congressional hearing in March 2009, half a year after AIG's initial bailout. In his testimony, Bernanke emphasized the enormous exposure to AIG on the part of not only banks ($50 billion), but also state and local government retirement funds ($10 billion), 401(k) plans ($40 billion), money market funds (up to $20 billion), and insurance policy holders. These exposures were much greater than those in the case of Lehman Brothers. If Chairman Bernanke had publicly made the case at the time of the AIG bailout, rather than in congressional testimony months later, that the AIG bailout was not primarily a bailout of banks, but a bailout of individual citizens' retirement and savings funds—basically an extension of the deposit insurance safety net—it could well have affected the popular perception of the AIG bailout. The median voter who perceives the AIG bailout as a bailout of banks might react differently than the median voter who perceives the AIG bailout as a bailout of his 401(k), his pension fund, his savings in a money market fund, or his insurance policy. In short, transparency (including communication) and accountability are essential for legitimacy.

Transparency also ensures that those responsible for bailouts are in fact held politically accountable. While there were significant pension and insurance funds at stake in the AIG bailout, the largest beneficiaries appear to have been foreign banks, a fact not mentioned in Bernanke's testimony but apparent from the Special Inspector General for the Troubled Asset Relief Program's report on the AIG bailout. AIG had also underwritten huge amounts of credit default swaps with foreign banks. These swaps reduced the foreign banks' regulatory capital requirements. As of December 30, 2008, AIG had $234 billion in foreign regulatory capital CDS exposure, compared with roughly $68 billion in other CDS exposure. Thus, the largest beneficiaries of the AIG bailout were arguably foreign banks, which but for the bailout, would have found themselves needing to raise significant capital for regulatory purposes at a time when capital markets were frozen. The median U.S. voter would likely be most unsympathetic to funding a bailout of foreign banks. Had there been real-time transparency, it is unlikely that the AIG bailout would have proceeded as it did; using U.S. taxpayer funds to bail out foreign banks would have been politically impossible, even if it contributed to the stability of the U.S. financial system.

Neither Congress nor agencies offer perfect models of accountability. Although agency accountability can be focused through careful delegation, it would, as Professor Edward Morrison has observed, require "a massive regulatory apparatus to constrain agency discretion." For example, agency LOLR authority could be restricted in many ways, including requiring both independent and presidential agency coauthorization, permitting congressional override without presidential approval, enunciating an intelligible principle for guiding use of LOLR authority, prohibiting particular types of LOLR activity (for example, permitting open-market activities in support of entire market sectors, but not allowing discount window lending in support of individual firms), requiring that all bailout expenditures go on the federal government's balance sheet, and providing for some judicial review mechanism.

Although *ex ante* limitations on authority are more likely to be effective controls, even ex post oversight mechanisms have an effect. For example, the only effective controls on the TARP are ex post oversight through the Congressional Oversight Panel and the Special Inspector General for the TARP, both of which have contributed significantly to the transparency of the bailout, sometimes to the chagrin of Treasury and the Fed. Yet, to the extent that agency discretion is constrained, it could diminish the effectiveness of agency action. Discretion and efficacy are but one of the trade-offs involved in bailouts.

Political accountability is not necessarily a good thing. It can also make bailout policy driven by electoral concerns that do not reflect median voter preferences, but those of particular concentrations of voters or special interests. Consider the temptation to intervene if, during a closely contested presidential election, a large employer in a swing state were in financial distress. If the firm were allowed to fail and be resolved in bankruptcy, some employees would lose their jobs and a lot of local firm creditors would suffer losses. A bailout could ensure that employees kept their jobs (at least through the election) and that local creditors received 100 cents on the dollar. There would be great temptation to use resolution authority as a form of political patronage. This temptation could exist for both Congress and agencies.

Likewise, Congress and agencies are both susceptible to lobbying for bailouts. As Peter Wallison has noted, large companies and their management can exercise substantial influence on the government: "There will be pressure on regulators to rescue firms with influential managements, or from states or districts that are represented by influential lawmakers. If the resolution authority exists, it will be used to favor these companies, to the detriment of others, and probably the taxpayers."

The politicization of bailouts could come from within the government itself or from interest groups seeking to influence the government. In either case, the evaluation of systemic risk would not reflect social risk tolerance but narrow electoral rent-seeking by incumbents.

Despite the potential pitfalls of political accountability, it is, on the whole, a positive feature that should be of paramount importance in the institutional design of bailouts. Bailouts are inherently political, so it makes sense to maximize accountability, rather than to attempt to depoliticize the process.

There are some practical implications from an identification of political accountability as the paramount institutional design goal. While the question of whether Congress or agencies are more accountable is not easily resolved, there are notable differences in accountability among agencies. Independent agencies are less politically accountable than are cabinet agencies. Thus, resolution authority could be vested in more or less politically accountable agencies.

If greater accountability is sought, then the Fed in particular should not have resolution authority, as it is perhaps the most politically insulated agency. This makes the Fed largely immune from direct political pressure. The Fed releases only stylized minutes of its meetings and generally operates behind a veil from the public. Likewise, the FDIC has limited accountability by virtue of its status as an independent agency. In contrast, the Treasury Secretary serves at the pleasure of the President and is thus much more politically accountable.

Similarly, vesting resolution authority in a council of regulators would diminish, rather than increase, political accountability. To the extent that there are multiple regulators involved, none of them ends up bearing ultimate accountability, and they can easily point fingers at each other and turn to each other as support for their own decisions. Likewise, involving the Judiciary in authorizing a resolution only serves to diminish political accountability. Ultimately, the more complex a resolution authorization mechanism is, the less transparent it will be and the less political accountability there will be. Although regulators—and particularly bank regulators—often eschew transparency and accountability, these qualities are necessary to promote the political legitimacy, and hence the efficacy, of resolutions.

4. Speed of Response

Although it is not clear whether congressional or agency action offers greater accountability, or the extent to which political accountability is desirable in terms of expressing social risk tolerance, agencies do have an advantage over Congress in terms of responsiveness. Agencies are likely to be able to respond faster than Congress to a crisis.

Agencies are always operating, while Congress is not always in session. Agencies' hierarchical organization structure facilitates quick decision making, while congressional bicameralism, majoritarian action requirements, and procedural rules act as brakes on the legislative process. Congressional action on an overnight basis is difficult, if not impossible. Witness the difference in the Fed and congressional responses to the financial crisis in 2008. The Fed was able to act nearly instantaneously through meetings of its governors (and even without the full Fed in attendance), whereas Congress took two weeks to enact the Emergency Economic Stabilization Act of 2008 (EESA) that authorized the TARP. When the Act passed, it was as part of a compromise bill that contained the Energy Improvement and Extension Act of 2008, the Tax Extenders and Alternative Minimum Tax Relief Act of 2008, and the Paul Wellstone and Pete Domenici Mental Health Parity and Addiction Equity Act of 2008.

As the EESA shows, congressional action is likely to be slowed by rent-seeking holdups and by ideological opposition to any bailouts, regardless of the consequences (which sometimes plays to electoral constituencies in some districts). Yet it is not clear which way greater agency responsiveness cuts . . .

The choice between ad hoc and institutionalized bailouts involves trade-offs between political accountability and responsiveness. Congressional action is not easy to achieve, but this is the virtue (and risk) of an ad hoc bailout system. While it poses the risk that Congress will fail to act when it should, it diminishes moral hazard because no firm has a guaranteed bailout, and it imposes at least the possibility of direct electoral political accountability for distributional and appropriations decisions. Institutionalized LOLR bailout systems, on the other hand, offer relatively greater flexibility and responsiveness than ad hoc systems, but their political accountability is less direct.

The trade-offs involved with congressional or agency action are clear; the proper resolution is not. Whether an ad hoc or institutionalized bailout system is preferable in any individual case may depend on the particular features of the systems. The choice between bailout systems must be made in the abstract, however, without knowing either the particular details of either system (which are amendable) or the circumstances in which they would be invoked.

B.   HAIRCUTS

. . . Regardless of which bailout system is preferable, a second and distinct question is whether the bailout should be combined with a bankruptcy-type "haircut" mechanism that enables the distressed TBTF firm to legally pay off its creditors for less than 100 cents on the dollar without their consent. The bailout mechanism question is one of authorizing use of government funds to limit losses stemming from a firm's actual or anticipated failure. The haircut mechanism question is about the distribution of the losses and the extent to which failed firms' counterparties benefit from government intervention.

Discussions of bailouts generally fail to distinguish between the bailout mechanism and the haircut mechanism. Both raise distributional questions, but the issues are independent. The question of whether to authorize a bailout is a question about whether to opt out of the loss allocation that would result from the default bankruptcy resolution. The question of whether to have a haircut is a secondary question about what the distributional impact of the opt out should be. The choice of whether to impose a haircut and, if so, what kind of a haircut, is a choice about distributional schemes. Without a haircut mechanism, a bailout's distributional impact is to shift all losses from the failed firm's counterparties to the government. With a haircut mechanism, however, some or all of those losses are still borne by the counterparties, thereby reducing the government's exposure.

The issues involved in haircuts become clear when bailouts are conceived as a form of insurance. Counterparties of TBTF firms are "insured" against the firms' failure by bailouts. The counterparties are the true bailout beneficiaries, as without the bailout, they would take losses either through delay or haircuts in a bankruptcy-type resolution. Requiring a haircut is equivalent to requiring a copayment at the haircut percentage rate. Requiring a copayment is an effective way to reduce moral hazard, but it is self-defeating when the insured party cannot afford the copayment.

There are three reasons to support a haircut mechanism. First, it reduces the cost of bailouts for the federal government. Haircuts mean that more losses are borne by private parties.

Second, a haircut mechanism would limit moral hazard for TBTF firms because they will bear the price of the haircut mechanism in their dealings with counterparties. TBTF firms themselves do not take haircuts. Instead, they are likely to have to repay funds loaned to them in a bailout or accept a stock investment that dilutes existing shareholders' holdings. Furthermore, TBTF firms bear the cost in their dealings with counterparties that are exposed to potential haircuts, not just in bankruptcy, but also in bailouts. Put differently, a haircut mechanism would add a default risk premium for TBTF firms' borrowing costs. This risk premium, in turn, would offset some of TBTF firms' competitive advantage by reducing the value of the implied government guarantee of their obligations.

Third, haircuts are crucial for maintaining the public legitimacy of bailouts. The haircut mechanism in bankruptcy-type resolution systems reflects a social loss-sharing norm. Deviation from that norm makes the loss allocation in bailouts suspect, not least because the loss allocation is to put 100% of the losses on taxpayers. Shared pain is the core fairness norm in resolutions, and violation of that norm undermines bailouts' legitimacy.

Combining a haircut mechanism with a bailout system, however, raises considerable fairness concerns. The reason for engaging in a bailout is often to protect certain counterparties of the TBTF firm from losses. Imposing haircuts on these critical counterparties is self-defeating. The whole point of the bailout is to avoid the consequences of these parties taking losses. It might be that they are able to incur a certain level of losses without triggering systemic problems, but it is hard to know that level at the time of the bailout. Critical counterparties might not be able to afford a non-nominal bailout "insurance" copayment at the time of the bailout. For example, in the first round of AIG's bailout, when it received an $85 billion line of credit from the Federal Reserve Bank of New York, the imposition of a haircut on Goldman Sachs could have triggered a run on Goldman. Therefore, it does little good to impose haircuts at the time of the bailout on critical counterparties.

If critical counterparties do not take haircuts, what about other noncritical counterparties that are too-small-to-matter? Imposing a haircut on them reduces the cost of a bailout and might help mitigate moral hazard. Applying haircuts only to noncritical counterparties violates a core principal of resolutions, namely that equity is equality—similarly situated creditors are to be treated alike—and losses should be shared pro rata, except when provided otherwise by statute. Violating this principal undermines the public legitimacy of bailouts because the loss allocations appear as naked interest group subsidies with public funds. Moreover, imposing haircuts only on the too-small-to-matter rewards counterparties that are themselves TBTF, exacerbating moral hazard problems.

* * *

16E. *The Creation of the Financial Stability Board*

This excerpt brings us back to the Financial Stability Forum (FSF), which we studied in Chapter 10, and its transformation into the Financial Stability Board (FSB). The excerpt shows how a sleepy international body was transformed into an important international player in the resolution of the crisis. In what ways did the FSF become relevant? Why transform the forum into the Financial Stability Board? Is the story set out in this article the best that can be done on an international level to strengthen financial stability? Remember that the law of international finance is "soft." The question is to what extent does the existence of the FSB "harden" it.

E. Carrasco, "The Global Financial Crisis and the Financial Stability Forum: The Awakening and Transformation of an International Body," *Transnational Law and Contemporary Problems* (2010)

I. INTRODUCTION

On November 15, 2008, leaders of the Group of Twenty ("G-20") met in Washington, D.C. to address the worst global financial and economic crisis since the Great Depression. One of the primary purposes of the summit, dubbed by some as "Bretton Woods II," was to begin discussions on reforms of the global financial architecture that would prevent a recurrence of another devastating global crisis. There was some initial anticipation that Bretton Woods II would produce a framework of fundamental reforms of the global financial system that was created in July 1944 during a three-week conference in Bretton Woods, New Hampshire. However, during the weekend summit, the most G-20 leaders could agree upon was a set of principles that would guide future reform of the financial markets.

One of the principles addressed reforming international financial institutions ("IFIs"), with a focus on giving developing and emerging countries greater voice and representation in such institutions. The G-20 leaders predictably pointed the finger of reform at the International Monetary Fund ("IMF"), which has been struggling with governance issues for a number of years. They also named another body that has not received the type of high-profile attention devoted to the IMF—the Financial Stability Forum ("FSF")—calling upon it to expand its emerging-country membership.

Formed in the wake of the Asian financial crisis, the FSF is an intergovernmental forum whose purpose is to promote the stability of the international financial system, with an eye towards reducing the type of financial contagion that marked the Asian crisis. In particular, its mandate is to "identify and oversee actions needed to address" the "vulnerabilities affecting the [international] financial system." Comprised of representatives of national financial authorities, IFIs, international regulatory and supervisory groups, committees of central bank experts, and the European Central Bank, the FSF has established a number of working groups to pursue its mandate, producing reports setting forth observations, guidance, and recommendations relating to the stability of domestic financial systems and the international financial system as a whole.

Thus, in a world lacking a global financial regulator, the FSF's function is to promote the development and adoption of standards and codes that, when adopted into domestic regulatory frameworks, will reduce vulnerabilities in the international financial system that may lead to global crises. Prior to the current global financial crisis, the FSF's work had few, if any, concrete results. Indeed, given the occurrence of the crisis, the FSF arguably failed its mandate to the extent it failed to identify, ex ante, the vulnerabilities that have led to the greatest global financial and economic crisis since the Great Depression. However, once it focused on the developing crisis in the fall of 2007, the FSF played a major role in addressing the causes of the crisis, recommending measures that should be taken to resolve it, and preventing future financial crises with global repercussions. Having demonstrated its relevance throughout 2008, the FSF was transformed into the Financial Stability Board ("FSB") with a broader mandate in April 2009.

This Article chronicles the awakening of the FSF and its transformation into the FSB. Part II describes the origins of the FSF and its relatively obscure work prior to the current crisis. Part III chronicles the FSF's significant rise in visibility throughout the crisis via its reports analyzing the crisis and setting forth recommendations relating to reforms of law and regulation of the financial markets. Part IV explains the FSF's transformation into the FSB, a move to give the FSF a more robust institutional grounding capable of coordinating its work with the IMF. Part V concludes that while the global financial crisis brought the FSF out of obscurity and resulted in its transformation into the FSB, it is still too early to tell whether the FSB will have a significant impact on global governance of international finance, especially with respect to the needs and interests of emerging economies.

II. THE FSF'S CREATION AND ITS WORK PRIOR TO THE GLOBAL FINANCIAL CRISIS

The FSF was created in 1999 to address vulnerabilities in the international financial system, identify and oversee action needed to address these vulnerabilities, and improve cooperation and information exchange among authorities responsible for financial stability. The FSF's mandate and its organizational structure grew out of a report commissioned by the G-7 in 1998 and written by Bundesbank President Dr. Hans Tietmeyer.

Tietmeyer presented his report to the G-7 finance ministers and central bank governors in February 1999, and the FSF convened for the first time in April 1999 under Chairman Andrew Crockett.

The FSF's initial members consisted of the finance minister, central bank governor, and a supervisory authority from each of the G-7 countries, as well as representatives from the IMF, World Bank, Bank for International Settlements ("BIS"), Organization for Economic Cooperation and Development ("OECD"), Basel Committee on Banking Supervision ("BCBS"), International Accounting Standards Board ("IASB"), International Association of Insurance Supervisors ("IAIS"), International Organization of Securities Commissions ("IOSCO"), Committee on Payment and Settlements Systems ("CPSS"), and Committee on the Global Financial System ("CGFS"). After its creation, the FSF added the European Central Bank, and additional national members Australia, Hong Kong, the Netherlands, and Switzerland.

A persistent criticism of the FSF was that it excluded developing or emerging economies. Chairman Crockett's explanation for this lack of representation was that the FSF could be more effective if it was "homogenous." The representatives met biannually or as needed in a plenary session, as well as convened in regional meetings and working groups. There were three initial working groups, focusing on HighlyLeveraged Institutions, Offshore Financial Centers, and Capital Flows, along with two additional groups, the Implementation Task Force and the Deposit Insurance Study Group. Though the FSF invited additional participants from developing and developed countries to join in the work of the additional groups, these were not considered formal working groups and participants were not members of the FSF.

The FSF initially convened to respond to failures in the financial regulatory system. In the wake of the financial crises of the 1990s, there was a push to create a New International Financial Architecture that would better address problems as they arose and better coordinate financial supervision and regulation on an international scale. The FSF was part of this push, with the particular goal of promoting the harmonization of standards among international financial organizations and institutions.

The FSF's work prior to the current crisis was underwhelming, despite the existence of an Implementation Task Force. The most ambitious project was the adoption of a Compendium of Standards, intended to harmonize and make the many sets of standards published by standard-setting bodies more workable. The Compendium was comprised of sixty-four standards that sought to harmonize the work of the FSF's institutional members. Because the FSF recognized that implementing so many standards would be an arduous task for most countries, the FSF flagged "Twelve Key Standards" for priority in implementation, such as the IMF's Code of Good

Practices on Fiscal Transparency, the IASB's International Accounting Standards, and IOSCO's Objectives and Principles of Securities Regulation. The standards take a sectoral (e.g., banking) as well as functional (e.g., regulation and supervision) approach, and differ between principles (e.g., Basel Committee's Core Principles for Effective Banking Supervision), practices (e.g., Basel Committee's Sound Practices for Loan Accounting), and methodologies or guidelines (e.g., implementation guidance).

Though the standards are available online, they have not been regularly updated, are not entirely transparent, and contain inconsistencies. There is also no means of ensuring adherence to the standards. Though it is unlikely that a single international body will ever close the "control gap" that divergent institutions have created, an effective Compendium could ensure informal coordination between institutions to make activities more coherent and effective. The present problem is that the national economies, which are ultimately responsible for implementation, have not implemented the standards or have not done so sufficiently.

The three working groups have also published reports on more limited areas, but difficulty coming to agreement on tough issues—always a major hurdle in international harmonization of law—means that the reports are similarly toothless. They include recommendations that are repetitive of others' work, basic frameworks that need elaboration on the details, and entreaties for the various players to cooperate. They also tend to point to substantial future work that needs to be done, positioning the FSF as a body that has potential rather than one that is actually achieving solutions to the problems it identifies. The Implementation Task Force has been somewhat more successful in focusing on implementation strategies for the twelve key standards in the Compendium, laying out piece-by-piece how institutions such as the IMF can actually take a role in putting the standards into practice. In sum, despite the FSF's visibility at its inception within the context of the New International Financial Architecture, its work thereafter did not figure prominently in international finance, and its presence on the global financial stage was slight compared to the IMF.

III. THE FSF'S ROLE IN THE GLOBAL FINANCIAL CRISIS

The FSF's obscure existence changed when it issued a high profile report on the global financial crisis in April 2008 and follow-up reports thereafter. The deliberations that led to the April report commenced in the fall of 2007.

A. *The FSF's September 2007 Meeting*

The FSF met in September 2007 in New York to discuss "the implications for financial stability of recent turbulence in global financial markets and what might need to be done going forward to strengthen financial system stability and resilience." At that meeting, the FSF, at the request of the G-7 Treasury Deputies, formed the Working Group on Market and

Institutional Resilience to analyze the underlying causes of the crisis and to make proposals to enhance market stability and resilience. The group was comprised of representatives of the BCBS, IOSCO, IASB, CPSS, CGFS, IMF, BIS, Joint Forum, and European Central Bank, as well as national regulators in key financial centers and private sector market participants.

B.   The FSF Working Group's Preliminary Report

In October 2007, the Working Group provided an outline of its work plan in the form of a Preliminary Report to the G-7 Finance Ministers and Central Bank Governors. The report noted that since June 2007, a reduction in risktaking, risk re-pricing, and a liquidity squeeze adversely affected the global financial markets. It identified the U.S. subprime mortgage market and related structured products as the triggers of the crisis that was affecting a wide range of markets, including the broader market for structured credit products, the leveraged loan markets, as well as the commercial paper and interbank funding markets. The crisis was being spread by, among other things, rating downgrades of mortgage-backed securities, a lack of confidence in ratings and valuations of other structured credit, and the drop in funding for many asset-backed commercial paper conduits. Although market participants had begun to take measures to rebuild confidence in the structured finance market, the report stated that there were a number of weaknesses in the financial markets—some of which were apparent beforehand—that required the attention of national and international financial policymakers. Accordingly, the Working Group agreed that it would provide an analysis of the recent events and recommend actions needed to enhance market discipline and institutional resilience. In so doing, it would focus on risk management practices; valuation, risk disclosure, and accounting; the role of credit rating agencies; and principles of prudential oversight. The Working Group also took upon itself an examination of issues relating to regulators' ability to coordinate their reactions to market turbulence on a national and international level.

C.   The FSF's Interim Report

In February 2008, the Working Group issued its Interim Report to the G-7 Finance Ministers and Central Bank Governors. It contained three main sections. First, it reviewed the prevailing conditions and adjustments in the financial system. Noting that the adjustment period would likely be prolonged and difficult, the Interim Report recommended a series of shortterm actions, including: (i) realistic asset pricing market liquidity and credit intermediation; (ii) further work to "provide confidence to markets that valuation practices and related loss estimates are adequate;" (iii) the need to have supervisors "continue to work closely with individual financial institutions to ensure" adequate levels of capital and liquidity; and (iv) the importance of having central banks continue to respond to developments effectively and in a coordinated fashion.

Second, the Interim Report preliminarily identified the now well-known factors that contributed to the credit crisis, ranging from fraudulent practices in the U.S. subprime mortgage sector to poor disclosure by financial firms of risks associated with their on- and off-balance sheet exposures. It also set forth considerations that regulators should take into account when considering policy responses. For instance, although policy prescriptions might be necessary, adjustments should be market-driven and monitored for discipline. Moreover, although regulators should attempt to identify emerging problems and mitigate them, it may be difficult to foresee and prevent financial crises. Hence, regulatory efforts should focus on ensuring resilience when markets come under stress. Similarly, the Report warned that although regulators should consider expanding the scope of regulatory coverage in the event of market failure, additional regulations can give rise to regulatory arbitrage or promote moral hazard when supervisors and regulators are stretched too far.

Finally, the Interim Report delineated policy measures agreed upon by the Working Group that would form the basis of the April report. Specifically, the Working Group addressed: (i) supervisory framework and oversight, which encompassed capital arrangements, liquidity buffers, risk management practices, and off-balance sheet activities; (ii) strengthening the underpinnings of the originate-to-distribute model; (iii) the uses and role of credit rating agencies; (iv) market transparency; (v) supervisory and regulatory responsiveness to risks; and (vi) authorities' ability to respond to crises.

D.   The FSF's April 2008 Report

On April 11, 2008, the FSF submitted its report ("April 2008 Report") to the G-7. The report, which received global press coverage, so identified the major causes of the crisis and proposed "concrete actions in . . . five areas: [1] strengthened prudential oversight of capital, liquidity and risk management; [2] enhancing transparency and valuation; [3] changes in the role and uses of credit ratings; [4] strengthening the authorities' responsiveness to risks; and [5] robust arrangements for dealing with stress in the financial system."

The April 2008 Report set forth a number of recommendations with respect to the five areas. For instance, as to strengthened prudential oversight of capital management, a key aspect of the crisis, it recommended: (i) raising Basel II capital requirements for "certain complex structured credit products;" (ii) introducing additional capital charges for default and event risk in the trading books of banks and securities firms; and (iii) strengthening the capital treatment of liquidity facilities to off-balance sheet conduits. As for enhancing transparency and valuation, the report strongly encouraged financial institutions to make robust risk disclosures using the leading disclosure practices set forth in the report and called upon standard setters to improve and converge financial reporting standards for off-balance sheet vehicles.

With respect to the role and use of credit ratings, the Report recommended that credit rating agencies should: (i) implement the revised IOSCO Code of Conduct Fundamentals for Credit Rating Agencies to manage conflicts of interest in rating structured products and improve the quality of the rating process; and (ii) differentiate ratings on structured credit products from those on bonds and expand the amount of information they provide. To strengthen the authorities' responsiveness to risks, the report called for a college of supervisors to be put in place by the end of 2008 for each of the largest global financial institutions. Regarding robust arrangements for dealing with stress in the financial system, the report called upon central banks to enhance their operational frameworks and strengthen their cooperation to deal with stress.

E.   Follow-Up Reports

In October 2008, the FSF issued a follow-up report ("October Report"), which stated that a substantial amount of work was underway to implement the recommendations of the FSF's April 2008 Report. Still, in view of market developments, implementation of certain recommendations had to be accelerated, including putting in place central counterparty clearing for overthe-counter ("OTC") credit derivatives and harmonizing guidance on valuation of instruments in inactive markets. The October Report also stated the FSF would address other issues, such as: (i) international interaction and consistency of emergency arrangements and responses being put in place to address the financial crisis; (ii) mitigation of the sources of pro-cyclicality in the financial system; (iii) and reassessment of the scope of financial regulation, with a special emphasis on unregulated institutions, instruments, and markets.

In April 2009, the FSF issued another update ("April 2009 Report") to coincide with the G-20's London Summit. The Report noted that extensive progress had been made in the implementation of the recommendations set forth in FSF's April 2008 Report. For instance, banking supervisors had published proposals for improving risk coverage under Basel II, especially with regard to credit-related risks in the trading book. They had also published revised capital charges for liquidity commitments to off-balance sheet entities and for the re-securitized instruments. Central counterparty clearing for OTC credit derivatives had been launched in the United States and Europe. The IASB and the U.S. Financial Accounting Standards Board had issued consistent guidance on fair valuation when markets are illiquid. Several Credit Rating Agencies ("CRAs"), including the three largest agencies, substantially implemented the 2008 revisions of IOSCO's Code of

Conduct Fundamental for Credit Rating Agencies. Also, supervisory colleges have been established for most of the global financial institutions.

IV. TRANSFORMATION OF THE FSF

With the crisis spreading to emerging economies and the increased prominence of the FSF came calls to broaden the FSF's membership. A key voice in this regard was the G-20, a forum created in the wake of the Asian financial crisis, in which finance ministers and central bank governors from systemically important industrialized and developing countries discuss issues relating to the global economy. In November 2008 and April 2009, the G-20 held summits in Washington, D.C. and London, respectively, to address the global crisis. The summits resulted in the transformation of the FSF into a Board and a broadening of the scope of policy deliberation to include emerging and developing countries.

A. The November Summit

On November 15, 2008, leaders of the G-20 met in Washington, D.C. to address what had become the worst global financial and economic crisis since the Great Depression. There was some initial anticipation that the meeting, dubbed by some as "Bretton Woods II," would produce a framework of fundamental reforms of the global financial system created in July 1944 during a three-week conference in Bretton Woods, New Hampshire. This was, of course, highly unrealistic, especially since George Bush was in the twilight of his presidency—President-elect Obama did not attend the summit, sending instead former Secretary of State Madeleine Albright and former Representative Jim Leach on his behalf to meet informally with G-20 leaders. While G-20 leaders took "immediate steps" to continue vigorous efforts to stabilize the financial system, to use fiscal measures as appropriate to stimulate domestic demand, and to help emerging and developing countries gain access to finance, reform efforts were limited to agreement upon a set of principles that would guide future reform of the financial markets.

Recognizing that strengthening of international standards and promoting international cooperation among national regulators—who form the first line of defense—are necessary in today's global financial markets, the G-20 leaders set forth five principles that would guide policy implementation: (i) strengthening transparency and accountability; (ii) enhancing sound regulation; (iii) promoting integrity in financial markets; (iv) reinforcing international cooperation; and (v) reforming international financial institutions. As to the fifth principle, the summit's leaders declared they were committed to reforming the Bretton Woods Institutions in order to give emerging and developing countries greater voice and representation. Moreover, the FSF (as well as other major standard setting bodies) had to be expanded "urgently to a broader membership of emerging economies." The leaders also called upon the IMF, in collaboration with the expanded

FSF and other bodies, "to better identify vulnerabilities, anticipate potential stresses, and act swiftly to play a key role in crisis response." The Action Plan attached to the Declaration set forth measures to be implemented by March 31, 2009 as well as in the medium term. With respect to the fifth principle, the Action Plan, among other things, called upon the FSF and the IMF to conduct "early warning exercises" by the March deadline. This collaboration anticipates that the IMF will assess macro-financial risks and systemic vulnerabilities, while the FSF will assess financial system vulnerabilities, drawing on the analyses of its member bodies, including the IMF. Where appropriate, the IMF and FSF may provide joint risk assessments and mitigation reports.

B.   London Summit

Given the November summit's March 31, 2009 deadlines for immediate actions, the international community quickly shifted its attention after the Washington, D.C. summit to London, the host for the next summit on April 2, 2009. Like the November summit, participants had high hopes during the lead up to the London summit, with U.K. Prime Minister Gordon Brown claiming the summit would launch a "grand bargain" among countries that would help end the global recession and set in motion reforms that would prevent future crises. However, after a reality check, particularly with respect to differences between the United States and Europe over additional stimulus measures, participants lowered their expectations.

Nevertheless, participants concluded the London summit with great fanfare, with a number of "announceables," even though participants had agreed upon a good number of measures before the summit and left a number unresolved. In addition to agreement on various financial measures intended to combat the crisis, the leaders declared they were "determined" to reform international financial institutions, such as the IMF, to ensure that emerging and developing economies have greater voice and representation. The declaration, however, lacked any newly agreed upon reforms. By contrast, with respect to strengthening financial supervision and regulation, the leaders agreed to establish a new Financial Stability Board ("FSB") as a successor to the FSF.

The purpose of the change was to give the FSF "a stronger institutional basis," so that it could more effectively assist and collaborate with national authorities, standard setting bodies ("SSBs") and international financial institutions in addressing vulnerabilities and implementing strong regulatory, supervisory, and other policies in the interest of financial stability.

Organizationally, the FSB consists of a Chairperson, a Steering Committee, the Plenary with member countries, SSBs, international financial institutions, and a Secretariat. The Chair oversees the Steering

Committee, the Plenary, and an enlarged Secretariat with a full-time Secretary General. The FSB Plenary is the decision-making organ of the FSB. The Steering Committee is an executive organ that provides operational guidance between plenary meetings (twice per year) to carry forward the directions of the FSB.

Plenary membership, which will be reviewed periodically, includes the current FSF members, plus the rest of the G-20, Spain, and the European Commission. FSB members are obligated to pursue the "maintenance of financial stability, maintain the openness and transparency of the financial sector, implement international financial standards (including the [twelve] key International Standards and Codes), and agree to undergo periodic peer reviews, using among other evidence IMF/World Bank public Financial Sector Assessment Program reports."

In addition to the FSF's current mandate—to assess vulnerabilities affecting the financial system, identify and oversee action needed to address them, and promote coordination and information exchange among authorities responsible for financial stability—the FSB will: (i) "monitor and advise on market developments and their implications for regulatory policy"; (ii) "advise on and monitor best practice in meeting regulatory standards"; (iii) "undertake joint strategic reviews of the policy development work of the international SSBs to ensure their work is timely, coordinated, focused on priorities and addressing gaps"; (iv) "set guidelines for and support the establishment of supervisory colleges"; (v) "manage contingency planning for cross-border crisis management, particularly with respect to systemically important firms"; and (vi) "collaborate with the IMF to conduct Early Warning Exercises."

To promote the broader mandate, the FSB Plenary will establish the following Standing Committees: (i) Vulnerabilities Assessment, (ii) Supervisory and Regulatory Cooperation (including for supervisory colleges and cross-border crisis management), and (iii) Implementation of Standards and Codes. It may establish other Standing Committees and ad hoc working groups, which can include non-FSB member countries, as necessary.

In an effort to promote its institutional legitimacy, the FSB's mandate includes increased regional outreach activities to broaden the circle of countries engaged in promoting international financial stability. Moreover, the FSB will engage in stronger public relations outreach to raise the visibility of its work and role in the international financial system.

Thus reconstituted, the FSB will play an integral role in strengthening the global financial system in the context of international cooperation (e.g., developing a framework for cross-border bank resolution arrangements), prudential regulation (e.g., working with accounting standard setters to implement recommendations to mitigate pro-cyclicality), and broadening the scope of regulation (e.g., "developing effective oversight of hedge funds).

The FSB held its inaugural meeting on June 26–27, 2009 in Basel. There, it assessed the state of the financial markets and the progress made toward implementation of the recommendations to strengthen financial systems. To this extent, its deliberations were no different than the FSF's work.

V. CONCLUSION

The global financial crisis has exposed significant weaknesses in the domestic and international institutions that regulate or monitor the financial markets, which today are global in scope. The FSF was created to coordinate the implementation of standards and codes that relate to the global markets, with the goal of preventing a financial crisis that, like the Asian financial crisis, has global repercussions. However, in the years after its creation, the FSF worked in relative obscurity, and failed to sound the alarm warning against "the perfect storm" that led to the current crisis.

Still, after the onset of the crisis, the FSF diligently analyzed the complex: causes of the crisis and made recommendations seeking to remedy the weaknesses in interconnected regulatory frameworks. The FSF's April 2008 Report was key to recovery efforts, and its follow-up reports usefully monitored progress made in implementing its recommendations.

Will the newly constituted FSB make a difference? It is hard to say at this point. The expanded membership that now includes emerging economies is long overdue. But this move alone will not guarantee the FSB's effectiveness—much will depend on the G-20. One thing is certain: the FSB's legitimacy will depend significantly on whether the Early Warning Exercises performed in conjunction with the IMF have real substance and utility.

16F. *It Ain't Going to Happen to Me! Really?*

This except is taken from a widely-read book published by two economists on the tail end of the crisis. Carmen Reinhard is with the Harvard Kennedy School and Kenneth Rogoff is also at Harvard. From 2001 to 2003, he was the Chief Economist and Director of Research at the International Monetary Fund. The idea behind the "this time is different syndrome" is that economists and policymakers mistakenly thought that the United States would be spared a tremendous economic crisis because the U.S. financial and regulatory system was superior to all others—the "conceit" of U.S. exceptionalism. What is the lesson you draw from this excerpt? Is it that if you put ten economists in a room to assess an economic problem or situation, you'll get eleven different opinions?

C. Reinhart & K. Rogoff, *The U.S. Subprime Crisis:*
An International and Historical Comparison in
<u>This Time Is Different</u> (2009)

* * *

The Time-Is-Different Syndrome and the Run-up to the Subprime Crisis

The global financial crisis of the late 2000s, whether measured by the depth, breadth, and (potential) duration of the accompanying recession or by its profound effect on asset markets, stands as the most serious global financial crisis since the Great Depression. The crisis has been a transformative moment in global economic history whose ultimate resolution will likely reshape politics and economics for at least a generation.

Should the crisis have come as a surprise, especially in its deep impact on the United States? Listening to a long list of leading academics, investors, and U.S. policy makers, one would have thought the financial meltdown of the late 2000s was a bolt from the blue, a "six-sigma" event. U.S. Federal Reserve Chairman Alan Greenspan frequently argued that financial innovations such as securitization and option pricing were producing new and better ways to spread risk, simultaneously making traditionally illiquid assets, such as houses, more liquid. Hence higher and higher prices for risky assets could be justified.

We could stop here and say that a lot of people were convinced that "this time is different" because the United States is "special." However, given the historic nature of the recent U.S. and global financial collapse, a bit more background will help us to understand why so many people were fooled.

Risks Posed by Sustained U.S. Borrowing from the Rest of the World: The Debate before the Crisis

Chairman Greenspan was among the legion that branded as alarmists those who worried excessively about the burgeoning U.S. current account deficit. Greenspan argued that this gaping deficit, which reached more than 6.5 percent of GDP in 2006 (over $800 billion), was, to a significant extent, simply a reflection of a broader trend toward global financial deepening that was allowing countries to sustain much larger current account deficits and surpluses than in the past. Indeed, in his 2007 book, Greenspan characterizes the sustained U.S. current account deficit as a secondary issue, not a primary risk factor, one that (along with others such as soaring housing prices and the notable buildup in household debt) should not have caused excessive alarm among U.S. policy makers during the run-up to the crisis that began in 2007.

The Federal Reserve chairman was hardly alone in his relatively sanguine view of American borrowing. U.S. Treasury Secretary Paul O'Neill famously argued that it was natural for other countries to lend to the United States given this country's high rate of productivity growth and that the current account was a "meaningless concept."

Greenspan's successor, Ben Bernanke, in a speech he made in 2005, famously described the U.S. borrowing binge as the product of a "global savings glut" that had been caused by a convergence of factors, many of which were outside the control of U.S. policy makers. These factors included the strong desire of many emerging markets to insure themselves against future economic crises after the slew of crises in Latin America and Asia during the 1990s and early 2000s. At the same time, Middle Eastern countries had sought ways to use their oil earnings, and countries with underdeveloped financial systems, such as China, had wanted to diversify into safer assets. Bernanke argued that it was also natural for some developed economies, such as Japan and Germany, to have high savings rates in the face of rapidly aging populations. All these factors together conspired to provide a huge pool of net savings in search of a safe and dynamic resting place, which meant the United States. Of course, this cheap source of funding was an opportunity for the United States. The question authorities might have wrestled with more was "Can there be too much of a good thing?" The same this-time-is-different argument appears all too often in the speeches of policy makers in emerging markets when their countries are experiencing massive capital inflows: "Low rates of return in the rest of the world are simply making investment in our country particularly attractive."

As money poured into the United States, U.S. financial firms, including mighty investment banks such as Goldman Sachs, Merrill Lynch (which was acquired by Bank of America in 2008 in a "shotgun marriage"), and the now defunct Lehman Brothers, as well as large universal banks (with retail bases) such as Citibank, all saw their profits soar. The size of the U.S. financial sector (which includes banking and insurance) more than doubled, from an average of roughly 4 percent of GDP in the mid-1970s to almost 8 percent of GDP by 2007. The top employees of the five largest investment banks divided a bonus pool of over $36 billion in 2007. Leaders in the financial sector argued that in fact their high returns were the result of innovation and genuine value-added products, and they tended to grossly understate the latent risks their firms were taking. (Keep in mind that an integral part of our working definition of the this-time-is-different syndrome is that "the old rules of valuation no longer apply.") In their eyes, financial innovation was a key platform that allowed the United States to effectively borrow much larger quantities of money from abroad than might otherwise have been possible. For example, innovations such as securitization allowed U.S. consumers to turn their previously illiquid housing assets into ATM machines, which represented a reduction in precautionary saving.

Where did academics and policy economists stand on the dangers posed by the U.S. current account deficit? Opinions varied across a wide spectrum. On the one hand, Obstfeld and Rogoff argued in several contributions that the outsized U.S. current account was likely unsustainable. They observed that if one added up all the surpluses of the countries in the world that were net savers (countries in which national savings exceed national investment, including China, Japan, Germany, Saudi Arabia, and Russia), the United States was soaking up more than two out of every three of these saved dollars in 2004–2006. Thus, eventually the U. S. borrowing binge would have to unwind, perhaps quite precipitously, which would result in sharp asset price movements that could severely stress the complex global derivatives system.

Many others took a similarly concerned viewpoint. For example, in 2004 Nouriel Roubini and Brad Setser projected that the U.S. borrowing problem would get much worse, reaching 10 percent of GDP before a dramatic collapse. Paul Krugman (who received a Nobel Prize in 2008) argued that there would inevitably be a "Wile E. Coyote moment" when the unsustainability of the U.S. current account would be evident to all, and suddenly the dollar would collapse. There are many other examples of academic papers that illustrated the risks.

Yet many respected academic, policy, and financial market researchers took a much more sanguine view. In a series of influential papers, Michael Dooley, David Folkerts-Landau, and Peter Garber—"the Deutschebank trio"—argued that the gaping U.S. current account deficit was just a natural consequence of emerging markets' efforts to engage in export-led growth, as well as their need to diversify into safe assets. They insightfully termed the system that propagated the U.S. deficits "Bretton Woods II" because the Asian countries were quasi-pegging their currencies to the U.S. dollar, just as the European countries had done forty years earlier.

Harvard economist Richard Cooper also argued eloquently that the U.S. current account deficit had logical foundations that did not necessarily imply clear and present dangers. He pointed to the hegemonic position of the United States in the global financial and security system and the extraordinary liquidity of U.S. financial markets, as well as its housing markets, to support his argument. Indeed, Bernanke's speech on the global savings glut in many ways synthesized the interesting ideas already floating around in the academic and policy research literature.

It should be noted that others, such as Ricardo Hausmann and Federico Sturzenegger of Harvard University's Kennedy School of Government, made more exotic arguments, claiming that U.S. foreign assets were mismeasured, and actually far larger than official estimates. The existence of this "dark matter" helped explain how the United States could finance a seemingly unending string of current account and trade deficits. Ellen McGrattan of Minnesota and Ed Prescott of Arizona (another Nobel Prize winner) developed a model to effectively calibrate dark matter and found that the explanation might plausibly account for as much as half of the United States' current account deficit.

In addition to debating U.S. borrowing from abroad, economists also debated the related question of whether policy makers should have been concerned about the explosion of housing prices that was taking place nationally in the United States (as shown in the previous section). But again, top policy makers argued that high home prices could be justified by new financial markets that made houses easier to borrow off of and by reduced macroeconomic risk that increased the value of risky assets. Both Greenspan and Bernanke argued vigorously that the Federal Reserve should not pay excessive attention to housing prices, except to the extent that they might affect the central bank's primary goals of growth and price stability. Indeed, prior to joining the Fed, Bernanke had made this case more formally and forcefully in an article coauthored by New York University professor Mark Gertler in 2001.

On the one hand, the Federal Reserve's logic for ignoring housing prices was grounded in the perfectly sensible proposition that the private sector can judge equilibrium housing prices (or equity prices) at least as well as any government bureaucrat. On the other hand, it might have paid more attention to the fact that the rise in asset prices was being fueled by a relentless increase in the ratio of household debt to GDP, against a backdrop of record lows in the personal saving rate. This ratio, which had been roughly stable at close to 80 percent of personal income until 1993, had risen to 120 percent in 2003 and to nearly 130 percent by mid-2006. Empirical work by Bordo and Jeanne and the Bank for International Settlements suggested that when housing booms are accompanied by sharp rises in debt, the risk of a crisis is significantly elevated. Although this work was not necessarily definitive, it certainly raised questions about the Federal Reserve's policy of benign neglect. On the other hand, the fact that the housing boom was taking place in many countries around the world (albeit to a much lesser extent if at all in major surplus countries such as Germany and Japan) raised questions about the genesis of the problem and whether national monetary or regulatory policy alone would be an effective remedy.

Bernanke, while still a Federal Reserve governor in 2004, sensibly argued that it is the job of regulatory policy, not monetary policy, to deal with housing price bubbles fueled by inappropriately weak lending standards. Of course, that argument begs the question of what should be done if, for political reasons or otherwise, regulatory policy does not adequately respond to an asset price bubble. Indeed, one can argue that it was precisely the huge capital inflow from abroad that fueled the asset price inflation and low interest rate spreads that ultimately masked risks from both regulators and rating agencies.

In any event, the most extreme and the most immediate problems were caused by the market for mortgage loans made to "subprime," or low-income, borrowers. "Advances" in securitization, as well as a seemingly endless run-up in housing prices, allowed people to buy houses who might not previously have thought they could do so. Unfortunately, many of these borrowers depended on loans with variable interest rates and low initial "teaser" rates. When it came time to reset the loans, rising interest rates and a deteriorating economy made it difficult for many to meet their mortgage obligations. And thus the subprime debacle began.

The U.S. conceit that its financial and regulatory system could withstand massive capital inflows on a sustained basis without any problems arguably laid the foundations for the global financial crisis of the late 2000s. The thinking that "this time is different"—because this time the U.S. had a superior system—once again proved false. Outsized financial market returns were in fact greatly exaggerated by capital inflows, just as would be the case in emerging markets. What could in retrospect be recognized as huge regulatory mistakes, including the deregulation of the subprime mortgage market and the 2004 decision of the Securities and Exchange Commission to allow investment banks to triple their leverage ratios (that is, the ratio measuring the amount of risk to capital), appeared benign at the time. Capital inflows pushed up borrowing and asset prices while reducing spreads on all sorts of risky assets, leading the International Monetary Fund to conclude in April 2007, in its twice-annual *World Economic Outlook*, that risks to the global economy had become extremely low and that, for the moment, there were no great worries. When the international agency charged with being the global watchdog declares that there are no risks, there is no surer sign that this time is different.

Again, the crisis that began in 2007 shares many parallels with the boom period before an emerging market crisis, when governments often fail to take precautionary steps to let steam out of the system; they expect the capital inflow bonanza to last indefinitely. Often, instead, they take steps that push their economies toward greater risk in an effort to keep the boom going a little longer.

Such is a brief characterization of the debate surrounding the this-time-is-different mentality leading up to the U.S. subprime financial crisis. To sum up, many were led to think that "this time is different" for the following reasons:

- The United States, with the world's most reliable system of financial regulation, the most innovative financial system, a strong political system, and the world's largest and most liquid capital markets, was special. It could withstand huge capital inflows without worry.

- Rapidly emerging developing economies needed a secure place to invest their funds for diversification purposes.
- Increased global financial integration was deepening global capital markets and allowing countries to go deeper into debt.
- In addition to its other strengths, the United States has superior monetary policy institutions and monetary policy makers.
- New financial instruments were allowing many new borrowers to enter mortgage markers.
- All that was happening was just a further deepening of financial globalization thanks to innovation and should not be a great source of worry.

The Episodes of Postwar Bank-Centered Financial Crisis

As the list of reasons that "this time is different" (provided by academics, business leaders, and policy makers) grew, so did the similarities of U.S. economic developments to those seen in other precrisis episodes.

To examine the antecedents of the 2007 U.S. subprime crisis (which later grew into the "Second Great Contraction"), we begin by looking at data from the eighteen bank-centered financial crises that occurred in the post-World War II period. For the time being, we will limit our attention to crises in industrialized countries to avoid seeming to engage in hyperbole by comparing the United States to emerging markets. But of course, as we have already seen . . . financial crises in emerging markets and those in advanced economies are not so different . . .

Among the eighteen bank-centered financial crises following World War II, the "Big Five" crises [Spain 1977, Norway 1987, Finland 1991, Sweden 1991, Japan 1992] have all involved major declines in output over a protracted period, often lasting two years or more. The worst postwar crisis prior to 2007, of course, was that of Japan in 1992, which set the country off on its "lost decade." The earlier Big Five crises, however, were also extremely traumatic events.

The remaining thirteen financial crises in rich countries [United Kingdom 1974, Germany 1977, Canada 1983, United States 1984, Iceland 1985, Denmark 1987, New Zealand 1987, Australia 1989, Italy 1990, Greece 1991, United Kingdom 1991, France 1994, United Kingdom 1995] represent more minor events that were associated with significantly worse economic performance than usual, but were not catastrophic. For example, the U.S. crisis that began in 1984 was the savings and loan crisis. Some of the other thirteen crises had relatively little impact, but we retain them for now for comparison purposes. It will soon be clear that the run-up to the

U.S. financial crisis of the late 2000s really did not resemble these milder crises, though most policy makers and journalists did not seem to realize this at the time.

A Comparison of the Subprime Crisis with Past Crises in Advanced Economies

In choosing the variables we used to measure the U.S. risk of a financial crisis we were motivated by the literature on predicting financial crises in both developed countries and emerging markets. This literature on financial crises suggests that markedly rising asset prices, slowing real economic activity, large current account deficits, and sustained debt buildups (whether public, private, or both) are important precursors to a financial crisis. Recall also the evidence on capital flow "bonanzas" . . . which showed that sustained capital inflows have been particularly strong markers for financial crises, at least in the post-1970 period of greater financial liberalization. Historically, financial liberalization or innovation has also been a recurrent precursor to financial crises . . .

. . . [C]ase studies have shown . . . that a massive run-up in housing prices usually precedes a financial crisis. It is a bit disconcerting to note that, according to this figure, the run-up in housing prices in the United States exceeded the average of the "Big Five" financial crises, and the downturn appears to have been sharper . . .

. . . [G]oing into the crisis, U.S. equity prices held up better than those in either comparison group, perhaps in part because of the Federal Reserve's aggressive countercyclical response to the 2001 recession and in part because of the substantial "surprise element" in the severity of the U.S. crisis. But a year after the onset of the crisis . . . , equity prices had plummeted, in line with what happened in the "Big Five" financial crises.

. . . [T]he U.S. current account deficit . . . was far larger and more persistent than was typical in other crises . . . The fact that the U.S. dollar remained the world's reserve currency during a period in which many foreign central banks (particularly in Asia) were amassing record amounts of foreign exchange reserves certainly increased the foreign capital available to finance the record U.S. current account deficits . . .

In 2008, developments took a turn for the worse, and the growth slowdown became more acute. At the beginning of 2009, the consensus—based on forecasts published in the *Wall Street Journal*—was that this recession would be deeper than the average "Big Five" experience. Note that in severe Big Five cases, the growth rate has fallen by more than 5 percent from peak to trough and has remained low for roughly three years . . .

. . . Increasing public debt has been a nearly universal precursor of other postwar crises . . .

One caveat to our claim that the indicators showed the United States at high risk of a deep financial crisis in the run-up to 2007: compared to other countries that have experienced financial crises, the United States performed well with regard to inflation prior to 2007. Of course, the earlier crises in developed countries occurred during a period of declining inflation in the rich countries.

Summary

Why did so many people fail to see the financial crisis of 2007 coming? As to the standard indicators of financial crises, many red lights were blinking brightly well in advance. We do not pretend that it would have been easy to forestall the U.S. financial crisis had policy makers realized the risks earlier. We have focused on macroeconomic issues, but many problems were hidden in the "plumbing" of the financial markets, as has become painfully evident since the beginning of the crisis. Some of these problems might have taken years to address. Above all, the huge run-up in housing prices—over 100 percent nationally over five years—should have been an alarm, especially fueled as it was by rising leverage. At the beginning of 2008, the total value of mortgages in the United States was approximately 90 percent of GDP. Policy makers should have decided several years prior to the crisis to deliberately take some steam out of the system. Unfortunately, efforts to maintain growth and prevent significant sharp stock market declines had the effect of taking the safety valve off the pressure cooker. Of course, even with the epic proportions of this financial crisis, the United States had not defaulted as of the middle of 2009. Were the United States an emerging market, its exchange rate would have plummeted and its interest rates soared. Access to capital markets would be lost in a classic Dornbusch/Calvo-type sudden stop. During the first year following the crisis (2007), exactly the opposite happened: the dollar appreciated and interest rates fell as world investors viewed other countries as even riskier than the United States and bought Treasury securities copiously. But buyer beware! Over the longer run, the U.S. exchange rate and interest rates could well revert to form, especially if policies are not made to re-establish a firm base for long-term fiscal sustainability.

CHAPTER 17

THE GFC EXPOSES CRACKS IN THE EUROPEAN MONETARY UNION: THE EUROPEAN SOVEREIGN DEBT CRISIS

■■■

On January 1, 1999, eleven member states of the European Union (EU) began Stage Three of the European Economic and Monetary Union (EMU). They adopted a single currency, the euro, and agreed that monetary policy in the Eurozone would be run through a single entity, the European Central Bank (ECB). It was an epic day politically and economically, as it marked yet another milestone in the long and evolving process toward European economic integration under a supranational framework of governance that you can't find anywhere else. Except for some bumps in the road, all seemed to be good with the Eurozone and the euro.

Then came the global financial crisis. European governments had to spend big time to keep their economies afloat. Ireland's debt went through the roof when it nationalized its debts. Fiscal deficits jumped up, and when they did, people could see flaws in the EMU. Starting with Greece and then moving to Ireland, Portugal, Spain, and Italy, governments found themselves unable or nearly unable to repay the bonds they issued to foreign investors. Thus was born the European sovereign debt crisis.

This chapter will tell you about it. You'll see familiar themes, such as screwed up economies and contagion. But the crisis differs from other crises we've looked at to the extent that it threatened the viability of the monetary union (although there's a long history of monetary unions that have collapsed), and tested the ability of the EU to preserve the idea of a united Europe. We're going to cover a lot here, but as with all other chapters, we're just giving you the basics.

> "[T]he currency union is our common destiny. It is a question, no more or less, of the preservation of the European idea. That is our historical task: for if the euro fails, then Europe fails."
>
> —Chancellor Angela Merkel, quoted in B. Hall and Q. Peel, "Europe: Adrift amid rift," *Financial Times* (2010)

And we're going to tell you the story of the crisis through 2012—the best part of the drama—and then give you an update. Let's begin with a primer on the EU.

701

I. THE FORMATION OF THE EMU

Part One: The Basics About the EU

The EU is all about peace and prosperity through integration—stop the bloody wars among neighbors. It started after World War II with the 1951 treaty that established the European Coal and Steel Community, which sought to achieve the free movement of coal and steel. Then came the European Economic Community (EEC), established in 1957 via a treaty known popularly as the Treaty of Rome. The EEC aimed to create a common market for the free movement of goods, services, capital, and labor. These two Communities along with the 1957 treaty that established the European Atomic Energy Community (to pursue peaceful uses of nuclear energy) formed the troika known as the European Community (EC) or EU. The treaties that established the European Communities have been amended several times. We're going to focus on the Treaty on European Union of 1992, also known as the Maastricht Treaty, which established the EU (currently 28 member countries) and laid down a roadmap for a monetary union.

In this chapter you're going to see references to the key EU institutions, especially the European Commission and the European Council. So let's talk briefly about the EU institutions. Let's start with the Commission. It's the executive branch of the EU and its primary responsibilities are to propose legislation and to make sure member states implement EU law. Then you have your Council of Ministers, which enacts legislation proposed by the Commission. (Don't confuse the Council of Ministers with the European Council, comprised of heads of state who decide on political aspects of the EU.)

"The European parliament is powerful. We can wake up [German finance minister] Wolfgang Schäuble at 5.30am—and he actually made concessions [over the EU banking union]."

> —Sven Giegold, Green MEP, quoted in A. Barker, "Marathon talks seal EU banking union," *Financial Times* (2014)

The European Parliament is also involved in legislation. Back in the day it had very little power—it basically played a consultative role. Today, the Parliament has real power: it can amend and even adopt legislation. What a concept! In some areas, including financial legislation, the Council and the Parliament have to work together to enact legislation.

"Wait just a darn second there fella," you might say. "How exactly do you implement EU legislation in them member countries? Huh, fella? Huh?" you might ask after too many energy drinks. You do it via directives or regulations. Directives bind member states but not citizens directly. They give states a general framework but states have to implement the directives through domestic legislation. Regulations, on the other hand, are directly binding on citizens and they become domestic law as soon as they are made. In a bit we'll talk about the Stability and Growth Pact, which is implemented via regulations. "Are you satisfied, sir or ma'am? Huh?"

Now let's see how the EU judiciary is put together. First you have the European Court of Justice (ECJ), which has original jurisdiction in cases where, say, the Commission claims that a member country has failed to do what it's supposed to do under EU law, or where an EU country (or the Council, Commission, or in some cases the Parliament) claims that an EU law is illegal and should be annulled. If there's an action in a national court, it might be referred to the ECJ for a preliminary ruling on EU law. Then there's the General Court. It has jurisdiction in a number of matters ranging from actions for damages brought by persons or companies that claim they've been harmed by action or inaction of the EU to EU staff claiming damages. The ECJ has appellate jurisdiction over these cases.

Okay, this should be enough. Let's get started on the EMU, starting with basics about monetary unions.

Part Two: Monetary Unions, Optimal Currency Area, and the EMU

Monetary Unions

Monetary unions go way back, well before the idea of an integrated Europe. A monetary union is an agreement among countries to adopt a common currency and allow a central authority run monetary policy. Why would they do this? First, let's talk transaction costs related to the exchange of goods and focus on currency-exchange costs. When countries don't share a common currency, fluctuations in their exchange rates can be a cost of doing business. Let's look at an example: Prior to the creation of the euro, if a French merchant wanted to purchase a product in Germany to sell in France, the merchant had to take French francs and exchange them for German deutschmarks to pay for the product. If a fluctuation in the exchange rate between the franc and the deutschmark caused the deutschmark to be valued higher than the franc—e.g., a change of 3FF/1DM to 5FF/1DM in the exchange rate—the French merchant would lose profit since it would have to convert more francs into deutschmarks to buy the product. And on top of that, the merchant would also have to pay service fees when exchanging the currencies. You can see that this cost can deter business transactions.

Another reason countries might be down for a monetary union is price transparency. When you have a common currency, producers and consumers can easily compare prices across the union without worrying about exchange rates. This will promote competition among sellers in union, which ultimately benefits the consumer. Another example: If a good is more expensive in country A than in country B, consumers will buy more of that good from country B because they won't incur transaction the costs we talked about. To compete with country B, the producer in country A will have to become more efficient to be able to reduce its prices so that it doesn't lose business. This gives consumers more purchasing power.

That's all good but there are downsides to monetary unions. A big one is that countries lose control over monetary policy. So a member country can't unilaterally decide to pump money into the economy to stimulate it and create jobs. And it can't suck money out of the economy to fight inflation. Here's another biggie: A country that's not in a monetary union can devalue its currency if it needs to—say, to promote exports. In a monetary union with a common currency that's no longer possible. Lots of folks said that if Greece had not adopted the euro and still used the drachma, it could have devalued its currency to boost its anemic exports.

The Optimal Currency Area Theory

Even though monetary unions might come with cool benefits, not just any group of countries can successfully form a union. Economists often ask whether the grouping constitutes an "optimal currency area." According to optimal currency area theory monetary unions will work when (i) there's lots of flexibility in wages and prices, allowing money and goods to be distributed according to region-wide supply and demand; (ii) labor is highly mobile across the region; (iii) intra-regional trade is high; and (iv) there's a system that can deal with "asymmetric shocks"—shocks that affect one part of the region more than the rest—through the transfer of funds or tax adjustments across the region.

The United States (one of the longest-lasting monetary unions) is an example of an optimal currency area. Wages are highly flexible (wages adjust to changes in demand for labor) and labor is highly mobile (it shifts to areas with high demand). This is important when a state or region of the U.S. experiences an economic downturn: if, say, the state of California experiences a downturn marked by increased unemployment, people without jobs can move relatively easily to other states to find jobs. This will result in a drop in wage levels in California (which helps companies cope with the crisis) until the state economy reverses course. States also do a lot of trade with each other. Fiscal federalism, meaning fiscal policies (taxing and spending) set at both the national and state levels, also helps. It allows the national government to respond better to asymmetric shocks— economic downturns in a state or region. And states can set their own fiscal policies to spur or slow growth when needed. The national government will have the states' back with fiscal transfers—increased spending in certain areas (e.g., unemployment benefits) when states' actions alone won't cut it.

The EMU

What about the EMU? Regarding the arguments for and against monetary unions, those in favor of the EMU threw down a number of arguments. First, it would promote efficiency and growth in the Eurozone by eliminating exchange rate uncertainty and transactions costs. Second, price stability and a single market would lead to low inflation and pump business. Third, the EMU would bring valuable gains for many countries' national budgets through reduced interest rates that would make it cheaper for a nation to borrow to fund its national budget. You'll see that the last argument will come back to bite the EU in the butt.

Critics of the idea pointed to a country's loss of control over monetary policy and the exchange rate, tools they could use in bad times. "And, hey," they said, "what if in bad times a country wants to use fiscal policy—spending, to return to good times?" The EMU would be predicated on a common low inflation rate. As we'll see, to do this EMU rules put limits on how much a country can spend by putting limits on fiscal deficits (3% of GDP). But deficit spending might be necessary to prevent the country from falling into a deep hole, so the argument goes.

And what about optimal currency area theory? Some economists have compared the U.S. to the EMU and concluded that the EMU doesn't meet all of the optimal currency area criteria. It doesn't have a common fiscal policy. Individual countries are responsible for setting their own fiscal policies to respond to asymmetric shocks. This raises the possibility that a country that goes on a spending spree can destabilize the monetary union. This is what gave rise to the European crisis despite the spending limits. What's more, the EMU can't make fiscal transfers to a country or region in crisis. And labor isn't as mobile in the EMU as it is in the U.S. due to language and cultural barriers. This makes wages less flexible to changes in demand, which prevents prices from adjusting easily to market changes.

But all this misses the point. It's ultimately all about politics. The EMU was another step toward political unification in Europe. The two key actors were Germany and France—Europe's largest economies. Germany's was down for the monetary union because it would secure Germany's place in a united Europe. Chancellor Helmut Kohl was determined to show that German unification and European integration were both in Europe's best interest. Kohl also wanted to stay cool with France.

> *"If a Chancellor is trying to push something through, he must be a man of power. And if he's smart, he knows when the time is ripe. In one case—the euro—I was like a dictator . . . The euro is a synonym for Europe. Europe, for the first time, has no more war."*
> —Former German Chancellor Helmut Kohl, quoted in J. Vasagar, "Helmut Kohl: I acted like a dictator to bring in the euro," *The Telegraph* (2013)

French leaders, on the other hand, viewed the currency union as a key step to increasing French influence within Europe. France was concerned that the deutschmark would become much stronger following the reunification of Germany, which would help Germany become the leading power in Europe. France thought more European integration would keep Germany under control. As we write this, Germany is playing France in the World Cup. But we don't know the score yet.

Anyway, there also was the peace thing. Europe's leaders were convinced that developing stronger economic ties through the EMU would deter European countries from going to war with one another since the costs of war would mess with the economic well-being of the entire region.

Part Three: The Establishment of the EMU

The drive to establish the EMU goes back to the fall of the Bretton Woods System in 1971—we covered it in Chapter 3. Remember that the BWS's collapse resulted in rough waters for exchange rates. Europe acted quickly to achieve exchange rate stability: In March 1972 member countries put together a "snake" where a number of countries agreed to limit the fluctuations of their currencies to a band of plus or minus 2.25%. But the snake couldn't survive the exchange rate turbulence of the 1970s. Its successor was the European Monetary System (EMS), established in 1979. The EMS was based on an Exchange Rate Mechanism (ERM) that was identical to the snake's bands. Meanwhile the drive for a monetary union culminated in Delors Report in 1988, the product of a committee of central bank governors chaired by Commission President Jacques Delors. The Report set out a three-stage process to achieve a monetary union, which many central bankers favored. A few years later the need for a monetary union was confirmed by the **1992–93 crisis of the EMS**, which was marked by severe turbulence that forced some countries to drop out. In 1989, Europe's leaders agreed to begin the first stage in 1990. But they weren't all of one mind on some important issues:

The Negotiations

Setting: Europe 1989–1991, a conference room somewhere in Europe

Chair: Are we agreed that there should be a single entity to manage monetary policy of participating countries under an agreed set of rules?

Country 1: Speaking on behalf of most member states, especially France and Italy, we believe that policy judgments should be based on the economic conditions of all the participating countries, not just on the economic conditions and views of the great country of Germany.

Country 2: Yes, of course.

Country 3: A most wise approach.

Country 4: Indeed!

Country 5: Where is the wine!

Country 4: Food without wine? Are we not civilized in Europe?

(big noises of approval)

Chair: As we pour, I put before you another question: Should entering the third stage of the EMU, adopting the euro, be optional?

Country 2: Most of us want a fixed timeline for joining the EMU. Why would we make the sacrifices to enter the EMU only to find that other countries have second thoughts about going forward?

Country 5: With all respect, not all of us, especially the United Kingdom and Denmark, agree with our brethren. We oppose setting a fixed timeline. Those countries that seek to be part of the union should be able to choose when they wish to join.

(rumbling)

Chair: Very well. The next question we must consider is whether the monetary union should require limits on member states' borrowing and indebtedness, and the flexibility of those limits.

Country 6: Let us not discount Germany's position that there should be permanent constraints on borrowing. Irresponsible fiscal policies would make it difficult for the European Central Bank to control monetary policy. Nor should we forget that if one or more member countries run excessive fiscal deficits as a result of excessive spending, doing so would negatively affect other members if the ECB were forced to impose higher interest rates to control the inflation. Borrowing would become more expensive, reducing long-term growth.

Country 3: Respectfully, many of us oppose this restriction. What would happen to our political affairs if we were forced to cut spending or raise taxes? Aside from crass politics, we must be able to use fiscal policy to combat economic stagnation via government spending.

* * *

Ultimately, as you'll see in a minute, the EMU's framers agreed on the three-stage timetable for the implementation of the EMU as well as a set of rules to constrain borrowing and spending. The third stage would begin automatically in 1999 with those countries that had fulfilled the necessary economic criteria, called "convergence criteria," established by the European Council. Let's go to the stages.

Stage One

During stage one, which lasted from July 1, 1990 until December 1993, member countries eliminated internal barriers to the free movement of capital and exchange rate controls, and more closely cooperated on economic and monetary policy. The most important aspect of this phase was the Maastricht Treaty on European Union, which was signed in February 1992 and entered into force in November 1993. It set out the necessary economic conditions for countries to fulfill if they wanted to join the EMU.

The Maastricht Treaty set forth a set of economic criteria—the convergence criteria—that European Union members had to meet to join the EMU. The four main criteria are:

Criteria	Description
Price Stability	Countries could not have an annual inflation rate of more than 1.5% higher than the average inflation rate of the three member countries with the lowest inflation.
Limiting government borrowing and debt	Governments' annual budget deficits could not exceed 3% of GDP and total outstanding debt could not be more than 60% of GDP. There were some exceptions to these rules. For instance, the deficit limit would not apply in cases where exceptional circumstances cause the excessive deficit such as a severe downturn in the economy or a fall in GDP of at least 2% in one year. And the 60% limit on debt would not apply when the debt was diminishing at a satisfactory pace.
Exchange rate stability	The exchange rate of applicant countries had to be within the normal fluctuation margins of the ERM for at least two years. During those two years, the country's currency could not have been devalued.
Durable long-term interest rates	Long-term interest rates could not be more than 2% higher than the interest rates of the three member states with the lowest inflation.

The Maastricht Treaty also created the ECB, which is responsible for setting monetary policy for the Eurozone. The primary objective of the ECB is to maintain price stability within the Eurozone. The ECB is also responsible for intervening in the foreign exchange market through the purchase or sale of foreign currencies to maintain a target inflation rate, holding and managing the foreign reserves of the member states, and promoting the smooth operations of payment systems—how transfers of money are handled. And only the ECB can issue euro banknotes and coins.

But understand this: The creation of the ECB didn't wipe out member countries' central banks. Central banks are responsible for implementing policy in their respective countries according to the guidelines the ECB establishes. And national central banks carry out other traditional functions such as overseeing banking supervision and regulation in their own countries.

Now let's talk fiscal policy. Unlike monetary policy, each national government retained control over its fiscal policy. Hmmm . . . why might that be? Basically because fiscal policy serves several economic and social objectives, such as providing social security, healthcare, and education. By allowing countries to retain control over fiscal policy, each country could tailor its spending priorities and response to economic shocks and structural problems in a way that it deemed best. In other words, the agreement regarding fiscal policy was based on a consensus that the task of smoothing asymmetric shocks—shocks that affect one country's economy more than the rest—should fall to national fiscal policy.

"The Union shall not be liable for or assume the commitments of central governments, regional, local or other public authorities, other bodies governed by public law, or public undertakings of any Member State, without prejudice to mutual financial guarantees for the joint execution of a specific project. A Member State shall not be liable for or assume the commitments of central governments, regional, local or other public authorities, other bodies governed by public law, or public undertakings of another Member State, without prejudice to mutual financial guarantees for the joint execution of a specific project."
—Article 125, Treaty on the Functioning of the European Union

But to guard against too much borrowing and spending, the framers of the Maastricht Treaty included a "no bailout" clause prohibiting member states from offering financial support to other member states (unless there are "severe difficulties caused by natural disasters or exceptional occurrences beyond the control of a member state") as well as financing another government's debt. The ECB's rules prohibiting it from purchasing bonds directly from member governments reinforce the no bailout constraint. We're back to moral hazard, folks: These prohibitions were designed to counter the risk that countries would act recklessly if they knew they would be bailed-out if necessary.

Stage Two

The second stage in the creation of the EMU spanned from January 1, 1994 to December 31, 1998. During this stage, the European Monetary Institute (EMI, which eventually became the European Central Bank in 1998) was established. The EMI was in charge of setting up the procedures and policy instruments to establish the single monetary policy for the EMU. The EMI was also responsible for reviewing the economic plans of the countries that wanted to join the EMU.

Remember the fiscal thing? (We just talked about it!) Stage Two witnessed the adoption of the Stability and Growth Pact (SGP) in 1997, legislation intended to make sure that member countries abided by the Maastricht Treaty's limits on deficits and debt—annual budget deficits would not exceed 3% of GDP and national debts would not exceed 60% of GDP. The Pact has a preventive and corrective arm. Under the preventive arm, member states submit plans (called stability or convergence programs) showing how the country intends to achieve or safeguard its fiscal stability and avoid excessive deficits. The corrective applies sanctions (up to 0.5% of GDP) against a country that has breached the SGP's deficit ceiling and hasn't done much about it for over a year.

Before the European sovereign debt crisis erupted, you could see that the SGP had no teeth. Check this out: In 2002, Germany exceeded the 3% fiscal deficit limit and projected that it would run a 3.4% deficit in 2003. The European Council basically shrugged. It did the same thing with France. In 2004, the French government approved a budget with a deficit of 3.6% of GDP. The Council once again shrugged its shoulders. This isn't surprising, considering that soon after the SGP took effect member countries criticized the Pact for being too stringent.

In 2005, the Eurozone Finance Ministers announced a set of reforms to the Pact. The changes included a requirement that countries lower their deficits and debts during periods of economic growth. Countries also would be able to claim factors such as spending on development aid as a justification for small breaches of the deficit limit. And a country could claim that it was the victim of a severe economic downturn, defined as a "negative growth rate," as opposed to –2% growth in the previous version. The deficit limit of 3% of GDP and 60% debt limit remained the same. As you'll see in a bit, the Pact was revised again in 2011 to give it some spine.

Stage Three

The final step toward establishing the EMU began in January 1999. It included the introduction of the euro as the Union's single currency and the transfer of the member states' monetary policy power to the ECB. At the end of this stage, eleven countries adopted the euro: Belgium, Germany, Spain, France, Ireland, Italy, Luxembourg, the Netherlands, Austria, Portugal, and Finland. In January 2001, the European Council found that Greece had also fulfilled the criteria and could join the EMU. But check this out regarding the convergence criteria. Some countries, such as Belgium, Italy, Ireland, and Greece, had big time debts—above 100% of GDP—during the 1980s and the early 1990s and deficits around 10% of GDP.

Denmark and the United Kingdom secured opt-outs, which legally exempts them from joining unless they decide otherwise. Sweden has a de facto opt out. As of this writing, the Eurozone has 18 members. In addition to the original 11 and Greece, we have: Slovenia (2007), Cyprus, (2008), Malta (2008), Slovakia (2009), Estonia (2011), and Latvia (2014). The remaining members of the EU, Bulgaria, Czech Republic, Hungary, Lithuania, Poland, and Romania, Croatia, are expected to adopt the euro as soon as they meet the economic policy targets.

The Flaws Exposed

The whole point of the convergence game was to get eurozone countries to come together economically so that the monetary union would function smoothly. Then things would rock. But actually the opposite happened: divergence. You had your northern European countries—Austria, Belgium, Germany, Finland, France, Luxembourg, and the Netherlands. Then you had your group of southern European countries, including Greece, Ireland, Italy, Portugal, and Spain, collectively referred to as the GIIPS.

The divergence was bad news for the GIIPS and eventually for the entire Eurozone. Let's look at a few divergences. Although the GIIPS had higher average economic growth rates than the northern European countries, they suffered from inflation, which reduced their competitiveness. The GIIPS ran trade deficits; northern European countries generally had pretty large trade surpluses. The GIIPS ran larger fiscal deficits and higher levels of government debt than the northern European countries.

And how did the GIIPS finance their trade and budget deficits? By issuing bonds to foreign investors. And why not borrow? Because they were members of the Eurozone, they could borrow cheaply—and investors saw the bonds as a safe bet. It's all good, right?

The global financial crisis erupts. And there's no EMU-wide fiscal policy.

II. SPREAD OF THE EUROPEAN SOVEREIGN DEBT CRISIS

You know all about "contagion" now that you've looked at the Asian financial crisis. The same kind of thing happened in this crisis. It all started with Greece. Most of this stuff should sound familiar.

Part One: The First Domino

Greece joined the EU in 1981. At the time, the economy was heavily controlled by the state. As the decade progressed, the government spent heavily on public sector wages and social benefits. Clientelism was widespread: Politicians used public sector jobs and benefits to secure political support. And tax evasion was rampant. Still, between 1997 and 2007 Greece boasted an average of 4% GDP growth annually—almost twice the EU average. Hmmm . . . How could that happen? Like we said just a bit ago, as Greece played the convergence game, interest rates on Greek bonds dropped dramatically—by 18% between 1993 and 1999. Investors gobbled up Greek bonds, thinking that the convergence criteria, the common monetary policy anchored by the European Central Bank, and the Stability and Growth Pact made Greece a safe bet.

But, like other countries we've seen hurdling towards a crisis, Greece didn't use the capital influx wisely. Instead of using the money to improve Greece's competitiveness, the government used the money to pay for its government spending—tax receipts sure weren't going to support the spending. The government also used the money to pay for imports while its exports sagged. Result: ballooning fiscal and trade deficits and a stagnant economy that was unable to generate the income to repay its debt.

Then the global financial crisis hit. Greece, like many advanced economies had to increase government spending to cope. Its reported public debt rose from 106% of GDP to 126% of GDP in 2009. In 2008, Greece's growth dropped to 2% of GDP. By 2009, Greece's economy dove into a recession.

What made things worse was that it turned out that the government had been falsely reporting data to cover up how bad things were. The government originally reported its 2009 deficit at 3.7%, but later revised it to 12.5% of GDP—the final number for 2009 was 15.4%. Then things went to hell in a handbasket:

- The major credit rating agencies downgraded Greece's sovereign debt rating.
- Spooked investors began demanding higher interest rates for Greek bonds.
- Greece was on the brink of default.
- A default would cause investors to dump the bonds of other Eurozone countries with high debt.
- Banks throughout Europe with exposure to Greek bonds and bonds of other Eurozone countries faced potentially debilitating blows.
- The end of the Eurozone and the euro?

> *"An uncontrolled default or exit of Greece from the euro zone would cause enormous economic and social damage, not only to Greece but to the European Union."*
>
> —Ollie Rehn (Finland), EU Economic and Monetary Affairs Commissioner, quoted in http://online.wsj.com/news/articles/SB10001424052970203716204577018383688667576?cb=logged0.3046858479437428 (2011)

News Alert May 2, 2010:

In a preemptive move to save the Greek government from defaulting on its sovereign bonds, the leaders of the Eurozone and the International Monetary Fund have announced a three-year package of €110 billion, or about $158 billion, in loans to Greece. Eurozone countries will contribute €80 billion, with the IMF providing the rest. Greece has agreed to implement austerity measures, including wage cuts, cuts in military spending, pension freezes, and increased taxes.

Part Two: The Contagion

The Greek bailout wasn't enough to calm jittery investors. They worried about other highly indebted Eurozone countries. So what if they weren't carbon copies of Greece. Investors began demanding higher interest rates on governments' bonds to compensate for the perceived increased risk, whether justified or not. Some investors withdrew from these markets altogether.

Ireland

The next domino to fall was Ireland, even though it wasn't "a Greece." It didn't have a tax evasion problem, it didn't suffer from a lack of competitiveness, and didn't falsify its fiscal data. Not only that, but it made spending cuts pretty quickly after its debt rose in the aftermath of the global financial crisis and before it had to ask for help in November 2010 to cover the cost of rescuing its banking sector. But it's not like Ireland didn't have problems. When it received the rescue package in 2010, its deficit was 32% of GDP, and its budget cuts didn't reassure investors that its debt was sustainable. Interest rates on its bonds soared in October 2010.

So what went wrong? Ireland's problems stemmed from a construction and housing boom. Irish banks financed mortgage loans by borrowing from foreign lenders, who were happy to provide funding to banks in a country that seemed stable and posed little financial risk. In 2008, Irish banks' combined debt from making loans for property purchases had reached over 60% of GDP. The banks relied on interest payments from their borrowers to repay the loans they received from foreign lenders.

You know what happened next, right? The housing bubble burst in 2008. Unemployed property owners began falling behind on loan payments and defaulting on loans, leaving Irish banks unable to repay their lenders. The government was forced to rescue the banking sector—you know, investor guarantees, purchasing bad loans from the banks, that kind of thing. It borrowed to finance its rescue of the banking sector, which caused its debt to rise from 24.8% to 44.5% of GDP between 2007 and 2009. By 2010, the writing was on the wall. As things worsened economically, investors lost confidence in Ireland's ability to repay its debts. It got so bad that the government couldn't issue bonds on the international markets to raise funds.

News Alert November 2010:

Ireland has agreed on a three-year €85 billion rescue package to help with government funding and the rescue of failing banks. Ireland's Treasury and National Pension Fund Reserve have contributed €17.5 billion, with the remainder coming from the International Monetary Fund and other European sources. In return for the rescue, Ireland has committed to reducing its deficit to 3% of GDP in four years by cutting at least €15 billion from its budget.

Investors weren't convinced that Ireland was out of the woods. As news of the rescue package spread, interest rates on Irish bonds increased. Standard & Poor's and Moody's downgraded Ireland's credit rating.

European leader 1: How can this be? The whole point of this rescue is to stop the contagion.

European leader 2: Calm the markets.

European leader 1: We can't let them attack Portugal.

European leader 2: Portugal's banks are not like Ireland's. But that won't stop them. They see slow economic growth. Large budget deficit. Another rescue. But that's not really the problem, is it?

European leader 1: The Spanish are outraged. "We're not Greece. We're not Ireland. And we're certainly not Portugal. We're healthy."

European leader 2: They can tear their beautiful hair out. But they can't hide their exposure to Portuguese debt. If Portugal falls . . .

European leader 1: My god.

European leader 2: And let's not forget Spain's housing-market crisis. Its high unemployment.

European leader 1: This is a nightmare. What more can we do?

European leader 2: *We* can have another glass. Premier cru. It calms the nerves, my friend.

Portugal

European leader 2 saw the problems with Portugal. Since joining the euro in 1999, Portugal had the lowest growth in the Eurozone. Like Greece, joining the Eurozone gave Portugal access to cheap funding via the international markets but it didn't use the capital to increase productivity and competitiveness. Between 2001 and 2007, Portugal's average annual growth rate was a measly 1.1%.

Meanwhile, increased government spending and decreasing tax revenue caused the fiscal deficit to shoot up. While Portugal's deficit was under 3% between 2002 and 2004, it rose to 5.9% in 2005 and reached a high of 10.1% of GDP in 2009, due in part to a drop in tax revenue when the global financial crisis hit. With less revenue coming in, the government had to rely on borrowed funds to finance its spending on social programs.

To finance the growing debt, Portugal issued new bonds. But investors demanded higher interest rates, which just added to the country's debt. Investors saw this and became increasingly unwilling to lend to Portugal. By the spring of 2011, it became clear that the Portuguese government wouldn't be able to repay its debt. In the beginning of the year, it had €2 billion in cash reserves and was due to repay investors €4.2 billion on government bonds in April and another €4.9 billion in June.

News Alert May 17, 2011:

Portugal has agreed to a €78 billion rescue package on the condition that it reduce its deficit and implement a number of other economic reforms. The International Monetary Fund's share of the package is €26 billion. The European Financial Stability Facility will contribute €16 billion.

As Portugal implemented austerity measures to try to bring its deficit under control, the economy contracted further. It didn't help that its exports dropped because of the crisis—70% of its exports went to the EU, including 24% to Spain. Portugal was in a real hole.

What were the European leaders really worried about?

Spain

At first glance, Spain was all good. It enjoyed substantial economic growth prior to 2007. And check this out: In 2007, Spain had a budget *surplus*— yeah, you heard right, a surplus of 1.9%.

So what happened to Spain? In a nutshell, Spain, like Ireland, experienced a housing boom. Like other Eurozone countries, Spain enjoyed low borrowing rates. Spain's banks and other lending institutions like the cajas de ahorros (Spain's savings and loan banks) borrowed from abroad and used the money to fund loans that households and businesses used to buy real estate. By 2008, Spain had borrowed the equivalent of 9.1% of GDP.

> *"The most important thing at this moment is that Spain stays solvent."*
> —Prime Minister Jose Luis Rodriguez Zapatero (Spain), quoted in http://online.wsj.com/news/articles/SB10001424052970203716204577018383688667576?cb=logged0.3046858479437428 (2011)

Then the housing bubble burst. Spanish banks all of sudden were sitting on a bunch of bad loans. Uh, oh. How were they going to pay back their lenders? Enter stage left: Spain's government. "We're here to rescue the banking sector!" That budget surplus in 2007? Uh . . . yeah, it turned into a deficit real quick: 4.5% of GDP in 2008, growing to 9.7% in 2010. Spain's debt rose from 39.6% of GDP in 2007 to 40.2% of GDP by 2009. By April 2012, Spain's debt was equivalent to 78% of GDP, up from 68% in 2011.

In March 2012, the government announced that it would not meet the 4.4% of GDP budget deficit target set by the European Commission for 2012. It also disclosed that its 2011 numbers were off; things were worse than originally forecasted. Following the announcement, interest rates on Spanish ten-year bonds spiked, reaching 5.81% in April 2012—their highest level since the beginning of December 2011. Brutal.

Italy

Really? Italy wasn't in the midst of a banking crisis like Ireland and Spain.

Although it had the fourth highest sovereign debt in the world (119% of GDP as of November 2011), its fiscal deficit—3.7% of GDP as of November 2011—was low compared to the Eurozone average of 6%. But it had a slow-growing economy and high debt, much like Greece and Portugal.

> *"A serious crisis of confidence has emerged towards our country, in Europe and not only in Europe. We must be aware of this and, more than feel wounded, we must feel spurred on in our pride and our determination to respond."*
> —President Giorgio Napolitano (Italy), quoted in http://online.wsj.com/news/articles/SB10001424052970203716204577018383688667576?cb=logged0.3046858479437428 (2011)

When the global financial crisis hit, Italy's economy took a hit: In 2008, the economy shrank by 1.3% followed by a 5.2% contraction in 2009. The government increased spending to try and stimulate the economy. Consequence? Italy's debt increased to over €1.88 trillion in 2011—120% of GDP—the second-highest in Europe behind Greece. The austerity measures to reduce the deficit were slow going due to political opposition.

The markets are unforgiving—so what if austerity measures are painful. Spain's long-term borrowing costs neared 7% in late 2011, which most economists regarded as too high to sustain.

Who's next?

<u>News Alert Early 2012</u>:

Standard & Poor's has downgraded France's sovereign bond rating.

European leader 1: This is a nightmare. What more can we do?

European leader 2: *We* can have another glass. Premier cru. It calms the nerves, my friend.

European leader 1: It's our second bottle.

European leader 2: Hmmm . . .

III. CONTAINING THE CRISIS

As the crisis spread, it became clear that extraordinary measures were required to stop further contagion. As the EU grappled to contain the crisis, fundamental ideological disagreements arose. Germany and the northern European countries called for "fiscal consolidation," meaning, "Get rid of your deficits and get your economy in order. You might suffer at first but then you'll grow responsibly." The GIIPS responded that stringent austerity measures were too brutal and that pro-growth policies were needed.

With that in mind, let's look broadly at four major initiatives to contain the crisis and prevent further such episodes. Let's start with the ECB.

Part One: The European Central Bank

Before we look at what the ECB did to save the euro, let's remember that it's the backbone of the EMU. The Maastricht Treaty created it as a politically-independent EU institution, and made it responsible for implementing monetary policy for the Eurozone with the key objective of maintaining price stability (capping inflation at 2%). Its integrity is critical to the stability of the Eurozone. Also keep in mind that the ECB is prohibited from playing a role typical of central banks—being a "lender of last resort," meaning that the central bank will only lend when there's nowhere else to turn. So the ECB can't lend funds directly to the governments of member states or make bond purchases directly from them. Let's see what it did and you can judge for yourself how compliant it was with EU rules.

> *"Monetary policy alone is not enough to deal with the situation . . . . We cannot have a common currency, a common monetary policy, and leave everything else to the states involved. That's why the 17 will have to go further."*
> —Herman Van Rompuy, President of the EU, quoted in http://online.wsj.com/news/articles/SB10 001424052970203716204577018383688667 576?cb=logged0.3046858479437428 (2011)

Collateral Standards

The ECB hardly stood on the sidelines in the crisis. It made a series of moves that were as critical as they were controversial. First, it relaxed its stringent collateral requirements for its lending to banks, many of which were in trouble. When Greece was tanking, the ECB announced that it would start accepting as collateral bonds with credit ratings as low as BBB-, the lowest investment grade credit rating. Lots of folks saw this as a bad move: What if borrowing banks don't repay their loans? Would that collateral be worth anything? It also started accepting asset-backed securities as collateral. Now how exactly do you price those securities in a severe crisis? Hmmm . . .

Bond Buying Program

What really got people all riled up was the ECB's announcement on May 14, 2010 that it would buy unlimited amounts of Eurozone debt under the newly created Securities Markets Programme (SMP). Although the ECB is prohibited from buying bonds directly from member states (in the biz, making primary market purchases), it began making secondary market purchases (where investors buy and sell securities from other investors rather than from the issuing entity) of bonds issued by the Eurozone countries that were in trouble. The idea was to increase the demand for the bonds, which **pushed interest rates down** and helped keep the cost of borrowing affordable for those countries. As of January 9, 2012, the ECB had purchased €213 billion worth of bonds under the program.

The critics pounced. German President Christian Wulff said the ECB was violating the EU Treaty's prohibition on the ECB buying debt directly from governments. Germany suggested that the bond-buying program violated the Maastricht Treaty's "no bail-out" provision. Check it out: Citizen groups in Germany lodged a series of complaints with the German Constitutional Court. Germany's highest court ruled that it was cool for the country to participate in the bailouts and it refused to invalidate the SMP. All along, the ECB maintained that there is no prohibition against the ECB purchasing sovereign debt in the secondary market.

Long-term Refinancing Operations

On December 23, 2011, the ECB loaned €489 billion worth of three-year loans at an interest rate of 1% to 523 banks in an unprecedented loan program designed to encourage lending to businesses and consumers and prevent a credit crunch. The loans, referred to as "long-term refinancing operations" (LTROs), also allowed some banks to borrow cheaply from the ECB, invest in high-yield bonds, and realize a profit from the difference in the two interest rates. The ECB hoped that investment in high-yield bonds of countries like Greece, Italy, Portugal, and Spain would help reduce the fears of default by increasing demand for the bonds. Increased demand would push down interest rates and reduce the cost of borrowing for these countries.

In February 2012, the ECB again offered the LTRO's and 800 financial institutions borrowed €529.5 billion, bringing the December and February total to nearly €1 trillion. Although the LTRO's gave a boost to the economy, there were those warned that the ECB's action would stoke inflation. Critics also pointed to the massive increase in the ECB's balance sheet and the risks that created.

Part Two: EU's Rescue Mechanisms

While the ECB was doing its part to save the euro, EU's leaders had to figure out how to come up with a supranational rescue facility that would help fund rescues and otherwise erect a firewall to stop the contagion. Let's have a look.

The European Financial Stability Facility

The Greek bailout and ECB interventions failed to contain the crisis. Greek's economy was descending into hell, dragging other Eurozone countries with it. In May of 2010, the Eurozone member countries announced a €750 billion Eurozone rescue package that included the creation of the European Financial Stability Facility (EFSF), a special purpose vehicle (SPV) with a lending capacity of €440 billion. The EFSF was authorized, among other things, to issue bonds and other debt instruments to finance loans to Eurozone countries in trouble and to finance recapitalization of banks via loans to EU governments, not just Eurozone countries. The EFSF's issues were backed by guarantees given by the Eurozone countries. The guarantees plus a funding cushion gave the EFSF a high credit rating that translated into cheaper borrowing costs.

(The cushion meant that the EFSF could only lend €250 billion—peanuts. The guarantees were upped to €780 billion to give the EFSF €440 billion in lending power.)

Another part of the rescue package was the creation of the European Financial Stabilization Mechanism (EFSM), which operated in tandem with the EFSF. Backed by the EU budget, the EFSM was an emergency funding mechanism authorized to borrow (or issue bonds) up to €60 billion. The final part of the €750 billion package was an IMF loan of €250 billion.

Of the EFSF's €440 billion lending capacity, €192 billion was allotted to Greece, Ireland, and Portugal, reducing the available lending capacity to €248 billion. The News Alert you read when we covered Portugal indicated that the EFSF contributed €16 billion to the rescue package. To finance a portion of Ireland's rescue package, the EFSF contributed €5 billion.

The EFSF didn't exist when Greece was first rescued. After the Portuguese rescue, all attention turned back to Greece with renewed fears of a sovereign default. In a desperate effort to save Greece (or the Eurozone?), the ECB started accepting Greek government bonds as collateral even though they had been downgraded to junk. After another downgrade, the ECB hung up its "We're closed, Greece. No more of your crap bonds as collateral" sign. Time for a second rescue package in February 2012: Greece would receive €109 billion in loans from the EFSF as well as €28 billion from the IMF in exchange for austerity measures. Part of the EFSF loan was to recapitalize Greek banks.

The EFSF and the EFSM were created as temporary rescue facilities. In October 2010, the European Stability Mechanism (ESM), a permanent rescue facility, replaced the EFSF and the EFSM.

The European Stability Mechanism

After a year of bailouts and rescue plans, it was pretty clear that the Eurozone was still in trouble. The EU needed something more comprehensive to contain the crisis. Fears of further contagion prompted leaders to create a firewall to insulate other struggling member countries like Spain and Italy, and convince the markets that the Eurozone could bailout these larger economies if necessary. On March 25, 2011, finance ministers of the seventeen Eurozone countries reached agreement on establishing a permanent EU bailout fund, the European Stability Mechanism (ESM). The ESM, a treaty, came into force, in September 2012. Unlike the EFSF, which relied on guarantees from member states, the ESM is funded by paid-in capital. The ESM's proposed lending capacity was €500 billion—double that of the EFSF.

Enter stage right, the critics: They argued that the lending capacity was inadequate. Some speculated that Europe needed up to €2 trillion to adequately contain the crisis. Jean-Claude Trichet, President of the ECB,

Italian Prime Minister Mario Draghi and IMF Managing Director, Christine LaGarde, were joined by French President Nicolas Sarkozy in calling for Germany to increase its contribution to the ESM. On March 30, 2012, after Germany agreed, European finance ministers announced the expansion of the firewall to €700 billion by temporarily combining the EFSF and the ESM. Originally, the EFSF's lending capacity was to count against the ESM's lending capacity, meaning that any loans made by the EFSF would have reduced the ESM's lending capacity. By running the EFSF and ESM in tandem (the EFSF would continue to fund the lending agreements with Portugal, Ireland, and Greece), the Eurozone's total lending capacity increased to €700 billion.

The ESM has been used twice thus far. In July 2012, Spain secured a €100 billion loan from the ESM to help the country recapitalize its banking sector in return for reforms of the sector. Its only other disbursement to date was a lending facility of up to €10 billion for Cyprus in June 2012 to help the country with macroeconomic adjustments, which include structural reforms to its financial sector.

Part Three: Fiscal Discipline

"The global financial crisis erupts. And there's no EMU-wide fiscal policy." We just had to repeat that for this part. After, or as, they stopped the bleeding, EU went about repairing the chink in the amour of the monetary union via the "six-pack" and a fiscal union. Let's start with the beer.

The Six-Pack

On September 28, 2011, the European Parliament approved six legislative measures. The six-pack is comprised of five regulations and one directive. It came into force on December 11, 2011 and applies to twenty-seven EU member states, with some provisions focused on the Eurozone countries. In the fiscal area, the six-pack attempts to strengthen the SGP. As to the preventive arm, it monitors EU member countries' fiscal positions. And regarding the corrective arm, it cracks down on countries with a debt ratio above 60% of GDP, which previously had been reserved for breaching the 3% deficit ratio. What's really interesting is what the six-pack does with fines for Eurozone countries: To ensure enforcement, a "reverse voting mechanism" is used. In practice this means that the Commission's proposal for a sanction will be considered adopted unless the Council turns it down by qualified majority. All this stuff is in the regulations. To give you an example of the difference between a reg and a directive, the six-pack contains a directive that sets out minimum requirements for reporting fiscal policy in national budgetary frameworks. Member countries have to adopt domestic legislation that implements the general framework of the directive.

The Fiscal Compact

As the euro crisis reached epic proportions, European leaders came under intense pressure to act with a purpose. Despite mounting pressures, they couldn't reach agreement on changes to EU treaties that would have created a fiscal union after the U.K. opposed the changes. After marathon talks in Brussels aimed at solving the crisis, Eurozone members and six other EU member states committed to entering their own fiscal pact. German Chancellor Angela Merkel proposed a European Union fiscal pact that would require each country to introduce legal limits on budget deficits or a "debt brake." "Uh . . . no!" said Britain. It refused to take part in any fiscal pact and critics questioned the legitimacy of the proposal because EU institutions may only act on a consensus of all twenty-seven-member states.

At the EU summit in Brussels on January 30, 2012, all EU member states except Britain and the Czech Republic agreed on a Treaty on Stability, Coordination and Governance (TSCG) in the Economic and Monetary Union, commonly called the "fiscal compact." It's not EU law but instead an "intergovernmental agreement" that binds the contracting parties (CPs). The TSCG is only binding on Eurozone countries; other CPs will be bound when they adopt the euro or earlier if they want to. It entered into force on January 1, 2013.

Keeping in mind the distinction between Eurozone and non-Eurozone parties made in the TSCG, it requires CPs to adopt a binding balanced-budget rule as part of their constitutions or national law. If a CP fails to adopt binding legislation, the European Commission may report it to the European Court of Justice, which can fine the offending CP up to 1% of GDP. A budget in surplus or having a deficit of less than 0.5% of GDP is considered balanced. The Treaty permits CPs whose debt-to-GDP ratio is significantly below 60% to have a structural deficit of up to 1%, and allows CPs to temporarily deviate from the balanced-budget rule in exceptional circumstances.

Part Four: A Banking Union

The crisis has brought home the need to further integrate the financial sector, including the banks. The crisis exposed the vicious circle that made things worse: The crisis deepens→ vulnerable banks need support from their national government→ the national government fiscal position worsens→ borrowing from the international markets for refinancing debt becomes more expensive→ banks' balance sheets worsen→ the crisis deepens, and over and over again. This vicious cycle fed the contagion.

To break the vicious circle, in June 2012, EU leaders committed to forming a banking union, with three components: a Single Supervisory Mechanism (SSM), a Single Resolution Mechanism (SRM), and a Deposit Guarantee

Scheme (DGS). The Commission set up a roadmap for creating the banking union, which would at some point be open to all EU member states but in the first instance to the Eurozone countries. In November 2013, the Single Supervisory Mechanism Regulation entered into force. In April 2014, the European Parliament adopted the Commission's proposals on the SRM regulation, a Bank Recovery & Resolution Directive (BBRD), and a Deposit Guarantee Schemes Directive (DGS). Both directives (the DGS was modified) must now be transposed into national law.

We'll just look at the SSM, the SRM, and the BBRD. The SSM gives the ECB new supervisory powers over all of the Eurozone's 6000 banks and ensures that there's consistent application of the **single rulebook**—a bunch of legislative acts that cover all financial actors and products in the Single Market. It will directly supervise "significant banks," that is, banks having assets of more than €30 billion or constituting at least 20% of their home country's GDP. "Less significant banks" (isn't it hurtful to be labeled "insignificant"?) will be supervised by national authorities but with the ECB watching them like a hawk. The SRM, which will be operational in 2016, complements the SSM. If a bank is subject to the SSM and a cross-border or domestic bank tanks, the SRM will manage its resolution. The BBRD saves taxpayer money by "bailing in" shareholders (they get wiped out first) followed by other creditors, such as holders of convertible (to equity) bonds and junior bonds.

Two years to put a banking union together? Pretty impressive, although you'll always find critics.

> "Take, for example, the mechanism for resolving a bank in trouble. In theory, this process should happen over a weekend, so as to avoid the risks of market turmoil and bank runs. The final arrangement, however, will involve multiple panels and more than 100 decision makers. National governments, which have the least incentive to shut down a bank in trouble since this might provoke a political backlash, will retain a say."
>
> —Editorial, "A highly imperfect banking union," *Financial Times* (2014)

Epilogue

Well, the euro and the Eurozone have survived. Greece is still part of the club, although there were big bets against it staying in. But the crisis was brutal. Don't forget that the rescue packages came with conditionality that forced the countries in question to implement painful and controversial austerity measures. While other countries didn't receive rescue money, they still had to tighten their belts—until it hurt. People took to the streets in protest.

> "Swarms of violent groups overtook a general protest against austerity measures in the city center on Wednesday, lashing out at the government and security forces and hurling gasoline bombs that, according to the police, set fire to a bank building and killed three workers. The demonstration had drawn tens of thousands of people near the central square in front of Parliament as part of a general strike that paralyzed airline flights, ferries, schools and hospitals . . . While the focus of blame was on the violent fringe group or groups, the dark turn had an immediate effect on world markets. The euro sank to a 14-month low of $1.28 as fears grew that unrest could spread to Europe's other debt-ridden economies."
>
> —D. Bilefsky, "Three Reported Killed in Greek Protests," *New York Times* (2010)

Today, unemployment is still widespread, with Greece and Spain coping with a jobless rate over 25%. Youth unemployment is staggeringly high, over 50% in Greece and Spain. People in the GIIPS streamed out of their countries looking for work.

Things are turning around slowly. In the first quarter of 2014, the Eurozone's economy expanded just 1.2%. The ECB has forecast that Eurozone will grow only 1% in 2014. In June, the ECB cut its main interest rate to 0.15 from .025% and its deposit rate (overnight deposits with the ECB) from zero to minus 0.1%, the first major central bank to go negative. And we're back to LTROs: The ECB announced that it will offer four "targeted longer-term refinancing operations" worth up to €400 billion. The

> "We aren't seeing the type of recovery that we should be seeing given the scale of the slowdown [during the sovereign debt crisis] . . . The data are not strong enough to tell us that we are even in a recovery."
>
> —Lucrezia Reichlin, former head of research at the ECB, quoted in C. Jones, "Surveys damp hopes of eurozone recovery," *Financial Times* (2014)

cheap loans are intended to encourage banks to lend to smaller firms in the periphery.

But there's some good news, considering that at one point some said the Eurozone and even the EU were headed for the history books. As we speak, Greece is expected to start growing—barely—this year after a recession the likes of which the country hadn't witnessed since World War II. Killer spending cuts and boosted tax collection has resulted in a budget surplus. But not everybody's happy. Workers have gone on strike at the state-controlled electric utility over the government's plan to privatize it. Things are looking up for Ireland. Unemployment is dropping and consumer spending is coming back. And check it out: Ireland was the first "rescued" country to pay back the money the "troika" (IMF, ECB, and EU) gave it.

European leader 1: We survived.

European leader 2: Did you really doubt we wouldn't?

European leader 1: Yes, I suppose I did. Yes.

European leader 2: When was the last time you read the treaty?

European leader 1: This morning. Why?

European leader 2: Did you notice something?

European leader 1: It was dark in the bathroom.

European leader 2: It doesn't say how a Eurozone country would leave the bloc. It doesn't envision an exit. Or a break up.

European leader 1: Shall we drink to that?

European leader 2: We've emptied the case.

European leader 1: A fate worse than losing the euro.

You Gotta Know Something About Them!

Jean-Claude Trichet

Image of Jean-Claude Trichet is licensed by CC BY 3.0, 2.5, 2.0 and 1.0.

Born in Lyon, France, Jean-Claude Trichet was appointed Governor of the Banque de France in 1993 where he earned a reputation for being an inflation hawk. In 2003, he was appointed President of the European Central Bank, where he steered the ECB and the Eurozone through the debt crisis by lowering the key policy rate from 4.25% to 2%—and then to 1%. He also increased the ECB's lending flexibility by allowing banks to borrow more and relaxing rules governing collateral, which helped to avoid a sharper economic downturn. Jean-Claude was a strong supporter of European integration. Check it out: He was one of the chief French negotiators that worked the Maastricht treaty. Jean-Claude likes to sail and is into other "sea" sports. While ECB Governor—he left in 2011—Jean-Claude grew fond of German white wine and Weisswurst, a sausage that some Germans eat for breakfast paired with beer. Beer for Jean-Claude in the morning? Gross! Maybe he needed it to get through the crisis.

Nicolas Sarkozy

Image of Nicolas Sarkozy by ℵ (Aleph) is licensed under CC BY 2.5.

Nicolas Sarkozy grew up in Paris and began his political career as mayor of an affluent Paris suburb. In 2007, he was elected President of France and quickly walked into controversy, like his strict immigration policies that angered human rights activists (the policies included the forced expulsion of Roma gypsies as well as legislation that would strip immigrants of their French nationality if they attacked police). Despite his controversies, Nicolas was crucial in the response to the global economic crisis, helping to establish G20 summits. Nicolas was buds, most of the time, with Germany's Chancellor Angela Merkel. They both pushed for austerity during the crisis. The French people didn't like this: he was voted out of office in 2012. Nicolas reentered public life in 2014 determined to run for president again. But in July he was arrested and held by police for 15 hours as part of an investigation into alleged campaign funding crimes associated with his 2007 campaign. Despite the French tradition of downplaying a politician's personal life, Nicolas's private life consistently made headlines during his time in office. He's been married three times, and his third and current wife, Carla Bruni, is a former supermodel who now has a career as a singer.

Angela Merkel

Image of Angela Merkel by ℵ (Aleph) is licensed under CC BY 2.5.

Angela Merkel grew up in East Germany. She studied physics at Leipzig University and became a research scientist. In 1990, Angela joined the Christian Democratic Union (CDU) and became a member of the German Bundestag in the same year. She held different positions with the CDU until she was elected Chancellor of the Federal Republic of Germany, the first woman to hold the position and the first person from the former East Germany. She'll be one of the longest serving German leaders, having won reelection to a third term in 2013. Although she's popular at home, folks in other countries, such as Greece and Spain, are not as wild about her. They're still smarting from the austerity measures she pushed during the crisis. Angela Merkel is known for having a very dry sense of humor. When she's not cracking the whip on austerity, she bakes. In college, she studied physics because she relished the challenge. The only class she ever failed was a physics course. Go figure . . .

What's Up with That?

The EMS and Its Crisis

The EMS functioned through the Exchange Rate Mechanism (ERM), which allow fluctuations within the band described in the text. If the foreign exchange rate reached upper or lower limits of the band, the central banks at issue had to intervene. For example, once the Irish punt appreciated to its upper limits against the Dutch guilder, the central banks of both countries had to intervene to support the depreciation of the guilder.

The crisis began when investors started to wonder whether the convergence under the EMU would actually come about. In 1990, West Germany reunified with East Germany. Conversion of East German money led to a significant growth in West Germany's deutsche mark money supply. Massive deficit spending stoked inflation. It was pretty clear that the German economy was overheating. So the Bundesbank raised interest rates.

In June 1992, Denmark rejected the Maastricht treaty. Players in the foreign exchange market expected a devaluation of the weak currencies. Speculators first attacked the Finnish markka and the Swedish krona. The markka depreciated significantly. Sweden beat back the attack by shooting up interest rates. The central bank increased its lending rate from 13% to 75%. The rate reached 500% on September 16. Brutal.

Britain and Italy struggled to keep their currencies within the band. By September 11, Germany had spent nearly $16 billion to support the lira under the EMS rules. Italy was then allowed to devalue the lira. This increased the speculators' feeding frenzy.

Then there was the Britain—Germany showdown: Britain, suffering at the time from a severe recession, refused to follow a country contractionary monetary policy. Germany refused to follow an expansionary monetary policy.

Speculators concluded that the value of the pound sterling would have to decline vis-à-vis the mark. This led to a massive selloff of pounds. Britain then raised its interest rates to 15%. On Black Wednesday, September 16, Britain withdrew from the EMS. Italy followed suit.

The crisis was expensive: the central bank spent billions of dollars in intervention. And the speculators profited. George Soros became known as "the man who broke the Bank of England." He made a cool $1 billion.

The crisis continued into 1993. After a furious attack on the French franc in July, the ERM band was widened to plus or minus 15%, except for the deutsche mark/dutch guilder rate.

The first attempt to create a European monetary union came about in October 1970 with the Werner Plan. The Plan sought to create an economic and monetary union in three stages starting in March 1971. The Plan's goal was to limit fluctuations between different European currencies by creating a currency band that required European countries to keep their currencies within a 2.25% fluctuation margin of each other, thus stabilizing exchange rates among the currencies. Shortly after the system was established, certain external shocks, such as the rise in oil prices in 1973, resulted in differing levels of inflation throughout the region, which impeded several countries' abilities to remain within the 2.25% fluctuation limits. In 1974, European countries opted to abandon the system and allow their currencies to float.

Bond Price and Yield

The text might have confused you. Why would interest rates go down if there's greater demand for a bond? Here's the relationship: When the yield on a bond goes up, the bond's price goes down, and vice versa. Why does this relationship hold? Because of the formula: yield = coupon/price.

Keep in mind that lots of people, especially professional traders, don't hold on to bonds when they buy them. They buy and sell bonds well before they mature in the secondary market. So let's take a bond with a "par" or face value of $1000 and an interest rate of 5% (its "coupon"). When that bond matures, say in thirty years, the holder of the bond will get the $1000 plus $50. But let's say that in the secondary market that bond is selling for $700—because a drop in demand—and you buy it for that price. If you hold on to that bond, you'll get the $1000 in principal plus the $50 in interest. That's pretty sweet for you because you bought the bond when the price went *down* and you're still going to get the $1050, meaning that your return or "yield" has gone *up*. 7.1% = $50/$700. The vice versa: If that bond is trading at $1500, that is, its price has gone *up*—because of increased demand, and you buy that bond, when it matures you're still going to get the $1050. Do the numbers and you'll see that your return or yield has gone *down*. 3.3% = $50/$1500. Bad for you, but good for the GIIPS.

EU Financial Regulation

The global financial crisis prompted the EU to improve its supervisory framework for the financial sector. To this end, three European supervisory authorities were created in 2011: (i) the European Banking Authority (EBA), which focuses on bank supervision, including bank capitalization; (ii) the European Securities and Markets Authority (ESMA), which works on the supervision of capital markets and directly supervises credit rating agencies; and (iii) the European Insurance and Occupational Pensions Authority (EIOPA), which deals with insurance supervision.

Member states' supervisors are represented in all three bodies. They help develop the single rulebook for financial regulation in Europe, and work on cross-border problems.

As to systemic risk, the EU created a European Systemic Risk Board (ESRB) to monitor potential threats to financial stability that arise from macro-economic problems in member countries and from system-wide financial developments There's a European Systemic Risk Board that provides early warnings of system-wide risks and may issue recommendations to address the risks.

QUESTIONS FROM YOUR TALKING DOG

1.   Where we going today? Ice cream? Okay, I have to earn it, huh? The EMU? What is this Maastricht treaty you talking about? Why is it so important?

2.   Hey, slow down! What about these EU institutions? The Commission? Council? Regulations? Directives?

3.   Let me guess. A monetary union is where there are unions of money? All right then, tell me about them, you know, why they might be worthwhile or not.

4.   Optimal currency area? I won't even try that one. What makes a currency area optimal? Is the EMU an optimal currency area? It's all about politics?

5.   I thought we were talking about the EMU. What's with this EMS?

6.   Three stages to the EMU, you say? Why have three stages and what's the point?

7.   Wait, wait, wait. Member countries would still control their own fiscal policy? Why? Couldn't a member country decide to spend as much as it wants to?

8.   Stability and Growth Pact. That sounds like something you agree to in a psych ward. So tell me about it. Was it effective?

9.   When are we going to get to the ice cream store? In stages? Okay, fine. Fine! So tell me about stage III of the EMU.

10.   Divergence rather than convergence? What?

11.   Yeah, I remember we talked about contagion on one of our walks. Okay, tell me about the contagion in this crisis, starting with Greece. But just give me the low lights, you know, why they got into trouble and how they were rescued.

12.   Yeah, I do wanna know how the EU kept everything together. Okay, let's start with the ECB. Talk to me.

13.   Some said the ECB was breaking the law? How so?

14. LTROs? Like UFOs?

15. Are we almost there? I gotta get some 'scream in my stomach, you know what I'm sayin'? Fine. Fine! Tell me about the European Financial Stability Facility and the European Financial Stabilization Mechanism. How were they put together? What was their purpose?

16. European this, European that. Now the European Stability Mechanism. Why did they need that when they had the other two facilities? What was different about the ESM?

17. 500 billion euros wasn't enough for the ESM? Are you kidding me? Okay, they were trying to save entire economies. What did they do about it?

18. I was wondering when you would get around to the fiscal disciple stuff. Seems like that's pretty important.

19. Six-pack? Sure, I could use a little brew before a vanilla cone. I know you meant something else. I'm just trying to drop some hints. So tell me about the six-pack. Was it same ole', same ole'?

20. Fiscal Compact. Another treaty? All EU member countries were part of it? What was the point of it? Give me some specifics.

21. NO, no, no! I need a rescue package . . . of ice cream. This is it. Banking union. Why is that necessary?

22. SSM? SRM? BBRD? Remember, I'm just a DOG. Give it to me, then. How did all that stuff work?

23. Hey, forget about the ice cream. Let's check out this wine bar.

<u>Chapter 17: Supplement</u>

17A. *Optimum Currency Area*

Here's a piece by a staunch liberal economist and Nobel Laureate. So, he says, most economists saw that the EMU didn't meet the criteria for an optimum currency area (OCA). What, in his view, is the purpose of asking whether a proposed monetary union constitutes an OCA? What is a major disadvantage of a monetary union? What was the major "assymetric shock" and the major problem(s) with the EMU? What banking issues does he raise? Why is a lender of last resort so important? What do you think of his proposals to improve the EMU? Does the banking union meet some of his concerns? Most would agree that the EMU is at bottom a political project.

P. Krugman, "Revenge of the Optimum Currency Area,"
The New York Times (2012)

The creation of the euro was supposed to be another triumphant step in the European project, in which economic integration has been used to foster political integration and peace; a common currency, so the thinking went, would bind the continent even more closely together. What has happened instead, however, is a nightmare: the euro has become an economic trap, and Europe a nest of squabbling nations. Even the continent's democratic achievements seem under threat, as dire economic conditions create a favorable environment for political extremism. Who could have seen such a thing coming?

Well, the answer is that lots of economists could and should have seen it coming, and some did. For we have a long-established way to think about the prospects for currency unions, the theory of optimum currency areas— and right from the beginning, this theory suggested serious concerns about the euro project.

These concerns were largely dismissed at the time, with many assertions that the theory was wrong, irrelevant, or that any concerns it raised could be addressed with reforms. Recent events have, however, very much followed the lines one might have expected given good old-fashioned optimum currency area theory, even as they have suggested both that we need to expand the theory and that some aspects of the theory are more important than we previously realized.

In what follows, I'll start with a very brief and selective review of what I consider the key points of optimum currency area theory, and what that theory seemed, some two decades ago, to say about the idea of a single European currency. Next up is the crisis, and the continuing refusal of many leaders to see it for what it is. Finally, some thoughts on possible futures.

Mundell, Kenen, and currencies

The advantages of a common currency are obvious, if hard to quantify: reduced transaction costs, elimination of currency risk, greater transparency and possibly greater competition because prices are easier to compare. Before the creation of the euro, some statistical work on the limited number of country pairs sharing a currency suggested that the common European currency might produce an explosion in intra-European trade; that hasn't happened, but trade does seem to have risen modestly as a result of the single currency, and presumably that corresponds to an increase in mutually beneficial and hence productive exchanges.

The disadvantages of a single currency come from loss of flexibility. It's not just that a currency area is limited to a one-size-fits-all monetary policy; even more important is the loss of a mechanism for adjustment. For it seemed to the creators of OCA, and continues to seem now, that changes in relative prices and wages are much more easily made via currency depreciation than by renegotiating individual contracts. Iceland achieved a 25 percent fall in wages relative to the European core in one fell swoop, via a fall in the krona. Spain probably needs a comparable adjustment, but that adjustment, if it can happen at all, will require years of grinding wage deflation in the face of high unemployment.

But why should such adjustments ever be necessary? The answer is "asymmetric shocks". A boom or slump everywhere in a currency area poses no special problems. But suppose, to take a not at all hypothetical example, that a vast housing boom leads to full employment and rising wages in part, but only part, of a currency area, then goes bust. The legacy of those boomtime wage increases will be an uncompetitive tradable sector, and hence the need to get at least relative wages down again.

So the advantages of a single currency come at a potentially high cost. Optimum currency area theory is about weighing the balance between those advantages and those potential costs.

Now, what we need to say right away is that this "weighing" takes place only in a qualitative sense: at this point nobody says that the benefits of joining the euro are x percent of GDP, the costs y, and x>y, so the euro it is. Instead, it's more along the lines of arguing that Florida is a better candidate for membership in the dollar zone than Spain is a candidate for membership in the euro zone. This doesn't necessarily say that Spain made a mistake by joining the euro—nor does it necessarily refute the argument that Florida would be better off with its own currency! But the theory does at least give us some insight into the tradeoffs.

We also need to say that in practice very little of optimum currency area theory is concerned with the benefits of a single currency area. Obviously these benefits depend on potential economic interactions; there would be no point in sharing a currency with, say, a colony on Mars that did almost no trade with Earth, and joining the euro makes a lot more sense for, say, Slovakia than it would for Mongolia. But almost all the interesting stuff comes from looking at factors that might mitigate the costs arising from the loss of monetary flexibility that comes with adopting someone else's currency—which brings us to the two big ideas of OCA.

First up, Mundell, whose classic 1961 paper argued that a single currency was more likely to be workable if the regions sharing that currency were characterized by high mutual labor mobility. (He actually said factor mobility, but labor is almost surely the one that matters). How so?

Well, suppose—to take a not at all hypothetical example—that the state of Massachusetts takes a major asymmetric hit to its economy that sharply reduces employment—which is, in fact, what happened at the end of the 1980s. If Massachusetts workers can't or won't leave the state, the only way to restore full employment is to regain the lost jobs, which will probably require a large fall in relative wages to make the state more competitive, a fall in relative wages that is much more easily accomplished if you have your own currency to devalue. But if there is high labor mobility, full employment can instead be restored through emigration, which shrinks the labor force to the jobs available. And that's what actually happened. Table 1 shows snapshots of the Massachusetts economy at three dates: 1986, the height of the "Massachusetts miracle" centered on minicomputers, 1991, after the shift to PCs and the bursting of a housing bubble had brought a severe local recession, and 1996. Notice that Massachusetts never regained the employment share it lost in the late-80s bust. Nonetheless, by the mid-90s it once again had an unemployment rate below the national average, because workers moved elsewhere.

So that's one main theme of optimum currency area theory. But it isn't the only one. There's also Peter Kenen's argument that fiscal integration—a large "federal" component to spending at the regional or local level—can help a lot in dealing with asymmetric shocks.

Let's once again take a not at all hypothetical example, Florida after the recent housing bust. America may have a small welfare state by European standards, but it's still pretty big, with large spending in particular on Social Security and Medicare—obviously both a big deal in Florida. These programs are, however, paid for at a national level. What this means is that if Florida suffers an asymmetric adverse shock, it will receive an automatic compensating transfer from the rest of the country: it pays less into the national budget, but this has no impact on the benefits it receives, and may even increase its benefits if they come from programs like unemployment benefits, food stamps, and Medicaid that expand in the face of economic distress.

How big is this automatic transfer? Table 2 shows some indicative numbers about Florida's financial relations with Washington in 2007, the year before the crisis, and 2010, in the depths of crisis. Florida's tax payments to DC fell some $33 billion; meanwhile, special federally funded unemployment insurance programs contributed some $3 billion, food stamp payments rose almost $4 billion. That's about $40 billion in de facto transfers, some 5 percent of Florida's GDP—and that's surely an understatement, since there were also crisis-related increases in Medicaid and even Social Security, as more people took early retirement or applied for disability payments.

You might argue that since Florida residents are also U.S. taxpayers, we really shouldn't count all of this as a transfer. The crucial point, however, is that the federal government does not currently face a borrowing constraint, and has very low borrowing costs. So all of this is a burden that would be a real problem if Florida were a sovereign state, but is taken off its shoulders by the fact that it isn't.

Wait, there's more: Florida banks benefit from federal deposit insurance; many mortgage losses fell on Fannie and Freddie, the federally-sponsored lending agencies. More on this financial backing shortly.

In summary, optimum currency area theory suggested two big things to look at—labor mobility and fiscal integration. And on both counts it was obvious that Europe fell far short of the U.S. example, with limited labor mobility and virtually no fiscal integration. This should have given European leaders pause—but they had their hearts set on the single currency.

Why did they believe it would work? I won't try for a detailed historiography; let me just say that what I recall from discussions at the time was the belief that two factors would make the adjustment problems manageable. First, countries would adopt sound fiscal policies, and thereby reduce the incidence of asymmetric shocks. Second, countries would engage in structural reforms that would make labor markets—and, presumably, wages—flexible enough to cope with such asymmetric shocks as occurred despite the soundness of the fiscal policies.

Even at the time, this sounded to many American economists like wishful thinking. After all, asymmetric shocks don't have to arise from unsound policies—they can come from shifts in relative product demand or, of course, such things as real estate bubbles. And European leaders seemed to believe that they could achieve a degree of wage flexibility that would be more or less unprecedented in the modern world.

Nonetheless, the project went ahead. Exchange rates were locked at the beginning of 1999, with the mark, the franc and so on officially becoming just denominations of the euro. Then came actual euro notes—and they all lived happily ever after, for values of "ever after" < 11 years.

The euro crisis

As I just suggested, the architects of the euro, to the extent that they took optimum currency area theory at all seriously, chose to believe that asymmetric shocks would be a relatively minor problem. What happened instead was the mother of all asymmetric shocks—a shock that was, in a bitter irony, caused by the creation of the euro itself.

In essence, the creation of the euro led to a perception on the part of many investors that the big risks associated with cross-border investment within Europe had been eliminated. In the 1990s, despite the absence of formal capital controls, capital movements and hence current-account imbalances within Europe were limited. After the creation of the euro, however, there was massive capital movement from Europe's core—mainly Germany, but also the Netherlands—to its periphery, leading to an economic boom in the periphery and significantly higher inflation rates in Spain, Greece, etc. than in Germany.

This movement was itself a large asymmetric shock, but a relatively gradual one, and one that the European Central Bank was willing to accommodate with slightly above-target inflation. Matters were quite different, however, when private capital flows from the core to the periphery came to a sudden stop, leaving the peripheral economies with prices and unit labor costs that were well out of line with those in the core. Suddenly the euro faced a major adjustment problem.

This was the kind of problem optimum currency area theory warned would be very difficult to handle without currency devaluation; euro optimists had believed that reforms would make labor markets sufficiently flexible to deal with such situations. Unfortunately, the pessimists were right. "Internal devaluation"—restoring competitiveness through wage cuts as opposed to devaluation—has proved extremely hard. Table 3 shows hourly labor costs in the business sectors of several peripheral economies that, by common account, entered the crisis with very flexible labor markets; even so, and despite very high unemployment, they have achieved at best small declines.

So optimum currency area theory was right to assert that creating a single currency would bring significant costs, which in turn meant that Europe's lack of mitigating factors in the form of high labor mobility and/or fiscal integration became a very significant issue. In this sense, the story of the euro is one of a crisis foretold.

Yet there have been some surprises—unfortunately, none of them favorable.

First, as far as I know nobody or almost nobody foresaw that countries hit by adverse asymmetric shocks would face fiscal burdens so large as to call government solvency into question. As it turned out, the adjustment problems of the euro area quickly turned into a series of fiscal emergencies as well. In this sense, Kenen has turned out to dominate Mundell: lack of labor mobility has not played a major role in euro's difficulties, at least so far, but lack of fiscal integration has had an enormous impact, arguably making the difference between the merely bad condition of America's "sand states", where the housing bubble was concentrated, and the acute crises facing Europe's periphery.

Second, traditional optimum currency area theory paid little attention to banking issues; little thought was given to the importance of national as opposed to regional bank guarantees in the United States. In retrospect, however, we can see just how crucial such guarantees have actually been. Deposits in U.S. banks are guaranteed at the federal level, so that bank bailouts have not been a burden on state governments; in Europe, bank bailouts have helped cause sudden jumps in government debt, most notably in Ireland, where the government's assumption of bank debts abruptly added 40 points to the ratio of public debt to GDP.

The combination of concerns about sovereign debt and the absence of federal bank backing have produced the now-famous phenomenon of "doom loops", in which fears of sovereign default undermine confidence in the private banks that hold much sovereign debt, forcing these banks to contract their balance sheets, driving the price of sovereign debt still lower.

Then there's the lender of last resort issue, which turns out to be broader than even those who knew their Bagehot realized. Credit for focusing on this issue goes to Paul DeGrauwe, who pointed out that national central banks are potentially crucial lenders of last resort to governments as well as private financial institutions. The British government basically can't face a "rollover" crisis in which bond buyers refuse to purchase its debt, because the Bank of England can always step in as financier of last resort. The government of Spain, however, can face such a crisis—and there is always the risk that fears of such a crisis, leading to default, could become a self-fulfilling prophecy.

As DeGrauwe has pointed out, Britain's fiscal outlook does not look notably better than Spain's. Yet the interest rate on British 10-year bonds was 1.7% at the time of writing, whereas the rate on Spanish 10-years was 6.6%; presumably this liquidity risk was playing an important role in the difference.

An even more striking comparison is between euro area countries and those nations that have pegged to the euro but not actually adopted the currency. Denmark, Austria, and Finland are all, by common agreement, in pretty good fiscal shape. But where Austria and Finland are euro nations, Denmark is merely pegged to the euro. You might have thought that this lack of full commitment on Denmark's part would exact a price in the form of higher interest rates—after all, someday Denmark might choose to devalue. In fact, however, Danish borrowing costs are significantly lower than those in Finland and Austria. To be fair, this could reflect fears that all euro countries will end up being contaminated by the problems of the periphery—say, by suffering large losses on loans between central banks. But a more likely explanation is that Denmark is seen as a safer bet because it could, in a liquidity squeeze, turn to its own central bank for financing, ruling out the self-fulfilling crises that pose risks even to relatively strong euro area governments.

The bottom line here would seem to be that concerns about the euro based on optimum currency area theory were actually understated. Members of a currency area, it turns out, should have high integration of bank guarantees and a system of lender of last resort provisions for governments as well as the traditional Mundell criterion of high labor mobility and the Kenen criterion of fiscal integration. The euro area has none of these.

Making the euro workable

I won't try here to project the likely outcome of the euro crisis, since any such discussion will surely be overtaken by events. Instead, let me ask what it might take to make the euro workable even if it isn't optimal.

One answer would be full integration, American-style—a United States of Europe, or at least a "transfer union" with much more in the way of automatic compensation for troubled regions. This does not, however, seem like a reasonable possibility for decades if not generations to come.

What about more limited fixes? I would suggest that the euro might be made workable if European leaders agreed on the following:

1.   Europe-wide backing of banks. This would involve both some kind of federalized deposit insurance and a willingness to do TARP-type rescues at a European level—that is, if, say, a Spanish bank is in trouble in a way that threatens systemic stability, there should be an injection of capital in return for equity stakes by all European governments, rather than a loan to the Spanish government for the purpose of providing the capital injection. The point is that the bank rescues have to be severed from the question of sovereign solvency.

2.   The ECB as a lender of last resort to governments, in the same way that national central banks already are. Yes, there will be complaints about moral hazard, which will have to be addressed somehow. But it's now painfully obvious that removing the option of emergency liquidity provision from the central bank just makes the system too vulnerable to self-fulfilling panic.

3.   Finally, a higher inflation target. Why? As I showed in Table 3, euro experience strongly suggests that downward nominal wage rigidity is a big issue. This means that "internal devaluation" via deflation is extremely difficult, and likely to fail politically if not economically. But it also means that the burden of adjustment might be substantially less if the overall Eurozone inflation rate were higher, so that Spain and other peripheral nations could restore competitiveness simply by lagging inflation in the core countries.

So maybe, maybe, the euro could be made workable. This still leaves the question of whether the euro even should be saved. After all, given everything I said, it looks increasingly as if the whole project was a mistake. Why not let it break up?

The answer, I think, is mainly political. Not entirely so—a euro breakup would be hugely disruptive, and exact high "transition" costs. Still, the enduring cost of a euro breakup would be that it would amount to a huge defeat for the broader European project I described at the start of this talk—a project that has done the world a vast amount of good, and one that no citizen of the world should want to see fail.

That said, it's going to be an uphill struggle. The creation of the euro involved, in effect, a decision to ignore everything economists had said about optimum currency areas. Unfortunately, it turned out that optimum currency area theory was essentially right, erring only in understating the problems with a shared currency. And now that theory is taking its revenge.

Table 1: Labor mobility in action MA share in US employment MA unemployment rate US unemployment rate			
1986	2.70	4.0	7.0
1991	2.48	8.8	6.8
1996	2.43	4.6	5.4

Table 2: Florida and the Feds		
	2007	2010
Revenue paid to DC	136.5	111.4
Special unemployment benefits	0	2.9
Food stamps	1.4	5.1

Table 3: Hourly labor costs in the business sector, 2008=100						
	2006	2007	2008	2009	2010	2011
Estonia	73.1	87.8	100.0	98.2	96.2	100.7
Ireland	91.5	95.7	100.0	103.1	102.4	100.7
Latvia	62.8	81.7	100.0	99.9	97.1	100.3

CHAPTER 18

DEVELOPMENT ISSUES IN THE NEW MILLENNIUM

■ ■ ■

Before we talk about what development means today and the rise of emerging market economies, we need to look at two really important topics in development and finance: the Millennium Development Goals (MDGs), and the debt relief movement. Both arose in the 1990s but continued to be a big deal today, especially the MDGs. The two topics are very much inter-related. The MDGs are all about making life better for millions of humans trying to eke out an existence. But it's kind a hard to do that when countries are struggling under a mountain of debt.

So let's start with the MDGs.

I. THE MILLENNIUM DEVELOPMENT GOALS

Just as we make New Year's resolutions to become better people (not necessarily by losing the holiday pounds), a new millennium prompts grand resolutions, such as the Millennium Development Goals. The MDGs are a frontal assault on conditions that strip away human dignity. Since they're "goals," that's it—they're just goals. Not binding in any sense—not law. You know, an aspirational thing. But a big and good—shall we say, ethical?—aspiration.

Let's look at how it all started and the MDGs themselves.

Part One: The Goals

Back in the day—December 1998—the U.N. General Assembly voted to hold a Millennium Summit, which was held in September 2000. It was a really collaborative effort—facilitators, round tables, lots of bad coffee and stale tuna sandwiches, which contributed to lots of bad breath. Actually, we're not sure about the coffee, sandwiches, and bad breath. Whatever they ate, it kept them pumped enough to issue a resolution called the Millennium Declaration. It's quite a lofty document. Check part of it out (take a look at supplement 18A):

> 6. We consider certain fundamental values to be essential to international relations in the twenty-first century. These include:

- **Freedom.** Men and women have the right to live their lives and raise their children in dignity, free from hunger and from the fear of violence, oppression or injustice. Democratic and participatory governance based on the will of the people best assures these rights.

- **Equality.** No individual and no nation must be denied the opportunity to benefit from development. The equal rights and opportunities of women and men must be assured.

- **Solidarity.** Global challenges must be managed in a way that distributes the costs and burdens fairly in accordance with basic principles of equity and social justice. Those who suffer or will benefit least deserve help from those who benefit most.

> *"Many human beings live in severe poverty, lacking secure access to basic necessities. This is nothing new. What is new is that global inequality has increased to such an extent that such poverty is now completely avoidable at a cost that would barely be felt in the affluent countries."*
> —T. Pogge. "The First U.N. Millennium Development Goal: A Cause for Celebration?" (2003)

- **Tolerance.** Human beings must respect one another, in all their diversity of belief, culture and language. Differences within and between societies should be neither feared nor repressed, but cherished as a precious asset of humanity. A culture of peace and dialogue among all civilizations should be actively promoted . . .

- **Shared responsibility.** Responsibility for managing worldwide economic and social development, as well as threats to international peace and security, must be shared among the nations of the world and should be exercised multilaterally. As the most universal and most representative organization in the world, the United Nations must play the central role.

* * *

11. We will spare no effort to free our fellow man, women and children from the abject and dehumanizing conditions of extreme poverty, to which more than 1 billion of them are currently subjected. We are committed to making the right to development a reality for everyone and to freeing the entire human race from want.

* * *

19. We resolve further:

- To halve, by the year 2015, the proportion of the world's people whose income is less than one dollar a day and the proportion of people who suffer from hunger and, by the same date, to halve the proportion of people who are unable to reach or to afford safe drinking water.

- To ensure that, by the same date, children everywhere, boys and girls alike, will be able to complete a full course of primary schooling and that girls and boys will have equal access to all levels of education.

- By the same date, to have reduced much maternal mortality by three quarters, and under-five child mortality by two thirds, of their current rates.

- To have, by then, halted, and begun to reverse, the spread of HIV/AIDS, the scourge of malaria and other major diseases that afflict humanity . . .

20. We also resolve:

- To promote gender equality and the empowerment of women as effective ways to combat poverty, hunger and disease and to stimulate development that is truly sustainable . . .

* * *

24. We will spare no effort to promote democracy and strengthen the rule of law, as well as respect for all internationally recognized human rights and fundamental freedoms, including the right to development.

Wow! "We are committed to . . . freeing the entire human race from want." Holy, moly! Time to roll up the sleeves and stock up on the energy drinks . . .

The Declaration gave rise to the MDGs: eight Goals, and eighteen targets, and over sixty indicators (to assess progress—check out supplement 18B). Here they are with selected indicators for two Goals:

Goal	Targets (Selected Indicators)
Goal 1: Eradicate extreme poverty and hunger *"Ending extreme poverty may seem utopian, but it is not. In fact, extreme poverty is an anachronism in the 21st century, since we now [have] the know-how, experience, and overall lift of world markets, to bring the curtain down on extreme poverty where it still exists. A realistic timeline would be 2030, as the World Bank has just adopted for the end of extreme poverty."* —J. Sachs, Interview with Ann Paisley Chandler on Integrated Development for Global Impact (2013)	• Halve, between 1990 and 2015, the proportion of people whose income is less than US$1.25 a day (PPP) • Achieve full and productive employment and decent work for all, including women and young people • Halve, between 1990 and 2015, the proportion of people who suffer from hunger • Indicators: Proportion of population below $1 (PPP) per day; poverty gap ratio; share of poorest quintile in national consumption

Goal 2: Achieve universal primary education

- Ensure that, by 2015, all children everywhere, boys and girls alike, will be able to complete a full course of primary schooling

Goal 3: Promote gender equality and empower women

- Eliminate gender disparity in primary and secondary education, preferably by 2005, and in all levels of education no later than 2015

- Indicators: Ratio of girls to boys in primary, secondary and tertiary education; share of women in wage employment in non-agricultural sector; proportion of seats held by women in national parliament

Goal 4: Reduce child mortality

- Reduce by two-thirds, between 1990 and 2015, the under-five mortality rate

Goal 5: Improve maternal health

- Reduce by two thirds, between 1990 and 2015, the maternal mortality ratio

- Achieve, by 2015, universal access to reproductive health

Goal 6: Combat HIV/AIDS, malaria and other diseases

- Have halted by 2015 and begun to reverse the spread of HIV/AIDS

- Achieve, by 2010, universal access to treatment for HIV/AIDS for all those who need it

- Have halted by 2015 and begun to reverse the incidence of malaria and other major diseases

Goal 7: Ensure environmental sustainability	• Integrate principles of sustainable development into country policies and programmes and reverse the loss of environmental resources
	• Reduce biodiversity loss, achieving, by 2010, significant reduction in the rate of loss
	• Halve, by 2015, the proportion of people without sustainable access to safe drinking water and basic sanitation
	• Achieve, by 2020, a significant improvement in the lives of at least 100 million slum dwellers
Goal 8: Develop a global partnership for development	• Develop further an open, rule-based, predictable, non-discriminatory trading and financial system
	• Address the special needs of least developed countries
	• Address the special needs of landlocked and small island developing States
	• Deal comprehensively with the debt problems of developing countries
	• In cooperation with pharmaceutical companies, provide access to affordable essential drugs in developing countries
	• In cooperation with the private sector, make available the benefits of new technologies, especially information and communications

While the emphasis is on the changes and improvements that poorer countries have to do (reduce poverty, child mortality, etc.), richer countries are asked to share resources. This is not limited to foreign aid, but also extends to sharing technologies and reducing trade barriers.

A pretty impressive agenda, huh? Well, that depends on who you talk to. Enter stage left: the critics. They have trashed the MDGs for a number of reasons. Some say they are too narrow because they don't address political and civil issues. Others say they're not ambitious enough. For example, Goal 1 should aim to cut the number, not just the proportion, of people living in extreme poverty by half (see supplement 18C for Pogge's biting critique). Similarly, critics slam the narrow indicators used to measure progress towards the MDGs. They don't consider indicators such as school enrollment gaps to be a meaningful measurement of human development progress. The underlying concern is that just because countries may lack a certain number of telephones or statistically have an equal number of boy and girl students enrolled in school, it doesn't necessarily mean that the goal to which the indicators relate is being met (or that a country is falling short).

The MDGs' supporters respond that the indicators can't be taken out of context, viewing the indicators not as ends in themselves, bur rather as benchmarks of progress towards the broader Goal to which they relate. Maybe the MDGs most effective function has been to promote political freedom and open debate, which lead civil society to demand more government accountability. And then there's the shame factor: countries that haven't set up programs to reach the MDGs get publicly shamed every year in the United Nations Development Programme (UNDP) progress reports. Haiti got the thumbs down for not having any women in its highest parliament. Shame! Sub-Saharan Africa countries were singled-out for their slow progress in getting more girls to school. Shame!

But some countries get a thumbs up. Check out Brazil: Former Brazilian President Luiz Inácio da Silva embraced the MDGs in his political platform for his first successful presidential election. He vowed to eradicate hunger and lift many Brazilians out of poverty, declaring that "[n]o other goals are more just or appropriate." The Brazilian government focused its initiatives on hunger, jobs, racial and gender equality, and environmental preservation—all of which directly relate to MDGs. It met Goal 1 by 2008 through social welfare programs such as *Zero Hunger*, which includes a family stipend that helps cover food costs.

Part Two: How Progress Is Measured

The United Nations Development Programme (UNDP) coordinates efforts to achieve the MDGs at both the global and national levels and tracks their progress. Under its plan, each developing country submits annual reports to the UNDP, which combines that information with information it receives from agencies like UNICEF and the World Bank, and publishes an annual progress report. Many governments and regional commissions are compiling regional and sub-regional MDGs reports to expand on certain topics—for example, special reports on education or maternal mortality.

The UNDP is present in 166 countries and acts in a cooperative capacity to implement MDG actions plans tailored to the needs of each individual country. Among other things, the UNDP works with other U.N.

organizations to provide hands-on support to countries to help them achieve the Goals, implement initiatives, and get the finances necessary to implement their cooperative efforts. Take Colombia—there, the UNDP helped to implement the MAF (MDG Acceleration Framework) at regional, sub-regional, and municipal levels. Niger is another great example. In that region, the UNDP coordinated donor support from the European Commission and Japan International Cooperation Agency to implement Niger's acceleration plan to address poverty and hunger.

To further help countries work towards the Goals, the UNDP created the United Nations Development Assistance Framework (UNDAF). The UNDAF is a strategic planning framework—a set of instructions—that facilitates cooperation between the U.N., country governments and other development partners. For example, the UNDP provided China with a UNDAF to address that region's unique needs in terms of achieving the MDGs, particularly in the areas of health, education, and poverty.

Part Three: Regional Progress

Now let's check out the status of some Goals in different parts of the world. Just so that we don't get confused, the U.N. breaks the developing world down into nine regions and keeps track of their individual progress towards each of the eight Goals: Northern Africa, Sub-Saharan Africa, Caucasus and Central Asia, Western Asia, Southern Asia, Eastern Asia, South-Eastern Asia, Latin America and the Caribbean, and Oceania.

North Africa and Sub-Saharan Africa

In the last two decades, North Africa has made impressive progress in a number of Goals. Enrollment in primary education increased by seventeen percent between 1990 and 2010; the number of people living on less than 1.25 USD per day fell from five percent to one; and the rate of new HIV infections per year per 100 people, though it actually increased, stayed pretty low (from 0.01 in 2001 to 0.02 in 2011).

Sub-Saharan Africa's progress is less impressive. One of the targets the U.N. set was to reduce maternal mortality rates by three-fourths. In 1990, that number was at 850 women out of every 100,000. By 2010, the number had been reduced to 500. Cool. But one-fourth of 850 is just above 212. In 2013, the U.N. noted that regarding reduction of child mortality: "Despite determined global progress in reducing child deaths, an increasing proportion of child deaths are in sub-Saharan Africa where one in nine children die before the age of five . . ." You take what you can get, even if it still hurts.

Eastern Asia and Southern Asia

Before we get started on these two regions, keep in mind that the U.N. takes Southern Asia to mean the area that encompasses India,

Bangladesh, and Nepal, and that extends westward through Iran. Eastern Asia, then, includes China, Mongolia, and the Koreas.

So check it out. Goal 7 looks at environmental sustainability, right? But at the same time, development and industry, which can do a great deal to help meet the other Goals, often come with environmental costs. For instance, Eastern Asia increased its CO_2 output by six billion metric tons (from three to nine billion) between 1990 and 2010 while Southern Asia's output increased by only two billion metric tons (from one to three billion) over the same period of time.

At the same time, Eastern Asia saw 70 percent employment in 2012, 15 deaths per thousand children in 2011, only 37 deaths per 100,000 in terms of maternal mortality in 2010, and (looking at China alone) an eye-popping reduction in the number of people living on less than $1.25 USD per day from 60 percent in 1990 to 12 percent in 2010. Southern Asia, on the other hand, still had 30 percent of its population living on less than $1.25 USD per day in 2010, only 54 percent employment in 2012, 61 deaths per thousand children in 2011, and 220 deaths per 100,000 in terms of maternal mortality in 2010.

South-Eastern Asia

We've been throwing around a bunch of numbers thus far—numbers that can be manipulated. Even people at the U.N., including Jan Vandemoortele, co-architect of the MDGs, have said that some of these Goal-related numbers can be a bit misleading.

So, according to the U.N., South-Eastern Asia has been doing great in terms of the percent of its population that has access to a safe water source.

> "*Development cannot be reduced to a set of technical recipes imported from abroad. The way a country develops is always shaped and influenced by its own specific circumstances. Those who claim that the MDGs should spell out the strategy for reaching the targets merely want to impose their own worldview onto others.*"
> —J. Vandemoortele, "Advancing the UN development agenda post-2015: some practical suggestions," 4 (2012)

In 1990, 71 percent of the population had access to safe water. By 2011, that number was up to 89 percent—that surpassed their target number by 3.5 percent! Looks pretty good, right?

But here's where Vandermoortele starts asking some tough questions. What exactly do we mean by safe water? And what counts as access to that water? Well, for starters, rainwater counts as a source of safe water. And while there are definitely methods for collecting rainwater that can make it a viable source of fresh water, it's not exactly what we tend to think of when we hear the phrase "source of fresh water." On top of that, the numbers-folk assume that a single source of water will necessarily cover all persons within a certain radius. But is that always the case? What about a faucet in someone's home? Are all the individuals in the radius going to have access to that faucet? Maybe so. Maybe not. But let's not end on so cynical a note. Whether the numbers are spot on or not, given a consistent methodology, we can safely say that there are at least more sources of safe water in the area. Again, you take what you can get.

Latin America and the Caribbean

Finally, let's look at gender equality in Latin America and the Caribbean. In primary, secondary, and tertiary education in this region, the ratio of boys to girls is very nearly equal. In fact, the farthest we get from equality is in tertiary education where there are actually more females than there are males (1.27:1 in 2011). In the area of employment, the region saw an increase of six percent in the number of women employees in non-agricultural jobs (1990 to 2011). And in the political realm, the number of women in parliamentary seats rose from 15 to 24.5 percent (2000 to 2013). Very cool.

But before we give this region a thumbs up, let's take a minute to pause and think about women in parliament. Not only in Latin America, but in regions throughout the world, increases in the number of women holding parliamentary seats have been the result, at least in part, of quota systems. So what's the deal with these quotas? They've done a great deal to provide representation to a historically unrepresented group in the political sphere, but as you can well imagine they raise some justified concerns.

Part Four: Financing Development

So, who is going to pay for all this awesome development? Look to Goal 8. The poorest countries can't achieve Goals 1–7 if the rich countries don't first change their domestic policies relating to foreign aid, debt relief, trade and technology transfers. The Monterrey Consensus, the result of the Monterrey International Conference on Financing for Development, covers the commitments the Member States made on financing the MDGs. The Monterrey Consensus was a pledge by developed countries, reaffirmed at many other conferences that came later, to increase foreign aid and focus on using that aid more effectively. The U.N. General Assembly, via the Monterrey Consensus, agreed that a combination of foreign investment, debt relief (we'll get to this in a moment), Official Development Assistance (ODA), and remittances (e.g., expats sending money back home to family) would help fund development (whether via the MDGs or the next phase) and stabilize the economies of developing and least developed countries.

But this whole ODA thing—it's got some issues. First, what is it? ODA is comprised of medium- and long-term concessional loans (including a grant element of at least twenty-five percent—effectively a ten percent discount rate) and grants from multilateral (e.g., the World Bank) and bilateral (U.S. government) sources. It's intended to promote economic development in the countries and territories in the Development Assistance Committee's (DAC) list of ODA recipients. The DAC is part of the Organisation for Economic Co-operation and Development, and its list includes a range of countries, from "least developed countries," such as Benin, to "upper middle income countries and territories," such as Jordan.

Getting back to ODA's issues, here's one: The Goal 8 indicator set for ODA is for developed countries to provide a proportion of their GNP to developing and least developed countries. The U.N. suggests 0.7 of their GNP to developing countries, and 0.15–0.20 of their GNP to least developed countries by 2015. But, besides the EU's commitment to reach 0.56 of their GNP in assistance by 2015, most developed countries (the United States being one of them) have skirted around the issue, affirming their generalized commitment to development financing in conferences like Monterrey, while not making a concrete and measurable commitment. Same ole, same ole, right?

Here's another issue: possible corruption. We talked about the c word in Chapter 6. Since one of the biggest concerns with ODA is that the receiving country's political elite or public officials might divert ODA money for their personal benefit, every U.N. resolution on financing MDGs clarifies that ODA will only be given to countries that exercise good governance. Well . . . you have to say it, at least.

But the issue that really makes you scratch your head is that because part of the ODA consists of loans (yeah, concessional, but still), the assistance merely adds to the external debt that many recipient countries struggle with. Donor countries and multilateral organizations such as the IMF and the World Bank, at the suggestion of the U.N. General Assembly, are now focusing on other avenues of aid that don't involve loans. For instance, donor countries can assist developing countries in their quest to accomplish Goals 1–7 by facilitating their access to advanced technologies designed to improve human health. They could also increase access to their markets by decreasing tariffs on goods from developing countries. But some observers are concerned that the expenses of these initiatives will cause developed countries to lower their ODA, which could bring everything back to square one.

The U.N. knows that relying on ODA only is not a good idea, so they have brainstormed several suggestions, including a global lottery, taxing currency flows, and global taxes (i.e. global income tax, ocean fishing tax, international air transport tax). But most of these funding ideas have their downsides. Take a global income tax, for example. Those better off would bear the burden. Have you heard of the one percent? Well, the problem here is global. In most OECD countries, the top one percent of the population receives a disproportional amount of the country's income. In the United Kingdom, for example, the top one percent received approximately 11.7 percent of the national income. In the United States, the one percent takes over 20 percent of the nation's income. As a result, countries end up in a "tax competition," trying to get these people (or corporations) to move to their country and pay them taxes. Instead, the countries could band together and grant global tax permits, which would allow these "one-percenters" to pay one flat tax rate, no matter what country they live in or how mobile they are. The tax collected would then be divided between the taxpayer's home country, other countries that belong to this organization, and funding for the MDGs, or the next global development initiative.

On September 25, 2013, the U.N. General Assembly convened to follow-up on efforts to achieve the MDGs. The communique noted the uneven progress in achieving the Goals and despaired that "immense challenges . . . remain," especially in most African countries. The U.N. pledged to "particularly target the most off-track MDGs and those where progress has stalled: including those relating to poverty and hunger, universal access to primary education, child mortality, universal access to reproductive health, including maternal health, environmental sustainability and access to water and sanitation. In each of these areas, we are determined to take the purposeful and coordinated action required."

"$1.25"

Setting: A cab pulling away from the United Nations

Characters:

> James: movie star
>
> Eyo: cabbie

Scene One

James: Pele's Churrascaria, please.

Eyo: Nice place. Lot's a food.

James: I need it. I've been living on just $1.25 a day for a week.

Eyo: Why?

James: $1.25 is the extreme poverty line. Millions of people live on less than that. I'm heading an anti-poverty campaign. Just spoke at the U.N.

Eyo: You're an important man, are you?

James: Nah . . . Just your run-of-the-mill movie star.

Eyo: Movie star. I don't watch movies.

James: No worries. But, hey, I've told you something about myself. Now it's your turn.

Eyo: I don't know what to say.

James: Well, just tell me where you're from. I know it's some place in Africa, right?

Eyo: Niger. How did you know?

James: I've been all over Africa . . . with my crew, filming poverty. Been in Niger.

Eyo: For your campaign?

James: Yup. The stuff we shot is awesome. Debuted tonight.

Eyo: What's the name of your campaign?

James: "Freeing the entire human race from want." Pretty gripping name, don't you think?

(pause)

Eyo: Was it hard?

James: What?

Eyo: Living on $1.25 a day.

James: Hell, yes. I could barely move by the third day.

Eyo: Hmmm . . .

James: I have to lose weight anyway for my next gig.

(James looks at the dashboard and sees a worn, blurry photo of a little girl with a faint smile)

James: Who's that? The girl in the photo?

Eyo: My daughter.

James: Cute.

(cab pulls up to the restaurant)

Eyo: One dollar and twenty-five cents.

James: What?

Eyo: My way of remembering her . . . No Churrascarias in Niger.

II. DEBT RELIEF

Achieving the MDGs and promoting continued equitable development is a pipe dream if the countries that most need the help are struggling under a mountain of foreign debt. It's time to forgive the debt! Well . . . let's not get ahead of ourselves. This section focuses on debt forgiveness by official creditors—such as a loan from the United States to Zambia or a loan to the country from the African Development Bank. You know this is a controversial topic (forgiveness of student debt?). But let's control ourselves and start with getting a sense of the debt problem. Then we'll see how different actors, ranging from non-governmental organizations (NGOs) to the World Bank (WB) and the International Monetary Fund (IMF), tried to do something about it and the reactions to those efforts. This story began in the 1990s and continued to unfold in the new millennium.

Part One: The Debt Relief Movement

The Debt

In Chapter 5 we told you about the debt crisis of the 1980s, focusing on Latin America. In this section we focus mostly on African countries. One commonality between the 1980s crisis and the debt relief movement of the 1990s is that countries ran up a lot of debt that eventually they couldn't repay. Check out the numbers for the countries that became identified as "heavily indebted poor countries" (HIPC): long-term debt ballooned from $7 billion in 1970 to $169 billion in 2000. But unlike the Latin American debt of the 1980s, the HIPC debt was owed largely to foreign governments (bilateral debt) or multilateral lending institutions such as the World Bank and the IMF (multilateral debt). When it's time to restructure bilateral debt, the countries go to the **Paris Club**. There isn't an established "club" to work out multilateral debt. Here we primarily discuss multilateral debt relief.

The Movement

In the 1990s, the Global North got real and decided that something had to be done about "unsustainable" debt, particularly in Africa (check out supplement 18D on Africa). Creditor nations such as the U.S., Japan, and European countries tried to provide debt relief through concessional rescheduling and even cancellation, but they quickly realized that debtor countries needed more to ease the debt burden—this put pressure on the World Bank and the IMF to take action. At the same time, non-governmental organizations (NGOs) and civil society organizations such as religious and advocacy groups created a movement to raise global awareness of developing countries' staggering debt problems.

> *"Debt relief for the most heavily indebted poor countries is one of the major challenges facing all of us. This is a major opportunity for Europe to take a strong political lead on one of the great moral issues of our time."*
> —Gordon Brown, Chancellor of the U.K.. *The Guardian* (1999)

The movement resulted in a campaign known as Jubilee 2000 (a play on the "Jubilee Year" described in Leviticus where those enslaved by debt are freed, and the call for the cancellation of all unsustainable debt by the year 2000). It eventually attracted the support of celebrities such as Bono of U2, Muhammad Ali, and Bob Gedolf. (Gotta have the celebrities . . .) Through demonstrations and lobbying, Jubilee 2000 was able to successfully put pressure on the countries that represent the world's largest economies to support developing country debt relief. Result: the HIPC Initiative.

> *"This initiative is a breakthrough . . . It deals with debt in a comprehensive way to give countries the possibility of exiting from unsustainable debt. It is very good news for the poor of the world."*
> —James D. Wolfensohn, President, World Bank, "HIPC—Debt Relief For Sustainable Development"

The Arguments

The argument in favor of debt relief is moral to the core. One slice of the argument is that it's morally wrong to saddle the people of a country with debt incurred by a previous corrupt and otherwise evil government or ruler (see supplement 12F on "odious debt'). The other slice is that, while borrowing countries are not blameless for running up debt, they do so within a global system that implicates all of us. And if that's the case, then it's immoral for us to allow children to die because money that could be used for health care and nutrition is going instead to pay foreign creditors (countries) that in most cases are very well off and don't need the money.

> *"Conditions of life anywhere on earth are today deeply affected by international interactions of many kinds and thus by the elaborate regimes of treaties and conventions that profoundly and increasingly shape such interactions. Those who participate in this regime especially in its design and imposition, are morally implicated in any contribution it make to ever-increasing global economic inequality and to the consequent persistence of severe poverty."*
>
> —T. Pogge, Politics As Usual: What Lies Behind the Pro-Poor Rhetoric, 13 (2010).

There's pushback, of course. Critics argue that debt forgiveness is not enough to fix the economic problems engulfing debtor countries—without effective political and economic reforms, debt relief just can't provide long-term economic stability. Some economists fear that debt forgiveness actually perpetuates corrupt governments because there's no guarantee that those in power will use the saved money (money is fungible) for legitimate social or development programs. And who is to say that governments who didn't use original loans for helping the poor will suddenly see the light and use new financial resources to support their impoverished citizens? Another fear, referred to as the "moral hazard," is that countries relieved of their debts will engage in reckless over-borrowing with the expectation that, once their debts once again reach unsustainable levels, their foreign creditors will simply forgive them again. For more, see supplement 18E.

> *"Poor nations suffer poverty not because of high debt burdens but because spendthrift governments constantly seek to redistribute the existing economic pie to privileged political elites rather than try to make the pie grow larger through sound economic policies. The debt-burdened government of Kenya managed to find enough money to reward President Moi's home region with the Eldoret International Airport in 1996, a facility that almost no one uses."*
>
> —W. Easterly, "Think Again: Debt Relief" (2001)

Nothing like a good debate—with real consequences.

Part Two: The HIPC Initiative and the MDRI

But something had to be done. Enter stage right: the World Bank and the IMF, each pulling along a conflicted white knight.

The Heavily Indebted Poor Countries (HIPC) Initiative

The Bank and the Fund launched the Heavily Indebted Poor Countries (HIPC) Initiative in 1996 in response to the growing global pressure. It was a pretty big deal, not only for debt relief, but also for the procedure involved in securing the relief. We've talked about debt restructuring of bilateral debt via the Paris Club. But prior to the Initiative, there was no forum for debt relief from multilateral lenders or a forum to bring together bilateral and multilateral lenders to provide comprehensive debt-relief solutions. The HIPC Initiative has come a long way since 1996 but the ride's been bumpy. Let's start with how it was originally conceived.

The basic idea behind the Initiative was to reduce "unsustainable" debt, meaning unsustainable debt levels despite full application of traditional bilateral debt relief. Well, okay, but what does that mean? HIPC considered debt unsustainable when the ratio of debt-to-exports exceeded 200–250% or when the ratio of debt-to-government revenues exceeded 280%. Once a country qualified under these ratios, it started a six-year program, split into two three-year phases, designed to generate a track record of good fiscal and economic performance. During Phase I, the country would work with the IMF to implement an Enhanced Structural Adjustment Facility (ESAF). The ESAF originally provided concessional loans (non-market rates) to poor nations and required countries to comply with a broad range of detailed reforms and conditions, such as privatization of state industries or cuts in domestic spending. (Yeah, basically restructuring the whole economy.) The purpose of the restruc—sorry, *reforms* was to ensure that the countries could use future funding effectively. The conclusion of Phase I was termed the "decision point;" it was then that the World Bank and IMF would review the country's debt level and determine how much debt forgiveness they would provide to enable the country to maintain sustainable debt levels. Phase II required continued implementation of the ESAF and culminated in the "completion point," where creditors would forgive the country's debts in the amount they promised at the decision point. What a ritual, huh?

Critics soon trashed the ritual. (They always spoil the fun, don't they?) They criticized the Initiative's definition of debt sustainability, arguing that the debt-to-export and debt-to-government-revenues criteria were arbitrary and too restrictive. As evidence, they highlighted that by 1999 only four countries, Uganda, Bolivia, Guyana, and Mozambique, had received any debt relief. They also claimed the six-year program was too long and too inflexible to meet the individual needs of debtor nations. Not only that but the Fund and Bank didn't cancel any debt until the completion point, leaving countries to struggle with crushing debt while at the same time trying to put into place the required structural reforms. Ironically, the ESAF conditions often undermined poverty-reduction efforts. For example, privatization of

> "We very much welcome the actions of the World Bank and IMF in making Bolivia eligible for HIPC debt relief . . . This relief will enable us to make major improvements in the health, education and living standards of those below the poverty line."
> —.E. Jorge Quiroga, Bolivian Vice President (1997)

utilities tended to raise the cost of services beyond the citizens' ability to pay. The criticism that really bites is that the Initiative was designed by creditors to protect their interests, leaving countries with unsustainable debt burdens even upon reaching the decision point.

The Enhanced HIPC

Then came the G-7's Cologne Debt Initiative ("CDI"), which was unveiled at the Cologne Economic Summit in June 1999. The CDI's thrust was "let's get serious about debt reduction for countries that are serious about structural reforms that will reduce poverty." In response to the criticism of the ESAF, the Fund retired that facility and introduced the **Poverty Reduction and Growth Facility**, which is designed to give countries more "ownership" of economic reforms. The thinking is that ownership will increase the chances that debt relief will actually contribute to poverty reduction. The quid pro quo for ownership is having a track record of policy reforms needed to get to the decision and completion points.

The CDI also modified the HIPC Initiative to provide faster relief and deeper relief! Let's start with the fast-relief pill. To recognize ambition, the CDI introduced a "floating completion point" to allow countries that met policy targets early on to progress towards completion in less than six years. And because debt service payments were a bit of a strain on HIPC countries (please tell us you got that sarcasm), they could qualify for "interim relief" before reaching the completion point—which the Paris Club had already been doing.

Now for the deeper relief! The CDI revisited the threshold requirements. As before, a country needed to show its debt was unsustainable. But to free up more poverty-reducing resources the targets for determining sustainability decreased to a debt-to-export ratio of 150% and a debt-to-government-revenues ratio of 250%.

The Global North, primarily the G-7, actually delivered on their pledges. But here come the critics—again! They argued that the enhanced HIPC Initiative eligibility criteria were flawed. Using debt-to-export ratios to determine eligibility and to determine debt sustainability was off-the-mark because this metric did not take into consideration poverty levels in evaluating the financial resources needed to reduce poverty. Excluding the social and development perspectives in the eligibility equation and focusing only on debt-to-export ratios excluded a number of countries, hosting the majority of the world's poor, from participation in the Initiative. Another major criticism related to the conditionality that came with the debt relief. Critics argued that the pace of the required reforms, which focused on fiscal management and market-based reforms such as privatization, was self-defeating because the timeframe made it difficult to make the process truly participatory. These critiques prompted calls for bringing in the U.N. as a counter-weight to the Fund and the Bank. Uh . . . yeah, right . . .

Another Try: Topping Up

In 2001, the IMF introduced another important tool to increase the Initiative's effectiveness—"topping up." If countries unexpectedly suffer economic setbacks after the decision point due to external factors, such as rising interest rates or falling commodity prices, they're eligible for increased debt assistance at the completion point. Five countries—Burkina Faso, Ethiopia, Malawi, Niger and Rwanda—have received topping up assistance.

Let's take a look at how topping up worked with Burkina Faso. By its HIPC completion point in 2002, Burkina Faso had 50% of its debt stocks eliminated but, because of poor export performance, its debt-to-export ratio exceeded the 150% target set under the 1999 revision. The external circumstances? Minor things, like falling world cotton prices (Burkina Faso's main cash crop is cotton) due in part to subsidies provided to cotton farmers in industrialized economies; political and economic events in neighboring countries; and crop damage caused by agricultural parasites. The Fund and the Bank decided to provide Burkina Faso with an additional $129 million as topping up assistance, to get its debt-to-export ratio down to the target.

In April 2013, the IMF and the World Bank staff concluded that the HIPC Initiative is nearly complete. Thirty-five out of thirty-nine countries have reached the completion point. The four countries that haven't reached the completion point, Chad, Eritrea, Somalia and Sudan, haven't done so for reasons ranging from poor economic performance to political instability. The Initiative wasn't intended to be a permanent mechanism for debt relief—entrance into the program was cut off to other countries in 2006, when its sunset clause went into effect.

Multilateral Debt Relief Initiative

In a G-8 Summit in 2005 held in Gleneagles, Scotland, the leaders agreed to establish a supplement to the HIPC Initiative: the Multilateral Debt Relief Initiative ("MDRI"), which provides 100 percent debt cancellation of multilateral debt owed to the IMF, the World Bank's International Development Association, and the African Development Bank (AfDB). The Initiative's purpose is to help HIPC countries that have reached or are likely to reach their completion points to achieve the MDGs. This forgiveness automatically applies to countries that reach the HIPC completion point, but only counts for debt incurred by the end of 2004. And countries who already reached the decision point before 2005 weren't excluded—they became eligible for full debt forgiveness once their lending agency confirmed they'd continued to maintain the reforms implemented during the duration of HIPC Initiative.

While the World Bank and AfDB limit the MDRI to only countries that complete the HIPC Initiative, the IMF's MDRI eligibility criteria are more inclusive. The Fund allows any country with annual per capita income of $380 or less (an amount close to the eligibility requirement of the HIPC Initiative) to qualify for MDRI debt cancellation. Countries must be current on their obligations to the IMF, and show satisfactory performance in macroeconomic policies, implementation of a poverty reduction strategy, and public expenditure management. The Fund has extended MDRI assistance to two non-HIPC countries: $82 million to Cambodia, and $99 million to Tajikistan. So far the MDRI has provided assistance to the thirty-four countries that have reached the HIPC Initiative completion point, in addition to Cambodia and Tajikistan.

Impact of HIPC and MDRI

Opinions on the success of the HIPC Initiative and the MDRI (which cost $112.9 billion) depend, of course, on the source. Duh. Let's take a look at the Fund and the Bank. They report that the HIPC and MDRI have reduced the debt stocks of the thirty-six post-decision-point countries by over 90 percent. They also say that the debt relief initiatives have alleviated debt burdens for the beneficiary countries, enabling them to increase their poverty-reducing expenditures. According to their numbers, the average debt service payment has dropped from 2.9 percent of GDP in 2001 to 0.9 percent of GDP in 2011 for the thirty-six countries who reached the post-decision point. And, in 2011, the Bank estimated that health expenditures rose from 5.2 percent of GDP in the period 1995–2000, to 6.6 percent in the period 2006–2009 for the thirty-two countries that had reached the HIPC completion point.

But everyone knows you can play around with numbers, right? So let's take a look at what the U.N. has to say. A 2013 Human Rights Council report is less optimistic than the Bank and the Fund. It concludes that it's kind of hard to find a link between debt relief and an increase in poverty-reducing expenditures. There might be other factors that increase those expenditures besides reduction in debt service payments, like higher prices for commodity exports. Even if reduction of debt service payments allows a government to spend more on social services, the result doesn't necessarily mean that poverty will disappear. Let's take a look at Zambia. In 2005, Zambia completed the HIPC Initiative and received $6.6 billion in debt relief through the HIPC and MDRI. It used savings from debt payments to eliminate school fees, eliminate user fees in rural health centers, and to fund infrastructure. Yet, approximately 64% of the population still lives on less than $1 per day. In fact, the HIPC Initiative conditions might have adverse effects. Seventy-five percent of Zambia's foreign exchange earnings

> *"Some stakeholders [from government to civil society in Zambia] noted that there were people in society who regarded street children to be the result of uncaring, irresponsible or reckless parents who spent time enjoying themselves at the expense of their children. As a result, many people perceived street children to be . . . 'unsightly if not incurable sores on the skin of society'."*
> —Report on Survey and Analysis of the Situation of Street Children in Zambia," 71 (2007)

come from copper mining, but as a condition for debt relief through the HIPC Initiative, Zambia had to adopt reforms like privatization of copper mining, which diverted earnings to foreign companies.

Scene Two

<u>Setting</u>: Pele's Churrascaria

James: Reservations for two under James.

Receptionist: It'll be about fifteen minutes before your table is ready, okay?

(James sees a jar with a piece of paper affixed to it: "Please contribute to Third World Debt Relief!" He stares at it.)

James: Don't worry about my reservation.

Receptionist: Are you sure you can't stay? We'll seat you very soon.

James: No thanks. I have to find a cabbie.

(fade to black)

You Gotta Know Something About Them!

Kofi Atta Annan

Image of Kofi Annan by Harry Wad is licensed under CC BY 2.5.

Born in Ghana (while it was still a British colony), Annan served as the United Nation's Secretary-General from 1997–2006. Kofi, whose name means "born on a Friday," had a twin sister, Efua Atta, who died in 1991. They were born into an aristocratic family—his grandfathers and uncle were tribal chiefs; his father was a governor of the Asante province. As he studied economics in Ghana, the Ford Foundation noticed his potential and sponsored his undergraduate studies in economics at Macalester College in Minnesota. Kofi was just twenty when he arrived at St. Paul. In his first winter there he refused to wear earmuffs because they cramped his style. Yeah, well, how long does it take for frostbite to set in? He bought, like, *huge* earmuffs. While at Macalester, he became a state champion orator (no wonder he's so eloquent) and ran on the track team—he was jacked. Kofi loved the school so much that he autographed a ping-pong table there. Dubbed by some as "the secular pope," in 2001 he won a Nobel Peace Prize along with the United Nations.

Jeffrey Sachs

Image of Jeffrey D. Sachs by Sikarin Thanachaiary, Copyright World Economic Forum, is licensed under CC BY 2.0.

Born in Detroit, Michigan, Sachs' passion for alleviating poverty can be traced to his father, a lawyer who fought for improved working conditions for public sector employees. A passionate youth, Jeffrey became president of his high school's student council, and while there became fascinated with the world's different economic systems. Check it out: He started his undergraduate studies at Harvard in 1972 and by 1980 he was a prolific professor there. Jeffrey thinks Kofi Annan is the world's greatest political leader, and shares Annan's passion for fixing the world's poverty problem. He once told a reporter, "I'm still fighting against the incredible capacity of the so-called international community to stare intense human disaster in the face and not flinch from ignoring it." Jeffrey was a Special Advisor to the United Nations and directed the U.N. Millennium Development Project, which was active from 2002–2006. He's currently the Director of the U.N. Sustainable Development Solutions Network.

Bono

Image of Bono by David Shankbone, editing by User:Megapixie, is licensed under CC BY 3.0.

Bono (or Paul David Hewson, his non-stage name) is the lead singer of the Irish band U2. He was a precocious child who was once kicked out of school for throwing dog feces at his Spanish teacher. Bono initially wanted to be an actor, but after responding to a community notice calling for musicians, he met his future U2 bandmates. And the rest is history. In addition to winning an incredible twenty-two Grammy Awards, Bono is also an extraordinary activist. He's truly committed to making the world a better place—he's been involved with Amnesty International and Greenpeace, and co-founded both DATA (Debt, Aid, Trade, Africa) and the ONE Campaign to Make Poverty History.

Kalombo

Kalombo is a ten-year-old boy who lives on the streets of Lusaka, Zambia. When he was eight, his father died of AIDS, along with 94,000 other Zambians who die annually from the disease. After burying his father, his mother told him to go to the streets and beg for money so they could eat. She disappeared a year later. His favorite place to sleep is in the doorway of a boutique that sells tapestries to Western tourists. He dreams of going to school, where he won't be beaten by the police. Kalombo doesn't know Bono.

Composite profile based on the Report on Survey and Analysis of the Situation of Street Children in Zambia, Ministry of Community Development and Social Services, Ministry of Sport, Youth and Child Development, Supported by UNICEF, Project Concern International and RAPIDS, 2006

What's Up with That?

$1.25 a Day (PPP)

The World Bank set the International Extreme Poverty Line in 2005. To get there, they first analyzed poverty in the 10–20 poorest countries to find national "poverty lines" by adding the cost of food (only the minimum daily caloric intake needed to survive, also called the "food poverty line") to non-food spending (found by looking at spending of people near the food poverty line). Then the Bank adjusted these lines using purchasing power parity (PPP)—comparing how much of a country's currency is needed in that country to buy what $1 would get you in the U.S.—and averaged them to find the $1.25 International Extreme Poverty Line. PPP allows the $1.25 line to be converted into a country's local currency. Sure, we could just use currency exchange rates, right? Well, actually, we can't. If the comparative costs of goods aren't measured, we don't realize that $1.25 in, say, Chad, might buy a different amount of goods than that same $1.25 would in the Czech Republic. The Bank has periodically adjusted the line.

Paris Club

It's not about wine and baguettes. The Paris Club is a forum in which sovereign borrowers on an ad hoc basis can restructure loans made by governments or by private lenders with a creditor-government guarantee. Government agencies, such as the Agency for International Development, the Export-Import Bank, and the Commodity Credit Corporation in the United States, typically provide such public sector credit. Private debt to official creditors (e.g., Ex-Im Bank loan to a private borrower through a supplier credit program) can also be restructured under the auspices of the

Paris Club if the government in which the private borrower is located cannot provide the borrower with foreign exchange to service the debt.

Poverty Reduction and Growth Facility (PRGF)

The PRGF, which replaced the HIPC Initiative's Enhanced Structural Adjustment Facility (ESAF) in 1999, aimed to reduce poverty and increase economic growth of the IMF's poorest member countries. PRGF programs were built from Poverty Reduction Strategy Papers, which were prepared by governments and other domestic development partners like NGOs and civil society groups. These papers were designed to create ownership of the targets and policies a country had to follow to meet the goals of the PRGF. They outlined the vision and the link between the means and ends the country hoped to achieve. The PRGF has since been replaced by the Extended Credit Facility, which provides for more flexible and tailored programs for specific member countries.

QUESTIONS FROM YOUR TALKING DOG

1.   Millennium Development Goals. Sounds grand. Ambitious. Stuff of dreams. A better world. Yeah, it sounds like I'm writing speech. Okay, let's start with the Millennium Declaration. What will I say in my speech? In the meantime, change the channel. I'm tired of listening to these clueless talking heads.

2.   The eight goals make sense. What do you think? And how about those targets? Give me something to talk about.

3.   Which way should I cut with the reactions to the MDG's? Critics or supporters?

4.   It seems like keeping track of all this stuff is a huge pain in the neck. How is progress measured?

5.   What's the word on North Africa and Sub-Saharan Africa? How about Eastern Asia and Southern Asia? Southeastern Asia? And let's not forget Latin America and the Caribbean.

6.   I need something on financing the MDG's. Give me some stuff, starting with the Monterrey Consensus. And I want to say something about ODA.

7.   Okay, I'm done with the speech. Now what? The debt relief movement. Forgive all student debt! Yeah! Oh, multilateral debt relief. Not quite the same. Shoot.

8.   I can imagine that debt relief is pretty controversial. Tell me about it.

9.   So the Heavily Indebted Poor Countries Initiative was about "unsustainable" debt? What does that mean?

10. So what was the process under HIPC?

11. Is it time for the critics yet? I thought so. Let's talk about it.

12. Cologne? I don't need it. I smell just fine. Okay, the Cologne Debt Initiative. Why was it an enhanced version of the HIPC?

13. Wow! So the Multilateral Debt Relief Initiative was all about 100% debt cancellation? Tell me more, man!

14. Can we wrap this up? I've got an appointment to get my nails trimmed. So just tell me about the opinions on the success or failure of the HIPC Initiative and the MDRI.

Chapter 12: Supplement

18A. *Millennium Declaration*

What a grand statement. In many ways it's a continuation of the New International Economic Order (NIEO) themes, which we studied in Chapter 4, only with a much greater and direct emphasis on the vulnerable groups. Can you find the NIEO themes? What do you think of the first bullet under paragraph 20?

U.N. Resolution, "United Nations Millennium Declaration" (2000)

Resolution adopted by the General Assembly
[without reference to a Main Committee (A/55/L.2)]
55/2. United Nations Millennium Declaration

The General Assembly

Adopts the following Declaration:

United Nations Millennium Declaration

I.   Values and principles

1.   We, heads of State and Government, have gathered at United Nations Headquarters in New York from 6 to 8 September 2000, at the dawn of a new millennium, to reaffirm our faith in the Organization and its Charter as indispensable foundations of a more peaceful, prosperous and just world.

2.   We recognize that, in addition to our separate responsibilities to our individual societies, we have a collective responsibility to uphold the principles of human dignity, equality and equity at the global level. As leaders we have a duty therefore to all the world's people, especially the most vulnerable and, in

particular, the children of the world, to whom the future belongs.

3. We reaffirm our commitment to the purposes and principles of the Charter of the United Nations, which have proved timeless and universal. Indeed, their relevance and capacity to inspire have increased, as nations and peoples have become increasingly interconnected and interdependent.

4. We are determined to establish a just and lasting peace all over the world in accordance with the purposes and principles of the Charter. We rededicate ourselves to support all efforts to uphold the sovereign equality of all States, respect for their territorial integrity and political independence, resolution of disputes by peaceful means and in conformity with the principles of justice and international law, the right to self-determination of peoples which remain under colonial domination and foreign occupation, non-interference in the internal affairs of States, respect for human rights and fundamental freedoms, respect for the equal rights of all without distinction as to race, sex, language or religion and international cooperation in solving international problems of an economic, social, cultural or humanitarian character.

5. We believe that the central challenge we face today is to ensure that globalization becomes a positive force for all the world's people. For while globalization offers great opportunities, at present its benefits are very unevenly shared, while its costs are unevenly distributed. We recognize that developing countries and countries with economies in transition face special difficulties in responding to this central challenge. Thus, only through broad and sustained efforts to create a shared future, based upon our common humanity in all its diversity, can globalization be made fully inclusive and equitable. These efforts must include policies and measures, at the global level, which correspond to the needs of developing countries and economies in transition and are formulated and implemented with their effective participation.

6. We consider certain fundamental values to be essential to international relations in the twenty-first century. These include:

•   **Freedom**. Men and women have the right to live their lives and raise their children in dignity, free from hunger and from the fear of violence, oppression or injustice. Democratic and participatory governance based on the will of the people best assures these rights.

- **Equality**. No individual and no nation must be denied the opportunity to benefit from development. The equal rights and opportunities of women and men must be assured.

- **Solidarity**. Global challenges must be managed in a way that distributes the costs and burdens fairly in accordance with basic principles of equity and social justice. Those who suffer or who benefit least deserve help from those who benefit most.

- **Tolerance**. Human beings must respect one other, in all their diversity of belief, culture and language. Differences within and between societies should be neither feared nor repressed, but cherished as a precious asset of humanity. A culture of peace and dialogue among all civilizations should be actively promoted.

- **Respect for nature**. Prudence must be shown in the management of all living species and natural resources, in accordance with the precepts of sustainable development. Only in this way can the immeasurable riches provided to us by nature be preserved and passed on to our descendants. The current unsustainable patterns of production and consumption must be changed in the interest of our future welfare and that of our descendants.

- **Shared responsibility**. Responsibility for managing worldwide economic and social development, as well as threats to international peace and security, must be shared among the nations of the world and should be exercised multilaterally. As the most universal and most representative organization in the world, the United Nations must play the central role.

7. In order to translate these shared values into actions, we have identified key objectives to which we assign special significance.

* * *

III. Development and poverty eradication

11. We will spare no effort to free our fellow men, women and children from the abject and dehumanizing conditions of extreme poverty, to which more than a billion of them are currently subjected. We are committed to making the right to development a reality for everyone and to freeing the entire human race from want.

12. We resolve therefore to create an environment—at the national and global levels alike—which is conducive to development and to the elimination of poverty.

13. Success in meeting these objectives depends, inter alia, on good governance within each country. It also depends on good governance at the international level and on transparency in the financial, monetary and trading systems. We are committed to an open, equitable, rule-based, predictable and non-discriminatory multilateral trading and financial system.

14. We are concerned about the obstacles developing countries face in mobilizing the resources needed to finance their sustained development. We will therefore make every effort to ensure the success of the High-level International and Intergovernmental Event on Financing for Development, to be held in 2001.

15. We also undertake to address the special needs of the least developed countries. In this context, we welcome the Third United Nations Conference on the Least Developed Countries to be held in May 2001 and will endeavour to ensure its success. We call on the industrialized countries:

   o To adopt, preferably by the time of that Conference, a policy of duty- and quota-free access for essentially all exports from the least developed countries;

   o To implement the enhanced programme of debt relief for the heavily indebted poor countries without further delay and to agree to cancel all official bilateral debts of those countries in return for their making demonstrable commitments to poverty reduction; and

   o To grant more generous development assistance, especially to countries that are genuinely making an effort to apply their resources to poverty reduction.

16. We are also determined to deal comprehensively and effectively with the debt problems of low- and middle-income developing countries, through various national and international measures designed to make their debt sustainable in the long term.

* * *

19. We resolve further:

   o To halve, by the year 2015, the proportion of the world's people whose income is less than one dollar a day and the proportion of people who suffer from hunger and, by the same date, to halve the proportion of people who are unable to reach or to afford safe drinking water.

o To ensure that, by the same date, children everywhere, boys and girls alike, will be able to complete a full course of primary schooling and that girls and boys will have equal access to all levels of education.

o By the same date, to have reduced maternal mortality by three quarters, and under-five child mortality by two thirds, of their current rates.

o To have, by then, halted, and begun to reverse, the spread of HIV/AIDS, the scourge of malaria and other major diseases that afflict humanity.

o To provide special assistance to children orphaned by HIV/AIDS.

o By 2020, to have achieved a significant improvement in the lives of at least 100 million slum dwellers as proposed in the "Cities Without Slums" initiative.

20. We also resolve:

o To promote gender equality and the empowerment of women as effective ways to combat poverty, hunger and disease and to stimulate development that is truly sustainable.

o To develop and implement strategies that give young people everywhere a real chance to find decent and productive work.

o To encourage the pharmaceutical industry to make essential drugs more widely available and affordable by all who need them in developing countries.

o To develop strong partnerships with the private sector and with civil society organizations in pursuit of development and poverty eradication.

o To ensure that the benefits of new technologies, especially information and communication technologies, in conformity with recommendations contained in the ECOSOC 2000 Ministerial Declaration, are available to all.

* * *

V. Human rights, democracy and good governance

24. We will spare no effort to promote democracy and strengthen the rule of law, as well as respect for all internationally recognized human rights and fundamental freedoms, including the right to development.

25. We resolve therefore:

o To respect fully and uphold the Universal Declaration of Human Rights.

o To strive for the full protection and promotion in all our countries of civil, political, economic, social and cultural rights for all.

o To strengthen the capacity of all our countries to implement the principles and practices of democracy and respect for human rights, including minority rights.

o To combat all forms of violence against women and to implement the Convention on the Elimination of All Forms of Discrimination against Women.

o To take measures to ensure respect for and protection of the human rights of migrants, migrant workers and their families, to eliminate the increasing acts of racism and xenophobia in many societies and to promote greater harmony and tolerance in all societies.

o To work collectively for more inclusive political processes, allowing genuine participation by all citizens in all our countries.

o To ensure the freedom of the media to perform their essential role and the right of the public to have access to information.

* * *

18B. *Millennium Development Goals: Progress Report 2013*

Compare Sub-Sarahan Africa to Latin America & the Caribbean. Big contrast, right? Come with me to parts of Latin America to ask people living in favelas in Brazil or to the shantytowns you see when flying into Caracas what they think of this report card.

U.N. Millennium Development Goals:
2013 Progress Chart (2013)

Goals and Targets	Africa		Asia				Oceania	Latin America & the Caribbean	Caucasus & Central Asia
	Northern	Sub-Saharan	Eastern	South-Eastern	Southern	Western			
GOAL 1 | Eradicate extreme poverty and hunger									
Reduce extreme poverty by half	low poverty	very high poverty	moderate poverty*	moderate poverty	very high poverty	low poverty	very high poverty	low poverty	low poverty
Productive and decent employment	large deficit in decent work	very large deficit in decent work	large deficit in decent work	large deficit in decent work	very large deficit in decent work	large deficit in decent work	very large deficit in decent work	moderate deficit in decent work	moderate deficit in decent work
Reduce hunger by half	low hunger	very high hunger	moderate hunger	moderate hunger	high hunger	moderate hunger	moderate hunger	moderate hunger	moderate hunger
GOAL 2 | Achieve universal primary education									
Universal primary schooling	high enrolment	moderate enrolment	high enrolment	high enrolment	high enrolment	high enrolment	—	high enrolment	high enrolment
GOAL 3 | Promote gender equality and empower women									
Equal girls' enrolment in primary school	close to parity	close to parity	close to parity	parity	parity	close to parity	close to parity	parity	parity
Women's share of paid employment	low share	medium share	high share	medium share	low share	low share	medium share	high share	high share
Women's equal representation in national parliaments	low representation	moderate representation	moderate representation	low representation	low representation	low representation	very low representation	moderate representation	low representation
GOAL 4 | Reduce child mortality									
Reduce mortality of under-five-year-olds by two thirds	low mortality	high mortality	low mortality	low mortality	moderate mortality	low mortality	moderate mortality	low mortality	moderate mortality
GOAL 5 | Improve maternal health									
Reduce maternal mortality by three quarters	low mortality	very high mortality	low mortality	moderate mortality	high mortality	low mortality	high mortality	low mortality	low mortality
Access to reproductive health	moderate access	low access	high access	moderate access	moderate access	moderate access	low access	high access	moderate access
GOAL 6 | Combat HIV/AIDS, malaria and other diseases									
Halt and begin to reverse the spread of HIV/AIDS	low incidence	high incidence	low incidence	low incidence	low incidence	low incidence	low incidence	low incidence	intermediate incidence
Halt and reverse the spread of tuberculosis	low mortality	moderate mortality	low mortality	moderate mortality	moderate mortality	low mortality	high mortality	low mortality	moderate mortality
GOAL 7 | Ensure environmental sustainability									
Halve proportion of population without improved drinking water	high coverage	low coverage	high coverage	moderate coverage	high coverage	high coverage	low coverage	high coverage	moderate coverage
Halve proportion of population without sanitation	high coverage	very low coverage	moderate coverage	low coverage	very low coverage	moderate coverage	very low coverage	moderate coverage	high coverage
Improve the lives of slum-dwellers	moderate proportion of slum-dwellers	very high proportion of slum-dwellers	moderate proportion of slum-dwellers	high proportion of slum-dwellers	high proportion of slum-dwellers	moderate proportion of slum-dwellers	moderate proportion of slum-dwellers	moderate proportion of slum-dwellers	—
GOAL 8 | Develop a global partnership for development									
Internet users	high usage	moderate usage	high usage	high usage	moderate usage	high usage	low usage	high usage	high usage

The progress chart operates on two levels. The words in each box indicate the present degree of compliance with the target. The colours show progress towards the target according to the legend below:

- ▓ Target already met or expected to be met by 2015.
- ▓ No progress or deterioration.
- ▓ Progress insufficient to reach the target if prevailing trends persist.
- ▓ Missing or insufficient data.

* Poverty progress for Eastern Asia is assessed based on China's data only.

18C. *The First Millennium Development Goal: A Cause for Celebration?*

Thomas Pogge is a philosopher who writes about global justice. One of his arguments is that, because of the oppressive global order that the rich countries have perpetrated, they have moral duty to assist the Global South.

And to do this will take very little from the rich countries to help many impoverished people in poor countries. In this excerpt he picks apart MDG Goal 1. What shell games does he identify?

T. Pogge, *The First Millennium Development Goal:*
A Cause for Celebration? in <u>Politics as Usual: What Lies
Behind the Pro-Poor Rhetoric</u> (2010)

3.0 Introduction

In the *UN Millennium Declaration* of the year 2000, the 191 member states of the UN committed themselves to the goal "to halve, by the year 2015, the proportion of the world's people whose income is less than one dollar a day and the proportion of people who suffer from hunger." This is the first and most prominent of what have come to be known as the eight UN Millennium Development Goals (MDGs).

The commitment to this goal, in such a prominent text, has been widely celebrated. The governments of the world have finally united behind the goal of eradicating hunger and extreme poverty, defined as the inability to afford "a minimum, nutritionally adequate diet plus essential non-food requirements." And they have not merely endorsed this goal in a vague and general way, but have committed themselves to a concrete path with a precise intermediate target. Given the abject poverty in which so many human beings subsist today, this highly official and highly visible commitment is surely reason for celebration.—Isn't it?

I am not so sure. In any case, I want to offer some skeptical reflections that we might ponder before judging the goal our governments have set in our names.

3.1 Reflection one—on halving world poverty

The goal of halving extreme poverty and hunger by 2015 is not new. It was very prominently affirmed, for instance, four years earlier, at the World Food Summit in Rome, where the 186 participating governments declared: "We pledge our political will and our common and national commitment to achieving food security for all and to an ongoing effort to eradicate hunger in all countries, with an immediate view to reducing the number of undernourished people to half their present level no later than 2015." An "immediate" view that budgets 19 years to solve merely half a problem is not especially ambitions, to be sure, but at least the pledge seemed definite and firm.

Is the first MDG then merely a reaffirmation of a commitment made earlier? Well, not exactly. Looking closely at the two texts, we find a subtle but important shift. While the earlier *Rome Declaration* spoke of halving by 2015 the *number* of undernourished, the later *Millennium Declaration* speaks of halving by 2015 the *proportion* of people suffering from hunger and extreme poverty.

Substituting "proportion" for "number" makes a considerable difference. The relevant proportion is a fraction consisting of the number of poor people in the numerator and "the world's people" in the denominator. With world population expected to increase by 2015 to about 120 percent of what it was in 2000, a reduction in the number of poor to 60 percent of what it was in 2000 suffices to cut the proportion in half. The *Rome Declaration* promised a 50 percent reduction in the number of poor by 2015. The *Millennium Declaration* promises only a 40 percent reduction in this number.

In highlighting this revision, I attach no importance to whether governments focus on the number of poor people or their proportion. My concern is with the dilution of the 2015 goal and with the effort to obscure this dilution. The dilution can be expressed in either idiom: the number of poor is to be reduced by 50 percent according to *Rome Declaration* and by only 40 percent according to the *Millennium Declaration*. Or: the proportion of poor is to be reduced by 58.33 percent according to the *Rome Declaration* and by only 50 percent according to the *Millennium Declaration*. Either formulation makes apparent that the goalposts were moved.

The significance of the dilution can be gauged in terms of the World Bank's current poverty statistics. These figures show 1,656 million extremely poor people in 1996, and the *Rome Declaration* thus promised that this number will be no more than 828 million in 2015. The same figures show that there were 1,665 million extremely poor people in 2000—27.2 percent of world population then. And the Millennium Declaration thus promised that this number will be no more than 993 million in 2015—13.6 percent of the expected world population in 2015. The subtle shift in language quietly adds 165 million to the number of those whose extreme poverty in 2015 will be deemed morally acceptable—an extra 165 million human beings for whom "a minimum, nutritionally adequate diet plus essential nonfood requirements" will be out of reach. This dilution was successfully obscured from the public, and kept out of the media, by opaquely switching from "number" to "proportion" while retaining the language of "halving poverty by 2015."

Since its celebrated adoption by the UN General Assembly, the poverty promise has undergone further revision, in two respects. The current UN statement and tracking of MDG-1 express the poor not as a "proportion of the world's people," but as a "proportion of people in the developing world." This change is significant because the population of the developing world grows faster than that of the world at large. Because such faster population growth accelerates the rise in the denominator of the proportion, a smaller reduction in the numerator suffices to halve the proportion.

The other change is that the current UN statement of MDG-1 backdates the baseline to 1990, thus envisioning that the halving should take place "between 1990 and 2015" rather than between 2000 and 2015. This change is significant because, lengthening the period in which population growth occurs, it further inflates the denominator and thereby diminishes even more the needed reduction in the number of poor. The population of the developing countries in 2015 is expected to be 146 percent of what it was in 1990. Therefore a reduction of the number of poor to 73 percent of what it was in 1990 suffices to cut that proportion in half.

It is worth noting that the creative accounting is not confined to MDG-1. The most recent MDG report states quite generally that "the baseline for the assessment is 1990, but data for 2000 are also presented, whenever possible, to provide a more detailed picture of progress since the Declaration was signed." The year "1990" occurs 62 times in the *Report 2008* and not even once in the *UN Millennium Declaration.* As the UN is now phrasing MDG-4 and MDG-5, they require us to "reduce by two thirds, between 1990 and 2015, the underfive mortality rate" and to "reduce by three quarters, between 1990 and 2015, the maternal mortality ratio." What the UN General Assembly had actually agreed to promise is rather different: "By the same date [2015], to have reduced maternal mortality by three quarters, and under-five child mortality by two thirds, of their *current* rates.

One remarkable consequence of the UN's backdating of the MDG baselines is that China's massive poverty reduction in the 1990s—the number of Chinese living in extreme poverty reportedly declined by 264 million during that decade—can now be counted as progress toward achieving the MDGs. The revision of MDG-1 thus led UN Secretary-General Kofi Annan tragicomically to report to the General Assembly that for the world's most populous region—East Asia and the Pacific—the 2015 poverty target was met already in 1999, a full year before this goal had even been adopted.

How does the dual revision of MDG-1 affect the allowable number of extremely poor people in 2015? According to the current World Bank statistics, there were 1,813.4 million extremely poor people in 1990 (43.8 percent of the 1990 population of the developing countries). The new target for 2015 is therefore to reduce the number of extremely poor persons to 1,324 million (21.9 percent of the 2015 population of the developing countries). By revising MDG-1, the UN has thus raised the number of those whose extreme poverty in 2015 will be deemed morally acceptable by 331 million (from 993 to 1,324 million). Relative to the *Rome Declaration,* the target was raised by 496 million and the promised reduction in the number of extremely poor people correspondingly lowered by nearly three-fifths: from 828 to 332 million. How are Kofi Annan and the rest of us going to explain to those 496 million people that we changed our minds and that consequently they shall not have a minimum, nutritionally adequate diet plus essential non-food requirements?

Let me sum up my first reflection. MDG-1 is taken to supersede commitment the world's governments had made years earlier, notably in the 1996 *Rome Declaration*. There they promised to reduce, by 2015, the *number* of extremely poor people to half its *present* (1996) level. The current statement of MDG-1 retains the language of halving world poverty by 2015 but also deforms this goal through three highly deliberate dilutions. First, it aims to halve the *proportion* of extremely poor people, not their number, thus taking advantage of population growth. Second, it redefines this proportion, replacing "the world's people" by "the population of the developing world," thereby taking advantage of faster growth in the latter population (and also detracting from the global moral responsibility of the affluent countries. Third, it extends the plan period backward in time, having it start in 1990 rather than at the time the commitment was made, thereby increasing population growth in the denominator and taking advantage of a reported massive poverty reduction in China.

. . . Compared to the 1996 World Food Summit commitment, MDG-1 as now stated by the UN *raises* the number of extremely poor people deemed morally acceptable in 2015 by 496 million (from 828 to 1,324 million) and thereby *shrinks* by more than half (from 837 to 341 million) the reduction in this number which governments pledge to achieve during the 2000–15 period. Had we stuck to the promise of Rome, our task for 20015 would have been to reduce the extremely poor by 837 million or 50.3 percent. MDG-1 as revised envisages a reduction by only one fifth or only 341 million: from 1,665 million in the year 2000 to 1,324 million in 2015.

With the World Bank's 2005 figure already down to 1,376.7 million, there is little doubt that the UN will be able to announce in 2015 that the goal of halving world poverty has been achieved. But this success will depend decisively on having replaced the promise of the *Rome Declaration*—to halve between 1996 and 2015 the number of people in extreme poverty— with the promise of MDG-1 as subsequently diluted: to halve between 1990 and 2015 the proportion of people in the developing world who live in extreme poverty.

The story of the sly revisions of the grand commitment of Rome and, more generally, of how the world's governments are managing the "halving of world poverty by 2015" illustrates one main reason for the persistence of massive poverty: the poor have no friends among the global elite. Hundreds of officials in many governments and international agencies were involved in shifting the goalposts to the detriment of the poor. Thousands of economists, statisticians, and other academics understood what was happening. So did thousands of people in the media, who had been reporting on the Rome Summit and the MDGs—with some of them expressly denying that the revisions were worth reporting. Most of these privileged harbor no ill will toward poor people. They merely have other priorities. And they don't care how their pursuit of these other priorities is affecting the global poor.

3.2   Reflection two—on tracking poverty by counting the poor

My first reflection may have been a little discomforting. But are the clever revision really such a big deal? Should we not also appreciate that poverty is declining, albeit not at the once envisioned rate?

Before answering this question, let us think a little more about whether poverty really is declining, that is, whether the Bank's figures provide an accurate portrait of the evolution of extreme poverty.

The Bank's portrait centrally involves counting the poor. It there relies on a binary criterion that categorizes each person as either poor or non-poor according to the per capita cost of the consumption the household to which she or he belongs. This criterion is an international poverty line (IPL), which the Bank currently defines in terms of average daily consumption whose cost in local currency has the same purchasing power as $1.25 had in the US in 2005 (henceforth $1.25 PPP 2005). Persons whose average daily consumption (of goods and services) costs less than $1.25 PPP 2005 are poor; persons whose average daily consumption costs $1.25 PPP 2005 or more are non-poor.

This method of tracking world poverty is problematic insofar as it wholly disregards information about how far above or below the IPL particular persons are living. Intuitively, the world poverty problem is alleviated when people manage to raise their average daily consumption from $1.00 to $1.20 PPP 2005, say, or from $1.30 to $1.69 2005—and such gains constitute more significant progress, actually, than gains from $1.24 to $1.25 PPP 2005.

It may be said in response that this is just a technicality. In the real world (in contrast to worlds imagined by philosophers), counting the number of poor people relative to *any* reasonable poverty line is going to give us an adequate picture of the global poverty problem and its evolution over time.

This response can be rebutted in two ways. One rebuttal points out that the Bank's poverty index serves not merely as a passive instrument of observation, but also as a guide for the policies of governments, international agencies, and NGOs. Insofar as such agents care about their perceived performance in regard to poverty, they will take account of how their policies are likely to affect future poverty figures reported by the Bank. Doing so, they will focus their efforts on people living just below the poverty line because such efforts produce the most cost-effective reductions in the poverty count. Such incentives are obviously undesirable; and their effect may cause the Bank's poverty statistics to deliver an overly rosy picture of the evolution of world poverty.

The other rebuttal points out that the response fails empirically. Thanks to Chen and Ravallion, the key World Bank researchers in charge of the poverty count, we know exactly how sensitive the Bank's portrait of the evolution of poverty is to the level at which the IPL is set. Chen and Ravallion provide headcounts not only for their own chosen IPL of $1.25 PPP 2005 (average daily consumption), but also for three other poverty lines likewise denominated in 2005 international dollars . . .

. . . No matter what time period one may wish to examine, the change in the poverty count during this period looks better the lower the IPL is set. Choosing the UN's newly favored 1990 benchmark, for instance, the number of poor people has, in the 1990–2005 period, fallen *86 percent more than required* to be "on track" for meeting MDG-1 as diluted—when poverty is defined in terms of average daily consumption of $1.00 PPP 2005. On this definition, the world had already in 2005 exceeded the 2015 target of a 27 percent reduction from the 1990 baseline. Yet, if poverty is defined in terms of average daily consumption of $2.50 PPP 2005, then there has been *no reduction at all,* during 1990–2005, in the number of poor people; on the contrary, this number has actually increased very slightly. More generally, if one of the two lower poverty lines is chosen, we are well on schedule for realizing the 27 percent headcount reduction required for reaching the diluted MDG-1. If one of the two higher poverty lines is chosen, we are very far behind schedule for realizing that 27 percent reduction by 2015.

In the preceding reflection we saw that MDG-1 will probably be achieved, but that this achievement depends decisively on the promise of the *Rome Declaration*—to halve between 1996 and 2015 the number of extremely poor people—having been replaced at the UN with the promise of MDG-1 as diluted: to halve between 1990 and 2015 the proportion of people in the developing world who are living in extreme poverty. The present reflection shows that even the achievement of this greatly diluted goal depends decisively on fixing the IPL at a sufficiently low level. The steady stream of happy news the World Bank delivers from the poverty front—worked into the titles lest anyone miss the paint—is not robust with respect to the level at which the IPL is set. This discredits the method the Bank and the UN are using to track world poverty by counting the poor. It also raises with urgency the question how the Bank decides to fix the level of the IPL where it does.

3.3 Reflection three—on where the line is drawn

Haw then does the World Bank decide the level of its IPL? It is widely accepted that the IPL should express a narrow conception of absolute poverty that is closely tied to hunger. The UNDP, for instance, affirms that people should be counted as poor only if they fall short of "the income or expenditure level below which a minimum, nutritionally adequate diet plus essential non-food requirements are not affordable." It is only on this minimalist understanding that the world's governments have agreed that poverty is to be eradicated.

How does the Bank convert this shared minimalist understanding of poverty into a specific level for its IPL? We have a rich historical record for answering this question, because the Bank has in fact successively employed and defended four distinct IPLs denominated in international dollars of three different base years: 1985, 1993, and 2005. The Bank has done so while contending that it is desirable to change the poverty line from time to time to keep it up to date. It is indeed true that an IPL denominated in international dollars of a recent base year leads to a more accurate picture of poverty around that year—but it is also true that such an updated poverty line gives us a less accurate picture of poverty in earlier years. So periodic switching of IPLs is not needed for the sake of attaining a more accurate picture of the long-term poverty trend.

The Bank has defended all four of its successive IPLs as "anchored to what 'poverty' means in the poorest countries." How do they know what "poverty" means in the poorest countries? The Bank infers its answer from one single piece of information: from the official domestic poverty lines used in poor countries. Thus, its latest IPL of $1.25 PPP 2005 is calculated as the mean of the official poverty lines—converted at 2005 PPPs into 2005 international dollars—used in the world's 15 poorest countries: Malawi, Mali, Ethiopia, Sierra Leone, Niger, Uganda; Gambia, Rwanda, Guinea-Bissau, Tanzania, Tajikistan, Mozambique, Chad, Nepal, and Ghana. It is unclear why political decisions made by rulers or bureaucrats in these 15 countries—9 of which have very small populations and 13 of which are located in sub-Saharan Africa—should be thought a reliable indicator of what "poverty" means to poor people all over the world. Nor can the Bank's involvement in setting domestic poverty lines for many poor countries increase confidence in the exercise: mere consistency of the Bank's judgments is no substitute for their justification.

To make matters worse, the most recent anchoring exercise—using the mean of the domestic poverty lines of the world's 15 poorest countries—is at variance with previous anchoring exercises. In 2000, the Bank introduced a revised IPL of $1.08 PPP 1993 while defending this level as the median of the 10 lowest official poverty lines—converted at 1993 PPPs into 1993 international dollars. And in 1990 the Bank had unveiled its first IPL of $1.02 PPP 1985 while defending this level with the argument that eight poor countries had official poverty lines that, converted at 1985 PPPs into 1985 international dollars, were close to this amount. This first IPL was then, by the way, quickly "rounded off" to the more memorable $1.00 PPP 1985 figure which, also enshrined in the text of the *Millennium*

Declaration, survives in the still frequent colloquial associations of extreme poverty with living below a dollar a day.

The Bank's successive substitutions have resulted in a tightening of the poverty criterion in most countries and a broadening in a few . . . A US household would count as poor by the Bank's new standard only if the cost of its entire 2009 consumption of goods and services had been below $506 per person.

Perhaps it is obvious that the Bank's latest IPL is absurdly low. But we should confirm this judgment. The US Department of Agriculture has for many decades published data about what it costs to adhere to an elaborately designed low-cost food plan that has variously been called the "Restricted Food Plan for Emergency Use," the "Economy Food Plan . . . developed as a nutritionally adequate diet for short-term or emergency use," and the "Thrifty Food Plan." In 2005, the cost of purchasing this minimal diet for a household of two to four people was (depending on household size and children's ages) between $3.59 and $4.97 per person per day. If this was the cost of a minimal or emergency diet in the US, then we can safely conclude that the Bank's IPL of $1.25 PPP 2005 is absurdly low in its base country and base year: in the US in 2005—especially if we remember that the $1.25 per day would need to cover not merely nutrition, but also minimal requirements of clothing, shelter, medical care, water and other utilities.

What can be said to justify the Bank's chosen IPL level? It is obvious that the Bank cannot justify its decision by saying that the IPL must be set at such a low level in order to show the world to be on track toward achieving MDG-1. A lower IPL entails lower poverty headcounts and also, as we have seen, much prettier trend figures than would be derived from higher IPLs. But this cannot be a *justification* for choosing a low IPL.

One also cannot defend the Bank's chosen IPL level by pointing out that the blatant insufficiency of $1.25 per day in the US in 2005 proves nothing, because, in the locations where in 2005 very poor people actually lived, dollars bought much more than they did in the United States. This attempted defense involves a common misunderstanding of the Bank's procedure. Dollars converted at going currency exchange rates in 2005 did indeed buy more in poor countries than in the US. But the Bank is using for its conversions not exchange rates but PPPs, which supposedly preserve purchasing power. Thus the Bank counts someone who, in 2005 in India or Vietnam, was living on the exchange rate equivalent of $0.40 or $0.45 per day as non-poor because this amount, converted at 2005 PPPs, equals or exceeds $1.25.

This raises the question whether the general household consumption PPPs employed by the Bank are an adequate guide to what poor people must actually pay for necessities. Can we conclude from the fact that $1.25 per day was not enough to meet the basic needs of a human being in the US in 2005 that the PPP equivalent of $1.25 per day in any other currency was similarly insufficient? As the following chapter shows, PPP conversions indeed fail to preserve command over basic necessities. But this does not help the Bank's case. For one thing, the prices of foodstuffs are, in every poor country, *higher* than PPPs suggest, and this by a whopping 50 percent on average . . . Moreover, the Bank cannot defend the level of its IPL by disqualifying as inadequate the PPPs it is using because, by doing so, it would fatally undermine the very methodology it employs, which assumes that PPPs provide suitable conversion rates for comparing incomes and consumption expenditures of poor people worldwide and for fixing the level of the IPL.

Let me restate this point a little more elaborately. I have shown in this third reflection that consumption expenditure of $1.25 per person per day was much too low to access even the most basic subsistence minimum in the US in 2005. It follows that the use of 2005 PPPs to convert this amount into another currency cannot be relied upon to yield an amount sufficient to purchase in 2005 the most basic subsistence minimum in the territory of that other currency. This follows from considering two jointly exhaustive possibilities. Suppose PPPs reliably preserve purchasing power with respect to basic necessities. Then any 2005 foreign currency equivalent of $1.25 per person per day was as inadequate abroad as $1.25 per person per day was in the US. Alternatively, suppose PPPs do not reliably preserve purchasing power with respect to basic necessities. Then a person's position relative to the IPL—calculated through PPP conversion into 2005 international dollars—does not tell us whether this person has access to a minimally adequate set of basic necessities.

3.4 Reflection four—on relating the IPL to the global product

There is one more possible justification for the very low IPL chosen by the Bank and employed by the UN for tracking MDG-1. This justification invokes the IPL's normative significance. We are monitoring the evolution of extreme poverty not merely out of curiosity, but also with the aim of its reduction and eventual eradication. Given this aim, one might say, we ought to define the IPL in such a way that the magnitude of the world poverty problem implied by this definition is reasonably related to the world's resources: we should not define poverty so broadly that its eradication becomes wholly impractical. Doing so might even be counterproductive by discouraging efforts to reduce poverty to the extent that we can.

. . . Using the PIL favored by the Bank and the UN, we find that the aggregate shortfall of the 1,377 million people living below this IPL amounts to merely 0.17 percent of the global product—or about $76 billion per annum or one-ninth of US military spending. It is *this* poverty problem that the world's privileged see themselves as reducing at the stately pace of 1.25 percent per annum, with the affluent states contributing some $12 billion annually in official development assistance for basic social services . . .

Were we to double the Bank's IPL, both the number of poor and their average shortfall from the poverty line would greatly increase. A seven times larger 1.13 percent change in the distribution of the global product would then be required to eradicate poverty so defined. Yet, even this shift would hardly be discouragingly large—not when one considers that poverty causes some 18 million premature deaths annually, thus killing at more than twice the rate of World War II during its worst period. Winning that war cost the lives of some 15 million Allied soldiers as well as half or more of the gross domestic products of the US, the UK, and the USSR during the war years. Ending world poverty would not require sending any young people into battle. And it would not—even on a broader definition of $2.50 PPP 2005 per day—seriously affect the economies of the affluent countries. It would lower the growth path of these countries a bit so that they would reach any future standard of living a little later than would otherwise be the case—perhaps half a year, or a year later on the $2.50 PPP 2005 per day definition of poverty. It is for the sake of comparatively trivial gains, then, that we let poverty destroy billions of human lives.

3.5 Concluding thoughts

In 2015, the world's privileged will likely be able to celebrate the achievement of MDG-1: of the goal to halve world poverty by 2015. But this achievement will owe much more to the clever shifting of goalposts than to reductions in poverty. It crucially depends on two revisions that effected a triple dilution of the goal. These revisions have raised the number of those whose extreme poverty in 2015 will be deemed morally acceptable from 828 million to 1,324 million—and they have shrunk the reduction in the number of poor that is to occur during 1996–2015 from 50 percent to 20 percent. The foreseeable achievement of MDG-1 also crucially depends on choosing an absurdly low IPL. Were we to track poverty by reference to a broader poverty criterion, more commensurate to basic human needs and human rights, then we would find that world poverty has been either rising or else decreasing much more slowly than would be required for achieving MDG-1.

Recall the genocide in Rwanda, when the UN and nearly all the rest of the world stood idly by while some 800,000 people were hacked to death . . . Suppose some Western politician had said, in April 1994, that the slaughter in Rwanda is morally unacceptable and that the world's governments ought to commit themselves to reducing the slaughter by 1.25 percent per annum. Or imagine Franklin Roosevelt in 1942 preparing a speech about the German atrocities in Europe: a speech promising that the

US would lead a collective effort to achieve a 20 percent reduction of these atrocities by 1957. Add to this hypothetical scenario a shrewd White House advisor urging Roosevelt to express his promise more appealingly in terms of a larger percentage reduction in the *proportion* of the world's population, or of the world's non-Aryan population, being victimized by the Nazis. And imagine Roosevelt making this reformulated promise to widespread celebration and self-congratulations in the media and among the general public.

This imagined response to the Nazi menace may seem horrifying. But this just *is* our actual response to world poverty. Or are there morally relevant differences that render our actual response to world poverty less bad than the imagined US response to fascist atrocities? There are such differences—but they actually weigh in the opposite direction: making our response to world poverty morally worse than the imagined US response to the fascist atrocities.

I have already stated two such differences: world poverty produces substantially more harm than the fascists ever did (more each year, and this over much longer periods than the fascists could have sustained), and the cost of ending world poverty is tiny in comparison to the cost of ending fascist rule. These two points combine to show a large discrepancy in the moral cost-benefit ratios associated with the two scenarios. In the 1942 scenario, the great moral urgency of fighting the axis powers is balanced by the huge losses in blood and treasure that such a fight would predictably involve. Yet, there are no morally significant costs that come anywhere near balancing the great moral urgency of ending world poverty. Instead, there is a morally grotesque incongruity between the human and the economic magnitude of world poverty. The problem is so large that it causes one third of all human deaths and blights well over half of all human lives with hunger, disease, oppression, exclusion, and abuse. Yet, global inequality has increased to such an extent that such poverty is now avoidable at a cost that would barely be felt in the affluent countries.

There is yet a third morally significant reason why our actual response to world poverty is worse than the imaginary Roosevelt response to fascism. The US was not a substantial contributor to the harms the fascist states were inflicting in Europe. By letting these harms continue, the US would have failed to live up to its positive duties to protect and to aid people in mortal distress. The governments; and citizens of today's affluent countries like to conceive of their relation to world poverty analogously: most of us believe that we bear no significant responsibility for the persistence of this problem and that our only moral reason to help alleviate it is our positive duty to assist innocent persons caught in a life-threatening emergency . . . . [T]his belief is highly questionable. The governments of the world's more powerful countries negotiate the design of the global institutional architecture with an eye to their own advantage and convenience, and they collaborate with one another and with the elites of the less powerful countries to impose this order on the world. They know that this regime maintains severe poverty on a massive scale and that such poverty is avoidable. But they are willing to bear the small opportunity costs that a poverty-avoiding global institutional architecture would impose upon them.

Avoiding most of the severe poverty existing in the world today is not expensive. But making progress through gimmickry is much cheaper still. It is not especially difficult to see through these statistical gimmicks and, more generally, to appreciate the ways in which the picture of world poverty widely held in the affluent countries is false. But the prevailing picture is more attractive than the truth, and so it is reaffirmed by the media and uncritically absorbed by the public. Beholding the Millennium Development Goals, we are moved by the loftiness of our goals and the selfless nobility of our effort—and happily continue to take from Africans their natural resources while paying their oppressors, and happily continue to consume the rapidly diminishing fish stocks in African waters. We celebrate ourselves for the thousands of lives we figure we are saving here and there through one or another generous initiative, without noticing that most of these lives need saving only because of the gravely unjust global institutional order our countries design and impose.

Perhaps the most fundamental obstacle to the eradication of poverty is such stunning thoughtlessness of the affluent in the face of a problem that destroys vastly more lives than many problems we do pay at least pay some attention to—such as the conflicts in the Middle East, the massacres in Rwanda and East Timor, or the 2004 tsunami. Our inattention to world poverty is all the more remarkable because we may bear a far greater responsibility for it than for those local eruptions of violence and also because we can actually do a great deal, even as individuals, toward reducing world poverty, while most of us can do very little toward protecting innocent people from violence in the world's trouble spots.

In a sense, such thoughtlessness in the affluent countries is not really surprising. Of course people do not like to think too hard about harms that they themselves may share responsibility for and can do something about. Many Germans in my parents' generation avoided moral reflection under the Nazis. But were they innocent merely because they did not think? Or wasn't their very lack of thought a great moral failing? The latter judgment is now widely held. Germans who could truthfully say that they had never thought about the fate of those whom state agents were taking from their neighborhoods and about the foreigners crushed by the Nazi war machine were not therefore innocent. Rather, they were guilty of violating their most fundamental moral responsibility: to work out for oneself what one's moral responsibilities are in the circumstances in which one finds oneself. In this respect, we are in the same boat with those Germans. They could not possibly have judged it obvious that Nazi conquests and mass arrests required no further thought from them. And we cannot possibly judge it obvious that we need give no further thought to world poverty. Apart from our involvement in the perpetuation of world poverty, we commit a separate crime of thoughtlessness. The global poor pose a morally inescapable question: what responsibilities do we have in regard to the social conditions that blight their lives? We owe them a reflective answer.

18D. *Why Foreign Aid Is Hurting Africa*

Moyo, a former economist at Goldman Sachs, condemns the cycle of aid that, in her view, keeps much of Africa impoverished. Is aid really, as Moyo says, an "unmitigated political, economic and humanitarian disaster"? Most would agree that aid may well be stolen by corrupt officials. Isn't the solution to make aid targeted and non-fungible to prevent this from happening? How would you do that? Moyo, who favors market solutions to break out of the cycle, proposes that African countries access the bond markets, the markets in the Middle East and China in particular. Is this realistic? What is the prerequisite? Are we dealing with a "chicken or the egg" problem? Is Moyo suggesting a sort of conspiracy theory to keep African countries indebted and poor? Is she justified?

D. Moyo, "Why Foreign Aid Is Hurting Africa,"
The Wall Street Journal (2009)

A month ago I visited Kibera, the largest slum in Africa. This suburb of Nairobi, the capital of Kenya, is home to more than one million people, who eke out a living in an area of about one square mile—roughly 75% the size of New York's Central Park. It is a sea of aluminum and cardboard shacks that forgotten families call home. The idea of a slum conjures up an image of children playing amidst piles of garbage, with no running water and the rank, rife stench of sewage. Kibera does not disappoint.

What is incredibly disappointing is the fact that just a few yards from Kibera stands the headquarters of the United Nations' agency for human settlements which, with an annual budget of millions of dollars, is mandated to "promote socially and environmentally sustainable towns and cities with the goal of providing adequate shelter for all." Kibera festers in Kenya, a country that has one of the highest ratios of development workers per capita. This is also the country where in 2004, British envoy Sir Edward Clay apologized for underestimating the scale of government corruption and failing to speak out earlier.

Giving alms to Africa remains one of the biggest ideas of our time—millions march for it, governments are judged by it, celebrities proselytize the need for it. Calls for more aid to Africa are growing louder, with advocates pushing for doubling the roughly $50 billion of international assistance that already goes to Africa each year.

Yet evidence overwhelmingly demonstrates that aid to Africa has made the poor poorer, and the growth slower. The insidious aid culture has left African countries more debt-laden, more inflation-prone, more vulnerable to the vagaries of the currency markets and more unattractive to higher-quality investment. It's increased the risk of civil conflict and unrest (the fact that over 60% of sub-Saharan Africa's population is under the age of 24 with few economic prospects is a cause for worry). Aid is an unmitigated political, economic and humanitarian disaster.

Few will deny that there is a clear moral imperative for humanitarian and charity-based aid to step in when necessary, such as during the 2004 tsunami in Asia. Nevertheless, it's worth reminding ourselves what emergency and charity-based aid can and cannot do. Aid-supported scholarships have certainly helped send African girls to school (never mind that they won't be able to find a job in their own countries once they have graduated). This kind of aid can provide band-aid solutions to alleviate immediate suffering, but by its very nature cannot be the platform for long-term sustainable growth.

Whatever its strengths and weaknesses, such charity-based aid is relatively small beer when compared to the sea of money that floods Africa each year in government-to-government aid or aid from large development institutions such as the World Bank.

Over the past 60 years at least $1 trillion of development-related aid has been transferred from rich countries to Africa. Yet real per-capita income today is lower than it was in the 1970s, and more than 50% of the population—over 350 million people—live on less than a dollar a day, a figure that has nearly doubled in two decades.

Even after the very aggressive debt-relief campaigns in the 1990s, African countries still pay close to $20 billion in debt repayments per annum, a stark reminder that aid is not free. In order to keep the system going, debt is repaid at the expense of African education and health care. Well-meaning calls to cancel debt mean little when the cancellation is met with the fresh infusion of aid, and the vicious cycle starts up once again.

In 2005, just weeks ahead of a G8 conference that had Africa at the top of its agenda, the International Monetary Fund published a report entitled "Aid Will Not Lift Growth in Africa." The report cautioned that governments, donors and campaigners should be more modest in their claims that increased aid will solve Africa's problems. Despite such comments, no serious efforts have been made to wean Africa off this debilitating drug.

The most obvious criticism of aid is its links to rampant corruption. Aid flows destined to help the average African end up supporting bloated bureaucracies in the form of the poor-country governments and donor-funded non-governmental organizations. In a hearing before the U.S.

Senate Committee on Foreign Relations in May 2004, Jeffrey Winters, a professor at Northwestern University, argued that the World Bank had participated in the corruption of roughly $100 billion of its loan funds intended for development.

As recently as 2002, the African Union, an organization of African nations, estimated that corruption was costing the continent $150 billion a year, as international donors were apparently turning a blind eye to the simple fact that aid money was inadvertently fueling graft. With few or no strings attached, it has been all too easy for the funds to be used for anything, save the developmental purpose for which they were intended.

In Zaire—known today as the Democratic Republic of Cong—Irwin Blumenthal (whom the IMF had appointed to a post in the country's central bank) warned in 1978 that the system was so corrupt that there was "no (repeat, no) prospect for Zaire's creditors to get their money back." Still, the IMF soon gave the country the largest loan it had ever given an African nation. According to corruption watchdog agency Transparency International, Mobutu Sese Seko, Zaire's president from 1965 to 1997, is reputed to have stolen at least $5 billion from the country.

It's scarcely better today. A month ago, Malawi's former President Bakili Muluzi was charged with embezzling aid money worth $12 million. Zambia's former President Frederick Chiluba (a development darling during his 1991 to 2001 tenure) remains embroiled in a court case that has revealed millions of dollars frittered away from health, education and infrastructure toward his personal cash dispenser. Yet the aid keeps on coming.

A nascent economy needs a transparent and accountable government and an efficient civil service to help meet social needs. Its people need jobs and a belief in their country's future. A surfeit of aid has been shown to be unable to help achieve these goals.

A constant stream of "free" money is a perfect way to keep an inefficient or simply bad government in power. As aid flows in, there is nothing more for the government to do—it doesn't need to raise taxes, and as long as it pays the army, it doesn't have to take account of its disgruntled citizens. No matter that its citizens are disenfranchised (as with no taxation there can be no representation). All the government really needs to do is to court and cater to its foreign donors to stay in power.

Stuck in an aid world of no incentives, there is no reason for governments to seek other, better, more transparent ways of raising development finance (such as accessing the bond market, despite how hard that might be). The aid system encourages poor-country governments to pick up the phone and ask the donor agencies for next capital infusion. It is no wonder that across Africa, over 70% of the public purse comes from foreign aid.

In Ethiopia, where aid constitutes more than 90% of the government budget, a mere 2% of the country's population has access to mobile phones. (The African country average is around 30%.) Might it not be preferable for the government to earn money by selling its mobile phone license, thereby generating much-needed development income and also providing its citizens with telephone service that could, in turn, spur economic activity?

Look what has happened in Ghana, a country where after decades of military rule brought about by a coup, a pro-market government has yielded encouraging developments. Farmers and fishermen now use mobile phones to communicate with their agents and customers across the country to find out where prices are most competitive. This translates into numerous opportunities for self-sustainability and income generation—which, with encouragement, could be easily replicated across the continent.

To advance a country's economic prospects, governments need efficient civil service. But civil service is naturally prone to bureaucracy, and there is always the incipient danger of self-serving cronyism and the desire to bind citizens in endless, time-consuming red tape. What aid does is to make that danger a grim reality. This helps to explain why doing business across much of Africa is a nightmare. In Cameroon, it takes a potential investor around 426 days to perform 15 procedures to gain a business license. What entrepreneur wants to spend 119 days filling out forms to start a business in Angola? He's much more likely to consider the U.S. (40 days and 19 procedures) or South Korea (17 days and 10 procedures).

Even what may appear as a benign intervention on the surface can have damning consequences. Say there is a mosquito-net maker in small-town Africa. Say he employs 10 people who together manufacture 500 nets a week. Typically, these 10 employees support upward of 15 relatives each. A Western government-inspired program generously supplies the affected region with 100,000 free mosquito nets. This promptly puts the mosquito net manufacturer out of business, and now his 10 employees can no longer support their 150 dependents. In a couple of years, most of the donated nets will be torn and useless, but now there is no mosquito net maker to go to. They'll have to get more aid. And African governments once again get to abdicate their responsibilities.

In a similar vein has been the approach to food aid, which historically has done little to support African farmers. Under the auspices of the U.S. Food for Peace program, each year millions of dollars are used to buy American-grown food that has to then be shipped across oceans. One wonders how a system of flooding foreign markets with American food, which puts local farmers out of business, actually helps better Africa. A better strategy would be to use aid money to buy food from farmers within the country, and then distribute that food to the local citizens in need.

Then there is the issue of "Dutch disease," a term that describes how large inflows of money can kill off a country's export sector, by driving up home prices and thus making their goods too expensive for export. Aid has the same effect. Large dollar-denominated aid windfalls that envelop fragile developing economies cause the domestic currency to strengthen against foreign currencies. This is catastrophic for jobs in the poor country where people's livelihoods depend on being relatively competitive in the global market.

To fight aid-induced inflation, countries have to issue bonds to soak up the subsequent glut of money swamping the economy. In 2005, for example, Uganda was forced to issue such bonds to mop up excess liquidity to the tune of $700 million. The interest payments alone on this were a staggering $110 million, to be paid annually.

The stigma associated with countries relying on aid should also not be underestimated or ignored. It is the rare investor that wants to risk money in a country that is unable to stand on its own feet and manage its own affairs in a sustainable way.

Africa remains the most unstable continent in the world, beset by civil strife and war. Since 1996, 11 countries have been embroiled in civil wars. According to the Stockholm International Peace Research Institute, in the 1990s, Africa had more wars than the rest of the world combined. Although my country, Zambia, has not had the unfortunate experience of an outright civil war, growing up I experienced first-hand the discomfort of living under curfew (where everyone had to be in their homes between 6 p.m. and 6 a.m., which meant racing from work and school) and faced the fear of the uncertain outcomes of an attempted coup in 1991—sadly, experiences not uncommon to many Africans.

Civil clashes are often motivated by the knowledge that by seizing the seat of power, the victor gains virtually unfettered access to the package of aid that comes with it. In the last few months alone, there have been at least three political upheavals across the continent, in Mauritania, Guinea and Guinea Bissau (each of which remains reliant on foreign aid). Madagascar's government was just overthrown in a coup this past week. The ongoing political volatility across the continent serves as a reminder that aid-financed efforts to force-feed democracy to economies facing ever-growing poverty and difficult economic prospects remain, at best, precariously vulnerable. Long-term political success can only be achieved once a solid economic trajectory has been established.

Proponents of aid are quick to argue that the $13 billion ($100 billion in today's terms) aid of the post-World War II Marshall Plan helped pull back a broken Europe from the brink of an economic abyss, and that aid could work, and would work, if Africa had a good policy environment.

The aid advocates skirt over the point that the Marshall Plan interventions were short, sharp and finite, unlike the open-ended commitments which imbue governments with a sense of entitlement rather than encouraging innovation. And aid supporters spend little time addressing the mystery of why a country in good working order would seek aid rather than other, better forms of financing. No country has ever achieved economic success by depending on aid to the degree that many African countries do.

The good news is we know what works; what delivers growth and reduces poverty. We know that economies that rely on open-ended commitments of aid almost universally fail, and those that do not depend on aid succeed. The latter is true for economically successful countries such as China and India, and even closer to home, in South Africa and Botswana. Their strategy of development finance emphasizes the important role of entrepreneurship and markets over a staid aid-system of development that preaches hand-outs.

African countries could start by issuing bonds to raise cash. To be sure, the traditional capital markets of the U.S. and Europe remain challenging. However, African countries could explore opportunities to raise capital in more non-traditional markets such as the Middle East and China (whose foreign exchange reserves are more than $4 trillion). Moreover, the current market malaise provides an opening for African countries to focus on acquiring credit ratings (a prerequisite to accessing the bond markets), and preparing themselves for the time when the capital markets return to some semblance of normalcy.

Governments need to attract more foreign direct investment by creating attractive tax structures and reducing the red tape and complex regulations for businesses. African nations should also focus on increasing trade; China is one promising partner. And Western countries can help by cutting off the cycle of giving something for nothing. It's time for a change.

Dambisa Moyo, a former economist at Goldman Sachs, is the author of "Dead Aid: Why Aid Is Not Working and How There Is a Better Way for Africa."

Corrections & Amplifications

In the African nations of Burkina Faso, Rwanda, Somalia, Mali, Chad, Mauritania and Sierra Leone from 1970 to 2002, over 70% of total government spending came from foreign aid, according to figures from the World Bank. This essay on foreign aid to Africa incorrectly said that 70% of government spending throughout Africa comes from foreign aid.

18E. *Getting Debt Relief Right*

Is Thomas describing a circus? Perhaps a farce? What's the script? Why don't you have a crack at it? How does his thesis relate to part of Chapter 6? Do you find his argument persuasive? What does he think of rock stars?

M. A. Thomas, "Getting Debt Relief Right," *The Council on Foreign Relations* (2001), Reprinted by permission of FOREIGN AFFAIRS, (October 2001). Copyright (2001) by the Council on Foreign Relations, Inc. www.ForeignAffairs.com

BLESSED ARE THE POOR?

Today 41 of the world's poorest countries are bankrupt. These nations, identified by the World Bank as "heavily indebted poor countries" (HIPCS), owe some $170 billion to foreign creditors, while half of their 600 million citizens get by on less than $1 a day. Nine out of ten HIPCS cannot sustain their debts, given their low export earnings and GNPs. Unless some of this debt is forgiven, they will be paying in perpetuity. Their creditors, on the other hand, include the wealthiest countries in the world, as well as the international financial institutions that are meant to support economic development.

In the spirit of the Jubilee (a semicentennial forgiveness of debts described in the Old Testament), a diverse and powerful coalition of political and religious leaders, Nobel Peace Prize winners, economists, rock stars, and rioting activists has rallied for a complete debt write-off. Arguing that high interest payments "crowd out" government spending on the poor, these advocates claim that forgiving national debts will help relieve the world's worst poverty. Using powerful emotional rhetoric, they offer heart-wrenching descriptions of the millions of people lacking security, adequate food, clean water, and basic health care and education. But as moving as this testimony may be, the reality is that the windfall of the current HIPC Initiative—a $28 billion debt-relief package administered by the International Monetary Fund (IMF) and the World Bank—does not go to the poor. Instead, it goes to the same governments that racked up the debt in the first place, many of which are weak, corrupt, and authoritarian—hardly the best intermediaries to carry out a philanthropic agenda.

IN THE RED

During the late 1970s, many HIPCS experienced a surge in the prices of their primary export commodities, such as oil, cocoa, tin, and coffee. Based on exceptionally strong export earnings, these countries borrowed from private banks and official export credit associations and then dramatically expanded government spending. But commodity prices quickly tumbled in the 1980s, and as a result, many HIPCs suffered dramatic downturns in their terms of trade (the prices of exports relative to imports). Ethiopia, for example, suffered a 90 percent degradation in its terms of trade between

1980 and 1993, while Cote d'Ivoire's terms of trade fell by nearly half. Meanwhile, a serious drought persisted in the Sahel, and high population growth continued across the board.

Under such circumstances, many HIPCS had trouble paying their creditors, both foreign and domestic. Borrowers and lenders alike initially saw this setback as temporary; HIPCS continued to borrow to make up the shortfall and stimulate economic growth based on optimistic predictions of recovering export prices. But even when it became clear that prices would not return to their previous highs, some countries were reluctant to cut government spending. They continued to borrow from other governments and multilateral institutions such as the IMF, the World Bank, and the African Development Bank. During the 1980s, long-term HIPC debt more than tripled before peaking in 1995. In 1997, 42 percent of this debt was owed to other governments, 22 percent to the World Bank and the IMF, and 10 percent to other multilateral institutions.

Still, the debt crisis might have been avoided if not for the bad economic policies and poor governance of many HIPCS. Many of them maintained money-losing public enterprises, created government posts to provide employment, imposed artificially high exchange rates and formidable trade barriers, and unduly concentrated on the production of just a few commodities. Many HIPC governments, moreover, have been riddled with corruption. In Transparency International's 2000 survey, which ranks countries according to perceived corruption, 9 out of the 15 HIPCS included were ranked in the bottom quartile.

Although total losses due to high-level corruption are impossible to estimate, individual cases indicate losses in the millions and billions of dollars. Foreign creditors continued to lend to Zaire, for example, even while President Mobutu Sese Seko amassed a personal fortune estimated to be as much as $5 billion; to Cote d'Ivoire, even after President Felix Houphouet-Boigny built a basilica that cost an estimated $300 million of his "own money"; and to Kenya, even as government officials siphoned up to $1.1 billion from the national treasury and central bank.

Studies of petty corruption also present troubling results. A 1996 budget-tracking exercise in Uganda showed that in 1991, only 2 percent of nonwage public spending on education actually arrived at the schools; in 1995, only 20 percent did. Although the country has since addressed this problem, a contemporaneous study found that Ugandan health-care workers were stealing and selling 78 percent of drug supplies for their personal profit, dramatically reducing public health care for the poor.

What percentage of foreign aid is lost to such corruption? That is the wrong question to ask. Because money is fungible, aid dollars that are actually spent on social services can free up government money for other purposes. That is why so many people looked askance last year when Uganda concluded the purchase of a presidential jet within days of receiving HIPC debt relief. The only way to determine whether earmarked funds add to or substitute for government spending is to track all poverty-related spending and social-service provision. But according to a recent report by the IMF and the International Development Association (IDA), none of the HIPCS currently receiving debt relief are capable of doing so. These countries lack the practices and procedures necessary for budgeting, monitoring, and reporting on the use of public resources. More fundamentally, they lack basic institutions of accountability.

BREAKING ALL THE RULES

Good budget execution starts with a good budget. But many HIPCS are unable to formulate good budgets because they lack access to reliable information. In Uganda, for example, official figures indicate that primary school enrollment remained stagnant from 1991to 1995, even though it actually increased by 60 percent. Many HIPCS do not account for foreign aid that is controlled and spent by donors because the donors fail to provide them with the necessary information. And many HIPCS deliberately keep certain revenues off-budget.

This weakness in budgeting contributes to what the IMF/IDA report calls the "significant differences between planned and actual expenditures" in more than a third of the countries now receiving debt relief. What is budgeted is often not disbursed, and what is disbursed often does not arrive. Salaries go unpaid for months, operating funds do not materialize, and government debts remain unsettled. At the same time, the executive branch makes unbudgeted expenditures throughout the year. These loose practices make public spending data extremely spotty—and the data that does exist is often inaccurate or even falsified.

When making government purchases, moreover, HIPCS routinely violate the rules of public contracting. Officials award contracts to favored companies, despite laws requiring competitive bidding; manipulate bid criteria; violate the confidentiality of bid documents, which are not standardized; and privately negotiate the terms of contracts after the contracts are already awarded. As a result, these governments persistently purchase unnecessary, inappropriate, overpriced, or low-quality goods and services. Many HIPCS do not archive contract documents, making subsequent audits impossible. And complicated spending procedures prompt even well-intentioned officials to evade the rules.

HIPCS also fail to follow standard procedures of human-resource management. Recruitment is not transparent and does not correspond to actual staffing needs. Minimum qualifications for positions often do not exist, and where they do, they are not respected. Orders jump the official hierarchy, so that supervisors do not know what their subordinates are doing or to whom they are reporting. Bosses do not evaluate the performance of their employees, or they do so based on punctuality and dress rather than the quality and quantity of work. Promotions are given without regard to objective criteria, even where laws establish them. Records of work performance and of disciplinary sanctions are either incomplete or missing. Governments perpetually struggle with the problem of "ghost workers"—people collecting salaries without actually working for the government—and some HIPCS do not even know how many civil servants they have.

OUT OF CONTROL

In many HIPCS, procedures and laws are violated in part because systems of monitoring and sanction are either weak or nonexistent. In many government agencies, supervisors do not visit, and inspections are not performed. And without reliable means of communication and transportation, remote local administrative units become isolated, independent fiefdoms. Audit offices are typically understaffed, undertrained, and underfunded. According to the IMF/IDA report, only a third of the HIPCS currently receiving debt relief have active audit systems—and even these are ineffective. Many governments do not close their books at the end of the fiscal year, and some government units— particularly local ones—keep no books at all.

When government officials violate the law, justice systems often cannot hold them accountable. Police forces are untrained and unequipped, subject to political interference, and no match for sophisticated white-collar criminals. Judiciaries are weak, underfunded, and corrupt. Case files are heaped in dirty corners or kept in rooms open to the public, making them easy to lose or manipulate. Judges lack access to law books and even paper on which to write opinions. The application of laws varies from city to city, based on the availability of texts. The executive branch firmly controls judicial appointments and promotions and constantly interferes in the judicial process. Administrative law—the basis on which orders from the executive branch are challenged—is underdeveloped, and most citizens do not know that the government is subject to the law, even if just in theory.

To make matters worse, legislatures cannot hold the rest of the government accountable. According to the IMF/IDA report, audited accounts are forwarded to legislatures within 12 months of the end of the fiscal year in fewer than one-fifth of the HIPCS now receiving debt relief. And even when legislators do see the accounts, they usually do nothing about them. With few exceptions, legislatures are firmly controlled by the president's party. Even those that strive to act independently are hampered by weak capacity. Many legislators are unable to read budgets, understand government documents, or draft legislation. Some cannot even communicate in the government's official language. And many legislatures have only a few technical staff.

Finally, the ultimate guarantor of accountability—the electoral process—is either weak or nonexistent in many HIPCS. Of the 41 HIPCS, 11 do not hold multiparty democratic elections. Of the other 30, fewer than 10 have been able to vote governments out of office. As a consequence, most HIPC government officials do not fear losing an election if they fail to respond to the people's needs. This lack of accountability plays out in the theft and waste of public resources, in routine torture and extrajudicial killings, and in the prevalence of government impunity.

WATER IN A SIEVE

The lack of procedures and institutions to ensure accountability is not simply a technical problem to be fixed with more money and more training. Rather, the root of the problem lies with the nature of governance itself. In many HIPCS, illegality permeates the highest levels of government, implicating presidents, ministers, legislators, and supreme court justices. These officials fill posts with cronies and pressure them to grant personal favors and remit money (often collected through bribes and embezzlement). This top-down pressure for illegal activity trickles down to all levels of government, creating hierarchies of wrongdoing.

At the same time, government officials protect themselves by deliberately destroying the fabric of accountability. It is misleading to say simply that systems of accountability are weak or nonexistent: rather, someone is actively weakening or neglecting them. People charged with maintaining records falsify or destroy them; people responsible for nominating judges choose those who are obedient rather than those who are independent and honest; people allocating resources underfund judiciaries and audit offices. In the absence of control, all types of abuses become possible, from petty corruption to human rights violations. When most of the government is corrupt, the government is unable to sanction its own members or reform itself.

Such corruption is fueled by the public's demand for private goods rather than public policies, supporting a system of "patronage politics." The very definition of corruption—the abuse of public office for private gain—assumes the existence of public purposes for which the office should be used. But in the HIPCs that were forged under colonialism, many citizens do not yet have a sense of belonging to a public larger than their families, villages, or clans. Familial roles and social obligations take precedence over formal roles and legal obligations, which do not carry the authority of either tradition or legitimate government. People look to the government as a collection of resources for private consumption, and those aspiring to public office must satisfy the demands of their constituents—the army, the civil service, or their own ethnic clans. If systems of planning, public resource management, and service delivery are exceptionally weak in HIPC governments, it is because the constituencies they serve do not demand public accountability or public services.

Despite all this, debt-relief advocates continue to press the international community to forgive HIPC debt in the name of the poor. One advocacy Web site states, for example, that "more than 18,000 children die each day because loan repayments to rich countries come before health care to the poor." This statement assumes that high interest payments trade off with government spending on social services, and that low spending is the principal cause of poor service delivery. But in the case of some HIPCS, where the largest part of every dollar spent can "go missing," bad governance—not low spending—is the immediate cause of poor service delivery. Increasing social spending will not necessarily improve service delivery because water cannot be carried in a sieve. Moreover, interest payments do not necessarily "crowd out" social spending; left to their own devices, HIPC governments would not necessarily use the funds now allocated to debt payments to tackle the problems of the poor. In fact, some HIPCS had no policy responses to poverty, AIDS, or corruption until they were required to develop them as conditions for debt relief under the HIPC Initiative.

Ensuring the proper use of debt-relief dollars requires HIPC governments not only to commit those funds to poverty-reducing programs but also to address the serious governance problems that hamper effective resource management and social-service delivery. The necessary reforms are deep and painful and unlikely to be taken voluntarily. Therefore, unless debt forgiveness is effectively conditioned on both the proper use of funds and the pursuit of structural reforms, it is unlikely to help the poor. Even worse, debt-relief funds may be used to support activities that actually aggravate poverty, such as war. Or they may get illegally diverted by government officials, who protect themselves by further undermining institutions of accountability.

Although conditions alone cannot guarantee sustainable reform, they can establish new precedents, catalyze local constituencies for change, and open public dialogues about social and policy issues—provided that the conditions are well chosen and enforced. Unfortunately, the current political pressure for faster debt relief undermines the design and enforcement of such conditions.

FASTER, FASTER

Although public attention to debt relief peaked last year because of the Jubilee 2000 campaign, debt payments were already being rescheduled in the 1980s. And as the crisis deepened in the late 1980s and the 1990s, debt-relief efforts continued on increasingly concessional terms. In 1996, the IMF and the World Bank launched the HIPC Initiative, under which individual creditors pledged to reduce debt to sustainable levels. Three years later they introduced the Enhanced HIPC Initiative, which more than doubled the amount of relief to be provided. This expanded program had two objectives: to accelerate the delivery of debt relief and to link it more closely to poverty reduction. Unfortunately, pursuing the first goal has made the second one more difficult to achieve.

Under the Enhanced HIPC Initiative, countries seeking debt forgiveness are required to develop poverty-reduction strategies outlining specific goals and programs. HIPCS qualify for temporary debt relief (known as "passing the decision point") after they have formulated interim poverty-reduction strategies; they receive permanent relief (known as "passing the completion point") after they have "implemented a set of key, pre-defined social and structural reforms and maintained good macroeconomic performance." No fixed date is set for the completion point, but the interim period is expected to last an average of 15 months.

This ambitious schedule leaves little time for HIPCS to effectively develop multisector poverty-reduction strategies. Because countries receive interim debt relief before they finalize their plans for some sectors or even start to develop programs for others, they are unable to use the strategies to prioritize their spending for poverty reduction. As a result, they are unlikely to use their debt-relief dollars effectively. In the absence of good planning, for example, governments have strong incentives to spend on infrastructure, given the profitability of public contracting. But putting a hospital in every village and a court in every town is not necessarily the best way to improve the quality and quantity of health and judicial services, particularly where fundamental institutional problems remain unaddressed, local demand is unknown, and funds for staffing, operation, and maintenance are unavailable.

Under the Enhanced HIPC Initiative, moreover, the HIPCS themselves are responsible for managing debt-relief funds. They are also responsible for monitoring their own poverty-reducing spending, even though none of the HIPCS currently receiving debt relief is capable of doing so. The IMF/IDA report estimates that only two HIPCS—with the proper technical assistance—could be brought up to speed within a year; seven others could be ready within two years. Sixteen will require "substantial upgrading," for which no time estimate is ventured. In other words, most HIPCS will not be able to report on their use of debt-relief funds before the end of the anticipated interim period. And after they pass the completion point and receive irrevocable debt relief, they will no longer have incentives to monitor and report on spending or to pursue reforms.

Nevertheless, some debt-relief advocates are pressuring the IMF and the World Bank to speed up their schedules. But accelerating interim debt relief will only further reduce the time available to develop meaningful poverty-reduction strategies, negotiate substantive conditions, implement monitoring mechanisms, and establish oversight institutions. By the same token, expediting permanent debt relief will reduce the number of reforms and the amount of benefits to the poor that can be monitored and assured. For some HIPCS, accelerating disbursements will serve no purpose, as they are already receiving money faster than they can spend it.

Unfortunately, both donors and recipients of debt relief have gotten the message that speed should take precedence over assuring benefits for the poor. The IMF and the World Bank initially envisioned that countries would become eligible for debt relief only after they had established a three-year good track record. But this requirement has been subsumed by arbitrary numerical targets: in 2000, the two organizations announced that they would see 20 HIPCS pass the decision point by the end of the year. And instead of considering conditions that will provide the greatest benefits for the poor, some staff are now looking for conditions that can be easily satisfied in six months.

HIPCS are also aware of the political pressure for fast debt relief. Some governments—particularly those that are not reform-minded—may well predict that they can pass the completion point by simply making pro forma reforms and stalling for a few months. One HIPC that recently qualified for interim debt reliefs already falling far behind schedule—even on easy, inexpensive measures. Very shortly, the international community will have to decide how serious it really is about tying debt relief to poverty reduction. But so far, no one has even discussed what will happen to countries that fail to meet conditions.

The indebtedness of the world's poorest countries is untenable. A long-term response to the problem must involve changes to the system of international aid, including the curbing of lending to heavily indebted countries and the establishment of minimum accountability requirements for governments managing aid money. But fresh lending to HIPC governments continues today—even as they benefit from debt relief.

A short-term response to the problem must entail debt relief, whether or not it has any impact on poverty. After all, poverty reduction is just one reason for forgiving HIPC debt. But if debt relief is to help the poor, advocates must give HIPC governments enough time to develop credible spending plans before interim debt relief is granted. They must monitor the implementation of key reforms and the delivery of social services to the poor. They must allow more time for the poor to realize gains before debt relief is made irrevocable. And they must send early and consistent signals that countries will not pass the completion point unless they use their debt-relief dollars to help the poor and satisfy their reform commitments. Having demanded and obtained debt relief in the name of the poor, advocates have a special responsibility to make sure that the needy actually benefit from it. The hardest work is still ahead—and the poor are watching.

18F. *Dilemma of Odious Debts*

We've decided to look at the concept of "odious debt" in this supplement rather than in the text. It's not that we think it's not important. But after Saddam Hussein was hanged, people wanted to talk about something else. The excerpt explains the evolution of the "odious debt" doctrine. According to the authors, unlike death and corporate bankruptcy, under the doctrine of state succession, "debt is congenital, adhesive, and ineradicable." But then an exception was formulated; the authors note William Howard Taft and Alexander Sack. Do you agree with the authors that Sack's test is impossible to apply? Why not just say that if the regime *is odious, then all the debt it has incurred can be repudiated by the successor government? Doesn't that sound cool? Or no? We've given you a short excerpt of a long but compelling article. In the conclusion, the authors argue that because creditors can now sue governments in court—they can't claim total sovereign immunity from being sued—we don't have to deal with the difficult task of applying the Sack test. Nor do we have to adhere to the (mistaken?) idea that debts of an odious regime—as opposed to odious debt by a regime—is per se repudiable. Let the creditors sue in court on specific loans, and let the government argue its defenses. What do you think?*

L. Buchheit, G. Mitu Gulati, & R. Thompson, "The Dilemma of Odious Debts," *Duke Law Journal* (2007)

INTRODUCTION

"If we were all responsible for the misdeeds of the governments that represent us, thought Isabel, then the moral burden would be just too great."

Public international law requires that states and governments inherit ("succeed to") the debts incurred by their predecessors, however ill-advised those borrowings may have been. There are situations in which applying this rule of law strictly can lead to a morally reprehensible result. Example: forcing future generations of citizens to repay money borrowed in the state's name by, and then stolen by, a former dictator.

Among the purported exceptions to the general rule of state succession are what have been labeled "odious debts," defined in the early twentieth century as debts incurred by a despotic regime that do not benefit the people bound to repay the loans. The absconding dictator is the classic example.

The removal of Iraq's Saddam Hussein in 2003 sparked a resurgence of interest in this subject. By enshrining a doctrine of odious debts as a recognized exception to the rule of state succession, some modern commentators have argued, a successor government would be able legally to repudiate the loans incurred by a malodorous prior regime. This, they contend, would have two benefits: it would avoid the morally repugnant consequence of forcing an innocent population to repay debts incurred in their name but not for their benefit, and it would simultaneously force prospective lenders to an odious regime to rethink the wisdom of advancing funds on so fragile a legal foundation.

In this recent debate, the adjective "odious" has quietly migrated away from its traditional place as modifying the word "debts" (as in "odious debts"), so that it now modifies the word "regime" (as in "debts of an odious regime"). This is a major shift. If this new version of the odious debt doctrine is to be workable, someone must assume the task of painting a scarlet letter "O" on a great many regimes around the world. Who will make this assessment of odiousness and on what criteria? The stakes are high. An unworkable or vague doctrine could significantly reduce cross-border capital flows to sovereign borrowers generally.

We are skeptical that this definitional challenge can be met. Rather than jettison the initiative as quixotic, however, we investigate how far principles of private (domestic) law could be used to shield a successor government from the legal enforcement of a debt incurred by a prior regime under irregular circumstances. A wholesale repudiation of all contracts signed by an infamous predecessor may be more emotionally and politically satisfying for a successor government, but establishing defenses to the legal enforcement of certain of those claims based on well-recognized principles of domestic law may be the more prudent path. Such defenses exist under United States law (and presumably elsewhere) and could be used to address many, although admittedly not all, cases of allegedly odious debts.

I.   THE INTERGENERATIONAL TENSION IN SOVEREIGN BORROWING

Imagine a not-unimaginable legal regime in which the debts of deceased persons pass automatically to their children or, failing offspring, to the nearest blood relative. Under such a regime, debt collection would not be restricted to the assets of the estate of the deceased. The debts would instead be collectible from the surviving blood relatives as personal obligations of those survivors.

Born into such a regime, might you not watch with mounting alarm mother's fondness for Capri in September? Or father's routine capitulations in the face of advertisements for the latest in computer technology? Or perhaps Uncle Otto's acquaintance with his turf accountant?

And when your turn came to receive unsolicited credit card applications, would you be able to resist that devastating Gucci handbag, secure in the knowledge that your niece will only have to work slightly harder during her career to pay for it? As the victim of the extravagance of your predecessors, can you be sure that mercy alone would instruct your behavior toward your progeny?

Under such a system, debts, once incurred, would be carried by each generation in the bloodline and passed on to each succeeding generation like a bucket brigade at a house fire. Naturally, the members of each generation would be sorely tempted to defer the repayment of their inherited debts for as long as possible in the hopes that final payment could be delayed to a date, any date, falling after they have managed to shuffle off this mortal coil. Whenever and wherever feasible, bucket carriers might also be tempted to top up the bucket with their own new liabilities before passing it on.

Every once in a while virtuous bucket carriers may resolve to repay the debts of their ancestors, and to refrain from new borrowing themselves, in order to pass on a light and empty bucket to the next generation. Human nature, however, counsels that such examples of virtue will be rare. Whenever the act of borrowing money is physically detached from the disagreeable task of receiving and paying the bill, virtue and temptation struggle on unequal ground. Ask any parent who has ever given a credit card to a teenage child as a birthday present.

The inheritance laws in the United States do not operate in this way. The debts of a natural person are personal in the sense that they may be collected from the individual while alive and from the estate of that individual upon death. They do not, however, trickle down some path of consanguinity to be visited upon innocent relatives. Stated differently, if someone dies owing more money than can be collected from the assets of their estate, the creditors attending the funeral will weep for reasons that go beyond simple bereavement. As the Bard would have it: "He that dies pays all debts."

This may not be the system that has been adopted for the transmission of personal debts, but it is precisely the system that public international law imposes with respect to sovereign debts. Under the public international law doctrine of "state succession," a government automatically inherits the debts of its predecessor governments, regardless of how dissimilar the forms of government may be. The state, together with its rights and obligations, continues; its governments come and go.

"State succession" is somewhat misleading. A line is often drawn, sometimes drawn very sharply, between governmental succession (when the state itself remains intact) and state succession (when the state undergoes some territorial change). Public international law is particularly strict in requiring successor governments to shoulder the debt obligations of their predecessors. So in the United States, it does not matter whether the Democrats or the Republicans win a presidential election: the massive national debt comes strapped to the keys to the White House. Corazon Aquino (a democratically elected leader of the Philippines in the mid-1980s) may have displaced a dictator, Ferdinand Marcos, but that did not give her the ability under international law to disavow the debts incurred under the Marcos regime.

The doctrine of state succession also applies, although in a more checkered way, to situations in which the state itself undergoes a major change. This occurs both in cases of cession of territory as well as in cases of secession or the disintegration of a state. When the Republic of Texas joined the United States in 1845, for example, the United States inherited (and had to settle) the debts of Texas. When the USSR disintegrated in 1991, the international community pressured the dominant successor state, Russia, to assume all of the debts of the former Soviet Union. A squabble over the appropriate division of the assets and liabilities of the former Yugoslavia among its various provinces is only now being resolved.

In the sovereign context, therefore, debts are congenital (in that each generation of citizens inherits a responsibility to contribute toward repayment of the old debts merely by being born in the state) and astonishingly adhesive. The obligations will remain legally glued to the territory notwithstanding changes of government (constitutional or extraconstitutional), a churning population, or even the disintegration of the state itself.

Contrast this to corporate debts. Acme Corporation borrows money. Over the years, the management and the board of directors of Acme may change many times. Over a long enough period of time, the entire corpus of Acme shareholders will change. But the debt remains. In that sense, corporate debts are also adhesive.

There are two important differences, however, between corporate debts and sovereign debts. If Acme Corporation becomes indebted beyond its capacity to repay, it may seek to have its obligations legally reduced or expunged in a bankruptcy proceeding. Moreover, the corporate planners of Acme are relying on the venerable corporate law principle of limited liability to block creditors' efforts to collect their claims, absent unusual circumstances, from Acme's shareholders. So, in the final extremity, the debts of an individual and the debts of a corporation are treated similarly: the debts do not pass involuntarily to those surviving the demise of the individual or the company.

Not so with sovereign debts. Sovereigns cannot look to death, dissolution, or bankruptcy for liberation from the consequences of imprudent borrowing. Sovereign debts devolve involuntarily on subsequent generations of citizens, long after the people who borrowed the money have departed and, in many cases, long after anyone can even remember why the debts were incurred in the first place. When a sovereign sins in this context, it therefore does so without hope of absolution or redemption, apart from whatever debt relief the sovereign may be able to negotiate or impose on its creditors down the road.

Under a strict application of the doctrine of state succession, sovereign debt is thus congenital, adhesive, *and* ineradicable. It is the combination of these three attributes that sets the stage for intergenerational conflict. The incumbent government of a country may incur debts that successor governments will be obliged to pay off. By the very nature of things, those successor governments and the citizens they represent are not consulted when the money is borrowed. They lie somewhere in offing—mute, disenfranchised and wholly reliant on the forbearance of their ancestors. They are, in fact, perfect victims of the linear progression of time.

When these new citizens finally appear on the scene, they will inherit many things: a territory, a history, and the infrastructure of a society. They may also inherit a stock of unpaid debts—debts that public international law requires them to assume as their own obligations. The obvious question is whether there are any circumstances in which such a bequest can legally be declined, with the consequence that the old debts will not bind successor generations of citizens. Stated differently, are there any exceptions to the strict rule of state succession?

II.   A TAXONOMY OF SOVEREIGN DEBT

Of all the people who have pondered the intergenerational conflict inherent in sovereign borrowing, only one has ever offered a truly crisp solution: Thomas Jefferson. On September 6, 1789, Jefferson wrote a letter to his friend James Madison in which he declared: " '[T]he earth belongs in usufruct to the living': . . . the dead have neither powers nor rights over it."

Jefferson was then ending his stint as the American Minister in France and was poised to return home soon to become the nation's first Secretary of State. He had been in France long enough to see the early ravages of the French Revolution. Jefferson wrote this sentence with particular reference to what he had come to see as the pernicious practice of sovereigns incurring debts that had to be repaid by succeeding generations. He called this principle—that the earth belongs in usufruct to the living—a principle of natural law. He described it as "self evident" (a phrase with which he had some success earlier in his career).

The solution he proposed was splendidly Jeffersonian. After studying life expectancy tables, Jefferson had determined that if a person of his time reached the age of twenty-one, that person was likely to live another thirty-four years. Jefferson's conclusion was that each generation may contract debts or, for that matter, may pass laws or enact constitutions, that must automatically expire within that generation's thirty-four-year average tenure. Thus, when a generation comes into its majority, it may legitimately contract a debt in the first year having a duration of no more than thirty-four years, and in the second year, thirty-three years, and so forth. In this way, one generation can never burden a successive generation with its own debts, its own laws, or its own constitutions.

This was, of course, one of Jefferson's more wobbly ideas. Generations are not born on the same day nor do they depart the world at precisely the same moment in the future. A Jeffersonian "shelf life" approach to public debt obligations therefore becomes, in practice, impossible to administer.

If one abandons the hope for a solution that absolves each succeeding generation of liability for *all* previously contracted debts, the task becomes one of deciding which types of inherited debts, if any, are candidates for repudiation by the involuntary heirs. The task is complicated at every turn by the patchwork, ad hoc nature of international law.

* * *

3.   *Odious Debts.* By the early twentieth century, therefore, the doctrinal cauldron was bubbling. The concept of hostile debts had embraced two propositions. First, not all borrowings by a government will bind the state as a whole; under certain circumstances, a loan to a government will be treated as a personal debt of the rulers who contracted the loan. The loan may indeed be repaid out of state funds, but only if those politicians retain power over the public fisc long enough to cause this to happen. If the rulers depart, the liability to repay the debt follows them. Second, if a lender knowingly advances funds in these circumstances, it cannot later claim surprise and injury if the regime changes and the new government refuses to treat the loan as a continuing charge against public revenues.

Both of these ideas received an important boost as a result of a 1923 arbitration involving Great Britain and Costa Rica. William Howard Taft (a former Yale law professor, colonial administrator of the Philippines, president of the United States and then Chief Justice of the United States Supreme Court) served as the sole arbitrator. The facts were these: In January 1917, the government of Costa Rica was overthrown by Frederico Tinoco and his brother. Frederico Tinoco's government lasted two years. Before he left the country, however, Tinoco managed to borrow some money from the Royal Bank of Canada. That money also left the country . . . in the company of Messrs. Tinoco.

In a subsequent arbitration, Great Britain claimed that the successor government of Costa Rica was bound to honor the loans extended by the Royal Bank of Canada. Costa Rica argued that the Tinoco government was neither the de facto nor the *de jure* government of Costa Rica and thus could not, under international law, bind successor Costa Rican governments. Taft disagreed. Citing various commentators, Taft held that under general principles of international law, a change of government has no effect upon the international obligations of the state.

That said, however, Taft refused to order Costa Rica to repay the Tinoco loans. These were, Taft said, not transactions "in regular course of business" but were "full of irregularities." Taft ruled that the bank

> must make out its case of actual furnishing of money to the government for its legitimate use. It has not done so. The bank knew that this money was to be used by the retiring president, F. Tinoco, for his personal support after he had taken refuge in a foreign country. It could not hold his own government for the money paid to him for this purpose.

Costa Rica's ability to disown responsibility for the Royal Bank of Canada loans therefore had nothing to do with the questionable legal status or legitimacy of the Tinoco government. Taft expressly rejected this line of argument as being inconsistent with the doctrine of state succession. Costa Rica *could* avoid responsibility for repaying the debts, Taft held, because the Royal Bank of Canada knew that the proceeds of its loans would benefit only Tinoco himself, not the state or the people of Costa Rica.

The lessons of Cuba, the Boer War settlement, and the Tinoco Arbitration were not lost on the international lawyers of this era. Lenders were repeatedly warned about extending loans that might, following a regime change in the debtor country, be portrayed as hostile to the citizens of that country, personal to a departing dictator, or otherwise lacking the consent of the people ultimately bound to repay the loans.

In 1927, a Russian jurist, Alexander Sack, stirred this cauldron once again and defined a class of what he called "odious" debts. In Sack's formulation, a sovereign debt is presumptively odious if

- the debt is contracted by a "despotic" power,
- for a purpose that is not in the general interests or needs of the state, and
- the lender knows that the proceeds of the debt will not benefit the nation as a whole.

Under Sack's theory, the consequence of tarring a debt with the label "odious" is that the debt is deemed to be personal to the despotic regime that contracted it and can only be collected from that regime. It follows that successor governments of the country can legally repudiate the debt once the despot is removed.

The odious debt exception to the general rule of state succession, at least as Alexander Sack defined it, comprised a very narrow corner of what we have called Profligate Debts. The three attributes of Sack's odious debt definition are conjunctive: the debt must be incurred by a despot (that is, without the consent of the population) *and* it must not benefit the state as a whole *and* the lender must be aware of these facts. Like a Las Vegas slot machine, all three cherries must simultaneously come into alignment before the Sackian odious debt bell starts to ring.

Under this definition, therefore, a Virtuous Debt (one that benefits, however remotely, the people obliged to repay the debt), even if incurred by a tyrannical regime, cannot be branded odious. A Profligate Debt, no matter how harebrained the intended use of proceeds, is not odious if it is contracted by a representative government. Finally, a Profligate Debt borrowed by a detestable regime is not odious if the lender genuinely believes that the proceeds will be used for a purpose that benefits the country.

Indeed, the contours of the odious debt category begin to blur almost as soon as one moves beyond debts incurred to suppress the people expected to repay them (the Cuban example) and loans to a dictator, for the dictator, and stolen by the dictator (the Tinoco case). This is not to say that there is any shortage of debts falling under those two descriptions; sadly, there are too many candidates. But pushing the concept of odious debt into more gauzy factual situations reveals its limits as a legal diagnostic tool.

For example, the Tinoco case was remarkable only to the extent that Tinoco appears to have appropriated for his own use the *entire* proceeds of the Royal Bank of Canada loans. Modern dictators do not behave in this way, and even the most indulgent lender might balk at a credit proposal whose "use of proceeds" line reads "corruption—high, wide and handsome." The modern technique is to steal only part of a loan, not the whole of it. So, the construction of a new hospital for children with terminal diseases requires financing of $50 million. The dictator *du jour* demands (indirectly, of course) a modest 5 percent commission, perhaps a level just below what an open-eyed lender would be forced to confront in its due diligence investigation. Is the loan odious? Partially odious (a new concept)? Does the overwhelmingly virtuous purpose of the loan justify, in a moral sense, a small blemish of transactional corruption? How would the terminally ill children vote on that question?

Most of the elements of the odious debt idea were already in play before Alexander Sack added his contribution in 1927. Among these was the notion that if a country (meaning the population of the country over time) must assume the burden of repaying a debt, it should have realized some benefit from the loan when the debt was incurred. Debts imposed on a country without the consent of the citizens are suspect. A creditor that advances money to a ruling regime knowing that the proceeds will not benefit the nation or its people can expect repayment only from the individuals contracting the debt.

Did the odious debt formulation therefore add anything new to this debate, or was it intended merely as a summary and restatement of the discussion as it stood in the late 1920s? We believe that the odious debt doctrine was just a summary and restatement. From the War-Debt and Hostile-Debt exceptions, Professor Sack drew the idea of loans that were used only to "strengthen" the governing regime, "suppress a popular insurrection" or were otherwise "hostile" to the interest of the people of the country. From Taft's decision in the Tinoco Arbitration, Sack gleaned the requirement that the lender know about the illegitimate purpose of the borrowing before the loan could be branded objectionable, as well as the notion that such a debt was "personal" to the ruler who commissioned it.

Alexander Sack did, however, contribute two highly emotive adjectives to the debate: "despotic" and "odious." Had he been less colorful in his choice of adjectives, perhaps this topic would have attracted less public attention than it has in this century.

A.   The Rebirth of the Odious Debt Debate

The concept of odious debts languished in something of a doctrinal backwater for many years. The phrase was occasionally enlisted for its emotive force to describe the pillaging of state treasuries by dictators such as Marcos in the Philippines, the Duvaliers (*père* and *fils*) in Haiti, Mobutu in the Congo, or the Abachas in Nigeria. Only rarely was the legal significance of the doctrine tested in municipal courts of law as a defense to the repayment of a sovereign debt, or in an international arbitration.

This changed abruptly, however, following the American invasion of Iraq in 2003 to oust the regime of Saddam Hussein. During the roughly twenty-five years that Saddam controlled Iraq, his regime managed to rack up approximately $125 billion of unpaid debts. Following the invasion, a number of commentators argued that most of these liabilities, in light of their provenance and their purpose (which was in large part to finance domestic tyranny and military aggression), should be declared odious and written off. This in turn kindled a significant resurgence in the literature and debate surrounding the topic of odious debt. This Article is a specimen of that resurgent literature.

Much of this renewed interest in odious debt enlists the terminology, but not the actual content, of the conventional doctrine. An odious debt, à la Alexander Sack, called for a loan-by-loan analysis. Some of the recent commentators are prepared to assume that all odious regimes behave odiously all the time and therefore all of their debts must be odious. The emphasis is thus placed on the odious nature of the regime, not on the circumstances surrounding each loan. All loans to a dictatorial regime are thus presumptively odious and liable to repudiation if the regime collapses.

This approach circumvents much of the definitional swamp that this Article has previously discussed. Sack's formulation calls for difficult judgments about whether a particular loan "benefits" the country, how the "consent" of the population to the incurrence of a debt is established, and what standards are applied in assessing the lender's "knowing" involvement in the transaction. These questions are largely irrelevant if the only significant criterion for identifying an odious debt is that the loan was extended to an opprobrious regime. From Sack's original list, therefore, only one significant criterion remains—deciding whether the borrowing regime is "despotic" (or at least *was* despotic at the time the loan was made).

To some modern commentators, therefore, the debate no longer involves odious debts; it involves debts of an odious regime. This is a major shift. It is curious that some of these commentators do not appear to be aware of how far they have left Alexander Sack and Chief Justice Taft behind.

Indeed, it would astonish Alexander Sack to learn that his catchy adjective "odious" had, in the twenty-first century, become the rallying cry of groups advocating the wholesale forgiveness of the sovereign debt of countries victimized by despotic or kleptomaniacal regimes. Sack himself would have recoiled at casually branding debts as odious. Sack envisioned the formation of an international tribunal charged with making the determination of odiousness. In a proceeding before that tribunal, the burden of persuasion would rest with the new government seeking to disavow responsibility for the debt. A new government would be required to establish that the proceeds of the borrowing were used for purposes contrary to the interests of the population of the country and that the lender, at the time the loan was extended, knew this to be the case. Even then, Sack's tribunal would afford the lender an opportunity to rebut the inference of an odious purpose to the loan.

Throughout the balance of his long career as a law teacher, Alexander Sack advocated a very strict application of the doctrine of government succession to debt obligations. State public debts, he later wrote, are a *"charge upon the territory of the State,"* by which he meant the entire financial resources of the state within its territorial limits. He openly ridiculed the argument of the Soviet government in 1918 that it, as the government of the " 'workers and peasants,' " had the legal right to repudiate the debts incurred by prior Russian governments of the " 'landlords and bourgeoisie.' "

* * *

CONCLUSION

It would never have occurred to Alexander Sack to suggest that successor governmental regimes should rely exclusively on municipal courts of law to invalidate the infamous debts incurred by their predecessors. There was a good reason for this. At the time Sack was writing in the 1920s, most countries recognized an "absolute" theory of sovereign immunity: sovereigns could not be sued in foreign courts without their consent. Commercial creditors were therefore compelled to seek the diplomatic assistance of their own governments in protesting debt defaults by foreign sovereign borrowers. If commercial loans could not become the subject of lawsuits in municipal courts, there was no reason to spend much time speculating about what defenses the sovereign defendants might have run in such cases.

All of that changed dramatically in the middle of the last century. The prevailing notion of absolute sovereign immunity gave way to a "restrictive" theory under which sovereigns could be held accountable in municipal courts for their commercial activities abroad. This restrictive theory was eventually codified into law in the late 1970s in both the United States and the United Kingdom.

For Alexander Sack and for all other interested commentators in the fifty years following him, therefore, the only possible countermeasure to the mandatory inheritance of debts incurred by a despotic regime lay in achieving an international consensus that such obligations should not, as a matter of international law, continue to burden the citizens of the country once the despot had been removed. But lenders now have legal remedies in municipal courts to pursue their debt recovery efforts. For the last thirty years in the United States, the legal enforcement of foreign sovereign debt obligations has been the province of U.S. federal judges applying conventional doctrines of state contract law. In those lawsuits, the sovereign defendants are perfectly at liberty to assert defenses based on principles of that same contract law or on U.S. public policy generally.

In short, the dream of Alexander Sack and many others since—to achieve an international consensus about what constitutes an odious sovereign debt—has been overtaken by events. This is probably just as well. As a putative doctrine of public international law, it faced an El Capitan of definitional obstacles. Had it flown at all (which we doubt), it probably would have flown very low, far beneath the level of near-universal consensus required to make it a binding norm of international law.

The prospect of yoking innocent generations of citizens to the repayment of *any* Profligate Debt causes an audible grinding of the moral teeth; the prospect of forcing this result on people already victimized by a corrupt and despotic regime is even more distasteful. This sense of moral outrage fueled the attempt over all these years to enshrine a public international law doctrine of odious debts. Strong moral imperatives, however, have a way of embodying themselves in principles of domestic law as well as public international law. We have suggested that the entrenched hostility of American law to bribery, litigants with unclean hands, faithless agents, and public officials embezzling state funds under the cover of what we have called the "governmental veil," is adequate to allow a sovereign defendant to defend itself in an American court against the attempted enforcement of what Alexander Sack would have recognized as an odious debt.

Establishing legal defenses on a loan-by-loan basis will achieve some, but certainly not all, of the objectives that modern champions of a doctrine of odious debt are seeking to promote. This approach will certainly have an *in terrorem* effect on prospective lenders that are toying with the idea of lending to disreputable regimes. It will not, however, provide a legal pretext for wholesale debt cancellation for emerging market countries previously ruled by kleptomaniacal regimes, nor will it permit a legal repudiation of Profligate Debts incurred for hare-brained projects.

A country weighed down by a history of imprudent borrowings is not, however, wholly without recourse. It is not necessary to repudiate (in a legal sense) every loan whose payments the country can no longer afford. Even in the absence of a transnational bankruptcy code applicable to sovereign debtors, overindebted countries have been able to approach their creditors (bilateral and commercial) for consensual debt relief when the accumulated debt burden becomes unsustainable, or is sustainable only at the cost of diverting all public financial resources away from other necessary expenditures. The sovereign debt restructuring process as it has evolved over the last twenty-five years is often not pleasant—indeed, it is frequently exasperating, contentious, and attenuated—but it is a recognized feature of the international financial system.

CHAPTER 19

"DEVELOPMENT" TODAY: THE CAPABILITIES APPROACH

■ ■ ■

We build upon our discussion of the Millennium Development Goals and debt relief by taking a look at what "development" means today, which is dominated by the "Capabilities Approach." As you know, the narrative of development began in Chapter 2 with an encounter between Rachel, a third-year law student, and Mitch, a cabbie who sees everything. You know from their conversation in the cab that the idea of development didn't exist way back in the day. But by the time the World Bank was established in 1946, Keynesian economics gave rise to a state-led framework of development that used economic growth, measured by Gross Domestic Product (GDP), as a metric for evaluating development policy—i.e., a country's aggregate well-being. Top down, statist policies were the rage in the 1970s, as we talked about in Chapter 4 regarding McNamara's Bank and the New International Economic Order (NIEO).

Things changed by the 1990s, with development coming to mean a people-centered, grassroots concept in the context of a market-based economy. Then in 1999, Amartya Sen, an Indian-born Nobel Laureate economist, theorist and basically the smartest person in the world, published Development As Freedom. In that book, which incorporates much of his previous technical publications, Sen makes the argument that development is not about aggregate economic growth but rather about expanding an individual's freedom to choose her path in life from as many paths as possible. Sen's take, along with the writings of the philosopher Martha Nussbaum, is known as the Capabilities Approach (CA). It competes with the philosophical writings of John Rawls when it comes to contemporary theory addressing social justice. The CA is embodied in the United Nations Development Programme's Human Development Reports and its Human Development Index. The MDGs we just looked at in Chapter 18 also reflect the CA. Despite some of its problems, the CA has generated a significant body of literature addressing theory and application, with notable contributions to public policy debate regarding health, disability, and education.

As with most of the topics in this textbook, this stuff can get really complicated, so we'll keep it as simple as possible. Rachel and Mitch are back, but we also introduce other individuals. You may want to skim

Chapter 2 before you read this one, if only for the subtext—what's really going on beneath the dialogue.

"Of Violence and Freedom"

Settings:

Chicago, Saturday evening, O'Hare Airport, December 2014

Mixteca, Mexico, two days earlier

Characters:

>Rachel: lawyer

>Mitch: cabbie

>Miguel: twenty-four years old

>Raul: twenty-seven years old

(lights up)

(4 a.m. in Mixteca, Mexico, the dialogue is in Spanish)

Raul: Did you give them a hug and a kiss?

Miguel: I did. I don't want to leave them.

Raul: We do what we have to do . . . as men . . . as fathers.

Miguel: We have no choice.

Raul: That word has no meaning for me. (pause) Let's go. He said to meet him behind the store.

(two days later, Rachel slips into the back seat of a cab)

Rachel: 350 Blarry Street, please.

Mitch: You got it.

Rachel: How long do you think it will take?

Mitch: Are you in a rush or something?

Rachel: Kind of.

Mitch: We've hit the rush hour. It'll be slow going. Okay?

Rachel: I don't have much of a choice.

Mitch: No, you don't.

(long pause)

Mitch: How've you—

Rachel: You look—

Mitch: been—

Rachel: I mean, I thought I . . .

(pause)

Mitch: Four years ago, am I right?

Rachel: I think so, maybe . . .

(pause)

Mitch: Well?

Rachel: What?

Mitch: How—

Rachel: I went to Rio, to a favela.

Mitch: Really. Are you a better person for it?

Rachel: I don't know. That's irrelevant anyway.

Mitch: You think?

Rachel: Yes, I think, thank you very much.

Mitch: Still sassy.

Rachel: But I tip well.

Mitch: Hah!

(pause)

Rachel: New cab?

Mitch: Got it last year. Sweet, yeah?

Rachel: Better than that . . . that—

Mitch: Piece of crap. Just say it, piece of crap.

Rachel: Piece of crap.

Mitch: You're a better person for saying that. Liberated.

Rachel: Well . . . I do feel a certain . . . inner peace.

Mitch: Speaking of crap.

Rachel: You walked into it.

Mitch: I couldn't see. Too dark.

Rachel: Imagine it then.

(Mitch looks in the rear view mirror, Rachel is smiling)

Mitch: How's the NGO?

Rachel: I changed jobs.

Mitch: Gave up on humanity?

Rachel: The opposite.

Mitch: A Dominican nun! Right on! Not as good as Jesuit priests, but—

Rachel: I'm an atheist.

Mitch: Okay, okay. There's a place for heathens. For sure.

Rachel: In the trenches. Where life happens.

Mitch: Excuse me. Life happens in a cab!

Rachel: Depends on the cabbie.

Mitch: I'm not gonna step in it again.

Rachel: Don't. It stinks.

Mitch: But I have a Little Tree air freshener.

Rachel: Is that what burns?

Mitch: Want my shovel?

Rachel: It's deep enough, isn't it?

Mitch: How about I start over.

Rachel: Please.

Mitch: So, new job, huh! Tell me about it!

Rachel: I work with the United Nations Development Programme, UNDP.

Mitch: Still development.

Rachel: Still.

Mitch: But United Nations. That rocks.

Rachel: I think so.

Mitch: And what may I ask do you do at the UNDP?

Rachel: I'm an advisor on the Capabilities Approach.

Mitch: Capabilities . . . making people more capable, that sort of thing, right?

Rachel: Sort of. It's about giving people the freedom to be capable of whatever they want to be capable of.

Mitch: You're making me dizzy.

Rachel: Have you heard of Amartya Sen? Martha Nussbaum?

Mitch: I just had dinner with them. Good people.

Rachel: So you must have read their books.

Mitch: On my nightstand.

Rachel: That's right. You read a lot. So which books?

Mitch: Oh, look! A flying pig!

Rachel: Sen—

Mitch: A Nobel Laureate economist.

Rachel: So you know about him.

Mitch: We're Facebook friends. Of course I know who he is.

Rachel: Why do you always play stupid with me?

Mitch: It helps pass the time.

Rachel: Well, stop. (pause) Have you read his book <u>Development As Freedom</u>?

Mitch: A while ago.

Rachel: Nussbaum?

Mitch: The philosopher. I dabble.

Rachel: You cabbies. That's all you do. Dabble.

Mitch: Here and there.

Rachel: Have you dabbled in the Capabilities Approach?

Mitch: Like I said, I read Sen's book back in the day.

Rachel: It can get pretty complicated but I can keep it simple for you.

(Mitch looks at the rearview mirror, Rachel is smiling)

Mitch: I'm all ears. Hold on.

(Mitch checks his ears in the rearview mirror)

Mitch: Still there. Shoot.

Rachel: When you think of well-being, what comes to mind?

Mitch: A gin martini, very dry, very dirty, and a smoke.

Rachel: I'm going to ignore that. Sen says you can best figure out a person's well-being by seeing how much freedom she has to choose the life she feels is worth living—her capabilities.

Mitch: Are we back to Mel Gibson, "FREEEEDOMMM!"

Rachel: He's bipolar. Remember?

Mitch: So what.

Rachel: You're throwing me off track.

Mitch: Freedom to choose the life worth living. See? I'm paying attention. Go.

Rachel: What he wants to show is that his approach is better at assessing well-being than other ways, like the traditional economic measurement of GDP per capita.

> *"For example, the citizens of Gabon or South Africa or Namibia or Brazil may be much richer in terms of per capita GNP than the citizens of Sri Lanka or China or the state of Kerala in India, but the latter have very substantially higher life expectancies than do the former."*
> —A. Sen, <u>Development As Freedom</u>, 6 (1999)

Mitch: Gross Domestic Product.

Rachel: Right.

Mitch: So you basically take the income and wealth of a country and divide it by the number of people in the country.

Rachel: Right again.

Mitch: You said other ways.

Rachel: Yeah, like measuring well-being by seeing if there's equality of resources, or the liberties you have, or how much happiness, pleasure you have and whether your desires have been fulfilled.

Mitch: Ooo, desires . . .

Rachel: Get your mind out of the gutter.

Mitch: But I like it there. Most cabbies do.

Rachel: And then there's Rawls's use of primary goods.

Mitch: Lou Rawls?

Rachel: What did I say, Mr. Cabbie!

Mitch: How stupid of me. John Rawls, the big-time philosopher. Justice as fairness. Political liberalism.

Rachel: So as you may recall, Sen asks: What level of capability does a person have to pursue the beings and doings she values? He calls them "functionings."

Mitch: Functionings.

Rachel: I know. Pretty funky lingo.

Mitch: Remind me of the funky functioning.

Rachel: It can be really basic. Eating, reading or seeing, being well nourished.

Mitch: Like eating a box of Frosted Crunchy Cornies?

Rachel: No. Do that and you would die before you should have. That's another functioning—avoiding premature mortality.

Mitch: Premature death by Frosted Crunchy Cornies.

Rachel: I knew that was coming.

Mitch: More than just that basic stuff, if I remember right.

Rachel: You remember right. Functionings can get more complex, like having self-respect.

Mitch: No such thing in a gutter.

Rachel: Being able to participate in community life.

Mitch: Like cabbies hanging out and trading stories.

Rachel: Sure. Why not.

Mitch: Any other complex ones?

Rachel: Appearing in public without shame.

Mitch: You mean like wearing a nose ring?

Rachel: More like everyone wears a nose ring but you're too poor to buy one.

Mitch: Everybody stares at you. Spits on you.

Rachel: I don't know about the spitting. That's gross.

Mitch: Do you spit when you talk?

Rachel: What? No!

Mitch: Just asking. Trying to get to know you better.

Rachel: Uh . . . no. Sen says a person's capability is all about the alternative combinations of functionings she's capable of achieving—what he calls "functioning vectors." A person's "capability set" is made up of alternative functioning vectors from which she can choose. And this is important. Listen. You might take a look at someone with a combination of functionings—her actual achievements, say a scuba diving instructor, that went to graduate school, plays the violin, and writes plays when she's deliriously happy—and say that's cool. But the capability set represents the level of freedom she enjoys to choose from the alternative functioning combinations. So to Sen, freedom is two-dimensional. First is the opportunity the individual has to choose the life she values. Second is the process of choice—what Sen calls a "comprehensive outcome." It's not good enough to ask if the individual actually is able to pursue an end she might have chosen—a "culmination outcome." Because choosing is a part of living—it may itself be an important functioning—and because freely choosing may promote well-being, you also have to ask if the culmination outcome was achieved by the individual choosing freely among various alternatives. Take two people who feel starved. We might not worry about rich people who have the capability to be well nourished and choose to fast—by choice they don't have the achieved functioning of being well nourished. But we should worry about poor people who lack that capability and are forced to starve.

(Mitch rolls his window down and sticks his head out)

Rachel: What are you doing? It's freezing!

Mitch: I'm choosing to freeze my face off. It's very comprehensive.

Rachel: Well I'm not choosing to freeze. So get your cabbie head back in here.

Mitch: Fine. Fine! But you've taken away some of my freedom. You freedom-thief! Sen wouldn't like this. Not at all. Shame on you.

Rachel: True, he's all about expanding freedom.

Mitch: Then give me some.

Rachel: Sen'll give you two kinds. He says freedom plays a "constitutive role" in the expansions of substantive freedoms.

Mitch: Translation, please.

Rachel: Substantive freedoms are elementary capabilities like not starving to death, not dying prematurely, being able to read, being able to participate in the political process, freedom of speech, that kind of thing.

Mitch: Right, right.

Rachel: He also says there's another type of freedom, instrumental freedom, actually five types. They're the drivers of development—they help a person develop his capabilities.

Mitch: Just give me the highlights.

Rachel: The five are political freedoms, economic facilities, social opportunities, and transparency guarantees.

Mitch: That's four.

Rachel: Oh, and protective security. But I'll just tell you something about the first three.

Mitch: I can guess the political freedoms. Voting, etc.

Rachel: It's broader than that. It's about being able to participate in a democratic dialogue with dissent and critiques.

Mitch: Gotcha.

Rachel: Economic facilities are basically economic resources.

Mitch: Yup.

Rachel: Yup?

Mitch: Yup.

Rachel: Is that a word?

Mitch: Yup.

Rachel: That's so lame.

Mitch: Yup.

Rachel: Enough. Social opportunities are about education and health care. They help increase a person's ability to participate in a country's economic and political activities.

Mitch: Yu—

Rachel: Say it again and I'll stab you with my glasses.

Mitch: You're not wearing glasses.

Rachel: Well, if I were—

Mitch: You bring glasses to a fight, I bring a gun.

Rachel: You have one?

Mitch: No. But if I did.

Rachel: If you did?

Mitch: You were supposed to let that one go.

Rachel: Oh, sorry, I lost the script.

Mitch: Life writes it for us every moment.

Rachel: What a Hallmark-thing of you to say. I think I'm going to sneeze.

Mitch: No snot in my cab.

Rachel: Oh, that's so gross!

Mitch: You started it.

(long pause)

Mitch: Are we still friends?

Rachel: Dream on.

Mitch: I've always been a dreamer. Sen?

Rachel: In a way, he's a dreamer, too.

Mitch: Tell me more.

Rachel: Remember I mentioned Rawls.

Mitch: Jonnie Boy, the philosopher king. Talk to me.

Rachel: In a nutshell, Rawls comes up with principles that try to make sure that—

Mitch: Justice is basic fairness. He asks you to put a bag over your head just before the beginning of society or something like that.

Rachel: He calls it a "veil of ignorance"—so that you don't know whether in the actual society you'll be rich or poor or any identity for that matter.

Mitch: So if I don't know what my identity will be, I'll want fair rules that'll give me a chance in the real world. Right?

Rachel: Not bad.

Mitch: Are you talking down to me?

Rachel: Never.

(Mitch looks at the rearview mirror, Rachel is smiling)

Rachel: Sen is critical of Rawls's use of "primary goods" as a metric for assessing social justice. Rawls says primary goods include rights and liberties, opportunities, income and wealth, and social bases of self-respect. He posits—

Mitch: Posits. Getting fancy on me, professor?

Rachel: He *says* that rational persons pursuing their own conception of the good life will want more rather than less of these goods. Social justice is advanced to the extent that people have a fair share of primary goods. But Sen says that Rawls's emphasis on primary goods, especially income and wealth, is mistaken because income and wealth are merely a *means* of living—a "means to other things, in particular freedom."

Mitch: Hey, give me income and wealth any day of the week.

Rachel: But hold on.

Mitch: I'm trying my best. Losing my grip, though.

Rachel: To really understand Sen's critique is the Capability Approach's emphasis on the ability of the individual to *convert* income and commodities into functionings. The conversion part of the equation will depend on personal characteristics, like metabolism, physical condition, and intelligence, and on social stuff, like infrastructure, institutions, public policies, and social norms. So a disabled person or a woman bound by social norms might not be able to convert a bicycle, a commodity, into the functioning of mobility.

> "If people were basically very similar, then an index of primary goods might be quite a good way of judging advantage. But, in fact, people seem to have very different needs varying with health, longevity, climatic conditions, location, work conditions, temperament, and even body size (affecting food and clothing requirements)."
> —A. Sen, "Equality of What?", *The Tanner Lectures on Human Values*, 215–216 (1979)

Mitch: It's all about conversion.

Rachel: That's it.

Mitch: If you and I have the same income and with that income we get the same bikes, I can ride the bike pretty easily but you can't because of your leg braces. Your legs are too weak. You need something more.

(long pause)

Mitch: You still there?

Rachel: Sen gives this example. Given varying conversion factors, Sen instead focuses on the "actual opportunities" of the individual to pursue what he values as the good life. By way of illustration, Sen says that a person with high income—one of Rawls's means to justice—who is prone to illness might not have the capabilities to translate the high income into the ability to choose what she values as the good life.

Mitch: If you're always sick and the health care system sucks, you might not ever be able to do what you want to do. Income alone doesn't cut it. Look at what you can actually achieve.

(long pause)

Mitch: Sorry.

Rachel: Here's a big word for you. Non-commensurability.

Mitch: Huge. Won't fit in the cab.

Rachel: I'll slim it down. Remember I said Sen doesn't criticize just Rawls. He critiques other approaches, such as measuring well-being based on how much happiness or pleasure you have and whether your desires have been fulfilled.

Mitch: Yeah, I remember that. My mind in the gutter.

Rachel: That's utilitarianism, but today we refer to utility instead of sex— I mean—

Mitch: Whose mind is in the gutter now!

Rachel: I'm getting out. How much?

Mitch: Oh, gee, my brakes are gone!

(long pause)

Rachel: I'm embarrassed.

Mitch: There's no such thing as shame in this cab, lady. Utilitarianism. Tell me.

Rachel: Sen says that the utilitarian tradition assumes homogeneous utility. So all you ask is, if a person has various alternatives, which alternative offers the most utility. That sense of security in using commensurable homogeneity has led to people using gross national product (GNP) to figure out the economic well-being of a nation and its citizens— GNP per capita. One commensurable metric is used.

Mitch: The value of all goods and services produced in an economy.

Rachel: Precisely. So the citizens of Brazil are better off than, say, the citizens of Mozambique because Brazil has a higher GNP per capita. Sen thinks that's too simplistic. Capabilities are non-commensurable because they are so diverse. A person in Uruguay might value the capability to become an accomplished symphony conductor—maybe the country's culture promotes that capability. A person in South Africa might value the capability to become a computer engineer. And a person in Spain might value the capability to be a yoga instructor.

Mitch: So if you have a country with citizens that value what seem to be infinite types of capabilities, you can't just add them up and then do a per capita on them.

Rachel: Exactly. You can't. And there's no morally objective way of rank ordering capabilities and their functionings in terms of value.

Mitch: What then? Pure chaos?

Rachel: No. People with reason have to have public discussions about how to rank capabilities.

Mitch: I'm guessing those discussions might take a long time. Like a century.

Rachel: Maybe not all the time. Sen says that "basic capabilities" wouldn't take much discussion.

Mitch: What might they be?

Rachel: Things like the ability to move around, to be healthy, have clothes and shelter, stuff like that. And if you're living in a country or a part of a country where human survival is at stake, you can be pretty sure that people would highly value the capabilities of nutrition, health, and safety.

Mitch: At least officially.

Rachel: Yeah. At least officially.

(a van is travelling the opposite direction of Mitch and Rachel, the dialogue is in Spanish)

Miguel: It's cold.

Raul: It's Chicago. December. What do you expect?

Miguel: How long to Iowa?

Raul: Not sure. I heard four or five hours.

Miguel: We're packed in here like a bunch of cows. It stinks.

Raul: Wait until we get to the meatpacking plant. That will stink, my friend. This is nothing.

(pause)

Miguel: Why are we doing this?

Raul: Because we have families . . . And we're not part of what the radio says.

Miguel: What?

Raul: Mexico's growing middle class.

Miguel: Middle class . . . That's where I want to be. That's where I want Juanita and Julio to be. (pause) A nice house. Two floors, maybe. A big kitchen and living room.

Raul: Don't dream too much.

Miguel: Why not? I like it.

Raul: We're here to work. Not dream. Send our money back. Maybe after a few years . . . A house . . . For our families.

Miguel: God willing.

(pause)

Raul: He's driving too fast and drinking too much.

Miguel: He wants a paycheck, too. Desperate, I guess.

Raul: Aren't we all.

(Mitch and Rachel in the cab)

Mitch: Coming up on a convenience store. Hungry?

Rachel: No, not really. Had a pretzel at the airport.

Mitch: Good?

Rachel: Very.

Mitch: Mustard?

Rachel: Is there any other way?

Mitch: Wash it down with an ice cold beer. Would that be a functioning?

Rachel: I suppose. But if you drink some of that ice cold horse urine, you're subhuman.

Mitch: I'm what?

Rachel: It's Martha Nussbaum's way of looking at capabilities.

Mitch: Remind me.

Rachel: She's like Sen but not. He uses the approach for comparison of quality-of-life assessment. Nussbaum, the philosopher, has spun a universalistic philosophical theory of social justice. She's all about human dignity. I quote, "My approach does this in an Aristotelian/Marxian way, thinking about the prerequisites for living a life that is fully human rather than subhuman, a life worthy of the dignity of the human being."

Mitch: Oh, so that's where the subhuman comes in.

Rachel: She wants to guarantee that all persons can claim ten central human capabilities.

Mitch: Oh, a top ten list.

Rachel: Want to hear it?

> "Sen's primary concern has been to identify capability as the most pertinent space of comparison for purposes of quality-of-life assessment . . . His version of the approach does not propose a definite account of basic justice...In consequence, Sen does not employ a threshold or a specific list of capabilities, although it is clear that he thinks some capabilities (for example, health and education) have a particular centrality. Nor does he make central theoretical use of the concept of human dignity, though he certainly acknowledges its importance. At the same time, Sen does propose that the idea of capabilities can be the basis for a comprehensive quality-of-life assessment in a nation, in that sense departing from the deliberately limited aims of my political liberalism."
>   —M. Nussbaum, *The Central Capabilities* in Creating Capabilities: The Human Development Approach, 19–20 (2011)

Mitch: To avoid being subhuman? Are you kidding me? Yes!

Rachel: Okay. But each one can get pretty long. I'll cut them short.

Mitch: Edit away!

Rachel: First, you got life. Not having to die prematurely or having such a miserable life it's not worth living.

Mitch: You mean if I go a day with lousy tips.

Rachel: Something like that. Second, bodily health.

Mitch: A no brainer.

Rachel: It includes reproductive health.

Mitch: Gotta procreate.

Rachel: Fourth—

Mitch: You mean third.

Rachel: That's what I said. Third is bodily integrity. Be free of violent assault, including sexual assault and domestic violence.

Mitch: For sure.

Rachel: You'll like this. Having opportunities for sexual satisfaction.

Mitch: Wait. Are you reading from Fifty Shades of Grey?

Rachel: Fourth is senses, imagination, and thought. In a nutshell, to imagine, think, and reason in a truly human way, which includes being able to have pleasurable experiences and to avoid non-beneficial pain.

Mitch: Non-beneficial pain . . . non-beneficial pain . . . I can't wrap my mind around that.

Rachel: You're not a woman.

Mitch: Last time I checked, no.

Rachel: Fifth is emotions.

Mitch: I think I'm going to cry because I'm bipolar—deliriously happy and desperately depressed at the same time.

Rachel: I think you got that one. Sixth is practical reason, which basically means being able to think critically about what you want in life.

Mitch: Let me think. Money. Yes, upon critical reflection I want to be filthy rich.

Rachel: Seventh is affiliation.

Mitch: I hang around with cabbies, the salt of the earth.

Rachel: Then you don't discriminate on the basis of race, sex, sexual orientation, ethnicity, caste, religion, or national origin.

Mitch: I pledged on my knees that I wouldn't.

Rachel: Nussbaum would be proud of you. Eight and nine are about being one with nature and being able to laugh and play.

Mitch: So I can't be a bore?

Rachel: You can choose to do that. Last but not least is control over your environment. It runs the gamut from political participation to being able to work as a human being.

Mitch: So this top ten list. It sound like it applies to everybody in the world.

Rachel: It does, doesn't it. Nussbaum says that even though it's universal, the capabilities can be realized in different ways based on local beliefs.

Mitch: Not sure that makes sense. I think I might like Sen better.

Rachel: Nussbaum has called upon Sen to have more backbone, so to speak—give a more objective "normative account of human functioning." He replied, no thanks. I'm happy with an incomplete approach so that other plausible takes on capabilities can be taken into account.

(the van swerves violently)

Miguel: What the hell!

Raul: Shut up!

Miguel: He's going to kill us!

Raul: I said shut up! Do you want us to get pulled over? Is that what you want?

Miguel (to the driver): Stop drinking, you fool! (to Raul) He's the one who's going to get us pulled over!

Raul: I'll take care of him. (to the driver) Hey, pull over. I have to take a piss.

Miguel: He's speeding up!

Raul: Idiot.

Miguel: I want to go back to Mixteca! I want to go back! I never should have done this!

Raul: Too late, my fellow illegal.

(Mitch and Rachel in the cab)

Mitch: Starting to rain.

Rachel: I'm surprised it's not snow.

Mitch: Rain, snow. Doesn't matter. There's always some idiot who overdrives the road conditions.

Rachel: It's coming down pretty hard.

Mitch: Getting back to this capabilities approach—

Rachel: Clever, Mr. Cabbie, try to distract me.

Mitch: I can see some real problems with it.

Rachel: You're not the only one. (*See supplement 19A.*) Rawls thinks the capabilities approach is a comprehensive moral view—contrary to liberalism. He also says it's too complex for public discussion.

Mitch: I can see that.

Rachel: There's another critic who says Sen's emphasis on the freedom to choose is wrongheaded. What really matters is whether a person's basic needs have been met, regardless of whether she exercised her freedom to choose. For example, being free from malaria due to the acts of others.

Mitch: This freedom to choose thing—

> "[Sen's] thought is that society must look to the distribution of citizen's effective basic freedoms, as these are more fundamental for their lives than what they possess in primary goods, since citizens have different capabilities and skills in using those goods to achieve desirable ways of living their lives. The reply from the side of primary goods is to grant this claim—indeed, any use of primary goods must make certain simplifying assumptions about citizen's capabilities—but also to answer that to apply the idea of effective basic capabilities without those or similar assumptions calls for more information than political society can conceivably acquire and sensibly apply. Instead, by embedding primary goods into the specification of the principles of justice and ordering the basic structure of society accordingly, we may come as close as we can in practice to a just distribution of Sen's effective freedoms."
>
> —J. Rawls, The Law of Peoples, 13 note 3 (1999)

Rachel: It sounds good but another problem is how to make it work on the ground. (*See supplement 19C.*) Sure, it makes for neat philosophical discussion—

Mitch: With a bourbon.

Rachel: Not a martini?

Mitch: Bourbon for philosophy.

Rachel: Well, have a sip and ask, how do you deal with its counterfactual nature? You know, contrasting what you can see with what you might otherwise see in a different situation resulting from your choice.

Mitch: And that non-commensurability thing.

Rachel: So much of the approach is so complex that it's hard to translate it into a way that can be practically applied for policymaking purposes.

Mitch: With Nussbaum, it's not the complex thing.

Rachel: She's gotten slammed. Critics say her universal list—a list single-handedly drawn up by a Western scholar—mistakenly assumes there is a global consensus on the nature of the human good. The list, they say, is paternalistic, procedurally illegitimate, and offensive. (*See supplement 19A.*)

Mitch: Just another form of Western imperialism, right?

Rachel: Actually, Sen doesn't think so. He got into a debate in the 1990s about whether his approach was incompatible with "Asian values" that supposedly don't put freedom to choose at the top of the list. The long and short of his argument is that you can find notions of freedom and tolerance—and lack of freedom and non-tolerance—in all societies. Ultimately, freedom and tolerance are human rights that transcend any distinction between Western and non-Western societies.

> "*Nussbaum's approach is more deeply troubling when it is placed back into the context in which it originated—that of international development . . . In the context of international development, this appeal to what is "truly human" is particularly problematic for historical reasons. The demarcation of "the human" as against what is not has been a typical colonialist discursive strategy. This was the very type of distinction that enabled the de-development of Central and South America, Africa, and parts of Asia that international development is currently attempting to counteract. This is not to say that once can never distinguish the human from that which is not. It is just that given its history, one might want to avoid this approach, particularly if others are available.*"
>
> —P. McReynolds, "Nussbaum's Capabilities Approach: A Pragmatist Critique," *The Journal of Speculative Philosophy*, New Series, Volume 16, 148–149 (2002)

Mitch: Human rights. Hmmm . . . So they transcend?

Rachel: Yes, they do.

Mitch: So let's say you got dirt poor families in Mexico. The men, the husbands of these families, they make the choice to immigrate illegally to the United States to realize their capabilities, the capabilities of their wives and children. That's okay with you?

Rachel: Yes.

Mitch: Why?

Rachel: They have no choice. They don't choose to be poor.

Mitch: That's Mexico's problem. Mexico has to give them choices.

Rachel: And if it can't or won't?

Mitch: We have an obligation to our own. What about South Side Chicago? Talk about lack of freedom and non-existent capabilities. You're a North Side elite.

Rachel (becoming increasingly impassioned): I'm a human being, Mr. Condescending Cabbie. A human being who believes we have a moral obligation to *all* families, to *all* women and children, no matter what country, to help them realize their capabilities. It would take a *sliver* of our wealth to create freedoms for so many around the world, including families on the South Side. So if the husbands of those dirt-poor families in Mexico can come to our county and send *not even a sliver* of wealth to their families, so be it. It's the morally right thing to do.

(long pause as hard rain pelts the cab)

Mitch: What's your name?

Rachel: Do you know where Mixteca is?

Mitch: No. Sorry.

Rachel: A really poor rural area in Mexico. Go there and ask that—

(the van crosses the median and slams head-on into the cab)

(fade to black)

You Gotta Know Something About Them!

Amartya Sen

Image of Amartya Sen, 2007 by Elke Wetzig is licensed under CC BY 3.0, 2.5, 2.0 and 1.0.

Amartya Sen was born in Santiniketan, India. His passion for welfare economics stemmed in part from what he saw as a young man: starving people going to Calcutta to find charities to help them. Amartya went on to receive his B.A. at Trinity College in Cambridge, followed by an M.A. and then a Ph.D in 1959. Amartya became the head of the department of economics at Calcutta's Jadavpur University at the age of 23, becoming the youngest teacher in the country. He's taught at some decent schools, such as Oxford, Harvard and

Trinity College. Oh, and yeah, in 1998 he won the Nobel Prize in Economic Sciences. But much more important is that in 2010 Amartya made Time's list of 100 most influential people.

Amartya is known for being very relaxed and unassuming, and a nice guy all around. He enjoys taking long bike rides. When he's not on his bike, he reads and argues with people. And he takes his civic duty very seriously: the 80-year-old recently hopped on a flight from New York to New Delhi, followed by another flight to Kolkata and then a taxi ride to his hometown to vote in the 2014 Indian election.

Martha Nussbaum

Image of Martha Nussbaum by Robin Holland is licensed under CC BY 3.0.

Martha Nussbaum was born in New York, New York and then moved to the Philadelphia suburbs. In high school, she participated in drama club, and had ambitions to be a professional actress. Even today she's into performing her own scripts. Martha received her B.A. from NYU, and then both her M.A. and Ph.D. from Harvard University. Like Amartya, she's taught at some decent schools, such as Harvard, Brown, and Oxford. These days she's the Ernst Freund Distinguished Service Professor of Law and Ethics at the University of Chicago Law School—along with other appointments at the university.

Check this out: Rather than listening to music when she goes for a run she tunes into a "mental soundtrack." Martha describes this soundtrack as being fully memorized excerpts from "The Marriage of Figaro" which she "listens" to in her mind. No earbuds. No Spotify or Pandora? And wrap your mind around this one: Rather than have a dog or cat as a pet, she'd prefer a genetically-engineered baby elephant the size of a dog. Hmmm . . . Did she get this idea from Aristotle?

QUESTIONS FROM YOUR TALKING DOG

1.   Spring has sprung. Happiness returns. Hope dawns. And I can go for walks without that stupid striped sweater. C'mon, let's check out the grass. Who? Rachel? She's back, huh? What's she talking about now? Capabilities Approach. Sen and who? Nussbaum. Okay, so Sen's all about freedom. To do what?

2.   How do you measure freedom? Speaking of which, can you ease up on the leash? Thanks.

3.   A what? Functioning? What's that? Like me lifting my leg on a tree? Functioning vectors? What? Capability set? Comprehensive outcome? Hey, I'm not moving until you explain this stuff.

4.   Two kinds of freedom? There's just one: Let me off this leash and let me run.

5.   Is that an insult? I'm behind a veil of ignorance? Alright, then tell me about this guy Rawls and Sen's problem with him. By the way, I don't look good in a veil. Returned one I bought online.

6.   It's all about conversion for Sen, huh? I understand that—that we're all different. So what? I kinda like that. Makes it fun in a dog park.

7.   Non . . . noncom . . . noncommen . . . ability. Non-commensurability. I want an ice cream cone for this one. Tell me.

8.   You know, this fancy stuff is just that, fancy. If a street person can end up with a decent apartment, food, and clothing, isn't that what we should worry about?

9.   Now Nussbaum. Okay. But, hey, I'm getting tired. Long winter. Didn't use the treadmill enough. So, quickly, my despot of a pet owner, how's Nussbaum's capabilities approach any different from Sen's?

10.   A top ten list of capabilities. Why ten? Why a list? What are they? Is Sen good with the list? Are we home yet?

11.   Okay, fine. Fine! Tell me what the critics say the Capabilities Approach. But please no more lingo, unless you make me a martini. You haven't checked your bottle, have you? Hey, jerk that leash one more time and I'll give you a taste of my capability!

19A. *A Critique of Nussbaum's Approach to Capabilities*

Here we give you a postcolonial critique of Martha Nussbaum's approach to capabilities. Postcolonial literature is huge, compelling, and provocative. The introduction to this piece gives you a pretty good idea of the essence of the postcolonial critique. Charusheela asks whether Nussbaum can have her cake and eat it too—i.e., can Nussbaum argue for a universalistic approach to capabilities that is still appropriately sensitive to cultural differences? Can you in your own words restate the author's postcolonial critique of development as it relates to literacy? How is literacy "institutionalized?" In Charusheela's view, is "development" actually disempowering? What precisely is Charusheela's critique of Nussbaum's interpretation of Nzegwu's argument? Do you agree with it? Does Nussbaum's approach to capabilities merely reinforce structural inequality? Is her approach a product of white privilege?

S. Charusheela, "Social analysis and the capabilities approach: a
limit to Martha Nussbaum's universalist ethics" Cambridge
Journal of Economics (2009)

1. Introduction

Postcolonial scholars ask how analysis and judgement work across
differences of culture and power. They locate the consolidation of ideas
about the 'modern' West and 'traditional' non-West in the dynamics of
colonial and neocolonial dominance, and show that certain characteristic
'Western' ways of talking about and representing the non-West are better
understood as ideological projections than as knowledge about specific
people and places. Going further, postcolonial scholars argue that a certain
complex of ideas, variously labelled as liberalism, modernism, essentialism
or universalism, are better understood as the self-constituting ideologies of
a dominant group than as altruistic, impartial bases for knowledge and
judgment.

In response to these and other critiques of ethnocentric universalism,
Martha Nussbaum argues that abandoning liberal universalism leads to
moral relativism. She accepts the criticism of certain universalisms (such
as the naive asocial rationalism of neoclassical economics), but contends
critics are wrong to believe that these defects are endemic to universalism.
She argues that the universalist project of political liberalism can be
salvaged by constructing universals more carefully. To do this, she has
developed a modified universalism based on Amartya Sen's capabilities
approach with, she claims, safeguards against the ethnocentric disrespect
and paternalism that marked previous forms of universalist thinking.

As one of those safeguards, Nussbaum set up cross-cultural conversations
with scholars and activists across the globe. This paper takes as its point
of departure the failure of a conversation between Nussbaum and
Africanist feminist philosopher Nkiru Nzegwu, one of the scholars she
invited to contribute to this dialogue. I use Nzegwu's contribution,
alongside Nussbaum's misinterpretation of it, to excavate the central role
of *social analysis* in Nussbaum's approach. Social analysis, as used here,
refers to cognitive frameworks used to understand and analyse society,
including ontological and epistemological presuppositions about the nature
of the social world. This paper shows that Nussbaum's framework does not
avoid ethnocentrism, but simply shifts it into social analysis . . .

2. Nussbaum's universalist framework

In her search for a non-ethnocentric universalism, Nussbaum asks whether
there exists an approach that is both robust enough to provide universal
ethics, yet flexible enough to ensure that we avoid the racism,
ethnocentrism, orientalism and paternalism of discredited universalisms.
She argues that the capabilities approach pioneered by Amartya Sen fits
the bill. In this framework . . . , *entitlements* are the set of things a person

can access or command given their current rights and opportunities. Entitlements set the level of functionings and capabilities a person may enjoy. *Functionings* are the actual combinations of things a person may value doing or being—such as having enough food to eat, getting a job or reading a book. *Capabilities* are alternate combinations of functionings that a person can achieve. The purpose of public policy is to secure and extend entitlements so that everyone's set of capabilities includes such basic functionings as health, good nutrition, adequate shelter and dignity.

Because it focuses on the feasible functionings and capabilities of individuals in a given context, says Nussbaum, this approach can provide a situationally sensitive, contextual mode of making ethical judgments and interventions. Further, by sharply distinguishing between functionings and capabilities, the approach allows universalists to both promote social good *and* leave open the particular ways in which individuals may use that good, avoiding the pitfalls of a homogenising paternalism.

However, listing a set of functionings and capabilities to be promoted by public policy is not universalist enough . . . :

> The capability view is in principle compatible with cultural relativism—with, that is, the view that the proper criteria for ethical and political choice are those given in each culture's traditions. It would always be possible to construct culturally varying lists of the most important functions and the associated capabilities, and to measure the life quality of individuals against such standards in each society. That, however, is not the direction in which the capability view has been developed by Sen and others . . . Instead, the view has taken a stand, indeed an increasingly specific stand, on what functions of human beings are most worth the care and attention of public planning, the world over . . . This universalist non-relative aspect of the view needs further development, however, if it is to prove possible to answer the legitimate worries of those who have seen all too much paternalistic imposition of some people's ways upon others.

Thus, Nussbaum's concern is to develop philosophical underpinnings for a universal list. In this project she draws on Aristotelian conceptions . . . of human nature and human experience, which, she argues, incorporate caring and connection as well as attention to local context—features that are absent in the rationalist Cartesian forms of universalist essentialism and whose absence has allowed some essentialist universalist approaches to be critiqued as androcentric and masculinist. She links the Aristotelian concepts to Marxian insights, which see human social and personal experience emerging out of social interaction. Nussbaum contends that this broad ontology, with its attention to caring and social interaction, is both universalist enough to form the basis for a trans-social approach to human nature, yet flexible enough to be adapted to the great diversity of local contexts that shape people's lived experiences.

Going further, Nussbaum argues that there remain limits to the framework as developed by Sen, when considered from the perspective of a universalist ethic . . . :

> Not surprisingly, I endorse these [Sen's] arguments. But I think that they do not take us very far in thinking about social justice. They give us a general sense of what societies ought to be striving to achieve, but because of Sen's reluctance to make commitments about substance (which capabilities a society ought most centrally to pursue), even that guidance remains but an outline.

Thus, as the next step in the development of this framework, Nussbaum uses the Aristotelian vision to ground a specific conception of the core features of human experience that let us identify the basic functionings that we will agree are universal, that is, essential for each individual to have in their capabilities set, regardless of their social location or cultural background. These key functionings are also called *central human functional capabilities* (or simply functional capabilities) in Nussbaum's approach.

Her process for generating this list is explicitly cross-cultural: what, asks Nussbaum, are the functionings through which *all* societies and cultures evaluate human life? This question has three parts. First, what are the functionings that all societies use to recognise themselves and others as functioning as *human*? Second, what are the functionings through which all societies assess the functioning of peoples as at an *adequate* level of human experience, in an ethical sense? Finally, having discerned those functionings we demarcate as universal based on the above principles, Nussbaum adds the concept of a 'threshold'—a minimum level for each of the functionings identified in her approach that needs to be available for each person conceived as an individual, and an end in his or her own right . . .

This process produces a list of ten central human functional capabilities . . . Nussbaum argues that all items on the list are valuable in themselves and should not be traded off against each other. Social ethics, and a society's practices, are to be assessed based on how well each member of society manages to attain these functional capabilities.

Indeed, Nussbaum contends that one can think of capabilities as fundamental political entitlements . . . She claims that the capabilities framework, as developed by her, provides a clearer way of thinking about rights . . .

Nussbaum takes care to ensure that this universalist ethic is sensitive to cultural difference. Nussbaum . . . describes six ways in which she has worked toward this end. First, she continues to view the list as flexible, 'open-ended and subject to revision'. Second, the items on the list are specified in abstract and general ways, so as to leave room for local interpretations. Third, the list is viewed as a free-standing 'partial moral conception', that is, 'it is explicitly introduced for political purposes only, and without any grounding in metaphysical ideas of the sort that divide people along the lines of culture and religion' . . . Thus, people can connect such a list to their own religious or secular comprehensive doctrines in their own ways. Fourth, Nussbaum maintains a strong division between capabilities and functionings that should, in principle, avoid the problem of ethnocentric control: By focusing on capabilities (focusing on the *ability* to attain these key functionings by ensuring they enter the capabilities set of each individual) rather than specific functionings (focusing on whether an individual actually *chose* this functioning out of the capabilities set), we should be able to intervene in ways that leave room for diversity and freedom of choice. Fifth, she argues that the major liberties that protect pluralism are themselves items on her list (she highlights freedom of speech, freedom of association and freedom of conscience). And finally, she argues for a strong distinction between justification and implementation— that is, she holds the list as a basis for persuasion, 'but I hold that military and economic sanctions are justified only in certain very grave circumstances involving traditionally recognized crimes against humanity' . . .

To ensure contemporary trans-social applicability of the emergent approach, Nussbaum invited a number of non-Western scholars to assess the applicability of the approach to a variety of settings in *Women, Culture and Development*. Whether the issues raised by scholars in that early engagement had an impact on the way the universalist approach was deployed will be a key question for this paper. To get at this, the next section is devoted to pulling out the social analysis embedded in Nussbaum's development of her approach. With that background, we will then return to the question of the impact of cross-cultural conversations on Nussbaum's universalist approach.

3.   The role of social analysis in Nussbaum's approach

Since the list of central human functional capabilities is only a general guide to ethical practice, one must still determine how individuals can attain capabilities in a specific social context. This requires a *social analysis* of how a society is organised and functions. This analysis in turn grounds a discussion of what social institutions and practices need to be changed in order to ensure that every individual attains these functional capabilities.

To examine the social analysis that lies behind Nussbaum's applications of the universal framework, it is necessary to move from its abstract shape to a specific application. Since Nussbaum claims that the merit of her system can be shown in the contextual fluidity of its application to specific places, this move is essential for exploring the universality, or lack thereof, of her approach. For the purposes of focusing discussion in this paper, I have selected the capability of literacy. This selection is dictated both by the specific debate between Nussbaum and one of her non-Western interlocutors used as the point of departure for my argument . . . , and by the fact that this capability should represent strong ground for Nussbaum: literacy is not, in general, controversial, and in her lead article for the 2003 *Signs* special issue on gender and globalisation, Nussbaum emphasises women's education, especially literacy, as the key task for feminism today. But though I develop my argument via the example of literacy, the general point about the role of social analysis made here would apply to *any* effort to give shape to and apply the capabilities approach to a specific place and time.

Literacy enters Nussbaum's approach in three principal ways. First, it enters the universal list under the central human functional capability of senses, imagination and thought, described as 'Being able to use the senses, to imagine, think, and reason—and do these things in a "truly human" way, a way informed and cultivated by an adequate education, including, but by no means limited to, literacy and basic mathematical and scientific training . . .' (. . . quotation marks in original).

Second, literacy is linked to the central functional capability of control over one's material environment . . . In the capabilities approach, this includes 'having the right to seek employment on an equal basis with others' . . . In her 2003 article on women's education, Nussbaum links literacy to women's employment: 'If there was a time when literacy was not a barrier to employment, that time has passed. The nature of the world economy is such that illiteracy condemns a woman (or man) to a small number of low-skilled types of employment' . . . Because literacy opens the door to better jobs, it permits women to attain numerous other advantages associated with higher incomes . . . : 'These concrete factors suggest some less tangible connections. Literacy (and education in general) is very much connected to women's ability to form social relationships on a basis of equality with others and to achieve the important social good of self-respect' . . .

Third, Nussbaum connects literacy to political activity: if women in particular want to organise in pursuit of political or institutional change, the ability to read and write is of practical value. Literacy is . . . also 'connected to the ability of women to meet and collaborate with other women', especially in larger political movements. It 'enhances women's access to the political process' and facilitates their 'access to the legal system' . . .

All of these arguments rest on implicit *social analyses*. Specifically, they assume the existence of a layer of institutions that organise the production of knowledge and culture, and assume that literacy is needed to engage with those institutions. To fully think, reason, and use one's senses one must be literate, and literate *in ways appropriate to those institutions*. These assumptions deny even the *possibility* that 'literacy' has been used, and indeed organised via these institutions, to exclude subaltern groups and privilege educated elites. Thus, at the heart of Nussbaum's approach is a social analysis that makes strong assumptions about how the institutions of state and civil society operate. To point out this leap in logic is not to deny that Nussbaum's implicit analysis may be correct for certain places and times, and it is certainly not to deny that literacy, just like mathematical knowledge or an appreciation of music or an understanding of foreign languages, is a good thing in itself. But Nussbaum is making an argument about literacy in terms of its universally emancipatory role in the contemporary world, and because of the universality of the claim being made, providing a universal social analysis of the causes for women's failure to flourish in the contemporary social world.

It is this central issue of social analysis—and the concomitant question of what type of social analysis we use—that, I argue, postcolonial theory foregrounds for us. To get there, we now turn to a conversation that was initiated as part of Nussbaum's effort to guard against ethnocentrism.

4. Nkiru Nzegwu's 'Recovering Igbo traditions': an alternate social analysis

To guard against ethnocentrism, Nussbaum drew on a diversity of voices in developing her framework . . . Among these voices is that of Africanist feminist philosopher Nkiru Nzegwu, whose 'Recovering Igbo traditions: a case for indigenous women's organizations in development', is the final article in Nussbaum and Glover's 1995 edited volume, *Women, Culture, and Development*. To pin down the failure of communication between Nzegwu and Nussbaum it will be necessary to establish the core elements of Nzegwu's critique . . .

Nzegwu uses a fascinating historical study of Igbo women's right to work in Nigeria to present a nuanced and sophisticated critique of Nussbaum's implicit social analysis, as described in the previous section. Nzegwu writes in the article's introduction:

> To some . . . [this discussion] would sound like nativism, a romantic re-creation of a pre-colonial reality that is of little relevance to Africa's postcolonial condition. But viewed critically, it is a *radical critique of foundational assumptions* about gender that underlie current development programs. (. . . emphasis added)

She goes on to argue that this critique applies not only to the types of modernisation programmes associated with the World Bank and International Monetary Fund (IMF), but equally to 'the conceptual biases of the participatory-models of Non-Governmental Agencies (NGOs)' . . .

Nzegwu agrees that women should earn independent incomes—indeed, she notes that Ndiya (Ibibio) women had advocated this as early as 1946, in a critique of British policies . . . But she disputes the notion that illiteracy is a fundamental cause of women's inadequate incomes or unequal job-access. Nonetheless, it is true that illiterate women have difficulty finding employment or getting the resources necessary for independent income-generating activities. Why?

Have they internalised their culture's norms of inequality, and remain unequal because they are not educated enough to comprehend and challenge these norms? Nzegwu provides a detailed historical discussion of Igbo traditions to show that this is not the case. Nzegwu shows that women had strong political and economic roles in Igbo society, and that they valued this role and took action to ensure that their roles and position were not eroded. Their actions to maintain their role show that Igbo women had a strong cognitive ability to perceive inequality and a robust set of institutional mechanisms to maintain that valued equality. They also had a vigorous tradition of organised political protest aimed at maintaining gender equality. In her words, the 1929 Women's War (to protest British policies) showed

> . . . their political acumen, foresight and vision, and revealed the existence of a powerful, highly efficient political structure with networks that transcended ethnic boundaries. The women displayed an incisive grasp of the colonial agenda, an ability to perform rapid and accurate analyses of the fluid, complex situation, and a remarkable capacity for formulating and deploying appropriate strategies . . .

Interestingly, Nzegwu also shows that it was *literate* privileged women from the emerging upper classes who showed a lack of political consciousness through an internalisation of Western patriarchal norms in the colonial period. She argues that this remains the case today. "At the upper-tier level, educated middle-class Igbo women find themselves shackled to a sexist system that leaves them politically disadvantaged to this day" . . . Hence,

> When development planners assume that rural women must lack organizational skills, and conclude that they should devote their resources to funding 'awareness workshops,' they illicitly transpose the apathy of the middle-class women on to rural women who have in fact continued to be politically active; they

illegitimately suppose that lack of literacy skills is equivalent to lack of organizational skills . . .

Thus, Nzegwu sharply rejects the argument that literacy is an *intrinsic* value necessary for the flourishing of senses, imagination, thought, for demonstrating practical reason, for being able to recognise inequality, or for enhancing women's consciousness.

Do illiterate women fail to attain jobs because they lack the skills and productivity needed to compete effectively or to undertake income-generating activities as equals? Nzegwu notes that increased literacy does not translate into increased productivity in agriculture, so that we cannot attribute poorer income-generating ability to lower skills or lower productivity on the part of the illiterate . . . Further, she convincingly argues that in terms of a wide variety of jobs and income-generating activities—the bulk of the jobs and income-generating activities in this context—illiterate women in this society have the skills and capabilities necessary to work and earn an income.

Thus, we cannot attribute the unequal work status of poor, illiterate, Igbo women to their traditional norms, to cognitive impairment and political apathy created by a lack of education, or to reduced levels of skills and productivity due to illiteracy. Nor can we presume that literacy and education will result in increased rather than decreased feminist consciousness and activism, since literate upper class women show far fewer signs of such cognitive recognition and consciousness than the illiterate poor women.

However, there is little doubt that in the data on Nigeria we see that empirically, economic inequality is linked to illiteracy. Why? Nzegwu argues that employers, government institutions and aid programs, including 'participatory' non-governmental organisation (NGO) efforts, have institutionalised literacy as a filter for access to a variety of social and economic entitlements, including employment. This is because of their *adherence to the conceptual frame in which the causal links between literacy, work skills, and cognitive capacity are presumed* . . . By assuming that those without literacy are not yet equipped for or capable of undertaking income-generating work at a level equal to those with literacy, they institutionalise literacy as a criterion for attaining equal access to jobs or resources. Not surprisingly, our data then show that the unlettered are disproportionately unemployed, underpaid and stuck at the bottom of the job structure.

Why do we still focus on making the illiterate literate as a precondition for equal access to jobs, instead of seeing literacy requirements as a mode of justifying the unequal labour market, which rewards some groups at the expense of others? Nzegwu's analysis suggests that when we use cognitive frameworks that uncritically privilege literacy, we naturalise the higher value (and concomitant material and political privileges) accorded to the literate, and legitimise the very power structure we are trying to undo. Thus, she shows that in a context where literacy acts as a job-filter to legitimise upper-class dominance in the labour market, 'participatory-NGO' efforts end up maintaining and promoting, rather than undoing, this structural barrier. These approaches simply assume a causal relationship between illiteracy and gender-inequality, as Nussbaum's social analysis above did, and in the process slip in an *ethnocentric normative assessment* of the capabilities of the illiterate. The ethnocentric framework they use not only institutionalises the inequality, it justifies it through the ethnocentric and classist presumptions about non-Western illiterate women, presumptions that are in-built into our social analysis ('explanation') of why they fare poorly. It also has the effect of *reducing* these women's sense of self-worth, as the illiterate, internalising the dominant frame that gives more value to the literate, begin to see themselves as less capable, and feel less able to protest these approaches as a result of such internalisation . . .

Our examination of Nzegwu's alternate social analysis of literacy not only provides us with a different way of thinking about the politics of literacy. It lets us see that *each particular application* of the universal approach requires—usually assumes—a social analysis. And, for each instance of application that makes a claim about what is necessary for promoting universal flourishing, we can ask—indeed, *need to ask* if we come from a critical perspective committed to ending oppression—whether ideological claims that uphold power are embedded in the analysis being used, and whether alternate social analyses may lead us to different conclusions.

5.   Nussbaum's misreading of structural critique

Nzegwu's critique of both the intrinsic and instrumental value of literacy appears in a volume co-edited and introduced by Nussbaum. Nussbaum has described the inclusion of non-Western scholars in the books that develop her project as part of a concerted effort to avoid ethnocentrism, which she acknowledges as a danger to universalist thinking. This section examines Nussbaum's response to Nzegwu in her editor's introduction to the volume in which Nzegwu's piece appeared. My purpose is not just to show that Nussbaum did not grasp Nzegwu's critique, but to examine the *nature* of Nussbaum's misreading.

As demonstrated in the previous section, Nzegwu argues that, historically, literacy in Nigeria has been a means to institutionalise the prestige of the upper, educated classes. In this context, literacy projects cannot simply be treated as an uncomplicated means of empowerment, since they serve to legitimate the structures of power that are responsible for poor women's current state of inequality. Nussbaum not only fails to register this argument, but writes that 'Because it is not her theme, Nzegwu does not place emphasis on the obstacles to women's full equality that surely exist in the Nigerian context' . . . That is, Nussbaum ignores Nzegwu's extended discussion of the historical institutionalisation of literacy *as an obstacle to women's equality*. Nussbaum then proceeds . . . to rectify the presumed omission by providing statistical data on inequality in employment and literacy in Nigeria. She implies a causal link between illiteracy and unemployment, apparently failing to register that it is precisely the nature and status of this causal link that Nzegwu has disputed.

How is Nussbaum able to ignore Nzegwu's theme—the institutional role of literacy as an obstacle to equality—and instead write that obstacles to equality are not her theme? The powerful framing that produces this misreading is that of 'modernity' versus 'tradition'. Nussbaum chooses to introduce Nzegwu's article as 'a vigorous defense of one traditional conception of women's role'. She says . . . : 'we end with a non-Western female voice that speaks with pride of its own traditions, viewing these as valuable resources in the critical social thought and action of women the world over' . . .

What is wrong with this framing? It is certainly true that Nzegwu writes positively about 'tradition' when she tells us about the organisational and cognitive capacities of specific Nigerian women. Writing about the 1929 Igbo Women's War (to protest British policies), she writes:

> . . . their political acumen, foresight and vision, and revealed the existence of a powerful, highly efficient political structure with networks that transcended ethnic boundaries. The women displayed an incisive grasp of the colonial agenda, an ability to perform rapid and accurate analyses of the fluid, complex situation, and a remarkable capacity for formulating and deploying appropriate strategies . . .

But if we look carefully, we see that here, and elsewhere, Nzegwu emphasises the flexibility and adaptability of these (illiterate) women *in the face of a changing world* that threatens their social position, *not* their repetition or reenactment of 'tradition'. As the previous section showed, Nzegwu was acutely aware of the danger that her discussion *'would sound like nativism, a romantic re-creation of a pre-colonial reality'*, (emphasis added) insisting that 'viewed critically, it is *a radical critique of foundational assumptions about gender that underlie current development programs*' (. . . emphasis added). That is, the radical critique depends precisely on *not* consigning these capacities and actions to 'tradition', as Nussbaum . . . does:

> The volume ends with a vigorous defense of one traditional conception of women's role . . . It is appropriate that we should end on this note, for we would not wish to be read as saying that all good ideas about women's equality come from the Western

Enlightenment. The cultures of the Enlightenment have frequently been unjustly contemptuous of the traditions of the people they have colonised, and obtuse about discovering that those traditions are [sic]. Nzegwu is surely right that the Victorian wife (or even the contemporary American professional woman) might profit from acquaintance with the remarkable tradition of 'sitting on a man'. She might also study with profit its associated patterns of women's group affiliation and self-definition, strikingly at variance with Western customs in which women's social identity derives primarily from that of a male head of household. These recognitions are in no way incompatible with the sort of universalism we wish to defend, as we have emphasised throughout. We want to take good ideas where we find them, and then think about how they might be implemented in a variety of concrete contexts. Having been, on the whole, highly critical of traditions, both non-Western and Western, we end with a non-Western female voice that speaks with pride of its own traditions, viewing these as valuable resources in critical social thought and action of women the world over.

Once the modern/traditional binary is set as the *interpretive* frame, it overrides Nzegwu's argument *despite* her request at the start of her article that we *not* read her as a romantic nativist. Every affirmation by Nzegwu of something done by non-Westernised Nigerian women is simply read as a proud affirmation of tradition, and therefore as something that, in a generous spirit, women everywhere might draw inspiration from. But while one can value it (that is, say nice things about the 'tradition'), once consigned to the category of 'tradition' as it is used here, it can no longer be read as *social analysis*. It is not surprising that, given this framing, Nussbaum also fails to take on board Nzegwu's commentary on the 'apathy' of the literate 'middle-class women' who often run NGOs, or 'the conceptual biases of the participatory-models of Non-Governmental Agencies (NGOs)'. Instead, Nzegwu's rich historical discussion of the structural and causal mechanisms that produce inequality for illiterate women is registered by Nussbaum via dismay about neglect of women's managerial knowledge.

The issue here is not whether one is 'for' or 'against' tradition. Rather, the question is about the *analytical status* of the concept of tradition in Nussbaum's framework. Once a nuanced historical analysis of social institutions has been collapsed into a defense of colourful 'tradition', the issues raised in Nzegwu's discussion can only resurface as discrete and isolable skills, rituals and practices that we might want to draw on or recover in a generous multicultural spirit. When 'tradition' means anything *more* serious or integrated than this, in Nussbaum's thought, it registers as obstinate nativism or thinly-disguised apologetics for women's oppression. Thus, Nussbaum . . . assigns all criticisms of her approach to literacy to the categories of nativism, relativism, apologia for women's oppression, an instance of argument from economic necessity and/or internalised oppression and false consciousness or 'poor implementation'. There is simply no *category* among these within which Nzegwu's social critique could fit.

The next section of this paper concludes by showing that the absence of a category where Nzegwu's critique could fit and the reading of Nzegwu as a defender of her tradition are part of the underlying ethnocentric modernist framework that Nussbaum has used in developing her universal approach.

6. Modernist developmentalism and the limits of universalist ethics

Although Sen's critique of Nussbaum's adaptation of his approach differs from mine, he says, arguing against 'the fixing of a cemented list of capabilities', that:

> I am a great believer in theory, . . . But pure theory cannot 'freeze' a list of capabilities for all societies . . . That would be not only a denial of the reach of democracy, but also a misunderstanding of what pure theory can do, completely divorced from the particular social reality that any particular society faces . . .

We can read this as two related questions: what is entailed in the construction of a list 'for all societies', and what is assumed in the move between a universal list and a 'particular social reality'?

So far, I have developed my discussion around the second question. I have shown that the move from a universal list to a 'particular social reality' requires social analysis. The social analysis Nzegwu uses, and that I used to raise questions about political voice toward the end of Section 4, comes from the framework used by a large body of scholarship that raises the question of *structural power and its relation to cognitive frameworks used to understand and organise the world*. This is the question raised by Marx, by critics of developmentalism, and by postcolonial scholars. What sets the terms of participation in the raced and gendered logics of contemporary capitalist markets? What authorises power and respect and legitimates, or renders invalid and delegitimates, alternate perspectives on our social order and competing modes of entering the social world? These questions can only be taken up in a social analysis that examines ethnocentrism not as an *attitude*, but as an *ideology*. Only when approached in this way—that is, as a cognitive framework that emerges out of a power dynamic—can we see how ethnocentric ideology legitimates and naturalises power, reproducing unequal relations while rendering them invisible.

What our discussion shows is that at the center of Nussbaum's and Nzegwu's competing positions on literacy are *divergent social analyses* of the causes and sources of women's inequality. Nussbaum's efforts to address the problem of ethnocentrism by carving out universalist ethics at an 'abstract' or general level thus prove inadequate, since the 'locus' of ethnocentrism *shifts* to the *social analysis* used to 'apply' the universal framework to various concrete social realities. In short Nussbaum has not *addressed* ethnocentrism, but instead has pushed it into the social analysis used to apply the framework to diverse settings. Since any effort to apply the universal approach to a concrete social reality entails social analysis, our discussion of literacy raises a *general* point or potential problem with Nussbaum's framework.

But this social analysis is not just deployed at the moment of deciphering why specific capabilities are not attained in a given society—the point of application discussed so far. It also underlies the prior choice of measures used to assess whether people have attained an adequate level of functioning in a particular capability. This may be less problematic for some kinds of capabilities and functionings, primarily those that pertain to the body, such as health and nutrition. But assessment is quite difficult for functionings that are properties of people's social and mental lives, their psychic states or the qualities of their inter-subjective relationships. We have already examined the difficulty of assuming that literacy is linked to, and is thus a proxy measure for, more fundamental capacities or qualities of psychic or social life. Similar points can be made about the continued use of labour force participation rates as a convenient measure of women's control over material environments despite the obvious Marxist objections to using wage labour as a measure of emancipation . . .

Thus, even though it presents itself as two separate stages—one stage of measuring to discern if key capabilities have been met, and another of applying social analysis to decipher the causes for failures to attain key capabilities—social analysis is already implicit in the measurement stage. We cannot assess different societies in terms of 'senses, imagination, and thought' without a social analysis that grounds the appropriate traces or measures of those things. And if we believe that the cross-cultural comparisons based on the measures we choose are meaningful, we must believe we are using a social analysis that has universal application.

The social analysis implicit in both the measurement and application stages of Nussbaum's framework is *modernist*. As used here, modernism (or modernity) is first of all a social vision that includes a liberal-democratic nation-state, an industrial capitalist economy, and a series of other specific institutions of public life and 'civil society', requiring a particular mode of interaction between individuals, individual and state, and individual and society. This conception is generally offered as a normative ideal.

Built into this vision are assumptions about the appropriate institutional unit for cultural or social organisation—the nation-state—and the appropriate institutional modes by which participation and voice should be expressed (constitutions and parliaments, legal forms and court structures, private and public spheres, political parties and civic organisations, rallies and petitions and writs, contract forms and state adjudication of them). Also built into this is an underlying set of assumptions about human nature that masquerades as universal—cognition expressed in particular ways, decisions made in specific ways, reason and voice deployed *in ways appropriate to these institutions.*

By deploying this vision of state policy as a universal normative ideal, Nussbaum has converted the ideal vision of what the state and civil society *should* be into a *social ontology.* That is, she assumes that *existing institutions* can usefully be understood *by reference to* the modern ideal— as fully modern, incompletely modern, or not modern at all (i.e., 'traditional'). With this framing, people's problems with modern institutions are always understood in terms of lack of access to, or participation in, those institutions, not as fundamental, in-built properties of real-life institutional structures. It thus becomes impossible to conceive that institutions that present themselves as modern might *generate* structural inequality.

Modernist ideologues assume, axiomatically, that women's problems lie elsewhere—in the sphere of family, or in a non-modern 'traditional' culture, or in something *else* that generates lack of participation in and exclusion from these institutions, never in the actual politics of institutionalisation itself. The hallmark of a modernist approach is its use of a traditional/modern split to organise *analysis* of social institutions. We have seen Nussbaum deploy this framework in her analysis of capabilities, and in her reading of Nzegwu. In her view women fail to flourish because of their lack of access to, or inadequate participation in, modernist institutions. These institutions are understood via the categories of liberal political philosophy, which results in conflating the normative just-so stories about the origins of liberal polities with the actual histories of liberal institutions.

The same framework filters responses to criticism. Nussbaum interprets critique of her perspective in terms of 'tradition', whether she understands it as benign multiculturalism (Nzegwu) or malign nativism (cultural relativists and apologists for patriarchy). The category of 'tradition' seals off institutional history and ideological politics: traditions may be respected or reviled since they call forth a *moral* or *ethical* positioning from the modernist, but they are not objects whose history, institutionalisation and operation in a contemporary world calls for *social analysis.* Similarly, identities (the counterpart category for 'tradition') can be valued, rejected or otherwise *assessed.* But, despite the Aristotelian framing, there is scant attention to the sexed, gendered, raced and classed social histories, to the discursive framings and struggles over meaning by which nation-states have been constituted and national and ethnic identities consolidated.

Thus, while Nussbaum defends her universalism from charges that she sees as coming from the argument from culture, the value of diversity and paternalism . . . , she has no category for critiques of universalism coming from a perspective on structural power that she even recognises, let alone responds to.

The only other category for critique that Nussbaum . . . allows, is 'poor implementation'. Using this perspective, the focus becomes one of fixing the problems of application, rather than exploring the power dynamics embedded in real-life institutions that may be responsible for the 'implementation' problems. Here, political liberalism acts as a counterpart to the neoliberal 'good governance' discourse. While their policy agendas differ, the response to failures turns out to be similar when it comes to the specific institutions—free markets in one case, state and 'civil society' in the other—that are at the centre of their respective modernist imaginations.

We can now see more fully the reasons for the failure of the process of the cross-cultural conversation that Nussbaum set up as a guard against the ethnocentric tendencies of modernism . . .

In these terms, Nussbaum reads Nzegwu as answering the question of what is useful in Nigerian tradition, not as responding to the question of the causes for women's inequality, which sets the parameters for the entire exchange. More generally, linking our discussion of modernist social analysis with Babbitt's critique of the way stories are read for moral meanings . . . , Nussbaum's effort to find commonalities across cultures is flawed because she 'listens' with the ear of the modern political liberal looking for commonalities, that is, *agreement.* All stories that indicate dissent are then 'heard' and 'explained' via the categories allowed for critique in her framework. She thus does not hear dissenting stories as anything other than affirmation of tradition (or alternately, as paternalism, nativism, cultural relativism, apologetics for oppression, false consciousness, the argument from economic necessity and implementation), and so fails to register criticisms of the historical role of power in, and hence the problems with, the institutions on which she rests her hopes for emancipation.

Modernist *ideology* becomes invisible to someone using a modernist *analytical framework,* as it shapes not only their own approach, but also how they understand and interpret others. Nzegwu shows how a modernist ideology that posits poor women as ontologically lacking enables oppression and blocks their access to important functionings. The inability of Nussbaum's framework to accommodate this kind of institutional reality is mirrored by Nussbaum's inability to register Nzegwu's critique. This inability is, as postcolonial feminist critics of ethnocentric modernism have noted, related to structural privilege. The ethnocentrism that attributes poverty to a lack of education rests on an unexamined counterpart assumption that the privileges enjoyed by educated people are appropriate and merited. Thus, the normalisation of privilege within modernist ideology has a dual action—it both creates inequality and makes mechanisms that institutionalise inequality invisible to us.

Modernist ideology either reduces structural critique to a technocratic—managerial problem of application, or misreads it as defence of tradition or particularism. I hope it is now clear that a critique of modernist universalism is not tantamount to relativism or to atavistic, uncritical celebration of the local and the traditional. This simplistic binary of critique is itself a product of modernism . . . , and acts to guard modernist approaches from critical self-revaluation, leaving us unable to attain in practice the hoped-for open-ended critical revision that liberalism promises in theory.

Thus, at each step of Nussbaum's development of the capabilities approach—in 'listening' to diverse stories for commonalities and deciding which capabilities to highlight, coming up with appropriate measures for them, and deciphering what the source of the problems are and how to address them—assumptions about social life and social analysis are already embedded. The question becomes—what social analysis should we use? My discussion above suggests that we need a theory that can help us *guard against the difficulty of embedded modernist assumptions, given that such assumptions can simultaneously authorise power and render it invisible.* Poststructuralist feminist and postcolonialist perspectives offer such a framework. They begin by seeing society as shaped by power, and argue that given the *historical* legacies of the structures of patriarchal power, class, race, orientalism and ethnocentrism, we should not be surprised to find that these systems have ramified into our cognitive frameworks.

We have come back full circle to the postcolonial critique of modernist universals that we began this paper with. Nussbaum's rejection of such postcolonial critique and argument for universalism rested on a two-fold move: (i) suggesting that postcolonial critique necessarily leads to a corrosive ethical relativism, and (ii) arguing that her reconstituted universalism escaped the problems of ethnocentric modernism that beset previous forms of universalism. I have shown that Nussbaum's approach is no more automatically safe from ethnocentric universalism, or automatically capable of addressing the hold of structural power on our discourses and social analyses, than previous renditions of modernist political liberalism.

Indeed . . . postcolonial thought explicitly seeks to explore the limits of not only modernism but also of relativism and nativism, in carving out its perspective on social power in its ontology and ethics. Because of its refusal to regard questions of social analysis as settled, and because of its refusal to regard the idealised modernist institutions of political liberalism as beyond the purview of structural critique, postcolonial critiques, far from being relativist, reflect a deeper commitment to liberatory practice than developmentalist modernism.

19B. *The Capabilities Approach and Feminism*

This excerpt by Ingrid Robeyns is a feminist's take on Sen's Capability Approach. The author explores whether Sen avoids false gender-neutral and androcentric theory. She does this by testing Sen's focus on functionings and capabilities, as well as the role Sen's approach gives to human diversity. How does Sen's emphasis on the conversion factor relate to the feminists concern? In Chapter 25, one of the selections focuses on racism and Critical Race Theory. That reading will tell you about "intersectionality," a term in CRT. The idea is "anti-essentialist," meaning that a person has more than one identity that may be the situs for oppression—for example a black woman with a physical disability. Is there a similar concept in feminist theory? Does Sen's approach adequately address this concept?

I. Robeyns, *Sen's capability approach and feminist concerns* in
The Capability Approach: Concepts, Measures And Applications
(2010), reprinted with the permission of
Cambridge University Press

Introduction

There is by now a vast feminist literature arguing that mainstream normative theories (whether they focus on inequality, poverty, wellbeing, social justice or policy reform) are often false gender-neutral and androcentric. Theories are false gender-neutral and androcentric when they pretend to be theories which apply equally to men and women, but upon closer scrutiny they are focusing mainly on male experiences and interests, thereby ignoring aspects of social institutions, or dimensions of well-being, that are of special importance to women and children. Often these theories have a poor underlying notion of gender, or implicitly rely upon sexist or androcentric assumptions, or incorporate empirical claims about gender issues that are highly contested . . .

This chapter is situated in this tradition. My aim is to analyse Amartya Sen's capability approach through a feminist lens. How far does Sen's capability approach address, or have the potential to address, feminist concerns regarding well-being and social justice? Or are there androcentric biases in the capability approach? I will frame my analysis in the context of affluent and technologically advanced societies. In such societies the biological differences between men and women have been reduced mainly to their different roles in the reproductive process (at least, if a person is able and chooses to engage in reproduction). The biological roots of the sexual division of labour have been weakened substantially in these societies, and can be eliminated almost completely in individual cases. Moreover, in these countries average living standards are well beyond those of physical survival. Empirically these countries often coincide with (imperfect) liberal democracies, where every person's idea of the good life would, at least in principle, be respected by the government, and where state and religion are constitutionally separated. In short, I will limit my analysis to countries where cultural, religious and gender norms are relatively liberal compared with other countries. This caveat does not imply that the analysis is irrelevant for societies or communities that are not affluent and technologically advanced and chat do not have a liberal constitution and laws. But it seems reasonable chat for these countries additional concerns will have to be taken into consideration. For example, a feminist analysis of the capability approach in poor and explicitly non-liberal societies would require extra attention for the impact of cultural, religious and gender norms on human well-being, and for how extreme poverty influences those norms and social institutions . . .

The first question that we need to ask is which aspects of the capability approach make it a framework sensitive to feminist concerns. There are at least three aspects of the capability approach that make it a gender-sensitive evaluative framework: its focus on functionings and capabilities; the key role given to human diversity; and its relation to individualism. We will analyse the first and second aspect in the following section and discuss the particular individualist nature of thc capability approach in the next section.

Human diversity and the evaluation of functionings and capabilities

The main characteristic of the capability approach is its focus on doings and beings and the freedom to achieve them, instead of the goods and resources that people can access or possess. In philosophical discussions on social or distributive justice, resources as a focal variable are advocated by many major normative theorists. In normative welfare economics, empirical analyses mostly focus on income, or sometimes consumption or wealth. Sen's aim is to criticise both subfields simultaneously, by proposing to focus on functionings and capabilities, instead of commodities.

Why does Sen advocate capabilities as the relevant evaluative space instead of resources? Capabilities are intrinsically important to people's well-being, whereas resources or commodities are only means to reach a valuable life. In other words, the capability approach focuses on the ends instead of the means of well-being. Why is this important?

People differ in their ability to convert resources or commodities into valuable functionings, hence a similar bundle of commodities will generate different capability sets for different people. While many theories of social justice and well-being acknowledge the importance of human heterogeneity, they either recognise only a limited number of dimensions in which people differ, such as handicaps, or they are unable to sufficiently translate this concern for diversity into their theoretical framework. Sen, however, gives human diversity a central place in his framework. For feminists this is very important, because all too often the agents in mainstream theories are very androcentric, in the sense that, either explicitly or implicitly, this person' s characteristics are 'masculine' characteristics, i.e. characteristics which are positively valued by the masculinity norms in dominant gender ideologies. For affluent western societies, these 'masculine' characteristics include that the person would be employed or at least be willing and able to be employed, and has no attachments to other people which might prevent him or her from holding a job. For many women (and very slowly an increasing number of 'new fathers'), this is a model that has never applied to their lives, as they often had to struggle to combine caring responsibilities for children, the infirm and the elderly with their wish and need to have a paid job. Care responsibilities have often been invisible and neglected in mainstream theories of well-being and justice, in particular the constraints which the world of care and the world of paid employment impose on one another, and how these constraints are different for men and women . . .

The capability approach accounts for human diversity in at least two ways. First, as pointed out above, it focuses on functionings and capabilities as the evaluative space, hence taking into account several dimensions of well-being instead of only one, such as income. Income might reveal much of the well-being of an idealised independent individual who is working full time, who is in good health and good physical and psychological condition, and who has no major caring responsibilities. But for an unemployed person, or a caretaker, or a dependent person, other dimensions of well-being might be much more important for their overall well-being. This is not to deny that income *is* an important determinant of well-being and can serve as a proxy in case other information is lacking or too costly to collect. The point is rather that the more a person deviates from the idealised model of an unattached healthy worker who has substantial control over his life, the more other factors influence the mapping from income into well-being. Femininist theorists have argued that accounting for this kind of diversity is crucial if one wants to develop theories which take into account both men's *and* women's lives, hence if one wants to avoid theories to be androcentric or gender biased. For example, for a young mother the availability of good quality subsidised child care might, next to her income level, be an important determinant of her functionings wellbeing, whereas this hardly affects the well-being of a single childless person or a parent whose caring responsibilities are taken care of by another person, such as his partner. Public goods, and the social networks on which we can rely, are just two of the aspects that can have a profound effect on our well-being levels. The well-being of diverse people should therefore be based on a *multidimensional metric* that can account for non-financial and non-material constituents—and the capability approach offers this.

The second way in which the capability approach accounts for human diversity is by acknowledging that the conversion of the characteristics of the commodities into functionings can also differ between people. Some of these differences will be individual, whereas others will be structural differences in society, related to gender, class, race, caste and so on. In the case of gender, discrimination is one of those factors influencing conversion, not only for income but for other commodities as well. Suppose a man and a woman have equal access to higher education and receive the same scholarship. Both eventually obtain the same educational degree and both want to use this degree to enable some functionings (like the functioning to lead an interesting life by means of one's profession, the functioning to develop self-esteem, to secure financial autonomy, to be able to provide support for dependent others, to develop interesting social contacts, to reach one's professional ambitions and so on). But since women are discriminated against in the labour market, it will be more difficult for a woman to use her degree to achieve all those functionings, compared with a man with the same degree. More generally, group-dependent constraints, like prejudices, social norms, habits and traditions, can affect the conversion of the characteristics of the commodities into capabilities. The capability approach thus acknowledges the importance of societal structures that impact differently on different groups.

It is important to recognize that the capability approach is not limited to the market but looks at people's beings and doings in market and nonmarket settings. Feminist economists have argued at length that economics needs to pay attention to processes and outcomes in the nonmarket economy too . . . This argument applies equally to inequality or poverty analysis; we need to take into account aspects of people's well-being and advantage related to both the market and non-market aspects of life. This is crucial for the assessment of gender inequality, as women are spending much more time outside the market economy than men . . . By making inequality or poverty assessments based on aspects of the market economy only, like income, earnings, or job-holding, we exclude from our analysis some aspects of well-being and advantage that affect women's lives more than men's, such as care labour, household work or how much one can rely on non-professional social networks.

Gendered social structures and constraints are important for *all* theories of well-being and justice, but not all theories are equally capable to include those constraints, nor are all theorists equally willing to take these gendered constraints into account. Most justice theorists do not make their account of gender relations explicit and do not respond to feminist critiques, but are implicitly relying on androcentric and gender-biased assumptions. This is strongly at odds with recent social theorising on gender, which generally tends to state that virtually all societal institutions have a gendered character and that for most areas of life this works to the disadvantage of girls and women and to the advantage of boys and men . . . It is striking that so little of this empirical and theoretical work on gender d differences and gender inequalities has been taken on board by social justice theorists. The important question which the capability approach faces is whether its further specification and operationalisation will be equally vulnerable to these androcentric biases.

* * *

19C. *The Capabilities Approach and HIV/AIDS*

This excerpt addresses the complexity of operationalizing the capabilities approach. In particular, Unterhalter looks at the problems associated with promoting capabilities in South Africa's educational system, in particular the gendered dimensions of the HIV/AIDS epidemic. According to the author, what at bottom is the problem with Sen's treatment of education to promote freedom? Is it really possible in the real world to obtain a nuanced and useful evaluation of capabilities? In other words, is Sen's theory just that—theory, which really can't be used effectively on the ground?

E. Unterhalter, *The capability approach and gendered education: some issues of operationalisation in the context of the HIV/AIDs epidemic in South Africa* in The Capability Approach Concepts, Measures And Applications (2010), reprinted with the permission of Cambridge University Press

Education appears untheorised in Amartya Sen's writings about the capability approach. In a brief section in the closing chapter of *Development as Freedom* the contrast is drawn between human capital theory, long the dominant trend in analyses of education in the third world, with human capability:

> the substantive freedom of people to lead the lives they have reason to value and enhance the real choices they have . . .

Sen describes the way human capital theory and the capability approach emphasise different elements of what is valued. Within a framework of human capital there is a narrow conception of the contribution of education to a limited range of indirect benefits for individuals, for example improving production or family income over generations.

The notion of capability, however, implies a larger scope of benefits from education which includes enhancing wellbeing and freedom of individuals and peoples, improving economic production and influencing social change . . . The problematic, but unstated, assumption in this passage and repeated in Sen's writing on education in India with Jean Dreze . . . is that the form of education linked with substantive freedom can unproblematically be equated with schooling. As stated, it is implied that evaluating only a very limited range of functionings that relates to the domain of schooling, such as enrolment and retention or a narrow notion of literacy, capabilities relating to education can be metonymically assessed.

Sen's writing on capability and justice is concerned with inequality and difference, and he is particularly sensitive to the ways certain social formations may entail women's complicity with gender injustice through adaptive preference . . . Given these concerns, his consideration of education, which fails to take sufficient account of contestations and complicities predicated on unequal social relations within schools, is surprising. The analysis he makes in much of his writing where education is mentioned often takes no account of differences in form or outcome of education. It is not concerned, for example, with the questions raised by curriculum in different education systems, particularly issues of the hierarchy of subjects. These are frequently associated with assumptions about learning linked to gender identities, for example that girls cannot or should not learn mathematics or other high status subjects, or boys should not learn about childcare. Nor is his writing concerned with the different modalities of education—processes of learning, teaching, assessment and management—and their differing and sometimes contradictory consequences for different groups. There is a remarkable homogeneity in the way Sen discusses education, a homogeneity that raises problems and leads to difficulties particularly when the passages are read as examples of the capabilities approach operationalised.

In this chapter I want to draw out some of the difficulties with these assumptions on the uniformity of education. This is not because I am hostile to the aspirations entailed in Sen's writing on capability, which I share, but because of the considerable empirical evidence that education, or at least formal schooling in particular contexts, may as much be a case of capability deprivation, as of human capability in development. In thinking about operationalising the capability approach I am concerned with the specific consideration given to complementary social theories that enable us to understand relations entailed by education and schooling. These theories need to be viewed not just as background context to an evaluative space but as having profound implications for how that space is understood.

I want to examine these issues at two levels. In the first part of the chapter I detail the ways in which Sen positions education in his exposition of capabilities. In the second part I look at a policy approach to HIV/AIDS initiated in 2000 by the Department of Education in South Africa and try to consider how the capability approach might be operationalised in evaluating this and what additional information might be needed. In the concluding section I return to a consideration of the capability approach in an attempt to explore how thinking about education raises not only the importance of capability for political and social analysis, which is the way in which Sen has framed the argument . . . A more refined theorisation of education raises questions that remain unresolved in the capability approach, questions that entail a consideration of how the approach locates and defines its relationship to political and social analysis.

Education and capabilities

* * *

Education appears in *Development as Freedom* in three guises. First, it appears as a feature of capability space, a very loosely defined set of facilities or arrangements that *enable* freedom. *Facilities* for education, Sen outlines, are a feature of 'the social and economic *arrangements*' on which freedom depends (. . . my italics). Here education is an uncontoured space, unmarked by contested power, history, or social division. Education merges into schooling. But this is a problematic assumption. There are some forms of schooling on which freedom does not depend, or where the relationship to freedom is complex. For example, schooling linked to indoctrination into a racial hierarchy, such as what occurred under apartheid in South Africa, could not simply be understood as the social arrangements on which freedom depended. Although undoubtedly that form of schooling, for all its inadequacies, did contribute to the conditions out of which a democratic society emerged, but for many decades it also contributed to the reproduction of repression . . .

Elsewhere, Sen makes clear that both opportunities (facilities) and processes, for example regarding education, are necessary to give substance to his view of freedom . . . But again this formulation does not distinguish between education and schooling. It does not take account of education facilities or processes that might not enhance freedom, such as those evident in village schools within some states in India where girls might learn subordination. This may be because they are forced to sit at the back of classrooms in the dark or because the ways in which they are portrayed in text books are always demeaning and derogatory . . . In a number of autobiographical texts written by South African women it is evident that they learn aspects of subordination through schooling. They depict themselves as gaining a wider education about social inequalities through participation in political opposition movements and reflections on the ways their bodies were racialised and gendered . . .

* * *

The capability approach and policy on gender, HIVIAIDs and education in South Africa

South Africa provides an interesting example of complexities and ambiguities in education and thus provides a wide scope for illustrating some of the difficulties in the positioning of education in Sen's writing on capabilities. In this section I want to look at what happens when one attempts to apply the capabilities approach to evaluating policies of the South African government for dealing with some of the gender dimensions of the HIV/AIDS epidemic.

The apartheid regime had used education as a major component of strategies for segregation and inequality . . . With its end the 1996 Constitution gave all those living in South Africa the right to basic education, including adult basic education, and committed the state 'through reasonable measures' to make education, beyond four years of basic education, 'available and accessible to all' . . . The 1996 Schools Act abolished the different departments of education of the apartheid era that had perpetuated inequity in provision. A range of funding mechanisms, a national qualifications framework, a common curriculum approach and extensive in service training of teachers (in contrast to the previous era) have been used to try to redress some of the inequities in provision from the past. But their impact has been relatively slow to take effect.

The racialised injustices of apartheid education were preeminent for those formulating education policy for the new democratic society, but gender injustices in education were not ignored. However, with the exception of some pol icy in higher education, the national Department of Education has been much less attentive to issues of gender justice than other aspects of equality. It has been particularly slow in implementing the recommendations of its Gender Equity Task Team which reported in 1997 . . .

Into this climate of slow but nonetheless significant reform, the scale of the HIV/AIDS epidemic came as a major shock. In the 1980s South Africans saw HIV/AIDS as primarily a disease of gay white men. At the time of the first democratic election the rate of HIV infection was still relatively low in South Africa, compared with central and eastern Africa. However, by the end of the decade infection rates had escalated dramatically. In 2000 it was estimated that 4.2 million people were HIV positive. This meant that at that time South Africa had the largest numbers of people with HIV in the world . . . The numbers infected represented nearly one quarter of the population (24.8 per cent) . . . However, the numbers affected as partners, children, family members, friends, community members, professionals, political representatives, workmates or employers were much larger. Women were estimated to comprise approximately 56 percent of those infected, with the single largest group of women comprising those aged 15–34 . . .

Treatment for those who were HIV positive in South Africa had been very limited until the government announced it would make antiretroviral drugs available in 2003. While access to cheaper treatment will make a difference in the future, to date the time span between infection and death associated with AIDs has been very short. Researchers for the South African Medical Research Council have described the epidemic as a series of waves. The number of people infected with AIDS peaked in 1998 with approximately 930,000 infections a year; the highest number of people living with AIDS was expected to peak around 2006 with 78 million infected. The wave of deaths from AIDS related illnesses is expected to reach a high point in 2010 with an estimated 800,000 deaths a year, although improved access to treatment might have a dramatic effect on this. The numbers of HIV/AIDS orphans is estimated to peak in 2015 with nearly 2 million orphaned children . . .

The level of HIV infection in schools is unknown as of yet. The HIV/ AIDS database of the US Bureau of Census using population based HIV survey evidence for 2002 estimated that in the 15–19 age range in South Africa 7.3 per cent of young women and 4 per cent of young men were HIV positive . . . A study in 2000 in Kwazulu Natal province estimated that amongst 15–19 years olds, the vast majority of whom are in school, 15.64 per cent of African girls were likely to be HIV positive compared with 2.58 per cent of African boys . . . The equivalent figures for other racialised groups were infection rates of 1.25 per cent for teenage white and Coloured school girls, 0.26 per cent for white and Coloured school boys of the same age and 1.29 per cent for Indian teenage schoolgirls and 0.26 per cent of Indian teenage school boys. The dramatic differences are the result partly of teenage African girls having or being coerced into sex with older men, also a group with high infection rates.

This information on the gendered dimension of HIV infection must be read in conjunction with related material on the high levels of sexual violence in South Africa. In 1998, according to Rape Crisis, there were 49,280 rapes reported. This was the highest rate of reported rape in the world, representing 115.6 rapes for every 100,000 of the population. These reports use a narrow definition of sexual violence when classifying rape. In addition, it is estimated that only 29 per cent of rapes are reported to the police. Extrapolating from these figures and using a wider definition of rape to include oral sex and rape with objects, the Rape Crisis Centre has arrived at a figure of 1,086,200 rapes per year, or an estimated one rape every 23 seconds somewhere in the country . . .

Sexual violence is a significant feature of South African schools. In a Human Rights Watch study published in April 2001, the considerable anecdotal evidence of high levels of rape and other forms of sexual violence in schools collected over many years . . . was confirmed and augmented . . . This large-scale study based on extensive interviews with learners, teachers, parents and school administrators in three provinces of South Africa documented how widespread sexual violence is and how it takes place in schools and on the way to school. Male teachers and young male pupils were frequently major perpetrators. The report acknowledges efforts by the government and women's rights organisations to try to deal with this long-existing pattern, but says that in practice the education departments and school governance bodies rarely do anything. The procedures and practices that exist for dealing with sexual violence in schools are grossly inadequate . . . This work is corroborated by other surveys. A study in Johannesburg in 1998 found that one schoolgirl in three had been raped . . . A survey on the frequency of rape amongst South African women conducted in 1998 with a large nationally representative sample of 11,735 women aged 15–49 by the Medical Research Council found that 159 women (1.6 per cent) had had forced sex before they were 15. Of these, 33 per cent reported the perpetrator as a teacher . . .

Qualitative ethnographic work confirms these findings. A study of two secondary schools in Durban in Kwazulu Natal, to which I have contributed, found that of fifteen girls participating, three reported a personal experience of rape involving teachers or fellow pupils. All fifteen reported firsthand knowledge of a friend or relative who had been . . . In roleplay activities dealing with gender undertaken with sixty learners, every single group, when asked to portray a gendered interaction, acted a scene involving a form of violence . . . In both schools, despite reasonably well functioning management structures, there was failure to respond at a whole-school level to cases of sexual violence involving teachers and learners. These were seen as individual aberrant examples . . .

A number of studies worldwide are pointing to the links between sexual violence and HIV infection . . . Research in South Africa confirms what has been noted elsewhere: unequal gender relations and extensive sexual violence often make it impossible for women to insist on condom use, and exposes them to increased risks of infection because of coerced sex . . . In South Africa discourses of masculinity which invoke violence or the ability to enjoy unprotected sex to demonstrate being a 'real man' are commonplace . . . However, some alternative discourses of masculinity linked to care and compassion have also been noted . . .

Thus side by side with South Africa's record on gender equity with regard to adult literacy and access to schooling, we must place the recognition of dangerous social divisions in schools, 'facilities for education', as a key part of the capability space and the conditions that facilitate freedom in Sen's analysis. Going to school for young black South African women may well not provide openings for what they are able to do or be, but may be placing them at grave risk of severe trauma, infection and early death. Education for these young girls may represent a key freedom, the capability to lead a fuller life, to realise themselves as ends not means. But it may, at the same time, signal a different and more sinister meaning of end. The process of education, in an unregulated social facility, literally ends the girl's life, destroying her capability. The high national figures on rape and sexual violence indicate profound gender inequities, and that girls are at risk even when they are not at school. But the failure of management in schools with regard to providing a safe environment for education places the assumption of education simply and unproblematically on enhancing capabilities in question.

The South African government now has ample evidence on the high levels of sexual violence in schools and the extent of HIV infection. The strategies it is putting in place attempt to address some of the links between gender, violence and HIV. Can the capability approach be used to evaluate this response?

Sen's writing on using the capability approach for evaluative purposes stresses that the space for evaluation is neither that of aggregated utilities, that is, the sum benefits for a whole society, nor that of primary goods, the resources needed to realise Rawls' difference principle. Evaluations are to be made in the capability space and what is to be evaluated is substantive freedom of an individual, his or her active empowered capability to choose a valued life. In practice what might be evaluated is realised functionings, that is what a person is and does, but evaluating functionings cannot serve as a substitute for evaluating the capability set of alternatives that a person is substantively free to do . . . Generally in much of the work that builds from Sen, and in Sen's own writing, functionings are taken as proxies for capabilities. But in the case of South Africa, given the history of a racialised and gendered education system, evaluating functionings is very limited. While evaluating capabilities has wider scope, this task needs to draw on history and social theory to provide an appropriate understanding and thus an adequate form of operationalisation.

A clear statement of the importance given to addressing gender issues in response to the HIV/AIDs epidemic occurs in the Tirisano plan adopted in 2000 by the new Minister of Education. The Tirisano initiative of the Department of Education was directed at consolidating the gains made in the early period of democratic reform in South Africa, where the focus had largely been on changing the legislative framework and creating a deracialised education system. Tirisano has been directed at deepening the quality of reform, paying attention to curriculum change, teacher development and measures to address poverty. Tirisano used an approach to planning that entailed setting clear objectives and implementation paths to translate generalised policy goals into outcomes. Addressing the HIV pandemic through work in schools was a major goal of the Tirisano plan.

Its first strategic objective was to incorporate learning about HIV/AIDS in the school curriculum, generally through the subject called Life Skills and to plan for the effects of the pandemic on the educational system . . .

Now we can try to evaluate implementation of this policy in terms of its success in securing achieved functionings—that is, firstly, whether certain values promoted throughout the school that enhance respect for women and girls have been put in place, and secondly, whether girls and women consider they are able to reject sexual harassment. We could assess success in achieving these by an outside measure of success. For example, an examination in the subject Life Skills could be conducted, or an assessment could be made by an inspector on the competence of the teachers and the school management in delivering the Life Skills syllabus and building a school community that supports this. Or we could assess the ways in which Life Skill s is working to enhance the status of women and girls in the school through participatory methodologies developed by those inside the school and by working with an outside facilitator. However, an attempt to undertake a combination of these two forms of evaluation in a study of an HIV/AIDs intervention in Durban schools I have participated in demonstrated how limited evaluation of functionings was. Pupils and teachers had a schooled response to the messages about HIV/AIDS, they knew the 'right' answers to provide . . .

If we use the capabilities approach for evaluation and consider not simply achieved functionings, but also the vectors of functionings, capabilities—the sets of alternatives girls and boys, men and women associated with the school are free to choose in response to the new curricular initiative—we will be looking for very different elements. At issue here are the feasible alternatives to the given policy. There are many feasible and different ways the policy could be framed and these need to be explored in relation to capabilities. Some public process of evaluation and selection of relevant capabilities would have to take place . . . In this process we would need to ask questions about whether the life skills curriculum enhances freedom and valued choices concerning life and protection from HIV infection or whether it just encourages a superficial understanding of the nature of the epidemic. We would need to consider whether gender differences in agency with regard to sexuality are enhanced or diminished by the new curriculum relative to some earlier baseline ideas about agency, gender and sexuality. We would also need to look at capabilities and approaches to health care and consider whether for many girls their capabilities are enhanced relative to a baseline of no formal schooling, which might be less risky. But it is unlikely that selecting these most relevant capabilities one would pay attention to the crucial area of the structures of gender inequality in the society that so profoundly conditions attitudes to sexuality, use of health services and responses to curriculum development initiatives. Just as with evaluating achieved functioning, it is difficult to make sense of the information without a social theory, so too for analysing capabilities. The capability approach to evaluation is likely to be extremely limited in fostering social change without some notion of gender injustice and the ways in which rape and other forms of sexual violence have been normalised in South Africa . . .

* * *

Refining the understanding of education in the capabilities approach

The very loose way that Sen identifies social space and education as a social facility or an enlargement of capability . . . could encourage a lack of critical edge entailed in evaluation utilising the capability approach as I have just sketched. In this final section I want to look at the relation between capabilities and political and social analysis, drawing particularly on what we know of the sociology and politics of schooling.

Sen argues persuasively on the importance of the theorisation of capabilities for political and social analysis. However, he is relatively silent about the relationship of political and social analysis to capabilities, leaving most of his comments gestural and associated with particular cases. See for example his discussion on the need to evaluate markets and their contribution to freedoms together with an assessment of democracy and the delivery of equity and efficiency . . . The way in which this assessment is to be made is left unspecified.

How are we to understand 'social arrangements' without an adequate social theory? As I outlined above, it might be possible to claim one was utilising the capability approach and view schooling as a space free of contestation, unmarked by race or gender inequalities, whose outcomes were always an expansion of human capabilities. In this reading the South African government policy would be an entirely adequate response predicated on aspects of the notion of capabilities. But schools are not outside society. It seems to me that political and social analysis are crucial to make the capability approach 'real' and that without an explicit acknowledgement of the salience of social theories of inequality, the capability approach lays itself open to becoming a hollow mantra.

Education is difficult to theorise because the word connotes ideas and aspirations, social relations, institutions and specific forms of understanding and skill. It is a process that is socially constructed, reproducing social inequalities and constantly contested, seeking to transform these. Different social theories looking at schooling will emphasised different aspects of these tensions. The importance of education for developing an understanding of the freedom to do and to be and for establishing our humanity is beyond question. But without appropriate social theories that allow us to understand what happens in the socially constructed spaces, in which the capability approach is applied, the reach of the approach can be limited.

Social theories themselves are not beyond critique, but those concerned with questions of egalitarianism have a commitment to social change in common. Social change is powerfully linked with human agency, which is itself central to the capability approach. In taking thinking about the capability approach and education further it seems crucial to consider the ways in which capabilities interface with the social and the political at a theoretical as well as an empirical level.

CHAPTER 20

THE RISE OF EMERGING MARKET ECONOMIES

■ ■ ■

We close the textbook with a look at rise of emerging market economies (EMEs) in the final two chapters. Today's world differs radically from the state of the world in 1944 when the Bretton Woods Institutions were established. Since the Bretton Woods Conference, countries of the Global South were "underdeveloped," "lesser-developed," "developing" or "Third World" countries, the last label having a negative connotation even though the term originally related to countries that didn't align themselves with NATO (U.S. and Europe) or the Communist bloc. But over time, some of the economies of the Global South, such as Brazil, India, Indonesia, Korea, Malaysia, the Philippines, South Africa, and Turkey, have grown big time. They, and some other countries, are referred to as EMEs today.

Check it out: According to two prominent economists, Ayhan Kose and Eswar Prasad, from the 1960s to 2008, EME's share of global GDP measured by purchasing power parity (PPP) grew from 17% to 39%. And if you look at the three big ones, Brazil, China, and India, their share of global GDP jumped from 9% in the 1970s to 23% in 2008. During the 2008–2009 global financial crisis, EMEs accounted for 86% of global growth, compared to 6% for the advanced economies. That's why when the crisis hit, people were saying that the adage "when advanced economies sneeze, developing countries catch a cold" no longer applied. In other words, the economies of the EMEs were becoming "decoupled" from the advanced economies. Eventually, though, the EMEs did get hit and people disputed the merits of the decoupling theory.

Still, it's important to know the story of the evolution of the EMEs because sooner or later they'll be in your face. So in this chapter we're going to tell you how the label EMEs came about and then we're going to take a look at Brazil as an example of an EME. By the way, we're going to use "emerging market economy" and "emerging economy" interchangeably.

I. WHAT'S AN "EMERGING MARKET ECONOMY"?*

Antoine van Agtmael of the World Bank's International Finance Corporation (IFC) coined the term "emerging market" in 1981. At the time, he was attempting to start a "Third World Equity Fund," but he had to come up with a more dynamic name to attract investors. Emerging markets were characterized by growing economies and increased wealth with low-to-middle per capita income. The basic notion was that emerging economies, such as the East Asian Tigers of the 1980s (South Korea, Singapore, Hong Kong, and Taiwan), were "emerging" because they were becoming significant players in the modern global economy.

The IFC's origination of the term indicates that it was investor driven. In 1992, the IFC's Farida Khambata coined the term "frontier markets" for economies that hadn't reached the status of emerging markets (because of, say, small market capitalization), but still looked like promising investment opportunities. Then in 2001, Goldman Sachs singled out Brazil, Russia, India, and China—the "BRICs"—as countries that, because of their increased global clout, should be considered for inclusion in the G-7.

Although "emerging economy" lacks a precise definition, common themes have emerged since the term's inception. Emerging market economies are characterized by significant and rapid economic growth that shows up in rising GDP in an aggregate and per capita basis, increased trade volumes, as well as increased foreign investment. The "market" part of the EME relates to orthodox economic policies that you'll usually find in most of them. The policies include, among other things, privatization of state-owned businesses, liberalization of domestic banking systems and stock markets to allow foreigners easier access, and decreased debt. As for trade, EMEs are generally more open to international trade than other economies, including advanced economies. While this openness is spurred initially by export-led growth models, it functions to diversify the goods countries export.

Economic factors are not the only criteria used to designate EMEs. Significant economic growth can translate into increased political influence on a regional and international scale. The level of international political clout varies from country to country, but EMEs generally are gaining power and influence internationally, especially compared to other developing countries. They're leaders in their respective regions, and lots of times are responsible for representing the interests of that entire region in global economic affairs.

The term EME suggests that a country so labeled is close to joining the club of advanced economies. But it's "emerging," and that suggests that an EME

---

*   This chapter was adapted closely from a previous publication of the author. See E. Carrasco & S. Williams, "Emerging Economies After the Global Financial Crisis: the Case of Brazil," Northwestern Journal of International Law & Business (2012).

still can't join the club because it has problems, such as policy failures, weak institutional structures, as well as weak financial sectors. You can throw in gross inequality, too. Policy failures might include ineffective monetary and exchange rate policies and poorly allocated investments in infrastructure, education, and health. Weak institutional structures relate to the regulatory regime, the judiciary, and political bodies. So the future looks positive but uncertain. (Isn't this picture condescending?)

> "The desire to be an influential nation drove much of the debate regarding slavery prior to its abolishment. Abolitionists feared that Brazil could not become a powerful, modern nation if it was the last country to abolish slavery, while the pro-slavery politicians argued that Brazil could not become a global power unless it was perceived as a white nation. The country eventually settled on a compromise: slavery was abolished and European immigrants were recruited to serve as cheap labor and reinforce the white population."
>
> —R. Roett, <u>The New Brazil</u>, 28–29 (2010)

Let's take a look at Brazil. It epitomizes the strengths and weaknesses typically associated with EMEs. Since 2003, it has pursued an orthodox macroeconomic framework that brought inflation under control, produced primary budget surpluses, decreased foreign debt, and increased foreign reserves. Its economic growth reached a peak in 2010, when it registered a 7.5% annual GDP growth rate. In 2011, Brazil overtook the U.K. as the sixth-largest economy in the world. Since then, though, its economic growth, like other EMEs, has stagnated.

II. BRAZIL

Part One: "Pre-emergent" Brazil

Yeah, it sounds like something you throw into the laundry machine. Anyway, Brazil went through of number of periods before it emerged. Let's have a look.

Post-Independence Brazil

Unlike its Spanish-American peers, Brazil didn't gain its independence from Portugal through an armed revolution, but rather by becoming a separate empire headed by a member of the Portuguese royal family. The country and its economy was dominated by the land-owning class and propelled by the free labor of African slaves that had dominated during the colonial period. In 1822, just before the establishment of the new empire, Brazil had the lowest GDP per capita of any New World colony and depended largely on sugar and cotton exports. By the end of the nineteenth century, coffee had supplanted sugar and cotton as the country's principal export. Industrialization? Forget it.

The monarchy outlawed slavery in 1888, and the country peacefully transitioned to a republic the following year. When the political climate stagnated during the first quarter of the twentieth century, it was young military officers who first challenged the old politics of the ruling elite in both the military and civilian world. The movement started by those officers came to a head in 1930 when a democratically-elected president was forced out of office in favor of the man who had been runner up in the election—former finance minister Getúlio Vargas.

Early Twentieth Century to the Debt Crisis of the 1980s

Although the Brazilian economy experienced its first stretch of sustained growth in the last years of the First Republic, it was under Getúlio Vargas that the Brazilian economy began to modernize. Under Vargas, the focus of Brazil's economic policies was to achieve self-sufficiency and economic independence through state-led development initiatives. Sound familiar? Brazil averaged 4% percent annual growth throughout the 1930s while most of the developed world was mired in the Great Depression. In 1937, Vargas consolidated his reforms after a self-coup of sorts allowed him to retain executive power despite a constitutional limit to one term as president. Vargas branded the new political reality the *"Estado Novo"* ("New State").

> *"For the next eight years [1937–1945]—until the end of the Second World War—they were to live under an authoritarian dictatorship, the state of siege or war made permanent. President Getúlio Vargas, backed by the military, exercised practically unlimited power. Indeed the Estado Novo represented the greatest concentration of power in the history of Brazil since independence."*
> —L. Bethell, "Politics in Brazil Under Vargas, 1930–1945," *The Cambridge History of Latin America*, 54 (ed. 2008)

After announcing the "New State," Vargas pushed the drive for industrialization by focusing state investment in the steel and oil sectors. Still, Brazil's economy continued to be largely dependent on coffee, and industrialization took its time. Then came President Juscelino Kubitschek (1956–1961), who made import substitution the cornerstone of an economic policy he claimed would produce fifty years of development during his five-year term. Go for it, Juscelino!

Actually, it was the Banco do Brasil that pushed the import substitution policies specifically targeted at industrialization. It issued a decree in 1955 that allowed entrepreneurs easy access to foreign capital if the government deemed their proposed investments desirable for Brazil's development. Brazil also changed its "Law of Similars" to make it easier for domestic producers to successfully apply for tariff protection against foreign competition. The government invested heavily in the automotive, shipbuilding, and petrochemical industries as part of the *"Programa de Metas"* ("Goals Program"). These import substitution policies had mixed results: economic growth but accompanied by inflation and regional inequality.

The 1960s were marked by political instability and military takeovers. When in power, the military regime used economic policies aimed at getting inflation and the budget deficit under control. The military regime also invested heavily in infrastructure and state-owned enterprises (parastatals). Their policies worked. The budget deficit steadily fell from 4.3% of GDP in 1963 to 0.3% in 1971, and inflation fell to about 20%. These adjustments set the stage for the so-called "Brazilian Miracle," lasting from 1968 to 1973, when the country's economy grew more than 10% each year. Changes to capital market regulations increased investment, which the government then directed towards specific industries through tax incentives. The policies helped dramatically diversify the country's exports. But the Miracle had a bad side effect: income inequality skyrocketed to one of the highest levels in the world—an issue that persists today.

Brazil's Debt Crisis of the 1980s

You know all about the debt crisis of the 1980s from Chapter 5 so we'll keep this short and sweet. The military government's drive to industrialize Brazil led the country to spend lots of borrowed money on infrastructure. When oil prices went through the roof in the 1970s, Brazil had to double the amount it spent on imported oil—money it borrowed at floating interest rates from foreign (mostly U.S.) commercial banks flush with petrodollar deposits from OPEC countries. The interest rates went through the roof. Mexico defaulted in 1982, followed by Brazil.

What's next? Yes, the IMF. Brazil had to devalue its currency, cut public spending, freeze all wages, reduce the level of subsidized credit available, raise taxes, and cut the amount of foreign borrowing by state-owned enterprises. After beginning to implement these measures in 1983, Brazil's GDP fell 4%, employment fell 12%, and inflation rose above 200%.

In 1985, the military regime handed power to a civilian government led by José Sarney, whose main economic task was to control inflation. Although IMF conditionality successfully lowered Brazil's budget deficit and restored growth by 1984, it did squat to control inflation. In fact, inflation quadrupled from 1982 to1986. In the hope of curbing inflation as quickly as possible, Sarney introduced the "*Cruzado* Plan" in early 1986. The plan introduced a new currency (the *cruzado*), and froze prices and exchange rates after de-indexing the economy (prices were no longer pegged to the rate of inflation). Though originally successful, the *Cruzado* Plan had unraveled by February 1987, and inflation returned as strong as ever. By the time Sarney's term ended in 1990, prices were increasing by 80% per month. Is that crazy or what?

Brazil in the 1990s

The 1990s was a critical decade of reform that set the stage for Brazil's phenomenal growth in the new millennium. In 1990, Fernando Collor de Mello became the first democratically-elected president of Brazil in nearly thirty years. His main economic policy goals were price stabilization, privatization, and increasing market competition. He quickly adopted a liberal international trade regime by lowering barriers to imports and privatizing many state-owned businesses—the first of a decade of reform that set the stage for Brazil's current growth. But, darn it, his policies still couldn't kill inflation, which continued to be a problem until 1994 when Collor's successor Itamar Franco announced the "*Real* Plan" designed by Minister of Finance, and future President, Fernando Henrique Cardoso.

> "On 15 March 1990 Fernando Collor de Mello took office as president for a five-year term. Few presidents were less well equipped by personality, background and training for the task. In addition, the challenges that he would face were not small. The economy was out of control: during the month of February, the Sarney administration's last month in office, inflation reached 84 percent."
>
> —L. Bethell and J. Nicolau "Politics in Brazil, 1985–2002," *The Cambridge History of Latin America*, 250 (ed. 2008)

The *Real* Plan introduced a new currency (the *real*), tightened monetary policy, introduced a managed-float exchange rate system, lowered tariffs, cut spending, and increased taxes. Inflation fell from just over 50% in June 1994 to less than 1% in September 1994. Happy days! Lower inflation has the practical effect of raising real wages by reducing prices, which in turn increases the buying power of wage earners and effectively reduces poverty. No surprise, then, that the vast majority of Brazilians propelled Fernando Henrique Cardoso to victory in the 1994 presidential election.

In his first term in office, Cardoso continued the privatization process started by President Collor, stabilized a weak banking sector, and started a conditional income transfer program to help the poor. Though the *Real* Plan is widely considered a success, and President Cardoso is credited with stabilizing the Brazilian economy, he failed to properly address the country's ever-growing fiscal deficit. Concerns over the sustainability of Brazil's debt began to arise just as the Asian financial crisis of the late 1990s hit the country. Go back to Chapter 10 to refresh your memory about what happened to Brazil. Henry's still there . . .

The crisis didn't last long. Cardoso's macroeconomic policies had proven to be successful—public sector revenues were rising, which gave Brazil more money to pay its debts, privatization had reduced the losses borne by the state, and increased agricultural production kept food prices stable—all of which helped blunt the effect of the crisis. The crisis quickly subsided and the *real* stabilized . . . Cardoso was constitutionally barred from running for a third term, and was replaced by Luiz Inácio "Lula" da Silva in 2002.

> " 'My presidency', Cardoso has written, 'was, at its most basic level, about trying to turn Brazil into a stable country'. Besides macroeconomic stability (and a greater engagement in international affairs, a more activist approach to multilateral institutions, in the post–Cold War period), his fundamental legacy was indeed political stability through the consolidation of Brazilian democracy."
>
> —L. Bethell and J. Nicolau, "Politics in Brazil, 1985–2002," *The Cambridge History of Latin America*, 267 (ed. 2008)

Part Two: Brazil Emerges!

Lula's Presidency and the Global Financial Crisis

It was under Lula that Brazil joined the ranks of EMEs. Yeah, his politics were generally left-of-center, but Lula calmed foreign investors during his campaign by promising to honor contracts, protect private property, assert fiscal discipline, and pay off debts! Once in office, he eliminated nearly all concerns by following the orthodox economic path of his predecessor. Interest rates fell to 6%, which made it cheaper for Brazilians to borrow money to expand businesses inside and outside Brazil. He also fostered greater ties with other developing countries to help decrease Brazil's dependence on the Global North as a source of consumers for Brazilian products.

> "The issues at the core of our concerns—the financial crisis, new global governance and climate change—have a strong common denominator. It is the need to build a new international order that is sustainable, multilateral and less asymmetric, free of hegemonies and ruled by democratic institutions. This new world is a political and moral imperative. We cannot just shovel away the rubble of failure; we must be midwives to the future! This is the only way to make repairs for so much injustice and to prevent new collective tragedies."
>
> —Statement by H. E. Luiz Inácio Lula da Silva, President of the Federative Republic of Brazil, at the General Debate of the 64th session of the United Nations General Assembly, (2009)

Like his predecessors, Lula faced a financial crisis when the 2008 U.S. financial crisis went global. But the crisis didn't last long. Brazil's GDP shrank slightly in 2009 before returning to booming growth in 2010, while the U.S. economy was still barely growing in 2011.

So how did Brazil handle the crisis so well? For one, like other EMEs, Brazilian banks had low exposure to the U.S. mortgage-backed securities market. Brazil also benefited from low unemployment and less dependence on trade with the Global North. Low unemployment and trade ties with the developing world meant that Brazil had access to a large number of consumers to keep demand for Brazilian exports high. Those increased ties were a focal point of Lula's foreign policy. No surprise, then, that China overtook the United States as Brazil's largest trading partner in 2009.

None of this is to say that Brazil went through the crisis completely unscathed. The government had to provide a stimulus package amounting to 1.5% of its GDP to spur the economy, but that paled in comparison to the stimulus packages in Japan (15% of a much larger GDP) and the United States (7% of an even larger GDP). Brazil's unemployment rate also rose slightly during the crisis.

President Lula da Silva's greatest success may have been his ability to increase Brazil's influence internationally. He led calls for a greater voice for the Global South in the IMF and to shift the main forum for global economic policy discussions from the G-7 to the G-20, which includes EMEs such as Brazil. Both of these calls were successful—the IMF is shifting more voting power to EMEs (including Brazil), and the G-20 became the main global economic forum in 2009.

Policies that Have Contributed to Brazil's Emergence

Several policies have played, and continue to play, an important role in Brazil's status as an EME. We've already talked about policies that have increased trade and foreign investment. Let's take a look at Brazil's emphasis on building the infrastructure. The most important infrastructure project is the "Growth Acceleration Plan" (known by its Portuguese acronym, PAC), put together by current President Dilma Rousseff while she was a member of Lula's cabinet.

> *"So I am here stating my first post-election commitment: to honour Brazilian women so that this fact—unprecedented until now—becomes something normal and can be repeated and expanded in companies, public institutions, and organisations that are representative of our entire society . . . I reiterate my fundamental promise: the eradication of poverty . . . We must not rest while there are Brazilians going hungry."*
> —"Brazil President-elect Rousseff pledges gender equality," at http://www.bbc.co.uk/news/world-latin-america-11666013 (2010)

The "Growth Acceleration Plan" is an umbrella term for thousands of economic development projects across Brazil that began in 2007. The program has several components, but the main goal is to improve the poor infrastructure that's led to social exclusion. The poor are more likely to live in areas with bad roads, poor public transportation, few available jobs, limited or no access to credit, and no mail or commercial delivery services. Surprising? PAC tries to remedy this problem by building or rebuilding homes and roads, and improving sanitation, sewage, water, and electrical services in the poorest areas of Brazil's cities. To maximize the program's impact, the government hires people living in those neighborhoods to perform the work. PAC's effectiveness had mixed reviews. In 2010, Lula announced an $872 billion extension of PAC—PAC II. Check this out: One of PAC II's goals was to make infrastructure improvements for the 2014 World Cup and 2016 Olympics to be held in Brazil, including building a high-speed rail to connect Brazil's two largest cities, Rio de Janeiro and São Paulo. Hmmm . . .

Let's mention one other policy. As Brazil has grown, it's tried hard to improve government institutions to make them more efficient for both Brazilians and foreign investors. Most important among these reforms, at least as far as encouraging investment is concerned, has been reforming the judicial system. A 2006 constitutional amendment mandated judicial reform and made judicial expeditiousness a constitutional guarantee—an important step for a traditionally slow legal system. A good start.

Part Three: Challenges Ahead

Being an EME means there are still challenges for the country. Let's look at something we're familiar with, the C word. Corruption in Brazil is a major challenge. Transparency International ranks Brazil the seventy-second least corrupt country out of one hundred eighty-three countries. The roots of corruption are too complex to fully explain here, but politics is partly to blame. Political parties are in a constant scramble for government money in the form of welfare benefits, government jobs, and contracts that would help influence voters.

Then there are the issues with Brazil's regulatory and legal framework. They impede foreign investment by making it riskier and more expensive to do business in Brazil. The National Federation of Industries termed these extra costs of doing business in Brazil the "*Custo Brasil*" ("Brazil Cost"). The cost includes high taxes and a tax code that's extremely complex, making compliance a lengthy and expensive process. Brazil ranked 116th in the World Bank's "Doing Business" ranking in terms of ease of paying taxes. It took the World Bank's hypothetical company 2,600 hours to fully comply with the tax laws. Add to that a slow and inefficient judiciary. Custo!

What really bites is inequality. In spite of Brazil's phenomenal growth, inequality is still an impediment: the World Bank has estimated that for every ten percent increase in poverty there is a corresponding one percent reduction in economic growth. For Brazil, this means that economic growth could increase by two or three percentage points each year by eliminating poverty. Today, the top 10% of the population accounts for 43% of total consumption, while the bottom 10% makes up just under 1% of Brazil's total consumption. While CEOs in São Paulo make more money than CEOs in New York City, over ten million Brazilians live on less than $1.25 per day. Brutal.

Land distribution is a real problem. In Brazil's largest cities squatters have illegally taken up residence on any open space they can find. The settlements have grown into entire neighborhoods, called "favelas," where hundreds of thousands of people live with almost no government services, including schools. The people in these neighborhoods (usually minorities) don't have title to their land—they lack what many people consider their most valuable asset. They also face gross discrimination from employers, banks, and oftentimes the police just because of their address. The favelas are often overrun by drug gangs and usually lack basic services like running water and electricity. Brutal.

When you see inequality, you'll see lots of people with no or poor education. It's bad in Brazil. What marginal improvements there've been in education can be attributed to President Cardoso's decision to mandate minimum per-pupil spending and teacher salaries along with the "*Bolsa Família*" ("Family Scholarship") program. Speaking of that program, President Cardoso designed the program—with technical and financial support from the World Bank—as a way to break the cycle of poverty. Through the program, poor families receive money each month (about $35) on the condition that they keep their children in school and take them for regular health checkups. Millions of families benefit from the program. And it trickles up: 94% of the funds go to the poorest 40% of Brazilian society—most of whom had never benefited from social programs before. The program has given a large boost to rural economies. From 2001 to 2008, the inequality gap shrank by 6%—the largest improvement in Latin America. Sweet.

You Gotta Know Something About Them!

Dilma Rousseff

Image of Dilma Rousseff by official photographer Roberto Stuckert Filho is licensed under CC BY 3.0 Brazil.

When Brazil's first female President, Dilma Rousseff, was a girl, she wanted to be a ballerina. Instead, she became a left-wing guerilla in 1969—her names were Estela, Luiza, and Wanda. She was part of the National Liberation Command, which aimed to take the government over by force. Dilma was caught in 1970—when she was just twenty-two—and spent three brutal years in prison, during which time interrogators used electrical shocks on her feet and ears, and hanged her upside down naked and bound. As President, she has led the nation without dwelling on those dark days of military rule, which has become the subject of a truth commission.

Luiz Inacio "Lula" Da Silva

Image of Luiz Inácio Lula da Silva by Ricardo Stuckert Fiho is licensed under CC BY 3.0 Brazil.

Luis Inacia "Lula" Da Silva was born in 1945 to an agriculture worker father and a seamstress mother. He didn't learn to read until age ten because his father didn't believe in education. Luis was forced to leave school after fifth grade to help support his family. He was a metalworker (he lost a pinky in a factory accident) before he became involved in politics and founded Brazil's only socialist party. Luis was elected Brazil's President in 2002, reelected in 2006, and was voted number one—yeah, number *one*—in Time magazine's 100 Most Influential People in the World for 2010. He goes by Lula—a nickname he formally added to his name in 1982.

QUESTIONS FROM YOUR TALKING DOG

1.   You're going to give me a ride in the car? Awesome! Let's go to the beach! Yeah, sure, we can talk about emerging market economies. What countries are considered EMEs?

2.   How could EMEs have accounted for 86% of global growth during 2008–2009? That's, like, fantastic.

3.   Can you put my window down, please? I don't care if it's bad for my eyes. Thanks. Sure, tell me how this term "emerging market" came about?

4.   Frontier markets. Sounds pretty neat. What are they?

5.   Can you look at these countries and see that they have some basic things in common? Like, what I have in common with all the doggies of the world.

6.   Of course, I want to hear about Brazil. Neymar rocks!

7.   So how does this story start with post-independence Brazil?

8.   Yeah, I've heard of import substitution, you talk about it in your sleep. How did it work in Brazil? Was it successful?

9.   Isn't that something. The military regime and its policies led to the "Brazilian Miracle." What did they do?

10.   Do I know about the debt crisis? Am I a dog? Seems like Brazil has always had a problem with inflation. What about this *"cruzado* plan"?

11.   Seems like most countries in the 1990s were into market-based reforms. Sure, tell me about what Brazil did, especially the "*real* plan" you just mentioned.

12.   So Brazil emerged because of President Lula. Why? Wasn't he a socialist?

13.   Can we stop here? You can get gas while I get a hotdog in my belly. Okay, when I'm back you can tell me about Brazil's experience in the global financial crisis. Happy?

14.   So what policies have made Brazil an EME?

15.   But Brazil still has problems? Corruption, of course. The what? *Custo Brasil*? What's that?

16.   Everyone's heard about inequality in Brazil. Give me some numbers.

17.   Yeah, I've heard of the favelas. How bad is it?

18.   This was fun. Are we finished? Okay then, tell me about *Bolsa Familia*.

Chapter 20: Supplement

20A. *Brazil's Economic Growth Hits Headwinds*

The excerpt in the text was written before Brazil experienced a considerable slowdown in economic activity. As we now know, the IMF's forecasted economic growth for 2012 was way off. In 2012, the economy grew just 0.9 percent. Growth for 2013 looks better, with economists forecasting 2.40 percent for the year. Note that the reasons for Brazil's slowdown are both internal and external. What factor exposes Brazil to global economic developments? Note the worrisome rise in consumer credit. Can you figure out what the Fund-speak, "capital flow management measures" means? What about the last question about the World Cup and the Olympics? Brazilians have protested over the building of stadiums when the money could be better spent on other projects. Can you figure out what Haksar is saying? Fund-speak . . .

IMF, "Brazil: Higher Savings and Investment Needed to Sustain
Expected Recovery" *IMF Survey Magazine:
Countries & Regions* (2012)

July 20, 2012

- Recovery expected later this year, reflecting substantial policy stimulus
- Brazil has buffers to absorb risks from European crisis and commodity shocks

- Domestic rebalancing would help secure strong, balanced growth
- Brazil's financial system is strong, but household credit expansion a concern

After strong growth in 2010, the Brazilian economy has slowed down, reflecting past policy tightening to contain inflation risks and, more recently, the weaker external environment.

The IMF is expecting a gradual recovery starting later this year as policies have been eased. Growth for the whole year is now expected at about 2.5 percent. But economic momentum is expected to pick up in the next months, with growth in the fourth quarter projected at about 4 percent compared with the same period in 2011.

Brazil, a member of the Group of Twenty leading advanced and emerging economies, has undergone a remarkable social and economic transformation over the past decade. Income inequality has decreased and the government has adopted a strong policy framework—most notably, fiscal responsibility laws, inflation targeting, and a flexible exchange rate.

But building on these gains will require higher investment and savings. Rebalancing demand from consumption to investment and net exports will help to secure strong, balanced growth going forward and support overall competitiveness.

In an interview with the *IMF Survey online*, to coincide with the publication of the IMF's regular annual health check of Latin America's largest economy, IMF mission chief for Brazil Vikram Haksar discusses the outlook for the country's economy and goes over the findings of his team's analysis.

IMF Survey: Why has growth slowed, and is the economy losing steam?

Haksar: Growth in Brazil had been expected to slow last year as policies were tightened to contain inflationary pressures, which had been a concern since the beginning of 2011. The combination of several economic policy levers—including fiscal, monetary, and credit—being tightened at the same time had larger than anticipated effects. Also, during the second half of last year the worsening external environment added to the drag on growth, including on confidence and investment. Investment has been particularly weak in Brazil during this cycle.

But policies have been eased since then and we expect growth to pick up in the second half of this year.

IMF Survey: Brazil's policymakers have responded to slower growth with a range of measures, including lower interest rates. Will this work?

Haksar: We support the policy mix that the authorities have put in place—easy monetary policy and fiscal policy focused on the primary surplus target to bring debt down.

Monetary policy is powerful in Brazil, as has been shown by various studies. There has already been a substantial 450 basis point reduction in the policy rate since last August. But there are lags with which monetary policy affects the economy. These lags are normally from 9 to 12 months.

We therefore expect the policy easing that started in 2011 to start having more significant effects by the second half of this year. Also, the exchange rate has weakened quite a bit since last year, which should gradually be more supportive of growth.

IMF Survey: The IMF has said that the risks to the global outlook have risen. What are the key risks for Brazil, and what is the best way to address them?

Haksar: Our analysis shows that the main risks for Brazil arise from the prospect of lower commodity prices, the possibility of tighter external financial conditions, and a potential drop in demand from Europe, which is a major trading partner for Brazil.

As has been documented in the IMF's recent World Economic Outlook and Global Financial Stability Report updates, global risks have increased. That said, we believe that the authorities have substantial room for maneuver. Brazil has built strong policy frameworks and increased its policy buffers. International reserves are at record high levels and liquidity buffers at commercial banks are very large. Both of these buffers can be used to support orderly liquidity assistance in the event of unexpected shocks that might hit.

Furthermore, if the global crisis were to intensify, there is substantial scope for further monetary policy easing, especially now that the implicit floor on the policy rate has been removed with the important recent reform of savings accounts.

IMF Survey: Capital flows to and from emerging markets have been extremely volatile recently. What has been the impact of such flows on Brazil?

Haksar: We believe that Brazil has appropriately used all available policy tools to manage volatile capital flows. In 2010 and 2011 when Brazil was receiving very large capital inflows, the exchange rate appreciated quite substantially, the authorities increased their reserves, and fiscal policy began to be tightened.

Additionally, when capital inflow pressures have been very strong, capital flow management measures (CFMs) have been deployed to offset this pressure. By the same token, when capital outflow pressures have arisen because of, for example, increased global risk perceptions, CFMs were eased in order to smooth the effects of this volatility.

The CFM framework in Brazil has been used in a countercyclical manner, which we believe has been appropriate.

IMF Survey: Bank credit has grown very fast in the past decade, particularly in the housing sector. Are you concerned about the impact this may have on the stability of the banking system?

Haksar: The expansion of credit that Brazil has seen in the last decade—both in terms of the rate of growth of credit and the duration of time for which credit has been expanding—has been quite high by international standards. Naturally, we looked at this quite carefully in our report and it was also an important focus of the Financial Sector Assessment Program analysis that was conducted at the same time as our review.

The financial system in Brazil has many strengths that mitigate risks—banks have high levels of good quality capital and large liquidity buffers. The supervisory and prudential framework is also strong and proactive.

However, consumer credit has risen to high levels. With interest rates in Brazil quite high, the debt service burden on households has gone up. This is a concern. Close monitoring will be needed to ensure that households have a manageable debt burden going forward.

Another area of concern is the rapid expansion of lending in the housing sector. But here it is important to note that, while overall credit has grown rapidly, including in housing, both have grown from low levels. The Brazilian financial system is small relative to the financial systems in many other emerging markets and certainly relative to advanced economies. Moreover, a large part of the lending has been to priority areas, especially in low-income housing through public sector banks. Again, this is an area that will require close monitoring, particularly as house price increases have been quite sizeable.

IMF Survey: How can Brazil build on the substantial progress made in terms of inclusive growth over the last decade?

Haksar: Brazil has had an impressive growth performance in the last decade, in part reflecting its gains on macroeconomic stabilization as well as higher commodity prices. This has supported the government's social agenda for more inclusive growth, which has resulted in sizeable reductions in poverty, inequality, and greater formalization of the economy, all of which have improved the standard of living and human development in Brazil.

Going forward, however, we believe that additional measures will be needed to ensure that stable, balanced growth can continue in Brazil. In this regard, it will be important to raise the level of aggregate savings and investment in the economy, both of which are low by comparison with emerging market peers. Beyond this, strengthening the business environment will also be crucial. This will not only create greater incentives for private investment, but also support gains on productivity and competitiveness, which are needed to ensure sustained growth.

IMF Survey: Brazil is embarking on two important projects, hosting the 2014 soccer World Cup and the 2016 Olympics. How can the country ensure a lasting and positive economic legacy from these events?

Haksar: These are two very important events and they do provide the country with a unique opportunity to support development in important areas. There is a need for increased investment by the public sector, which is low compared to emerging market peers, especially in infrastructure.

But public investment increases should also be matched by increased public savings to pay for this higher level of investment. One way to achieve this would be to find increased space within the budget to fund and prioritize investment as opposed to consumption spending. In this context, steps could be taken to increase the flexibility of the budget, which would make it easier to increase investment within the established fiscal targets. By leveraging these important international events, Brazil can provide a lasting economic legacy that will support productivity and growth.

20B. *Brazil's Middle Class*

An indicator of a country entering into EME status is the rise of a middle class—with spending power. But, as this Wall Street article shows, the middle class can overspend—on credit cards. Brazil's economic history is marked by periods of brutal inflation. With inflation once again raising its ugly head, Brazil's central bank is taking no chances. But raising interest rates has negative repercussions. According to the article, are Brazil's banks in a good position to absorb a wave of defaults? If you were a Brazilian policymaker, would you make the same choices?

L. Chao & J. Lyons, "Bill Comes Due for Brazil's Middle Class:
Debt Woes Help Explain Why the Country's Once-Dazzling
Growth Has Fizzled," *The Wall Street Journal* (2013)

SÃO PAULO, Brazil—Like millions of poor people during Brazil's decadelong boom, Odete Meira da Silva took out loans to speed her rise to the middle class. The single mom bought a computer, a flat-screen TV and started building a concrete home on the rough southern edge of this sprawling city.

Now, her spending spree is over. The 56-year-old small-business owner is today concerned with a less glamorous side of middle-class life: paying off debt. After her ballooning credit-card bills exceeded what she could afford, she cut back on everything and stopped home construction. On a recent day, a bare concrete staircase rose from her living room to an unfinished second floor. It is a reminder of her own halfway climb up Brazil's economic ladder.

"I still plan to finish the house, but it will have to be done bit by bit, maybe in three more years," she said, sitting in her living room, the only part of the house completed before she ran out of money.

Ms. Silva's debt woes help explain why Brazil's once-dazzling growth has fizzled and isn't expected to blast off again soon. Most people think of Brazil—among the world's biggest producers of iron ore and soybeans—as a poor country that lives or dies on sales of commodities. But aspiring shoppers like Ms. Silva fueled much of the country's recent boom, as consumer loans more than doubled to around $600 billion in five years.

Odete Meira da Silva borrowed to buy household goods and to build a home in São Paulo. *Rodrigo Marcondes for The Wall Street Journal*

Odete Meira da Silva had to stop construction amid ballooning credit-card bills. *Rodrigo Marcondes for The Wall Street Journal*

Now, many of these new shoppers are suffering from credit-card fatigue—or worse. Some are defaulting on Brazilian credit cards that can charge 80% annual interest or more. Facing more defaults, banks are now warier about lending.

As a result, consumption is expanding at its lowest rate since 2004. That is compounding other problems, including weaker exports to China and a manufacturing slump caused by a strong currency, that were already slowing Brazil down. With consumer confidence declining, Brazil's gross domestic product is expected to post 2.4% growth this year, after reaching 7.5% in 2010.

Complicating matters, Brazil's consumption boom sparked 6% inflation as demand for goods outpaced the economy's ability to supply them. That has put Brazil's central bank in the uncomfortable position of raising interest rates to control inflation amid a sluggish economy, a move that could slow growth even more. Economists expect the central bank to raise its already high 9% benchmark rate by a half percentage point during a policy meeting Wednesday.

Brazil's troubles offer a warning to emerging markets caught up in one of the most enticing economic stories of the past decade: the rise of middle-class consumers in the developing world.

From Brazil to Indonesia to South Africa, faster growth rates lifted millions from poverty in the last 10 years, bringing more people into the middle class and introducing many of them to credit for the first time. But while economists mostly view such credit expansion as a good thing, the case of

Brazil shows how middle-class growth can also be knocked off track by too much debt.

In Thailand, household debt soared 88% between 2007 and 2012, in part due to government stimulus programs that encouraged car sales. In South Africa, consumer loans have reached nearly 40% of gross domestic product, more than twice the average of its developing world peers. Russian consumers put nearly 80% more on their credit cards last year than the year before.

While workers in China are known as savers, not borrowers, the country is now trying to push its population to consume more to extend its recent boom.

But Brazil's consumer credit troubles stand out among big developing economies. Consumer lending rose at an annual average rate of 25% in the four years after the global financial crisis of 2008. As of June 2013, some 5% of Brazilian consumer loans were 90 days overdue, twice the rate of India and more than Mexico, South Africa and Russia, according to Fitch Ratings.

"All these people have been spending more than they have, creating an illusion of economic growth," said Vera Remedi, an executive at Procon São Paulo, a Brazilian government agency that advises people like Ms. Silva on how to manage or renegotiate their debts.

Part of the problem, some economists say, is that Brazil focused too heavily on policies designed to increase consumption instead of completing ports and roads to help economic production in the long term. Brazilians bought a lot of flat screens during the boom, but the country's ports are still so clogged some ships turn away instead of waiting.

"Brazil's external borrowing was spent on trips to Disneyland, suitcases packed with goods straight from New York or Miami," said Paulo Leme, who runs Goldman Sachs' business in Brazil. "That will have consequences in the future."

Finance Minister Guido Mantega and others say Brazil's economy is getting caught in a global slowdown and that matters would be even worse without measures to increase consumption.

Brazil's credit problems aren't expected to return the country to the kinds of crises that destroyed middle classes of generations past, economists say. Brazil's total outstanding bank loans, including commercial and consumer debt, are around 55% of GDP, which is low by international standards.

The country's banks are sitting on large capital reserves, which should help Brazil weather any deeper downturn. The central bank's reserves of $372 billion are a tenfold jump from a decade ago.

All the same, consumer-debt worries have prompted a rethink on how far Brazil's new middle class will climb, and how fast. The percentage of household income that goes to pay off debts is unusually high: In Brazil, it is more than a fifth of household income compared with 10% in the U.S., according to both countries' central banks. That is largely because Brazil's lending rates are sky-high, a leftover from years of economic crashes. The interest on an average loan is 37%.

Plus, the profile of Brazilian debt isn't as healthy as it is in countries like the U.S. A big chunk of U.S. borrowing is home loans, seen as healthier since home prices can rise. But Brazil's mortgage market is tiny. Brazil's consumer debt went largely to appliances and cars—items that lose value.

Car sales are an example of how the credit boom played out. Auto loans more than tripled between 2004 and 2010 to around $70 billion a year, as consumers clamored to own a key symbol of middle-class life. Banks were lending with no money down, a previously unthinkable concept in the country.

Last year, there were 2.9 million new cars registered in Brazil, a 130% increase from a decade ago. Economists started pointing to massive traffic jams of entry-level hatchbacks as symbols of development.

"At one point, I was selling cars with 80-month financing to people who made $500 a month," said Adalberto Fava, sales manager of a Hyundai dealership that serves a working-class neighborhood on the outskirts of São Paulo. "I knew there was no way they could afford it," with monthly payments as high as $200. Many of these cars were repossessed, he said.

One such buyer was Jorge Luiz Bispo, a married 44-year-old father of one. With an elementary education and few prospects, Mr. Bispo saw a chance to leave his poor childhood in the northern state of Bahia behind. He borrowed money from a bank to buy his family's first car, a used Volkswagen.

For a while, credit financed Mr. Bispo's climb into the entrepreneurial class. He also borrowed $4,200 to start a small business, a beauty salon. He borrowed more to send his wife to a four-year beauty program.

Within six months, the family was behind on loan payments, largely because it had underestimated how much debt it could afford. Ms. Bispo had to drop her college classes. The bank took their car. The couple is trying to hang on to the salon, but it is bleeding money as neighborhood customers, some grappling with their own debt problems, shy away, Mr. Bispo said. The Bispos are defaulting on some bills.

"Each month, we have to decide which bills we can pay. We're having a financial crisis," he said.

Political leaders worked hard to expand consumption, hoping to close the historically wide gap between rich and poor in Brazil. Under Luiz Inacio Lula da Silva, a poor union leader elected president in 2002, and his successor, President Dilma Rousseff, Brazil hired tens of thousands of new government workers and expanded its welfare system. It subsidized gasoline and electricity prices and directed government banks to unleash billions in consumer loans.

The strategy helped lift living standards and spurred growth. In 2009, Mr. da Silva cited the growing middle class in a successful pitch to hold the 2016 Olympic Games in Rio de Janeiro, an event he said would help correct inequality and inspire a poor continent. But policy makers failed to match their consumer-friendly steps with measures to improve productivity and long-term growth, many economists say.

Plans to improve ports, roads and sanitation stalled. In 2007, Brazil announced a $250 billion infrastructure investment program to make the economy more efficient. But many of the most important projects—new roads in the poor Northeast, new trains, irrigation canals and better ports—have been delayed by years amid poor planning and execution, analysts say.

The result: Consumption kept growing even as the rest of the economy was showing strains from weakening commodity prices and an overvalued currency. Brazilian tourists, many of them flying overseas for the first time, were among the biggest spenders among foreign tourists to New York City last year, city officials said.

Back at home, industrial production shrank as Brazilian factories lost ground to global rivals. This mismatch between consumer demand and economic output fueled rising inflation, economists say.

"The government insists on trying to get people to consume, but on the other hand, the supply, the industries, the companies, haven't produced that much," said Samy Dana, a professor at Fundação Getulio Vargas university in São Paulo.

Ms. Rousseff, who faces elections next year and gets many of her votes from the country's poor, has signaled plans to keep pushing more consumption. She recently announced a minimum-wage increase and a plan to provide an additional $8 billion in credit to low-income families.

Brazil's development bank, BNDES, said disbursements will rise 22% this year, after a 12.3% rise in 2012.

Ms. Rousseff announced Sept. 2 that Brazil's government lent around $500 million in three months so people in a subsidized home mortgage program could buy home appliances, too. Through the program, called "My Better House," the government extended credit lines to participants to spend on a list of approved items such as refrigerators, televisions and beds.

All the same, people like Ms. Silva in the unfinished house in São Paulo have to find ways to cut back. Her family keeps the lights off and takes short showers to save on utilities. She worries cold drafts from the dusty unfinished second floor are aggravating her youngest son's asthma, she said.

Though Ms. Silva's income of about $26,000 per year makes her a solid member of the middle class, her gains are precarious.

The family doesn't have a lot of education. Her eldest son went to work in his teens. Her youngest wants to go to college, but Ms. Silva is concerned he won't get in. The teachers at his public school are often on strike, creating gaps in his learning.

Crime is her biggest concern. They live in a rough neighborhood in a country with one of the highest murder rates in the world. Almost everyone in her family has had cars they financed stolen. Her eldest son recently lost a used $15,000 Volkswagen. He still has to make payments on the car, even though it was stolen.

Ms. Silva is an energetic woman who took advantage of government subsidies and credit to climb up the ladder. Barely getting by as a store clerk a decade ago, she heard that the government was hiring drivers to offer free school busing.

She decided to buy a bus and go into business. She sold her small apartment to raise half the $28,000 she needed. She borrowed the rest through bank loans and credit cards.

She racked up debts on three credit cards, buying household goods and $5,000 worth of building materials. At high interest rates, the debt on the construction materials alone more than doubled to about $11,000.

Now Ms. Silva is digging out from her debt. She cut deals with her lenders who agreed to lower her interest payments, reducing what she owed by several thousand dollars.

But other challenges loom. She must buy a new school van next year to keep her contract as part of a government rule designed to increase vehicle consumption. In Brazil's tightening lending market, getting a loan this time will be harder.

She says she isn't worried: "I believe things are getting better."

CHAPTER 21

EMERGING MARKET ECONOMIES: SELECTED TOPICS

■ ■ ■

Our final chapter explores a number of topics that you need to know about relating to EMEs. Unlike the rest of the textbook, here we provide you with excerpts of various pieces. You can think of this chapter as a bunch of interesting supplements. First we look at racism, using Brazil as an example. We follow that with a discussion of inequality in the context of Asia. Then we'll read about possible links between violence, free markets, democracy, and ethnicity in EMEs. Next we'll explore the right to information movement, looking at India's experience. The concept of financial inclusion follows—the movement to bring millions of people into the formal financial system, starting with banking. Wait a second. These topics are equally applicable to the United States!

We continue the chapter by covering remittances, you know, when, say, a worker in the United States sends money back to his family in Mexico. You should know something about securities markets in EMEs, so we'll look at China's markets. How about Islamic finance—for sure you should be familiar with the basics. Then we take a glimpse at the evolving global economic order after the global financial crisis. We end the chapter with a gripping epic battle pitting a U.S. district court judge against Argentina in the context of a suit by so-called "vulture funds." They hold some of Argentina's bonds and are insisting on recovering 100 cents on the dollar even though other bondholders agreed to receive only a fraction of what was due to them after Argentina defaulted in 2001.

Thanks for sticking with us throughout the textbook. It's been a good ride . . .

A. RACISM

Racial Democracy in Brazil: Pele is White

Exploitation sucks and it's everywhere, not just in EMEs. Racism is only one form of exploitation. This selection, written by Professor Hernandez, takes us back to Brazil. As the introduction indicates, Professor Hernandez's piece is a response to Professor Crenshaw's piece that examines the future of Critical Race Theory (CRT) in a supposedly post-racial society in the United States.

The CRT literature is enormous today. Put simply, CRT focuses on the relationship between race and power. Race-crits argue that racism is an ordinary fact of life—not aberrational. Another CRT concept is what is called "interest convergence," which argues that it's hard to lose racism when both white elites and working class people come together to preserve the status quo. Race-crits also believe that racism is a social construct, not based solely on skin color. In fact, the dominant sectors of society have racialized different groups of people depending on the period in question. Take, for example, the internment of Japanese Americans during World War II. Another very important concept is the idea of intersectionality or "anti-essentialism." CRT rejects the idea that a person has one essential identity. A Latina may be lesbian and have a physical disability. So there may be multiple forms of oppression of that individual or people with similar multiple identities.

CRT made its debut of sorts in 1989 at a summer convention in Madison Wisconsin. Some of the early CRT writers are Derrick Bell, Alan Freeman, and Richard Delgado. Other well-known figures are Kimberlé Crenshaw, Angela Harris, Charles Lawrence, Mary Matsuda, and Patricia Williams. The CRT movement has spun off a number of other critical approaches to law and society, such as queer-crits, LatCrits (focusing on Latina/os) and critical race feminists.

In this piece, Professor Hernandez takes a comparative approach to examine post-racialism. In so doing, she peels away Brazil's "official" identity as a racial democracy to uncover a system of "branquemento" and "mestiçagem" which has sought to preserve white supremacy.

In Part V of the article, Professor Hernandez discusses the Tiririca case as an example of intersectionality, oppression based on gender and race, and how constituencies seeking to promote social justice can use the law to expose Brazil as anything but a racial democracy.

T. K. HERNANDEZ, "THE VALUE OF INTERSECTIONAL
COMPARATIVE ANALYSIS TO THE 'POST-RACIAL' FUTURE
OF CRITICAL RACE THEORY: A BRAZIL-U.S.
COMPARATIVE CASE STUDY"

Connecticut Law Review (2011)

I.   INTRODUCTION

In her article in this volume, *Twenty Years of Critical Race Theory: Looking Back To Move Forward*, Kimberlé Williams Crenshaw turns her attention to considering the "contemporary significance of CRT's trajectory in light of today's 'post-racial' milieu." Post-racialism is characterized by a public policy agenda of colorblind universalism rooted in the assertion that society has transcended racism. Post-racialism incorporates colorblindness but is distinct in extending beyond the colorblindness retreat from race as primarily an aspiration for eliminating racism. In contrast, the rhetoric of post-racialism contends that racism has already been largely transcended.

In Crenshaw's consideration of post-racialism she notes that the present challenge to Critical Race Theory (CRT) is to preclude an "overinvestment in the symbolic significance" of post-racialism as a racial frame that disregards manifestations of racial inequality in its celebration of formal equality and a colorblindness that equates the articulation of racial concerns with an act of racism. Crenshaw convincingly demonstrates the fallacy of post-racialism and the simultaneous difficulty in dispelling it, given the contemporary racial fatigue and public desire to foreclose any discussions of race. To combat the Obama mania that Crenshaw notes sanctions all talk of racism as a racial grievance itself, Crenshaw urges CRT to develop a broader project "to remap the racial contours in the way that people see the world that we live in—then in so doing . . . create a new set of possibilities for racial-justice advocates." Crenshaw urges that the "next turn in CRT should be decidedly interdisciplinary, intersectional and cross-institutional." In this Commentary Article, I would like to suggest that the next turn in CRT also focus more deeply on comparative law.

Because the post-racialism racial frame casts a veil which hinders the ability to see racial disparities and understand them as connected to various forms of racial discrimination, what is needed is a mechanism for refocusing the U.S. racial lens. Comparative law can make a useful contribution in the effort to refocus the racial lens. A key insight from comparative law is its "potential for sharpening, deepening and expanding the lenses through which one perceives law," because of its ability to "challenge entrenched categorizations and fundamental assumptions in one's own and others' legal cultures." Indeed, anthropologists have long noted that we cannot fully see and appreciate our own "culture" until we have compared it to that of another. A number of CRT scholars and related LatCrit scholars have started the project of incorporating a comparative law component into CRT and the associated endeavor of applying CRT to non-U.S. legal jurisdictions. What I am underscoring in this Article is the particular usefulness that comparative law presents for the specific project of combating the post-racialism racial frame . . .

As a vehicle for illustrating the value of comparative law to the CRT project of dismantling the post-racialism racial frame, I shall provide a comparative analysis of an instructive Brazilian intersectionality case. Because Brazil is a country that has long claimed that all racial distinctions were abandoned with the abolition of slavery, it is an instructive platform from which to assess the viability of contemporary assertions of post racialism in the United States. Yet, as shall be discussed below, growing discrimination jurisprudence in Brazil shows the longstanding post-racial assertion to be false. To the extent that a century-old claim to a form of post-racialism in Brazil is shown to be a fallacy, the many parallels that exist between Brazil and the United States enable a salient critique of U.S. post-racialism. In particular, because of their objectified and denigrated status, examining the treatment of Black women as an intersectional matter, helps to demystify the barriers to productive transnational comparisons of racial ideologies between the United States and Latin America. In order to be concrete, I shall focus on a recent intersectional discrimination case that was litigated in Brazil. But before discussing the case, it will be helpful to first explain the contours of the "post-racial" Brazilian racial ideology.

II. BRAZILIAN "POST-RACIAL" RACIAL DISCOURSE

Like the United States, Brazil is a racially diverse nation with a significant number of persons of African descent stemming from the country's history of slavery. Yet Brazil's involvement in the African slave trade was even longer and more intense than that of the United States. This accounts for the fact that, aside from Nigeria, Brazil is the nation with the largest number of people of African descent in the world. After emancipation, Brazil continued to be a racially divided nation, but occasionally provided social mobility for a few light-skinned mixed-race individuals.

> "Of the 9.5 million people captured in Africa and brought to the New World between the 16th and 19th century, nearly 4 million landed in Rio [de Janeiro], 10 times more than all those sent to the United States."
>
> —N. Bourcier, "Brazil Comes to Terms with Its Slave Trading Past," at http://www.theguardian.com/world/2012/oct/23/brazil-struggle-ethnic-racial-identity (2012)

This social mobility was directly tied to the racist nationbuilding concepts of *branqueamento* (whitening) and *mestiçagem* (racial mixing/miscegenation), which can best be described as campaigns to whiten the population through a combination of European immigration incentives and the encouraging of racial mixture in order to diminish over time the visible number of persons of African decent [*sic*]. Indeed, the social recognition of the racially-mixed racial identity of *mulato/pardo* was a mechanism for buffering the numerical minority of white-identified elite Brazilians from the discontent of the vast majority of persons of African descent. Greater symbolic social status and occasional economic privilege were accorded based on one's light skin color and approximation of a European phenotype, which simultaneously denigrated Blackness and encouraged individuals to disassociate from their African ancestry. It should be noted that in terms of concrete economic benefits, few mulattoes radically superseded the status of those Afro-descendants viewed as "Black." Rather, the recognition of mulattoes as racially distinctive from Blacks served primarily as a kind of "psychological wage" associated with the prestige of approximating whiteness without any significant groupwide monetary benefit for such status. As a result, Brazil was able to maintain a rigid racial hierarchy that served white supremacy in a demographically-patterned society where people of African descent approximated and sometimes even outnumbered the white elite. This is in marked contrast to the demographic pattern in the United States, where, with just a few exceptions, Blacks have always been a numerical minority and have thus been more vulnerable to the white majority's enforcement of Jim Crow racial segregation after emancipation from slavery. In Brazil, with its greater population of people of African descent, the ideological use of the "mulatto escape hatch" was such an effective tool of racial subordination that Jim Crow legal segregation was never needed and all racial justice movements were efficiently hindered. But it was the absence of Jim Crow in Brazil that later enabled the nation to promote itself as a country in which racial mixture had created a racially harmonious society. In fact, until recently, it has been a firmly entrenched notion that Brazil was a model of race relations that could be described as a "racial democracy" exemplified by racial fluidity in its racial classification practices. Hence, post-racialism in Brazil, and much of Latin America is characterized by a negation that racism exists after the abolition of slavery. The denial of racism is justified by the racial mixture of the population which has presumably "transcended" racism. Existing racial disparities are instead attributed to the cultural deficiencies and socio-economic disadvantages of Afro-Brazilians. As a result, those who raise the issue of racial discrimination are viewed as racist themselves. These facets of Brazilian post-racialism closely parallel the rhetoric of post-racialism in the United States and the related fascination with racial mixture as emblematic of racial harmony.

Today, racial fluidity in Brazil is rhetorically based upon the premise that racial classifications are determined more closely by how one phenotypically appears rather than strictly by one's genetic history or ancestors. For instance, before a racial designation of Black/"negro" is deemed appropriate, custom dictates that an informal visual assessment of an individual's hair texture, nose width, thickness of lips, and degree of dark pigmentation be compared with what are stereotypically viewed as the characteristics of a Black person. Accordingly, individuals with identical racial heritage are often identified socially or informally by distinct racial designations based on their phenotype. For this reason, Brazilian and Latin American racial classification practices have been termed a "prejudice of mark," in contrast to the "prejudice of origin" which has traditionally guided racial classification in the United States, with its focus on familial and ancestral origins as the determination of racial identification. Contemporary scholars, however, note that the distinctions between prejudice of mark and prejudice of origin are overstated given the Latin American use of ancestry to inform phenotype assessments and the use of phenotype to inform assessments of ancestry. Brazilian social etiquette may permit the use of a wide spectrum of color and racial categories—but Blackness is still disfavored. While the United States has traditionally relegated all persons of African ancestry regardless of skin color shade to a single racial category of Black, there is a commonality with the Brazilian disregard for Blackness itself.

To a certain extent, prejudice of mark practices also permit economic and social status to mediate the determination of racial classification. As a result, dark-skinned Afro-Brazilians with higher socioeconomic standing may feel more entitled to claim a racial classification invoking greater whiteness than more impoverished individuals with the same skin-color. The interplay between social class and racial classification is rooted in the *branqueamento* (and Latin American/Caribbean *blanqueamiento)* whitening ideal which continues to be central to Brazilian, Latin American, and Caribbean race ideology. *Branqueamento* refers to the aspiration of transforming one's social status by approaching whiteness. An individual can become symbolically lighter by marrying a lighter-skinned partner, or by becoming wealthy or famous. For instance, a popular legend that is consistently recounted is that the dark-skinned soccer icon from Brazil, Pele, successfully deployed the *branqueamento* ideology when he had his birth certificate amended to reflect a White racial classification after achieving world fame.

In concert with the prejudice of mark and *branqueamento* approaches to racial identification, the Brazilian and Latin American/Caribbean race model advances the cultural practice known as *mestiçagem,* which asserts that race mixture has made racial identification a very indeterminate and unnecessary practice. In turn, racial mixture is rhetorically idealized and promoted as the national norm. But the national representation of racial mixture that Brazilians prefer is closer to White than to Black, and individuals are overtly discouraged from identifying along racial lines in order to maintain the national myth of racial democracy.

An examination of the census context in Brazil reinforces the importance of this transnational comparison. Unlike most of Spanish America, Brazil has included a color identity question on the vast majority of their censuses. The color terms used are White, Yellow, Brown, and Black. Although the Brazilian census schedules use the term "color categories," the color categories utilized correspond directly with racial categories. The "Yellow" color category corresponds with an Asian racial category, while "Black" corresponds with African ancestry, and "Brown" represents persons with mixed Black and White ancestry.

Demographers have noted that since the Brazilian census instituted self-classification for collecting racial data in 1950, a significant number of individuals have changed their color classification from one census enumeration to another. The racial alterations fell into a specific pattern in which a large proportion of those who classified themselves as Black *(preto)* on the 1950 census, reclassified themselves as brown *(pardo)* on the

1980 census. Similar reclassification patterns occurred in the census years that followed.

Sociological studies of other data collections in Brazil with racial data from both the respondent and an interviewer have more closely examined the practice of fluidity in racial classification, and have noted that the "whitening effect" corresponds to a very specific pattern. Seventy-nine percent of the time interviewers and respondents chose the same color classification for the respondent. While persons at the light end of the color continuum tend to be consistently classified, ambiguity is greater for those at the darker end. But even that ambiguity has limitations. Interviewers tended to whiten the classification of higher-educated self-identified brown *(pardo)* persons particularly when they lived in nonWhite regions. In contrast, there is much greater consistency in the classification of Whites living in White-dominated regions. Furthermore, the whitening effect of higher educational status on racial classification is similarly constrained. In the case of the darkest males, education does not vary the color classification. It is people at the lighter end of the color spectrum living in predominantly non-White areas whose classification is more prone to be lightened. In short, racial democracy rhetoric theoretically enables anyone to whiten themselves, but in practice predetermined social norms circumscribe it. It would seem that only in regions (such as the northeast) where few "actual whites" live, are light skinned persons of African ancestry with higher-education socially permitted to whiten themselves statistically. Where "actual whites" predominate in a region (such as the south), there is little flexibility for persons of African ancestry to whiten themselves—regardless of their skin shade or educational status. This pattern is even starker for men of African ancestry than for women of African ancestry.

Similarly, the intergenerational whitening of children follows a specific pattern. In a study of the 2005 Brazilian National Household Survey, collected by the Brazilian Institute of Geography and Statistics—the agency also responsible for the census—it was found that a non-White parent with secondary school or primary school education is unlikely to whiten his child from a marriage to a White person. It is primarily among the infrequent intermarriages between those with higher education in which a child is often statistically whitened. Intermarriage alone, and thus "one drop of white blood," is not sufficient to whiten a mixed-race child. Rather, it is the educational status within a mixed marriage that facilitates whitening.

What all these studies of the malleability of racial/color categories in Brazil demonstrate is that while factors other than racial ancestry influence the selection of census color categories, the actual practice of symbolic racial fluidity is restricted to lighter-skinned persons with higher education. For those with unambiguous white and black pigmentation and features, racial classification is more fixed and polarized. Even those studies which have examined the plethora of informal color categories that exist in Brazil have concluded that in practice the variation is all centered on denoting racial mixture, while simultaneously maintaining the polarities in meaning of whiteness and Blackness. Central to the Brazilian celebration of racial mixture is the notion that African ancestry is inferior and needs to be mixed with whiteness in order to be ameliorated. The Latin American trope of racial mixture as racial utopia continues to have whiteness as the ideal and the presumed locus of power, even while racial mixture is purportedly celebrated.

The White supremacist underpinnings of the racial mixture as racial utopia concept are made even more evident when one considers the intersectional gender and race specificity regarding the discourse of racial mixture. White elite women are completely precluded from the idealization of racial mixture. Their racial purity and class status are not implicated in the *mestiçagem*/cult of racial mixture; they are meant to continue the production of an elite white class. Instead, it is the intimacy of black women with white men that is the focus of national racial mixture and its presumed ability to decrease the Black presence within the nation. Further, while interracial intimacy is viewed as the prerogative of all white men, only working-class men are viewed as the appropriate marriage partners of black women. The gendered racism of the trope of racial mixture is also prevalent across Latin America.

Challenging the narrative of the Brazilian "post-racial" utopia is the work of Black feminists and Black social justice movement participants. Both have contributed a great deal to the production of knowledge about the historical and contemporary existence of racial stratification. With the growth of the Black social movement, social scientists have begun to document the existing racial disparities in Brazil that contradict the platitudes of post-racial rhetoric.

III. QUANTITATIVE AND QUALITATIVE INDICATORS OF DISCRIMINATION IN BRAZIL

While there are White Brazilians who continue to contend that the absence of Jim Crow segregation in Brazil has obviated the existence of racial discrimination in Brazil, a plethora of social science research indicates the contrary. This dichotomy is well exemplified by a study indicating that while eighty-seven percent of non-Black Brazilians manifest racial bias in their response to survey questions, only ten percent admit to having any racial prejudice. Similarly, while eighty-nine percent of all Brazilians admit that racism against Blacks exists, only ten percent admit to harboring anti-Black bias. In a later study, eighty-nine percent of Brazilians stated that racism exists in Brazil, while at the same time only four percent conceded harboring racial prejudice. Nor can Brazilians imagine an Afro-Brazilian equivalent of President Barack Obama being elected president of Brazil as a self-professed Afro Brazilian.

Despite its repute as a land of "cordial" race relations, Brazilians, like others in Latin America, are acutely aware of color distinctions and their hierarchical significance . . .

Socioeconomic indicators show considerable inequalities between black and white Brazilians, despite the fact that Afro-Brazilians were reported as 51.1% of the population in the Census Bureau data for 2009. Whites on average earn almost two times what non-Whites earn. Illiteracy among the non-white population is more than double that of Whites. Even with the advent of university affirmative action policies in the 1990s, Whites today are still admitted to universities at twice the rate of non-Whites. In addition, there is a consistent pattern of Afro-Brazilian investments in education providing less of an improvement in labor market opportunities as compared to white Brazilians. To be specific, with just two additional years in the average rate of schooling for Whites (8.5 years as compared to 6.4 years for Afro-Brazilians), white Brazilians average a monthly salary 3.6 times the minimum wage as compared to Afro Brazilians, who only average a monthly salary of 1.9 times the minimum wage. When Afro-Brazilians and white Brazilians have the same years of schooling, Whites earn forty percent more than Afro-Brazilians. Wage inequality exists even amongst Afro-Brazilians with the highest level of education, and the disparity is more accentuated in the higher income Brackets. In fact, Brazil's own Census Bureau, *Instituto Brasileiro de Geografia e Estatística* ("IBGE"), specifically states that "education cannot be characterized as a sufficient factor for overcoming racial inequalities in income in Brazil."

Clearly, the unsatisfactory life circumstances of Afro-Brazilians cannot be attributed solely to an issue of class status. As family income decreases, the differential disadvantage in access to schooling between students of European and African ancestry increases. Despite expectations to the contrary, economic development has not improved racial disparities in the educational system. Some commentators even suggest that periods of socio-economic national development have increased rather than decreased racial inequality, especially for those at the higher end of the social structure. This matter is only made worse by the racial disparities in university enrollment rates.

Examining Brazilian racial disparity in the educational context reveals startling patterns. A study holding per capita family income constant

showed that (1) non-Whites have a lower rate of schooling than Whites, (2) non-white students have a higher likelihood of falling behind in school than white students, and (3) non-white students attend schools that are apt to offer fewer classroom hours than schools attended by white students. Students of African descent achieved educational levels consistently inferior to those achieved by Whites from the same socioeconomic level, and African-descended students' returns to education were disproportionately lower. Whites have a greater, and vastly disproportionate, likelihood of completing college compared to non-Whites.

The deficiency of the public primary and secondary school content is magnified by the racialized treatment Afro-Brazilian children receive in school. For example, social scientists have documented that the majority of Brazilian teachers view Afro-Brazilian students as lacking the potential to learn. As one such teacher stated, "[t]hey can't learn, they're not disciplined, they're lazy and they give up too soon. All they want is soccer and samba. *It's in the blood."* Racialized attitudes are also manifested in the textbooks children are assigned, in which Black people are consistently depicted as animal-like, as socially subordinate, and in other stereotyped manners. When Black children are targeted with racist behavior by classmates who have internalized the societal bias against those with dark skin, school authorities condone the behavior by characterizing it as harmless teasing and joking. These racialized attitudes may in turn help explain the reasons for the neglect of public education by the government, and may also help explain why educational specialists observe that in Brazil, the "benefits of 'universally' designed programs to improve educational outcomes do not reach the poor adequately."

Yet, children of African descent encounter in Brazil not only an environment inhospitable for learning, but also racialized access to schooling. Even though it is compulsory for children aged seven to fourteen to attend school, it is common for Brazilian families to informally adopt children of color—in an unstated exchange for their unpaid labor—and prevent them from attending primary school, for school officials do not enforce the compulsory nature of education. The Afro-Brazilian students who do manage to stay in school often encounter a substandard quality of instruction. For example, in the rural Northeast where the majority of residents are Afro-Brazilian, less than half of the primary school teachers have themselves completed primary schooling. Furthermore, even middle-class Afro-Brazilian children encounter barriers in enrolling in the private schools their parents are able to afford. For instance, when an Afro-Brazilian college-educated professional woman sought to enroll her six-year old in an exclusive Sao Paulo neighborhood school, another mother asked, "Do you see any other black child here?" as an explanation as to why the child had been rejected.

The statistical racial disparity in levels of education is paralleled by the racial segregation of Brazil's educational system, in which students of African descent are relegated to underfinanced public schools for primary and secondary education, while economically privileged white children attend private schools. This schooling disparity results in a racially segregated public university setting as well, because the public primary and secondary schools fail to prepare their students for the public university entrance examination. In contrast, the white children whose parents are better able to pay the fees for the racially exclusive private primary and secondary schools are then better trained for the public university entrance examination. This all results in the free, elite, and well-funded public universities of Brazil disproportionately attended by white students. In turn, the major companies who recruit heavily from the elite public universities for their trainees end up with a racially exclusive white trainee pool . . .

* * *

IV. THE INTERSECTIONAL POSITION OF AFRO-BRAZILIAN WOMEN

The social indicators for Afro-Brazilian women paint a devastating picture of intersectional racial exclusion and bias, as is also the case for African American women in the United States. Afro-Brazilian women have the worst socio-economic indicators given the more intensive social barriers at the intersection of race and gender. The most recent government statistics reveal that Afro-Brazilian women are worse off in the labor market than white women and men of all races because they disproportionately work in the informal labor market without rights to unemployment insurance and maternity leave. Indeed, they are the most indigent group of the entire population. The median salary for Afro-Brazilian women is half that of white women. Even when Afro-Brazilian women have the same years of schooling as white women, white women still earn forty percent more than they do. Moreover, Afro-Brazilian women have the highest unemployment rate in the nation, despite the fact that they enter the labor market earlier than all other groups and retire the latest. Analyses of labor market changes during periods of rapid industrialization demonstrate that white women still gain access to higher education and better-paying occupations in much greater numbers than Afro-Brazilian women. In addition, white women continue to be paid higher wages in every occupation. In fact, when socio-demographic differences such as educational level and occupational placement are controlled in statistical studies, Afro-Brazilian women are still shown to be paid less than similarly qualified white women. Furthermore, "Afro Brazilian women who rose to the top of the occupational hierarchy experienced increased inequality . . ."

For Afro-Brazilian women, racial discrimination often takes the form of sexual objectification as prostitutes or direction to service entrances as presumed domestic servants despite the apparel and trappings of middle class status. They also experience exclusion from job positions explicitly and implicitly requiring "boa aparência" (a good appearance), widely understood as a white appearance. Even in the context of the Afro-Brazilian dominated domestic service sector, Afro-Brazilian applicants find that "[t]hey prefer white [empregadas] over black ones (pretas)." For those Afro-Brazilians who do get hired as domestic servants, they observe a pattern of white employers designating separate plates, utensils, and foods, seemingly motivated by a fear of racial contamination. In fact, the racial motivation of the employers is often quite explicit as demonstrated by such employer comments as: " 'No, you can't [work here]. No, my husband doesn't like black people' " and " 'Oh, I don't want you [here], no, because my children don't get along with negras . . .' "

* * *

In short, a wealth of qualitative and quantitative research confirms that Brazil is a racially stratified society in which Afro-Brazilians experience both explicit and subtle discrimination, and Afro-Brazilian women experience intersectional discrimination. The Organization of American States has stated that the pervasive existence of racial discrimination in Brazil will hinder its ability to meet the goals of the United Nations Millennium Development Goals for 2015, which it committed to as a precise and measurable manner of diminishing social exclusion in the nation. In the attempt to address the pervasive racial inequality of Brazilian society, the law has become an arena for change in Brazil. The *Tiririca* case, discussed in the next section, is one example of the ways in which social justice organizations are using the law to respond to the Brazilian post-racial myth of racial democracy.

V.   THE INTERSECTIONAL CASE OF TIRIRICA

Francisco Everado Oliveira Silva, whose stage name is Tiririca, is a Brazilian entertainer who in 1996 released a song with the Sony Music company entitled *Veja os Cabelos Dela (Look at Her Hair)*. The song was in essence a long tirade against the inherent distasteful animal smell of Black women and the ugliness of their natural hair. The lyrics stated in significant part:

> *"Tiririca . . . ran for Brazil's House of Deputies in 2010. Campaigning under the slogan 'It Can't Get Any Worse' and wearing a women's blonde wig, Tiririca took satirical aim at Brazil's reviled Congress . . . Tiririca was elected—with the most votes of any candidate in the history of Brazil's lower house."*
> —B. Winter, "What a Brazilian Clown Reveals About the Crisis in Legislatures," at http://www.reuters.com/article/2013/01/21/us-reutersmagazine-davos-legislator-clow-idUSBRE 90K0F620130121 (2013)

> When she passes she calls my attention, but her hair, there's no way no. Her *catinga* [African] (body odor) almost caused me to faint. Look, I cannot stand her odor. Look, look, look at her hair! It looks like a scouring pad for cleaning pans. I already told her to wash herself. But she insisted and didn't want to listen to me. This smelly *negra* (Black woman) . . . Stinking animal that smells worse than a skunk.

The lyrics struck a violent cord with Afro-Brazilian feminists. This is because the lyrics embody an absolute denigration of Black women. Moreover, the public message of disgust for Black women was a reflection of the troublesome but longstanding disinterest in Black women as marriage partners. The Black feminist NGO Criola, and a number of other social justice organizations, sued the singer and Sony Music company.

The civil action was filed pursuant to Article Three of Brazil's Constitution, which states the national objective is "to promote the well being of all, without prejudice as to origin, race, sex, color, age and any other form of discrimination." The case was a civil action to protect the diffuse and collective rights of Black women to be free of discrimination. Free of the criminal context which in Brazil requires a finding of demonstrated intent to discriminate, the civil court held that the defendant's authorship of the lyrics was discriminatory in and of itself because the words inherently provoke feelings of humiliation in black women. The court took note that because the singer Tiririca, who was often nationally televised in a clown costume, was a popular entertainer for children, the insulting and injurious content of the song was also prejudicial to the formation of Black youth. As compensation for the moral damages of collective emotional harm to dignity, in 2008, the court ordered payment of 300,000 *reais* in addition to attorney's fees and costs (approximately USD 162,000).

The monetary payment for the damage to the collective equality interest of Black women was directed towards the Ministry of Justice's Fund for the Defense of Diffuse Rights, for "the creation of educational anti-racism youth programs disseminated through radio, television, film, and printed materials for elementary schools in the state."

With the judge's conclusion that the popular song lyrics were inherently discriminatory, the official image of Brazil as a post-racial democracy begins to erode. What the case immediately begins to deconstruct is the notion that Brazil's racial situation is less severe than that of the United States due to its predisposition for recognizing racial mixture and fluidity in racial identity, in contrast to the restrictive black white racial binary of the United States. In other words, how significant is it to live in Brazil's "racial democracy" or racially mixed paradise, when Black women are targeted as objects of ridicule because of deeply racialized stereotypes regarding their Blackness?

Thus, by looking at the operation of Brazilian racial democracy from the intersectional position of Black women, the mystique of its own "post racialism" is dispelled, and the common subordinated plight of Afrodescended women in the United States and Brazil is revealed. In effect, a critical intersectional examination of Brazilian post-racial/racial democracy, diminishes the promise of post-racialism as the end of U.S. racism. Bluntly stated, a critical examination of the Brazilian "racial democracy" delivers the powerful message of "don't believe the hype," for a U.S. audience otherwise subject to the deceptive allure of "postracial" discourse. Furthermore, the Brazilian case study also illustrates how resistance to post-racialism can be possible even after decades of postracial rhetoric. In short, comparative CRT clarifies the commonalities in subordination that varied racial ideologies can share, but appear opaque in isolation. Comparative law can be yet another CRT tool for revealing and addressing racial subordination.

You Gotta Know Something About Them!

Criola

This Brazilian non-profit organization, set up 1992, has Afro-Brazilian women's back by confronting racism, sexism, and homophobia via various projects and collaborations. Most of Criola's work is in Rio de Janeiro where it works on a bunch of stuff with black women, including health and jobs. Check it out: It holds an annual Festival of Art, Culture, Health and Citizenship where professionals consult with the public about women's health issues and preventive care. Rock on.

QUESTIONS FROM YOUR TALKING DOG

1.   You know, people always talk about Brazilian soccer as the beautiful game. It's really not that way anymore. It looks more like a European game . . . I don't sleep on your lap all the time that you're watching games. No, I don't know much about race and racism in Brazil. Sounds like this is going to be a

heavy conversation. I'm ready. *Branqueamento* and *mestiçagem*. What's that all about?

2.   No Jim Crow laws in Brazil. Okay. So what? Phenotype? Huh? Slow down and explain.

3.   What did you say about Pele? He's a soccer god! A white God? Why would he do that?

4.   Whitening? Is that like toothpaste? Then what is it?

5.   Gender always comes up, doesn't it? Tell me more.

6.   Sure, give me some numbers on inequality. But not too many. I'm a dog, remember?

7.   Education is, like, super important—at least that's what most people say. What about ed in Brazil?

8.   What happens if you're an Afro-Brazilian woman?

9.   Yeah, sure, tell me about the Tiririca case.

10.   So what race is the national team?

B. INEQUALITY

It's Not All About Morality

As you know from studying Brazil, one of the markers of an EME is inequality. This paper looks at rising inequality in Asia. Note that poverty reduction doesn't necessarily mean reduction in inequality. Predictably, inequality of opportunity is one of the main culprits of inequality. The paper indicates that inequality can impede the rise of the middle class. A robust middle class in the EMEs and developing countries is key to sustained development. Another compelling issue for policymakers is "pure luck." In other words, as the paper indicates, an individual can't control where she will be born or what her gender will be. Should government policy take this into account? Notice also that global financial integration increases inequality. If increased inequality is a form of violence, then once again we see that international finance is violence. What do you think of the recommended policy responses? Do you see anything new?

J. ZHUANG, R. KANBUR, & C. RHEE, ASIAN DEVELOPMENT
BANK INSTITUTE, "RISING INEQUALITY IN ASIA
AND POLICY IMPLICATIONS"

(2014)

1.   INTRODUCTION

Poverty reduction in developing Asia over the past two decades has happened faster than in any other region of the world, at any other time in history. Still, the bulk of the region's population lives in countries with rising inequality. This is in contrast to both the "growth with equity" story that marked the transformation of the newly industrialized economies in the 1960s and 1970s, and to recent trends in some other parts of the developing world, in particular Latin America, where income inequality has been narrowing since the 1990s.

The drivers of Asia's rapid growth—technological change, globalization, and market-oriented reform—have had significant distributional consequences. These drivers have favored owners of capital over labor, skilled over unskilled workers, and urban and coastal areas over rural and inland regions. Furthermore, unequal access to opportunity caused by institutional weaknesses and social exclusion has compounded the impacts of these forces. All these combined have led to a falling share of labor income in national income, increasing premiums on human capital, and growing spatial disparity—all contributing to rising inequality.

This dilemma presents a huge challenge for Asian governments. The three drivers of rising inequality cannot and should not be blocked, because they are the same forces that drive productivity and income growth. This paper outlines a number of policy options for Asian policy makers to consider in addressing rising inequality. These options, aiming to equalize opportunity and, thereby, reduce inequality, include efficient fiscal measures that reduce inequality in human capital, policies that work toward more and high-quality jobs, interventions that narrow spatial disparity, and reforms that strengthen governance, level the playing field, and eliminate social exclusion.

2.   RECENT TRENDS IN INEQUALITY IN DEVELOPING ASIA

In the last two decades, many countries in Asia and the Pacific have achieved remarkable growth and poverty reduction. From 1990 to 2010, the average annual growth rate of gross domestic product (GDP) for developing Asia reached 7% in 2005 purchasing power parity (PPP) terms—more than double the 3.4% for Latin America and the Caribbean (Figure 1). This growth was driven mainly by the People's Republic of China (PRC) and India—the world's two most populous countries—with annual GDP growth of 9.9% and 6.4%, respectively.

The rapid growth has dramatically improved living standards and greatly reduced poverty.

> "Take South Korea. In the early 1960s, the country's per capita income was similar to that of Sudan. Today an O.E.C.D. economy, South Korea turns out smartphones, chips and cars, and a taxi ride from the airport to central Seoul costs as much as anywhere in the world. Other economies, having hit their stride slightly later, are in the process of delivering equally impressive gains in prosperity."
> —F. Neumann, "Asia's Perilous Inequality," The New York Times, at http://www.nytimes.com/2012/03/07/opinion/asias-perilous-inequality.html (2012)

> "The main cause of increased inequality, especially in China, is the differing fortunes of rural and urban households. Productivity—and hence income—is growing much more slowly in agriculture, on which most of the poor depend, than in manufacturing services."
> —"For Whosoever Hath, To Him Shall Be Given, and He Shall Have More," The Economist, at http://www.economist.com/node/9616888 (2007)

During 1990–2010, the region's average per capita GDP in 2005 PPP terms increased from $1,633 to $5,133. The percentage of the population living at or below the $1.25-a-day poverty line fell from 53% in 1990 to 21% in 2010, as about 700 million people were lifted out of poverty. Seventeen countries reduced poverty by more than 15 percentage points in the period.

Figure 1: Gross Domestic Product Growth and Poverty Reduction

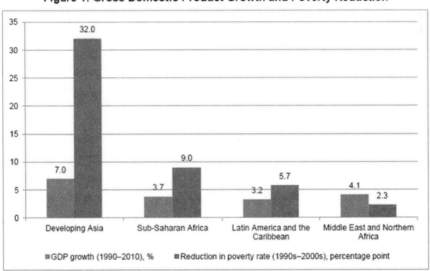

GDP = gross domestic product.

Source: Kanbur, R., C. Rhee, and J. Zhuang. 2014. *Inequality in Asia and the Pacific: Trends, Drivers, and Policy Implications*. London: Routledge / Asian Development Bank.

Growth and poverty reduction have, however, been accompanied by rising inequality in many countries. Of the 28 economies that have comparative data between the 1990s and 2000s, 12—accounting for more than 80% of developing Asia's population in 2010—experienced rising inequality (see Figure 2).

- The Gini coefficient of per capita expenditure worsened in 12 economies, including the PRC, India, and Indonesia. From the early 1990s to the late 2000s, the Gini coefficient increased from 32 to 43 in the PRC, from 33 to 37 in India, and from 29 to 39 in Indonesia. There appears to be a positive, statistically significant relationship between the increase in the Gini coefficient and GDP growth.

- The change in the quintile ratio is more pronounced than the change in the Gini for all 12 economies. This suggests that rising inequality has been driven by the rich getting richer much faster than the poor.

- The expenditure shares of the richest 1% and 5% of population also show rising gaps between the rich and the poor. For many of the countries with available data, the expenditure share of the richest 1% was in the range of 6–9% and the share of the richest 5% was in the range of 17–22%. For the Pacific countries, the shares of the richest 1% and 5% are higher with wider variation, at 5–16% and 15–28%, respectively.

- Although Asia's inequality levels are generally below those in other developing regions—developing Asia's range of Gini coefficients is 28–51, compared with 30–66 for Sub-Saharan Africa and 45–60 for Latin America and the Caribbean—incquality declined elsewhere, with the exception of the Organisation for Economic Co-operation and Development (OECD) countries. The majority of the OECD countries—with Gini coefficients in the range of 25–40—also experienced rising inequality in the last two decades.

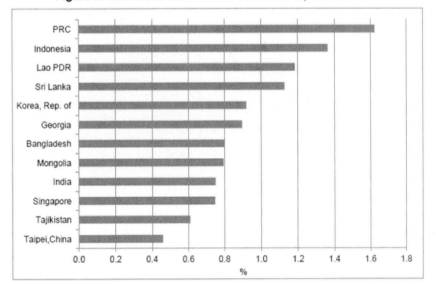

Figure 2: Annual Growth of Gini Coefficients, 1990s–2000s

PRC = People's Republic of China, Lao PDR = Lao People's Democratic Republic.

Source: Asian Development Bank. 2012. *Asian Development Outlook 2012*. Manila, Philippines: Asian Development Bank.

Another challenge facing developing Asia is inequality of opportunity, which is a crucial factor in widening income inequality. Huge disparities exist in the means to raise one's living standards, such as physical assets (e.g., capital and land), human capital (e.g., education and health), and market access (e.g., labor and finance). Inequality of opportunity also derives from unequal access to public services, especially education and health. National household surveys conducted in the mid to late 2000s revealed many facets of diverging opportunities:

- School-age children from households in the poorest income quintile were three to five times as likely to be out of primary and secondary school as their peers in the richest quintile in some countries. The situation was worse for tertiary education where poorer college-age individuals were 10–20 times more likely not to attend college than their better-off peers.

- Infant mortality rates among the poorest households in some countries were double or triple the rates among the richest households. In the most extreme examples, the chance of a poor infant dying at birth was more than 10 times higher than for an infant born to a rich family.

- With few exceptions, the region's economies have made significant progress toward gender parity in primary and secondary education. Yet, high gender disparities in tertiary education remain in South Asia and the Pacific.

> *"Even before the recent economic and financial crisis, Asia was estimated to be losing 42 to 47 billion dollars a year because of limits on women's access to employment opportunities and another 16 to 30 billion dollars a year as a result of gender gaps in education..."*
> —"Asia Leads World In Gender Inequality," at http://www.dawn.com/news/625141/asia-leads-world-in-gender-inequality (2011); based on estimates from the United Nations.

Inequality of opportunity and income can lead to a vicious circle as unequal opportunities create income disparities, which in turn lead to differences in future opportunities for individuals and households.

3.   WHY INEQUALITY MATTERS

Rising inequality hampers poverty reduction. Economic growth will generate a lower rate of poverty reduction when inequality is increasing than when it remains unchanged or is decreasing. Simulations reveal how rising inequality holds back poverty reduction (Figure 3). Had inequality not increased, the poverty headcount rate at the $1.25-a-day poverty line would have been:

- 29.5% instead of the actual 32.7% in 2010 in India;
- 4.9% instead of the actual 13.1% in 2008 in the PRC; and
- 6.1% instead of the actual 16.3% in 2011 in Indonesia.

Figure 3: Actual and Simulated Poverty Rates at the $1.25-a-Day Poverty Line, 1990s–2000s

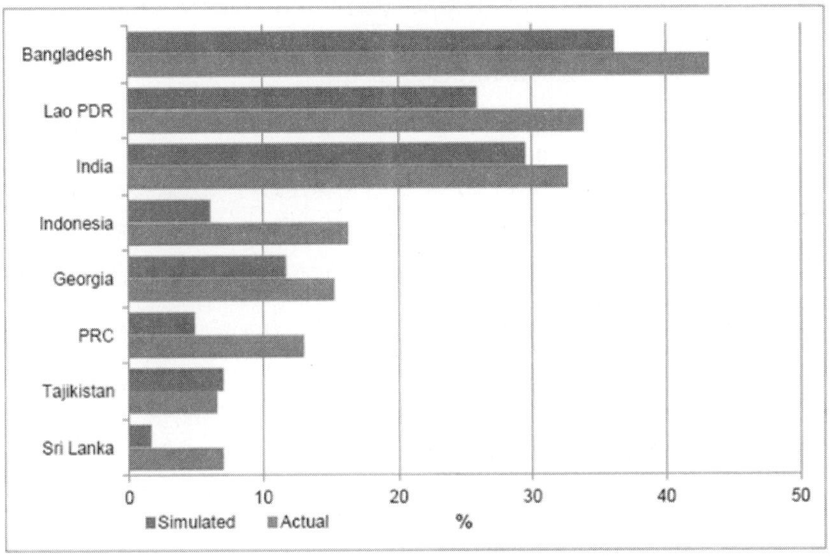

PRC = People's Republic of China, Lao PDR = Lao People's Democratic Republic.

Note: The simulated poverty rate is the poverty rate that would have been observed in the final year (with the same mean per capita expenditure) had inequality remained at its level during the initial year.

Source: Simulations using PovcalNet (accessed 9 March 2012) and synthetic expenditure data derived from household surveys.

For the 12 economies, the cost of rising inequality equates to 240 million more people being trapped under the $1.25-a-day poverty line—6.5% of the region's current population.

Inequality can weaken the basis of growth itself. High and rising inequality can affect growth through a number of economic, social, and political mechanisms. Inequality of wealth and income can lead to large divergences in human capital. Those with little wealth or low income face formidable challenges in investing in human capital, or wealth- and income-enhancing activities, and will remain poor. In principle they may be able to borrow for investment purposes, but imperfect financial markets, coupled with other market failures, often heavily constrain their ability to borrow and invest.

Widening inequality—leaving more people at the top and bottom of the income distribution—can mean a smaller middle class. Growth driven by and benefiting a middle class is more likely to be sustained; both economically, to the extent that the rent seeking and corruption associated with highly concentrated gains to growth are avoided; and politically, to the extent that conflict and horizontal inequalities between racial and ethnic groups are easier to manage.

In fact, there is a broad consensus among researchers on the link between inequality and the quality of institutions. On several dimensions, ranging from political stability, through to institutional stability and property rights, the negative impact of inequality on institutional quality seems to be well established, although the two-way causality is also widely accepted. Similarly, the effect of inequality on crime and violence and, through that, on the investment climate is also recognized.

Finally, greater inequality may lead to a political backlash, in which pressure for governments to enact populist policy measures grows. In response to the rising demands, the political process may favor policies that benefit the lower end of the income distribution in the short term, but also hold back efficiency and growth in the long run. Under such conditions, the interests of the political system diverge from the interests of the economy as a whole. This is a widespread concern in developing and developed countries alike.

> *"The rice pledging scheme uses taxpayer funds to subsidise government purchase of rice at prices 30 to 40 per cent above the market price. The benefit received by a farmer depends on the quantity of rice sold, not the quantity produced, some of which farmers consume themselves. The effect is that larger farmers, who sell the most, receive a disproportionate share of the benefits . . . . These populist interventions focus on short-term political benefits to the government, through gaining votes and economic benefits to favoured special interests, while ignoring the need to craft long-term solutions to the country's problems."*
> —P. Warr, "The Changing Face of Thai Populism," at http://www.eastasiaforum.org/2013/06/12/the-changing-face-of-thai-populism/ (2013)

Asian governments are responding to rising inequality, as seen in their development plans, which include explicit goals to make growth more inclusive. In India, the government made an explicit commitment to inclusive growth in the Eleventh Five-Year Plan (2007–2012). The central vision of the plan is "not just faster growth but also inclusive growth, that is, a growth process which yields broad based benefits and ensures equality of opportunity for all." The development goal in the PRC's Eleventh Five-Year Plan (2006–2010) is to build a harmonious society. This goal has been reaffirmed in the Twelfth Five-Year Plan (2011–2015), with greater emphasis on the quality—not just the rate—of growth, and making growth inclusive. In Indonesia, Malaysia, and the Philippines, inclusive growth or development is at the heart of current medium-term development strategies.

The distinction between inequality of opportunity and inequality of outcome is important in guiding public policy. Inequality of opportunity—access to education, health care, public services, or jobs—often arises from differences in individual circumstances that are outside the control of individuals, such as gender, ethnic origin, parental education, or location of birth. Such inequality largely reflects institutional weaknesses and social exclusion, and should be the target of public policy. On the other hand, given an individual's circumstances, efforts in the labor market or in education will also influence his or her outcomes—such as income or consumption. Inequality of outcomes arising from differences in individual efforts reflects and reinforces the market-based incentives that are needed to foster innovation and growth. The general public and policy makers in Asia seem to be aware of this distinction, as shown by the results from the World Values Survey and the Asian Development Bank's survey of Asian policy makers.

4.   WHAT DRIVES INEQUALITY IN DEVELOPING ASIA

The key drivers of developing Asia's rapid growth in the last two decades—technological progress, globalization, and market-oriented reform—have had huge distributional consequences. Combined, they have favored skilled over unskilled labor, capital over labor, and urban and coastal areas over rural and inland regions. These forces can explain a large part of the movements in income distribution and inequality in many countries in Asia.

Technological change can influence the distribution of income among different factors of production. If it favors skilled labor (more educated or more experienced) over unskilled labor by increasing its relative productivity, we can expect the skill premium—the ratio of skilled to unskilled wages—to rise, which would most likely increase income inequality. Technological change can also affect the distribution of income between labor and capital. If it is biased in favor of capital—leading to an increasing share of capital income in national income—it can also increase inequality, since capital incomes in general are less equally distributed and accrue more to the rich than to the poor.

Similarly, globalization can affect income distribution. Trade integration, for example, can change relative demand for and hence relative wages of skilled and unskilled workers. It can also affect income distribution between capital and labor because capital and skills often work together due to their complementarity. Financial integration can broaden access to finance by the poor, but can also increase the risk of financial crises and hurt the poor more than the rich. Globalization can also magnify the distributional impact of technological progress.

Existing literature has yet to provide a clear-cut answer toward understanding the impacts of trade integration, financial integration, and technological change on income distribution. One complication is that there are several, closely linked, confounding factors. A cross-country study by the International Monetary Fund (IMF) in 2007 finds that global trade integration helps reduce inequality while global financial integration increases it. The IMF also finds that technological progress was the most important contributor to rising global inequality in the last two decades. The analysis suggests that these impacts are particularly pronounced in developing Asia.

Lastly, market-oriented reform is an important driver of growth, but can also have significant distributional consequences. Trade policy reform is often part of the driving forces of globalization. Labor market reforms can change the bargaining position of labor in relation to owners of capital, impacting on wage rates and income distribution between labor and capital. Economic transition from a command to a market economy can improve efficiency and make returns to assets more closely reflective of resource scarcity, which can affect income distribution among different productive assets.

Moreover, the impacts of the three drivers of growth—technological progress, globalization, and market-oriented reform—can be geographically uneven, leading to a further channel of changing income distribution: spatial inequality. This is because new economic opportunities, released by these drivers, are often most easily seized by locations closer to the existing trade routes—coastal areas, for example, not inland ones—and areas with better public infrastructure—such as urban locations, not rural areas. Agglomeration economies also facilitate a self-perpetuating process of increasing concentration. These lead to shifts in income distribution among different geographic locations.

> *"Despite the continued growth in urbanization, some 50.3% of China's mainland population (or 674.15 million people) continue to live in rural areas. In 2010, rural residents had an annual average per capita disposable income of 5,900 yuan ($898). That's less than a third of the average per capita disposable income of urban residents, which stood at 19,100 yuan ($2,900)."* —Dr. D. Tobin, "Inequality in China: Rural Poverty Persists as Urban Wealth Balloons," at http://www.bbc.com/news/business-13945072

In sum, the three key drivers of growth can affect income distribution through three channels: capital, skill, and spatial bias. The bias toward capital reduces labor's share of national income while increasing the income share of the owners of capital. Similarly, the heightened demand for better skilled workers raises the premium on their earnings. And spatial disparities are becoming more acute; locations with superior infrastructure, market access, and scale economies are more able to benefit from changing circumstances. Moreover, inequality of opportunity magnifies the distributional consequences of the three drivers of growth. Those individuals and groups excluded from the market because of discrimination or individual circumstances beyond their control would certainly not benefit from these opportunities.

Figures 4, 5, and 6 provide empirical evidence on three key sources of rising inequality in developing Asia, corresponding to the three channels described above: shifts in income distribution between skilled and unskilled labor, between labor and capital, and between different locations.

Figure 4: Income Inequality Decomposition by Educational Attainment of Household Head

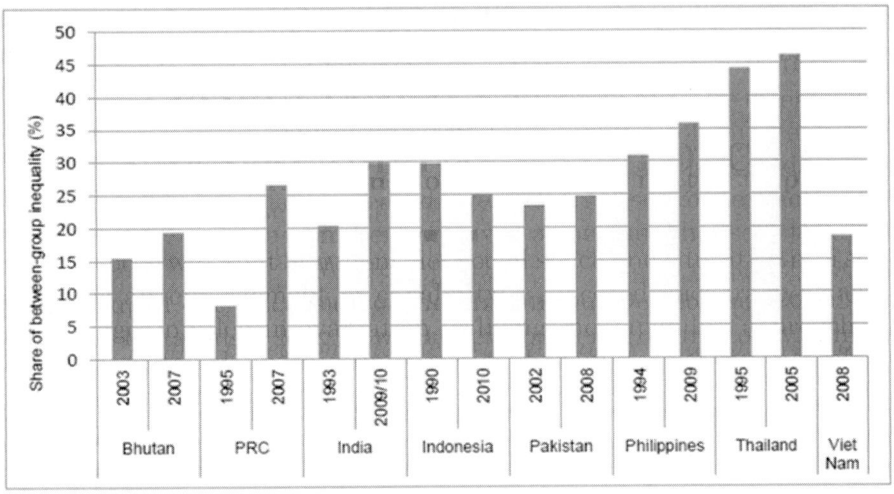

PRC = People's Republic of China.

Source: Asian Development Bank estimates using unit-level data.

- *Rising skill premiums.* The share of inequality accounted for by differences in educational attainment increased in all the countries with available data during the periods looked at, with the increase most significant in the PRC, from 8.1% in 1995 to 26.5% in 2007, followed by India, from 20% in 1993 to 30% in 2010. In the late 2000s, as much as 25–35% of the total inequality can be explained by inter-person differences in human capital and skill endowments in most Asian countries with available data (Figure 4).

- *Labor's falling share of total income.* Between the mid-1990s and the mid-2000s, labor income as a share of manufacturing output in the formal sector fell from 48% to 42% in the PRC and from 37% to 22% in India (Figure 5). The employment intensity of growth in Asia has also declined in the last two decades. Being less equally distributed, capital has contributed to rising inequality.

- *Increasing spatial inequality.* Inequalities between rural and urban areas and across provinces/states have increased significantly in many Asian countries during the last two decades. In the late 2000s, about 25–50% of total inequality can be explained by spatial inequality—between urban and rural and inter-province/state inequalities combined—in some countries, including the PRC, India, and Indonesia (Figure 6).

Figure 5: Share of Labor Income in Industrial/Manufacturing Value Added in Selected Asian Economies

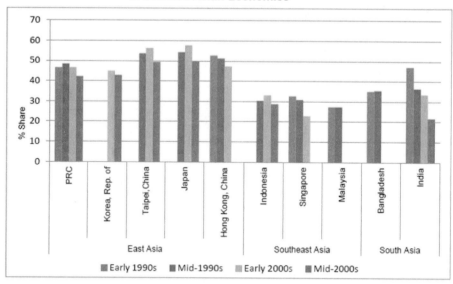

PRC = People's Republic of China.

Note: Early 1990s (1990–1992), mid-1990s (1994–1996), early 2000s (2000–2002), and mid-2000s (2004–2006) for the PRC; India; Singapore; Malaysia; India; Hong Kong, China; and Bangladesh.

Sources: OECD Stat database for Japan; Republic of Korea; Taipei,China; and Indonesia (accessed 1 March 2012); Felipe and Sipin (2004) for Singapore; Malaysia; Hong Kong, China; and Bangladesh; Bai and Qian (2009) for the PRC; and Felipe and Kumar (2010) for India's organized manufacturing sector.

Figure 6: Combined Contribution of Spatial Inequality to Overall Inequality in Selected Asian Countries

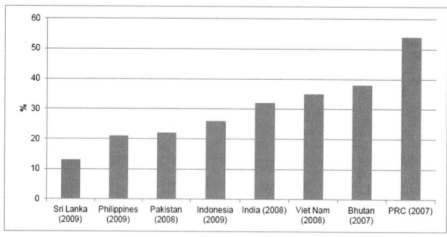

PRC = People's Republic of China.

Source: Asian Development Bank estimates using unit level data.

5.   HOW TO RESPOND TO RISING INEQUALITY

Because the forces behind rising inequality are also the engines of productivity and income growth, policy makers should not hinder their progress. A distinction needs to be made between the income differences that arise as economies and individuals take advantage of the new opportunities from technology, trade, and efficiency-enhancing reforms, and those that are generated by unequal access to market opportunities and public services. This latter source of inequality requires a policy response since it gets magnified by the driving forces of growth, leads to inefficiency, and undermines the sustainability of growth.

The Asian Development Outlook 2012 (ADB 2012) highlights three sets of policy responses to rising inequality in Asia: (i) efficient fiscal policies to reduce inequality in human capital with a view to addressing rising skill premiums relative to low wages of unskilled workers; (ii) interventions to reduce spatial inequality; and (iii) policies to make growth more employment-friendly with a view to increasing labor demand and hence labor's share in national income. These measures cannot eliminate inequality, but will go a long way toward reducing it and, at the same time, not endanger development and hurt growth.

- *Efficient fiscal policies.* These include: (i) spending more on education and health, especially for poorer households; (ii) developing and spending more on better-targeted social protection schemes, including conditional cash transfers that target income to the poor but also incentivize the buildup of human capital; (iii) switching fiscal spending from general price subsidies (such as on fuel) to targeted transfers; and (iv) broadening the tax base and strengthening tax administration for greater and more equitable revenue mobilization.

- *Interventions to address lagging regions.* These include: (i) improving transport and communications networks between more developed and poorer regions; (ii) creating growth poles in lagging areas; (iii) strengthening fiscal transfers for greater investment in human capital and better access to public services in lagging regions; and (iv) removing barriers to within-country migration.

- *Policies to make growth more employment-friendly.* These include: (i) facilitating structural transformation to create a greater number of productive jobs, and maintaining a balanced sectoral composition of growth between manufacturing, services, and agriculture; (ii) supporting development of small and medium-sized enterprises; (iii) removing factor market distortions that favor capital over labor; (iv) establishing or strengthening labor market institutions; and (v) introducing public employment schemes as a temporary bridge to address pockets of unemployment and underemployment.

SUMMARY: TOWARD INCLUSIVE GROWTH IN ASIA

Driven by globalization, technological progress, and market-oriented reform, developing Asia has had a remarkable period of growth and poverty reduction. However, the drivers of growth are also magnifying the effects of inequalities in physical and human capital, leading to rising income inequality. These forces require Asian policy makers to redouble their efforts to generate more productive jobs; equalize opportunities in employment, education, and health; and address spatial inequality. Without such growth-enhancing policies, Asia may be pulled into inefficient populist policies that benefit neither growth nor equity.

The policy options outlined constitute key elements of a strategy for inclusive growth. Broadly, inclusive growth can be defined as "growth coupled with equality of opportunity," supported by three policy pillars: sustained growth to create productive jobs for a wide section of the population; social inclusion to equalize access to opportunity; and social safety nets to mitigate vulnerability and risks and prevent extreme poverty (see Figure 7 and also Zhuang and Ali [2010]). Such a strategy would ensure that all members of society can participate in the development process productively and benefit equitably from the opportunities generated by economic growth.

Figure 7: Policy Pillars of Inclusive Growth

Source: Adapted from Zhuang (2010).

More and more developing Asian countries are embracing the concept of inclusive growth, with an increasing number of countries—including the PRC, India, and many Southeast Asian countries—placing inclusive growth at the heart of their development policy. Indeed, the entire development community is embracing the concept of inclusive growth. These developments will go a long way toward reducing poverty and inequality and making the world a more equitable place.

You Gotta Know Something About Them!

Iam Apiwatnawa

Iam is a typical Thai rice farmer. He's 45 years old, and has worked as a rice farmer for over 20 years. Popular Thai culture paints a brutal picture of farming: a sordid and dirty lifestyle. Bangkok rocks by comparison. Result: young peeps think farming sucks. In fact, only 12 percent of Thai farmers are younger than 25—that's down from 35% in 1985. Iam's looking at about $3,000 in debt that he's incurred to run his farm. That $3,000 is equivalent to nearly five years of income. Brutal. Although some of his neighbors carry less debt, they also earn more of their money from additional off-farm work. How will Iam make ends meet? Maybe migrant work . . .

Composite profile based on statistics from the government of Thailand, as compiled and reported in T. Fuller, "Thai Youth Seek a Fortune Away From the Farm" (2012), at http://www.nytimes.com/2012/06/05/world/asia/thai-youth-seek-a-fortune-off-the-farm.html?_r=0.

QUESTIONS FROM YOUR TALKING DOG

1.   Why don't I get the dog food that's on TV? That's not right. I have to eat this rat food and that dog gets to eat steak and chicken? Inequality. It's wrong. I'm gonna start a revolution! What about Asia? Hasn't that region been rocking economically? Then why do they have rising inequality?

2.   I don't get it. If poverty has gone way down in Asia, why's inequality rising? How bad is it?

3.   Yeah, I've heard about equality of opportunity. We're in America, right? Okay, tell me about Asia, then.

4.   You know, just like most people don't want to hear me gripe about my dog food, I wouldn't be surprised if most people don't really want to talk about inequality. Why does it matter?

5.   Seems like technology almost always comes up during our walks. So tell me, how exactly does technology affect inequality?

6.   Okay. Stop. It seems like globalization is always the bad guy. Same story with inequality?

7.   I thought market-oriented reform is always a good thing. Am I wrong?

8.   Spatial inequality? Not sure I get that one.

9.   This is all bad stuff. But how do you fix it? It's all about inclusive growth?

10. I'm still going to start a revolution for equal opportunity to eat that good stuff.

C. VIOLENCE

Maybe This Free Markets and Democracy Thing May Kill People

Think about the narrative of international finance and development we've presented in this textbook. From the 1950s through the 1970s, finance and development created a state-led model of development in most parts of the world. Democratic governance was hardly widespread and huge gaps between the rich and the poor were common in many countries, as illustrated by Brazil and Asia.

During the 1980s, neoliberalism began its ascent, in many cases aided by the International Monetary Fund and the World Bank. In the 1990s, the market-friendly framework of development, embodied in the Washington Consensus, went viral. Market economies married with democratic, corruption-free, and transparent governance was seen as the nirvana of development. Francis Fukuyama's 1989 essay, "The End of History?" followed three years later by this book, End of History and the Last Man Standing, stated: There's no system better than liberalism. It's the best way to achieve equitable development.

> "The triumph of the West, of the Western idea, is evident first of all in the total exhaustion of viable systematic alternatives to Western liberalism. In the past decade, there have been unmistakable changes in the intellectual climate of the world's two largest communist countries, and the beginnings of significant reform movements in both. But this phenomenon extends beyond high politics and it can be seen also in the ineluctable spread of consumerist Western culture in such diverse contexts as the peasant's markets and color television sets now omnipresent throughout China, the cooperative restaurants and clothing stores opened in the past year in Moscow, the Beethoven piped into Japanese department stores, and the rock music enjoyed alike in Prague, Rangoon, and Tehran."
> —F. Fukuyama, "The End of History," National Interest, 3 (1989)

We've also seen throughout the textbook instances when the worlds of finance and violence collide. In Chapter 10 on the Asian financial crisis, we saw how violence erupted in Indonesia, resulting in the deaths of many ethnic Chinese. This piece by Professor Amy Chua presents a provocative thesis that challenges the proposition that free market and democracy are, like, a no-brainer. Professor Chua cautions us to look more closely at the socio-economic conditions in countries before we push free markets and democracy as the panacea for peace and prosperity. A year after she published this piece she published the widely read book, World on Fire. Do you agree with her thesis? If so, do you agree with her recommendations? Would the Capabilities Approach be the most effective framework for development in light of Professor Chua's thesis?

A. CHUA, "A WORLD ON THE EDGE," *THE WILSON QUARTERLY*

Vol. 26, No. 4, 62–77, excerpted from World on Fire: How Free Market Democracy
Breeds Ethnic Hatred and Global Instability (Doubleday, 2002)

One beautiful blue morning in September 1994, I received a call from my mother in California. In a hushed voice, she told me that my Aunt Leona, my father's twin sister, had been murdered in her home in the Philippines, her throat slit by her chauffeur. My mother broke the news to me in our native Hokkien Chinese dialect. But "murder" she said in English, as if to wall off the act from the family through language.

The murder of a relative is horrible for anyone, anywhere. My father's grief was impenetrable; to this day, he has not broken his silence on the subject. For the rest of the family, though, there was an added element of disgrace. For the Chinese, luck is a moral attribute, and a lucky person would never be murdered. Like having a birth defect, or marrying a Filipino, being murdered is shameful.

My three younger sisters and I were very fond of my Aunt Leona, who was petite and quirky and had never married. Like many wealthy Filipino Chinese, she had all kinds of bank accounts in Honolulu, San Francisco, and Chicago. She visited us in the United States regularly. She and my father—Leona and Leon—were close, as only twins can be. Having no children of her own, she doted on her nieces and showered us with trinkets. As we grew older, the trinkets became treasures. On my 10th birthday she gave me 10 small diamonds, wrapped up in toilet paper. My aunt loved diamonds and bought them up by the dozen, concealing them in empty Elizabeth Arden face moisturizer jars, some right on her bathroom shelf. She liked accumulating things. When we ate at McDonald's, she stuffed her Gucci purse with free ketchups.

According to the police report, my Aunt Leona, "a 58-year-old single woman," was killed in her living room with "a butcher's knife" at approximately 8 P.M. on September 12, 1994. Two of her maids were questioned, and they confessed that Nila Abique, my aunt's chauffeur, had planned and executed the murder with their knowledge and assistance. "A few hours before the actual killing, respondent [Abique] was seen sharpening the knife allegedly used in the crime." After the killing, "respondent joined the two witnesses and told them that their employer was dead. At that time, he was wearing a pair of bloodied white gloves and was still holding a knife, also with traces of blood." But Abique, the report went on to say, had "disappeared," with the warrant for his arrest outstanding. The two maids were released.

Meanwhile, my relatives arranged a private funeral for my aunt in the prestigious Chinese cemetery in Manila where many of my ancestors are buried in a great, white-marble family tomb. According to the feng shui monks who were consulted, my aunt could not be buried with the rest of the family because of the violent nature of her death, lest more bad luck strike her surviving kin. So she was placed in her own smaller vault, next to—but not touching—the main family tomb.

After the funeral, I asked one of my uncles whether there had been any further developments in the murder investigation. He replied tersely that the killer had not been found. His wife explained that the Manila police had essentially closed the case.

I could not understand my relatives' almost indifferent attitude. Why were they not more shocked that my aunt had been killed in cold blood, by people who worked for her, lived with her, saw her every day? Why were they not outraged that the maids had been released? When I pressed my uncle, he was short with me. "That's the way things are here," he said. "This is the Philippines—not America."

My uncle was not simply being callous. As it turns out, my aunt's death was part of a common pattern. Hundreds of Chinese in the Philippines are kidnapped every year, almost invariably by ethnic Filipinos. Many victims, often children, are brutally murdered, even after ransom is paid. Other Chinese, like my aunt, are killed without a kidnapping, usually in connection with a robbery. Nor is it unusual that my aunt's killer was never apprehended. The police in the Philippines, all poor ethnic Filipinos themselves, are notoriously unmotivated in these cases. When asked by a Western journalist why it is so frequently the Chinese who are targeted, one grinning Filipino policeman explained that it was because "they have more money."

My family is part of the Philippines' tiny but entrepreneurial and economically powerful Chinese minority. Although they constitute just one percent of the population, Chinese Filipinos control as much as 60 percent of the private economy, including the country's four major airlines and almost all of the country's banks, hotels, shopping malls, and big conglomerates. My own family in Manila runs a plastics conglomerate. Unlike taipans Lucio Tan, Henry Sy, or John Gokongwei, my relatives are only "third-tier" Chinese tycoons. Still, they own swaths of prime real estate and several vacation homes. They also have safe deposit boxes full of gold bars, each one roughly the size of a Snickers bar, but strangely heavy. I myself have such a gold bar. My Aunt Leona express-mailed it to me as a law school graduation present a few years before she died.

Since my aunt's murder, one childhood memory keeps haunting me. I was eight, staying at my family's splendid hacienda-style house in Manila. It was before dawn, still dark. Wide-awake, I decided to get a drink from the kitchen. I must have gone down an extra flight of stairs, because I literally stumbled onto six male bodies. I had found the male servants' quarters, where my family's houseboys, gardeners, and chauffeurs—I sometimes imagine that Nilo Abique was among them—were sleeping on mats on a dirt floor. The place stank of sweat and urine. I was horrified.

Later that day I mentioned the incident to my Aunt Leona, who laughed affectionately and explained that the servants—there were perhaps 20 living on the premises, all ethnic Filipinos—were fortunate to be working for our family. If not for their positions, they would be living among rats and open sewers, without a roof over their heads. A Filipino maid then walked in; I remember that she had a bowl of food for my aunt's Pekingese. My aunt took the bowl but kept talking as if the maid were not there. The Filipinos, she continued—in Chinese, but plainly not caring whether the maid understood or not—were lazy and unintelligent and didn't really want to do much. If they didn't like working for us, they were free to leave at any time. After all, my aunt said, they were employees, not slaves.

Nearly two-thirds of the roughly 80 million ethnic Filipinos in the Philippines live on less than $2 a day. Forty percent spend their entire lives in temporary shelters. Seventy percent of all rural Filipinos own no land.

> "The richest man in the Philippines, Henry Sy, is a shopping mall magnate who is worth approximately $12 billion."
> —*Forbes*, at http://www.forbes.com/profile/henry-sy/ (2014)

Almost a third have no access to sanitation. But that's not the worst of it. Poverty alone never is. Poverty by itself does not make people kill. To poverty must be added indignity, hopelessness, and grievance. In the Philippines, millions of Filipinos work for Chinese; almost no Chinese work for Filipinos. The Chinese dominate industry and commerce at every level of society. Global markets intensify this dominance: When foreign investors do business in the Philippines, they deal almost exclusively with Chinese. Apart from a handful of corrupt politicians and a few aristocratic Spanish mestizo families, all of the Philippines' billionaires are of Chinese descent. By contrast, all menial jobs in the Philippines are filled by Filipinos. All peasants are Filipinos. All domestic servants and squatters are Filipinos. My relatives live literally walled off from the Filipino masses, in a posh, all-Chinese residential enclave, on streets named Harvard, Yale, Stanford, and Princeton. The entry points are guarded by armed private-security forces.

Each time I think of Nila Abique—he was six-feet-two and my aunt was four-feet-eleven—I find myself welling up with a hatred and revulsion so intense it is actually consoling. But over time I have also had glimpses of how the vast majority of Filipinos, especially someone like Abique, must see the Chinese: as exploiters, foreign intruders, their wealth inexplicable, their superiority intolerable. I will never forget the entry in the police report for Abique's "motive for murder." The motive given was not robbery, despite the jewels and money the chauffeur was said to have taken. Instead, for motive, there was just one word—"revenge."

My aunt's killing was just a pinprick in a world more violent than most of us have ever imagined. In America, we read about acts of mass slaughter and savagery—at first in faraway places, now coming closer home. We do not understand what connects these acts. Nor do we understand the role we have played in bringing them about.

In the Serbian concentration camps of the early 1990s, the women prisoners were raped over and over, many times a day, often with broken bottles, often together with their daughters. The men, if they were lucky, were beaten to death as their Serbian guards sang national anthems; if they were not so fortunate, they were castrated or, at gunpoint, forced to castrate their fellow prisoners, sometimes with their own teeth. In all, thousands were tortured and executed.

In Rwanda in 1994, ordinary Hutus killed 800,000 Tutsis over a period of three months, typically hacking them to death with machetes. Bill Berkeley writes in *The Graves Are Not Yet Full* (2001) that young children would come home to find their mothers, fathers, sisters, and brothers on the living room floor, in piles of severed heads and limbs.

In Jakarta in 1998, screaming Indonesian mobs torched, smashed, and looted hundreds of Chinese shops and homes, leaving more than 2,000 dead. One who survived—a 14-year-old Chinese girl—later committed suicide by taking rat poison. She had been gang-raped and genitally mutilated in front of her parents.

In Israel in 1998, a suicide bomber driving a car packed with explosives rammed into a school bus filled with 34 Jewish children between the ages of six and eight. Over the next few years such incidents intensified, becoming daily occurrences and a powerful collective expression of Palestinian hatred. "We hate you," a senior aide to Yasir Arafat elaborated in April 2002. "The air hates you, the land hates you, the trees hate you, there is no purpose in your staying on this land."

On September 11, 2001, Middle Eastern terrorists hijacked four American airliners, intent on using them as piloted missiles. They destroyed the World Trade Center and the southwest side of the Pentagon, crushing or incinerating more than 3,000 people. "Americans, think! Why you are hated all over the world," proclaimed a banner held by Arab demonstrators.

There is a connection among these episodes apart from their violence. It lies in the relationship—increasingly, the explosive collision—among the three most powerful forces operating in the world today: markets, democracy, and ethnic hatred. There exists today a phenomenon—pervasive outside the West yet rarely acknowledged, indeed often viewed as taboo—that turns freemarket democracy into an engine of ethnic conflagration. I'm speaking of the phenomenon of market-dominant minorities: ethnic minorities who, for widely varying reasons, tend under market conditions to dominate economically, often to a startling extent, the "indigenous" majorities around them.

Market-dominant minorities can be found in every corner of the world. The Chinese are a market-dominant minority not just in the Philippines but throughout Southeast Asia. In 1998 Chinese Indonesians, only three percent of the population, controlled roughly 70 percent of Indonesia's private economy, including all of the country's largest conglomerates. In Myanmar (formerly Burma), entrepreneurial Chinese recently have taken over the economies of Mandalay and Yangon. Whites are a marketdominant minority in South Africa—and, in a more complicated sense, in Brazil, Ecuador, Guatemala, and much of Latin America. Lebanese are a market-dominant minority in West Africa, as are the Ibo in Nigeria. Croats were a market-dominant minority in the former Yugoslavia, as Jews almost certainly are in post-communist Russia.

Market-dominant minorities are the Achilles' heel of free-market democracy. In societies with such a minority, markets and democracy favor not just different people or different classes but different ethnic groups. Markets concentrate wealth, often spectacular wealth, in the hands of the market-dominant minority, while democracy increases the political power of the impoverished majority. In these circumstances, the pursuit of free-market democracy becomes an engine of potentially catastrophic ethnonationalism, pitting a frustrated "indigenous" majority, easily aroused by opportunistic, voteseeking politicians, against a resented, wealthy ethnic minority. This conflict is playing out in country after country today, from Indonesia to Sierra Leone, from Zimbabwe to Venezuela, from Russia to the Middle East.

Since September 11, the conflict has been brought home to the United States. Americans are not an ethnic minority (although we are a national-origin minority, a close cousin). Nor is there democracy at the global level. Nevertheless, Americans today are everywhere perceived as the world's market-dominant minority, wielding outrageously disproportionate economic power relative to our numbers. As a result, we have become the object of the same kind of mass popular resentment that afflicts the Chinese of Southeast Asia, the whites of Zimbabwe, and other groups.

Global anti-Americanism has many causes. One of them, ironically, is the global spread of free markets and democracy. Throughout the world, global markets are bitterly perceived as reinforcing American wealth and dominance. At the same time, global populist and democratic movements give strength, legitimacy, and voice to the impoverished, frustrated, excluded masses of the world—in other words, precisely the people most susceptible to anti-American demagoguery. In more non-Western countries than Americans would care to admit, free and fair elections would bring to power anti-market, anti-American leaders. For the past 20 years,

Americans have been grandly promoting both marketization and democratization throughout the world. In the process, we have directed at ourselves what the Turkish writer Orhan Pamuk calls "the anger of the damned."

The relationship between free-market democracy and ethnic violence around the world is inextricably bound up with globalization. But the phenomenon of market-dominant minorities introduces complications that have escaped the view of both globalization's enthusiasts and its critics.

To a great extent, globalization consists of, and is fueled by, the unprecedented worldwide spread of markets and democracy. For more than two decades now, the American government, along with American consultants and business interests, has been vigorously promoting free-market democracy throughout the developing and post-communist worlds. Both directly and through powerful international institutions such as the World Bank, International Monetary Fund, and World Trade Organization (WTO), it has helped bring capitalism and democratic elections to literally billions of people. At the same time, American multinationals, foundations, and nongovernmental organizations (NGOs) have touched every corner of the world, bringing with them ballot boxes and Burger Kings, hip-hop and Hollywood, banking codes and American-drafted constitutions.

The prevailing view among globalization's supporters is that markets and democracy are a kind of universal elixir for the multiple ills of underdevelopment.

Market capitalism is the most efficient economic system the world has ever known. Democracy is the fairest political system the world has ever known, and the one most respectful of individual liberty. Together, markets and democracy will gradually transform the world into a community of prosperous, war-shunning nations, and individuals into liberal, civic-minded citizens and consumers. Ethnic hatred, religious zealotry, and other "backward" aspects of underdevelopment will be swept away.

Thomas Friedman of *The New York Times* has been a brilliant proponent of this dominant view. In his best-selling *book The Lexus and the Olive Tree* (1999), he reproduced a Merrill Lynch ad that said "the spread of free markets and democracy around the world is permitting more people everywhere to turn their aspirations into achievements," erasing "not just geographical borders but also human ones." Globalization, Friedman elaborated, "tends to tum all friends and enemies 'into competitors.' " Friedman also proposed his "Golden Arches Theory of Conflict Prevention," which claims that "no two countries that both have McDonald's have ever fought a war against each other." (Unfortunately, notes Yale University historian John Lewis Gaddis, "the United States and its NATO allies chose just that inauspicious moment to begin bombing Belgrade, where there was an embarrassing number of golden arches.")

For globalization's enthusiasts, the cure for group hatred and ethnic violence around the world is straightforward: more markets and more democracy. Thus, after the September 11 attacks, Friedman published an op-ed piece pointing to India and Bangladesh as good "role models" for the Middle East and citing their experience as a solution to the challenges of terrorism and militant Islam: "Hello? Hello? There's a message here. It's democracy, stupid!"—" . . . multiethnic, pluralistic, freemarket democracy."

I believe, rather, that the global spread of markets and democracy is a principal aggravating cause of group hatred and ethnic violence throughout the non-Western world. In the numerous societies around the world that have a market-dominant minority, markets and democracy are not mutually reinforcing. Because markets and democracy benefit different ethnic groups in such societies, the pursuit of free-market democracy produces highly unstable and combustible conditions. Markets concentrate enormous wealth in the hands of an "outsider" minority, thereby fomenting ethnic envy and hatred among often chronically poor majorities. In absolute terms, the majority may or may not be better off—a dispute that much of the globalization debate revolves around—but any sense of improvement is overwhelmed by its continuing poverty and the hated minority's extraordinary economic success. More humiliating still, marketdominant minorities, along with their foreign-investor partners, invariably come to control the crown jewels of the economy, often symbolic of the nation's patrimony and identity-oil in Russia and Venezuela, diamonds in South Africa, silver and tin in Bolivia, jade, teak, and rubies in Myanmar.

Introducing democracy under such circumstances does not transform voters into open-minded co-citizens in a national community. Rather, the competition for votes fosters the emergence of demagogues who scapegoat the resented minority and foment active ethnonationalist movements demanding that the country's wealth and identity be reclaimed by the "true owners of the nation."

Even as America celebrated the global spread of democracy in the 1990s, the world's new political slogans told of more ominous developments: "Georgia for the Georgians," "Eritreans out of Ethiopia," "Kenya for Kenyans," "Venezuela for Pardos," "Kazakhstan for Kazakhs," "Serbia for Serbs," "Hutu Power," "Jews out of Russia." Vadim Tudor, a candidate in Romania's 2001 presidential election, was not quite so pithy. "I'm Vlad the Impaler," he declared, and referring to the historically dominant Hungarian minority, he promised, "We will hang them directly by their Hungarian tongue!"

When free-market democracy is pursued in the presence of a market-dominant minority, the result, almost invariably, is backlash. Typically, it takes one of three forms. The first is a backlash against markets that targets the market-dominant minority's wealth. The second is an attack against democracy by forces favorable to the market-dominant minority. And the third is violence, sometimes genocidal, directed against the market-dominant minority itself.

Zimbabwe today is a vivid illustration of the first kind of backlash—an ethnically targeted anti-market reaction. For several years now, President Robert Mugabe has encouraged the violent seizure of 10 million acres of white-owned commercial farmland. As one Zimbabwean explained, "The land belongs to us. The foreigners should not own land here. There is no black Zimbabwean who owns land in England. Why should any European own land here?" Mugabe has been more explicit: "Strike fear in the heart of the white man, our real enemy." Most of the country's white "foreigners" are third-generation Zimbabweans. They are just one percent of the population, but they have for generations controlled 70 percent of the country's best land, largely in the form of highly productive 3,000-acre tobacco and sugar farms.

Watching Zimbabwe's economy take a free fall as a result of the mass land grab, the United States and United Kingdom, together with dozens of human rights groups, urged President Mugabe to step down and called resoundingly for "free and fair elections." But the idea that democracy is the answer to Zimbabwe's problems is breathtakingly naive. Perhaps Mugabe would have lost the 2002 elections in the absence of foul play. But even if that's so, it's important to remember that Mugabe himself is a product of democracy.

The hero of Zimbabwe's black liberation movement and a master manipulator of the masses, he swept to victory in the closely monitored elections of 1980 by promising to expropriate "stolen" white land. Repeating that promise has helped him win every election since. Moreover, Mugabe's land-seizure campaign was another product of the democratic process. It was deftly timed in anticipation of the 2000 and 2002 elections, and deliberately calculated to mobilize popular support for Mugabe's teetering regime. According to The Economist, 95 percent of Zimbabwe's largely white-owned commercial farms are now earmarked for confiscation without compensation, and many farmers have been ordered off the land.

In the contest between an economically powerful ethnic minority and a numerically powerful impoverished majority, the majority does not always prevail. Rather than a backlash against the market, another possible outcome is a backlash against democracy that favors the market-dominant minority. Examples of this dynamic are extremely common.

The world's most notorious cases of "crony capitalism" have all involved partnerships between a market-dominant ethnic minority and a cooperative autocrat. Ferdinand Marcos's dictatorship in the Philippines, for example, sheltered and profited from the country's wealthy Chinese before he was driven from office in 1986. In Kenya, President Daniel arap Moi, who had once warned Africans to "beware of bad Asians," is sustained by a series of "business arrangements" with a handful of local Indian tycoons. And the bloody tragedy of Sierra Leone's recent history can be traced in significant part to the regime of President Siaka Stevens, who converted his elective office into a dictatorship during the early 1970s and promptly formed a shadow alliance with five of the country's Lebanese diamond dealers.

In Sierra Leone, as in many other countries, independence (which came in 1961) had been followed by a series of anti-market measure sand policies that took direct aim at market-dominant minorities. People of "European or Asiatic origin," including the Lebanese, were denied citizenship. Stevens's approach thus represented a complete about-face—a pattern that's been repeated in country after country. Stevens protected the economically powerful Lebanese, and in exchange, they—with their business networks in Europe, the Soviet Union, and the United States— worked economic wonders, generating enormous profits and kicking back handsome portions to Stevens and other officials. (It is just such webs of preexisting relationships with the outside world that have given economically dominant minorities their extraordinary advantages in the current era of globalization.)

Stevens was succeeded by other autocrats, who struck essentially the same deal while also successfully courting foreign investment and aid. In 1989 and 1990, the International Monetary Fund championed a "bold and decisive" free-market reform package that included a phase-out of public subsidies for rice and other commodities. Already living in indescribable poverty, Sierra Leoneans watched the cost of rice nearly double, and many blamed the Lebanese. In any event, the rebel leader Foday Sankoh had little trouble finding recruits for his insurgency. Some 75,000 died in the ensuing chaos.

The third and most ferocious kind of backlash is majority-supported violence aimed at eliminating a market-dominant minority. Two recent examples are the "ethnic cleansing" of Croats in the former Yugoslavia and the mass slaughter of Tutsi in Rwanda. In both cases, sudden, unmediated democratization encouraged the rise of megalomaniacal ethnic demagogues and released long-suppressed hatreds against a disproportionately prosperous ethnic minority.

Of course, markets and democracy were not the only causes of these acts of genocide, but they were neglected factors. In the former Yugoslavia, for example, the Croats, along with the Slovenes, have long enjoyed a strikingly higher standard of living than the Serbs and other ethnic groups. Croatia and Slovenia are largely Catholic, with geographical proximity and historical links to Western Europe, while the Eastern Orthodox Serbs inhabit the rugged south and lived for centuries under the thumb of the Ottoman Empire. By the 1990s, per capita income in northern Yugoslavia had risen to three times that in the south. The sudden coming of Balkan electoral democracy helped stir ancient enmities and resentments. In Serbia, the demagogue and future "ethnic cleanser" Slobodan Milosevic swept to power in 1990 as supporters declared to hysterical crowds, "We will kill Croats with rusty spoons because it will hurt more!" (In the same year, Franjo Tudjman won a landslide victory in Croatia preaching anti-Serb hatred; the subsequent mass killing of Croatia's Serbs shows that market-dominant minorities aren't always the victims of persecution.)In a now-famous speech delivered in March 1991—which contains a telling allusion to Croat and Slovene market dominance—Milosevic declared: "If we must fight, then my God we will fight. And I hope they will not be so crazy as to fight against us. Because *if we don't know how to work well or to do business*, at least we know how to fight well!" (Emphasis added.)

To their credit, critics of globalization have called attention to the grotesque imbalances that free markets produce. In the 1990s, writes Thomas Frank in *One Market under God* (2000), global markets made "the corporation the most powerful institution on earth," transformed "CEOs as a class into one of the wealthiest elites of all time," and, from America to Indonesia, "forgot about the poor with a decisiveness we hadn't seen since the 1920s." A host of strange bedfellows have joined Frank in his criticism of "the almighty market": American farmers and factory workers opposed to the North American Free Trade Agreement, environmentalists, the American Federation of Labor-Congress of Industrial Organizations, human rights activists, Third World advocates, and sundry other groups that protested in Seattle, Davos, Genoa, and New York City. Defenders of globalization respond, with some justification, that the world's poor would be even worse off without global marketization, and recent World Bank studies show that, with some important exceptions, including most of Africa, globalization's "trickle down" has benefited the poor as well as the rich in developing countries.

More fundamentally, however, Western critics of globalization, like their pro-globalization counterparts, have overlooked the ethnic dimension of market disparities. They tend to see wealth and poverty in terms of class conflict, not ethnic conflict. This perspective might make sense in the advanced Western societies, but the ethnic realities of the developing world are completely different from those of the West. Essentially, the anti-globalization movement asks for one thing: more democracy. At the 2002 World Social Forum in Brazil, Lori Wallach of Public Citizen rejected the label "anti-globalization" and explained that "our movement, really, is globally for democracy, equality, diversity, justice and quality of life." Wallach has also warned that the WTO must "either bend to the will of the people worldwide or it will break." Echoing these voices are literally dozens of NGOs that call for "democratically empowering the poor majorities of the world." But unless democratization means something more than unrestrained majority rule, calling for democracy in the developing world can be shortsighted and even dangerous. Empowering the Hutu majority in Rwanda did not produce desirable consequences. Nor did empowering the Serbian majority in Serbia.

Critics of globalization are right to demand that more attention be paid to the enormous disparities of wealth created by global markets. But just as it is dangerous to view markets as the panacea for the world's poverty and strife, so too it is dangerous to see democracy as a panacea. Markets and democracy may well offer the best long-run economic and political hope for developing and post-communist societies. In the short run, however, they're part of the problem.

In the West, terms such as "market economy" and "market system" refer a broad spectrum of economic systems based primarily on private property and competition, with government regulation and redistribution ranging from substantial (as in the United States) to extensive (as in the Scandinavian countries). Yet for the past 20 years the United States has been promoting throughout the non-Western world raw, laissez-faire capitalism—a form of markets that the West abandoned long ago. The pro-capitalism measures being implemented today outside the West include privatization, the elimination of state subsidies and controls, and free-trade and foreign investment initiatives. As a practical matter they rarely, if ever, include any substantial redistribution measures.

"Democracy," too, can take many forms. I use the term "democratization" to refer to the political reforms that are actually being promoted in the nonWestern world today—the concerted efforts, for example, largely driven by the United States, to implement immediate elections with universal suffrage. It's striking to note that at no point in history did any Western nation ever implement laissez-faire capitalism and overnight universal suffrage simultaneously—though that's the precise formula for free-market democracy currently being pressed on developing countries around the world. In the United States, the poor were totally disenfranchised by formal property qualifications in virtually every state for many decades after the Constitution was ratified, and economic barriers to participation remained well into the 20th century.

It is ethnicity, however, that gives the combination of markets and democracy its special combustibility. Ethnic identity is not a static, scientifically determinable status but shifting and highly malleable. In Rwanda, for example, the 14 percent Tutsi minority dominated the Hutu majority economically and politically for four centuries, as a kind of cattle-owning aristocracy. But for most of this period, the lines between Hutus and Tutsi were permeable. The two groups spoke the same language, intermarriage occurred, and successful Hutus could "become Tutsi." That was no longer true after the Belgians arrived and, steeped in specious theories of racial superiority, issued ethnic identity cards on the basis of nose length and cranial circumference. The resulting sharp ethnic divisions were later exploited by the leaders of Hutu Power.

"When the Belgian colonists arrived [in Rwanda], they produced identity cards classifying people according to their ethnicity. The Belgians considered the Tutsis to be superior to the Hutus. Not surprisingly, the Tutsis welcomed this idea, and for the next 20 years they enjoyed better jobs and educational opportunities than their neighbours."
—"Rwanda: How the Genocide Happened," *BBC News*, at http://www.bbc.com/news/world-africa-13431486 (2011)

Along similar lines, all over Latin America today—where it is often said that there are no "ethnic divisions" because everyone has "mixed" blood—large numbers of impoverished Bolivians, Chileans, and Peruvians are suddenly being told that they are Aymaras, Incas, or just *indios*, whatever identity best resonates and mobilizes. These indigenization movements are not necessarily good or bad, but they are potent and contagious.

At the same time, ethnic identity is rarely constructed out of thin air. Subjective perceptions of identity often depend on more "objective" traits assigned to individuals based on, for example, perceived morphological characteristics, language differences, or ancestry. Try telling black and white Zimbabweans that they are only imagining their ethnic differences—that "ethnicity is a social construct"—and they'll at least agree on one thing: You're not being helpful. Much more concretely relevant is the reality that there is roughly zero intermarriage between blacks and whites in Zimbabwe, just as there is virtually no intermarriage between Chinese and Malays in Malaysia or between Arabs and Israelis in the Middle East. That ethnicity can be at once an artifact of human imagination and rooted in the darkest recesses of history—fluid and manipulable, yet important enough to kill for—is what makes ethnic conflict so terrifyingly difficult to understand and contain.

The argument I am making is frequently misunderstood. I do not propose a universal theory applicable to every developing country. There are certainly developing countries without market-dominant minorities: China and Argentina are two major examples. Nor do I argue that ethnic conflict arises only in the presence of a market-dominant minority.

There are countless instances of ethnic hatred directed at economically oppressed groups. And, last, I emphatically do not mean to pin the blame for any particular case of ethnic violence—whether the mass killings perpetuated by all sides in the former Yugoslavia or the attack on America—on economic resentment, on markets, on democracy, on globalization, or on any other single cause. Many overlapping factors and complex dynamic—religion, historical enmities, territorial disputes, or a particular nation's foreign policy—are always in play.

The point, rather, is this: In the numerous countries around the world that have pervasive poverty and a market-dominant minority, democracy and markets—at least in the raw, unrestrained forms in which they are currently being promoted—can proceed only in deep tension with each other. In such conditions, the combined pursuit of free markets and democratization has repeatedly catalyzed ethnic conflict in highly predictable ways, with catastrophic consequences, including genocidal violence and the subversion of markets and democracy themselves. That has been the sobering lesson of globalization over the past 20 years.

Where does this leave us? What are the implications of marketdominant minorities for national and international policymaking? Influential commentator Robert D. Kaplan offers one answer: Hold off on democracy until free markets produce enough economic and social development to make democracy sustainable. In *The Coming Anarchy* (2000), Kaplan argues that a middle class and civil institutions—both of which he implicitly assumes would be generated by market capitalism—are preconditions for democracy. Contrasting Lee Kuan Yew's prosperous authoritarian Singapore with the murderous, "bloodletting" democratic states of Colombia, Rwanda, and South Africa, Kaplan roundly condemns America's post-Cold War campaign to export democracy to "places where it can't succeed."

"The number of people he caused to be killed has been tabulated by exiles and international human rights groups as close to 300,000 out of total population of 12 million. Those murdered were mostly anonymous people: farmers, students, clerks and shopkeepers who were shot or forced to bludgeon one another to death by members of death squads, including the chillingly named Public Safety Unit and the State Research Bureau."

—M. Kaufman, "Idi Amin, Murderous and Erratic Ruler of Uganda in the 70's, Dies in Exile," *The New York Times*, at http://www.nytimes.com/2003/08/17/world/idi-amin-murderous-and-erratic-ruler-of-uganda-in-the-70-s-dies-in-exile.html (2003)

This is a refreshingly unromantic view, but ultimately unsatisfactory. As one writer has observed, "If authoritarianism were the key to prosperity, then Africa would be the richest continent in the world." Ask (as some do) for an Augusto Pinochet or an Alberto Fujimori, and you may get an Idi Amin or a Papa Doc Duvalier. More fundamentally, Kaplan overlooks the global problem of market-dominant minorities. He stresses the ethnic biases of elections but neglects the ethnic biases of capitalism. He is overly optimistic about the ability of markets alone to lift the great indigenous masses out of poverty, and he fails to see that markets favor not just some people over others but, often, hated ethnic minorities over indigenous majorities. Overlooking this reality, Kaplan blames too much of the world's violence and anarchy on democracy.

The best economic hope for developing and post-communist countries does lie in some form of market-generated growth. Their best political hope lies in some form of democracy, with constitutional constraints, tailored to local realities. But if global free-market democracy is to succeed, the problem of market-dominant minorities must be confronted head-on. If we stop peddling unrestrained markets and overnight elections as cure-alls—both to ourselves and others—and instead candidly address the perils inherent in both markets and democracy, there is in many cases room for optimism.

The first and most obvious step is to isolate, where possible, and address, where appropriate, the causes of the market dominance of certain groups. In South Africa, expanding educational opportunities for the black majority—restricted for more than 70 years to inferior Bantu schooling— is properly a national priority and should be vigorously supported by the international community. Throughout Latin America, educational reform and equalization of opportunities for the region's poor indigenous-blooded majorities are imperative if global markets are to benefit more than just a handful of cosmopolitan elites.

Yet we must be realistic. The underlying causes of market dominance are poorly understood, difficult to reduce to tangible factors, and in any event highly intractable. Research suggests, for example, that additional spending on education, if not accompanied by major socioeconomic reforms, produces depressingly few benefits. Political favoritism, though often a sore point with the majority in many societies with a market-dominant minority, tends to be more the consequence than the cause of market dominance. Most market-dominant minorities, whether the Bamileke in Cameroon or Indians in Fiji, enjoy disproportionate economic success at every level of society down to the smallest shopkeepers, who can rarely boast of useful political connections. Indeed, many of these minorities succeed despite official discrimination against them. Any explanation of their success will likely include a host of intangibles such as the influence of religion and culture.

To "level the playing field" in developing societies will thus be a painfully slow process, taking generations if it is possible at all. More immediate measures will be needed to address the potentially explosive problems of ethnic resentment and ethnonationalist hatred that threaten these countries.

A crucial challenge is to find ways to spread the benefits of global markets beyond a handful of market-dominant minorities and their foreign investor partners. Western-style redistributive programs—progressive taxation, social security, unemployment insurance—should be encouraged, but, at least in the short run, they have limited potential. There simply is not enough to tax, and nearly no one who can be trusted to transfer revenues. Other possibilities are somewhat more encouraging. The Peruvian economist Hernando de Soto makes a powerful case in *The Mystery of Capital* (2000) for the benefits of giving the poor in the developing world formal, legally defensible property rights to the land they occupy but to which, because of underdeveloped legal systems and the tangles of history, they very often lack legal title.

A more controversial strategy consists of direct government intervention in the market designed to "correct" ethnic wealth imbalances. The leading example of such an effort is Malaysia's New Economic Policy (NEP), a program established after violent riots in 1969 by indigenous Malays angry over the economic dominance of foreign investors and the country's ethnic Chinese minority. The Malaysian government adopted sweeping ethnic quotas on corporate equity ownership, university admissions, government licensing, and commercial employment. It also initiated large-scale purchases of corporate assets on behalf of the *bumiputra* (Malay) majority.

In many respects, the results have been impressive. While the NEP has not lifted the great majority of Malays (particularly in the rural areas) out of poverty, it has helped to create a substantial Malay middle class. Prime Minister Mahathir Mohamad, who frankly concedes that the NEP has tended to favor elite, well-connected Malays, nevertheless contends that it serves an important symbolic function: "With the existence of the few rich Malays at least the poor can say their fate is not entirely to serve rich non-Malays. From the point of view of racial ego, and this ego is still strong, the unseemly existence of Malay tycoons is essential."

Efforts like the NEP, however, are far from a universal solution. Few countries enjoy the degree of prosperity that makes them feasible, and even Malaysia has not achieved its goal of eradicating poverty. Moreover, such programs may well exacerbate ethnic tensions rather than relieve them, especially when government leaders are themselves ethnic partisans. In his own mind Serbia's Slobodan Milosevic was conducting a form of affirmative action on behalf of long-exploited majorities, as Zimbabwe's Robert Mugabe doubtless feels he is doing now.

For better or worse, the best hope for global free-market democracy lies with market-dominant minorities themselves. This is adamantly not to blame these groups for the ethnonationalist eruptions against them. But it is to suggest that they may be in the best position to address today's most pressing challenges. To begin with, it must be recognized that market-dominant minorities often engage in objectionable practices—bribery, discriminatory lending, labor exploitation—that reinforce ethnic stereotypes and besmirch the image of free-market democracy. In

Indonesia, the notorious "crony capitalism" of President Suharto depended on a handful of Chinese magnates and fueled massive resentment of the Chinese community generally.

More affirmatively, if free-market democracy is to prosper, the world's market-dominant minorities must begin making significant and visible contributions to the local economies in which they are thriving. Although such efforts have been relatively few and by no means always successful in promoting goodwill, some valuable models can be found. The University of Nairobi, for example, owes its existence to wealthy Indians in Kenya. The Madhvani family, owners of the largest industrial, commercial, and agricultural complex in East Africa, not only provide educational, health, housing, and recreational opportunities for their African employees, but also employ Africans in top management and offer a number of wealth-sharing schemes. In Russia, there is the unusual case of the Jewish billionaire Roman Abramovich, whose generous philanthropy and ambitious proposals won him election as governor of the poverty-stricken Chukotka region in the Russian Far East. More typically, however, building ethnic goodwill would require collective action. Fortunately, most economically successful minorities do have the resources for such action, in the form of local ethnic chambers of commerce, clan associations, and other organizations.

What of the world's largest economically dominant minority? What are Americans to do? It's obviously true that antiAmericanism, including the virulent Islamicist strain, doesn't stem from economic deprivation alone. As others have pointed out, the Islamicists themselves rarely even speak of a desire for prosperity. And it is fantasy to think that U.S. economic aid can do anything more than make a small dent in world poverty, at least in the near future. Yet those who call for increases in U.S. aid to the world's poor do seem to have wisdom on their side. The United States now devotes only 0.1 percent of its gross domestic product to foreign aid, a smaller share than any other advanced country. Rightly or wrongly, for millions around the world the World Trade Center symbolized greed, exploitation, indifference, and cultural humiliation. By extending themselves to the world's poor, Americans could begin to send a different sort of message. Retreating into isolationism or glorifying American chauvinism holds no longterm promise. It is difficult to see, in any event, how a little generosity and humility could possibly hurt.

You Gotta Know Something About Them!

Ferdinand Marcos

Ferdinand Marcos was born in Ilocos Norte, Philippines. He wanted to be a lawyer but a slight problem: In 1935, following the defeat of his father in his bid for a seat in the National Assembly, the winner, Julio Nalundasan, was found murdered in his home. The cops arrested Ferdinand for murder, suspecting him of offing Nalundasan. He went to prison. But he appealed to the Supreme Court and won—and he argued his own case before the Supreme Court. Once free he became a trial lawyer in Manila.

Ferdinand ran for president of the Philippines in 1965 and won. Although he was cool at first, he started using his power to hook up his friends and family. As Ferdinand became increasingly unpopular, he declared martial law in 1972, claiming that communist guerillas threatened the nation. He became increasingly authoritarian, suppressing popular dissent and jailing opposition leaders. But it all came home to roost. Filipinos got sick of corruption and economic stagnation and booted Ferdinand out in 1986 after a sham election. He and his family decided to check out Hawaii. Imelda, a shopping queen, left behind over 1,000 pairs of shoes and 800 designer purses.

QUESTIONS FROM YOUR TALKING DOG

1.   Do we really have to talk about violence? It's such a nice day! Look at all the pretty butterflies! Okay, fine! Tell me about the Chinese Filipinos. Why the violence against them?

2.   All of this violence in different places. Seems like they're not connected, but you say they are. How so?

3.   I think I understand this market-dominant minority theory. But how does the minority become dominant?

4.   On one of our walks, we talked about how the law and development movement crumbled because of the cookie-cutter approach. You know, whatever works in the Western world can easily be replicated in developing countries. Yeah, it sounds like I'm giving a lecture. Anyway, it seems like the export of free markets and democracy is kind of the same thing. Am I right? So tell me again why markets and democracy are tied to ethnic violence.

5.   Okay, I got the quote "markets concentrate enormous wealth in the hands of an outsider minority." But I still don't understand how that happens.

6.   How can democracy be a bad thing?

7.   So, sure, there's violence in the country. But what do foreigners have to do with that?

8.   This dynamic you talking about, it can trigger crony capitalism? Really? Tell me about Sierra Leone.

9.   Hold on a second. I have to roll in the stuff . . . Okay. So what's the problem with Western critics of globalization?

10.   Wait, wait. Ethnic identity is not static? What do you mean?

11.   So how do you go about stopping this ethnic violence? Education? Government intervention? Quotas?

12.   Shouldn't the market-dominant minorities do something, too?

13.   Let's not forget the United States. What can it do?

14.   Yeah, I smell. Deal with it! Thanks for the walk.

D. THE RIGHT TO INFORMATION

A Critical View of India's Right to Information Act: What's Really Going On

We have seen how transparency became all the rage in the 1990s. When India passed the Right to Information Act in 2005, the legislation was hailed as a milestone in the transparency movement in EMEs. By 2008, seventy-eight countries had passed similar laws. Today we throw around the word without thinking much about it. But as this piece indicates, transparency is a contested term. In other words, it's a loaded term that can have complicated and conflicting subtexts. It becomes even more contested when you start talking about the "right" to information. And as this author argues, the term has to be understood in context. Once transparency is situated in the space between citizen and government, its meaning and effectiveness become a major battleground with real consequences for citizens who want answers to their questions. And in this battleground you should take into account how the global transparency movement affects the local movement.

A. SHARMA, "STATE TRANSPARENCY AFTER THE NEOLIBERAL TURN: THE POLITICS, LIMITS, AND PARADOXES OF INDIA'S RIGHT TO INFORMATION LAW"

Political and Legal Anthropology Review (2013), reproduced by permission of the American Anthropological Association from PoLAR: *Political and Legal Anthropology Review*, Volume 36, Issue 2, pages 308–325, November 2013.
Not for sale or further reproduction.

Introduction

What first caught my attention about India's Right to Information (RTI) law was the public reaction to it: the excitement and hope were palpable. Nearly every English-language Indian daily I read quoted people who hailed the passage of this law in 2005 as the most important step in state and democratic reform in five decades and as India's final liberation from colonialism. Consider this, for instance: "It is on October 12, 2005, [that India] got . . . actual independence, since it is the day when the RTI Act was enforced . . . . It is a true people's Act. It explains properly what democracy is" . . . The RTI law signified the decisive undoing of colonial rule because it challenged the British Official Secrets Act of 1889 that established a regime of state secrecy inherited by the postcolonial state. When I began my study of the everyday life of the RTI law in August 2008, many activists I interacted with described it as a tool for empowering ordinary citizens and changing the culture of governance by making it transparent, less corrupt, participatory, and accountable. But along with celebration came caution. Precisely because it augurs such important changes in governance and a shift in the balance of power between citizens and the state, the law faces ongoing challenges from officialdom. Shekhar Singh, a leading RTI figure, writes that "the RTI movement, though it has its own victims and levels of . . . violence, promises a much more benign method [as compared to Maoist groups] of making governments answerable . . . . The worrying thing is that the government . . . continues to try and weaken the RTI regime" . . .

> "The Indian fight for a right to information law emerged out of a series of struggles for survival by poor people. One challenge was to get payment of a statutory minimum wage for peopling working in the public sector. My organization, for the empowerment of workers and peasants, called the Mazdoor Kisan Shakti Sangathan (MKSS), unearthed startling discrepancies between official records and what was actually happening, including dead people's names being added to labour lists, people being entered as working in more than one place at the same time, and people who had never done manual work listed as manual workers. In one landmark hearing, 40 "ghost" workers were discovered. Their money was being pocketed by corrupt middle men. Disclosing records has significantly controlled such blatant fraud and malpractice."
> —A. Roy, "How the UK Can Learn From India's Right to Information Act," *The Guardian*, at http://www.theguardian.com/society/2012/apr/10/india-freedom-of-information (2012)

In this article, I show how the RTI law is being both implemented *and* subverted in India through routine bureaucratic proceduralism, and tease out the limits and contrary logic of state transparency in the neoliberal age.

Why do I invoke neoliberalism here? Primarily because this transnational policy context disappears in most popular accounts about the Indian RTI law, where, according to one of my interlocutors, only "certain factors get hearing space" . . . The RTI story is largely told as a tale of a homegrown fight undertaken by local groups, which successfully overturned state secrecy. I present a translocal picture that includes the larger context of neoliberal "good governance" (of which transparency is a centerpiece) against which the Indian story unfolds. My intention is neither to undermine the local part of the RTI tale nor to suggest that the global forces of neoliberalism tightly script the outcomes of governmental transparency in India. Rather, I attend to how the good governance mantra *articulates* with the RTI act and how it conditions the law's field of possibility. I consider where and in what manner dominant transnational meanings and practices of state transparency intersect with and color popular mobilizations of the RTI law in India . . . My contention is that the technocratic casting of transparent and good governance under neoliberalism lends a formalized and procedural hue to the ground-level workings of Indian RTI law. This ends up hemming in activist aspirations for fundamental changes in democratic governance, bureaucratizing social life and, paradoxically, reinforcing state opacity.

The turn toward good governance happened in the late 1980s, when mainstream development institutions, such as the World Bank, blamed the negative impact of structural adjustment programs on bad governance in the developing world . . . Fostering a facile and instrumentalist form of good governance-as-liberal democracy became the order of the day as a means for achieving development success. International agencies have since pushed a standard political liberalization package . . . across the globe, which includes top-down, technocratic reforms that formalize market-based freedom; civil society empowerment and participation; and governmental efficiency, minimalism, accountability, and transparency . . . Governance, here, is not seen as an exercise in power but as apolitical administration, which can be improved through expert restructuring. However, even as the global development regime works as an antipolitics machine . . . to depoliticize rule, it also spawns unpredictable forms of political struggles that challenge state power and keep the meaning of good governance and democracy in play . . . In the case of India's RTI law, bureaucratic paper archives and communication practices have emerged as critical arenas where this political contest is unfolding.

Government documents are the primary site of state transparency in both mainstream and populist imaginaries. Sunshine laws enable citizens to access these apparently faithful and comprehensive repositories of government work through formal petitioning. Official records, however, are not just annals of state facts but are also political artifacts that do not compile truths as much as conjure them. Bureaucratic documents are not simply products of statework but also produce the state. Official files, signatures, letterheads, and seals are routine objects that actualize state authority and rule in people's lives . . . The RTI law focuses on these symbols of political power, politicizing the relationship between writing, records, and governmental domination in new ways . . . Where burning documents was an important form of subaltern resistance against governmental authority in colonial India . . . , retrieving official papers through bureaucratic means is now emerging as a common mode of citizen protest against unaccountable state power.

This increasingly technocratic and formalized method of challenging the state has paradoxical consequences, at once empowering and disciplinary. The RTI law works as a governmental mechanism . . . that forces people to engage and audit the state in its own idiom. As petitioners learn how to make their demands legible by learning the ways and words of the state, however, the language of administration morphs. Officials shift the interplay between writing and orality in their daily work, change what they record and how they do so, and strategically use bureaucratic techniques to avert accountability and preserve anonymity. They thus ensure that the state remains vertically authoritative . . . and continues to be written under erasure . . . , even in the age of horizontality and transparency.

I proceed by first situating India's RTI law against a translocal context and explaining how it is supposed to work. I then draw upon ethnographic vignettes to elaborate my arguments about the limits and paradoxical effects of the RTI law. My stories are culled from a specific time and place, but they have wider relevance for understanding the relationship between secrecy and state power. I conclude this article by considering what makes the very idea of a transparent state a contradiction in terms.

Situating Information Freedom in India

The worlding of information as a "highly valued commodity" . . . and information freedom as a governance ideal have much to do with late capitalism, the end of the Cold War, neoliberal development discourse, and the information technology revolution. I found out, during an RTI workshop in New Delhi in December 2008, that while only 12 countries had sunshine laws in 1980, 78 countries had such laws by 2008. The gentleman conducting the workshop pointed out the protransparency countries, colored green on a map that he was using, and informed us that, "All countries that have comprehensive RTIs in place are democratic." . . . He explained that the global mushrooming of sunshine laws in the 1990s happened because of economic liberalization, which increased the threat of corporate and government corruption. In order to secure a proinvestment environment, many states had to downsize licensing regimes and enact disclosure laws.

The end of the Cold War also aided the worldwide spread of transparency. The collapse of the USSR reinforced the ideological equations between secrecy and authoritarianism, on the one hand, and freedom and Western liberal democracy, on the other. The democratic credentials and legitimacy of some post-Soviet states, like Ukraine, depended upon formally establishing information-sharing as a governance principle. Indeed, the international development regime has played a key role in scripting economic and political liberalization plans for the former Soviet world, in addition to the so-called Third World.

Organizations like the World Bank and the Asian Development Bank proliferate the neoliberal good governance agenda by tying loans and guarantees to administrative and judicial reforms . . . Transparency is a key variable in the calculus by which government efficiency and "goodness" is rated; it is a powerful instrument of global governmentality by which state conduct and practices are managed and normalized by multilateral institutions and international NGOs alike . . . The Millennium Challenge Corporation and Transparency International, for example, are nongovernmental actors that use accounting and audit technologies to rate the performance of governments according to standardized transparency and corruption indexes . . . These indexes are powerful regulatory tools that impact the political-economic present and future of nations. Institutionalizing transparency in this context sends an important signal that a country is a legitimate sovereign on the transnational capitalist stage, deserving of aid and investment.

Another factor that helped globalize transparency is the growth in information technology. The idea that information ought to be freely available and that "knowledge should be at my fingertips," as one of my elite male interlocuters unselfconsciously put it . . . , had arrived by the 1990s. Indeed, the World Bank coined the phrase "knowledge economy" to underscore the role that scientific education and information technology play in development and made India the poster child for its "Knowledge for Development" strategy . . . The Indian state's active promotion of this strategy reinforced the professional middle class's belief in the integral connection between information, knowledge, and power, and its unquestioned entitlement to all three.

While it is important to situate India's RTI law against these entangled global trends, the story of its passage is adamantly translocal. Grassroots movements in India, in opposition to narrow and instrumentalist definitions of good governance, compelled the Indian state to pass a progressive sunshine law that was not centered on capitalist profits or middle-class entitlement, but on the empowerment and survival rights of marginalized groups. During the 1980s and 1990s, there were prominent instances, such as the Union Carbide gas leak and Narmada Dam cases, where the Indian state invoked the Official Secrets Act and denied critical information to activists. Justice for the disenfranchised clearly required a law that overturned state secrecy.

The *Mazdoor Kisan Shakti Sangathan* (MKSS) (Worker Peasant Power Coalition), a people's movement founded in 1990 in the state of Rajasthan, took up the issue of transparency and mobilized the popular slogan, *Hum janenge, hum jeeyenge* (we will know, we will live). It fought and won a protracted battle against state corruption and injustice, and for information as a human right. MKSS organized around state-sponsored famine relief. Rajasthan is a drought prone area, and public works programs offer a key survival mechanism for the poor. The money slated for these programs, however, found its way into the pockets of the powerful. Accessing state records was the only way to trace this corruption. The government maintains "muster rolls" that list, among other things, the names of people who labor on public works projects and the wages paid to them. MKSS representatives were able to obtain muster rolls for famine relief work in certain areas and held *jan sunvais* (public hearings) to which they invited residents, officials, and other well-known personalities. Muster rolls were read out loud and those named were asked to verify if the recorded information was correct. The wrongdoings of administrators and local bigwigs were easily revealed: some laborers' names were made up; some names were those of people long dead; some of those listed as being paid were never paid; others who were paid got less than the recorded minimum wage; and so on. The officials present were questioned directly by residents and activists. In some cases, the intended beneficiaries of famine relief were paid retroactively. In other cases, a fear of public shaming pushed officials to settle accounts with individuals in advance of scheduled hearings. These "social audits" brought home the message that poor people's livelihoods and prospects for justice rested on obtaining state documents. Unlike the subaltern rebels . . . who resisted authority by destroying records, the peasants and workers representing MKSS confronted state power by demanding government records. Information, for them, was a human right, and necessary for survival and for building a just democracy.

The tenacious 15 year-long struggle led by MKSS, working alongside human rights activists, environmentalists, and the National Campaign for People's Right to Information, bore fruit in 2005 when the Indian parliament passed the RTI Act. According to this law, any citizen acting in the public interest can submit a written application for any information held by the government, as long as it does not pose a national security risk. For example, an individual can request details about how a member of Parliament used her or his annual quota of development funds, or ask for a list of the names and quantities of medicines stocked by a local government health clinic. Every government department designates Public Information Officers (PIOs), who constitute the first tier of the information bureaucracy. The PIOs have 30 days to process an RTI query. If they delay or refuse disclosure without providing written justification or if they release wrong or partial information, applicants can appeal to higher officials, First Appellate Authorities (FAAs), in the same department. If an FAA upholds a PIO's decision, applicants can turn to the highest tier of the information bureaucracy, Information Commissioners, at the state and central government levels, who have the power to decide whether a PIO and FAA acted in accordance with the law, and to penalize any PIO 250 Rupees (roughly US$4) per day up to a maximum of 25,000 Rupees or just over US$400 for wrongfully withholding or destroying information, or giving incomplete or incorrect information.

Mimicking the Words and Ways of the State

In August 2008, I began my research into the symbolic and material shifts in the imaginations and practices of citizenship, the state, and democracy that the RTI law represents. My project combined documentary research on legislative debates surrounding the Official Secrets and RTI acts with an ethnographic study of the everyday life of the RTI law, and I focused on three overlapping groups of actors: activists, citizen-users, and officials.

I entered the RTI field in New Delhi as a volunteer, working mainly with two NGOs that promote RTI education and usage among slum dwellers. I did specific projects for these organizations and assisted their employees in routine activities, such as awareness raising, filing RTI applications and appeals, and meeting officials. My volunteer work gave me access to RTI users of various class backgrounds, to the larger network of activists, and also to PIOs and Information Commissioners. Between August 2008 and August 2010, I interviewed several activists, applicants, lawyers, officials, and public intellectuals, and participated in workshops, conferences, public hearings, information commission proceedings, social audits, and rallies connected to the RTI act.

One of the NGOs I volunteered for was *Parivartan* (Change), which was founded by Arvind Kejriwal, a bureaucrat-turned-RTI activist. I first met Arvind at his home on a rain-soaked monsoon morning toward the end of August 2008. We discussed my research proposal and volunteering details over cups of hot, milky tea prepared by his mother. I found him warm and energetic, handling phone calls and work alongside our meeting without skipping a beat. He gave me useful suggestions about my research questions and also described a "right to food" project for which he sought my assistance. Parivartan was using the RTI law to expose corruption in the government's Public Distribution System, which dispenses subsidized food to people living below the poverty line, but which is also notorious for not delivering what it promises. We agreed that working on this project would allow me to understand how marginalized citizens were using the law to obtain entitlements from the state. Arvind also asked me to pick up a pamphlet about the RTI act from his office and to look it over carefully. It would be a quick read, he said, because the activists who drafted the law took pains to use simple and accessible language.

I obtained the RTI pamphlet later that day and began reading it on the metro ride home. While some parts of the law were straightforward, others were confusing. I was full of questions for Arvind at our next one-on-one meeting and sought clarification on the meaning of "public interest," the exemption clause that allows the state to withhold information, and the RTI application and appeals process. Arvind answered my queries patiently but also advised that the best way to understand how the law works and what its various clauses mean in practice was to submit an information request: "Just file an RTI application." "About what?" I wondered aloud. "Oh, about anything," replied Arvind. "MTNL [a government-owned telephone company] service, potholes in your neighborhood streets, anything at all" . . .

I chose to tackle an issue at home. My grandfather, a retired civil servant, had made an out-of-pocket payment for an emergency surgery. He was covered by the government's health plan and filed for reimbursement, but the health department had not processed his claim after nearly a year. "The government is dragging its feet because they know he is old," my mother confided in me. "They are just waiting for him to die" . . . We decided to make an RTI intervention.

I asked my grandfather what he wanted to say in his RTI petition. "That I am 91 years old and a retired government servant," he began, establishing his social legitimacy and claim on state services, and proceeded to narrate in elaborate detail why he could not seek prior permission for an emergency surgery. I produced a cleaned-up version of his story on my laptop and ended the application by asking why his claim had not been processed after nearly a year . . .

My activist colleague, Nisha, took one look at my two and a half-page, single-spaced letter and told me to edit it. She also asked me to delete the final question that I had posed, "Why has no action been taken?" and word it exactly as follows:

1. Please give me the daily progress made on my application so far: on which date my medical claim application reached which officer and what did this officer do.
2. Please give me the names of the officers who were supposed to take action on my medical claim reimbursement and have not done so.
3. What action will be taken against these officers and by when?
4. By when will I get my reimbursement of medical claim? . . .

Why did Nisha instruct me to shorten this petition when the law did not prescribe any word limit? And why did she substitute my simply worded "why" question with four new ones? I did not quiz Nisha right then as she was busy, but followed her advice and mailed the now single-page application, along with the required 10 Rupee fee (US$0.15) to the relevant PIO.

My perplexity was cleared a few weeks later when I participated in an RTI workshop organized for PIOs. Approximately 200 government officers, of whom barely a tenth were women, were in attendance. A senior civil servant opened the proceedings:

> For sixty years we were told not to give out any information—a continuation of the colonial mindset. [It is] not so now . . . . There is a lack of awareness among PIOs . . . . Their attitude seems to be: Find some exemption provision to deny information. This attitude must change . . . . Whatever might be the motivation of this law—whether it is grassroots activism or pressure from the World Bank—this Act is a milestone . . . . Everything *has* to be disclosed . . .

This was followed by a rapid clause-by-clause exposition of the law by two male facilitators, until they reached section eight. This section details the exemption clause of the RTI Act, specifying when information may be legally withheld for national security, sovereignty, and related reasons. Despite the repeated message of the facilitators that the new bureaucratic ethos ought to focus on releasing information, not hiding it, they were bombarded with questions about how PIOs could use section eight to reject RTI requests and avoid paying a penalty.

"I think we need to remember here that a point of view brought under public scrutiny and discussion in an isolated manner may sometimes present a distorted or incomplete picture of what really happened in the processes of making the final decisions. The Right to Information [Act] should not adversely affect the deliberative processes in the government."
—Manmohan Singh, Prime Minister of India, as quoted in "RTI Needs Critical Review: Manmohan Singh," at http://indiatoday.intoday.in/story/rti-act-prime-minister-manmohan-singh/1/154834.html (2011)

I found this discussion provocative, but also unsurprising. A PIO I had interviewed prior to the workshop told me that his was a "harassed lot" . . . The PIOs are directed to take on RTI duties in addition to their routine work and are mandated to share information in a timely and appropriate manner; otherwise their salaries can be docked. A fine of 25,000 Rupees is no small amount for PIOs, many of whom are lower-level government employees. The senior bureaucrats I interacted with largely supported the law and welcomed *RTI ka zamana* (the age of RTI). However, as an activist commented, these upper-class elite officers are "free to take a liberal, positive attitude" because they are not held personally liable for nondisclosure . . . For PIOs, however, the law has meant increased work, recordkeeping, and answerability to their bosses and, ostensibly, to the public. Because the law affects them directly, PIOs often seek clarification about its various sections and especially about the exemption clause. Vineet, an NGO representative who ran a helpline to assist citizens in understanding the RTI law and in filing applications, told me that a large proportion of the calls he received were from PIOs seeking advice on how to either appropriately respond to information requests or deny them without breaking the law . . .

At the above-mentioned workshop, I got a taste of the PIO interest in lawful nondisclosure. Among other questions, PIOs asked when they could label a petition "voluminous" or "frivolous and vexatious," or "not in the public interest," or a national security risk and reject it. Could they decline a query because it was noninformational? And could they refuse to answer "why" questions? I was taken aback. The law did not exclude "why" or any other questions as "noninformational" that did not merit response.

Later that evening I met up with Sunil, an NGO colleague, and shared my bafflement: "What does 'why' have to do with anything!" Sunil smiled knowingly and explained that the law defines information broadly as "anything that exists in government records" in any form, including documents, files, images, and computer data . . . However, many RTI applications are denied because the question a person asks cannot be answered given the form in which information is documented. Sunil gave me an example. If a person files an RTI application asking, "Why was my passport denied," but there is no official record of the reasons behind that denial, her request can be refused because the information she asked for is nonexistent. She cannot exert her right because she asked an unanswerable "why" question. If there were a "noting" in her passport file that specified the reasons for rejection, then "information" would exist and she could access it. Hence, what gets recorded in files and how it gets recorded makes a difference. State representatives lean toward not documenting the reasons behind their decision-making. Why questions, therefore, run aground in the RTI world. Sunil's explanation helped me understand the dynamics of the PIO workshop. I also realized that Nisha had reworded the why question on my grandfather's application to prevent its rejection: There was probably no note in his health department file that indicated why his reimbursement was being held up.

Sunil continued. "The reasons why . . . should be recorded!" he exclaimed passionately and shook his head in frustration. "We have been fighting to have such information included in files." I intervened: "Well, maybe you could pose the informational query in a more creative manner, without using 'why'." I mused about the possible ways one could phrase an RTI petition, quite like Nisha did, using what, who, and when questions. "But that just says that if you can use words and the English language better, then your petition will be heard," interjected Sunil angrily. "The [RTI] law is not about the creative use of language, Anu!"

Even as he chastised me, Sunil admitted that this was indeed happening. State functionaries were compromising the spirit of the law by narrowly interpreting the letter of the law and miring it in technicalities. If people want information from the government, they have to appeal to it primarily in writing, in a formalized and abbreviated idiom that mimics statist use of words. Vineet, who ran the RTI helpline mentioned above, had told me earlier that a simple RTI petition is not enough; people must use certain "key phrases [and] the right language" . . . He and other activists I worked with instructed applicants to format their information petitions in a formulaic manner, using institutionally appropriate language and asking a standardized set of what one of them called "magical questions" . . . , quite like the ones I had been told to pose on my grandfather's application.

Many RTI users I interviewed narrated their cases and complaints against the government in great detail. Their stories, like my grandfather's, partook in broader criticisms of governmental failure and corruption that suffuse the Indian public sphere . . . RTI applications constitute a recent form these criticisms take, through which people can grumble against the state and rightfully demand redress. Bureaucrats, however, tend to treat these applications as formulaic and concise petitions made by supplicants to a higher power, and not as creative critiques of that very power. The rich intricacies of my grandfather's case, which he composed into a moral story about his career in the government, retirement, old age, ill health, and rightful claims on the state, had no place in his official RTI letter. That letter had to be a dry and standard document that spoke to the state in its own specialized language. Walter Benjamin . . . blamed the thin and abbreviated information age for a decline in the art of storytelling; the technocratic narrowing of information under neoliberalism deals it a further blow.

The neoliberal emphasis on formalized transparency bureaucratizes and juridifies its workings. The language, interpretation, and procedures of the law become ends unto themselves. This focus on technical details tends to work against the more expansive popular agenda for state openness, inclusiveness, and accountability that MKSS and other activist groups strive for. Vineet told me that 60 percent of the RTI appeals made to Information Commissioners in Delhi are rejected on meaningless procedural grounds; for example, appeals are not typed or not written in English, or lack an index of the papers attached or a list of dates. He claimed that state's fixation on such bureaucratic minutiae has given new life to lawyers in Delhi, who compose suitable RTI applications and appeals for those who can afford them . . .

Official insistence on formal rules and words in the context of the RTI law normalizes statist languages of protest. It bureaucratizes social lives and activism, forcing ordinary individuals to become competent in a specific kind of technical literacy: "official-ese." The law acts as a governmental tool, dispersing "modalities and spaces of rule" . . . across society. This proliferation of cultures of audit and expertise . . . promotes activist citizenship of a documentary sort. The law's formal textual workings also tend to advantage middle- and upper-class "citizen-auditors" who have the requisite bureaucratic literacy, economic and cultural capital, as well as time to navigate the RTI world. As one of my elite informants commented:

> [The RTI law] has more power to work at the middle-class level: the people who know how to do this, the people who persist. The man who is uneducated . . . has to depend on somebody who can file an RTI form . . . . Even educated people have difficulty . . . in how to phrase questions . . . . I think [RTI] is going to be far more effective in the middle-class sector than anywhere else . . .

Those not fluent in statist words and ways, regardless of their formal schooling, have to rely upon others, like NGO workers and lawyers, to tackle the state's information labyrinth (Webb 2010). And those subalterns who have neither bureaucratic literacy nor contacts with NGOs or activists face obstacles in exercising a right that was, ironically, enacted in the name of empowering the ordinary citizen or *aam aadmi* (common man). The law's increasingly technocratic workings, in other words, can undermine democratic inclusivity and participation.

Interestingly, while officialdom insists that people must learn the language of the state and rigidly follow rules to access information, it is changing its own recording and communication practices in order to thwart disclosure. By changing what they document and how, state functionaries effectively alter records and, hence, the substance of information that may be available to the public. Predictably, therefore, government files and documentary practices have become more fetishized and fought over in the RTI age.

The State in a Mode of Erasure

Written records are deeply entangled with state power . . . Files are iconic of rationalized bureaucratic administration . . . , and play an important role in materializing the state as a vertically dominant entity . . . The Indian state's *kaghazi raj* (paper rule) . . . , put in place by the British, relies on an elaborate system of organizing and circulating files. These "paper shrines" . . . , built with the occult-like force of official inscriptions, are capable of manipulating lives . . . "To most laypersons the government file is a musty compilation of important papers. Almost all of India, even the illiterate . . . knows the significance and power the file holds to control the destiny of many people" . . . Official files, as mysterious fetish objects, symbolize and carry hidden and inexplicable powers. Their religico-magical force is sustained by the authoritative and just-out-of-reach nature of the "paperealities" . . . they construct. The RTI law politicizes these files by promising to make their contents knowable.

Every government file contains two sections: the substantive papers relating to a particular project on the right-hand side, and official notes, written or typed, on the left. "File notings" constitute a specific form of statist writing, documenting the flow of work between different levels of a departmental bureaucracy, the opinions and oral deliberations of functionaries at each level, and the final decision on a particular issue and its implementation process. The British created this noting system for "internal transparency and oversight" . . . , not public accountability. The Official Secrets law protected the identities, written recommendations, and acts of colonial administrators. Signed or initialed bureaucratic notes carry a different significance, however, under transparent postcolonial democracy. File notings become a dangerous and unsecured paper trail for bureaucrats—a potentially enduring record of their past actions and communication, which can reveal the why, who, and how of state decisionmaking to citizens. The very thing that enacts state verticality, sovereignty, and mystique when hidden—an official note—can threaten to unravel state reason and power when exposed.

Predictably, the bureaucratic establishment in India fought to keep notings out of the RTI act. The activists who drafted the act pointedly used the phrase "including file notings" when defining information, but it was deleted in the version of the bill debated and passed by the parliament . . . Activists nonetheless believed that notings were unquestionably covered under the law. The state agency charged with implementing the RTI legislation, however, declared that notings do not count as public information because they record "internal" bureaucratic discussions on an issue prior to a final decision . . . Citizens appealed to information commissions, which upheld the activist interpretation that notings constitute a "paper trail, vital to establish a chain of transparency and accountability," and excluding them was tantamount to "taking the life out of the RTI Act" . . . In 2006 and 2009, officials tried to amend the law and take out notings but failed in their efforts; the battle, however, is far from over.

This struggle over file notings reveals the accepted truisms regarding state records that underwrite India's RTI law and the mainstream logic of transparency. This logic . . . relies on a straightforward relationship between "the signifier and the signified, or between representation and reality" . . . Files are assumed to faithfully reproduce backstage realities of statework and to serve as permanent inscribed chronicles of administrative facts and oral decision-making. Official notes, moreover, are sanctified as stand-ins for state officials; they give power a face. People can get a hold on the state and rein in arbitrary power by accessing files and notings. That, at least, is the presumed ideal.

In practice, however, bureaucratic documents rarely function as unchanging and legible stores of administrative work, disinterestedly constructed through rational rules. Even bureaucrats know and decry this, as the following memo, circulated by the vice chairman of the Slum Department of the Delhi Development Authority, makes obvious:

> Not much care is being taken for proper up-keep of files and papers. Many times files become so bulky that corners of pages are torn and previous notings become totally illegible. In the majority of files, the correspondence and noting portions are not page numbered, leading to a situation where any paper can be taken out if somebody had mala fide intentions . . .

Where files are malleable, notings can obfuscate . . . . [R]epresentatives of the Pakistani bureaucracy inscribe notes so as to avoid personal responsibility. They confuse agency by using passive voice and quoting words from previous notes rather than naming particular individuals . . . They duplicate a certain mode of writing rather than referring to a specific decision-maker. Thus notings operate as authorless bureaucratic texts and reproduce a mimicked and enclosed knowledge economy where agency, intentionality, and originality are mystified.

The internal administrative scripts of Indian government bodies are now under the public gaze, and officials are altering the form and content of file notings to further complicate legibility, authorship, and accountability. A mid-level government employee told me in confidence that instead of writing detailed comments on note sheets included in files, some of his coworkers use separate notepads that circulate alongside files but are not included in the official record . . . Neel, a researcher who was part of a study on the impact of the RTI law, reported during a meeting that officials increasingly write notes on sticky papers, which can be removed; he called this the new "Post-it" culture of bureaucracy. Neel added that even when officials inscribe and initial a note on a note sheet, they often write "see me" or "discuss with me." Discussions largely happen in person or over phones and what gets recorded in the file is the phrase, "seen, discussed, deliberated" and the final decision. Aruna Roy, a prominent RTI activist and former bureaucrat, who was in attendance at this meeting, criticized these practices: "If seen, what was seen! If discussed, what was discussed! Whenever there is a difficult decision to take, bureaucrats choose a scapegoat and make this person write the note" . . . In other words, officials either use meaningless words that do not convey anything or calculatingly document information to frame particular individuals and circumvent responsibility for bad judgments. Both these procedural tactics largely preserve state inscrutability and unaccountability.

Thus, when ordinary bureaucratic records and forms of writing are redefined as "information" and become objects of public concern, they are made to morph. Government representatives are able to maintain state verticality, elusiveness, and unanswerability by simply changing how they communicate and what they record. Bureaucratic writing atrophies and remains only partly legible. The use of ephemeral Post-it notes in files or of the phrase "seen, discussed, deliberated," as a chain of empty words that refuse to signify, guarantee neither the transparency of meaning nor the traceability of power . . . Additionally, the emphasis on oral deliberations, in person or over the phone, which often go unrecorded, makes official notings and files even more partial and evanescent.

These instances force us to contend with the mutuality of and exchange between writing and orality in administrative rule . . . Writing is commonly understood as the script of the state because of its supposed certitude in conveying meaning, portability, and permanence as a mode of recording information. However, a singular focus on the fact of writing occludes the form and content of official inscriptions and how they intertwine with spoken words to enact state authority. The examples I have recounted demonstrate that ephemeral forms of writing and orality work in tandem to keep state power arbitrary and opaque. Administrative writing, albeit never entirely intelligible, can signify even less as government documents are made accessible. And orality's "jelly fish like" . . . quality—manipulable and fleeting—makes it valuable for exerting bureaucratic state power. Orality is not just a powerful mode of antistate resistance and horizontality . . . ; it can equally well serve to enforce hierarchy and subvert substantive democratization when used by those in power.

Vanishing bureaucratic scripts and atrophied records, which are rendered more powerful for what they do not say rather than for what they do, ensure that the state continues to be spoken and written under erasure in the era of transparency. Accessing a file in this context becomes akin to making one's way through more puzzles and fictions . . . rather than following a certain path to the truth of state authority and reason. The face of state power is more liable to disappear just when you think you can grasp it through its records. This perpetual deferral makes the work of citizens, particularly activists, difficult. They must learn statist languages and simultaneously fight to transform them. RTI activists demand literality: faithful documentation of oral discussions and meticulous notes that make bureaucratic realities and authors unambiguously present and the state decipherable. This, however, is proving difficult to achieve given the very nature of bureaucracy and sovereign state power, as I next discuss.

State Power and Transparency: Concluding Thoughts

I received an initial reply to my grandfather's RTI petition within two weeks, informing me that it was being forwarded to the correct PIO.

Around two weeks later I got a letter from the appropriate PIO requesting some case-related details, which were, in fact, already included in the original document. Interpreting this as an object lesson in official foot-dragging, I wrote a frustrated but proper response restating the required facts and my four questions. After nearly eight weeks, well past the 30-day deadline for PIOs to respond to RTI queries, a health department functionary told us over the phone that my grandfather's reimbursement had been approved and would be disbursed after the new federal budget was passed in February 2009. The payment arrived in May 2009. Interestingly, whereas the RTI law helped my grandfather receive his entitled due in a "timelier" manner, it failed to deliver on his right to information. We did not find out the answers to the questions we had asked on his application, including the names of the officials who processed his file.

Many users of the law I interacted with had similar experiences. *RTI se kaam ho jata hai* (RTI gets work done) was a common refrain I heard.

Activists also applauded the law's success as a "grievance redress" mechanism, but some felt that this undermined the larger aim of information disclosure. Limited improvement in governmental efficiency on an individual basis could dangerously trump the norm of state transparency, which, for many activists, is the main goal of the law. Ashish, for example, while discussing the findings of a national RTI-impact study then under way in 2008–09, expressed optimism about the reported increase in the number of RTI petitions. He saw this as a sign of growing public empowerment but stated that the ultimate measure of the law's success would be a decline in RTI queries . . . This would happen when the government shared information proactively, thus rendering it unnecessary for citizens to use their right to information. The RTI law, in other words, would triumph when it obviated its own need.

> *"RTI naysayers may breathe easy. India's bureaucracy is already choking the RTI Act to a slow death. According to a forecast by Shailesh Gandhi, one of India's leading Information Commissioners (IC), the Central Information Commission (CIC) is likely to be saddled with over 90,000 pending complaints by 2015. Gandhi believes that the Act is losing steam because there are not enough people to handle the number of pending complaints. If Gandhi's forecast is accurate, a waiting period of at least three years is to be expected before a complaint can be taken up. This because all the commissioners together can at best solve just about 30,000 cases in a year."*
> —U. Misra, "The Slow Death of the RTI Act," *Forbes India,* at http://forbesindia.com/article/resolutio n/the-slow-death-of-the-rti-act/22182/1 (2011)

This aim, as I have illustrated above, is proving tough to achieve in practice and is being subverted through procedural tactics and technicalities. State transparency in contemporary India is a checkered terrain, in part because of its transnational articulations with neoliberal development discourse. This discourse promotes a form of good democratic governance that is technocratic and instrumentalist. Governance, in the neoliberal imagination, concerns neither rule nor power but is reduced to administrative and judicial reforms. Democracy is promoted not for its radical potential but for the veneer of representation and legitimacy that it lends to antipoor austerity measures . . . This seemingly apolitical, formalized approach conditions the workings of the Indian RTI law; it tussles with and constrains popular understandings of transparency as "engaged political activity" . . . aimed at fundamentally altering the institutions and modes of democratic governance.

The ground level dynamics of the Indian RTI act are paradoxical. The law, enacted in the name of the ordinary citizen, furthers cultures of expertise and audit among the public that are empowering for some but not necessarily horizontal or inclusive. It governmentalizes social life and fosters bureaucratized activism and procedural citizenship. It also ends up reifying opacity as the core of state power, as officials tactically alter their modes of decision-making, communication, and documentation to confuse accountability and preclude information sharing.

By highlighting the inconsistencies and obstacles that arise in the workings of the RTI act, I do not wish to mark the exceptionalism of the Indian state or use it as a typical example of Third World corruption. Indeed, the Indian case has broader theoretical relevance for understanding transparency, secrecy, and state power. It reveals that secrecy is not a distortion of a liberal democratic state, but constitutive of it. My contention is that bureaucratic and sovereign modes of state power . . . are at odds with the ideal of transparent governance and subvert it from within.

Bureaucracy, as depersonalized, hierarchical, and rationalized rule, is premised on procedures and structures that keep the authorless governmental machine working precisely and predictably. This Weberian-type state body—where bureaucrats are entirely defined by their function, personal ties do not matter, and the public can access everything efficiently—is presumed normative by the neoliberal governance mantra. Indeed, every charge of corruption and every rating of countries on standardized governance and transparency scales reinforce the ideal bureaucratic state—streamlined, calculable, and impersonal . . . This onstage rationality, visibility, and liberality of bureaucratic bodies, however, is made possible by whisking arbitrariness, opacity, and illiberality out of sight. For example:

> On the one hand, bureaucratic institutions accentuate their rational side . . . in the form of transparent criteria . . . . The flip side of the transparency of bureaucratic institutions . . . is the public erasure of irrational actions and decisions . . . . This is done by hiding what goes on inside . . . through a whole range of naturalized and logical strategies . . .

Bureaucratic state power and transparency exert contrary pulls on each other. Transparency relies on making state representatives accountable for their actions by publicizing government paper archives that supposedly reveal how decisions were made and by whom. Agency and accountability run into trouble with the principle of anonymity, which also lies at the heart of rationalized bureaucracy and is reproduced through banal procedures that depersonalize authority. Making a bureaucratically organized state transparent through the very languages and rules that keep power faceless is bound to run aground at some point.

Furthermore, these languages and procedures can be bent at random by state agents to keep bureaucratic operations opaque. Arbitrariness, after all, is a key aspect of state sovereignty. This prerogative or illiberal mode of state power . . .—what defines the raison d'être of a state—is "expressed as the armed force of the police or as vacillating criteria for obtaining welfare benefits" . . . Random changes in bureaucratic policies and rules articulate the sovereign will of the state as much as spectacular displays of might. The Indian case revels how procedural tactics and bureaucratic discretion allow for the routine exertion of sovereign state power; they are used by officialdom to reify its authority and water down the RTI law. In fact, before this act was passed, a section of the bureaucracy argued that transparency was anathema because "government would become too rigid and rule-bound as no officer would like to exercise discretion which could later be questioned" . . . On the one hand, officials want to preserve their authority to arbitrarily ignore rules, but on the other hand, they force the public to follow tedious rules in order to obtain information. Indeed, on July 31, 2012, the government issued new rules regarding the RTI law, which dictate that applications cannot exceed 500 words and appeals to the Information Commissions must contain all required documents in order to prevent delays or rejection . . . Significantly, these rules were made in a nonparticipatory and opaque manner.

Secrecy and arbitrary discretion are not marks of bad or corrupt government, as dichotomous understandings of state transparency tend to assume, but of government-as-usual. Secrecy is the other face of the open, democratic state. Indeed, "bureaucratic administration always tends to be an administration of 'secret sessions'; in so far as it can, it hides its knowledge and action" . . . And Indian officials who opposed the RTI law from the start argued that secrecy is "the bedrock of governance" . . . These bureaucrats lost, but only partially. The connection between state sovereignty and secrecy is institutionalized in the law. Section eight of the RTI act excludes from disclosure any information that "would prejudicially affect the sovereignty and integrity of India [and] the security, strategic, scientific or economic interests of the State" . . . This clause establishes sovereignty as the limit of transparency and as an exception; it cannot do otherwise.

The global regime of neoliberal governmentality challenges state sovereignty and verticality by attempting to downsize governments; by enabling certain modes of participatory and self-government; and by compromising, to lesser or greater degrees, states' control over domestic policymaking . . . Additionally, popular demands for state accountability and openness in India also contest state power by challenging governmental impenetrability. The RTI law does augur danger for governmental secrecy, which has been in place for a very long time. It threatens to respatialize the state's distinction from and domination over society by allowing those on the outside to question and partake in inside decisions. This gets to the heart of state sovereignty—that backstage, privatized recess that symbolizes the "why" of rule and the sheer "prestige of domination" . . . This is the space where illiberality, arbitrariness, and unaccountability reign. It is this face of the state that citizens threaten to unravel and implode when they retrieve official records as information. Some escape hatches are needed if the state's sovereign prerogative is to be maintained in the age of participatory and transparent governance. The exemption clause in the RTI law, the expanding bureaucratic procedures that citizens must follow to actualize their right to information, and emergent modes of official communication and documentation that routinely frustrate disclosure, serve as those escape hatches; they prevent the transgression of the state-nonstate boundary and hierarchy, and keep the why and who of state power illegible.

You Gotta Know Something About Them!

Aruna Roy

Image of Aruna Roy by V. Malik, modifications by Ekabhishek, is licensed under CC BY 2.0.

Aruna Roy was born in Chennai, India and then moved with her parents to New Delhi when she was four. She was a kind of "renaissance student." Five years at the Convent of Jesus and Mary. Then off to Kalakshetra (a renowned art school) where she studied art, dance, and classical music. Throw in some religious studies and a major in English literature. Interesting story about how Aruna helped make the RTI a reality: She joined the prestigious Indian Administrative Services (IAS), which is the civil service that supports all aspects of Indian governance. She then left the government and joined a social work group started by her husband, which led her to establish the Mazdoor Kisan Shakti Sangathana (MKSS). Aruna helped steer a nationwide debate regarding the public's right to view official records and demand transparent government.

Check this out: Aruna and her hubby agreed to a number of marriage covenants of sorts: no kids; they had to be financially independent of each other; they wouldn't cram their beliefs down each other's throat; and to be free as individuals to do what they wanted. Did they shake hands on this stuff?

QUESTIONS FROM YOUR TALKING DOG

1.   Yeah, I'm a pretty critical thinker. I bet I can score higher on the LSAT than you . . . Sorry, I suppose that was a little out of line. So, India's Right to Information Act. I'm up for a discussion of it. So how did it come about?

2.   This article. Pretty cool. Fetishized? What does that mean and how does it relate to the RTI?

3.   You've always told me that transparency is cool, especially between us. But then how does government mess it up?

4.   Yeah, I get what global neoliberalism means. I'm hip. Well, maybe you should remind me . . . So how does the author relate neoliberalism to governance and transparency?

E. FINANCIAL INCLUSION:
EXCLUSION SUCKS IN LOTS OF WAYS

"The stark reality is that most poor people in the world still lack access to sustainable financial services . . . The great challenge before us is to address the constraints that exclude people from full participation in the financial sector," said Kofi Annan, then the Secretary General of the United Nations, declaring 2005 as the International Year of Microcredit. Other international development organizations, as well as policymakers in developing countries, have been increasingly emphasizing the need to build more inclusive financial systems as the essential part of development agenda. This excerpt looks at financial inclusion in Africa. As you'll see, the extent of aggregate financial exclusion in the continent is staggering. And differences in inclusion/exclusion among, and within, countries are equally staggering. Why should financial inclusion matter? For one, channeling savings into the formal financial sector (e.g., banking) will increase savings that can be invested to promote growth. But from a broader perspective, financial inclusion is yet another aspect of today's bottom-up, participatory framework of development. Financial

> *"Globally, 2.5 billion adults have no mechanisms to save money, let alone pay bills through a transactional account or through a mobile phone. We believe we can chart a path toward universal financial access by bringing together multiple approaches and technologies. This is exactly the type of ambitious project that can help lift many people, especially women, out of poverty."*
> —World Bank Group President Jim Yong Kim quoted in B. Nolan, "Quotable: Universal Financial Access By 2020 Is Possible," at http://www.globalenvision.org/2013/10/30/quotable-universal-financial-access-2020-possible (2013)

> *"Now, we in the Obama Administration have made financial inclusion a priority. Last year, President Obama announced a new Microfinance Growth Fund, which has committed more than $100 million to provide credit to individuals and small businesses, especially those run by women. Beyond that, we are encouraging partnerships to open up new opportunities for mobile banking."*
> —Secretary of State Hillary Clinton, Speaking at the Millennium Development Goals Summit, 2010.

inclusion, then, is really about increasing the capabilities of individuals (and businesses). Is financial inclusion a human right? Hmmm ... But even if you don't want

> *"But economic inclusion also implies a kind of belonging and membership in the economy that goes beyond employment. In the financial and regulatory world, "economic inclusion" refers to efforts to expand public access to, and participation in, mainstream financial services. This effective inclusion in the financial marketplace depends upon a strong regulatory framework, active market participation, and an expansion in public financial literacy. [Financial inclusion] ... is indispensably important to effective navigation of the twists and turns of life in the American economy. Imagine what it would be like, even with a job, if you had no access to banking or credit; if you did not understand how mortgages or credit cards work; or if you had no way to save a portion of your earnings. Sadly, there are millions of Americans lingering in these margins."*
> —Speech by Governor Sarah Bloom Raskin, "Economic and Financial Inclusion in 2011: What it Means for Americans and our Economic Recovery," at the New America Foundation Forum, Washington, D.C. (2011)

to go there, financial inclusion makes a whole lot of sense when it comes to economic development, both on a national and global level. Still, there are roadblocks, ranging from lack of infrastructure—especially in rural areas—to lack of confidence in the banking industry. Oh, and if you think financial inclusion is only important for EMEs (and developing countries), think again.

A. HANNIG & S. JANSEN, *FINANCIAL INCLUSION AND FINANCIAL STABILITY: CURRENT POLICY ISSUES* IN FINANCIAL MARKET REGULATION AND REFORMS IN EMERGING MARKETS

Kawai, Masahiro, and Eswar S. Prasad, eds. Financial Market Regulation and Reforms in Emerging Markets. pp. 285–305. © 2011 The Brookings Institution and ADBI.

* * *

What Is Financial Inclusion?

Financial inclusion aims at drawing "unbanked" populations into the formal financial system so that they have the opportunity to access financial services ranging from savings, payments, and transfers to credit and insurance. Financial inclusion neither implies that everybody should make use of the supply, nor that providers should disregard risks and other costs when deciding to offer services. Both voluntary exclusion and unfavorable risk-return characteristics may preclude a household or a small firm, despite unrestrained access, from using one or more of the services. Such outcomes do not necessarily warrant policy intervention. Rather, policy initiatives should aim to correct market failures and to eliminate nonmarket barriers to accessing a broad range of financial services.

Despite the considerable progress made by microfinance institutions, credit

> *"Eventually, you should unleash domestic savings because of the domestic resources that should be put back in to productive loans so that people can actually make the investment, grow the production, and increase employment."*
>
> —Her Majesty Queen Maxima of the Netherlands, U.N. Special Advocate for Financial Inclusion quoted in M. van der Wolf, "UN Utilizing Financial Inclusion Programs to Fight Rural Poverty," at http://www.voanews.com/content/un-utilizing-financial-inclusion-programs-fight-rural-poverty/1811039.html (2013)

unions, and savings cooperatives over the last two decades, the majority of the world's poor remain unserved by formal financial intermediaries that can safely manage cash and intermediate between net savers and net borrowers. According to the Consultative Group to Assist the Poor (CGAP), the absolute number of savings accounts worldwide is reported to exceed the global population. And yet half of the world's adult population—2.5 billion people—does not, in fact, have access to savings accounts and other formal financial services . . .

Financial sector policies have evolved through three styli stages: first, fostering state-let industrial and agricultural development through direct a credit; second, market-led development through liberalization and deregulation; and third, institution building that aims at balancing market and government failures.

At least until the 1980s, many developing countries channeled public funds to target groups like farmers and small enterprises, and regulated the scope of activities for which these funds could be used. These "directed credit" programs assume that the rural poor were unable to save or to afford market rates of interest and therefore needed loans at subsidized rates to build capital. Hence development banks lent at below-market rates to selected target groups. To find cheap loans, deposit rates were often subject to regulatory ceilings, undermining domestic resource mobilization. The results of "financial repression" were typically shallow financial systems and institutions that have little capacity to allocate resources efficiently according to risk-return characteristics . . .

At the end of the 1980s, a new approach emerged that focused on the performance of financial institutions in delivering their services to segments of the population with little or no access to finance. The changes were substantial: the new approach shifted the discussion away from individual firms and households to institutions and their ability to provide services on a sustainable and widespread basis. Initial experiences in Indonesia, Bangladesh, Bolivia, and some other countries demonstrated that micro finance and rural finance conceived as "banking with the poor" are indeed financially viable and made us increase our reach unsustainable basis. These encouraging examples led to a new view called the "financial system" paradigm . . .

Over the past few years, micro finance has undergone a rapid transformation as it links to the formal financial system have been expanded. Growing theoretical and empirical evidence suggests that financial systems that serve low-income people promote pro-poor growth. Lack of access to finance, therefore, adversely affects growth and poverty alleviation. It makes it more difficult for the poor to accumulate savings and build assets to protect against risks, as well as to invest in income-generating projects. As a result, the interest in financial sector development has increasingly focused on the factors that determine not only the depth but also breadth of access, in a move toward inclusive financial systems . . .

How to Measure Progress?

Reliable and comprehensive data that capture various dimensions of financial inclusion are a critical condition for evidence-based policymaking . . .

Broadly speaking, financial inclusion can be measured through the following lenses in order of complexity:

- Access: the ability to use available financial services and products from formal institutions . . .

- Quality: the relevance of the financial service or product to the lifestyle needs of the consumer . . .

- Usage: beyond the basic adoption of banking services, usage focuses more on the permanence and depth of financial service and product use . . .

- Impact: measuring changes in the lives of consumers that can be attributed to the usage of a financial device or service poses serious methodological challenges to survey design . . .

Financial Inclusion Trends

There has been significant but uneven progress toward financial inclusion around the world in recent years. Some of the steps have been driven by market-friendly policies . . .

Some countries in Asia, such as India and Indonesia, have a long tradition of emphasizing access to finance. At the regional level, these policy priorities have paid off: 25% of households living on less than two dollars a day now have access to formal or semiformal financial services, compared to 40 to 50% of the population as a whole.

Other success stories include:

> *"We, in India, are currently engaged in a massive exercise to enable our large population in rural areas to have access to banks. This is being achieved through the use of a bio-metric unique identification system which establishes identity and enables the individual to access her bank account through a network of banking correspondents using information technology and mobile connectivity. In this way, modern technology and institutional innovation will help add hundreds of millions of individuals as customers of banks in the short space of a few years."*
> —Dr. Manmohan Singh, Prime Minister of India, Second Working Session of the St. Petersburg G-20 Summit, "Financial Inclusion Essential for Inclusive Growth: PM," at https://in.news.yahoo.com/financial-inclusion-essential-inclusive-growth-pm-114238720.html (2013)

- Mongolia a successful turnaround of a state bank increased the number of deposits by over 1.4 million since 2006, now reaching 62 percent of households.

- Philippines: mobile phone banking has expanded to serve four million clients since 2002 . . .

- Bangladesh: Four to six million new microcredit clients have been added since 2006; financial services have reached about 55% of poor households, substantially expanding access to savings . . .

Particularly in Asia, the poor are often served by public banks or non-bank entities, including nongovernmental (NGOs), with private sector banks playing a smaller role. Key examples of these public banks and non-bank entities include:

- Pakistan: post-Savings Bank, with 3.6 million accounts in 2006 . . .

- Thailand: Government Savings Bank, with thirty-six million accounts in 2006 . . .

However, despite this outreach, service quality is inferior, and most institutions depend on subsidies . . .

Africa faces substantially larger challenges than most of Asia, mostly due to a much higher incidence of poverty . . . While across Asia 25 percent of poor households have access to formal financial services, individual countries in Africa rarely demonstrate such a level of household access.

In Africa, Kenya has pioneered an interesting process of financial inclusion through leapfrogging to mobile phone payment solutions . . . As of 2009, with only three years of its initial startup, the Kenyan telecommunications provider Safaricom has attracted 7.9 million subscribers to its short message service-based transfer scheme, with significant positive impacts on users.

Latin America is home to some of the best regulatory environments for microfinance, such as Peru and Bolivia. In these two countries, rapid growth over the past seven years has included six million clients in the formal financial system . . .

Despite these impressive achievements, half of the world's population is still without access to savings accounts, insurance, and other financial services, and about 95 percent of the unbanked are in developing countries.

Impact of Financial Inclusion: Recent Evidence

. . . Most countries are only beginning to track financial inclusion, so data for projecting longer-term trends are not yet available . . .

Macroeconomic Evidence

Financial institutions contribute to growth by reducing information asymmetries that would otherwise hinder the efficient intermediation of resources among savers and investors. There is substantial evidence that financial development has a causal impact on growth . . . . Along these lines, access to finance for new entrepreneurs is an important ingredient in the finance-growth nexus.

More recently, the focus has shifted to links between finance and income inequality . . . [T]he aggregate usage financial services, that is, deeper financial systems, appears to reduce Gini coefficients, a measurement of inequality.

There is also evidence at the macroeconomic level that broader financial systems enhance economic growth . . .

Microeconomic Evidence

. . . In Kenya, a randomly selected group of rural poor were offered savings accounts. The impact was found to be highly positive: uptake was very significant for female clients, and female market vendors reached higher daily expenditure levels within six months of opening an account. There was no evidence that savings accounts crowd out other investments, and neither was there evidence that the savings accounts allow for more efficient smoothing over bad shocks, particularly sickness. This study also shows a more significant positive impact of savings accounts for women than for men . . .

Recent research in South Africa highlights the risk management benefits of financial inclusion. Loan applicants that have been declined "at the margin" were randomly offered loans and turned out to be significantly less likely to report leaving a job after entering the experiment than those rejected clients without loans. Treated households earn more and were more likely to move out of poverty. Overall, increased access to credit appears to improve welfare. The study does present evidence that short-term loans are an important cash flow management tool and that they have largely positive impacts on people's welfare, particularly in the area of employment and income. The study also found that loans to customers at (or slightly beyond) the margin were actually profitable . . .

Financial Inclusion Policies: Recent Innovations

The financial sector is prone to market failure and, therefore, is generally heavily regulated. The low-income segment is particularly plagued by information asymmetries, as participants of the demand side often lack a track record or collateral to pacify lenders concerns. In addition, lenders lack experience in new markets at the bottom of the pyramid and face adjustment costs regarding business processes. At the same time, the limited size of both individual transactions and the overall market pose challenges to suppliers that need to recover fixed costs.

> "One key innovation which I believe has as much potential to transform the lives of the poor as a new vaccine or yielding crop, is digital payments. Digital payments give the poor a foothold [to escape poverty] by freeing them from one of their biggest obstacles to financial security: cash."
>
> —Bill Gates, Speaking at the United Nations General Assembly event Partnerships for Digital Financial Inclusion, as quoted at http://betterthancash.org/news-releases/digital-payments-and-financial-inclusion-key-to-poverty-alleviation-and-economic-growth-say-world-leaders/ (2013)

However, once the pioneers of the microfinance revolution demonstrated tangible market opportunities, substantial business model innovation has expanded the "access possibilities frontier." More recently, technological innovation has dramatically lower the fixed costs of reaching the low-income segment in attracted a broader range of new suppliers.

Agent Banking

Policies that enable banks to contract with nonbank retail agents as outlets for financial services have proven highly successful in advancing financial inclusion where bank branches are not economically viable. Such policies leverage existing retail infrastructure as delivery channels and turn pharmacies, post offices, or supermarkets not only into agents of banks but agents of financial inclusion.

Collaboration among banks and agents has become possible as technology has reduced the cost and risks of the remote exchange of information to carry out financial transactions. Coupled with simplified account opening procedures and other incentives to use this channel, such as the delivery of cash transfers, financial system outreach and numbers of users can increase explosively, as recently observed in Brazil.

Brazil was the early leader in agent banking through the large-scale introduction of "banking correspondents" to distribute welfare grants to unbanked Brazilians. This solution addressed a key physical access barrier: Only 1,600 municipalities had bank branches in 2000. Today, some

95,000 correspondents cover all of the 5,500 municipalities, and nearly twelve million accounts were opened at agents over three years. The Brazilian success has inspired similar approaches in Colombia, Peru, Mexico, and Chile . . .

Mobile Payments

Globally, four billion mobile phone subscriptions were projected for 2009, well over half of them in the developing world. Mobile phone penetration in developing countries has almost tripled in the past five years, with Asia in particular showing high growth rates . . . In Kenya, for example, 47 percent of adults own a mobile phone, and the rate of ownership rises to 73 percent in urban areas and 80 percent in Nairobi . . .

In Kenya, the e-money transfer service M-PESA offered by mobile network operator Safaricom has achieved the most impressive outreach of mobile payments thus far. The service has experienced rapid growth and currently enjoys a subscription base of more than seven million registered customers, many previously unbanked. A recent national survey illustrates the positive impact on financial inclusion: the usage of semiformal services including M-PESAhas increased from 8.1 percent in 2006 to 17.9 percent in 2009, while the proportion of the population with access to only informal financial services decreased from 35 percent to 26.8 percent, respectively. Most important, the share of the population excluded from financial service decreased from 38.3 percent to 32.7 percent over the same time frame . . .

Formalizing Microsavings

Policymakers have adopted various regulatory and supervisory strategies to manage the risks of licensing a wider range of institutions to offer deposit and insurance products. Strategies to adapt banking regulations to the specific nature of micro-finance include:

> *"Long before the crisis of 2008, when financial institutions were crumbling all over the world, many of us had been saying that we need to redesign the financial system [which] only serves the top one-third of the world; two-thirds are left out. Microcredit has shown how you can reach out to people that conventional banking cannot. It has demonstrated that it's a doable proposition."* Muhammad Yunus as quoted in D. Bornstein, "Beyond Profit: A Talk With Muhammad Yunus,"*
> *—The New York Times,* at http://opinionator.blogs.nytimes.com/2013/04/17/beyond-profit-a-talk-with-muhammad-yunus/?_php=true&_type=blogs&_r=0 (2013)

- licenses for specialized institutions dedicated to taking microdeposits,

- bank licenses for successfully transforming financial NGOs, or

- licenses for nonbank financial institutions . . .

In Bolivia, two microfinance NGOs that transformed into banks and six nonbank deposit-taking micro finance institutions (known as private financial funds) operating under a special regulatory framework held a combined $955 million in deposits as of June 2008. Of this amount, $458 million were held by the private financial funds, which opened almost

136,000 new savings accounts in the first half of 2008. New laws, specially designed for previously unregulated NGOs, were passed in 2008. The main difference from the preceding model is that NGOs will not need to be transformed into private financial funds. Instead, they will keep their nonprofit status and be allowed to collect deposits and offer extra financial services. NGOs will have the nature of nonbanking financial intermediaries but will be under the same rules as banks and financial entities.

State Bank Reform

In many countries, state-owned banks still play a major role in the banking system, and in providing financial services to the poor . . . [S]ome governments have closed down poorly performing state banks as the least-cost choice, as did Benin, Brazil, and Peru, while others continue to suffer from political interference and mediocre performance. More interestingly, however, some policymaker-pushed reforms have demonstrated the potential to turn financial inclusion into a new, profitable business for state banks.

Rather than restructuring the whole bank, Bank Rakyat Indonesia (BRI) and Banco do Nordeste in Brazil, for example, created separate lines of business to introduce profitable microfinance operations, key success factors were governance reform and state-of-the-art microcredit technologies.

BRI has over 4,200 village units that serve 3.5 million borrowers and twenty-one million savers. The profit of BRI's microfinance operations (27 percent of total loan portfolio) cross-subsidized the less successful banking operations during the Asian crisis.

Banco do Nordeste's "CrediAmigo" has grown rapidly, becoming the second largest microcredit program in Latin America since it was launched in the late 1990s. CrediAmigo is a microfinance line of business that operates in 2,000 municipalities, providing microcredit to 400,000 clients for a total portfolio of $155 million.

* * *

You Gotta Know Something About Them!

Grameen Bank & Professor Yunus

Image of Muhammad Yunus by Chaudhry Azan, modification by World Economic Forum, is licensed under CC BY 2.0.

The Grameen Bank is legendary. It's a micro-lending institution that provides credit—small, uncollaterized loans—to poor individuals in rural Bangladesh. It all started with Muhammad Yunus, the Bank's founder. A prof at the University of Chittagong and Head of the Rural Economics Program, he first launched an action research project in 1976 to figure out whether a credit delivery system targeted at the rural poor would work. The original Grameen Bank Project (so named because "grameen" means "rural" or "village" in Bangla language) did some cool financial inclusion stuff, such as extending banking to the poor, empowering the disadvantaged—especially women—and increasing savings. It rocked so much that in 1983 the government gave the thumbs up to the creation of Grameen Bank. Since 1983, the Bank has issued tons of loans worth billions of dollars. And check it out: the loan recovery rate is 96.67%. Why so high? In part because borrowers must belong to a five-member group, whose purpose is make sure everything remains copasetic—but the borrower is solely responsible for repayment. In 2006, the Nobel Peace Prize was awarded jointly to the Grameen Bank and Professor Yunus.

Muhummad was the third of fourteen children, five of whom died in infancy. He was a Boy Scout when he was a kid, and traveled to Pakistan, India, and Canada to represent. Fast forward to 2009: President Obama bestowed upon Muhammad the Presidential Medal of Freedom. Two years later, the government of Bangladesh declared that Muhammad, then 72 years old, was twelve years past the legal retirement age for civil servants—too old to continue leading the Grameen Bank. They booted him out. Two years later, he received the Congressional Medal of Honor. Not bad for a Boy Scout.

QUESTIONS FROM YOUR TALKING DOG

1.   Let's go in. It's a beautiful park. I want to run free. I can't? I'm excluded? That's not right. What did you say? About 2.5 billion people don't have access to banks and stuff like that? That's staggering! How did this financial inclusion thing get started?

2.   For me, I measure inclusion by how many parks I can run around in. Is it the same thing for financial inclusion? How many people have bank accounts?

3.   You know, this is all theoretical. Parks aren't theoretical. Give me some real-life examples of financial inclusion.

4.   Is financial inclusion just about feeling warm inside? You know, like I feel for you (as long as you rub my belly). All right, then, tell me why it's a good thing.

5.   What are you doing? That phone of yours, it does everything but make you a bologna sandwich. Yeah, technology rocks. Then tell me how it relates to financial inclusion.

6.   I read about Kenya in The Economist. Tell me more about what's happening there with financial inclusion.

7.   Financial inclusion is cool, but how do you regulate this whole thing? Are we talking lots of government involvement?

8.   What's going on in Brazil? Take me there someday, okay? That's inclusion, right?

F. REMITTANCES

It's Not Chump Change

Over the past decade, remittances, typically migrants sending money back to their families in their home countries, have become an important aspect of development. In 2012, migrant workers sent home $401 billion to their families to help them pay for food, housing, education, healthcare, and other expenses. The impact of remittances on the development of the receiving country can be significant. In 2012, remittances comprised 10% or more of GDP in twenty-two countries. Substantial inflows of money can only be a good thing, right? By now you should know that's not necessarily the case. The first piece discusses the upsides and downsides of remittances and how governments can manage them effectively.

The second piece deals with a micro-level issue: the costs of remittances. The World Bank monitors remittance costs via a database called "Remittance Prices Worldwide." The data indicates that remittance prices average 9% of the total that's being transferred. In some parts of the world the costs are lower, such as 4% in the United Arab Emirates. But in other regions, such as Africa, the remittance charge averages about 12%. In 2012, about $60 billion in remittances flowed to Africa. The fees? $7 billion. That's not chump change. In 2007, the World Bank tried to get a handle on costs by articulating five general principles to promote safety and efficiency in international remittance services. The third piece is an excerpt from the Bank's report. There's now an international effort led by the G8 called "5x5 Objective," whose goal is to bring down remittance prices to 5% by 2014.

R. CHAMI & C. FULLENKAMP, "BEYOND THE HOUSEHOLD"
Finance & Development (2013)

Remittances—private income transfers from migrants to family members in their home country—are good news for the families that receive them. Often sent a few hundred dollars at a time, the remittances increase disposable income and are generally spent on consumption—of food, clothing, medicine, shelter, and electronic equipment. They have been growing for decades . . . Remittances help lift huge numbers of people out of poverty by enabling them to consume more than they could otherwise. They also tend to help the recipients maintain a higher level of consumption during economic adversity. Recent studies report that these flows allow households to work less, take on risky projects they would avoid if they did not receive this additional source of income, or invest in the education and health care of the household. In other words, remittances are a boon for households.

But what is good for an individual household isn't necessarily good for an entire economy. Whether remittances are also good for the economies that receive them is an important question because remittances are one of the largest sources of financial flows to developing countries. In 2012, workers sent home an estimated $401 billion or more through official channels, and it is likely that billions more were transferred through unofficial ones. These flows are often large relative to the economies that receive them. In 2011, for example, remittances were at least 1 percent of GDP for 108 countries; and 5 percent of GDP or more for 44 countries. For 22 countries, remittances represented 10 percent or more of GDP . . . Moreover, remittance flows are typically stable and, from the perspective of the recipient, countercyclical—helping offset a turn of bad luck.

> "Remittances are a larger source of money to Latin America than official foreign aid. In 2011, when foreign aid to Spanish-speaking Latin American nations totaled $6.2 billion, formal remittances were more than eight times that—$53.1 billion."
>
> —D. Cohn et al, "Remittances to Latin America Recover—but Not to Mexico," at http://www.pewhispanic.org/2013/11/15/remittances-to-latin-america-recover-but-not-to-mexico/ (2013)

It is not only important to examine whether remittances have a positive or a negative impact on the overall (or macro) economy. Because policymakers and international organizations have come to view these flows as a possible source of funding for economic development, it is also important to examine whether remittances do, indeed, facilitate economic development and, if so, how. For example, have some countries that receive a great deal of remittances been able to develop faster as a result? This article assesses the macroeconomic effects of these flows, highlighting issues in managing their effects and providing policy advice on how to harness their developmental potential. Finding answers is not straightforward, because remittances affect an economy in many different ways. And, ultimately, their net effect depends on how they are used by the recipients.

A source of government revenue

Besides households, there is one other economic actor that benefits from remittances and whose actions are important to the economy—the government. Remittances spent on the consumption of both domestically produced goods and imports increase the tax base, which in turn increases revenues from sales taxes, value-added taxes, and import duties. In other words, remittances can provide much-needed fiscal space—which allowed some countries to increase spending, lower taxes, or both, to fight the effects of the recent global recession.

As we have suggested, the economic impact of remittances depends in part on how governments choose to use them. For example, governments can sustain higher levels of debt when the ratio of remittances to domestic income is high—which reduces country risk. Indeed, the IMF and the World Bank (2009) recently recognized the increased significance of remittances as a stable and countercyclical source of external financing in its assessment of how much debt low-income countries can safely handle. Remittances enable countries to borrow more, which permits them to use that extra borrowing power to fund investments that facilitate economic growth.

On the other hand, [there is some] evidence that remittances hurt the quality of institutions in recipient countries, precisely because they increase the ability of governments to spend more or tax less. By expanding the tax base, remittances enable a government to appropriate more resources and distribute them to those in power. At the same time, remittances mask the full cost of government actions. Remittances can give rise to a moral hazard problem because they allow government corruption to be less costly for the households that receive those flows. Recipients are less likely to feel the need to hold the authorities accountable, and, in turn, the authorities feel less compelled to justify their actions. This reduces the likelihood that the fiscal space created by remittances will be used for productive social investments. In other words, the interactions that determine the impact of remittances on the overall economy are complex, which is why it is difficult to make generalizations regarding their net effects.

The business cycle

The complex effect of remittances on the economy is also apparent when the business cycle is taken into account. Because remittances increase household consumption, fluctuations in remittance flows can cause changes in output in the short term. But a shock that reduces economic output is also likely to induce workers abroad to send more remittances home, which then has the effect of reducing output volatility.

However, the increase in remittances is also likely to weaken the incentive to work, which could lead to a more volatile business cycle.

Recipient countries also are affected by economic conditions in the countries that are the sources of remittances. Remittance flows increase the simultaneous occurrence of business cycles in remittance-sending and remittance-receiving countries. This effect is likely to be especially pronounced during economic downturns in the sending countries, which tend to be wealthier than the recipient countries.

So, again, the evidence is mixed. Remittances do stimulate consumption, which for some economies will help reduce the size of the swing between recession and growth by putting a floor under total demand. But for other economies, remittances may increase the severity of business cycles, by inducing workers to stay home when the economy turns down, as well as by linking the business cycles of some developing economies more strongly to the business cycles of remittance-sending countries.

Remittances and growth

Over the past decade, the most studied aspect of remittances has been their impact on economic growth, partly because of the policy importance of this issue and partly because of the many and complex ways remittances might affect economic growth. A useful way to organize the large and diverse body of findings on this question is to use a growth-accounting approach in which the effect of remittances on capital accumulation, labor force growth, and total factor productivity (TFP) growth is studied. TFP is essentially growth that is not accounted for by increases in traditional inputs such as labor and capital and encompasses such things as technology and finance.

Capital accumulation: Worker remittances can affect the rate of capital accumulation in recipient economies in various ways. First, they can directly finance investment. Remittance inflows can also facilitate the financing of investments by improving the creditworthiness of households, effectively augmenting their capacity to borrow. Remittances may also reduce the risk premium that lenders demand, because they reduce output volatility.

But if remittances are perceived to be permanent income, households may spend them rather than save them—significantly reducing the amount of flows directed to investment. And, in fact, the amount of remittances devoted to investment tends to be low. For example, remittance flows into the Middle East and North Africa region fuel the consumption of domestic and foreign goods, with very little going to investment. In addition, many households save part of the remittances by purchasing assets such

> *"Somalis living in the UK send more than £100 million a year for food, healthcare and education to relatives in the Horn [of Africa]. Somalia is particularly dependent on money-service businesses as it lacks a formal banking system after decades of war."*
>
> —M. Tran, "Somali Remittances: Dahabshiil granted Barclays Reprieve," *The Guardian*, at http://www.theguardian.com/global-development/2013/nov/05/somali-remittances-dahabshiil-barclays-bank (2013)

as real estate, which generally doesn't increase the capital stock.

Remittances could stimulate increases in so-called human capital by enabling younger members of a household to continue schooling rather than having to work to contribute to household income. For example, evidence from the Philippines and from Mexico suggests that receiving remittances leads to increased school attendance. However, that extra education would likely have little effect on domestic economic growth if it simply makes it possible for the recipients to emigrate.

Labor force growth: Remittances may also influence growth by affecting the rate of growth of labor inputs. One channel through which remittances could affect labor inputs is in labor force participation—the percentage of the population that is working or seeking work. But as has been noted, those effects can be negative. Remittances enable recipients to work less and maintain the same living standard, regardless of how the distant sender intended them to be used (say, to increase household consumption or investment). Anecdotal evidence of this negative labor effort effect is abundant, and academic studies have detected such an effect as well. Thus, remittances appear to serve as a drag on labor supply.

Total factor productivity: Researchers have identified two main ways through which remittances may affect the growth of TFP. First, remittances may enhance the efficiency of investment by improving domestic financial intermediation (channeling funds from savers to borrowers). That is, they may affect *the ability of the recipient economy's formal financial system to allocate capital.* For example, remittances may help GDP growth when the financial markets are relatively underdeveloped because remittances loosen the credit constraints imposed on households by a small financial sector. In addition, regardless of the state of the financial sector's development, remittances are likely to increase the amount of funds flowing through the banking system. This, in turn, may lead to enhanced financial development and thus to higher economic growth through increased economies of scale in financial intermediation.

The business cycle

A second way remittances may affect TFP growth is *through the exchange rate* . . . [R]emittances can lead to real exchange rate appreciation, which in turn can make exports from remittance-receiving countries less competitive. The industries or companies that produce the exports may be transferring know-how to the rest of the economy or providing opportunities for other local companies to climb up the value chain. This is often the case, for example, with manufacturing. Therefore, if these companies become less competitive owing to exchange rate changes (which are themselves caused by remittances), then these firms must scale back or close, and their beneficial impact on productivity is reduced.

There have been many attempts to estimate the impact of remittances on growth. The earliest such study . . . found that whereas domestic investment and private capital flows were positively related to growth, the ratio of workers' remittances to GDP either was not statistically significant or was negatively related to growth. Since then, many studies have been performed, and their main findings vary widely. Some find remittances help growth and others find they hurt growth—and some find no discernible effects. When a positive effect of remittances on growth is found, it tends to be conditional, suggesting that other factors must be present for remittances to enhance economic growth. For example, some studies have found that remittances tend to boost economic growth only when social institutions are better developed.

Perhaps most disappointing is the lack of a remittances-growth success story: a country in which remittances-led growth contributed significantly to its development. Given that in some countries remittances exceeded 10 percent of GDP for long periods of time, one would have hoped to find at least one example of remittances serving as a catalyst for significant economic development. It is worth noting, however, that researchers have also failed to find clear and consistent evidence that other financial flows, such as capital flows and official aid, enhance economic growth and development.

Whither remittances?

The mixed evidence regarding the macroeconomic impact of remittances reflects a number of underlying truths about their role in an economy. First, they are unequivocally good for recipient households because they alleviate poverty and provide insurance against economic adversity. Second, there are many different paths through which remittances affect an economy. Third, none of these paths is necessarily active at any given time—that is, many economic and social conditions determine whether any given path is active or significant. And, finally, many of these paths have opposing or conflicting economic effects.

These realities shape the challenge faced by policymakers who wish to maximize the development potential of remittances. To make the most of remittances, governments will have to strengthen or facilitate the channels through which remittances benefit the overall economy while limiting or weakening others. This task is challenging not only because economists still do not fully understand all the ways that remittances affect the economy, but also because this task may put policymakers in conflict with households, which are used to utilizing remittances in particular ways. Nonetheless, there are several promising approaches for policy.

Each country wishing to make better use of remittances must study how the recipients actually use them. This is essential to ensuring that policymakers understand the specific obstacles that prevent remittances from being used to facilitate development, and the kinds of development-friendly activities (such as education, business formation, or investment) remittance recipients would be most likely to engage in. Obstacles to using remittances for development and opportunities for such use are likely to vary with the particular economic, social, and legal environment of each country.

Policymakers must take advantage of the fiscal space created by remittance flows by investing more in social institutions and public infrastructure. For example, the increased tax revenues that remittances generate can finance initiatives to increase the professionalism of civil servants and improve the enforcement of rules and regulations. Likewise, the government can take advantage of its increased borrowing capacity to finance improvements in infrastructure. One potential use would be to upgrade a country's financial system at all levels, including improvements in the payment system, availability of banking services, and financial literacy.

Policymakers must design programs that are responsive to the needs of individual households and that give recipients the proper incentives to use remittances productively. Promoting the acceptance of remittance income as collateral for private loans used to finance productive investments is one way to direct remittance income into growth-enhancing investments. In addition, governments could subsidize education or business loans for which remittances are pledged as collateral. Policymakers will have to work closely with remittance recipients—and senders—to make these efforts work.

Increasing globalization and demographic changes, such as the aging of developed-economy workforces, mean that remittances are likely to increase in size and importance in the future. It is clear that remittances improve the welfare of households that receive them and, as such, should be encouraged. But, to be more helpful to recipient economies, governments must design policies that promote remittances and increase their benefits while limiting or offsetting any counterproductive side effects. Getting the most value possible out of remittances will require significant, thoughtful effort from national governments and the assistance of international organizations. For example, a review of governance and institutional quality is routinely undertaken as a part of the IMF's annual consultations. The incentive effects of remittance flows suggest that such reviews are of particular importance in remittance-receiving economies. Efforts like these enable countries to tailor their development strategies to the role that remittances actually play, which in turn increases the chance that they can be utilized to enhance development and growth.

D. RATHA, "REMITTANCES: FUNDS FOR THE FOLKS BACK HOME"

Finance & Development (2012)

When migrants send home part of their earnings in the form of either cash or goods to support their families, these transfers are known as workers' or migrant remittances. They have been growing rapidly in the past few years and now represent the largest source of foreign income for many developing countries.

In the past several years, the average amount of remittances sent per migrant worker in the U.S. increased among women relative to men. In 2009, male migrant workers sent an average of 12 remittances per year worth $232 each, while female workers sent remittances worth $229 each. In 2013, the value of remittances from male workers had dropped to $189 while remittances from female workers averaged $207.
—M. Jordan, "Migrant Women Lift Remittances," at http://online.wsj.com/news/articles/SB100014240527023038478 04579479690660408488 (2014)

It is hard to estimate the exact size of remittance flows because many transfers take place through unofficial channels. Worldwide, officially recorded international migrant remittances were projected to exceed $483 billion in 2011, with $351 billion flowing to developing countries. These flows are recorded in the balance of payments; exactly how to record them is being reviewed by an international technical group. Unrecorded flows through informal channels are believed to be at least 50 percent larger than recorded flows. Not only are remittances large but they are also more evenly distributed among developing countries than capital flows, including foreign direct investment, most of which goes to a few big emerging markets. In fact, remittances are especially important for low-income countries. Remittance flows to low-income countries are nearly 6 percent of their gross domestic product (GDP), compared with about 2 percent of GDP for middle-income countries.

Getting the money there

A typical remittance transaction takes place in three steps:

- Step 1: The migrant sender pays the remittance to the sending agent using cash, check, money order, credit card, debit card, or a debit instruction sent by e-mail, phone, or through the Internet.
- Step 2: The sending agency instructs its agent in the recipient's country to deliver the remittance.
- Step 3: The paying agent makes the payment to the beneficiary.

For settlement between agents, in most cases, there is no real-time fund transfer; instead, the balance owed by the sending agent to the paying agent is settled periodically according to an agreed schedule, through a commercial bank. Informal remittances are sometimes settled through goods trade.

The costs of a remittance transaction include a fee charged by the sending agent, typically paid by the sender, and a currency-conversion fee for delivery of local currency to the beneficiary in another country. Some smaller money transfer operators require the beneficiary to pay a fee to collect remittances, presumably to account for unexpected exchange-rate movements. In addition, remittance agents (especially banks) may earn an indirect fee in the form of interest (or "float") by investing funds before delivering them to the beneficiary. The float can be significant in countries where overnight interest rates are high.

Remittances are typically transfers from a well-meaning individual or family member to another individual or household. They are targeted to meet specific needs of the recipients and thus tend to reduce poverty. Cross-country analyses generally find that remittances have reduced the share of poor people in the population. In fact, World Bank studies, based on recent household surveys, suggest that international remittance receipts helped lower poverty (measured by the proportion of the population below the poverty line) by nearly 11 percentage points in Uganda, 6 percentage points in Bangladesh, and 5 percentage points in Ghana. Between a fifth and half of the 11 percent reduction in poverty in Nepal between 1995 and 2004, a time of political conflict, has been attributed to remittances.

In poorer households, remittances may finance the purchase of basic consumption goods, housing, and children's education and health care. In richer households, they may provide capital for small businesses and entrepreneurial activities. They also help pay for imports and external debt service, and in some countries, banks have been able to raise overseas financing using future remittances as collateral . . .

High transaction costs

Transaction costs are not usually an issue for large remittances (those made for the purpose of trade, investment, or aid), because, as a percentage of the principal amount, they tend to be small, and major international banks are eager to offer competitive services for large-value remittances. But for smaller remittances—under $200, say, which is often typical for poor migrants—remittance fees typically average 10 percent, and can be as high as 15–20 percent of the principal in smaller migration corridors (see table).

Transfer costs

Remittance fees could be reduced significantly if they were a flat fee instead of a percentage of the principal transferred. Approximate cost of remitting $200 (as a percent of principal) between[:]

	MTOs[1]	Banks	Hawala[2]
Australia-Papua New Guinea	15.3	18.1	—
Germany-Serbia	6.6	20.9	—
Japan-Brazil	10.1	18.1	—
Malaysia-Indonesia	1.9	7.1	—
New Zealand-Tonga	9.4	18.2	—
Russia-Ukraine	2	—	1–2
South Africa-Mozambique	11.8	22.4	—
South Africa-Zimbabwe	15.8	19.2	—
Saudi Arabia-Pakistan	3.3	3	—
United Arab Emirates-India	2.5	13.1	1–2
United Kingdom-India	2.4	5	—
United Kingdom-Philippines	6.2	4.9	—
United States-Colombia	6.2	17.5	—
United States-Mexico	6.7	3.6	—
United States-Philippines	6.5	10	—

Source: World Bank Remittance Prices Worldwide database; and World Bank Global Economic Prospects 2006: Economic Implications of Remittances and Migration.

Notes: — denotes that data are not available. Data are for the third quarter of 2011. Figures include currency-conversions charge, except for Russia-Ukraine.

[1] MTOs: money transfer operators.

[2] Hawala is an informal remittance transfer system that operates outside traditional financial channels—largely in the Middle East and other parts of Africa and Asia.

Cutting transaction costs would significantly help recipient families. A number of factors could reduce transactions costs:

First, *the remittance fee should be a low fixed amount*, not a percentage of the principal, because the cost of remittance services does not depend on the amount of principal. Indeed, the real cost of a remittance transaction—including labor, technology, networks, and rent—is estimated to be significantly below the current level of fees.

Second, *greater competition would bring prices down*. Entry of new market players can be facilitated by harmonizing and lowering bond and capital requirements, and avoiding overregulation (such as requiring full banking licenses for money transfer operators). The intense scrutiny of money service businesses for money laundering or terrorism financing since the 9/11 attacks on the World Trade Center has made it difficult for them to maintain accounts with their correspondent banks, forcing many in the United States to close. While regulations are necessary to curb money laundering and terrorism financing, they should not make it difficult for legitimate money service businesses to maintain accounts with correspondent banks. Using a risk-based approach to regulation—in which only suspicious transactions are checked and small transactions below, say, $1,000 are exempt from requiring proof of identity and address—can reduce remittance costs and facilitate flows.

> "Barclays made a legitimate decision to exit these businesses based upon the well-known risks of money-laundering and terrorist financing in the money service business sector. The risk of financial crime is an important regulatory concern and we take our responsibilities in relation to this very seriously."
>
> —Barclays spokesman following a UK court decision granting an injunction against the bank prohibiting it from ending its remittance business with Dahabshiil, a firm dealing with remittances to Somalia. M. Tran, "Somali Remittances: Dahabshiil granted Barclays Reprieve," The Guardian, at http://www.theguardian.com/global-development/2013/nov/05/somali-remittances-dahabshiil-barclays-bank (2013)

An example where competition has spurred reductions in fees is in the U.S.-Mexico corridor, where remittance fees have fallen by more than 50 percent from over $26 (to send $300) in 1999 to about $12 in 2005. Fees appear to have leveled off since then. In addition, some commercial banks have recently started providing remittance services for free, hoping that would attract customers for their deposit and loan products. And in some countries, new remittance tools—based on cell phones, smart cards, or the Internet—have emerged.

Third, *establishing nonexclusive partnerships between remittance-service providers and existing postal and other retail networks* would help expand remittance services without requiring large fixed investments to develop payment networks.

Fouth, *poor migrants could be given greater access to banking*. Banks tend to provide cheaper remittance services than money transfer operators. Both sending and receiving countries can increase banking access for migrants by allowing origin-country banks to operate overseas; by providing identification cards (such as the Mexican *matricula consular*) that are accepted by banks to open accounts; and by facilitating participation of microfinance institutions and credit unions in the remittance market.

Boosting flows

Governments have often offered incentives to increase remittance flows and to channel them to productive uses. But such policies are more problematic than efforts to expand access to financial services or reduce transaction costs. Tax incentives may attract remittances, but they may also encourage tax evasion. Matching-fund programs to attract remittances from migrant associations may divert funds from other local funding priorities, while efforts to channel remittances to investment have met with little success. Fundamentally, remittances are private funds that should be treated like other sources of household income. Efforts to increase savings and improve the allocation of expenditures should be accomplished through improvements in the overall investment climate, rather than by targeting remittances.

THE WORLD BANK, COMMITTEE ON PAYMENT AND
SETTLEMENT SYSTEMS, "GENERAL PRINCIPLES FOR
INTERNATIONAL REMITTANCE SERVICES"

(2007)

* * *

Key issues concerning remittance services and the General Principles

14. In any market, full information—ie transparency—is important because it enables individuals to make informed decisions about which services to use and helps to make the market as a whole more efficient. Transparency in the market for remittances is arguably particularly important because the price to the consumer depends on two elements, the exchange rate used and any fees charged, and combining these to calculate which service is cheapest is difficult for most consumers. Transparency, as well as adequate consumer protection, is also important because, as low-income migrants in a foreign country, many senders may have difficulties in understanding the local language or in providing adequate identification to open a bank account, or lack the time and financial literacy to search out and compare different remittance services. *General Principle 1 is therefore that the market for remittance services should be transparent and have adequate consumer protection.* (See Box 1 for a list of the five General Principles and related roles.) RSPs should therefore be encouraged to provide relevant information about their own services in easily accessible and understandable forms. Authorities or other organisations may want to provide comparative price information. They may also wish to undertake

educational campaigns to give senders and receivers sufficient background knowledge to be able to understand the information provided.

15. The infrastructure needed to support remittance services is sometimes inadequate. Many services require RSPs to cooperate to create a network of access points and it may not always be easy for potential RSPs to identify suitable partners to do this, particularly in other countries. Moreover, underdevelopment of the domestic financial infrastructure, particularly in receiving countries, may mean that transferring funds to the access points is slow and unreliable; in some cases non-cash payment services may only be available in urban locations. Another important aspect of the infrastructure is correspondent banking, which is widely used for cross-border transfers of funds but which can be expensive for small-value payments such as remittances. *General Principle 2 is therefore that improvements to payment system infrastructure that have the potential to increase the efficiency of remittance services should be encouraged.* The safety and efficiency of remittance services can be affected by payment systems in the relevant markets and the way that these systems are accessed and used by RSPs or by banks acting for RSPs. Remittance services may be improved by initiatives aimed at facilitating greater interoperability of systems and straight through processing. In many receiving countries, expanding the payment system infrastructure in under-served areas and improving access to it, although a huge task, could be of benefit for delivering financial services of all kinds, including remittances.

16. The remittance industry is likely to flourish best under appropriate laws and regulations. As already noted, remittances may be regulated for various reasons including, perhaps most importantly, prevention of their misuse for purposes such as money laundering or terrorist financing. However, as with all laws and regulations, there is the possibility that those for remittances are badly designed with unintended side effects, that they are disproportionate to the problem they are designed to tackle, or that they continue to be applied even when no longer useful. Moreover, regulating remittances solely by type of entity, as is sometimes the case (eg when the regulations are applied only to the services provided by licensed institutions such as banks), may make regulation less effective (by creating loopholes which can be exploited for illegal activities) and distort markets (by enabling some RSPs to inappropriately avoid the costs of regulation and thus offer artificially cheaper services). National regulations should aim to create a level playing field between equivalent remittance services. *General Principle 3 is therefore that remittance services should be supported by a sound, predictable, non-discriminatory and proportionate legal and regulatory framework in relevant jurisdictions.*

Box 1

The General Principles and related roles

The General Principles are aimed at the public policy objectives of achieving safe and efficient international remittance services. To this end, the markets for the services should be contestable, transparent, accessible and sound.

Transparency and consumer protection

General Principle 1.   The market for remittance services should be transparent and have adequate consumer protection.

Payment system infrastructure

General Principle 2.   Improvements to payment system infrastructure that have the potential to increase the efficiency of remittance services should be encouraged.

Legal and regulatory environment

General Principle 3.   Remittance services should be supported by a sound, predictable, non-discriminatory and proportionate legal and regulatory framework in relevant jurisdictions.

Market structure and competition

General Principle 4.   Competitive market conditions, including appropriate access to domestic payment infrastructures, should be fostered in the remittance industry.

Governance and risk management

General Principle 5.   Remittance services should be supported by appropriate governance and risk management practices.

Roles of remittance service providers and public authorities

A.   *Role of remittance service providers.* Remittance service providers should participate actively in the implementation of the General Principles.

B.   *Role of public authorities.* Public authorities should evaluate what action to take to achieve the public policy objectives through implementation of the General Principles.

---

17. The efficiency of remittance services depends on there being a competitive business environment. *General Principle 4 is therefore that competitive market conditions, including appropriate access to domestic payment infrastructures, should be fostered in the remittance industry.*

Competition can be assisted by various steps such as discouraging exclusivity conditions, whereby an RSP allows its agents or other RSPs to offer its remittance service only on condition that they do not offer any other remittance service. And it is important that RSPs without direct access to the domestic payment infrastructure needed to provide remittance services should be able to use, on an equitable basis, the payment services provided by institutions that do have direct access.

18.   The relatively small values involved in remittance transfers mean that it is unlikely that there will be systemic risk involved. However, RSPs do face financial, legal, operational, fraud and reputational risks. *General Principle 5 is therefore that remittance services should be supported by appropriate governance and risk management practices.* Governance and risk management practices that are appropriate for the size and type of an RSP's business and the level of risks can improve the safety and soundness of remittance services and help protect consumers.

19.   The importance of remittance flows varies from country to country so, although these principles are designed to be generally applicable, some countries may decide that the size of the remittance market does not justify significant action or that there is no need for any action. In addition, the principles are in most cases likely to be applied in sending countries regardless of the destination of the funds and in receiving countries regardless of their origin. However, in applying some aspects of the principles (such as the education programmes discussed under General Principle 1), authorities may want to prioritise their efforts in the most important bilateral corridors or corridors where they believe their efforts will be most productive. Authorities in sending countries should also bear in mind that, even if remittances are not a priority for them, they may be important for the receiving countries and the latter may be unable to implement the principles effectively without the cooperation of the sending countries.

20.   Where it is decided that action should be taken to implement the principles, both RSPs and public authorities will need to be involved. Authorities should evaluate what action to take to achieve the public policy objectives through implementation of the principles, and the implementation itself will also need the active participation of RSPs. Because of the links between remittances, access to financial services and poverty alleviation, and thus the relevance of remittances to the implementation of the Millennium Development Goals, international financial institutions (such as the World Bank, regional development banks and the International Monetary Fund) have a role to play in supporting both authorities and market participants in the application of the principles.

* * *

You Gotta Know Something About Them!

Hector Castillejos

Hector is a legal migrant worker who works on U.S. farms. These days he's working in Iowa picking melons and detasseling corn for farmers. The work is grueling: 14 or more hours a day in the hot summer sun. Hector sleeps in a barracks-type building with rows of bunks. No air-conditioning. Running water, but not enough for the hundreds of workers. Portable restrooms and handwashing stations outside.

Hector makes $10.44 an hour, which is far more than he could make in Mexico. That's why he left, lured by the promise that he would be able to make almost $6,000 for Sonia, his wife, and his three children, Maria, Carmen, and Jose. Hector wakes up at 5:30 a.m. A cool breeze runs through the cornfield, though Hector knows the day will be hot and humid. Just one more day's work and Sonia will have enough for a refrigerator.

Composite based on the experience of various migrant workers as detailed in "Labor Pains: Migrant Workers in Conesville Say They've Been Left Stranded," at http://muscatinejournal.com/news/local/labor-pains-migrant-workers-in-conesville-say-they-ve-been/article_b0f6cf72–7c4c–5a 35–955f–076db72529aa.html (2008).

QUESTIONS FROM YOUR TALKING DOG

1.   Yeah, I know Carlos, the maintenance guy at the apartments. I thought I heard him say he's from Mexico. Says he's married but I never see his wife or kids, if he has any . . . He sends money back. Nice of him. Didn't mean to be flip, sorry. Where're we going today? The Latino Festival? I'm down for that.

2.   Carlos sends money back? Remittances. What does that mean?

3.   How much money are we talking about?

4.   It's obvious that remittances help families. But what about governments?

5.   No, I don't know how the business cycle affects remittances. Do I look like an economist to you? Explain, please.

6.   Can we take a break? No? Then give me a treat . . . Okay, I'm ready. Let's go to remittances and economic growth. Tell me.

7.   Wait, wait, wait. Remittances can hurt exports? You gotta explain that one.

8.   With all these pros and cons, especially the cons, what should be done to manage remittances? It's so condescending when you say, "good question."

9.   Hold on a second. Will you stop? Haven't we put the cart before the horse? How exactly does Carlos get the money back to his family? How does his family use the money?

10.   It seems like it's all about fees in finance. Same here with remittances. So what's being done, or what could be done, to reduce the costs?

11.   Not surprised that the World Bank is involved. Tell me about the General Principles.

12.   How about another treat for being so conversational with you. What do you mean you'll send me some??

G. SECURITIES MARKETS

Of Stock and Bonds: Check Out China

In Chapter 8, we talked about the importance of securities markets, a form of finance that, if properly regulated, efficiently allocates capital via direct contractual links between savers, the investors, and borrowers, the issuing companies. Back in the day, most securities markets were domestic, meaning they linked up domestic investors with domestic issuers. That's no longer the case—domestic markets are becoming increasingly internationalized as we speak. The U.S. securities markets, which are the largest in the world, are an example of this phenomenon: U.S. investors hold trillions of dollars in foreign stocks and debt securities, and foreign investors are doing the same the opposite way.

In EMEs, the banking sector traditionally provided financing for private or state-owned companies. Securities markets began to develop in the 1990s as EMEs began to privatize state-owned sectors in the 1990s. In the past fifteen years, EME's financial markets have grown substantially.

Good thing, right? Lots of economists agree that foreign investors, in most cases led by professional fund managers, can have a positive effect on securities markets by increasing pricing efficiency. To build the markets, governments have had to deal with a number of issues. If there's political instability, foreign investors will demand a premium, effectively raising the cost of funding for issuers. Then you got your corruption, which kind of scares investors. And governments have to make sure that the regulatory framework meets international standards which safeguard shareholders rights and provide efficient dispute resolution. Liquidity is also important to stock exchanges because traders want to make trades quickly at a reasonable cost.

Having said all this, developing securities markets and opening them up to the world has its costs. Today, pension funds, insurance companies and mutual funds scour EMEs to make money. But it's hot money and its movement depends on monetary policy in different parts of the world, particularly the monetary policy of the United States.

Let's take the U.S. Fed's monetary policy to kick-start the U.S. economy. In September 2012, the Fed started a program called "quantitative easing" (QE). With the key interest rate (the Fed funds rate) at practically zero, the Fed couldn't use interest rates to stimulate the economy. Solution? On a monthly basis, it started buying massive amounts of bonds—long-term treasury bonds and mortgage-backed securities per month, up to $85 billion monthly. This flooded the monetary base, lowering interest rates with the hope of stimulating the economy.

But don't forget about institutional investors always on the yield hunt. Where did they go? EMEs. Their stock markets climbed as did the value of their currencies—not a good thing for their exports. Then came Fed Chair Bernanke's Congressional testimony in May 2013 where he said the Fed might start cutting back on its purchase of bonds. The announcement sparked chaos in EMEs. Stock markets plummeted as did currencies— between 3% and 15% against the dollar. In December 2013, Bernanke announced that the Fed would start tapering the program by reducing the monthly bond buying by $10 billion. In late January 2014, the Fed announced it would reduce its bond buying by an additional $10 billion to $65 billion a month. Institutional investors, especially mutual funds, unloaded emerging markets stocks and bonds like hot potatoes. And they did this even though the host country's economic fundamentals were just fine. Remember the buffalo? Herd behavior.

Is the solution to close off emerging market financial markets? Most policymakers think that would be a mistake. Instead, they say EMEs have to continue to develop their markets so they can withstand external shocks— like the global impact of the Fed's QE program—in an increasingly globalized financial landscape.

With all this in mind, we're going to take a look at China's securities markets. Since implementing market reforms in 1979, China has been one of the fastest-growing economies in the world. Average annual GDP growth was nearly 10% through 2013. With a population of 1.3 billion, it's the world's second-largest economy, with some economists forecasting that China will move into the #1 spot within a few years (as measured by purchasing power parity—you know what that means by now). Still, in many ways it's still a developing country. For instance, nearly 100 million people live below the national poverty line of RMB 2,300 per year as measured in 2012.

For these reasons, we've picked China for our look at securities markets in an EME. You'll see many of the markers of an EME: impressive development of the financial sector, but still underdeveloped compared to its bank-centered financial sector; gradual liberalization of its segmentation scheme but with trading dominated by state-owned entities; thin, volatile and mispriced trading: a legal framework that looks good on paper but in reality doesn't do that much to protect investors via enforcement.

W. ALLEN & H. SHEN, "ASSESSING CHINA'S
TOP-DOWN SECURITIES MARKETS"

National Bureau of Economic Research (2011)

It is widely observed that, despite its remarkable economic progress over the last thirty years, the economy of China continues to require substantial development of its legal and financial infrastructure. In that connection, this essay seeks to assess an important part of that infrastructure: the securities markets of China. We assess those markets, both in terms of their size and composition and in terms of their economic function and importance to the Chinese economy. In doing so, we also review and assess the regulatory regime within which these markets function and the corporate governance mechanisms that operate upon the firms that are listed on the Chinese stock exchanges . . .

The Shanghai and Shenzhen Stock Exchanges represent an effort initiated in the early 1990s to centralize and develop securities trading in modern China. Since that time those exchanges have grown rapidly in terms of listings, trading, products and regulatory structures. They remain, however, a work in progress. While quite large by some measures, these markets do not yet play a very important role in the finance of the Chinese economy. The finance of the Chinese economy continues to be dominated, on large scale

> *"In the traditional bank-based system, the partial privatization of the large state-owned banks is beginning to erode the availability of cheap and easy credit and thus constrains the main source of capital for mainland Chinese firms . . . As a result, the importance of stock markets and equity financing as an additional source of external finance is rapidly increasing."*
> —B. Karreman and B. van der Knaap, "The Geography of Equity Listing and Financial Centre Competition in Mainland China and Hong Kong," *Journal of Economic Geography*, 903 (2012)

projects, primarily by bank finance and direct and indirect government support and, on entrepreneurial finance level, primarily by foreign direct investment and a range of less formal arrangements including friends and family, trade credit, business alliances and, importantly, local government support . . . The securities markets serve as a secondary source of finance to the Chinese economy. Access to securities markets in China has been tightly controlled by the state and these markets have largely played the role of a supplemental source of finance for large state-owned enterprises (SOEs). The resulting markets are comparatively small in terms of the size of the general economy. Prices of securities traded on them are volatile and

EMERGING MARKET ECONOMIES: SELECTED TOPICS CH. 21

do not appear to price securities very well. Because prices on these markets do not appear to be efficiently set and because, as we show, the governance standards of the legal system they incorporate are ineffective, the market's prices do not provide either a positive signaling function or a disciplinary function for the corporate management of listed firms. Finally, because they have not yet evolved developed futures markets or a large capacity to create derivative securities, the Chinese securities markets do not yet provide adequate opportunities for the management of financial risks. For all of these reasons, the Chinese securities markets do not presently appear to deliver to the Chinese economy the principle allocative or disciplinary functions that a developed securities markets can provide.

If these markets do not provide the fundamental economic benefits that securities markets can provide, one may ask, why do they exist and grow? In this essay we suggest that they flourish because they provide valuable benefits both to investors, and to the Chinese state. Even without substantial legal system protection from exploitation, these markets do provide investors a way to participate in the rapid growth of [the] Chinese economy. In addition, these markets provide the following significant benefits to the country and its leadership: (1) they provide a mechanism through which foreign capital can flow to support the SOEs that comprise the largest part of the firms listed on the mainland exchanges; (2) they provide a channel through which can flow a limited amount of investment from the very large reservoir of domestic family savings in order to do the same thing; (3) they serve as means to induce improvements in the management and governance of listed SOEs; (4) they provide to the leadership a possible option for future expansion of the role of private sector in financing enterprise, including both the existing state sector and the entrepreneurial sector of the economy; and finally (5) they provide in some measure the non-economic satisfaction of locating a globally important center of finance on mainland China.

Thus, despite the limited economic importance of Chinese securities markets to the nation's economy at the moment, they continue to command both international investors' interest and the support of the country's leadership. The leadership has demonstrated its continuing commitment to building out the infrastructure that might allow Chinese securities markets to play a greater role in the future in its extended effort to restructure the Chinese share segmentation system . . . and in facilitating the continued development of instruments of modern finance . . . The following essay aims to assist interested readers in thinking about the future of these markets.

* * *

PART I. THE CHARACTERISTICS OF THE CHINESE SECURITIES MARKETS TODAY

The Chinese securities markets constitute an impressive accomplishment. The technological, legal and human infrastructure supporting these markets has been created from almost nothing two decades ago. While they remain a work in progress, that progress has been remarkable.

In assessing these markets, we begin by placing them in context of the formal system that finances business activity in China today. China's system of formal finance is essentially a bank-centered system primarily dominated by its four largest state-owned banks. China's economy has a substantially higher ratio of bank credit to GDP (1.27 at the close of 2009 according to the National Bureau of Statistic of China), than even the German, bank-centered system of finance (.99). Securities markets by comparison, while large by some measures, are small in economic terms. Moreover[,] when assessing the reported size of these markets, it is important to understand that what actually trades on the mainland exchanges (and in fact what, until quite recently was legally tradable on them) is in almost all cases a very small percent of the outstanding shares. (See e.g. the analysis of the holdings of the shares in ICBC bank, China's largest bank, reported below).

Expressed in terms of proportion of financial assets rather than percentage of GDP, data for 2006, confirms the relatively undeveloped state of the mainland securities markets. According to CSRC [(Chinese Securities Regulatory Commission)] data for that year the total value of securities in the PRC (equities and bonds, including treasury bonds) constituted just 22% of total financial assets, while in the U.S., U.K., Japan and Korea those percentages were far higher (82%, 71%, 62% and 75%, respectively) . . . More recent data compiled by McKinsey & Co for year 2008 reported in Table 1 below is consistent with this view. China appears on this data to have a substantially higher proportion of financial assets in bank deposits than any other region. Moreover[,] this table most probably exaggerates the importance of securities markets in China by using market capitalization data without adjusting for the very thin float of listed firms, which we discuss below.

Table 1

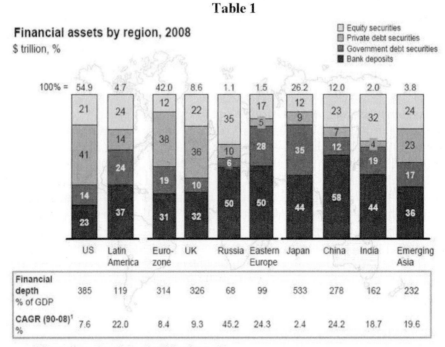

Financial assets by region, 2008
$ trillion, %

Legend:
☐ Equity securities
▦ Private debt securities
▨ Government debt securities
■ Bank deposits

	US	Latin America	Euro-zone	UK	Russia	Eastern Europe	Japan	China	India	Emerging Asia
Financial depth % of GDP	385	119	314	326	68	99	533	278	162	232
CAGR (90-08)[1] %	7.6	22.0	8.4	9.3	45.2	24.3	2.4	24.2	18.7	19.6

1 Compound annual growth rate using 2008 exchange rates.
Note: Some numbers do not sum due to rounding.
Source: McKinsey Global Institute Global Financial Stock database

As we noted, an accurate understanding of the scale and scope of the Chinese securities markets must take into consideration the on-going effects of the now reformed share segmentation system that until recently limited the number of shares of each listed SOE that could be traded on an exchange. Therefore, we begin our discussion of the markets with a brief description of that reform. Those familiar with the well-known share segmentation system and its now largely completed reform, may safely move directly to Section 1.3.

1.1 Background: The Share Segmentation System and Its Reform

Among the signal marks of the program of liberalization that was initiated in 1978 under the leadership of Deng Xiaoping was its pragmatism and gradualism. Among the steps taken to ensure that corportization [*sic*] of certain state sector production facilities could be safely tried, while not engendering unforeseen complication, was the adoption of a plan strictly to limit the potential non-state ownership of shares of the corporations that were to be formed from state and province production facilities. Thus newly incorporated enterprises carved from state assets in the 1990s were authorized by the State Council to issue shares pursuant to an elaborate share segmentation plan.

Under the share segmentation scheme that governed the listing of shares on securities exchanges, a majority of shares of SOEs (which from the beginning and today constitute most of the companies listed on the exchanges) would be non-tradable and held by institutions that were directly or indirectly controlled by the government. The minority of shares that were to be tradable were themselves broken down into A shares and B shares on both Shanghai Stock Exchange and Shenzhen Stock Exchange. The A shares constitute the vast majority of shares traded on these exchanges, are traded in renminbi on the Shanghai or Shenzhen stock exchanges and originally could be purchased only by Chinese nationals or institutions. B shares are traded on the same exchanges but were listed in US dollars in Shanghai and HK dollars in Shenzhen; they could be purchased originally only by foreign nationals or institutions (now they can be purchased by Chinese nationals as well). In addition to A and B shares, some larger Chinese firms, seeking access to foreign capital, have received (from the CSRC) permission to list on foreign exchanges. Stocks traded on these exchanges are denominated H shares (Hong Kong Stock Exchange), N shares (NYSE), L shares (LSE) and S shares (Singapore Exchange) and carry the same voting and cash flow rights as A shares.

> "Both Shanghai and Shenzhen run a pure order-driven trading mechanism on electronic systems without official market makers. Trading is conducted from Monday to Friday, except holidays. For each trading day, there is a morning session and afternoon session. The morning session includes one pre-trading auction 9:15–9:25 AM and one continuous trading period 9:30–11:30 AM. The afternoon session includes only one continuous trading period 13:00–15:00."
>
> —H. Chung et al, "An Empirical Analysis of the Shanghai and Shenzhen Limit Order Books," *Economic Modelling*, 37 (2013)

Importantly, in addition to the segmentation of shares into A and B shares, Chinese shares were distinguished by the nature of the holder. Shares could be either (1) pre-IPO shares issued in connection with the "corporitization" of the assets to (a) instrumentalities of the state—such as a Ministry, the State-owned Assets Supervision and Administration Commission ("SASAC") or a provincial or municipal governments; or (b) to certain legal persons (principally the parent of the listed SOE, which itself will generally be controlled by a province or municipal body; or (2) shares issued in or after the IPO to Chinese nationals or institutions (for example, the Qualified Foreign Institutional Investors, "QFIIs"). At least prior to the recent reform described below, the pre-IPO shares issued to state or municipal entities or to SOE management as part of the IPO process were generally classified as "C shares" and were not tradable on the exchange. Non-tradable shares ("NTSs") could only be transferred to legal persons (including in recent years foreign strategic investors) in private placements with the prior approval of both SASAC and the CSRC.

Prior to the completion of share segmentation reform, significantly, with respect to every listed SOE—and, most of the firms listed on the Shanghai

Stock Exchange are SOEs, recent estimates varying between 70% and 80% . . . —NTSs significantly outnumbered the proportion of shares that are tradable. According to CSRC data, for example, at the end of 2004, there were 714.9 billion shares outstanding of all listed Chinese companies of which 454.3 billion or 64% were non-tradable. Thus, a fact of fundamental importance is that the trading market on the Chinese securities exchanges has represented only minority interests. Generally for most listed firms control exists in one or more state affiliated firms or entities. For a relatively small minority of listed firms control exists in an individual, family or small group.

The non-tradability of control blocks has been deemed undesirable and the CSRC attempted for several years to reform this structure. After several failed attempts to do so, the CSRC has now largely completed its program in which most NTSs have been converted to shares that may be traded on the exchanges. The state-owned shares are now legally capable of being gradually floated to the open market according to relevant rules.

The completion of the share segmentation reform raises a new series of economically interesting questions, however: will the state in fact dissolve its control blocks through secondary market sales of formerly NTSs? If so, the control of which firms will be put on the market and when? It seems highly unlikely that the state will allow control over key elements of the economy, e.g., finance, transportation, energy, communications, and natural resources, to pass into the market. And with respect to less vital SOEs, the state may raise capital by sale of state-owned shares while retaining blocks of 20%–25% which ordinarily would be deemed sufficient to thwart a market based change in corporate control.

Thus while the completion of the NTSs reform removes a formidable impediment to the development of an effective securities market, it remains to be seen if, when and with respect to which firms the reform will be operationalized.

1.2 Growth in Market for Large Company (SOEs) Shares

The mainland Chinese stock exchanges are now quite large. By close of June 2010, the Shanghai and Shenzhen Stock Exchanges together listed 1,891 companies. The majority listed companies were SOEs. Using the market capitalization metric, with its weaknesses, the two mainland Chinese exchanges would have together constituted the fourth largest exchange in the world at the close of June 2010. At that time, total market capitalization of both markets equaled US$2,877.6 trillion, about one quarter of the size of the NYSE. While in the context of the Chinese securities markets, market capitalization figures may mislead as much as inform, still the numbers are impressive. Daily trading volume on both markets averaged US$33.4 billion as of April 30, 2010. Again, measured in total market capitalization, the comparative recent growth rates of these exchanges and their volatility appears remarkable. Comparative data for the periods of 2006 through 2009 is set forth in Table 2.

Table 2
Global Stock Market Capitalizations and Percent Changes

Stock Exchange	Stock Market Capitalization				Percent Changes		
	2009	2008	2007	2006	2009 vs. 2008	2008 vs. 2007	2007 vs 2006
	(US$ in millions)						
NYSE	11,837,793.30	9,208,934.10	15,650,832.50	15,421,167.90	↑28.5%	↓41.2%	↑1.5%
Nasdaq	3,239,492.44	2,396,344.30	4,013,650.30	3,865,003.60	↑35.2	↓40.3	↑3.8
London SE	2,796,444.32	1,868,064.80	3,851,705.90	3,794,310.30	↑49.7	↓51.5	↑1.5
Hong Kong SE	2,305,142.79	1,328,768.50	2,65,416.1	1,714,953.30	↑73.5	↓49.9	↑54.8
Shanghai SE	2,704,778.45	1,425,354.00	3,694,348.00	917,507.50	↑89.8	↓61.4	↑302.7
Shenzhen SE	868,373.99	353,430.00	784,518.60	227,947.30	↑145.7	↓54.9	↑244.2
Singapore SE	481,246.70	264,974.40	539,176.60	384,286.40	↑81.6	↓50.9	↑40.3
Korea SE	834,596.47	470,797.30	1,122,606.30	834,404.30	↑77.3	↓58.1	↑34.5
Bombay SE	1,306,520.21	647,204.80	1,819,100.50	818,878.60	↑101.9%	↓64.4%	↑122.1%

Source: World Federation of Exchanges

In recent years, the mainland exchanges have been active sites for raising new capital. Indeed, according to data collected by the World Federation of Exchanges, the Shanghai Stock Exchange raised more capital during the period of 2006–2009 than any other global market.

Table 3
Market Capitalization of Newly Listed Shares

	2004	2005	2006	2007	2008	2009
			(US$ in millions)			
Shanghai SE	14,438	3,140	223,322	1,576,732	92,118	99,924
Shenzhen SE	8,536	1,634	23,691	74,655	38,769	71,450
Hongkong SE	37,347	98,292	102,941	155,199	28,767	95,235
NYSE	118,944	135,719	192,412	244,515	207,612	64,810
LSE	52,468	322,269	131,137	144,674	77,560	24,437
Tokyo SE	87,832	110,399	81,982	35,969	40,106	18,062

Source : www.world-exchanges.org/statistics

1.3 Concentration, Liquidity and Pricing Efficiency of the Shanghai Stock Exchange

The largest SOEs dominate trading on the Shanghai Stock Exchange. Of more than 800 listed firms as of June 2010, the ten largest firms represent 39.5% of the exchange's total market capitalization. The two largest listed firms—PetroChina Company Limited ("PetroChina") and Industrial and Commercial Bank of China ("ICBC") together account for approximately 20% of the market capitalization of the entire exchange as of the end of June 2010. The Shanghai Exchange is substantially more concentrated than either the New York Stock Exchange or the Tokyo Exchange, but currently about the same as the London Exchange.

Table 4
Market Concentration
Percentages of Total Market Capitization Represented by Largest Ten Firms

	2004	2005	2006	2007	2008	2009
NYSE	19.6%	16.4%	16.1%	19.3%	20.1%	15.7%
London SE	40.2%	40.9%	37.1%	38.2%	46.3%	41.3%
Shanghai SE	29.0%	32.6%	56.6%	51.6%	49.0%	41.2%
Tokyo SE	18.1%	18.1%	20.1%	18.5%	18.3%	17.6%

Source : World Federal of Exchanges: www.wfe.org/statistics

As we suggested earlier, market capitalization figures of the Chinese exchanges must be interpreted carefully because of the large blocks of untraded (albeit now legally tradable) shares in virtually every listed firm. Consider, for example, the share ownership structure of ICBC Bank, the second largest market cap listing on the Shanghai stock exchange. In October 2006, ICBC, the state-owned bank, simultaneous [sic] listed and distributed a minority block of its shares on the Shanghai Stock Exchange and the Hong Kong Stock Exchange, in what proved at the time to be the world largest IPO, generating approximately US$21.9 billion in proceeds.

As of June 30, 2010, ICBC bank had more than 334 billion shares outstanding; 24.87% of its outstanding shares are H shares listed and traded on the Hong Kong Stock Exchange. The reminder of its shares, following the completion of share segmentation reform are A shares technically tradable on the Shanghai Stock Exchange. But how much of this equity is actually public [sic] floated and controlled by non-state affiliate entities? Table 5 sets forth shareholding of the top five shareholders of ICBC as of June 30, 2010.

Table 5
Top Five Shareholders of ICBC as of June 30, 2010

Name of Shareholder	Nature of Shareholder	Type of shares	Total number of shares held	Shareholding Percentage
Central Huijin Investment Limited [1]	State-owned	A shares	118,316,816,139	35.4%
Ministry of Finance of the PRC	State-owned	A shares	118,006,174,032	35.3%
HKSCC Nominees Limited [2]	Foreign corporation	H shares	68,577,667,687	20.5%
The Goldman Sachs Group, Inc.	Foreign corporation	H shares	13,180,811,324	3.9%
American Express Company	Foreign corporation	H shares	638,061,117	0.2%

(1) Central Huijin Investment Limited is a wholly-owned subsidiary of China Investment Corporation, the Chinese state sovereign investment company.

(2) Most retail and institutional investors hold their shares through a bank, broker or custodian who in turn hold them in an account with the Central Clearing and Automated Settlement System (CCASS) operated by Hong Kong Securities Clearing Co., Ltd. (HKSCC), a subsidiary of HKEx. HKSCC Nominees Ltd., a subsidiary of HKSCC, is the registered shareholder of listed companies and acts as nominee for the account holders of CCASS. The total number of shares held by HKSCC also included H shares held by PRC National Council for Social Security Fund.

From the table, we conclude the *publicly owned* ICBC shares tradable on the Shanghai Stock Exchange constitute less than 4.3% of ICBC A shares (since most of the 75.13% of ICBC shares that could in theory be traded on the Shanghai Stock Exchange are actually held by Central Huijin Investment Limited or the Ministry of Finance). One must look to the Hong Kong Stock Exchange to find more substantial private investment in ICBC shares. There we find listed ICBC H shares constitute 24.87% of all outstanding ICBC shares. One obvious conclusion from these figures is that in the case of ICBC Bank, the Hong Kong Stock Exchange has been much more important than Shanghai as a source of new capital. Specifically, more than six times the capital raised by ICBC from investors on the Shanghai Exchange was raised by it on the Hong Kong Exchange.

ICBC's share trading structure is not unique among the largest SOEs. The proportion of shares not controlled by state-affiliated entities of the largest firms on the Shanghai Stock Exchange is typically quite small. For example, as of June 30, 2010, 67.53% of the A shares of Bank of China was owned by Central Huijin Investment Ltd. and less than 2.35% A shares were public floated and controlled by domestic non-state owned entities or individuals . . .

The upshot of the fact that the trading markets in Shanghai are relatively thin and are more highly concentrated than most developed markets and that Chinese investors have highly restricted alternative investment opportunities, is that there is good reason to suppose that the prices reflected on the mainland markets are not a good signal of fundamental value of the shares or the firms listed on the exchange. In fact, Chinese stock markets are frequently described as highly volatile; price movements are notably synchronous . . . and when market prices are compared to prices at which control transactions occur it has been found that the control of a listed firm is traded by private contract on average at almost a 20% *discount* to market price . . . The reasonable conclusion is that traded prices are likely not a good signal of fundamental firm value.

* * *

1.5 Institutional Investors

Retail investors dominated China's stock markets from their inception. This fact has doubtlessly contributed to the relative price volatility of these markets. The dominance of retail investors, however, has gradually eroded in China, as QFIIs and domestic institutional investors, such as insurance companies, a variety of managed investment funds, and the national social security fund have grown in importance. In fact, by the end of 2008, the CSRC could report that institutional investors had for the first time became the dominant force in the market, by holding 54.6% of market capitalization of all tradable shares in the domestic markets. By comparison we note that institutional investors have been reported to represent seventy percent of the Hong Kong stock exchange and eighty percent of the New York Stock Exchange.

The participation of QFIIs in the two mainland exchanges, however, remains quite limited. These foreign institutional investors, would no doubt be interested in channeling increasing amounts of foreign investment into the Chinese securities markets. But their ability to do so is limited. Following the initiation of the QFII program in 2003, qualifying institutions were permitted to invest in the A-share and the government bond markets. According to the State Administration of Foreign Exchange, as of June 30, 2010, there were eighty-eight QFIIs approved in China, with an approved investment amount of US$17.1 billion, which represented only about 1% of the A shares market capitalization . . .

1.6 Market Access for "Private" Firms: The SME Board & the GEM Board.

To a large extent, the growth of the Chinese economy is attributable not to the SOEs that dominate the Shanghai Stock Exchange, but to private and hybrid firms, that is those firms with private as well as local government involvement (as lenders, minority owners or business partners). But formal sources of finance either bank loans or securities markets are difficult for private firms in China . . . These firms have largely, but not completely, been excluded by the CSRC from listing on the stock exchanges. While there are about 570 private companies listed on the two Chinese stock exchanges, representing 34.8% of the total number of all listed companies, those firms represent only 12.2% of the market capitalization . . .

Private firms have tended not been [sic] approved for listing by the CSRC for a variety of reasons. First, of course, is the fact that the fundamental mission of the securities markets at least for the first fifteen years of their existence has been to support SOEs with additional capital. Especially in the first years of the exchanges, allocation of listings were heavily influenced by the capital needs of inefficient province level SOEs. Second, the CSRC deems itself charged to protect investors from excessively risky companies. Thus an unwillingness to approve listings for private firms may, in part, reflect a belief that these firms will on average be more risky than existing state-affiliated enterprises. Third, these smaller more entrepreneurial enterprises may lack political patrons, which in a system (and a culture) that is inevitably affected by political and personal networks, may be a significant disadvantage. Finally, the under representation of small and growing private firms may in part reflect an ideological bias against "private" wealth building. Whatever the source of the bias, given the fact that, as a class, private or hybrid firms represent the greatest prospect for substantial economic growth, the failure of the securities markets to provide finance to this segment must be deemed as a substantial current weakness. The leadership has recognized this fact and approved substantial steps to address it. The CSRC has two initiatives in that respect. In 2004, a Small and Medium Enterprises Board (the "SME Board") was opened in Shenzhen and more recently a Growth Enterprise Board ("GEB Board") was opened on the same exchange.

The SME Board has met with some success. Private enterprises have a very significant presence on the SME Board. They are said to represent approximately 76% listed companies as of October 2005. By June 2010, 437 firms had listed shares on this board. Moreover, reportedly the annual average revenue growth rate of these firms was 30 percent and growth rate of net profit was reportedly 18.5%. However, in many respects the listing standards for the SME board are similar to those of the bigger boards. The SME Board requires companies to have a minimum RMB30 million of accumulated net profits in the three years prior to listing. This rather importantly limits its utility to smaller entrepreneurial firms.

The CSRC's second, more recent and more substantial step to try to begin to afford better access to capital markets to non-state enterprises was reflected in the first IPO in October 2009 on the new Growth Enterprise Board ("GEB" also sometimes referred to as "ChiNext") of the Shenzhen Stock Exchange. This Board has been designed to function much as the NASDAQ market does in the U.S., providing public capital to entrepreneurial, especially high tech firms. One aspect of this initiative is to provide a potential exit channel for venture capital funded enterprises, thus further encouraging the development of a PRC venture capital business. Access to the GEB market will be overseen by a special review committee, which committee will presumably be professionally familiar with the special character of entrepreneurial and venture financed backed firms. The standards for listing on the GEB are lower than the SME Board: a minimum RMB10 million in retained earnings. Nevertheless, in contrast to similar markets in other countries, companies that apply for the listing on the GEB must already be profitable, a test that neither Amazon nor Ebay, for example, would have been able to satisfy. Thus even these innovative small company boards may reflect a strong regulatory bias against more risky enterprises. This bias may be appropriate in a system with a weak information environment, but it does limit the benefits that entrepreneurial activity can provide.

The first batch of twenty-eight selected firms selected for listing on the GEB went public on October 30, 2009 to warm market acceptance. As of June 2010, ninety companies were listed on the GEB.

1.7 The Absence of a Substantial Market for Commercial Bonds

From the perspective of more highly developed financial markets, a notable feature of the Chinese securities markets is the practical absence of a market for commercial bonds and indeed a very small bond market even when government bonds are included.

For example, at the close of 2006, the PRC bond market was reported to equal just 35.3% of China's GDP. Comparable international bond market numbers demonstrate the undeveloped nature of the Chinese bond market: Japan (201.0%), the U.S. (188.5%), U.K. (140.5%), Korea (125.1%), and Germany (69.0%). The existing bond market is heavily dominated by treasury bonds and financial institutions bonds. Huang and Zhu report that there are primarily four types of bonds in the domestic Chinese bond markets: Treasury bonds (they estimate at 2,149 billion yuan in late 2006), central bank notes (2,931 billion yuan), financial bonds (2.097 billion yuan), and commercial bonds (170 billion yuan). Thus the bond market supplies only a tiny portion of the capital available to non-financial firms . . .

China's lack of a substantial bond market does not make it an outlier among developing nations, however. As Table 1 shows, India, and Russia both have small bond markets. But neither of these countries has developed their economy or the formal institutions of capital markets as consistently as has China. Therefore, one is entitled to wonder why this aspect of capital market development has not made more progress in China? A possible answer might involve a desire to protect the large, state owned banks from bond or money market competition. Should a substantial bond market be available for long or short term debt, presumably the strongest credits would tend to migrate there, leaving weaker creditors for the subsidized banking system. In addition[,] bank lending may appear to the leadership to be superior to a [*sic*] commercial bond markets because bank lending is arguably more easily susceptible to influence by government officials than would be a bond market—both with respect to allocating capital in the first place and with respect to controlling the consequences of a default.

PART II.   THE REGULATORY ENVIRONMENT: THE CSRC.

Prior to 1992, China's infant securities markets had been lightly regulated by local governments and the local branch offices of the People's Bank of China (the "PBOC"). Following the establishment of the Shanghai and Shenzhen Stock Exchanges in 1990 and 1991, respectively, the State Council, in order to consolidate the complex, multilayered and fragmented institutional framework for securities trading, in fall 1992 formed the Securities Committee of the State Counsel (the "SCSC") and the CSRC, as the SCSC's executive arm. These new entitles were charged to create a centralized supervisory framework for securities issuance and trading in China.

2.1 CSRC's Dual Mandate: Advance State Policy While Also Protecting Investors.

As an executive arm of State Council, the CSRC has a primary obligation to advance state policy and programs. These state aims importantly include successful implementation of the state corporitization program, the development of the securities markets and the modernization of management of corporatized state-owned firms. In connection with its effort to supervise and guide the development of modern securities markets, the CSRC has adopted approaches that in some respects appear to have been influenced by the structure and policies of the U.S. Securities Exchange Commission ("SEC"). In other respects, however, the CSRC's mission and the nature of the PRC governmental structure requires quite different treatment of problems than that of western securities regulators.

As set forth in the PRC Securities Law of 2006, the CSRC's functions are broad indeed. They are to: (1) formulate relevant rules and regulations to supervise and administer the securities markets and exercise the power of examination or verification; (2) supervise and administer the issuance, offering, trading, registration, custody and settlement of securities (including granting or withholding permission to issuers to distribute shares); (3) supervise and administer securities activities of securities issuers, listed companies, securities firms, securities investment funds, securities trading service institutions, stock exchanges and securities registration and clearing institutions; (4) formulate the standards for securities practice qualification and code of conduct and carry on the supervision and implementation; (5) supervise and examine information disclosure relating to securities issuance, offering and trading; (6) offer guidance for and supervise activities of securities industries associations; (7) investigate and punish violations of any securities laws and administrative rules; and (8) perform any other functions and duties in accordance with law or administrative rules.

The CSRC is widely regarded as one of China's most highly professional regulatory bodies. It has been an active and effective participant in guiding market development, improving market transparency and in encouraging the development of modern management techniques. Perhaps its role differs from that of the SEC most fundamentally in that, as an executive arm of the State Council of the PRC, it has assumed the power to control access to the securities markets by all potential issuers of shares. Thus it acts as a gatekeeper to public finance available both in the IPO and the secondary issuance markets . . .

* * *

2.3. Enforcement

It is a commonplace for legal scholars to note the critical role of enforcement in effective securities regulation . . . The difference between law as written on a page and law as implemented by active agents and courts can be great.

Securities law enforcement is one of the CSRC's major regulatory functions. Prescribed market misconduct includes: illegal stock offerings, misrepresentation and omission in connection with the offer or sale of securities, insider trading, market manipulation and professional (securities firm/accounting firm/law firm) misconduct in connection with the offer or sale of securities. Among the recurring matters that give rise to enforcement activities of the CSRC are disclosure violations, securities firm misconducts such as misappropriation of client funds and market manipulation. Authorized penalties against public companies or securities firms include disgorgement, fines, revocations of business licenses, orders of business suspension and internal correction, and warnings or censure. Fines, an up-to a lifelong bar from the industry, and warnings are available against individuals, including directors and senior management in listed companies.

While it is empowered, it is difficult to say that the CSRC is as an effective enforcement body. For the most part, CSRC enforcement activities are limited and its penalties are mild. While the number of CSRC enforcement actions has grown as the markets has grown, the number of such actions does not seem large . . .

In all events, the result in most CSRC enforcement cases in which a listed company is accused of wrongdoing is censure; fines are quite rare . . . Yet Donald Clark wisely notes that where senior officers of SOEs are state officials, as may be the case in many large SOEs, a censure may be an effective remedy because it is likely to have serious career effects.

In recent years private actions by mislead investors have been permitted. Enforcement of securities private litigation in the PRC courts is a recent phenomenon. The PRC courts have faced a problem similar to that of the CSRC: they need to provide access to investors claiming fraud often in connection with SOE issuance of shares, while at the same time considering the interests of state in front of massive private securities litigations.

* * *

3.4 Chinese Courts and Shareholders' Right to Sue

3.4.1   The Institutional Contributions That Courts Can Provide.

While administrative agencies such as CSRC can act as powerful instruments in structuring and operating a system of market regulation, courts could supplement such activity in useful ways. Courts can give force and effect to abstract statements of law by determining contested facts and declaring and enforcing rights and duties of managers, shareholders or directors in those factual contexts. Among the institutional advantages of courts are the following: (1) well-functioning courts offer a professional commitment to make decisions only in accordance with pre-existing law and to be unaffected by other matters; (2) they have expertise in the content of pre-existing law and in accepted professional techniques of interpretation of it; (3) they make decisions grounded in the facts of a particular case, which are determined in an unbiased manner; and (4) they often or usually provide written justification for their results. In a judicial system in which courts function in this way, citizens know after a litigation has been determined that they have been heard by a disinterested judge with expertise who has ruled according to law. In this way well-functioning courts can provide a form of satisfaction even to parties who lose their disputes. The reliable provision of these services can *ex ante* facilitate investment and more broadly contracting among strangers.

As an arbiter of disputes between shareholders and those controlling the management of the firm, courts could serve a corporate governance function either at the instance of government actors (e.g. administrative agencies) or at the instance of shareholders directly. In fact since the 2006 amendment of the Company Law, Chinese courts have been authorized to adjudicate claims of director wrongdoing in so-called "derivative" lawsuits—that is a suit brought by a shareholder in the name and for the benefit of the corporation itself. Such suits are brought against the corporate directors or officers who are alleged to have violated their duty and injured the company in some way.

Derivative lawsuits can be subject to abuse, but they can serve as an important constraint on corrupt behavior. Generally, these suits can be useful even if directors are not frequently required to pay damages for wrongs in such lawsuits. In the U.S., most such suits are settled through the payment of a relatively small payment from an insurance underwriter. Nevertheless, such suits are useful to investors because, *ex ante*, directors adjust their behavior knowing that in certain types of transactions they face a high probability that their conduct will be subject to derivative litigation and thus close judicial review. Thus the existence of this types [*sic*] of lawsuit and the legal infrastructure that permits them to be brought, [*sic*] can serve an important chilling effect on violations of the corporate directors fiduciary duties.

* * *

PART IV.   THE   FUTURE   OF   CHINA'S   "TOP   DOWN" SECURITIES MARKETS

4.1 Assessing a Great Accomplishment

The creation in less than twenty years of the complex technological, financial and legal infrastructure necessary to operate the two mainland securities exchanges is unquestionably a great achievement. With these exchanges, and the corporatization effort that is their premise, the people of China have created one of the essential working parts of a world-class economy. They have successfully organized the former state and provincial production facilities into individual firms in which professional managers can direct activities with an eye to market-oriented production. They have created embryonic corporate governance structures and a structure of legal rights and duties that might

> "*China's capital markets are still not mature, and some systemic problems still exist. New problems are continually appearing. We will persevere with market-based and rule of law-based orientation and uphold open, equal, and fair market order.*"
>
> —Statement of China's State Council, as reported in "China Pledges to Push Ahead with Capital Market Reforms," at http://www.reuters.com/article/2014/05/09/us-china-markets-reform-idUSBREA 4807H20140509 (2014)

be used to create more highly elaborated investor based corporate governance protections in the future. They have created a means for the corporatized firms to access domestic household savings and world global investment pools. They have created the option to institute some forms of stock or stock price related incentive compensation for professional senior managers. And they have made initiating some forms of capital markets based disciplinary methods such as takeovers, a policy option for the future, as well.

Nevertheless in their present state these markets represent more potential value to China than realized value. They are not economically highly important yet. While the equity markets have grown rapidly in terms of market capitalization and in terms of listings, when compared to the securities markets in more developed financial systems, they appear as quite small relative to the Chinese economy. They lack deep liquidity and are excessively volatile; there is good evidence that they do not price equities very efficiently. An economically significant market for non-governmental bonds has not yet arisen in China and is important. Financial risk management has been severely limited in part because hedging opportunities are constricted by a prohibition, now to be eased, on borrowing shares. Futures markets for securities are in their infancy. Quite significantly the public markets continue to offer little assistance in funding growth in the important non-governmental sector of the economy. And by most accounts there is [a] significant level of managerial and other forms of corruption and virtually little investor corporate governance remedies available.

* * *

There are two updates we want to bring to your attention: relaxation of bans on short sales and margin trading, and the importance of the Hong Kong Exchange. Although the paper notes that bans on short sales and margin trading were relaxed in 2010, and that a trial project had commenced, no information was yet available regarding the success or failure of the trial. Since then, a study was published that explores the effects of the trial program. The study finds that the use of margin trading is almost non-existent on the mainland exchanges. But some investors have used short sales, although the volume of such transactions is small, with short sale activity occurring only on 8% of trading days. One of the study's hypotheses is that the availability of short sales would lead to better priced securities, as stocks on the mainland exchanges are often overpriced when compared to similar listings on the Hong Kong Exchange, given that pessimistic traders had no ability to affect stock price. The study concludes that although the trial-program stocks were better priced, the effect was due more to lower volume of trade as uninformed investors sought to reduce the risk associated with more informed investors willing to short sell. See S. Sharif et al, "Against the Tide: The Commencement of Short Selling and Margin Trading in Mainland China," Accounting and Finance (2013).

As to the importance of the Hong Kong Exchange to mainland China, the HKEX provides mainland firms with a more mature stock market on which to list and with greater access to foreign capital. Because of more stringent reporting requirements, a mainland firm that lists in Hong Kong can create greater investor interest by signaling to investors that it has higher standards of reporting and corporate governance. See Bas Karreman and Bert van der Knapp. "The Geography of Equity Listing and Financial Centre Competition in Mainland China and Hong Kong", Journal of Economic Geography, 2012. Also, as part of China's 12th five year plan, created in 2011, the government aims to make the renminbi (RMB) a global reserve currency. To reach this goal, China has increased the availability of RMB to Hong Kong banks, as well as spurred the growth of RMB-denominated bonds sold in Hong Kong and the availability of RMB denominated stocks. In essence, China is using Hong Kong as an offshore market for RMB, allowing Hong Kong to act as a buffer zone for the rest of the mainland. This allows foreign capital to flow into and out of China without the adverse impacts that can result from such flows. See H. Fung and J. Yau. "Chinese Offshore RMB Currency and Bond Markets: The Role of Hong Kong," China & World Economy (2012).

You Gotta Know Something About Them!

Deng Xiaoping

Deng Xiaoping rose through the ranks of the communist party but ran into trouble with Mao. Deng was all about material incentives and skills to spur economic development. Mao didn't like that, preferring egalitarianism and revolutionary enthusiasm to grow the economy. Because of Deng's views, radical Mao supporters stripped him of his positions during the Cultural Revolution (1966–76). He came back, though. In 1978, the Communist Party of China came around to Deng's reform agenda and in December the Party officially adopted it. This marked the beginning of a long road of market-based reforms—"market socialism with Chinese characteristics."

Although Deng was down for economic reforms, he wasn't down for political reforms or political liberalism. The Party had to stay in control of China. Heard of Tiananmen Square? In June 1989, the Chinese military descended upon the Square where millions of people were protesting against corruption and calling for democracy. The military shot dead hundreds of civilians. Deng gave the thumbs up to the military. Brutal. But he liked to play bridge and ate cheese. Doesn't that count for anything?

QUESTIONS FROM YOUR TALKING DOG

1.   What? We're going to another Chinese buffet? I'm gonna get an egg roll out of this. No, I really haven't had time to bone up on China's securities markets. So tell me the story. When did they begin to develop?

2.   Bank-centric financial system? What you mean by that? Well then tell me, how big is China's banking sector compared to the US?

3.   I don't like playing this game. Throw me a shrimp, then. Okay, the stock market is in Peking, right? Wrong? Like I said, I don't like playing this game. Another one? I'd say that the stock markets trade shares . . . of . . . of private companies? Wrong again? Not completely? Can we play another game? Like go fetch?

4.   Stop shoveling in the fried rice. I can't understand you. Did you say segmentation? What the heck does that mean? There was segmentation reform, huh?

5.   No, I don't want another piece of sweet-and-sour chicken. Just tell me why China's stock markets are inefficient.

6.   From retail to institutional investors. Wow! That's very . . . very interesting. Care to tell me a bit more?

7.   Yeah, I know what a bond is. That warm feeling between a master and his pet. Oh, bond markets. They're underdeveloped? Why is that?

8.   The CSRC? Regulation? Enforcement? Chinese courts? Fine. Tell me. But then we're going to the park. I told you not to feed me the sweet-and-sour stuff.

H. ISLAMIC FINANCE

Ethically Based Finance: What A Concept!

You need to know something about Islamic finance because it's been growing by leaps and bounds over the past few decades, with global assets totaling more than $1 trillion today. Most of you have probably heard the term Sharī'a. It's usually translated as "Islamic law." But it's more accurate to describe it as the Divine mandate of the "Duty of Man." The two pieces below give you some of the basics and how Islamic finance has developed in the United Kingdom, the major market for Sharī'a-compliant transactions.

> *"Shariah banking may still grow about 50 percent faster in coming years than the overall financial sector in several major markets . . . Indonesia's industry may expand fivefold to $83 billion by 2015, while Turkey's may triple in size in the next decade to more than $100 billion…"*
>
> —Y. Ho, "Profit Shortfall Slows Shariah Bank Expansion: Islamic Finance," at http://www.bloomberg.com/news/2013-03-05/profit-gap-slows-shariah-bank-growth-islamic-finance-correct-.html (2013)

> *"Britain is home to 22 Islamic banks, of which six are fully sharia-compliant. This is substantially more than in any other Western country or offshore center and is more than double the number in the United States."*
>
> —S. Kern, "Britain: 'A World Capital for Islamic Finance,'" at http://www.gatestoneinstitute.org/4042/britain-islamic-finance (2013)

Given all of the financial crises you've read about in this book, especially the global financial crisis, which many folks on the street feel was caused by "casino" finance, we want to say a few things here about finance, and risk in particular. Under Sharī'a principles, financial risks are divided into three categories. First, you got your essential risk, which is the risk inherent in all profit-making activity. Essential risk is cool unless the risk involves paying interest. And it's not allowed if the essential risk is related to a business venture that's prohibited—e.g, a deal involving the purchase and sale of alcohol. Then you're looking at prohibited risk, or gharar, which involves an ambiguity that may result in injustice. For example, a contract with an ambiguous term that would clearly benefit one party and leave the other one in the hole depending how that term is interpreted, is prohibited. All other risks, such as liquidity risks, credit risks, or market risks, are permissible. Check it out: Generally, money acquired from activities that don't comply with Islamic guidelines and rules is considered spiritual poison and illicit, meaning contracts based on poisoned transactions, including those that include prohibited risks—e.g. speculation (gambling)—might be struck down.

After you read these pieces, ask yourselves whether we'd be better served with a financial system, both domestic and global, informed by strong ethical principles. What challenges do you think you would face trying to construct such a system?

Oh, one last thing. Lest you think Islamic finance is limited to the Middle East and other Islamic countries, the United States is a major market for Sharī'a-compliant transactions. Islamic finance got started in 1986 by two California companies, Muslim Savings and Investments, and American Finance House—LARIBA. Today the U.S. gets most of its business from foreign investors doing transactions in a number of sectors, ranging from real estate to corporations.

> *"Unlike the secularist market paradigm, human well-being is not considered to be dependent primarily on maximizing wealth and consumption; it requires a balanced satisfaction of both the material and the spiritual needs of the human personality. The spiritual need is not satisfied merely by offering prayers; it also requires the moulding of individual and social behaviour in accordance with the Shari'ah (Islamic teachings), which is designed to ensure the realization of the maqasid al-Shari'ah (the goals of the Shari'ah hereafter referred to as the maqasid), two of the most important of which are socio-economic justice and the well-being of all God's creatures."*
>
> —M. Umer Chapra, What is Islamic Economics?, Jeddah, IRTI/IDB, No. 9 in the IDB Prize Winners' Lecture Series, 1996, 22, available at http://www.iiibf.org/elibrary/muchapra/A8%20What%20is%20Islamic%20Economics.pdf.

Z. IQBAL, "ISLAMIC FINANCIAL SYSTEMS"
Finance and Development (2007)

Islamic finance is emerging as a rapidly growing part of the financial sector in the Islamic world. Islamic finance is not restricted to Islamic countries, but is spreading wherever there is a sizable Muslim community . . .

What is Islamic finance?

Islamic finance was practised predominantly in the Muslim world throughout the Middle Ages, fostering trade and business activities with the development of credit. In Spain and the Mediterranean and Baltic states, Islamic merchants became indispensable middlemen for trading activities. In fact, many concepts, techniques, and instruments of Islamic finance were later adopted by European financiers and businessmen.

In contrast, the term "Islamic financial system" is relatively new, appearing only in the mid-1980s. In fact, all the earlier references to commercial or mercantile activities conforming to Islamic principles were made under the umbrella of either "interest-free" or "Islamic" banking. However, describing the Islamic financial system simply as "interest-free" does not provide a true picture of the system as a whole. Undoubtedly, prohibiting the receipt and payment of interest is the nucleus of the system, but it is supported by other principles of Islamic doctrine advocating risk sharing, individuals' rights and duties, property rights, and the sanctity of contracts. Similarly, the Islamic financial system is not limited to banking but covers capital formation, capital markets, and all types of financial intermediation.

Interpreting the system as "interest free" tends to create confusion. The philosophical foundation of an Islamic financial system goes beyond the interaction of factors of production and economic behavior. Whereas the conventional financial system focuses primarily on the economic and financial aspects of transactions, the Islamic system places equal emphasis on the ethical, moral, social, and religious dimensions, to enhance equality and fairness for the good of society as a whole. The system can be fully appreciated only in the context of Islam's teachings on the work ethics, wealth distribution, social and economic justice, and the role of the state.

The Islamic financial system is founded on the absolute prohibition of the payment or receipt of any predetermined, guaranteed rate of return. This closes the door to the concept of interest and precludes the use of debt-based instruments. The system encourages risk-sharing, promotes entrepreneurship, discourages speculative behavior, and emphasizes the sanctity of contracts (Box 1).

An Islamic financial system can be expected to be stable owing to the elimination of debt-financing and enhanced allocation efficiency. A "two-windows" model for Islamic financial intermediaries has been suggested in which demand deposits are backed 100 percent by reserves, and investment deposits are accepted purely on an equity-sharing basis. Analytical models demonstrate that such a system will be stable since the term and structure of the liabilities and the assets are symmetrically matched through profit-sharing arrangements, no fixed interest cost accrues, and refinancing through debt is not possible. Allocation efficiency occurs because investment alternatives are strictly selected based on their productivity and the expected rate of return. Finally, entrepreneurship is encouraged as entrepreneurs compete to become the agents for the suppliers of financial capital who, in turn, will closely scrutinize projects and management teams.

Box 1: Principles of an Islamic Financial System

The basic framework for an Islamic financial system is a set of rules and laws, collectively referred to as *shariah*, governing economic, social, political, and cultural aspects of Islamic societies. *Shariah* originates from the rules dictated by the *Quran* and its practices, and explanations rendered (more commonly known as *Sunnah*) by the Prophet Muhammad (P.B.U.H). Further elaboration of the rules is provided by scholars in Islamic jurisprudence within the framework of the *Quran* and *Sunnah*. The basic principles of an Islamic financial system can be summarized as follows:

Prohibition of interest. Prohibition of *riba*, a term literally meaning "an excess" and interpreted as "any unjustifiable increase of capital whether in loans or sales" is the central tenet of the system. More precisely, any positive, fixed, predetermined rate tied to the maturity and the amount of principal (i.e., guaranteed regardless of the performance of the investment) is considered *riba* and is prohibited. The general consensus among Islamic scholars is that *riba* covers not only usury but also the charging of "interest" as widely practiced.

This prohibition is based on arguments of social justice, equality, and property rights. Islam encourages the earning of profits but forbids the charging of interest because profits, determined ex post, symbolize successful entrepreneurship and creation of additional wealth whereas interest, determined ex ante, is a cost that is accrued irrespective of the outcome of business operations and may not create wealth if there are business losses. Social justice demands that borrowers and lenders share rewards as well as losses in an equitable fashion and that the process of wealth accumulation and distribution in the economy be fair and representative of true productivity.

Risk sharing. Because interest is prohibited, suppliers of funds become investors instead of creditors. The provider of financial capital and the entrepreneur share business risks in return for shares of the profits.

Money as "potential" capital. Money is treated as "potential" capital—that is, it becomes actual capital only when it joins hands with other resources to undertake a productive activity. Islam recognizes the time value of money, but only when it acts as capital, not when it is "potential" capital.

Prohibition of speculative behavior. An Islamic financial system discourages hoarding and prohibits transactions featuring extreme uncertainties, gambling, and risks.

Sanctity of contracts. Islam upholds contractual obligations and the disclosure of information as a sacred duty. This feature is intended to reduce the risk of asymmetric information and moral hazard.

Shariah-*approved activities.* Only those business activities that do not violate the rules of *shariah* qualify for investment. For example, any investment in businesses dealing with alcohol, gambling, and casinos would be prohibited.

An Islamic financial system can be expected to be stable owing to the elimination of debt-financing and enhanced allocation efficiency. A "two-windows" model for Islamic financial intermediaries has been suggested in which demand deposits are backed 100 percent by reserves, and investment deposits are accepted purely on an equity-sharing basis. Analytical models demonstrate that such a system will be stable since the term and structure of the liabilities and the assets are symmetrically matched through profit-sharing arrangements, no fixed interest cost accrues, and refinancing through debt is not possible. Allocation efficiency occurs because investment alternatives are strictly selected based on their productivity and the expected rate of return. Finally, entrepreneurship is encouraged as entrepreneurs compete to become the agents for the suppliers of financial capital who, in turn, will closely scrutinize projects and management teams.

Basic instruments

Islamic markets offer different instruments to satisfy providers and users of funds in a variety of ways: sales, trade financing, and investment (Box 2). Basic instruments include cost-plus financing (*murabaha*), profit-sharing (*mudaraba*), leasing (*ijara*), partnership (*musharaka*), and forward sale (*bay' salam*). These instruments serve as the basic building blocks for developing a wide array of more complex financial instruments, suggesting that there is great potential for financial innovation and expansion in Islamic financial markets.

Box 2: Islamic Financial Instruments

Some of the more popular instruments in Islamic financial markets are ***Trade with markup or cost-plus sale*** **(murabaha).** One of the most widely used instruments for short-term financing is based on the traditional notion of purchase finance. The investor undertakes to supply specific goods or commodities, incorporating a mutually agreed contract for resale to the client and a mutually negotiated margin. Around 75 percent of Islamic financial transactions are cost-plus sales.

Leasing **(ijara).** Another popular instrument, accounting for about 10 percent of Islamic financial transactions, is leasing. Leasing is designed for financing vehicles, machinery, equipment, and aircraft. Different forms of leasing are permissible, including leases where a portion of the installment payment goes toward the final purchase (with the transfer of ownership to the lessee).

Profit-sharing agreement **(mudaraba).** This is identical to an investment fund in which managers handle a pool of funds. The agent-manager has relatively limited liability while having sufficient incentives to perform. The capital is invested in broadly defined activities, and the terms of profit and risk sharing are customized for each investment. The maturity structure ranges from short to medium term and is more suitable for trade activities.

Equity participation **(musharaka).** This is analogous to a classical joint venture. Both entrepreneur and investor contribute to the capital (assets, technical and managerial expertise, working capital, etc.) of the operation in varying degrees and agree to share the returns (as well as

---

the risks) in proportions agreed to in advance. Traditionally, this form of transaction has been used for financing fixed assets and working capital of medium and long-term duration.

Sales contracts. Deferred-payment sale (*bay' mu'ajjal*) and deferred-delivery sale (*bay'salam*) contracts, in addition to spot sales, are used for conducting credit sales. In a deferred-payment sale, delivery of the product is taken on the spot but delivery of the payment is delayed for an agreed period. Payment can be made in a lump sum or in installments, provided there is no extra charge for the delay. A deferred-delivery sale is similar to a forward contract where delivery of the product is in the future in exchange for payment on the spot market.

Market trends

Banking is the most developed part of the Islamic financial system. The state constitutions of Iran and Pakistan, for example, require their banking systems to be fully compatible with Islamic law. In Egypt, Indonesia Malaysia, Sudan, and the Gulf Cooperation Council (GCC) countries Islamic banking exists alongside conventional banking. Islamic banking is currently practiced through two channels: "specialized" Islamic banks and "Islamic windows." Specialized Islamic banks are commercial, and investment banks, structured wholly on Islamic principles, and they deal only with Islamic instruments. Islamic windows are special facilities offered by conventional banks to provide services to Muslims who wish to engage in Islamic banking. Both Western banks and banks headquartered in Islamic countries provide Islamic windows.

Traditionally, specialized Islamic banks have been well positioned to attract deposits from Muslims, but these institutions have generally lacked the technical ability to invest efficiently. This gap has been bridged by the services of Western banks that swiftly and efficiently deploy funds into Islamically acceptable channels. But this has often meant lower returns for Islamic investors owing to the second layer of intermediation. This trend is changing. Islamic banks are becoming resourceful and are going global, in part owing to their increased integration with international markets. At the same time, aware of the potential of Islamic markets, Western banks are reaching out to investors directly and eliminating the middleman—the Islamic banks or Islamic windows of banks in Muslim countries. For example, Citibank opened its first Islamic bank subsidiary in Bahrain in 1996.

Historically, Islamic financial markets have lacked liquidity-enhancing instruments, thus eliminating a large segment of potential investors. However, more liquid instruments are emerging through securitization; Islamic funds, with a current market size of $1 billion, represent the initial application of securitization (see table). There are three types of Islamic funds: equity, commodity, and leasing. Equity funds, the largest share of the Islamic funds market, are the same as conventional mutual funds but with an Islamic touch that requires a unique "filtration" process to select appropriate shares. The filtration process ensures that the mode, operation, and capital structure of each business the fund invests in are compatible with Islamic law, eliminating companies engaged in prohibited activities and those whose capital structure relies heavily on debt financing (to avoid dealing with interest). For this reason, companies with a negligible level of debt financing (10 percent or less) may be selected, provided that the debt does not remain a permanent feature of the capital structure. The future of Islamic equity funds is bright in part because of a new wave of privatization under way in Muslim countries such as Egypt and Jordan, and in high-growth Islamic countries such as Indonesia and Malaysia, where the demand for Islamic financial products is growing rapidly. Commodity and leasing funds are other forms of Islamic funds. Commodity funds invest in base metals. Leasing funds pool auto, equipment, and aircraft leases and issue tradable certificates backed by the leases.

International and regional institutions are working with Islamic finance and are contemplating the introduction of derivative products and syndication to enhance project finance. The International Finance Corporation (IFC) has successfully executed several transactions in the Middle East and Pakistan that conform to Islamic principles. While the introduction of derivative products is being cautiously studied, it is suspected that these incorporate interest and may also support speculative activities. Simple derivatives, such as forward contracts, are being examined because their basic elements are similar to those of the Islamic instrument of deferred sale. Project finance, which puts emphasis on equity participation, is another natural fit for Islamic finance. The successful experimentation with long-term project financing in the construction industry in Malaysia is a positive development in this area.

Table 1 Emerging Islamic funds

Fund	Type	Year launched	Financial institution	Size (million dollars)
IIBU Fund II Plc	Leasing	1994	United Bank of Kuwait	51.5
Faysal Saudi Real Estate Fund		1995	Faysal Islamic Bank of Bahrain	27.0
GCC Trading Fund		1996	Faysal Islamic Bank of Bahrain	10.0
Oasis International Equity Fund	Equity	1996	Robert Fleming & Co. (United Kingdom)	16.6
Faisal Finance Real Estate Income Fund II	Real estate	1996	Faisal Finance (Switzerland) S.A.	100.0
Unit Investment Fund (all tranches)	Income/ mudaraba syndication	1996	Islamic Development Bank (Saudi Arabia)	500.0
Al Safwa International Equity Fund	Equity unit trust	1996	Al-Tawfeed Company for Investment Funds Ltd..	27.0
Ibn Khaldun International Equity Fund	Equity	1996	PFM Group (United Kingdom)	25.0
Adil Islamic Growth Fund	Equity	1996	Faisal Finance Switzerland) S.A.	10.0

Source: Islamic Banker, 1995–96, various issues.

Issues and challenges

Islamic financial markets are operating far below their potential because Islamic banking by itself cannot take root in the absence of the other necessary components of an Islamic financial system. A number of limitations will have to be addressed before any long-term strategy can be formulated:

A uniform regulatory and legal framework supportive of an Islamic financial system has not yet been developed. Existing banking regulations in Islamic countries are based on the Western banking model. Similarly, Islamic financial institutions face difficulties operating in non-Islamic countries owing to the absence of a regulatory body that operates in accordance with Islamic principles. The development of a regulatory and supervisory framework that would address the issues specific to Islamic institutions would further enhance the integration of Islamic markets and international financial markets.

There is no single, sizable, and organized financial center that can claim to be functioning in accordance with Islamic principles. Although stock markets in emerging Islamic countries such as Egypt, Jordan, and

Pakistan are active, they are not fully compatible with Islamic principles. The stock markets in Iran and Sudan may come closest to operating in compliance with Islamic principles. Moreover, the secondary market for Islamic products is extremely shallow and liquid, and money markets are almost nonexistent, since viable instruments are not currently available. The development of an interbank market is another challenge.

The pace of innovation is slow. For years, the market has offered the same traditional instruments geared toward short and medium-term maturities, but it has not yet come up with the necessary instruments to handle maturities at the extremes. There is a need for risk-management tools to equip clients with instruments to hedge against the high volatility in currency and commodities markets. In addition, the market lacks the necessary instruments to provide viable alternatives for public debt financing.

An Islamic financial system needs sound accounting procedures and standards. Western accounting procedures are not adequate because of the different nature and treatment of financial instruments. Well-defined procedures and standards are crucial for information disclosure, building investors' confidence, and monitoring and surveillance. Proper standards will also help the integration of Islamic financial markets with international markets.

Islamic institutions have a shortage of trained personnel who can analyze and manage portfolios, and develop innovative products according to Islamic financial principles. Only a limited number of Islamic institutions can afford to train their staffs and deploy resources in product development. There is lack of uniformity in the religious principles applied in Islamic countries. In the absence of a universally accepted central religious authority, Islamic banks have formed their own religious boards for guidance. Islamic banks have to consult their respective religious boards, or *shariah* advisors, to seek approval for each new instrument. Differences in interpretation of Islamic principles by different schools of thought may mean that identical financial instruments are rejected by one board but accepted by another. Thus, the same instrument may not be acceptable in all countries. This problem can be addressed by forming a uniform council representing different schools of thought to define cohesive rules and to expedite the process of introducing new products.

Future directions

The further growth and development of the Islamic financial system will depend largely on the nature of innovations introduced in the market. The immediate need is to deploy human and financial resources to develop instruments to enhance liquidity; develop secondary, money, and interbank markets; perform asset/liability and risk management; and introduce public finance instruments. The Islamic financial system can also offer alternatives at the microfinance level.

Securitization is a step in the right direction but even this requires more sophistication. The scope of securitization, the process of unbundling and repackaging a financial asset to enhance its marketability, negotiability, and liquidity in Islamic financial markets is very promising, because current market operations are restricted by the dearth of liquidity-enhancing products; secondary markets lack depth and breadth; and, more important, instruments for asset/liability management are simply nonexistent. With the expansion of securitization, the customer base of Islamic financial systems will grow as institutional investors, who have access to broader maturity structures, are attracted to the market; the secondary market will develop; and asset/liability management will become a reality. Other strong candidates for securitization include real estate, leasing, and trade receivables because of the collateralized nature of their cash flows.

Microfinance is another candidate for the application of Islamic finance. Islamic finance promotes entrepreneurship and risk sharing, and its expansion to the poor could be an effective development tool. The social benefits are obvious, since the poor currently are often exploited by lenders charging usurious rates.

An Islamic financial system can play a vital role in the economic development of Islamic countries by mobilizing dormant savings that are being intentionally kept out of interest-based financial channels and by facilitating the development of capital markets. At the same time, the development of such systems would enable savers and borrowers to choose financial instruments compatible with their business needs, social values, and religious beliefs.

R. WILSON, *ISLAMIC BANKING IN THE UNITED
KINGDOM* IN ISLAMIC BANKING AND FINANCE
IN THE EUROPEAN UNION

(2010) © **IRTI**

This chapter examines the experience of Islamic banking in the United Kingdom since 1980 . . . serving the British Muslim community of over 1.8 million people . . .

SHARI'AH-COMPLIANT LIQUIDITY MANAGEMENT

Initially the major Islamic finance activity involved wholesale operations, with banks in London providing overnight deposit facilities for the newly established Islamic banks in the Gulf. These Islamic banks could not hold liquid assets such as treasury bills, which paid interest, but the joint venture Arab banks in London, such as Saudi International Bank and the

United Bank of Kuwait, accepted deposits on a *murabaha* mark-up basis, with the associated short term trading transaction being conducted on the London Metal Exchange.

Although the staffs of the joint venture banks were mainly British and non-Muslims, they became increasingly well informed about *Shari'ah* requirements regarding finance, and were able to respond to the demands of their Muslim clients in an imaginative manner. There was considerable interaction between British bankers involved with Gulf clients, *Shari'ah* scholars and the British Pakistani community, notably through the Institute of Islamic Banking and Insurance (IIBI) that had been established in 1976 by Muzzam Ali, a former journalist and head of the Press Association of Pakistan. Muzzam Ali worked closely with Prince Mohammed Bin Faisal of Saudi Arabia, a leading advocate of Islamic finance, and became Vice Chairman of Dar Al Maal Al Islami in Geneva, the international Islamic finance organisation established by Prince Mohammed in 1982. The IIBI was initially located in the Kings Cross area, near to the City of London where the Arab joint venture banks operated, and in 1990 moved to more prestigious premises in Grosvenor Crescent in the West End of London.

THE AL BARAKA INTERNATIONAL BANK

The next milestone in 1982 was when the Jeddah-based Al Baraka Investment Company bought Hargrave Securities, a licensed deposit taker, and converted it into an Islamic bank. This served the British Muslim community to a limited extent, but its main client base was Arab visitors of high net worth who spent the summer months in London. Its business expanded from 1987 when it opened a branch on the Whitechapel Road in London, followed by a further branch on the Edgeware Road in 1989, and a branch in Birmingham in 1991, as by then the bank had between 11,000 and 12,000 clients. It offered current accounts to its customers, the minimum deposit being £150, but a balance of £500 had to be maintained to use cheque facilities, a much higher requirement than that of other United Kingdom banks. These conventional banks usually allow current accounts to be overdrawn, although then clients are liable for interest charges, which Al Baraka, being an Islamic institution, did not levy.

Al Baraka also offered investment deposits on a *mudaraba* profit sharing basis for sums exceeding £5000, with 75 per cent of the annually declared rate of profit paid to those deposits subject to three months' notice, and 90 per cent paid for time deposits of over one year. Deposits rose from £23 million in 1983 to £154 million by 1991. Initially much of Al Baraka's assets consisted of cash and deposits with other banks, which were placed on an Islamic basis, as the institution did not have the staff or resources to adequately monitor client funding. Some funds were used to finance commodity trading through an affiliate company, as Al Baraka was not a specialist in this area.

Al Baraka's major initiative was in housing finance, as it started to provide long-term Islamic mortgages to its clients from 1988 onwards. Al Baraka and its clients would sign a contract to purchase the house or flat jointly, the ownership share being determined by the financial contribution of each of the parties. Al Baraka would expect a fixed predetermined profit for the period of the mortgage, the client making either monthly or quarterly repayments over a 10–20 year period, which covered the advance plus the profit share. There was some debate if the profit share could be calculated in relation to the market rental value of the property, but this was rejected, as frequent revaluation of the property would be expensive and administratively complicated, and given the fluctuating prices in the London property market, there would be conservable risk for the bank.

Although Al Baraka provided banking services in London, its most profitable area was investment management, and in many respects it functioned more like an investment company than a bank. It lacked the critical mass to achieve a competitive cost base in an industry dominated by large institutions, and the possibility of expanding through organic growth was limited. In these circumstances when the Bank of England tightened its regulatory requirements after the demise of BCCI the bank decided that it was not worth continuing to hold its banking licence, as it would have meant a costly restructuring of the ownership and a greater injection of shareholder capital. Consequently in June 1993 Al Baraka surrendered its banking licence and closed its branches, but continued operating as an investment company from Upper Brook Street in the West End of London . . . Depositors received a full refund, and many simply transferred their money to the investment company. This offered greater flexibility, as it was no longer regulated under the 1987 Banking Act but under financial services and company legislation.

THE UNITED BANK OF KUWAIT

By the late 1980s there was an increasing demand from the United Bank of Kuwait's Gulf clients for Islamic trade based investment, and the decision was taken in 1991 to open a specialist Islamic Banking Unit within the bank. Employees with considerable experience of Islamic finance were recruited to manage the unit, which enjoyed considerable decision-making autonomy. In addition to being a separate unit, accounts were segregated from the main bank, with Islamic liabilities on the deposit side matched by Islamic assets, mainly trade financing instruments. The unit had its own *Shari'ah* advisors, and functioned like an Islamic bank, but was able to draw on the resources and expertise of the United Bank of Kuwait as required. In 1995 the renamed Islamic Investment Banking Unit (IIBU) moved to new premises in Baker Street, and introduced its own logo and brand image to stress its distinct Islamic identity. Its staff of 16 in London included asset and leasing managers and portfolio traders and administrators, and by the late 1990s investment business was generated from throughout the Islamic World, including South East Asia, although the Gulf remained the major focus of interest. Assets under management exceeded $750 million by the late 1990s, just prior to the merger with Al Ahli Bank, which resulted in the bank being renamed the Al Ahli United Bank.

After Al Baraka pulled out of the Islamic housing market the United Bank of Kuwait entered the market in 1997, with its Manzil home ownership plan based on a *murabaha* instalment structure. A double stamp duty was incurred on *murabaha* transactions, firstly when the bank purchased the property on behalf of the client, and secondly when it resold the house to the client at a mark-up. This was felt by many in the Muslim community to be discriminatory, and following effective lobbying by the Muslim Council of Britain, and a report by a committee charged with investigating the issues, the double stamp duty was abolished in the 2003 budget, with the change taking effect from December of that year. The double stamp duty also applied to the *ijara* mortgages introduced under the Manzil plan in 1999.

THE ISLAMIC BANK OF BRITAIN

The development that has attracted the greatest interest in recent years has been the establishment of the Islamic Bank of Britain: It had long been felt by many in Britain's Muslim community, especially since the withdrawal of Al Baraka from the retail Islamic banking market, that the United Kingdom should have its own exclusively Islamic Bank. A group of Gulf businessmen, with its core investors based in Bahrain but with extensive business interests in the United Kingdom, indicated that they were prepared to subscribe to the initial capital of £50 million. A business plan was formulated in 2002, and a formal application made to the Financial Services Authority (FSA) for the award of a banking licence.

The FSA was well disposed towards the application; indeed its staff charged with regulating the London operations of banks from the Muslim World were knowledgeable about Islamic banking and believed that in a multicultural and multi-faith society such as that of Britain in the twenty-first century, Islamic banking was highly desirable to extend the choice of financial product available to the Muslim community. There was no objection to the new bank being designated as Islamic, as this was not felt to be a sensitive issue in the UK, unlike in some countries where there are large Christian populations such as Nigeria, where the terms Muslim and Islamic cannot be used to designate banks. In Saudi Arabia, a wholly Muslim country, the term Islamic bank also cannot be used, as the major commercial banks and many *Shari'ah* scholars object to religion being used as a marketing tool.

The major concern of the FSA was that the new Islamic bank should be financially secure by being adequately capitalised, and that the management had the capability to adhere to the same reporting requirements as any other British bank. The emphasis was on robustness of the accounting and financial reporting systems, and in proper auditing procedures being put in place. Systems of corporate governance were also scrutinised, including the responsibilities of the *Shari'ah* advisory committee, and their role in relation to the management and the shareholders of the Islamic Bank of Britain. The FSA cannot of course provide assurance of *Shari'ah* compliance, as that is deemed to be a matter for the Islamic Bank of Britain and its *Shari'ah* committee. However the FSA wishes to satisfy itself that the products offered are clearly explained to the clients, and that full information on their characteristics is provided in the interest of consumer protection.

The Islamic Bank of Britain opened its first branch on the Edgware Road in London in September 2004, less than one month after regulatory approval was given. Its operational headquarters are in Birmingham, where costs are lower, and it has opened other branches in Birmingham, Leicester, Manchester, Southall, Whitechapel and East Ham. The size of the Muslim population in the immediate locality is one factor determining the choice of branch location, the socio-economic status of the potential clients being another factor, as middle class Muslims in professional occupations with regular monthly salaries are obviously more profitable to service than poorer groups. The bank stresses the Islamic values of faith and trust, as these are fundamental, but it also emphasises value and convenience, the aim being to have standards of service and pricing at least comparable with British conventional banks.

The opening of the first branch attracted much media attention, and therefore free publicity for the bank. The bank has a well designed website to attract business, offers 24-hour online and telephone services, and has produced informative and attractive leaflets and other publicity material outlining its services. All the material at present is in English rather than Urdu or Arabic, as the costs of translation and printing have to be seen in the context of promotional benefits. Some staff members are fluent in Urdu and Arabic, but at varying levels of proficiency, and foreign language ability is not a prerequisite for appointing staff, but good English is important. Many staff members have previous banking experience, and most, but not all, are Muslim.

The Islamic Bank of Britain offers current, savings and treasury accounts, all of which are *Shari'ah* compliant. No interest payments or receipts are made with current accounts, but a chequebook and a multifunctional bankcard is provided, these initially being simply cheque guarantee cards. Savings accounts operate on a *mudaraba* basis with £1 being the minimum balance. Profits on savings accounts are calculated monthly and have been held at around 3 per cent since October 2004 (the rate on fixed term deposits of 12 months at September 2009 wall 2.8 per cent). No notice is required for withdrawals from basic savings accounts, which in other words can be designated as instant access accounts. Term deposit savings accounts, which are subject to a minimum deposit of £5000, pay higher rates: In March 2005 deposits for one, three or six months earned 3.5 per cent, 3.75 per cent and 4 per cent respectively. Unique amongst Islamic banks, the Islamic Bank of Britain offers treasury deposits, with a minimum £100,000 for 1, 3 or 6 months being invested. These operate on a *murabaha* basis, with funds invested on the London Metal Exchange. This type of account in other words replicates for the retail market the type of wholesale or inter-bank deposit facilities first operated on a *Shari'ah* compliant basis in London in the early 1980s.

"Islamic Bank of Britain (IBB), the country's only sharia-compliant retail lender, has received a 75.8 million pound ($124 million) injection from it new Qatari owner to support the bank's expansion plans. The investment bring IBB's capital to 100 million pounds, after it was acquired . . . by Masraf Al Rayan, Qatar's largest Islamic bank by market value."

—B. Vizcaino, "Islamic Bank of Britain Gets Fresh Capital, Plans Expansion," at http://www.reuters.com/article/2014/02/04/islamic-finance-britain-idUSL5N0L902 F20140204 (2014)

The Islamic Bank of Britain offers personal finance, with amounts ranging from £1000 to £20,000 made available for 12 to 36 months. This operates through *tawarruq* with the bank buying *Shari'ah*-compliant commodities that are sold to the client on a cost plus profit basis. The client's agent, who is conveniently recommended by the bank, in turn buys the commodities and the proceeds are credited to the client's account. The client then repays the bank through deferred payments. Home purchase plans are now available, which are halal alternatives to mortgages.

ISLAMIC HOME FINANCE AND CURRENT ACCOUNTS OFFERED BY CONVENTIONAL BANKS

It is a challenge for a new entrant such as the Islamic Bank of Britain to compete in a mature market for banking services with the major conventional banks offering Islamic products, notably HSBC through its dedicated Amanah Islamic finance division and Lloyds TSB, which has entered the market through Cheltenham and Gloucester, the former building society that it bought to create a focused mortgage and retail savings subsidiary.

It was the abolition of double stamp duty, as already discussed, that encouraged new entrants into the market for Islamic home finance, notably, HSBC Amanah in 2004 and Lloyds TSB from March 2005. At the same time the Al-Ahli United Bank, the successor of the United Bank of

Kuwait, reached agreement with the West Bromwich Building Society for the distribution of Islamic mortgages through its extensive branch network. A similar agreement was concluded between the London based Islamic finance subsidiary of Arab Banking Corporation, Alburaq, and the Bank of Ireland, for the distribution of Islamic mortgages through its English subsidiary, the Bristol and West Building Society.

There are a number of different structures for Islamic home finance in the United Kingdom, the original Al Baraka and the United Bank of Kuwait Manzil scheme being *murabaha*-based with fixed monthly repayments to cover the cost of the house purchase that the bank undertook, plus the mark-up profit margin. In 1999 a second Manzil scheme was introduced based on *ijara,* with the United Bank of Kuwait, and its successor the Al Ahli United Bank, purchasing the property, but with the client paying a monthly rent, as well as a monthly repayment. The rent varied, but rather than being calculated on the rental value of the property, which would have implied frequent expensive revaluations, the rent was simply benchmarked to LIBOR, the London Inter-Bank Offer Rate. As this was an interest-based rate, this was potentially controversial from an Islamic perspective, but the Bank's *Shari'ah* board approved its use as a benchmark, as LIBOR is often used in Islamic finance calculations because of its widespread acceptance in the banking community. The HSBC Amanah monthly home finance payments are also calculated in this way, as are those of the ABC Alburaq home financing facility marketed through the Bristol and West, although the latter is designated as a diminishing *musharaka* scheme, as over the life of the mortgage, the client's ownership share increases as repayments are made, and the share of the bank in the equity of the house correspondingly reduces.

One factor that appears to be limiting the uptake of Islamic home finance is that the cost is higher than conventional mortgages. For Islamic financing worth £135,000 from Lloyds TSB over a period of 25 years the monthly repayments were £883 plus £21 a month for buildings insurance in March 2005. This comprised a rental payment of £693 plus a capital repayment of £190. The total monthly payment was over £100 per month more than the cost of a Lloyds TSB conventional mortgage. With HSBC Amanah for the same loan of £135,000 over 25 years the monthly repayments were £857, only £7 per month more than the bank's conventional mortgage, but the buildings insurance of £34 per month was obligatory with the Islamic financing as the property itself is owned by the bank, unlike with a conventional mortgage where the bank simply has a charge on the property so that it can be repossessed in the case of payments default.

A survey of 503 Muslims in ten cities throughout England undertaken by Dr. Humayon Dar of Loughborough University showed that many respondents had little knowledge of *Shari'ah* compliant finance, but those who had enquired about Islamic home finance were deterred from proceeding by the higher costs. These, however, partly reflect the limited scale of the market, and hence the higher costs per mortgage approved, as well as the costs involved in *Shari'ah* compliance, not least paying the fees and expenses of members of the *Shari'ah* committee. Of course the cost of a mortgage is not the only factor determining the level of business, as those Muslims who have signed contracts for Islamic finance have been prepared to pay a premium for *Shari'ah* compliance. Rather the issue seems to be the size of the premium, which greater competition in the market should reduce.

A further factor inhibiting the uptake of Islamic home finance is that a significant proportion of the Muslim population in the UK is in a low socio-economic position and cannot afford to buy property. This applies in areas such as East London where many of those in the Bangladeshi community are quite poor, but property prices are relatively high. One solution might be co-ownership through Islamic housing associations, with the tenant, association and bank all owning a share in the property, but at present these do not exist in the UK.

Both HSBC Amanah and Lloyds TSB offer Islamic current accounts, these being linked to the Islamic home finance being offered, as clients make their repayments through these accounts. Neither HSBC Amanah nor Lloyds TSB pay or charge interest on these accounts, but the accounts offer normal transactions facilities such as cheque books, standing orders and direct debit facilities, monthly statements and multifunctional cards that serve as cheque guarantee and debit cards. With HSBC Amanah a minimum balance of £1000 is required to maintain the account, but with Lloyds TSB there is no minimum. At present savings and investment accounts based on *mudaraba* are not offered by either bank in the UK, as the liabilities to match the Islamic mortgage assets are generated elsewhere, notably in the case of HSBC Amanah through *Shari'ah*-compliant deposits in the Gulf.

FUTURE PROSPECTS FOR ISLAMIC FINANCE IN THE UNITED KINGDOM

Although the UK has the most active and developed Islamic banking sector in the European Union, most activity until recently has been related to the role of the city of London as an international financial centre, rather than serving the retail banking needs of British Muslims. This is however likely to change in the years ahead, especially if other major UK based mortgage banks, notably Halifax Bank of Scotland (HBOS) and Royal Bank of Scotland (RBS, which owns NatWest) enter the market for Islamic mortgages. UNB Bank launched an Islamic mortgage product in 2004 aimed at the Scottish market, with the international law firm, Norton Rose, providing advice on *Shari'ah* issues, and the mortgages being based on the diminishing *musharaka* principle. HBOS and RBS have already sent representatives to several Islamic finance conferences in London, and it seems likely that the UNB Islamic mortgage aimed at the Scottish market, even though UNB is a minor player, may encourage the larger Edinburgh-based institutions such as Standard Life to bring forward their launch plans for Islamic financial products.

HSBC Amanah launched an Islamic pension fund in May 2004, where the assets held in the fund are screened for *Shari'ah* compliance, shares of companies involved in alcohol production and distribution, pork products and conventional banking being excluded, including ironically HSBC shares. The pension fund is marketed to individuals and small Muslim family businesses. This may be a more promising way forward in the UK market than Islamic mutual funds, where there has been a history of failure, from the Kleinwort Benson Islamic unit trust of the 1980s to Flemings Oasis Fund and the Halal Mutual Fund of the 1990s, all of which failed to attract sufficient investors to ensure sustainability.

The UK government is determined to create a level playing field for *Shari'ah-compliant* products. In the 2005 budget statement the same treatment was extended for *ijara* leasing mortgages and diminishing *musharaka* co-ownership mortgages as had already been applied to *murabaha* mortgages in the 2003 budget, with only a single stamp duty levy applying. The then Chancellor of the Exchequer, Gordon Brown, announced at the Muslim News Awards for Excellence in March 2005 that a consultation paper would be issued concerning equal treatment for Muslim council tenants under the 'right to buy scheme', that at present is restricted to interest-based mortgages. All this bodes well for the future, as a non-discriminatory system of taxation and regulation will encourage more competition in the market for Islamic financial services, reduce prices and margins, and make Islamic products more affordable. There is much that other European Union member states can learn from the quarter of century of experience in the UK, and even if some of the lessons are cautionary, many in the Muslim community now believe that British Islamic finance is really taking off.

You Gotta Know Something About Them!

Sayyid Muhammad Baqir Al Sadr

Born in Kadhimiya, Iraq, Sayyid Muhammad Baqir Al-Sadr became a big time Islamic scholar who wrote about pretty much everything: politics, Islamic culture, Qu'ran commentary, logic, law, philosophy, jurisprudence, and economics. Check it out: The Kuwaiti government, which was swimming in money, commissioned the Ayatolla (he was an Ayatolla, too) to check out the country's compliance with Islamic principles. The consulting job led to a major work on Islamic banking that still's the basis for modern Islamic banks: *Al-Bank al-la Ribawi fi al-Islam* ("Usury-free Banking in Islam"). Sayyid Muhammad Baqir Al Sadr's ancestry can be traced back to the Holy Prophet Muhammad through the Seventh Imam, Imam Musa al-Kadhim. Hence, "Sayyid." He helped found the Islamic Dawa Party in 1958, and established the Islamist movement in Iraq. He made enemies with Saddam Hussein, never a good thing: Saddam had him hanged in 1980.

QUESTIONS FROM YOUR TALKING DOG

1.   We always pass this place. What is it? A mosque. Nice. Islamic finance, huh? Interesting. Isn't that all about no interest? More? Tell me. Okay, let's start with Sharī'a and the basic principles of this Islamic financial system you're talking about.

2.   Stop a second. I need a drink of water. Yeah, I know it looks pretty gross but it's wet. So tell me more about some of these Islamic financial instruments while I wet my whistle.

3.   No kidding? Western banks want some of the action? How so?

4.   Financial innovation is what it's all about these days. Big article on it. Financial Times. You read it too, huh. Pretty interesting what's happening with Islamic finance, isn't it? Especially securitization. I sound like an investment banker, don't I? But I don't look the part.

5.   This all sounds pretty neat. But how popular can Islamic financing get outside of Islamic countries? Lots of problems, right?

6.   Yeah, the article talked about the UK. Pretty interesting how it got started, don't you think? You got Al Baraka, then the Islamic Bank of England. Interesting how the UK dealt with it from a regulatory point of view. Your thoughts?

7.   Islamic home financing is pretty fascinating. What do you think about how they got around using the London Interbank Offer Rate? Isn't that always the case, only the well-to-do can afford the premium. But the UK is still happening place for the stuff.

8.   Hey . . . uh . . . the drink I had. Is the water that bad in the UK?

I. THE GLOBAL ECONOMIC ORDER

Will EMEs Gain More Clout?

Now we look at what some might say is a new international economic order or the beginnings of it. The journey began with the Bretton Woods Conference in 1944, where the United States and the United Kingdom established the Bretton Woods System (BWS). Developing countries had little voice in fashioning the key pillars of the system—it was John Maynard Keynes and Harry Dexter White who took the main stage.

During the 50s, 60s, and 70s, developing countries "developed" primarily by becoming suppliers of commodities to the advanced countries in exchange for manufactured goods. The structuralists argued that developing countries were spinning their wheels and that to really develop traction they had to industrialize via the import substitution model of development. Development at that state was "statist" in that the government, supported by World Bank lending, played a central role in all facets of the economy, the view being that the private markets were too weak and underdeveloped to push the country forward.

The collapse of the BWS in the early 70s created a space, however small, for the Global South to assert itself. It did so via a call for a New International Economic Order (NIEO), which at bottom was a call for reform of the world economic order based on economic sovereignty. The Global South said (maybe yelled), "We need resources from the Global North and a change in rules that will give us more voice in multilateral institutions, including the International Monetary Fund."

Well, that didn't happen. Instead many developing countries, especially in Latin America were hit with a debt crisis in the 1980s. During that decade, debtor countries received loans from the IMF and the World Bank in exchange for market-based reforms that envisioned a much smaller role for the state. It was the age of neoliberalism and the Washington Consensus. It was the age of conditionality.

The 1990s was a critical decade in many respects. The "market-friendly" model of development went viral. Countries that had adopted market-based reforms were starting to grow again. Still, when the 50th anniversary of the IMF and World Bank (BWIs) came around, NGOs around the world condemned the BWIs for making people all over the world miserable. Down with conditionality! Hell, down with the BWIs! Okay, well, if we're not going to raze them we should at least address the democratic deficit, proclaimed the NGOs and others. What they meant was that developing countries kept the BWIs in business, yet the Global South had relatively little say in the institutions.

The 1990s also witnessed two major financial crises: the 1994–1995 Mexican crisis and the Asian financial crisis in the latter part of the decade. They demonstrated the explosive combination of portfolio investment, prematurely liberalized financial markets, and domestic economic distortions. The IMF was involved in both crises, but in the Asian financial crisis the Fund went nuts with conditionality, literally restructuring entire economies—but often prescribing the wrong medicine. This led to calls for "country ownership" of reforms, the idea being that reforms mandated by the BWIs would be more realistic and successful if the country undergoing the reforms had more input in fashioning the reforms. What a concept!

As we began the new Millennium, countries in the Global South were growing again—at a healthy pace. Although the term "emerging market" was coined in 1981, it really became a topic of much conversation in the 2000s. There were "emerging market economies"—the BRICs—that were becoming important players in the global economy. Maybe, just maybe, the global economic order was poised for a significant transformation. The Global South might finally capture the voice in global economic affairs it had been seeking since the 1970s.

Then came the global financial crisis. This time, the crisis was caused by the United States, the global superpower. This was the opening the Global South needed. Here is the story of its success . . . or lack thereof.

E. CARRASCO, "AN OPENING FOR VOICE IN THE GLOBAL
ECONOMIC ORDER: THE GLOBAL FINANCIAL CRISIS
AND EMERGING ECONOMIES"

Oregon Review of International Law, Vol. 12, Number 2, 179 (2010)

* * *

IV

THE GLOBAL FINANCIAL CRISIS

Just one year after the IEO issued its report on structural conditionality, the world experienced the worst financial and economic crisis since the Great Depression. Throughout history, calls for reform have followed in the wake of major financial or economic crises. The extent and nature of reforms depend, of course, on the players that control the discourse over establishing the new order. In 1944, in Bretton Woods, New Hampshire, the controlling players were the United States and the United Kingdom. Developing countries were on the sidelines and "emerging economies" did not exist. The global financial crisis of 2008 occurred in a vastly different world, a world where the economic power of (white) Americans and Europeans is being challenged by (non-white) nonWestern countries such as China and India. Consequently, as this Part will show, in the Summits that occurred during the crisis, new players demanded to be included in the discourse regarding the postcrisis financial and economic order. First, I briefly address the impact of the crisis on emerging economies.

A.   Emerging Economies and the Crisis

The global financial crisis was triggered by subprime loans in the United States and, due in part to lax or no regulation over certain financial instruments and institutions, spread throughout the world via securitization. At the outset of the crisis, most observers believed that emerging economies would not be significantly affected by the crisis, which appeared to be concentrated in the United States and Europe. This is because most emerging economies did not hold toxic assets. Moreover, after the economic/financial crises in the 1980s and 1990s, many emerging economies engaged in significant reform of their financial sectors, including significant increases in foreign exchange reserves, which would make them less vulnerable to external shocks. Thus, they were becoming "decoupled" from developed countries' economies and not dependent on them for economic growth and stability. Indeed, in the midst of the financial crisis in the summer of 2008, it appeared that growth in emerging economies, amounting to half of all global economic growth in a given year, could help avert a global meltdown.

Nevertheless, emerging economies were not immune from the crisis. Despite their progress, they still depend greatly on foreign capital and investment, which is problematic when, during a crisis, foreign investors withdraw their money to perceived safer investments. Moreover, much of the double-digit growth seen throughout the developing world has depended on the availability of foreign credit, a stable currency, and sustainable global demand for exports, all of which were put in jeopardy because of the crisis. Thus, emerging economies experienced decreased capital and investment flows, currency depreciation, stock market crashes, and drops in exports and commodity prices.

Still, while emerging and developing countries were not spared from the global financial crisis, for the most part their economies recovered more quickly in 2009 than the economies of the United States and Europe. Therefore, the concept of decoupling cannot be summarily dismissed, and the possibility of it has at least one very significant impact: it has given emerging economies a voice that, unlike the NIEO of the 1970s, is capturing the attention of the developed world.

B.   The Drumbeat for Governance and Accountability Reform

Even prior to the global financial crisis and the decoupling debate, there was a post-NIEO "governance and accountability reform" movement to give developing and emerging economies greater voice in international monetary affairs. The movement's roots can be traced to 1994, when the World Bank and the International Monetary Fund marked the fiftieth year of their existence. The anniversary prompted hundreds of religious, labor, human rights, and environmental organizations across the globe to declare that "Fifty Years Is Enough." Critics claimed the two institutions contributed to human rights abuses, social injustice, and environmental degradation in developing countries.

Only a few years following the controversial anniversary, the IMF and the World Bank had to cope with the outbreak of the Asian financial crisis. The Fund's handling of the crisis gave critics yet another opportunity to denounce it. Among other things, critics claimed the Fund was an opaque institution that suffered from a "democratic deficit"—i.e., that member countries most affected by the Fund's programs had little voice in an institution controlled by a handful of industrialized countries. In particular, the Fund's Board of Directors has been dominated by members of industrialized countries. Moreover, its quota-based weighted voting system has given the G-7 countries approximately forty-five percent of the voting power in the Fund. Industrialized-country domination of the Fund has also been reflected in the tradition that has allowed the Europeans to name the institution's managing director (whereas the United States has traditionally named the president of the World Bank).

The Fund responded to its critics with a number of limited measures. Among other accountability-related measures, in July 2001, it established the Independent Evaluation Office to perform "objective and independent" evaluations of issues relating to the Fund's mandate. As to voice-related governance measures, in 2006 the Fund made an *ad hoc* quota adjustment for China, Turkey, Korea, and Mexico. In April 2008, it proposed a series of voice-related reforms, which included, *inter alia,* adopting a revised quota formula, a second round of *ad hoc* quota increases for "dynamic economies," and a tripling of basic votes intended to increase the voice of low-income countries. As to the selection of the IMF's Managing Director, a consensus has developed that the Fund should abandon the tradition of allowing the Europeans to choose the Managing Director behind closed doors and instead adopt a process of appointment that is "open, transparent, and merit-based." The G-20 endorsed this proposition in the summits held during the global financial crisis, which I turn to next.

C.   The Summits

A key voice that arose during the global financial crisis was the G-20, a forum created in the wake of the Asian financial crisis in which finance ministers and central bank governors from systemically important industrialized and developing countries discuss issues relating to the global economy. In November 2008, April 2009, September 2009, and

November 2010, the G-20 held summits in Washington, D.C., London, Pittsburgh, and Seoul respectively, to address the global crisis. The summits resulted in a number of decisions that reflected the increased voice of emerging and developing countries within the IMF and in global financial governance generally.

1.   The November Summit

On November 15, 2008, leaders of the G-20 met in Washington, D.C., to address what had become the worst global financial and economic crisis since the Great Depression. There was some initial anticipation that the meeting, dubbed by some as "Bretton Woods II," would produce a framework of fundamental reforms of the global financial system created in July 1944 during a three-week conference in Bretton Woods, New Hampshire. However, while G-20 leaders took "immediate steps" to stabilize the financial system, to use fiscal measures as appropriate to stimulate domestic demand, and to help emerging and developing countries gain access to finance, reform efforts were limited to agreement upon a set of principles that would guide future reform of the financial markets.

One of the principles was reforming international financial institutions. The summit's leaders declared they were committed to reforming the Bretton Woods Institutions in order to give emerging and developing countries greater voice and representation. Moreover, the FSF (as well as other major standard-setting bodies) had to be expanded "urgently to a broader membership of emerging economies." The leaders also called upon the IMF, in collaboration with the expanded FSF and other bodies, "to better identify vulnerabilities, anticipate potential stresses, and act swiftly to play a key role in crisis response." The Action Plan accompanying the Declaration set forth measures to be implemented by March 31, 2009, as well as in the medium term. With respect to reforming international financial institutions, the Action Plan, *inter alia,* called upon the FSF and the IMF to conduct "early warning exercises" by the March deadline.

The Declaration's reference to the FSF was an important one. Created in 1999 in the wake of the Asian financial crisis, the FSF mandate was to address vulnerabilities in the international financial system, identify and oversee action needed to address these vulnerabilities, and improve cooperation and information exchange among authorities responsible for financial stability.

The FSF's initial members consisted of the finance minister, central bank governor, and a supervisory authority from each of the G-7 countries, as well as representatives from the IMF, World Bank, Bank for International Settlements, Organization for Economic Cooperation and Development, Basel Committee on Banking Supervision, International Accounting Standards Board, International Association of Insurance Supervisors,

International Organization of Securities Commissions, Committee on Payment and Settlements Systems, and Committee on the Global Financial System. After its creation, the FSF added the European Central Bank, and additional national members Australia, Hong Kong, the Netherlands, and Switzerland.

A persistent criticism of the FSF was that it excluded developing or emerging economies. FSF's chairman Crockett's explanation for this lack of representation was that the FSF could be more effective if it was "homogeneous." While that explanation was arguably defensible in 1999, it clearly lacked legitimacy nearly a decade later in the context of a global crisis that emanated from the United States and significantly affected emerging and developing economies. Thus, the November summit's leaders understood that emerging economies could no longer remain voiceless in matters relating to the international financial system.

2.   IMF Announcements Prior to the London Summit

Given the November summit's March 31, 2009, deadline for implementation of various measures to address the crisis and the deepening of the crisis itself, constituencies throughout the world greatly anticipated the April G-20 summit in London. However, just prior to the summit, two developments, both related to IMF conditionality, drew considerable attention.

First, the IMF announced reforms to its conditionality regime, reforms that responded to the critiques of conditionality addressed above. Recognizing that IMF loans were overloaded with conditions that did not focus on the IMF's core areas of expertise, it announced that it would rely on "pre-set qualification criteria (ex-ante conditionality) where appropriate rather than on traditional (ex-post) conditionality." This change in the Fund's approach to conditionality is embodied in a new lending instrument: the Flexible Credit Line (FCL). As stated by the IMF, the FCL is intended for

> countries with very strong fundamentals, policies, and track records of policy implementation . . . . FCL arrangements would be approved for countries meeting pre-set qualification criteria. Access under the FCL would be determined on a case-by-case basis. Disbursements under the FCL would not be phased or conditioned to policy understandings as is the case under a traditional Fund-supported program.

Thus far, Mexico, Colombia, and Poland have secured FCL arrangements.

Second, in addition to announcing the creation of the FCL, the Fund announced that it is discontinuing the use of structural performance criteria in all Fund arrangements, opting instead to monitor structural policies via program reviews. The Fund stated, "[w]hile structural reforms will continue to be integral to Fundsupported programs where needed, their monitoring will be done in a way that reduces stigma, as countries will no longer need formal waivers if they fail to meet a structural reform by a particular date."

As the IMF's carefully crafted language indicates, while these developments do not eliminate Fund involvement in structural transformations of member countries' economies, they do hold promise that borrowers will gain more ownership of reform measures.

3.   *The London Summit*

Like the November summit, participants had high hopes during the lead up to the London summit. U.K. Prime Minister Gordon Brown claimed the summit would launch a "grand bargain" among countries that would help end the global recession and set in motion reforms that would prevent future crises. However, after a reality check, particularly with respect to differences between the United States and Europe over additional stimulus measures, participants lowered their expectations.

Nevertheless, participants concluded the London summit with great fanfare, with a number of "announceables" of significance to emerging and developing countries. Through a creative use of numbers, the summit leaders declared that, in addition to a fiscal stimulus of $5 trillion, they had agreed upon "an additional $1.1 trillion programme of support to restore credit, growth and jobs in the world economy." Recognizing that global recovery must include emerging and developing economies—the engines of recent world growth—the leaders agreed 1) to triple the resources available to the IMF to $750 billion, 2) to support a new SDR allocation of $250 billion, 3) to support at least $100 billion of additional lending by the multilateral development banks, 4) to ensure $250 billion of support for trade finance, and 5) to use additional resources from agreed IMF gold sales for concessional finance for the poorest countries. The leaders also reiterated that they were "determined" to reform international financial institutions, such as the IMF, to ensure that emerging and developing economies have greater voice and representation. The declaration, however, lacked any newly agreed upon reforms.

By contrast, with respect to strengthening financial supervision and regulation, the leaders agreed to establish a new Financial Stability Board (FSB) as a successor to the FSF.

The purpose of the change was to give the FSF "a stronger institutional basis," so that it could more effectively assist and collaborate with national authorities, standard setting bodies, and international financial institutions in addressing vulnerabilities and implementing strong regulatory, supervisory, and other policies in the interest of financial stability.

Importantly, the membership of the FSB's Plenary, the decision-making organ of the body, includes the current FSF members, in addition to the rest of the G-20, Spain, and the European Commission. This

> "[T]o be an effective monitor for all countries pursuing financial stability, the FSB needs a loud whistle, and the authority, expertise and support of its members to blow the whistle, even if the offender is a powerful country . . . If rapid efforts are not made to address weaknesses, the FSB may suffer the fate of its predecessor, the FSF, an institution that clearly failed to meet the high hopes of many of its creators, even though it produced often excellent studies warning of systemic risks that were not acted upon. If these challenges are met effectively, then the FSB will stand a better chance of emerging into the role of a more substantial fourth pillar of global economic governance . . ."
> —S. Griffith-Jones, Eric Helleiner and N. Woods, eds., "The Financial Stability Board: An Effective Fourth Pillar of Global Economic Governance?," The Center for International Governance Innovation, 12 (2010)

means that in addition to the FSF's mandate to assess vulnerabilities affecting the financial system, identify and oversee action needed to address them, and promote coordination and information exchange among authorities responsible for financial stability, emerging economies that are members of the FSB will:

- Monitor and advise on market developments and their implications for regulatory policy;
- Advise on and monitor best practice in meeting regulatory standards;
- Undertake joint strategic reviews of the policy development work of the international standard setting bodies to ensure their work is timely, coordinated, focused on priorities, and addressing gaps;
- Set guidelines for, and support the establishment . . . of . . . , supervisory colleges;
- Support contingency planning for cross-border crisis management, particularly with respect to systemically important firms; and
- Collaborate with the IMF to conduct Early Warning Exercises.

Thus, emerging economies now have the potential to play an integral role in strengthening the global financial system in the context of international cooperation (e.g., developing a framework for cross-border bank resolution arrangements), prudential regulation (e.g., working with accounting standard setters to implement recommendations to mitigate pro-cyclicality), and broadening the scope of regulation (e.g., developing effective oversight of hedge funds).

4. *The Pittsburgh Summit*

At the Pittsburgh summit held in September 2009, the participants declared that, because of the globally coordinated efforts to stem the crisis, the world's economy was in the "midst of a critical transition from crisis to recovery." Accordingly, the summit's leaders agreed to a number of measures of importance to both developed and developing countries. They ranged from "a Framework for Strong, Sustainable and Balanced Growth," to "Strengthening the International Financial Regulatory System," to "Energy Security and Climate Change."

> "[M]ember countries have been effective in moving together to stabilize financial markets, coordinate regulatory reform and launch a global economic stimulus. In doing so, they succeeded in averting grievous harm to the global economy . . . The group has been largely effective in financial re-engineering to mitigate the financial effects of the crisis, and in maintaining global capital flows. It has put issues on the table that were once regarded as largely being the province of sovereign governments, thereby bringing greater recognition of the 'spillover' effects of national policies into the domain of the broader international community . . . Beyond financial regulation, the G20 has, thus far, struggled in addressing the highly political tasks of resolving the current account, trade and budget imbalances conundrum, the roots of which run deep into the national economic and political philosophies of the world's largest economic players, and touch their respective concepts of sovereignty . . ."
>
> —P. Heinbecker, "The Future of the G20 and Its Place in Global Governance," CIGI G20 Papers, No.5, 3 (2011)

They also agreed to measures specifically intended to increase the voice of emerging and developing countries international financial and economic matters. First, in recognition of the multipolar economic world that has developed since the collapse of the Bretton Woods system, the leaders agreed to abandon the G-7/8 as the principal forum for discussion [of] global economic and financial issues. Henceforth, the G-20 will be the "premier forum" for international economic cooperation.

Second, in response to the drumbeat for governance reform at the IMF, the summit leaders made the following statement:

> Modernizing the IMF's governance is a core element of our effort to improve the IMF's credibility, legitimacy, and effectiveness. We recognize that the IMF should remain a quota-based organization and that the distribution of quotas should reflect the relative weights of its members in the world economy, which have changed substantially in view of the strong growth in dynamic emerging market and developing countries. To this end, we are committed to a shift in quota share to dynamic emerging market and developing countries of at least five percent from over-represented to underrepresented countries using the current IMF quota formula as the basis to work from. We are also committed to protecting the voting share of the poorest in the IMF. On this basis

and as part of the IMF's quota review . . . we urge an acceleration of work toward bringing the review to a successful conclusion. As part of that review, we agree that a number of other critical issues will need to be addressed, including: the size of any increase in IMF quotas, which will have a bearing on the ability to facilitate change in quota shares [and] the size and composition of the Executive Board . . . . As part of a comprehensive reform package, we agree that the heads and senior leadership of all international institutions should be appointed through an open, transparent and merit-based process. We must urgently implement the package of IMF quota and voice reforms agreed in April 2008.

This is a significant statement. But it does not represent a revolution in IMF governance. As to the quota shift, the BRIC (Brazil, Russia, India, and China) countries pushed for a seven percent shift, which would have given developing countries, currently holding about forty-four percent of the quotas, a majority share. The proposed shift hardly indicates that the United States and European nations have agreed to cede control of the IMF. Changing the composition of the Executive Board is key to giving emerging and developing countries greater voice in the Fund's governance, but actually accomplishing a change, such as reducing the over representation of European countries on the Board, is easier said than done. And while it is significant that there is now a consensus that choosing the leaders of the IMF and World Bank should be accomplished in a transparent and merit-based procedure, it is not clear how the process will work in practice.

5.   *The Seoul Summit*

In November 2010, leaders of the G-20 summit went to Seoul to tackle global trade imbalances, currency values—particularly the value of the yuan, and financial regulation. The summit took place amid observations that global cooperation to solve economic problems had weakened considerably since the first summit and that the G-20 was in "serious difficulties." Not surprisingly, then, the leaders made little progress with respect to the first two issues, which are particularly important to emerging and developing countries. The United States sought to reach agreement on numerical limits for current account deficits and surpluses (no more than four percent of gross domestic product), but the most the leaders could agree on was to formulate "indicative guidelines" to measure "large imbalances that require preventive and corrective actions to be taken." Regarding currency values and the United States' view of the undervaluation of the yuan, the leaders made the tepid commitment to move "toward more market-determined exchange rate systems," enhance exchange rate flexibility, and avoid competitive devaluations. As to the last issue, however, the leaders claimed success in endorsing a "landmark agreement reached by the [Basel Committee on Banking Supervision] on the new bank capital and liquidity framework . . . ." Dubbed "Basel III," the framework addresses the weaknesses of Basel II that became evident as a result of the global financial crisis. Although Basel III is not currently of great significance to the Global South, the rules on capital adequacy and liquidity will become increasingly important as the banking sectors of emerging and developing countries become more sophisticated.

Although giving emerging and developing economies greater voice in global economic and financial affairs was not high on the agenda, the Seoul summit resulted in what appeared to be further gains on this critical issue, especially with respect to IMF governance. The gains included 1) a shift "in quota shares to dynamic emerging market and developing and to under-represented countries of over 6% while protecting the share of the poorest," 2) a "doubling of quotas, with a corresponding rollback of the New Arrangements to Borrow (NAB) preserving relative shares," 3) "[g]reater representation for emerging market and developing countries at the Executive Board through two fewer advanced European chairs, and the possibility of a second alternate for all multi-country constituencies," and 4) "[m]oving to an all-elected Board, along with a commitment by the IMF's membership to maintain the Board size at 24 chairs . . . ."

> *"In order for the proposed amendment on reform of the Executive Board to enter into force, acceptance by three-fifths of the Fund's 188 members (or 113 members) having 85 percent of the Fund's total voting power is required. As of [June 19, 2014], 145 members having 76.97 percent of total voting power had accepted the amendment . . . For the quota increases under the 14th General Review of Quotas to become effective, the entry into force of the proposed amendment to reform the Executive Board is required, as well as the consent to the quota increase by members having not less than 70 percent of total quotas (as of November 5, 2010). As of June 19, 2014, 160 members having 79.43 percent of total quota had consented."*
> —The United States hasn't yet accepted the amendments. "Acceptances of the Proposed Amendment of the Articles of Agreement on Reform of the Executive Board and Consents to 2010 Quota Increase," International Monetary Fund, at http://www.imf.org/external/np/sec/misc/consents.htm#a2 (2014)

Dominique Strauss-Kahn, the IMF's Managing Director, declared that summit leaders' commitments constituted "the most important reform in the governance of the institution since its creation." He also stated: "We put an end to a discussion which has been in the headlines for decades about the legitimacy of the institution." India's finance minister was more circumspect: "The legitimacy of the IMF is increasing." The increased legitimacy is reflected in the voting power of important emerging economies. China will become the third largest shareholder, behind the United States and Japan. Russia, India, and Brazil will be among the top ten shareholders.

Although the reforms are important, one must be cautious about claiming that a profound change in favor of emerging economies is about to occur at the IMF. The United States, with approximately seventeen percent of the IMF's voting power, still retains the veto over key decisions, which require an eighty-five percent vote. Moreover, two-thirds of the six percent quota shift comes from developing countries, resulting in only a two percent shift to developing countries. Ultimately, the proof will be in the pudding. The question remains whether the IMF's operations will reflect the voices of emerging and developing countries, even when decisions may run contrary to the interests of the United States and other developed member countries.

CONCLUSION

As a result of the global financial crisis, emerging economies are on the verge of acquiring voice—i.e., meaningful and effective representation in discourse at key "table[s]" relating to global economic and financial affairs. This has led some to exclaim that we are at the threshold of a new New International Economic Order!

Part of this new NIEO envisions a reformed IMF. Prior to the crisis, the IMF took steps to improve its governance and accountability vis-a-vis emerging and developing economies. The measures were limited, however. Consequently, the Fund's clients abandoned it. The Fund was once again on the brink of irrelevance. In August 2008, IMF lending totaled SDR 11.65 (approximately $16.65 billion) as compared to SDR 76.84 (approximately $116 billion) in September 2003, resulting in a significant drop in income (because of a drop in interest payments). The crisis not only revived the IMF, but it also created an opening for emerging economies to demand greater voice within the institution. Moreover, emerging economies demanded and obtained representation in fora that determine global economic and financial policy, as reflected in the shift in global economic policymaking from the G-7 to the G-20 and the expansion of the Financial Stability Forum (FSF) membership to include emerging economies.

These developments must not be overblown, however. As this Article has demonstrated, change in favor of emerging and developing countries has come only incrementally. Much work remains for the IMF to achieve governance reforms that will persuade its borrowers (and many critical observers) of its legitimacy. Moreover, not all observers believe the reforms are in the best interests of emerging and developing countries. Even if the reforms are worthy, we have yet to see whether they will be effective in practice. For instance, will emerging economies and the G-20 generally be able to articulate economic policy coherently or is the forum too unwieldy? And even if emerging economies such as China and India exercise their newfound voice, will they represent the interests of developing countries or will they be co-opted by the rich countries in the club? Only time will tell.

You Gotta Know Something About Them!

Gordon Brown

Born in Glasgow, Scotland, Gordon was a pretty precocious kid: he went to high school when he was 10 years old and was off to Edinburgh University age 16. He became a member of parliament in 1983, running on the Labour Party ticket—that's where he became buds with Tony Blair. Gordon went on to become Chancellor of the Exchequer and then Prime Minister in 2007. And then the global financial crisis came knocking on his door. Gordon was a good athlete in his youth. But check this out: while playing rugby, he was kicked in the head and tore his retinas. He's blind in his left eye and has lost most of his sight in his right eye. Brutal.

Dominique Strauss-Kahn

Dominique Strauss-Kahn became the tenth Managing Director of the IMF on November 1, 2007 after a career as a corporate lawyer and economics prof. Just before that he was a member of the French National Assembly. As Managing Director, Dominque kept the Fund relevant. He increased total loans outstanding from a low point of $10 billion to $84 billion by the time he left the IMF. Total capital quadrupled under his leadership, from approximately $250 billion to $1 trillion. While Gordon was holding down the fort in the U.K., Dominique was doing his part at the IMF, making billions of dollars of loans available during the financial crisis. Overall, he was a pretty respected guy.

Now let's talk personal life. In May of 2011, Dominique resigned as Managing Director after allegations that he raped a hotel maid in Manhattan. He was put in cuffs and made to do the perp walk—you know, when the police officers pull the arrested suspect out of the cop car and make him walk into the courthouse with his arms cuffed behind him. With cameras recording every second of it. Downright humiliating. The rape charges were eventually dropped over concern about the woman's credibility. The maid filed suit in civil court, but eventually settled with Dominique. But that's not all! When he returned to France, Dominique was investigated for alleged involvement in a prostitution ring. Yeah, something about orgies at the Carlton Hotel in Lille, France. What high finance will do to a person . . .

QUESTIONS FROM YOUR TALKING DOG

1.   "Ridi Pagliaccio . . ." Okay, so I'm not another Pavarotti. But don't you think I have a pretty good voice for a dog? So you want to talk about a different kind of voice, huh. Emerging economies? Fine. I'll drop the opera for now. What did you say? Decoupled? What does that have to do with emerging economies and the financial crisis?

2.   It's all about democracy these days. So how does that apply to the IMF and the World Bank?

3.   You can't stop there. How did the IMF respond to the democratic deficit argument?

4.   So these summits you're talking about—that's a lot of traveling. I hate planes, even though I've never been on one. Tell me about the November summit from the point of view of emerging economies.

5.   A reform of conditionality? Again? Now what did they do?

6.   Now to London? What happened there that was important for emerging economies? Tell me more about this Financial Stability Board.

7.   How did they pick Pittsburgh for a summit? Some significant stuff. Like what? A redistribution of quotas? Are you kidding me? And changing how the leaders of the IMF and the World Bank are chosen? Are you kidding me? We gotta stop for a second. I'm stunned.

8.   Now we jump over to Seoul. Boy, South Korea has come a long way since the Asian financial crisis, don't you think? So what happened there that was important for emerging economies?

9.   So bottom line this for me. Are we really transforming into a new global economic order? Or is it the same ole, same ole, with just some tinkering here and there?

J. ARGENTINA'S BONDS AND THE *PARI PASSU* CLAUSE

OR THE JUDGE WHO BROUGHT ARGENTINA TO ITS KNEES

UNITED STATES DISTRICT COURT

SOUTHERN DISTRICT OF NEW YORK

NML CAPITAL, LTD.,

Plaintiff,	08 Civ. 6978 (TPG)
	09 Civ. 1707 (TPG)
—against—	09 Civ. 1708 (TPG)
REPUBLIC OF ARGENTINA,	**ORDER**
Defendant.	

Upon consideration of the motion by NML Capital, Ltd. ("NML") for partial summary judgment pursuant to Rule 56(a) of the Federal Rules of Civil Procedure ("FRCP") and for injunctive relief and/or specific performance pursuant to FRCP 65(d) and the court's inherent equitable powers, the response of the Republic of Argentina (the "Republic") thereto, NML's reply, and all other arguments submitted to the court in the parties' papers and at the hearing held on September 28, 2011;

WHEREAS the uncontested facts establish that:

1.   The Republic issued bonds pursuant to a 1994 Fiscal Agency Agreement ("FAA").

2.   Paragraph 1(c) of the FAA provides, among other things, that:

The Securities [i.e., the bonds] will constitute . . . direct, unconditional, unsecured and unsubordinated obligations of the Republic and shall at all times rank <u>pari passu</u> and without any preference among themselves. The payment obligations of the Republic under the Securities shall at all times rank at least equally with all its other present and future unsecured and unsubordinated External Indebtedness (as defined in this Agreement).

3.   The bonds issued pursuant to the FAA contain the following clause, as quoted in <u>EM Ltd. v. The Republic of Argentina</u>, 720 F.Supp.2d 273, 278 (S.D.N.Y. 2010):

The Republic has in the Fiscal Agency Agreement irrevocably submitted to the jurisdiction of any New York state or federal court sitting in the Borough of Manhattan, The City of New York and the courts of the Republic of Argentina (the "Specified Courts") over any suit, action, or proceeding against it or its properties, assets or revenues with respect to the Securities of this Series or the Fiscal Agency Agreement (a "Related Proceeding") except with respect to any actions brought under the United States federal securities laws. The Republic has in the Fiscal Agency Agreement waived any objection to Related Proceedings in such courts whether on the grounds of venue, residence or domicile or on the ground that the Related Proceedings have been brought in an inconvenient forum. The Republic agrees that a final nonappealable judgment in any such Related Proceeding (the "Related Judgment") shall be conclusive and binding upon it and may be enforced in any Specified Court or in any other courts to the jurisdiction of which the Republic is or may be subject (the "Other Courts"), by a suit upon such judgment.

4.   NML owns bonds issued pursuant to the FAA ("NML's Bonds").

5.   The Republic issued other bonds in its 2005 and 2010 Exchange Offers ("Exchange Bonds"), thereby creating new unsecured and unsubordinated External Indebtedness.

6.   The Republic has satisfied the payment obligations that have come due to date under the Exchange Bonds.

7.   The Republic has not paid principal or interest on NML's Bonds since December, 2001.

8.   NML has brought the captioned actions to recover on the defaulted bonds, pursuant to its legal rights, and also pursuant to the express undertakings in the bonds.

9.   On February 10, 2005, Argentina enacted Law 26,017, providing that the "national State shall be prohibited from conducting any type of in-court, out-of-court or private settlement with respect to bonds" that were eligible to participate in the 2005 Exchange Offer.

10.   On December 9, 2009, Argentina enacted Law 26,547, which, *inter alia,* suspended the effect of Law 26,017 for a period of time during which the 2010 Exchange Offer was launched, closed, and consummated. Law 26,547 also provides that the "Republic of Argentina . . . is prohibited to offer holders of government bonds [including those issued pursuant to the FAA] who may have initiated judicial, administrative, arbitration or any other type of action [to enforce their rights], more favorable treatment than what is offered to those who have not done so."

WHEREAS NML claims that the Republic breached (and continues to breach) its contractual duty to rank its payment obligations under NML's Bonds at least equally with all its other present and future unsecured and unsubordinated External Indebtedness, NML seeks summary judgment on the Republic's liability for that breach, and NML seeks an injunction that would restore it to its bargained-for position among other creditors;

It is HEREBY ORDERED that:

1.   The motion for partial summary judgment pursuant to Rule 56(a) is GRANTED.

2.   It is DECLARED, ADJUDGED, and DECREED that the Republic is required under Paragraph 1(c) of the FAA at all times to rank its payment obligations pursuant to NML's Bonds at least equally with all the Republic's other present and future unsecured and unsubordinated External Indebtedness.

3.   It is DECLARED, ADJUDGED, and DECREED that the Republic's payment obligations on the bonds include its payment obligations to bondholders who have brought actions to recover on their defaulted bonds, and on judgments entered pursuant to judicial action brought by bondholders.

4.   It is DECLARED, ADJUDGED, and DECREED that the Republic violates Paragraph 1(c) of the FAA whenever it lowers the rank of its payment obligations under NML's Bonds below that of any other present or future unsecured and unsubordinated External Indebtedness, including (and without limitation) by relegating NML's bonds to a non-paying class by failing to pay the obligations currently due under NML's Bonds while at the same time making payments currently due to holders of other

unsecured and unsubordinated External Indebtedness or by legislative enactment.

5.   It is DECLARED, ADJUDGED, and DECREED that the Republic lowered the rank of NML's bonds in violation of Paragraph 1(c) of the FAA when it made payments currently due under the Exchange Bonds, while persisting in its refusal to satisfy its payment obligations currently due under NML's Bonds.

6.   It is DECLARED, ADJUDGED, and DECREED that the Republic lowered the rank of NML's bonds in violation of Paragraph l(c) of the FAA when it enacted Law 26,017 and Law 26,547.

7.   It is DECLARED, ADJUDGED, and DECREED that the aforesaid laws were in direct violation of the right of NML under the FAA and the bond agreements to bring a legal action in court to recover on the defaulted bonds.

8.   The motion for injunctive relief and/or specific performance pursuant to FRCP 65(d) and the court's inherent equitable powers is DENIED at the present time to permit further consideration by the court regarding the means of enforcement of the present ORDER.

SO ORDERED.

Dated: New   York,   New
            York

            December 7, 2011

                        Thomas P. Griesa

                        U.S. District Judge

                   * * *

And that's how it started . . .

We finish the textbook with Argentina's December 2001 heart-stopping sovereign default on $100 billion of external debt that included sovereign bonds. Since the default, a story worth a Broadway musical has played out, pitting a New York federal district court judge, Thomas Griesa, against a sovereign state that has produced two of the best soccer players ever.

The developments that led to the default will sound familiar to you. Like Brazil, Argentina's path to becoming an EME is marked by policy failures. Let's look at its development path first.

Argentina's Development Path

Through much of the 20th century, Argentina pursued fiscal deficit spending and an expansive monetary policy to cover the deficit. This led to periods of high inflation and by the late 1990s, Argentina was in the throes of hyperinflation.

In 1989 Carlos Menem became president of Argentina and named Domingo Cavallo Minister of Economy. In 1991, the government put in place a currency board—known in Argentina as the "convertibility plan"—that guaranteed a one dollar-one peso exchange rate. What's a currency board? It's a monetary authority that issues notes and coins (Argentine pesos) that are convertible on an unlimited basis into a foreign anchor currency (U.S. dollars) at a fixed rate on demand. Approximately 70 countries have used currency boards. The idea originated in Britain in the early 1800s and reached its apex in the late 1940s—about 50 countries used currency boards. They disappeared after that, but enjoyed a revival of sorts in the 1990s.

Countries adopt currency boards in many cases to kill hyperinflation and to assure foreign investors that they'll follow prudent macroeconomic policies that'll avoid defaults. Currency boards have to hold sufficient reserves to make sure that all holders of its notes and coins can convert them into the reserve or anchor currency. We've talked about how countries that adopt a fixed exchange rate give up control over monetary policy. Well, a currency board is the ultimate fixed exchange rate. The board acts in a passive and automatic fashion. Its sole function is to exchange its notes and coins for the anchor currency at a fixed rate. So under a currency board system, the government can't finance its spending by printing money—it can only tax or borrow. Cool, but a major disadvantage of a currency board is that it can't engage in the balance of payments adjustments by devaluing its currency.

Getting back to Argentina, the currency board worked pretty well at first. Fiscal and monetary policies were under control, and this led to economic growth and a drop in inflation. But like other countries we've studied, it eventually had a problem with fiscal deficits. And just two years after the establishment of the convertibility plan, Argentina's debt started rising—from 1995 to 2001, the debt service ratio grew from 30% to 66%. It didn't help that the dollar was strengthening, that Argentina's regional trading powers—especially Brazil—were more competitive, and that commodity prices were falling. By 1999, Argentina's economy was in recession.

It was at that time that the currency board posed problems. Like the euro zone countries we've looked at, because of the currency board, Argentina couldn't devalue the peso to increase exports, and it couldn't engage in fiscal stimulus to fight the economic downturn. We know by now that it's never solely the country's poor policy choices that lead to an economic crisis. There was the yield hunt: global investors chased after higher yield and were more than happy to lend to Argentina despite risks. And many blamed the IMF for lending to Argentina during the 1990s without pushing Argentina to make policy changes. The IMF later admitted that it made mistakes that helped push Argentina to the brink of crisis.

Argentina's Default and Its Bondholders

In December 2001, the government defaulted on its sovereign debt, abandoned the currency board, and devalued the peso. At the time of the default, Argentina owed Paris Club countries $6.3 billion and the IMF $9.5 billion. But the real problem would be the debt owed to private investors holding bonds with a face value of $81.8 billion.

In January 2005, Argentina made a unilateral—and hardline—offer of a bond exchange to deal with debt having a face value of that $81.8 billion (plus past-due interest). Negotiations went nowhere, with creditors arguing that Argentina could afford to pay more than what it was offering. To pressure bondholders into accepting the exchange offer, Argentina's legislature passed the "Lock Law,' which prohibits the government from (i) reopening the 2005 exchange offer, and (ii) conducting "any type of in-court, out-of-court or private settlement with respect to the bonds . . ." The offering's prospectus also warned that the government had "no intention" to pay on the bonds that weren't tendered. Uh-oh . . .

The exchange resulted in $62.3 billion being exchanged for $35.2 billion in new bonds. All told, bondholders agreed to a "haircut" between 70 and 75% of the debt they held. Brutal. But check this out: $18.6 billion of bonds were not tendered in the exchange. Hmmm . . .

In 2010, Argentina temporarily suspended the Lock Law and did another bond exchange, where approximately $12.4 billion of the eligible $18.4 billion in bonds were exchanged—approximately $6.0 billion in bonds were not tendered. Like the 2005 prospectus, the 2010 prospectus warned that non-participating bondholders wouldn't be paid and that Argentina would oppose any litigation to collect on the bonds not exchanged. Uh-oh . . .

The total participation rate for both bond exchanges (Exchange Bonds) totaled 91.3% of total defaulted debt. Still, what about the untendered debt? Answer: global lawsuits.

The Hold-Outs Sue

After the default, the Argentine bonds plummeted in value. This opened up an opportunity for hedge funds specializing in distressed debt to buy it up really cheaply and then litigate—they're popularly called "vulture funds." They are the "hold-outs" and present the hold-out problem in debt restructuring. They're creditors that for strategic reasons don't agree to a debt restructuring deal. They do this hoping that by suing the government, they can get paid in full or get better treatment than the creditors who took the restructuring deal. And it's worked, as explained in the article we selected below. It's called a problem because it prevents a comprehensive restructuring of sovereign debt.

Remember the hmmm . . . a few secs ago? A vulture fund, NML Limited, along with other hedge funds and individuals, collectively holding $1.33

billion worth of 2001 bonds (FAA Bonds), sued Argentina in the Southern District of New York, which resulted in Judge Griesa's order you've just read. A couple of months after that order, the judge granted injunctive relief and ordered Argentina to abide by the *pari passu* provision and to provide plaintiffs a "ratable payment" whenever it paid on the Exchange Bonds. The order also prohibited Bank of New York and other agent banks—the banks that pay the Argentina's bondholders—from paying on the Exchange Bonds. Bringing third parties into this on the basis of the *pari passu* clause? Hmmm . . . In March 2012, Judge Griesa issued a stay on the carrying out of the order.

On appeal in October 2012, the Second Circuit Court of Appeals disagreed with Argentina's argument that according to most experts the *pari passu* prohibits only *legal* subordination, and that it didn't violate the provision because it didn't give the holders of the Exchange Bonds a *legally* enforceable preference over the FAA Bonds. Citing to a slew of sources indicating the clause's meaning is far from clear, the appeals court said the *pari passu* clause not only prohibited Argentina from subordinating debt by *issuing* superior debt, but also prohibited it from *paying* on the Exchange Bonds without paying on the FAA Bonds. The Court held that Argentina violated the clause by paying on the Exchange Bonds while refusing to pay on the FAA Bonds. It also violated the clause by enacting the Lock Law, which barred Argentina from paying on the bonds and forbade its courts from recognizing plaintiffs' judgments. Exchange bondholders faced no such barrier. The Court affirmed the summary judgment granted to plaintiffs on their claims of breach of the *pari passu* clause. It remanded to have the district court better explain how a "ratable payment" would work and how the injunction would work against third-party banks—a part of Judge Griesa's injunction that bothered the appeals court.

A month later, all hell broke loose. On November 21, in addition to issuing an opinion clarifying the two remanded issues, Judge Griesa issued an opinion vacating the March stay, essentially because President Cristina Kirchner gave him the finger. "Surely an extraordinary circumstance of the most serious nature arises from continuous declarations by the President of Argentina and cabinet officers, that Argentina will not honor or carry out the current rulings of the District Court and Court of Appeals in litigation to which Argentina is a party," the judge fumed. Bottom line: Given the way the judge explained "ratable payment," Argentina would have to pay plaintiffs 100 cents on the dollar or $1.33 billion—the amount "currently due" to the plaintiffs because the default accelerated unpaid principal plus interest on the FAA Bonds—when it made its December 2012 interest payments of about $3.14 billion to the Exchange Bondholders. Oh, s___!

On November 21, the Court of Appeals stayed Judge Giesa's orders and set oral arguments for February 27, 2013. An epic battle loomed before the appellate court, pitting plaintiff NML Capital's lawyer Theodore Olson of Gibson, Dunn & Crutcher against Argentina's lawyer, Jonathan Blackman of Cleary Gottlieb Steen & Hamilton. All international finance freaks emptied groceries stores of their chips, salsa, and beer. Furniture stores' easy chairs sold out.

* * * * *

Blackman: Good afternoon. May it please the court, Jonathan Blackman representing the Republic of Argentina. The court remanded to have the District Court address two critical remedial issues so that you could then, uh, determine the merits of the remedy. And the District Court's determination of both of those issues was erroneous. The two issues are very much related. The District Court's version of ratable payments is an order to pay the full amount of plaintiff's monetary claims. And the unprecedented injunctions are concededly a device to enforce that payment . . .

Judge Raggi: Well, let's deal with what the District Judge did. The rate that the District Judge set, which is full payment, is based on the conclusion that, having been in default, Argentina triggered the acceleration provision of the original bonds. And so what would be improper about the judge saying that when you have to pay your obligations, you have to pay the full obligation, um, existing as of this time? Because that's effectively what the judge did.

Blackman: Well, ratable payments, I think, we believe—and I think you believed—you believed that was a separate obligation from the payment obligation, which clearly is for the full amount of accelerated principal and interest. Ratable payments, uh, you remanded because you wanted clarification of what that meant. And you gave two examples. One was the example of every time a single interest payment is made under restructured debt to pay 100% of what was due and owing on the unrestructured debt. The other example that was given was an example that if the total amount paid on the restructured debt would be a percentage of the total of that, then that similar percentage would be paid on the unrestructured debt. And the formula we've proposed, which we think is actually the only one that is truly an equal treatment, is a formula that takes, as the baseline, the defaulted debt—that's where we started— and says the exchange bond holders, Mr. Boies's clients, are getting on a given interest payment a fraction of the original amount they were owed on the, uh, unrestructured debt. And that same fractions of the unrestructured debt should be the ratable payment. That would satisfy ratable payment . . .

[B]ut it does drive the definition of equal treatment in the default context. Otherwise what Your Honor is really saying is this: that we—if there's a default—and the default was certainly caused by, you know, lots of circumstances beyond Argentina's control, the debtor only has two choices. It can stay in default forever, which no one would want, and they would have more judgments, not fewer. Or, if it restructures, uh, the restructuring, uh, becomes impossible because of the first mover problem. None of Mr. Boies's clients would've agreed to take this quite dramatic haircut if they knew that after some period of time, Mr. Olson's clients could say, "Well, we didn't restructure. We want 100%, and moreover"—this gets to the injunction point—"we can prevent you from getting, uh, your discounted amount, uh, unless we get paid in full." . . .

Judge Raggi: Same percentage. Okay. Um, and you're also telling us that despite the District Court's order and despite the possibility that we might affirm it, you would not obey any order other than the one you've just proposed.

Blackman: We—we—uh, public policy is firm on that issue, and I don't want to be—

Judge Raggi: So the answer is yes? [OVERLAY]

Blackman: Yes, there is—

Judge Raggi: That you will—you will not obey anything other than what you've just proposed?

Blackman: We—we—we would not voluntarily obey such an order, but I'd like to explain, because that's a—that's a red flag.

Judge Raggi: What does that mean, voluntarily obey? I mean, we would issue an order, and—I—I just want to be sure you're telling—you're telling us it wouldn't be obeyed?

Blackman: I'm telling you it wouldn't be voluntarily obeyed, and that gets me to a fundamental point. And I don't want to wave a red—

Judge Raggi: What does voluntarily mean?

Blackman: Please would—

Judge Raggi: I mean, we're not gonna send out the marshals, you know.

Blackman: Well, that's the point, that's—

Judge Raggi: Okay, so—

Blackman: You can't send out the marshals—

Judge Raggi:—there will be no compliance except basically you're dictating what the court [OVERLAY] would order.

Jonathan Blackman: We're not trying to dictate. We're trying to persuade the court to do something which is workable and doesn't create a terrible confrontation.

* * * * *

HALFTIME

Commercial: Are you in debt up to your eyeballs? Is it so bad you can't sleep, eat, or play with your dogs? We can help. Sovereigns R Us can register you as a sovereign country. You can come up with your own country name, such as the Republic of Gotohell. Call us at 800-stick-it-to-em.

* * * * *

Theodore Olson: Thank you. May it please the court, my name is Theodore Olson on behalf of NML . . . And I must say that Argentina never made any proposal except this. And—and this is very telling. This is what the President of Argentina said on November 4, 2012, eight days or so after your decision. "Not one dollar to the vulture funds." That is my clients. That is the President of Argentina. "Not one dollar." So as—as—as distinguished from making any proposal with respect to the ratable payment provision, not one dollar. The minister, the Economic Minister of—of Argentina said, uh, "We are never going to pay the vulture funds, uh, and it doesn't matter what the courts of the United States say; we are never going to do that. We will not pay one peso to the vulture funds."

Judge Pooler: So what we heard, um, Argentina, Mr. Blackman, say that if they found a percentage payment that they thought was fair, they would go to the legislature, the administration, and try to get approval for that payment.

Theodore Olson: That's squarely contradicted by the statements of the President of Argentina, the economic—Economy Minister of Argentina, and the Ambassador to the United States.

Judge Pooler: Well, sometimes politicians say things and then they change their minds.

Theodore Olson: Well, the—they may—[laughter]

Judge Pooler: Did you ever hear of that?

Theodore Olson: I never heard of anything like that. [laughter] I think we should take the words of the—that have been repeated over and over again, you heard them again here today. Basically, it's not the policy of Argentina to pay any money to the so-called "hold-out" funds, the funds of the—and—and—and you were quite correct, I submit, in saying that in Footnote 15 of your opinion, they had no responsibility or any obligation to accept the reduced amount under the exchange proposals. Um, the—the equity of the ratable formula—and I think some of your questions touched on this—it is exactly what is owed. Uh, Mr. Boies [representing Exchange Bondholder Group] said 300 cents on the dollar. This is exactly what is owed under the instruments that were drafted and created by Argentina, submitting to the jurisdiction of the United States, waiving sovereign immunity, submitting to the jurisdiction of the court, and putting in an equal payment provision that quite literally squares completely with what Judge Griesa [PH 00:58:24] owes [sic], the acceleration provision, the interest provisions which have already been litigated again. So what my clients are seeking, and what Judge Griesa ordered is, if you're going to pay 100% of what is owed tomorrow to the exchange bond holders, the ratable payment provision or the equal treatment provision requires that you pay the same percentage, 100% of what is owed, to the, um, N—NML and the—and the other bond holders that are here before you—

Judge Raggi: Which effectively means that your client only needs to get one payment out of this, if they pay 100%. Then you're done. Is that what you're saying?

Theodore Olson: Well, that is what is required by the agreement . . . I think it's very important that what's happening here, is Argentina saying, "We will continue to default on our obligations, to stick it to the people that we borrowed money from invoking the laws of the United States, that— and—and the—and—and the courts of the United States. Uh, and we will not only do that but we will violate other obligations to other people to force this court to back down, from the lawful decision of the courts of the United States with respect to the continued default by Argentina." The court—and the court cannot give in to that. Um, this is a lawful obligation of Argentina. It has been defying it for years. This court has affirmed that the equal treatment provision means what Judge Griesa determined that it meant. This court has affirmed that there's been a breach of the equal treatment provision. This court has decided and affirmed that an equitable remedy is appropriate in the form of the ratable payment provision. Is the ratable payment provision equitable and appropriate? Argentina can afford to pay it. It is what's owed. It's equal. It's a literal interpretation. It's consistent with the fact that the exchange bond holders imposed—helped participate in the imp—imposition of the lock law, which is a part of the violation itself, because they don't want others to receive payments.

And the court must assume that Argentina, notwithstanding these statements—I—I take your point that they may change their mind; I hope they do. Everyone here, I think, hopes that Argentina will repudiate or change its mind with respect to the statements its officials have made that they don't care what the courts of the United States do, they're going to keep doing what they're doing anyway. I submit that its the law of this circuit—and the Higgins case and other cases, that Argentina will comply, and must comply and must be assumed to comply, and then all of this will be unnecessary . . .

* * * * *

Promising international finance freak: Well? What did you think?

Not-so-promising international finance freak: (belch) Yeah, man . . . that was . . . like . . . kickass. (belch)

Promising international finance freak: Someday we'll be like them, huh!

Not-so-promising international finance freak: DUDE, DID YOU EAT ALL THE CHIPS?

On August 23, the Second Circuit issued its opinion (NML Capital, Ltd. v. Republic of Arg., 727 F.3d 230 (2d Cir. N.Y. 2013)). Argentina got slammed. Not even Messi could save it. The Court portrayed Argentina as an outlier sovereign debtor—a "uniquely recalcitrant debtor." For that reason, its decision was limited to Argentina—it wasn't providing a definitive interpretation of the *pari passu* clause: "We simply affirm the district court's conclusion that Argentina's extraordinary behavior was a violation of the particular *pari passu* clause found in the FAA." As to the arguments that Judge Griesa's orders improperly restrained third parties, especially Bank of New York, the appeals court said essentially, "Don't worry about that now—you can make your arguments if and when you're hauled into court for violating the injunctions." Banks: "Oh, great. Thanks, judges. That gives us lots of comfort . . ." The Second Circuit stayed the enforcement of the injunctions pending an appeal to the Supremes.

Argentina did appeal, arguing that the Foreign Sovereign Immunities Act (it wouldn't have much luck with the *pari passu* issue because that's state law) insulated it from subpoenas demanding post-judgment discovery of global assets from two nonparty banks, including Bank of America. The high court rejected the appeal on June 16, 2014. Argentina's subsequent negotiations with the holdouts went nowhere. On June 30, 2014, Argentina's payment to restructured bondholders was due. It failed to pay, which started a 30-day grace period. As of this writing, Argentina is in default.

In August, Argentina petitioned the International Court of Justice to bring a case against the United States, arguing that U.S. courts have violated its sovereignty. But that request won't go anywhere because the U.S. has to consent to jurisdiction and it ain't gonna do that.

While you're discussing the end of global capital markets as we know it, here's a piece that addresses the *pari passu* clause in the context of Argentina's saga.

You Gotta Know Something About Them!

The Honorable Thomas (Don't Mess With Me) Griesa

Judge Thomas Griesa was born in 1930 in Kansas City, Missouri. After graduation from Stanford Law School, he joined Davis Polk & Wardwell LLP in New York, eventually making partner. Thomas was appointed to the bench in 1972 and a few years later let loose his fury, holding U.S. Attorney General Griffin Bell in contempt of court in 1978. To calm his nerves, he plays the harpsichord. His lunch ritual: soup, orange, and a cookie. No Argentine steak for Thomas!

President Cristina (You See This Griesa?) Fernandez de Kirchner

 The daughter of a bus driver, President Cristina Fernandez de Kirchner became Argentina's President in 2007 after her husband, President Néstor Kirchner (elected 2003), kicked the bucket. After practicing law with Néstor in the firm they both founded, Cristina went political, elected first to Santa Cruz's legislature and then to the National Congress. Known as the "Iron Lady of the South," she has enjoyed (at times) lots of support in Argentina—she was re-elected in 2011. But she has lots of political enemies who blame her for many of Argentina's ills, ranging from inflation to corruption. Still, check it out: In 2008, Forbes ranked her as the 13th most powerful woman out of 100.

R. OLIVARES-CAMINAL, "THE PARI PASSU CLAUSE IN SOVEREIGN DEBT INSTRUMENTS: DEVELOPMENTS IN RECENT LITIGATION," IN "SOVEREIGN RISK: A WORLD WITHOUT RISK-FREE ASSETS?"

BIS Papers No. 72, Monetary and Economic Department (2013)

1. Introduction

The pari passu clause is a standard clause in public or private international unsecured debt obligations (syndicated loan agreements and bond issuances). To understand the pari passu clause, it is first necessary to understand the meaning of the short Latin phrase "pari passu". Literally, this means "with equal step", from *pari*, ablative of *par*, "equal" and *passu*, ablative of *passus*, "step". That is to say, pari passu refers to things that are in same situation, things that rank equally. This notwithstanding, the pari passu clause, as brilliantly noted . . . , "is short, obscure and sports a bit of Latin; all characteristics that lawyers find endearing".

In 1900, an opinion was given that "[t]here is no special virtue in the words 'pari passu', 'equally' would have the same effect or any other words showing that the [bonds] were intended to stand on the same level footing without preference or priority among themselves . . ." . . . However, more recently, the pari passu clause has been described as a harmless relic of historical evolution . . .

The reason why the pari passu clause returned to the limelight is a lawsuit that is currently taking place in New York against Argentina (*NML Ltd. v Republic of Argentina*) which is basically the background of this paper on the interpretation of the pari passu clause.

This lawsuit has resulted in some important developments that are worth analysing, namely: (i) the real meaning and the novel interpretation of the pari passu clause; and (ii) the remedies recently proposed by the New York District Court for the enforcement of the clause, which pose a real threat to the future of sovereign debt restructuring—and especially to New York's future as an international financial centre. This paper will focus only on substantial aspects of the interpretation of the clause and will not address the details of the judicial processes.

2.   The ad hoc scenario and the use of contractual sweeteners

Currently, there is no statutory regime to deal with a sovereign in distress. We are thus left with two main options. One is the use of collective action clauses (CACs), provided that such clauses have already been included in the bonds. The other option is to use an exchange offer, which is a voluntary process whereby the bondholders accept a "new" bond in exchange for the "original" or "old" instrument. The most pertinent aspect of an exchange offer is that the new bond will usually offer less attractive financial and legal terms.

Sometimes, exchange offers incorporate so-called legal or financial "sweeteners" to increase the rate of bondholders' participation in the offer; or are combined with the use of exit consents,[2] which have been used in a number of restructurings (eg those of Ecuador in 2000, Uruguay in 2003 and the Dominican Republic in 2005). These sweeteners can be seen as an ad hoc approach to addressing the lack of a formal insolvency-like regime to force bondholders to accept a restructuring exercise. Some examples of these contractual sweeteners include mandatory prepayment clauses or mandatory restatement of principal clauses, ie clauses that can be included in the new terms of the bonds when the exchange offer is launched, with

---

[2]   Exit consent is the technique by which holders of bonds who decide to accept an exchange offer, at the moment of accepting said offer, grant their consent to be represented by a third party to amend certain non-payment terms of the (old) bonds that are being exchanged. By using the exit consent technique, the exchange offer is conditioned to a minimum threshold of creditors' acceptance and the amendments to the terms are performed once the required majority to amend the terms has been obtained. Some of these amendments include delisting the bonds, reinstating sovereign immunity provisions or changing the governing law of the bonds. By means of these amendments, the (old) bonds subject to the exchange offer become less attractive (in legal and financial terms), forcing a greater number of bondholders to accept the exchange offer. Hence, if holdout bondholders do not accept the exchange offer, they will end up holding an impaired bond without some of the original contractual protections.

the aim of convincing the bondholders that they will continue to be protected, either by a reduction in the outstanding stock of debt (ie via mandatory prepayment clauses) or by a reinstatement of the accepted face value reduction in the event of a new default (mandatory restatement of principal clauses). Still others include the use of credit-linked notes (eg as in Argentina 2005); a guarantee (eg as in Seychelles in 2010, where a guarantee was provided by the African Development Bank); the use of a principal defeasance (eg as mooted in an early stage of the Greek PSI); or the use of collateral (eg as in the Brady Plan).

One kind of sweetener that is of particular relevance to the interpretation of the pari passu clause in the ongoing Argentine litigation is the "most favoured creditor clause" (MFCC), as used by Argentina in 2005 . . . Say a sovereign—after an initial exchange offer—decides to enter into a repurchase, a new exchange offer, or to enter into a *settlement* (pertinent here) on better terms than the exchange offer made to the original bondholders. Including an MFCC in the new terms of the bond being issued as a result of the exchange offer means that the "more beneficial" terms subsequently offered will also be extended to those that that accepted the initial exchange offer. This is usually intended to show that an exchange offer is definitive and, in the event that there is a holdout creditor, the sovereign is not willing to enter into any kind of settlement agreement with more beneficial terms. Why? Because if it enters into a settlement to put an end to ongoing litigation and pays the holdouts 100% of the value of the claim, then bondholders who accepted a reduction in the face value of the original or old bonds will be entitled to that same treatment. When Argentina included an MFCC in the prospectus with a view to enhancing the degree of investor participation, it forgot to include the word "settlement", rendering the MFCC inadequate since it failed to protect bondholders who accepted the 2005 exchange offer from the possibility that a separate settlement might be reached with a holdout creditor. As result of this gaffe, Argentina passed what is known as a "Lock Law" which prevents the Argentine government from reopening the exchange process or making any kind of court, out-of-court or private transaction or settlement with respect to the bonds that were subject to the exchange offer.

The cases of Pakistan (1999), Ukraine (1999), Ecuador (2000), Uruguay (2003), Argentina (2005–10) and Belize (2006) can be used to evaluate whether such exchange offers work. These six different countries have been selected because they serve as an adequate sample of different types of restructuring episodes, including a pre-emptive debt reprofiling, default (with and without nominal value reductions) and the use of CACs and exit consents. In all these cases, the degree of participation in the exchange offers, which means the rate of acceptance, was above 90% (Ukraine 95%,

Ecuador 97%, Pakistan 99%, Uruguay 93%, Argentina 93% after two rounds of exchanges, and Belize 97%) . . .

Despite the fact that these exchange offers did not achieve 100% participation, none of them experienced the degree of belligerent litigation that has been witnessed in the Argentina case. Argentina's experience is slightly different because it followed a coercive approach and took more than 36 months to launch an exchange offer. In addition, it touches upon another clause, which is the pari passu clause—a clause that even now causes legal professionals to disagree as to its meaning or purpose and even origin.

3.   Understanding the pari passu clause

A pari passu clause included in sovereign bond issuances usually reads that the bonds rank pari passu with each other and with other unsecured (payment) obligations of the issuer.[3] This can be read as "equal among equals" and that bondholders are in the same ranking as other unsecured creditors.

From a close reading of the clause, it can be argued that it has two elements:

(i)   an internal element, ie that the bonds will rank pari passu with each other; and

(ii)   an external element, ie that the bonds will rank pari passu with other unsecured (present or future) indebtedness of the issuer.

Sometimes the term "payment" is included before "obligations", which adds nothing since we are talking about a bond—which cannot be anything other than a payment obligation . . . . [A]dding "payment" means nothing, while rank means rank. It does not mean "will pay", nor does it mean "will give equal treatment to creditors". "If a clause adopts a variant such as rank pari passu in priority of payment, then the result should be the same."

3.1 The (in)famous Elliott case

The meaning of the pari passu clause in the sovereign debt context was first discussed in the *Elliott* case, which was brought by Elliott Associates LP against Peru. The peculiarity of this case was the lack of assets to attach in the United States when the claimants sought to enforce a payment obligation. This forced the claimant to resort to the courts of Belgium,

---

[3]   The pari passu clause included in Argentina's 1994 Fiscal Agency Agreement (Clause 1(c)) reads as follows: "The Securities will constitute [. . .] direct, unconditional, unsecured and unsubordinated obligations of the Republic and shall at all times rank pari passu and without any preference among themselves. The payment obligations of the Republic under the Securities shall at all times rank at least equally with all its other present and future unsecured and unsubordinated External Indebtedness (as defined in this Agreement)."

Canada, England, Germany, Luxembourg and the Netherlands to seek enforcement of the decision.

In September 2000, Elliott obtained a restraining order from a Brussels Court of Appeals prohibiting Chase Manhattan (the financial agent) and Euroclear from paying interest on the Republic of Peru's Brady bonds (approximately USD 80 million that was due on October 2000). The Brussels Court of Appeals resolution stated that "[t]*he basic agreement regulating the reimbursement of the Peruvian foreign debt, also indicates that the different creditors enjoy a 'pari passu clause', which has as a result that the debt should be paid down equally towards all creditors in proportion to their claim.*"

Confronted by the judicial order not to make any payment, Peru faced default on restructured bonds totalling USD 3,837 million. In response, the country attempted to create a trust to make twice-yearly payments of interest due on the Brady bonds in order to keep servicing interest due and to avoid disrupting the flow of funds. Shortly after, however, Peru decided not to implement the trust structure because payments were curtailed through Euroclear, as well as through the Depository Trust Company (DTC) as result of attachment orders in different states in the United States. The only window that was left open—albeit temporarily—was to make the payments through Clearstream . . . This would have implied that only those bondholders holding an account with Clearstream would be paid or that bondholders not holding an account with Clearstream should open an account there (which implied an additional cost and several practical difficulties for Peru). As it was, it was only a matter of time before Elliott obtained a restraining order in Luxembourg (where Clearstream is headquartered).

This scenario forced Peru to reach an agreement with Elliott in order to avoid a new default on its recently restructured debt under the auspices of the Brady Plan. The final settlement agreement implied a payment in the total amount of USD 58.45 million. In the end, after the settlement, Peru was able to pay the due interest in time, avoiding a new default. The decision of the Brussels Court of Appeals that forced the parties to reach a settlement was based on the violation of the principle of equal treatment of creditors under the pari passu clause. The Belgian court mistakenly opened a door that permanently changed sovereign debt practices, as is explained below.

3.2 The ongoing Argentine litigation

Most practitioners and legal scholars thought that it would be just a matter of time until a New York court passed an interpretation of the pari passu clause. As a side note, it is worth pointing out that the Belgian court had to interpret the *pari passu* clause not under Belgian law but under New York law. The interpretation of the pari passu clause under New York law by experts in New York law finally occurred in the wake of the current Argentine litigation (*NML Ltd. v Republic of Argentina*). The first great surprise occurred when the District Court ruled that "*it is declared, adjudged and decreed that the Republic* [of Argentina] *violates Paragraph 1(c) of the FAA whenever it lowers the rank of its payment obligations . . . including (and without limitation) by relegating NML's bonds to a non-paying class . . .*". The salient point here is to understand why NML's bonds have been relegated to a non-paying class. The answer to this is the Lock Law. This is why the District Court finds that there has been a form of subordination. It says: " . . . *that the Republic lowered the rank of NML's bonds in violation of Paragraph 1(c) of the FAA when it enacted* [the Lock law]".

In the Argentine restructuring case, the bonds that were restructured did not include CACs. Argentina was unable to use exit consents because, in one of the bond series, bondholders managed to get a blocking holding curtailing any possible amendments to the non-payment terms. Therefore, Argentina had to resort to the MFCC. After the above-mentioned gaffe in the drafting of the MFCC (forgetting to include the word "settlement"), the government then passed the Lock Law to persuade bondholders who were in the process of tendering their original or old bonds that Argentina would not settle with holdouts. Otherwise, holding out might have eventually paid off.

However, it was the Lock Law that provided a basis for judging that there had been an alteration in the legal ranking. For, by means of the Lock Law, Argentina opened the way for an interpretation of the pari passu clause in the narrow or payment interpretation and not in the broad payment interpretation as in the Belgian case. Why? Because now there was a basis for subordination. It can be argued that Argentina *formally* subordinated a class of creditors lowering holdouts to a non-performing class by means of the Lock Law. In addition, in its US Securities and Exchange Commission filings (Form 18K, which is an annual report), Argentina has stated that holdouts are a category separate from its regular debt-holders and that since 2005 it has "not [been] in a legal . . . position to pay" that category. Emphasis should be put on the "*legal position*", which can be read as an indirect acknowledgment by Argentina that holdout creditors are a different category created by law. In this line of thinking, . . . "*you can do pretty much whatever you want in discriminating among creditors (in terms of who gets paid and who does not) but do not try to justify your behavior by taking steps that purport to establish a legal basis for discrimination*". This is precisely what happened in the case of Argentina.

More worrying is that now, when the New York courts were faced with the need to interpret the pari passu clause, we find ourselves in the same position that we were in the year 2000 with the Belgian courts. The District Court found that: "*Argentina lowered the rank of the plaintiff bonds in two ways: when it made payments currently due under the exchange bonds while persisting in its refusal to satisfy its payment obligations currently due under the bonds; and when it enacted the Lock Law.*" This clearly denotes that it is not just the actual subordination but something else.

The decision of the District Court was appealed to the US Court of Appeals for the Second Circuit. Surprisingly, the Court of Appeals understood that "*. . . in pairing the two sentences of its Pari Passu Clause, the FAA manifested an intention to protect bondholders from more than just formal subordination*". Again, as the District Court found, it is not just the actual subordination (which took place as result of the Lock Law) but something else.

According to the Court of Appeals, the pari passu clause protects against: (i) "the issuance of other superior debt (first sentence)";[4] and (ii) "the giving of priority to other payment obligations (second sentence)".[5] This confirms the broad interpretation of the pari passu clause along similar lines to the Belgian court's opinion and that as result of this we might be witnessing the opening of a Pandora's box. This means that the courts can order: (i) the debtor not to pay other debts of equal rank without making a rateable payment under the debt benefiting from the clause; (ii) other creditors: (a) not to accept a payment from the debtor unless the pari passu-protected lender receives a rateable payment; or, (b) if they have knowingly received and accepted a non-rateable payment, they are answerable to the pari passu-protected creditor for a rateable share of the funds; and (iii) a financial intermediary (eg a fiscal agent or a bond clearing system) can be ordered to freeze any non-rateable payment received from the debtor and to turn over to the pari passu-protected creditor its rateable share of the funds . . .

In January 2012 the District Court issued a temporary restraining order enjoining Argentina from altering the payment process (including the use of different firms or other vehicles). In addition, in February 2012, the same court issued an injunctive relief order requesting that, each time that a payment is made on exchanged bonds, the same fraction of the amount due on them should be paid to holdouts. The latter decision is based on principles of equitable relief, given that Argentina had formally made clear its intention not to pay. Since Argentina might refuse to comply with the injunctive order, the District Court extended its applicability not only to Argentina but also to its officers, agents, servants, employees and attorneys as well as other persons who are in active concert or participation with them. The injunctive order expressly prohibited Argentina's agents

---

[4]   The first sentence of the pari passu clause included in the Argentine bonds reads: ". . . shall at all times rank pari passu and without any preference among themselves".

[5]   The second sentence of the pari passu clause included in the Argentine bonds reads: "y(3)27 shall at all times rank at least equally with all its other present and future unsecured and unsubordinated [e]xternal [i]ndebtedness".

from aiding and abetting any further violation of the order by the court.[6] This clearly falls under point (iii) in the previous paragraph. These procedural orders (ie the temporary restraining order and the injunctive relief order) are currently under scrutiny by the Court of Appeals.

3.3 A serious threat to New York as a leading financial centre for sovereign debt

The broad interpretation of the pari passu clause will affect New York as an international financial centre because sovereign issuers will fear that it opens the way to litigation on such clauses. In addition, the injunctive relief order enjoining other parties (ie financial intermediaries) has several operational ramifications that threaten to impair the functioning of the payment systems. On the other hand, if the injunctive order is reversed by the Court of Appeals, creditors' enforcement rights will be affected. In both scenarios, New York stands to lose as an international financial centre, particularly in the sovereign debt arena.

To follow this line of thinking, it is worth noting that in the 1990s, in the *Pravin* and *Elliott* cases, the Court of Appeals for the Second Circuit was faced with balancing two important considerations, namely: (i) granting US-resident bondholders scope to pursue the repayment of their credit, although this would limit the chances of achieving a debt restructuring under the auspices of the IMF; and (ii) disallowing such claims because they would prejudice New York's status as a financial centre. Both issues were important for US foreign policy. For the Court of Appeals, however, the priority lay with the protection of investors and the sanctity of contracts.

4. Concluding remarks

The broad interpretation of the pari passu clause is a very delicate issue because we are opening a Pandora's box without knowing what might emerge. If we consider the aftermath of the *Elliott* case, which was the first time that there was a broad interpretation, and despite the fact that it was by a less authoritative court (many of the sovereign debt issuances are governed by New York law), there were several developments: the sovereign debt restructuring mechanism proposal of the IMF; the private sector reaction, ie the use of CACs and exit consent; increased NGO activism clamouring for debt forgiveness; increased investment by distressed debt funds; "vulture" repudiation by means of legislation in the United States and the United Kingdom; the erroneous re-emergence of the odious debt principle and its mutation into the debts of odious regimes and illegitimate debts; and an increased aggressiveness on the part of debtors and creditors.

---

[6]   This conflicts with another norm that states that intermediaries cannot be affected (Art. 4–A of the UCC).

As indicated above, this will seriously affect the future of the sovereign debt market in New York. The harm has been done; one way or another, there will be damage.

The interpretation of the pari passu clause in the pre-Argentine litigation was incorrect. It was based on the Belgian court's interpretation of the pari passu clause in the broad sense. Post-Argentine litigation, the interpretation could have been based on the correct reading of the clause based on an actual breach of it due to the ranking or narrow form as a result of the legal subordination from the Lock Law. Unfortunately this was not the case. This was a great missed opportunity, and it will trigger a new round of litigation.

. . . [T]he clause has little or no meaning in the sovereign debt context. However, it is a boilerplate and boilerplates are sticky. After the decision of the Second Circuit Court of Appeals it will become even stickier. Looking forward, it is the task of lawyers—as guardians of the purity of language in contracts—to clearly state whether the pari passu clause should read as "rank" or "rateable payment" instead of the not very clear Latin phrase "pari passu". In the meantime, there are still many contracts with Frankenstein-like pari passu clauses that will be litigated.

* * * * *

Hector: Hey, wait a second, man!!! This is so crazy!!! Crazier than me! Isn't there some kind of global court that can take care of bond defaults? You know, like U.S. bankruptcy courts? I really need to know, man! Really!

Oh, Hector, we didn't expect to see you here. Good question, though. The short answer is that there's no global bankruptcy court. You see, when lending to developing countries switched from loans by foreign banks to issuance of sovereign bonds in the 1990s, debtor countries faced a "collective action" problem, meaning it was hard to have widely dispersed bondholders to act collectively. Some would inevitably hold out: they would refuse to participate in a restructuring, hoping to recover 100 cents on the dollar. This made it harder for debtor countries to restructure bond debt. In the early 2000s, the IMF proposed a Sovereign Debt Restructuring Mechanism (SDRM) where debtors could get a stand-still on payments and a stay on creditor litigation. It didn't go anywhere because the U.S. and emerging market economies opposed it. The EMEs didn't like it because they thought the SDRM would make raising capital more expensive if the creditors knew that restructuring would be easy.

But what about changing the payment provision in the bond, which is a contract after all. The problem was that bonds issued under New York law (but not under U.K. law) by convention required unanimous consent to change payment terms. This encouraged the holdouts. But in 2003, Mexico issued bonds that departed from the convention and allowed payment terms to be modified by bondholders holding 75% of the bonds' outstanding principal. Today, virtually all bonds issued under New York law have adopted super-majority collective action clauses (CACs).

Hector: Will CACs eliminate the @#$%* hold-outs? Tell me, man!

An epic question, Hector. How about some beer, chips, and salsa.

Epilogue

The not-so-promising international finance freak

 He went on to become Managing Director of the International Monetary Fund. And he took his talking dog with him.

Peace out.

SELECTED READINGS

. . .

There's enough literature regarding everything in this textbook that would choke ten million horses. So here we provide a relatively few number of sources that we've relied upon and that otherwise might make interesting reading for you. The readings are broken down by chapter. You might see repeated citations throughout various chapters—the sources are relevant to a bunch of stuff.

Chapter 1: The Bretton Woods Institutions

M. Bordo & B. Eichengreen, <u>A Retrospective on the Bretton Woods System</u> (1993)

D. Bradlow & D. B. Hunter, eds., <u>International Financial Institutions and International Law</u> (2010)

C. Brummer, <u>Soft Law and the Global Financial System: Rule Making in the 21st Century</u> (2012)

J. M. Chwieroth, <u>Capital Ideas: The IMF and the Rise of Financial Liberalization</u> (2010)

E. Denters, <u>Law and Policy of IMF Conditionality</u> (1996)

R. W. Edwards, Jr., <u>International Monetary Collaboration</u> (1985)

M. Garritsen de Vries et al., <u>The International Monetary Fund 1945–1965</u>, vols. I–III (1969)

J. Gold, <u>Conditionality (Pamphlet Series - International Monetary Fund no. 31)</u> (1979)

J. Gold, <u>The International Monetary Fund and International Law: An Introduction</u> (1965)

J. Gold, <u>Legal and Institutional Aspects of the International Monetary System: Selected Essays</u> (1981)

J. K. Horsefield, <u>The International Monetary Fund 1945–1965: Twenty Years of International Monetary Cooperation</u>, vols. II, III (1969)

H. James, <u>International Monetary Cooperation Since Bretton Woods</u> (1996)

O. Kirshner, <u>The Bretton-Woods Gatt System: Retrospect and Prospect After Fifty Years</u> (1996)

A. F. Lowenfeld, <u>The International Monetary System</u>, vol. IV (1984)

<u>Proceedings and Documents of United Nations Monetary and Financial Conference: Bretton Woods, New Hampshire</u>, July 1–22, vols. I, II, (1948)

B. Steil, <u>The Battle of Bretton Woods</u> (2013)

Chapter 2: Development

R. Chilcote, ed., <u>Development in Theory and Practice</u> (2003)

J. M. Chwieroth, <u>Capital Ideas: The IMF and the Rise of Financial Liberalization</u> (2010)

E. Dosman, <u>The Life and Times of Raúl Prebisch</u> (2008)

A. Frank, <u>Dependent Accumulation and Underdevelopment</u> (1979)

D. Hunt, <u>Economic Theories of Development: An Analysis of Competing Paradigms</u> (1989)

J. Sachs, <u>The End of Poverty</u> (2005)

M. Todaro & S. Smith, <u>Economic Development: Eleventh Edition</u> (2012)

Chapter 3: The Fall of the Bretton Woods System

M. Bordo et al., "U.S. Intervention during the Bretton Woods Era: 1962–1973" (2007)

J. M. Chwieroth, <u>Capital Ideas: The IMF and the Rise of Financial Liberalization</u> (2010)

K. W. Dam, <u>The Rules of the Game: Reform and Evolution in the International Monetary System</u> (1982)

M. Garritsen de Vries, <u>The International Monetary Fund 1966–1971</u>, vols. I, II (1976)

H. James, <u>International Monetary Cooperation Since Bretton Woods</u> (1996)

H. G. Johnson, "The Case for Flexible Exchange Rates" (1969)

L. B. Johnson, <u>The Vantage Point: Perspectives of the Presidency, 1963–1969</u> (1971)

R. Triffin, <u>Gold and the Dollar Crisis</u> (1960)

R. Triffin, <u>Our International Monetary System: Yesterday, Today, and Tomorrow</u> (1968)

Chapter 4: Rise of the WB and NIEO

J. Bhagwati, ed., <u>The New International Economic Order: The North-South Debate</u> (1977)

I. Garcia-Chafardet, *Sexism as an Obstacle to Development*, in Social and Cultural Issues of the New International Economic Order (1981)

M. Garritsen de Vries, The International Monetary Fund 1972–1978: Cooperation on Trial, vols. I–III (1985)

D. Halberstam, The Best and the Brightest (1972)

D. Kapur et al., The World Bank: Its First Half Century, vols. I, II (1997)

J. Kraske et al., Bankers with a Mission: The Presidents of the World Bank, 1946–1991 (1996)

E. Mason & R. Asher, The World Bank Since Bretton Woods (1973)

The McNamara Years at the World Bank: Major Policy Addresses of Robert S. McNamara 1968–1981 (1981)

Chapter 5: The 1980s Debt Crisis and The Lost Decade

D. Beek, "Commercial Bank Lending to the Developing Countries," *Federal Reserve Bank of New York Quarterly Review* (summer 1977)

J. Boughton, Silent Revolution: The International Monetary Fund 1979–1989 (2001)

R. P. Buckley & D. W. Arner, From Crisis to Crisis: The Global Financial System and Regulatory Failure (2011)

E. Carrasco, "Chile, Its Foreign Commercial Bank Creditors and Its Vulnerable Groups: An Assessment of the Cooperative Case-By-Case Approach to the Debt Crisis," *24 Law & Pol'y Int'l Bus. 273* (1992–1993)

E. Carrasco & M. Kose, "Income Distribution and the Bretton Woods Institutions: Promoting an Enabling Environment for Social Development," *6 Transnat'l L. & Contemp. Probs. 1* (1996)

T. Curry, *The LDC Debt Crisis*, in "FDIC: History of the Eighties—Lessons for the Future," vol. I (1997)

H. James, International Monetary Cooperation Since Bretton Woods (1996)

C. P. Kindleberger & R. Aliber, Manias, Panics, and Crashes: A History of Financial Crises (2005)

J. B. Treaster, Paul Volcker: The Making of a Financial Legend (2004)

Chapter 6: Development in the 1990s

L. Hass et al., World Bank, "Setting Standards for Communication and Governance: The Example of Infrastructure Projects" (2007)

N. Serra & J. Stiglitz, "The Washington Consensus Reconsidered: Towards a New Global Governance" (2008)

I. Shihata, <u>The World Bank in a Changing World</u>, vols. I (1991), II (1995), III (2000)

I. Shihata, <u>The World Bank Legal Papers</u> (2000)

J. Stiglitz, <u>Globalization and Its Discontents</u> (2002)

Transparency International, "Global Corruption Report 2005: Corruption in Construction and Post-Conflict Reconstruction" (2005)

D. Trubek & M. Galanter, "Scholars in Self-Estrangement: Some Reflections on the Crisis in Law and Development Studies in the United States," *1974 Wis. L. Rev. 1062* (1974)

J. Williamson, *What Washington Means by Policy Reform*, in <u>Latin American Adjustment: How Much Has Happened?</u> (1990)

World Bank, "Governance and Development" (1992)

World Bank, "Legal and Judicial Reform: Strategic Directions" (2003)

World Bank, "The State in a Changing World" (1997)

Chapter 7: The BWIs 50th Anniversary

J. M. Boughton, <u>Tearing Down Walls: The International Monetary Fund 1990–1999</u> (2012)

J. M. Boughton and K. S. Lateef, eds., <u>Fifty Years After Bretton Woods: The Future of the IMF and the World Bank</u> (1995)

D. Bradlow, "Should the International Financial Institutions Play a Role in the Implementation and Enforcement of International Humanitarian Law?" *50 U. Kan. L. Rev. 695* (2001–2002)

D. Bradlow, "The World Bank, the IMF, and Human Rights," *6 Transnat'l L. & Contemp. Probs. 47* (1996)

J. Cavanagh, D. Wysham, & M. Arruda, eds., <u>Beyond Bretton Woods: Alternatives to the Global Economic Order</u> (1994)

D. Clark, J. Fox, & K. Treakle, eds., <u>Demanding Accountability: Civil-Society Claims and the World Bank Inspection Panel</u> (2003)

K. Danaher, ed., <u>50 Years is Enough: The Case Against the World Bank and the International Monetary Fund</u> (1994)

M. Darrow, <u>Between Light and Shadow: The World Bank, the International Monetary Fund and International Human Rights Law</u> (2003)

D. Kapur, J. P. Lewis, & R. Webb, <u>The World Bank: Its First Half Century</u>, vols. I, II (1997)

O. Kirshner, ed., <u>The Bretton Woods-GATT System: Retrospect and Prospect After Fifty Years</u> (1996)

I. Shihata, <u>The World Bank in a Changing World</u>, vols. I (1991), II (1995), III (2000)

I. Shihata, <u>The World Bank Legal Papers</u> (2000)

S. I. Skogly, <u>The Human Rights Obligations of the World Bank and the International Monetary Fund</u> (2001)

J. D. Wolfensohn, <u>A Global Life: My Journey Among Rich and Poor, from Sydney to Wall Street to the World Bank</u> (2010)

Chapter 8: Capital Markets

D. Folkerts-Landau & T. Ito et al., <u>International Capital Markets: Developments, Prospects, and Policy Issues</u> (1995)

Chapter 9: The Mexican Crisis

E. Carrasco, "Encouraging Relational Investment and Controlling Portfolio Investment in Developing Countries in the Aftermath of the Mexican Financial Crisis," *34 Colum. J. Transnat'l L. 539* (1996)

J. M. Chwieroth, <u>Capital Ideas: The IMF and the Rise of Financial Liberalization</u> (2010)

C. P. Kindleberger & R. Aliber, <u>Manias, Panics, and Crashes: A History of Financial Crises</u> (2005)

J. Sachs et al., "The Mexican peso crisis: Sudden death or death foretold?" *41 J. Int'l Econ. 265* (1996)

Chapter 10: The Asian Financial Crisis

R. P. Buckley & D. W. Arner, <u>From Crisis to Crisis: The Global Financial System and Regulatory Failure</u> (2011)

J. J. Choi, ed., <u>International Finance Review vol. 1, The Asian Crisis: Financial, Structural and International Dimensions</u> (2000)

J. M. Chwieroth, <u>Capital Ideas: The IMF and the Rise of Financial Liberalization</u> (2010)

S. Haggard, <u>The Political Economy of the Asian Financial Crisis</u> (2000)

K. D. Jackson, ed., <u>Asian Contagion: The Causes and Consequences of a Financial Crisis</u> (1999)

S. Jwa & I. K. Lee, eds., <u>Competition and Corporate Governance in Korea</u> (2004)

C. P. Kindleberger & R. Aliber, <u>Manias, Panics, and Crashes: A History of Financial Crises</u> (2005)

P. Krugman, <u>The Return of Depression Economics and the Crisis of 2008</u> (2009)

R. S. Milne & D. K. Mauzy, <u>Malaysian Politics Under Mahathir</u> (1999)

J. Stiglitz, <u>Globalization and Its Discontents</u> (2003)

J. Strauss et al., <u>Indonesia Living Standards Before the After the Financial Crisis: Evidence from the Indonesia Family Life Survey</u> (2004)

M. Tsurumi, ed., <u>Financial Big Bang in Asia</u> (2001)

Chapter 11: Capital Adequacy

D.K. Tarullo, <u>Banking on Basel: The Future of International Financial Regulation</u> (2008)

Chapters 12–16: Global Financial Crisis Chapters

E. J. Balleisen & D.A. Moss, <u>Government and Markets: Toward a New Theory of Regulation</u> (2010)

R. P. Buckley & D. W. Arner, <u>From Crisis to Crisis: The Global Financial System and Regulatory Failure</u> (2011)

W. D. Cohan, <u>House of Cards: A Tale of Hubris and Wretched Excess on Wall Street</u> (2009)

J. M. Chwieroth, <u>Capital Ideas: The IMF and the Rise of Financial Liberalization</u> (2010)

N. Dobos, C. Barry, & T. Pogge, eds., <u>Global Financial Crisis: The Ethical Issues</u> (2011)

T. Frankel & M. Fagan, <u>Law and the Financial System: Securitization and Asset Back Securities: Law, Process, Case Studies, and Simulations</u> (2009)

J. Friedman, ed., <u>What Caused the Financial Crisis</u> (2011)

W. Grant & G. K. Wilson, eds., <u>The Consequences of the Global Financial Crisis</u> (2012)

P. Krugman, <u>The Return of Depression Economics and the Crisis of 2008</u> (2009)

R. Rajan, <u>Fault Lines: How Hidden Fractures Still Threaten the World Economy</u> (2010)

Y. V. Reddy, <u>India and the Global Financial Crisis: Managing Money and Finance</u> (2009)

C. Reinhart & K. S. Rogoff, <u>This Time is Different: Eight Centuries of Financial Folly</u> (2009)

G. Rosas, <u>Curbing Bailouts: Bank Crises and Democratic Accountability in Comparative Perspectives</u> (2009)

P. Savona, J. J. Kirton, & C. Oldani, eds., <u>Global Financial Crisis: Global Impact and Solutions</u> (2011)

P. Shu & C. Adressen, eds., <u>Australia, China and the Global Financial Crisis</u> (2010)

A. S. Sisodiya & N. J. Rao, eds., <u>Economic Decoupling: Insights and Experiences</u> (2008)

J. Stiglitz, <u>Freefall: America, Free Markets, and the Sinking of the World Economy</u> (2010)

L. B. Thomas, <u>The Financial Crisis and Federal Reserve Policy</u> (2011)

M. Wolf, <u>Fixing Global Finance</u> (2008)

M. Zandi, <u>Financial Shock: A 360° Look at the Subprime Mortgage Implosion, and How to Avoid the Next Financial Crisis</u> (2009)

Chapter 17: The GFC Exposes Cracks in the European Monetary Union: The European Sovereign Debt Crisis

C. Alessi, "The Role of the European Central Bank," *Council on Foreign Relations* (2012)

P. Bofinger, "The European Monetary System (1979–1988) Achievements, Flaws, and Applicability to Other Regions of the World," *Background Paper for Special Session IV*, United Nations Economic Commission for Europe (2000)

R. Jenkins, "Europe's Present Challenge and Future Opportunity," Speech, Jean Monnet Lecture (1977)

L. Kühnhardt, *The Fall of the Berlin Wall and European Integration*, in <u>20 Years After the Fall of the Berlin Wall</u> (2009)

F. P. Mongelli, "European Economic and Monetary Integration, and the Optimum Currency Area Theory," *European Economy, Economic Papers 302* (2008)

R. Mundell, "A Theory of Optimum Currency Areas," *The American Economic Review* (1968)

J. Priewe, *Reconsidering the Theories of Optimum Currency Area—A Critique*, in <u>European Integration in Crisis</u> (2007)

H. Rockoff, "How Long Did It Take the United States to Become an Optimal Currency Area?" *NBER Working Paper Series, Historical Paper 124* (2000)

M. E. Sarotte, "Eurozone Crisis as Historical Legacy: The Enduring Impact of German Unification, Twenty Years On," *Crisis in the Eurozone* (2010)

H. Z. de Sousa, "The Future of the Stability and Growth Pact as a Tool For Economic Policy Co-Ordination," *Notre Europe, Policy Paper No. 9* (2004)

"The United States as a Monetary Union," *EMU Study*, HM Treasury (2003)

A. Sen, Inequality Reexamined (1992)

Chapter 20: The Rise of Emerging Market Economies

M. Ayhan Kose & E. S. Prasad, Emerging Markets: Resilience and Growth Amid Global Turmoil (2010)

L. Beridze, ed., Economics of Emerging Markets (2008)

D. Folkerts-Landau and T. Ito et al., International Capital Markets: Developments, Prospects, and Policy Issues (1995)

M. Kawai & E. S. Prasad, eds., Financial Market Regulation and Reforms in Emerging Markets (2011)

Organisation for Economic Co-operation and Development, Globalisation and Emerging Economies: Brazil, Russia, India, Indonesia, China, and South Africa (2008)

P. Reddy, Global Innovation in Emerging Economies (2011)

Chapter 21: Emerging Market Economies: Selected Topics

A. Al-Roubaie & S. Alvi, eds., Islamic Banking and Finance (2010)

S. Archer, R. Ahmed, & A. Karim, Islamic Finance: The New Regulatory Challenge (2013)

J. M. Boughton & D. Lombardi, eds., Finance, Development, and the IMF (2009)

M. Bradley & M. Gulati, "Collective Action Clauses for the Eurozone: An Empirical Analysis," *Review of Finance* (2013)

W. Bratton, "Pari Passu and a Distressed Sovereign's Rational Choices," *53 Emory L.J. 823* (2004)

L. Buchheit, "The Pari Passu Clause Sub Specie Aeternitatis," *10 Int'l L. Rev. 11* (1991)

L. Buchheit & J. Pam, "The Pari Passu Clause in Sovereign Debt Instruments," *53 Emory L.J. 869* (2004)

R. P. Buckley & D. W. Arner, From Crisis to Crisis: The Global Financial System and Regulatory Failure (2011)

A. Buira, ed., Reforming the Governance of the IMF and the World Bank (2005)

A. Chua, World On Fire: How Exporting Free Market Democracy Breeds Ethnic Hatred and Global Instability (2003)

S. K. Das, India's Rights Revolution: Has It Worked for the Poor? (2013)

U. Das et al., "Sovereign Debt Restructurings 1950–2010: Literature Survey, Data and Stylized Facts," IMF Working Paper 12/203 (August 2012)

J. Faundez & C. Tan, eds., <u>International Economic Law, Globalization and Developing Countries</u> (2010)

M. Gulati & K. Klee, "Sovereign Piracy," *56 Bus. Law 635, 646* (2001)

T. K. Hernández, <u>Racial Subordination in Latin America: The Role of the State, Customary Law, and the New Civil Rights Response</u> (2013)

C. P. Kindleberger & R. Aliber, <u>Manias, Panics, and Crashes: A History of Financial Crises</u> (2005)

P. Krugman, <u>The Return of Depression Economics and the Crisis of 2008</u> (2009)

R. M. Lastra & L. Buchheit, eds., <u>Sovereign Debt Management</u> (2014)

M. Mussa, <u>Argentina and the Fund: From Triumph to Tragedy</u> (2002)

M. Pastor & C. Wise, "From Poster Child to Basket Case," *Foreign Affairs* (Nov./Dec. 2001)

C. A. Primo Braga & G. A. Vincelette, eds., <u>Sovereign Debt and the Financial Crisis: Will This Time Be Different?</u> (2011)

J. Stiglitz, <u>Globalization and Its Discontents</u> (2003)

D. Vines & C. L. Gilbert, eds., <u>The IMF and Its Critics: Reform of Global Financial Architecture</u> (2004)

INDEX

References are to Pages